Windows® 2000 GRAPHICS API

Black Book

Damon Chandler
Michael Fötsch

President and CEO
Keith Weiskamp

Publisher
Steve Sayre

Acquisitions Editor
Kevin Weeks

Development Editor
Michelle Stroup

Product Marketing Manager
Tracy Rooney

Project Editor
Sean Tape

Technical Reviewer
Luis Alejandro Allegretti

Production Coordinator
Laura Wellander

Cover Designer
Jody Winkler

Layout Designer
April Nielsen

CD-ROM Developer
Chris Nusbaum

Windows® 2000 Graphics API Black Book

The Coriolis Group, LLC
14455 N. Hayden Road
Suite 220
Scottsdale, Arizona 85260

(480) 483-0192
FAX (480) 483-0193
www.coriolis.com

Library of Congress Cataloging-in-Publication Data
Chandler, Damon
Windows 2000 graphics API black book / by Damon Chandler and Michael Fötsch.
p. cm.
Includes index.
ISBN 1-57610-876-7
1. Computer graphics. 2. Microsoft Windows (Computer file) I. Fötsch, Michael. II. Title.
T385 .C452 2001
006.6'8--dc21 00-069419
CIP

Printed in the United States of America
10 9 8 7 6 5 4 3 2 1

The Coriolis Group, LLC • 14455 North Hayden Road, Suite 220 • Scottsdale, Arizona 85260

Dear Reader:

Coriolis Technology Press was founded to create a very elite group of books: the ones you keep closest to your machine. Sure, everyone would like to have the Library of Congress at arm's reach, but in the real world, you have to choose the books you rely on every day *very* carefully.

To win a place for our books on that coveted shelf beside your PC, we guarantee several important qualities in every book we publish. These qualities are:

- *Technical accuracy*—It's no good if it doesn't work. Every Coriolis Technology Press book is reviewed by technical experts in the topic field, and is sent through several editing and proofreading passes in order to create the piece of work you now hold in your hands.
- *Innovative editorial design*—We've put years of research and refinement into the ways we present information in our books. Our books' editorial approach is uniquely designed to reflect the way people learn new technologies and search for solutions to technology problems.
- *Practical focus*—We put only pertinent information into our books and avoid any fluff. Every fact included between these two covers must serve the mission of the book as a whole.
- *Accessibility*—The information in a book is worthless unless you can find it quickly when you need it. We put a lot of effort into our indexes, and heavily cross-reference our chapters, to make it easy for you to move right to the information you need.

Here at The Coriolis Group we have been publishing and packaging books, technical journals, and training materials since 1989. We're programmers and authors ourselves, and we take an ongoing active role in defining what we publish and how we publish it. We have put a lot of thought into our books; please write to us at **ctp@coriolis.com** and let us know what you think. We hope that you're happy with the book in your hands, and that in the future, when you reach for software development and networking information, you'll turn to one of our books first.

Keith Weiskamp
President and CEO

Jeff Duntemann
VP and Editorial Director

To my mother and sister.
—Damon Chandler

❧

To my mother, Dagmar Fötsch.
—Michael Fötsch

❧

About the Authors

Damon Chandler holds a B.S. in biomedical engineering from the Johns Hopkins University and a M.Eng in electrical engineering from Cornell University. He currently develops Windows and X-Windows applications at the Cornell Visual Communications Lab. Damon's research includes medical image compression, psychology, and color science. He has been developing graphics applications since the early days of MS-DOS. Damon is also a member of Team Borland, a select group of software developers who provide support to the online development community. Damon currently resides in Ithaca, NY; contact him at dmc27@ee.cornell.edu.

Michael Fötsch is a freelance software developer who specializes in DirectX technology. He has more than 15 years experience in developing games and other graphics-intensive applications. Michael is a regular contributor to Mr. Gamemaker, and he is an active member of Microsoft's DirectX newsgroups. Michael currently resides in Seiersberg, Austria; contact him at foetsch@crosswinds.net.

Acknowledgments

This text is a collaborative effort of many dedicated individuals whose technical and moral support have made such a book possible.

First, I'd like to thank my sister, Katherine Chandler, who spent many sleepless nights proofreading bulky chapters, deriving new equations, and addressing (and, in many cases, correcting) much of the technical and grammatical content. Your hard work and dedication is much appreciated.

Many thanks to the folks at Coriolis who have played a pivotal role in seeing this project to its completion. I'd particularly like to thank Kevin Weeks, who's responsible for this book's original conception, and Sean Tape, for his top-notch dedication as a project editor. You guys have shown true professionalism throughout the entire process. An author could not ask for better editors. I'd also like to thank Catherine Oliver and Luis Allegretti who have worked hard to make this text grammatically and technically accurate. Catherine's dedication as a copy editor truly reflects her command of the English language; thanks for teaching me so much.

Special thanks to Dave Richards, Jared "EZJ" Bish, and Tak Cheng for keeping me on my toes during the writing process. And, thanks to the many mentors—Sheila Hemami, Claudia Wortman, Brett Simon, Catherine Marcucci, Irvin Smoot, Paul Willoughby, and Michael Buonviri—who have shaped me both academically and spiritually.

Lastly, I'd like to thank my mother, Shizue Chandler, for providing so much encouragement and moral support. I am—and always will be—in your debt.

—Damon Chandler

Contents at a Glance

Table of Contents

Immediate Solutions

Chapter 6
The Bitmap Object 287

Chapter 7
Device-Independent Bitmaps 355

Part II DirectDraw

Immediate Solutions

Part IV Appendixes

Introduction

Application development is one of the most rewarding, yet frustrating fields to work in. It really is amazing how one profession can send you on such an emotional roller-coaster ride. One minute you're pulling your hair out, cursing the engineers at Microsoft. The next minute you're ready to pop open a bottle of champagne. Most of the time, however, you're staring at the progress of the compiler, waiting in anticipation as if the results will make or break you. And when you do finally get things working, you realize that either you learned a great deal in the process, or you'll never again trust Microsoft's documentation.

Admit it—how many times have you read a cryptic explanation of a function or a technique and wasted so many hours simply because someone neglected to mention a common pitfall? It's completely frustrating! Unfortunately, it seems as if too many things are explained in hieroglyphics—all too often without code examples. (In many cases, I personally find examples more explanatory than the text itself.) Think about it for a moment. The ultimate goal of documentation is to exchange information; and if you can't get this information across, what's the point? Would the TV Food Network be so popular if Emeril just sat in front of the camera reading from a cookbook? No, of course not! On the other hand, if Emeril is cooking, but you have your TV muted, you're still not going to know exactly what to do. Whatever the task at hand is—whether you're preparing a gourmet meal, solving a difficult equation, or, in our case, developing applications—the point is, your source of information must contain a good mix of background information and hands-on examples.

Nowadays—with the increasing availability of high-end processing power and the rapid decrease in the cost of video-display components—more and more applications are including graphics-based content. This trend places a great demand on the contemporary developer and makes a basic understanding of graphics programming a vital part of any curriculum. Perhaps more than any other programming interface, the Windows graphics API doesn't leave room for error; many of the techniques require a strict procedure that must be followed to the letter. Often this scheme forces you to memorize a specific set of function calls that are easily forgotten.

We've written *Windows 2000 Graphics API Black Book* with two primary goals in mind: First, as a definitive problem-solver, this text is designed to alleviate the chore of rote memorization. As you'll soon discover, many graphics-based techniques aren't all that difficult—there's certainly no rocket science or magic to it. The fact remains, however, that if you've forgotten which functions to call, or if you've never before attempted the solution, there's a good chance that you'll waste several hours just trying to get this—conceptually simple—technique to work. Well, we've learned (from personal experience) that this is an all too common situation. As a result, each chapter of this text contains an "Immediate Solutions" section that provides systematic answers, or "recipes," that you can follow to get the task accomplished quickly. When you're in a bind, who cares about a lengthy explanation? You simply follows the recipe, learn from the example, cut and paste the code from the CD-ROM, and then move on to the next task. (Don't get us wrong; we're not trying to endorse bad habits, but we've all done our fair share of cutting and pasting.) Second, and perhaps more importantly, this text aims to answer the *whys*. "Why do I use function X instead of function Y? Why is this technique faster than the others? Why is this function named so and so?" To answer these questions, each chapter opens with a thorough "In Depth" section that provides the theory behind the solutions. In this way, *Windows 2000 Graphics API Black Book* serves as both a reference and an explanatory guide.

Is This Book for You?

Windows 2000 Graphics API Black Book was written with the intermediate or advanced user in mind. This book's topics include:

- *The Windows Graphics Device Interface (GDI)*—The GDI is the foundation of the Windows user interface. Use of the GDI can be seen throughout Windows—from simple controls, such as the Start button, to complex images, such as the thumbnail previews in Explorer. Designed primarily for business and desktop-publishing applications, the GDI is used, to some extent, by every Windows application. Despite its prevalence, the GDI is one of the most difficult Windows-based technologies to work with; it presents many pitfalls that oftentimes leave developers scratching their heads. For this reason, Chapters 1 through 10 provide a comprehensive treatment of the Windows GDI, presenting effective solutions to the most commonly encountered problems.
- *DirectDraw*—DirectDraw is a component of the DirectX library that allows applications to take advantage of enhanced video hardware capabilities. Many display adapters, for example, possess specific integrated circuits designed to handle the task of rendering textures. Using DirectDraw, an application can access such capabilities for enhanced performance. When specific hardware is absent, DirectDraw emulates the functionality through its HEL (Hardware Emulation Layer). Though DirectDraw is designed primarily

for games, it can be used in any application and even in conjunction with the GDI. In Chapters 11 through 15, we provide a task-oriented treatment of DirectDraw, often drawing parallels to corresponding GDI-based approaches.

- *Image Color Management (ICM) 2*—Microsoft's Image Color Management technology gives applications the ability to control the way an image will appear on a specific device. For example, the ICM services can be used to ensure that the printed version of a Web page will appear as close as possible to what appears on the screen. Such functionality is most often required when the range of printable colors is only a subset of the range capable of being displayed by the monitor, as is the case for most printers. This argument holds true for image acquisition devices as well. In Chapter 16, we'll take an in-depth look at the motivation behind Image Color Management, and we'll examine how you easily incorporate ICM 2 technology into your applications.
- *Image processing*—Manipulating the pixels of an image to achieve a special effect is easier said than done. Sure, it's simple enough to manipulate the color of each pixel, but what if you want to alter an image's frequency components? What if you want to change the shape of only a particular object within an image? Or what if you want to morph two images? In Chapter 17, we address these questions and a whole lot more. We'll discuss intensity-based manipulations, geometrically based manipulations, and frequency-based manipulations. We'll also discuss a bit of signal processing theory, and we'll demonstrate how to compute the discrete cosine transform and the discrete wavelet transform.
- *Image file formats*—Although the Windows API provides native support for bitmaps, most applications aren't limited to only this format. In Chapter 18, we examine two of the most common types of compressed images: JPEGs and PNGs. We'll discuss the differences between the types' compression schemes, and we'll discuss how you can read and write JPG and PNG files.

The companion CD-ROM contains numerous code examples, demo applications, utility functions, and useful C++ classes that reinforce the concepts from the text. We've included projects for both Microsoft Visual C++ and Borland C++Builder.

An Overview of Windows Graphics

Back in the command-line era, there was little need for any type of standard graphics interface. Most applications were completely text-based, and the idea of painting a control to the screen often seemed unnecessary or beyond the scope of an application. Those applications that did require a graphics-based display employed the use of a proprietary graphics interface. In the early 1990s, the release of Windows 3 necessitated the inclusion of a standard graphics interface. The idea was to provide a common means by which an application could render its controls so as to conform to the rest of the graphics environment. The Windows *Graphics Device Interface*, or GDI for short, filled this role and, at the same time, reduced most third-party interfaces to obsolescence. You can probably imagine the chaos that might result when separate interfaces attempt to simultaneously access the display device driver. Eliminating the developer's role of delegating these interfaces was a primary motivation for developing the GDI.

Conceptually, the GDI is nothing more than an abstract layer between the developer of a Windows-based application and a device driver. This statement lacks a device specification because the GDI can be used to render graphical representations to a whole slew of different devices. For example, you can use the GDI to produce graphical output on a plotter or printer, as well as on the display monitor. In fact, you rarely have to worry about the specifics of how the interface communicates with separate devices. Instead, you can think of the GDI as a common set of structures and functions that can be used for drawing and painting. There are, of course, some limitations to this rule; rarely is Microsoft technology so straightforward. Don't worry, though—we give you a heads-up when things get nasty. And if the Windows GDI just isn't your cup of tea, you can quickly refer to a DirectDraw-based solution.

DirectDraw was introduced in 1995 as part of the DirectX set of APIs. This set of APIs was developed to facilitate the creation of games and multimedia applications for the Microsoft Windows operating system. With the help of DirectX, Windows 95 soon replaced MS-DOS as the premier platform for PC games. However, you'll notice that DirectX is useful not only for games but for other applications as well.

DirectDraw, as the 2D graphics component of DirectX, gives applications low-level access to the display hardware. With DirectDraw, it's possible to use special hardware features that are not exposed through the Windows GDI. DirectDraw was also designed to be compatible with the widest possible variety of display devices. DirectDraw is even capable of emulating features when the hardware does not support them directly.

In the past few years, DirectDraw has been under constant development. With version 7 of the DirectX runtime (DirectX 7 is an integral part of the Windows 2000 operating system), the DirectDraw API is finally complete. DirectX 8, which was released in November 2000, continues to support DirectDraw. This book is the complete guide to high-performance 2D graphics in Windows 2000 and future operating systems. We'll cover everything from DirectDraw initialization to setting up full-screen applications, taking advantage of hardware acceleration, gaining direct access to the video memory, using stereo vision, and much more.

How to Use This Book

Most of the chapters of this text are independent. You don't need to read the book in a serial fashion. And, when applicable, we'll refer you to the related chapters. To understand the code, however, you will need at least a basic understanding of general Windows programming, pointers, C++ references, and exception handling. In most cases, whatever language you use, if you're familiar with general programming, it's not too difficult to translate.

A Note on Common Windows Entities

Although we provide an explanation for most of the graphics-API-related types, structures, and macros, you should be familiar with those that are common to general Windows development. Some of the more ubiquitous ones are: **HANDLE**, **HGLOBAL**, **HINSTANCE**, **HWND**, **MSG**, **LPARAM**, **WPARAM**, **BYTE**, **WORD**, **DWORD**, **POINT**, **RECT**, **SIZE**, **COLORREF**, **RGB**, and **PALETTERGB**.

A Note on Exception Handling

Because we want to endorse good programming practices (and thus reliable code), we've strived to use exception handling wherever it's needed (and in some cases, even when it's not). We've also tried to avoid using specific exception classes that might be ambiguous to non-C++ developers (and even some C++ compilers). To this end, whenever you see code like the following:

```
memory_buffer = some_memory_allocation_function();
try
{
   if (some_function() == SOME_ERROR_CONDITION)
   {
      throw;  // or, throw "some error message";
   }
}
catch (...)
{
   // error-handling/clean-up code...
   some_memory_deallocation_function(memory_buffer);
   some_error_reporting_function();
}
some_memory_deallocation_function(memory_buffer);
```

you should replace the generic **throw** statement with one that's more applicable to your code, and you should replace the generic **catch** statement with one that's designed to handle the type of exception that you raised. For example, if you were using the Standard C++ Library's **runtime_error** class, you'd do the following:

```
memory_buffer = some_memory_allocation_function();
try
{
   if (!some_function())
   {
      throw std::runtime_error("argh!");
   }
}
catch (std::runtime_error& e)
{
   // error-handling/clean-up code...
   some_memory_deallocation_function(memory_buffer);
   MessageBox(
      GetForegroundWindow(),
      TEXT(e.what()),
      TEXT("Runtime Error!"),
      MB_OK | MB_ICONERROR
      );
}
some_memory_deallocation_function(memory_buffer);
```

Also, if you haven't done so already, familiarize yourself with the documentation that accompanies your specific development environment and compiler. In particular, know how to include the required header files and how to link with static and dynamic libraries. (If you're having problems with these issues, feel free to contact us via email; our email addresses are provided at the end of this introduction.)

The *Black Book* Philosophy

Written by experienced professionals, Coriolis *Black Books* provide immediate solutions to global programming and administrative challenges, helping you complete specific tasks, especially critical ones that are not well documented in other books. The *Black Book*'s unique two-part chapter format—thorough technical overviews followed by practical immediate solutions—is structured to help you use your knowledge, solve problems, and quickly master complex technical issues to become an expert. By breaking down complex topics into easily manageable components, this format helps you quickly find what you're looking for, with the diagrams and code you need to make it happen.

We welcome your feedback on this book. You can either email The Coriolis Group at **ctp@coriolis.com** or email us directly at **dmc27@ee.cornell.edu** and **foetsch@crosswinds.net**. Errata, updates, and more are available at **www.coriolis.com**.

Part I

The Windows GDI

Chapter 1

Device Contexts

If you need an immediate solution to:	See page:

In Depth

Whether you're rendering a complex animation or simply drawing the outline of a button, you'll need some type of surface to draw on. If you're a cartoonist, this surface is usually a piece of drawing paper. If you're a painter, this surface is usually a canvas. If you're a graffiti artist, this surface is more often than not the side of a building. And if you're a Windows developer, this surface is a *device context*.

As it turns out, a device context, or *DC* for short, is much more than a simple drawing surface. Technically, a device context is a data structure that defines the attributes and associated graphic objects that will affect graphical representations on a device. For most applications, this device is the display monitor. Conceptually, however, a device context is very much like a painter's canvas.

In this chapter, we'll examine the various types of device contexts, their uses, and the techniques and rules governing the use of a device context's associated graphic objects. We'll also discuss several rendering modes and how you can adjust these modes to suit your specific needs. In addition, we'll examine how to retrieve device-specific information from a device context and how this information is used to influence the approach you'll take when rendering. Finally, we'll discuss how to speed up the rendering process, and we'll explore some approaches that can be used to eliminate flicker.

Types of Device Contexts

The GDI (Graphics Device Interface) provides four types of device contexts. These are listed in Table 1.1. Here we'll limit our discussion to the first three types.

As with most Windows objects, you never work directly with a device context itself; instead, you manipulate a device context through its handle of type **HDC**.

Table 1.1 Types of GDI device contexts.

DC Type	Device
Display	Used for video display monitors
Memory	Created to be compatible with other devices
Information	Yields information on any device
Printer	Used for hard-copy printing devices—laser, ink jet, dot matrix, plotters

The **HDC** handle type is used for all types of device contexts. Indeed, the *type* of device context that you'll want to use depends on the type of device that you're interested in rendering to.

Display Device Contexts

A display device context is used to render graphical output to the display monitor, often referred to as the *video display*. This is the most commonly used type of device context because it's typically associated with a specific window. There are five kinds of display device contexts: *common*, *private*, *class*, *parent*, and *window*. Aside from private and class device contexts, all display device contexts are maintained by Windows in an exclusive GDI device-context cache. Because of this fact, any changes made to a display device context are lost when it is released.

Common Device Contexts

Device contexts are an integral part of the Windows user interface, and as such, they are used ubiquitously throughout Windows. Undoubtedly, the most frequent use of a DC is that of rendering a window. Most windows that are rendered to the video display are rendered through the use of a *common device context* or *common DC*. A common device context is a type of display DC that is used to render graphical output to the client area of a window. The common DC is the default type of device context for all windows (i.e., it requires no specification in the **WNDCLASS::style** or **WNDCLASSEX::style** data member).

Typically, rendering to a common DC is performed in response to the **WM_ERASEBKGND** and **WM_PAINT** messages. With the **WM_ERASEBKGND** message, a handle to the corresponding window's common DC is indicated by the associated **wParam** argument. Therefore, you are free to render to this device context without any extra work. However, with the **WM_PAINT** message, a handle to the common DC of the corresponding window is generally not provided. Here you must manually obtain a handle to the window's common DC. You can do this by using the **GetDC**, **GetDCEx**, or **BeginPaint** functions. We'll return to this issue shortly.

Private Device Contexts

A *private device context* is similar to a common device context except that the former is *not* retrieved from the GDI device-context cache. Instead, Windows allocates separate memory for a private device context so that any attribute changes (of graphic object associations and modes) are maintained throughout the lifetime of the corresponding window. Because of this memory allocation, private device contexts are useful for graphics-intensive applications and can significantly reduce the time required to produce a graphical representation A window whose class is registered with the **CS_OWNDC** class style is created with a private device context.

As with the common DC, rendering to a private DC is usually performed in response to the **WM_ERASEBKGND** and **WM_PAINT** messages. We'll examine private DCs more closely later in this chapter—when we examine how to use a private DC for enhanced performance (see the section called "Using a Private Device Context for Speed").

Class Device Contexts

A *class device context* is similar to a private device context in that neither is retrieved from the GDI device-context cache. The difference is that a class DC is shared by all windows of a particular class. Specifically, when a class is registered with the **CS_CLASSDC** class style, a single class DC is created when a window of that class is created. All subsequent windows of the same class share this single class DC. Rendering to this type of device context is no different from rendering to a common or private device context. In addition, as is the case with a common or private DC, rendering to a class DC is most often performed in response to the **WM_ERASEBKGND** and **WM_PAINT** messages.

Parent Device Contexts

A *parent device context* is used by some child windows to eliminate expensive clipping initializations. A parent DC is identical to a common DC except that renderings made to a parent DC are not clipped to the bounds of the control itself; rather, output is clipped to the bounds of the control's *parent* window. A parent DC is used by a control whose class is registered with the **CS_PARENTDC** class style. As with a common DC, output to a parent DC is typically performed in response to the **WM_ERASEBKGND** and **WM_PAINT** messages.

Window Device Contexts

A *window device context* is identical to a common device context. The only difference is that when you render to a window DC your output is not clipped to the client area of the corresponding window. Because of this fact, you can draw in the non-client areas of the window as well. For example, a window's title bar and system menu icon are rendered to its window DC. Moreover, all window DCs are retrieved from the GDI device-context cache even if the window itself uses a private or class DC. Typically, rendering to a window DC is performed in response to the **WM_NCPAINT** message.

The Memory Device Context

A *memory device context*, as its name suggests, is used with a bitmap object to render graphical representations off screen. When you perform a painting or drawing operation to a display DC, the result is immediately visible on the video display. In many situations, however, this is not necessarily desirable. If you render to a memory DC, the GDI will not display the results to the screen; rather, the rendering is directed to a bitmap object.

Moreover, anything that you do render to a display DC is only temporary. This is one of the main reasons that most painting and drawing routines are performed in response to the **WM_PAINT** message. For example, if you draw an ellipse to the display DC of your window in response to the click of a button, two things will happen: First, unless your window was created with a private device context, any changes made to your window's device context will be lost when the DC is released. Second, the next time your window is refreshed (via **WM_ERASEBKGND** and/or **WM_PAINT**), some or all of your drawing might be lost.

A memory device context is created via the **CreateCompatibleDC** function. The name of this function comes from the fact that a memory device context is often called a *compatible* or *virtual* device context. The compatibility element comes from the fact that memory device contexts are always created to be compatible with a specific device. In addition, because you can direct most of the same GDI functions to a memory DC just as you would to a non-memory DC, you can think of a memory DC as a virtual representation of a device context.

Memory device contexts have two frequent uses. First, for rendering windowed controls, memory DCs are used when direct output to a common DC would otherwise result in flicker. Second, memory DCs are used to manipulate bitmap objects. Although it's entirely possible to change the pixels of a bitmap (i.e., a DIB section bitmap) via direct memory manipulation, the GDI provides several high-level functions that can be used to easily render graphical primitives to a device context. Imagine the hassle of drawing even a simple ellipse via direct memory manipulation. We'll return to these issues later in this chapter (see "Memory Device Contexts"). For more information on bitmaps, see Chapters 6 and 7.

The Information Device Context

When a device context is created, it's given certain default graphic objects and modes (discussed next). Often it's necessary to access information about a specific device from these default values. Instead of performing the costly operation of creating a device context and its default objects, you can use a special type of device context known as an *information device context* (or simply *information context*). By using an information context, you can access default device information faster and more efficiently than you can by creating, for example, a display or printer device context.

Device Context Attributes

A device context is more than just a drawing surface—it also contains information that governs how rendering operations will be represented on its corresponding device. This information is stored via a device context's associated *graphic objects*, *text* and *background colors*, and *graphic modes*.

Graphic Objects

The GDI provides seven graphic objects that can be associated with a device context. These are listed in Table 1.2.

Each of these graphic objects provides different types of output to the target device. The *brush* object is used primarily for filling and painting operations. The *pen* object is used for line drawing and outlining operations. The *font* object is used to render textual output. *Bitmaps* are used to render bitmapped images. *Palettes* are used to map color indices to colors that are available on the device. *Regions* and *paths* are used for both clipping and defining specialized figures.

If you think of a device context as a page from a coloring book, we can build a familiar correspondence between each of these graphic objects and their real-world counterparts. Following this analogy, the brush object represents a particular physical brush (e.g., bristle, foam, sponge, and roller) and a particular color of paint. The pen object represents a physical pen (or crayon) and the color of its ink (wax). The font object represents a set of rubber stamps, in which each stamp represents a character from a particular alphabet. The bitmap object represents a picture clipping (e.g., from a magazine article) or photograph. The palette object defines the colors that the paper can accurately retain. The region object represents the interior of an outlined figure (i.e., the objects in the picture), and the path object represents the boundary of this outline.

It's not my intention here to explore each of these graphic objects in depth; I'll examine all of these objects more closely in their respective chapters. The take-home message is that graphic objects can be used to render various types of graphical output to a device via a device context. In this chapter, I'll focus on issues specifically related to the interaction of graphic objects and device contexts.

Table 1.2 A device context's corresponding graphic objects.

Graphic Object	Handle Type	Related Structure
Brush	**HBRUSH**	**LOGBRUSH**
Pen	**HPEN**	**LOGPEN**, **EXTLOGPEN**
Font	**HFONT**	**LOGFONT**, **EXTLOGFONT**
Bitmap	**HBITMAP**	**BITMAP**, **DIBSECTION**
Palette	**HPALETTE**	**LOGPALETTE**
Region	**HRGN**	**RGNDATA**
Path	None	None

Associating a Graphic Object with a Device Context

In most cases, before you can use a graphic object for a drawing or painting operation, you'll need to associate your graphic object with the target device context. This task is accomplished with the **SelectObject** function:

```
HGDIOBJ SelectObject(
    IN HDC hdc,               // handle to the target device context
    IN HGDIOBJ hgdiobj        // handle to the graphic object to associate
  );
```

The **SelectObject** function simply associates a particular graphic object with a device context. This association process is commonly referred to as ***selecting an object into a device context***—thus the name **SelectObject**. This process is also called *realization* because the target device must *realize* (make real) a physical object that corresponds to the specified logical object. If you imagine selecting a yellow pen into a device context that corresponds to an ink jet printer, the printer realizes the yellow pen by using its yellow-colored ink.

Because only one instance of each type of graphic object can be selected into a device context at any given time, if the **SelectObject** function is successful, it returns a handle to the previously selected object of the same type. (**HGDIOBJ** is a generic type that indicates a handle to any graphic object.) If the **SelectObject** function fails, however, the return value is **NULL**. Moreover, the return value differs if you select a region into a device context. In this case, the return value is one of the constants listed in Table 1.3.

WARNING! Do not use the SelectObject function for palettes. Palettes are selected via the SelectPalette function (see Chapter 9).

TIP: *If you're interested in filling a rectangular area with a particular color, you do not necessarily have to select a brush into a device context—both the* ***FillRect*** *and* ***FillRgn*** *functions accept a handle to a brush object.*

Table 1.3 Return values of the SelectObject function when selecting a region into a device context.

Return Value	Value	Description
SIMPLEREGION	2	The selected region comprises only a single rectangle
COMPLEXREGION	3	The selected region comprises more than one rectangle
NULLREGION	1	The selected region has zero dimensions
GDI_ERROR	–1	The **SelectObject** function has failed

If the graphic object that you're selecting into a device context is not a region, you should save the returned value so that you can restore the device context to its original state before releasing it. You perform this restoration by calling the **SelectObject** function again, this time specifying the handle of the original (stored) graphic object (i.e., the return value of the first call to the **SelectObject** function):

```
HDC hDC = GetDC(hWnd);
HPEN hPen = CreatePen(PS_SOLID, 5, PALETTERGB(0, 0, 255));
HPEN hOldPen = static_cast<HPEN>(SelectObject(hDC, hPen));
try
{
   //
   // perform rendering to hDC...
   //
}
catch (...)
{
   SelectObject(hDC, hOldPen);
   DeleteObject(hPen);
   ReleaseDC(hWnd, hDC);
}
SelectObject(hDC, hOldPen);
DeleteObject(hPen);
ReleaseDC(hWnd, hDC);
```

Selecting the original graphic object back into the device context does two things. First, it deselects the new graphic object from the device context, giving you an opportunity to free the object by using the **DeleteObject** function. This is important because you shouldn't free a brush or pen while it is selected into a device context. (This is not an issue with bitmap objects, but it's a good habit to get into nonetheless.) Second, if you're given the device context from, for example, a third-party library, restoring the device context will ensure that an unaltered version is returned to the supplier.

NOTE: *If you've retrieved a DC from the GDI device-context cache, you don't necessarily have to store, and then select, the original graphic object back into the DC before you release it. Because a "clean" DC is one that has only stock graphic objects selected into it, you can alternatively select a stock object (of the appropriate type) back into the DC before you release it. This scheme, of course, may not be well suited if you've retrieved your DC from another source (e.g., a third-party library).*

It's customary to see the restoration and deletion steps performed via a composite of the **SelectObject** and **DeleteObject** functions:

```
DeleteObject(SelectObject(hDC, hOldPen));
```

This technique is valid because the **SelectObject** function returns a handle to the previously selected object. Moreover, because the return value is of type **HGDIOBJ**, during your *initial* call to the **SelectObject** function, you'll need to cast the return value to the type of graphic object you are storing. In the previous example, we used the **static_cast** typecast operator:

```
HPEN hOldPen = static_cast<HPEN>(SelectObject(hDC, hPen));
```

To avoid the hassle of casting the return value, one approach is to store the return value in a generic **HGDIOBJ**-type variable:

```
HGDIOBJ hOldPen = SelectObject(hDC, hPen);
```

Another technique is to use the appropriate GDI-related macro as defined in the windowsx.h header file. For object selection, you use the macro specifically tuned to the type of graphic object that you're working with. These macros include:

```
SelectPen(hdc, hpen);        // for pen objects
SelectBrush(hdc, hbr);       // for brush objects
SelectFont(hdc, hfont);      // for font objects
SelectBitmap(hdc, hbm);      // for bitmap objects
```

Also note that, unlike the **dynamic_cast** operator, the **static_cast** operator has no runtime cost associated with its use. Using the macros just mentioned, however, can enhance the readability of your code.

Retrieving a Graphic Object from a Device Context

As I mentioned, device contexts are inherently linked to graphic objects. When you use the **SelectObject** function to select a new graphic object into a device context, you are returned a handle to the currently selected object of the same type (note that this statement does not apply when the graphic object is a region). There might be times, however, when you need to retrieve information about an object that is currently selected into a device context. For example, if a third-party library function gives you a handle to a display device context, and you'd like to render a solid blue rectangle to this device context, you might want to determine if the device context already contains the appropriate brush.

Given a handle to a device context, you can obtain a handle to any of its currently associated graphic objects by using the **GetCurrentObject** function:

```
HGDIOBJ GetCurrentObject(
    IN HDC hdc,             // handle to target device context
    IN UINT uObjectType     // predefined constant that identifies the
                            // type of graphic object to retrieve
   );
```

The **GetCurrentObject** function takes two parameters. The **hdc** parameter is simply the handle to the device context from which you want to retrieve the handle to the selected graphic object. The type of graphic object whose handle you want to retrieve is indicated by the **uObjectType** parameter. This parameter can be specified as one of the constants listed in Table 1.4.

When the **OBJ_BITMAP** identifier is used, the **hdc** parameter must correspond to a memory device context. This is because bitmaps can be selected only into memory device contexts. For other graphic objects, the **hdc** parameter can indicate a memory *or* non-memory device context. For example, to retrieve a handle to the selected brush, you call the **GetCurrentObject** function, specifying the handle to the target device context and the **OBJ_BRUSH** identifier:

```
HBRUSH hCurrentBrush = static_cast<HBRUSH>(
   GetCurrentObject(hDC, OBJ_BRUSH)
   );
```

Note that the handle to the graphic object returned by the **GetCurrentObject** function is not a handle to a copy; it is a handle to the actual graphic object. Therefore, you should use this handle with care. For example, you should never pass the returned handle to the current pen or brush object to the **DeleteObject** function.

Once you have a handle to a particular graphic object, you can determine its attributes by using the **GetObject** function:

Table 1.4 Possible values for the uObjectType parameter.

Identifier Constant	Value	Effect
OBJ_BRUSH	2	The return value is a handle to the current brush
OBJ_PEN	1	The return value is a handle to the current pen
OBJ_FONT	6	The return value is a handle to the current font
OBJ_BITMAP	7	The return value is a handle to the current bitmap
OBJ_PAL	5	The return value is a handle to the current palette
OBJ_COLORSPACE	14	The return value is a handle to an ICM (Image Color Management) color space

```
int GetObject(
    IN HGDIOBJ hgdiobj,     // handle to the graphic object to query
    IN int cbBuffer,        // number of bytes that the buffer indicated via
                            // the lpvObject parameter can hold
    OUT LPVOID lpvObject    // pointer to a buffer in which the graphic
                            // object information will be stored
   );
```

The **hgdiobj** parameter is specified as a handle to the graphic object whose information you want to retrieve. This information is placed in the buffer indicated by the **lpvObject** parameter. The size of this buffer is specified by the **cbBuffer** argument. The **GetObject** function will return the number of bytes that it copies into the **lpvObject** buffer.

The type of information returned in the **lpvObject** parameter varies according to the type of object indicated by the **hgdiobj** parameter. For example, if the **hgdiobj** parameter is specified as a handle to a brush object, then the buffer is filled with information from a corresponding **LOGBRUSH** structure. Therefore, the **lpvObject** is typically specified as the address of a variable of the appropriate type. For example, when retrieving information about a brush object, you pass the address of a **LOGBRUSH**-type variable as the **lpvObject** parameter:

```
HBRUSH HCurrentBrush = static_cast<HBRUSH>(
   GetCurrentObject(hDC, OBJ_BRUSH)
   );

LOGBRUSH lb;
if (GetObject(HCurrentBrush, sizeof(LOGBRUSH), &lb) == sizeof(LOGBRUSH))
{
   // ...
}
```

Similarly, to retrieve the width and height of the selected bitmap object, you pass the address of a **BITMAP**-type variable as the **lpvObject** parameter:

```
HBITMAP hCurrentBmp = static_cast<HBITMAP>(
      GetCurrentObject(hMemDC, OBJ_BITMAP)
      );

BITMAP bmp;
if (GetObject(hCurrentBmp, sizeof(BITMAP), &bmp) == sizeof(BITMAP))
{
   int bitmap_width = bmp.bmWidth;
   int bitmap_height = bmp.bmHeight;
   // ...
}
```

When the **GetObject** function is called with the **hgdiobj** parameter specified as the handle of a palette, the **lpvObject** function is filled with a 16-bit value indicating the number of entries in the palette:

```
HPALETTE hPal = static_cast<HPALETTE>(
   GetCurrentObject(hDC, OBJ_PAL)
   );

WORD num_pal_entries;
if (GetObject(hPal, sizeof(WORD), &num_pal_entries))
{
   // ...
}
```

TIP: *If you're interested in the palette entries themselves, use the* ***GetPaletteEntries*** *function (see Chapter 9).*

A special situation arises when you're working with a handle to a pen returned by the **GetCurrentObject** function. Although you can indeed obtain a handle to the pen by specifying the **OBJ_PEN** identifier, you don't know whether this pen is a normal or extended pen. Therefore, you won't know whether to pass the address of a **LOGPEN**-type variable or the address of a **EXTLOGPEN**-type variable as the **lpvObject** parameter to the **GetObject** function. Fortunately, the answer to the problem is as simple as a single call to the **GetObjectType** function.

Classifying a Graphic Object Based on Its Handle

The GDI provides the **GetObjectType** function, which can be used to distinguish between different types of graphic objects (including a pen and an extended pen) based solely on the object's handle:

```
DWORD GetObjectType(
    IN HGDIOBJ h        // handle to the graphic object to query
   );
```

The single parameter, **h**, is a handle to the graphic object whose type you want to determine. If the function is successful, it returns one of the constants listed in Table 1.5. (If the **GetObjectType** function fails, it returns zero.)

If you pass the **GetObjectType** function a handle to an object other than those listed in Table 1.5, the return value is zero. To use the **GetObjectType** function for distinguishing between a pen and an extended pen, you test the return value for equality with **OBJ_PEN** and **OBJ_EXTPEN**, respectively:

Table 1.5 Possible return values of the GetObjectType function.

Identifier Constant	Value	Interpretation
OBJ_BRUSH	2	The handle refers to a brush object
OBJ_PEN	1	The handle refers to a pen object
OBJ_EXTPEN	11	The handle refers to an extended pen object
OBJ_FONT	6	The handle refers to a font object
OBJ_BITMAP	7	The handle refers to a bitmap object
OBJ_PAL	5	The handle refers to a logical palette
OBJ_REGION	8	The handle refers to a region
OBJ_DC	3	The handle refers to a non-memory DC
OBJ_MEMDC	10	The handle refers to a memory DC
OBJ_METAFILE	9	The handle refers to a metafile
OBJ_METADC	4	The handle refers to a metafile DC
OBJ_ENHMETAFILE	13	The handle refers to an enhanced metafile
OBJ_ENHMETADC	12	The handle refers to an enhanced metafile DC
OBJ_COLORSPACE	14	The handle refers to an ICM color space

```
DWORD dwType = GetObjectType(hCurrentPen);
if (dwType == OBJ_PEN)
{
   LOGPEN lp;
   GetObject(hCurrentPen, sizeof(LOGPEN), &lp);
   // ...
}
else if (dwType == OBJ_EXTPEN)
{
   EXTLOGPEN xlp;
   GetObject(hCurrentPen, sizeof(EXTLOGPEN), &xlp);
   // ...
}
```

Text and Background Colors

In addition to the various graphic objects, a device context also maintains two color quantities: *text color* and *background color*.

Text Color

A device context's *text color*, as its name suggests, defines the foreground color in which all textual output will be rendered. This value is important because, as we'll discuss in Chapter 4, the GDI font object does not store any color information. Again, if you think of a font object as a set of rubber stamps, the stamps alone are not linked to a particular color; rather the color depends on the color of the dye in whatever stamp pad is used. Following this analogy, a device context's text color is the color of the dye in the stamp pad.

The current text color is retrieved via the **GetTextColor** function and specified via the **SetTextColor** function. The default text color of a display device context is governed by the current system text-color setting. For more information on text color, refer to Chapter 4.

Background Color

While the value of the text color defines the foreground color of all rendered characters, the value of the *background color* defines the color behind these characters and many other drawing operations. For example, when you're rendering a dashed line with a non-extended pen, the background color is used to fill in the gaps between each dash. When you're rendering with a font object, the background color is the color that appears behind the characters. A device context's background color is also the color that is used to fill in the spaces between the hatch marks of a hatch brush object. Again, relating a device context to a page from a coloring book, the background color is analogous to the color of the paper itself.

A device context's current background color is retrieved via the **GetBkColor** function and changed via the **SetBkColor** function. Display device contexts are created with a default background color identical to the current system background-color setting.

Graphic Modes

While its associated graphic objects are used for drawing and painting, and its text and background colors govern the coloration of certain renderings, a device context also stores information about how rendering operations will affect the final output. This information is contained in a device context's *graphic modes*. Table 1.6 lists the five graphic modes that are associated with a device context.

Background Mode

The *background mode* of a device context, also called the *background mixing mode*, determines how the background color is mixed with the device context's existing drawings. As it turns out, this mode is not quite as sophisticated as it may sound. Simply put, the background mode governs whether or not the background color is used when you're drawing to a device context.

If you've ever used Microsoft Paint to draw text, you've probably worked with the background mode without even knowing it. If you check the Draw Opaque option

Table 1.6 A device context's graphic modes.

Graphic Mode	Effect
Background	Determines how the background color is mixed with colors of any existing drawings
Drawing	Determines how the foreground color is mixed with colors of any existing drawings
Filling	Determines which areas of a complex shape are filled with the current brush
Stretching	Determines which pixels are discarded and/or altered when a bitmap is compacted (rendered smaller than its actual dimensions)
Mapping	Determines how logical coordinates are mapped to device coordinates

in the Options menu, the background of any rendered text is automatically filled with the currently selected background color. Unchecking this menu item causes the program to draw the text transparently—so that the letters are visible but the background is not filled.

The GDI defines two background modes: **OPAQUE** and **TRANSPARENT**. When the background mode is set to **OPAQUE**, the current background color is used to fill the background when you're rendering with a hatched brush, a non-solid pen, or a font object. When the background mode is set to **TRANSPARENT**, the current background color is ignored, meaning that the background is not altered when you're rendering with any of the aforementioned graphic objects.

The current background mode of a device context is retrieved via the **GetBkMode** function and altered via the **SetBkMode** function. This latter function is particularly helpful for creating transparent controls. The default background mode of a display device context is **OPAQUE**.

Drawing Mode

A device context's *drawing mode* determines how the foreground color is mixed with colors of any existing drawings. This mode is also called the *foreground mixing mode*, but it's most commonly referred to as the *binary-raster-operation mode* or simply *ROP2 mode*. This name arises from the fact that the drawing mode governs how the GDI combines bits of the destination bitmap (memory device context) with the color of the current pen. The "binary" prefix comes from the fact that there are two *operands*—the current pen (or brush) and the destination memory. The drawing mode determines which *operator* (**AND**, **NOT**, **OR**, or **XOR**) is used to combine the bits of each operand. When a filled shape is rendered, the drawing mode also determines how the bits of the current brush and the bits of the destination bitmap are combined.

WARNING! Do not confuse the drawing mode with the polygon-filling mode. The latter is used only to define which areas of a complex polygon are filled.

The drawing mode is retrieved via the **GetROP2** function and specified via the **SetROP2** function. The default drawing mode of a display device context is **R2_COPYPEN**.

NOTE: *The drawing mode is relevant for only those devices that support binary raster operations.*

When you're rendering filled shapes, the drawing mode also determines how the existing colors are mixed with the current brush object. This feature also applies to filled shapes rendered via the **FillPath** and **StrokeAndFillPath** functions. However, the drawing mode is not used when a brush object is used to manually fill an area via the **FillRect** function. For example, when you're using the **Rectangle** function to render a filled rectangle, the drawing mode *will* influence the appearance of the filled area:

```
HDC hDC = GetDC(hWnd);
HBRUSH hBrush =
   CreateSolidBrush(PALETTERGB(0, 0, 255));
HBRUSH hOldBrush =
   static_cast<HBRUSH>(SelectObject(hDC, hBrush));
try
{
   SetROP2(hDC, R2_NOT);
   Rectangle(hDC, 0, 0, 100, 100);
}
catch (...)
{
   DeleteObject(SelectObject(hDC, hOldBrush));
   ReleaseDC(hWnd, hDC);
}
DeleteObject(SelectObject(hDC, hOldBrush));
ReleaseDC(hWnd, hDC);
```

This is in contrast to using the **FillRect** function to fill a rectangle. In this case, even if the current brush is used, the output is *not* affected by the drawing mode:

```
HDC hDC = GetDC(hWnd);
HBRUSH hBrush =
   CreateSolidBrush(PALETTERGB(0, 0, 255));
HBRUSH hOldBrush =
   static_cast<HBRUSH>(SelectObject(hDC, hBrush));
try
{
   SetROP2(hDC, R2_NOT);
```

```
    HBRUSH HCurrentBrush =
        static_cast<HBRUSH>(
            GetCurrentObject(hDC, OBJ_BRUSH)
            );
    RECT R = {0, 0, 100, 100};
    FillRect(hDC, &R, HCurrentBrush);
}
catch (...)
{
    DeleteObject(SelectObject(hDC, hOldBrush));
    ReleaseDC(hWnd, hDC);
}
```

Filling Mode

When you're rendering a simple shape via the **Polygon** function, for example, typically the interior area is filled with the current brush. This results from the fact that **Polygon** and its related functions are designed for drawing filled shapes. However, when you draw a complex shape that comprises several different interior shapes, you might want to control how the interior is filled—this is where the filling mode of the target device context comes into play.

When you're filling a complex polygon with a brush object, a device context's *filling mode* determines which areas of the shape are filled. The GDI defines two filling modes: alternate mode (**ALTERNATE**) and winding-number mode (**WINDING**). When the device context is set to use the alternate filling mode, the GDI fills only the areas that lie between odd- and even-numbered sides of the polygon. When the device context is set to use the winding-number filling mode, the GDI fills an area only if a horizontal ray extending from within the area to the outer-left edge of the polygon crosses an unequal number of directionally (upward/downward) drawn sides.

A device context's filling mode is retrieved via the **GetPolyFillMode** function and changed via the **SetPolyFillMode** function. The default filling mode of a display device context is **ALTERNATE**. For more information on the filling mode, refer to Chapter 5.

Stretching Mode

Imagine that you need to draw a bitmap such that the rendered version is smaller than the actual image size. In this case, you need to scale the bitmap down. Suppose, for the moment, that the GDI did not provide the **StretchBlt** function. If this were the case, you would need to manually implement an algorithm for removing some of the bitmap's pixels. The question now would be: which pixels do you want to remove? For a simple line drawing, you could probably just throw out X out of every N pixels. Yet if you were rendering a picture of a human face, for example, simply discarding pixels would probably result in poor image quality. Indeed, in this case, you'd want to use a halftoning technique. In other words, the compacting (scaling down) method that you'd want to use would depend heavily on the *type* of image that you were rendering. This is the purpose of a device context's stretching mode—it governs how the **StretchBlt** function performs its compaction.

The GDI defines four stretching modes: **BLACKONWHITE**, **WHITEONBLACK**, **COLORONCOLOR**, and **HALFTONE**. The **BLACKONWHITE** and **WHITEONBLACK** stretching modes are typically used only for stretching monochrome bitmaps. For color bitmaps, the **BLACKONWHITE** stretching mode uses the Boolean **AND** operator to combine the colors of preserved and eliminated pixels; the **WHITEONBLACK** stretching mode uses the Boolean **OR** operator to combine these colors. The **COLORONCOLOR** stretching mode is used when colors must be preserved. With this mode, pixels are simply discarded and no colors are combined. The **HALFTONE** stretching mode is used for rendering natural images. In this mode, an average color value is computed from a block of pixels, the computed color is assigned to the preserved pixel, and then the surrounding pixels are discarded.

WARNING! When using a dithered, hatched, or patterned brush object, you must track and reset the brush origin after setting the stretching mode to HALFTONE (see Chapter 2).

The current stretching mode is retrieved via the **GetStretchBltMode** function and specified via the **SetStretchBltMode** function. The default stretching mode of a display device context is **BLACKONWHITE**.

NOTE: *Windows 95 and Windows 98 have a bug that prevents the stretching mode from being adjusted. On these platforms, the stretching mode is always* ***COLORONCOLOR****. This bug is not present in Windows NT and Windows 2000.*

Mapping Mode

Because a device context, in part, represents a device-specific drawing surface, when you're rendering to a DC, logical coordinates need to be mapped to device coordinates before output can be directed to the device. This mapping is defined by the device context's *mapping mode*, which affects nearly all output to the DC.

Two rectangles are used to define the mapping from logical space to device space—the *window* for logical space and the *viewport* for device space. Each of these rectangles, in turn, is represented by four values: an *origin* (X, Y) and a pair of *extents* (dX, dY). When the window origin differs from the viewport origin, the GDI performs a translation. Likewise, when the window extents differ from the viewport extents, a scaling operation is performed.

The GDI presents eight mapping modes; these are listed in Table 1.7. The default mapping mode for a display device context is **MM_TEXT**, and the window and viewport origins are both (0, 0). In all cases, you can adjust the window origin and viewport origins. For some mapping modes, however, the window extents and viewport extents remain fixed (by design).

The current mapping mode is retrieved via the **GetMapMode** function and changed via the **SetMapMode** function.

To adjust the window or viewport origin, use the **SetWindowOrgEx** or **SetViewportOrgEx** function, respectively. To adjust the window or viewport extent, use the **SetWindowExtEx** or **SetViewportExtEx** function, respectively. For more information on mapping modes, origins, and extents, refer to Chapter 10.

Table 1.7 A device context's eight mapping modes.

Mapping Mode	Value	Effect
MM_TEXT	1	The window and viewport extents are fixed at one (i.e., no scaling). The positive x-axis points rightward, and the positive y-axis points downward.
MM_LOMETRIC	2	The window and viewport extents are fixed such that one logical unit maps to 0.1 millimeters on the target device. The positive x-axis points rightward, and the positive y-axis points upward.
MM_HIMETRIC	3	The window and viewport extents are fixed such that one logical unit maps to 0.01 millimeters on the target device. The positive x-axis points rightward, and the positive y-axis points upward.
MM_LOENGLISH	4	The window and viewport extents are fixed such that one logical unit maps to 0.01 inches on the target device. The positive x-axis points rightward, and the positive y-axis points upward.
MM_HIENGLISH	5	The window and viewport extents are fixed such that one logical unit maps to 0.001 inches on the target device. The positive x-axis points rightward, and the positive y-axis points upward.
MM_TWIPS	6	The window and viewport extents are fixed such that one logical unit maps to 0.0006944 inches on the target device. The positive x-axis points rightward, and the positive y-axis points upward.
MM_ISOTROPIC	7	The window and viewport extents can be specified by the user. However, the extents are scaled such that one logical unit maps to the same device distance in both the horizontal and vertical directions.
MM_ANISOTROPIC	8	The window and viewport extents can be specified by the user.

The WM_PAINT Message

Windows sends the **WM_PAINT** message to a window when some portion of that window's client area needs to be painted. This portion is called the *invalidated region* of the window. In addition, the **WM_PAINT** message is a *queued message*. That is, it passes through an application's main message pump before it is sent to a particular window within the application. Because painting messages are considered low-priority messages, **WM_PAINT** is sent to a window only when there are no other messages in the queue. This scheme helps reduce unnecessary rendering because multiple painting messages can be combined into a single message, thus reducing the number of times a window needs to repaint its contents.

The **WM_PAINT** message is simply a signal between Windows and a window indicating that some operation has taken place that may have disturbed the contents of a window's appearance. Yet you may ask: "Why does a windowed control need to be painted more than once?" Indeed, this is a common consideration when you're first working with custom controls or the GDI because most of the predefined control classes are *self-refreshing*. Let's explore this topic further by examining the nature of the underlying rendering-delegation mechanism.

Why Use the WM_PAINT Message?

Many users examine the behavior of Windows itself and are quickly convinced that there is, in fact, some depth to the screen. For example, one may think that when an application is activated and placed in front of all the other windows, it is actually "on top" of the other windows. Indeed, our visual system is accustomed to the idea of depth perception; in many instances what we perceive is not actually what is physically present.

Although we all know that the screen of our display monitor is actually a two-dimensional surface, Windows does a good job of simulating the third dimension. In fact, the entire screen can be thought of as a single large bitmap in which each window occupies a defined area. When a window is "on top" of another window, the top window actually occupies some, or all, of the bottom window's screen bitmap portion. Neither window is actually on top; rather, the window lower in z-order is instructed not to paint in the area occupied by any window higher in z-order. Because the single screen bitmap must be shared by all windows, each window must be capable of constantly rendering any portion that is not obscured by other windows. This task is accomplished by rendering in response to the **WM_PAINT** message.

Using the GetDC and ReleaseDC Functions in Response to the WM_PAINT Message

The **WM_PAINT** message is typically handled explicitly within a window's window procedure. Using the **GetDC** function, you can get a handle to the device context on which to perform any rendering. Let's examine such a message handler by considering the example depicted in Figure 1.1.

Here our goal is simply to render the words "Persistent Text" to the client area of our window. The rendered text will indeed be persistent because we'll perform the rendering in response to the **WM_PAINT** message. The code for this example is provided in Listing 1.1.

Listing 1.1 Using the GetDC and ReleaseDC functions in response to the WM_PAINT message.

```
// ——————————————————————————
// Windows 2000 Graphics API Black Book
// Chapter 1 - Listing 1.1 (GetDC/ReleaseDC WM_PAINT Demo)
// ——————————————————————————

#include <windows.h>

const char* WndClassName = "GMainWnd";
LRESULT CALLBACK MainWndProc(HWND hWnd, UINT msg, WPARAM wParam,
   LPARAM lParam);

int APIENTRY WinMain(HINSTANCE hInstance, HINSTANCE HPrevInstance,
    LPTSTR lpCmdLine, int nCmdShow)
{
   WNDCLASS wc;
   memset(&wc, 0, sizeof(WNDCLASS));

   wc.style = CS_VREDRAW | CS_HREDRAW | CS_DBLCLKS;
   wc.lpfnWndProc = MainWndProc;
   wc.hInstance = hInstance;
   wc.hCursor = LoadCursor(NULL, IDC_ARROW);
   wc.hbrBackground =
      reinterpret_cast<HBRUSH>(COLOR_BTNFACE + 1);
```

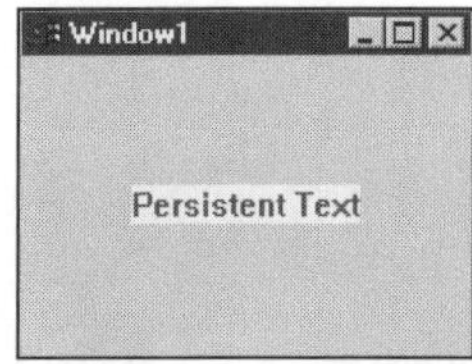

Figure 1.1 Rendering in response to the WM_PAINT message.

```
    wc.lpszClassName = WndClassName;

    if (RegisterClass(&wc))
    {
       HWND hWnd =
          CreateWindow(WndClassName, "Window1",
                       WS_OVERLAPPEDWINDOW | WS_CAPTION | WS_VISIBLE,
                       CW_USEDEFAULT, CW_USEDEFAULT, 200, 150,
                       NULL, NULL, hInstance, NULL);

       if (hWnd)
       {
          ShowWindow(hWnd, nCmdShow);
          UpdateWindow(hWnd);

          MSG msg;
          while (GetMessage(&msg, NULL, 0, 0))
          {
              TranslateMessage(&msg);
              DispatchMessage(&msg);
          }
       }
     }
     return 0;
}

LRESULT CALLBACK MainWndProc(HWND hWnd, UINT msg, WPARAM wParam,
   LPARAM lParam)
{
   switch (msg)
   {
      case WM_PAINT:
      {
         // determine the invalidated area of the window
         RECT RUpdate;
         GetUpdateRect(hWnd, &RUpdate, false);  // note!

         //
         // grab a handle to our window's
         // common display device context
         //
         HDC hDC = GetDC(hWnd);
         try
         {
            RECT RClient;
            GetClientRect(hWnd, &RClient);
```

```
            // set the clipping region
            IntersectClipRect(hDC, RUpdate.left, RUpdate.top,
                              RUpdate.right, RUpdate.bottom);  // note!

            // fill the client area with the background brush
            HBRUSH hBrush =
               reinterpret_cast<HBRUSH>(
                  GetClassLong(hWnd, GCL_HBRBACKGROUND)
                  );
            FillRect(hDC, &RClient, hBrush);

            // render the persistent text
            const char* text = "Persistent Text";
            SetTextColor(hDC, PALETTERGB(0, 0, 255));
            DrawText(hDC, text, strlen(text), &RClient,
                  DT_CENTER | DT_VCENTER | DT_SINGLELINE);
         }
         catch (...)
         {
            // release the device context
            ReleaseDC(hWnd, hDC);
            // validate the update area
            ValidateRect(hWnd, &RUpdate);  // note!
         }
         // release the device context
         ReleaseDC(hWnd, hDC);
         // validate the update area
         ValidateRect(hWnd, &RUpdate);  // note!

         break;
      }
      case WM_DESTROY:
      {
         PostQuitMessage(0);
         return 0;
      }
   }
   return DefWindowProc(hWnd, msg, wParam, lParam);
}
```

The bulk of the code in Listing 1.1 is used for the window creation and application setup. The key routine follows the **case** statement for the **WM_PAINT** message. Specifically, you use the **GetDC** function to retrieve a handle to the device context of the target window, perform any necessary rendering to this device context (in this case, we simply filled the background of our window, then rendered some text), and then release the device context via the **ReleaseDC** function. And, although it's not entirely necessary for our simple example, you should use an appropriate means of error handling to ensure that the **ReleaseDC** function will indeed be called. (In this case, we used ordinary exception handling.)

For general rendering, use of the **GetDC** and **ReleaseDC** combination is appropriate. However, in specific response to the **WM_PAINT** message, these functions are cumbersome to use. In Listing 1.1, note that we first used the **GetUpdateRect** function to retrieve a rectangle defining the invalidated portions of our window; we then used this result in an explicit call to the **ValidateRect** function. As its name suggests, the **ValidateRect** function is used to validate an arbitrary portion of a window's client area. Validation simply removes the specified area from the window's update region. In fact, this function call is absolutely necessary because Windows will continue to send **WM_PAINT** messages until the entire update region is validated. If you fail to validate the invalidated areas, your application's message pump will receive a continuous stream of **WM_PAINT** messages. It is the hassle of this validation procedure that the **BeginPaint** and **EndPaint** functions relieve.

Using the BeginPaint and EndPaint Functions in Response to the WM_PAINT Message

As I just mentioned, any invalidated portions of a window's client area must be validated to avoid a flood of **WM_PAINT** messages. In the previous example, we used the **ValidateRect** function to accomplish this chore. In fact, the **ValidateRect** function need not be called explicitly. Instead, typical **WM_PAINT** handlers use the **BeginPaint** and **EndPaint** functions to ease many of the tasks that we performed in our example. Each of these functions accepts a handle to a window as its first parameter and accepts the address of a **PAINTSTRUCT** structure as its second parameter:

```
typedef struct tagPAINTSTRUCT {
    HDC  hdc;
    bool fErase;
    RECT rcPaint;
    bool fRestore;
    bool fIncUpdate;
    BYTE rgbReserved[32];
} PAINTSTRUCT;
```

The **PAINTSTRUCT::hdc** data member holds the handle to the device context on which the rendering operation will be performed. This member is identical to the handle returned by the call to **BeginPaint**. The **fErase** data member is simply a flag that indicates whether or not the background should be erased. If this flag is set, the **BeginPaint** function will send the corresponding window the **WM_ERASEBKGND** message before proceeding. The **rcPaint** data member is a rectangle defining the update area, and it is identical to the rectangle filled by a call to the **GetUpdateRect** function. The last three data members—**fRestore**, **fIncUpdate**, and **rgbReserved**—are used internally by Windows.

Because the **BeginPaint** function fills the supplied **PAINSTRUCT** variable's **rcPaint** data member, use of this function removes the need to call the **GetUpdateRect** function. In fact, the **rcPaint** data member isn't really needed because the **BeginPaint** function automatically validates the update region and sets the appropriate clipping region. In addition, the **EndPaint** function automatically releases the device context, which means that there's no need to call the **ReleaseDC** function. Let's redefine the code (of Listing 1.1) that follows the **case** statement for the **WM_PAINT** message by using the **BeginPaint** and **EndPaint** functions in Listing 1.2.

Listing 1.2 Using the BeginPaint and EndPaint functions in response to the WM_PAINT message.

```
// ————————————————————————————
// Windows 2000 Graphics API Black Book
// Chapter 1 - Listing 1.2 (BeginPaint/EndPaint WM_PAINT Demo)
// ————————————————————————————
case WM_PAINT:
{
   //
   // grab a handle to our window's
   // common display device context
   //
   PAINTSTRUCT ps;
   HDC hDC = BeginPaint(hWnd, &ps);
   try
   {
      RECT RClient;
      GetClientRect(hWnd, &RClient);

      const char* text = "Persistent Text";
      SetTextColor(hDC, PALETTERGB(0, 0, 255));
      DrawText(hDC, text, strlen(text), &RClient,
               DT_CENTER | DT_VCENTER | DT_SINGLELINE);
   }
   catch (...)
   {
      //
      // release the device context
      // and validate the update area
      //
      EndPaint(hWnd, &ps);
   }
```

```
    //
    // release the device context
    // and validate the update area
    //
    EndPaint(hWnd, &ps);
    break;
}
```

The single call to the **BeginPaint** function in Listing 1.2 allows us to remove many of the previous function calls. First, notice that **BeginPaint** returns a handle to the device context of our window. This eliminates the need for the **GetDC** function. Next, **BeginPaint** automatically selects the clipping region into the device context, eliminating the need for the **GetUpdateRect** and **IntersectRect** function calls. Finally, the **BeginPaint** function automatically validates the entire client area, eliminating the need for the **ValidateRect** function.

The painting operation is closed via the **EndPaint** function. **EndPaint** releases the device context returned by **BeginPaint**, eliminating the need for an explicit call to the **ReleaseDC** function. Because a call to **BeginPaint** must be followed by a call to **EndPaint**, we use exception handling to guarantee that the **EndPaint** function will be called.

Using the BeginPaint and EndPaint Functions in General

Because the **BeginPaint** and **EndPaint** functions are extremely helpful for use in rendering a window's client area, you might be wondering if you can use these functions elsewhere. Although you can indeed use the **BeginPaint** and **EndPaint** functions anywhere in your code, these functions are designed primarily for use in response to the **WM_PAINT** message. In fact, if you call the **BeginPaint** function elsewhere and then render to the returned device context, you will not see any output. This can be explained by recalling that the **BeginPaint** function automatically sets the clipping region of the returned device context to the area indicated by the invalidated portions of your window's client area. Yet if you do not call **BeginPaint** in response to the **WM_PAINT** message, there are, in fact, no invalidated areas (unless explicitly forced). Therefore, the clipping region has zero dimension (**NULLREGION**), and your rendering operation will have no effect. You can convince yourself that this is indeed the case by examining the width and height of the **rcPaint** data member of the **PAINTSTRUCT** structure that is passed into the **BeginPaint** function.

The WM_ERASEBKGND Message

Typically, the default window procedure handles the **WM_ERASEBKGND** message and fills the background with the brush object specified in the **hbrBackground** data member of the **WNDCLASS** structure that is used to initially register the window's class. However, if this data member is specified as **NULL**, the **WM_ERASEBKGND** message can be handled to fill the background manually. Explicitly handling this message can be useful if further customization is needed when the window's background must be drawn.

Unlike the **WM_PAINT** message, the **WM_ERASEBKGND** message is not a queued message. It is sent directly to the window procedure whenever the **BeginPaint** function is called. This provides an opportunity for the background to be filled with a certain color, pattern, or image before any primary rendering takes place. If the **WM_ERASEBKGND** message is not explicitly handled, and the **hbrBackground** data member is **NULL**, the background will not be erased, and remnants from underlying windows might remain visible. In most situations, the **hbrBackground** data member is specified, informing Windows that the background should be filled. In some situations, however, it is undesirable to have the background filled because subsequent drawing or painting operations will obscure the background. Also, recall that the **hbrBackground** data member is a class-wide specification. That is, the brush object indicated by this member will be used to fill the background of all windows of the class. For some classes, this might not be appropriate because you might want to give the user the ability to change the background color of only a single instance of the class.

Why Use the WM_ERASEBKGND Message?

Although it's possible to render the background of a window from within a handler for the **WM_PAINT** message, this approach can often lead to flicker. Suppose that you specify the handle to a gray brush object as the **hbrBackground** data member, but you fill a window's client area with a red brush object in response to the **WM_PAINT** message. Each time the **BeginPaint** function is called, the default window procedure receives the **WM_ERASEBKGND** message and fills the window's background with the gray brush object. Then the code following the **BeginPaint** function call executes; now the background is again filled, this time with the red brush object. We can see here that this scheme is rather inefficient, and on slower systems the initial background filling operation might be visible. Typically, if the rendering code of the **WM_PAINT** message handler fills the entire client area, then the **hbrBackground** is set to **NULL** or the **WM_ERASEBKGND** message is trapped.

Rendering a Background Image in Response to the WM_ERASEBKGND Message

An ideal time to render a background image to a window is in response to the **WM_ERASEBKGND** message. Because this message is sent whenever the window's background needs updating, you can safely render a background image without worrying about it conflicting with any previous drawings that might have been performed in response to the **WM_PAINT** message. Moreover, because a handle to the common device context of the corresponding window is supplied by the **wParam** argument, all that's required is a simple typecast. (That is, you do not have to call the **BeginPaint** or **GetDC** function.) Moreover, you don't need to release this device context—the caller (the sender of the message) is responsible for this task.

Saving and Restoring a Device Context

When you're rendering to a device context with multiple graphic objects, it's often cumbersome to store the current graphic object, replace it, perform the drawing operation, and then restore the original graphic object. In addition to being a hassle, this process is error-prone. Fortunately, the GDI provides a way to make this task easier. By using the **SaveDC** function before changing a device context, you can effectively instruct the GDI to remember the current state of the device context. Later, when you need to restore the device context back to its saved state, you simply use the **RestoreDC** function.

Consider a common situation, when handling the **WM_PAINT** message, in which a custom brush, a pen, and a font object need to be selected into a device context. Recall that before you release the device context you need to restore the previously selected graphic objects. Therefore, you always need to store the return values of the initial calls to the **SelectObject** function (or select a stock object back into the DC):

```
HDC hDC = GetDC(hWnd);
HBRUSH hBrush =
   CreateSolidBrush(PALETTERGB(0, 0, 255));
HPEN hPen =
   CreatePen(PS_SOLID, 2, PALETTERGB(255, 0, 0));
HFONT hFont =
   static_cast<HFONT>(GetStockObject(OEM_FIXED_FONT));

HBRUSH hOldBrush =
   static_cast<HBRUSH>(SelectObject(hDC, hBrush));
HPEN hOldPen =
   static_cast<HPEN>(SelectObject(hDC, hPen));
SelectObject(hDC, hFont);  // stock font
try
{
   //
   // render to hDC...
   //
}
```

```
catch (...)
{
   SelectObject(hDC, hOldBrush);
   SelectObject(hDC, hOldPen);
   DeleteObject(hBrush);
   DeleteObject(hPen);
   ReleaseDC(hWnd, hDC);
}
SelectObject(hDC, hOldBrush);
SelectObject(hDC, hOldPen);
DeleteObject(hBrush);
DeleteObject(hPen);
ReleaseDC(hWnd, hDC);
```

The **SaveDC** function, in effect, takes a "snapshot" of the device context, and the **RestoreDC** function uses this "picture" to reinstate the device context. Utilizing these functions, you can rewrite the previous code as follows:

```
HDC hDC = GetDC(hWnd);
HBRUSH hBrush =
   CreateSolidBrush(PALETTERGB(0, 0, 255));
HPEN hPen =
   CreatePen(PS_SOLID, 2, PALETTERGB(255, 0, 0));
HFONT hFont =
   static_cast<HFONT>(GetStockObject(OEM_FIXED_FONT));

const int save_id = SaveDC(hDC);

SelectObject(hDC, hBrush);
SelectObject(hDC, hPen);
SelectObject(hDC, hFont);
try
{
   //
   // render to hDC...
   //
}
catch (...)
{
   RestoreDC(hDC, save_id);
   DeleteObject(hBrush);
   DeleteObject(hPen);
   ReleaseDC(hWnd, hDC);
}
```

```
RestoreDC(hDC, save_id);
DeleteObject(hBrush);
DeleteObject(hPen);
ReleaseDC(hWnd, hDC);
```

The **SaveDC** function takes only a single parameter, a handle to the device context whose current attributes are to be saved:

```
int SaveDC(
    IN HDC hdc         // handle to device context to be saved
   );
```

If the **SaveDC** function is successful, the return value is an integer identifying the saved state. This value is an ordinal number indicating how many restoration operations are required. The restoration is accomplished via the **RestoreDC** function:

```
BOOL RestoreDC(
    IN HDC hdc,         // handle to device context to be restored
    IN int nSavedDC     // specifies saved state-identifier
   );
```

This function takes as its first parameter a handle to a previously saved device context, and takes as its second parameter the return value of the corresponding **SaveDC** function. You can also pass a value of –1 as the **nSavedDC** parameter to revert to the most recent saved state. The **RestoreDC** function returns a Boolean value indicating success or failure.

The **SaveDC** function stores nearly all attributes of the device context. For example, the current brush, pen, font, bitmap, palette, and region are stored. The function also saves the current background and text colors, background mode, drawing mode, and mapping mode. The viewport origin, brush origin, and (if applicable) window origin are also preserved, as are the viewport and (if applicable) window extents. However, don't expect the **SaveDC** function to save what's drawn to the device context. The **SaveDC** and **RestoreDC** functions are designed to preserve only the *attributes* of a device context, not its rendered content. Use a memory device context and a bitmap object to save a device context's current drawings (appearance).

Note that calls to the **SaveDC** and **RestoreDC** functions can be nested. You just need to ensure that each call to the **SaveDC** function has a corresponding call to the **RestoreDC** function:

```
const int save_id = SaveDC(hDC);
try
{
   // ...
   const int save_id2 = SaveDC(hDC);
   try
   {
      // ...
   }
   catch (...)
   {
      RestoreDC(hDC, save_id2); // or RestoreDC(hDC, -1);
      throw;
   }
   RestoreDC(hDC, save_id2); // or RestoreDC(hDC, -1);
}
catch (...)
{
   RestoreDC(hDC, save_id); // or RestoreDC(hDC, -1);
}
RestoreDC(hDC, save_id); // or RestoreDC(hDC, -1);
```

As a final note, there is a downside to using the **SaveDC** and **RestoreDC** functions. Because the GDI must store the state of the device context to the GDI stack and then use this memory to reinstate the device context, there is both a memory cost and a performance cost. Fortunately, the GDI provides an alternative approach—the use of the private device context—that eliminates the performance overhead.

Using a Private Device Context for Speed

A *private device context* is a type of display device context that's strictly associated with a specific window. Recall that, unlike a common or window device context, a private device context is not retrieved from the GDI device-context cache. This means that any attribute changes (in modes, colors, origins, and graphic objects) that you make to a private device context are preserved until you explicitly modify them. This also means that you never have to use the **ReleaseDC** function to explicitly release a private device context; it is automatically freed when the associated window is destroyed. Moreover, because a private device context is preserved throughout the lifetime of its associated window, you need to retrieve its handle only once.

***NOTE:** Because a private device context is stored in memory until its associated window is destroyed, its use will increase the memory requirements of your application. Although this increase is rarely significant (on the order of 1K of memory), you should use a private device context only when increased performance is required.*

How can a private device context help speed up your painting process? Well, it won't speed up the actual rendering. That is, the rendering routines are not executed any faster when directed to a private device context versus, say, a common device context. What a private device context can do, however, is reduce the number of times you need to perform any initializations. For example, if you need to draw to a common device context by using a custom brush, a pen, a font, and a bitmap object, you'll need to explicitly associate these objects with the device context each time it's retrieved from the GDI device-context cache. This same argument applies for any changes that you need to make in the modes, colors, or origins of the common device context. Often these initializations are performed in response to the **WM_PAINT** message, which is sent many times throughout the lifetime of a window. Clearly, this scheme is less than optimal. Using a private device context, on the other hand, you need to perform these initializations only once. That is, you can store the handle to a window's private device context in response to, for example, the **WM_CREATE** message, carry out any necessary initializations, and then perform only the key rendering routines in response to the **WM_PAINT** message. Because the initialization process is executed only once, the speed of the overall painting process can be increased.

***TIP:** If you perform only minimal initializations, you won't see a significant increase in performance when using a private device context instead of a common device context. If you're experiencing flicker, use a double-buffering approach instead.*

Creating a Window That Uses a Private Device Context

To create a window that uses a private device context, you add the **CS_OWNDC** bit to the **style** data member of the **WNDCLASS** structure that is used during registration of the window's class:

```
WNDCLASS wc;
memset(&wc, 0, sizeof(WNDCLASS));
wc.style = /* other style bits | */ CS_OWNDC;
```

After the window's class is registered and the window is created, you can use the **GetDC** function to retrieve a handle to its private device context. You should also store this value for use in subsequent rendering operations:

```
HDC hPrivateDC;
LRESULT CALLBACK MainWndProc(HWND hWnd, UINT msg, WPARAM wParam,
   LPARAM lParam)
```

```
{
   switch (msg)
   {
      case WM_CREATE:
      {
         hPrivateDC = GetDC(hWnd);
         //
         // perform any initializations...
         //
         break;
      }
      // use hPrivateDC elsewhere...
   }
   // ...
}
```

After a handle to your window's private device context is stored, you'll never need to call the **GetDC** function again. The return value of subsequent calls will be identical to that of the first call to the **GetDC** function (i.e., the value of the stored handle).

Rendering to a Private Device Context

There is nothing special about rendering to a private device context as opposed to a common device context. The techniques for both types are identical. In fact, you can think of a private device context as a *static* common device context.

You won't need to call the **BeginPaint** function in response to the **WM_PAINT** message to retrieve a handle to your window's private device context (because you've already stored this value). You might, however, want to use the **BeginPaint** function for the purpose of clipping and validation. Although the GDI automatically clips a private device context to the client area of its associated window, you'll most likely want to clip your output to only the update area (the area that requires repainting). Moreover, to avoid a continuous stream of **WM_PAINT** messages, you'll still need to validate this update area. Either you can carry out the clipping and validation tasks manually (with **GetUpdateRect** and **ValidateRect**, for example), or you can delegate these tasks to the **BeginPaint** function. Note that in this case, the **BeginPaint** function is used *only* for the purpose of clipping and validation—the handle that the **BeginPaint** function returns is identical to the stored handle (i.e., the handle to the private DC that you retrieved earlier). The stored private-device-context handle is also the same handle indicated by the **wParam** parameter associated with the **WM_ERASEBKGND** message. This means that once you've stored a handle to your window's private device context, there's no need to use the supplied **wParam** argument in response to the **WM_ERASEBKGND** message.

Obtaining a Handle to a Common Device Context

Should you ever need a handle to the common device context of a window that uses a private device context, you can use the **GetDCEx** function with the **DCX_CACHE** flag. This flag instructs the function to return a handle to a common device context, regardless of the specified window's current setup. In this case, because the returned device context is retrieved from the GDI device-context cache, you need to ensure that the DC is released via the **ReleaseDC** function:

```
HDC hCommonDC = GetDCEx(hWnd, NULL, DCX_CACHE);
try
{
   // ...
}
catch (...)
{
   ReleaseDC(hWnd, hCommonDC);
}
ReleaseDC(hWnd, hCommonDC);
```

The process of creating and using a private device context is straightforward. In fact, once the window itself is created, you'll most likely find that working with a private device context is *easier* than working with a common device context. This results from the fact that you don't need to repeatedly perform any rote initializations.

Bit-Block Transfer

When the output of a rendering operation is directed to a display device context, that output is immediately visible on the video display. In contrast, when the output of a rendering operation is directed to a *memory* device context, that output is *not* immediately visible on the video display. Instead, the results are stored in memory; specifically, the memory associated with the pixels of a bitmap object. When you want to display these pixels on the screen, you'll need a way to transfer them to a display device context. To do this, you can use any of the bit-block transfer functions. This technique of transferring bits is commonly referred to as *blitting*.

The BitBlt Function

The **BitBlt** function is the most commonly used method for blitting. The name "BitBlt" originates from the purpose of the function—it performs a BIT-BLock Transfer. When you use the **BitBlt** function to render output from a memory device context to a display device context, this transfer entails copying the bits of a bitmap object to the section of video display memory associated with the target display DC (i.e., a portion of the screen bitmap). When you use the **BitBlt** function to render output to and from a memory device context, the bits of the source bitmap are copied to those of the destination bitmap. You can also use the **BitBlt** function to transfer the bits associated with a display device context (video display memory) to those associated with a memory device context (its currently selected bitmap) or even to those associated with another display device context.

The StretchBlt Function

The **StretchBlt** function is much like the **BitBlt** function—the result is a transfer of memory. Most often, this transfer entails copying the bits of a bitmap object to a portion of video display memory that is associated with a specific section of the screen (i.e., to a display device context). Other times, this transfer is performed strictly between user-defined bitmap objects or strictly between display device contexts. The **StretchBlt** function, however, offers more functionality than does the **BitBlt** function. As its name suggests, the **StretchBlt** function can be used to render a bitmap image in an expanded (stretched) or compressed (compacted) fashion.

The **StretchBlt** function is ideal when you need to display a bitmap image so that the entire bitmap is drawn to fit within the bounds of a given rectangular area. For example, if you need to add zooming capabilities to your application, you'll want to render the image in a larger or smaller fashion. Instead of manually replicating or deleting pixels, you can simply use the **StretchBlt** function, in which the zooming factor is determined by the ratio between the size of the destination rectangle and the size of the original image. The **StretchBlt** function can also be used to resize an image.

Recall that the **StretchBlt** function operates according to the target device context's current stretching mode. Specifically, when the size of the destination rectangle is less than that of the source image, some pixels need to be discarded. Therefore, the current stretching mode of the destination device context governs exactly which pixels are deleted.

Ternary Raster Operations

The **BitBlt** and **StretchBlt** functions can perform more than a simple bitwise copy operation. They also let you specify how the bits of the source bitmap are combined with those of the destination bitmap. This is similar to the drawing mode of a device context except that the **BitBlt** and **StretchBlt** functions use a *ternary raster operation* (*ROP3*) instead of a binary raster operation (ROP2).

When a binary raster operation is used, the GDI is instructed on how to combine the color of the current pen (or brush) with colors of the target bitmap. There are only two operands—a pen (or brush) and a bitmap. A ternary raster operation specifies how the colors of *three* operands are combined—the source bitmap, the target device context's current brush, and the destination bitmap. Because a ternary raster operation involves three operands and four operators (**NOT**, **AND**, **OR**, and **XOR**), there are a total of 256 different combinations (ROP3 codes) as opposed to the 16 binary-raster-operation codes.

Rarely are all 256 ternary-raster-operation codes used. The GDI assigns only 17 identifiers to the most commonly used ROP3 codes. These identifiers are listed in Table 1.8.

Mismatched Color Formats

What happens when the destination device context has a color format different from that of the source device context? The resulting color format is always that of the destination device context. That is, the **BitBlt** or **StretchBlt** function

Table 1.8 Ternary-raster-operation constants.

ROP3 Identifier	Effect
SRCCOPY	Destination = source
SRCPAINT	Destination = source **OR** destination
SRCAND	Destination = source **AND** destination
SRCINVERT	Destination = source **XOR** destination
SRCERASE	Destination = source **AND** (**NOT** destination)
NOTSRCCOPY	Destination = **NOT** source
NOTSRCERASE	Destination = (**NOT** source) **AND** (**NOT** destination)
MERGECOPY	Destination = (source **AND** brush)
MERGEPAINT	Destination = (**NOT** source) **OR** destination
PATCOPY	Destination = brush
PATPAINT	Destination = destination **OR** (brush **OR** (**NOT** source))
PATINVERT	Destination = brush **XOR** destination
DSTINVERT	Destination = **NOT** destination
BLACKNESS	Destination = black
WHITENESS	Destination = white
NOMIRRORBITMAP	Windows 98 and 2000 only: Do not mirror the image
CAPTUREBLT	Windows 98 and 2000 only: Consider layered windows

automatically adjusts the colors of the result so that they match the color format of the destination device context. Often, however, this conversion is less than optimal. If necessary, you should make a copy of the original bitmap, and then manually adjust its colors to match the color format of the destination device context before blitting (see Chapter 16).

Memory Device Contexts

Unlike other graphic objects, bitmaps can be selected into only a memory device context. To direct any GDI rendering functions to a memory device context, you must first provide the memory DC with an associated bitmap. Therefore, memory device contexts and bitmap objects are used together almost exclusively. Although you can also select other graphic objects into a memory device context and perform drawing or painting functions, a bitmap object must be selected into the memory device context for these rendering operations to be stored. In short, the bitmap object serves as the “memory” of the memory device context.

Bitmaps

When a memory device context is created, it’s given most of the same default attributes as those of a non-memory device context. However, unlike non-memory device contexts, memory device contexts are created with a default “placeholder” bitmap object. This bitmap is monochrome (one bit per pixel) and contains exactly one pixel (it is one pixel wide and high). You can convince yourself of this fact by using the **GetCurrentObject** function to retrieve a handle to the placeholder bitmap and then using the **GetObject** function to fill an associated **BITMAP** structure:

```
// ...
HBITMAP hBmp =
    static_cast<HBITMAP>(GetCurrentObject(hMemDC, OBJ_BITMAP));
BITMAP bmp;
GetObject(hBmp, sizeof(BITMAP), &bmp);
// ...
```

After executing this code, you can examine the **BITMAP::bmWidth**, **bmHeight**, and **bmBitsPixel** data members—they will all indicate one.

Most often, you’ll want to replace the default bitmap with one that can hold more bits. To do this, you first use the **CreateCompatibleBitmap** function to create a bitmap object (i.e., a device-dependent bitmap) that is compatible with the same device as that of the memory device context.

NOTE: *The* ***CreateCompatibleBitmap*** *function always creates a device-dependent bitmap. As we'll discuss in Chapter 6, device-dependent bitmaps suffer from the fact that they're always limited to the color format of a specific device (e.g., the screen). In Chapter 7, we'll discuss the DIB section bitmap, which does not suffer from this limitation.*

After you create the memory device context and the compatible bitmap object, you use the **SelectObject** function to select the bitmap object into the memory device context. This technique is similar to that of selecting other graphic objects into a display device context; however, bitmaps can be selected only into memory device contexts and into only one memory device context at any given time. Again, the bitmap serves as the underlying memory of the memory device context; therefore, any drawing or painting directed to the memory device context will be stored in the bitmap. It is commonplace to see references to "rendering to a bitmap" instead of "rendering to a memory device context," but both of these statements are accurate.

Although the **CreateCompatibleBitmap** function is commonly used to create a bitmap for a memory device context, you are not restricted to this function. For example, you can use the **LoadImage** function to load a bitmap object from a file, and then select this bitmap into the memory device context:

```
// create a memory DC compatible with the screen
HDC hMemDC = CreateCompatibleDC(NULL);

// load a bitmap from a file
HBITMAP hBmp =
   static_cast<HBITMAP>(
      LoadImage(hInst, "MYBITMAP.BMP", IMAGE_BITMAP,
                0, 0, LR_LOADFROMFILE)
                );

// select the bitmap into the memory DC
HBITMAP hOldBmp = SelectObject(hMemDC, hBmp);
// ...
```

Flicker Reduction

Whether you're working with something as simple as an owner-drawn control or as complex as a three-dimensional animation, you're bound to run into flicker. Not only is this phenomenon annoying, but it might also conflict with the intended functionality of your application.

Flicker originates from our ability to perceive a difference between two images, and it's governed by the temporal frequency at which these images are displayed. For example, most modern monitors are refreshed 75 times per second. In this case, the first image is a blank display, and the second image consists of what you normally see on the screen. Clearly, there is a noticeable difference between a blank surface and the Windows desktop. However, because the image of the desktop is displayed at a frequency beyond that at which we can perceive the intermediate blank screen, we do not notice the flicker.

In an application, flicker typically results when a drawing needs to be erased and subsequently changed—this might be a change in location or a change in the image itself. When these two operations cannot be performed fast enough (at a high enough frequency), the result is a flickering effect.

The most widely used approach to flicker elimination is a technique called *double-buffering*. The idea behind this approach can best be appreciated by considering the following analogy:

> Our friend John is hired to paint a picture of a penguin on the ceiling of his neighbor's office. After obtaining a ladder and the proper painting supplies, John looks up at the ceiling and realizes that such a task will take quite a while. Hastily concluding that a cramped neck and a sore arm are bound to result, he decides to contract the job out. While gathering his supplies and preparing to leave, John notices that his neighbor has a blank canvas sitting in the corner of the room—he is then struck with a moment of inspiration. Quickly grabbing the canvas and propping it up against the ladder, John easily paints the feathered friend in no time at all. He pins the masterpiece to the ceiling and hands his neighbor an invoice shortly thereafter.

In the same way that it's more time-consuming for John to paint the penguin directly on the ceiling, drawing or painting directly to a display device context is generally slower than rendering to a memory device context. As you direct rendering operations to a display device context, the GDI must communicate with the display device driver so that the results are represented on the video display. For this reason, drawing or painting operations that are performed off screen (on a canvas leaned against a ladder) usually require less work than rendering directly to the screen (ceiling). Here you can think of John's canvas as a *back-buffer* (a memory device context with an associated bitmap), and think of the ceiling as a display surface (a display device context). When you're actually ready to display the contents of the bitmap, you can simply block-transfer the bits (pin the canvas) to the target display device context (the ceiling).

To reinforce the idea behind this procedure, and its advantages, let's consider two approaches to rendering a series of concentric ellipses to the device context of a window. First, let's examine the classical approach that does not use a memory device context. Here the output is rendered directly to the target display device context:

```
RECT RWork;
if (SystemParametersInfo(SPI_GETWORKAREA, 0, &RWork, NULL))
{
   // resize to full work area of the primary screen
   const int width = RWork.right - RWork.left;
   const int height = RWork.bottom - RWork.top;
   MoveWindow(hWnd, 0, 0, width, height, true);

   // grab a handle to the display DC
   HDC hDC = GetDC(hWnd);
   try
   {
      // paint it black (see also PatBlt)
      HBRUSH hBlackBrush =
         static_cast<HBRUSH>(GetStockObject(BLACK_BRUSH));
      FillRect(hDC, &RWork, hBlackBrush);

      // perform the rendering to the display DC
      for (int index = 0; index < 200; ++index)
      {
         Ellipse(hDC, RWork.left, RWork.top,
                 RWork.right, RWork.bottom);
         InflateRect(&RWork, -2, -2);
      }
   }
   catch (...)
   {
      ReleaseDC(hWnd, hDC);
   }
   ReleaseDC(hWnd, hDC);
}
```

If you execute the code from this first technique, the area of the rendered ellipses will gradually decrease as each ellipse is immediately drawn to the screen in response to the **Ellipse** function call. If you wrap the previous code into a single function and then call this function repetitively, you're bound to experience flicker. To avoid this, let's rewrite the implementation to use a double-buffered approach:

```
RECT RWork;
if (SystemParametersInfo(SPI_GETWORKAREA, 0, &RWork, NULL))
{
   // resize to full work area of the primary screen
   const int width = RWork.right - RWork.left;
   const int height = RWork.bottom - RWork.top;
   MoveWindow(hWnd, 0, 0, width, height, true);

   // grab a handle to the display DC
   HDC hDC = GetDC(hWnd);

   // create the back-buffer
   HDC hMemDC = CreateCompatibleDC(hDC);
   HBITMAP hBmp =
      CreateCompatibleBitmap(hDC, width, height);
   HBITMAP hOldBmp =
      static_cast<HBITMAP>(SelectObject(hMemDC, hBmp));
   try
   {
      // paint it black (see also PatBlt)
      HBRUSH hBlackBrush =
         static_cast<HBRUSH>(GetStockObject(BLACK_BRUSH));
      FillRect(hMemDC, &RWork, hBlackBrush);

      // perform the rendering to the back-buffer
      for (int index = 0; index < 200; ++index)
      {
         Ellipse(hMemDC, RWork.left, RWork.top,
                 RWork.right, RWork.bottom);
         InflateRect(&RWork, -2, -2);
      }

      //
      // bit-block transfer the bits of
      // the back-buffer to the display DC
      //
      BitBlt(hDC, 0, 0, width, height, hMemDC, 0, 0,
             SRCCOPY);
   }
   catch (...)
   {
      // clean up
      DeleteObject(SelectObject(hMemDC, hOldBmp));
      DeleteDC(hMemDC);
      ReleaseDC(hWnd, hDC);
   }
```

```
    // clean up
    DeleteObject(SelectObject(hMemDC, hOldBmp));
    DeleteDC(hMemDC);
    ReleaseDC(hWnd, hDC);
}
```

In contrast to the first technique, the double-buffered approach does not display the result to the screen until all ellipses are rendered. That is, the drawing is first directed to the back-buffer and then transferred to the screen in one shot. Specifically, because the memory device context and the bitmap object together serve as the back-buffer, the ellipses are stored in the bits of the bitmap. When the final ellipse is drawn, these bits are transferred to the display device context via the **BitBlt** function.

In addition to using double-buffering, you should also get rid of any unnecessary erasing routines. The process of erasing involves replacing the pixels of the rendered object with those from the appropriate background area. When the background is a solid color, this manipulation simply involves filling the background with a brush object. In fact, this procedure is exactly what most windows do in response to the **WM_ERASEBKGND** message. Yet when the entire client area of a window is completely obscured by a drawing, as is often the case, there is no need to fill the background. For example, it would make little sense to call the **FillRect** function in response to the **WM_ERASEBKGND** message only to fill this same area with a drawing in response to the **WM_PAINT** message.

Immediate Solutions

Obtaining a Handle to a Display Device Context

In this section, we'll examine the methods that are used to obtain a handle to a display device context.

Grabbing a Handle to the Common Device Context of a Window

To obtain a handle to the common device context of a window, you use either the **GetDC** function or the **BeginPaint** function. The **GetDC** function is used primarily for general rendering, and the **BeginPaint** function is used strictly in response to the **WM_PAINT** message.

The GetDC and ReleaseDC Functions

The **GetDC** function requires only one parameter: a handle to a window. The handle that is passed into the function determines which window's client area the output will be clipped to:

```
HDC GetDC(
   IN HWND hWnd      // handle to the target window
   );
```

By default, all windows are created with a common device context. Because common DCs are retrieved from an internally maintained cache, you must be sure to release the device context when you no longer need it. This task is accomplished with the **ReleaseDC** function:

```
int ReleaseDC(
    IN HWND hWnd,      // handle to the target window
    IN HDC hDC         // handle to the device context to release
   );
```

The **ReleaseDC** function takes two parameters. The **hWnd** parameter identifies the handle of the window whose device context will be released. The handle of the device context itself is specified by the **hDC** parameter. Note that the **hWnd** parameter of the **ReleaseDC** function contains the value passed to the **GetDC** function:

```
HDC hDC = GetDC(hWnd);
//
// perform any rendering to hDC...
//
ReleaseDC(hWnd, hDC);
```

NOTE: *After a device context is released, any changes that you make to it are lost. For example, if you use the* ***SetTextColor*** *function to change the text color of the device context, this alteration is not preserved after the device context is returned to the system. This is not the case, however, when the* ***GetDC*** *function is used to retrieve a handle to a private device context (i.e., the device context of a window created with the* ***CS_OWNDC*** *class style). In this case, the* ***ReleaseDC*** *function has no effect.*

When you're working with a window that uses a common device context, the **GetDC** and **ReleaseDC** functions are almost always used together. That is, 99 percent of the time, you will follow a call to the **GetDC** function with a subsequent call to the **ReleaseDC** function.

The BeginPaint and EndPaint Functions

An alternative technique to obtaining a handle to the common device context of a window is to use the **BeginPaint** function. This function is usually used with the **EndPaint** function, and both are designed for use in response to the **WM_PAINT** message. Specifically, typical **WM_PAINT** handlers use these functions to make validation easier:

```
HDC BeginPaint(
    IN HWND hWnd,              // handle to the target window
    OUT LPPAINTSTRUCT lpPaint  // pointer to a PAINTSTRUCT structure
   );

bool EndPaint(
    IN HWND hWnd,                    // handle to the target window
    IN const PAINTSTRUCT *lpPaint    // pointer to a PAINTSTRUCT structure
   );
```

Both the **BeginPaint** and **EndPaint** functions require two parameters: a handle to a window (**hWnd**) and a pointer to a **PAINTSTRUCT** structure (**lpPaint**). The **hWnd** parameter of the **BeginPaint** function identifies the window whose common device context you want to retrieve a handle to. The **hWnd** parameter of the **EndPaint** function identifies the window whose common device context you want to release. For example:

```
PAINTSTRUCT ps;
HDC hDC = BeginPaint(hWnd, &ps);
//
//  perform any rendering to hDC...
//
EndPaint(hWnd, &ps);
```

If successful, the **BeginPaint** function returns a handle to the common device context of the window indicated by its **hWnd** parameter; otherwise, the return value is **NULL**. The **EndPaint** function always returns **TRUE**.

Like the **GetDC** function, the **BeginPaint** function automatically sets the clipping region of the returned common device context. With **BeginPaint**, however, the clipping region is not set to the region defined by the client area of the corresponding window; rather, the clipping region is limited to the window's update (invalidated) areas. This scheme prevents superfluous painting. The **BeginPaint** function also validates the update region and, if necessary, sends the window the **WM_ERASEBKGND** message.

Related solutions:	*Found on page:*
Obtaining the Clipping Region of a Device Context	480
Adjusting the Clipping Region of a Device Context	482
Retrieving the Bounds of a Device Context's Clipping Region	485

Grabbing a Handle to the Window Device Context of a Window

You can obtain a handle to a window's window device context by using the **GetWindowDC** function:

```
HDC GetWindowDC(
    IN HWND hWnd        // handle to the target window
  );
```

The single **HWND**-type parameter identifies the handle of the window whose window device context you want to retrieve a handle to. This DC's handle will be returned by **GetWindowDC** if the function is successful; otherwise, the return value is **NULL**. In contrast to the common device context retrieved by the **GetDC** function, here the origin of the returned device context is the top-left corner of the window itself, not of the window's client area.

Window device contexts are always retrieved from the GDI device-context cache, whether or not the window uses a private device context. Therefore, any attribute changes made to a window device context are lost after it is released. As with the

GetDC function, you use the **ReleaseDC** function to release a window device context:

```
HDC hWindowDC = GetWindowDC(hWnd);
try
{
   //
   // perform any rendering to HWindowDC...
   //
}
catch (...)
{
   ReleaseDC(hWnd, hWindowDC);
}
ReleaseDC(hWnd, hWindowDC);
```

An alternative to the **GetWindowDC** function is to use the **GetDCEx** function with the **DCX_WINDOW** flag. This flag instructs the function to return a handle to the window device context of the specified window:

```
HDC GetDCEx(
     IN HWND hWnd,        // handle to the target window
     IN HRGN hrgnClip,    // handle to the region to clip output to
     IN DWORD flags       // flags that determine the type and attributes
                          // of the returned device context
   );
```

When you're handling the **WM_NCPAINT** message, the **GetDCEx** function is more versatile than the **GetWindowDC** function. Because the **GetDCEx** function accepts a handle to a clipping region, and the **wParam** parameter associated with the **WM_NCPAINT** message is a handle to the clipping region of the window, you can simply add the **DCX_INTERSECTRGN** flag and then specify the supplied update-region handle (**wParam**) as the **hrgnClip** argument to the **GetDCEx** function. This approach eliminates the need to explicitly set the clipping region via the **SelectClipRgn** function:

```
case WM_NCPAINT:
{
   HRGN hClipRgn = reinterpret_cast<HRGN>(wParam);
   HDC hWindowDC =
      GetDCEx(hWnd, hClipRgn, DCX_WINDOW | DCX_INTERSECTRGN);
   try
   {
      //
```

```
      // render non-client areas...
      //
   }
   catch (...)
   {
      ReleaseDC(hWnd, hWindowDC);
   }
   ReleaseDC(hWnd, hWindowDC);
}
```

Grabbing a Handle to the Device Context of the Screen

You can retrieve a handle to the device context of the desktop window via the **GetDC**, **GetDCEx**, **GetWindowDC**, or **CreateDC** functions. For the first two functions, you can specify **NULL** as the **hWnd** parameter. When you do this, the returned device context handle will correspond to the window device context of the desktop window on the primary display monitor. This device context is often referred to as the device context of the screen because any rendering made to this device context is displayed on top of all other windows, including the Taskbar. For example, to render a red ellipse that spans the entire primary display screen:

```
HDC hScreenDC = GetDC(NULL);
HBRUSH hBrush = CreateSolidBrush(PALETTERGB(255, 64, 64));
HBRUSH hOldBrush =
   static_cast<HBRUSH>(SelectObject(hScreenDC, hBrush));
try
{
   const int screen_width =
      GetDeviceCaps(hScreenDC, HORZRES);
   const int screen_height =
      GetDeviceCaps(hScreenDC, VERTRES);

   Ellipse(hScreenDC, 0, 0, screen_width, screen_height);
}
catch (...)
{
   DeleteObject(SelectObject(hScreenDC, hOldBrush));
   ReleaseDC(NULL, hScreenDC);
}
DeleteObject(SelectObject(hScreenDC, hOldBrush));
ReleaseDC(NULL, hScreenDC);
```

An alternative technique is to use the **GetWindowDC** function with the **GetDesktopWindow** function. The results of this combination are identical to the results of the previous technique, but the code is slightly easier to read and understand:

```
HDC hScreenDC = GetWindowDC(GetDesktopWindow());
try
{
   //
   // perform any rendering to hScreenDC...
   //
}
catch (...)
{
   ReleaseDC(GetDesktopWindow(), hScreenDC);
}
ReleaseDC(GetDesktopWindow(), hScreenDC);
```

A third approach is to use the **CreateDC** function, specifying **"DISPLAY"** as the **lpszDriver** parameter (or **NULL** for Windows 95 or 98) and specifying the literal **"\\.\Display#"**—where # represents the ordinal number of the display monitor whose device context you want to retrieve a handle to—as the **lpszDevice** parameter:

```
HDC hScreenDC = CreateDC("DISPLAY", "\\\\.\\Display1", NULL, NULL);
try
{
   //
   // perform any rendering to hScreenDC...
   //
}
catch (...)
{
   DeleteDC(hScreenDC);
}
DeleteDC(hScreenDC);
```

Grabbing a Handle to the Device Context of the Desktop List-View Control

The GDI provides several techniques for retrieving a handle to the device context of the screen, in which case, any rendering is done on top of all windows. Indeed, because all top-level windows are children of the desktop window, this result is not surprising. However, in some situations you might want to render behind other windows on the desktop. In these situations, you don't want to work with the device context of the desktop window; rather, you need access to the device context of the desktop's list-view control.

***NOTE:** Using a tool such as Microsoft's Spy++, you can easily determine the setup of a typical desktop display. This scheme consists of a main desktop window (of class **#32769**) whose handle is the return value of the **GetDesktopWindow** function. All other windows are children of this desktop window. The Taskbar (of class **Shell_TrayWnd**), for example, is a child of the desktop window. Another well-known child of the desktop window is the Program Manager (of class **Progman**). The Program Manager window contains a single child window of class **SHELLDLL_DefView**, which in turn contains a child list-view control. It is this list-view control that contains the familiar desktop icons and wallpaper.*

You can obtain a handle to the desktop's list-view control by using a combination of the **FindWindow** and **GetWindow** functions. Once you have a handle to the list view, you can use the familiar **GetDC** or **GetDCEx** function to retrieve a handle to its common device context. In this way, any rendering is limited to the client area of the list view. Moreover, this output will appear behind all top-level windows:

```
HWND hProgMan = FindWindow("ProgMan", 0);
HWND hShellView = GetWindow(hProgMan, GW_CHILD);
HWND hListView = GetWindow(hShellView, GW_CHILD);

HDC hDC = GetDC(hListView);
HBRUSH hBrush = CreateSolidBrush(PALETTERGB(255, 64, 64));
HBRUSH hOldBrush =
   static_cast<HBRUSH>(SelectObject(hDC, hBrush));
try
{
   RECT RClient;
   GetClientRect(hListView, &RClient);
   Ellipse(hDC, RClient.left, RClient.top,
           RClient.right, RClient.bottom);
}
catch (...)
{
   DeleteObject(SelectObject(hDC, hOldBrush));
   ReleaseDC(hListView, hDC);
}
DeleteObject(SelectObject(hDC, hOldBrush));
ReleaseDC(hListView, hDC);
```

Extracting Information from a Device Context

In this section, we'll look at a few techniques for retrieving information from a device context.

Retrieving a Window Handle from a Device Context

You can obtain a handle to a display device context's associated window by using the **WindowFromDC** function:

```
HWND WindowFromDC(
    IN HDC hDC          // handle to the display device context
   );
```

The single **HDC**-type parameter is the handle of the display device context whose associated window handle will be returned. You can then use this window handle to retrieve attributes of the corresponding window. For example, using the return value of the **WindowFromDC** function, you can use the **GetClientRect** function to determine the coordinates of the client area of the device context's corresponding window:

```
HDC hDC = library_func();
HWND hWndFromDC = WindowFromDC(hDC);

RECT RClient;
GetClientRect(hWndFromDC, &RClient);
HBRUSH hBrush = reinterpret_cast<HBRUSH>(
   GetClassLong(hWndFromDC, GCL_HBRBACKGROUND)
   );
FillRect(hDC, &RClient, hBrush);
```

Retrieving Device-Specific Information from a Device Context

The **GetDeviceCaps** function is designed to yield device-specific information from a device context. As its name suggests, given a device context, this function literally **get**s the **cap**abilities of the corresponding **device**:

```
int GetDeviceCaps(
    IN HDC hdc,         // handle to target device context
    IN int nIndex       // index of device capability to retrieve
   );
```

The **hdc** parameter identifies the device context whose capabilities you want to query. The specific capability to be retrieved is specified by the **nIndex** parameter. This parameter can be assigned one of the identifiers listed in Table 1.9.

If the **GetDeviceCaps** function fails, the return value is zero; otherwise, the return value indicates the result of the capability that was queried. Let's now examine a few examples of retrieving some commonly queried capabilities.

Table 1.9 Capability identifiers for use with the GetDeviceCaps function.

Capability ID	Value	Returned Information
DRIVERVERSION	0	The version number of the device driver
TECHNOLOGY	2	The classification of the device
HORZSIZE	4	The horizontal size (in millimeters)
VERTSIZE	6	The vertical size (in millimeters)
HORZRES	8	The horizontal size (in pixels)
VERTRES	10	The vertical size (in pixels)
BITSPIXEL	12	The number of bits used to represent the color of a pixel
PLANES	14	The number of color planes
NUMBRUSHES	16	The number of brushes that the device can realize
NUMPENS	18	The number of pens that the device can realize
NUMMARKERS	20	The number of markers that the device can realize
NUMFONTS	22	The number of fonts that the device can realize
NUMCOLORS	24	The number of colors that the device supports
PDEVICESIZE	26	The size required for the device's descriptor fields
CURVECAPS	28	The device's curve rendering capabilities
LINECAPS	30	The device's line rendering capabilities
POLYGONALCAPS	32	The device's polygonal rendering capabilities
TEXTCAPS	34	The device's text rendering capabilities
CLIPCAPS	36	The device's clipping capabilities
RASTERCAPS	38	The device's bit-block transfer capabilities
ASPECTX	40	The width of a device pixel, relative to its height
ASPECTY	42	The height of a device pixel, relative to its width
ASPECTXY	44	The diagonal length of a device pixel
SHADEBLENDCAPS	45	The device's shading and blending capabilities (Win98/2000 only)
LOGPIXELSX	88	The number of logical pixels per inch in the horizontal direction
LOGPIXELSY	90	The number of logical pixels per inch in the vertical direction
SIZEPALETTE	104	The number of entries in the device's physical palette
NUMRESERVED	106	The number of reserved palette entries
COLORRES	108	The color resolution of the device
PHYSICALWIDTH	110	The physical width in device units (printer-specific)
PHYSICALHEIGHT	111	The physical height in device units (printer-specific)
PHYSICALOFFSETX	112	The physical width of the left margin (printer-specific)

(continued)

Table 1.9 Capability identifiers for use with the GetDeviceCaps function *(continued)*.

Capability ID	Value	Returned Information
PHYSICALOFFSETY	113	The physical height of the top margin (printer-specific)
SCALINGFACTORX	114	The x-axis scaling factor (printer-specific)
SCALINGFACTORY	115	The y-axis scaling factor (printer-specific)
VREFRESH	116	The current vertical refresh rate in Hz (display-specific; WinNT/2000 only)
DESKTOPVERTRES	117	The horizontal width of the entire desktop (in pixels; display-specific; WinNT/2000 only)
DESKTOPHORZRES	118	The vertical height of the entire desktop (in pixels; display-specific; WinNT/2000 only)
BLTALIGNMENT	119	The preferred horizontal blitting alignment (display-specific; WinNT/2000 only)

Determining the Dimensions of the Screen

Using the **GetDeviceCaps** function with the **HORZRES** and **VERTRES** capability identifiers, you can determine the width and height of the screen, in pixels, respectively:

```
HDC hScreenDC = GetDC(NULL);
const int width = GetDeviceCaps(hScreenDC, HORZRES);
const int height = GetDeviceCaps(hScreenDC, VERTRES);
//...
ReleaseDC(NULL, hScreenDC);
```

Computing the Number of Display Colors

You can use the **GetDeviceCaps** function with the **BITSPIXEL** capability identifier to determine how many bits per color plane are used to represent a screen pixel color. Multiplying this value by the number of color planes (**PLANES**), you can compute the number of available colors:

```
HDC hScreenDC = GetDC(NULL);
const int bpp =
   GetDeviceCaps(hScreenDC, BITSPIXEL) *
   GetDeviceCaps(hScreenDC, PLANES);
ReleaseDC(NULL, hScreenDC);

char value[12];
wsprintf(value, "%d", static_cast<int>(pow(2, bpp)));
MessageBox(hWnd, value, "Num Colors...", MB_OK);
```

WARNING! Even if the display device is set to a color depth of 15 bits per pixel, the GetDeviceCaps function (with the BITSPIXEL identifier) will return a value of 16.

Determining the Number of Pixels Per Inch

The number of screen pixels used to represent a logical inch is determined by the size of the system font (such as Small Fonts or Large Fonts). This quantity is especially important when you need to customize your application's appearance for proper display under various font size settings. Using the **GetDeviceCaps** function with the **LOGPIXELSX** capability identifier, you can determine the number of pixels per inch:

```
HDC hScreenDC = GetDC(NULL);
const int ppi = GetDeviceCaps(hScreenDC, LOGPIXELSX);
ReleaseDC(NULL, hScreenDC);

char buffer[13];
switch (ppi)
{
   case 72: lstrcpy(buffer, "Large Fonts"); break;
   case 96: lstrcpy(buffer, "Small Fonts"); break;
   default: lstrcpy(buffer, "User-Defined"); break;
}
MessageBox(hWnd, buffer, "Font Setting...", MB_OK);
```

Retrieving and Manipulating a Device Context's Attributes

In this section, we'll discuss how to retrieve and adjust some common attributes of a device context, including the background color, the background mode, the drawing mode, the filling mode, the stretching mode, and the mapping mode. For more information on mapping modes, see Chapter 10. For information on how to change a device context's text color, refer to Chapter 4. If you're looking for information on how to change a device context's arc direction, see Chapter 5.

Changing the Background Color of a Device Context

To retrieve a device context's current background color, you use the **GetBkColor** function:

```
COLORREF GetBkColor(
    IN HDC hdc        // handle to the target device context
   );
```

The **GetBkColor** function accepts only a single parameter—a handle to the device context whose background color you want to retrieve. This can be a handle to either a memory or a non-memory device context. If the function is successful, it returns a **COLORREF** value that indicates the current background color. If the function fails, the return value is **CLR_INVALID** (–1):

```
COLORREF clrBk = GetBkColor(hDC);
```

To change the background color of a device context, you use the **SetBkColor** function:

```
COLORREF SetBkColor(
    IN HDC hdc,                // handle to the target device context
    IN COLORREF crColor        // new background color
   );
```

The **hdc** parameter designates the device context whose background color you want to change. This color value is specified by the **crColor** parameter. If the function is successful, it returns a **COLORREF** value of the previous background color. Otherwise, the return value is **CLR_INVALID**:

```
COLORREF clrOriginal = SetBkColor(hDC, PALETTERGB(255, 0, 0));
```

Don't confuse a device context's background color with the color of its brush. The background color defines the color that appears behind the drawings created with graphic objects. The color of a device context's brush object is used only for filling predefined areas (ellipses, rectangles, and so on). In addition, a device context's background mode governs whether or not the background color is used. Specifically, the background color is relevant only when the background mode is set to **OPAQUE**.

Changing the Background Mode of a Device Context

The current background mode is retrieved via the **GetBkMode** function:

```
int GetBkMode(
    IN HDC hdc          // handle to the target device context
   );
```

The single **hdc** parameter identifies the device context whose background mode is returned. This return value is either **OPAQUE** or **TRANSPARENT**, as described in Table 1.10.

Table 1.10 A device context's background modes.

Background Mode	Value	Effect
OPAQUE	2	The device context's current background color is used
TRANSPARENT	1	The device context's current background color is ignored

```
HDC hDC = GetDC(hWnd);
try
{
   int BkMode = GetBkMode(hDC);
   if (BkMode == OPAQUE)
   {
      // ...
   }
   else // if (BkMode == TRANSPARENT)
   {
      // ...
   }
}
catch (...)
{
   ReleaseDC(hWnd, hDC);
}
ReleaseDC(hWnd, hDC);
```

You can adjust a device context's current background mode by using the **SetBkMode** function:

```
int SetBkMode(
    IN HDC hdc,         // handle to target device context
    IN int iBkMode      // identifier of new background mode
   );
```

Here the **hdc** parameter identifies the device context whose background mode you want to change. The new mode is identified by the **ibkMode** parameter, which is specified as **OPAQUE**, as **TRANSPARENT**, or as a device-driver-specific value.

***NOTE:** The background mode has no effect for extended pens.*

If successful, the **SetBkMode** function returns the previous background mode; otherwise, the return value is zero:

```
int OldBkMode = SetBkMode(hDC, TRANSPARENT); // set to transparent
```

Changing the Drawing Mode of a Device Context

The current drawing mode is retrieved via the **GetROP2** function:

```
int GetROP2(
    IN HDC hdc          // handle to the target device context
   );
```

The **hdc** parameter indicates the device context whose current drawing-mode value you want to retrieve:

```
int rop2_code = GetROP2(hDC);
```

If the function fails, the return value is zero; otherwise, the current drawing mode is signified by one of the return values listed in Table 1.11.

The current drawing mode is changed via the **SetROP2** function:

```
int SetROP2(
    IN HDC hdc,         // handle to the target device context
    IN int fnDrawMode   // new drawing mode identifier
   );
```

Table 1.11 Binary-raster-operation constants.

Drawing Mode	Value	Effect
R2_BLACK	1	Destination = black
R2_NOTMERGEPEN	2	Destination = **NOT**(destination **OR** pen)
R2_MASKNOTPEN	3	Destination = destination **AND** (**NOT** pen)
R2_NOTCOPYPEN	4	Destination = **NOT** pen
R2_MASKPENNOT	5	Destination = pen **AND** (**NOT** destination)
R2_NOT	6	Destination = **NOT** destination
R2_XORPEN	7	Destination = destination **XOR** pen
R2_NOTMASKPEN	8	Destination = **NOT**(destination **AND** pen)
R2_MASKPEN	9	Destination = destination **AND** pen
R2_NOTXORPEN	10	Destination = **NOT**(destination **XOR** pen)
R2_NOP	11	Destination = destination
R2_MERGENOTPEN	12	Destination = destination **OR** (**NOT** pen)
R2_COPYPEN	13	Destination = pen
R2_MERGEPENNOT	14	Destination = pen **OR** (**NOT** destination)
R2_MERGEPEN	15	Destination = destination **OR** pen
R2_WHITE	16	Destination = white

If the **SetROP2** function is successful, it returns the previous drawing mode. If the function fails, the return value is zero. The **hdc** parameter indicates the device context whose drawing mode will be changed. The new drawing mode is specified by the **fmDrawMode** parameter, which can be specified as any one of the aforementioned 16 ROP2 codes.

```
int old_rop2 = SetROP2(hDC, R2_XORPEN);  // used for rubber-banding
```

NOTE: *The drawing mode affects the appearance of the current brush object only when it is used for rendering the interior of filled polygons via one of the filled-shape functions or via a region- or path-based filling function. For example, the filling effect of the* ***Rectangle*** *function is governed by the current drawing mode of the target device context, but this is not the case for the* ***FillRect*** *or* ***PatBlt*** *functions.*

If your application relies on the manipulation of the drawing mode, you should ensure that the target device is a raster device, not a vector device. Indeed, it would make little sense to change the raster-operation mode of a non-raster device. Some output devices, namely plotters, do not support raster operations. You can determine if your target device is a raster device by using the **GetDeviceCaps** function with the **TECHNOLOGY** capability index. For example, to test whether the video display is a raster device, use the following code:

```
bool is_raster_display =
   (GetDeviceCaps(hScreenDC, TECHNOLOGY) == DT_RASDISPLAY);
```

Changing the Filling Mode of a Device Context

The GDI defines two filling modes: *alternate mode* and *winding mode* (also called *winding-number* mode). To retrieve a device context's current filling mode, you use the **GetPolyFillMode** function:

```
int GetPolyFillMode(
    IN HDC hdc    // handle to the target device context
);
```

The **GetPolyFillMode** function accepts only a single parameter—a handle to the device context whose filling mode you want to retrieve. The return value identifies the current filling mode:

```
switch (GetPolyFillMode(hDC))
{
   case ALTERNATE:
      /* alternate filling mode */
      break;
```

```
        case WINDING:
            /* winding-number filling mode */
            break;
}
```

The **GetPolyFillMode** function returns **ALTERNATE** for alternate filling mode or **WINDING** for winding-number mode. For more information on these filling modes, refer to Chapter 5.

To change a device context's filling mode, you pass either **ALTERNATE** or **WINDING** to the **SetPolyFillMode** function:

```
int SetPolyFillMode(
    IN HDC hdc,                // handle to the target device context
    IN int iPolyFillMode       // new filling mode
   );
```

The **SetPolyFillMode** function accepts, as its first parameter, a handle to the device context whose filling mode will be changed. The new filling mode is specified by the **iPolyFillMode** parameter. If the **SetPolyFillMode** function is successful, the return value identifies the previous filling mode; otherwise, the function returns zero:

```
// change filling mode to alternate
int old_fill_mode = SetPolyFillMode(hDC, ALTERNATE);
```

Changing the Stretching Mode of a Device Context

The GDI provides four stretching modes for use with the **StretchBlt** function when you're rendering a scaled-down version of an image. The stretching mode has no effect when the **StretchBlt** function is used to render an image in its actual size or larger. Table 1.12 lists the four stretching modes that can be assigned to the target device context.

WARNING! The HALFTONE stretching mode can produce the best-looking results for natural images, but because an averaging computation is involved, it is also the slowest of the stretching modes.

Table 1.12 A device context's stretching modes.

Stretching Mode	Value	Effect
BLACKONWHITE	1	Discards white pixels to preserve black pixels
WHITEONBLACK	2	Discards black pixels to preserve white pixels
COLORONCOLOR	3	Used to preserve colors; simply discards pixels
HALFTONE	4	Used for natural images; averages blocks of pixels

To retrieve a device context's current stretching mode, you use the **GetStretchBltMode** function:

```
int GetStretchBltMode(
    IN HDC hdc        // handle to the target device context
  );
```

The single **hdc** parameter indicates the device context whose stretching mode you want to retrieve. If the **GetStretchBltMode** function is successful, this mode is identified by the return value, which is one of the constants listed in Table 1.12. If the function fails, the return value is zero:

```
int stretching_mode = GetStretchBltMode(hDC);
```

You can change the stretching mode of a device context by using the **SetStretchBltMode** function:

```
int SetStretchBltMode(
    IN HDC hdc,                 // handle to the target device context
    IN int iStretchMode         // new stretching mode
  );
```

The **hdc** parameter is a handle to the device context whose stretching mode will be changed. The new stretching mode is specified by the **iStretchMode** parameter. This parameter can be assigned one of the values from Table 1.12.

WARNING! The SetStretchBltMode function is ignored on systems running Windows 95 or Windows 98. On these platforms, the stretching mode is always COLORONCOLOR.

If the **SetStretchBltMode** function succeeds, the return value identifies the previous stretching mode; otherwise, the function returns zero:

```
int old_stretching_mode = SetStretchBltMode(hDC, COLORONCOLOR);
```

There is a caveat to remember when you set the stretching mode to **HALFTONE**. In this mode, the brush origin of the target device context's current brush is not tracked. Therefore, the brush might become misaligned when used for filling purposes. Although misalignment is not an issue when you're working with a solid brush, it can produce undesirable results when you're using, for example, a pattern brush. To track and reset the brush origin in this situation, perform the following steps:

1. Retrieve and store the current brush origin by using the **GetBrushOrgEx** function.
2. Change the stretching mode of the target device context to **HALFTONE**.
3. Deselect the brush by selecting a stock object into the target device context.
4. Reset the brush origin to the stored value by using the **SetBrushOrgEx** function.
5. Instruct the device to re-realize the brush by using the **UnrealizeObject** function.
6. Select the brush back into the target device context by using the **SelectObject** function.

```
// 1. Get the current brush origin
POINT POrg;
GetBrushOrgEx(hMemDCDest, &POrg);

// 2. Change to HALFTONE stretching mode
SetStretchBltMode(hMemDCDest, HALFTONE);

// 3. Deselect the brush to track
HBRUSH hStockBrush = static_cast<HBRUSH>(
   GetStockObject(BLACK_BRUSH)
   );
HBRUSH hTrackBrush = static_cast<HBRUSH>(
   SelectObject(hMemDCDest, hStockBrush)
   );

// 4. Reset the brush origin
SetBrushOrgEx(hMemDCDest, POrg.x, POrg.y, NULL);

// 5. Re-realize the brush the next time it's selected
UnrealizeObject(hTrackBrush);

// 6. Select the brush back into the DC
SelectObject(hMemDCDest, hTrackBrush);
```

Note that Steps 3, 5, and 6 are not required for Windows NT and Windows 2000. On these platforms, the **SetBrushOrgEx** function affects the origin of the current brush. On systems running Windows 95 or Windows 98, however, this function changes the origin of the *next* brush that is realized. This is why you need to use the **UnrealizeObject** function. For more information on the brush origin, refer to Chapter 2.

As previously mentioned, due to a bug in the GDI (see Microsoft Knowledge Base article Q138105), only the **COLORONCOLOR** stretching mode is supported in

Windows 95 and Windows 98. Although it might seem unnecessary to change the stretching mode to **HALFTONE** (when applicable) and to reset the brush origin as described in Steps 1 through 6, you cannot be sure whether Microsoft will release a service pack that fixes this behavior at some later date—better safe than sorry.

Changing the Mapping Mode of a Device Context

To retrieve a device context's current mapping mode, use the **GetMapMode** function. This function takes a handle to a device context as its only parameter:

```
int GetMapMode(
    IN HDC hdc          // handle to the target device context
   );
```

If the **GetMapMode** function is successful, the return value indicates the current mapping mode via one of the identifiers listed in Table 1.7. If the function fails, the return value is zero:

```
int map_mode = GetMapMode(hDC);
```

To change a device context's current mapping mode, use the **SetMapMode** function. This function takes two parameters—a handle to a device context, and an identifier for the new mapping mode:

```
int SetMapMode(
    IN HDC hdc,         // handle to the target device context
    IN int fnMapMode    // new mapping mode
   );
```

If the **SetMapMode** function is successful, it returns the previous mapping mode identifier; otherwise, the function returns zero:

```
int old_map_mode = SetMapMode(hDC, MM_ANISOTROPIC);
```

For more information on mapping modes, origins, and extents, see Chapter 10.

Working with Memory Device Contexts

In this section, we'll discuss memory device contexts. We'll examine how to create a memory DC, how to associate a device-dependent bitmap with it, and how to use this combination to reduce flicker.

Creating a Memory Device Context

To create a memory device context, you use the **CreateCompatibleDC** function. This function takes a single **HDC**-type parameter, which identifies the device with which the memory device context will be compatible:

```
HDC CreateCompatibleDC(
    IN HDC hdc          // handle to the device context that is used
                        // for compatibility
   );
```

If you want to create a memory device context that is compatible with the screen, as is most often the case, you can specify the **hdc** parameter as **NULL**.

Memory device contexts are created with an associated default single-pixel, monochrome bitmap object. You should use the **CreateCompatibleBitmap** function, the **CreateDIBSection** function, or another appropriate bitmap-related function to get a handle to a bitmap object of the desired size. Then use the **SelectObject** function to replace the default bitmap with the new one.

As we'll discuss in Chapter 7, the **CreateDIBSection** function is preferred over the **CreateCompatibleBitmap** function since **CreateDIBSection** creates a DIB section bitmap. The **CreateCompatibleBitmap** function, on the other hand, creates a device-dependent bitmap, which is limited in size on both Windows 95/98 and Windows NT/2000 (see Chapter 6). Here, we'll focus on the **CreateCompatibleBitmap** function:

```
HBITMAP CreateCompatibleBitmap(
    IN HDC hdc,         // handle to the device context that is used
                        // for compatibility
    IN int nWidth,      // width of returned bitmap, in pixels
    IN int nHeight      // height of returned bitmap, in pixels
   );
```

The **hdc** parameter of the **CreateCompatibleBitmap** function serves a similar role as that of the **CreateCompatibleDC** function. That is, this parameter indicates the device with which the returned bitmap should be compatible. Yet, unlike with the **CreateCompatibleDC** function, you can't specify **NULL** as the **hdc** parameter of the **CreateCompatibleBitmap** function to achieve compatibility with the screen. This is a rather irksome implementation oversight because it requires you to use the **GetDC** function to manually obtain a handle to the screen's device context and then later use the **ReleaseDC** function to release it.

WARNING! One of the mistakes made most frequently after creating a memory DC (and before selecting a bitmap into it) is to specify its handle as the hdc parameter of the CreateCompatibleBitmap function. Unfortunately, doing this will always create a monochrome bitmap. Remember, once a memory device context is created, it is given a one-bit, one-pixel bitmap by default. If you then pass the handle to this memory DC to the CreateCompatibleBitmap function, the newly created bitmap will also be monochrome.

After you're done with the memory device context, you don't release it as you would a non-memory device context. Instead, you must free it by using the **DeleteDC** function. (Remember, use the **ReleaseDC** function only for a display device context that was retrieved from the GDI device-context cache.) Similarly, once you're done with the bitmap, you must free it by using the **DeleteObject** function. You can't rely on the **DeleteDC** function to also free the bitmap object:

```
// grab a handle to the DC of the screen
HDC hScreenDC = GetDC(NULL);

// create a memory DC compatible with the screen
HDC hMemDC = CreateCompatibleDC(hScreenDC);

// create a bitmap compatible with the screen
HBITMAP hBmp =
    CreateCompatibleBitmap(hScreenDC, width, height);

// release the screen DC
ReleaseDC(hScreenDC);

// select the bitmap into the memory DC
HBITMAP hOldBmp = static_cast<HBITMAP>(SelectObject(hMemDC, hBmp));
try
{
    //
    // perform rendering to hMemDC...
    //


    //
    // optionally transfer the bits to the video display...
    //
}
catch (...)
{
    // free the bitmap
    DeleteObject(SelectObject(hMemDC, hOldBmp));
```

```
    // free the memory DC
    DeleteDC(hMemDC);
}
// free the bitmap
DeleteObject(SelectObject(hMemDC, hOldBmp));

// free the memory DC
DeleteDC(hMemDC);
```


Related solutions:	Found on page:
Creating a Monochrome Device-Dependent Bitmap	307
Creating a Color Device-Dependent Bitmap	311
Rendering a Device-Dependent Bitmap	338

Using a Memory Device Context to Eliminate Flicker

There are two classic approaches to reducing flicker. The first involves optimizing the rendering process via double-buffering, and the second entails eliminating any superfluous erasing operations.

Double-Buffer Multiple or Expensive Rendering Operations

To implement a double-buffered solution, you perform the following steps:

1. Use the **CreateCompatibleDC** function to create a memory device context that is compatible with the target display device.
2. Create an appropriately sized device-dependent bitmap or DIB section bitmap that will serve as the "memory" of the memory device context. You can use the **CreateCompatibleBitmap** function to create a device-dependent bitmap or the **CreateDIBSection** function to create a DIB section bitmap.
3. Use the **SelectObject** function to select the bitmap into the memory device context.
4. Direct any rendering to the memory device context. You can simply modify your existing code by replacing all references to the original target device context with references to the memory device context.
5. When the rendering is complete, use the **BitBlt** function to transfer the bits of the bitmap to the original target device context.

The following code snippet demonstrates the previous steps:

```
// (1) Create a memory DC compatible with the screen
HDC hMemDC = CreateCompatibleDC(NULL);

// (2) Create a bitmap object compatible with the screen
HDC hScreenDC = GetDC(NULL);
HBITMAP hBmp =
   CreateCompatibleBitmap(hScreenDC, 300, 300);
ReleaseDC(NULL, hScreenDC);

// (3) Associate the bitmap with the memory DC
HBITMAP hOldBmp = static_cast<HBITMAP>(
   SelectObject(hMemDC, hBmp)
   );

// (4) Perform the rendering to the memory DC
RECT R = {0, 0, 300, 300};
for (int index = 0; index < 100; ++index)
{
   InflateRect(&R, -2, -2);
   Rectangle(hMemDC, R.left, R.top, R.right, R.bottom);
}

// (5) Transfer the results to a display DC
HDC hDC = GetDC(hWnd);
BitBlt(hDC, 0, 0, 300, 300, hMemDC, 0, 0, SRCCOPY);
ReleaseDC(hWnd, hDC);

// Clean up...
DeleteObject(SelectObject(hMemDC, hOldBmp));
DeleteDC(hMemDC);
```

Erase Only When Necessary

When the entire client area of your window is to be covered by a drawing, you should instruct the default window procedure not to fill the background with the class background-brush object. You can do this by assigning **NULL** (or the **NULL_BRUSH** stock object) to the **WNDCLASS::hbrBackground** data member before the window's class is registered:

```
WNDCLASS wc;
// ...
WNDCLASS::hbrBackground = NULL;
```

An equivalent technique is to always return non-zero in response to the **WM_ERASEBKGND** message:

```
LRESULT CALLBACK MainWndProc(HWND hWnd, UINT msg, WPARAM wParam,
   LPARAM lParam)
{
   switch (msg)
   {
      case WM_ERASEBKGND: return 1;
      // ...
   }
   return DefWindowProc(hWnd, msg, wParam, lParam);
}
```


Related solutions:	Found on page:
Creating a Monochrome Device-Dependent Bitmap	307
Creating a Color Device-Dependent Bitmap	311
Rendering a Device-Dependent Bitmap	338

Transferring Bits

In this section, we'll focus on two functions—**BitBlt** and **StretchBlt**—that can be used to transfer bits from one device context to another.

Rendering to a Device Context by Using the **BitBlt** Function

The **BitBlt** function takes a total of nine parameters and returns a Boolean value indicating success or failure:

```
BOOL BitBlt(
    IN HDC hdcDest,     // handle to the target device context
    IN int nXDest,      // horizontal position of the top-left corner
                        // of the destination rectangle
    IN int nYDest,      // vertical position of the top-left corner
                        // of the destination rectangle
    IN int nWidth,      // width of the destination rectangle
    IN int nHeight,     // height of the destination rectangle
    IN HDC hdcSrc,      // handle to the source device context
    IN int nXSrc,       // horizontal position of the top-left corner
                        // of the source rectangle
    IN int nYSrc,       // horizontal position of the top-left corner
                        // of the source rectangle
    IN DWORD dwRop      // ternary-raster-operation code
   );
```

The **hdcDest** parameter indicates the device context to which the bits associated with the source device context (**hdcSrc**) should be transferred (copied). The **nXDest**, **nYDest**, **nWidth**, and **nHeight** parameters together designate the dimensions of the destination rectangle. The **hdcSrc** parameter identifies the source device context. The **nXSrc** and **nYSrc** parameters indicate the top-left coordinates of the source rectangle. The **dwRop** parameter specifies the ternary-raster-operation code (see Table 1.8).

Of the 17 GDI-assigned ROP3 identifiers, only a small subset of these is used frequently. In fact, the most commonly specified ROP3 code is **SRCCOPY**, where the source bits are copied directly to the destination:

```
BitBlt(hDC, x, y, target_width, target_height, hMemDC, 0, 0, SRCCOPY);
```

As mentioned, the **BitBlt** function can take on many roles. It's the fastest GDI-based function for rendering the contents of a memory device context, but its use is not limited to this aspect. Indeed, the best way to understand the use of the **BitBlt** function is by example.

WARNING! You should never use the BitBlt function to transfer bits to different devices. That is, the device contexts indicated by the hdcSrc and hdcDest parameters must both correspond to the same device. Blitting across device contexts associated with different devices is not supported. Even when you're working with only a single device, you should ensure that the BitBlt function is supported. You can do this by using the GetDeviceCaps function with the RASTERCAPS capability index.

Example 1—Rendering a Bitmap Image

Undoubtedly, the most common use of the **BitBlt** function is to display the contents of a bitmap image. For example, if you load a bitmap from a file, you can use the **BitBlt** function to display the bitmap in the client area of a window. Listing 1.3 illustrates this idea.

Listing 1.3 Using the BitBlt function to render a bitmap.

```
// ————————————————————————————————
// Windows 2000 Graphics API Black Book
// Chapter 1 - Listing 1.3 (BitBlt Bitmap Rendering Demo)
// ————————————————————————————————

#include <windows.h>

HINSTANCE hInst;
const char* WndClassName = "GMainWnd";
LRESULT CALLBACK MainWndProc(HWND hWnd, UINT msg, WPARAM wParam,
   LPARAM lParam);
```

```
int APIENTRY WinMain(HINSTANCE hInstance, HINSTANCE HPrevInstance,
    LPTSTR lpCmdLine, int nCmdShow)
{
   hInst = hInstance;

   WNDCLASS wc;
   memset(&wc, 0, sizeof(WNDCLASS));

   wc.style = CS_VREDRAW | CS_HREDRAW | CS_DBLCLKS;
   wc.lpfnWndProc = MainWndProc;
   wc.hInstance = hInstance;
   wc.hCursor = LoadCursor(NULL, IDC_ARROW);
   wc.hbrBackground = reinterpret_cast<HBRUSH>(COLOR_BTNFACE + 1);
   wc.lpszClassName = WndClassName;

   if (RegisterClass(&wc))
   {
      HWND hWnd =
         CreateWindow(WndClassName, "BitBlt Bitmap Rendering Demo",
                      WS_OVERLAPPEDWINDOW | WS_CAPTION |
                      WS_VISIBLE | WS_CLIPSIBLINGS,
                      0, 0, 675, 560,
                      NULL, NULL, hInst, NULL);

      if (hWnd)
      {
         ShowWindow(hWnd, nCmdShow);
         UpdateWindow(hWnd);

         MSG msg;
         while (GetMessage(&msg, NULL, 0, 0))
         {
             TranslateMessage(&msg);
             DispatchMessage(&msg);
         }
      }
    }
    return 0;
}

// image related
BITMAP bmp;
const char* filename = "LENA.BMP";
HDC hMemDC = NULL;
HBITMAP hOldBmp = NULL;
```

```
// main window procedure
LRESULT CALLBACK MainWndProc(HWND hWnd, UINT msg, WPARAM wParam,
   LPARAM lParam)
{
   switch (msg)
   {
      case WM_CREATE:
      {
         // create a memory DC
         hMemDC = CreateCompatibleDC(NULL);
         if (hMemDC)
         {
            // load a bitmap from file
            HBITMAP hBmp =
               static_cast<HBITMAP>(
                  LoadImage(hInst, filename, IMAGE_BITMAP,
                            0, 0, LR_LOADFROMFILE)
                            );
            if (hBmp)
            {
               // extract dimensions of the bitmap
               GetObject(hBmp, sizeof(BITMAP), &bmp);

               // associate the bitmap with the memory DC
               hOldBmp = static_cast<HBITMAP>(
                  SelectObject(hMemDC, hBmp)
                  );
            }
         }
      }
      case WM_PAINT:
      {
         PAINTSTRUCT ps;
         const HDC hDC = BeginPaint(hWnd, &ps);
         try
         {
            //
            // TODO: add palette support...
            //

            BitBlt(hDC, 0, 0,
                   bmp.bmWidth, bmp.bmHeight,
                   hMemDC, 0, 0,
                   SRCCOPY);
         }
```

```
            catch (...)
            {
               EndPaint(hWnd, &ps);
            }
            EndPaint(hWnd, &ps);
            break;
         }
         case WM_DESTROY:
         {
            // clean up
            DeleteObject(SelectObject(hMemDC, hOldBmp));
            DeleteDC(hMemDC);

            PostQuitMessage(0);
            return 0;
         }
      }
      return DefWindowProc(hWnd, msg, wParam, lParam);
   }
```

Example 2—Copying a Bitmap

As mentioned, the **BitBlt** function can also be used to transfer bits of one bitmap to those of another. For example, if you need to copy a bitmap, you can use the **BitBlt** function as demonstrated in Listing 1.4.

Listing 1.4 Using the BitBlt function to copy a bitmap.

```
// ----------------------------------------------
// Windows 2000 Graphics API Black Book
// Chapter 1 - Listing 1.4 (BitBlt Bitmap Copying Demo)
// ----------------------------------------------

#include <windows.h>
#include <cassert>

HBITMAP CopyBitmap(HBITMAP hBmpSrc, HPALETTE HPal = NULL)
{
   assert(hBmpSrc != NULL);

   BITMAP bmp;
   if (GetObject(hBmpSrc, sizeof(BITMAP), &bmp) == sizeof(BITMAP))
   {
      const int src_width = bmp.bmWidth;
      const int src_height = bmp.bmHeight;

      HBITMAP hBmpDest = NULL;
      HDC hMemDCSrc = NULL, hMemDCDest = NULL;
```

```
HDC hScreenDC = GetDC(NULL);
bool blits_supported =
   (GetDeviceCaps(hScreenDC, RASTERCAPS) & RC_BITBLT);
try
{
   if (!blits_supported) throw;

   //
   // create two memory DCs - one for the source
   // bitmap and one for the destination bitmap
   //
   hMemDCSrc = CreateCompatibleDC(hScreenDC);
   hMemDCDest = CreateCompatibleDC(hScreenDC);

   // create the destination bitmap
   hBmpDest = CreateCompatibleBitmap(
      hScreenDC, src_width, src_height
      );
}
catch (...)
{
   ReleaseDC(NULL, hScreenDC);
   if (hBmpDest) DeleteObject(hBmpDest);
   if (hMemDCDest) DeleteDC(hMemDCDest);
   if (hMemDCSrc) DeleteDC(hMemDCSrc);
   return NULL;
}
ReleaseDC(NULL, hScreenDC);

// select the source bitmap into the source memory DC
HBITMAP hOldBmpSrc = static_cast<HBITMAP>(
   SelectObject(hMemDCSrc, hBmpSrc)
   );
// select the dest. bitmap into the dest. memory DC
HBITMAP hOldBmpDest = static_cast<HBITMAP>(
   SelectObject(hMemDCDest, hBmpDest)
   );

HPALETTE hOldPal;
if (HPal)
{
   // select and realize the bitmap's palette
   hOldPal = static_cast<HPALETTE>(
      SelectPalette(hMemDCDest, HPal, false)
      );
```

```
            RealizePalette(hMemDCDest);
        }

        //
        // use the BitBlt function to copy
        // the bitmap's pixels
        //
        BitBlt(hMemDCDest, 0, 0,
               src_width, src_height,
               hMemDCSrc, 0, 0,
               SRCCOPY);

        // clean up
        if (HPal)
        {
            SelectObject(hMemDCDest, hOldPal);
        }
        SelectPalette(hMemDCDest, hOldPal, false);
        DeleteObject(SelectObject(hMemDCSrc, hOldBmpSrc));
        DeleteDC(hMemDCDest);
        DeleteDC(hMemDCSrc);

        // return copy
        return hBmpDest;
    }
    return NULL;
}
```


Related solution:	Found on page:
Rendering a Device-Dependent Bitmap	338

Rendering to a Device Context by Using the StretchBlt Function

Unlike the **BitBlt** function, the **StretchBlt** function accepts 11 parameters, 9 of which are identical to those of the **BitBlt** function. The two that differ—**nWidthSrc** and **nHeightSrc**—are used to specify the size of the source image. In this way, the **StretchBlt** function is informed of the size of both the destination rectangle and the source rectangle (image):

```
BOOL StretchBlt(
    IN HDC hdcDest,        // handle to the destination device context
    IN int nXOriginDest,   // horizontal position of the top-left
                           // corner of the destination rectangle
    IN int nYOriginDest,   // vertical position of the top-left
                           // corner of the destination rectangle
```

```
    IN int nWidthDest,       // width of the destination rectangle
    IN int nHeightDest,      // height of the destination rectangle
    IN HDC hdcSrc,           // handle to the source device context
    IN int nXOriginSrc,      // horizontal position of the top-left
                             // corner of the source rectangle
    IN int nYOriginSrc,      // vertical position of the top-left
                             // corner of the source rectangle
    IN int nWidthSrc,        // width of the source rectangle
    IN int nHeightSrc,       // height of the source rectangle
    IN DWORD dwRop           // ternary-raster-operation code
  );
```

The **hdcDest** parameter indicates the device context to which the bits associated with the source device context (**hdcSrc**) should be transferred (copied). The dimensions of the destination rectangle are specified by the **nXDest**, **nYDest**, **nWidth**, and **nHeight** parameters. The **hdcSrc** parameter identifies the source device context. The **nXSrc**, **nYSrc**, **nWidthSrc**, and **nHeightSrc** parameters specify the bounds of the source rectangle. Finally, the **dwRop** parameter specifies the ternary-raster-operation code.

NOTE: *It is important to realize that the GDI performs the stretching operation in memory first and then transfers the manipulated bits to the destination device context. Therefore, the ternary raster operation is performed with the compacted or stretched bits, not with the original bits.*

The most commonly used ROP3 code is **SRCCOPY**, where the brush or bitmap of the destination device context is ignored. That is, specifying **SRCCOPY** as the **dwRop** parameter instructs the **StretchBlt** function to copy the source bitmap bits directly to the destination:

```
StretchBlt(hDC, x, y, target_width, target_height,
           hMemDC, 0, 0, source_width, source_height,
           SRCCOPY);
```

Similar to the **BitBlt** function, the **StretchBlt** function can best be appreciated by inspecting examples that demonstrate its usefulness. It should be noted, however, that when no compaction or stretching is required, it's best to use the faster **BitBlt** function instead. Some drivers might default to the **BitBlt** function when the area of the destination rectangle is identical to that of the source rectangle, but this is not guaranteed. Moreover, you can check whether the **StretchBlt** function is supported at all by using the **GetDeviceCaps** function with the **RASTERCAPS** capability index:

```
bool stretch_supported =
     (GetDeviceCaps(HTargetDC, RASTERCAPS) & RC_STRETCHBLT);
```

Figure 1.2 Using StretchBlt for zooming support.

Listing 1.5 demonstrates the use of the **StretchBlt** function for adding zooming functionality. The result is depicted in Figure 1.2.

Listing 1.5 Using the StretchBlt function to provide zooming capabilities.

```
// ——————————————————————————————
// Windows 2000 Graphics API Black Book
// Chapter 1 - Listing 1.5 (StretchBlt Zooming Demo)
// ——————————————————————————————

#include <windows.h>

HWND hListBox = NULL;
const int ID_LISTBOX = 101;

HINSTANCE hInst;
const char* WndClassName = "GMainWnd";
LRESULT CALLBACK MainWndProc(HWND hWnd, UINT msg, WPARAM wParam,
   LPARAM lParam);

int APIENTRY WinMain(HINSTANCE hInstance, HINSTANCE HPrevInstance,
    LPTSTR lpCmdLine, int nCmdShow)
{
   hInst = hInstance;

   WNDCLASS wc;
   memset(&wc, 0, sizeof(WNDCLASS));
```

```
wc.style = CS_VREDRAW | CS_HREDRAW | CS_DBLCLKS;
wc.lpfnWndProc = MainWndProc;
wc.hInstance = hInstance;
wc.hCursor = LoadCursor(NULL, IDC_ARROW);
wc.hbrBackground = reinterpret_cast<HBRUSH>(COLOR_BTNFACE + 1);
wc.lpszClassName = WndClassName;

if (RegisterClass(&wc))
{
   HWND hWnd =
      CreateWindow(WndClassName, "StretchBlt Zooming Demo",
                   WS_OVERLAPPEDWINDOW | WS_CAPTION |
                   WS_VISIBLE | WS_CLIPSIBLINGS,
                   0, 0, 675, 560,
                   NULL, NULL, hInst, NULL);

   if (hWnd)
   {
      hListBox =
         CreateWindowEx(WS_EX_CLIENTEDGE, "LISTBOX", "",
                        LBS_NOTIFY | WS_CHILD | WS_VISIBLE,
                        530, 5, 130, 150, hWnd,
                        reinterpret_cast<HMENU>(ID_LISTBOX),
                        hInst, NULL);
      if (hListBox)
      {
         SNDMSG(hListBox, LB_ADDSTRING, 0,
                reinterpret_cast<LPARAM>("Zoom 25%"));
         SNDMSG(hListBox, LB_ADDSTRING, 0,
                reinterpret_cast<LPARAM>("Zoom 50%"));
         SNDMSG(hListBox, LB_ADDSTRING, 0,
                reinterpret_cast<LPARAM>("Zoom 75%"));
         SNDMSG(hListBox, LB_ADDSTRING, 0,
                reinterpret_cast<LPARAM>("Zoom 100%"));
         SNDMSG(hListBox, LB_ADDSTRING, 0,
                reinterpret_cast<LPARAM>("Zoom 125%"));
         SNDMSG(hListBox, LB_ADDSTRING, 0,
                reinterpret_cast<LPARAM>("Zoom 150%"));
         SNDMSG(hListBox, LB_ADDSTRING, 0,
                reinterpret_cast<LPARAM>("Zoom 200%"));
         SNDMSG(hListBox, LB_ADDSTRING, 0,
                reinterpret_cast<LPARAM>("Zoom 300%"));
      }
```

```
            ShowWindow(hWnd, nCmdShow);
            UpdateWindow(hWnd);

            MSG msg;
            while (GetMessage(&msg, NULL, 0, 0))
            {
                TranslateMessage(&msg);
                DispatchMessage(&msg);
            }
         }
      }
      return 0;
}

// image related
BITMAP bmp;
const char* filename = "LENA.BMP";
HDC hMemDC = NULL;
HBITMAP hOldBmp = NULL;

// zooming related
float zoom_factor = 0.5;
RECT RDest = {5, 5, 0, 0};
enum {ID_ZOOM25, ID_ZOOM50, ID_ZOOM75, ID_ZOOM100,
      ID_ZOOM125, ID_ZOOM150, ID_ZOOM200, ID_ZOOM300};

// main window procedure
LRESULT CALLBACK MainWndProc(HWND hWnd, UINT msg, WPARAM wParam,
   LPARAM lParam)
{
   switch (msg)
   {
      case WM_CREATE:
      {
         // create a memory DC
         hMemDC = CreateCompatibleDC(NULL);
         if (hMemDC)
         {
            // load a bitmap from file
            HBITMAP hBmp =
               static_cast<HBITMAP>(
                  LoadImage(hInst, filename, IMAGE_BITMAP,
                            0, 0, LR_LOADFROMFILE)
                            );
            if (hBmp)
            {
```

```
            // extract dimensions of the bitmap
            GetObject(hBmp, sizeof(BITMAP), &bmp);

            // associate the bitmap with the memory DC
            hOldBmp = static_cast<HBITMAP>(
               SelectObject(hMemDC, hBmp)
               );
         }
      }
   }
   case WM_COMMAND:
   {
      if (wParam == MAKEWPARAM(ID_LISTBOX, LBN_SELCHANGE))
      {
         switch (SNDMSG(hListBox, LB_GETCURSEL, 0, 0))
         {
            case ID_ZOOM25: zoom_factor = 0.25; break;
            case ID_ZOOM50: zoom_factor = 0.50; break;
            case ID_ZOOM75: zoom_factor = 0.75; break;
            case ID_ZOOM100: zoom_factor = 1.00; break;
            case ID_ZOOM125: zoom_factor = 1.25; break;
            case ID_ZOOM150: zoom_factor = 1.50; break;
            case ID_ZOOM200: zoom_factor = 2.00; break;
            case ID_ZOOM300: zoom_factor = 3.00; break;
         }

         // calculate the new width and height
         const int new_width =
            static_cast<int>(zoom_factor * bmp.bmWidth);
         const int new_height =
            static_cast<int>(zoom_factor * bmp.bmHeight);

         // is zooming in?
         bool zoom_in = (new_width > RDest.right - RDest.left);

         // calculate the area that needs to be updated
         RECT RUpdate = {
            RDest.left, RDest.top,
            RDest.left + max(new_width, RDest.right - RDest.left),
            RDest.top + max(new_height, RDest.bottom - RDest.top)
            };

         //
         // adjust the dimensions of the
         // destination rectangle
         //
```

```
            RDest.right = RDest.left + new_width;
            RDest.bottom = RDest.top + new_height;

            // invoke a repaint
            InvalidateRect(hWnd, &RUpdate, zoom_in ? false : true);
         }
         break;
      }
      case WM_PAINT:
      {
         PAINTSTRUCT ps;
         const HDC hDC = BeginPaint(hWnd, &ps);
         try
         {
            //
            // TODO: add palette support...
            //

            if (RDest.right - RDest.left > 0)
            {
               // use BitBlt when not zooming
               if (zoom_factor == 1.0)
               }
               else
               {
                  if (zoom_factor < 1.0)
                  {
                     // use the COLORONCOLOR stretching mode
                     SetStretchBltMode(hDC, COLORONCOLOR);
                  }
                  BitBlt(hDC, RDest.left, RDest.top,
                         RDest.right - RDest.left,
                         RDest.bottom - RDest.top,
                         hMemDC, 0, 0,
                         SRCCOPY);
               }

               // render the zoomed image
               StretchBlt(hDC, RDest.left, RDest.top,
                          RDest.right - RDest.left,
                          RDest.bottom - RDest.top,
                          hMemDC, 0, 0,
                          bmp.bmWidth, bmp.bmHeight,
                          SRCCOPY);
            }
         }
```

```
            catch (...)
            {
                EndPaint(hWnd, &ps);
            }
            EndPaint(hWnd, &ps);
            break;
        }
        case WM_DESTROY:
        {
            // clean up
            DeleteObject(SelectObject(hMemDC, hOldBmp));
            DeleteDC(hMemDC);

            PostQuitMessage(0);
            break;
        }
    }
    return DefWindowProc(hWnd, msg, wParam, lParam);
}
```


Related solution:	Found on page:
Rendering a Device-Dependent Bitmap in a Scaled Fashion	341

Chapter 2

The Brush Object

In Depth

When you create a Windows-based application, your primary goal is to convey information to the application's users. You accomplish this task via a user interface. Physically, this interface is nothing more than a smaller image that is drawn to the larger desktop image. Exactly *how* this smaller image is drawn is up to you—this image defines the appearance (and to some extent the use) of your application. *What* you use to draw this image is also your choice. You can render your user interface a pixel at a time, or you can use the tools provided by the GDI. Most developers choose the latter method, and for a good reason: the GDI provides high-level graphic objects that can easily be used to render different colors, shapes, and figures to the target device. The *brush object* is perhaps the most frequently used of all GDI graphic objects, and as you will soon discover, brushes are one of the easiest graphic objects to work with.

In this chapter, we'll cover the GDI brush object. We'll discuss the differences between a logical brush and a physical brush, and we'll discuss how and when each one is used. In addition, we'll examine the process of creating different types of brushes and even discuss how to use the same brushes that Windows uses for its own windows, captions, and menus. We'll also discuss the new way of changing the color of a brush object in Windows 2000, and we'll contrast this technique with the classic approach. Finally, we'll look at a practical example of using a brush object and touch on the advantages of a brush over other GDI graphic objects.

Types of Brushes

Brushes are used primarily to fill defined areas. So you can think of a brush as a patch of wallpaper. When you need to paint the background of a particular area, you can paste this patch in a tiled fashion until the area is covered. In fact, this is exactly what most applications do to paint the background of their windows.

A *logical brush* is nothing more than a representation of a bitmap object. This being the case, brushes aren't really needed at all because you can accomplish the same effect by using a bitmap object and the **BitBlt** function. Logical brushes, however, provide a high-level, intuitive means of working with colors and patterns. Each type of logical brush is manipulated via its handle of type **HBRUSH**. This type is declared, right after the declaration for the **HBITMAP** type, in the windef.h header file.

Imagine that you need to fill an area with a particular color. Without a logical brush object, you'd need to create a memory device context, create a bitmap object, associate the bitmap with the memory device context, manipulate the bits of this bitmap to accurately represent the desired color, and then use the **BitBlt** function to fill the area. While not impossible, this is clearly a cumbersome way to proceed, not to mention that it's far from intuitive. This is where the logical brush object comes into play. Instead of working directly with a bitmap object, you can create a logical brush that represents the bitmap, and then simply use this brush to fill the area by using the more friendly **FillRect** or **FillRgn** functions. That's all a logical brush is—a high-level representation of a bitmap object; its related "filling" functions are simply an abstraction of the **BitBlt** function.

What's a Physical Brush?

A *physical brush* is a bitmap object. Specifically, a physical brush is the bitmap that the device driver creates according to the attributes of a logical brush. In this way, you can also think of a logical brush as a representation of a physical brush, and think of a physical brush as a device-specific bitmap object. Device drivers work with physical brushes, and applications work with logical brushes. A physical brush is created when a logical brush is associated with a device context. Indeed, this makes sense because a device context and a physical brush are both device-dependent entities.

The GDI defines four types of logical brushes. The type of brush governs how the bits of the corresponding bitmap are defined and how these bits are used during the filling process. Table 2.1 lists the four types of logical brushes.

Solid Brushes

Solid brushes represent a 64-pixel bitmap object that is 8 pixels high and 8 pixels wide. Solid brushes are used to fill an area with a particular color. The color itself might be truly solid, or it might be dithered. For a truly solid color, all 64 pixels of the corresponding bitmap are assigned the value of this color. Manipulating one or more of these 64 pixels creates a dithered color. The device driver performs this manipulation during the process of realization, and whether or not a color is dithered is governed by the color capabilities of the target device. Figure 2.1 depicts an array of rectangles rendered via a set of solid brushes.

Table 2.1 The four types of GDI logical brushes.

Brush Type	Effect
Solid	Fills an area with a solid or dithered color
Stock	Fills an area with a predefined color or with the color of a window element
Hatch	Fills an area with a predefined pattern
Pattern	Fills an area with a user-defined pattern

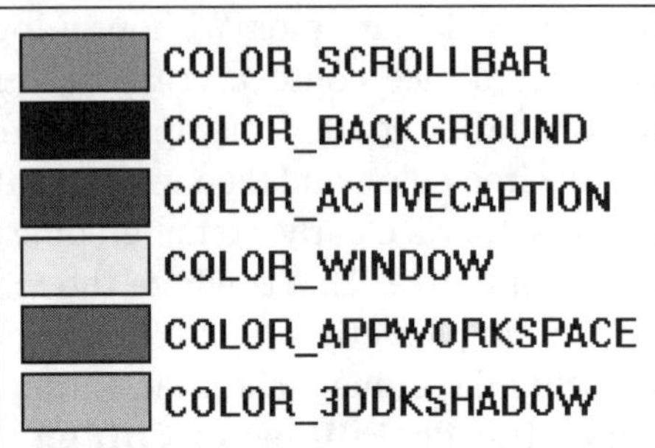

Figure 2.1 Colored blocks created using different-colored solid brushes.

To create a solid brush, you use the **CreateSolidBrush** function, which simply takes a **COLORREF** value, and then returns a handle to a new logical solid brush object of the specified color. When a solid brush is no longer needed, you destroy it by using the **DeleteObject** function.

Stock Brushes

Stock brushes aren't strictly a separate type of brush; rather, they represent a set of 35 (32 on Windows 95 and Windows NT) logical brushes that Windows creates during initialization. Seven of these brushes are maintained by the GDI itself, and the remaining 28 (25 on Windows 95 and Windows NT) stock brushes are used by the Windows user-interface system. Brushes from this latter set are frequently referred to as *system brushes* because they are used to paint various standard window elements, including windows, menus, scroll bars, and buttons. Figure 2.2 depicts some of the stock system brushes used for the "Eggplant" system color scheme in Windows.

A handle to one of the seven GDI stock brushes is obtained via the **GetStockObject** function. A handle to a system brush is retrieved via the **GetSysColorBrush** function. You are not required to destroy a stock brush after you're done with it. Although you can call the **DeleteObject** function on a GDI stock brush (it has no effect), you should not use this function on a *system* stock brush.

Hatch Brushes

Hatch brushes are useful for filling an area with a predefined pattern. Hatch brushes are identical to pattern brushes except that with hatch brushes the pattern itself is limited to one of the six predefined hatch styles depicted in Figure 2.3.

Figure 2.2 Various stock system brushes used for the "Eggplant" color scheme.

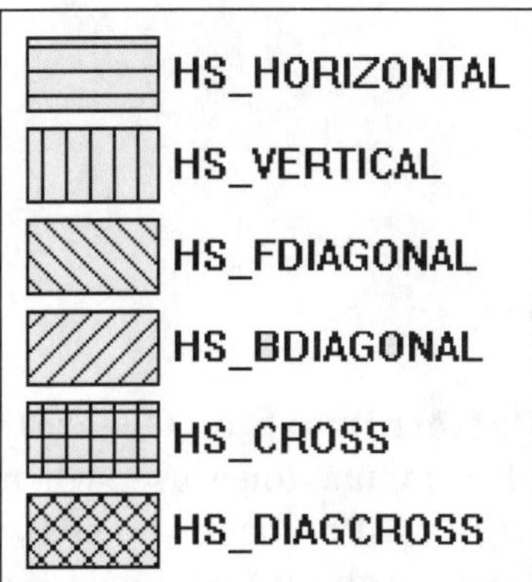

Figure 2.3 The six predefined styles of hatch brushes.

A hatch brush is created via the **CreateHatchBrush** function. This function takes a hatch style identifier (depicted in Figure 2.3) and a **COLORREF** value. If the **CreateHatchBrush** function is successful, it returns a handle to the newly created logical hatch brush object. As with solid brushes, hatch brushes are destroyed via the **DeleteObject** function.

An interesting thing to note about hatch brushes is that when you're using a filled-shaped function such as **Rectangle**, the background (i.e., the areas between the hatch marks) might or might not be filled. Specifically, this behavior is governed by the target device context's current background mode (**OPAQUE** or **TRANSPARENT**). This is not the case when you're rendering with a pattern brush or with the **FillRect** function, which will always fill the areas between pattern marks with the current background color. The adjustable filling-behavior of hatch brushes occurs because devices drivers provide specific support for hatch brushes. We'll examine this issue more closely in Chapter 5.

Pattern Brushes

Pattern brushes are similar to hatch brushes in that they both represent a specific pattern. However, with a pattern brush, the pattern is not limited to one of the six predefined styles depicted in Figure 2.3. Instead, pattern brushes are created according to a design described by the pixels of a user-defined (template) bitmap. Therefore, pattern brushes are also commonly referred to as *custom brushes*. Figure 2.4 depicts rectangles that were filled using various custom brushes.

The bitmap that is used to describe the custom brush pattern can be a device-dependent bitmap (DDB) or a device-independent bitmap (DIB). However, on systems running Windows 95, the pattern of the resulting logical brush is determined by only the top-left 64 pixels (8 pixels wide and high) of this bitmap. Other platforms (Windows 98, NT, 2000) do not impose this limitation.

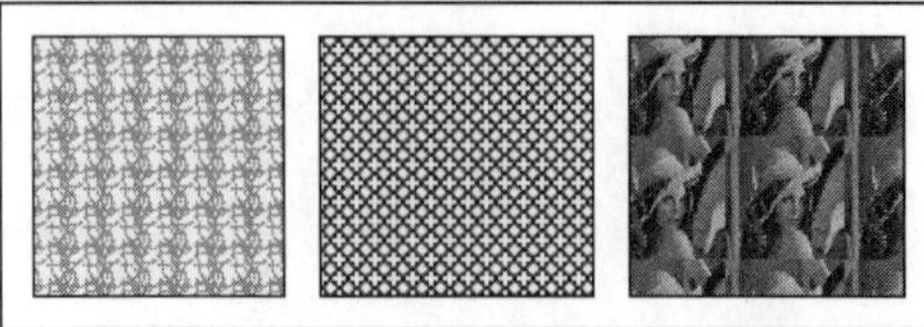

Figure 2.4 Rectangles filled with custom brush patterns.

A pattern brush is created via the **CreatePatternBrush** or **CreateDIB-PatternBrushPt** function. The **CreatePatternBrush** function is used when the template bitmap is a DDB; the **CreateDIBPatternBrushPt** function is used when the template bitmap is a DIB. (For a code example of these functions, see the Immediate Solutions section.) Like solid and hatch brushes, pattern brushes must be destroyed via the **DeleteObject** function when no longer needed.

The LOGBRUSH Structure

The **LOGBRUSH** type is a special GDI-defined structure that is designed to hold the attributes of a logical brush:

```
typedef struct tagLOGBRUSH {
    UINT lbStyle;
    COLORREF lbColor;
    ULONG_PTR lbHatch;
} LOGBRUSH, *PLOGBRUSH, NEAR *NPLOGBRUSH, FAR *LPLOGBRUSH;
```

The **lsStyle** data member identifies the type or "style" of brush. This member can be assigned one of the identifiers listed in Table 2.2.

The **lbColor** data member identifies the color of the brush. For solid brushes, this value indicates the solid or dithered color. For hatch brushes, this value indicates the color of the hatch marks. For pattern brushes whose patterns

Table 2.2 Possible values of the LOGBRUSH::lsStyle data member.

Identifier	Value	Style
BS_SOLID	0	Indicates a solid brush
BS_NULL	1	Indicates a transparent (hollow) brush
BS_HATCHED	2	Indicates a hatch brush
BS_PATTERN	3	Indicates a pattern brush whose pattern is defined by a device-dependent bitmap
BS_DIBPATTERNPT	6	Indicates a pattern brush whose pattern is defined by a device-independent bitmap; the **lbHatch** data member specifies a pointer to this DIB

are defined by a device-independent bitmap, the **lbColor** data member identifies the format of the bitmap's color table (**DIB_PAL_COLORS** or **DIB_RGB_COLORS**).

For hatch brushes, the **lbHatch** data member identifies the hatch style. This style is indicated by one of the identifiers listed in Table 2.3 (see also Figure 2.3). For solid brushes, the **lbHatch** data member is ignored. For pattern brushes, this data member indicates the bitmap that defines the brush's pattern. In this case, the **lbHatch** data member identifies either a handle to a device-dependent bitmap object or a direct pointer to a packed device-independent bitmap.

The **LOGBRUSH** structure can hold the attributes of all types of logical brushes and therefore can be used to create any type of logical brush. Recall from the previous section that to create a logical brush, you have to call the brush-creation function that is specific to the type of brush you're creating. For example, to create a solid brush, you use the **CreateSolidBrush** function. To create a hatch brush, you use the **CreateHatchBrush** function. To create a pattern brush, you use one of its related creation functions. Instead of requiring that you memorize each of these function names, however, the GDI provides a more generalized brush-creation function, **CreateBrushIndirect**, which can be used to create a solid, hatch, or pattern brush:

```
HBRUSH CreateBrushIndirect(
    IN CONST LOGBRUSH *lpclb    // pointer to a const LOGBRUSH structure
   );
```

The single **lpclb** parameter points to a **LOGBRUSH** structure that describes the type and attributes of the brush that you're creating. If the **CreateBrushIndirect** function is successful, the return value is a handle to the new logical brush object; otherwise, the function returns **NULL**.

Table 2.3 Possible values of the LOGBRUSH::lbHatch data member for hatch brushes.

Identifier	Value	Style
HS_HORIZONTAL	0	Pattern consists of parallel lines that run horizontally
HS_VERTICAL	1	Pattern consists of parallel lines that run vertically
HS_FDIAGONAL	2	Pattern consists of parallel lines that run northwest to southeast
HS_BDIAGONAL	3	Pattern consists of parallel lines that run southwest to northeast
HS_CROSS	4	Pattern consists of two sets of parallel lines that run horizontally and vertically
HS_DIAGCROSS	5	Pattern consists of two sets of parallel lines that run northwest to southeast and southwest to northeast

The Brush Origin

When a brush object is used to fill an area of a window, the GDI maps the origin of this window's client area to a specific pixel in the brush's underlying bitmap. A device context's *brush origin* simply determines which pixel in this bitmap is mapped to the window origin (in device units).

Think back to the analogy between a brush object and a patch of wallpaper. If the pattern of the wallpaper is not random, then before you cut out a certain patch, you'll need to decide from which area of the wallpaper this patch should be extracted so that when you do finally paste it on the wall, the patch will blend in with the surrounding areas that have already been covered. A device context's brush origin is similar to the location within the wallpaper from which the patch was cut. Following this notion, it should be clear that the brush origin is relevant for hatch and pattern brushes but has little meaning for solid brushes. To retrieve a device context's current brush origin, you use the **GetBrushOrgEx** function:

```
BOOL GetBrushOrgEx(
    IN HDC hdc,          // handle to the target device context
    OUT LPPOINT lppt     // pointer to a POINT structure that receives
                         // the current brush origin
  );
```

The **hdc** parameter identifies the device context whose brush origin you want to retrieve. This value is placed in the **POINT** structure specified by the **lppt** parameter. The **GetBrushOrgEx** function returns a Boolean value indicating success or failure.

To change the current brush origin, you use the **SetBrushOrgEx** function:

```
BOOL SetBrushOrgEx(
    IN HDC hdc,           // handle to the device context
    IN int nXOrg,         // horizontal location of the new brush origin
    IN int nYOrg,         // vertical location of the new brush origin
    OUT LPPOINT lppt      // pointer to a POINT structure that receives
                          // the previous brush origin
  );
```

The **hdc** parameter identifies the device context whose brush origin will be changed. The **nXOrg** and **nYOrg** parameters specify the new brush origin, while the **lppt** parameter points to a **POINT** structure that receives the previous brush origin. Like the **GetBrushOrgEx** function, **SetBrushOrgEx** returns **TRUE** if successful and **FALSE** otherwise.

The **SetBrushOrgEx** function works differently on systems running Windows 95 or Windows 98. On these platforms, the brush origin is not automatically tracked, so the **SetBrushOrgEx** function does not change the origin of the device context's currently associated brush; rather, it changes the origin of the *next* brush that is realized. This is especially cumbersome because the GDI caches all realized brushes. This being the case, you need to use the **UnrealizeObject** function to force the GDI to re-realize the brush. The following code snippet demonstrates this process:


```
// 1. Deselect the brush to track by replacing
// it with a stock brush object
HBRUSH hStockBrush = static_cast<HBRUSH>(
   GetStockObject(BLACK_BRUSH)
   );
HBRUSH hTrackBrush = static_cast<HBRUSH>(
   SelectObject(hDC, hStockBrush)
   );

// 2. Change the brush origin of the next brush
// that is realized with this device context
SetBrushOrgEx(hDC, new_x, new_y, NULL);

// 3. Instruct the GDI to re-realize the brush
// the next time it is selected
UnrealizeObject(hTrackBrush);

// 4. Select the brush back into the DC (the brush will
// be re-realized with the new origin)
SelectObject(hDC, hTrackBrush);
```

Rendering with a Brush Object

As I pointed out earlier, brushes are used primarily to fill defined areas. All of the GDI functions that render a filled shape carry out the "filling" portion by using the target device context's currently selected brush object. For example, if you use the **Rectangle** function, the interior of the specified rectangle is filled with whatever brush object is selected into the destination device context. Moreover, **Rectangle** and its related filled-shaped functions are governed by the target device context's current drawing mode. (These functions are also governed by the target device context's current background mode when you're using a hatch brush object.)

To supplement the filled-shape functions, the GDI provides the **FillRect** and **PatBlt** functions, which are specifically designed for use with brush objects. The **FillRect** function can be used to fill a rectangular area with a brush object, without requiring that the brush be explicitly selected into the target device context. This function is useful when you don't want to manually select, then deselect, the desired brush and when you don't want the filling operation to be affected by the device context's current drawing (ROP2) mode. The **PatBlt** function is handy when you do want to use the currently selected brush, but you do not want to explicitly change the current drawing mode.

The FillRect Function

The **FillRect** function is designed to fill a rectangular area with a particular brush object. This function is equivalent to the **Rectangle** function, in which a transparent pen object is used to outline the rectangle, and in which the drawing mode is set to **R2_COPYPEN**.

The **FillRect** function takes three parameters:

```
int FillRect(
    IN HDC hDC,              // handle to the target device context
    IN CONST RECT *lpcrc,    // pointer to const RECT structure that
                             // defines the area to fill
    IN HBRUSH hbr            // handle to the logical brush object
                             // to fill with
  );
```

The **hDC** parameter identifies the destination device context. The **lpcrc** parameter is a pointer to a **RECT** structure whose data members define the rectangular area that's to be filled with the brush object identified by the **hbr** parameter. For example:

```
HBRUSH hBrush = static_cast<HBRUSH>(GetStockObject(WHITE_BRUSH));
RECT RDest = {0, 0, 100, 200};
FillRect(hDC, &RDest, hBrush);
```

TIP: *The* ***hbr*** *parameter need not be a handle to a logical brush object; you can also specify a system-element color index that is offset by 1 (e.g.,* ***COLOR_WINDOW + 1****).*

Note that when the target DC's graphic mode (see Chapter 10) is set to **GM_COMPATIBLE**, the width and height of the filled area is one device unit within the right and bottom edges of the specified rectangle, respectively. If successful, the **FillRect** function returns a non-zero value; otherwise, the return value is zero.

The PatBlt Function

The **PatBlt** function is similar to the **BitBlt** function—both perform a bit-block transfer. The **PatBlt** function, however, does not include a parameter that specifies the source device context; rather, the "source" is the target device context's currently selected brush object. In this way, the **PatBlt** function is useful for filling an area with the current brush. "PatBlt" stands for PATtern BLock Transfer.

Like the **FillRect** function, **PatBlt** ignores the target device context's current drawing mode. Yet, unlike the former function, the **PatBlt** function is not limited to the **R2_COPYPEN** mode:

```
BOOL PatBlt(
    IN HDC hdc,             // handle to the target device context
    IN int nXLeft,          // horizontal position of the top-left corner
                            // of the destination rectangle
    IN int nYLeft,          // vertical position of the top-left corner
                            // of the destination rectangle
    IN int nWidth,          // width of the destination rectangle
    IN int nHeight,         // height of the destination rectangle
    IN DWORD dwRop          // ternary-raster-operation code
  );
```

The **hdc** parameter identifies the destination device context. It is the currently selected brush object of this device context that is used as the source "image." The destination rectangle is specified by the **nXLeft**, **nYLeft**, **nWidth**, and **nHeight** parameters, in logical units. The **dwRop** parameter is used to specify the ternary-raster-operation (ROP3) code. However, because there is no source device context, and thus there are only two operands (the target device context and its associated brush), only a subset of the 256 standard ROP3 codes are valid. Specifically, this subset includes only those codes that do not involve the bits of the source bitmap. Table 2.4 lists the predefined ROP3 codes that are valid with the **PatBlt** function.

Table 2.4 The predefined ternary-raster-operation constants that are valid for the PatBlt function.

ROP3 Identifier	Effect
PATCOPY	Destination = brush
PATPAINT	Destination = brush **XOR** destination
PATINVERT	Destination = (brush **OR** (**NOT** destination)) **OR** destination
DSTINVERT	Destination = **NOT** destination
BLACKNESS	Destination = black
WHITENESS	Destination = white

The **PatBlt** function returns a Boolean value indicating success or failure.

Interestingly, calling the **PatBlt** function is equivalent to calling the **BitBlt** function with a **NULL hdcSrc** parameter. Because the former relies on the latter, the results are identical. The **PatBlt** function, however, requires fewer parameters, and it's commonly used as a quick way to clear a bitmap that's selected into a memory device context:

```
PatBlt(hMemDC, 0, 0, bmp.bmWidth, bmp.bmHeight, BLACKNESS);
```

Another common use of the **PatBlt** function is for rendering a tracking rectangle. Typically, such a scheme is handled by a technique called *rubber banding*, in which the "moving" effect is accomplished by repetitively drawing, then erasing, a rectangle. The task of "erasing" is done by changing the drawing mode of the destination device context, typically the device context of the screen. But, because the rendering is most often performed in response to mouse-related messages (e.g., **WM_LBUTTONDOWN**, **WM_MOUSEMOVE**), it's quite burdensome to store, then restore, the drawing mode and/or pen of the target device context. However, if you use the **DSTINVERT** ROP3 code with the **PatBlt** function, there's no need to alter the drawing mode or graphic objects of the destination device context. Listing 2.1 demonstrates how to create an application that allows the user to move an image by using the mouse. The "moving" operation is signified by a tracking rectangle that is drawn using the **PatBlt** function.

Listing 2.1 Rendering a tracking rectangle by using the PatBlt function.

```
// ----------------------------------------------------------------
// Windows 2000 Graphics API Black Book
// Chapter 2 - Listing 2.1 (PatBlt Tracking Rect Demo)
// ----------------------------------------------------------------

#include <windows.h>

HINSTANCE hInst;
const char* WndClassName = "GMainWnd";
LRESULT CALLBACK MainWndProc(HWND hWnd, UINT msg, WPARAM wParam,
   LPARAM lParam);

int APIENTRY WinMain(HINSTANCE hInstance, HINSTANCE, LPTSTR,
   int nCmdShow)
{
   hInst = hInstance;

   WNDCLASS wc;
   memset(&wc, 0, sizeof(WNDCLASS));
```

```
    wc.style = CS_VREDRAW | CS_HREDRAW;
    wc.lpszClassName = WndClassName;
    wc.lpfnWndProc = MainWndProc;
    wc.hInstance = hInstance;
    wc.hCursor = LoadCursor(NULL, IDC_ARROW);
    wc.hbrBackground = static_cast<HBRUSH>(
       GetStockObject(BLACK_BRUSH)
       );

    if (RegisterClass(&wc))
    {
       HWND hWnd =
          CreateWindow(WndClassName, "Move the Penguin! ",
                       WS_OVERLAPPEDWINDOW | WS_CAPTION |
                       WS_VISIBLE | WS_CLIPCHILDREN,
                       CW_USEDEFAULT, CW_USEDEFAULT, 640, 480,
                       NULL, NULL, hInst, NULL);

       if (hWnd)
       {
          ShowWindow(hWnd, nCmdShow);
          UpdateWindow(hWnd);

          MSG msg;
          while (GetMessage(&msg, NULL, 0, 0))
          {
              TranslateMessage(&msg);
              DispatchMessage(&msg);
          }
       }
     }
     return 0;
}

// image related
HDC hMemDC = NULL;
HBITMAP hOldBmp = NULL;
const char* filename = "PENGUIN.BMP";
RECT RImage = {225, 110, 225, 110};

// tracking related
bool is_tracking = false;
HDC hScreenDC = NULL;
POINT PMouse = {0, 0};
RECT RTrack = {0, 0, 0, 0};
const int line_width = 5;
```

```
// utility function to map to/from window coordinates
void MapRect(IN HWND hWndFrom, IN HWND hWndTo, IN OUT RECT& RMap)
{
   MapWindowPoints(
      hWndFrom, hWndTo,
      reinterpret_cast<LPPOINT>(&RMap), 2
      );
}

//
// utility function that uses the PatBlt function to
// render a tracking rectangle
//
void RenderTrackingRect(IN HDC hDestDC, IN RECT& RRender)
{
   const int width = RRender.right - RRender.left;
   const int height = RRender.bottom - RRender.top;
   const DWORD dwROP3 = DSTINVERT; // experiment with others

   // render top bar
   PatBlt(hDestDC,
          RRender.left, RRender.top,
          width, line_width,
          dwROP3);
   // render bottom bar
   PatBlt(hDestDC,
          RRender.left, RRender.bottom - line_width,
          width, line_width,
          dwROP3);
   // render left bar
   PatBlt(hDestDC,
          RRender.left, RRender.top + line_width,
          line_width, height - (2 * line_width),
          dwROP3);
   // render right bar
   PatBlt(hDestDC,
          RRender.right - line_width, RRender.top + line_width,
          line_width, height - (2 * line_width),
          dwROP3);
}

LRESULT CALLBACK MainWndProc(HWND hWnd, UINT msg, WPARAM wParam,
   LPARAM lParam)
{
   switch (msg)
   {
```

```
case WM_CREATE:
{
   // create a memory DC
   hMemDC = CreateCompatibleDC(NULL);
   if (hMemDC)
   {
      // load the penguin bitmap
      HBITMAP hBmp = static_cast<HBITMAP>(
         LoadImage(hInst, filename, IMAGE_BITMAP, 0, 0,
                   LR_LOADFROMFILE | LR_DEFAULTSIZE)
         );
      if (hBmp)
      {
         // get the bitmap's dimensions
         BITMAP bmp;
         if (GetObject(hBmp, sizeof(BITMAP), &bmp))
         {
            RImage.right += bmp.bmWidth;
            RImage.bottom += bmp.bmHeight;

            // realize the bitmap
            hOldBmp = static_cast<HBITMAP>(
               SelectObject(hMemDC, hBmp)
               );
         }
         else DeleteObject(hBmp);
      }
   }
   break;
}
case WM_LBUTTONDOWN:
{
   PMouse.x = LOWORD(lParam);
   PMouse.y = HIWORD(lParam);

   RECT RClient;
   if (PtInRect(&RImage, PMouse) &&
        GetClientRect(hWnd, &RClient))
   {
      MapRect(hWnd, HWND_DESKTOP, RClient);
      ClipCursor(&RClient);

      //
      // grab a handle to the screen DC and clip
      // all output to the client area of our window
      //
```

```
            hScreenDC = GetDC(NULL);
            HRGN hClipRgn = CreateRectRgnIndirect(&RClient);
            SelectClipRgn(hScreenDC, hClipRgn);
            DeleteObject(hClipRgn);

            CopyRect(&RTrack, &RImage);
            MapRect(hWnd, HWND_DESKTOP, RTrack);

            // render the first tracking rect
            RenderTrackingRect(hScreenDC, RTrack);
            is_tracking = true;
         }
         break;
      }
      case WM_MOUSEMOVE:
      {
         if (HScreenDC && is_tracking)
         {
            POINT PCurrent = {LOWORD(lParam), HIWORD(lParam)};
            const int dX = PCurrent.x - PMouse.x;
            const int dY = PCurrent.y - PMouse.y;

            // erase the previous rectangle
            RenderTrackingRect(hScreenDC, RTrack);
            // update the position
            OffsetRect(&RTrack, dX, dY);
            // render the new tracking rectangle
            RenderTrackingRect(hScreenDC, RTrack);

            // update the mouse position
            memcpy(&PMouse, &PCurrent, sizeof(POINT));
         }
         break;
      }
      case WM_LBUTTONUP:
      {
         // clean up
         if (is_tracking)
         {
            is_tracking = false;
            SelectClipRgn(hScreenDC, NULL);
            ReleaseDC(NULL, hScreenDC);

            InvalidateRect(hWnd, &RImage, true);
            CopyRect(&RImage, &RTrack);
```

```
            MapRect(HWND_DESKTOP, hWnd, RImage);
            InvalidateRect(hWnd, &RImage, true);

            ClipCursor(NULL);
         }
         break;
      }
      case WM_PAINT:
      {
         PAINTSTRUCT ps;
         HDC hDC = BeginPaint(hWnd, &ps);
         try
         {
            //
            // TODO: Add palette support...
            //

            // render the penguin
            BitBlt(hDC, RImage.left, RImage.top,
                   RImage.right - RImage.left,
                   RImage.bottom - RImage.top,
                   hMemDC, 0, 0,
                   SRCCOPY);
         }
         catch (...)
         {
            EndPaint(hWnd, &ps);
         }
         EndPaint(hWnd, &ps);
         break;
      }
      case WM_DESTROY:
      {
         // clean up
         DeleteObject(SelectObject(hMemDC, hOldBmp));
         DeleteDC(hMemDC);

         PostQuitMessage(0);
         break;
      }
   }
   return DefWindowProc(hWnd, msg, wParam, lParam);
}
```

Immediate Solutions

Creating a Solid Brush

If you need to fill an area with a particular color, you'll want to use a logical solid brush object. To create a solid brush, you use the **CreateSolidBrush** function:

```
HBRUSH CreateSolidBrush(
    IN COLORREF crColor     // desired color of solid brush
   );
```

The single **crColor** parameter is a **COLORREF**-type (32-bit) value that identifies the color of the solid brush. If the **CreateSolidBrush** function is successful, the return value is a handle to the new logical brush object. If the **CreateSolidBrush** function fails, the return value is **NULL**.

TIP: *You need to create a solid brush object only if you require a unique color that the system has not already defined. If you want to render an object in the system window background color, for example, use a stock brush object instead.*

After the brush is created, you can use it directly (e.g., with the **FillRect** function), or you can select it into a device context via the **SelectObject** function. The following code snippet demonstrates how to create a solid red logical brush object (**hBrush**) and how to use it with the **FillRect** function to paint the client area of a window (**hWnd**) :

```
HDC hDC = GetDC(hWnd);
try
{
   // create a solid red brush object
   COLORREF clrRed = PALETTERGB(255, 0, 0);
   HBRUSH hBrush = CreateSolidBrush(clrRed);
   if (hBrush)
   {
      RECT RClient;
      if (GetClientRect(hWnd, &RClient))
      {
         FillRect(hDC, &RClient, hBrush);
      }
      DeleteObject(hBrush);
```

```
    }
}
catch (...)
{
    ReleaseDC(hWnd, hDC);
}
ReleaseDC(hWnd, hDC);
```

As demonstrated in the previous code snippet, when you're finished using the brush, you must destroy it by using the **DeleteObject** function.

WARNING! Do not call the DeleteObject function for a brush that is selected into a device context—you must disassociate the brush from the device context before you destroy it.

An alternative to using the **CreateSolidBrush** function is to use the "general-purpose" **CreateBrushIndirect** function. In this case, you assign the **BS_SOLID** identifier to the **LOGBRUSH::lbStyle** data member, and assign the desired brush color to the **lbColor** data member. In the previous example, we created a logical solid red brush object; we'll do the same thing here, but do it by using the **CreateBrushIndirect** function:

```
HDC hDC = GetDC(hWnd);
try
{
    LOGBRUSH lb;
    lb.lbStyle = BS_SOLID;
    lb.lbColor = PALETTERGB(255, 0, 0);

    // create a solid red brush
    HBRUSH hBrush = CreateBrushIndirect(&lb);
    if (hBrush)
    {
        RECT RClient;
        if (GetClientRect(hWnd, &RClient))
        {
            FillRect(hDC, &RClient, hBrush);
        }
        DeleteObject(hBrush);
    }
}
catch (...)
{
    ReleaseDC(hWnd, hDC);
}
ReleaseDC(hWnd, hDC);
```

Creating a Hatch Brush

If you need to fill an area with one of the six predefined patterns depicted in Figure 2.3 (see the "In Depth" section), you'll want to use a logical hatch brush.

***TIP:** If you need a pattern other than those represented by the six standard hatch styles, use a pattern brush instead.*

To create a logical hatch brush, you use the **CreateHatchBrush** function:

```
HBRUSH CreateHatchBrush(
    IN int fnStyle,        // hatch style identifier
    IN COLORREF clrref     // color of the hatch lines
   );
```

The **fnStyle** parameter is specified as one of the six hatch-style identifiers listed in Table 2.3 (see the "In Depth" section). This parameter governs the pattern that the new logical brush object will contain. The **clrref** parameter is used to specify the color of the hatch marks. If the **CreateHatchBrush** function is successful, it returns a handle to the new logical hatch brush object. Otherwise, the return value is **NULL**.

***NOTE:** The **clrref** parameter of the **CreateHatchBrush** function determines the color of the brush's hatch marks, but the background color of the destination device context governs the color that will appear in between these hatches.*

As with all non-stock logical brush objects, when you're finished with a hatch brush, you must destroy it by using the **DeleteObject** function. However, do not call the **DeleteObject** function on a brush that is currently selected into a device context; you must deselect the brush before destroying it.

The following code snippet demonstrates how to create a logical hatch brush object for the purpose of rendering a filled rectangle:

```
HDC hDC = GetDC(hWnd);
try
{
   // create a hatch red brush
   const COLORREF clrRed = PALETTERGB(255, 0, 0);
   HBRUSH hHatchBrush =
      CreateHatchBrush(HS_CROSS, clrRed);
   if (hHatchBrush)
   {
      RECT RDest = {0, 0, 100, 100};
      FillRect(hDC, &RDest, hHatchBrush);
```

```
        DeleteObject(hHatchBrush);
    }
}
catch (...)
{
    ReleaseDC(hWnd, hDC);
}
ReleaseDC(hWnd, hDC);
```

Instead of using the **CreateHatchBrush** function, you can use the more general **CreateBrushIndirect** function. Here, you specify the **LOGBRUSH::lbStyle** data member as **BS_HATCHED**, specify the **lbHatch** data member as the desired hatch style identifier, and specify the **lbColor** data member as the desired hatch mark color:

```
HDC hDC = GetDC(hWnd);
try
{
    LOGBRUSH lb;
    lb.lbStyle = BS_HATCHED;
    lb.lbHatch = HS_CROSS;
    lb.lbColor = PALETTERGB(255, 0, 0);

    // create a hatch red brush
    HBRUSH hHatchBrush = CreateBrushIndirect(&lb);
    if (hHatchBrush)
    {
        RECT RDest = {0, 0, 100, 100};
        FillRect(hDC, &RDest, hHatchBrush);

        DeleteObject(hHatchBrush);
    }
}
catch (...)
{
    ReleaseDC(hWnd, hDC);
}
ReleaseDC(hWnd, hDC);
```

Creating a Pattern Brush from a DDB

If you need to fill an area with a custom pattern, you'll want a pattern brush. The pattern itself must be defined by the bits of a bitmap. Here, we'll focus on the case when this bitmap is a device-dependent bitmap (DDB).

To create a pattern brush from a DDB, you use the **CreatePatternBrush** function:

```
HBRUSH CreatePatternBrush(
    IN HBITMAP hbmp     // handle to the template DDB
   );
```

The function requires only one parameter: a handle to the bitmap object whose bits govern the pattern of the new logical brush object. If the **CreatePatternBrush** function is successful, it returns a handle to this brush object. If the function fails, the return value is **NULL**.

WARNING! In Windows 95, the size of the template bitmap is limited to 64 pixels (8 pixels wide and high). Although you can pass the CreatePatternBrush a larger bitmap, the resultant pattern will be based upon only the upper-left 64 pixels.

The following code snippet demonstrates how to create a pattern brush from a device-dependent bitmap that is loaded from a file:

```
const char* filename = "PATTERNBITMAP.BMP";
HBITMAP hBmp = static_cast<HBITMAP>(
   LoadImage(hInst, filename, IMAGE_BITMAP, 0, 0,
             LR_LOADFROMFILE | LR_DEFAULTSIZE)
   );

if (hBmp)
{
   HBRUSH hPatternBrush = CreatePatternBrush(hBmp);
   DeleteObject(hBmp);

   if (hPatternBrush)
   {
      // ...
      DeleteObject(hPatternBrush);
   }
}
```

Instead of the aforementioned approach, you can use the **CreateBrushIndirect** function to create a pattern brush from a DDB. To accomplish this, you need to first initialize a **LOGBRUSH** structure appropriately. Namely, you specify the **lpStyle** data member as **BS_PATTERN** and specify the **lbHatch** data member as the handle to the DDB.

As with all non-stock brush objects, you must destroy a pattern brush by using the **DeleteObject** function when the brush is no longer needed. However, do not call the **DeleteObject** function on a brush that is currently selected into a device context. You can destroy the template bitmap (also via **DeleteObject**) any time after the pattern brush is created.

Related solutions:	Found on page:
Creating a Monochrome Device-Dependent Bitmap	307
Creating a Color Device-Dependent Bitmap	311
Loading a Device-Dependent Bitmap from a File	323

Creating a Pattern Brush from a DIB

To create a pattern brush from a device-independent bitmap (DIB), you use the **CreateDIBPatternBrushPt** function:

```
HBRUSH CreateDIBPatternBrushPt(
    IN CONST VOID *lpcPackedDIB,    // pointer to a packed DIB
    IN UINT iUsage                  // information about the format of the
                                    // DIB's color table
   );
```

The **lpcPackedDIB** parameter is used to specify the address of a packed DIB. Recall, a packed DIB is nothing more than a DIB whose bits immediately follow the associated **BITMAPINFO** structure. By using a packed DIB, you can pass the **CreateDIBPatternBrushPt** function information about the attributes of the DIB, and its bits, via a single parameter.

WARNING! In Windows 95, the size of the template bitmap is limited to 64 pixels (8 pixels wide and high). Although you can pass CreateDIBPatternBrushPt a larger DIB, the resultant pattern will be based upon only the upper-left 64 pixels.

The **iUsage** parameter is used to specify how the bitmap's color-table entries (if present) should be used. If the color table contains raw red, green, and blue (RGB) intensity values, this parameter must be set to **DIB_RGB_COLORS** (0). If, instead, the entries of the bitmap's color table are palette indices, **iUsage** should be set to **DIB_PAL_COLORS** (1). If no color table is provided, this parameter is ignored.

If the **CreateDIBPatternPt** function succeeds, the return value is a handle to the new logical brush object. If the function fails, it returns **NULL**. The following code snippet demonstrates the use of the **CreateDIBPatternPt** function to create a logical pattern brush with a densely striped green pattern:

```
const int bpp = 24;
const int width = 100;
const int height = 100;
const int bytes_per_scanline =
   (((width * bpp) + 31) & ~31) / 8;

const long size =
   sizeof(BITMAPINFO) +
   height * bytes_per_scanline;

unsigned char* data = new unsigned char[size];
try
{
   memset(data, 0, size);
   LPBITMAPINFO lpbi =
      reinterpret_cast<LPBITMAPINFO>(data);

   lpbi->bmiHeader.biSize = sizeof(BITMAPINFOHEADER);
   lpbi->bmiHeader.biWidth = width;
   lpbi->bmiHeader.biHeight = -height; // top-down
   lpbi->bmiHeader.biPlanes = 1;
   lpbi->bmiHeader.biBitCount = bpp;
   lpbi->bmiHeader.biCompression = BI_RGB;

   unsigned char* bits =
      reinterpret_cast<unsigned char*>(
         lpbi->bmiColors + lpbi->bmiHeader.biClrUsed
      );

   for (int y = 0; y < height; ++y)
   {
      const int row = bytes_per_scanline * y;
      for (int x = 0; x < bytes_per_scanline; x += 3)
      {
         if (y % 4 == 0)
         {
            *(bits + (x + 0) + row) = 0;   // blue
            *(bits + (x + 1) + row) = 255; // green
            *(bits + (x + 2) + row) = 0;   // red
         }
         else
         {
            *(bits + (x + 0) + row) = 255; // blue
            *(bits + (x + 1) + row) = 255; // green
            *(bits + (x + 2) + row) = 255; // red
```

```
            }
        }
    }

    HBRUSH hPatternBrush =
        CreateDIBPatternBrushPt(lpbi, DIB_RGB_COLORS);
    delete [] data; data = NULL;
    if (hPatternBrush)
    {
        // ...
        DeleteObject(hPatternBrush);
    }
}
catch (...)
{
    delete [] data;
}
```


An equivalent method to creating a pattern brush from a DIB is to use the general **CreateBrushIndirect** function. Here, you initialize the corresponding **LOGBRUSH** structure by setting the **lbStyle** data member to **BS_DIBPATTERNPT**, setting the **lbColor** data member to **DIB_RGB_COLORS** or **DIB_PAL_COLORS**, and setting the **lbHatch** data member to the address of the packed DIB.

When you're done with the pattern brush, you must destroy it by using the **DeleteObject** function. If the brush is selected into a device context, you must deselect it before passing its handle to **DeleteObject**. You can free the memory associated with the DIB any time after the pattern brush is created.

Related solutions:	Found on page:
Creating a Device-Independent Bitmap	391
Loading a Device-Independent Bitmap from a File	405

Creating a Transparent Brush

A transparent or "hollow" brush is useful when you need to render by using a filled-shape function, but you do not want the interior of the shape to be filled. In fact, you don't need to create a transparent brush because the GDI automatically creates one during its initialization process. Therefore, you can simply use the **GetStockObject** function to retrieve a handle to the logical stock transparent brush object:

```
HBRUSH hHollowBrush = static_cast<HBRUSH>(
   GetStockObject(HOLLOW_BRUSH)
   );
```

You instruct the **GetStockObject** function to retrieve a handle to the stock transparent brush by specifying the **HOLLOW_BRUSH** or **NULL_BRUSH** type identifier. Moreover, because the returned handle is a handle to a GDI stock object, there's no need to call the **DeleteObject** function. For more information on the **GetStockObject** function, refer to the section called "Obtaining a Handle to a Stock Brush."

An alternative approach is to create a transparent brush via the **CreateBrushIndirect** function. Here, you specify the **LOGBRUSH::lbStyle** data member as **BS_HOLLOW**; all other data members are ignored:

```
LOGBRUSH lb;
lb.lbStyle = BS_HOLLOW;

HBRUSH hHollowBrush = CreateBrushIndirect(&lb);
if (hHollowBrush)
{
   // ...
   DeleteObject(hHollowBrush);
}
```

In this latter case, because you're actually creating a new logical brush object, you must explicitly destroy it by using the **DeleteObject** function. However, as with other non-stock brush objects, do not destroy a transparent brush until it is appropriately deselected from a device context.

Obtaining a Handle to a Stock Brush

To obtain a handle to a logical stock brush object, you use the **GetStockObject** function:

```
HGDIOBJ GetStockObject(
    IN int fnObject        // identifier of the stock object
   );
```

The value that is passed as the **fnObject** parameter determines which stock brush object the function will return. **GetStockObject** is a general function and therefore can be used to retrieve a handle to non-brush stock objects as well. For the

Table 2.5 Stock brush object identifiers for use with the **GetStockObject** function.

Identifier	Value	Stock Brush Variety
WHITE_BRUSH	0	Solid white stock brush
LTGRAY_BRUSH	1	Solid light-gray stock brush
GRAY_BRUSH	2	Solid gray stock brush
DKGRAY_BRUSH	3	Solid dark-gray stock brush
BLACK_BRUSH	4	Solid black stock brush
NULL_BRUSH	5	Transparent stock brush
HOLLOW_BRUSH	5	Same as **NULL_BRUSH**
DC_BRUSH	18	Solid brush of a variable color; white is the default (Windows 2000 only)

purpose of retrieving a handle to one of the GDI's seven stock brushes, you specify the **fnObject** parameter as one of the identifiers listed in Table 2.5. For example:

```
HBRUSH hStockBrush = static_cast<HBRUSH>(
   GetStockObject(WHITE_BRUSH)
   );
```

***TIP:** If you merely want to fill an area with a black or white color, consider using the **PatBlt** function with the **BLACKNESS** or **WHITENESS** ternary-raster-operation code, respectively.*

Although it does no harm, there is no need to call the **DeleteObject** function on a GDI stock brush object. The function will actually do nothing. Note, however, that you should never call the **DeleteObject** function on a *system* stock brush.

Obtaining a Handle to a System Brush

If you need to paint a control or fill an area with the color that Windows itself uses for one of its standard window elements, you'll want to use a system stock brush. To obtain a handle to one of the 28 predefined system brushes, you use the **GetSysColorBrush** function:

```
HBRUSH GetSysColorBrush(
    IN int nIndex        // system color index
   );
```

The single **nIndex** parameter is specified as the color index of one of the 28 window elements. This value can be assigned any one of the identifiers listed in Table 2.6. For example:

```
HBRUSH hMDIBrush = GetSysColorBrush(COLOR_APPWORKSPACE);
```

Table 2.6 Color-index identifiers for standard window elements.

Color Identifier	Value	Window Element Color
COLOR_SCROLLBAR	0	The color of the background area (gutter) of a scroll bar
COLOR_BACKGROUND	1	The color of the desktop
COLOR_ACTIVECAPTION	2	The color of the title bar of an active window
COLOR_INACTIVECAPTION	3	The color of the title bar of an inactive window
COLOR_MENU	4	The background color of a menu
COLOR_WINDOW	5	The background color of a window
COLOR_WINDOWFRAME	6	The color of a window's frame
COLOR_MENUTEXT	7	The text color of a menu item
COLOR_WINDOWTEXT	8	The text color of a window
COLOR_CAPTIONTEXT	9	The text color of an active window's title bar
COLOR_ACTIVEBORDER	10	The color of the border of an active window
COLOR_INACTIVEBORDER	11	The color of the border of an inactive window
COLOR_APPWORKSPACE	12	The background color of an MDI (Multiple Document Interface) client window
COLOR_HIGHLIGHT	13	The background color of a control's selected items
COLOR_HIGHLIGHTTEXT	14	The text color of a control's selected items
COLOR_BTNFACE	15	The background color of a button
COLOR_BTNSHADOW	16	The color of a three-dimensional control's shadow
COLOR_GRAYTEXT	17	The color of disabled text
COLOR_BTNTEXT	18	The color of a button's caption
COLOR_INACTIVECAPTIONTEXT	19	The text color of an inactive window's title bar
COLOR_BTNHIGHLIGHT	20	The color of a three-dimensional control's highlights
COLOR_3DDKSHADOW	21	The dark color of a three-dimensional control's shadow
COLOR_3DLIGHT	22	The light color of a three-dimensional control's shadow

(continued)

Table 2.6 Color-index identifiers for standard window elements *(continued)*.

Color Identifier	Value	Window Element Color
COLOR_INFOTEXT	23	The text color of a tool-tip control
COLOR_INFOBK	24	The background color of a tool-tip control
COLOR_HOTLIGHT	26	The hot-tracking color of a control (Windows 98 and 2000 only)
COLOR_GRADIENTACTIVECAPTION	27	The faded (right-side) color of an active window's title bar (Windows 98 and 2000 only)
COLOR_GRADIENTINACTIVECAPTION	28	The faded (right-side) color of an inactive window's title bar (Windows 98 and 2000 only)

TIP: *If you plan to use a system brush with the* ***FillRect*** *function, you do not need its handle. The* ***hbr*** *parameter of the* ***FillRect*** *function can accept any of the color indices listed in Table 2.6, offset by positive one (e.g.,* ***COLOR_BTNFACE + 1****).*

Because system stock brushes are used by Windows to paint standard window elements, you should not destroy a system brush via the **DeleteObject** or any other function. Moreover, because a window's class assumes ownership of any brush object whose handle is assigned to the **hbrBackground** data member of the **WNDCLASS** structure used to initially register the class, you should not assign the return value of the **GetSysColorBrush** function to this data member. Instead, because the default window procedure will use the **FillRect** function to paint the window's background, you can set the **hbrBackground** data member to one of the color indices listed in Table 2.6 offset by a value of positive one (e.g., **COLOR_WINDOW + 1**).

Retrieving the Attributes of a Brush

Given only a handle to a logical brush object, you can retrieve its attributes by using the **GetObject** function. This function can be used to fill an associated **LOGBRUSH** structure whose data members can then be read to extract information about the brush:

```
int GetObject(
    IN HGDIOBJ hgdiobj,        // handle to the logical brush object
    IN int cbBuffer,           // number of bytes in the LOGBRUSH structure
    OUT LPVOID lpvObject       // address of a LOGBRUSH structure
  );
```

The **GetObject** function is actually more general than what is described in my earlier parameter comments. Here we'll focus specifically on the use of this function with logical brush objects. For a more general discussion of the **GetObject** function, refer to Chapter 1.

***TIP:** To obtain a handle to a device context's currently selected brush object, you can use the **GetCurrentObject** function with the **OBJ_BRUSH** identifier (see Chapter 1).*

The **hgdiobj** parameter is assigned the handle to the brush object whose attributes you want to retrieve. These attributes are stored in a **LOGBRUSH** structure, whose address is passed as the **lpvObject** parameter. The **cbBuffer** parameter is used to tell the function how many bytes the **lpvObject** parameter can hold. Here, you can simply pass the return value of the **sizeof** operator, specifying the **LOGBRUSH** type name. For example:

```
LOGBRUSH lb;
const size_t lbSize = sizeof(LOGBRUSH);
if (GetObject(hBrush, lbSize, &lb) == lbSize)
{
   switch (lb.lbStyle)
   {
      case BS_SOLID: // solid brush
         // ...
         break;
      case BS_HATCHED: // hatch brush
         // ...
         break;
      case BS_HOLLOW: // transparent brush
         // ...
         break;
   }
}
```

If successful, the **GetObject** function returns the number of bytes that were copied into the **lpvObject** parameter, namely the **sizeof(LOGBRUSH)**. If the function fails, the return value is zero. Typically, this function fails as a result of passing a handle to a non-brush object as the **hgdiobj** parameter. You can verify that a GDI object is indeed a logical brush object by using the **GetObjectType** function (see Chapter 1).

Changing the Color of a Brush

On systems running Windows 95, Windows 98, or Windows NT, there is no way to automatically change the color of a device context's selected brush object. On these platforms, you have no choice but to create a new brush of the appropriate color. In Windows 2000, however, you can achieve a similar effect by using the **SetDCBrushColor** function:

```
COLORREF SetDCBrushColor(
    IN HDC hdc,              // handle to the target device context
    IN COLORREF crColor      // COLORREF value of the new brush color
   );
```

The **SetDCBrushColor** function does not change the color of just any logical brush object that's selected into the target device context. Instead, this function affects the device context's brush color only when the stock **DC_BRUSH** is used. In this way, the function is somewhat limited.

The **hdc** parameter is specified as the handle to the device context whose current brush color you want to change. The new color is specified by the **crColor** parameter. If the **SetDCBrushColor** function is successful, the return value identifies the device context's previous brush color; otherwise, the function returns **CLR_INVALID**. For example:

```
COLORREF clrOld = SetDCBrushColor(hDC, PALETTERGB(0, 0, 255));
```

To select the stock **DC_BRUSH** brush into a device context, you use a combination of the **SelectObject** and **GetStockObject** functions:

```
SelectObject(hDC, GetStockObject(DC_BRUSH));
```

To verify that the color of a device context's **DC_BRUSH** does need to be changed, you can first use the **GetDCBrushColor** function:

```
COLORREF GetDCBrushColor(
    IN HDC hdc        // handle to the target device context
   );
```

If the **GetDCBrushColor** function is successful, the **hdc** parameter is specified as the handle to the device context whose brush color is returned. If the function fails, the return value is **CLR_INVALID**:

```
COLORREF clrDCBrush = GetDCBrushColor(hDC);
```

Chapter 3

The Pen Object

In Depth

Pens are used primarily to draw lines and curves. For example, if you're developing a statistics-based application, you can use a pen object to render a line that represents the least-squares fit of a set of points. In other cases, you might simply want to render the outline of a button or a list-box control—a pen object is useful for this as well. In short, if you need to draw any type of line-based representation to a device context, the GDI pen object is the tool of choice.

In fact, pens are used for much more than simple line drawings. As I mentioned, you can use a pen to render curves as well. Moreover, all of the filled-shape functions rely on a pen object to outline the boundaries of rectangles, ellipses, and other polygons. You can even use a pen to trace a device context's current path. That's what this chapter is about: the GDI pen object. We'll examine the different types and styles of pens, and we'll discuss how and when to use each type and even how to create a transparent pen when you don't want a shape outlined. In addition, we'll look at the new Windows 2000–based technique of changing a device context's pen color, and we'll discuss the advantages of this approach over the traditional method. Finally, we'll revisit the "tracking rectangle" example of Chapter 2, here using a pen instead of a brush.

Types of Pens

In Chapter 2, we related a logical brush object to a patch of wallpaper. What, then, does a logical pen object represent? Well, an ink pen, of course! In fact, you can think of a GDI pen object as an ink pen, a colored pencil, or a marker. Like its physical counterparts, a pen object can have varying widths, colors, and styles. For example, you can render a dotted line by simply using a dotted logical pen object. Similarly, if you need to render a wide blue line, you can create a blue-colored pen that is multiple pixels wide.

What Is a Physical Pen?

All GDI graphic objects come in two flavors: *logical* and *physical*. Recall, a physical graphic object is created when its logical counterpart is selected into a device context. This process of realization (i.e., the conversion of the logical to the physical) holds true for pens as well. For example, when you select a cyan-colored pen into a plotter's device context, you can think of the realization process as the plotter physically switching to a new cyan-colored ink marker.

When developing an application, you can, for all intents and purposes, forget about the notion of a physical pen. Unless you're creating a device driver, you'll work strictly with logical pens. Therefore, in this chapter, we'll focus exclusively on the logical variety.

The GDI defines two types of logical pen objects: *cosmetic* and *geometric*. Each of these types, in turn, defines two subtypes: *non-extended* and *extended*. All logical pen objects are manipulated through their handle of type **HPEN**.

Cosmetic vs. Geometric Pens

A *cosmetic pen* is a pen whose width is fixed to one device unit. When used to render an output primitive to the video monitor, this unit is one pixel. The width of a cosmetic pen is not influenced by the target device context's mapping mode, nor is it affected by any coordinate-space transformations. The width of a *geometric pen*, on the other hand, is not limited to one device unit. Instead, a geometric pen's width is defined in logical units. Therefore, when you draw a line with a geometric pen, the width of this line is governed by the mapping mode and/or the coordinate space transformations of the target device context.

In short, a geometric pen differs from a cosmetic pen only in that the width of the former depends on the "geometry" of the target device context. For this reason, drawing with a cosmetic pen is generally about five times faster than drawing with a geometric pen.

Stock Pens

During initialization, the GDI creates three *stock pens*. These aren't actually a new type of pen; rather, each is a non-extended pen. Specifically, these three pens are a non-extended cosmetic solid black pen (**BLACK_PEN**), a non-extended cosmetic solid white pen (**WHITE_PEN**), and a non-extended geometric transparent pen (**NULL_PEN**). On systems running Windows 98 or Windows 2000, there is also a fourth stock pen, known as the *DC pen* (**DC_PEN**). This latter type is also a non-extended solid cosmetic pen; it differs from the other three stock pens only in that its color can be changed (see "Changing the Color of a Pen," later in this chapter).

NOTE: *The **BLACK_PEN** stock object is the default pen for all display device contexts.*

As with other GDI stock objects, you obtain a handle to a stock pen by using the **GetStockObject** function. When you're done using a stock pen, there's no need to explicitly destroy it. In fact, if you pass the **DeleteObject** function a handle to a stock pen, the function will simply return **TRUE** without actually doing anything.

Extended and Non-Extended Pens

Recall, both cosmetic and geometric pens come in two varieties: extended and non-extended. After you've decided whether you need a cosmetic or a geometric pen, you'll still need to decide which subtype is better suited for your drawing. To this end, let's now examine both of these subtypes and explore the main differences between them.

Non-Extended Pens

Non-extended pens, whether cosmetic or geometric, allow you to specify two attributes: *style* and *color*. For geometric pens, you can also specify a third attribute: *width*. You must specify these attributes when you create the pen. The single exception to this rule involves specifying the color of the **DC_PEN** stock object (see "Changing the Color of a Pen," later in this chapter).

To create a non-extended pen, you use either the **CreatePen** function or the **CreatePenIndirect** function. A cosmetic non-extended pen is created when you specify a pen width of zero. (This signifies a pen width of one device unit.) A geometric non-extended pen is created when you specify a pen width greater than zero. (This signifies a logical width.)

Pen Style

Non-extended cosmetic and geometric pens can be created with one of seven predefined *pen styles*. Five of these are depicted in Figure 3.1.

The two styles that are not illustrated in Figure 3.1—the inside-frame (**PS_INSIDEFRAME**) and transparent (**PS_NULL**) styles—will be discussed when we examine the **LOGPEN** structure (see Table 2.1).

Unfortunately, when the width of the pen is more than one device unit, only the solid (**PS_SOLID**), inside-frame, and transparent styles are valid. In Windows NT and Windows 2000, you can bypass this limitation by using an extended pen. On systems running Windows 95 or Windows 98, however, you'll have to simulate the line via other means (see "Filling the Interior of a Path" in Chapter 8).

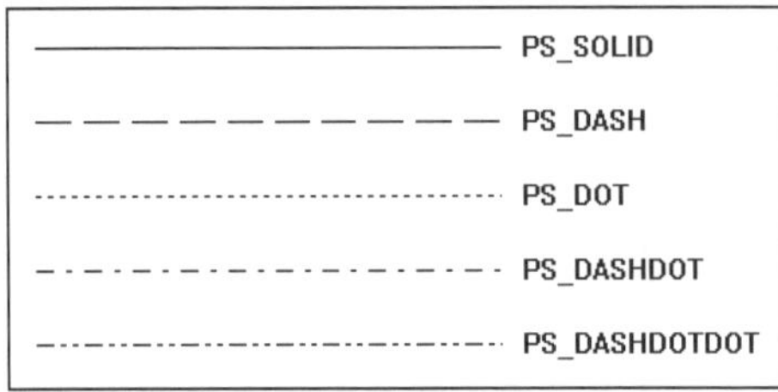

Figure 3.1 Five of the seven predefined pen styles.

Pen Color

In addition to a particular style, each non-extended pen can be created with a specific *color*. Figure 3.2 depicts several lines that were drawn using non-extended pens of various colors.

For all but the inside-frame-style pens, the specified color is a truly solid color, and if a device cannot represent the specified color, its closest match is used. For inside-frame-style pens with a width greater than one device unit, however, if a color cannot be represented, its dithered counterpart is used.

Pen Width (Geometric Pens Only)

As I mentioned, cosmetic pens are fixed in width to one device unit. In contrast, the width of a geometric pen is not fixed; rather, you can specify its width in logical units. Figure 3.3 portrays a series of lines that were drawn using geometric pens of varying widths.

For lines that are significantly wide, display device drivers typically implement the rendering via a combination of primitives and a correctly colored brush object. From a development standpoint, however, you seldom need to worry about the specifics of how this is implemented.

Extended Geometric Pens

What's the difference between an extended and a non-extended pen? The simple answer is that extended pens allow you to specify "extended" (additional) attributes, such as the pattern that will be used to fill a rendered line, the geometry of a line's ends (*end cap*), and the geometry of how two lines are joined (*join*).

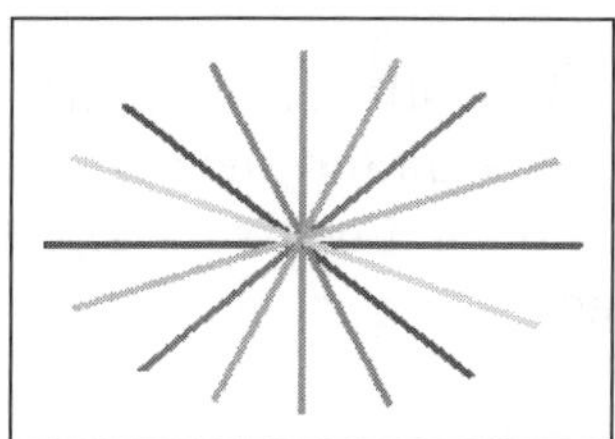

Figure 3.2 Lines rendered using different-colored pens.

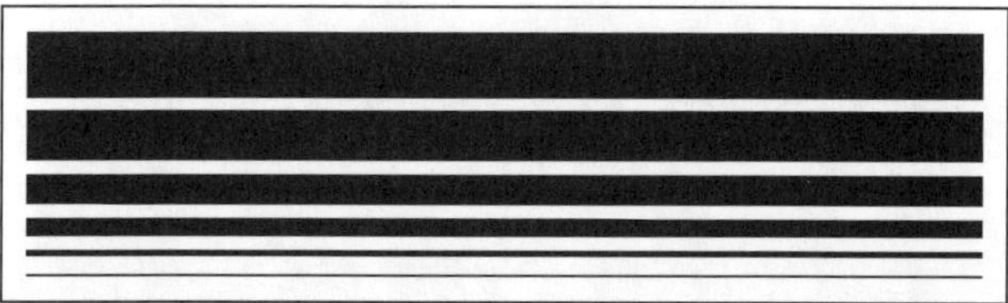

Figure 3.3 Lines rendered using several geometric pens of varying widths.

Notice the use of the word "geometry" in these latter two descriptions. As you may have guessed, these extended attributes are applicable only to extended *geometric* pens. Although you can indeed create an extended cosmetic pen, it is still limited to one device unit and cannot contain a custom fill pattern, end cap, or join.

What's the Purpose of an Extended Cosmetic Pen?

In addition to the aforementioned extended attributes, on systems running Windows NT or Windows 2000, extended cosmetic pens can be created with one additional style: **PS_ALTERNATE**. As the name implies, lines rendered with a pen of this style will have every other pixel highlighted. Moreover, in Windows NT and Windows 2000, both cosmetic and geometric extended pens can be created with a *custom* style (**PS_USERSTYLE**). Therefore, you're not limited to the styles depicted in Figure 3.1; you can specify exactly which pixels you want highlighted.

Extended pens are created via the **ExtCreatePen** function. Because extended pens inherit all of the attributes of non-extended pens, this function allows you to specify the pen type (i.e., cosmetic or geometric), style, color, and width (for geometric pens only). The function also accepts extended style parameters such as pattern, end cap, and join. Again, all of these latter styles are applicable only to extended geometric pens.

NOTE: *The specified join style is used only when the extended pen is used to trace (i.e., stroke) a path. In Windows 95 and Windows 98, this limitation applies to the end cap as well.*

The Extended Pen's Pattern

Using an extended pen, you can render a line that is filled with a specific *pattern*. For example, instead of rendering a solid line, you may want the line to be filled with a custom pattern that is defined by a separate bitmap. Figure 3.4 depicts a circle that was drawn using a patterned extended pen.

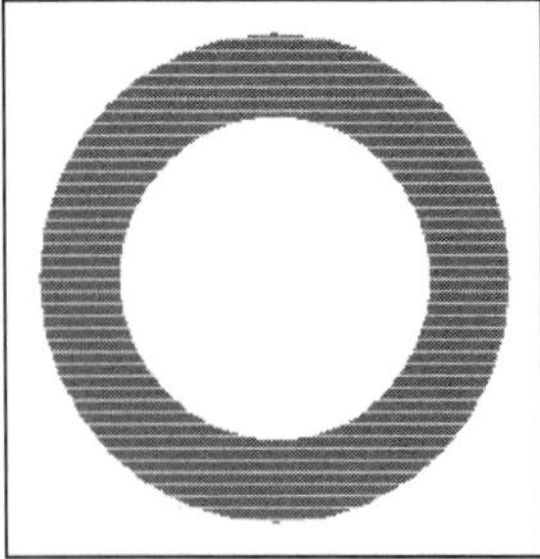

Figure 3.4 A circle rendered using an extended geometric pen with a custom pattern.

The pattern depicted in Figure 3.4 was defined by a packed device-independent bitmap (DIB), but you can also use a device-dependent bitmap (DDB) to describe the fill pattern. However, because you use a **LOGBRUSH** structure to specify the pattern (and the color) of an extended pen, you don't always have to use a custom pattern; you can, in fact, use any one of the six predefined hatch-brush styles (see Chapter 2).

The Extended Pen's End Cap

An extended pen's *end cap* governs the shape that a rendered line's ends will take on. For example, if you think of a line as a tube, you can cap the ends of this tube by using either a flat or a round cap. It's easiest to understand the effect of the end cap by examining the lines depicted in Figure 3.5.

Each of the lines shown in Figure 3.5 was rendered to extend from one edge of the box to the next. The first line was drawn using an extended pen with a *round* end cap. The third line was drawn using an extended pen with a *square* end cap. In both of these cases, the cap protrudes beyond the ends of the line (and thus the box). The middle line was rendered using an extended pen with a *flat* end cap. In this case, the cap is flush with the ends of the line.

NOTE: *Extended cosmetic pens and non-extended cosmetic or geometric pens always use a rounded end cap.*

The Extended Pen's Join

When two lines intersect, you may want to control the appearance of this intersection. The *join* of an extended pen determines the shape of the intersection between the ends of two lines.

Imagine yourself as a carpenter. Say, for example, that you'd like to use three 2x4's to create the letter "Z." When you glue the ends of two of these boards together, you have a choice of how to leave the ends. You could leave them as is, you could sand the ends down in a rounded fashion, you could sand the ends to create a perfect corner, or you could sand the ends at an angle. This process of "sanding" is the role of an extended pen's join. Figure 3.6 depicts the letter "Z" rendered with different joins.

Figure 3.5 Lines rendered using various end caps: **PS_ENDCAP_ROUND, PS_ENDCAP_FLAT,** and **PS_ENDCAP_SQUARE.**

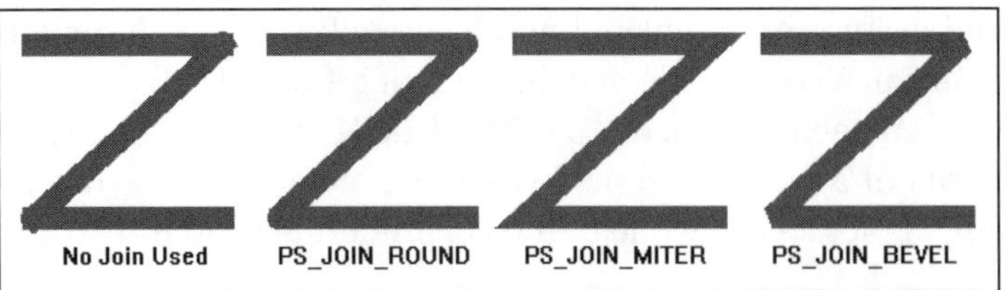

Figure 3.6 Lines rendered using various joins: **PS_JOIN_ROUND**, **PS_JOIN_MITER**, and **PS_JOIN_BEVEL**.

As previously mentioned, an extended pen's join is used only when you're rendering via a filled-shape function (e.g., **Rectangle**; Windows NT/2000 only) or when you're tracing a path (i.e., *stroking;* see Chapter 8). In fact, the first "Z" of Figure 3.6 was rendered without using a path object. Indeed, without the notion of a shape or a path, the GDI has no idea how these lines are supposed to intersect. Following this notion, for the join to have an effect, the lines must be rendered in a continuous fashion.

Logical Pen Structures

Most GDI graphic objects have a corresponding structure that can be used to describe the object's attributes. For logical non-extended pens, this structure is **LOGPEN**.

The LOGPEN Structure

As previously mentioned, the attributes of a non-extended pen include a style, a color, and—for non-extended geometric pens—a width. Not surprisingly, the **LOGPEN** structure contains a data member for each of these features:

```
typedef struct tagLOGPEN {
    UINT lopnStyle;
    POINT lopnWidth;
    COLORREF lopnColor;
} LOGPEN, *PLOGPEN, NEAR *NPLOGPEN, FAR *LPLOGPEN;
```

The **lopnStyle** data member indicates the pen's style. This style is specified by one of the identifiers listed in Table 3.1. Note that only the **PS_SOLID**, **PS_NULL**, and **PS_INSIDEFRAME** identifiers are valid when the pen width is greater than one device unit.

The **lopnWidth** data member is a **POINT** structure whose **x** data member indicates the width of the pen in logical units (the **y** data member has no meaning). If this data member is zero, the pen is a cosmetic pen. If **lopnWidth.x** is greater than zero, the pen is a geometric pen.

Table 3.1 Possible values for the LOGPEN::lopnStyle data member.

Identifier	Value	Style
PS_SOLID	0	The pen renders a solid line in a truly solid color.
PS_DASH	1	The pen renders a series of dashes in a truly solid color.
PS_DOT	2	The pen renders a series of dots in a truly solid color.
PS_DASHDOT	3	The pen renders a series with each dash followed by a dot in a truly solid color.
PS_DASHDOTDOT	4	The pen renders a series with each dash followed by two dots in a truly solid color.
PS_NULL	5	The pen is transparent (i.e., it produces no output).
PS_INSIDEFRAME	6	The pen renders a solid line that, when used by a filled-shape function, is enclosed entirely within the specified bounding rectangle. The color might be truly solid or it might be dithered. This style is meaningful for geometric pens only.

The **lopnColor** data member is a **COLORREF** (32-bit) value that indicates the color of the pen. When a logical pen is selected into a device context, if the target device cannot represent the specified color, the closest matching color is used. This is not the case when the style is **PS_INSIDEFRAME**. Here, if the color cannot be represented, the device driver might use a dithered color.

***TIP:** You can use the **RGB** macro to generate a **COLORREF** value from individual red, green, and blue intensities.*

The **LOGPEN** structure can be passed to the **CreatePenIndirect** function as a more convenient means of creating a logical pen:

```
HPEN CreatePenIndirect(
    IN CONST LOGPEN *lpclgpn    // pointer to a const LOGPEN structure
   );
```

The single **lpclgpn** parameter points to a **LOGPEN** structure that describes the attributes of the pen that is created. If the **CreatePenIndirect** function is successful, a handle to this pen is returned. Upon failure, **CreatePenIndirect** returns **NULL**.

The EXTLOGPEN Structure

Whereas the **LOGPEN** structure is used for non-extended pens, the **EXTLOGPEN** structure is used to describe the attributes of an extended pen. Because an extended pen can possess more features than a non-extended pen can, the **EXTLOGPEN** structure naturally contains more data members:

```
typedef struct tagEXTLOGPEN {
    DWORD elpPenStyle;
    DWORD elpWidth;
    UINT elpBrushStyle;
    COLORREF elpColor;
    ULONG_PTR elpHatch;
    DWORD elpNumEntries;
    DWORD elpStyleEntry[1];
} EXTLOGPEN, *PEXTLOGPEN, NEAR *NPEXTLOGPEN, FAR *LPEXTLOGPEN;
```

The **elpPenStyle** data member indicates the style of the extended pen. This member can be assigned a combination of one of the identifiers listed in Table 3.1 or **PS_USERSTYLE** (7), one of the identifiers listed in Table 3.2, one identifier from Table 3.3, and one from Table 3.4.

When you use the **GetObject** function to retrieve information about an extended pen, the function fills the specified **EXTLOGPEN** structure. In this case, you'll probably want to isolate an individual identifier from the **elpPenStyle** data member. You can accomplish this task by using the bitwise **AND** operator (&) to combine this data member with one of the appropriate mask identifiers listed in Table 3.5.

Table 3.2 Extended-pen type identifiers for the EXTLOGPEN::elpPenStyle data member.

Identifier	Value	Style
PS_COSMETIC	0	The pen is a cosmetic pen.
PS_GEOMETRIC	65536	The pen is a geometric pen.

Table 3.3 Extended-pen end-cap identifiers for the EXTLOGPEN::elpPenStyle data member.

Identifier	Value	Style
PS_ENDCAP_ROUND	0	The end cap is rounded.
PS_ENDCAP_SQUARE	256	The end cap is square.
PS_ENDCAP_FLAT	512	The end cap is flat.

Table 3.4 Extended-pen join identifiers for the EXTLOGPEN::elpPenStyle data member.

Identifier	Value	Style
PS_JOIN_ROUND	0	The join is round.
PS_JOIN_BEVEL	4096	The join is beveled.
PS_JOIN_MITER	8192	The join is mitered to a corner. The amount of mitering is determined by the target device context's current miter limit.

Table 3.5 Mask identifiers that can be used to isolate a specific identifier from the EXTLOGPEN::elpPenStyle data member.

Identifier	Value	Style
PS_STYLE_MASK	15	Used to isolate a pen style identifier.
PS_ENDCAP_MASK	3840	Used to isolate an extended-pen end-cap identifier.
PS_JOIN_MASK	61440	Used to isolate an extended-pen join identifier.
PS_TYPE_MASK	983040	Used to isolate an extended-pen type identifier.

The **elpWidth** data member indicates the width of the extended pen. This value is reported in logical units if the pen is a geometric pen, and in device units if the pen is a cosmetic pen. When specified in device units, **elpWidth** always contains a value of 1.

Recall, the pattern of an extended pen is defined by a **LOGBRUSH** structure. Therefore, some of the data members of the **EXTLOGPEN** structure are used to describe particular data members of the corresponding **LOGBRUSH** structure that was used to create the extended pen. This is the role of the **EXTLOGPEN::elpBrushStyle**, **elpColor**, and **elpHatch** data members. Specifically, the **elpBrushStyle** data member corresponds to the **LOGBRUSH::lbStyle** data member. You can assign the **elpBrushStyle** data member any one of the identifiers listed in Table 2.2 (see Chapter 2). Similarly, the **elpColor** data member corresponds to the **LOGBRUSH::lbColor** data member and can be assigned the desired **COLORREF** value. Finally, the **elpHatch** data member corresponds to the **LOGBRUSH::lbHatch** data member and can be assigned any one of the identifiers listed in Table 2.3 (see Chapter 2), or can be assigned the handle to a device-dependent bitmap (or a pointer to a packed DIB) that describes the fill pattern.

***NOTE:** Because cosmetic pens cannot have a pattern, the **elpBrushStyle** data member always specifies **BS_SOLID** for a cosmetic pen.*

The **elpNumEntries** and **elpStyleEntry** data members are used only when the **elpPenStyle** data member contains the **PS_USERSTYLE** identifier. Using this latter style, you can define a custom series of dashes to define the pen's style. The **elpNumEntries** data member indicates the number of entries in the **elpStyleEntry** data member. The even-indexed entries of **elpStyleEntry** indicate the lengths of the dashes, while the odd-indexed entries indicate the lengths of the spaces.

Rendering with a Logical Pen

Just as the GDI provides the **FillRect** and **PatBlt** functions to be used specifically with logical brush objects, the GDI provides several functions that are specific to pens. Because all of these functions are designed for rendering lines and curves (covered in Chapter 5), we will not discuss them here. Instead, let us revisit the "tracking rectangle" example of Chapter 2, but here we'll use a non-extended geometric pen instead of a brush. Before we can realize this goal, however, we'll need to first examine how to render a rectangle by using a pen object.

Outlining a Rectangle

In addition to rendering lines and curves, pens are used to render the boundaries of polygons. That is, when a filled-shape function is used to render a polygon, the target device context's current pen is used to outline this shape. Undoubtedly, the most commonly rendered shape is a rectangle. The most common means of drawing a rectangle is to use the **Rectangle** function:

```
BOOL Rectangle(
    IN HDC hdc,      // handle to the target device context
    int nLeftRect,   // horizontal position of bounding rectangle's
                     // top-left corner
    int nTopRect,    // vertical position of bounding rectangle's
                     // top-left corner
    int nRightRect,  // horizontal position of bounding rectangle's
                     // bottom-right corner
    int nBottomRect  // vertical position of bounding rectangle's
                     // bottom-right corner
   );
```

The **hdc** parameter identifies the device context to which the rectangle will be rendered. The bounds of this rectangle are specified by the **nLeftRect**, **nTopRect**, **nRightRect**, and **nBottomRect** parameters. The **Rectangle** function returns a Boolean value indicating success or failure.

If you use the **Rectangle** function to draw a rectangle, the boundary of the rectangle is drawn using the destination device context's current pen. In addition, this device context's current brush is used to fill the interior of the rectangle. Because we're interested in rendering only the rectangle's boundary, we'll need to prevent the **Rectangle** function from filling the interior. We do this by simply selecting a hollow brush into the target device context. The following example demonstrates how to render only the outline of a rectangle:

```
#include <cassert>
BOOL OutlineRect(IN HDC hDestDC, IN const RECT& RDest)
{
   assert(hDestDC != NULL);

   // select a hollow brush into the target DC
   HBRUSH hhOldBrush = static_cast<HBRUSH>(
      SelectObject(hDestDC, GetStockObject(HOLLOW_BRUSH))
      );

   // render the outline of the rectangle
   BOOL result =
      Rectangle(
         hDestDC,
         RDest.left, RDest.top,
         RDest.right, RDest.bottom
         );

   // restore the original brush
   SelectObject(hDestDC, hhOldBrush);

   return result;
}
```

Rendering a Tracking Rectangle

To render a tracking rectangle, we'll need to use a technique called *rubber banding*, in which the rectangle is "moved" via a series of draw-and-erase operations. The "erasing" operation is typically carried out by using an **XOR**-type raster operation. In Chapter 2, we accomplished this feat by using the **PatBlt** function with the **DSTINVERT** ternary-raster-operation code. One of the advantages of this function is that you can specify the raster-operation code that will be used. Unfortunately, **PatBlt** operates using the target device context's current brush, not the current pen.

In Chapter 1, I mentioned that a device context's drawing mode governs how colors drawn with the current pen are combined with the device context's existing colors. Here, for the purpose of rubber banding, we'll change this drawing mode to **R2_XORPEN**. Using this mode and the **OutlineRect** function of the previous code snippet, we can rewrite the implementation of Listing 2.1 to use a non-extended geometric pen instead of a brush. The code for this revised example is provided in Listing 3.1.

Listing 3.1 Rendering a tracking rectangle by using a non-extended pen and the Rectangle function.

```
// ---------------------------------------------------------------------
// Windows 2000 Graphics API Black Book
// Chapter 3 - Listing 3.1 (Non-Extended Pen Tracking Rect Demo)
// ---------------------------------------------------------------------

#include <windows.h>

HINSTANCE hhInst;
const char* WndClassName = "GMainWnd";
LRESULT CALLBACK MainWndProc(HWND hhWnd, UINT msg, WPARAM wParam,
   LPARAM lParam);

int APIENTRY WinMain(HINSTANCE hhInstance, HINSTANCE, LPTSTR,
   int nCmdShow)
{
   hhInst = hInstance;

   WNDCLASS wc;
   memset(&wc, 0, sizeof(WNDCLASS));

   wc.style = CS_VREDRAW | CS_HREDRAW;
   wc.lpszClassName = WndClassName;
   wc.lpfnWndProc = MainWndProc;
   wc.hInstance = hInstance;
   wc.hCursor = LoadCursor(NULL, IDC_ARROW);
   wc.hbrBackground = static_cast<HBRUSH>(
      GetStockObject(BLACK_BRUSH)
      );

   if (RegisterClass(&wc))
   {
      HWND hWnd =
         CreateWindow(WndClassName, "Move the Penguin, Again!",
                      WS_OVERLAPPEDWINDOW | WS_CAPTION |
                      WS_VISIBLE | WS_CLIPCHILDREN,
                      CW_USEDEFAULT, CW_USEDEFAULT, 640, 480,
                      NULL, NULL, hInst, NULL);

      if (hWnd)
      {
         ShowWindow(hWnd, nCmdShow);
         UpdateWindow(hWnd);
```

```
            MSG msg;
            while (GetMessage(&msg, NULL, 0, 0))
            {
                TranslateMessage(&msg);
                DispatchMessage(&msg);
            }
        }
    }
    return 0;
}

// image related
HDC hMemDC = NULL;
HBITMAP hOldBmp = NULL;
const char* filename = "PENGUIN.BMP";
RECT RImage = {225, 110, 225, 110};

// tracking related
bool is_tracking = false;
HPEN hTrackPen = NULL, hOldPen = NULL;
HDC hScreenDC = NULL;
POINT PMouse = {0, 0};
RECT RTrack = {0, 0, 0, 0};
const int line_width = 5;

// utility function to map to/from window coordinates
void MapRect(IN HWND hWndFrom, IN HWND hWndTo,
   IN OUT RECT& RMap)
{
   MapWindowPoints(
      hWndFrom, hWndTo,
      reinterpret_cast<LPPOINT>(&RMap), 2
      );
}

//
// utility function that uses the Rectangle function to
// render the outline of a rectangle
//
#include <cassert>
BOOL OutlineRect(IN HDC hDestDC, IN const RECT& RDest)
{
   assert(hDestDC != NULL);
```

```
    // select a hollow brush into the target DC
    HBRUSH hOldBrush = static_cast<HBRUSH>(
       SelectObject(hDestDC, GetStockObject(HOLLOW_BRUSH))
       );

    // render the outline of the rectangle
    BOOL result =
       Rectangle(
          hDestDC,
          RDest.left, RDest.top,
          RDest.right, RDest.bottom
          );

    // restore the original brush
    SelectObject(hDestDC, hOldBrush);

    return result;
 }

 //
 // utility function that uses the OutlineRect function to
 // render a tracking rectangle
 //
 void RenderTrackingRect(IN HDC hDestDC, IN const RECT& RRender)
 {
    int OldROP2 = SetROP2(hDestDC, R2_XORPEN);
    OutlineRect(hDestDC, RRender);
    SetROP2(hDestDC, OldROP2);
 }

 LRESULT CALLBACK MainWndProc(HWND hWnd, UINT msg, WPARAM wParam,
    LPARAM lParam)
 {
    switch (msg)
    {
       case WM_CREATE:
       {
          // create a memory DC
          hMemDC = CreateCompatibleDC(NULL);
          if (hMemDC)
          {
             //
             // load the penguin bitmap
             // (see Chapter 6 for info on loading bitmaps w/ palettes)
             //
```

```
        HBITMAP hBmp = static_cast<HBITMAP>(
           LoadImage(hInst, filename, IMAGE_BITMAP, 0, 0,
                 LR_LOADFROMFILE | LR_DEFAULTSIZE)
           );
        if (hBmp)
        {
           // get the bitmap's dimensions
           BITMAP bmp;
           if (GetObject(hBmp, sizeof(BITMAP), &bmp) == sizeof(BITMAP))
           {
              RImage.right += bmp.bmWidth;
              RImage.bottom += bmp.bmHeight;

              // realize the bitmap
              hOldBmp = static_cast<HBITMAP>(
                 SelectObject(hMemDC, hBmp)
                 );
           }
           else DeleteObject(hBmp);
        }
     }

     //
     // create the non-extended geometric pen
     //
     const COLORREF clrWhite = RGB(255, 255, 255);
     hTrackPen =
        CreatePen(PS_INSIDEFRAME, line_width, clrWhite);
     assert(hTrackPen != NULL);

     break;
  }
  case WM_LBUTTONDOWN:
  {
     PMouse.x = LOWORD(lParam);
     PMouse.y = HIWORD(lParam);

     RECT RClient;
     if (PtInRect(&RImage, PMouse) &&
         GetClientRect(hWnd, &RClient))
     {
        MapRect(hWnd, HWND_DESKTOP, RClient);
        ClipCursor(&RClient);
```

```
            //
            // grab a handle to the screen DC, and clip
            // all output to the client area of our window
            // (see Chapter 8 for more info on clipping regions)
            //
            hScreenDC = GetDC(NULL);
            HRGN hClipRgn = CreateRectRgnIndirect(&RClient);
            SelectClipRgn(hScreenDC, hClipRgn);
            DeleteObject(hClipRgn);

            CopyRect(&RTrack, &RImage);
            MapRect(hWnd, HWND_DESKTOP, RTrack);

            // select the pen into the screen DC
            hOldPen = static_cast<HPEN>(
               SelectObject(hScreenDC, hTrackPen)
               );

            // render the first tracking rect
            RenderTrackingRect(hScreenDC, RTrack);
            is_tracking = true;
         }
         break;
      }
      case WM_MOUSEMOVE:
      {
         if (hScreenDC && is_tracking)
         {
            POINT PCurrent = {LOWORD(lParam), HIWORD(lParam)};
            const int dX = PCurrent.x - PMouse.x;
            const int dY = PCurrent.y - PMouse.y;

            // erase the previous rectangle
            RenderTrackingRect(hScreenDC, RTrack);
            // update the position
            OffsetRect(&RTrack, dX, dY);
            // render the new tracking rectangle
            RenderTrackingRect(hScreenDC, RTrack);

            // update the mouse position
            memcpy(&PMouse, &PCurrent, sizeof(POINT));
         }
         break;
      }
```

```
case WM_LBUTTONUP:
{
   // clean up
   if (is_tracking)
   {
      is_tracking = false;
      SelectObject(hScreenDC, hOldPen);
      SelectClipRgn(hScreenDC, NULL);
      ReleaseDC(NULL, hScreenDC);

      InvalidateRect(hWnd, &RImage, true);
      CopyRect(&RImage, &RTrack);
      MapRect(HWND_DESKTOP, hWnd, RImage);
      InvalidateRect(hWnd, &RImage, true);

      ClipCursor(NULL);
   }
   break;
}
case WM_PAINT:
{
   PAINTSTRUCT ps;
   HDC hDC = BeginPaint(hWnd, &ps);
   try
   {
      //
      // TODO: Add palette support (see Chapter 9)...
      //

      // render the penguin
      BitBlt(hDC, RImage.left, RImage.top,
             RImage.right - RImage.left,
             RImage.bottom - RImage.top,
             hMemDC, 0, 0,
             SRCCOPY);
   }
   catch (...)
   {
      EndPaint(hWnd, &ps);
   }
   EndPaint(hWnd, &ps);
   break;
}
```

```
        case WM_DESTROY:
        {
            // clean up
            if (hTrackPen)
            {
                DeleteObject(hTrackPen);
            }
            DeleteObject(SelectObject(hMemDC, hOldBmp));
            DeleteDC(hMemDC);

            PostQuitMessage(0);
            break;
        }
    }
    return DefWindowProc(hWnd, msg, wParam, lParam);
}
```

Immediate Solutions

Working with Non-Extended Pens

Non-extended pens are useful when you need to render simple lines whose ends are always rounded and whose color is always solid. As you will discover in this section, the process of creating a non-extended pen is straightforward; this is not always the case with extended pens.

Creating a Non-Extended Cosmetic Pen

If you want to render a solid line or a dashed or dotted line whose width is fixed to one device unit and whose ends are always rounded, and if speed is a primary issue, you'll want to use a non-extended cosmetic pen. To create a non-extended cosmetic pen, you use the **CreatePen** function. If successful, this function returns a handle to a logical non-extended pen object:

```
HPEN CreatePen(
    IN int fnPenStyle,     // the pen's style
    IN int nWidth,         // the pen's width
    IN COLORREF crColor    // the pen's color
   );
```

The **fnPenStyle** parameter is used to specify the pen's style. This parameter can be assigned any one of the values from Table 3.1. (These styles are depicted in Figure 3.1.) The **nWidth** parameter is used to specify the pen's width. To create a non-extended cosmetic pen, you must set this parameter to zero. The **crColor** parameter is used to specify the pen's color. It is the responsibility of the device driver to match the parameter-specified color to the closest color that the device can represent. If the **CreatePen** function fails, the return value is **NULL**.

The following code snippet demonstrates how to use **CreatePen** to create a non-extended, solid blue, cosmetic pen for use in rendering the border of a circle:

```
HPEN hBluePen = CreatePen(PS_SOLID, 0, RGB(0, 0, 255));
if (hBluePen)
{
   HDC hDC = GetDC(hWnd);
   HPEN hOldPen = static_cast<HPEN>(
      SelectObject(hDC, hBluePen)
      );
```

```
    try
    {
        Ellipse(hDC, 10, 10, 210, 210);
    }
    catch (...)
    {
        DeleteObject(SelectObject(hDC, hOldPen));
        ReleaseDC(hWnd, hDC);
    }
    DeleteObject(SelectObject(hDC, hOldPen));
    ReleaseDC(hWnd, hDC);
}
```


Another way to create a non-extended cosmetic pen is to use the **CreatePenIndirect** function. Here you initialize the **LOGPEN::lopnStyle** data member to any one of the identifiers listed in Table 3.1. You set the **x** data member of the **LOGPEN::lopnWidth** data member to zero, and set the **LOGPEN::lopnColor** data member to the desired color. For example, to create a non-extended, dotted, green cosmetic pen:

```
LOGPEN lp;
lp.lopnStyle = PS_DOT;
lp.lopnWidth.x = 0;
lp.lopnColor = RGB(0, 255, 0);

HPEN hGreenDotPen = CreatePenIndirect(&lp);
// ...
```

As with most non-stock GDI graphic objects, when a pen is no longer needed, you must destroy it by using the **DeleteObject** function. However, be sure to deselect the pen from any associated device contexts before passing its handle to this function.

Creating a Non-Extended Geometric Pen

When you need to render a solid line whose width is not fixed to one device unit and whose ends are always rounded, you'll want to use a non-extended geometric pen. To create a non-extended geometric pen, you use the **CreatePen** function:

```
HPEN CreatePen(
    IN int fnPenStyle,      // the pen's style
    IN int nWidth,          // the pen's width
    IN COLORREF crColor     // the pen's color
   );
```

The **fnPenStyle** parameter is used to specify the pen's style. This parameter can be assigned any one of the values from Table 3.1. (These styles are depicted in Figure 3.1.) The **nWidth** parameter is used to specify the pen's width in logical units. To create a non-extended geometric pen, you must set this parameter to a value greater than zero.

WARNING! Although you can specify the fnPenStyle parameter as any one of the values from Table 3.1, the pen style is limited to PS_SOLID, PS_NULL, or PS_INSIDEFRAME when the nWidth parameter is greater than one device unit. If this condition is not met, the style defaults to PS_SOLID.

The **crColor** parameter is used to specify the pen's color. It is the responsibility of the device driver to match the parameter-specified color to the closest color that the device can represent.

If the **CreatePen** function is successful, it returns a handle to a newly created logical pen object. If the function fails, the return value is **NULL**. The following code snippet demonstrates how to use **CreatePen** to create a non-extended, solid red, geometric pen, with a width of 10 logical units, for use in rendering the border of an ellipse:

```
HPEN hRedPen = CreatePen(PS_SOLID, 10, RGB(255, 0, 0));
if (hRedPen)
{
   HDC hDC = GetDC(hWnd);
   HPEN hOldPen = static_cast<HPEN>(
      SelectObject(hDC, hRedPen)
      );
   try
   {
      Ellipse(hDC, 5, 10, 200, 100);
   }
   catch (...)
   {
      DeleteObject(SelectObject(hDC, hOldPen));
      ReleaseDC(hWnd, hDC);
   }
   DeleteObject(SelectObject(hDC, hOldPen));
   ReleaseDC(hWnd, hDC);
}
```

If you prefer, you can use the **CreatePenIndirect** function to create a non-extended geometric pen. In this case, you initialize the **LOGPEN::lopnStyle** data member to any one of the identifiers listed in Table 3.1. As it is with the **CreatePen** function, with the **CreatePenIndirect** function, the **lopnStyle** data member is limited to **PS_SOLID**, **PS_NULL**, or **PS_INSIDEFRAME**. To create a non-extended geometric pen, you must set the **x** data member of the **LOGPEN::lopnWidth** data member to a value greater than zero. The **LOGPEN::lopnColor** data member is simply assigned the desired color. For example, to create a non-extended, solid blue, geometric pen with a width of 15 logical units:

```
LOGPEN lp;
lp.lopnStyle = PS_SOLID;
lp.lopnWidth.x = 15;
lp.lopnColor = RGB(0, 0, 255);

HPEN HBluePen = CreatePenIndirect(&lp);
// ...
```

When the pen is no longer needed, you must destroy it by using the **DeleteObject** function. However, do not destroy a pen while it is selected into a device context. You must deselect the pen from any associated device contexts before you destroy it.

Retrieving a Handle to a Stock Pen

To obtain a handle to a logical stock pen object, you use the **GetStockObject** function:

```
HGDIOBJ GetStockObject(
    IN int fnObject         // identifier of the stock object
   );
```

The **fnObject** parameter is used to specify which stock pen object you want to retrieve. Because **GetStockObject** is a general function, it can be used to retrieve a handle to non-pen stock objects as well. However, to retrieve a handle to one of the GDI's four stock pens, you specify the **fnObject** parameter as one of the identifiers listed in Table 3.6.

***NOTE:** All stock pens are non-extended solid pens. If you need a pen of another style, a pen with a width of more than one device unit, or an extended pen, you must create it manually.*

If successful, the **GetStockObject** function returns a handle to the logical stock object that is requested; otherwise, the return value is **NULL**. For example, to retrieve a handle to the stock white pen:

```
HPEN hStockPen = static_cast<HPEN>(
   GetStockObject(WHITE_PEN)
   );
```

Table 3.6 Stock-pen-object identifiers for use with the GetStockObject function.

Identifier	Value	Stock Brush Variety
WHITE_PEN	6	Solid white non-extended cosmetic pen
BLACK_PEN	7	Solid black non-extended cosmetic pen
NULL_PEN	9	Transparent non-extended geometric pen
DC_PEN	19	Solid non-extended cosmetic pen of a variable color (Windows 98/2000 only)

Unlike non-stock objects, with stock pen objects there's no need to call the **DeleteObject** function. The function will do nothing.

Related solution:	*Found on page:*
Obtaining a Handle to a Stock Brush	108

Working with Extended Pens

Extended pens are useful when you need superior control of the appearance of the lines that you're going to draw. As opposed to non-extended pens, extended pens allow you to specify features such as the end cap, the join, and the pattern that's used to fill the lines.

Creating an Extended Cosmetic Pen

If you need to render a line with a custom style or with every other pixel set, and you need the line's width to be fixed to one device unit, you'll want to use an extended cosmetic pen.

NOTE: *On systems running Windows 95 or Windows 98, there is no advantage to using an extended cosmetic pen. Because these platforms do not support the* ***PS_ALTERNATE*** *or* ***PS_USERSTYLE*** *styles, you might as well use a non-extended cosmetic pen.*

To create an extended cosmetic pen, you use the **ExtCreatePen** function:

```
HPEN ExtCreatePen(
    DWORD dwPenStyle,      // pen's style
    DWORD dwWidth,         // pen's width
    CONST LOGBRUSH *lplb, // pen's brush attributes
    DWORD dwStyleCount,    // number of elements in the custom style array
    CONST DWORD *lpStyle  // pen's custom style array (in device units)
   );
```

The **dwPenStyle** parameter specifies the pen's style. For a cosmetic pen, this is set to a combination of **PS_COSMETIC** and any of the identifiers listed in Table 3.1 or **PS_ALTERNATE** or **PS_USERSTYLE**. The **dwWidth** parameter is used to specify the pen's width. This parameter must be set to 1 for cosmetic pens. The **lplb** parameter is assigned the address of a **LOGBRUSH** structure, which specifies the pen's pattern and color. For cosmetic pens, the **LOGBRUSH::lbStyle** data member must be set to **BS_SOLID**. The pen's color is specified by the **LOGBRUSH::lbColor** data member. The **dwStyleCount** and **lpStyle** parameters are used only when the **dwPenStyle** parameter is set to **PS_USERSTYLE**.

If the **ExtCreatePen** function is successful, it returns a handle to the newly created logical pen. If the function fails, the return value is **NULL**. The following code snippet demonstrates how to create an extended cosmetic pen with the **PS_ALTERNATE** style:

```
const DWORD style = PS_COSMETIC | PS_ALTERNATE;

LOGBRUSH lb;
lb.lbStyle = BS_SOLID;
lb.lbColor = RGB(255, 255, 255);

HPEN HExtWhitePen = ExtCreatePen(style, 1, &lb, 0, NULL);
if (HExtWhitePen)
{
   // ...
}
```

When the **PS_USERSTYLE** identifier is assigned to the **dwPenStyle** parameter, you need to assign proper values to the **dwStyleCount** and **lpStyle** parameters. The **lpStyle** parameter points to an array of **DWORD** values, where each even-indexed entry specifies the length of a dash (in device units), and each odd-indexed entry specifies the length of a space (in device units). The **dwStyleCount** parameter specifies the number of elements in this array. For example, the following code snippet demonstrates how to create an extended cosmetic pen where the first dash is of length 3, the first space is of length 2, the second dash is of length 10, and the second space is of length 5:

```
const DWORD style = PS_COSMETIC | PS_USERSTYLE;

LOGBRUSH lb;
lb.lbStyle = BS_SOLID;
lb.lbColor = RGB(0, 0, 255);
```

```
const DWORD dash1 = 3;
const DWORD space1 = 2;
const DWORD dash2 = 10;
const DWORD space2 = 5;

const DWORD num_elements = 4;
const DWORD styles[] = {dash1, space1, dash2, space2};

HPEN hExtBluePen =
   ExtCreatePen(style, 1, &lb, num_elements, styles);
// ...
```

When the pen is no longer needed, you must destroy it by using the **DeleteObject** function. However, don't try to destroy the pen while it is selected into a device context. You must deselect the pen before passing its handle to **DeleteObject**.

Creating an Extended Geometric Pen

If you need to render a line with a specific end cap, a specific join, or a custom style or pattern, you'll want to use an extended geometric pen. To create a pen of this type, you use the **ExtCreatePen** function:

```
HPEN ExtCreatePen(
    DWORD dwPenStyle,      // pen's style
    DWORD dwWidth,         // pen's width
    CONST LOGBRUSH *lplb, // pen's brush attributes
    DWORD dwStyleCount,    // number of elements in the custom style array
    CONST DWORD *lpStyle  // pen's custom style (in logical units)
   );
```

The **dwPenStyle** parameter specifies the pen's style. For the geometric pens, this parameter is set to a combination of **PS_GEOMETRIC** and any of the identifiers listed in Tables 3.1 (or **PS_USERSTYLE**), 3.3, and 3.4 (one value from each table).

WARNING! In Windows 95 and Windows 98, the PS_DOT, PS_DASH, PS_DASHDOT, and PS_DASHDOTDOT identifiers are not supported for extended geometric pens. Moreover, on these platforms, the end cap and join styles are valid only when the pen is used to outline a path.

The **dwWidth** parameter is used to specify the pen's width. For geometric pens, this value is specified in logical units. The **lplb** parameter is assigned the address of a **LOGBRUSH** structure, which specifies the pen's pattern and color. For geometric pens, the **LOGBRUSH::lbStyle** data member can be assigned any of the values listed in Table 2.2 (see Chapter 2). Similarly, the **LOGBRUSH::lbHatch** data member can be assigned any one of the identifiers listed in Table 2.3 (see

Chapter 2), a handle to a bitmap object, or a pointer to a packed DIB. The pen's color is specified by the **LOGBRUSH::lbColor** data member. The **dwStyleCount** and **lpStyle** parameters are used only when the **dwPenStyle** parameter is set to **PS_USERSTYLE** (see "Creating an Extended Cosmetic Pen" for an example that uses these parameters).

If the **ExtCreatePen** function is successful, it returns a handle to a logical extended pen object; if the function fails, it returns **NULL**. The following code snippet demonstrates how to create an extended geometric pen with a solid fill style, a flat end cap, a beveled join, and a width of 12 logical units. (For an example of creating an extended geometric pen with a custom fill pattern, see "Creating an Extended Pen with a Custom Pattern.")

```
const DWORD style =
   PS_GEOMETRIC | PS_SOLID | PS_ENDCAP_FLAT | PS_JOIN_BEVEL;

LOGBRUSH lb;
lb.lbStyle = BS_SOLID;
lb.lbColor = RGB(255, 0, 172);

HPEN hExtPinkPen = ExtCreatePen(style, 12, &lb, 0, NULL);
if (hExtPinkPen)
{
   // ...
}
```

When the pen is no longer needed, you must destroy it by using the **DeleteObject** function. However, don't try to destroy the pen while it is selected into a device context. You must deselect the pen before passing its handle to **DeleteObject**.

Creating an Extended Geometric Pen with a Custom Pattern

If you need to render a line that is filled with a custom pattern, you'll want to create an extended geometric pen. You do this by using the **ExtCreatePen** function, whose specifics are described in "Creating an Extended Geometric Pen." Here we'll focus on the special case of using this function to create an extended geometric pen that can be used to draw lines containing a custom fill pattern.

The **lplb** parameter of the **ExtCreatePen** function is a pointer to a **LOGBRUSH** structure (see Chapter 2 for a description of this structure). To create an extended geometric pen whose fill pattern is described by a device-dependent bitmap (DDB), you set the **LOGBRUSH::lbStyle** data member to **BS_PATTERN**. If the fill pattern will be described by a packed DIB, you set the **lbStyle** data member to **BS_DIBPATTERNPT**. In this latter case, you must also set the **LOGBRUSH::lbColor** data member to a value that describes how the color table of the DIB should be interpreted (**DIB_PAL_COLORS** or **DIB_RGB_COLORS**). The **LOGBRUSH::lbHatch** data member is assigned either the handle to a bitmap object or a pointer to a packed DIB.

The following code snippet demonstrates how to create an extended geometric pen whose fill pattern is described by a device-dependent bitmap that is loaded from a file:

```
const char* filename = "MYBITMAP.BMP";
HBITMAP hBmp = static_cast<HBITMAP>(
   LoadImage(hInst, filename, IMAGE_BITMAP, 0, 0,
             LR_LOADFROMFILE | LR_DEFAULTSIZE)
   );
if (hBmp)
{
   try
   {
      const DWORD style =
         PS_GEOMETRIC | PS_ENDCAP_ROUND | PS_JOIN_ROUND;

      LOGBRUSH lb;
      lb.lbStyle = BS_PATTERN;
      lb.lbHatch = reinterpret_cast<LONG>(hBmp);

      HPEN hExtBmpPen =
         ExtCreatePen(style, 20, &lb, 0, NULL);
      DeleteObject(hBmp);
      hBmp = NULL;

      if (hExtBmpPen)
      {
         HDC hDC = GetDC(hWnd);
         HPEN hOldPen = static_cast<HPEN>(
            SelectObject(hDC, hExtBmpPen)
            );
         try
         {
            Rectangle(hDC, 10, 10, 200, 200);
         }
         catch (...)
         {
            DeleteObject(SelectObject(hDC, hOldPen));
            ReleaseDC(hWnd, hDC);
         }
         DeleteObject(SelectObject(hDC, hOldPen));
```

```
            ReleaseDC(hWnd, hDC);
        }
    }
    catch (...)
    {
        DeleteObject(hBmp);
    }
}
```

The following code snippet demonstrates how to create an extended geometric pen whose fill pattern is described by a packed DIB (this code was used to create the circle depicted in Figure 3.4):

```
const int bpp = 24;
const int width = 35;
const int height = 35;
const int bytes_per_scanline =
    (((width * bpp) + 31) & ~31) / 8;

const size_t size =
    sizeof(BITMAPINFO) +
    height * bytes_per_scanline;

unsigned char* data = new unsigned char[size];
try
{
    memset(data, 0, size);
    LPBITMAPINFO lpbi =
        reinterpret_cast<LPBITMAPINFO>(data);

    lpbi->bmiHeader.biSize = sizeof(BITMAPINFOHEADER);
    lpbi->bmiHeader.biWidth = width;
    lpbi->bmiHeader.biHeight = -height; // top-down
    lpbi->bmiHeader.biPlanes = 1;
    lpbi->bmiHeader.biBitCount = bpp;
    lpbi->bmiHeader.biCompression = BI_RGB;

    unsigned char* bits =
        reinterpret_cast<unsigned char*>(
            lpbi->bmiColors + lpbi->bmiHeader.biClrUsed
        );

    for (int y = 0; y < height; ++y)
    {
        const int row = bytes_per_scanline * y;
```

```
    for (int x = 0; x < bytes_per_scanline; x += 3)
    {
       if (y % 5 == 0)
       {
          *(bits + (x + 0) + row) = 255; // blue
          *(bits + (x + 1) + row) = 255; // green
          *(bits + (x + 2) + row) = 128; // red
       }
       else
       {
          *(bits + (x + 0) + row) = 0;   // blue
          *(bits + (x + 1) + row) = 0;   // green
          *(bits + (x + 2) + row) = 255; // red
       }
    }
 }

 const DWORD style =
    PS_GEOMETRIC | PS_ENDCAP_SQUARE | PS_JOIN_MITER;

 LOGBRUSH lb;
 lb.lbStyle = BS_DIBPATTERNPT;
 lb.lbColor = DIB_RGB_COLORS;
 lb.lbHatch = reinterpret_cast<LONG>(lpbi);

 HPEN hExtDIBPen = ExtCreatePen(style, 35, &lb, 0, NULL);
 delete [] data;
 data = NULL;

 if (hExtDIBPen)
 {
    HDC hDC = GetDC(hWnd);
    HPEN hOldPen = static_cast<HPEN>(
       SelectObject(hDC, hExtDIBPen)
       );
    try
    {
       Ellipse(hDC, 30, 30, 200, 200);
    }
    catch (...)
    {
       DeleteObject(SelectObject(hDC, hOldPen));
       ReleaseDC(hWnd, hDC);
    }
    DeleteObject(SelectObject(hDC, hOldPen));
```

```
        ReleaseDC(hWnd, hDC);
    }
}
catch (...)
{
    delete [] data;
}
```


Related solutions:	Found on page:
Creating a Monochrome Device-Dependent Bitmap	307
Creating a Color Device-Dependent Bitmap	311
Loading a Device-Dependent Bitmap from a File	323
Creating a Device-Independent Bitmap	391
Loading a Device-Independent Bitmap from a File	405

Obtaining and Changing Pen Attributes

When you create a logical pen, you determine which attributes this pen will have. Yet, when you're provided with a logical pen from a third-party library, or when it's not practical to store the specified attributes, you'll need a method of obtaining these attributes afterward. In this section, we'll discuss some techniques for obtaining a pen's attributes given only its handle. We'll also examine the new way of changing a device context's pen color in Windows 2000.

Retrieving the Attributes of a Pen

Given a handle to a logical pen object, you can use the **GetObject** function to retrieve the pen's attributes. This function can be used to fill a **LOGPEN** or **EXTLOGPEN** structure for non-extended or extended pens, respectively.

TIP: *To determine whether you have a handle to a non-extended pen or an extended pen, see "Determining Whether a Pen is Non-Extended or Extended," later in this section.*

```
int GetObject(
    IN HGDIOBJ hgdiobj,        // handle to the logical brush object
    IN int cbBuffer,           // number of bytes in the LOGPEN
                               // or the EXTLOGPEN structure
    OUT LPVOID lpvObject       // address of a LOGPEN or an
                               // EXTLOGPEN structure
);
```

Although the **GetObject** function can be used for other graphic objects, here we'll focus specifically on the task of filling a **LOGPEN** or **EXTLOGPEN** structure (as reflected in the previous parameter comments). For a more general discussion of the **GetObject** function, see Chapter 1.

***TIP:** To obtain a handle to a device context's currently selected pen object, use the **GetCurrentObject** function with the **OBJ_PEN** identifier (see Chapter 1).*

The **hgdiobj** parameter is specified as the handle to the pen object whose attributes you want to retrieve. If the **GetObject** function is successful, it stores these attributes in the **LOGPEN** structure whose address is passed as the **lpvObject** parameter. The **cbBuffer** parameter indicates how many bytes are available in the buffer indicated by **lpvObject**. You specify this parameter as **sizeof(LOGPEN)** or **sizeof(EXTLOGPEN)** for non-extended or extended pens, respectively. For example:

```
EXTLOGPEN elp;
const size_t elpSize = sizeof(EXTLOGPEN) - sizeof(elp.elpStyleEntry);
if (GetObject(hExtPen, sizeof(EXTLOGPEN), &elp) >= elpSize)
{
   switch (elp.elpPenStyle & PS_ENDCAP_MASK)
   {
      case PS_ENDCAP_ROUND:
         /* rounded end cap */
         break;
      case PS_ENDCAP_SQUARE:
         /* square end cap */
         break;
      case PS_ENDCAP_FLAT:
         /* rounded end cap */
         break;
   }
}
```

If the **GetObject** function is successful, it returns the number of bytes (of the buffer indicated by **lpvObject**) that have been filled. If the function fails, the return value is zero.

Determining Whether a Pen Is Cosmetic or Geometric

If you're working with an extended pen, you can determine whether it's a cosmetic or geometric pen by using the **GetObject** function. Specifically, you use the **GetObject** function to fill a corresponding **EXTLOGPEN** structure, then use the bitwise **AND** operator (&) to combine the **EXTLOGPEN::elpPenStyle** data member with the **PS_TYPE_MASK** identifier, and then test this combination for equality with either **PS_COSMETIC** or **PS_GEOMETRIC**.

TIP: *To determine whether you have a handle to a non-extended or extended pen, see "Determining Whether a Pen is Non-Extended or Extended."*

The following example demonstrates this process:

```
bool IsExtendedPenCosmetic(IN HPEN hExtPen)
{
   EXTLOGPEN elp;
   const size_t elpSize = sizeof(EXTLOGPEN) - sizeof(elp.elpStyleEntry);
   if (GetObject(hExtPen, sizeof(EXTLOGPEN), &elp) >= elpSize)
   {
      return ((elp.elpPenStyle & PS_TYPE_MASK) == PS_COSMETIC);
   }
   return false;
}
```

If you're working with a non-extended pen, you can use a technique similar to the one just demonstrated. Recall, a non-extended cosmetic pen is created by specifying zero as the **nWidth** parameter of the **CreatePen** function or as the **lopnWidth.x** data member of the **LOGPEN** structure that's used with the **CreatePenIndirect** function. Therefore, you can use the **GetObject** function to fill a **LOGPEN** structure, and then test whether or not the **lopnWidth.x** data member is zero. For example:

```
bool IsNonExtendedPenCosmetic(IN HPEN hPen)
{
   LOGPEN lp;
   const size_t lpSize = sizeof(LOGPEN);
   if (GetObject(hPen, lpSize, &lp) == lpSize)
   {
      return (lp.lopnWidth.x == 0);
   }
   return false;
}
```

Determining Whether a Pen Is Non-Extended or Extended

The GDI provides a function, **GetObjectType**, which can be used to classify a type of graphic object based on its handle. This function can be used to distinguish between non-extended and extended pens. For more information on **GetObjectType**, refer to Chapter 1.

If the handle that you pass to the **GetObjectType** function identifies a non-extended pen, the return value is **OBJ_PEN**. If this handle indicates an extended pen, the return value is **OBJ_EXTPEN**. The following example demonstrates this process:

```
enum PenType {PT_NONEXTENDED, PT_EXTENDED, PT_UNKNOWN};

PenType GetPenType(IN HPEN hPen)
{
   switch (GetObjectType(hPen))
   {
      case OBJ_PEN: return PT_NONEXTENDED;
      case OBJ_EXTPEN: return PT_EXTENDED;
      default: return PT_UNKNOWN;
   }
}
```

An alternative technique is to use the **GetObject** function. If you pass **NULL** as the **lpvObject** parameter, **GetObject** returns the number of bytes required. You can then test this value for equality with the size of the **LOGPEN** structure to determine if the pen is non-extended. However, this latter technique cannot guarantee that the object whose handle is passed to the **GetObject** function is indeed a pen object.

Changing the Color of a Pen

In Windows 95, Windows 98, and Windows NT, the only way to "change" the color of a pen is to create a new one. For example, you can *retrieve* the attributes of a pen by using the **GetObject** function, but the GDI does not provide a "SetObject" function that can be used to change these attributes. In Windows 2000, on the other hand, the GDI offers the **SetDCPenColor** function:

```
COLORREF SetDCPenColor(
    IN HDC hdc,              // handle to the target device context
    IN COLORREF crColor      // COLORREF value of the new DC_PEN color
   );
```

The **hdc** parameter is specified as the handle to the device context whose current pen color you want to change. The **crColor** parameter is used to specify the new color. If the **SetDCPenColor** function succeeds, the return value indicates the device context's previous pen color. If the function fails, the return value is **CLR_INVALID**. For example:

```
COLORREF clrOld = SetDCPenColor(hDC, PALETTERGB(255, 128, 255));
```

Unfortunately, the **SetDCPenColor** function changes the color of only the stock **DC_PEN** object. You can't use this function to change the color of some random pen, even if that pen is selected into the target device context.

The **SetDCPenColor** function can be used at any time, even if the **DC_PEN** object is not selected into the target device context. However, before any rendering operation will use the specified pen color, the **DC_PEN** object must be selected. You can accomplish this by using a combination of the **SelectObject** and **GetStockObject** functions:

```
SelectObject(hDC, GetStockObject(DC_PEN));
```

To retrieve a device context's current **DC_PEN** color, you use the **GetDCPenColor** function:

```
COLORREF GetDCPenColor(
    IN HDC hdc        // handle to the target device context
   );
```

The **hdc** parameter is specified as the handle to the device context whose **DC_PEN** color you want to retrieve. If the **GetDCPenColor** function is successful, the return value is this color. If the function fails, it returns **CLR_INVALID**.

Related solution:	Found on page:
Changing the Color of a Brush	113

Chapter 4

The Font Object

In Depth

Think back to the last application that you installed on your system, and recall the first thing that you tried to familiarize yourself with. If you're like most users, you probably said the toolbar, the control that was likely filled with a multitude of buttons, each with an "intuitive" glyph. But as eloquent as these images may have been, did you instantly know what function each button served? Admit it—like the rest of us, you probably held the mouse pointer over the button, waiting for the tooltip to appear. Yes, a picture is worth a thousand words, and yes, most of this book is indeed focused on creating image-based representations, but in reality, very few applications can survive without some form of textual communication.

No one will argue with the fact that Windows, with its colorful icons and fancy bitmaps, is a huge improvement over the lifeless, text-based interface that we were all forced to work with under DOS. Likewise, save for a few mildly insane Unix fanatics, you'd be hard-pressed to find anyone who prefers typing a half-dozen keywords just to copy a few files. The fact remains, however, that the vast majority of information interchange is still performed through textual means. Because of this fact, Windows provides support for a wide variety of fonts; this support itself is based on the GDI font object.

This chapter is dedicated to fonts and text. We'll begin with a brief overview of the types of fonts that are supported by Windows and how each one is used. We'll then connect these fonts to the GDI font object and examine the structures that are used to describe the font object. Next, we'll discuss several functions that are designed to work with font objects for the purpose of rendering text. We'll also examine various methods for rendering formatted text, and even some techniques for drawing disabled and textured text.

Windows Font Support

Perhaps more than any other graphics-based platform, Windows provides superb support for a wide variety of fonts. Each of these fonts falls under one of the four core font technologies: *raster*, *vector*, *TrueType*, and *OpenType*. Before we examine these types, let's briefly cover some of the terminology that's commonly used to describe each technology.

A *character* is a graphic symbol that conveys information. A character often holds linguistic value, in which case you can think of a character as a letter in an alphabet. The image of a character is called a *glyph*. A *font* is simply a specific collection of characters that share the same design. For example, when the letters A through Z are rendered in a particular font, each letter (character), while represented by a unique image (glyph), will have the same overall look. A *font family* is a set of fonts that share the same basic design, and a *typeface* is used to collectively describe the characteristics of a particular font's design. Most of us are familiar with typeface names such as *Arial*, *Courier*, and *Times New Roman*.

In addition to these terms, you're likely to come across the adjectives *proportional*, *fixed*, and *scalable*. The former two are strictly related to the width of each character. Specifically, each character of a proportional font has a variable width, and all characters of a fixed font share the same width. Because of this fact, most developers choose to program in a fixed-width font so that blocks of code align properly. A scalable font is one that can be stretched or compacted to any arbitrary size without loss of legibility.

Raster, vector, TrueType, and OpenType fonts all share one thing in common: in all of these types, every character is represented by a glyph. In fact, each of these technologies differs mainly in the way each glyph is represented and the fashion in which the corresponding character is rendered.

Raster Fonts

If you've ever browsed the Web under X-Windows, you've probably noticed how terrible some Web pages look. This occurs because many X-servers strictly use *raster* fonts such as *Courier* and *Helvetica*.

In a raster font, each glyph is represented by a bitmap that's designed for a specific device and resolution. When Windows or X-Windows needs to display a line of text, each bitmap is simply drawn to the target device. For this reason, raster fonts are rendered faster than most other types of fonts. However, because each glyph in a raster font is a bitmap of a specific size, when you scale a raster font to a size for which there is no corresponding bitmap, the image itself must be scaled. Therefore, text rendered in a scaled raster font is often illegible. Raster fonts are sometimes referred to as *bitmapped fonts* because the glyph data is actually the pixels of each character bitmap; this data is stored in a font-resource file identified by the .fot extension.

Vector Fonts

Unlike glyphs of a raster font, each glyph of a *vector* font is represented by a series of vector operations. When Windows renders a character in a vector font, the process is very much like drawing a character manually via a series of **MoveToEx** and **LineTo** function calls. Because of this fact, the rendering process is generally slower than for other font types. The advantage, however, is that vector fonts are easily scaled and rotated. A vector font is often referred to as a *stroked font*. Some common typeface names include *Roman* and *Script*. As it is with raster fonts, the glyph data for a vector font is stored in a .fot font-resource file.

TrueType and OpenType Fonts

A *TrueType* font is a type of scalable font in which each glyph is represented by an outline whose contours are defined by a set of points and *hints*. The points describe straight-line segments and second-order Bézier curves. The hints describe how the outline should be scaled, when necessary. In this way, TrueType fonts provide better scales and rotations than do other font types.

Because a TrueType font is described by an outline, you're probably thinking that the rendering process is incredibly slow. As it turns out, this isn't the case. Because each character in a TrueType font is initially drawn to a bitmap, and each bitmap is stored in a special font cache, only the *initial* rendering process is slow. For subsequent rendering operations, Windows simply copies the stored bitmap to the target device. In this way, TrueType fonts are drawn nearly as fast as raster fonts.

OpenType fonts are extended TrueType fonts that support Adobe PostScript CFF (Compact File Format) outlines. From a distribution standpoint, OpenType fonts are superior because the font files are typically smaller than those used for TrueType fonts. From the designer's point of view, OpenType fonts are more flexible because they provide increased typographic control. For application developers, however, an OpenType font is just another TrueType variety. The outline data for both TrueType and OpenType fonts are stored in a .ttf font-resource file.

Logical Fonts

Like other GDI graphic objects, a *logical* font object is a description of a physical font (e.g., the physical fonts that are installed on the target system or device). You create a logical font by using the **CreateFont** function or the **CreateFontIndirect** function (see the solution "Creating a Logical Font"). Each of these functions returns a value a type **HFONT**, a handle to a logical font object.

During the process of realization, the GDI uses the information described by a logical font object to locate the closest matching *physical* font; the GDI font mapper performs this matching. It's important to know that a logical font is only an ideal description of a physical font. A physical font is deemed an "exact" match when the typeface name, character set, height, weight, and italic status are all identical. If an exact match cannot be found, the font mapper chooses the closest matching physical font by penalizing each attribute by a certain weight. The physical font with the least demerits is then deemed the "closest" match. If a tie occurs, the font mapper chooses a winner based on the specified output-precision attribute (see Table 4.4).

We'll examine the attributes of a logical font more closely when we discuss the **LOGFONT** structure later in this chapter (see "The **LOGFONT** Structure"). For now, let's examine how the GDI describes the size of a logical font.

Font Metrics

Because a raster font is represented by a set of bitmaps—with each bitmap designed for a specific device and resolution—the size of a rendered character depends on the device itself. The true size of a raster font is the size of the glyph bitmap. A similar argument can be made for vector fonts. In general, however, the size of a raster or vector font is estimated by the "g-to-M" height, which is the vertical distance between the bottom of a lowercase "g" to the top of an uppercase "M." TrueType fonts, on the other hand, offer precise metric data.

TrueType and OpenType Metrics

As I mentioned, the outline of a TrueType or OpenType font is described by a set of points and hints. For our current discussion of metrics, let's focus strictly on the points.

Recall that the glyph data for a font is stored in a font-resource file. For TrueType and OpenType fonts, these data consist of contour points. Because these types of fonts are not designed for a specific device or resolution, the points in the font-resource file are provided not in device units but in *font units*, which are commonly referred to as *FUnits*.

What exactly is an FUnit? It's the resolution of the font's *em square*. What is the em square? It's nothing more than an imaginary bounding square that surrounds each character. Typical em squares are designed so that rendered characters and lines do not collide even when they're drawn in a condensed fashion. The em square itself is divided into an imaginary grid whose granularity is defined by the font's FUnit. Figure 4.1 depicts an em square.

In short, the points in a font's glyph data are specific locations within an imaginary grid that's bounded by the font's em square. The font's FUnit, then, is simply the spacing of this grid (i.e., the width or height of a grid block).

A font's typographic *ascent* is a measure of how far (in FUnits) each character is located above the font's designated baseline. A font's typographic *descent* is a measure of how far (in FUnits) each character is located below this baseline. The sum of these two quantities yields the typographic *body* of the font. This value is the TrueType and OpenType equivalent of the aforementioned "g-to-M" height.

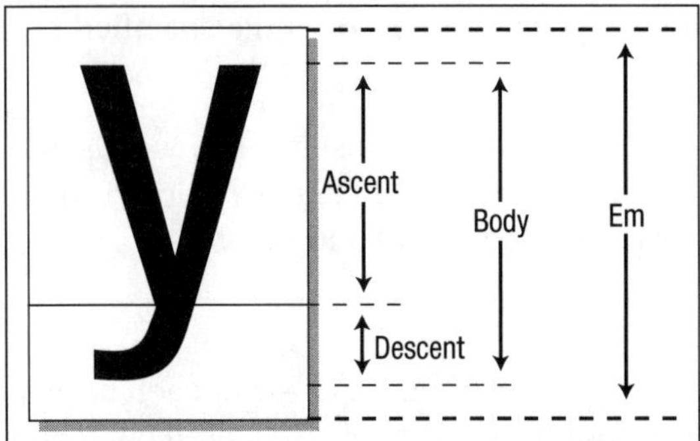

Figure 4.1 A TrueType or OpenType font's em square.

Character Cells

A *character cell* is an imaginary rectangle that encompasses each font character. The height of this cell is the "g-to-M" height (or body), plus a value known as a font's *internal leading*. The internal leading height is typically occupied by diacritical characters such as accent marks, but it's not required that this height be a positive value.

The GDI defines the width of a character cell by three values, *A*, *B*, and *C*, as depicted in Figure 4.2. The sum of these widths (A+B+C) is a quantity known as the *advance width*, which is simply the length that the target device's output apparatus (e.g., a plotter pen) must advance before the next character in a string is rendered.

In many cases, the character's glyph will be wider than its advance width (e.g., B is greater than advance width), in which case the outlying portions are referred to as *underhang* and *overhang*, for the left and right edges of the cell, respectively.

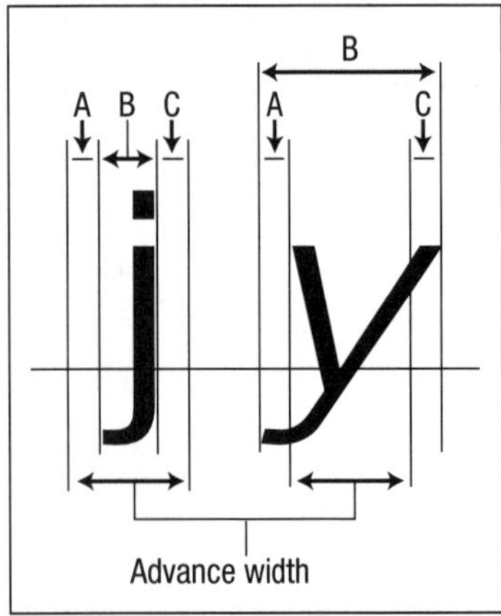

Figure 4.2 A font's ABC width.

Due to the presence of underhang and overhang, the A and C widths can be negative.

Point Sizes

Rarely is the size of a font object described in terms of device units; rather, font sizes are typically defined in terms of *points*. A point is defined as approximately 0.013837 inches and is commonly approximated as 1/72 of an inch. To convert from pixels to points, you use the following formula:

```
point_size = (cell_height - internal_leading) * (72 / vertical_resolution)
```

In this formula, **cell_height** and **internal_leading** are specified in pixels, and **vertical_resolution** is specified in pixels-per-inch. In this way, units of pixels multiplied by units of pixels-per-inch divided by units of pixels-per-inch will yield a value in units of points. To convert from points to inches, you use the following formula:

```
cell_height = ((vertical_resolution * point_size) / 72) + internal_leading
```

Using the **DPtoLP** and **LPtoDP** functions with these two formulae, you can easily convert from points to logical units and vice versa. The problem, however, is that the true vertical resolution of a video display cannot be programmatically determined. The most commonly used technique is to approximate a real inch as a device-specific *logical inch*. This value is obtained via the **GetDeviceCaps** function, specifying the **LOGPIXELSY** capability index:

```
const int pixels_per_inch = GetDeviceCaps(hScreenDC, LOGPIXELSY);
```

An alternative technique is to estimate the number of pixels per physical inch by using the **VERTRES** and **VERTSIZE** capability indices. When the **GetDeviceCaps** function is called with the **VERTRES** index as the **nIndex** parameter, the result is the height of the screen in pixels. When you specify the **VERTSIZE** index, **GetDeviceCaps** returns the (estimated) height of the screen in millimeters. You can use these values to approximate the number of pixels per physical inch:

```
const int mm_per_inch = 25.4;
const int pixels_per_mm =
   GetDeviceCaps(hDestDC, VERTRES) /
   GetDeviceCaps(hDestDC, VERTSIZE);

const int pixels_per_inch = pixels_per_mm * mm_per_inch + 0.5;
```

Although the result of this latter approach might be more accurate, it's still an estimate because Windows itself has no notion of the actual physical dimensions of the end user's monitor. In fact, on systems running Windows 95 or Windows 98, the two techniques yield the same result: typically 96 when the system display properties are set to Small Fonts, and 120 when set to Large Fonts.

Stock Fonts

As with other graphic objects, the GDI creates seven stock logical font objects during initialization. Some of these are used by Windows itself for user-interface elements such as dialog-box controls and window captions. Table 4.1 lists the seven identifiers that can be used with the **GetStockObject** function to retrieve a handle to a stock font object; see the solution "Obtaining the Handle to a Stock Font" for the specifics of the **GetStockObject** function.

All display devices contexts are created with the **SYSTEM_FONT** stock font object, by default. In addition, although it does no harm, there is no need to destroy a stock font object via the **DeleteObject** function. The GDI is responsible for destroying stock fonts.

The LOGFONT Structure

As previously mentioned, a logical font is a description of a physical font. This description itself is represented by a special GDI type: the **LOGFONT** structure.

```
typedef struct tagLOGFONT {
    LONG lfHeight;
    LONG lfWidth;
    LONG lfEscapement;
    LONG lfOrientation;
```

Table 4.1 Seven stock-font identifiers for use with the GetStockObject function.

Identifier	Value	Description
OEM_FIXED_FONT	10	A device-driver-defined fixed-pitch font that's set by the original equipment manufacturer (OEM).
ANSI_FIXED_FONT	11	A device-driver-defined fixed-pitch font, typically Courier, that uses the Windows character set.
ANSI_VAR_FONT	12	A device-driver-defined variable-pitch font, typically MS Sans Serif, that uses the Windows character set.
SYSTEM_FONT	13	A GDI-defined variable-pitch font, typically MS Sans Serif (Windows 95/98/NT) or Tahoma (Windows 2000), that uses the Windows character set.
DEVICE_DEFAULT_FONT	14	A device-dependent font. It's the preferred font of a specific device.
DEFAULT_GUI_FONT	17	A GDI-defined variable-pitch font that's used for user-interface elements.

```
    LONG lfWeight;
    BYTE lfItalic;
    BYTE lfUnderline;
    BYTE lfStrikeOut;
    BYTE lfCharSet;
    BYTE lfOutPrecision;
    BYTE lfClipPrecision;
    BYTE lfQuality;
    BYTE lfPitchAndFamily;
    CHAR lfFaceName[LF_FACESIZE];
} LOGFONT, *PLOGFONT, NEAR *NPLOGFONT, FAR *LPLOGFONT;
```

The **lfHeight** data member specifies the height of the font's cell, or the height of the font's character, in logical units. When the **LOGFONT** structure is used to create a logical font, or when you fill a **LOGFONT** structure by using the **GetObject** function, the **lfHeight** data member is interpreted in different ways, depending on its sign. Specifically, when the **lfHeight** data member is positive, its value represents the font's cell height. When **lfHeight** is negative, its value represents the font's character height. When **lfHeight** is zero, its value represents the font's default character height (typically a point size of 12).

Most often, you'll want to create a font of a specific point size, in which case you might think to use the aforementioned points-to-logical-units conversion formula. The problem is that you don't know the font's internal leading height. However, following the previous sign-related logic, you can assign **lfHeight** a negative value, and the font mapper will take its absolute value as the desired character height. So, 99 percent of the time, you'll want to use the following modified version of the points-to-logical-units conversion formula:

```
lf.lfHeight = static_cast<int>(
   (point_size * pixels_per_inch / points_per_inch) + 0.5
   );
```

The typecast and the addition of the 0.5 (bias) round the result to the nearest integer. This is more concisely written using the **MulDiv** function (which does the rounding for you):

```
lf.lfHeight = -MulDiv(point_size, pixels_per_inch, points_per_inch);
```

The **lfWidth** data member specifies the average width of each character in logical units. When you use the corresponding **LOGFONT** structure to create a logical font (i.e., with the **CreateFontIndirect** function), this data member is usually set to zero. In this case, the font mapper will choose the closest matching font based on the aspect ratio of the target device. For most situations, the **lfWidth** data member is specified as zero.

The **lfEscapement** data member specifies the amount of rotation of a line of text in tenths of a degree. For example, if you need to render the caption of a button in a vertical fashion, you can create a font that's rotated by either positive or negative 90 degrees. In this case, you'd set the **lfEscapement** data member to either positive or negative 900 (i.e., 90 × 10 tenths of a degree), respectively.

The **lfOrientation** data member is similar to the **lfEscapement** data member except that **lfOrientation** specifies the rotation of each character. This is true only on systems running Windows NT or Windows 2000 when the graphics mode is set to **GM_ADVANCED** (see Chapter 10). In all other cases, the **lfOrientation** data member is identical to the **lfEscapement** data member and can either be assigned the same value as the latter or be ignored.

The **lfWeight** data member specifies the weight of each character. You can think of the weight as the thickness of each curve that's used to depict a particular character. Along these same lines, the **lfWeight** data member is what's used to create a boldface font. Table 4.2 lists the various identifiers that can be assigned to the **lfWeight** data member. When the **lfWeight** data member is set to **FW_DONTCARE**, the font's default weight is used. This is the most commonly used initialization value.

NOTE: *For raster and vector fonts, or for TrueType and OpenType fonts that do not have a boldface variety, the GDI will mimic a bold appearance by rendering each character twice (the second one is drawn one pixel to the right).*

The **lfItalic**, **lfUnderline**, and **lfStrikeOut** data members are Boolean values that specify whether the font's characters are italicized, underlined, and/or struck out. The GDI will synthesize the indicated effect when the **lfUnderline** and/or

Table 4.2 Possible values for the LOGFONT::lfWeight data member.

Identifier	Value
FW_DONTCARE	0
FW_THIN	100
FW_EXTRALIGHT	200
FW_LIGHT	300
FW_NORMAL	400
FW_MEDIUM	500
FW_SEMIBOLD	600
FW_BOLD	700
FW_EXTRABOLD	800
FW_HEAVY	900

lfStrikeOut data members are **TRUE**. For raster and vector fonts, or for TrueType and OpenType fonts that do not have an italic variety, the GDI will mimic the italic effect by rendering each character in a slanted fashion.

The **lfCharSet** data member specifies the character set that the font will use. This data member can be assigned any one of the identifiers listed in Table 4.3.

Some of the identifiers provided in Table 4.3 are specific to certain language-specific versions of Windows. You must make sure that the **lfCharSet** data member is assigned an appropriate character-set identifier according to the typeface name of the font. In some cases, you can use **DEFAULT_CHARSET**, but do so only if you're sure that the specified font does indeed exist on the target machine. On systems running Windows NT or Windows 2000, the **DEFAULT_CHARSET** identifier is based on the current locale.

The **lfOutPrecision** data member specifies how precisely the logical font matches its description. This data member is used by the font mapper during its matching

Table 4.3 Possible values for the LOGFONT::lfCharSet data member.

Identifier	Value
ANSI_CHARSET	0
DEFAULT_CHARSET	1
SYMBOL_CHARSET	2
MAC_CHARSET	77
SHIFTJIS_CHARSET	128
HANGEUL_CHARSET	129
JOHAB_CHARSET	130
GB2312_CHARSET	134
CHINESEBIG5_CHARSET	136
GREEK_CHARSET	161
TURKISH_CHARSET	162
VIETNAMESE_CHARSET	163
HEBREW_CHARSET	177
ARABIC_CHARSET	178
BALTIC_CHARSET	186
RUSSIAN_CHARSET	204
THAI_CHARSET	222
EASTEUROPE_CHARSET	238
OEM_CHARSET	255

process; this data member is also used to indicate a font technology during an enumeration process (see Listing 4.1 for an example of enumerating fonts). Table 4.4 lists the various identifiers that can be assigned to the **lfOutPrecision** data member.

Table 4.4 Possible values for the LOGFONT::lfOutPrecision data member.

Identifier	Value	Description
OUT_DEFAULT_PRECIS	0	The font mapper follows its normal matching scheme.
OUT_STRING_PRECIS	1	This identifier is indicated during the enumeration of raster fonts.
OUT_STROKE_PRECIS	3	On systems running Windows 95 or Windows 98, when multiple fonts of the same typeface name are available, the font mapper chooses the vector or TrueType variety. This identifier is also indicated during the enumeration of vector, TrueType, and OpenType fonts. On systems running Windows NT or Windows 2000, this identifier is indicated only during the enumeration process.
OUT_TT_PRECIS	4	When multiple fonts of the same typeface name are available, the font mapper chooses the TrueType variety.
OUT_DEVICE_PRECIS	5	When multiple fonts of the same typeface name are available, the font mapper chooses the device-specific variety (e.g., a font supplied by a printer manufacturer).
OUT_RASTER_PRECIS	6	When multiple fonts of the same typeface name are available, the font mapper chooses the raster variety.
OUT_TT_ONLY_PRECIS	7	The font mapper chooses from only the available TrueType fonts.
OUT_OUTLINE_PRECIS	8	When multiple fonts of the same typeface name are available, the font mapper chooses the TrueType or other outline-based variety.
OUT_SCREEN_OUTLINE_PRECIS	9	When multiple fonts of the same typeface name are available, the font mapper chooses the TrueType or other outline-based variety, but chooses from only those fonts available for the display monitor.
OUT_PS_ONLY_PRECIS	10	The font mapper chooses from only the available OpenType fonts.

The **OUT_DEFAULT_PRECIS** identifier is used in most situations; assigning this identifier to the **lfOutPrecision** data member instructs the font mapper to use its default matching scheme. The **OUT_TT_ONLY_PRECIS** or **OUT_PS_ONLY_PRECIS** identifier is used when strictly TrueType or OpenType fonts are needed, respectively. When one of these identifiers is used, the font mapper chooses either from the available TrueType (**OUT_TT_ONLY_PRECIS**) fonts or from the available OpenType (**OUT_PS_ONLY_PRECIS**) fonts. If no matching fonts are available, the font mapper defaults to its normal matching scheme.

When multiple fonts of the same typeface name are available, you can assign the **lfOutPrecision** data member the **OUT_DEVICE_PRECIS**, **OUT_RASTER_PRECIS**, **OUT_STROKE_PRECIS**, **OUT_OUTLINE_PRECIS**, or **OUT_TT_PRECIS** identifier, depending on the specific font technology that's desired. When any one of these identifiers is used, the font mapper chooses a match according to the specified technology. On systems running Windows NT or Windows 2000, however, the **OUT_STROKE_PRECIS** identifier is used only during enumeration; this identifier is not used by the font mapper.

The **lfClipPrecision** data member specifies the font's clipping behavior. This governs how the GDI should draw characters that fall partially beyond the target device context's clipping region. Table 4.5 lists the possible identifiers for this data member.

The **lfQuality** data member specifies the quality of the rendered characters. You can use this data member to control the appearance of rendered text in much the same way that you would adjust the quality of a print job. Table 4.6 lists the identifiers that can be assigned to the **lfQuality** data member.

The **lfPitchAndFamily** data member specifies the font's pitch and family. The pitch (i.e., fixed- or variable-pitch), which can be assigned one of the identifiers listed in Table 4.7, is specified by the two low-order bits.

Table 4.5 Possible values for the LOGFONT::lfClipPrecision data member.

Identifier	Value	Description
CLIP_DEFAULT_PRECIS	0	The default clipping behavior is used.
CLIP_STROKE_PRECIS	2	This identifier is returned only during enumeration.
CLIP_LH_ANGLES	16	When this identifier is specified, the direction of the rotation of all non-device fonts is governed by the current coordinate system.
CLIP_EMBEDDED	128	This identifier is used for embedded read-only fonts.

Table 4.6 Possible values for the LOGFONT::lfQuality data member.

Identifier	Value
DEFAULT_QUALITY	0
DRAFT_QUALITY	1
PROOF_QUALITY	2
NONANTIALIASED_QUALITY	3
ANTIALIASED_QUALITY	4

Table 4.7 Possible values for the two low-order bits of the LOGFONT::lfPitchAndFamily data member.

Identifier	Value
DEFAULT_PITCH	0
FIXED_PITCH	1
VARIABLE_PITCH	2
MONO_FONT	8

The **MONO_FONT** identifier is only used when the **LOGFONT** structure is used with the **EnumFontFamiliesEx** function to enumerate fonts on systems with Arabic or Hebrew languages.

The family of the font is specified by the fourth through seventh bits of the **lfPitchAndFamily** data member. These bits can be assigned any of the identifiers listed in Table 4.8.

The **lfFaceName** data member specifies the typeface name. Because this member is a character array of length **LF_FACESIZE** (32), you can use the **lstrcpy** or **lstrcpyn** function to specify a **NULL**-terminated string that indicates the desired typeface name.

Table 4.8 Possible values for bits four through seven of the LOGFONT::lfPitchAndFamily data member.

Identifier	Value
FF_DONTCARE	0
FF_ROMAN	16
FF_SWISS	32
FF_MODERN	48
FF_SCRIPT	64

Text Color

You may have noticed that the **LOGFONT** structure does not contain a data member that identifies a font's color. Indeed, the GDI font object does not maintain a color quantity. Instead, the color in which a font's characters will appear is defined by the *text color* of the device context to which the text is rendered.

A device context's text color defines the foreground color that the font's characters will take on. Likewise, the color that appears behind these characters is governed by the device context's background color (see Chapter 1).

You can determine a device context's current text color by using the **GetTextColor** function:

```
COLORREF GetTextColor(
    IN HDC hdc        // handle to the target device context
   );
```

The single **hdc** parameter is specified as the handle to the device context whose text color (a **COLORREF** value) is returned if the **GetTextColor** function is successful. If the function fails, the return value is **CLR_INVALID**.

Similarly, you can change the text color of a device context by using the **SetTextColor** function. When this function is successful, it returns the previous background color:

```
COLORREF SetTextColor(
    IN HDC hdc,           // handle to the target device context
    IN COLORREF crColor   // new text color
   );
```

The **hdc** parameter identifies the device context whose text color will be changed to the color specified by the **crColor** parameter. Like **GetTextColor**, when the **SetTextColor** function fails, it returns **CLR_INVALID**. For example, to change the text color to white, you use the **SetTextColor** function this way:

```
COLORREF clrWhite = PALETTERB(255, 255, 255);
COLORREF clrOld = SetTextColor(hDC, clrWhite);
```

Rendering with a Font Object

As with other graphic objects, the GDI provides a set of functions that render textual output by using a logical font object. Although the use of these functions is relatively straightforward, achieving a specific look is not always easy. Still, with a general understanding of the various text-output functions, and by using the aforementioned techniques to determine the width and height of a string, rarely will you find an appearance that can't be achieved. Of the text-output functions, **TextOut** is the most commonly used.

General Output: The TextOut Function

The **TextOut** function is the simplest, and most popular, GDI text-output function. It can be used to render a string to a specific location on the target device. The signature of the function is as follows:

```
BOOL TextOut(
    IN HDC hdc,           // handle to the target device context
    IN int nXStart,       // x-coordinate of the string
    IN int nYStart,       // y-coordinate of the string
    IN LPCSTR lpString,   // a pointer to the string
    IN int cbString       // length of the string
   );
```

The **hdc** parameter identifies the destination device context. The **nXStart** and **nYStart** parameters specify the location within the associated device where the text should appear. The **lpString** parameter is a pointer to the desired string, and the **cbString** parameter specifies how many characters this string contains. On systems running Windows 95 or Windows 98, the length is limited to 8,192 characters. If the **TextOut** function is successful, the return value is **TRUE**; otherwise, the function returns **FALSE**:

```
const POINT PText = {10, 20};
TCHAR text[] = TEXT("This is a single line of text\0");
BOOL success = TextOut(hdc, PText.x, PText.y, text, lstrlen(text));
```

By default, the **TextOut** function renders text that is aligned to the top left. That is, the **nXStart** and **nYStart** parameters describe the location of the top-left edge of the text's bounding rectangle. Rarely, however, will you need to draw text that is aligned only to the left. For example, if you're manually rendering the items in a report-view list-view control, you might want to right-align the caption of each item in a particular column. To this end, the GDI allows you to specify a device context's text-alignment attributes. Specifically, using the **SetTextAlign** function, you can modify the device context's interpretation of the x- and y-coordinate parameters of many text-output functions, including **TextOut**. In this way, you can easily control the text's horizontal and vertical alignment. Tables 4.9, 4.10, and 4.11 list the various text-alignment attributes that can be specified for a device context. For more information on the **SetTextAlign** function, see the solution "Rendering Aligned Text."

***NOTE:** The text-alignment settings are used only by the **TextOut**, **ExtTextOut**, **PolyTextOut**, and **TabbedTextOut** functions. In Tables 4.9, 4.10, and 4.11, the x- and y-coordinate descriptions refer to the x- and y-coordinate parameters of each of these functions when the **TA_NOUPDATECP** attribute is set, or to the current position when the **TA_UPDATECP** attribute is set. The default text alignment is a combination of **TA_LEFT**, **TA_TOP**, and **TA_NOUPDATECP**.*

Whereas the identifiers of Tables 4.9 and 4.10 govern the way the x- and y-coordinate parameters are interpreted, the two identifiers listed in Table 4.11 simply determine if these parameters are used. The default setting is **TA_NOUPDATECP**, which simply means that output will be placed according to whatever values you specify as the x- and y-coordinate parameters. For example, when you use the **TextOut** function with this default setting, the **nXStart** and **nYStart** parameters describe an "absolute" logical location. On the other hand, when the **TA_UPDATECP** identifier is specified, the target device context's current position (a.k.a., the DC's pen position) is used as the x- and y-coordinate parameters. In this

Table 4.9 Horizontal-alignment identifiers used with the SetTextAlign function.

Identifier	Value	Effect
TA_LEFT	0	The x-coordinate specifies the left edge of the string's bounding rectangle.
TA_RIGHT	2	The x-coordinate specifies the right edge of the string's bounding rectangle.
TA_CENTER	6	The x-coordinate specifies the horizontal center of the string's bounding rectangle.

Table 4.10 Vertical-alignment identifiers used with the SetTextAlign function.

Identifier	Value	Effect
TA_TOP	0	The y-coordinate specifies the top edge of the string's bounding rectangle.
TA_BOTTOM	8	The y-coordinate specifies the bottom edge of the string's bounding rectangle.
TA_BASELINE	24	The y-coordinate specifies the base line of the string.

Table 4.11 Current-position-behavior identifiers used with the SetTextAlign function.

Identifier	Value	Effect
TA_NOUPDATECP	0	The current position is not updated after each string is rendered.
TA_UPDATECP	8	The current position is updated after each string is rendered. Subsequent text output will use the current position instead of any specified x- and y-coordinates.

case, the **nXStart** and **nYStart** parameters of the **TextOut** function are ignored. This latter setting is useful for rendering a string in segments via multiple calls to a text-output function. For example, if you need to render a string where each word is a different color, you can use the **TA_UPDATECP** setting as follows:

```
const POINT PText = {10, 20};
const TCHAR text[] = TEXT(
   "Using the TextOut function when the TA_UPDATECP option is set.\0"
   );
HDC hDC = GetDC(hWnd);
try
{
   SetBkMode(hDC, TRANSPARENT);
   SetTextAlign(hDC, TA_LEFT | TA_TOP | TA_UPDATECP);
   MoveToEx(hDC, PText.x, PText.y, NULL);

   int pos = 0;
   int word_start = 0;
   while (text[pos++] != '\0')
   {
      if (text[pos] == ' ' || text[pos] == '\0')
      {
         SetTextColor(hDC, PALETTERGB(0, 0, rand() % 255));
         const int word_len = pos - word_start;
         TextOut(hDC, -1, -1, text + word_start, word_len);
         word_start = pos;
      }
   }
}
catch (...)
{
   ReleaseDC(hWnd, hDC);
}
ReleaseDC(hWnd, hDC);
```

Formatted Output

In addition to the **TextOut** function, the GDI provides several other text-output functions that can be used to render text. Most of these are simple variations of the **TextOut** function that provide extended control over the format of the output. For example, the **ExtTextOut** function extends the **TextOut** function by providing both clipping and opaquing control. Similarly, the **TabbedTextOut** function extends **TextOut** by providing the ability to render expanded tab characters. Likewise, the **PolyTextOut** function can be used to render multiple lines of text.

Aside from the **TextOut** function and its derivatives, the GDI provides an all-purpose text-output function: **DrawText**. The **DrawText** function is perhaps the most useful of all GDI text-output functions. Typically, this function is used when you're drawing a single block of text (i.e., a single line or a single paragraph) in one shot. Unlike the **TextOut** function, **DrawText** can perform formatted rendering without explicit manipulation of the target device context's alignment attributes:

```
int DrawText(
    IN HDC hDC,                // handle to the target device context
    IN LPCSTR lpString,        // pointer to the string
    IN int nCount,             // number of character in the string
    IN OUT LPRECT lpRect,      // target bounding rectangle
    IN UINT uFormat            // text-formatting parameters
  );
```

The **hDC** parameter identifies the destination device context. The **lpString** and **nCount** parameters are used to specify the desired string and the number of characters that it contains, respectively. As with the other text-output functions, on systems running Windows 95 or Windows 98, the length is limited to 8,192 characters. You use the **lpRect** parameter to specify the text's bounding rectangle. This rectangle is used to describe the area to which the text is formatted (e.g., aligned, opaqued, and clipped). The **uFormat** parameter is used to describe the actual formatting options. This parameter can be assigned a combination of the identifiers listed in Table 4.12.

***TIP:** If the string indicated by the **lpString** parameter is **NULL**-terminated, you can pass a value of **–1** as the **nCount** parameter.*

Table 4.12 Identifiers that can be assigned to the uFormat parameter of the DrawText function.

Identifier	Value	Effect
DT_TOP	0x00000000	The text is vertically aligned to the top of the specified bounding rectangle.
DT_LEFT	0x00000000	The text is horizontally aligned to the left of the specified bounding rectangle.
DT_CENTER	0x00000001	The text is horizontally aligned to the center of the specified bounding rectangle.
DT_RIGHT	0x00000002	The text is horizontally aligned to the right of the specified bounding rectangle.

(continued)

Table 4.12 Identifiers that can be assigned to the uFormat parameter of the DrawText function *(continued)*.

Identifier	Value	Effect
DT_VCENTER	0x00000004	The text is vertically aligned to the center of the specified bounding rectangle. Use of this option also requires the **DT_SINGLELINE** identifier.
DT_BOTTOM	0x00000008	The text is vertically aligned to the bottom of the specified bounding rectangle.
DT_WORDBREAK	0x00000010	The text is rendered such that words that fall beyond the edge of the specified bounding rectangle are wrapped to the next line.
DT_SINGLELINE	0x00000020	The text is rendered as a single line only.
DT_EXPANDTABS	0x00000040	The text is rendered with tab characters expanded.
DT_TABSTOP	0x00000080	Use this identifier when the **DrawText** function is used only to set the number of characters that are used for subsequent rendering with the **DT_EXPANDTABS** option. The high-order byte of the low-order word of the **uFormat** parameter is assigned the number of characters that will be used for each expanded tab stop.
DT_NOCLIP	0x00000100	The text is not clipped to the specified bounding rectangle. By default, any characters that fall outside the bounding rectangle are clipped. Use of this option can reduce the amount of time required for the rendering. This identifier cannot be combined with **DT_TABSTOP**.
DT_EXTERNALLEADING	0x00000200	The font's external leading metric is used in the line height calculation. This identifier cannot be combined with **DT_TABSTOP**.
DT_CALCRECT	0x00000400	Use this identifier when the **DrawText** function is used only to calculate the text's bounding rectangle. When this identifier is used with the **DT_SINGLELINE** option, the function modifies the bottom and right edges of the specified rectangle to encompass the entire string. When the **DT_SINGLELINE** option is not set (i.e., when you want to render multiple lines of text), you must set the width of the bounding rectangle; **DrawText** modifies the bottom edge of this rectangle to encompass the entire paragraph. This identifier cannot be combined with **DT_TABSTOP**.

(continued)

Table 4.12 Identifiers that can be assigned to the uFormat parameter of the DrawText function *(continued)*.

Identifier	Value	Effect
DT_NOPREFIX	0x00000800	This identifier prevents the function from interpreting the **&** prefix character as a hotkey combination. Without this option, the **DrawText** function underlines any character that follows the prefix character, and when the double prefix **&&** is specified, the **DrawText** function renders a single "&". This identifier cannot be combined with **DT_TABSTOP**.
DT_INTERNAL	0x00001000	The system font is used during the formatting calculations. This identifier cannot be combined with **DT_TABSTOP**.
DT_EDITCONTROL	0x00002000	The text is rendered in a fashion similar to that of a multiline edit control.
DT_PATH_ELLIPSIS	0x00004000	The text is rendered so that the entire string fits within the specified bounding rectangle. If necessary, an appropriate number of characters from the middle of the string are replaced with ellipses. The actual string is not modified unless the **DT_MODIFYSTRING** option is specified.
DT_END_ELLIPSIS	0x00008000	The text is rendered so that the entire string fits within the specified bounding rectangle. If necessary, an appropriate number of characters from the beginning of the string are replaced with ellipses. The actual string is not modified unless the **DT_MODIFYSTRING** option is specified.
DT_MODIFYSTRING	0x00010000	When used with the **DT_PATH_ELLIPSIS** or **DT_END_ELLIPSIS** identifier, this option causes the actual string to be modified to match the rendered version. You must allow enough space in the **lpString** buffer to accommodate any extra characters (up to four characters can be added).
DT_RTLREADING	0x00020000	The text is rendered with a right-to-left reading order. The target device context must have an Arabic or Hebrew font selected into it.
DT_WORD_ELLIPSIS	0x00040000	Any word that does not fit within the specified bounding rectangle is replaced with ellipses.

(continued)

Table 4.12 Identifiers that can be assigned to the uFormat parameter of the DrawText function *(continued)*.

Identifier	Value	Effect
DT_NOFULLWIDTHCHARBREAK	0x00080000	This identifier instructs the function not to break a line at a double-wide character string. Windows 98 and 2000 only.
DT_HIDEPREFIX	0x00100000	This identifier instructs the function to ignore the **&** prefix character. Without this option, the **DrawText** function underlines any character that follows the prefix character. The double prefix **&&** combination still produces a single "&" character. Windows 2000 only.
DT_PREFIXONLY	0x00200000	This identifier instructs the function to render only the underscore symbol at the location of the character that follows the **&** character. Without this option, the **DrawText** function underlines any character that follows the prefix character. The double prefix **&&** combination still produces a single "&" character. Windows 2000 only.

***TIP:** If you need additional control over the number of spaces that are used when tab characters are expanded, use the **DrawTextEx** function instead of the **DrawText** function. The **DrawTextEx** function is identical to **DrawText**, except that **DrawTextEx** accepts an additional parameter, which can be used to specify tab and margin lengths.*

If the **DrawText** function is successful, it returns the height of the text. When the **DT_VCENTER** or **DT_BOTTOM** options are set, the return value specifies the offset from the top of the specified bounding rectangle to the bottom of the text. If the function fails, the return value is zero. The following code snippet demonstrates the use of the **DrawText** function to render a right-aligned paragraph with proper word breaks:

```
const TCHAR text[] = TEXT(
   "A common example of the use of the DT_PATH_ELLIPSIS option "
   "can be seen in the (details-mode) folder view of Windows "
   "Explorer itself. If you reduce the width of a column header "
   "just enough to where the text of the longest caption is "
   "longer than the column width, Explorer will replace the end "
   "of the caption with ellipses. In fact, this is the normal "
   "behavior of a standard list-view control. Still, if you "
   "ever need to render the list items manually, consider using "
   "the DrawText function.\0"
   );
```

```
HDC hDC = GetDC(hWnd);
try
{
   RECT RParagraph = {10, 10, 350, 0};

   // calculate the proper rectangle height
   UINT format_options =
      DT_RIGHT | DT_WORDBREAK | DT_NOCLIP | DT_CALCRECT;
   DrawText(hDC, text, -1, &RParagraph, format_options);

   // render the border
   InflateRect(&RParagraph, 4, 4);
   DrawEdge(hDC, &RParagraph, EDGE_SUNKEN, BF_RECT);

   // fill the background
   InflateRect(&RParagraph, -2, -2);
   PatBlt(hDC, RParagraph.left, RParagraph.top,
          RParagraph.right - RParagraph.left,
          RParagraph.bottom - RParagraph.top,
          WHITENESS);
   SetBkMode(hDC, TRANSPARENT);

   // render the paragraph right-aligned
   InflateRect(&RParagraph, -2, -2);
   format_options &= ~DT_CALCRECT;
   DrawText(hDC, text, -1, &RParagraph, format_options);
}
catch (...)
{
   ReleaseDC(hWnd, hDC);
}
ReleaseDC(hWnd, hDC);
```

As previously mentioned, the **DrawText** function is extremely handy for rendering formatted text; namely, the **uFormat** parameter can be used to specify a multitude of formatting options. Still, when you're rendering repetitious blocks of aligned text, it's best to use a combination of the **SetTextAlign** and **TextOut** functions. Because the **DrawText** function modifies the alignment of the target device context each time, it's generally slower than the **TextOut** function. This is especially true when you need to set the text-alignment options (via the **SetTextAlign** function) only once. Moreover, the **DrawText** function will not work with rotated fonts. If you need to render a rotated font, you have to use **TextOut**, or one of its close relatives (e.g., **ExtTextOut** or **TabbedTextOut**).

Immediate Solutions

Creating a Logical Font

To create a logical font, you use the **CreateFontIndirect** function:

```
HFONT CreateFontIndirect(
    IN CONST LOGFONT lpclf*     // pointer to a LOGFONT structure that
                                // describes the logical font
   );
```

The **lpclf** parameter is assigned the address of a **LOGFONT** structure whose data members describe the attributes of the logical font. If the **CreateFontIndirect** function is successful, it returns a handle to a logical font. If the function fails, the return value is **NULL**.

Typically, most of the data members of the **LOGFONT** structure are initialized to zero, and only the **lfHeight**, **lfCharSet**, and **lfFaceName** members are assigned specific values. The following code snippet demonstrates how to create a boldface logical font object that uses the **ANSI_CHARSET** with a point size of 14 and a typeface name of "Times New Roman." Once created, this font is used to render the words "My Font!" via the **DrawText** function. The mapping mode of the target device context is assumed to be **MM_TEXT** with an identity matrix (i.e., one-to-one) world-transform; see Chapter 10 for more information on mapping modes and coordinate-space transformations. Here's the code:

```
const int point_size = 14;
const int points_per_inch = 72;
int pixels_per_inch = 0;

HDC hScreenDC = GetDC(NULL);
try
{
   pixels_per_inch = GetDeviceCaps(hScreenDC, LOGPIXELSY);
}
catch (...)
{
   ReleaseDC(NULL, hScreenDC);
}
ReleaseDC(NULL, hScreenDC);
```

```
LOGFONT lf;
memset(&lf, 0, sizeof(LOGFONT));
lf.lfHeight = -MulDiv(point_size, pixels_per_inch, points_per_inch);
lf.lfWeight = FW_BOLD;
lf.lfCharSet = ANSI_CHARSET;
lstrcpy(reinterpret_cast<LPTSTR>(&lf.lfFaceName),
        TEXT("Times New Roman"));

HFONT hFont = CreateFontIndirect(&lf);
if (hFont)
{
   HDC hDC = GetDC(hWnd);
   HFONT hOldFont = static_cast<HFONT>(
      SelectObject(hDC, hFont)
      );
   try
   {
      RECT RText = {10, 10, 300, 100};
      DrawText(hDC, TEXT("My Font!\0"), -1,
               &RText, DT_SINGLELINE | DT_VCENTER);
   }
   catch (...)
   {
      DeleteObject(SelectObject(hDC, hOldFont));
      ReleaseDC(hWnd, hDC);
   }
   DeleteObject(SelectObject(hDC, hOldFont));
   ReleaseDC(hWnd, hDC);
}
```

***NOTE:** In the previous example, the **LOGPIXELSY** capability index was used (with the **GetDeviceCaps** function) to compute the number of pixels per logical inch. You can also estimate the number of pixels per physical inch by using a combination of the **VERTRES** and **VERTSIZE** capability indices (see "Point Sizes" in the In Depth section).*

As demonstrated in this example, when a logical font is no longer needed, you must destroy it by using the **DeleteObject** function. Do not, however, call the **DeleteObject** function on a font that's currently selected into a device context. Be sure to deselect the font before you destroy it.

An alternative approach is to use the **CreateFont** function. Here, instead of passing the address of a **LOGFONT** structure, the function accepts parameters that correspond to each of the **LOGFONT** structure's data members. The following code snippet demonstrates how to create a logical font object for use with the primary display monitor, with a typeface name of "Courier New," a point size of

30, and an italic appearance. (The mapping mode of the target device context is assumed to be **MM_TEXT** with an identity matrix world-transform.) Here's the code:

```
const int point_size = 30;
const int points_per_inch = 72;
int pixels_per_inch = 0;

HDC hScreenDC = GetDC(NULL);
try
{
   pixels_per_inch = GetDeviceCaps(hScreenDC, LOGPIXELSY);
}
catch (...)
{
   ReleaseDC(NULL, hScreenDC);
}
ReleaseDC(NULL, hScreenDC);

const int logical_height =
   -MulDiv(point_size, pixels_per_inch, points_per_inch);

HFONT hFont =
   CreateFont(
      logical_height, 0, 0, 0, 0, true,
      0, 0, ANSI_CHARSET, 0, 0, 0, 0,
      TEXT("Courier New")
      );
if (hFont)
{
   // ...
}
```

Because the creation of a logical font object is a frequently performed task, it makes sense to wrap this process into a utility function. The following sample function can be used to create fonts of various attributes. Here, the current world-transform and mapping mode are effectively handled via the scaling (**xf.eM22**) that's computed using the **GetWorldTransform** function and the **DPtoLP** function, respectively:

```
namespace font
{
   const FS_NONE       = 0x00000000;
```

```
const FS_BOLD      = 0x00000001;
const FS_ITALIC    = 0x00000002;
const FS_UNDERLINE = 0x00000004;
const FS_STRIKEOUT = 0x00000008;

HFONT MakeFont(
   IN HDC hDestDC,
   IN LPCSTR typeface_name,
   IN int point_size,
   IN const BYTE charset = ANSI_CHARSET,
   IN const DWORD style = FS_NONE)
{
   XFORM xf;
   GetWorldTransform(hDestDC, &xf);
   const int pixels_per_inch = GetDeviceCaps(hDestDC, LOGPIXELSY);

   POINT PSize;
   PSize.x = 0;
   PSize.y = static_cast<LONG>(
      xf.eM22 * -MulDiv(point_size, pixels_per_inch, 72) + 0.5
      );

   HFONT hResult = NULL;
   if (DPtoLP(hDestDC, &PSize, 1))
   {
      LOGFONT lf;
      memset(&lf, 0, sizeof(LOGFONT));

      lf.lfHeight = PSize.y;
      lf.lfCharSet = charset;
      lstrcpyn(reinterpret_cast<LPTSTR>(&lf.lfFaceName),
               typeface_name, LF_FACESIZE);

      lf.lfWeight = (style & FS_BOLD) ? FW_BOLD : FW_DONTCARE;
      lf.lfItalic = (style & FS_ITALIC) ? true : false;
      lf.lfUnderline = (style & FS_UNDERLINE) ? true : false;
      lf.lfStrikeOut = (style & FS_STRIKEOUT) ? true : false;

      hResult = CreateFontIndirect(&lf);
   }
   return hResult;
}
}
```

Creating a Rotated Font

To create a rotated logical font, you use the **CreateFontIndirect** function:

```
HFONT CreateFontIndirect(
    IN CONST LOGFONT lpclf*     // pointer to a LOGFONT structure that
                                // describes the logical font
  );
```

The **lpclf** parameter is assigned the address of a **LOGFONT** structure whose data members describe the attributes of the logical font. You set the **lfEscapement** and **lfOrientation** data members of the **LOGFONT** structure to the angle of rotation, in tenths of a degree.

NOTE: *Only vector, TrueType, and OpenType fonts support rotation. Raster (bitmapped) fonts do not.*

If the **CreateFontIndirect** function is successful, it returns a handle to a logical font; otherwise, the return value is **NULL**. The following code snippet demonstrates how to create a logical font object that's rotated by an angle of positive 60 degrees, and that uses the **ANSI_CHARSET** with a point size of 32 and a typeface name of "Arial." (The mapping mode of the target device context is assumed to be **MM_TEXT** with an identity matrix world-transform.) Here's the code:

```
const int num_degrees = 60;
const int point_size = 32;
const int points_per_inch = 72;
int pixels_per_inch = 0;

HDC hScreenDC = GetDC(NULL);
try
{
   pixels_per_inch = GetDeviceCaps(hScreenDC, LOGPIXELSY);
}
catch (...)
{
   ReleaseDC(NULL, hScreenDC);
}
ReleaseDC(NULL, hScreenDC);

LOGFONT lf;
memset(&lf, 0, sizeof(LOGFONT));
lf.lfHeight = -MulDiv(point_size, pixels_per_inch, points_per_inch);
lf.lfEscapement = num_degrees * 10;
lf.lfOrientation = lf.lfEscapement;
```

```
lf.lfCharSet = ANSI_CHARSET;
lstrcpy(reinterpret_cast<LPTSTR>(&lf.lfFaceName),
        TEXT("Arial"));

HFONT hRotatedFont = CreateFontIndirect(&lf);
if (hRotatedFont)
{
   // ...
}
```

As with other GDI graphic objects, when a logical font is no longer needed, you must destroy it by using the **DeleteObject** function. However, be sure to deselect the font from any device contexts before you destroy it.

On systems running Windows NT or Windows 2000, when the graphics mode of the target device context is set to **GM_ADVANCED** (see Chapter 10), you can also rotate each character (versus the entire string). To do this, you assign the character rotation angle (in tenths of a degree) to the **LOGFONT::lfOrientation** data member. (The mapping mode of the target device context is assumed to be **MM_TEXT** with an identity matrix world-transform.) Here's the code:

```
const int num_degrees = 60;
const int num_char_degrees = 120;
const int point_size = 32;
const int points_per_inch = 72;
int pixels_per_inch = 0;

HDC hScreenDC = GetDC(NULL);
try
{
   pixels_per_inch = GetDeviceCaps(hScreenDC, LOGPIXELSY);
}
catch (...)
{
   ReleaseDC(NULL, hScreenDC);
}
ReleaseDC(NULL, hScreenDC);

LOGFONT lf;
memset(&lf, 0, sizeof(LOGFONT));
lf.lfHeight = -MulDiv(point_size, pixels_per_inch, points_per_inch);
lf.lfEscapement = num_degrees * 10;
lf.lfOrientation = num_char_degrees * 10;;
lf.lfCharSet = ANSI_CHARSET;
lstrcpy(reinterpret_cast<LPTSTR>(&lf.lfFaceName),
        TEXT("Arial"));
```

```
HFONT hRotatedCharFont = CreateFontIndirect(&lf);
if (hRotatedCharFont)
{
   // ...
}
```

Obtaining the Handle to a Stock Font

To retrieve a handle to one of the seven stock font objects, you use the **GetStockObject** function:

```
HGDIOBJ GetStockObject(
    IN int fnObject        // identifier of the stock object
   );
```

The **fnObject** parameter is used to specify which stock font object you want to retrieve. Because **GetStockObject** is a general function, it can be used to retrieve a handle to non-font stock objects as well. However, to retrieve a handle to one of the GDI's seven stock fonts, you specify the **fnObject** parameter as one of the identifiers listed in Table 4.1.

If the **GetStockObject** function is successful, it returns a handle to the logical stock object that is requested. If the function fails, the return value is **NULL**. For example, to retrieve a handle to the stock system fixed font:

```
HFONT hStockFont = static_cast<HFONT>(
   GetStockObject(SYSTEM_FIXED_FONT)
   );
```

Determining the Width of a Character

To determine the width of a particular font character (or a range of characters) in logical units, you use the **GetCharWidth32** function:

```
BOOL GetCharWidth32(
    IN HDC hdc,            // handle to the target device context
    IN UINT iFirstChar,    // first character in the range
    IN UINT iLastChar,     // last character in the range
    OUT LPINT lpBuffer     // pointer to an array of INTs that will
                           // receive the width of each character
   );
```

The **hdc** parameter identifies the device context whose currently selected font is used during the width calculation. The actual character whose width you want to determine is specified by the **iFirstChar** and **iLastChar** parameters (set them both to the same character). If you need to determine the width of a range of characters, assign the **iFirstChar** and **iLastChar** parameters the first and last characters in the range, respectively. The **lpBuffer** parameter identifies an array of integers that will be filled with the width of each character in the range. The **GetCharWidths32** function returns a Boolean value indicating success or failure.

TIP: *If you need a more precise width measurement, use the* ***GetCharWidthFloat*** *function instead.*

For example, to retrieve the width of the letter "Z," you use the **GetCharWidths32** function as follows:

```
int width;
if (GetCharWidth32(hDC, 'Z', 'Z', &width))
{
   // ...
}
```

Likewise, to retrieve the width of each character in the range from "A" to "Z", you use the **GetCharWidth32** function like so:

```
int widths[26];
if (GetCharWidth32(hDC, 'A', 'Z', widths))
{
   // ...
}
```

The **GetCharWidth32** function is handy when you need to render a line of text in which each character has a different attribute, or in other situations that might warrant the output of an individual character at a time (e.g., a word processor). The following code snippet demonstrates how to render a line of text in which each character has a random color:

```
int pos = 0;
const int extra = GetTextCharacterExtra(hDC);
LPCSTR text = TEXT("A random line of text\0");
const int length = lstrlen(text);
for (int index = 0; index < length; ++index)
{
```

```
        SetTextColor(
            hDC,
            PALETTERGB(rand() % 256, rand() % 256, rand() % 256)
            );
        TextOut(hDC, 10 + pos, 10, &text[index], 1);

        int width;
        if (GetCharWidth32(hDC, text[index], text[index], &width))
        {
            pos += width + extra;
        }
    }
```


Determining the Width and Height of a String

To determine the width and height of a line of text in logical units, you use the **GetTextExtentPoint32** function:

```
BOOL GetTextExtentPoint32(
    IN HDC hdc,           // handle to the target device context
    IN LPCSTR lpString,   // pointer to a string of characters
    IN int cbString,      // the number of characters in the string
    OUT LPSIZE lpSize     // pointer to a SIZE structure that will
                          // receive the width and height of the string
   );
```

The **hdc** parameter identifies the device context whose currently selected font object is used to determine the width and height of the string. This string is specified by the **lpString** parameter. The **cbString** parameter is used to specify the number of characters that the string contains. The actual height and width of the string, in logical units, are placed in the **cx** and **cy** data members of the **SIZE** structure whose address is indicated by the **lpSize** parameter. If the **GetTextExtentPoint32** function is successful, it returns **TRUE**; otherwise, the return value is **FALSE**.

WARNING! If your string contains tab characters, you should use the GetTabbedTextExtent function instead. Although the GetTextExtentPoint32 function takes into account any extra character spacing (set via the SetTextCharacterExtra function), it does not consider the width of expanded tab characters. The GetTabbedTextExtent function, on the other hand, was designed specifically for this task.

The following code snippet demonstrates how to determine the width and height of a string:

```
SIZE SText;
LPCSTR text = TEXT("My String\0");
if (GetTextExtentPoint32(hDC, text, lstrlen(text), &SText))
{
   const int width = SText.cx;
   const int height = SText.cy;
   // ...
}
```

Enumerating the Available Fonts for a Specific Device

To enumerate the currently installed fonts, you use the **EnumFontFamiliesEx** function:

```
int EnumFontFamiliesEx(
    IN HDC hdc,                           // handle to the target device
                                          // context
    IN LPLOGFONT lpLogfont,               // pointer to a LOGFONT structure
    IN FONTENUMPROC lpEnumFontFamExProc,  // pointer to a callback function
    IN LPARAM lParam,                     // optional user-defined data to
                                          // pass to the callback function
    IN DWORD dwFlags                      // used internally--set to zero
   );
```

The **hdc** parameter indicates the device context whose available fonts you want to enumerate. For example, to query the available screen fonts, you pass the device context of the screen as the **hdc** parameter. The **lpLogfont** parameter is used to specify the attributes of the fonts that you want enumerated. Only the **LOGFONT::lfCharSet**, **lfPitchAndFamily**, and **lfFaceName** data members are used by the **EnumFontFamiliesEx** function to narrow down the types of fonts that are enumerated. For example, you can set the **lfFaceName** parameter to a specific typeface name to query only those fonts with that typeface name. This parameter can be **NULL**, in which case all of the device's available fonts are enumerated. The **lpEnumFontFamExProc** parameter is the address of a callback function that will be called for each font. The **lParam** argument is used to supply the callback function with any user-defined data. This value is then supplied (as the **lParam** argument) to the callback function. The **dwFlags** parameter is reserved and must be set to zero.

As previously mentioned, the callback function indicated by the **lpEnumFontFamExProc** parameter is called for each font that's found. While the **lpEnumFontFamExProc** parameter is defined as type **FONTENUMPROC**, the signature of the callback function that's used with the **EnumFontFamiliesEx** function typically looks like the following:

```
int CALLBACK MyEnumFontFamExProc(
   ENUMLOGFONTEX* lpelfe,        // pointer to a ENUMLOGFONTEX structure
   NEWTEXTMETRICEX* lpntme,      // pointer to a NEWTEXTMETRICEX structure
   int FontType,                 // identifier of the font technology
   LPARAM lParam                 // optional user-defined data
);
```

The **lpelfe** parameter identifies an **ENUMLOGFONTEX** structure, which itself contains a **LOGFONT** structure (the **elfLogFont** data member) that describes the current font along with three other data members that indicate the font's full name (**elfFullName**), style (**elfStyle**), and script (**elfScript**). The **lpntme** parameter is a pointer to a **NEWTEXTMETRICEX** structure whose data members describe the attributes of the font. The **FontType** parameter identifies the font technology and indicates **DEVICE_FONTTYPE**, **RASTER_FONTTYPE**, or **TRUETYPE_FONTTYPE**. The **lParam** parameter is the value passed as the **lParam** parameter of the **EnumFontFamiliesEx** function. The return value of the callback function determines whether the enumeration process should continue (return a non-zero value) or terminate (return zero).The last value that you return is used as the return value of the **EnumFontFamiliesEx** function itself.

You can use the parameters of the callback function to filter out certain fonts. For example, to list only those fonts of a certain size, you can use the information contained in the **NEWTEXTMETRICEX** structure that's indicated by the **lpntme** parameter. Moreover, because the **ENUMLOGFONTEX** structure identified by the **lpelfe** parameter contains the **elfLogFont** data member, you can pass the address of this **LOGFONT**-type data member to the **CreateFontIndirect** function.

The example shown in Listing 4.1 demonstrates how to fill an owner-drawn list-box control with all TrueType and OpenType fonts available to the primary display monitor. This example then creates each associated logical font, which is then used to render each list-box item.

Listing 4.1 Filling an owner-drawn list-box control with all TrueType and OpenType fonts available to the primary display monitor.

```
// -------------------------------------------------------------------
// Windows 2000 Graphics API Black Book
// Chapter 4 - Listing 4.1 (Font Enumeration Demo)
// -------------------------------------------------------------------

#include <windows.h>
#include <cassert>
```

4. The Font Object

```
HWND hListBox = NULL;
const int ID_LISTBOX = 101;

HINSTANCE hInst;
const char* WndClassName = "GMainWnd";
LRESULT CALLBACK MainWndProc(HWND hWnd, UINT msg, WPARAM wParam,
   LPARAM lParam);

int APIENTRY WinMain(HINSTANCE hInstance, HINSTANCE, LPTSTR,
   int nCmdShow)
{
   hInst = hInstance;

   WNDCLASS wc;
   memset(&wc, 0, sizeof(WNDCLASS));

   wc.style = CS_VREDRAW | CS_HREDRAW;
   wc.lpszClassName = WndClassName;
   wc.lpfnWndProc = MainWndProc;
   wc.hInstance = hInstance;
   wc.hCursor = LoadCursor(NULL, IDC_ARROW);
   wc.hbrBackground = reinterpret_cast<HBRUSH>(
      COLOR_BTNFACE + 1
      );

   if (RegisterClass(&wc))
   {
      HWND hWnd =
         CreateWindow(WndClassName, "Screen Fonts",
                      WS_OVERLAPPEDWINDOW | WS_CAPTION |
                      WS_VISIBLE | WS_CLIPCHILDREN,
                      CW_USEDEFAULT, CW_USEDEFAULT, 295, 285,
                      NULL, NULL, HInst, NULL);
      if (hWnd)
      {
         ShowWindow(hWnd, nCmdShow);
         UpdateWindow(hWnd);

         MSG msg;
         while (GetMessage(&msg, NULL, 0, 0))
         {
             TranslateMessage(&msg);
             DispatchMessage(&msg);
         }
      }
    }
```

```
    return 0;
}

int CALLBACK MyEnumFontFamExProc(ENUMLOGFONTEX *lpelfe,
   NEWTEXTMETRICEX *lpntme, int FontType, LPARAM lParam)
{
   if (FontType == TRUETYPE_FONTTYPE)
   {
      // if the typeface name is not already in the list
      LPARAM name = reinterpret_cast<LPARAM>(lpelfe->elfFullName);
      if (SNDMSG(hListBox, LB_FINDSTRINGEXACT, -1, name) == LB_ERR)
      {
         // add each font to the list box
         int index = SNDMSG(hListBox, LB_ADDSTRING, 0, name);

         // fix the size of the font
         lpelfe->elfLogFont.lfHeight = -20;
         lpelfe->elfLogFont.lfWidth = 0;

         //
         // create a new font and store its handle
         // as the data of the newly added item
         //
         HFONT hFont = CreateFontIndirect(&lpelfe->elfLogFont);
         SNDMSG(hListBox, LB_SETITEMDATA, index,
               reinterpret_cast<LPARAM>(hFont));
      }
   }
   return 1;
}

void AddScreenFonts()
{
   // grab a handle to the screen's DC
   HDC hScreenDC = GetDC(NULL);
   try
   {
      // enumerate the current screen fonts
      EnumFontFamiliesEx(
         hScreenDC, NULL,
         reinterpret_cast<FONTENUMPROC>(MyEnumFontFamExProc),
         0, 0
         );
   }
   catch (...)
   {
```

```
        // release the screen's DC
        ReleaseDC(NULL, hScreenDC);
    }
    // release the screen's DC
    ReleaseDC(NULL, hScreenDC);
}

LRESULT CALLBACK MainWndProc(HWND hWnd, UINT msg, WPARAM wParam,
    LPARAM lParam)
{
    switch (msg)
    {
        case WM_CREATE:
        {
            hListBox =
                CreateWindowEx(WS_EX_CLIENTEDGE, "LISTBOX", "",
                               WS_CHILD | WS_VISIBLE | LBS_STANDARD |
                               LBS_HASSTRINGS | LBS_OWNERDRAWFIXED,
                               20, 10, 250, 250, hWnd,
                               reinterpret_cast<HMENU>(ID_LISTBOX),
                               hInst, NULL);
            if (hListBox)
            {
                AddScreenFonts();
            }
        }
        case WM_MEASUREITEM:
        {
            // grab a pointer to the MEASUREITEMSTRUCT structure
            LPMEASUREITEMSTRUCT lpmis =
                reinterpret_cast<LPMEASUREITEMSTRUCT>(lParam);

            //
            // test the identifier of the control that
            // the message is meant for
            //
            if (lpmis->CtlID == ID_LISTBOX)
            {
                // adjust the height
                lpmis->itemHeight = 25;

                return TRUE;
            }
            break;
        }
```

4. The Font Object

```
case WM_DRAWITEM:
{
   // grab a pointer to the DRAWITEMSTRUCT structure
   LPDRAWITEMSTRUCT lpdis =
      reinterpret_cast<LPDRAWITEMSTRUCT>(lParam);

   //
   // test the identifier of the control that
   // the message is meant for
   //
   if (lpdis->CtlID == ID_LISTBOX)
   {
      COLORREF OldColor = GetTextColor(lpdis->hDC);
      int stock = WHITE_BRUSH;

      // if the item is currently selected
      if (lpdis->itemState & ODS_SELECTED)
      {
         //
         // set the text color to white and
         // the background color to black
         //
         COLORREF clrWhite = PALETTERGB(255, 255, 255);
         OldColor = SetTextColor(lpdis->hDC, clrWhite);
         stock = BLACK_BRUSH;
      }
      FillRect(
         lpdis->hDC, &lpdis->rcItem,
         static_cast<HBRUSH>(GetStockObject(stock))
         );

      if (lpdis->itemID != -1)
      {
         // extract the item's text
         char text[MAX_PATH];
         SNDMSG(hListBox, LB_GETTEXT, lpdis->itemID,
                reinterpret_cast<LPARAM>(text));

         // extract the corresponding font handle
         DWORD value =
             SNDMSG(hListBox, LB_GETITEMDATA, lpdis->itemID, 0);
         HFONT hFont = reinterpret_cast<HFONT>(value);
```

```
            //
            // select the corresponding font
            // into the device context
            //
            HFONT hOldFont = static_cast<HFONT>(
               SelectObject(lpdis->hDC, hFont)
               );

            // render the text transparently
            SetBkMode(lpdis->hDC, TRANSPARENT);

            // render the text
            RECT RText = lpdis->rcItem;
            InflateRect(&RText, -2, -2);
            DrawText(lpdis->hDC, text, strlen(text), &RText,
                     DT_LEFT | DT_VCENTER | DT_SINGLELINE);

            // restore the previous font
            SelectObject(lpdis->hDC, hOldFont);
         }

         // render the focus rectangle
         if (lpdis->itemState & ODS_FOCUS)
         {
            DrawFocusRect(lpdis->hDC, &lpdis->rcItem);
         }

         // restore the previous color/mode
         SetTextColor(lpdis->hDC, OldColor);
         SetBkMode(lpdis->hDC, OPAQUE);

         return TRUE;
      }
      break;
   }
   case WM_DESTROY:
   {
      // delete each created font object
      int count = SNDMSG(hListBox, LB_GETCOUNT, 0, 0);
      for (int index = 0; index < count; ++index)
      {
         DWORD value = SNDMSG(hListBox, LB_GETITEMDATA, index, 0);
         DeleteObject(reinterpret_cast<HFONT>(value));
      }
```

```
            PostQuitMessage(0);
            break;
        }
    }
    return DefWindowProc(hWnd, msg, wParam, lParam);
}
```

Retrieving the Text Capabilities of a Device

To retrieve the text capabilities of a device, you use the **GetDeviceCaps** function:

```
int GetDeviceCaps(
    IN HDC hdc,         // handle to the target device context
    IN int nIndex       // index of device capability to retrieve
   );
```

The **hdc** parameter is specified as a handle to the device context that identifies the device whose text capabilities you want to query. The **nIndex** parameter is used to specify the capability to query. This parameter can be specified as **NUMFONTS** (22) to determine the number of available device-specific fonts or as **TEXTCAPS** (34) to determine the device's text-rendering capabilities.

When the **nIndex** parameter is set to **NUMFONTS**, the **GetDeviceCaps** function simply returns the number of fonts that are provided by the target device. When **nIndex** is set to **TEXTCAPS**, the return value is packed with bits that indicate whether or not a specific text-rendering-related capability is supported. To extract this data, you should use the bitwise **AND** operator (&) to combine the return value with one of the identifiers listed in Table 4.13.

For example, to determine if the primary display monitor can render vector fonts:

```
HDC hScreenDC = GetDC(NULL);
try
{
   bool does_vector_fonts =
      (GetDeviceCaps(hScreenDC, TEXTCAPS) & TC_VA_ABLE);
   // ...
}
catch (...)
{
   ReleaseDC(NULL, hScreenDC);
}
ReleaseDC(NULL, hScreenDC);
```

Table 4.13 Masks used with the return value of the GetDeviceCaps function when the TEXTCAPS capability index is specified.

Identifier	Value	Capability
TC_OP_CHARACTER	0x00000001	The device supports character output precision.
TC_OP_STROKE	0x00000002	The device supports stroke output precision.
TC_CP_STROKE	0x00000004	The device supports stroke clip precision.
TC_CR_90	0x00000008	The device supports 90-degree character rotation.
TC_CR_ANY	0x00000010	The device supports any character rotation.
TC_SF_X_YINDEP	0x00000020	The device supports individual horizontal and vertical scaling.
TC_SA_DOUBLE	0x00000040	The device supports doubled character scaling.
TC_SA_INTEGER	0x00000080	The device supports only integer-based scaling.
TC_SA_CONTIN	0x00000100	The device supports continuous scaling.
TC_EA_DOUBLE	0x00000200	The device can render double-weighted characters.
TC_IA_ABLE	0x00000400	The device can render italic characters.
TC_UA_ABLE	0x00000800	The device can render underlined characters.
TC_SO_ABLE	0x00001000	The device can render struck-out-style characters.
TC_RA_ABLE	0x00002000	The device can render raster fonts.
TC_VA_ABLE	0x00004000	The device can render vector fonts.
TC_SCROLLBLT	0x00010000	The device cannot be scrolled via a bit-block transfer.

Rendering Aligned Text

To render aligned text, you use a combination of the **SetTextAlign** function and the **TextOut** function. (For more information on the **TextOut** function, refer to the “In Depth” section “Rendering with a Font Object.”) The **SetTextAlign** function is used to adjust the text-alignment attributes of a device context:

```
UINT SetTextAlign(
    IN HDC hdc,           // handle to the target device context
    IN UINT fMode         // text-alignment options
  );
```

The **hdc** parameter identifies the device context whose text-alignment attributes you want to adjust. The new attributes are specified by the **fMode** parameter, which can be set to a combination of the identifiers listed in Tables 4.9, 4.10, and 4.11 (one from each). If the **SetTextAlign** function is successful, it returns the previous text-alignment settings; otherwise, the return value is **GDI_ERROR**.

For example, to render a single-line string that is aligned to the top-left edge of a given rectangle (**REdit**), you use the **SetTextAlign** and **TextOut** functions as follows:

```
RECT REdit = {10, 10, 200, 40};
DrawEdge(hDC, &REdit, EDGE_SUNKEN, BF_RECT);

LPCSTR text = TEXT("This is a line of text!\0");
SetTextAlign(hDC, TA_LEFT | TA_TOP | TA_NOUPDATECP);
TextOut(hDC, REdit.left, REdit.top, text, lstrlen(text));
```

Likewise, to render the same string aligned to the bottom-right edge, you use the **SetTextAlign** and **TextOut** functions like so:

```
RECT REdit = {10, 10, 200, 40};
DrawEdge(hDC, &REdit, EDGE_SUNKEN, BF_RECT);

LPCSTR text = TEXT("This is a line of text!\0");
SetTextAlign(hDC, TA_RIGHT | TA_BOTTOM | TA_NOUPDATECP);
TextOut(hDC, REdit.right, REdit.bottom, text, lstrlen(text));
```

And, to render text that is horizontally centered along the string's baseline, you use the **SetTextAlign** and **TextOut** functions like so:

```
RECT REdit = {10, 10, 200, 40};
DrawEdge(hDC, &REdit, EDGE_SUNKEN, BF_RECT);

LPCSTR text = TEXT("This is a line of text!\0");
SetTextAlign(hDC, TA_CENTER | TA_BASELINE | TA_NOUPDATECP);

const int center = static_cast<int>(
   0.5 * (REdit.right - REdit.left) + 0.5
   );
TextOut(hDC, center, REdit.bottom, text, lstrlen(text));
```

An alternative approach is to render the text by using the **DrawText** function. This is the easiest solution when you need to render only a single string, but it's generally slower than using the **SetTextAlign** and **TextOut** functions. For more information on the **DrawText** function, refer to the "In Depth" section "Rendering with a Font Object."

Rendering Disabled Text

To render disabled text, you use the **DrawState** function:

```
BOOL WINAPI DrawState(
    IN HDC hdc,                     // handle to the target device context
    IN HBRUSH hbr,                  // not used; set to NULL
    IN DRAWSTATEPROC lpOutputFunc,  // not used; set to NULL
    IN LPARAM lData,                // pointer to the string
    IN WPARAM wData,                // length of the string
    IN int x,                       // horizontal location of the string
    IN int y,                       // vertical location of the string
    IN int cx,                      // not used; set to zero
    IN int cy,                      // not used; set to zero
    IN UINT fuFlags                 // rendering flags; set to
                                    // DST_TEXT | DSS_DISABLED
   );
```


As you've likely guessed from its parameters, the **DrawState** function is used for more than rendering disabled text. Fortunately, when this function is used to render disabled text, many of its parameters are ignored. The only parameters that you need to specify are the following: the **hdc** parameter, which identifies the destination device context; the **lData** parameter, which is specified as the address of the string to render in a disabled fashion; the **wData** parameter, which specifies the number of characters in this string; the **x** and **y** parameters, which specify the text location in logical coordinates; and the **fuFlags** parameter, which is specified as the bitwise **OR** (|) combination of **DST_TEXT** (1) and **DSS_DISABLED** (32).

NOTE: *The **DrawState** function ignores any text-alignment attributes specified by the **SetTextAlign** function.*

If the **DrawState** function is successful, it returns **TRUE**; otherwise, the return value is **FALSE**. For example, to render a string in a location (10, 20):

```
HDC hDC = GetDC(hWnd);
try
{
   LPCSTR text = TEXT("This is the line of disabled text!\0");
   DrawState(hDC, NULL, NULL,
             reinterpret_cast<LPARAM>(text),
             lstrlen(text), 10, 20, 0, 0,
             DST_TEXT | DSS_DISABLED);
}
```

```
catch (...)
{
   ReleaseDC(hWnd, hDC);
}
ReleaseDC(hWnd, hDC);
```

Rendering a String Containing Multiple Fonts

To render a string that contains characters of different fonts, you use the **TextOut** function with the **GetTextExtentPoint32** function. The **TextOut** function is used for general text output (see "Rendering with a Font Object" in the "In Depth" section). The **GetTextExtentPoint32** function is used to determine the width and height of a string (see "Determining the Width and Height of a String" in this section).

Typically, you use the **TextOut** function to render a string that contains characters of all the same font. When the font of one or more of these characters needs to be adjusted, you must render the string in segments. The **GetTextExtentPoint32** function is used to determine how many units to advance before rendering the next string segment.

***NOTE:** If you're rendering text in a boldface raster font, subtract the overhang width from the width that the **GetTextExtentPoint32** function computes. This is necessary because boldface raster fonts are synthesized by rendering each character twice (the second character is offset to the right by one overhang width). For italic raster fonts, you must subtract the overhang before and after rendering because the italic attribute affects the beginning and the end of the string. You can retrieve the overhang width by using the **GetTextMetrics** function (**TEXTMETRIC::tmOverhang**).*

For example, the following code snippet demonstrates how to render a string that contains normal, boldface, italic, and vector font sub-strings—with each substring a different size. This example uses the **MakeFont** function (see "Creating a Logical Font"):

```
HDC hDC = GetDC(hWnd);

HFONT hNormalFont =
   font::MakeFont(hDC, TEXT("Tahoma"), 10);
HFONT hBoldFont =
   font::MakeFont(hDC, TEXT("Courier"), 12, 0, font::FS_BOLD);
HFONT hItalicFont =
   font::MakeFont(hDC, TEXT("Courier"), 16, 0, font::FS_ITALIC);
HFONT hVectorFont =
   font::MakeFont(hDC TEXT("Script"), 14);
```

```
HFONT hOldFont = static_cast<HFONT>(
    SelectObject(hDC, hNormalFont)
    );
try
{
    LPCSTR text_normal = TEXT("A line of text that contains\0");
    LPCSTR text_bold = TEXT("boldface text from a raster font, \0");
    LPCSTR text_italic = TEXT("italic text from a raster font, \0");
    LPCSTR text_vector = TEXT("and text from a vector font.\0");

    SetTextAlign(hDC, TA_LEFT | TA_BASELINE | TA_NOUPDATECP);
    POINT PText = {10, 150};
    TEXTMETRIC tm;

    SIZE STextNormal = {0, 0};
    int length_normal = lstrlen(text_normal);
    // render the normal text segment
    TextOut(hDC, PText.x, PText.y, text_normal, length_normal);
    // compute the width of the text segment
    GetTextExtentPoint32(hDC, text_normal, length_normal, &STextNormal);
    // advance by this width
    PText.x += STextNormal.cx;

    SelectObject(hDC, hBoldFont);
    SIZE STextBold = {0, 0};
    int length_bold = lstrlen(text_bold);
    // render the raster-bold text segment
    TextOut(hDC, PText.x, PText.y, text_bold, length_bold);
    // compute the width of the text segment
    GetTextExtentPoint32(hDC, text_bolded, length_bold, &STextBold);
    // advance by this width
    PText.x += STextBold.cx;
    // account for raster-bold overhang
    GetTextMetrics(hDC, &tm);
    PText.x -= tm.tmOverhang;

    SelectObject(hDC, hItalicFont);
    SIZE STextItalic = {0, 0};
    int length_italic = lstrlen(text_italic);
    // account for leading raster-italic overhang
    GetTextMetrics(hDC, &tm);
    PText.x -= tm.tmOverhang;
    // render the raster-italic text segment
    TextOut(hDC, PText.x, PText.y, text_italic, length_italic);
    // compute the width of the text segment
    GetTextExtentPoint32(hDC, text_italic, length_italic, &STextItalic);
```

```
    // advance by this width
    PText.x += STextItalic.cx;
    // account for ending raster-italic overhang
    PText.x -= tm.tmOverhang;

    SelectObject(hDC, hVectorFont);
    int length_vector = lstrlen(text_vector);
    // render the vector text segment
    TextOut(hDC, PText.x, PText.y, text_vector, length_vector);
}
catch (...)
{
    DeleteObject(SelectObject(hDC, hOldFont));
    DeleteObject(hBoldFont);
    DeleteObject(hItalicFont);
    DeleteObject(hVectorFont);
    ReleaseDC(hWnd, hDC);
}
DeleteObject(SelectObject(hDC, hOldFont));
DeleteObject(hBoldFont);
DeleteObject(hItalicFont);
DeleteObject(hVectorFont);
ReleaseDC(hWnd, hDC);
```


Instead of using the **GetTextExtentPoint32** function to manually adjust the position of subsequent text segments, you can instruct the **TextOut** function to update the current position after a text segment is rendered. You do this by using the **SetTextAlign** function, specifying the **TA_UPDATECP** flag instead of **TA_NOUPDATECP** as in the previous example. The current position is initially manipulated via the **MoveToEx** function. For example, the following code snippet demonstrates how to achieve the same functionality as that of the previous example, but here without using the **GetTextExtentPoint32** function:

```
HDC hDC = GetDC(hWnd);

HFONT hNormalFont = font::MakeFont(hDC, "Tahoma", 10);
HFONT hBoldFont = font::MakeFont(hDC, "Courier", 12, 0, font::FS_BOLD);
HFONT hItalicFont = font::MakeFont(hDC, "Courier", 16, 0, font::FS_ITALIC);
HFONT hVectorFont = font::MakeFont(hDC, "Script", 14);

HFONT hOldFont = static_cast<HFONT>(
    SelectObject(hDC, hNormalFont)
    );
try
```

```
{
   LPCSTR text_normal = TEXT("A line of text that contains\0");
   LPCSTR text_bold = TEXT("boldface text from a raster font, \0");
   LPCSTR text_italic = TEXT("italic text from a raster font, \0");
   LPCSTR text_vector = TEXT("and text from a vector font.\0");

   SetTextAlign(hDC, TA_LEFT | TA_BASELINE | TA_UPDATECP);
   POINT PText = {10, 200};
   MoveToEx(hDC, PText.x, PText.y, NULL);
   TEXTMETRIC tm;

   int length_normal = lstrlen(text_normal);
   // render the normal text segment
   TextOut(hDC, 0, 0, text_normal, length_normal);

   SelectObject(hDC, hBoldFont);
   int length_bold = lstrlen(text_bold);
   // render the raster-bold text segment
   TextOut(hDC, 0, 0, text_bold, length_bold);
   // account for raster-bold overhang
   GetTextMetrics(hDC, &tm);
   GetCurrentPositionEx(hDC, &PText);
   MoveToEx(hDC, PText.x - tm.tmOverhang, PText.y, NULL);

   SelectObject(hDC, hItalicFont);
   int length_italic = lstrlen(text_italic);
   // account for leading raster-italic overhang
   GetTextMetrics(hDC, &tm);
   GetCurrentPositionEx(hDC, &PText);
   MoveToEx(hDC, PText.x - tm.tmOverhang, PText.y, NULL);
   // render the raster-italic text segment
   TextOut(hDC, 0, 0, text_italic, length_italic);
   // account for ending raster-italic overhang
   GetCurrentPositionEx(hDC, &PText);
   MoveToEx(hDC, PText.x - tm.tmOverhang, PText.y, NULL);

   SelectObject(hDC, hVectorFont);
   int length_vector = lstrlen(text_vector);
   // render the vector text segment
   TextOut(hDC, 0, 0, text_vector, length_vector);
}
catch (...)
{
   DeleteObject(SelectObject(hDC, hOldFont));
   DeleteObject(hBoldFont);
```

```
        DeleteObject(hItalicFont);
        DeleteObject(hVectorFont);
        ReleaseDC(hWnd, hDC);
    }
    DeleteObject(SelectObject(hDC, hOldFont));
    DeleteObject(hBoldFont);
    DeleteObject(hItalicFont);
    DeleteObject(hVectorFont);
    ReleaseDC(hWnd, hDC);
```


Using Masking to Render Reverse-Colored Text

When rendering a string to a complex background, you're bound to run into the situation in which the colors of the background (image) conflict with the color of the text; in many cases, the result is illegible. For example, we've all seen those annoying Web pages where the author insists on presenting red text on a blue background. When legibility outweighs the need for exact text-color representation, you can render the text in a color that is the inverse of the background. Such a scheme is ideal when you're rendering text on a complex background image.

***NOTE:** The solution presented here uses a technique called* masking*, which relies on memory device contexts and bitmaps. For more information on memory device contexts, refer to Chapter 1. Further information on bitmaps can be found in Chapter 6.*

To render reverse-colored text, you use two bitmap objects. The first serves as an overlay image that contains a "snapshot" of the original destination image plus the desired text rendered in black. The second bitmap serves as a mask, which simply prevents the non-text areas of the destination image from being altered. The result is produced via a two-stage process: First, you draw the mask to the destination by using the **NOTSRCERASE** ternary-raster-operation code. At this point, the destination contains the reverse-colored text with a black background. Second, you draw the overlay to the destination (i.e., on top of the previous result) by using the **SRCPAINT** ternary-raster-operation. Because this latter ROP3 code is simply a bitwise **OR** (|) combination of the destination and the overlay, the destination's black background becomes the original background (remember, the original background is saved to the overlay), while the parts of the destination that contain the reverse-colored text are preserved. This process can be outlined via the following steps:

1. Create a memory device context (**hMaskDC**) that's compatible with the destination. This device context will be used with the mask bitmap.

2. Create a memory device context (**hOverlayDC**) that's compatible with the destination. This device context will be used with the overlay bitmap.
3. Create the mask bitmap (**hMaskBmp**), and select it into the first memory device context (**hMaskDC**).
4. Create the overlay bitmap (**hOverlayBmp**), and select it into the second memory device context (**hOverlayDC**).
5. Save the destination image to the overlay bitmap. Then, to this result, render the desired text in black.
6. Prepare the mask bitmap by filling it with a white background and rendering the desired text in black.
7. Render the mask to the destination by using the **NOTSRCERASE** ROP3 code.
8. Render the overlay to the destination by using the **SRCPAINT** ROP3 code.

TIP: *Consider caching the bitmaps for enhanced performance.*

The following utility function, **InverseTextOut**, demonstrates this process. If successful, the function returns **TRUE**; otherwise, the return value is **FALSE**. Refer to Chapter 9 for information on adding palette support to this function, and to Chapter 10 for information on supporting different mapping modes. Here's the code:

```
BOOL InverseTextOut(IN HDC hDestDC, IN int X, IN int Y,
   IN LPCSTR text, IN int text_len = -1)
{
   if (text_len == -1) text_len = lstrlen(text);

   // determine the width and height of the text
   SIZE SText = {0, 0};
   if (!GetTextExtentPoint32(hDestDC, text, text_len, &SText))
      return false;

   // create the mask memory DC
   HDC hMaskDC = CreateCompatibleDC(hDestDC);
   if (!hMaskDC)
   {
      return false;
   }

   // create the overlay memory DC
   HDC hOverlayDC = CreateCompatibleDC(hDestDC);
```

```
if (!hOverlayDC)
{
   DeleteDC(hMaskDC);
   return false;
}

// create the mask bitmap
HBITMAP hMaskBmp =
   CreateCompatibleBitmap(hDestDC, SText.cx, SText.cy);
if (!hMaskBmp)
{
   DeleteDC(hMaskDC);
   DeleteDC(hOverlayDC);
   return false;
}

// create the overlay bitmap
HBITMAP hOverlayBmp =
   CreateCompatibleBitmap(hDestDC, SText.cx, SText.cy);
if (!hOverlayBmp)
{
   DeleteDC(hMaskDC);
   DeleteDC(hOverlayDC);
   DeleteObject(hMaskBmp);
   return false;
}

BOOL result = false;
HBITMAP hOldMaskBmp = static_cast<HBITMAP>(
   SelectObject(hMaskDC, hMaskBmp)
   );
HBITMAP hOldOverlayBmp = static_cast<HBITMAP>(
   SelectObject(hOverlayDC, hOverlayBmp)
   );

// extract the current font of the target DC
HFONT hDestFont = static_cast<HFONT>(
   GetCurrentObject(hDestDC, OBJ_FONT)
   );
if (hDestFont)
{
   // match the font of the memory DCs
   // with that of the target DC
   HFONT hOldMaskFont = static_cast<HFONT>(
      SelectObject(hMaskDC, hDestFont)
      );
```

```
        HFONT hOldOverlayFont = static_cast<HFONT>(
            SelectObject(hOverlayDC, hDestFont)
            );

        // save the original background to the overlay
        result = BitBlt(hOverlayDC, 0, 0, SText.cx, SText.cy,
                        hDestDC, X, Y, SRCCOPY);

        // render the text to the overlay
        SetBkMode(hOverlayDC, TRANSPARENT);
        SetTextColor(hOverlayDC, PALETTERGB(0, 0, 0));
        result &= TextOut(hOverlayDC, 0, 0, text, text_len);

        // create the text mask
        result &= PatBlt(hMaskDC, 0, 0, SText.cx, SText.cy, WHITENESS);
        SetBkMode(hMaskDC, TRANSPARENT);
        SetTextColor(hMaskDC, PALETTERGB(0, 0, 0));
        result &= TextOut(hMaskDC, 0, 0, text, text_len);

        // blt the mask to the destination using NOTSRCERASE
        result &= BitBlt(hDestDC, X, Y, SText.cx, SText.cy,
                         hMaskDC, 0, 0, NOTSRCERASE);

        // blt the overlay to the destination using SRCPAINT
        result &= BitBlt(hDestDC, X, Y, SText.cx, SText.cy,
                         hOverlayDC, 0, 0, SRCPAINT);

        SelectObject(hOverlayDC, hOldOverlayFont);
        SelectObject(hMaskDC, hOldMaskFont);
    }
    DeleteObject(SelectObject(hOverlayDC, hOldOverlayBmp));
    DeleteObject(SelectObject(hMaskDC, hOldMaskBmp));

    DeleteDC(hOverlayDC);
    DeleteDC(hMaskDC);

    return result;
}
```


Related solutions:	***Found on page:***
Creating a Monochrome Device-Dependent Bitmap	307
Creating a Color Device-Dependent Bitmap	311
Loading a Device-Dependent Bitmap from a File	323

Using Masking to Render Textured Text

To render textured text, you use three bitmap objects. The first bitmap contains the texture that will be used to fill the interior of the characters. The second bitmap serves as an overlay image that contains a "snapshot" of the original destination image plus the desired text rendered in black. The third bitmap serves as a mask, which, in this case, contains white characters on a black background.

NOTE: *The solution presented here uses a technique called* masking, *which relies on memory device contexts and bitmaps. For more information on memory device contexts, refer to Chapter 1. Further information on bitmaps can be found in Chapter 6.*

Using the texture, overlay, and mask bitmaps, you can render the textured text via a three-stage process. First, you draw the texture to the mask by using the **SRCAND** ternary-raster-operation code. Because the background of the mask is black and the text is white, the result will be the textured text on a black background. Second, you draw the overlay to the mask by using the **SRCPAINT** ternary-raster-operation code. This combines the previous result with the overlay by using the bitwise **OR** operator. Because the original background is saved to the overlay, **OR**ing this with the mask's black background results in the original background (i.e., the background of the overlay). The textured text, on the other hand, remains intact. Third, you simply render the result (contained in the mask) to the target device context. The following steps outline this process:

1. Create a memory device context (**hMaskDC**) that's compatible with the destination. This device context will be used with the mask bitmap.
2. Create a memory device context (**hOverlayDC**) that's compatible with the destination. This device context will be used with the overlay bitmap.
3. Create the mask bitmap (**hMaskBmp**), and select it into the first memory device context (**hMaskDC**).
4. Create the overlay bitmap (**hOverlayBmp**), and select it into the second memory device context (**hOverlayDC**).
5. Save the destination image to the overlay bitmap. Then, to this result, render the desired text in black.
6. Prepare the mask bitmap by filling it with a black background and rendering the desired text in white.
7. Render the texture to the mask by using the **SRCAND** ROP3 code (tile the texture, if necessary).
8. Render the overlay to the mask by using the **SRCPAINT** ROP3 code.
9. Render the mask to the destination by using the **SRCCOPY** ROP3 code.

***TIP:** Consider caching the bitmaps for enhanced performance.*

The following utility function, **TextureTextOut**, demonstrates this process. Upon success, the function returns **TRUE**. If the function fails, the return value is **FALSE**. Refer to Chapter 9 for information on adding palette support to this function, and to Chapter 10 for information on supporting different mapping modes. Here's the code:

```
BOOL TextureTextOut(IN HDC hDestDC, IN HBITMAP hTextureBmp,
   IN int X, IN int Y, IN LPCSTR text, IN int text_len = -1)
{
   if (text_len == -1) text_len = lstrlen(text);

   // determine the width and height of the text
   SIZE SText = {0, 0};
   if (!GetTextExtentPoint32(hDestDC, text, text_len, &SText))
      return false;

   // create the mask memory DC
   HDC hMaskDC = CreateCompatibleDC(hDestDC);
   if (!hMaskDC)
   {
      return false;
   }

   // create the overlay memory DC
   HDC hOverlayDC = CreateCompatibleDC(hDestDC);
   if (!hOverlayDC)
   {
      DeleteDC(hMaskDC);
      return false;
   }

   // create the overlay memory DC
   HDC hTextureDC = CreateCompatibleDC(hDestDC);
   if (!hTextureDC)
   {
      DeleteDC(hMaskDC);
      DeleteDC(hTextureDC);
      return false;
   }

   // create the mask bitmap
   HBITMAP hMaskBmp =
      CreateCompatibleBitmap(hDestDC, SText.cx, SText.cy);
```

```
if (!hMaskBmp)
{
   DeleteDC(hMaskDC);
   DeleteDC(hOverlayDC);
   return false;
}

// create the overlay bitmap
HBITMAP hOverlayBmp =
   CreateCompatibleBitmap(hDestDC, SText.cx, SText.cy);
if (!hOverlayBmp)
{
   DeleteDC(hMaskDC);
   DeleteDC(hOverlayDC);
   DeleteObject(hMaskBmp);
   return false;
}

BOOL result = false;
HBITMAP hOldMaskBmp = static_cast<HBITMAP>(
   SelectObject(hMaskDC, hMaskBmp)
   );
HBITMAP hOldTextureBmp = static_cast<HBITMAP>(
   SelectObject(hTextureDC, hTextureBmp)
   );
HBITMAP hOldOverlayBmp = static_cast<HBITMAP>(
   SelectObject(hOverlayDC, hOverlayBmp)
   );

// extract the current font of the target DC
HFONT HDestFont = static_cast<HFONT>(
   GetCurrentObject(hDestDC, OBJ_FONT)
   );
if (HDestFont)
{
   // match the font of the mask and overlay
   // memory DCs with that of the target DC
   HFONT hOldMaskFont = static_cast<HFONT>(
      SelectObject(hMaskDC, HDestFont)
      );
   HFONT hOldOverlayFont = static_cast<HFONT>(
      SelectObject(hOverlayDC, HDestFont)
      );

   // save the original background to the overlay
   result = BitBlt(hOverlayDC, 0, 0, SText.cx, SText.cy,
                   hDestDC, X, Y, SRCCOPY);
```

```
        // render the text to the overlay
        SetBkMode(hOverlayDC, TRANSPARENT);
        SetTextColor(hOverlayDC, PALETTERGB(0, 0, 0));
        result &= TextOut(hOverlayDC, 0, 0, text, text_len);

        // create the text mask
        result &= PatBlt(hMaskDC, 0, 0, SText.cx, SText.cy, BLACKNESS);
        SetBkMode(hMaskDC, TRANSPARENT);
        SetTextColor(hMaskDC, PALETTERGB(255, 255, 255));
        result &= TextOut(hMaskDC, 0, 0, text, text_len);

        // blt the texture to the mask using SRCAND
        // TODO: tile if needed
        result &= BitBlt(hMaskDC, 0, 0, SText.cx, SText.cy,
                         hTextureDC, 0, 0, SRCAND);

        // blt the overlay to the mask using SRCPAINT
        result &= BitBlt(hMaskDC, 0, 0, SText.cx, SText.cy,
                         hOverlayDC, 0, 0, SRCPAINT);

        // blt the mask to the destination using SRCCOPY
        result &= BitBlt(hDestDC, X, Y, SText.cx, SText.cy,
                         hMaskDC, 0, 0, SRCCOPY);

        SelectObject(hOverlayDC, hOldOverlayFont);
        SelectObject(hMaskDC, hOldMaskFont);
    }
    SelectObject(hTextureDC, hOldTextureBmp);
    DeleteObject(SelectObject(hOverlayDC, hOldOverlayBmp));
    DeleteObject(SelectObject(hMaskDC, hOldMaskBmp));

    DeleteDC(hTextureDC);
    DeleteDC(hOverlayDC);
    DeleteDC(hMaskDC);

    return result;
}
```


Related solutions:	Found on page:
Creating a Monochrome Device-Dependent Bitmap	307
Creating a Color Device-Dependent Bitmap	311
Loading a Device-Dependent Bitmap from a File	323

Chapter 5

Lines, Curves, and Shapes

(continued)

If you need an immediate solution to:	*See page:*
Changing the Arc Direction	281
Retrieving the Line Capabilities of a Device	282
Retrieving the Curve Capabilities of a Device	283
Retrieving the Shape Capabilities of a Device	285

In Depth

Consider the task of rendering a straight line via direct pixel manipulation; if the line is purely horizontal or vertical, it's not much of a challenge. Yet if the line contains both vertical and horizontal elements, the job is not so easy. Now consider adding a custom join or end cap to two intersecting lines, or rendering an ellipse or a pie slice. Not to say that such a task is impossible, but you'll likely be spending a fair amount of time implementing a library of basic drawing functions. In fact, those who write device drivers are all too familiar with this task.

Whether you're creating a complex drawing application, a simple pie chart, or even an owner-drawn button, you're bound to run into a situation where you need to render a line, shape, or curve. One of the main advantages of using the GDI over the DirectDraw interface is that the GDI provides native support for a wide variety of two-dimensional lines, curves, and shapes, collectively referred to as *output primitives;* rarely will you need to resort to direct pixel manipulation.

In this chapter, we'll examine the various types of lines, curves, and shapes that the GDI supports. We'll cover each output primitive from a geometric and an analytic perspective, and discuss the functions that can be used to render each type. We'll also examine the method that the GDI uses to fill standard and complex shapes, and discuss how you can adjust the filling algorithm to better suit your needs. Finally, by investigating the art of hit-testing, we'll explore the process of interacting with these output primitives.

Output Primitives

The GDI supports seven types of two-dimensional output primitives: straight lines, arcs, Bézier curves, rectangles, ellipses, pie wedges, and chords. Actually, you can create almost any shape via a combination of one or more of these primitives. In this section, we'll examine how to render each of these output primitives. And, because rendering is based on an analytical description, we'll review some of the math behind each type.

A Peek under the Hood at the DDK Output Function

Like most Windows interfaces, the GDI serves as a mediator between an application developer and a device; namely, a graphics device. As developers, we communicate with the GDI through the functions presented in the GDI.DLL dynamic link library. The GDI, in turn, communicates with the graphics device through its device driver. It's not required that the device driver speak the same language as the developer, and it's certainly not required that we speak the same language as the device driver, but both parties *must* be able to speak with the GDI. This is one of the reasons why some applications won't work on certain versions of Windows and why device vendors must often supply separate drivers for Windows 9x, NT, and 2000.

When you call a GDI function to render something to a graphics device, the GDI translates this request into something that the device driver can understand. For lines, curves, and shapes, this request translates to the **Output** function. Every graphics device driver must provide an **Output** function, although not all of its functionality has to be supported.

While it's not my intention here to describe the ins and outs of the **Output** function, there are a few things that you should keep in mind as you read this chapter. First, **Output** draws all lines from the specified starting point up to, but not including, the specified ending point. This means that all of your lines will be drawn one logical unit short. Second, when the graphics mode of a DC is set to **GM_COMPATIBLE** (see Chapter 10), **Output** draws all rectangles (including rounded rectangles and all other shapes that are defined by a bounding rectangle) so that the width and height are one device unit within the right and bottom edges of the specified rectangle, respectively. This means that all of your rectangles will be one device unit skinny and short. Third, when used to render a custom polygon, **Output** will ignore the **PS_INSIDEFRAME** pen style. This means that when you call the **Polygon** or **PolyPolygon** function (see "Custom Polygons" later in this chapter), you should adjust the locations of the vertices accordingly (e.g., by half the width of the pen). Finally, and most importantly, when a device driver does not support a specific feature, the **Output** function is implemented to return –1. In this case, the GDI simulates the primitive by using a series of line segments (for lines, curves, and the boundary of shapes) and a scan-line-based filling algorithm (for the interior regions of filled shapes).

Lines

A straight *line* is a collection of points that satisfy the equation:

$$y = mx + b \qquad (5.1)$$

The *slope* of the line is the term m, and it's commonly defined as "the change in y (Δy) over the change in x (Δx)." This means that in order to stay on the line, you must move m units in the y-direction for every one unit that you move in the x-direction. The value of y at which x equals zero is represented by the term, b more commonly known as the *y-intercept*. Figure 5.1 illustrates these quantities.

Although it's hard to depict, the line in Figure 5.1 is not bounded (i.e., it extends indefinitely). The term *line segment* is used to describe a portion of a line that's

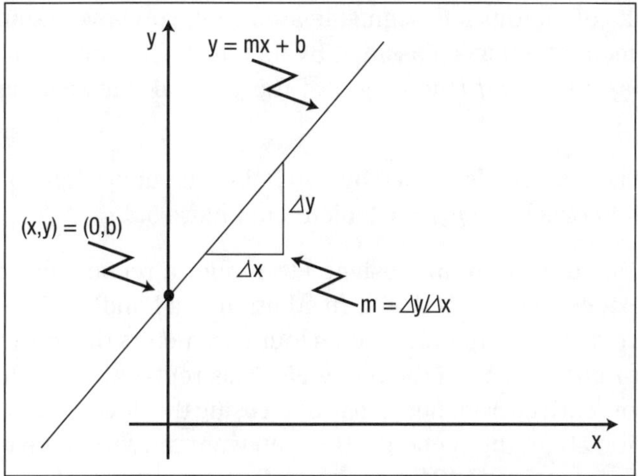

Figure 5.1 The equation of a line, its slope, and its y-intercept.

bounded by two endpoints. The term *polyline* is used to describe two or more line segments.

On a raster device, a line is represented by a set of highlighted pixels. If the line is neither purely horizontal nor purely vertical, it's represented by a staircase of highlighted pixels. The pitch of this staircase depends on the slope of the line.

Line segments and polylines are rendered, using the current pen of the target device context, via the GDI **LineTo**, **Polyline**, **PolylineTo**, or **PolyPolyline** functions. The **LineTo** function draws a line segment from the current position of the target device context up to, but not including, a specified point. The latter three functions require the specification of both the starting point and the ending point of each line segment. These coordinates are conveyed to each of these functions by an array of **POINT** structures:

```
typedef struct tagPOINT {
    LONG x;
    LONG y;
} POINT, *PPOINT, NEAR *NPPOINT, FAR *LPPOINT;
```

The **x** and **y** data members describe the horizontal and vertical locations of the point, respectively.

Rectangles

A *rectangle* is a type of quadrilateral (a four-sided polygon) that's composed of two sets of equal-length line segments. One set contains two line segments that are purely horizontal, and the other set contains two line segments that are purely vertical. When the lengths of all four line segments are equal, you have a square. Otherwise, you have a rectangle that's classified by its *width* (the length of the horizontal line segments), its *height* (the length of the vertical line segments), and its location.

In Windows, a rectangle is typically described by two points: its upper-left corner (x_1, y_1) and its lower-right corner (x_2, y_2), as depicted in Figure 5.2.

The GDI provides four functions that are designed to render a rectangle: **Rectangle**, **FillRect**, **FrameRect**, and **InvertRect**. In addition to a handle to the target device context, the **Rectangle** function accepts four parameters that describe the upper-left and lower-right corners of the rectangle. This rectangle is outlined using the target device context's current pen and is filled using the device context's current brush. Information about the rectangle that you want drawn is conveyed to each of the other three functions (**FillRect**, **FrameRect**, and **InvertRect**) by a **RECT** structure:

```
typedef struct tagRECT {
    LONG left;
    LONG top;
    LONG right;
    LONG bottom;
} RECT, *PRECT, NEAR *NPRECT, FAR *LPRECT;
```


The **left** data member describes the x-coordinate of the rectangle's top-left corner (x_1), while the **top** data member describes the y-coordinate of this corner (y_1). Similarly, the **right** and **bottom** data members describe the x- and y-coordinates of the rectangle's lower-right corner, respectively.

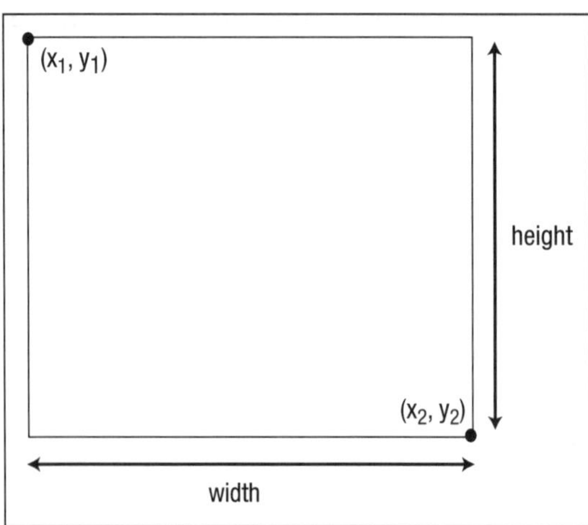

Figure 5.2 A rectangle is described by its top-left and bottom-right corners.

Ellipses

An *ellipse* is a collection of points that satisfy the equation:

$$\frac{(x - x_c)^2}{r_x^{\,2}} + \frac{(y - y_c)^2}{r_y^{\,2}} = 1 \qquad (5.2)$$

The quantities x_c and y_c describe the x- and y-coordinates of the ellipse's center, respectively. The term r_x represents half the ellipse's width, and r_y represents half the ellipse's height. When r_x and r_y are equal, you have a circle.

In Windows, an ellipse is described by its bounding rectangle—specifically, the upper-left (x_1, y_1) and lower-right corners (x_2, y_2) of its bounding rectangle, as depicted in Figure 5.3.

From Figure 5.3, we can see that the terms r_x and r_y can be computed as:

$$(r_x, r_y) = (\frac{x_2 - x_1}{2}, \frac{y_2 - y_1}{2}) \qquad (5.3)$$

Similarly, the center of the ellipse can be computed via the following equation:

$$(x_c, y_c) = (x_1 + \frac{x_2 - x_1}{2}, y_1 + \frac{y_2 - y_1}{2}) \qquad (5.4)$$

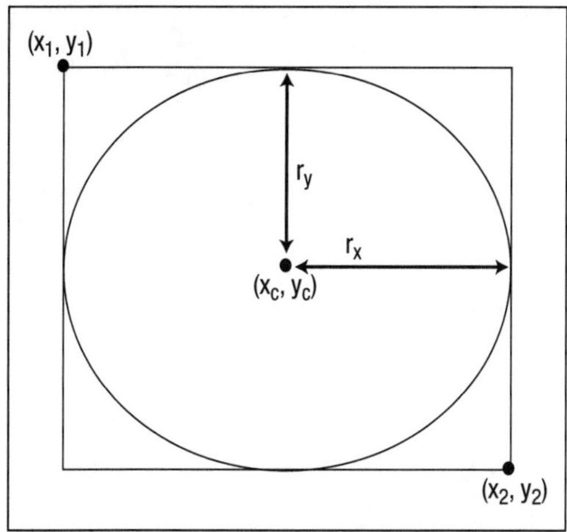

Figure 5.3 An ellipse is described by the top-left and bottom-right corners of its bounding rectangle.

Equation 5.4 can be more concisely written as:

$$(x_c, y_c) = (x_1 + r_x, y_1 + r_y) \qquad (5.5)$$

The GDI **Ellipse** function is designed to render a filled ellipse. The ellipse's outline is drawn using the target device context's current pen, and the ellipse's interior is filled using the target device context's current brush. In addition, ellipses are rendered in a clockwise or counterclockwise fashion, depending on the arc direction of the target device context. For more information on the arc direction, see "Changing the Arc Direction" in the "Immediate Solutions" section. The parameters of the **Ellipse** function are identical to those of the **Rectangle** function—they identify the upper-left and lower-right corners of the bounding rectangle.

Arcs

An *arc* is a continuous interval of a curved body—typically, of an ellipse. In Windows, an arc is always a portion of an ellipse, so we'll focus specifically on this type. The interval of the ellipse that's used to form the arc is defined by a *starting angle* (θ_1) and an *ending angle* (θ_2). The ellipse itself is defined, as usual, by the upper-left corner (x_1, y_1) and lower-right corner (x_2, y_2) of its bounding rectangle. These quantities are depicted in Figure 5.4.

Notice, in Figure 5.4, the points (x_{r1}, y_{r1}) and (x_{r2}, y_{r2}). The starting angle (θ_1) is defined by the line that's formed between the center of the ellipse (x_c, y_c) and the point (x_{r1}, y_{r1}). Similarly, the ending angle (θ_2) is defined by the line that's formed

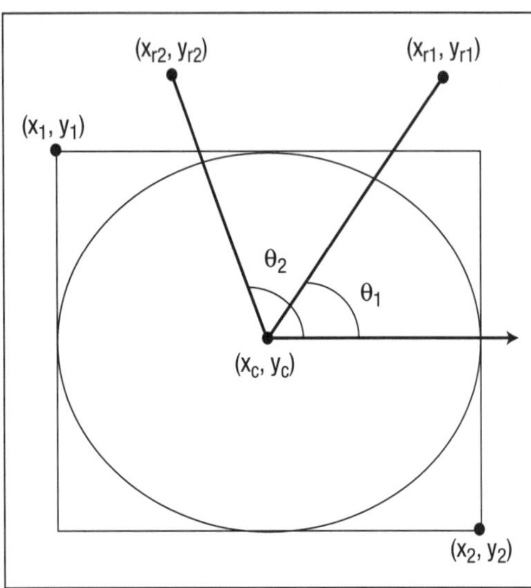

Figure 5.4 An arc is described by an interval of an ellipse.

between the ellipse's center (x_c, y_c) and the point (x_{r2}, y_{r2}). These interval-defining lines are sometimes called *radials*. The arc itself is the interval of the ellipse between θ_1 and θ_2.

The GDI **Arc** or **ArcTo** function is used to render an arc using the target DC's current pen. (The only difference between the two functions is that the latter one updates the target device context's current position.) In addition to the parameters of the **Ellipse** function, **Arc** and **ArcTo** also require the starting and ending angles. These values are not explicitly passed to either function; rather, you pass the x- and y-coordinates of the points (x_{r1}, y_{r1}) and (x_{r2}, y_{r2}). Note that when these points are collinear (i.e., when θ_1 is equal to θ_2), the **Arc** (and **ArcTo)** function will render an entire ellipse.

TIP: *The **Arc** and **ArcTo** functions are commonly used to render unfilled ellipses and circles.*

Like ellipses, arcs are rendered according to the target device context's current arc direction. For example, consider the ellipse and angles depicted in Figure 5.4. When the counterclockwise arc direction is specified (the default for display device contexts), the resulting arc is that illustrated in Figure 5.5.

And, when the clockwise arc direction is set, the arc depicted in Figure 5.6 is the result.

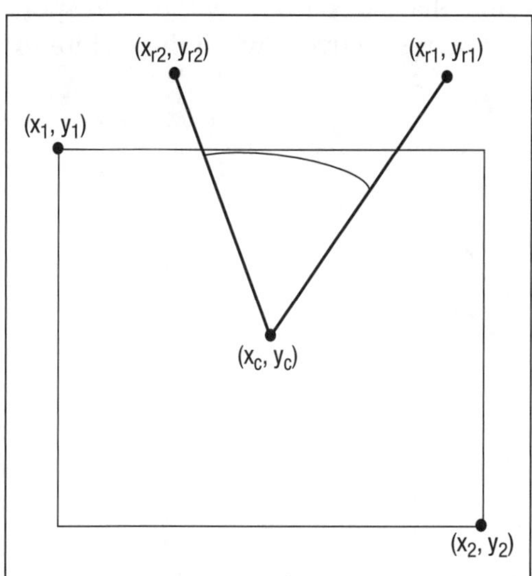

Figure 5.5 The arc described by the ellipse and angles of Figure 5.4 when the counterclockwise arc direction is set.

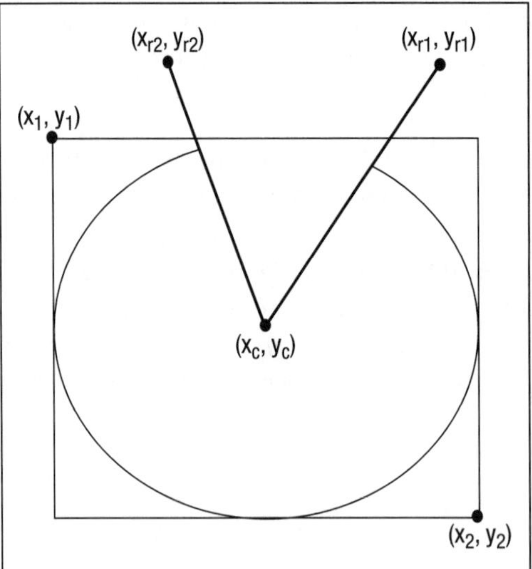

Figure 5.6 The arc described by the ellipse and angles of Figure 5.4 when the clockwise arc direction is set.

Pie Slices

A *pie slice* or *wedge* is a region of an ellipse that's bounded by the same lines that define an arc's interval (see Figure 5.4). For example, the shaded region of the ellipse in Figure 5.7 depicts the pie slice that's described by the corresponding arc's starting and ending angles, θ_1 and θ_2, respectively, when the counterclockwise arc direction is set.

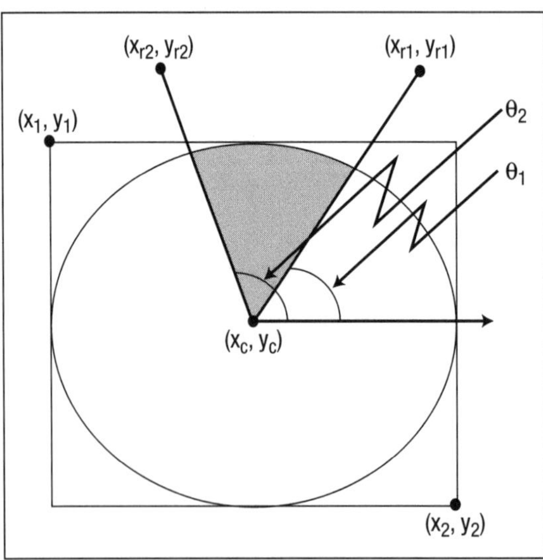

Figure 5.7 A pie slice is described by an interval of an ellipse.

Recall, θ_1 is defined by the line that's formed between the center of the ellipse (x_c, y_c) and the point (x_{r1}, y_{r1}), while θ_2 is defined by the line that's formed between the center of the ellipse and the point (x_{r2}, y_{r2}).

The GDI **Pie** function is used to render a pie section. This function accepts the same parameters as those of the **Arc** and **ArcTo** functions, and when the points (x_{r1}, y_{r1}) and (x_{r2}, y_{r2}) are collinear (i.e., when θ_1 is equal to θ_2), the result is an entire ellipse.

As with arcs, pie slices are rendered according to the target device context's current arc direction (see Figures 5.5 and 5.6). Moreover, like other shapes, pie slices are filled by using the target device context's current brush and are outlined by using this device context's current pen.

Chords

A *chord* is a line segment that joins two points on a curve. In Windows, this curve is an arc, and the two points are the points where the corresponding ellipse intersects the lines that define the arc's interval. The term "chord" is broadly used in GDI-related documentation to describe the region between an arc and its actual chord (commonly referred to as a *secant*). This "chord region" is depicted by the shaded portion of the pie slice in Figure 5.8 (for the counterclockwise arc direction).

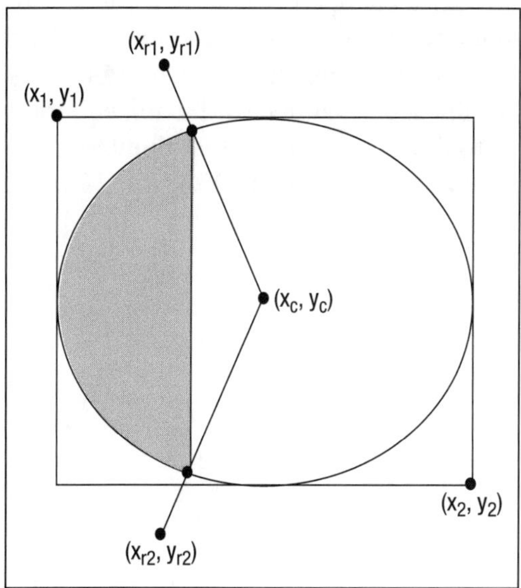

Figure 5.8 A chord is described by the intersection of an arc and its secant.

Chords are rendered via the GDI **Chord** function. This function's parameters are identical to those of the **Arc**, **ArcTo**, and **Pie** functions; when the points (x_{r1}, y_{r1}) and (x_{r2}, y_{r2}) are collinear (i.e., when θ_1 is equal to θ_2), the result is an entire filled ellipse. Like pies, chords are outlined using the current pen of the target device context and are filled using this device context's current brush. Moreover, as with pies and arcs, chords are rendered according to the target device context's current arc direction (see Figures 5.5 and 5.6).

Bézier Curves

Named after French engineer Pierre Bézier, a *Bézier* (pronounced "bayz-ee-yeh") *curve* is a special type of spline curve that's defined by three or more control points. Unlike other spline curves, Bézier curves do not necessarily touch each control point. Two of these control points, called *anchors*, define the endpoints of the Bézier curve; these are the only two points that the Bézier curve must intersect. The other points, called *nodes*, control the shape of the curve. The GDI provides native support for only cubic Bézier curves (four control points; two nodes), so we'll limit our discussion here to this type. Figure 5.9 depicts a cubic Bézier curve and its control points.

Geometrically, the curvature of a cubic Bézier curve results from the relationship between its endpoints and its nodes. Here's how it works. Given just the endpoints, we have a straight line segment. Now, if we place the nodes right on this line segment, we still have a straight line segment. What happens when we move the nodes? This is exactly how the curvature is generated. As the nodes are moved away from the initial straight line segment, the more curved this line segment (and thus the Bézier curve) becomes. Specifically, the line $\underline{P_1P_2}$ (defined by the first endpoint, P_1, and the first nodal point, P_2) is tangent to the Bézier curve at P_1. Similarly, the line segment $\underline{P_3P_4}$ is tangent to the Bézier curve at P_4 (see Figure 5.9). The Bézier curve

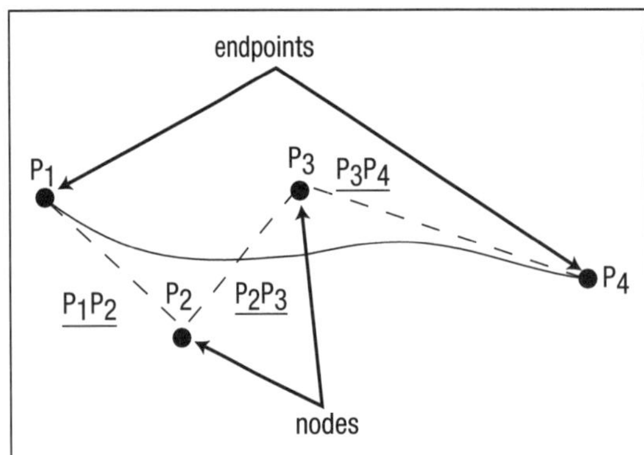

Figure 5.9 A cubic Bézier curve is described by four controls points: two *endpoints* and two *nodes*.

flips its direction at the point where it intersects the line that joins the two nodes ($\underline{P_2P_3}$). If this technical description is confusing, just think of the Bézier curve as a Slinky. The nodes are attached to this Slinky with several strings, and are used to shape the Slinky in much the same way that a puppeteer controls a marionette (see Figure 5.10).

Analytically, a cubic Bézier curve is defined by a linear combination of degree-three Bernstein polynomials. The x- and y-elements of the parameterized Bézier curve are shown in Equations 5.6 and 5.7; the parameter t runs from zero to one:

$$x(t) = x_1 c_1(t) + x_2 c_2(t) + x_3 c_3(t) + x_4 c_4(t) \qquad (5.6)$$

$$y(t) = y_1 c_1(t) + y_2 c_2(t) + y_3 c_3(t) + y_4 c_4(t) \qquad (5.7)$$

The terms x_i and y_i represent the x- and y-coordinates of the i-th control point (P_i), respectively. The Bernstein polynomials—$c_1(t)$, $c_2(t)$, $c_3(t)$, and $c_4(t)$—are defined as follows:

$$c_1(t) = (1 - t)^3 \qquad (5.8)$$

$$c_2(t) = 3t(1 - t)^2 \qquad (5.9)$$

$$c_3(t) = 3t^2(1 - t) \qquad (5.10)$$

$$c_4(t) = t^3 \qquad (5.11)$$

You can refer to the references in Appendix B for more information (and more math) on Bézier curves and Bernstein polynomials, but for general rendering,

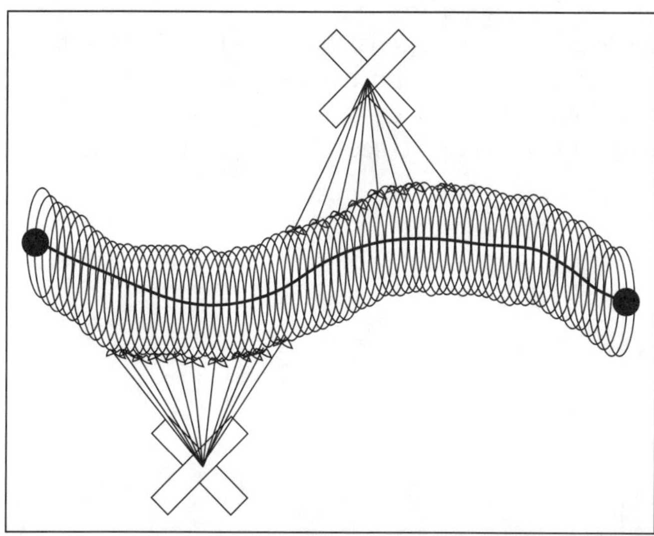

Figure 5.10 The position of a cubic Bézier curve's nodes define its curvature.

you don't need to worry about the specifics of these formulae. The GDI **PolyBezier** function, which is used to render cubic Bézier curves, is particularly straightforward. You simply supply the following: a handle to the target device context; an array of **POINT** structures that describe the control points; and an integer value that specifies the number of **POINT** structures that this array contains. The Bézier curve is drawn using the target device context's current pen.

Custom Polygons

In addition to the standard output primitives, the GDI allows you to render any arbitrary polygon. In fact, this mechanism is not as inviting as it may sound—the GDI allows you to specify a set of vertices from which a polygon is drawn in a "connect the dots" fashion. Figure 5.11 depicts a 10-sided polygon (a star) and its corresponding vertices.

The **Polygon** function is used to render a custom polygon. This function is very much like the **Polyline** function except that the **Polygon** function automatically connects the last vertex to the first (i.e., it draws a *closed polygon*). You pass the **Polygon** function a handle to the target device context, an array of **POINT** structures that describe the polygon's vertices, and an integer value that indicates the number of **POINT**s in this array.

To render a series of custom polygons, you use the **PolyPolygon** function. This function is identical to the **Polygon** function except that for the **PolyPolygon** function the vertex array contains the vertices for all of the polygons. Accordingly, **PolyPolygon** requires an additional array-type parameter whose entries indicate which vertices belong to which polygon.

Like the other predefined shapes, custom polygons are outlined using the target device context's current pen and are filled using this device context's current brush. However, unlike the other shapes, a custom polygon is filled according to the filling mode of the target device context (see "The Polygon Fill Mode" later in this chapter).

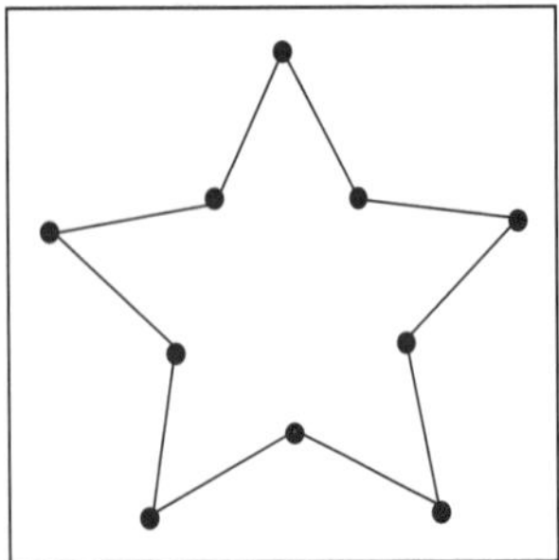

Figure 5.11 An arbitrary polygon is described by a set of vertices.

Listing 5.1 demonstrates the use of each of the aforementioned GDI output-primitive-related functions. The goal here is to render each shape to an owner-drawn list box as depicted in Figure 5.12.

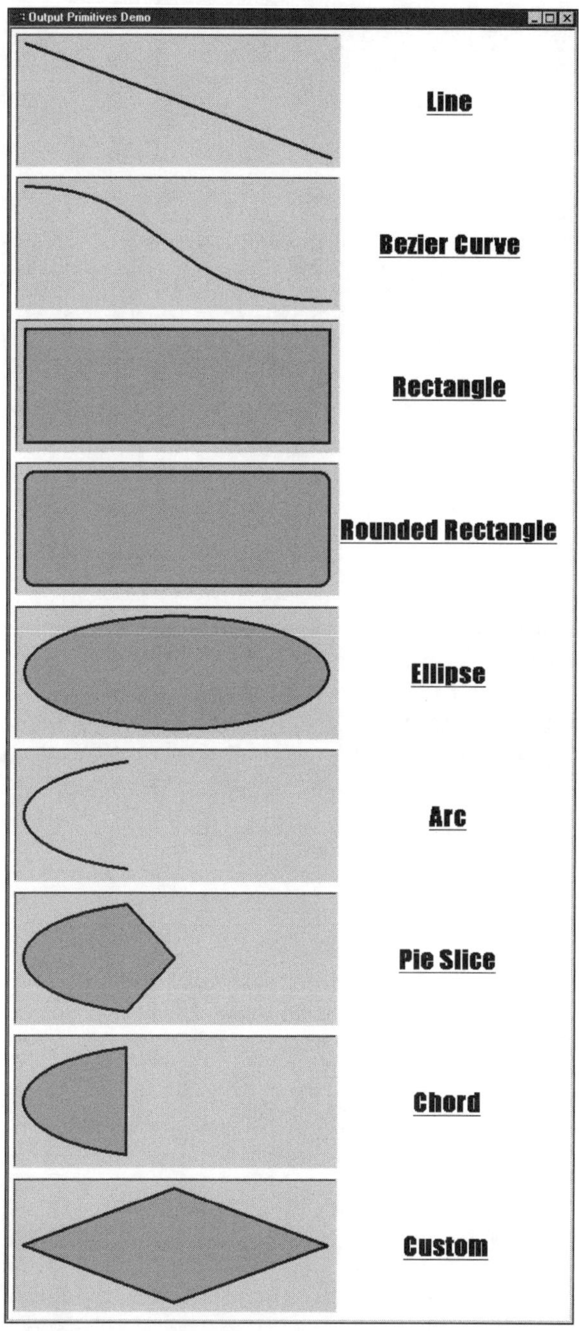

Figure 5.12 An owner-drawn list box whose items represent various output primitives.

Listing 5.1 An owner-drawn list box whose items consist of lines, curves, and shapes that are rendered via the GDI.

```
// ----------------------------------------------------------------
// Windows 2000 Graphics API Black Book
// Chapter 5 - Listing 5.1 (Output Primitives Demo)
// ----------------------------------------------------------------
#include <windows.h>
#include <cassert>

HINSTANCE hInst;
const char* WndClassName = "GMainWnd";
LRESULT CALLBACK MainWndProc(HWND hWnd, UINT msg, WPARAM wParam,
   LPARAM lParam);

int APIENTRY WinMain(HINSTANCE hInstance, HINSTANCE, LPTSTR,
   int nCmdShow)
{
   hInst = hInstance;

   WNDCLASS wc;
   memset(&wc, 0, sizeof(WNDCLASS));

   wc.style = CS_VREDRAW | CS_HREDRAW;
   wc.lpszClassName = WndClassName;
   wc.lpfnWndProc = MainWndProc;
   wc.hInstance = hInst;
   wc.hCursor = LoadCursor(NULL, IDC_ARROW);
   wc.hbrBackground = reinterpret_cast<HBRUSH>(
      COLOR_BTNFACE + 1
      );

   if (RegisterClass(&wc))
   {
      HWND hWnd =
         CreateWindow(WndClassName, "Output Primitives Demo",
                      WS_OVERLAPPEDWINDOW | WS_CAPTION |
                      WS_VISIBLE | WS_CLIPCHILDREN,
                      CW_USEDEFAULT, CW_USEDEFAULT, 640, 480,
                      NULL, NULL, hInst, NULL);

      if (hWnd)
      {
         ShowWindow(hWnd, nCmdShow);
         UpdateWindow(hWnd);
```

```
            MSG msg;
            while (GetMessage(&msg, NULL, 0, 0))
            {
                TranslateMessage(&msg);
                DispatchMessage(&msg);
            }
        }
    }
    return 0;
}

enum OutPrimitive {
   opLine, opBezier, opRectangle, opRoundRect,
   opEllipse, opArc, opPie, opChord, opCustom
   };

void DrawPrimitive(IN HDC hDC, IN const RECT& RPrimitive,
   IN OutPrimitive PrimitiveID)
{
   RECT R = RPrimitive;
   InflateRect(&R, -10, -10);

   switch (PrimitiveID)
   {
      case opLine:
      {
         const POINT PLine[] = {{R.left, R.top}, {R.right, R.bottom}};
         Polyline(hDC, PLine, 2);
         break;
      }
      case opBezier:
      {
         const POINT PControlPoints[] = {
            {R.left, R.top},
            {(R.right - R.left) / 2, R.top},
            {(R.right - R.left) / 2, R.bottom},
            {R.right, R.bottom}
            };
         PolyBezier(hDC, PControlPoints, 4);
         break;
      }
      case opRectangle:
      {
         Rectangle(hDC, R.left, R.top, R.right, R.bottom);
         break;
      }
```

```
case opRoundRect:
{
   RoundRect(hDC, R.left, R.top, R.right, R.bottom, 20, 20);
   break;
}
case opEllipse:
{
   Ellipse(hDC, R.left, R.top, R.right, R.bottom);
   break;
}
case opArc:
{
   const POINT PRads[] = {
      {(R.right - R.left) / 3 + R.left, R.top},
      {(R.right - R.left) / 3 + R.left, R.bottom}
      };
   Arc(hDC, R.left, R.top, R.right, R.bottom,
       PRads[0].x, PRads[0].y, PRads[1].x, PRads[1].y);
   break;
}
case opPie:
{
   const POINT PRads[] = {
      {(R.right - R.left) / 3 + R.left, R.top},
      {(R.right - R.left) / 3 + R.left, R.bottom}
      };
   Pie(hDC, R.left, R.top, R.right, R.bottom,
       PRads[0].x, PRads[0].y, PRads[1].x, PRads[1].y);
   break;
}
case opChord:
{
   const POINT PRads[] = {
      {(R.right - R.left) / 3 + R.left, R.top},
      {(R.right - R.left) / 3 + R.left, R.bottom}
      };
   Chord(hDC, R.left, R.top, R.right, R.bottom,
       PRads[0].x, PRads[0].y, PRads[1].x, PRads[1].y);
   break;
}
case opCustom:
{
   const POINT PVertices[] = {
      {R.left, (R.bottom - R.top) / 2 + R.top},
      {(R.right - R.left) / 2 + R.left, R.top},
      {R.right, (R.bottom - R.top) / 2 + R.top},
```

```
            {(R.right - R.left) / 2 + R.left, R.bottom}
            };
         Polygon(hDC, PVertices, 4);
         break;
      }
   }
}


HWND hListBox = NULL;       // handle to the list box
HBRUSH hListBrush = NULL;   // handle to the list-box brush
HPEN hListPen = NULL;       // handle to the list-box pen
HFONT hListFont = NULL;     // handle to the list-box font

LRESULT CALLBACK MainWndProc(HWND hWnd, UINT msg, WPARAM wParam,
   LPARAM lParam)
{
   switch (msg)
   {
      case WM_CREATE:
      {
         hListBox =
            CreateWindowEx(
               WS_EX_CLIENTEDGE, "LISTBOX", "",
               WS_CHILD | WS_VISIBLE | WS_VSCROLL |
               LBS_HASSTRINGS | LBS_NOINTEGRALHEIGHT |
               LBS_OWNERDRAWFIXED,
               0, 0, 640, 480,
               hWnd, NULL, hInst, NULL
               );
         assert(hListBox != NULL);

         SetWindowLong(
            hListBox, GWL_ID, reinterpret_cast<LONG>(hListBox)
            );

         SNDMSG(hListBox, LB_ADDSTRING, 0,
               reinterpret_cast<LPARAM>(TEXT("Line")));
         SNDMSG(hListBox, LB_ADDSTRING, 0,
               reinterpret_cast<LPARAM>(TEXT("Bezier Curve")));
         SNDMSG(hListBox, LB_ADDSTRING, 0,
               reinterpret_cast<LPARAM>(TEXT("Rectangle")));
         SNDMSG(hListBox, LB_ADDSTRING, 0,
               reinterpret_cast<LPARAM>(TEXT("Rounded Rectangle")));
         SNDMSG(hListBox, LB_ADDSTRING, 0,
               reinterpret_cast<LPARAM>(TEXT("Ellipse")));
```

```
      SNDMSG(hListBox, LB_ADDSTRING, 0,
            reinterpret_cast<LPARAM>(TEXT("Arc")));
      SNDMSG(hListBox, LB_ADDSTRING, 0,
            reinterpret_cast<LPARAM>(TEXT("Pie Slice")));
      SNDMSG(hListBox, LB_ADDSTRING, 0,
            reinterpret_cast<LPARAM>(TEXT("Chord")));
      SNDMSG(hListBox, LB_ADDSTRING, 0,
            reinterpret_cast<LPARAM>(TEXT("Custom")));

      hListBrush = CreateSolidBrush(PALETTERGB(64, 192, 64));
      hListPen = CreatePen(PS_SOLID, 3, PALETTERGB(0, 0, 0));
      HDC hScreenDC = GetDC(NULL);
      try
      {
         // MakeFont from Chapter 4
         hListFont = font::MakeFont(
            hScreenDC, "Impact", 20, ANSI_CHARSET,
            font::FS_BOLD | font::FS_UNDERLINE
            );
      }
      catch (...)
      {
         ReleaseDC(NULL, hScreenDC);
      }
      ReleaseDC(NULL, hScreenDC);
      break;
   }
   case WM_MEASUREITEM:
   {
      LPMEASUREITEMSTRUCT lpmis =
         reinterpret_cast<LPMEASUREITEMSTRUCT>(lParam);
      assert(lpmis != NULL);

      if (lpmis->CtlID == reinterpret_cast<UINT>(hListBox))
      {
         lpmis->itemHeight = 150;
         return TRUE;
      }
      break;
   }
   case WM_DRAWITEM:
   {
      LPDRAWITEMSTRUCT lpdis =
         reinterpret_cast<LPDRAWITEMSTRUCT>(lParam);
      assert(lpdis != NULL);
```

```
if (lpdis->CtlID == reinterpret_cast<UINT>(hListBox))
{
   SaveDC(lpdis->hDC);
   try
   {
      SelectObject(lpdis->hDC, hListBrush);
      SelectObject(lpdis->hDC, hListPen);
      SelectObject(lpdis->hDC, hListFont);

      bool selected = (lpdis->itemState & ODS_SELECTED);
      COLORREF clrText = GetSysColor(
         selected ? COLOR_HIGHLIGHTTEXT : COLOR_WINDOWTEXT
         );
      HBRUSH hListBrush = GetSysColorBrush(
         selected ? COLOR_HIGHLIGHT : COLOR_WINDOW
         );

      // fill the background
      FillRect(lpdis->hDC, &lpdis->rcItem, hListBrush);

      // render the output primitive
      RECT RPrimitive = lpdis->rcItem;
      InflateRect(&RPrimitive, -5, -5);
      RPrimitive.right = static_cast<int>(
         0.6 * lpdis->rcItem.right + 0.5
         );
      FillRect(
         lpdis->hDC, &RPrimitive,
         reinterpret_cast<HBRUSH>(COLOR_BTNFACE + 1)
         );
      DrawPrimitive(
         lpdis->hDC, RPrimitive,
         static_cast<OutPrimitive>(lpdis->itemID)
         );
      if (selected) InvertRect(lpdis->hDC, &RPrimitive);
      DrawEdge(lpdis->hDC, &RPrimitive, EDGE_SUNKEN, BF_RECT);

      // render the text
      TCHAR text[13];
      if (SNDMSG(hListBox, LB_GETTEXT, lpdis->itemID,
                 reinterpret_cast<LPARAM>(&text)) != LB_ERR)
      {
         RECT RText = RPrimitive;
         RText.left =  RPrimitive.right;
         RText.right = lpdis->rcItem.right;
```

```
                    SelectObject(lpdis->hDC, hListFont);
                    SetBkMode(lpdis->hDC, TRANSPARENT);
                    SetTextColor(lpdis->hDC, clrText);

                    DrawText(lpdis->hDC, text, -1, &RText,
                             DT_CENTER | DT_VCENTER | DT_SINGLELINE);
                 }

                 // indicate keyboard focus
                 if (lpdis->itemState & ODS_FOCUS)
                 {
                    RECT RFocus = lpdis->rcItem;
                    InflateRect(&RFocus, -1, -1);
                    DrawFocusRect(lpdis->hDC, &RFocus);
                 }
              }
              catch (...)
              {
                 RestoreDC(lpdis->hDC, -1);
              }
              RestoreDC(lpdis->hDC, -1);
              return TRUE;
           }
           break;
        }
        case WM_SIZE:
        {
           MoveWindow(
              hListBox, 0, 0, LOWORD(lParam), HIWORD(lParam), TRUE
              );
           return 0;
        }
        case WM_DESTROY:
        {
           if (hListBrush) DeleteObject(hListBrush);
           if (hListPen) DeleteObject(hListPen);
           if (hListFont) DeleteObject(hListFont);

           PostQuitMessage(0);
           break;
        }
     }
     return DefWindowProc(hWnd, msg, wParam, lParam);
  }
```

The Polygon Fill Mode

As I mentioned, when you use the GDI to draw a standard shape such as a rectangle, an ellipse, or a triangle, the interior of the shape is filled using the target device context's current brush. Typically, the method that's used to perform this filling operation is specific to each device driver. When a device driver does not support the filling of a standard shape (e.g., **Output** called for an ellipse returns –1), the GDI uses a standard scan-line-based polygon fill algorithm. On the other hand, when you render a custom polygon that contains closed interior regions (i.e., child polygons), the GDI must differentiate between those regions that belong to the polygon itself and those that are simply enclosed. To this end, the GDI provides an alternative, direction-based, polygon fill algorithm.

To determine which interior regions of a custom polygon should be filled, the GDI implements two types of polygon fill algorithms: *even-odd* (scan-line-based) and *winding-number* (direction-based). When the even-odd approach is used, the GDI identifies a point as an interior point if an imaginary line, drawn from that point to a distant point outside the polygon, crosses an odd number of edges. Typically, this line is drawn in the horizontal direction; hence the classification "scan-line-based." When the winding-number approach is used, the GDI counts the number of times each point is "wound" by the polygon edges in the counterclockwise direction. This technique involves associating a "direction" with each edge and then drawing an imaginary line from the point in question to a distant point that lies outside the polygon. Each time the line intersects an edge of the polygon that's drawn in the counterclockwise direction (right-to-left or bottom-to-top), the point's winding number is incremented. Each time the line intersects an edge of the polygon that's drawn in the clockwise direction (left-to-right or top-to-bottom), the point's winding number is decremented. Those points that have a non-zero winding number are classified as interior points. Figure 5.13 illustrates the results when each of these algorithms is used for a "box in a box in a box."

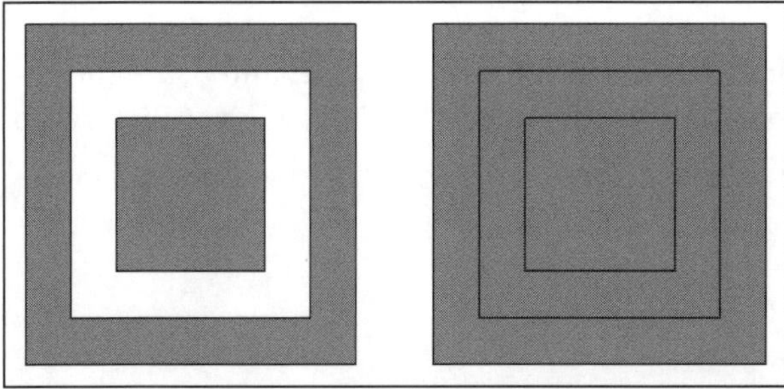

Figure 5.13 The result of interior region classifications made by the even-odd technique (left) and the winding-number technique (right).

A device context's *polygon fill mode* (also called the *filling mode*) governs which method (even-odd or winding-number) the GDI will use to determine which regions to fill when a complex and/or overlapping polygon is drawn via the **Polygon** or **PolyPolygon** function. The **ALTERNATE** (1) identifier is passed to the **SetPolyFillMode** function to specify the even-odd approach (the default). The **WINDING** (2) identifier is passed to the **SetPolyFillMode** function to specify the winding-number approach. For the specifics of the **SetPolyFillMode** function, see Chapter 1.

Hit-Testing

When you draw lines, curves, and shapes to a device context, rarely will these objects be fixed in position and size. In most cases, you'll want to provide a feature that lets the user interact with them. Moreover, you'll likely want to allow this interaction to be mouse-based. *Hit-testing* is the first step toward accomplishing this.

When you hit-test an object, your objective is to assess whether or not a specific point, typically the location of the mouse cursor, is within the bounds of the object. For some primitives, such as circles or rectangles, this task is fairly straightforward. For other, more complex, shapes, the process can become quite involved.

Hit-testing gets even more tricky when you need to control the sensitivity of the test. In many cases, it's nearly impossible to position the mouse cursor exactly over the object (e.g., a thin line). Unless the object is sufficiently large, it's always best to use a hit-testing algorithm that allows a bit of leeway. To this end, you'll need the distance from a point to a line. You can compute this quantity by using Equation 5.12 (from Donald Hearn and M. Pauline Baker, *Computer Graphics, C Version*, 2nd ed., Upper Saddle River, NJ: Prentice Hall, 1997):

$$d = \frac{(x_2 - x_1)(y - y_1) - (y_2 - y_1)(x - x_1)}{\sqrt{(x_2 - x_1)^2 + (y_2 - y_1)^2}} \qquad (5.12)$$

Here, x and y are the coordinates of the point, and x_1, y_1, x_2, and y_2 are the coordinates of the two points that define the line. The following utility function, **DistToLine**, uses Equation 5.12:

```
int DistToLine(
    IN const POINT& PPoint,     // the point
    IN const POINT* PLine       // the line
   )
```

```
{
   const int dXLine = PLine[1].x - PLine[0].x;
   const int dYLine = PLine[1].y - PLine[0].y;

   if (dXLine == 0 && dYLine == 0)
   {
      const int dX = PPoint.x - PLine[0].x;
      const int dY = PPoint.y - PLine[0].y;
      return sqrt((dX * dX + dY * dY));
   }

   const int numerator =
      (dXLine * (PPoint.y - PLine[0].y)) -
      (dYLine * (PPoint.x - PLine[0].x));
   const int denominator =
      sqrt((dXLine * dXLine) + (dYLine * dYLine));
   return (numerator / denominator);
}
```

In this section, we'll examine some techniques for hit-testing lines, curves, and shapes. After an object is "hit," you are free to provide feedback to the user. For example, you can render the object in a different color, or provide a series of markers or *control grips*. Let's start with the easiest of primitives, the rectangle.

Hit-Testing Rectangles

Rectangles are by far the simplest primitive to hit-test: you simply check whether the x-coordinate of the point in question lies between the rectangle's left and right edges, and whether the y-coordinate of the point lies between the rectangle's top and bottom edges. In fact, you don't even need to implement this scheme manually—simply use the **PtInRect** function. And to control the sensitivity of the test, you call the **InflateRect** function beforehand.

Hit-Testing Ellipses

Hit-testing an ellipse is nearly as simple as hit-testing a rectangle. Although there is no built-in Windows function to accomplish this task, we can simply rely on Equation 5.2. Specifically, if the point in question is exactly on the ellipse (i.e., on its boundary), the quantity

$$\frac{(x - x_c)^2}{r_x^{\,2}} + \frac{(y - y_c)^2}{r_y^{\,2}} = 1$$

will evaluate to one. If the point in question lies within the ellipse's interior region, this quantity will be less than one. And when the point in question lies exactly on the center of the ellipse, this quantity will be zero.

You control the sensitivity of the hit test for an ellipse in the same way you do for a rectangle. Because an ellipse is described by its bounding rectangle, you simply use the **InflateRect** function before performing the hit test. This is equivalent to adjusting the values of r_x and r_y.

Hit-Testing Pie Slices

After you can determine whether or not a point lies in or on an ellipse, hit-testing a pie slice is fairly straightforward. From Figure 5.7, recall two things: θ_1 is defined by the line that's formed between the center of the ellipse (x_c, y_c) and the point (x_{r1}, y_{r1}); and θ_2 is defined by the line that's formed between the center of the ellipse and the point (x_{r2}, y_{r2}). If the angle θ_{hit}—defined by the line that's formed between the center of the ellipse (x_c, y_c) and the point in question (x_{hit}, y_{hit})—is between θ_1 and θ_2, then (x_{hit}, y_{hit}) is in the pie slice defined by the ellipse, θ_1 and θ_2. This scheme is depicted in Figure 5.14.

The sensitivity for hit-testing the arc portion is automatically afforded from the hit test for the ellipse itself. To add sensitivity for the interval-defining lines (i.e., the radials), use either the distance formula or the technique that we'll build later in this section to hit-test lines (see "Hit-Testing Lines").

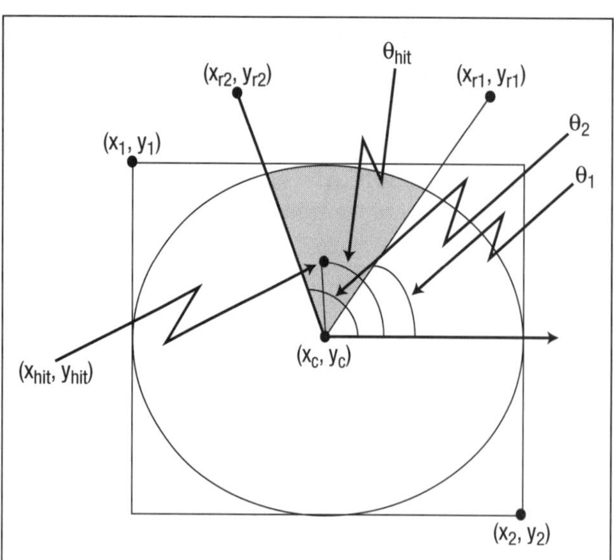

Figure 5.14 The point in question, (x_{hit}, y_{hit}), is in the pie slice if it is in the ellipse and if θ_{hit} is between the angles θ_1 and θ_2.

Hit-Testing Arcs

In the previous section, we discussed how to hit-test a pie slice. Well, hit-testing an arc is a simple extension of this technique. Given that a point is in a pie slice, you can determine if that point is on the corresponding arc by using Equation 5.2. Recall, if the following equality holds

$$\frac{(x - x_c)^2}{r_x^{\,2}} + \frac{(y - y_c)^2}{r_y^{\,2}} = 1$$

then the specified point is on the ellipse (i.e., on the boundary of the ellipse versus its interior). Following this logic, if the point is both in the pie slice and on the ellipse, the point is on the arc.

Unfortunately, controlling the sensitivity of this hit test is not so straightforward. For the curvature of the arc, we're afforded a sensitivity consideration from the hit test of the ellipse, but there is no easy way to get accurate results for the endpoints of the arc. Moreover, we can't revert to the distance formula because we don't know these endpoints. The solution, then, is to calculate these endpoints; to do this, we'll need to compute the intersection of a radial and an ellipse as depicted in Figure 5.15.

As in Figure 5.15, let's define the point of intersection as (x_e, y_e). Here, the subscript "e" stands for "ellipse" because the point of intersection is indeed on the ellipse. And, as usual, the radial is defined by the center of the ellipse, (x_c, y_c), and

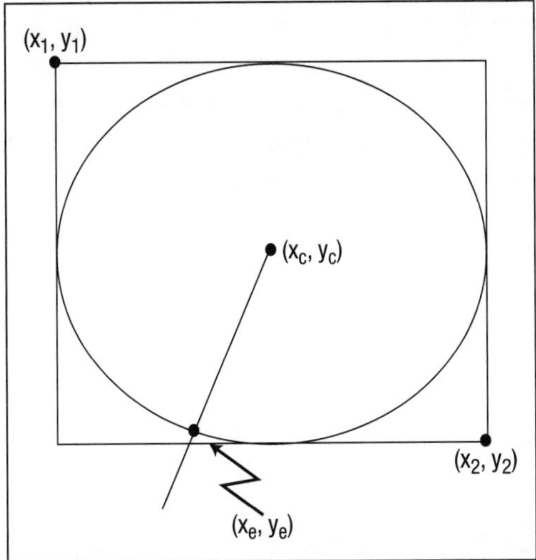

Figure 5.15 The intersection, (x_e, y_e), of a line and an ellipse.

by the radial point (x_r, y_r). Our goal, then, is to compute the point of intersection, (x_e, y_e), given the ellipse's bounding rectangle—from which we can compute (x_c, y_c)—and the radial point (x_r, y_r).

To make things easier, let's work with the point-slope form of the equation of a line, given here in Equation 5.13 for the radial:

$$(y_r - y_c) = m(x_r - x_c) \qquad (5.13)$$

Because we know the radial point (x_r, y_r) and the ellipse's center (x_c, y_c), the only unknown in this equation is the slope, m which we can easily solve for. Moreover, because the point of intersection (x_e, y_e) is on the radial, the line segment formed between (x_c, y_c) and (x_e, y_e) will have this same slope. That is, the m given in Equation 5.13 is the same m given in Equation 5.14:

$$(y_e - y_c) = m(x_e - x_c) \qquad (5.14)$$

Equation 5.14 is the point-slope form of the equation of the line joining the ellipse's center (x_c, y_c) and the point of intersection (x_e, y_e). Because we can compute the slope of this line from Equation 5.13, the only unknowns here are x_e and y_e. One equation and two unknowns? We'll need another equation. This we can get from Equation 5.2, the equation of an ellipse. Moreover, because we know that the point of intersection (x_e, y_e) is on the ellipse, we can plug the intersection's coordinates in for the x and y terms of Equation 5.2. Equation 5.15 depicts this modification:

$$\frac{(x_e - x_c)^2}{r_x^2} + \frac{(y_e - y_c)^2}{r_y^2} = 1 \qquad (5.15)$$

Once again, the only unknowns are the values of x_e and y_e (remember, r_x and r_y are simply half the width and half the height of the ellipse, respectively). We now have two equations and two unknowns—so let's solve for x_e:

$$\frac{(x_e - x_c)^2}{r_x^2} + \frac{(y_e - y_c)^2}{r_y^2} = 1$$

$$\rightarrow \frac{(x_e - x_c)^2}{r_x^2} + \frac{(m(x_e - x_c))^2}{r_y^2} = 1$$

$$\rightarrow \frac{(x_e - x_c)^2 r_y^2 + (m(x_e - x_c))^2 r_x^2}{r_x^2 r_y^2} = 1$$

$$\rightarrow (x_e - x_c)^2 r_y^2 + (m(x_e - x_c))^2 r_x^2 = r_x^2 r_y^2$$

$$\rightarrow (x_e - x_c)^2 (r_y^2 + m^2 r_x^2) = r_x^2 r_y^2$$

$$\rightarrow (x_e - x_c)^2 = \frac{r_x^2 r_y^2}{(r_y^2 + m^2 r_x^2)}$$

$$\rightarrow x_e = x_c \pm \sqrt{\frac{r_x^2 r_y^2}{(r_y^2 + m^2 r_x^2)}} \qquad (5.16)$$

Now that we have an equation for x_e, we can plug this into Equation 5.14 to solve for y_e:

$$\rightarrow y_e = y_c \pm m \sqrt{\frac{r_x^2 r_y^2}{(r_y^2 + m^2 r_x^2)}} \qquad (5.17)$$

Again, the value of m is computed from Equation 5.13.

Using Equations 5.16 and 5.17 for each radial point, you can compute the respective points of intersection, which are the endpoints of the arc. This process is demonstrated in the following code snippet:

```
void IntersectRadialAndEllipse(
    IN const POINT& PRadial,
    IN const RECT& RBounds,
    OUT POINT& PIntersect
    )
{
   const float a = 0.5 * (RBounds.right - RBounds.left);
   const float b = 0.5 * (RBounds.bottom - RBounds.top);
   const POINT PCenter = {a + RBounds.left, b + RBounds.top};

   const float dX = PRadial.x - PCenter.x;
   const float dY = PRadial.y - PCenter.y;
   if (dX == 0)
   {
      PIntersect.x = PCenter.x;
      PIntersect.y = (dY < 0) ? RBounds.top : RBounds.bottom;
      return;
   }
   if (dY == 0)
   {
      PIntersect.x = (dX < 0) ? RBounds.left : RBounds.right;
```

```
        PIntersect.y = PCenter.y;
        return;
    }

    const float m = dY / dX;
    const int a_sqrd = a * a;
    const int b_sqrd = b * b;
    const float x_offset =
        sqrt((a_sqrd * b_sqrd) / (b_sqrd + (m * m * a_sqrd)));

    const int x_pos = PCenter.x + x_offset + 0.5;
    const int x_neg = PCenter.x - x_offset + 0.5;
    if (abs(PRadial.x - x_pos) < abs(PRadial.x - x_neg))
    {
        PIntersect.x = x_pos;
        PIntersect.y = PCenter.y + (m * x_offset) + 0.5;
    }
    else
    {
        PIntersect.x = x_neg;
        PIntersect.y = PCenter.y - (m * x_offset) + 0.5;
    }
}
```


With the points of intersection (**PIntersect**), you can use the distance formula to compute the distance from the point in question to each endpoint, and then assess whether each distance is within the specified tolerance.

Hit-Testing Chords

Hit-testing a chord is a simple variation of hit-testing an arc. Once again, you need to compute the endpoints of the corresponding arc, except this time you use these points to define a line (i.e., the secant). Then the logic is as follows: If the point in question is in the pie slice and beyond the secant, then the point is in the chord region. This scheme is depicted in Figure 5.16.

As before, the sensitivity for hit-testing the arc portion is automatically provided by the hit test for the ellipse itself. And again, to add sensitivity for the radials (and the secant), you simply use the distance formula or the technique that we'll discuss for hit-testing lines (see "Hit-Testing Lines").

Hit-Testing Lines

To hit-test a straight line or a straight line segment, you use the following logic: If the slope of the line formed between one point on the line and the point in question is equal to the slope of the line formed between a different point on the line

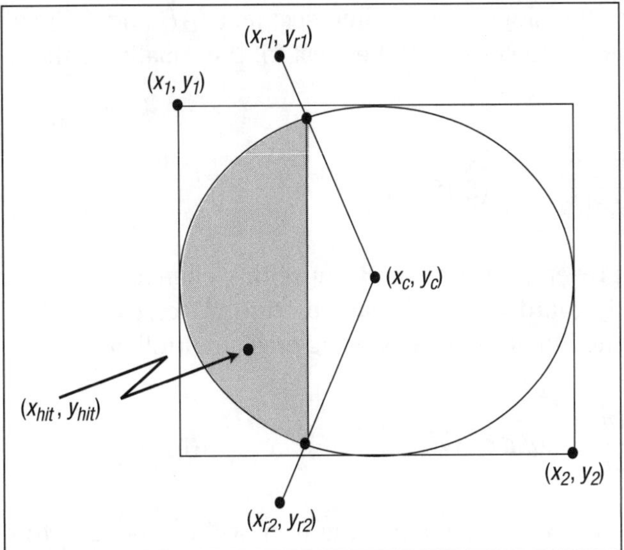

Figure 5.16 The point in question, (x_{hit}, y_{hit}), is in the chord region if it is in the pie slice and beyond the line segment connecting the corresponding arc's endpoints.

and the point in question, then the point in question is on the line. Moreover, if the point in question is within the bounds of the two initial "on-the-line" points, then the point in question lies on the line segment between those two points.

For example, consider a line segment, $\underline{AC}$, formed between two points: A and C as depicted in Figure 5.17. For a given point, B, to be on this line segment, the slope of the line segment $\underline{AB}$ must be equal to the slope of the line segment $\underline{BC}$. In addition, point B cannot lie beyond either point A or point C.

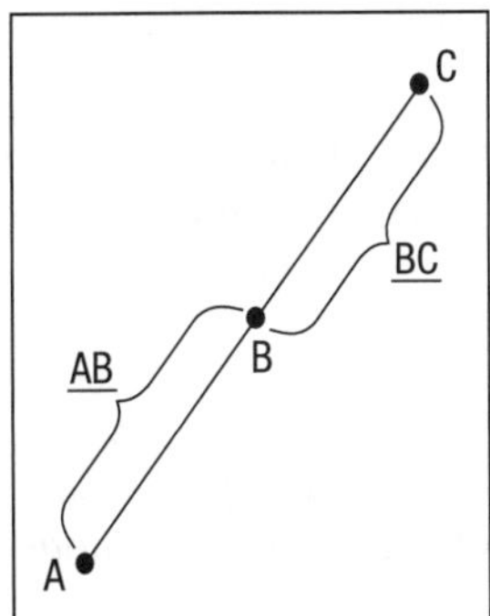

Figure 5.17 For the point B to be on the line segment $\underline{AC}$, the slope of $\underline{AB}$ must equal the slope of $\underline{BC}$, and B must be within A and C.

Typically, you'd calculate the slope of each line segment (<u>AB</u> and <u>BC</u>) as "the change in y divided by the change in x" and then test for the equality of these two quantities:

$$slope_1 = slope_2 \rightarrow \frac{dy_1}{dx_1} = \frac{dy_2}{dx_2} \qquad (5.18)$$

However, this approach presents a problem. Because the "change in x" might be zero, you have to explicitly guard against division by zero. We can avoid this situation by simply rearranging Equation 5.18 by using cross-multiplication:

$$slope_1 = slope_2 \rightarrow \frac{dy_1}{dx_1} = \frac{dy_2}{dx_2} \rightarrow dy_1 dx_2 = dy_2 dx_1 \qquad (5.19)$$

Often, when selecting a line with the mouse, the user will not be able to click exactly on the line. This is a particularly common problem when the line is thin or short. To incorporate a tolerance factor into this hit test (i.e., to add a bit of flexibility), we need to quantify the change that occurs to each slope when point B is offset from the line. We can do this by simply scaling the tolerance by the length of the line segment.

Consider the case when point B is offset from the line segment <u>AC</u> by a factor of Δx in the x-direction and Δy in the y-direction, as depicted in Figure 5.18. The error induced in the quantity $dy_1 dx_2 - dy_2 dx_1$ can be related to the tolerance by the following approximation:

$$\begin{aligned} error &\approx (tolerance)(line\ Segment\ Length) \\ &= \sqrt{\Delta x^2 + \Delta y^2}\sqrt{(dx_1 + dx_2)^2 + (dy_1 + dy_2)^2} \end{aligned} \qquad (5.20)$$

To see where the offset approximation relationship comes from, let's solve for the quantity $dy_1 dx_2 - dy_2 dx_1$, taking into account the offsets, Δx and Δy. Recall, for the ideal case, we'd simply test the following:

$$dy_1 dx_2 - dy_2 dx_1 = 0 \qquad (5.21)$$

However, if we test this relation for the lengths depicted in Figure 5.18, the test will always yield false. This occurs because point B is not on the line segment <u>AC</u>. What we actually need to test is the following relation:

$$(dy_1 - \Delta y)(dx_2 - \Delta x) - (dy_2 + \Delta y)(dx_1 + \Delta x) = 0 \qquad (5.22)$$

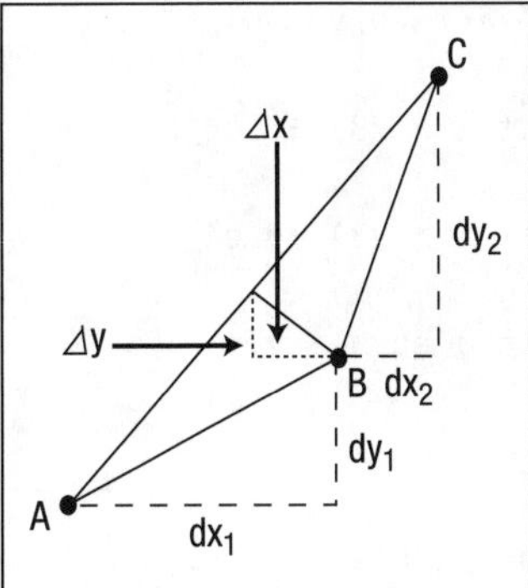

Figure 5.18 Point *B*, offset from the line segment *AC* by Δ*x* and Δ*y*.

Multiplying the right-hand side of this equation, we get the following:

$$(dy_1\, dx_2 - dx_2\, \Delta y - dy_1 \Delta x + \Delta x \Delta y) - (dy_2\, dx_1 + dx_1\, \Delta y + dy_2 \Delta x + \Delta x \Delta y) = 0$$

$$\rightarrow dy_1\, dx_2 - dy_2\, dx_1 - \Delta x(dy_1 + dy_2) - \Delta y(dx_1 + dx_2) = 0 \qquad (5.23)$$

Notice that this latter equation is simply the relation for the ideal case, $(dy_1\, dx_2 - dy_2\, dx_1)$, plus an error term, $(\Delta x(dy_1 + dy_2) + \Delta y(dx_1 + dx_2))$. It is this error term that is approximated as:

$$\Delta x\, (dy_2 + dx_2) + \Delta y(dx_1 + dx_2) \approx \sqrt{\Delta x^2 + \Delta y^2}\sqrt{(dx_1 + dx_2)^2 + (dy_1 + dy_2)^2} \qquad (5.24)$$

Hit-Testing Bézier Curves

The most straightforward approach to hit-testing a Bézier curve is to digitize the curve into *N* discrete points. You can do this by using the analytical form of a cubic Bézier curve, described by Equations 5.6 and 5.7. Specifically, you place these equations inside a loop that iterates over the parameter *t*, and you compute the x- and y-coordinates of each point on the Bézier curve at each value of *t*. After a point is computed, you test this point for, within tolerance, equality to the point in question. The following pseudo-code outlines this process:

```
for t = 0.0 to 1.0
begin
   // compute the values of the Bernstein polynomials at t
   c1_at_t = value of c1(t) computed using equation 5.8
   c2_at_t = value of c2(t) computed using equation 5.9
   c3_at_t = value of c3(t) computed using equation 5.10
   c4_at_t = value of c4(t) computed using equation 5.11
```

```
    // compute the x- and y-coordinates of the Bézier curve point at t
    x_at_t =
          (c1_at_t * x1) + (c2_at_t * x2) + (c3_at_t * x3) + (c4_at_t * x4)
    y_at_t =
          (c1_at_t * y1) + (c2_at_t * y2) + (c3_at_t * y3) + (c4_at_t * y4)

    // test x_at_t and y_at_t for (within tolerance) equality
    // to the point in question (hit_point)
    if x_at_t ≈ hit_point AND y_at_t ≈ hit_point
    begin
       // the point in question (hit_point) is on the Bézier curve
       break the loop and signal TRUE
    end

    // increment t and test the next point
    t = t + (1 / N)
end
// the point in question is not on the Bézier curve
signal FALSE
```

What value of N should you choose? For an exact representation of the points on the analytically described (analog) Bézier curve, you'll want the value of N to be at least the length of the curve. Unfortunately, raster-based devices can rarely represent a curve as exacting as its analytical form, so there's no point in computing a precise length (or more correctly, a close approximation). For digitizing purposes, you can estimate the length of a Bézier curve by adding the distances between its control points (i.e., $\underline{P_1P_2} + \underline{P_2P_3} + \underline{P_3P_4}$).

Immediate Solutions

Rendering Lines, Curves, and Shapes

The GDI provides several functions that can be used to render output primitives. In this section, we'll examine each of these functions, including their various parameters and return values.

Rendering a Single Line Segment

To render a single line segment, you use the **LineTo** function:

```
BOOL LineTo(
    IN HDC hdc,         // handle to the target device context
    IN int nXEnd,       // x-coordinate of line's ending point
    IN int nYEnd        // y-coordinate of line's ending point
   );
```

The **hdc** parameter identifies the device context to which the line will be rendered. The endpoint of this line is specified, in logical units, by the **nXEnd** and **nYEnd** parameters. If the **LineTo** function is successful, it returns **TRUE**; otherwise, the function returns **FALSE**.

The **LineTo** function renders a line from the target device context's current position up to, but not including, the point specified by the **nXEnd** and **nYEnd** parameters. The current position of the target device context is then updated to the point (**nXEnd**, **nYEnd**). To change the current position of the target device context without rendering a line, you use the **MoveToEx** function:

```
BOOL MoveToEx(
    IN HDC hdc,            // handle to the target device context
    IN int X,              // x-coordinate of the new current position
    IN int Y,              // y-coordinate of the new current position
    OUT LPPOINT lpPoint    // pointer to a POINT structure that will receive
                           // the old current position
   );
```

The **hdc** parameter identifies the device context whose current position will be changed to the point specified, in logical units, by the **X** and **Y** parameters. The previous current position is stored in the **POINT** structure indicated by the **lpPoint** parameter. If this information is not needed, you can set **lpPoint** to **NULL**. If the

MoveToEx function is successful, it returns **TRUE**; otherwise, the return value is **FALSE**.

For example, to render a line segment from logical coordinate (10, 10) up to, but not including, logical coordinate (100, 200), you use the **LineTo** and **MoveToEx** functions like so:

```
HDC hDC = GetDC(hWnd);
try
{
   const POINT PStart = {10, 10};
   const POINT PEnd = {100, 200};
   if (MoveToEx(hDC, PStart.x, PStart.y, NULL))
   {
      LineTo(hDC, PEnd.x, PEnd.y);
   }
}
catch (...)
{
   ReleaseDC(hWnd, hDC);
}
ReleaseDC(hWnd, hDC);
```


Rendering a Series of Line Segments

To render a series of connected line segments, you use the **Polyline** function:

```
BOOL Polyline(
    IN HDC hdc,              // handle to the target device context
    IN CONST POINT *lppt,    // array of POINT structures that define the
                             // ending point of each line (the first POINT
                             // is the starting point of the first line)
    IN int cPoints           // number of points in the array
   );
```

The **hdc** parameter identifies the device context to which the connected line segments will be rendered. The **lppt** parameter specifies the starting point of the first line and the ending point of each subsequent line via an array of **POINT** structures; the **cPoints** parameter specifies the number of **POINT** structures in this array. If the **Polyline** function is successful, it draws the polyline using the target DC's current pen, and then returns **TRUE**; otherwise, the return value is **FALSE**.

NOTE: *The **Polyline** function does not update the target device context's current position. If you need the current position updated, use the **PolylineTo** function instead. This latter function has the same signature and functionality as **Polyline**, but **PolylineTo** moves the target device context's current position to the endpoint of the last line.*

WARNING! On Windows 95 and Windows 98, the number of points is limited to 16,000. If you're rendering with a geometric pen, this limit can be much lower if the target device does not support wide lines (see "Retrieving the Line Capabilities of a Device"). The Polyline function won't fail, but the extra points won't be rendered.

The **Polyline** function renders the first line, starting at the first point in the array of **POINT** structures specified by the **lppt** array parameter, and extending up to, but not including, the second point in the **lppt** array. However, unlike the **LineTo** function, **Polyline** does not update the target device context's current position. When **Polyline** is used to draw multiple lines, the starting point of the next line is the ending point of the previous line (i.e., the lines are connected). For example, to render the letter "Z" via a series of line segments:

```
const int num_points = 4;
const POINT points[] = {
   {10, 10}, {200, 10}, {10, 200}, {200, 200}
   };

HDC hDC = GetDC(hWnd);
try
{
   Polyline(hDC, points, num_points);
}
catch (...)
{
   ReleaseDC(hWnd, hDC);
}
ReleaseDC(hWnd, hDC);
```

To render a series of line segments that are not connected, or to render a series of individually connected lines (i.e., a series of polylines), you use the **PolyPolyline** function:

```
BOOL PolyPolyline(
    IN HDC hdc,                     // handle to the target device context
    IN CONST POINT *lppt,           // array of POINT structures that
                                    // define the starting and ending
                                    // points of each line segment
    IN CONST DWORD *lpdwPolyPoints, // array of DWORDs that indicate the
                                    // number of points in the lppt array
                                    // that correspond to each polyline
    IN DWORD cCount                 // number of values in the
                                    // lpdwPolyPoints array
   );
```

5. Lines, Curves, and Shapes

The **hdc** parameter identifies the device context to which the polylines are rendered. The **lppt** parameter points to an array of **POINT** structures, in which each pair of points specifies the starting and ending points of each line segment. The **lpdwPolyPoints** parameter points to an array of **DWORDs**, in which each value specifies the number of points in the **lppt** array that correspond to each polyline. The position of each value in the **lpdwPolyPoints** array indicates the polyline to which the value itself refers. For example, the first **DWORD** value in the **lpdwPolyPoints** array indicates the number of points in the **lppt** array that correspond to the first polyline. So, for example, if this value is set to 12, the first polyline is composed of 6 line segments, where each pair of points defines the starting and ending points of each line segment. The **cCount** parameter specifies the number of **DWORDs** that the **lpdwPolyPoints** array contains (i.e., the number of polylines).

NOTE: *The **PolyPolyline** function does not update the target device context's current position. If you need the current position updated, use multiple calls to the **PolylineTo** function instead.*

WARNING! On Windows 95 and Windows 98, the number of points is limited to 16,000. If you're rendering with a geometric pen, this limit can be much lower if the target device does not support wide lines (see "Retrieving the Line Capabilities of a Device"). The PolyPolyline function won't fail, but the extra points won't be rendered.

If successful, the **PolyPolyline** function draws the polylines using the target DC's current pen, and then returns **TRUE**; otherwise, the return value is **FALSE**. For example, to render the letters "ZA" as a series of three polylines (one for the "Z," one for the upside-down "V" portion of the "A," and one for the center cross mark of the "A"):

```
const int num_polylines = 3;
const POINT points[] = {
   // the letter Z
   {10, 10}, {200, 10}, {10, 200}, {200, 200},
   // hat portion of the letter A
   {250, 200}, {345, 10}, {440, 200},
   // center mark portion of the letter A
   {300, 100}, {390, 100}
   };
const DWORD num_points_per_polyline[] = {4, 3, 2};

HDC hDC = GetDC(hWnd);
try
{
   PolyPolyline(hDC, points, num_points_per_polyline, num_polylines);
}
```

```
catch (...)
{
  ReleaseDC(hWnd, hDC);
}
ReleaseDC(hWnd, hDC);
```

Rendering a Bézier Curve

To draw a Bézier curve, you use the **PolyBezier** function:

```
BOOL PolyBezier(
    IN HDC hdc,             // handle to the target device context
    IN CONST POINT *lppt,   // pointer to an array of end and control points
    IN DWORD cPoints        // number of end and control points
  );
```

The **hdc** parameter identifies the destination device context. The **lppt** parameter specifies the curve's endpoints and control points. These points are stored in an array of **POINT** structures, in which each set of four points defines a single Bézier curve. For a single curve, the first set of four **POINT** structures in this array defines the curve's endpoints and control points: the first point indicates the coordinates of the starting point; the second and third points indicate the coordinates of the control points; and the fourth point indicates the coordinates of the ending point. For multiple curves, the ending point of the previous curve is used as the starting point of the next curve. For example, to render two Bézier curves, the **lppt** parameter must point to an array of seven points—the first four points define the first curve, while the fourth point and the remaining three points define the second curve (see Figure 5.19). The **cPoints** parameter specifies the number of **POINT** structures in the array. This parameter must be set to one more than three times the number of Bézier curves to be rendered.

***NOTE:** The **PolyBezier** function does not update the target device context's current position. If you need the current position updated, use the **PolyBezierTo** function instead. This latter function has the same signature and functionality as **PolyBezier**, but **PolyBezierTo** moves the target device context's current position to the endpoint of the last Bézier curve.*

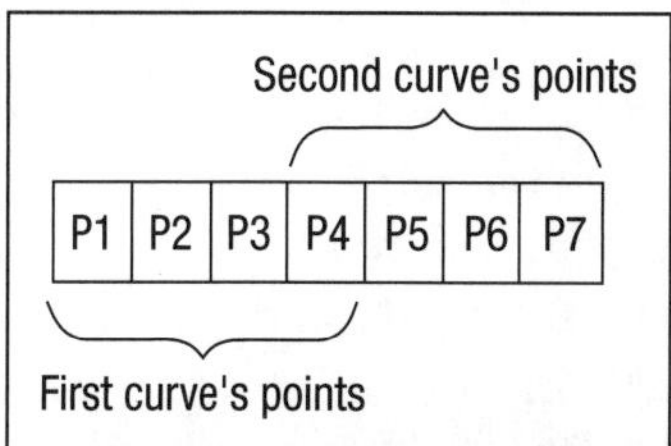

Figure 5.19 The layout of the points in the lppt array when you're rendering two Bézier curves.

WARNING! On Windows 95 and Windows 98, the number of points is limited to 16,000. If you're rendering with a geometric pen, this limit can be much lower if the target device does not support wide lines (see "Retrieving the Line Capabilities of a Device"). The PolyBezier function won't fail, but the extra points won't be rendered.

If successful, the **PolyBezier** function draws the Bézier curve(s) using the target DC's current pen, and then returns **TRUE**; otherwise, the return value is **FALSE**. For example, to render a single Bézier curve, you use the **PolyBezier** function as follows:

```
const int num_curves = 1;
const int num_points = (3 * num_curves) + 1;
const POINT points[] = {
   {100, 10},                  // starting point
   {10, 10}, {100, 100},       // control points
   {10, 100}                   // ending point
   };

HDC hDC = GetDC(hWnd);
try
{
   PolyBezier(hDC, points, num_points);
}
catch (...)
{
   ReleaseDC(hWnd, hDC);
}
ReleaseDC(hWnd, hDC);
```

Similarly, to render, for example, three Bézier curves, you use the **PolyBezier** function as follows:

```
const int num_curves = 3;
const int num_points = (3 * num_curves) + 1;
const POINT points[] = {
   {280, 10},                  // first curve starting point
   {235, 10}, {235, 100},      // first curve control points
   {190, 100},                 // first curve ending point and
                               // second curve starting point
   {145, 100}, {145, 190},     // second curve control points
   {100, 190},                 // second curve ending point and
                               // third curve starting point
   {55, 190}, {55, 280},       // third curve control points
   {10, 280},                  // third curve ending point
   };
```

```
HDC hDC = GetDC(hWnd);
try
{
   PolyBezier(hDC, points, num_points);
}
catch (...)
{
   ReleaseDC(hWnd, hDC);
}
ReleaseDC(hWnd, hDC);
```

Rendering a Rectangle

To render a rectangle, you use the **Rectangle** function:

```
BOOL Rectangle(
    IN HDC hdc,          // handle to the target device context
    IN int nLeftRect,    // x-coordinate of top-left corner
    IN int nTopRect,     // y-coordinate of top-left corner
    IN int nRightRect,   // x-coordinate of bottom-right corner
    IN int nBottomRect,  // y-coordinate of bottom-right corner
   );
```

The **hdc** parameter identifies the destination device context. The rectangle is outlined using this device context's current pen, and filled using its current brush.

***TIP:** If you don't want the rectangle filled, select the **NULL_BRUSH** stock object into the destination device context before calling the **Rectangle** function. Likewise, if you don't want the rectangle outlined, use the **NULL_PEN** stock object in a similar fashion.*

The top-left and bottom-right corners of the rectangle are specified, in logical units, by the **nLeftRect**, **nTopRect**, **nRightRect**, and **nBottomRect** parameters.

***NOTE:** The **Rectangle** function does not update the target device context's current position. If you need the current position updated, make an explicit call to the **MoveToEx** function.*

WARNING! On Windows 95 and Windows 98, the width and the height of the specified rectangle are limited to MAXSHORT.

If successful, the **Rectangle** function returns **TRUE**. If the function fails, the return value is **FALSE**. For example, to render a rectangle whose bounds are defined by the **RECT** structure **RBounds**:

```
HDC hDC = GetDC(hWnd);
try
{
   const RECT RBounds = {10, 10, 150, 100};
   Rectangle(
      hDC,
      RBounds.left, RBounds.top,
      RBounds.right, RBounds.bottom
      );
}
catch (...)
{
   ReleaseDC(hWnd, hDC);
}
ReleaseDC(hWnd, hDC);
```

Rendering a Rounded Rectangle

To render a rectangle whose corners are rounded, you use the **RoundRect** function:

```
BOOL RoundRect(
    IN HDC hdc,          // handle to the target device context
    IN int nLeftRect,    // x-coordinate of top-left corner
    IN int nTopRect,     // y-coordinate of top-left corner
    IN int nRightRect,   // x-coordinate of bottom-right corner
    IN int nBottomRect,  // y-coordinate of bottom-right corner
    IN int nWidth,       // horizontal extent of rounding
    IN int nHeight       // vertical extent of rounding
   );
```

The **hdc** parameter identifies the destination device context. The rectangle is outlined using this device context's current pen, and filled using its current brush.

***TIP:** If you don't want the rectangle filled, you can select the **NULL_BRUSH** stock object into the destination device context before calling the **RoundRect** function. Likewise, if you don't want the rectangle outlined, use the **NULL_PEN** stock object in a similar fashion.*

The top-left and bottom-right corners of the rectangle are specified, in logical units, by the **nLeftRect**, **nTopRect**, **nRightRect**, and **nBottomRect** parameters. The extent of the rectangle's corner-rounding is specified by the **nWidth** and **nHeight** parameters. These quantities specify the width and height of an ellipse whose curvature "shapes" the corners. Figure 5.20 illustrates the role of these parameters.

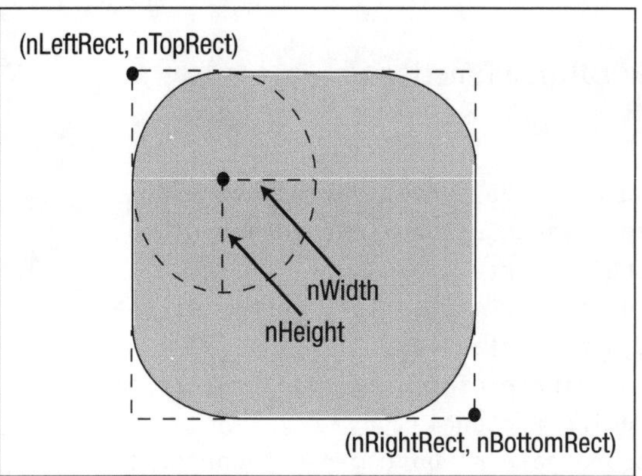

Figure 5.20 The effect (shaded region) of the RoundRect function and the role of its parameters.

NOTE: *The* ***RoundRect*** *function does not update the target device context's current position. If you need the current position updated, make an explicit call to the* ***MoveToEx*** *function.*

WARNING! On Windows 95 and Windows 98, the width and the height of the specified rectangle are limited to MAXSHORT.

If successful, the **Rectangle** function returns **TRUE**. If the function fails, the return value is **FALSE**. For example, to render a rectangle whose bounds are defined by the **RECT** structure **RBounds** and whose corners are rounded with a circle of radius 50 logical units:

```
HDC hDC = GetDC(hWnd);
try
{
   const RECT RBounds = {100, 100, 300, 300};
   const SIZE SCircle = {50, 50};
   RoundRect(
      hDC,
      RBounds.left, RBounds.top,
      RBounds.right, RBounds.bottom,
      SCircle.cx, SCircle.cy
      );
}
catch (...)
{
   ReleaseDC(hWnd, hDC);
}
ReleaseDC(hWnd, hDC);
```

Rendering an Ellipse

To render an ellipse, you use the **Ellipse** function:

```
BOOL Ellipse(
    IN HDC hdc,          // handle to the target device context
    IN int nLeftRect,    // x-coordinate of top-left corner of the
                         // bounding rectangle
    IN int nTopRect,     // y-coordinate of top-left corner of the
                         // bounding rectangle
    IN int nRightRect,   // x-coordinate of bottom-right corner of the
                         // bounding rectangle
    IN int nBottomRect,  // y-coordinate of bottom-right corner of the
                         // bounding rectangle
   );
```

The **hdc** parameter identifies the destination device context. The ellipse is outlined using this device context's current pen, and filled using its current brush.

TIP: *If you don't want the ellipse filled, you can select the* ***NULL_BRUSH*** *stock object into the destination device context before calling the* ***Ellipse*** *function. Likewise, if you don't want the ellipse outlined, use the* ***NULL_PEN*** *stock object in a similar fashion.*

The top-left and bottom-right corners of the ellipse's bounding rectangle are specified, in logical units, by the **nLeftRect**, **nTopRect**, **nRightRect**, and **nBottomRect** parameters. Figure 5.21 illustrates the role of these parameters; the shaded region depicts the rendered ellipse.

NOTE: *The* ***Ellipse*** *function does not update the target device context's current position. If you need the current position updated, make an explicit call to the* ***MoveToEx*** *function.*

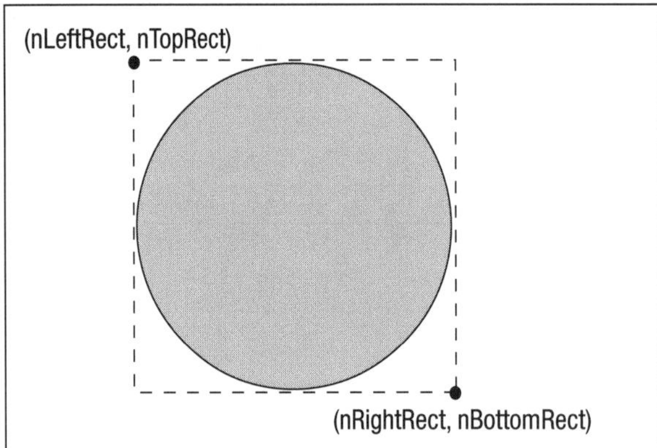

Figure 5.21 The effect (shaded region) of the **Ellipse** function and the role of its parameters.

WARNING! On Windows 95 and Windows 98, the width and the height of the specified bounding rectangle are limited to MAXSHORT.

If successful, the **Ellipse** function returns **TRUE**; otherwise, the function returns **FALSE**. For example, to render an ellipse whose bounding rectangle is specified by **RBounds**:

```
HDC hDC = GetDC(hWnd);
try
{
   const RECT RBounds = {10, 20, 200, 100};
   Ellipse(
      hDC,
      RBounds.left, RBounds.top,
      RBounds.right, RBounds.bottom
      );
}
catch (...)
{
   ReleaseDC(hWnd, hDC);
}
ReleaseDC(hWnd, hDC);
```

Rendering a Pie Slice

To render a pie slice (or the entire pie), you use the **Pie** function:

```
BOOL Pie(
    IN HDC hdc,          // handle to the target device context
    IN int nLeftRect,    // x-coordinate of top-left corner of the
                         // bounding rectangle
    IN int nTopRect,     // y-coordinate of top-left corner of the
                         // bounding rectangle
    IN int nRightRect,   // x-coordinate of bottom-right corner of the
                         // bounding rectangle
    IN int nBottomRect,  // y-coordinate of bottom-right corner of the
                         // bounding rectangle
    IN int nXRadial1,    // x-coordinate of the starting-radial ending point
    IN int nYRadial1,    // y-coordinate of the starting-radial ending point
    IN int nXRadial2,    // x-coordinate of the ending-radial ending point
    IN int nYRadial2     // y-coordinate of the ending-radial ending point
   );
```

The **hdc** parameter identifies the destination device context. The pie slice is outlined using this device context's current pen, and filled using its current brush.

*TIP: If you don't want the pie slice filled, you can select the **NULL_BRUSH** stock object into the destination device context before calling the **Pie** function. Likewise, if you don't want the pie outlined, use the **NULL_PEN** stock object in a similar fashion.*

The **nLeftRect**, **nTopRect**, **nRightRect**, and **nBottomRect** parameters specify, in logical units, the top-left and bottom-right corners of the bounding rectangle (of the ellipse from which the pie slice is cut). The starting point of the pie slice is determined by the intersection of the line drawn from the center of the ellipse to the point specified (in logical units) by the **nXRadial1** and **nYRadial1** parameters. Likewise, the ending point of the pie slice is determined by the intersection of the line drawn from the center of the ellipse to the point specified (in logical units) by the **nXRadial2** and **nYRadial2** parameters. Figure 5.22 illustrates the role of these parameters; the shaded region is the rendered pie slice when the target device context's arc direction is **AD_COUNTERCLOCKWISE**.

*NOTE: The **Pie** function does not update the target device context's current position. If you need the current position updated, make an explicit call to the **MoveToEx** function.*

WARNING! On Windows 95 and Windows 98, the width and the height of the specified bounding rectangle are limited to MAXSHORT.

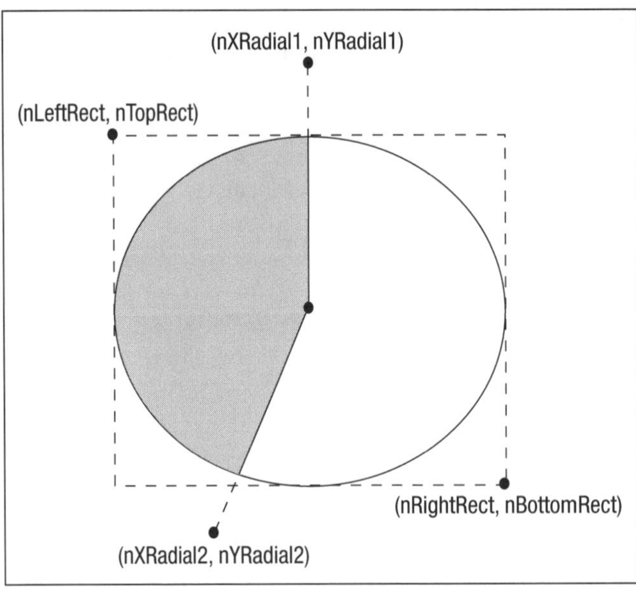

Figure 5.22 The effect (shaded region) of the **Pie** function and the role of its parameters when the **AD_COUNTERCLOCKWISE** arc direction is used.

The target device context's current arc direction governs the direction in which the arc of the pie slice is drawn. (See "Changing the Arc Direction.")

WARNING! On systems running Windows 95 or Windows 98, the arc direction cannot be changed; all arcs are drawn in a counterclockwise fashion.

If successful, the **Pie** function returns **TRUE**; otherwise, the return value is **FALSE**. For example, to render the pie slice cut from the lower half of a circle whose bounding rectangle is defined by **RBounds**:

```
HDC hDC = GetDC(hWnd);
try
{
   const RECT RBounds = {10, 10, 100, 100};
   const POINT PPie[] = {{10, 55}, {110, 55}};

   SetArcDirection(hDC, AD_COUNTERCLOCKWISE);
   Pie(
      hDC,
      RBounds.left, RBounds.top,
      RBounds.right, RBounds.bottom,
      PPie[0].x, PPie[0].y,
      PPie[1].x, PPie[1].y
      );
}
catch (...)
{
   ReleaseDC(hWnd, hDC);
}
ReleaseDC(hWnd, hDC);
```

Rendering an Arc

To render an arc, you use the **Arc** function:

```
BOOL Arc(
    IN HDC hdc,          // handle to the target device context
    IN int nLeftRect,    // x-coordinate of top-left corner of the
                         // bounding rectangle
    IN int nTopRect,     // y-coordinate of top-left corner of the
                         // bounding rectangle
    IN int nRightRect,   // x-coordinate of bottom-right corner of the
                         // bounding rectangle
    IN int nBottomRect,  // y-coordinate of bottom-right corner of the
                         // bounding rectangle
    IN int nXStartArc,   // x-coordinate of the starting-radial ending point
```

```
    IN int nYStartArc,  // y-coordinate of the starting-radial ending point
    IN int nXEndArc,    // x-coordinate of the ending-radial ending point
    IN int nYEndArc     // y-coordinate of the ending-radial ending point
  );
```

The **hdc** parameter identifies the destination device context. The **nLeftRect**, **nTopRect**, **nRightRect**, and **nBottomRect** parameters together specify the bounding rectangle of the ellipse from which the arc's curve is computed. The **nXStartArc** and **nYStartArc** parameters determine the arc's starting point, and the **nXEndArc** and **nYEndArc** parameters determine the arc's ending point.

***NOTE:** The **Arc** function does not update the target device context's current position. If you need the current position updated, use the **ArcTo** function instead. This latter function has the same signature and functionality as **Arc**, but **ArcTo** moves the target device context's current position to the endpoint of the arc.*

WARNING! On Windows 95 and Windows 98, the width and the height of the specified bounding rectangle are limited to MAXSHORT.

The starting and ending points of the arc are not directly specified by the **nXStartArc**, **nYStartArc**, **nXEndArc**, and **nYEndArc** parameters. Rather, these points are computed from the intersection of the ellipse's boundary and an imaginary line drawn from the center of the ellipse to the specified point (see Figure 5.23).

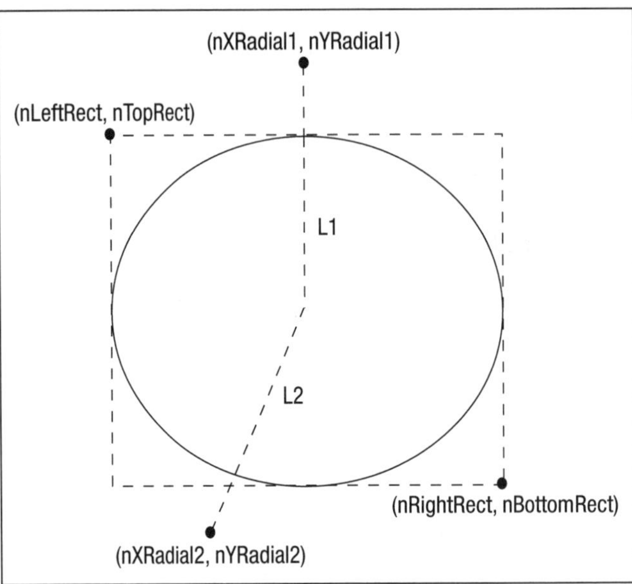

Figure 5.23 **The effect of the Arc function and the role of its parameters when the AD_COUNTERCLOCKWISE arc direction is used.**

The direction in which the arc is drawn is governed by the target device context's current arc direction. (See "Changing the Arc Direction.")

WARNING! On systems running Windows 95 or Windows 98, the arc direction cannot be changed; all arcs are drawn in a counterclockwise fashion.

Upon success, the **Arc** function returns **TRUE**; otherwise, the function returns **FALSE**. For example, to render the left half of a circle, you use the **Arc** function like so:

```
HDC hDC = GetDC(hWnd);
try
{
   RECT RBounds = {10, 10, 100, 100};
   const int center = static_cast<int>(
      0.5 * (RBounds.right - RBounds.left) +
      RBounds.left + 0.5
      );
   POINT PEnd1 = {center, RBounds.top};
   POINT PEnd2 = {center, RBounds.bottom};

   SetArcDirection(hDC, AD_COUNTERCLOCKWISE);
   Arc(
      hDC,
      RBounds.left, RBounds.top,
      RBounds.right, RBounds.bottom,
      PEnd1.x, PEnd1.y,
      PEnd2.x, PEnd2.y
      );
}
catch (...)
{
   ReleaseDC(hWnd, hDC);
}
ReleaseDC(hWnd, hDC);
```

Rendering a Chord

To render a chord, you use the **Chord** function:

```
BOOL Chord(
    IN HDC hdc,          // handle to the target device context
    IN int nLeftRect,    // x-coordinate of top-left corner of the
                         // bounding rectangle
    IN int nTopRect,     // y-coordinate of top-left corner of the
                         // bounding rectangle
```

```
    IN int nRightRect,  // x-coordinate of bottom-right corner of the
                        // bounding rectangle
    IN int nBottomRect, // y-coordinate of bottom-right corner of the
                        // bounding rectangle
    IN int nXRadial1,   // x-coordinate of the starting-radial ending point
    IN int nYRadial1,   // y-coordinate of the starting-radial ending point
    IN int nXRadial2,   // x-coordinate of the ending-radial ending point
    IN int nYRadial2    // y-coordinate of the ending-radial ending point
);
```

The **hdc** parameter identifies the destination device context. The chord is outlined using this device context's current pen, and filled using its current brush.

__TIP:__ If you don't want the chord filled, you can select the __NULL_BRUSH__ stock object into the destination device context before calling the __Chord__ function. Likewise, if you don't want the chord outlined, use the __NULL_PEN__ stock object in a similar fashion.

The **nLeftRect**, **nTopRect**, **nRightRect**, and **nBottomRect** parameters specify, in logical units, the bounding rectangle of the ellipse from which the chord is cut.

WARNING! On Windows 95 and Windows 98, the width and the height of the specified bounding rectangle are limited to MAXSHORT.

The starting point of the chord's parent pie section is determined by the intersection of the line (*L1*) drawn from the center of the ellipse to the point specified (in logical units) by the **nXRadial1** and **nYRadial1** parameters. Likewise, the ending point of the chord's parent pie section is determined by the intersection of the line (*L2*) drawn from the center of the ellipse to the point specified (in logical units) by the **nXRadial2** and **nYRadial2** parameters. The chord itself is cut from the outer portion of its parent pie section, defined by the intersection of this pie section and the line connecting the points where *L1* and *L2* intersect the ellipse. Figure 5.24 illustrates the role of these parameters; the shaded region depicts the chord that's rendered when the target device context's arc direction is **AD_COUNTERCLOCKWISE**.

__NOTE:__ The __Chord__ function does not update the target device context's current position. If you need the current position updated, make an explicit call to the __MoveToEx__ function.

The target device context's current arc direction governs the direction in which the arc of the chord's parent pie section is drawn. (See "Changing the Arc Direction.")

WARNING! On systems running Windows 95 or Windows 98, the arc direction cannot be changed; all arcs are drawn in a counterclockwise fashion.

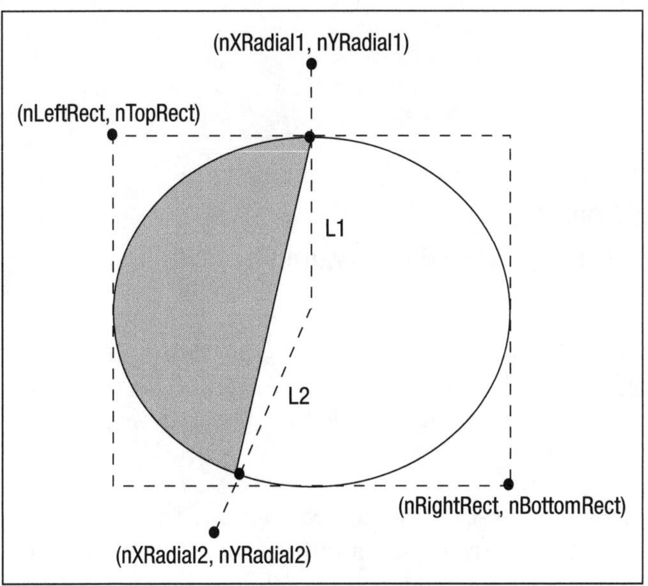

Figure 5.24 The effect (shaded region) of the Chord function and the role of its parameters when the AD_COUNTERCLOCKWISE arc direction is used.

Upon success, the **Chord** function returns **TRUE**; otherwise, the return value is **FALSE**. For example, to render the chord cut from the lower portion of an ellipse whose bounding rectangle is defined by **RBounds**, where the arc of the parent pie section is defined by the points **PPie**:

```
HDC hDC = GetDC(hWnd);
try
{
   const RECT RBounds = {10, 20, 200, 100};
   const POINT PPie[] = {
      {RBounds.left, RBounds.bottom},
      {RBounds.right, RBounds.bottom}
      };

   SetArcDirection(hDC, AD_COUNTERCLOCKWISE);
   Chord(
      hDC,
      RBounds.left, RBounds.top,
      RBounds.right, RBounds.bottom,
      PPie[0].x, PPie[0].y,
      PPie[1].x, PPie[1].y
      );
}
```

```
catch (...)
{
   ReleaseDC(hWnd, hDC);
}
ReleaseDC(hWnd, hDC);
```

Rendering a Custom Polygon

To render an arbitrary polygon, you use the **Polygon** function:

```
BOOL Polygon(
    IN HDC hdc,                  // handle to the target device context
    IN CONST POINT *lpPoints,    // pointer to an array of vertices
    IN int nCount                // number of POINTs in the vertex array
   );
```

The **hdc** parameter identifies the destination device context. The polygon is outlined using this device context's current pen, and filled using its current brush. For complex or overlapping polygons, the areas are filled according to the target device context's current filling mode.

*TIP: If you don't want the polygon filled, you can select the **NULL_BRUSH** stock object into the destination device context before calling the **Polygon** function. Likewise, if you don't want the polygon outlined, use the **NULL_PEN** stock object in a similar fashion.*

The vertices of the polygon are specified by the **lpPoints** parameter, which is a pointer to an array of **POINT** structures (one for each vertex). Because the **Polygon** function automatically closes the polygon, the last **POINT** structure in this array does not have to be identical to the first **POINT** structure. The **nCount** parameter specifies the number of **POINT** structures that the **lpPoints** array contains.

*NOTE: The **Polygon** function does not update the target device context's current position. If you need the current position updated, make an explicit call to the **MoveToEx** function.*

WARNING! On Windows 95 and Windows 98, the number of points is limited to 16,000. If you're rendering with a geometric pen, this limit can be much lower if the target device does not support wide lines (see "Retrieving the Line Capabilities of a Device"). The Polygon function won't fail, but the extra points won't be rendered.

If successful, the **Polygon** function returns **TRUE**; otherwise, the return value is **FALSE**. For example, to draw an isosceles triangle, you use the **Polygon** function like so:

```
HDC hDC = GetDC(hWnd);
try
{
   // triangle vertices
   const POINT vertices[] = {
      {10, 110}, {110, 10}, {210, 110}
      };
   // render the triangle
   Polygon(hDC, vertices, 3);
}
catch (...)
{
   ReleaseDC(hWnd, hDC);
}
ReleaseDC(hWnd, hDC);
```

Similarly, to render the color and shape of a stop sign (a red octagon), you use the **Polygon** function as follows:

```
const COLORREF clrRed = PALETTERGB(255, 0, 0);
HBRUSH hRedBrush = CreateSolidBrush(clrRed);

HDC hDC = GetDC(hWnd);
HBRUSH hOldBrush = static_cast<HBRUSH>(
   SelectObject(hDC, hRedBrush)
   );
try
{
   // octagon vertices
   const POINT vertices[] = {
      {10, 45}, {45, 10}, {95, 10}, {130, 45},
      {130, 95}, {95, 130}, {45, 130}, {10, 95}
      };
   // render the octagon
   Polygon(hDC, vertices, 8);
}
catch (...)
{
   DeleteObject(SelectObject(hDC, hOldBrush));
   ReleaseDC(hWnd, hDC);
}
DeleteObject(SelectObject(hDC, hOldBrush));
ReleaseDC(hWnd, hDC);
```

Rendering a Series of Custom Polygons

To render a series of arbitrary polygons, you use the **PolyPolygon** function:

```
BOOL PolyPolygon(
    IN HDC hdc,                    // handle to the target device context
    IN CONST POINT *lpPoints,      // pointer to an array of vertices
    IN CONST INT *lpPolyCounts,    // pointer to an array of INTs that
                                   // indicate the count of vertices for
                                   // each polygon
    IN int nCount                  // total number of polygons
   );
```

The **hdc** parameter identifies the destination device context. The polygons are outlined using this device context's current pen, and filled using its current brush. For complex or overlapping polygons, the areas are filled according to the target device context's current filling mode.

***TIP:** If you don't want the polygons filled, you can select the **NULL_BRUSH** stock object into the destination device context before calling the **PolyPolygon** function. Likewise, if you don't want the polygons outlined, use the **NULL_PEN** stock object in a similar fashion.*

The **lpPoints** parameter points to an array of **POINT** structures that define the vertices for all the polygons. The **PolyPolygon** function uses the values of the array specified by the **lpPolyCounts** parameter to identify which of these **POINT** structures corresponds to which polygon. Because the function automatically closes each polygon, the last **POINT** structure for a particular polygon does not have to be identical to its first **POINT** structure. The **nCount** parameter indicates the total number of polygons. For example, if you need to render a hexagon and a triangle, the **lpPoints** array should contain a total of nine **POINT**s: six for the hexagon and three for the triangle. In this case, the **lpPolyCounts** array should contain two entries, with a value of six in the first position and a value of three in the second position. Accordingly, you set **nCount** to two, the total number of polygons.

***NOTE:** The **PolyPolygon** function does not update the target device context's current position. If you need the current position updated, make an explicit call to the **MoveToEx** function.*

WARNING! On Windows 95 and Windows 98, the number of points is limited to 16,000. If you're rendering with a geometric pen, this limit can be much lower if the target device does not support wide lines (see "Retrieving the Line Capabilities of a Device"). The PolyPolygon function won't fail, but the extra points won't be rendered.

Upon success, the **PolyPolygon** function returns **TRUE**. If the function fails, the return value is **FALSE**. For example, to render a hexagon, a triangle, and a diamond, you use the **PolyPolygon** function as follows:

```
HDC hDC = GetDC(hWnd);
try
{
   const int num_polygons = 3;
   const POINT poly_vertices[] = {
      // hexagon vertices
      {10, 45}, {70, 10}, {130, 45},
      {130, 95}, {70, 130}, {10, 95},
      // triangle vertices
      {100, 100}, {150, 10}, {210, 110},
      // diamond vertices
      {180, 80}, {260, 0}, {340, 80}, {260, 160}
      };

   // the number of vertices for each polygon
   const int num_verts_per_polygon[] = {6, 3, 4};

   // set to fill each polygon completely
   SetPolyFillMode(hDC, WINDING);

   // render the polygons
   PolyPolygon(
      hDC,
      poly_vertices,
      num_verts_per_polygon,
      num_polygons
      );
}
catch (...)
{
   ReleaseDC(hWnd, hDC);
}
ReleaseDC(hWnd, hDC);
```

Filling the Interior of a Rectangle with a Custom Brush

To fill a rectangular area with a particular brush object, you use the **FillRect** function:

```
int FillRect(
    IN HDC hDC,             // handle to the target device context
    IN CONST RECT *lpcrc,   // pointer to const RECT structure that defines
                            // the area to fill
```

```
    IN HBRUSH hbr           // handle to the logical brush object
                            // to fill with
   );
```

The **hDC** parameter identifies the device context to which the rectangular area, defined (in logical units) by the **lprc** parameter, will be filled with the brush object whose handle is specified by the **hbr** parameter.

***NOTE:** The **FillRect** function fills up to, but not including, the right and bottom edges of the rectangle specified by the **lprc** parameter.*

Unlike the **Rectangle** function, the **FillRect** function only fills the specified rectangular area; it does not outline the rectangle with the current pen. Moreover, **FillRect** ignores the drawing mode of the destination device context; it always uses **R2_COPYPEN**. By far, however, the main advantage of using **FillRect** over the **Rectangle** or **PatBlt** functions comes from the fact that **FillRect** will fill an area with a *specific* brush, not with the brush that's currently selected into the target device context. This feature is especially useful when you need to fill multiple areas with various colors.

***TIP:** If you need to fill a rectangular area by using a specific raster-operation mode, use the **PatBlt** function. Before calling this function, you'll have to select the desired brush object into the target device context.*

Upon success, the **FillRect** function returns a non-zero value; otherwise, the return value is zero. For example, to fill a rectangular area, defined by **RBounds**, with a red solid brush object:

```
const COLORREF clrRed = PALETTERGB(255, 0, 0);
HBRUSH hRedBrush = CreateSolidBrush(clrRed);
HDC hDC = GetDC(hWnd);
try
{
   const RECT RBounds = {10, 10, 200, 150};
   FillRect(hDC, &RBounds, hRedBrush);
}
catch (...)
{
   DeleteObject(hRedBrush);
   ReleaseDC(hWnd, hDC);
}
DeleteObject(hRedBrush);
ReleaseDC(hWnd, hDC);
```

Recall, you can assign a system-element color index that's offset by 1 (e.g., **COLOR_WINDOW** + 1) to the **hbrBackground** data member of the **WNDCLASS** structure that's used to register a window class. This is possible because a window's default window procedure relies on the **FillRect** function to fill the background of the window. Following this logic, the **hbr** parameter does not have to be a handle to a brush object; you can, instead, pass a system element color index, offset by positive one. For example, to fill a rectangular area (**RBounds**) with the color that's used to paint the background of tooltip controls:

```
HDC hDC = GetDC(hWnd);
try
{
   const RECT RBounds = {10, 10, 100, 50};
   FillRect(hDC, &RBounds, reinterpret_cast<HBRUSH>(COLOR_INFOBK + 1));
}
catch (...)
{
   ReleaseDC(hWnd, hDC);
}
ReleaseDC(hWnd, hDC);
```

Outlining a Rectangle with a Custom Brush

To render the outline of a rectangle with a particular brush object, you use the **FrameRect** function:

```
int FrameRect(
    IN HDC hDC,              // handle to the target device context
    IN CONST RECT *lpcrc,    // pointer to const RECT structure that defines
                             // the area to frame
    IN HBRUSH hbr            // handle to the logical brush object that's
                             // used to render the outline
   );
```

The **hDC** parameter identifies the device context to which the outline of the rectangle, defined (in logical units) by the **lprc** parameter, will be rendered, using the brush object whose handle is specified by the **hbr** parameter.

***NOTE:** The **FrameRect** function draws an outline that's always one logical unit wide. If you need a thicker border, use the **FillRect** function four times (once for each edge).*

The **FrameRect** function uses the **R2_COPYPEN** binary-raster-operation mode to render the outline of the specified rectangle. The drawing mode of the destination device context is ignored.

***TIP:** If you need to outline a rectangle by using a specific raster-operation mode, use the **PatBlt** function for each edge. Before calling this function, you'll have to select the desired brush object into the target device context.*

If successful, the **FrameRect** function returns a non-zero value; otherwise, the return value is zero. For example, to draw the outline of a rectangle (**RFrame**) with a green solid brush object:

```
const COLORREF clrGreen = PALETTERGB(0, 255, 0);
const HBRUSH hGreenBrush = CreateSolidBrush(clrGreen);
const HDC hDC = GetDC(hWnd);
try
{
   const RECT RFrame = {10, 20, 100, 250};
   FrameRect(hDC, &RFrame, hGreenBrush);
}
catch (...)
{
   DeleteObject(hGreenBrush);
   ReleaseDC(hWnd, hDC);
}
DeleteObject(hGreenBrush);
ReleaseDC(hWnd, hDC);
```


Inverting the Pixels within a Rectangle

To invert the pixels that lie within a rectangular area, you use the **InvertRect** function:

```
BOOL InvertRect(
    IN HDC hDC,             // handle to the target device context
    IN CONST RECT *lprc     // pointer to const RECT structure that defines
                            // the area to invert
   );
```

The **hDC** parameter identifies the destination device context. The logical **NOT** operator is used to invert the colors within the rectangular area specified, in logical units, by the **lprc** parameter. This operation is equivalent to using the **PatBlt** function with the **DSTINVERT** ROP3 code.

If successful, the **InvertRect** function returns **TRUE**; otherwise, the return value is **FALSE**. For example, to invert the pixels within the rectangular area defined by the **RECT** structure **RInvert**:

```
HDC hDC = GetDC(hWnd);
try
{
```

```
   const RECT RInvert = {10, 10, 100, 50};
   InvertRect(hDC, &RInvert);
}
catch (...)
{
   ReleaseDC(hWnd, hDC);
}
ReleaseDC(hWnd, hDC);
```

Consequently, calling the **InvertRect** function again (for the same rectangle) results in the "inverse of the inverse," which produces the original colors. This result is useful if you need to momentarily highlight a particular area. For example, the following utility function, **FlashRect**, uses the **InvertRect** function to "flash" a rectangular area "on" and "off":

```
void FlashRect(IN const HDC hDC, IN const RECT& RHighlight,
   IN int num_times = 4, IN int ms_delay = 100)
{
   // ensure that we don't end on an inverse
   if (num_times % 2 != 0) ++num_times;

   for (int index = 0; index < num_times; ++index)
   {
      InvertRect(hDC, &RHighlight);

      // allow important queued messages to be processed
      MSG msg;
      if (PeekMessage(&msg, NULL, 0, 0, PM_REMOVE))
      {
         TranslateMessage(&msg);
         DispatchMessage(&msg);
      }
      Sleep(ms_delay);
   }
}
```


Shading a Rectangle (or a Triangle)

To render a shaded rectangle, you use the **GradientFill** function (Windows 98 and Windows 2000 only):

```
BOOL GradientFill(
   IN HDC hdc,              // handle to the target device context
   IN PTRIVERTEX pVertex,   // pointer to an array of vertices
   IN ULONG dwNumVertex,    // number of TRIVERTEXs in the vertices array
```

```
    IN PVOID pMesh,         // pointer to an array of GRADIENT_RECT
                            // structures that define the connectivity mesh
    IN ULONG dwNumMesh,     // number of GRADIENT_RECTs in the mesh array
    IN ULONG dwMode         // horizontal or vertical gradient fill mode
  );
```

The **hdc** parameter identifies the destination device context. The **pVertex** parameter specifies an array of **TRIVERTEX** structures, each of which defines the position and color intensity of the rectangle's vertices. To fill a single rectangle, this array should contain two **TRIVERTEX** structures: one for the rectangle's upper-left corner, and one for the rectangle's lower-right corner. For multiple rectangles, **pVertex** should contain two **TRIVERTEX** structures for each rectangle. The **dwNumVertex** parameter specifies the number of vertices (i.e., **TRIVERTEX** structures) that the **pVertex** array contains. The **pMesh** parameter specifies the indices of the **pVertex** array that contains the rectangle's corners. This parameter is specified as an array of **GRADIENT_RECT** structures, one for each rectangle. The **dwNumMesh** parameter specifies the number of **GRADIENT_RECT** structures that the **pMesh** array contains. The **dwMode** parameter controls the direction of the shading. When this parameter is set to **GRADIENT_FILL_RECT_H** (0), the rectangle is shaded in the horizontal direction. When this parameter is set to **GRADIENT_FILL_RECT_V** (1), the rectangle is shaded in the vertical direction.

The **GradientFill** function can also be used to render a shaded triangle. In this case, each set of three **TRIVERTEX** structures in the **dwVertex** array specifies a triangle. Also, the **dwMesh** parameter must point to an array of **GRADIENT_TRIANGLE** structures, and the **dwMode** parameter must be set to **GRADIENT_FILL_TRIANGLE**.

If successful, the **GradientFill** function returns **TRUE**; otherwise, the return value is **FALSE**. For example, to shade a rectangle from black to white in the vertical direction, you use the **GradientFill** function like so:

```
TRIVERTEX vertices[2];
vertices[0].x = 10;
vertices[0].y = 10;
vertices[0].Red = 0;
vertices[0].Green = 0;
vertices[0].Blue = 0;
vertices[0].Alpha = 0;

vertices[1].x = 200;
vertices[1].y = 100;
vertices[1].Red = 255;
```

```
vertices[1].Green = 255;
vertices[1].Blue = 255;
vertices[0].Alpha = 0;

GRADIENT_RECT gr = {0, 1};
GradientFill(hDC, vertices, 2, &gr, 1, GRADIENT_FILL_RECT_V);
```

Similarly, to shade this same rectangle in the horizontal direction, you use the **GradientFill** function as follows (here, passing the **GRADIENT_FILL_RECT_H** identifier as the **dwMode** parameter):

```
TRIVERTEX vertices[2];
vertices[0].x = 10;
vertices[0].y = 10;
vertices[0].Red = 0;
vertices[0].Green = 0;
vertices[0].Blue = 0;
vertices[0].Alpha = 0;

vertices[1].x = 200;
vertices[1].y = 100;
vertices[1].Red = 255;
vertices[1].Green = 255;
vertices[1].Blue = 255;
vertices[0].Alpha = 0;

GRADIENT_RECT gr = {0, 1};
GradientFill(hDC, vertices, 2, &gr, 1, GRADIENT_FILL_RECT_H);
```


Hit-Testing Lines, Curves, and Shapes

Hit-testing is the process of determining whether a point lies within or on the boundary of an output primitive. In this section, we'll look at several user-defined functions that can be used to hit-test each of the GDI's seven types of output primitives. Each of these functions assumes an **MM_TEXT** mapping mode.

Hit-Testing Lines

To determine if a specific point lies on a particular line segment, you use the **PtOnLineSegment** application-defined function:

```
#include <math.h>
BOOL PtOnLineSegment(
    IN const POINT& PHit,    // the point in question
```

```
    IN const POINT& PEnd1,    // first endpoint of the line segment
    IN const POINT& PEnd2,    // second endpoint of the line segment
    IN int tolerance = 0      // sensitivity
   )
{
   // precalculations
   const int dXLine = PEnd2.x - PEnd1.x;
   const int dYLine = PEnd2.y - PEnd1.y;

   // TEST 1A:
   // if the point is beyond the first endpoint of
   // the line segment, the point cannot be on the line
   const int dX1 = PEnd1.x - PHit.x;
   const int dY1 = PEnd1.y - PHit.y;
   if ((dXLine > 0 && dX1 > 0) || (dYLine < 0 && dY1 < 0) ||
       (dXLine < 0 && dX1 < 0) || (dYLine > 0 && dY1 > 0))
   {
      return (sqrt((dX1 * dX1) + (dY1 * dY1)) <= tolerance);
   }

   // TEST 1B:
   // if the point is beyond the second endpoint of
   // the line segment, the point cannot be on the line
   const int dX2 = PEnd2.x - PHit.x;
   const int dY2 = PEnd2.y - PHit.y;
   if ((dXLine > 0 && dX2 < 0) || (dYLine < 0 && dY2 > 0) ||
       (dXLine < 0 && dX2 > 0) || (dYLine > 0 && dY2 < 0))
   {
      return (sqrt((dX2 * dX2) + (dY2 * dY2)) <= tolerance);
   }

   // TEST 2:
   // if the slopes are equal, within
   // tolerance, the point is on the line
   tolerance *= sqrt((dXLine * dXLine) + (dYLine * dYLine));
   const int diff = (dY1 * dX2) - (dY2 * dX1);
   return (diff >= -tolerance && diff <= tolerance);
}
```

The **PHit** parameter is specified as the point that you want to test for inclusion on the line segment. The endpoints of this line segment are specified by the **PEnd1** and **PEnd2** parameters. The **tolerance** parameter is used to add a bit of leeway to the test; this leeway is especially important when the function is used in response to mouse messages. This parameter is specified as the allowable distance by which **PHit** can be offset from the line.

The **PtOnLineSegment** function returns **TRUE** if the point is on the line segment, and **FALSE** otherwise. For example, to determine if the point **PHit** is on the line segment defined by the points **PLine**:

```
const POINT PHit = {50, 50};
const POINT PLine[] = {{0, 0}, {100, 100}};
BOOL IsHit = PtOnLineSegment(PHit, PLine[0], PLine[1]);
```

In the implementation of the **PtOnLineSegment** function, the code marked **TEST 1A** and **TEST 1B** tests whether **PHit** is beyond the bounds of **PEnd1** and **PEnd2**, respectively, taking the **tolerance** specification into account. Specifically, if the point is beyond either endpoint, the function returns **TRUE** if the distance from the point to the closest endpoint is within tolerance, and **FALSE** otherwise. The code marked **TEST 2** tests the slopes for equality (within tolerance). For this comparison, the slopes aren't actually computed; rather, the relation presented in Equation 5.1 (see "Hit-Testing Lines" in the "In Depth" section) is tested to avoid division by zero. In addition, the value of the **tolerance** parameter is scaled according to Equation 5.2.

As I mentioned, the **tolerance** parameter is useful when the **PtOnLineSegment** function is used to hit-test a line segment (i.e., in response to mouse messages). Rarely will the user be able to click exactly on a line segment, so the **tolerance** parameter provides a bit of flexibility to the test; this is also handy when you're hit-testing wide lines.

Hit-Testing Bézier Curves

To determine if a point lies on a Bézier curve, you use the **PtOnBezierCurve** application-defined function:

```
#include <math.h>
BOOL PtOnBezierCurve(
    IN const POINT& PHit,      // the point in question
    IN const POINT* PCurve,    // the endpoints and control points
    IN int tolerance = 1,      // sensitivity
   )
{
   // TEST 1:
   // test for PHit near an endpoint or control point
   for (int index = 0; index < 4; ++index)
   {
      const int dX = PHit.x - PCurve[index].x;
      const int dY = PHit.y - PCurve[index].y;
      if (sqrt((dX * dX) + (dY * dY)) <= tolerance)
      {
```

```
      return TRUE;
   }
}

// compute the total (line-segmented) curve distance
double curve_dist = 0;
for (int seg = 0; seg < 3; ++seg)
{
   const int dXseg = PCurve[seg].x - PCurve[seg + 1].x;
   const int dYseg = PCurve[seg].y - PCurve[seg + 1].y;
   curve_dist += sqrt((dXseg * dXseg) + (dYseg * dYseg));
}
// base the number of time-steps on the curve distance
double time_step = 1.0 / curve_dist;

// TEST 2:
// test for PHit on the curve using the parametric equations
for (double t = 0.0; t < 1.0; t += time_step)
{
   // precalculations
   const double t_squared = t * t;
   const double one_minus_t = (1.0 - t);
   const double one_minus_t_squared = one_minus_t * one_minus_t;

   const double c1 = one_minus_t_squared * one_minus_t;
   const double c2 = 3 * t * one_minus_t_squared;
   const double c3 = 3 * t_squared * one_minus_t;
   const double c4 = t_squared * t;

   // compute x(t)
   const double xt =
      (c1 * PCurve[0].x) + (c2 * PCurve[1].x) +
      (c3 * PCurve[2].x) + (c4 * PCurve[3].x);

   // test for PHit.x equal to x(t), within tolerance
   const double dX = PHit.x - xt;
   if (dX >= -tolerance && dX <= tolerance)
   {
      // compute y(t)
      const double yt =
         (c1 * PCurve[0].y) + (c2 * PCurve[1].y) +
         (c3 * PCurve[2].y) + (c4 * PCurve[3].y);

      // test for PHit.y equal to y(t), within tolerance
      const double dY = PHit.y - yt;
      if (dY >= -tolerance && dY <= tolerance) return TRUE;
```

```
      }
   }
   return FALSE;
}
```

The **PHit** parameter is specified as the point that you want to test for inclusion on the Bézier curve. The endpoints and control points of this curve are specified by the **PCurve** parameter, which is a pointer to an array of four **POINT** structures. The first and last **POINT** structures in this array define the endpoints, while the second and third **POINT** structures define the curve's control points. The **tolerance** parameter is used to control the sensitivity of the test; this is useful when the function is used for hit-testing (i.e., in response to mouse messages). Because the **PtOnBezierCurve** function relies on floating-point arithmetic, the default value of this parameter is set to 1 (as opposed to zero for the **PtOnLineSegment** function).

If the specified point lines on the Bézier curve, the **PtOnBezierCurve** function returns **TRUE**; otherwise, the return value is **FALSE**. For example, to determine if point **PHit** lies on the Bézier curve defined by the points **PCurve**:

```
const POINT PHit = {50, 155};
const POINT PCurve[] = {
   {0, 20}, {20, 200}, {80, 200}, {100, 20}
   };
BOOL IsHit = PtOnBezierCurve(PHit, PCurve);
```

In the implementation of the **PtOnBezierCurve** function, the code marked **TEST 1** tests whether the distance from the point **PHit** to any of the curve's endpoints or control points is within tolerance. This test simply eliminates the (relatively expensive) parametric-equation-based test if **PHit** is close to any of the known points. If **TEST 1** fails, the function computes the **time_step** variable that's used in the code marked **TEST 2**. This value determines the "granularity" of the Bézier curve approximation (i.e., the number of discrete points that the Bézier curve is divided into). For each **time-step** variable, the code marked **TEST 2** computes the point on the Bézier curve, and then tests this point for (within tolerance) equality to **PHit**.

The **tolerance** parameter is useful when the **PtOnBezierCurve** function is used to hit-test a curve (i.e., in response to mouse messages). In most cases, the user won't be able to click exactly on the curve, so the **tolerance** parameter provides a bit of flexibility to the test; this is also useful when you're hit-testing wide curves. For more information on hit-testing curves, refer to "Hit-Testing Curves" in the "In Depth" section.

Hit-Testing Ellipses

To determine if a specific point lies in an ellipse (or on its boundary), you use the **PtInEllipse** application-defined function:

```
#include <math.h>
BOOL PtInEllipse(
    IN const POINT& PHit,         // the point in question
    IN const RECT& RBounds,       // the ellipse's bounding rectangle
    IN int tolerance = 0          // sensitivity
   )
{
   const float a = 0.5 * (RBounds.right - RBounds.left) + tolerance;
   const float b = 0.5 * (RBounds.bottom - RBounds.top) + tolerance;

   const int X = PHit.x - (a + RBounds.left - tolerance);
   const int Y = PHit.y - (b + RBounds.top - tolerance);

   return (((X * X) / (a * a)) + ((Y * Y) / (b * b)) <= 1);
}
```


The **PHit** parameter is specified as the point that you want to test for inclusion within the ellipse (or on its boundary). The bounding rectangle of this ellipse is specified by the **RBounds** parameter. The **tolerance** parameter is used to add a bit of leeway to the test. This parameter is specified as the allowable distance (in the x- or y-direction) by which **PHit** can be offset from the ellipse's boundary.

TIP: *The* ***tolerance*** *parameter is useful when the* ***PtInEllipse*** *function is used to hit-test an ellipse (i.e., in response to mouse messages). Specifically, you'll want to specify this parameter when the rendered ellipse is particularly small or when the ellipse is outlined with a thick pen.*

The **PtInEllipse** function returns **TRUE** if the point is in the ellipse or on its boundary, and **FALSE** otherwise. For example, to determine if the point **PHit** is on the ellipse defined by the rectangle **RBounds**:

```
const POINT PHit = {11, 11};
const RECT RBounds = {10, 10, 200, 100};
BOOL IsHit = PtInEllipse(PHit, REllipse);
```

The logic behind the **PtInEllipse** function comes from the standard equation of an ellipse (see Equation 5.2). The **tolerance** value is taken into account by "inflating" the ellipse's bounding rectangle before the equation is used. For more information on hit-testing ellipses, refer to "Hit-Testing Ellipses" in the "In Depth" section.

Hit-Testing Pie Slices

To determine if a specific point lies in a pie slice (or on its boundary), you use the **PtInPieSlice** application-defined function:

```
#include <math.h>
BOOL PtInPieSlice(
    IN const POINT& PHit,        // the point in question
    IN const RECT& RBounds,      // the ellipse's bounding rectangle
    IN const POINT& PRadial1,    // the endpoint of the starting radial
    IN const POINT& PRadial2,    // the endpoint of the ending radial
    IN int tolerance = 0,        // sensitivity
    IN BOOL clockwise = FALSE    // arc direction
   )
{
   const float a = 0.5 * (RBounds.right - RBounds.left) + tolerance;
   const float b = 0.5 * (RBounds.bottom - RBounds.top) + tolerance;

   const POINT PCenter = {
      a + RBounds.left - tolerance,
      b + RBounds.top - tolerance
      };
   const int X = PHit.x - PCenter.x;
   const int Y = PHit.y - PCenter.y;
   if (X == 0 && Y == 0) return TRUE;

   // if the point is in the ellipse
   if (((X * X) / (a * a)) + ((Y * Y) / (b * b)) <= 1)
   {
      // if the point is on either radial line segment
      const POINT PLine1[] = {
         {PRadial1.x , PRadial1.y},
         {PCenter.x, PCenter.y}
         };
      const POINT PLine2[] = {
         {PRadial2.x, PRadial2.y},
         {PCenter.x, PCenter.y}
         };
      if (PtOnLineSegment(PHit, PLine1, tolerance) ||
           PtOnLineSegment(PHit, PLine2, tolerance))
      {
         return TRUE;
      }

      double theta1 =
         atan2(
```

```
                PCenter.y - PRadial1.y,
                PRadial1.x - PCenter.x
                );
        double theta2 =
            atan2(
                PCenter.y - PRadial2.y,
                PRadial2.x - PCenter.x
                );
        double thetaHit = atan2(-Y, X);

        if (theta1 < 0) theta1 += (2 * M_PI);
        if (theta2 < 0) theta2 += (2 * M_PI);
        if (thetaHit < 0) thetaHit += (2 * M_PI);

        // determine if the point is within the region
        // defined by the starting and ending angles
        if (theta1 == theta2) return TRUE;
        if (theta2 < theta1) theta2 += (2 * M_PI);
        if (thetaHit < theta1) thetaHit += (2 * M_PI);
        return (clockwise ^ (thetaHit > theta1 && thetaHit < theta2));
    }
    return FALSE;
}
```


The **PHit** parameter is specified as the point that you want to test for inclusion within the pie slice (or on its boundary). The bounding rectangle of the pie's parent ellipse is specified by the **RBounds** parameter. The **PRadial1** and **PRadial2** parameters specify the endpoint of the starting and ending interval-defining line segments, respectively. (The starting point of each line segment is the ellipse's center point.)

WARNING! The PtInPieSlice function assumes that PRadial1 and PRadial2 are beyond the bounds of the parent ellipse.

The **tolerance** parameter is used to add a bit of leeway to the test. This parameter is specified as the allowable distance (in the x- or y-direction) by which **PHit** can be offset from the bounds of the pie slice.

__TIP:__ The __tolerance__ parameter is useful when the __PtInPieSlice__ function is used to hit-test a pie slice (i.e., in response to mouse messages). Specifically, you'll want to specify this parameter when the rendered wedge is particularly small or when the wedge is outlined with a thick pen.

The **PtInPieSlice** function returns **TRUE** if the point is in the ellipse or on its boundary, and **FALSE** otherwise. For example, to determine if the point **PHit** is in the pie slice whose parent ellipse is defined by the rectangle **RBounds** and whose interval is defined by **PRadial1** and **PRadial2**:

```
const POINT PHit = {190, 50};
const POINT PRadial1 = {400, 20};
const POINT PRadial2 = {200, 300};
const RECT RBounds = {40, 10, 300, 200};
BOOL IsHit = PtInPieSlice(PHit, RBounds, PRadial1, PRadial2);
```

The logic behind the **PtInPieSlice** function comes from the standard equation of an ellipse (see Equation 5.2) and the angles formed by the radials and the line segment that's defined by the ellipse's center point and the point in question. The **tolerance** value is taken into account by "inflating" the ellipse's bounding rectangle before the equation is used. For more information on hit-testing pie slices, refer to "Hit-Testing Pie Slices" in the "In Depth" section.

Hit-Testing Arcs

To determine if a specific point lies on an arc, you use the **PtOnArc** application-defined function:

```
#include <math.h>
BOOL PtOnArc(
    IN const POINT& PHit,           // the point in question
    IN const RECT& RBounds,         // the ellipse's bounding rectangle
    IN const POINT& PRadial1,       // the endpoint of the starting radial
    IN const POINT& PRadial2,       // the endpoint of the ending radial
    IN int tolerance = 0            // sensitivity
   )
{
   const float a_min =
      0.5 * (RBounds.right - RBounds.left) - tolerance - 1;
   const float b_min =
      0.5 * (RBounds.bottom - RBounds.top) - tolerance - 1;
   const float a_max =
      0.5 * (RBounds.right - RBounds.left) + tolerance;
   const float b_max =
      0.5 * (RBounds.bottom - RBounds.top) + tolerance;

   const POINT PCenter = {
      a_max + RBounds.left - tolerance,
      b_max + RBounds.top - tolerance
      };

   // find the arc's first endpoint and then
   // compute its distance from PHit
```

```
POINT PEnd1;
IntersectRadialAndEllipse(PRadial1, RBounds, PEnd1);
const int dX1 = PHit.x - PEnd1.x;
const int dY1 = PHit.y - PEnd1.y;
if (sqrt((dX1 * dX1) + (dY1 * dY1)) <= tolerance)
{
   return TRUE;
}

// find the arc's second endpoint and then
// compute its distance from PHit
POINT PEnd2;
IntersectRadialAndEllipse(PRadial2, RBounds, PEnd2);
const int dX2 = PHit.x - PEnd2.x;
const int dY2 = PHit.y - PEnd2.y;
if (sqrt((dX2 * dX2) + (dY2 * dY2)) <= tolerance)
{
   return TRUE;
}

const int X = PHit.x - PCenter.x;
const int Y = PHit.y - PCenter.y;

const float ellipse_min =
   ((X * X) / (a_min * a_min)) +
   ((Y * Y) / (b_min * b_min));
const float ellipse_max =
   ((X * X) / (a_max * a_max)) +
   ((Y * Y) / (b_max * b_max));

// if the point is on the ellipse (within tolerance)
if ((ellipse_min == ellipse_max) ||
    (ellipse_min >= 1.0 && ellipse_max <= 1.0))
{
   float theta1 =
      atan2(
         PCenter.y - PRadial1.y,
         PRadial1.x - PCenter.x
         );
   float theta2 =
      atan2(
         PCenter.y - PRadial2.y,
         PRadial2.x - PCenter.x
         );
   float thetaHit = atan2(-Y, X);
```

```
        if (theta1 < 0) theta1 += (2 * M_PI);
        if (theta2 < 0) theta2 += (2 * M_PI);
        if (thetaHit < 0) thetaHit += (2 * M_PI);

        if (theta1 == theta2) return TRUE;
        if (theta2 < theta1) theta2 += (2 * M_PI);
        if (thetaHit < theta1) thetaHit += (2 * M_PI);

        // if point is in the pie slice
        return (clockwise ^ (thetaHit > theta1 && thetaHit < theta2));
    }
    return FALSE;
}
```

The **PHit** parameter is specified as the point that you want to test for inclusion within the pie slice (or on its boundary). The bounding rectangle of the pie's parent ellipse is specified by the **RBounds** parameter. The **PRadial1** and **PRadial2** parameters specify the endpoint of the starting and ending interval-defining line segments, respectively. (The starting point of each line segment is the ellipse's center point.) The **tolerance** parameter is used to add a bit of leeway to the test. This parameter is specified as the allowable distance (in the x- or y-direction) by which **PHit** can be offset from the bounds of the pie slice.

TIP: *The* ***tolerance*** *parameter is useful when the* ***PtOnArc*** *function is used to hit-test a pie slice (i.e., in response to mouse messages). Specifically, you'll want to specify this parameter when the rendered wedge is particularly small or when the wedge is outlined with a thick pen.*

The **PtOnArc** function returns **TRUE** if the point is in the ellipse or on its boundary, and **FALSE** otherwise. For example, to determine if the point **PHit** is on the arc whose parent ellipse is defined by the rectangle **RBounds** and whose interval is defined by **PRadial1** and **PRadial2**:

```
const POINT PHit = {50, 70};
const POINT PRadial1 = {200, 100};
const POINT PRadial2 = {200, 300};
const RECT RBounds = {40, 10, 300, 200};
BOOL IsHit = PtOnArc(PHit, RBounds, PRadial1, PRadial2);
```

The logic behind the **PtOnArc** function comes from three things: the standard equation of an ellipse (see Equation 5.2); the angles formed by the radials and by the line segment that's defined by the ellipse's center point and the point in question; and the intersection of a radial and an ellipse (see Equations 5.16 and 5.17). The **tolerance** value is taken into account by "inflating" the ellipse's bounding rectangle before the equation is used. For more information on hit-testing arcs, refer to "Hit-Testing Arcs" in the "In Depth" section.

Hit-Testing Chords

To determine if a specific point lies in (or on) a chord, you use the **PtInChord** application-defined function:

```
#include <math.h>
BOOL PtInChord(
    IN const POINT& PHit,          // the point in question
    IN const RECT& RBounds,        // the ellipse's bounding rectangle
    IN const POINT& PRadial1,      // the endpoint of the starting radial
    IN const POINT& PRadial2,      // the endpoint of the ending radial
    IN int tolerance = 0           // sensitivity
   )
{
const float a = 0.5 * (RBounds.right - RBounds.left) + tolerance;
   const float b = 0.5 * (RBounds.bottom - RBounds.top) + tolerance;

   const POINT PCenter = {
      a + RBounds.left - tolerance,
      b + RBounds.top - tolerance
      };

   // find the arc's first endpoint and then
   // compute its distance from PHit
   POINT PEnds[2];
   IntersectRadialAndEllipse(PRadial1, RBounds, PEnds[0]);
   const int dX1 = PHit.x - PEnds[0].x;
   const int dY1 = PHit.y - PEnds[0].y;
   if (sqrt((dX1 * dX1) + (dY1 * dY1)) <= tolerance)
   {
      return TRUE;
   }

   // find the arc's second endpoint and then
   // compute its distance from PHit
   IntersectRadialAndEllipse(PRadial2, RBounds, PEnds[1]);
   const int dX2 = PHit.x - PEnds[1].x;
   const int dY2 = PHit.y - PEnds[1].y;
   if (sqrt((dX2 * dX2) + (dY2 * dY2)) <= tolerance)
   {
      return TRUE;
   }
```

```
const int X = PHit.x - PCenter.x;
const int Y = PHit.y - PCenter.y;
if (X == 0 && Y == 0) return TRUE;

// if the point is in the ellipse
if (((X * X) / (a * a)) + ((Y * Y) / (b * b)) <= 1)
{
   // compute the distance from PHit to PEnds
   const int dist_to_sec = DistToLine(PHit, PEnds);
   if (dist_to_sec <= tolerance && dist_to_sec >= -tolerance)
   {
      return TRUE;
   }

   if ((PCenter.x == PRadial1.x && PCenter.y == PRadial1.y) ||
       (PCenter.x == PRadial2.x && PCenter.y == PRadial2.y))
   {
      return FALSE;
   }

   float theta1 =
      atan2(PCenter.y - PRadial1.y, PRadial1.x - PCenter.x);
   float theta2 =
      atan2(PCenter.y - PRadial2.y, PRadial2.x - PCenter.x);
   float thetaHit = atan2(-Y, X);

   if (theta1 < 0) theta1 += (2 * M_PI);
   if (theta2 < 0) theta2 += (2 * M_PI);
   if (thetaHit < 0) thetaHit += (2 * M_PI);

   if (theta1 == theta2) return TRUE;
   if (theta2 < theta1) theta2 += (2 * M_PI);
   if (thetaHit < theta1) thetaHit += (2 * M_PI);

   // if the chord occupies more than half of the ellipse
   if (theta2 - theta1 > M_PI)
   {
      return (!PtInChord(PHit, RBounds, PRadial2, PRadial1, tolerance));
   }

   // if point is in the pie slice
   if (thetaHit > theta1 && thetaHit < theta2)
   {
      // compute the distance from PCenter to PHit
      const int dX = PHit.x - PCenter.x;
      const int dY = PHit.y - PCenter.y;
      const int dist_to_hit = sqrt((dX * dX) + (dY * dY));
```

```
            // if the distance from PHit to the secant is less
            // than the distance from PHit to the center, and
            // the sign of each distance is the same, then
            // PHit is within the chord region
            if ((dist_to_sec <= dist_to_hit) &&
                ((dist_to_hit > 0 && dist_to_sec > 0) ||
                 (dist_to_hit < 0 && dist_to_sec < 0)))
            {
               return TRUE;
            }
         }
      }
      return FALSE;
   }
```

The **PHit** parameter is specified as the point that you want to test for inclusion within the chord (or on its boundary). The bounding rectangle of the pie's parent ellipse is specified by the **RBounds** parameter. The **PRadial1** and **PRadial2** parameters specify the endpoint of the starting and ending interval-defining line segments, respectively. (The starting point of each line segment is the ellipse's center point.) The **tolerance** parameter is used to add a bit of leeway to the test. This parameter is specified as the allowable distance (in the x- or y-direction) by which **PHit** can be offset from the bounds of the chord.

__TIP:__ The __tolerance__ parameter is useful when the __PtInChord__ function is used to hit-test a pie slice (i.e., in response to mouse messages). Specifically, you'll want to specify this parameter when the rendered wedge is particularly small or when the wedge is outlined with a thick pen.

The **PtInChord** function returns **TRUE** if the point is in the ellipse or on its boundary, and **FALSE** otherwise. For example, to determine if the point **PHit** is in the chord whose parent ellipse is defined by the rectangle **RBounds** and whose interval is defined by **PRadial1** and **PRadial2**:

```
const POINT PHit = {190, 150};
const POINT PRadial1 = {400, 20};
const POINT PRadial2 = {200, 300};
const RECT RBounds = {40, 10, 300, 200};
BOOL IsHit = PtInChord(PHit, RBounds, PRadial1, PRadial2);
```

The logic behind the **PtInChord** function comes from three things: the standard equation of an ellipse (see Equation 5.2); the angles formed by the radials and by the line segment that's defined by the ellipse's center point and the point in question; and the intersection of a radial and an ellipse (see Equations 5.16 and 5.17).

The **tolerance** value is taken into account by "inflating" the ellipse's bounding rectangle before the equation is used. For more information on hit-testing chords, refer to "Hit-Testing Chords" in the "In Depth" section.

Output-Primitive-Related Modes and Capabilities

Many of the functions that are designed to render output primitives are governed by the arc direction of the target device context. In this section, we'll discuss how to change a device context's arc direction. In addition, we'll examine how to retrieve device-specific line-, shape-, and curve-related capabilities.

Changing the Arc Direction

The arc or "drawing" direction determines the direction in which primitives are rendered when any of the following functions are used: **Arc**, **ArcTo**, **Chord**, **Ellipse**, **Pie**, **Rectangle**, and **RoundRect**. To retrieve a device context's arc direction, you use the **GetArcDirection** function:

```
int GetArcDirection(
    IN HDC hdc,            // handle to the target device context
);
```

The **hdc** parameter identifies the device context whose current arc direction you want to retrieve. If the **GetArcDirection** function is successful, the return value is either **AD_COUNTERCLOCKWISE** (1) or **AD_CLOCKWISE** (2), for the counterclockwise or clockwise arc direction, respectively. The return value is zero if the function fails:

```
switch (GetArcDirection(hDC))
{
   case AD_COUNTERCLOCKWISE:
      /* counterclockwise arc direction */
      break;
   case AD_CLOCKWISE:
      /* clockwise arc direction */
      break;
   case 0:
      /* error */
      break;
}
```

The default arc direction is **AD_COUNTERCLOCKWISE**. On systems running Windows NT or Windows 2000, you can change the arc direction by using the **SetArcDirection** function:

```
int SetArcDirection(
    IN HDC hdc,          // handle to the target device context
    IN int ArcDirection  // new arc direction
   );
```

***NOTE:** The arc direction is respected only if the graphics mode of the target DC is set to **GM_COMPATIBLE**. When the graphics mode is set to **GM_ADVANCED**, the DC will always use the counterclockwise arc direction.*

***NOTE:** Although you can use the **SetArcDirection** function in Windows 95 and Windows 98, unfortunately, there's no point in doing so. Primitives will always be rendered in the counterclockwise direction.*

The **hdc** parameter identifies the device context whose arc direction will be changed to that specified by the **ArcDirection** parameter. This parameter can be set to either **AD_COUNTERCLOCKWISE** (1) or **AD_CLOCKWISE** (2) for the counterclockwise or clockwise arc direction, respectively. If the **SetArcDirection** function is successful, it returns the previous arc direction; otherwise, the return value is zero:

```
int old_arc_direction = SetArcDirection(hDC, AD_CLOCKWISE);
```


Retrieving the Line Capabilities of a Device

To retrieve the line capabilities of a device, you use the **GetDeviceCaps** function:

```
int GetDeviceCaps(
    IN HDC hdc,        // handle to the target device context
    IN int nIndex      // index of device capability to retrieve
   );
```

The **hdc** parameter is specified as a handle to the device context that identifies the device whose line capabilities you want to retrieve. The **nIndex** parameter specifies the capability to query. For line-related capabilities, you set this parameter to **LINECAPS** (30), in which case the return value is packed with bits that indicate whether or not a specific line-related capability is supported. To extract this data, you should use the bitwise **AND** operator (&) to combine the return value with one of the identifiers listed in Table 5.1.

***NOTE:** Even if a specific line-related capability is not supported, the GDI will normally simulate the effect by other means. The result, however, is typically less accurate and is produced more slowly than it would be if the capability were natively supported by the device.*

Table 5.1 Masks used with the return value of the GetDeviceCaps function when the LINECAPS capability index is specified.

Identifier	Value	Capability
LC_NONE	0	The device does not support lines.
LC_POLYLINE	2	The device supports polylines.
LC_MARKER	4	The device supports markers.
LC_POLYMARKER	8	The device supports polymarkers (e.g., points used to mark a curve).
LC_WIDE	16	The device supports wide lines.
LC_STYLED	32	The device supports styled lines.
LC_WIDESTYLED	64	The device supports wide styled lines.
LC_INTERIORS	128	The device supports figures with filled interiors.

For example, to determine if the primary display monitor is capable of rendering polylines:

```
HDC hScreenDC = GetDC(NULL);
try
{
   bool does_polylines =
      (GetDeviceCaps(hScreenDC, LINECAPS) & LC_POLYLINE);
   // ...
}
catch (...)
{
   ReleaseDC(NULL, hScreenDC);
}
ReleaseDC(NULL, hScreenDC);
```


Retrieving the Curve Capabilities of a Device

To retrieve the curve capabilities of a device, you use the **GetDeviceCaps** function:

```
int GetDeviceCaps(
    IN HDC hdc,        // handle to the target device context
    IN int nIndex      // index of device capability to retrieve
   );
```

The **hdc** parameter is specified as a handle to the device context that identifies the device whose curve capabilities you want to retrieve. The **nIndex** parameter specifies the capability to query; set this parameter to **CURVECAPS** (31) to determine curve-related capabilities. The return value is packed with bits that indicate whether or not a specific curve-related capability is supported. To query a specific capability, you use the bitwise **AND** operator (&) to combine the return value with one of the identifiers listed in Table 5.2.

NOTE: *Even if a particular curve-related capability is not supported, the GDI will normally simulate the effect by other means. The result, however, is typically less accurate and is produced more slowly than it would be if the capability were natively supported by the device.*

For example, to determine if the primary display monitor is capable of rendering rounded rectangles:

```
HDC hScreenDC = GetDC(NULL);
try
{
   bool does_round_rects =
      (GetDeviceCaps(hScreenDC, CURVECAPS) & CC_ROUNDRECT);
   // ...
}
catch (...)
{
   ReleaseDC(NULL, hScreenDC);
}
ReleaseDC(NULL, hScreenDC);
```


Table 5.2 Masks used with the return value of the GetDeviceCaps function when the CURVECAPS capability index is specified.

Identifier	Value	Capability
CC_NONE	0	The device does not support curves.
CC_CIRCLES	1	The device supports circles.
CC_PIE	2	The device supports pie sections.
CC_CHORD	4	The device supports chords.
CC_ELLIPSES	8	The device supports ellipses.
CC_WIDE	16	The device supports wide lines.
CC_STYLED	32	The device supports styled lines.
CC_WIDESTYLED	64	The device supports wide styled lines.
CC_INTERIORS	128	The device supports figures with filled interiors.
CC_ROUNDRECT	256	The device supports rounded rectangles.

Retrieving the Shape Capabilities of a Device

To retrieve the shape capabilities of a device, you use the **GetDeviceCaps** function:

```
int GetDeviceCaps(
    IN HDC hdc,          // handle to the target device context
    IN int nIndex        // index of device capability to retrieve
  );
```

The **hdc** parameter is specified as a handle to the device context that identifies the device whose shape capabilities you want to retrieve. The **nIndex** parameter specifies the capability to query; set this parameter to **POLYGONALCAPS** (32) to determine shape-related capabilities. When this identifier is used, the return value is packed with bits that indicate whether or not a specific shape-related capability is supported. To query a specific capability, use the bitwise **AND** operator (&) to combine the return value with one of the identifiers listed in Table 5.3.

***NOTE:** Even if a particular shape-related capability is not supported, the GDI will normally simulate the effect by other means. The result, however, is typically less accurate and is produced more slowly than it would be if the capability were natively supported by the device.*

Table 5.3 Masks used with the return value of the GetDeviceCaps function when the POLYGONALCAPS capability index is specified.

Identifier	Value	Capability
PC_NONE	0	The device does not support polygons.
PC_POLYGON	1	The device supports alternate-fill polygons.
PC_RECTANGLE	2	The device supports rectangles.
PC_WINDPOLYGON	4	The device supports winding-fill polygons.
PC_SCANLINE	8	The device supports single scan lines.
PC_WIDE	16	The device supports wide borders.
PC_STYLED	32	The device supports styled borders.
PC_WIDESTYLED	64	The device supports wide styled borders.
PC_INTERIORS	128	The device supports figures with filled interiors.
PC_POLYPOLYGON	256	The device supports multiple polygons.
PC_PATHS	512	The device supports paths (used only for PostScript printers).

For example, to determine if the primary display monitor is capable of rendering a polygon by using the winding-number filling mode:

```
HDC hScreenDC = GetDC(NULL);
try
{
   bool does_winding_fills =
      (GetDeviceCaps(hScreenDC, POLYGONALCAPS) & PC_WINDPOLYGON);
   // ...
}
catch (...)
{
   ReleaseDC(NULL, hScreenDC);
}
ReleaseDC(NULL, hScreenDC);
```

Chapter 6

The Bitmap Object

In Depth

The term *bitmap* was coined back when most display devices were capable of producing only binary output. Such devices are still prevalent even to this day, the most notable variety being the LCD (liquid crystal display) watch. Indeed, on these types of devices, a bitmap is literally a "map" of "binary digits." The device highlights those pixels that correspond to the "on" bits, and ignores each "off" bit. For devices that are capable of displaying more than one bit per pixel, the term *pixmap* is used instead. In fact, both of these terms refer to an area in memory that a device uses to store its display data; this area is more commonly known as the device's *frame buffer*.

In Windows, the term "bitmap" is used more loosely. Rarely will you hear a Windows developer use the word to refer to a frame buffer. Sometimes you'll see "bitmap" used to describe a digital image; most often, however, the term is used to refer to a *bitmap object*. (For the remainder of this chapter, the terms "bitmap" and "bitmap object" will be used interchangeably.) In fact, aside from device contexts, bitmaps are perhaps the most fundamental part of the GDI. You can see them used throughout Windows itself—from the image on the Start button to the background of your desktop. As you might have guessed, bitmap objects are used to display digital images.

In this chapter, we'll examine the GDI bitmap object. We'll discuss how to create both monochrome and color bitmaps and how to load and save a bitmap to and from a file. We'll examine how to draw to a bitmap object, and discuss the steps involved in displaying a bitmap. We'll even look at some methods for rendering a bitmap object in a scaled and transparent fashion. In addition, we'll discuss how to retrieve information about a bitmap object, and we'll discuss a technique that can be used to manipulate the bits (i.e., the pixels) of a bitmap.

A Compatible Bitmap

As Chapter 1 mentioned, a bitmap object is one of the seven GDI graphic objects that can be associated with a device context. Yet, unlike other graphic objects, a bitmap object has no logical variety. When you create a bitmap object, you're given (indirect) access to the physical bitmap that the device driver creates. Because of this fact, a bitmap object is commonly referred to as a *compatible bitmap* or *device-dependent bitmap* (DDB). The format of a DDB is *compatible* with only a specific device; that is, its format *depends* on the device. In fact, during the process of realization, the GDI simply performs a few error checks and some minor initializations. This is in contrast to the realization process of most other GDI graphic objects, for which realization consists of creating the physical version of a logical object.

There is an exception to the device dependency of a DDB; monochrome DDBs are stored in a format that's compatible with all devices. You create a monochrome bitmap by using the **CreateBitmap** or **CreateBitmapIndirect** function. The **CreateBitmapIndirect** function accepts a pointer to a **BITMAP** structure (discussed later in this chapter; see "The BITMAP Structure"). The **CreateBitmap** function accepts the parameters that correspond directly to the fields of this structure. Neither of these functions requires a handle to a device context because the device itself is irrelevant.

The GDI provides three functions for the creation of color DDBs: **CreateCompatibleBitmap**, **CreateDIBitmap**, and **CreateDiscardableBitmap**. Each of these functions requires a handle to a device context. The **CreateCompatibleBitmap** function is the most popular because it accepts a handle to a DC and two **int**-type parameters that specify the desired width and height of the bitmap. The **CreateDiscardableBitmap** function is obsolete. It's a remnant from the 16-bit days, when low-memory situations were common, in which case the GDI would destroy any so-called "discardable bitmaps" that were not selected into a device context. The **CreateDIBitmap** function is used to create a DDB from a device-independent bitmap (DIB).

As I just mentioned, the **CreateCompatibleBitmap**, **CreateDIBitmap**, and **CreateDiscardableBitmap** functions all require a handle to a device context. Why is this DC needed? Simply put, it's used to determine the device with which the DDB is to be compatible. For this reason, the color format of a color DDB is always the same as the color format of the device with which the DDB is compatible. For example, on an 8-bit display, all DDBs that are created to be compatible with the screen will also use 8 bits per pixel. (In Chapter 7, we'll examine the DIB section bitmap, which is not restricted by this limitation.)

As with other GDI graphic objects, you're never given direct access to a DDB; instead, you work with it through its handle (of type **HBITMAP**). And, after you're done with the DDB, you destroy it by passing its handle to the **DeleteObject** function.

Unfortunately, working only with a DDB's handle poses a major limitation: You don't have direct access to the bitmap's pixels. The memory is there; the GDI just won't let you (directly) access it. You can use the **GetPixel** and **SetPixel** functions, but these are so slow that unless your bitmap is extremely small, it's not even worth it. You can also manipulate the pixels of a DDB by filling it with information from a DIB. This, too, is less than optimal because the device driver must first translate the DIB before it can perform the conversion. Therefore, in order to manipulate a DDB efficiently, you must use an appropriate GDI drawing function. This is often the fastest approach because the GDI will delegate the work to the device driver.

What should you do when you need direct access to a DDB's pixels? The best approach is to abandon the DDB altogether and use a DIB section bitmap; we'll discuss DIB section bitmaps in Chapter 7.

The BITMAP Structure

In Chapter 2, we discussed the **LOGBRUSH** structure that's used to describe a logical brush. Similarly, in Chapter 3, we examined the **LOGPEN** structure, used for logical pens, and in Chapter 4, the **LOGFONT** structure, used for logical fonts. Not surprisingly, there is a special structure, **BITMAP**, that's used to describe DDBs. Note the lack of the "LOG" prefix because there is no "logical" bitmap object. Here's the declaration of the **BITMAP** structure:

```
typedef struct tagBITMAP {
    LONG bmType;
    LONG bmWidth;
    LONG bmHeight;
    LONG bmWidthBytes;
    WORD bmPlanes;
    WORD bmBitsPixel;
    LPVOID bmBits;
} BITMAP, *PBITMAP, NEAR *NPBITMAP, FAR *LPBITMAP;
```

The **bmType** data member identifies the DDB's format; this member is always zero. The **bmWidth** and **bmHeight** data members describe the DDB's width and height, in device units, respectively. The **bmWidthBytes** data member describes the number of bytes that occupy a single scan line. Because each scan line must be **WORD**-aligned, the value of this data member will always be an integer multiple of two, that is, an even number (i.e., 2 bytes = 16 bits = the size of a **WORD**). The **bmPlanes** data member identifies the number of color planes per pixel. Most DDBs will be created with only a single color plane per pixel. DDBs created on some devices (e.g., EGA and VGA) might yield a **bmPlanes** value that's greater than one. The **bmBitsPixel** data member identifies the number of bits that are used to represent a pixel. The **bmBits** data member is supposedly a pointer to the DDB's bits, but because the GDI does not give you access to the pixels of a DDB, this data member is always zero. (As we'll see in Chapter 7, **bmBits** is indeed valid for DIB section bitmaps.) The **bmBits** data member is rarely used for DDBs, although it can be used to initialize a monochrome DDB via the **CreateBitmapIndirect** function.

The **BITMAP** structure is most commonly used with the **GetObject** function to determine the color depth and/or dimensions of a DDB. For example, you can use the following approach to estimate the amount of global memory that a DDB requires:

```
size_t SizeOfDDB(IN HBITMAP hBmp)
{
   BITMAP bmp;
   if (GetObject(hBmp, sizeof(BITMAP), &bmp) == sizeof(BITMAP))
   {
      return (
         32 + bmp.bmHeight * bmp.bmWidthBytes *
         (bmp.bmPlanes * bmp.bmBitsPixel / 8.0)
         );
   }
   return 0;
}
```

As I mentioned, the **BITMAP** structure is also used with the **CreateBitmapIndirect** function to create a monochrome bitmap. In this case, instead of retrieving information *from* a **BITMAP** structure, you initialize its data members to pass information *to* the **CreateBitmapIndirect** function. For example, to create an uninitialized 100-by-100 monochrome DDB:

```
BITMAP bmp;
memset(&bmp, 0, sizeof(BITMAP));

bmp.bmWidth = 100;
bmp.bmHeight = 100;
bmp.bmWidthBytes = 100;
bmp.bmPlanes = 1;
bmp.bmBitsPixel = 1;

BITMAP hBmp = CreateBitmapIndirect(&bmp);
assert(hBmp != NULL);
try
{
   // ...
}
catch (...)
{
   DeleteObject(hBmp);
}
DeleteObject(hBmp);
```

Rendering DDBs

We first discussed DDBs in Chapter 1, when we examined the special type of device context known as a *memory* device context. Indeed, before you can render to a DDB, you must first select it into a memory device context. What's the point of using a memory device context? Remember, a device context is, in essence, a drawing surface. All GDI rendering functions require a handle to a device context; this handle tells the function where to place the output. For example, if you call the **Ellipse** function, specifying the handle to a display device context, the function will render the ellipse to the corresponding display device. If, on the other hand, you pass the **Ellipse** function the handle to a memory device context that has a DDB selected into it, the function will store the result in the bits of the DDB. It's the job of the DDB to serve as the "buffer" or "memory" of its associated memory device context.

Unlike other GDI graphic objects, you can't select a DDB into a display device context. A DDB can be selected into only a memory device context and only one memory device context at a time. A memory device context that doesn't have a DDB selected into it is, in a sense, a "memory-less" memory device context. On the other hand, the terms *memory bitmap* and *off-screen bitmap* are commonly used to refer to a DDB that's been selected into a memory device context.

Drawing to a DDB

Most GDI rendering functions regard a memory device context that has an associated DDB as a regular device context. If the destination device context is specified as a memory device context, the output will be drawn to the pixels of the memory device context's associated DDB, not to the display. For example, the following code demonstrates how to use the **PatBlt** function to set all the pixels of a color DDB (**hBmp**) to black. Here, **hDC** is a handle to a display device context:

```
// Step 1: Create the color DDB (assuming
// that hDC identifies a color device)
SIZE SBitmap = {100, 200};
HBITMAP hBmp = CreateCompatibleBitmap(hDC, SBitmap.cx, SBitmap.cy);

// Step 2: Create the memory DC
HDC hMemDC = CreateCompatibleDC(hDC);

// Step 3: Select the DDB into the memory DC
HBITMAP hOldBmp = static_cast<HBITMAP>(
   SelectObject(hMemDC, hBmp)
   );

// Step 4: Manipulate the DDB's bits via PatBlt
PatBlt(hMemDC, 0, 0, SBitmap.cx, SBitmap.cy, BLACKNESS);
```

```
// ...

// clean up
DeleteObject(SelectObject(hMemDC, hOldBmp));
DeleteDC(hMemDC);
```

In fact, because you're never given direct access to a DDB's pixels, the only way to manipulate its pixels is to use a GDI output function. This means that, in 99 percent of all cases, you'll need to select the bitmap into a memory device context. The remaining 1 percent is reserved for the **SetDIBits** function, which is used to initialize a DDB from a DIB (see the solution "Manipulating the Bits of a Device-Dependent Bitmap"). In general, to draw to a DDB, you first select it into a memory device context, and then you indirectly manipulate its pixels through this memory device context by using the appropriate rendering function.

Displaying a DDB

Note from the previous code snippet that, although we manipulated the DDB, we never displayed it to the screen. Displaying it to the screen also requires that the DDB be selected into a memory device context. In this way, you can specify this memory DC as the **hdcSrc** parameter to **BitBlt**, **StretchBlt**, and other bit-block-transfer-related functions. For example, the following code snippet is a modification (with exception handling) of the previous code, here using the **BitBlt** function to display the DDB to the display device context (**hDC**) of a window (**hWnd**):


```
// step 0: Grab a handle to hWnd's display DC
HDC hDC = GetDC(hWnd);
try
{
   // step 1: Create the color DDB (assuming that
   // hDC identifies a color device)
   SIZE SBitmap = {100, 200};
   HBITMAP hBmp = CreateCompatibleBitmap(hDC, SBitmap.cx, SBitmap.cy);

   // step 2: Create the memory DC
   HDC hMemDC = CreateCompatibleDC(hDC);

   // step 3: Select the DDB into the memory DC
   HBITMAP hOldBmp = static_cast<HBITMAP>(
      SelectObject(hMemDC, hBmp)
      );
   try
   {
      //
      // TODO: add palette code as needed
```

```
        // (see  Chapter 9)...
        //

        // step 4: Manipulate the DDB's bits via PatBlt
        PatBlt(hMemDC, 0, 0, SBitmap.cx, SBitmap.cy, BLACKNESS);

        // step 5: Copy the results to the display DC
        BitBlt(hDC, 0, 0,
               SBitmap.cx, SBitmap.cy,
               hMemDC, 0, 0,
               SRCCOPY);
        // ...
    }
    catch (...)
    {
        // clean up
        DeleteObject(SelectObject(hMemDC, hOldBmp));
        DeleteDC(hMemDC);
        throw;
    }
    // clean up
    DeleteObject(SelectObject(hMemDC, hOldBmp));
    DeleteDC(hMemDC);
}
catch (...)
{
    // clean up
    ReleaseDC(hWnd, hDC);
}
// clean up
ReleaseDC(hWnd, hDC);
```


Listing 6.1 provides a more practical example: rendering a background image to the channel of a trackbar by using a DDB and the Custom Draw service. The background bitmap used here is actually a fingerprint from the FBI's database. The result is depicted in Figure 6.1.

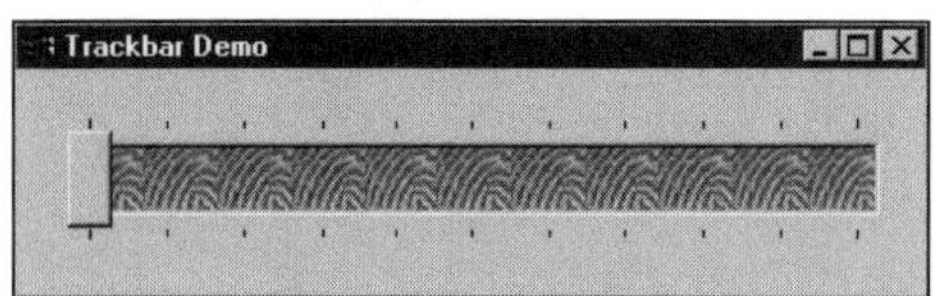

Figure 6.1 A DDB as a trackbar's background image.

Listing 6.1 Rendering a DDB to the device context of a trackbar by using the Custom Draw service.

```
// ---------------------------------------------------------------
// Windows 2000 Graphics API Black Book
// Chapter 6 - Listing 6.1 (Trackbar DDB Demo)
// ---------------------------------------------------------------

#include <windows.h>
#include <commctrl.h>

HINSTANCE hInst;
const char* WndClassName = "GMainWnd";
LRESULT CALLBACK MainWndProc(HWND HWnd, UINT Msg, WPARAM WParam,
   LPARAM LParam);

int APIENTRY WinMain(HINSTANCE hInstance, HINSTANCE, LPTSTR,
   int nCmdShow)
{
   hInst = hInstance;

   WNDCLASS wc;
   memset(&wc, 0, sizeof(WNDCLASS));

   wc.style = CS_VREDRAW | CS_HREDRAW;
   wc.lpszClassName = WndClassName;
   wc.lpfnWndProc = MainWndProc;
   wc.hInstance = hInst;
   wc.hCursor = LoadCursor(NULL, IDC_ARROW);
   wc.hbrBackground = reinterpret_cast<HBRUSH>(
      COLOR_BTNFACE + 1
      );

   if (RegisterClass(&wc))
   {
      HWND hWnd =
         CreateWindow(
            WndClassName, "Trackbar Demo",
            WS_OVERLAPPEDWINDOW | WS_CAPTION |
            WS_VISIBLE | WS_CLIPCHILDREN,
            CW_USEDEFAULT, CW_USEDEFAULT, 400, 120,
            NULL, NULL, hInst, NULL
            );
```

```
        if (hWnd)
        {
            ShowWindow(hWnd, nCmdShow);
            UpdateWindow(hWnd);

            MSG msg;
            while (GetMessage(&msg, NULL, 0, 0))
            {
                TranslateMessage(&msg);
                DispatchMessage(&msg);
            }
        }
    }
    return 0;
}

HDC hMemDC = NULL;
HBITMAP hOldBmp = NULL;
HWND hTrackBar = NULL;

LRESULT CALLBACK MainWndProc(HWND hWnd, UINT msg, WPARAM wParam,
    LPARAM lParam)
{
    switch (msg)
    {
        case WM_CREATE:
        {
            INITCOMMONCONTROLSEX icx;
            icx.dwSize = sizeof(INITCOMMONCONTROLSEX);
            icx.dwICC = ICC_BAR_CLASSES;

            InitCommonControlsEx(&icx);

            hTrackBar =
                CreateWindow(
                    TRACKBAR_CLASS, "",
                    TBS_HORZ | TBS_BOTH | TBS_AUTOTICKS |
                    TBS_FIXEDLENGTH | TBS_ENABLESELRANGE |
                    WS_CHILD | WS_VISIBLE,
                    10, 15, 375, 60,
                    hWnd, NULL, hInst, NULL
                    );

            if (hTrackBar)
            {
                SNDMSG(hTrackBar, TBM_SETTHUMBLENGTH, 40, 0);
                SNDMSG(hTrackBar, TBM_SETRANGEMAX, TRUE, 10);
```

```
        //
        // see Immediate Solution "Loading a
        // Device-Dependent Bitmap from a File"
        // for the CreateDDBFromFile definition
        //
        LPCSTR filename = TEXT("FINGER_PRINT.BMP\0");
        HBITMAP hBmp = CreateDDBFromFile(filename, NULL);

        if (hBmp)
        {
           hMemDC = CreateCompatibleDC(NULL);
           if (hMemDC)
           {
              hOldBmp = static_cast<HBITMAP>(
                 SelectObject(hMemDC, hBmp)
                 );
           }
           else DeleteObject(hBmp);
        }
     }
     break;
  }
  case WM_NOTIFY:
  {
     LPNMCUSTOMDRAW lpnmcd =
        reinterpret_cast<LPNMCUSTOMDRAW>(lParam);

     if (lpnmcd->hdr.code == NM_CUSTOMDRAW &&
         lpnmcd->hdr.hwndFrom == hTrackBar)
     {
        switch (lpnmcd->dwDrawStage)
        {
           // prior to drawing
           case CDDS_PREPAINT:
           {
              // tell Windows we want notification
              // of each portion being drawn
              return CDRF_NOTIFYITEMDRAW;
           }

           // upon drawing each portion
           case CDDS_ITEMPREPAINT:
           {
              // if we're currently drawing the channel
              if (lpnmcd->dwItemSpec == TBCD_CHANNEL)
```

```
{
   // get the handle to the target DC
   HDC hDC = lpnmcd->hdc;
   // get the rectangle of the channel
   RECT R = lpnmcd->rc;

   // store the current clipping region
   RECT RClip;
   GetClipBox(hDC, &RClip);

   // set the new clipping region
   IntersectClipRect(
      hDC, R.left, R.top,
      R.right, R.bottom
      );

   //
   // TODO: add palette code as needed
   // (see Chapter 9)...
   //

   // tile the bitmap
   for (int y = R.top; y < R.bottom; y += 32)
   {
      for (int x = R.left; x < R.right; x += 32)
      {
         BitBlt(
            hDC, x, y, 32, 32,
            hMemDC, 0, 0,
            SRCCOPY
            );
      }
   }

   // restore the old clipping region
   SelectClipRgn(hDC, NULL);
   IntersectClipRect(
      hDC, RClip.left, RClip.top,
      RClip.right, RClip.bottom
      );

   // draw the channel border
   DrawEdge(hDC, &R, EDGE_SUNKEN, BF_RECT);

   // tell Windows we drew the channel manually
   return CDRF_SKIPDEFAULT;
```

```
                }
                break;
            }
        }
        // otherwise have Windows draw it
        return CDRF_DODEFAULT;
    }
    break;
}

//
// see Chapter 9 for info on palette handling...
//

case WM_DESTROY:
{
    // clean up
    if (hMemDC)
    {
        if (hOldBmp)
        {
            DeleteObject(SelectObject(hMemDC, hOldBmp));
        }
        DeleteDC(hMemDC);
    }

    PostQuitMessage(0);
    break;
}
}
return DefWindowProc(hWnd, msg, wParam, lParam);
}
```


DDBs and Palettes

When displaying a DDB on a palettized device, you should first select the DDB's palette into the display device context, and instruct the display device context to realize the palette. This should be done before any blitting is performed. Why are these steps necessary? Remember, a DDB is always compatible with a specific device. If the screen's color format is, say, 8 bits-per-pixel, and your DDB is created to be compatible with the screen, then the DDB's color format will also be 8 bits-per-pixel. This means that each of the DDB's pixels refers to a palette index, not a literal RGB color value. For this reason, the DDB's palette must be selected into the target device context (and realized) to ensure that palette indices (i.e., the DDB's pixel values) are mapped to the correct RGB values.

When you're blitting from one memory DC that has a DDB selected into it, to another memory DC that has a DDB selected into it, and both of these DDBs use the *same palette*, then there's no need to select or realize this palette into the target memory DC before calling **BitBlt** or **StretchBlt**. This example, of course, is an ideal case because the source DDB (**hBmp**) and the new DDB (**hhResizedBmp**) both use the same palette. Things aren't so straightforward when the target DDB's palette differs from the source DDB's palette. For example, if you're blitting from a memory device context whose current DDB uses, say, palette "A", to another memory device context whose current DDB uses, say, palette "B", there's no way to correctly translate palette indices to RGB values. In this case, the best way to proceed is to use the **StretchDIBits** function (see Chapter 7).

There are actually more permutations when the source memory DC contains a DIB section bitmap or you're blitting to a memory DC that contains a DIB section bitmap. I'll save this discussion for Chapter 9. The take home message is, when blitting a DDB to a display device context, you should always select the DDB's palette into the display DC, and realize the palette. (Typically, the realization is performed in response to the **WM_QUERYNEWPALETTE** message, and the selection is performed just before blitting.) When you're blitting from one memory DC that has a DDB selected into it, to another memory DC that has a DDB selected into it, and both of these DDBs use the *same palette*, you don't need to bother with the palette at all. Again, for the details of when a palette is required for DDBs and DIB sections, see Chapter 9.

DDBs vs. DIBs

If you've followed the discussion on device-dependent bitmaps so far, you know that a DDB is a GDI graphic object. That is, it can be selected into a device context. A device-independent bitmap (DIB), on the other hand, is *not* a GDI graphic object. You can't associate a DIB with a device context, nor can you use any GDI function to render to a DIB. What, then, is a DIB, you ask? Simply put, it's the *description* of a bitmap. The "device-independence" results from the fact that this "description" is universally understood.

Advantages of DDBs

Although you can't use the GDI to render to a DIB itself, there are a couple of GDI functions that you can use to render a DIB to a device. However, because the device driver must translate a DIB from its universal format to one that's specific to the device before the DIB can be displayed, drawing a DIB can be slow. This is in contrast to drawing a DDB because the DDB is already in a device-specific format. Therefore, one advantage of using a DDB instead of a DIB is speed. The other advantage comes from the fact that a DDB is a true GDI graphic object.

Because you can select a DDB into a memory device context, you can use high-level GDI functions to draw to the DDB. A DIB, on the other hand, cannot be selected into a device context; therefore, if you need to draw anything to a DIB, you'll have to manipulate its bits directly.

Limitations of DDBs

Lack of portability is clearly one major disadvantage of device-dependence. Because a DDB is maintained by the device driver, and is therefore stored in a format known only by the device, you can't reliably transfer DDBs among different devices. For example, you can't draw to the printer a DDB that's compatible with the screen and simply assume that the printer's device driver will be able to decode it (although some are sophisticated enough to do this). In addition, DDBs are limited in size. In Windows 95 and Windows 98, 16MB is as big as you can get. In Windows NT and Windows 2000, you have a bit more headroom (48MB), but remember that these numbers are maximum limits. In practice, depending on the device driver and the amount of system memory available, these limits can be much lower. Still, for most developers, the greatest limitation imposed by a DDB's device-dependence is the lack of direct access to its bits. In Chapter 7, we'll introduce the DIB section bitmap, which does provide direct pixel access and is not as limited in size. For now, let's make the best of what we *can* do with a DDB's bits.

Obtaining a Copy of a DDB's Bits

As I mentioned, the GDI will never give you direct access to the bits of a DDB. It's not that the bits aren't there, but remember, a DDB is stored in a device-specific format. In order to provide access to a DIB's bits, the GDI would have to instruct the device driver to copy them to some universal format that both you and the device driver could understand. However, we do have such a format—a DIB. So, although you can't directly access the bits of a DDB, you can receive a *copy* of these bits through the use of a DIB. This is exactly the job of the **GetDIBits** function:

```
int GetDIBits(
    IN HDC hdc,                  // handle to the target device context
    IN HBITMAP hbmp,             // handle to the DDB
    IN UINT uStartScan,          // first scan line to copy
    IN UINT cScanLines,          // number of scan lines to copy
    OUT LPVOID lpvBits,          // array that will receive a copy of the
                                 // DDB's bits
    IN OUT LPBITMAPINFO lpbi,    // pointer to a BITMAPINFO structure that
                                 // describes the desired format of the bits
    IN UINT uUsage               // color table format identifier
   );
```

Alas, what do all these parameters mean? Let's start with the two that are most straightforward: **hbmp** and **lpvBits**. The **hbmp** parameter is simply a handle to the DDB whose bits you'll receive a copy of. This copy is placed in the buffer whose address you pass as the **lpvBits** parameter. With these two parameters, the function knows where to get the bits from (**hbmp**) and where to copy the bits to (**lpvBits**).

Now you need to tell the function *how many* bits to copy. This is done through the **uStartScan** and **cScanLines** parameters. The **uStartScan** parameter is a zero-based index of the first scan line to copy. The **cScanLines** parameter simply conveys the total number of scan lines that should be copied (note that your **lpvBits** buffer must be large enough to hold these bits). So, if you want to copy the entire DDB, you pass **GetDIBits** the following:

```
GetDIBits(???, hMyBitmap, 0, my_bitmap_height, my_buffer, ???, ???);
```

Okay, we've tackled four of the parameters; what about the other three? Let's proceed with the next most straightforward parameter: **lpbi**, which is a pointer to a **BITMAPINFO** structure. As we'll discuss in Chapter 7, this structure is composed of two parts: a **BITMAPINFOHEADER** structure that describes the format of the DIB; and an **RGBQUAD** or **WORD** array that holds the DIB's color table. (A color table is optional for DIBs with more than 8 bits per pixel.) The **lpbi** parameter tells the **GetDIBits** function what format you want to receive the bits in, and it provides a pointer to the DIB's color table. (A color table will be synthesized for bitmaps with 8, or fewer, bits per pixel; you must allocate enough space for this color table.) Remember, because the device driver has to perform the conversion anyway, you might as well have it convert to a format that's easy to work with. For example, it's much easier to work with a 24-bit bitmap in which each pixel is an **RGBTRIPLE**, versus a 16-bit bitmap in which you'd have to extract the red, green, and blue intensities from each 16-bit pixel value.

As it turns out, you have to specify only the first six fields of the **lpbi** parameter's **BITMAPINFOHEADER** structure; you can set the others to zero, and **GetDIBits** will do the rest. For most cases, you'll want to initialize these data members like so:

```
lpbi->bmiHeader.biSize = sizeof(BITMAPINFOHEADER);
lpbi->bmiHeader.biWidth = my_bitmap_width;
lpbi->bmiHeader.biHeight = my_bitmap_height * -1;
lpbi->bmiHeader.biPlanes = 1;
lpbi->bmiHeader.biBitCount = 24;
lpbi->bmiHeader.biCompression = BI_RGB;
```

The negative value for the **biHeight** data member instructs **GetDIBits** that you want the bits arranged in a top-down fashion (a DIB is usually stored upside-down).

That takes care of **lpbi**; what about the **hdc** and **uUsage** parameters? These two parameters are actually related. Recall that when you set the **BITMAPINFOHEADER::biBitCount** data member to a value of 8 or less, a color table is synthesized. The **uUsage** parameter tells the **GetDIBits** function what format to use for this color table. If you set **uUsage** to **DIB_RGB_COLORS** (0), the generated color table will consist of **RGBQUADs**. When **uUsage** is set to **DIB_PAL_COLORS** (1), the generated color table will consist of **WORD**-type palette indices. In the latter case, the palette that these indices refer to is the logical palette that's selected into (and realized by) the device context that's specified by the **hdc** parameter. When no color table is required, the **hdc** parameter is commonly passed a handle to the screen's device context, and the **uUsage** parameter is set to **DIB_RGB_COLORS**.

So there it is—you now know what all these parameters mean. However, there is a catch. As mentioned previously, you're responsible for allocating the memory for the buffer that's to hold a copy of the DDB's bits. How large should this buffer be? This depends on the format that you specify by the **lpbi** parameter's **BITMAPINFOHEADER** structure. You can call the **GetDIBits** function with a **NULL lpvBits** parameter to instruct the device driver to compute the number of bytes that are required. This value is placed in the **BITMAPINFOHEADER::biSizeImage** data member. For example:

```
BITMAPINFO bmi;  // no space for color table needed for 24-bit DIB
memset(&bmi, 0, sizeof(BITMAPINFO));

bmi.bmiHeader.biSize = sizeof(BITMAPINFOHEADER);
bmi.bmiHeader.biWidth = bmp.bmWidth;
bmi.bmiHeader.biHeight = -bmp.bmHeight;
bmi.bmiHeader.biPlanes = 1;
bmi.bmiHeader.biBitCount = 24;
bmi.bmiHeader.biCompression = BI_RGB;

HDC hScreenDC = GetDC(NULL);
bool success =
   GetDIBits(
      hScreenDC, hBmp, 0, abs(bmi.bmiHeader.biHeight),
      NULL,
      &bmi, DIB_RGB_COLORS
      );
ReleaseDC(NULL, hScreenDC);
```

```
const size_t buffer_size = bmi.bmiHeader.biSizeImage;
if (success && (buffer_size != 0))
{
   unsigned char* bits_buffer = new unsigned char[buffer_size];
   // ...
}
```

You might be thinking that you can just compute the size manually from the specified width, height, and color depth. For example, you might be tempted to use the following approach:

```
const size_t buffer_size = width * height * bytes_per_pixel;
```

Unfortunately, because the scan lines of a DIB are always **DWORD**-aligned, this formula won't always work. Say, for example, you have an 8-bit DDB that's 133 pixels wide. When the DDB is converted to a DIB, each scan line won't be 133 bytes long; rather, the scan lines are padded so that each line is an integer multiple of 4 bytes (the size of a **DWORD**). This means that the 133 would be rounded up to the next integer multiple of 4, 136. In this case, the previous computation of the required bytes would be too small. The correct approach is to account for the **DWORD** alignment like so:

```
const int padding_per_scanline =
   ((width * bytes_per_pixel) % 4 == 0) ?
   0 : 4 - ((width * bytes_per_pixel) % 4);

const size_t buffer_size =
   (width * height * bytes_per_pixel) +
   (padding_per_scanline * height);
```

This is more concisely computed directly from the **BITMAPINFOHEADER**'s data members via the following:

```
const size_t buffer_size =
   abs(bmi.bmiHeader.biHeight) *
   ((((bmi.bmiHeader.biWidth * bmi.bmiHeader.biBitCount)
      + 31) & ~31) >> 3);
```

In fact, you should manually compute the required size of the buffer if the device driver fails to fill the **biSizeImage** data member after the first call to **GetDIBits**. When you know how much space to allocate, you can call **GetDIBits** again, this time to actually get a copy of the bits. For example:

```
BITMAPINFO bmi;  // no space for color table needed for 24-bit DIB
memset(&bmi, 0, sizeof(BITMAPINFO));

bmi.bmiHeader.biSize = sizeof(BITMAPINFOHEADER);
bmi.bmiHeader.biWidth = bmp.bmWidth;
bmi.bmiHeader.biHeight = -bmp.bmHeight;
bmi.bmiHeader.biPlanes = 1;
bmi.bmiHeader.biBitCount = 24;
bmi.bmiHeader.biCompression = BI_RGB;

HDC hScreenDC = GetDC(NULL);
bool success =
   GetDIBits(
      hScreenDC, hBmp, 0, abs(bmi.bmiHeader.biHeight),
      NULL, &bmi, DIB_RGB_COLORS
      );
ReleaseDC(NULL, hScreenDC);

const size_t buffer_size =
   bmi.bmiHeader.biSizeImage != 0 ?
   bmi.bmiHeader.biSizeImage :
   abs(bmi.bmiHeader.biHeight) *
   ((((bmi.bmiHeader.biWidth * bmi.bmiHeader.biBitCount)
   + 31) & ~31) >> 3);

if (success)
{
   unsigned char* bits_buffer = new unsigned char[buffer_size];
   HDC hScreenDC = GetDC(NULL);
   try
   {
      //
      // when lpvBits is not NULL, GetDIBits returns
      // the number of scan lines that were copied
      //
      const int num_scanlines_copied =
         GetDIBits(
            hScreenDC, hBmp, 0, abs(bmi.bmiHeader.biHeight),
            bits_buffer, &bmi, DIB_RGB_COLORS
            );

      if (num_scanlines_copied == abs(bmi.bmiHeader.biHeight))
      {
         // ...
      }
```

```
    }
    catch (...)
    {
       ReleaseDC(NULL, hScreenDC);
       delete [] bits_buffer;
    }
    ReleaseDC(NULL, hScreenDC);
    delete [] bits_buffer;
}
```

Once you have a copy of the DDB's bits, you are free to manipulate them as desired. However, remember that you're only working with a copy. Any changes that you make won't be reflected in the DDB. One way around this is to copy the bits back to the DDB by using the **SetDIBits** function (see the Immediate Solution "Manipulating the Bits of a Device-Dependent Bitmap"). An alternative method is to use the **StretchDIBits** function to "draw" the DIB to the DDB. For a detailed discussion of the **GetDIBits** and **StretchDIBits** functions, and for an example of using the **GetDIBits** function for retrieving DIBs of other color formats, refer to Chapter 7.

Immediate Solutions

Creating a Monochrome Device-Dependent Bitmap

To create a monochrome device-dependent bitmap, you use the **CreateBitmap** function:

```
HBITMAP CreateBitmap(
    IN int nWidth,           // width of the bitmap, in pixels
    IN int nHeight,          // height of the bitmap, in pixels
    IN UINT cPlanes,         // number of color planes; set to one
    IN UINT cBitsPerPel,     // number of bits per pixel; set to one
    IN CONST VOID *lpvBits   // optional pointer to an array of bits
   );
```

The **nWidth** and **nHeight** parameters specify the desired width and height of the bitmap, in pixels, respectively. The **cPlanes** and **cBitsPerPel** parameters together specify the number of bits that are used to represent each color. You should set both of these parameters to 1.

WARNING! Although you can theoretically create a DDB of any width and height, beware that its size (width × height × color depth) is limited to 16MB on systems running Windows 95 or Windows 98, and 48MB on systems running Windows NT or Windows 2000. In practice, however, these limitations are set by the video device driver and are usually much lower.

The **lpvBits** parameter specifies optional initialization data. This parameter points to an array whose entries define the pixels of the bitmap; each bit corresponds to one pixel. A bit that's set to zero represents a pixel whose color is the foreground color (the text color) of the target device context. A bit that's set to one represents a pixel whose color is the target device context's background color. If you don't need to initialize the bitmap's pixels, set the **lpvBits** parameter to **NULL**.

NOTE: *The* ***lpvBits*** *array must be* ***WORD****-aligned. This means that each scan line of the bitmap must contain an integer multiple of 2 bytes (i.e., 16 bits—the size of a* ***WORD****). If your bitmap is not wide enough, pad each scan line with zeros.*

If successful, the **CreateBitmap** function returns a handle to the newly created monochrome DDB. If the function fails, the return value is **NULL**. Before you can render to the bitmap, you must select it into a memory device context. In addition, unlike other GDI graphic objects, you can select a bitmap into only one memory device context at a time. When the bitmap is no longer needed, destroy it by using the **DeleteObject** function. If you specify a pointer to an array as the **lpvBits** parameter, you can free the memory associated with this array any time after the bitmap is created.

TIP: *If you need access to the bits of the bitmap, use a DIB section bitmap instead. See Chapter 7 for information on how to create a DIB section bitmap.*

The following code snippet demonstrates how to create a monochrome device-dependent bitmap that's 105 pixels wide and 100 pixels high. Once created, the DDB is selected into a memory device context, its background is filled with a blue color, and then a red ellipse is drawn to it. Finally, the **BitBlt** function is used to display the bitmap:

```
const int bpp = 1;
const SIZE SBitmap = {150, 100};

// create a monochrome DDB
HBITMAP hBmp = CreateBitmap(SBitmap.cx, SBitmap.cy, 1, bpp, NULL);
if (hBmp)
{
   // create a memory DC and select the DDB into it
   HDC hMemDC = CreateCompatibleDC(NULL);
   HBITMAP hBmpOld = static_cast<HBITMAP>(
      SelectObject(hMemDC, hBmp)
      );

   HDC hDC = GetDC(hWnd);
   try
   {
      // fill the background with blue
      const COLORREF clrZeros = PALETTERGB(0, 0, 255);
      SetTextColor(hDC, clrZeros); // color of zero-valued bits
      PatBlt(hMemDC, 0, 0, SBitmap.cx, SBitmap.cy, BLACKNESS);

      // render a red ellipse
      const COLORREF clrOnes = PALETTERGB(255, 0, 0);
      SetBkColor(hDC, clrOnes); // color of one-valued bits
      Ellipse(hMemDC, 0, 0, SBitmap.cx, SBitmap.cy);

      // render the DDB to the display DC
      BitBlt(hDC, 10, 10,
             SBitmap.cx, SBitmap.cy,
```

```
                hMemDC, 0, 0,
                SRCCOPY);
    }
    catch (...)
    {
        DeleteObject(SelectObject(hMemDC, hBmpOld));
        DeleteDC(hMemDC);
        ReleaseDC(hWnd, hDC);
    }
    DeleteObject(SelectObject(hMemDC, hBmpOld));
    DeleteDC(hMemDC);
    ReleaseDC(hWnd, hDC);
}
```

Similarly, the following code snippet demonstrates how to use the **CreateBitmap** function to create a monochrome DDB (105 pixels wide and 100 pixels high) whose bits are initialized. Here, the top half of the bitmap's pixels are initialized to white, and the bottom half of the bitmap's pixels are initialized to black:

```
const int bpp = 1;
const SIZE SBitmap = {450, 100};

// compute the WORD-aligned size of the array of bits
const int padding_per_line = static_cast<int>(
    0.5 + ((((SBitmap.cx * bpp) + 15) & ~15) -
    (SBitmap.cx * bpp)) / 8.0
    );
const int bytes_per_line = static_cast<int>(
    0.5 + (SBitmap.cx / 8.0) + padding_per_line
    );
const long size = bytes_per_line * SBitmap.cy;

unsigned char* pBits = new unsigned char[size];
try
{
    // set the top half of the bits
    memset(pBits, 255, size / 2);
    // clear the bottom half of the bits
    memset(pBits + (size / 2), 0, size / 2);

    // create a monochrome DDB
    HBITMAP hBmp =
        CreateBitmap(SBitmap.cx, SBitmap.cy, 1, bpp, pBits);
    delete [] pBits;  pBits = NULL;
```

```
    if (hBmp)
    {
        // create a memory DC and select the DDB into it
        HDC hMemDC = CreateCompatibleDC(NULL);
        HBITMAP hBmpOld = static_cast<HBITMAP>(
            SelectObject(hMemDC, hBmp)
            );
        try
        {
            const COLORREF clrZeros = PALETTERGB(0, 0, 0);
            const COLORREF clrOnes = PALETTERGB(255, 255, 255);
            SetTextColor(hDC, clrZeros); // color of zero-valued bits
            SetBkColor(hDC, clrOnes);    // color of one-valued bits

            BitBlt(hDC, 10, 10,
                   SBitmap.cx, SBitmap.cy,
                   hMemDC, 0, 0,
                   SRCCOPY);
        }
        catch (...)
        {
            DeleteObject(SelectObject(hMemDC, hBmpOld));
            DeleteDC(hMemDC);
        }
        DeleteObject(SelectObject(hMemDC, hBmpOld));
        DeleteDC(hMemDC);
    }
}
catch (...)
{
    delete [] pBits;
}
delete [] pBits;
```

NOTE: *You can alternatively use the* ***CreateBitmapIndirect*** *function to create a monochrome DDB. For information on this function, see "The* ***BITMAP*** *Structure" in the In Depth section.*

Related solutions:	Found on page:
Creating a Memory Device Context	64
Creating a Device-Independent Bitmap	391
Creating a DIB Section Bitmap	424

Creating a Color Device-Dependent Bitmap

To create a color device-dependent bitmap whose color format is identical to that of a specific device, you use the **CreateCompatibleBitmap** function:

```
HBITMAP CreateCompatibleBitmap(
    IN HDC hdc,         // handle to the target device context
    IN int nWidth,      // width of the bitmap, in pixels
    IN int nHeight      // height of the bitmap, in pixels
   );
```

The **hdc** parameter identifies the device context that describes the device with which the bitmap will be compatible. This parameter can be assigned a handle to a memory device context, in which case the color format of the memory device context's current bitmap is used for compatibility.

WARNING! Unlike that of the CreateCompatibleDC function, the hdc parameter of the Create-CompatibleBitmap function cannot be specified as NULL to create a bitmap that's compatible with the primary display monitor. For this, you must explicitly pass a handle to the screen's DC as the hdc parameter.

The **nWidth** and **hHeight** parameters are used to specify the width and height of the DDB, in pixels.

WARNING! Although you can theoretically create a bitmap of any width and height, beware that the size of a DDB is limited to 16MB on systems running Windows 95 or Windows 98, and 48MB on systems running Windows NT or Windows 2000. In practice, however, these limitations are set by the video device driver and are usually much lower.

If the **CreateCompatibleBitmap** function succeeds, the return value is a handle to the newly created DDB. Upon failure, the function returns **NULL**. Before you can render to the bitmap, you must select it into a memory device context. In addition, unlike other GDI graphic objects, you can select a bitmap into only one memory device context at a time. When the bitmap is no longer needed, you must destroy it by using the **DeleteObject** function.

TIP: *If you need access to the bits of the bitmap, use a DIB section bitmap instead. See Chapter 7 for information on how to create a DIB section bitmap.*

The following code snippet demonstrates how to create a device-dependent bitmap (300 pixels wide and 400 pixels high) whose color format matches that of the primary display monitor. After the bitmap is created, it's selected into a memory device context, an ellipse is rendered to it, and then the **BitBlt** function is used to display the result:

```
HDC hMemDC = NULL;
HBITMAP hBmp = NULL;
const SIZE SBitmap = {300, 400};

HDC hScreenDC = GetDC(NULL);
try
{
   // create a memory DC compatible with the screen
   hMemDC = CreateCompatibleDC(hScreenDC);
   if (!hMemDC) throw;

   // create a DDB compatible with the screen
   hBmp = CreateCompatibleBitmap(hScreenDC, SBitmap.cx, SBitmap.cy);
   if (!hBmp) throw;
}
catch (...)
{
   DeleteDC(hMemDC);
   DeleteObject(hBmp);
   ReleaseDC(NULL, hScreenDC);
}
ReleaseDC(NULL, hScreenDC);

// select the bitmap into the memory DC
HBITMAP hOldBmp = static_cast<HBITMAP>(
   SelectObject(hMemDC, hBmp)
   );

HDC hDC = GetDC(hWnd);
try
{
   // clear the background
   PatBlt(hMemDC, 0, 0, SBitmap.cx, SBitmap.cy, BLACKNESS);

   // render an ellipse
   Ellipse(hMemDC, 0, 0, SBitmap.cx, SBitmap.cy);

   // transfer the results to the display DC
   BitBlt(hDC, 0, 0,
          SBitmap.cx, SBitmap.cy,
          hMemDC, 0, 0,
          SRCCOPY);
}
```

```
catch (...)
{
   DeleteObject(SelectObject(hMemDC, hOldBmp));
   DeleteDC(hMemDC);
   ReleaseDC(hWnd, hDC);
}
DeleteObject(SelectObject(hMemDC, hOldBmp));
DeleteDC(hMemDC);
ReleaseDC(hWnd, hDC);
```

Because the creation of a DDB and a memory DC is a frequently performed task, it's best to wrap this into a utility function (or a class). The following utility function can be used to create a memory device context and a DDB, both of which are compatible with the primary display monitor:

```
BOOL CreateDisplayDDB(
    OUT HDC& hMemDC,           // handle to the memory device context
    OUT HBITMAP& hOldBmp,      // handle to the original bitmap
    IN const SIZE& SBitmap     // desired width and height
   )
{
   hMemDC = NULL;
   hOldBmp = NULL;

   HDC hScreenDC = GetDC(NULL);
   try
   {
      hMemDC = CreateCompatibleDC(hScreenDC);
      if (!hMemDC) throw;

      hOldBmp = CreateCompatibleBitmap(
         hScreenDC, SBitmap.cx, SBitmap.cy
         );
      if (!hOldBmp) throw;

      hOldBmp = static_cast<HBITMAP>(
         SelectObject(hMemDC, hOldBmp)
         );
   }
   catch (...)
   {
      DeleteDC(hMemDC);
      ReleaseDC(NULL, hScreenDC);
      return FALSE;
   }
```

```
    ReleaseDC(NULL, hScreenDC);
    return (hOldBmp != NULL);
}
```

The **hMemDC** parameter refers to an **HDC**-type variable that will receive the handle to the newly created memory device context. Similarly, the handle to this device context's original "placeholder" bitmap is placed in the **hOldBmp** parameter. The **SBitmap** parameter specifies the desired size of the DDB. Once created, the DDB is selected into the memory device context. Note that a handle to this new DDB is not returned. If you need a handle to the DDB, use the **GetCurrentObject** function.

Upon success, the **CreateDisplayDDB** utility function returns **TRUE**; otherwise, the return value is **FALSE**. The caller is responsible for destroying the memory device context and the new DDB. The following code snippet demonstrates how to achieve the same effect as the previous example, here using the **CreateDisplayDDB** function:

```
HDC hMemDC;
HBITMAP hOldBmp;
const SIZE SBitmap = {300, 400};

if (CreateDisplayDDB(hMemDC, hOldBmp, SBitmap))
{
    HDC hDC = GetDC(hWnd);
    try
    {
        // clear the background
        PatBlt(hMemDC, 0, 0, SBitmap.cx, SBitmap.cy, BLACKNESS);

        // render an ellipse
        Ellipse(hMemDC, 0, 0, SBitmap.cx, SBitmap.cy);

        // transfer the results to the display DC
        BitBlt(hDC, 0, 0,
               SBitmap.cx, SBitmap.cy,
               hMemDC, 0, 0,
               SRCCOPY);
    }
    catch (...)
    {
        DeleteObject(SelectObject(hMemDC, hOldBmp));
        DeleteDC(hMemDC);
        ReleaseDC(hWnd, hDC);
    }
```

```
    DeleteObject(SelectObject(hMemDC, hOldBmp));
    DeleteDC(hMemDC);
    ReleaseDC(hWnd, hDC);
}
```

Related solutions:	Found on page:
Creating a Memory Device Context	64
Creating a Device-Independent Bitmap	391
Creating a DIB Section Bitmap	424

Creating a Device-Dependent Bitmap from a Device-Independent Bitmap

To create a device-dependent bitmap from a device-independent bitmap, you use the **CreateDIBitmap** function.

***TIP:** If you already have a DDB created and you simply need to initialize its color data with that of a DIB, use the **SetDIBits** function instead (see the solution "Manipulating the Bits of a Device-Dependent Bitmap").*

The **CreateDIBitmap** function creates a new DDB from a DIB and optionally sets its color data according to the bits and color table of the DIB:

```
HBITMAP CreateDIBitmap(
    IN HDC hdc,                          // handle to the target device
    IN CONST BITMAPINFOHEADER *lpbmih,   // context pointer to the DIB's
                                         // BITMAPINFOHEADER structure
    IN DWORD fdwInit,                    // pixel initialization flag
    IN CONST VOID *lpbInit,              // pointer to optional pixel
                                         // initialization data
    IN CONST BITMAPINFO *lpbmi,          // pointer to an optional bitmap
                                         // color format data
    IN UINT fuUsage                      // color table format identifier
  );
```

On palettized displays, a mapping is performed between the colors in the DIB's color-table entries and those of the logical palette that's selected into the device context identified by the **hdc** parameter. On non-palettized displays, the device context that's identified by the **hdc** parameter is used only when the DIB's color table contains palette indices. In this case, the device context's current palette is used to reverse-map these palette indices into literal RGB values. The **lpbih** parameter is a pointer to a **BITMAPINFOHEADER** structure that specifies the dimensions and color format of the DIB.

WARNING! Although you can theoretically create a DDB of any width and height, beware that its size (width × height × color depth) is limited to 16MB on systems running Windows 95 or Windows 98, and 48MB on systems running Windows NT or Windows 2000. In practice, however, these limitations are set by the video device driver and are usually much lower.

The **fdwInit** parameter is used to specify whether the pixels of the DDB should be initialized with those of the DIB. This parameter can be set to zero for no initialization, or to **CBM_INIT** to initialize the DDB's pixels. When the **fdwInit** parameter is specified as **CBM_INIT**, the **lpbInit** parameter is specified as a pointer to the DIB's bits, and the **lpbmi** parameter is specified as a pointer to the DIB's corresponding **BITMAPINFO** structure (mainly to supply the DIB's color table information).

NOTE: *Each scan line of the pixel data that's specified by the* ***lpbInit*** *parameter must be* ***DWORD****-aligned. This means that each scan line of the bitmap must contain an integer multiple of 4 bytes (i.e., 32 bits—the size of a* ***DWORD****). If your bitmap is not wide enough, pad each scan line with zeros.*

The **fuUsage** parameter specifies the format of the DIB's color table, if one exists. This parameter is ignored unless the **fdwInit** is specified as **CBM_INIT**. If the DIB's color table consists of literal RGB values via an array of **RGBQUAD** structures, set **fuUsage** to **DIB_RGB_COLORS** (0). If the DIB's color table is composed of **WORD**-type entries, not **RGBQUAD**s, specify the **DIB_PAL_COLORS** (1) identifier. Note that DIBs of this latter type are seldom used because the color table is no longer device-independent.

NOTE: *When you specify the* ***DIB_PAL_COLORS*** *identifier, the associated logical palette must be selected into the device context (whose handle you pass to the* ***CreateDIBitmap*** *function) before you call* ***CreateDIBitmap****. This must be done whether or not the device is palettized. To create a logical palette from a DIB's color table, refer to Chapter 7.*

If successful, the **CreateDIBitmap** function returns a handle to the newly created DDB. If the function fails, the return value is **NULL**. Before you can render to the bitmap, you must select it into a memory device context. In addition, unlike other GDI graphic objects, you can select a bitmap into only one memory device context at a time. When the bitmap is no longer needed, you should destroy it by using the **DeleteObject** function. The memory for the DIB can be freed at any time after the DDB is created.

The following code snippet demonstrates the use of the **CreateDIBitmap** function to create a DDB from a DIB (described by **lpbi**), without initializing the DDB's color data:

```
HGLOBAL hDIB = some_func_get_dib();
if (hDIB)
{
   const LPBITMAPINFO lpbi = static_cast<LPBITMAPINFO>(GlobalLock(hDIB));
   if (lpbi)
   {
      HBITMAP hBmp = NULL;
      HDC hDC = GetDC(hWnd);
      try
      {
         hBmp = CreateDIBitmap(NULL, &lpbi->bmiHeader, 0, NULL, NULL, 0);
         if (!hBmp) throw;

         GlobalUnlock(hDIB);
         GlobalFree(hDIB);
         hDIB = NULL;

         // ...
      }
      catch (...)
      {
         GlobalUnlock(hDIB);
         GlobalFree(hDIB);

         DeleteObject(hBmp);
         ReleaseDC(hWnd, hDC);
      }
      DeleteObject(hBmp);
      ReleaseDC(hWnd, hDC);
   }
   else GlobalFree(hDIB);
}
```

Similarly, the following code snippet shows how to use the **CreateDIBitmap** function to create a DDB from a packed DIB (described by **lpbi**) whose color table consists of literal RGB values. After the DDB is created, it's selected into a memory device context, and then it's displayed via the **BitBlt** function:

```
HGLOBAL hDIB = some_func_to_get_dib_with_RGBQUAD_color_table();
if (hDIB)
{
```

```
const LPBITMAPINFO lpbi = static_cast<LPBITMAPINFO>(GlobalLock(hDIB));
if (lpbi)
{
   HDC hMemDC = NULL;
   HBITMAP hBmp = NULL, hOldBmp = NULL;

   HDC hDC = GetDC(hWnd);
   try
   {
      HPALETTE hPal = NULL, hOldPal = NULL;
      bool palettized = (GetDeviceCaps(hDC, RASTERCAPS) & RC_PALETTE);
      if (palettized)
      {
         //
         // NOTE: The PaletteFromDIBColorTable function
         // comes from Chapter 7.
         //
         hPal = PaletteFromDIBColorTable(*lpbi);
         hOldPal = SelectPalette(hDC, hPal, false);
         RealizePalette(hDC);
      }

      //
      // NOTE: The PointerToDIBits function
      // comes from Chapter 7.
      //
      const unsigned char* bits = PointerToDIBits(lpbi);

      hBmp =
         CreateDIBitmap(
            hDC, &lpbi->bmiHeader, CBM_INIT,
            bits, lpbi, DIB_RGB_COLORS
            );
      GlobalUnlock(hDIB);
      GlobalFree(hDIB);

      if (hBmp)
      {
         hMemDC = CreateCompatibleDC(hDC);
         hOldBmp = static_cast<HBITMAP>(
            SelectObject(hMemDC, hBmp)
            );

         BitBlt(
            hDC, 0, 0,
```

```
                lpbi->bmiHeader.biWidth,
                abs(lpbi->bmiHeader.biHeight),
                hMemDC, 0, 0,
                SRCCOPY
                );
         }
         if (palettized)
         {
            DeleteObject(SelectPalette(hDC, hOldPal, false));
         }
      }
      catch (...)
      {
         GlobalUnlock(hDIB);
         GlobalFree(hDIB);

         DeleteObject(SelectObject(hMemDC, hOldBmp));
         ReleaseDC(hWnd, hDC);
      }
      DeleteObject(SelectObject(hMemDC, hOldBmp));
      ReleaseDC(hWnd, hDC);
   }
   else GlobalFree(hDIB);
}
```

Likewise, the following code snippet demonstrates the use of the **CreateDIBitmap** function to create a DDB from a packed DIB (described by **lpbi**) whose color table consists of **WORD**-type palette indices. In this case, the device's palettized status is not queried because we're using the **DIB_PAL_COLORS** identifier. A logical palette must be used, regardless. As before, after the DDB is created, it's selected into a memory device context, and then it's displayed via the **BitBlt** function:

```
HGLOBAL hDIB = some_func_to_get_dib_with_WORD_color_table();
if (hDIB)
{
   const LPBITMAPINFO lpbi = static_cast<LPBITMAPINFO>(GlobalLock(hDIB));
   if (lpbi)
   {
      HDC hMemDC = NULL;
      HBITMAP hBmp = NULL, hOldBmp = NULL;

      HDC hDC = GetDC(hWnd);
```

```
try
{
   //
   // NOTE: The PaletteFromDIBColorTable() function
   // comes from Chapter 7.
   //
   HPALETTE hPal = PaletteFromDIBColorTable(*lpbi);
   if (!hPal) throw;
   HPALETTE hOldPal = SelectPalette(hDC, hPal, false);
   RealizePalette(hDC);

   //
   // NOTE: The PointerToDIBits() function
   // comes from Chapter 7.
   //
   const unsigned char* bits = PointerToDIBits(lpbi);

   hBmp =
      CreateDIBitmap(
         hDC, &lpbi->bmiHeader, CBM_INIT,
         bits, lpbi, DIB_PAL_COLORS
         );
   if (!hBmp) throw;
   GlobalUnlock(hDIB);
   GlobalFree(hDIB);
   hDIB = NULL;

   if (hBmp)
   {
      hMemDC = CreateCompatibleDC(hDC);
      hOldBmp = static_cast<HBITMAP>(
         SelectObject(hMemDC, hBmp)
         );

      BitBlt(
         hDC, 0, 0,
         lpbi->bmiHeader.biWidth,
         abs(lpbi->bmiHeader.biHeight),
         hMemDC, 0, 0,
         SRCCOPY
         );
   }
   DeleteObject(SelectPalette(hDC, hOldPal, false));
}
```

```
        catch (...)
        {
            GlobalUnlock(hDIB);
            GlobalFree(hDIB);

            DeleteObject(SelectObject(hMemDC, hOldBmp));
            ReleaseDC(hWnd, hDC);
            throw;
        }
        DeleteObject(SelectObject(hMemDC, hOldBmp));
        ReleaseDC(hWnd, hDC);
    }
    else GlobalFree(hDIB);
}
```


Related solutions:	Found on page:
Creating a Memory Device Context	64
Creating a Device-Independent Bitmap	391
Creating a DIB Section Bitmap	424

Copying a Device-Dependent Bitmap

To copy a device-dependent bitmap on a non-palettized device, you use the **CopyImage** function:

```
HANDLE CopyImage(
    IN HANDLE hImage,     // handle to the bitmap to copy
    IN UINT uType,        // type of image; set to IMAGE_BITMAP
    IN int cxDesired,     // desired width; set to zero
    IN int cyDesired,     // desired height; set to zero
    IN UINT fuFlags       // copying flags; set to zero
  );
```

The **hImage** parameter is specified as the handle to the DDB that you want to copy. The **uType** parameter identifies the type of image; for DDBs, set this parameter to **IMAGE_BITMAP** (0). To make an exact copy, set all other parameters to zero.

Upon success, the **CopyImage** function returns a handle to the DDB's copy; otherwise, the return value is **NULL**. For example, to copy a 24-bpp (bits per pixel) DDB (**hBmp**), you use the **CopyImage** function like so:

```
HBITMAP hBmpCopy = static_cast<HBITMAP>(
   CopyImage(hBmp, IMAGE_BITMAP, 0, 0, 0)
   );
```

***TIP:** If you don't want an exact copy (in terms of dimensions), you can specify the desired width and the desired height as the **cxDesired** and **cyDesired** parameters, respectively. The copy will be scaled accordingly.*

Unfortunately, on devices that use a palette, the **CopyImage** function mangles the colors of the DDB. In this case, you need to perform the copying manually as demonstrated by the following example function:

```
HBITMAP CopyBitmap(
    IN const HBITMAP hBmp,   // handle to the DDB to copy
    IN const HPALETTE hPal   // handle to the DDB's palette
   )
{
   BITMAP bmp;
   const size_t bmpSize = sizeof(BITMAP);
   if (GetObject(hBmp, bmpSize, &bmp) != bmpSize)
   {
      return NULL;
   }

   HDC hScreenDC = GetDC(NULL);
   HDC hMemDC = CreateCompatibleDC(hScreenDC);
   HDC hCopyMemDC = CreateCompatibleDC(hScreenDC);

   HBITMAP hCopyBmp =
      CreateCompatibleBitmap(
         hScreenDC, bmp.bmWidth, bmp.bmHeight
         );
   HBITMAP hOldBmp = static_cast<HBITMAP>(
      SelectObject(hMemDC, hBmp)
      );
   HBITMAP hOldCopyBmp = static_cast<HBITMAP>(
      SelectObject(hCopyMemDC, hCopyBmp)
      );
   try
   {
      bool has_palette =
         (GetDeviceCaps(hScreenDC, RASTERCAPS) & RC_PALETTE);

      HPALETTE hOldPal;
      if (has_palette)
```

6. The Bitmap Object

```
        {
           hOldPal = SelectPalette(hCopyMemDC, hPal, false);
           RealizePalette(hCopyMemDC);
        }

        // render the bitmap to the copy
        BitBlt(hCopyMemDC, 0, 0,
               bmp.bmWidth, bmp.bmHeight,
               hMemDC, 0, 0,
               SRCCOPY);

        if (has_palette)
        {
           SelectPalette(hCopyMemDC, hOldPal, false);
        }
     }
     catch (...)
     {
        SelectObject(hMemDC, hOldBmp);
        SelectObject(hCopyMemDC, hOldCopyBmp);
        DeleteDC(hMemDC);
        DeleteDC(hCopyMemDC);
        ReleaseDC(NULL, hScreenDC);
        return NULL;
     }
     SelectObject(hMemDC, hOldBmp);
     SelectObject(hCopyMemDC, hOldCopyBmp);
     DeleteDC(hMemDC);
     DeleteDC(hCopyMemDC);
     ReleaseDC(NULL, hScreenDC);

     return hCopyBmp;
}
```


Loading a Device-Dependent Bitmap from a File

To load a device-dependent bitmap from a file, you use the application-defined **CreateDDBFromFile** function:

```
#include <ole2.h>
#include <olectl.h>
HBITMAP CreateDDBFromFile(
```

```
     IN LPCSTR filename,         // name of the image file to load
     OUT HPALETTE* pHPal = NULL  // receives the image's palette, if present
    )
{
    HBITMAP hBmp = NULL;

    // open the file for shared reading
    HANDLE hFile =
       CreateFile(
          filename, GENERIC_READ, FILE_SHARE_READ, NULL,
          OPEN_EXISTING, FILE_ATTRIBUTE_NORMAL, NULL
          );

    if (hFile != INVALID_HANDLE_VALUE)
    {
       // allocate a global memory object of the file's size
       const DWORD dwSize = GetFileSize(hFile, NULL);
       HGLOBAL hData = GlobalAlloc(GMEM_MOVEABLE, dwSize);
       if (hData)
       {
          LPVOID lpData = GlobalLock(hData);
          if (lpData)
          {
             // read the file
             DWORD dwRead = 0;
             bool read_ok = ReadFile(hFile, lpData, dwSize, &dwRead, NULL);
             if (read_ok && (dwRead == dwSize))
             {
                GlobalUnlock(hData);
                CloseHandle(hFile);
                hFile = NULL;

                // create an IStream object on hData
                LPSTREAM pStream;
                HRESULT hRes = CreateStreamOnHGlobal(
                   hData, false, &pStream
                   );
                if (SUCCEEDED(hRes))
                {
                   // load the picture (create an IPicture object)
                   LPPICTURE pPicture;
                   hRes =
                      OleLoadPicture(
                         pStream, 0, false, IID_IPicture,
                         reinterpret_cast<void**>(&pPicture)
                         );
```

```
if (SUCCEEDED(hRes))
{
   // if a palette was requested by the caller
   if (pHPal)
   {
      // grab a handle to its palette
      pPicture->get_hPal(
         reinterpret_cast<OLE_HANDLE*>(pHPal)
         );

      // copy the palette (because IPicture owns it)
      if (*pHPal)
      {
         const int num_entries =
            GetPaletteEntries(*pHPal, 0, 0, NULL);
         const long size =
            sizeof(LOGPALETTE) +
            (num_entries - 1) * sizeof(PALETTEENTRY);

         LPLOGPALETTE lpLogPal =
            reinterpret_cast<LPLOGPALETTE>(
               GlobalAlloc(GPTR, size)
               );
         if (lpLogPal)
         {
            const int num_got =
               GetPaletteEntries(
                  *pHPal, 0, num_entries,
                  lpLogPal->palPalEntry
                 );
            lpLogPal->palVersion = 0x300;
            lpLogPal->palNumEntries = num_got;

            *pHPal = CreatePalette(lpLogPal);
            GlobalFree(lpLogPal);
         }
      }
   }

   // retrieve the width and height of the picture
   SIZE SHiMetric = {0, 0};
   pPicture->get_Width(&SHiMetric.cx);
   pPicture->get_Height(&SHiMetric.cy);
```

```
// convert HIMETRIC units to pixels
HDC hScreenDC = GetDC(NULL);
const int width =
   MulDiv(
      SHiMetric.cx,
      GetDeviceCaps(hScreenDC, LOGPIXELSX),
      2540
      );
const int height =
   MulDiv(
      SHiMetric.cy,
      GetDeviceCaps(hScreenDC, LOGPIXELSY),
      2540
      );

// create a memory DC and a DDB
HDC hMemDC = CreateCompatibleDC(hScreenDC);
hBmp = CreateCompatibleBitmap(
   hScreenDC, width, height
   );
ReleaseDC(NULL, hScreenDC);

bool has_palette = (pHPal != NULL && *pHPal != NULL);
if (has_palette)
{
   *pHPal = SelectPalette(hMemDC, *pHPal, false);
   RealizePalette(hMemDC);
}
hBmp = static_cast<HBITMAP>(
   SelectObject(hMemDC, hBmp)
   );

// render the picture to the memory DC
pPicture->Render(
   hMemDC, 0, 0, width, height, 0, SHiMetric.cy,
   SHiMetric.cx, -SHiMetric.cy, NULL
   );

if (has_palette)
{
   *pHPal = SelectPalette(hMemDC, *pHPal, false);
}
hBmp = static_cast<HBITMAP>(
   SelectObject(hMemDC, hBmp)
   );
DeleteDC(hMemDC);
```

```
                    // release the IPicture object
                    pPicture->Release();
                }
                // release the IStream object
                pStream->Release();
            }
        }
        // clean up
        else GlobalUnlock(hData);
    }
    // free the global memory object
    GlobalFree(hData);
  }
  // clean up
  if (hFile) CloseHandle(hFile);
 }
 return hBmp;
}
```

The **filename** parameter is specified as a pointer to a **NULL**-terminated string that contains the full path of the image file from which the DDB is created. The **pHPal** parameter is specified as the address of a handle to a logical palette. You can set this parameter to **NULL** if a palette is not needed.

***NOTE:** You can alternatively use the **LoadImage** function if you're loading a bitmap that contains more than 256 colors.*

Upon success, the **CreateDDBFromFile** function returns a handle to a DDB that has been initialized with the color data (i.e., the "image") contained in the image file. If the function fails, the return value is **NULL**. If a palette is needed and the image exposes a corresponding palette, the variable specified by the **pHPal** parameter will contain a handle to the logical palette; if no palette is available, this variable is set to **NULL**.

The following code snippet demonstrates the use of the **CreateDDBFromFile** function to create a DDB (**hBmp**) from the information contained in a bitmap file (**filename**):

```
LPCSTR filename = TEXT("MYBITMAP.BMP\0");
HPALETTE hPal = NULL;
HBITMAP hBmp = CreateDDBFromFile(filename, &hPal);
if (hBmp)
{
   BITMAP bmp;
   if (GetObject(hBmp, sizeof(BITMAP), &bmp) == sizeof(BITMAP))
```

```
    {
        HDC hDC = GetDC(hWnd);
        HDC hMemDC = CreateCompatibleDC(hDC);
        HBITMAP hOldBmp = static_cast<HBITMAP>(
            SelectObject(hMemDC, hBmp)
            );
        try
        {
            if (hPal)
            {
                hPal = SelectPalette(hDC, hPal, false);
                RealizePalette(hDC);
            }

            BitBlt(
                hDC, 0, 0,
                bmp.bmWidth, bmp.bmHeight,
                hMemDC, 0, 0,
                SRCCOPY
                );

            if (hPal) DeleteObject(SelectPalette(hDC, hPal, false));
        }
        catch (...)
        {
            DeleteObject(SelectObject(hMemDC, hOldBmp));
            DeleteDC(hMemDC);
            ReleaseDC(hWnd, hDC);
        }
        DeleteObject(SelectObject(hMemDC, hOldBmp));
        DeleteDC(hMemDC);
        ReleaseDC(hWnd, hDC);
    }
    else DeleteObject(hBmp);
}
```


As it turns out, the **CreateDDBFromFile** function can be used to load more than just bitmaps—you can also use this function for JPEGs, GIFs, icons, and metafiles. The image decoding task is delegated to the **IPicture** OLE interface. For a non-OLE-based version of this function, see the implementation on the CD-ROM.

Related solutions:	*Found on page:*
Loading a Device-Independent Bitmap from a File	405
Loading a DIB Section Bitmap from a File	427

Saving a Device-Dependent Bitmap to a File

To save a device-dependent bitmap to a file, you use the application-defined **SaveDDBToFile** function:

```
#include <ole2.h>
#include <olectl.h>
BOOL SaveDDBToFile(
    IN const LPCSTR filename,       // name of the file to save as
    IN const HBITMAP hBmp,          // handle to the DDB
    IN const HPALETTE hPal = NULL   // handle to the logical palette
   )
{
   BOOL result = FALSE;

   // initialize the picture's description
   PICTDESC pd;
   pd.cbSizeofstruct = sizeof(PICTDESC);
   pd.picType = PICTYPE_BITMAP;
   pd.bmp.hbitmap = hBmp;
   pd.bmp.hpal = hPal;

   // create the IPicture object
   LPPICTURE pPicture;
   HRESULT hRes =
      OleCreatePictureIndirect(
         &pd, IID_IPicture, false,
         reinterpret_cast<void**>(&pPicture)
         );
   if (SUCCEEDED(hRes))
   {
      // create an IStream object
      LPSTREAM pStream;
      hRes = CreateStreamOnHGlobal(NULL, true, &pStream);
      if (SUCCEEDED(hRes))
      {
         // write the picture to the stream
         LONG bytes_streamed;
         hRes = pPicture->SaveAsFile(pStream, true, &bytes_streamed);
         if (SUCCEEDED(hRes))
         {
            // write the stream to the file
            HANDLE hFile =
```

```
                CreateFile(
                    filename, GENERIC_WRITE, FILE_SHARE_READ, NULL,
                    CREATE_ALWAYS, FILE_ATTRIBUTE_NORMAL, NULL
                    );
            if (hFile)
            {
                HGLOBAL hMem = NULL;
                GetHGlobalFromStream(pStream, &hMem);
                LPVOID lpData = GlobalLock(hMem);

                DWORD bytes_written;
                result =
                    WriteFile(
                        hFile, lpData, bytes_streamed,
                        &bytes_written, NULL
                        );
                result &=
                    (bytes_written == static_cast<DWORD>(bytes_streamed));

                GlobalUnlock(hMem);
                CloseHandle(hFile);
            }
        }
        pStream->Release();
    }
    pPicture->Release();
  }
  return result;
}
```


The **filename** parameter identifies the name of the file in which the DDB should be saved. If a file of the same name already exists, it is overwritten. The **hBmp** parameter is specified as the handle to the DDB that's to be saved. The **hPal** parameter is specified as this DDB's associated palette, if present. Upon success, the **SaveDDBToFile** function returns **TRUE**; otherwise, the return value is **FALSE**.

Note from the implementation of the **SaveDDBToFile** function that the bulk of the work is delegated to the **IPicture** OLE interface. For a non-OLE-based version of this function, see the implementation on the CD-ROM.

The following code snippet demonstrates the use of the **SaveDDBToFile** function to save a DDB (**hBmp**) and its associated palette (**hPal**) to a file (**out_filename**):

```
LPCSTR out_filename = TEXT("MYBITMAP.BMP\0");
BOOL save_ok = SaveDDBToFile(out_filename, hBmp, hPal);
```


Related solutions:	*Found on page:*
Saving a Device-Independent Bitmap to a File	409
Saving a DIB Section Bitmap to a File	432

Retrieving the Dimensions and Color Depth of a Device-Dependent Bitmap

To retrieve the attributes of a device-dependent bitmap, including its width, height, and color depth, you use the **GetObject** function:

```
int GetObject(
    IN HGDIOBJ hgdiobj,         // handle to the DDB
    IN int cbBuffer,            // number of bytes in the BITMAP structure
    OUT LPVOID lpvObject        // address of a BITMAP structure
   );
```

The **GetObject** function can also be used for other graphic objects, but here we'll focus specifically on the task of filling a **BITMAP** structure (as reflected in the previous parameter comments). For a more general discussion of the **GetObject** function, see Chapter 1.

TIP: *To obtain a handle to a device context's currently selected DDB, use the* ***GetCurrentObject*** *function with the* ***OBJ_BITMAP*** *identifier (see Chapter 1).*

The **hgdiobj** parameter is specified as the handle to the DDB whose attributes you want to retrieve. If the **GetObject** function is successful, these attributes are placed in the **BITMAP** structure whose address is specified by the **lpvObject** parameter. The **cbBuffer** parameter specifies how many bytes are available in the buffer indicated by **lpvObject**. Here you specify this parameter as **sizeof(BITMAP)**.

Upon success, the **GetObject** function will return the number of bytes that have been copied into the variable referred to by the **lpvObject** parameter. For DDBs, you want this return value to be **sizeof(BITMAP)**. If the function fails, the return value is zero.

The following code snippet demonstrates the use of the **GetObject** function to retrieve the width and height of a DDB (**hBmp**):

```
BITMAP bmp;
const size_t bmpSize = sizeof(BITMAP);
if (GetObject(hBmp, bmpSize, &bmp) == bmpSize)
{
   const int width = bmp.bmWidth;
   const int height = bmp.bmHeight;
   // ...
}
```

Similarly, to retrieve a DDB's color depth, you use the **GetObject** function like so:

```
BITMAP bmp;
const size_t bmpSize = sizeof(BITMAP);
if (GetObject(hBmp, bmpSize, &bmp) == bmpSize)
{
   const int bpp = bmp.bmPlanes * bmp.bmBitsPixel;
   // ...
}
```


Related solution:	Found on page:
Retrieving Information about a DIB Section Bitmap	432

Manipulating the Bits of a Device-Dependent Bitmap

The GDI does not provide direct access to the bits of a device-dependent bitmap (as it does with DIB section bitmaps). If you plan to manipulate a bitmap on a per-pixel basis, it's best to work with a DIB section bitmap instead. Nonetheless, you can retrieve a copy of a DDB's bits by using the **GetDIBits** function, manipulate the copy, and then use the **SetDIBits** function to send the changes to the DDB.

The **GetDIBits** function is designed to retrieve a copy of a DDB's bits in a device-independent format:

```
int GetDIBits(
    IN HDC hdc,                // handle to the target device context
    IN HBITMAP hbmp,           // handle to the DDB
    IN UINT uStartScan,        // first scan line to copy
    IN UINT cScanLines,        // total number of scan lines to copy
```

```
    OUT LPVOID lpvBits,          // array that will receive a copy of the
                                 // DDB's bits
    IN OUT LPBITMAPINFO lpbi,    // pointer to a BITMAPINFO structure that
                                 // describes the desired format of the bits
    IN UINT uUsage               // color table format identifier
);
```

The **hdc** parameter identifies the device context whose corresponding device driver is called to retrieve the DDB's bits. The **hBmp** parameter is specified as the handle to the DDB whose bits you want to copy.

WARNING! The DDB specified by the hBmp parameter must not be selected into a device context before you call GetDIBits.

The **uStartScan** and **cScanLines** parameters define the set of scan lines to copy. The **uStartScan** parameter is specified as the zero-based index of the first scan line. The **cScanLines** parameter indicates the desired number of scan lines to copy. The **lpvBits** parameter points to an array that will receive a copy of the DDB's bits. The **lpbi** parameter points to a **BITMAPINFO** structure that describes the desired format of these bits. The **GetDIBits** function will also fill this structure with information about the DDB, including a synthesized color table, if needed. Accordingly, the **uUsage** parameter specifies the desired format of this color table—either **DIB_RGB_COLORS** (0) for a color table that consists of **RGBQUAD**s, or **DIB_PAL_COLORS** (1) for a color table that consists of **WORD**-type palette indices.

The **GetDIBits** function requires that the caller initialize the first six data members of the **BITMAPINFOHEADER** structure that's contained in the specified **BITMAPINFO** structure (indicated by the **lpbi** parameter). Specifically, you should initialize these data members as follows:

```
BITMAPINFOHEADER::biSize = set to sizeof(BITMAPINFOHEADER)
BITMAPINFOHEADER::biWidth = the width of the DDB
BITMAPINFOHEADER::biHeight = negative the height of the DDB
BITMAPINFOHEADER::biPlanes = set to 1
BITMAPINFOHEADER::biBitCount = the desired number of bits per pixel
BITMAPINFOHEADER::biCompression = set to BI_RGB
```

WARNING! Be careful about setting the biBitCount data member to a value smaller than that of the DDB's color depth. Doing so will likely result in a loss of color information.

In addition, the **GetDIBits** function requires that sufficient memory be allocated for the **BITMAPINFO** structure's **bmiColors** data member; it must be large enough to hold the color table that will be synthesized, if required. Moreover, the array indicated by the **lpvBits** parameter must be large enough to hold the number of scan lines that are requested (by the **uStartScan** and **cScanLines** parameters). To this end, when the **lpvBits** parameter is specified as **NULL**, the **GetDIBits** function initializes the **BITMAPINFOHEADER::biSizeImage** data member and fills the color table (if required), but no bits are copied. (Remember, there's no place to copy them to yet.) You can then allocate exactly **biSizeImage** bytes for the **lpvBits** array, and then call the **GetDIBits** function again (this time with a non-**NULL** **lpvBits** parameter) to retrieve a copy of the DDB's bits.

NOTE: *Each scan line of the **lpvBits** array will be padded such that the scan line is **DWORD**-aligned.*

If the **GetDIBits** function is successful, and the **lpvBits** parameter is specified as **NULL**, the function returns non-zero (for systems running Windows NT or Windows 2000) or the total number of scan lines in the bitmap (for systems running Windows 95 or Windows 98). When **lpvBits** is non-**NULL**, and the **GetDIBits** function is successful, the function returns the number of scan lines that have been copied. In either case, the return value is zero if the function fails.

The following example demonstrates the use of the **GetDIBits** function to retrieve a copy of the bits of a DDB (**hBmp**) in a 24-bits-per-pixel format:

```
BOOL CopyBitsFromDDB24(
    IN const HBITMAP hBmp,          // handle to the DDB
    OUT unsigned char*& bits,       // array to retrieve the bits
    OUT LONG& bits_size,            // length of bits array
    OUT LONG& bytes_per_scanline    // number of bytes per scan line
   )
{
   BOOL result = FALSE;
   const int bpp = 24;

   BITMAP bmp;
   const size_t bmpSize = sizeof(BITMAP);
   if (GetObject(hBmp, bmpSize, &bmp) == bmpSize)
   {
      BITMAPINFO bmi;
      memset(&bmi, 0, sizeof(BITMAPINFO));

      // initialize the first six BITMAPINFOHEADER data members
      bmi.bmiHeader.biSize = sizeof(BITMAPINFOHEADER);
      bmi.bmiHeader.biWidth = bmp.bmWidth;
      bmi.bmiHeader.biHeight = -bmp.bmHeight; // "-" for top-down bits
      bmi.bmiHeader.biPlanes = 1;
      bmi.bmiHeader.biBitCount = bpp;
      bmi.bmiHeader.biCompression = BI_RGB;
```

6. The Bitmap Object

```
// use screen's DC for the call to GetDIBits
HDC hScreenDC = GetDC(NULL);
try
{
   //
   // call GetDIBits first with a NULL lpvBits
   // parameter so the device driver will calculate
   // the biSizeImage data member to tell us
   // how much memory to allocate for the bits
   //
   GetDIBits(
      hScreenDC, hBmp,
      0, bmp.bmHeight, NULL,
      &bmi, DIB_RGB_COLORS
      );

   //
   // if the driver didn't calculate the size,
   // let's estimate it ourselves
   //
   if (!bmi.bmiHeader.biSizeImage)
   {
      bmi.bmiHeader.biSizeImage =
         ((((bmp.bmWidth * bpp) + 31) & ~31) / 8) * bmp.bmHeight;
   }

   // allocate memory for, and copy, the bits
   bits = new unsigned char[bmi.bmiHeader.biSizeImage];
   try
   {
      result =
         GetDIBits(
            hScreenDC, hBmp,
            0, bmp.bmHeight, bits,
            &bmi, DIB_RGB_COLORS
            );
      if (!result) throw;

       //
       // fill in the length of the bits array
       // and compute the bytes per scan line
       //
       bits_size = bmi.bmiHeader.biSizeImage;
       bytes_per_scanline = bits_size / bmp.bmHeight;

   }
```

```
            catch (...)
            {
               delete [] bits;
               throw;
            }
         }
         catch (...)
         {
            ReleaseDC(NULL, hScreenDC);
            return FALSE;
         }
         ReleaseDC(NULL, hScreenDC);
      }
      return result;
   }
```

For more information on the **GetDIBits** function, especially for cases when a color table is required, refer to Chapter 7.

After you've retrieved a copy of the DDB's bits, you can manipulate them as desired. Then you can reflect the changes back to the DDB by using the **SetDIBits** function:

```
int SetDIBits(
    IN HDC hdc,                   // handle to the target device context
    IN HBITMAP hbmp,              // handle to the DDB
    IN UINT uStartScan,           // first scan line to copy
    IN UINT cScanLines,           // number of scan lines to copy
    IN LPVOID lpvBits,            // array that will be copied to the
                                  // DDB's bits
    IN LPBITMAPINFO lpbi,         // pointer to a BITMAPINFO structure that
                                  // describes the format of the bits
    IN UINT fuColorUse            // color-data usage flag
   );
```

The parameters of the **SetDIBits** function serve similar roles as those of the **GetDIBits** function. Here, however, the **hdc** parameter is used only when the **fuColorUse** parameter is specified as **DIB_PAL_COLORS**. Also note that none of the parameters are filled; they are all intended to convey information to the function (i.e., all parameters are declared as **IN**). Upon success, the **SetDIBits** function returns the number of scan lines that have been copied to the DDB. If the function fails, the return value is zero.

The following example demonstrates the use of the **SetDIBits** function to copy 24-bits-per-pixel data to a DDB:

```
BOOL CopyBitsToDDB24(
    IN const HBITMAP hBmp,          // handle to the DDB
    IN const unsigned char* bits,   // array of bits to copy
    IN LONG bits_size               // length of bits array
   )
{
   BOOL result = FALSE;
   const int bpp = 24;

   BITMAP bmp;
   const size_t bmpSize = sizeof(BITMAP);
   if (GetObject(hBmp, bmpSize, &bmp) == bmpSize)
   {
      BITMAPINFO bmi;
      memset(&bmi, 0, sizeof(BITMAPINFO));

      // initialize the BITMAPINFOHEADER data members
      bmi.bmiHeader.biSize = sizeof(BITMAPINFOHEADER);
      bmi.bmiHeader.biWidth = bmp.bmWidth;
      bmi.bmiHeader.biHeight = -bmp.bmHeight; // "-" for top-down bits
      bmi.bmiHeader.biPlanes = 1;
      bmi.bmiHeader.biBitCount = bpp;
      bmi.bmiHeader.biCompression = BI_RGB;
      bmi.bmiHeader.biSizeImage = bits_size;

      // copy the bits to the DDB
      result =
         SetDIBits(
            NULL, hBmp,
            0, bmp.bmHeight, bits,
            &bmi, DIB_RGB_COLORS
            );
   }
   return ((result == bmp.bmHeight) && (bmp.bmHeight != 0));
}
```

The following code snippet demonstrates the use of these example functions to make a DDB (**hBmp**) "brighter":

```
unsigned char* bits = NULL;
LONG bits_size = 0, bytes_per_scanline = 0;
```

```
// copy the bits from the DDB
if (CopyBitsFromDDB24(hBmp, bits, bits_size, bytes_per_scanline))
{
   try
   {
      // scale the intensity of bit
      for (int index = 0; index < bits_size; ++index)
      {
         bits[index] = min(2 * bits[index], 255);
      }
      //
      // we've changed our copy of the DDB's pixels,
      // now let's copy these pixels back to the DDB
      //
      CopyBitsToDDB24(hBmp, bits, bits_size);
   }
   catch (...)
   {
      delete [] bits;
   }
   delete [] bits;
}
```


Rendering a Device-Dependent Bitmap

To render a device-dependent bitmap in its actual size, or to render a portion of a device-dependent bitmap, you use the **BitBlt** function:

```
BOOL BitBlt(
    IN HDC hdcDest,     // handle to the target device context
    IN int nXDest,      // horizontal position of the top-left corner
                        // of the destination rectangle
    IN int nYDest,      // vertical position of the top-left corner
                        // of the destination rectangle
    IN int nWidth,      // width of the destination rectangle
    IN int nHeight,     // height of the destination rectangle
    IN HDC hdcSrc,      // handle to the source device context
    IN int nXSrc,       // horizontal position of the top-left corner
                        // of the source rectangle
    IN int nYSrc,       // horizontal position of the top-left corner
                        // of the source rectangle
    IN DWORD dwRop      // ternary-raster-operation code
   );
```

The **hdcDest** parameter specifies the target device context, that is, the DC to which the bits associated with the source device context (**hdcSrc**) should be transferred (copied). The **nXDest**, **nYDest**, **nWidth**, and **nHeight** parameters together designate the bounds of the destination rectangle, in logical units. The **hdcSrc** parameter identifies the source device context. To render a DDB, specify this parameter as the handle to the memory device context into which the bitmap object is selected. The **nXSrc** and **nYSrc** parameters indicate the top-left coordinates of the source rectangle, in logical units. The **dwRop** parameter specifies the ternary-raster-operation code, which is usually set to **SRCCOPY**, indicating that the destination will receive a COPY of the SouRCe (see Chapter 1).

NOTE: *Before you use the **BitBlt** function to render a DDB, you must select the DDB into a memory device context. The handle to this memory device context is then specified as the **hdcSrc** parameter.*

WARNING! You should never use the BitBlt function to transfer bits to different devices. That is, the device contexts indicated by the hdcSrc and hdcDest parameters must both correspond to the same device. Blitting across device contexts associated with different devices is not reliable.

If successful, the **BitBlt** function will return **TRUE**; otherwise, the return value is **FALSE**. For example, to render a DDB (**hBmp**) to a display device context (**hDC**) at the location **PDest** (on a non-palettized display), you use the **BitBlt** function as follows:

```
HDC hDC = GetDC(hWnd);
HDC hMemDC = CreateCompatibleDC(hDC);
HBITMAP hOldBmp = static_cast<HBITMAP>(SelectObject(hMemDC, hBmp));
try
{
   BITMAP bmp;
   const size_t bmpSize = sizeof(BITMAP);
   if (GetObject(hBmp, bmpSize, &bmp) != bmpSize) throw;

   const POINT PDest = {10, 20};
   BitBlt(
      hDC, PDest.x, PDest.y,
      bmp.bmWidth, bmp.bmHeight,
      hMemDC, 0, 0,
      SRCCOPY
      );
}
catch (...)
{
```

```
    DeleteObject(SelectObject(hMemDC, hOldBmp));
    DeleteDC(hMemDC);
    ReleaseDC(hWnd, hDC);
}
DeleteObject(SelectObject(hMemDC, hOldBmp));
DeleteDC(hMemDC);
ReleaseDC(hWnd, hDC);
```

Similarly, to render the lower-right (100-by-100) portion of a DDB (on a non-palettized display), you use the **BitBlt** function like so:

```
HDC hDC = GetDC(hWnd);
HDC hMemDC = CreateCompatibleDC(hDC);
HBITMAP hOldBmp = static_cast<HBITMAP>(SelectObject(hMemDC, hBmp));
try
{
    BITMAP bmp;
    const size_t bmpSize = sizeof(BITMAP);
    if (GetObject(hBmp, bmpSize, &bmp) != bmpSize) throw;

    const POINT PDest = {10, 20};
    BitBlt(
        hDC, PDest.x, PDest.y,
        100, 100,
        hMemDC,
        bmp.bmWidth - 100,
        bmp.bmHeight - 100,
        SRCCOPY
        );
}
catch (...)
{
    DeleteObject(SelectObject(hMemDC, hOldBmp));
    DeleteDC(hMemDC);
    ReleaseDC(hWnd, hDC);
}
DeleteObject(SelectObject(hMemDC, hOldBmp));
DeleteDC(hMemDC);
ReleaseDC(hWnd, hDC);
```

On a palettized display, the method is similar. In this case, you simply select (and realize) the bitmap's associated palette into the destination device context (not into the bitmap's associated memory device context) before calling **BitBlt**. Refer to Chapter 9 for more information on palettes. For more information on the **BitBlt** function, see Chapter 1.

Related solutions:	Found on page:
Creating a Memory Device Context	64
Rendering to a Device Context by Using the **BitBlt** Function	68
Rendering a Device-Independent Bitmap	412

Rendering a Device-Dependent Bitmap in a Scaled Fashion

To render a device-dependent bitmap (or a portion of a device-dependent bitmap) in a stretched or compacted fashion, you use the **StretchBlt** function:

```
BOOL StretchBlt(
    IN HDC hdcDest,         // handle to the destination device context
    IN int nXOriginDest,    // horizontal position of the top-left
                            // corner of the destination rectangle
    IN int nYOriginDest,    // vertical position of the top-left
                            // corner of the destination rectangle
    IN int nWidthDest,      // width of the destination rectangle
    IN int nHeightDest,     // height of the destination rectangle
    IN HDC hdcSrc,          // handle to the source device context
    IN int nXOriginSrc,     // horizontal position of the top-left
                            // corner of the source rectangle
    IN int nYOriginSrc,     // vertical position of the top-left
                            // corner of the source rectangle
    IN int nWidthSrc,       // width of the source rectangle
    IN int nHeightSrc,      // height of the source rectangle
    IN DWORD dwRop          // ternary-raster-operation code
  );
```

The **hdcDest** parameter specifies the target device context; that is, the DC to which the bits associated with the source device context (**hdcSrc**) should be transferred (copied). The **nXOriginDest**, **nYOriginDest**, **nWidthDest**, and **nHeightDest** parameters together specify the location and dimensions of the destination rectangle, in logical units. The **hdcSrc** parameter identifies the source device context. To render a DDB, pass a handle to the memory DC into which the DDB is selected as the **hdcSrc** parameter. The **nXOriginSrc**, **nYOriginSrc**, **nWidthSrc**, and **nHeightSrc** parameters specify the location and the dimensions of the source rectangle, in logical units. The **dwRop** parameter specifies a ternary-raster-operation code (see Chapter 1).

***NOTE:** Before you use the **StretchBlt** function to render a DDB, you must select the DDB into a memory device context. The handle to this memory device context is then specified as the **hdcSrc** parameter.*

When the area of the destination rectangle is smaller than that of the source rectangle (such that the image should be scaled down), the stretching mode of the target device context determines the fashion in which pixels are discarded. For more information on the stretching mode, see Chapter 1.

WARNING! You should never use the StretchBlt function to transfer bits to different devices. That is, the device contexts indicated by the hdcSrc and hdcDest parameters must both correspond to the same device. Blitting across device contexts associated with different devices is not reliable.

Upon success, the **StretchBlt** function returns **TRUE**; otherwise, the return value is **FALSE**. For example, to render a DDB (**hBmp**) to a display device context (**hDC**) stretched to twice its original width and height (on a non-palettized display), you use the **StretchBlt** function like so:

```
HDC hDC = GetDC(hWnd);
HDC hMemDC = CreateCompatibleDC(hDC);
HBITMAP hOldBmp = static_cast<HBITMAP>(SelectObject(hMemDC, hBmp));
try
{
   BITMAP bmp;
   const size_t bmpSize = sizeof(BITMAP);
   if (GetObject(hBmp, bmpSize, &bmp) != bmpSize) throw;

   const POINT PDest = {0, 0};
   StretchBlt(
      hDC, PDest.x, PDest.y,
      2 * bmp.bmWidth, 2 * bmp.bmHeight,
      hMemDC, 0, 0,
      bmp.bmWidth, bmp.bmHeight,
      SRCCOPY
      );
}
catch (...)
{
   DeleteObject(SelectObject(hMemDC, hOldBmp));
   DeleteDC(hMemDC);
   ReleaseDC(hWnd, hDC);
}
DeleteObject(SelectObject(hMemDC, hOldBmp));
DeleteDC(hMemDC);
ReleaseDC(hWnd, hDC);
```

Likewise, to render the lower-right (50-by-50) portion of a DDB (on a non-palettized display) scaled to one-and-a-half times its original size, you use the **StretchBlt** function like so:

```
HDC hDC = GetDC(hWnd);
HDC hMemDC = CreateCompatibleDC(hDC);
HBITMAP hOldBmp = static_cast<HBITMAP>(SelectObject(hMemDC, hBmp));
try
{
   BITMAP bmp;
   const size_t bmpSize = sizeof(BITMAP);
   if (GetObject(hBmp, bmpSize, &bmp) != bmpSize) throw;

   const POINT PDest = {0, 0};
   StretchBlt(
      hDC, PDest.x, PDest.y,
      1.5 * bmp.bmWidth, 1.5 * bmp.bmHeight,
      hMemDC,
      bmp.bmWidth - 50, bmp.bmHeight - 50,
      50, 50,
      SRCCOPY
      );
}
catch (...)
{
   DeleteObject(SelectObject(hMemDC, hOldBmp));
   DeleteDC(hMemDC);
   ReleaseDC(hWnd, hDC);
}
DeleteObject(SelectObject(hMemDC, hOldBmp));
DeleteDC(hMemDC);
ReleaseDC(hWnd, hDC);
```

When rendering to a palettized device, you should select the bitmap's associated palette into the destination device context (not into the bitmap's associated memory device context), and then realize this palette, before calling **StretchBlt**. For more information on palettes, see Chapter 9. For more information on the **StretchBlt** function, see Chapter 1.

Related solutions:	*Found on page:*
Creating a Memory Device Context	64
Rendering to a Device Context by Using the **StretchBlt** Function	74
Rendering a Device-Independent Bitmap in a Scaled Fashion	415

Rendering the Mirror Image of a Device-Dependent Bitmap

To render a device-dependent bitmap in a flipped or mirrored fashion, you use the **StretchBlt** function, specifying a negative value for the **nWidthDest** parameter and/or the **nHeightDest** parameter. For the specifics of the **StretchBlt** function, see Chapter 1.

Typically, the **nXOriginDest**, **nYOriginDest**, **nWidthDest**, and **nHeightDest** parameters of the **StretchBlt** function together specify a bounding rectangle for the destination image; the DDB is drawn to fit within this rectangle. However, when the **nWidthDest** or **nHeightDest** parameter is specified as a negative value, the bitmap is drawn in a mirrored fashion. Specifically, when you specify a negative value as **nWidthDest**, the bitmap is mirrored across its left edge (see Figure 6.2). Similarly, when you specify a negative value as **nHeightDest**, the bitmap is mirrored across its bottom edge (see Figure 6.3). When both **nWidthDest** and **nHeightDest** are passed negative values, the bitmap is flipped upside-down (i.e., it's rotated 180 degrees).

The following code snippet demonstrates the use of the **StretchBlt** function to mirror a bitmap (**hBmp**) across its left edge. For comparison purposes, the **StretchBlt** function is used a second time to render the original image. The result is depicted in Figure 6.2:

```
HDC hDC = GetDC(hWnd);
HDC hMemDC = CreateCompatibleDC(hDC);
HBITMAP hOldBmp = static_cast<HBITMAP>(SelectObject(hMemDC, hBmp));
try
{
   BITMAP bmp;
   const size_t bmpSize = sizeof(BITMAP);
   if (GetObject(hBmp, bmpSize, &bmp) != bmpSize) throw;
```

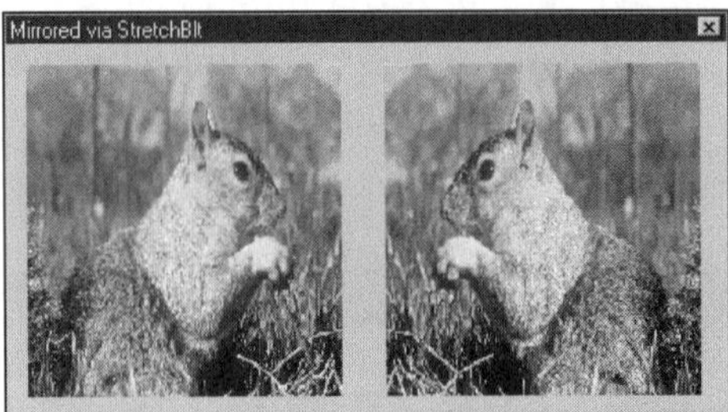

Figure 6.2 A bitmap that's rendered in a horizontally mirrored fashion (left) and its original (right).

```
    //
    // TODO: add palette support as needed...
    //

    POINT PDest = {10, 10};

    // render the DDB mirrored across its left edge
    StretchBlt(
        hDC, PDest.x + bmp.bmWidth, PDest.y,
        -bmp.bmWidth, bmp.bmHeight,
        hMemDC, 0, 0,
        bmp.bmWidth, bmp.bmHeight,
        SRCCOPY
        );

    PDest.x += bmp.bmWidth + 25;

    // render the original image (for comparison purposes)
    StretchBlt(
        hDC, PDest.x, PDest.y,
        bmp.bmWidth, bmp.bmHeight,
        hMemDC, 0, 0,
        bmp.bmWidth, bmp.bmHeight,
        SRCCOPY
        );
}
```


Likewise, the following code snippet demonstrates how to use the **StretchBlt** function to mirror a DDB (**hBmp**) across its bottom edge. As before, for comparison purposes, the **StretchBlt** function is used a second time to render the original image. The result is depicted in Figure 6.3:

```
HDC hDC = GetDC(hWnd);
HDC hMemDC = CreateCompatibleDC(hDC);
HBITMAP hOldBmp = static_cast<HBITMAP>(SelectObject(hMemDC, hBmp));
try
{
    BITMAP bmp;
    const size_t bmpSize = sizeof(BITMAP);
    if (GetObject(hBmp, bmpSize, &bmp) != bmpSize) throw;

    //
    // TODO: add palette support as needed...
    //
```

Figure 6.3 A bitmap that's rendered in a vertically mirrored fashion (bottom) and its original (top).

```
   POINT PDest = {10, 10};

   // render the original image (for comparison purposes)
   StretchBlt(
      hDC, PDest.x, PDest.y,
      bmp.bmWidth, bmp.bmHeight,
      hMemDC, 0, 0,
      bmp.bmWidth, bmp.bmHeight,
      SRCCOPY
      );

   PDest.y += bmp.bmHeight + 25;

   // render the DDB mirrored across its bottom edge
   StretchBlt(
      hDC, PDest.x, PDest.y + bmp.bmHeight,
      bmp.bmWidth, -bmp.bmHeight,
      hMemDC, 0, 0,
      bmp.bmWidth, bmp.bmHeight,
      SRCCOPY
      );
}
catch (...)
{
   DeleteObject(SelectObject(hMemDC, hOldBmp));
   SelectObject(hMemDC, hOldBmp);
```

```
    DeleteDC(hMemDC);
    ReleaseDC(hWnd, hDC);
}
DeleteObject(SelectObject(hMemDC, hOldBmp));
SelectObject(hMemDC, hOldBmp);
DeleteDC(hMemDC);
ReleaseDC(hWnd, hDC);
```

Rendering a Transparent Device-Dependent Bitmap

To render a device-dependent bitmap (or a portion of a device-dependent bitmap) in a transparent fashion, you use the **TransparentBlt** function (Windows 98 and Windows 2000 only):

```
BOOL TransparentBlt(
    IN HDC hdcDest,         // handle to the destination device context
    IN int nXOriginDest,    // horizontal position of the top-left
                            // corner of the destination rectangle
    IN int nYOriginDest,    // vertical position of the top-left
                            // corner of the destination rectangle
    IN int nWidthDest,      // width of the destination rectangle
    IN int nHeightDest,     // height of the destination rectangle
    IN HDC hdcSrc,          // handle to the source device context
    IN int nXOriginSrc,     // horizontal position of the top-left
                            // corner of the source rectangle
    IN int nYOriginSrc,     // vertical position of the top-left
                            // corner of the source rectangle
    IN int nWidthSrc,       // width of the source rectangle
    IN int nHeightSrc,      // height of the source rectangle
    IN UINT crTransparent   // color to use for transparency
  );
```

The **hdcDest** parameter identifies the target device context, that is, the DC to which the bits associated with the source device context (**hdcSrc**) should be transferred (copied). The **nXOriginDest**, **nYOriginDest**, **nWidthDest**, and **nHeightDest** parameters together specify the location and the dimensions of the destination rectangle, in logical units. The **hdcSrc** parameter identifies the source device context. To render a DDB, you specify a handle to the memory DC (into which the DDB is selected) as the **hdcSrc** parameter. The **nXOriginSrc**, **nYOriginSrc**, **nWidthSrc**, and **nHeightSrc** parameters specify the bounds of the source rectangle, in logical units. The **crTransparent** parameter specifies which pixels of the DDB should not be rendered (i.e., the transparent pixels). Any pixels of the DDB that represent this color value will not be displayed on the destination device.

NOTE: *Before you use the* ***TransparentBlt*** *function to render a DDB, you must select the DDB into a memory device context. The handle to this memory device context is then specified as the* ***hdcSrc*** *parameter.*

Unlike the **StretchBlt** function, the **TransparentBlt** function always uses the **SRCCOPY** ternary raster operation and the **COLORONCOLOR** stretching mode. Moreover, negative values for the **nWidthDest** and **nHeightDest** parameters cannot be used for a mirrored effect. Upon success, the **TransparentBlt** function returns **TRUE**; otherwise, the return value is **FALSE**.

WARNING! You should never use the TransparentBlt function to transfer bits to different devices. That is, the device contexts indicated by the hdcSrc and hdcDest parameters must both correspond to the same device. Blitting across device contexts associated with different devices is not reliable.

The following code snippet demonstrates how to transparently render a DDB (**hBmp**) to a display device context (**hDC**) in its original width and height (on a non-palettized display):

```
HDC hDC = GetDC(hWnd);
HDC hMemDC = CreateCompatibleDC(hDC);
HBITMAP hOldBmp = static_cast<HBITMAP>(SelectObject(hMemDC, hBmp));
try
{
   BITMAP bmp;
   const size_t bmpSize = sizeof(BITMAP);
   if (GetObject(hBmp, bmpSize, &bmp) != bmpSize) throw;

   const POINT PDest = {0, 0};
   const COLORREF clrTransparent = PALETTERGB(255, 0, 0);

   TransparentBlt(
       hDC, PDest.x, PDest.y,
       bmp.bmWidth, bmp.bmHeight,
       hMemDC, 0, 0,
       bmp.bmWidth, bmp.bmHeight,
       clrTransparent
       );
}
catch (...)
{
   DeleteObject(SelectObject(hMemDC, hOldBmp));
   DeleteDC(hMemDC);
```

```
    ReleaseDC(hWnd, hDC);
}
DeleteObject(SelectObject(hMemDC, hOldBmp));
DeleteDC(hMemDC);
ReleaseDC(hWnd, hDC);
```

The **TransparentBlt** function can also be used to transparently draw a DDB, or a portion of a DDB, in a stretched or compacted fashion. For example, to render the upper-left (100-by-100) corner of a DDB (**hBmp**) to a display device context (**hDC**) stretched to twice its original width and height (on a non-palettized display), you use the **TransparentBlt** function as follows:

```
HDC hDC = GetDC(hWnd);
HDC hMemDC = CreateCompatibleDC(hDC);
HBITMAP hOldBmp = static_cast<HBITMAP>(SelectObject(hMemDC, hBmp));
try
{
    BITMAP bmp;
    const size_t bmpSize = sizeof(BITMAP);
    if (GetObject(hBmp, bmpSize, &bmp) != bmpSize) throw;

    const POINT PDest = {0, 0};
    const COLORREF clrTransparent = PALETTERGB(255, 0, 0);

    TransparentBlt(
        hDC, PDest.x, PDest.y,
        2 * bmp.bmWidth, 2 * bmp.bmHeight,
        hMemDC, 0, 0,
        100, 100,
        clrTransparent
        );
}
catch (...)
{
    DeleteObject(SelectObject(hMemDC, hOldBmp));
    DeleteDC(hMemDC);
    ReleaseDC(hWnd, hDC);
}
DeleteObject(SelectObject(hMemDC, hOldBmp));
DeleteDC(hMemDC);
ReleaseDC(hWnd, hDC);
```

When rendering to a palettized device, you should select the bitmap's associated palette into the destination device context (not into the bitmap's associated memory device context) before calling **TransparentBlt**. For information on palettes, see Chapter 9.

Unfortunately, the **TransparentBlt** function is not available on systems running Windows 95 or Windows NT. For these systems, you must perform the masking manually. The following example demonstrates this process:

```
BOOL TransparentBlt95NT(
    IN HDC hdcDest,          // handle to the destination device context
    IN int nXOriginDest,     // horizontal position of the top-left
                             // corner of the destination rectangle
    IN int nYOriginDest,     // vertical position of the top-left
                             // corner of the destination rectangle
    IN int nWidthDest,       // width of the destination rectangle
    IN int nHeightDest,      // height of the destination rectangle
    IN HDC hdcSrc,           // handle to the source device context
    IN int nXOriginSrc,      // horizontal position of the top-left
                             // corner of the source rectangle
    IN int nYOriginSrc,      // vertical position of the top-left
                             // corner of the source rectangle
    IN int nWidthSrc,        // width of the source rectangle
    IN int nHeightSrc,       // height of the source rectangle
    IN UINT crTransparent    // color to use for transparency
   )
{
   //
   // NOTE: see Chapter 7 for information on
   // modifying this function to use DIB section
   // bitmaps instead of the size-limited DDBs
   //

   // create the mask memory DC
   HDC hMaskDC = CreateCompatibleDC(hdcDest);
   if (!hMaskDC)
   {
      return false;
   }
   SetStretchBltMode(hMaskDC, COLORONCOLOR);

   // create the overlay memory DC
   HDC hOverlayDC = CreateCompatibleDC(hdcDest);
   if (!hOverlayDC)
   {
      DeleteDC(hMaskDC);
      return false;
   }
```

```
// create a DC to hold the result
HDC hCompositeDC = CreateCompatibleDC(hdcDest);
if (!hCompositeDC)
{
   DeleteDC(hOverlayDC);
   DeleteDC(hMaskDC);
   return false;
}

// create the mask bitmap
HBITMAP hMaskBmp =
   CreateBitmap(nWidthDest, nHeightDest, 1, 1, NULL);
if (!hMaskBmp)
{
   DeleteDC(hMaskDC);
   DeleteDC(hOverlayDC);
   return false;
}

// create the overlay bitmap
HBITMAP hOverlayBmp =
   CreateCompatibleBitmap(hdcDest, nWidthDest, nHeightDest);
if (!hOverlayBmp)
{
   DeleteDC(hMaskDC);
   DeleteDC(hOverlayDC);
   DeleteObject(hMaskBmp);
   return false;
}

// create the composite bitmap
HBITMAP hCompositeBmp =
   CreateCompatibleBitmap(hdcDest, nWidthDest, nHeightDest);
if (!hCompositeBmp)
{
   DeleteDC(hMaskDC);
   DeleteDC(hOverlayDC);
   DeleteDC(hCompositeDC);
   DeleteObject(hMaskBmp);
   DeleteObject(hOverlayBmp);
   return false;
}

BOOL result = FALSE;
HBITMAP hOldMaskBmp = static_cast<HBITMAP>(
```

```
      SelectObject(hMaskDC, hMaskBmp)
      );
   HBITMAP hOldOverlayBmp = static_cast<HBITMAP>(
      SelectObject(hOverlayDC, hOverlayBmp)
      );
   HBITMAP hOldCompositeBmp = static_cast<HBITMAP>(
      SelectObject(hCompositeDC, hCompositeBmp)
      );

   // create the mask
   COLORREF crOld = SetBkColor(hdcSrc, crTransparent);
   SetStretchBltMode(hMaskDC, COLORONCOLOR);
   result = StretchBlt(hMaskDC, 0, 0,
                       nWidthDest, nHeightDest,
                       hdcSrc, nXOriginSrc, nYOriginSrc,
                       nWidthSrc, nHeightSrc,
                       NOTSRCCOPY);
   SetBkColor(hdcSrc, crOld);

   // create the overlay
   result &= BitBlt(hOverlayDC, 0, 0,
                    nWidthDest, nHeightDest,
                    hMaskDC, 0, 0,
                    NOTSRCCOPY);
   result &= BitBlt(hOverlayDC, 0, 0,
                    nWidthDest, nHeightDest,
                    hdcDest, nXOriginDest, nYOriginDest,
                    SRCAND);

   // copy the mask to the composite
   result &= BitBlt(hCompositeDC, 0, 0,
                    nWidthDest, nHeightDest,
                    hMaskDC, 0, 0,
                    SRCCOPY);
   // clean up
   DeleteObject(SelectObject(hMaskDC, hOldMaskBmp));
   DeleteDC(hMaskDC);

   // select that target's palette into the composite DC
   HPALETTE hPal = static_cast<HPALETTE>(
      GetCurrentObject(hdcDest, OBJ_PAL)
      );
   if (hPal)
   {
```

```
        hPal = SelectPalette(hCompositeDC, hPal, false);
        RealizePalette(hCompositeDC);
    }

    // AND the source with the composite
    SetStretchBltMode(hCompositeDC, COLORONCOLOR);
    result &= StretchBlt(hCompositeDC, 0, 0,
                         nWidthDest, nHeightDest,
                         hdcSrc, nXOriginSrc, nYOriginSrc,
                         nWidthSrc, nHeightSrc,
                         SRCAND);

    // OR the overlay with the composite
    result &= BitBlt(hCompositeDC, 0, 0,
                     nWidthDest, nHeightDest,
                     hOverlayDC, 0, 0,
                     SRCPAINT);
    // clean up
    DeleteObject(SelectObject(hOverlayDC, hOldOverlayBmp));
    DeleteDC(hOverlayDC);

    // copy the composite to the target
    result &= BitBlt(hdcDest, nXOriginDest, nYOriginDest,
                     nWidthDest, nHeightDest,
                     hCompositeDC, 0, 0,
                     SRCCOPY);
    // clean up
    SelectPalette(hCompositeDC, hPal, false);
    DeleteObject(SelectObject(hCompositeDC, hOldCompositeBmp));
    DeleteDC(hCompositeDC);

    return result;
}
```


Related solution:	Found on page:
Creating a Memory Device Context	64

Chapter 7

Device-Independent Bitmaps

In Depth

In Chapter 6, we discussed the differences between a device-dependent bitmap (DDB) and a device-independent bitmap (DIB). Recall that the device-dependence of a DDB, while beneficial for rendering speed, prevents us from directly accessing the DDB's pixels. Again, this limitation results from the fact that DDBs are stored in a device-specific format. The format of a DIB, on the other hand, is not device-specific.

Many references provide only a cursory treatment of DIBs or a DIB class. Think about it for a moment, though—a class serves two main roles: abstraction and encapsulation. Heck, DIBs are abstract enough; why hide the implementation? Encapsulation, on the other hand, is helpful because working with DIBs is a chore, to say the least. Still, the only way to learn is to get your hands dirty; in doing so, you'll become comfortable with DIBs.

In this chapter, we'll examine both DIBs and DIB section bitmaps. First, we'll look at how the DIB format is laid out, how it's stored in memory, and how you can access its individual elements. Next, we'll look at different types of DIBs and the techniques that are used to manipulate the pixels of each type. We'll also discuss how to render a DIB to a device context, and we'll discuss some of the advantages and limitations that result from device-independence. Next, we'll shift gears and focus on the DIB section bitmap. We'll contrast this special type of bitmap with normal DDBs and DIBs, and examine how DIB sections provide both speed and flexibility.

A "Universal" Format

What exactly is a DIB? Simply put, it's a composite entity—a multipart "structure," if you will. And, though not truly universal, the format of this "structure" is *well known;* that is, it's not specific to a particular device. In this way, a DIB is very much like a common language that both applications and device drivers can speak. By the end of this chapter, you, too, will be fluent in this language.

Before we get into the specifics of a DIB's format, here are a few key points that need to be made. The most important thing to understand is that a DIB is not a GDI graphic object. There's no such thing as a handle to a DIB, nor is there the notion of a logical or physical variety. Another thing to understand, which actually results from the first fact, is that unlike brushes, pens, fonts, or DDBs, you can't select a DIB into a device context, not even a memory device context. This means that if you need to draw something to a DIB, you can't use any GDI function that requires a handle to a device context. In fact, there are no GDI functions for drawing to a DIB, although there are a few that can be used to transfer a DIB to a device context. This leads us to the final fact: the GDI does provide a means of rendering a DIB to a device context. There are actually two functions, which we'll discuss later in this chapter (see "Rendering DIBs"), that are specifically designed for transferring DIBs among different devices.

To recap, you should keep the following things in mind throughout this chapter:

- A DIB is *not* a GDI graphic object.
- A DIB *cannot* be selected into a device context.
- A DIB *can* be rendered to a device context by using specialized GDI functions.

Because many developers fail to grasp these concepts early in the game, DIBs remain a great mystery to a majority of the development community. Most of this confusion, however, simply results from the fact that the format of a DIB is often intimidating.

A DIB is composed of three entities: a *header*, an optional *color table*, and an array of *pixels*. This layout is depicted in Figure 7.1.

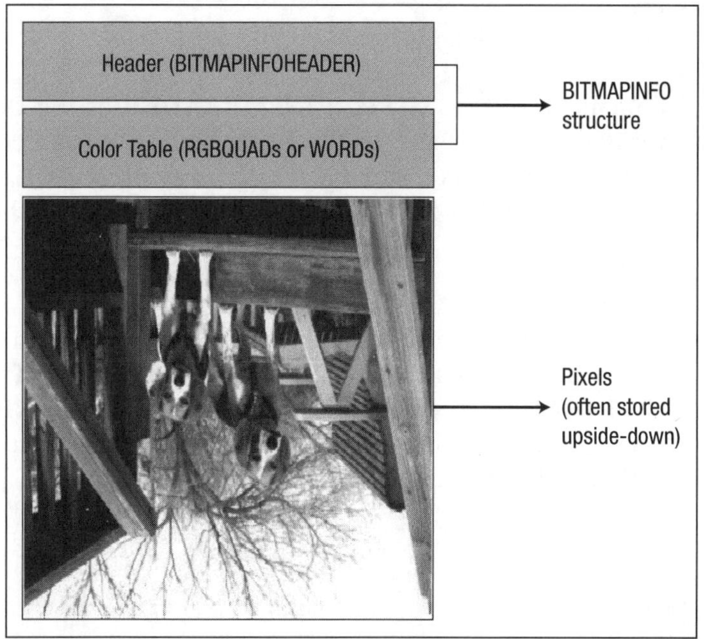

Figure 7.1 A DIB is defined by a header, a color table, and an array of pixels.

The header and the optional color table are always stored contiguously; the color table, if present, always follows the header. The memory for the pixels, however, can come from anywhere. Often a DIB's last scan line is stored first (i.e., the image itself is upside-down), and in many cases, the array of pixels immediately follows the color table. As we'll discuss shortly (see "The Pixels"), these varieties are known as *bottom-up* and *packed* DIBs, respectively.

Because a DIB is not a GDI graphic object, there's no predefined function that can be used to create one. In fact, when you see the phrase "create a DIB," this simply means: allocate a chunk of memory to hold the header and the color table; assign proper values to the fields of the header; and then fill the entries of the color table. In addition, you allocate memory for the pixels of the DIB as you would any other array of bytes. As it turns out, the most difficult part of this process is deciding how *much* memory to allocate for each part. Let's examine each of these parts more closely.

The BITMAPINFO Structure

The first two parts of a DIB consist of a header and a color table. These components are stored in a special structure, **BITMAPINFO**:

```
typedef struct tagBITMAPINFO {
    BITMAPINFOHEADER bmiHeader;
    RGBQUAD bmiColors[1];
} BITMAPINFO, FAR *LPBITMAPINFO, *PBITMAPINFO;
```

The **bmiHeader** data member, of type **BITMAPINFOHEADER**, is the DIB's header; it describes various attributes such as the DIB's dimensions and color depth. The **bmiColors** data member is a variable-length array of **RGBQUAD**s that holds the DIB's color-table entries. Let's take a closer look at each of these data members.

The Header

A DIB's header describes the attributes of a DIB. This information is stored in one of the following three structures: **BITMAPINFOHEADER**, **BITMAPV4-HEADER**, or **BITMAPV5HEADER**. The latter two structures are used with ICM (Image Color Management), which we'll cover in Chapter 16. Here we'll focus strictly on the **BITMAPINFOHEADER** structure:

```
typedef struct tagBITMAPINFOHEADER {
    DWORD      biSize;
    LONG       biWidth;
    LONG       biHeight;
    WORD       biPlanes;
```

```
    WORD        biBitCount;
    DWORD       biCompression;
    DWORD       biSizeImage;
    LONG        biXPelsPerMeter;
    LONG        biYPelsPerMeter;
    DWORD       biClrUsed;
    DWORD       biClrImportant;
} BITMAPINFOHEADER, FAR *LPBITMAPINFOHEADER, *PBITMAPINFOHEADER;
```

There's a somewhat intimidating number of data members, but don't worry; many of these are simply set to zero. The first five convey the most vital information. The **biSize** data member identifies the size of the DIB's header and is typically specified as **sizeof(BITMAPINFOHEADER)**. The **biWidth** and **biHeight** data members identify the horizontal and vertical dimensions of the DIB (in pixels), respectively. The **biPlanes** and **biBitCount** data members describe the color depth of the DIB. The **biPlanes** data member, which identifies the number of color planes, must be set to a value of 1. The **biBitCount** data member, which identifies the number of bits that are used for each pixel, can be set to 1, 4, 8, 16, 24, or 32.

The **biCompression** data member identifies the type of compression that's used, if any. Table 7.1 lists the possible identifiers that can be assigned to this data member. Note that run-length encoding (RLE) is rarely used—it provides poor compression ratios and slower rendering speeds.

The **biSizeImage** data member identifies the number of bytes that are required for the pixels of the DIB. This data member can be zero when the **biCompression**

Table 7.1 Possible identifiers for the BITMAPINFOHEADER::biCompression data member.

Identifier	Value	Meaning
BI_RGB	0	The DIB is not compressed.
BI_BITFIELDS	3	The DIB is not compressed, and its color table is composed of three **DWORD** values that are used as color masks. This identifier applies only to 16- or 32-bit DIBs.
BI_RLE4	2	The DIB is compressed using run-length encoding. This identifier applies only to 4-bit DIBs.
BI_RLE8	1	The DIB is compressed using run-length encoding. This identifier applies only to 8-bit DIBs.
BI_JPEG	4	The DIB is compressed in the same fashion as a JPEG image (Windows 98 and 2000 only).
BI_PNG	5	The DIB is compressed in the same fashion as a PNG image (Windows 98 and 2000 only).

data member is set to **BI_RGB**, but when you're creating a DIB, it's customary to initialize this data member to convey the size required by the array of pixels. We'll return to this issue shortly (see "The Pixels").

The **biXPelsPerMeter** and **biYPelsPerMeter** data members identify the number of pixels per meter in the horizontal and vertical directions, respectively. These data members are often ignored and simply initialized to zero.

The **biClrUsed** data member, which identifies the number of entries in the DIB's color table, was actually designed to reduce the size of the color table. Typically, the size of the color table depends on the number of bits per pixel. For example, the color table of an 8-bit DIB would normally contain 256 entries. However, if the image itself uses only, say, a dozen unique colors, there's no need for the color table to be that large. In this case, **biClrUsed** would be set to 12. The savings in space, however, are usually minimal, and this scheme won't work with packed DIBs. In most situations, **biClrUsed** is set to zero, indicating that the color table contains the maximum number of colors for its color depth.

The **biClrImportant** data member is used to optimize the appearance of the DIB when it's displayed on a device with a limited number of colors. This data member specifies the number of color-table entries that are required for the DIB to look "acceptable." Naturally, this value is subjective, and it's usually set by the creator of the image. Like the **biClrUsed** data member, **biClrImportant** is usually set to zero, indicating that all colors are important.

The Color Table

A DIB's color table, as its name suggests, is a lookup table that maps color indices to red, green, and blue intensities. A color table is required for 1-, 4-, or 8-bit DIBs and is optional for those of greater color depths.

Why is a color table needed in the first place? Well, consider the case of an 8-bit DIB. Here each pixel is represented by exactly eight bits, and somehow, a red, green, and blue intensity (RGB value) must be conveyed using only these bits. Because blue contributes least to the total luminance, one approach is to use three bits each for the red and green information, and the remaining two bits for blue. With three bits, you can represent a maximum of eight unique numbers. So, for example, if we map these eight numbers to the range [0, 255], using a spacing of 36 units, we get the following list of possible values for the red and green intensities:

```
  red = [0,  36,  72,  108,  144,  180,  216,  255]
green = [0,  36,  72,  108,  144,  180,  216,  255]
```

Note that the sum of 216 and 36 is not 255, but assume that we need pure red and pure green. Similarly, for the blue information, we have only two bits, or four unique numbers. Mapping the interval [0, 3] to [0, 255], using a spacing of 85 units, we get the following list of possible values for the blue intensity:

```
blue = [0, 85, 170, 255]
```

Using this scheme, we indeed have 256 (8x8x4) unique colors, but we're limited to only a discrete set of colors. That is, we can represent pure red (255, 0, 0), pure green (0, 255, 0), or pure blue (0, 0, 255), but we can't represent, for example, gray (128, 128, 128). This limitation is exactly what a color table alleviates. Using eight bits, you can represent any integer from 0 to 255. In this case, each pixel represents not an RGB value but a location within the color table. To retrieve the actual red, green, and blue intensities for a pixel, you *look up* the corresponding location in the color table:

```
location = pixel[x][y]
color = color_table(location)
```

Following this logic, the color table of an 8-bit DIB can contain a maximum of 256 entries because each pixel can represent only a value from 0 to 255. Similarly, the color table of a 4-bit DIB can contain up to 16 entries because, with only four bits, each pixel can represent a value from 0 to 15. And the color table of a 1-bit DIB can contain up to two entries because a single bit is either zero or one. For 1-, 4-, or 8-bit DIBs, you can determine the maximum number of entries in the color table by using the following shorthand formula:

```
unsigned short mum_color_table_entries = (1 << num_bits_per_pixel);
```

Each entry of a DIB's color table describes the intensities of the red, green, and blue channels. This is accomplished via an array of **RGBQUAD** structures:

```
typedef struct tagRGBQUAD {
    BYTE rgbBlue;
    BYTE rgbGreen;
    BYTE rgbRed;
    BYTE rgbReserved;
} RGBQUAD, FAR* LPRGBQUAD;
```

The **rgbBlue**, **rgbGreen**, and **rgbRed** data members indicate the blue, green, and red intensities, respectively. The **rgbReserved** data member is always zero. The counterintuitive ordering of the first three data members is a remnant of the OS/2 days.

Notice from the declaration of the **BITMAPINFO** structure that the color table is provided through the **bmiColors** data member. However, sometimes you'll be given just a pointer to a **BITMAPINFOHEADER** structure. In this case, you can grab a pointer to the color table (specifically, its first entry) by traversing exactly **BITMAPINFOHEADER::biSize** bytes from the beginning of the **BITMAPINFOHEADER** structure:

```
LPRGBQUAD pColorTable = reinterpret_cast<LPRGBQUAD>(
   reinterpret_cast<unsigned char*>(lpbiHeader) +
   lpbiHeader->biSize
   );
```

Finally, there's one more twist that you should be aware of: the color table of a DIB is not always an array of **RGBQUADs**. Sometimes a DIB's color table consists of an array of **WORDs**. In this case, each entry reveals not an RGB value but rather an index into a logical palette. You actually have two mappings—each pixel indicates a location within a color table, and each color-table entry indicates a location within a logical palette. This type of DIB is rare because the color table is inherently linked to a palette, a fact that obviates the DIB's device-independence. Retrieving a pointer to the color table, in this case, is accomplished by the same approach. Here you simply typecast the result to an **LPWORD**:

```
LPWORD pColorTable = reinterpret_cast<LPWORD>(
   reinterpret_cast<unsigned char*>(lpbiHeader) +
   lpbiHeader->biSize
   );
```

Things are a bit different for 16- and 32-bit DIBs because the first three entries of the color table might contain **DWORD**-type intensity masks. We'll return to this issue shortly (see "16-bit DIBs" and "32-bit DIBs").

The Pixels

Notice that the **BITMAPINFO** structure has no data member that corresponds to the pixels of a DIB. How, then, do you access its pixels? If you're given a DIB from a third-party library, for example, sometimes you'll be given a pointer to the pixels as well, in which case, there's no work involved. Usually, however, you're given only a pointer to a **BITMAPINFO** structure. In this case, you can assume one of two things: either the vendor of the library messed up, or the DIB is in the form of a *packed DIB*, in which the array of pixels is stored immediately after the color table. To retrieve a pointer to the pixels of a packed DIB, you traverse just past the last entry of its color table. For example, for a 1-, 4-, or 8-bit DIB, when the color table contains **RGBQUAD**-type entries:

```
const unsigned short num_color_table_entries =
   (lpbi->bmiHeader.biClrUsed > 0) ?
```

```
   lpbi->bmiHeader.biClrUsed :
   1 << lpbi->bmiHeader.biBitCount;

unsigned char* pBits = reinterpret_cast<unsigned char*>(
   lpbi->bmiColors + num_color_table_entries
   );
```

Similarly, when the color table contains **WORD**-type entries, you cast the **bmiColors** data member to an **LPWORD**:

```
const unsigned short num_color_table_entries =
   (lpbi->bmiHeader.biClrUsed > 0) ?
   lpbi->bmiHeader.biClrUsed :
   1 << lpbi->bmiHeader.biBitCount;

unsigned char* pBits = reinterpret_cast<unsigned char*>(
   reinterpret_cast<LPWORD>(lpbi->bmiColors) + num_color_table_entries
   );
```

Because a color table is optional for 16-, 24-, and 32-bit DIBs, for these types, you should rely solely on the **BITMAPINFOHEADER::biClrUsed** data member for the number of color-table entries, like so:

```
const unsigned short num_color_table_entries = lpbi->bmiHeader.biClrUsed;
unsigned char* pBits = reinterpret_cast<unsigned char*>(
   lpbi->bmiColors + num_color_table_entries
   );
```

Things get a bit more complicated when intensity masks are used for 16- and 32-bit DIBs. We'll examine this issue more closely when we discuss each of these types later in this section. Of course, if the DIB is not packed, then you should already have a pointer to the pixels, so the previous steps are irrelevant.

WARNING! Don't try to locate the pixels of an unpacked DIB by traversing past the last color-table entry. Unless the DIB is packed, the pixels can be stored anywhere. If the DIB isn't packed and you attempt to access the memory beyond its last color table entry, there's a good chance that you'll get an access violation error.

Once you have access to a DIB's pixels, working with them is similar to working with any other array of bytes. There are, however, a few caveats. The first thing to note is that each scan line must end on a **DWORD** boundary. This requirement is commonly referred to as ***DWORD**-alignment*. Because the size of a **DWORD** is exactly four bytes, the length of each scan line, in bytes, must be an integer multiple of four.

Consider a 24-bit DIB that's 199 pixels wide. In this case, each pixel occupies three bytes, so each scan line should be 597 (3x199) bytes long. But 597 is not a multiple of four, so each scan line must be padded with three extra bytes (597+3 = 600, which is a multiple of four). You can compute the length (in bytes) of each **DWORD**-aligned scan line by using the following approach:

```
unsigned int unaligned_bytes_per_scanline =
   static_cast<unsigned int>(width * (bits_per_pixel / 8.0) + 0.5);

unsigned char padding_per_scanline =
   (unaligned_bytes_per_scanline % 4 == 0) ?
   0 : 4 - (unaligned_bytes_per_scanline % 4);

unsigned int aligned_bytes_per_scanline =
   unaligned_bytes_per_scanline + padding_per_scanline;
```

These calculations can be written more compactly using bit-shifting:

```
unsigned int aligned_bytes_per_scanline =
   (((width * bits_per_pixel) + 31) & ~31) >> 3;
```

It's important to take into account the **DWORD**-alignment when you access a DIB's pixels. For example, when iterating over the pixels of an 4-bit DIB, you can use a scheme like the following (taking into account the padding):

```
unsigned char* pBits = // grab a pointer to the pixels
for (unsigned int y = 0; y < height; ++y)
{
   unsigned char* pScanLine =
      reinterpret_cast<unsigned char*>(
         pBits + (y * aligned_bytes_per_scanline)
         );
   for (unsigned int x = 0; x < unaligned_bytes_per_scanline; ++x)
   {
      pScanLine[x] = // ...
   }
}
```

Unfortunately, although this approach does account correctly for the **DWORD**-alignment, it doesn't account for the orientation of the image itself. This is precisely the second caveat; namely, the image of a DIB is often stored upside-down. DIBs of this type are commonly referred to as *bottom-up* DIBs. The previous code assumes that the DIB is a so-called *top-down* variety in which the image is oriented from top to bottom (as any sane person would expect). This counterintuitive upside-down storage is a carry-over from the OS/2 days.

How can you tell whether you have a top-down or bottom-up DIB? You examine the sign of the **biHeight** data member in the DIB's header. If this data member has a positive value, then the DIB is bottom-up, and if the value is negative, the DIB is top-down. If you do have a bottom-up DIB, you can modify the previous code like so:

```
unsigned char* pBits = // grab a pointer to the pixels
for (unsigned int y = 0; y < height; ++y)
{
   unsigned char* pScanLine =
      reinterpret_cast<unsigned char*>(
         pBits + ((height - y - 1) * aligned_bytes_per_scanline)
         );
   for (unsigned int x = 0; x < unaligned_bytes_per_scanline; ++x)
   {
      pScanLine[x] = // modify each pixel
   }
}
```

So much for the caveats; let's move on to actually decoding DIBs of different color depths. Indeed, working with an 8-bit DIB is simple because each pixel is exactly 1 byte—just remember that you're working with color-table indices, not actual RGB values—but what about a 4-bit DIB or even a 16-bit DIB? How are the pixels manipulated in these cases? Let's examine each of these types more closely.

1-Bit DIBs

A DIB that uses only one bit per pixel can represent a maximum of two (2^1) colors; each pixel reveals a location in the DIB's color table, which contains two entries. For each *set* ("on") bit, the value from the second color-table entry is used. For each *clear* ("off") bit, the value from the first color-table entry is used.

If you grab a pointer to the DIB's pixels as an **unsigned char*** (**LPBYTE**), each element is exactly one byte (eight bits). To determine whether each bit within a specific byte is set or clear, you first shift the byte to the right by N-1 bits, where N is the (one-based) position (from the right) of the bit in question; you then use the bitwise **AND** (&) operator to combine this result with the decimal value of one (00000001 in binary). For example, to query the sixth bit (from the right) of the first byte of each scan line, you'd do the following:

```
bool is_set = (pScanLine[0] >> 5) & 1;
```

To see what this operation is doing, let's consider a byte that contains the value 163, which is the following when written as a binary number:

```
1 0 1 0 0 0 1 1
```

Here, the sixth bit (from the right) is set. Now when you shift this number by five bits to the right, you get the following:

```
0 0 0 0 0 1 0 1
```

Now, when you use the bitwise **AND** operator to combine this result with 00000001, you get the desired result, like so:

```
    (0 0 0 0 0 1 0 1)
AND (0 0 0 0 0 0 0 1)
--------------------
     0 0 0 0 0 0 0 1
```

Going the other way around, to set an individual bit in a particular byte, you perform a bitwise **OR** (|) operation with the pixel value itself and the decimal value of 1 shifted to the left by N-1 bits, where N is the (one-based) position (from the right) of the bit that you want to set. For example, to set the third bit (from the right) of the first byte of each scan line, you'd do the following:

```
pScanLine[0] = pScanLine[0] | (1 << 2);
```

Again, let's see what this code is actually doing. Say that **pScanLine[0]** is 240. Written in binary notation, this value looks like so:

```
1 1 1 1 0 0 0 0
```

Similarly, the value 1 **<<** 2, which is 4 written as a decimal value, looks like the following in binary:

```
0 0 0 0 0 1 0 0
```

Now, when you combine these two values by using the bitwise **OR** operator, you get the desired result (244); namely, you've successfully set the third bit (from the right). That is:

```
   (1 1 1 1 0 0 0 0)
OR (0 0 0 0 0 1 0 0)
--------------------
    1 1 1 1 0 1 0 0
```

To clear a particular bit, you perform a similar technique, except this time, you combine the pixel value with the complement of 1 **<<** N by using the bitwise **AND** operator. Let's consider another example. Say that **pScanLine[0]** is 192, or in binary, the following:

```
1 1 0 0 0 0 0 0
```

If you want to clear the seventh bit (from the right) to get a decimal value of 128 (10000000), you'd use 1 **<<** 6 (a decimal value of 64), which looks like the following in binary:

```
0 1 0 0 0 0 0 0
```

Then take its complement (191) via the bitwise **NOT** (**~**) operator:

```
NOT(0 1 0 0 0 0 0 0)  =  1 0 1 1 1 1 1 1
```

Then combine this by using the **AND** operator with the original value to get the desired result (128). That is:

```
    (1 1 0 0 0 0 0 0)
AND (1 0 1 1 1 1 1 1)
--------------------
     1 0 0 0 0 0 0 0
```

In C(++) notation, this entire operation would be written like so:

```
pScanLine[0] = pScanLine[0] & ~(1 << 6);
```

There's another catch when you're setting the pixels of a 1-bit DIB. Because you have to traverse each scan line one *byte* at a time, you can't necessarily stop at the value of **unaligned_bytes_per_scanline**, as we did previously. For example, if your DIB is, say, 25 pixels (bits) wide, the previous computation of **unaligned_bytes_per_scanline** will yield a value of 3 (bytes). But, 3 bytes is only 24 bits (pixels), so in this case, you'll be missing the last pixel of each scanline. What you need to do is adjust **unaligned_bytes_per_scanline** by one byte. So, to traverse the pixels of a 1-bit top-down DIB, adjusting each bit along the way, you'd do something like the following:

```
unsigned int unaligned_bytes_per_scanline =
   static_cast<unsigned int>(width * (bits_per_pixel / 8.0) + 0.9);
unsigned int aligned_bytes_per_scanline =
   (((width * bits_per_pixel) + 31) & ~31) >> 3;

unsigned char* pBits = // grab a pointer to the pixels

// for each scan line
for (unsigned int y = 0; y < height; ++y)
{
   unsigned char* pScanLine =
```

```
         reinterpret_cast<unsigned char*>(
            pBits + (y * aligned_bytes_per_scanline)
            );

   // for each byte of each scan line
   for (unsigned int x = 0; x < unaligned_bytes_per_scanline; ++x)
   {
      // for each bit of each byte of each scan line
      for (unsigned char bit_pos = 0; bit_pos < 8; ++bit_pos)
      {
         bool new_value = // true or false
         pScanLine[x] = new_value ?
            pScanLine[x] | (1 << bit_pos) :
            pScanLine[x] & ~(1 << bit_pos);
      }
   }
}
```

That's all there is to working with a 1-bit DIB. Just remember, you're setting only color-table indices, not actual RGB values. Let's move on to the 4-bit case.

4-Bit DIBs

A DIB that uses 4 bits per pixel can contain up to 16 (2^4) colors. Specifically, the color table contains 16 entries, and each pixel indicates a location within this color table. As with a 1-bit DIB, when you grab a pointer to the pixels of a 4-bit DIB as an **unsigned char***, you're working with 8 bits at a time. This means that each entry in the array of pixels actually corresponds to two consecutive pixels. The last four bits of each byte (from the right) correspond to the first pixel, and the first four bits (from the right) correspond to the next pixel. As counterintuitive as this scheme might sound, getting and setting the bits of a 4-bit DIB isn't too bad, namely because you can use hexadecimal values.

To retrieve the value of the first pixel (i.e., the last four bits from the right) from a particular byte, you first combine the byte with the hexadecimal "mask" F0 by using the bitwise **AND** operator; you then shift this result to the right by four bits. Likewise, to retrieve the second pixel (i.e., the first four bits from the right) of a particular byte, you just **AND** the byte with the hexadecimal mask 0F. Note that there's no bit-shift required in the second case because the first four bits are already in the correct position.

To see why this scheme works, suppose that a particular byte contains the decimal value 155, which is 9B as a hexadecimal number, and the following when written in binary:

```
1 0 0 1  1 0 1 1
```

The masks, F0 and 0F, on the other hand, look like the following in binary:

```
F0  =  1 1 1 1  0 0 0 0
0F  =  0 0 0 0  1 1 1 1
```

You can see here that an **AND** operation with either mask will isolate just the desired portion of the original byte. For example, the operation (9B **&** F0) will yield the hexadecimal value 90. Let's look at this operation in binary notation:

```
    (1 0 0 1  1 0 1 1)
AND (1 1 1 1  0 0 0 0)
----------------------
     1 0 0 1  0 0 0 0
```

Now when you shift 90 to the right by 4 bits, you get only the "9" portion—that is, the first pixel. Note that in this case, the mask (F0) isn't really necessary because you're discarding the first four bits (from the right) anyway. Similarly, if you combine 9B with mask 0F, you'll extract only the "B" portion. In this case, there's no need to shift the bits because the "B" portion already occupies the first four bits (from the right) of the byte. Therefore, to traverse the pixels of a 4-bit DIB, reading the value of each pixel along the way, you'd do something similar to the following:

```
unsigned int unaligned_bytes_per_scanline =
   static_cast<unsigned int>(width * (bits_per_pixel / 8.0) + 0.5);
unsigned int aligned_bytes_per_scanline =
   (((width * bits_per_pixel) + 31) & ~31) >> 3;

unsigned char* pBits = // grab a pointer to the pixels

// for each scan line
for (unsigned int y = 0; y < height; ++y)
{
   unsigned char* pScanLine =
      reinterpret_cast<unsigned char*>(
         pBits + (y * aligned_bytes_per_scanline)
         );

   // for each byte of each scan line
   for (unsigned int x = 0; x < unaligned_bytes_per_scanline; ++x)
   {
      /* unsigned char first_mask = 0xF0;  // not really needed */
      unsigned char first_pixel = (pScanLine[x] /* & first_mask */) >> 4;

      unsigned char second_mask = 0x0F;
      unsigned char second_pixel = (pScanLine[x] & second_mask);
   }
}
```

Now let's go the other way around. Consider the situation where you need to set the first pixel of each scan line to a (color-table index) value of 9, and set the next pixel to 15. Here you can simply assign the first byte of each scan line a hexadecimal value of 9F (remember, F in hexadecimal notation is 15 when written as a decimal value):

```
pScanLine[0] = 0x9F;
```

Similarly, if you want to assign a value of 12 to the first pixel of each scan line and assign a value of zero to the next pixel, you do the following:

```
pScanLine[0] = 0xC0;
```

Things get a bit more complicated when you want to change only one of the pixels (i.e., only the first four or the last four bits of each byte). In this case, you must first **AND** the original pixel value with a hexadecimal mask, and then **OR** this result with the new value. For example, say that the original byte is 163, which is A3 when written as a hexadecimal value. In this case, if you want to change the last 4 bits from the right (i.e., the first pixel; the "A" portion) to a value of 5, you first combine A3 with the hexadecimal mask 0F by using the bitwise **AND** operator. Because (A **&** 0) yields 0, and (3 **&** F) yields 3, you'll get the following:

```
(A3) AND (0F) = 03
```

Now, you somehow need to change the "0" portion of 03 to the new value of 5. In this case, you simply combine 03 with the hexadecimal value 50 (i.e., the decimal value 5x16=80) by using the bitwise **OR** operator. Because (0 | 5) yields 5, and (3 | 0) yields 3, you get the desired hexadecimal result of 53 (83 in decimal notation):

```
(03) OR (50) = 53
```

When you want to change the second pixel (i.e., the first four bits from the right; the "3" portion), you simply swap the digits of the mask, and likewise the digits of the new value. That is, instead of using 0F, you use F0, and instead of using 50, you use 05. Again, when you combine A3 with the hexadecimal mask F0 by using the bitwise **AND** operator, you get the following:

```
(A3) AND (F0) = A0
```

Now, when you combine A0 with the hexadecimal value 05 by using the bitwise **OR** operator, you get the desired result:

```
(A0) OR (05) = A5
```

Using C(++) notation, you change the first pixel of each scan line (to a decimal value of 5, for example) via the following:

```
const unsigned char new_value = 0x50; // 5 * 16  (5 is the new pixel value)
const unsigned char mask = 0x0F;
pScanLine[0] = (pScanLine[0] & mask) | new_value;
```

And you change the second pixel of each scan line like so:

```
const unsigned char new_value = 0x05; // 5 * 1  (5 is the new pixel value)
const unsigned char mask = 0xF0;
pScanLine[0] = (pScanLine[0] & mask) | new_value;
```

Putting all of this together, you can traverse the pixels of a 4-bit top-down DIB, adjusting, for example, every second pixel to a decimal value of 11, via the following:

```
unsigned int unaligned_bytes_per_scanline =
   static_cast<unsigned int>(width * (bits_per_pixel / 8.0) + 0.5);
unsigned int aligned_bytes_per_scanline =
   (((width * bits_per_pixel) + 31) & ~31) >> 3;

unsigned char* pBits = // grab a pointer to the pixels

// for each scan line
for (unsigned int y = 0; y < height; ++y)
{
   unsigned char* pScanLine =
      reinterpret_cast<unsigned char*>(
         pBits + (y * aligned_bytes_per_scanline)
         );

   // for each byte of each scan line
   for (unsigned int x = 0; x < unaligned_bytes_per_scanline; ++x)
   {
      unsigned char new_value = 0x0B;
      unsigned char mask = 0xF0;
      pScanLine[x] = (pScanLine[0] & mask) | new_value;
   }
}
```

Again, keep in mind that each pixel of a 4-bit DIB indicates a color-table index, not an RGB value. Let's take a breather and tackle the relatively simple 8-bit case.

8-Bit DIBs

A DIB that uses 8 bits per pixel can contain up to 256 (2^8) colors. As with 1- and 4-bit DIBs, each pixel represents a color-table index. As you may have guessed, the color table of an 8-bit DIB contains a maximum of 256 entries. In fact, this variety is perhaps the easiest type of DIB to work with because each pixel is exactly one byte. To manipulate the pixels, you simply assign an 8-bit value to each entry in the array. Moreover, you don't have to worry about an **unaligned_bytes_per_width** calculation because this is exactly the width of the DIB itself. For example (assuming a top-down DIB):

```
unsigned int aligned_bytes_per_scanline =
   (((width * bits_per_pixel) + 31) & ~31) >> 3;

unsigned char* pBits = // grab a pointer to the pixels
for (unsigned int y = 0; y < height; ++y)
{
   unsigned char* pScanLine =
      reinterpret_cast<unsigned char*>(
         pBits + (y * aligned_bytes_per_scanline)
         );
   for (unsigned int x = 0; x < width; ++x)
   {
      pScanLine[x] = // modify each pixel
   }
}
```

The biggest question when you're working with an 8-bit DIB is not actually how to manipulate the pixels, but what value to assign to each pixel. You need to specify a color-table index, but which index do you use? We'll return to this issue in Chapter 16, when we discuss ICM.

16-Bit DIBs

A DIB that uses 16 bits per pixel can contain up to 65,536 (2^{16}) colors. Though a color table is optional, working with a 16-bit DIB is not entirely straightforward. Indeed, 16 bits is exactly the size of a **WORD**, but remember, because there's no color table, the intensities for the red, green, and blue channels are packed into each set of 16-bits.

There are actually two varieties of 16-bit DIBs. The default type, which is obtained when the **BITMAPINFOHEADER::biCompression** data member is set to **BI_RGB**, is actually a 15-bit DIB, with 5 bits for each color-channel (red, green, blue) intensity. The first five bits (from the left) are used to describe the blue intensity; the next five are for the green intensity; and the last five are for the red intensity. This is somewhat of a waste because the sixteenth bit is never used. Nonetheless, let's focus first on this type, which we'll refer to as a 15-bit DIB—we'll tackle the other variety (the true 16-bit version) afterward.

Again, the color table for a 15-bit DIB is optional. To determine whether a color table is present, you examine the **BITMAPINFOHEADER::biClrUsed** data member. If it's non-zero, then the color table contains exactly **biClrUsed** entries. But if **biClrUsed** is zero, then you can assume that there's no color table. In either case, if you're working with a packed DIB, you can grab a pointer to the pixels by using the following approach (for **RGBQUAD** entries):

```
unsigned char* pBits = reinterpret_cast<unsigned char*>(
   reinterpret_cast<unsigned char*>(lpbi->bmiColors) +
   lpbi->bmiHeader.biClrUsed * sizeof(RGBQUAD)
   );
```

Similarly, when the color table consists of **WORD** indices, you use the following:

```
unsigned char* pBits = reinterpret_cast<unsigned char*>(
   reinterpret_cast<unsigned char*>(lpbi->bmiColors) +
   lpbi->bmiHeader.biClrUsed * sizeof(WORD)
   );
```

Because, in this case, the **biClrUsed** data member is zero, either of these two methods will work when the DIB has no color table.

Each pixel of a 15-bit DIB occupies 16 bits, and the most significant bit (i.e., the sixteenth bit from the right) is simply ignored. Assume for the moment that you have a 16-bit value (one pixel). How do you extract the intensities of each color channel? As with a 4-bit DIB, it's easiest to use hexadecimal masks. Specifically, you use 001F to get the blue intensity, 03E0 for green, and 7C00 for red. It's easiest to visualize these masks by using binary notation:

```
pixel  =  r r r r r  g g g g g  b b b b b
 001F  =  0 0 0 0 0  0 0 0 0 0  1 1 1 1 1
 03E0  =  0 0 0 0 0  1 1 1 1 1  0 0 0 0 0
 7C00  =  1 1 1 1 1  0 0 0 0 0  0 0 0 0 0
```

Notice how the 1's for each mask line up with their respective portions of the pixel value. If you **AND** each mask with the pixel value, and then shift the bits to the right, you can extract the intensity for each color channel. Let's look at the red case first. Say the pixel value is 20,382, which, when written as a binary number, is the following:

```
 1 0 0 1 1  1 1 1 0 0  1 1 1 1 0
```

To extract just the red portion (the last five bits from the right; 10011), you first combine the pixel value with the red mask (7C00) by using the bitwise **AND** operator:

```
    (1 0 0 1 1  1 1 1 0 0  1 1 1 1 0)
AND (1 1 1 1 1  0 0 0 0 0  0 0 0 0 0)
-------------------------------------
     1 0 0 1 1  0 0 0 0 0  0 0 0 0 0
```

Now, to obtain just the last 5 bits from the right, you shift the result to the right by 10 bits:

```
0 0 0 0 0 0 0 0 0 0  1 0 0 1 1
```

Let's look at this process again—this time to get the green intensity. Taking the same pixel value, to extract just the green portion (the middle five bits; 11100), you first **AND** the pixel value with the green mask (03E0):

```
    (1 0 0 1 1  1 1 1 0 0  1 1 1 1 0)
AND (0 0 0 0 0  1 1 1 1 1  0 0 0 0 0)
-------------------------------------
     0 0 0 0 0  1 1 1 0 0  0 0 0 0 0
```

Now you shift the result to the right, this time by five bits:

```
0 0 0 0 0  1 1 1 0 0
```

For the blue intensity (the first five bits from the right; 11110), it's the same deal. You simply **AND** the original pixel value with the blue mask (001F):

```
    (1 0 0 1 1  1 1 1 0 0  1 1 1 1 0)
AND (0 0 0 0 0  0 0 0 0 0  1 1 1 1 1)
-------------------------------------
     0 0 0 0 0  0 0 0 0 0  1 1 1 1 0
```

In this case, there's no shifting required because the blue information is already in the first five bits (from the right) of the result.

Because each pixel of a 15-bit DIB contains 15 meaningful bits, when you grab a pointer to each scan line, it's easiest to cast the result to an **unsigned short*** (**LPWORD**), instead of an **unsigned char*** as we did before. In doing so, however, you need to compute the number of **shorts** per scan line, not the number of bytes. So, in C(++) notation, you'd read each color-channel intensity like so:

```
// NOTE: bits_per_pixel should be set to 16, not 15
unsigned int unaligned_shorts_per_scanline =
   static_cast<unsigned int>(
      0.5 * width * (bits_per_pixel / 8.0) + 0.5
      );
```

```
unsigned int aligned_bytes_per_scanline =
   (((width * bits_per_pixel) + 31) & ~31) >> 3;

unsigned char* pBits = // grab a pointer to the pixels
for (unsigned int y = 0; y < height; ++y)
{
   unsigned short* pScanLine =
      reinterpret_cast<unsigned short*>(
         pBits + (y * aligned_bytes_per_scanline)
         );
   for (unsigned int x = 0; x < unaligned_shorts_per_scanline; ++x)
   {
      unsigned char blue = (pScanLine[x] & 0x001F);
      unsigned char green = (pScanLine[x] & 0x03E0) >> 5;
      unsigned char red = (pScanLine[x] & 0x7C00) >> 10;
      // ...
   }
}
```

Now let's go the other way around—let's assign a value to each 5-bit portion. Again, the key here is to use masking. Consider the pixel value from before (20,382). Say you want to change the red portion to a decimal value of 21 (10101 in binary), but you want to leave the green and blue portions as they are. Here's what you know so far:

```
    (1 0 0 1 1  1 1 1 0 0  1 1 1 1 0)
?   (? ? ? ? ?  ? ? ? ? ?  ? ? ? ? ?)
?   (? ? ? ? ?  ? ? ? ? ?  ? ? ? ? ?)
-----------------------------------
     1 0 1 0 1  1 1 1 0 0  1 1 1 1 0
```

The problem is: how do you fill in the question marks? Well, if you **AND** the original pixel value with the complement of the red mask (7C00), you get the following:

```
    (1 0 0 1 1  1 1 1 0 0  1 1 1 1 0)
AND (0 0 0 0 0  1 1 1 1 1  1 1 1 1 1)
-----------------------------------
     0 0 0 0 0  1 1 1 0 0  1 1 1 1 0
```

Then, if you take this result and **OR** it with 101010000000000 (21 **<<** 10), you can change just the red portion:

```
    (1 0 0 1 1  1 1 1 0 0  1 1 1 1 0)
AND (0 0 0 0 0  1 1 1 1 1  1 1 1 1 1)
-----------------------------------
```

```
      0 0 0 0 0  1 1 1 0 0  1 1 1 1 0
  OR (1 0 1 0 1  0 0 0 0 0  0 0 0 0 0)
  -----------------------------------
      1 0 1 0 1  1 1 1 0 0  1 1 1 1 0
```

Similarly, to change just the green portion, you **AND** the original pixel value with the complement of the green mask (03E0), and then **OR** this result with 00000*ggggg*00000, where the *g*'s represent the binary digits of the new green intensity. For example, to change the green portion to a decimal value of 31 (11111 in binary), you **AND** the pixel with the complement of the green mask, and then **OR** this result with 000001111100000 (31 **<<** 5):

```
     (1 0 0 1 1  1 1 1 0 0  1 1 1 1 0)
 AND (1 1 1 1 1  0 0 0 0 0  1 1 1 1 1)
 -----------------------------------
      1 0 0 1 1  0 0 0 0 0  1 1 1 1 0
  OR (0 0 0 0 0  1 1 1 1 1  0 0 0 0 0)
 -----------------------------------
      1 0 0 1 1  1 1 1 1 1  1 1 1 1 0
```

In the same way, to change just the blue portion, you combine the original pixel value with the complement of the blue mask (001F) by using the bitwise **AND** operator, and then **OR** this result with 0000000000*bbbbb*, where the *b*'s represent the binary digits of the new blue intensity. So to change blue to 10 (01010 in binary), you **AND** the pixel with the complement of the blue mask, and then **OR** this result with 000000000001010 (10 **<<** 0, or just 10):

```
     (1 0 0 1 1  1 1 1 0 0  1 1 1 1 0)
 AND (1 1 1 1 1  1 1 1 1 1  0 0 0 0 0)
 -----------------------------------
      1 0 0 1 1  1 1 1 0 0  0 0 0 0 0
  OR (0 0 0 0 0  0 0 0 0 0  0 1 0 1 0)
 -----------------------------------
      1 0 0 1 1  1 1 1 0 0  0 1 0 1 0
```


For reference, the complement of the blue mask, written as a hexadecimal number, is 7FE0. The complement of the green mask is 7C1F, and the complement of the red mask is 03FF. So in C(++) notation, you'd change each color intensity like so:

```
unsigned int unaligned_shorts_per_scanline =
   static_cast<unsigned int>(
      0.5 * width * (bits_per_pixel / 8.0) + 0.5
      );
unsigned int aligned_bytes_per_scanline =
   (((width * bits_per_pixel) + 31) & ~31) >> 3;
```

```
unsigned char* pBits = // grab a pointer to the pixels
for (unsigned int y = 0; y < height; ++y)
{
   unsigned short* pScanLine =
      reinterpret_cast<unsigned short*>(
         pBits + (y * aligned_bytes_per_scanline)
         );
   for (unsigned int x = 0; x < unaligned_shorts_per_scanline; ++x)
   {
      unsigned char new_blue = 3;     // [0, 31]
      unsigned char new_green = 14;   // [0, 31]
      unsigned char new_red = 31;     // [0, 31]

      pScanLine[x] = (pScanLine[x] & 0x7FE0) | (new_blue);
      pScanLine[x] = (pScanLine[x] & 0x7C1F) | (new_green << 5);
      pScanLine[x] = (pScanLine[x] & 0x03FF) | (new_red << 10);
   }
}
```

You may have noticed that with only 15 bits, each color channel can range from 0 to 31. This range is mapped from 0 to 255, but with only 15 bits per color channel, you can represent only up to 32,768 ($32^3 = 2^{15}$) unique colors. This is only half of what can be represented with a full 16 bits! Indeed, ignoring the sixteenth bit can be detrimental to image quality. This detriment is exactly what the second type of 16-bit DIB avoids; it takes advantage of all 16 bits.

When a 16-bit DIB has its **BITMAPINFOHEADER::biCompression** data member set to **BI_BITFIELDS**, its color table is no longer optional. Instead, the first few entries of the color table are now used to hold three **DWORD** *intensity masks*, one for each color channel (red, green, and blue; in that order). These masks define the "fields of the bits" that correspond to each color channel. There are actually two variations of 16-bit DIBs that use **BI_BITFIELDS**. The type that's least used is actually another 15-bit variety, similar to that which we just discussed. The only difference is that the masks are now stored in the color table. In fact, on systems running Windows 95 or Windows 98, these masks must be identical to those that we used before: 001F for blue, 03E0 for green, and 7C00 for red. The other, more common, variation is a true 16-bit DIB. In Windows 95 and Windows 98, the extra bit is given to the green intensity. This is a good choice because humans are most sensitive to shades of green. In Windows NT and Windows 2000, you have a bit more flexibility because the masks aren't predefined; you can divvy up the bits as you want. For example, you can give a full byte to the green channel and four bits each to the red and blue channels. This scheme is rare, however, and in most cases, the predefined masks that are required for Windows 95/98 are used.

Again, most 16-bit DIBs allocate five bits for the red intensity, six bits for the green intensity, and five bits for the blue intensity. These *bit fields* are defined by the hexadecimal masks: F800 for red, 07E0 for green, and 001F for blue. You can probably guess what these values look like in binary:

```
pixel   =  r r r r r  g g g g g g  b b b b b
  001F  =  0 0 0 0 0  0 0 0 0 0 0  1 1 1 1 1

  07E0  =  0 0 0 0 0  1 1 1 1 1 1  0 0 0 0 0
  F800  =  1 1 1 1 1  0 0 0 0 0 0  0 0 0 0 0
```

As I mentioned, these masks are stored in the DIB's color table as **DWORD**s. To extract them from the color table, you cast the **BITMPINFO::bmiColors** data member to an **LPDWORD**, and then take the first three entries. The red mask is stored first, followed by the green mask, and finally the blue mask:

```
LPDWORD lpMasks = reinterpret_cast<LPDWORD>(lpbi->bmiColors);
// red_mask = lpMasks[0];
// green_mask = lpMasks[1];
// blue_mask = lpMasks[2];
```

Once you have a pointer to the masks, it's just like before—you extract the red, green, and blue intensities from each pixel by using the bitwise **AND** operator to combine the original pixel value with the appropriate mask:

```
unsigned int unaligned_shorts_per_scanline =
   static_cast<unsigned int>(
      0.5 * width * (bits_per_pixel / 8.0) + 0.5
      );
unsigned int aligned_bytes_per_scanline =
   (((width * bits_per_pixel) + 31) & ~31) >> 3;

unsigned char* pBits = // grab a pointer to the pixels
for (unsigned int y = 0; y < height; ++y)
{
   unsigned short* pScanLine =
      reinterpret_cast<unsigned short*>(
         pBits + (y * aligned_bytes_per_scanline)
         );
   for (unsigned int x = 0; x < unaligned_shorts_per_scanline; ++x)
   {
      unsigned char blue = (pScanLine[x] & lpMasks[2]);
      unsigned char green = (pScanLine[x] & lpMasks[1]) >> 5;
      unsigned char red = (pScanLine[x] & lpMasks[0]) >> 11;
      // ...
   }
}
```

Notice the extra bit-shift for the red intensity because we're working with a full 16 bits now.

Along these same lines, to set the RGB value of each pixel, you combine the original pixel value with the complement of each respective mask:

```
unsigned int unaligned_shorts_per_scanline =
   static_cast<unsigned int>(
      0.5 * width * (bits_per_pixel / 8.0) + 0.5
      );
unsigned int aligned_bytes_per_scanline =
   (((width * bits_per_pixel) + 31) & ~31) >> 3;

unsigned char* pBits = // grab a pointer to the pixels
for (unsigned int y = 0; y < height; ++y)
{
   unsigned short* pScanLine =
      reinterpret_cast<unsigned short*>(
         pBits + (y * aligned_bytes_per_scanline)
         );
   for (unsigned int x = 0; x < unaligned_shorts_per_scanline; ++x)
   {
      unsigned char new_blue = 15;   // [0, 31]
      unsigned char new_green = 63;  // [0, 63]
      unsigned char new_red = 28;    // [0, 31]

      pScanLine[x] = (pScanLine[x] & lpMasks[2]) | (new_blue);
      pScanLine[x] = (pScanLine[x] & lpMasks[1]) | (new_green << 5);
      pScanLine[x] = (pScanLine[x] & lpMasks[0]) | (new_red << 11);
   }
}
```

When you use all 16 bits per pixel, the green channel can range from 0 to 63. Again, this interval is mapped to the range 0 to 255. So if you want pure white, for example, you set both the red and blue intensities to 31, as before, but you set the green intensity to 63.

When you're working with a true 16-bit DIB, there's one more subtlety that actually has to do with grabbing a pointer to the pixels. Recall, when the **BI_BITFIELDS** identifier is used, the color table is no longer optional—it must contain at least three masks. What is optional, however, is what comes after these three masks. If the **BITMAPINFOHEADER::biClrUsed** data member is nonzero, then the true color-table entries are located just after the masks. (Note that the count indicated by **biClrUsed** does not include the masks.) In this case, you can grab a pointer to the true color-table entries by traversing past the masks (for **RGBQUAD** entries):

```
LPRGBQUAD lpColorTable = reinterpret_cast<LPRGBQUAD>(
   reinterpret_cast<unsigned char*>(lpbi->bmiColors) +
   3 * sizeof(DWORD)
   );
```

Similarly, when the color table consists of **WORD**-type entries, it's the same deal, just a different typecast:

```
LPWORD lpColorTable = reinterpret_cast<LPWORD>(
   reinterpret_cast<unsigned char*>(lpbi->bmiColors) +
   3 * sizeof(DWORD)
   );
```

Once you have a pointer to the true color table, you can traverse past its last entry to grab a pointer to the pixels (assuming that you're working with a packed DIB). Written as a single step, this can be accomplished like so, when the color table contains **RGBQUAD**s:

```
unsigned char* pBits = reinterpret_cast<unsigned char*>(
   reinterpret_cast<unsigned char*>(lpbi->bmiColors) +
   3 * sizeof(DWORD) +
   lpbi->bmiHeader.biClrUsed * sizeof(RGBQUAD)
   );
```

And it can be accomplished like so, when the color table consists of **WORD**s:

```
unsigned char* pBits = reinterpret_cast<unsigned char*>(
   reinterpret_cast<unsigned char*>(lpbi->bmiColors) +
   3 * sizeof(DWORD) +
   lpbi->bmiHeader.biClrUsed * sizeof(WORD)
   );
```


Either of these methods will work when the DIB has no true color table. In this case, because the **biClrUsed** data member is zero, the bits are located just after the three masks. Again, if your DIB is not packed, then you should already have a pointer to the pixels.

Whew! That's a lot of information to swallow just for one type of DIB. In fact, many device drivers have poor support for 16-bit DIBs, so it's not too surprising that this variety is rare. Let's move on to the more commonly used, more straightforward variety, the 24-bit DIB.

24-Bit DIBs

A 24-bit DIB can contain a maximum of 16,777,216 (2^{16}) colors. A color table is optional here because each pixel is represented by exactly 24 bits—8 for each color channel (red, green, and blue). Therefore, this type of DIB is undeniably the easiest to work with. In fact, there's a special structure that makes things even simpler, **RGBTRIPLE**:

```
#include <pshpack1.h>
typedef struct tagRGBTRIPLE {
    BYTE rgbtBlue;
    BYTE rgbtGreen;
    BYTE rgbtRed;
} RGBTRIPLE;
#include <poppack.h>
```

The **rgbtBlue**, **rgbtGreen**, and **rgbtRed** data members indicate the blue, green, and red intensities, respectively. Here, as with the **RGBQUAD** structure, the ordering of these data members is counterintuitive. As it turns out, the pixels of a 24-bit DIB are stored in this same reversed fashion. That is, for each pixel, the first byte (from the right) indicates the blue intensity, the second byte (from the right) indicates the green intensity, and the third byte (from the right) indicates the red intensity. In this way, the **RGBTRIPLE** structure is ideal for working with a 24-bit DIB. Also, notice the use of the **pshpack1.h** and **poppack.h** headers. These files call the (**#pragma**) **pack** directive to instruct the compiler to temporarily use single-byte alignment. This is needed because the size of the **RGBTRIPLE** structure is not an integer multiple of four bytes.

As with 15-bit and 16-bit DIBs, a color table is optional for a 24-bit DIB. You can examine the **BITMAPINFOHEADER::biClrUsed** data member to determine whether a color table is present and, if so, how many entries it contains. To retrieve a pointer to the pixels, you use the same approach as with a 15-bit DIB; namely, when the color table contains **RGBQUAD**s:

```
unsigned char* pBits = reinterpret_cast<unsigned char*>(
   reinterpret_cast<unsigned char*>(lpbi->bmiColors) +
   lpbi->bmiHeader.biClrUsed * sizeof(RGBQUAD)
   );
```

And when the color table contains **WORD**s, you do the following:

```
unsigned char* pBits = reinterpret_cast<unsigned char*>(
   reinterpret_cast<unsigned char*>(lpbi->bmiColors) +
   lpbi->bmiHeader.biClrUsed * sizeof(WORD)
   );
```

Now, when you iterate over each scan line, it's easiest to typecast the result to an **RGBTRIPLE***. When you do this, the previous computation of **unaligned_bytes_**

per_width becomes irrelevant; because you're taking three bytes at a time, you can simply iterate over the width of the DIB itself. For example, to set each pixel of a 24-bit DIB to yellow—that is, an RGB value of (255, 255, 0)—you'd do the following:

```
unsigned int aligned_bytes_per_scanline =
   (((width * bits_per_pixel) + 31) & ~31) >> 3;

unsigned char* pBits = // grab a pointer to the pixels
for (unsigned int y = 0; y < height / 2; ++y)
{
   RGBTRIPLE* pScanLine =
      reinterpret_cast<RGBTRIPLE*>(
         pBits + (y * aligned_bytes_per_scanline)
         );
   for (unsigned int x = 0; x < width; ++x)
   {
      pScanLine[x].rgbtBlue = 0;
      pScanLine[x].rgbtGreen = 255;
      pScanLine[x].rgbtRed = 255;
   }
}
```

With the lack of a color table, the ease of manipulation, and the intuitive nature of the **RGBTRIPLE** structure (save the ordering of its data members), 24-bit DIBs are the variety of choice for most developers. The only problem is that they have a potential to become extremely large. Moreover, for some types of images (namely, grayscale images), 24 bits per pixel is overkill; you end up with a lot of redundant information. On the flip side, some applications require more than 24 bits per pixel. In such cases, the 32-bit variety is warranted.

32-Bit DIBs

A DIB that uses 32 bits per pixel can contain up to 4,294,967,296 (2^{32}) colors. Usually, however, only the first 24 bits of each pixel are used to hold color information; the remaining byte often serves as an *alpha channel*, which is used for translucency. When alpha information is supplied, each pixel contains an RGBA (red, green, blue, alpha) value. In fact, on systems running Windows 95 or Windows 98, it's required that only the first 24 bits (from the right) are used to represent a color: 8 bits each for the red, green, and blue color channels. In Windows NT and Windows 2000, you can use all 32 bits for the color information, but keep in mind that many devices aren't capable of supporting 4,294,967,296 colors.

Like 16-bit DIBs, 32-bit DIBs have two varieties: those that have the **BITMAPINFOHEADER::biCompression** data member set to **BI_RGB**, and those that have this data member set to **BI_BITFIELDS**. When **BI_RGB** is specified, the color table is optional, and the color of each pixel is represented by 24 bits (a byte for each RGB intensity). As I mentioned, this is the most prevalent type and the easiest type to work with. When **BI_BITFIELDS** is specified, the color table contains three **DWORD** *bit-field* intensity masks, just as with 16-bit DIBs. In Windows 95 and Windows 98, these masks must define full byte-length fields: 000000FF for the blue intensity, 0000FF00 for the green intensity, and 00FF0000 for the red intensity. In Windows NT and Windows 2000, you can define your own masks; in this way, you can create a true 32-bit DIB. For example, if you want to give the extra byte to the green channel, you can use 000000FF for blue, 00FFFF00 for green, and FF000000 for red.

Working with a 32-bit DIB is similar to working with 16- and 24-bit DIBs. If the **BITMAPINFOHEADER::biClrUsed** data member is greater than zero, you grab a pointer to the **RGBQUAD**-type color table like so:

```
LPRGBQUAD lpColorTable = reinterpret_cast<LPRGBQUAD>(
   reinterpret_cast<unsigned char*>(lpbi->bmiColors) +
   3 * sizeof(DWORD)
   );
```

And when the color table consists of **WORD**s, you cast the result to an **LPWORD**:

```
LPWORD lpColorTable = reinterpret_cast<LPWORD>(
   reinterpret_cast<unsigned char*>(lpbi->bmiColors) +
   3 * sizeof(DWORD)
   );
```

To grab a pointer to the pixels, you use the same approach as that described for a 16-bit DIB. Namely, when the **BI_RGB** identifier is specified, you do the following (for **RGBQUAD**s in the color table):

```
unsigned char* pBits = reinterpret_cast<unsigned char*>(
   reinterpret_cast<unsigned char*>(lpbi->bmiColors) +
   lpbi->bmiHeader.biClrUsed * sizeof(RGBQUAD)
   );
```

And when the color table contains **WORD**s, you do the following:

```
unsigned char* pBits = reinterpret_cast<unsigned char*>(
   reinterpret_cast<unsigned char*>(lpbi->bmiColors) +
   lpbi->bmiHeader.biClrUsed * sizeof(WORD)
   );
```

Likewise, when the **biCompression** data member specifies **BI_BITFIELDS**, you grab a pointer to the intensity masks via the following:

```
LPDWORD lpMasks = reinterpret_cast<LPDWORD>(lpbi->bmiColors);
// red_mask = lpMasks[0];
// green_mask = lpMasks[1];
// blue_mask = lpMasks[2];
```

To grab a pointer to the true color table, you simply traverse past these three masks, like so for the **RGBQUAD** case:

```
unsigned char* pBits = reinterpret_cast<unsigned char*>(
   reinterpret_cast<unsigned char*>(lpbi->bmiColors) +
   3 * sizeof(DWORD) +
   lpbi->bmiHeader.biClrUsed * sizeof(RGBQUAD)
   );
```

And like so, when the color table contains **WORD**-type indices:

```
unsigned char* pBits = reinterpret_cast<unsigned char*>(
   reinterpret_cast<unsigned char*>(lpbi->bmiColors) +
   3 * sizeof(DWORD) +
   lpbi->bmiHeader.biClrUsed * sizeof(WORD)
   );
```

Instead of working with a byte at a time, for each scan line, you can cast the result to a pointer to a specialized structure. Here, instead of casting each scan line to an **RGBTRIPLE*** (as you do with 24-bit DIBs), it's easiest to use a pointer to an **RGBQUAD** because each pixel is 32 bits long. For example, to change the color of each pixel to orange, and to set the alpha value of each pixel to 60%—that is, an RGBA value of (255, 128, 0, 153)—you'd do the following (assuming that **BI_RGB** is used):

```
unsigned int aligned_bytes_per_scanline =
   (((width * bits_per_pixel) + 31) & ~31) >> 3;

unsigned char* pBits = // grab a pointer to the pixels
for (unsigned int y = 0; y < height; ++y)
{
   RGBQUAD* pScanLine =
      reinterpret_cast<RGBQUAD*>(
         pBits + (y * aligned_bytes_per_scanline)
         );
   for (unsigned int x = 0; x < width; ++x)
   {
```

```
        pScanLine[x].rgbBlue = 0;
        pScanLine[x].rgbGreen = 128;
        pScanLine[x].rgbRed = 255;
        pScanLine[x].rgbReserved = 153;
    }
}
```

This approach is valid even when the **biCompression** data member specifies **BI_BITFIELDS** (assuming the masks define full byte-length fields that denote BGR ordering) because the **RGBQUAD** structure itself defines the byte-length fields. If the masks are custom (e.g., on a system running Windows NT or Windows 2000), you need to inspect the masks to determine how many bits are given to each channel; this number will also tell you how many bits to shift to the right. To this end, the **bitset** class from the Standard C++ Library comes highly recommended. In fact, you might find this class helpful for all types of DIBs.

Rendering DIBs

The GDI provides two functions that can be used to render a DIB to a device context: **StretchDIBits** and **SetDIBitsToDevice**. The **StretchDIBits** function is designed to render a DIB in a scaled fashion. The **SetDIBitsToDevice** function simply transfers the image in its original size. Because **StretchDIBits** also accepts a **dwRop** parameter that specifies a ternary raster operation, this function is more popular than **SetDIBitsToDevice**, even when no stretching or compacting is required. However, be warned that many devices (namely, printers) support only the **SRCCOPY** ROP3 code.

The **StretchDIBits** function is similar to the **StretchBlt** function; the former accepts a pointer to a **BITMAPINFO** structure instead of accepting a handle to a source device context. In fact, neither **StretchDIBits** nor **SetDIBitsToDevice** accept a handle to a source device context because both functions transfer a DIB in a device-independent fashion. (Remember, a DIB is not a GDI graphic object.)

Unfortunately, when you're using the **StretchDIBits** or **SetDIBitsToDevice** functions, the device driver is responsible for decoding the DIB into a format the device can understand. This means that the results can vary significantly, depending on the device itself. Moreover, both of these functions are considerably slower than the **BitBlt** and **StretchBlt** functions. In fact, on some systems it's slower to use **StretchDIBits** than it is to convert the DIB to a DDB by using the **CreateDIBitmap** function (see "Creating a Device-Dependent Bitmap from a Device-Independent Bitmap" in Chapter 6) and then displaying the DDB via **StretchBlt**. In short, **StretchDIBits** is the preferred (and most reliable) way to transfer an image to another device. If you're just rendering images to the screen, stick with **StretchBlt**.

A Hybrid Object: The DIB Section Bitmap

You might have noticed that you're in somewhat of a catch-22 situation when you're working with bitmaps. On the one hand, you could use a DDB for optimal rendering speed, but unfortunately, you don't have direct access to its pixels. On the other hand, you could use a DIB for direct pixel access, but in this case, your application will likely suffer from poor rendering speeds.

It didn't take long for the folks at Microsoft to realize the limitations presented by DDBs and DIBs. As a result, Microsoft's engineers devised what's known as a *DIB section bitmap* (or just *DIB section*)—a hybrid object that contains both DDB and DIB components. You can think of a DIB section bitmap as a genetically engineered offspring that inherits only the positive qualities of both of its parents. In this way, you get the best of both worlds: optimal rendering speed from the DDB, and direct pixel access from the DIB.

From its DIB component, a DIB section bitmap inherits device-independence. You can create a DIB section bitmap of any of the bit depths that are valid for normal DIBs; namely, 1, 4, 8, 16, 24, or 32 bits per pixel. From its DDB component, a DIB section bitmap inherits the traits of a GDI graphic object. And, as with any other GDI graphic object, there is a function that's specifically designed to create a DIB section bitmap, **CreateDIBSection**:

```
HBITMAP CreateDIBSection(hdc, pbmi, iUsage, ppvBits, hSection, dwOffset);
```

In the simplest case, you pass this function a pointer to an initialized **BITMAPINFO** structure (**pbmi**), and it returns a handle to a DIB section bitmap (of type **HBITMAP**). When you need access to the pixels, you can use the **ppvBits** parameter, which is a pointer to a pointer that will refer to the DIB section's pixels. All of the other parameters are usually set to **NULL**. When the DIB section is no longer needed, you destroy it in the same way that you would a DDB; you pass its handle to the **DeleteObject** function.

Direct Pixel Access

As I mentioned, a DIB section offers direct access to its pixels. The format of these pixels depends on the value that was assigned to the **BITMAPINFOHEADER::biBiCount** data member when the DIB section was created. To gain access to the pixels, the most common technique is to pass the **CreateDIBSection** function, via the **ppvBits** parameter, the address of a pointer that the function will in turn point to the pixels. For example, to create a DIB section bitmap that uses 24 bits per pixel, and where **pBits** will point to its pixels, you'd do the following:

```
BITMAPINFO bmi;
memset(&bmi, 0, sizeof(BITMAPINFO));

bmi.bmiHeader.biSize = sizeof(BITMAPINFOHEADER);
bmi.bmiHeader.biWidth = 100;
bmi.bmiHeader.biHeight = -200; // top-down DIB section
bmi.bmiHeader.biPlanes = 1;
bmi.bmiHeader.biBitCount = 24;
bmi.bmiHeader.biCompression = BI_RGB;

unsigned char* pBits;
HBITMAP hDIBSection =
   CreateDIBSection(
      NULL, &bmi, 0,
      reinterpret_cast<LPVOID*>(&pBits),
      NULL, 0
      );

if (pBits)
{
   unsigned int aligned_bytes_per_scanline =
      (((bmi.bmiHeader.biWidth * bmi.bmiHeader.biBitCount)
        + 31) & ~31) >> 3;

   for (int y = 0; y < -bmi.bmiHeader.biHeight; ++y)
   {
      RGBTRIPLE* pScanLine = reinterpret_cast<RGBTRIPLE*>(
         pBits + (y * aligned_bytes_per_scanline)
         );
      for (int x = 0; x < bmi.bmiHeader.biWidth; ++x)
      {
         // orange is RGB value (255, 128, 64)
         pScanLine[x].rgbtBlue = 64;
         pScanLine[x].rgbtGreen = 128;
         pScanLine[x].rgbtRed = 255;
      }
   }

   //
   // ...
   //
   DeleteObject(hDIBSection);
}
```

Note that the **pBits** parameter was not initialized to **NULL** before it was passed to the **CreateDIBSection** function. This step wasn't necessary because **CreateDIBSection** will set **pBits** to **NULL** if something goes wrong during the creation process. Also note the use of the **DeleteObject** function to destroy the DIB section bitmap. Although, in the context of this code snippet, **DeleteObject** will also free the memory associated with the DIB section's pixels, this isn't always the case. Notice that the **CreateDIBSection** function was called with a **NULL hSection** parameter. This parameter can be specified as **NULL**, indicating that Windows should manage the memory for the DIB section's pixels. Alternatively, you can specify the **hSection** parameter as the handle to a file-mapping object. Now you're responsible for the pixels indirectly through the memory-mapped file. In this case, to free the memory for the pixels, you destroy your file-mapping object by using the **CloseHandle** function.

Most of the time, management of the memory that's used for the DIB section's pixels is left up to Windows (i.e., **hSection** is passed as **NULL**). And, because a DIB section's pixels are stored in user-mode paged memory, the size of a DIB section is limited only by the amount of virtual memory. In Windows 95 and Windows 98, **CreateDIBSection** will likely fail before the amount of virtual memory is exhausted because much of the bitmap-related implementation is still based on 16-bit code. Even on these platforms, however, it's not uncommon to see DIB sections on the order of tens of megabytes in size.

As the previous code snippet demonstrated, once you have a pointer to a DIB section's pixels, you can work with them as you would a true DIB's pixels. Specifically, the approach you take depends on the format of the pixels (i.e., the color depth of the DIB section's DIB component). Yet you may have noticed a limitation in this approach; namely, you can gain access to the pixels only if you're the creator of the DIB section. What happens when you're supplied a handle from, say, a third-party library? In this case, you'll need to use an alternative technique, which, as we'll discuss next, can be accomplished by using the **DIBSECTION** structure.

The DIBSECTION Structure

The **DIBSECTION** structure is designed to hold information about a DIB section bitmap—it's the DIB section equivalent of the **BITMAP** structure that's used with DDBs. In fact, the **DIBSECTION** structure contains both a **BITMAP** structure (for the DDB part) and a **BITMAPINFOHEADER** structure (for the DIB part):

```
typedef struct tagDIBSECTION {
    BITMAP dsBm;
    BITMAPINFOHEADER dsBmih;
    DWORD dsBitfields[3];
```

```
    HANDLE dshSection;
    DWORD dsOffset;
} DIBSECTION, FAR *LPDIBSECTION, *PDIBSECTION;
```

The **dsBm** data member is a **BITMAP** structure that describes the DIB section's DDB-type features. The **dsBmih** data member holds the associated **BITMAPINFOHEADER** structure that describes the DIB section's DIB-type features. The **dsBitfields** data member is valid only when the DIB section is a 16- or 32-bit variety. In this case, **dsBitfields** holds the three bit-field masks that define which bits of each pixel correspond with each color channel. The **dshSection** data member identifies the handle to the file-mapping object that was passed as the **hSection** parameter of the **CreateDIBSection** function. Similarly, the **dwOffset** data member identifies the value that was passed to the **CreateDIBSection** function's **dwOffset** parameter.

As with any other GDI graphic object, you can use the **GetObject** function to fill a **DIBSECTION** structure. Unfortunately, some of the data members don't always reveal the correct results, although most do. Specifically, in Windows NT and Windows 2000, the **dsBmih::biHeight** data member always yields a positive value, whether the DIB section is top-down or bottom-up. Furthermore, on systems running Windows 95, the **dshSection** and **dsOffset** data members always specify **NULL**, even if non-**NULL** values were passed as the corresponding parameters (**hSection** and **dwOffset**, respectively) to **CreateDIBSection**.

Again, notice that the **DIBSECTION** structure contains a **BITMAP** structure. When you use the **GetObject** function to fill the **DIBSECTION** structure, this **BITMAP** structure is also filled. This is exactly the approach to take to retrieve a pointer to a DIB section's pixels, given just its handle. The **BITMAP::bmBits** data member—that's accessible through the **DIBSECTION::dsBm** data member—is always **NULL** for DDBs, but actually points to the pixels for a DIB section bitmap—see the solution "Creating a DIB Section Bitmap from a Device-Dependent Bitmap" for a code snippet of this process.

Rendering DIB Section Bitmaps

Recall that a DIB section bitmap inherits, from its DDB component, features that are common to all GDI graphic objects. Because these features include the ability to be selected into a memory device context, you can render a DIB section bitmap as you would a normal DDB. Therefore, you can use the speedy **BitBlt** or **StretchBlt** functions instead of **StretchDIBits**.

Like a DDB, a DIB section can be selected into only a memory device context. And, as with DDBs, you can select a DIB section into only one memory device context at a time. To select a DIB section into a memory device context, you follow the same steps that you would for a DDB. Namely, you first use the **CreateCompatibleDC** function to create a memory device context, and you then use the **SelectObject** function to select the DIB section into the memory DC.

There's yet another advantage to using a DIB section. When you render to a memory device context that has a DIB section bitmap selected into it, Windows performs an automatic (albeit rudimentary) color conversion. This provides an easy way to convert between bitmaps of different color depths. For example, if you need to create a grayscale DIB from a color DDB, you can first create a grayscale DIB section, **BitBlt** the DDB to the DIB section, and then copy the DIB portion of the DIB section. Moreover, for DIB sections that require a color table, you no longer need to navigate through the often-confusing **BITMAPINFO::bmiColors** data member. Instead, you can use the much simpler **GetDIBColorTable** and **SetDIBColorTable** functions.

Immediate Solutions

Creating a Device-Independent Bitmap

There's no predefined function to create a device-independent bitmap. Instead, you allocate memory for the DIB's header (a **BITMAPINFOHEADER** structure) and, when required, memory for its color table (an array of **RGBQUADs** or **WORDs**). In addition, if you want to create a packed DIB, you also allocate enough memory for the pixels; otherwise, the pixels can be created as a separate array of bytes. Let's walk through a systematic example of creating an uncompressed 8-bit (133-by-225) packed DIB with **RGBQUAD**-type color-table entries.

Step 1: Compute the Number of Bytes Required for the DIB

The first step is to determine how much memory to allocate. This value must be large enough to hold a **BITMAPINFOHEADER** structure, all of the color-table entries, and all of the pixels:

```
const unsigned char bits_per_pixel = 8;

// compute the size of the color table
const short num_color_table_entries = (1 << bits_per_pixel); // 256
const size_t color_table_size =
   num_color_table_entries * sizeof(RGBQUAD);

// compute the size of the pixel array
const SIZE SBitmap = {133, 225};
const size_t pixels_size =
   SBitmap.cy * (((SBitmap.cx * bits_per_pixel) + 31) & ~31) >> 3;

// compute the total size of the packed DIB
const size_t total_DIB_size =
   sizeof(BITMAPINFOHEADER) +  color_table_size + pixels_size;
```

Step 2: Allocate the Memory

The next step is to allocate the memory for the packed DIB, which you can do via the **GlobalAlloc** function (or the **new []** operator). Then zero-out the memory, and then typecast the result to a pointer to a **BITMAPINFO** structure:

```
HGLOBAL hDIB = GlobalAlloc(GHND, total_DIB_size); // zero-init from GHND
if (hDIB)
{
   LPBITMAPINFO lpbi =
      reinterpret_cast<LPBITMAPINFO>(GlobalLock(hDIB));
   if (!lpbi)
   {
      GlobalFree(hDIB);
      return;
   }

   // on to the next step...
}
```

Step 3: Initialize the DIB's Header

Once you have a pointer to a **BITMAPINFO** structure, the next step is to properly initialize the fields of the **bmiHeader** data member. The value that you assign to each field depends on the type of DIB you want. Here, we'll initialize **bmiHeader** for an uncompressed 8-bit DIB:

```
HGLOBAL hDIB = GlobalAlloc(GHND, total_DIB_size);
if (hDIB)
{
   LPBITMAPINFO lpbi =
      reinterpret_cast<LPBITMAPINFO>(GlobalLock(hDIB));
   if (!lpbi)
   {
      GlobalFree(hDIB);
      return;
   }

   lpbi->bmiHeader.biSize = sizeof(BITMAPINFOHEADER);
   lpbi->bmiHeader.biWidth = SBitmap.cx;
   lpbi->bmiHeader.biHeight = -SBitmap.cy; // top-down DIB
   lpbi->bmiHeader.biPlanes = 1;
   lpbi->bmiHeader.biBitCount = bits_per_pixel;
   lpbi->bmiHeader.biCompression = BI_RGB;
   lpbi->bmiHeader.biSizeImage = pixels_size;

   // on to the next step...
}
```

Step 4: Fill the Color Table

After you've initialized the DIB's header, you need to set the entries of its color table. How you fill the color table depends on the colors that the image requires. Here, we'll create a grayscale color table:

```
HGLOBAL hDIB = GlobalAlloc(GHND, total_DIB_size);
if (hDIB)
{
   LPBITMAPINFO lpbi =
      reinterpret_cast<LPBITMAPINFO>(GlobalLock(hDIB));
   if (!lpbi)
   {
      GlobalFree(hDIB);
      return;
   }

   lpbi->bmiHeader.biSize = sizeof(BITMAPINFOHEADER);
   lpbi->bmiHeader.biWidth = SBitmap.cx;
   lpbi->bmiHeader.biHeight = -SBitmap.cy; // top-down DIB
   lpbi->bmiHeader.biPlanes = 1;
   lpbi->bmiHeader.biBitCount = bits_per_pixel;
   lpbi->bmiHeader.biCompression = BI_RGB;
   lpbi->bmiHeader.biSizeImage = pixels_size;

   for (int index = 0; index < num_color_table_entries; ++index)
   {
      lpbi->bmiColors[index].rgbRed = index;
      lpbi->bmiColors[index].rgbGreen = index;
      lpbi->bmiColors[index].rgbBlue = index;
   }

   // on to the next step...
}
```


Step 5: Initialize the Pixels, If Required

At this point, because you've previously zeroed-out the entire block of memory, all of the pixels will indicate the first color-table index (the color black for our grayscale color table). If you need to change the value of each pixel, now's the time to do so. For our 8-bit grayscale example, the following code creates a black-to-white horizontal grayscale gradient (left to right):

```
HGLOBAL hDIB = GlobalAlloc(GHND, total_DIB_size);
if (hDIB)
{
```

```
LPBITMAPINFO lpbi =
   reinterpret_cast<LPBITMAPINFO>(GlobalLock(hDIB));
if (!lpbi)
{
   GlobalFree(hDIB);
   return;
}

lpbi->bmiHeader.biSize = sizeof(BITMAPINFOHEADER);
lpbi->bmiHeader.biWidth = SBitmap.cx;
lpbi->bmiHeader.biHeight = -SBitmap.cy; // top-down DIB
lpbi->bmiHeader.biPlanes = 1;
lpbi->bmiHeader.biBitCount = bits_per_pixel;
lpbi->bmiHeader.biCompression = BI_RGB;
lpbi->bmiHeader.biSizeImage = pixels_size;

for (int index = 0; index < num_color_table_entries; ++index)
{
   lpbi->bmiColors[index].rgbRed = index;
   lpbi->bmiColors[index].rgbGreen = index;
   lpbi->bmiColors[index].rgbBlue = index;
}

// grab a pointer to the pixels
unsigned char* pBits = reinterpret_cast<unsigned char*>(
   lpbi->bmiColors + num_color_table_entries
   );

// compute the byte-width of each DWORD-aligned scan line
unsigned int aligned_bytes_per_scanline =
   (((SBitmap.cx * bits_per_pixel) + 31) & ~31) >> 3;

//
// set the pixels to create a horizontal grayscale gradient
//
const float dIntensity = 256.0 / SBitmap.cx;
for (int y = 0; y < SBitmap.cy; ++y)
{
   // grab a pointer to each scan line
   unsigned char* pScanLine =
      pBits + (y * aligned_bytes_per_scanline);

   for (int x = 0; x < SBitmap.cx; ++x)
   {
      pScanLine[x] = static_cast<unsigned char>(x * dIntensity);
   }
}
```

```
    // on to the next step...
}
```

Step 6: Clean Up

After you've created the DIB, you're free to use it as required. For example, you can render it to a device context by using **StretchDIBits**, or you can write it out to a file. In any event, unless you forfeit ownership of the DIB, you're required to free its associated memory. And, as for any other block of memory, you do this by using the complement of the allocation method. Remember, a DIB is not a GDI graphic object—there are no pitfalls—you simply free the memory. For example, if you allocate memory for the DIB via the **new []** operator, you use **delete []** to clean up. In this example, we used the **GlobalAlloc** and **GlobalLock** functions, so we need to use matching calls to the **GlobalUnlock** and **GlobalFree** functions:

```
HGLOBAL hDIB = GlobalAlloc(GHND, total_DIB_size);
if (hDIB)
{
   LPBITMAPINFO lpbi =
      reinterpret_cast<LPBITMAPINFO>(GlobalLock(hDIB));
   if (!lpbi)
   {
      GlobalFree(hDIB);
      return;
   }

   //
   // steps 3, 4, and 5...
   // use the DIB...
   //

   GlobalUnlock(hDIB);
   GlobalFree(hDIB);
}
```

Creating DIBs of other bit depths is accomplished via the same systematic procedure. However, note that a color table is required for 1-, 4-, and 8-bit DIBs, but it's optional for other types. Moreover, when you create a 16- or 32-bit DIB and assign the **BI_BITFIELDS** identifier to the **biCompression** data member of the DIB's header, you're required to supply three **DWORD** intensity masks as the first three entries of the color table. Whether or not a real color table follows these masks is up to you. (Just remember, if you do provide a color table for a 16-, 24-, or 32-bit DIB, be sure to set the **biClrUsed** data member appropriately and assign it the number of entries in the color table).

Creating a Device-Independent Bitmap from a Device-Dependent Bitmap

To create a device-independent bitmap from a device-dependent bitmap, you use the **GetDIBits** function:

```
int GetDIBits(
    IN HDC hdc,                   // handle to the target device context
    IN HBITMAP hbmp,              // handle to the DDB
    IN UINT uStartScan,           // first scan line to copy
    IN UINT cScanLines,           // number of scan lines to copy
    OUT LPVOID lpvBits,           // array that will receive a copy of the
                                  // DDB's bits
    IN OUT LPBITMAPINFO lpbi,     // pointer to a BITMAPINFO structure that
                                  // describes the desired format of the bits
    IN UINT uUsage                // color-table format identifier
   );
```

The **hdc** parameter identifies the device context whose currently realized logical palette is used to synthesize the DIB's color table, if required. The **hbmp** parameter identifies the DDB from which the DIB is created. This DDB must not be selected into a memory device context during the call to **GetDIBits**. The **uStartScan** and **uScanLines** parameters define the range of scan lines that will be initialized with the corresponding range of pixel values from the DDB. Typically, to create a DIB based on the entire DDB, you'd specify **uStartScan** as zero and specify **uScanLines** as the height of the DDB. The **lpvBits** parameter specifies the location of the DIB's pixel array that will be filled according to the pixels of the DDB. You're responsible for allocating this array—**GetDIBits** won't manage the memory for you. The **lpbi** parameter is specified as the address of an initialized **BITMAPINFO** structure. This structure is used to specify the desired format of the resulting DIB. If a color table is required, you must allocate enough memory for the color-table entries.

The **uUsage** parameter identifies the desired format of the color table that **GetDIBits** will synthesize, if required. When **uUsage** is passed as **DIB_RGB_COLORS** (0), the synthesized color table will consist of literal RGB values in the form of an **RGBQUAD** array. When **uUsage** is specified as **DIB_PAL_COLORS** (1), the synthesized color table will consist of **WORD**-type indices into **hdc**'s currently realized logical palette.

NOTE: *Technically, because you're still responsible for all of the memory (de)allocation, the* ***GetDIBits*** *function doesn't "create" a DIB. The function does, however, properly initialize the memory according to the DIB format that's specified by the* ***lpbi*** *parameter. That is, the function initializes (some of) the header, all of the color-table entries (if a color table is required), and the specified range of pixels, which are set according to those of the DDB.*

Note that the **GetDIBits** function does not create a DIB according to the color format of the specified DDB (**hbmp**) because this would obviate the device-independence. Instead, **GetDIBits** creates a DIB according to the data members of the **BITMAPINFOHEADER** structure that you specify through the **lpbi** parameter. For example, if **hbmp** refers to an 8-bit DDB, but the **BITMAPINFOHEADER::biBitCount** data member indicates a 24-bit DIB, the result is a 24-bit DIB.

When a color table is required, the **GetDIBits** function generates one according to the **uUsage** parameter. Specifically, the function creates a color table only when the **BITMAPINFOHEADER::biBitCount** data member (specified by the **lpbi** parameter) is assigned a value of 1, 4, or 8. When a 1-bit DIB is specified, the color table is filled with two entries: black and white (in that order). When a 4-bit DIB is specified, the color table is filled with colors from the standard 16-color VGA palette. When an 8-bit DIB is specified, the color table is filled with a general mix of 256 unique colors. Again, you're responsible for allocating the memory for the color table. You can compute the required size of the color table by using the following approach for a color table that contains **RGBQUAD**-type entries (i.e., **uUsage** is set to **DIB_RGB_COLORS**):

```
const short num_color_table_entries = (1 << bits_per_pixel);
const size_t color_table_size =
   num_color_table_entries * sizeof(RGBQUAD);
```

Use the following approach when you want a color table that contains **WORD**-type indices (i.e., **uUsage** is set to **DIB_PAL_COLORS**):

```
const short num_color_table_entries = (1 << bits_per_pixel);
const size_t color_table_size =
   num_color_table_entries * sizeof(WORD);
```

Once you've allocated enough memory for the header and the color table, you need to initialize the data members of the header. However, you aren't required to initialize all of the fields; you have to initialize only the first six. Typically, these data members are specified like so, and the rest are set to zero:

```
lpbi->bmiHeader.biSize = sizeof(BITMAPINFOHEADER)
lpbi->bmiHeader.biWidth = width_of_DDB;
lpbi->bmiHeader.biHeight = -height_of_DDB; ("-" for a top-down DIB)
lpbi->bmiHeader.biPlanes = 1;
lpbi->bmiHeader.biBitCount = 1, 4, 8, 16, 24, or 32;
lpbi->bmiHeader.biCompression = BI_RGB;
```

After you've allocated enough space for the header and the color table, and you've properly initialized the first six data members of **lpbi**'s **BITMAPINFOHEADER** structure, the next task is to allocate memory for the pixels. To determine how much memory to allocate, you first call the **GetDIBits** function with a **NULL lpvBits** parameter. This will instruct the function to fill in the **BITMAPINFOHEADER::biSizeImage** data member and the color-table entries; no pixels are copied because there's nowhere to put them yet. In this case, if the **GetDIBits** function is successful, it returns either the total number of scan lines in the DDB (for Windows 95 or Windows 98) or **TRUE** (for Windows NT or Windows 2000). If the function fails, the return value is zero.

After the **biSizeImage** data member is initialized, its value will tell you how many bytes to allocate for the pixels. If **biSizeImage** is still zero, you can compute the required size manually by using the following technique:

```
const size_t buffer_size =
   abs(bmi.bmiHeader.biHeight) *
   ((((bmi.bmiHeader.biWidth * bmi.bmiHeader.biBitCount)
      + 31) & ~31) >> 3);
```

After you allocate sufficient memory for the array of pixels, you call the **GetDIBits** function again, this time passing the address of your array as the **lpvBits** parameter. This will instruct the **GetDIBits** function to copy the value of each pixel from the DDB to your array. When the array of pixels has been filled, you're done. That is, you now have an initialized **BITMAPINFO** structure and an initialized array of pixels.

Let's work through a step-by-step example of creating a packed 8-bit DIB, with **RGBQUAD** color-table entries, from a 24-bit DDB (**hBmp**). Note that there will be a loss of color information because we're going from 24 bits per pixel down to 8 bits per pixel.

Step 1: Allocate Memory for the Header and the Color Table

The first step is to compute the required size of the header and the color table, and then allocate that many bytes. Note that, for DIBs with more than eight bits per pixel, **GetDIBits** won't synthesize a color table; in that case, you can ignore the color table. Here, we're going for an 8-bit DIB, so we'll indeed need to make room for a color table.

```
const unsigned char bits_per_pixel = 8;
const short num_color_table_entries = (1 << bits_per_pixel); // 256

// compute the size of the header and the color table
const size_t DIB_size_wo_pixels =
   sizeof(BITMAPINFOHEADER) +
   num_color_table_entries * sizeof(RGBQUAD);
```

```
//
// allocate memory for the header and the color table
// and initialize the memory to zero (here, via GHND)
//
HGLOBAL hDIB = GlobalAlloc(GHND, DIB_size_wo_pixels);
if (hDIB)
{
   // grab a pointer to the memory and cast it to a BITMAPINFO pointer
   LPBITMAPINFO lpbi =
      reinterpret_cast<LPBITMAPINFO>(GlobalLock(hDIB));
   if (!lpbi)
   {
      GlobalFree(hDIB);
      return;
   }

   // on to the next step...
}
```

Step 2: Initialize the First Six Fields of the Header

After you cast your block of memory to a pointer to a **BITMAPINFO** structure, the next step is to initialize only the first six fields of the header (the rest can be set to zero). You can use the **GetObject** function to determine the width and height of your DDB:

```
HGLOBAL hDIB = GlobalAlloc(GHND, DIB_size_wo_pixels);
if (hDIB)
{
   LPBITMAPINFO lpbi =
      reinterpret_cast<LPBITMAPINFO>(GlobalLock(hDIB));
   if (!lpbi)
   {
      GlobalFree(hDIB);
      return;
   }

   // determine the dimensions of the DDB
   BITMAP bmp;
   if (GetObject(hBmp, sizeof(BITMAP), &bmp) != sizeof(BITMAP))
   {
      GlobalUnlock(hDIB);
      GlobalFree(hDIB);
      return;
   }
```

```
    // initialize the first six data members of the header
    lpbi->bmiHeader.biSize = sizeof(BITMAPINFOHEADER);
    lpbi->bmiHeader.biWidth = bmp.bmWidth;
    lpbi->bmiHeader.biHeight = -bmp.bmHeight; // top-down DIB
    lpbi->bmiHeader.biPlanes = 1;
    lpbi->bmiHeader.biBitCount = bits_per_pixel;
    lpbi->bmiHeader.biCompression = BI_RGB;

    // on to the next step...
}
```

Step 3: Call GetDIBits to Determine the Required Size for the Pixels

After the header has been initialized, it's time to determine how much memory is required for the pixels. For this, you can use the **GetDIBits** function, passing a **NULL lpvBits** parameter. When **lpvBits** is passed as **NULL**, **GetDIBits** will initialize the header's **biSizeImage** data member and fill in the color table. If the device driver fails to initialize the **biSizeImage** data member, compute the size manually:

```
HGLOBAL hDIB = GlobalAlloc(GHND, DIB_size_wo_pixels);
if (hDIB)
{
    LPBITMAPINFO lpbi =
        reinterpret_cast<LPBITMAPINFO>(GlobalLock(hDIB));
    if (!lpbi)
    {
        GlobalFree(hDIB);
        return;
    }

    // determine the dimensions of the DDB
    BITMAP bmp;
    if (GetObject(hBmp, sizeof(BITMAP), &bmp) != sizeof(BITMAP))
    {
        GlobalUnlock(hDIB);
        GlobalFree(hDIB);
        return;
    }

    // initialize the first six data members of the header
    lpbi->bmiHeader.biSize = sizeof(BITMAPINFOHEADER);
    lpbi->bmiHeader.biWidth = bmp.bmWidth;
    lpbi->bmiHeader.biHeight = -bmp.bmHeight; // top-down DIB
    lpbi->bmiHeader.biPlanes = 1;
```

```
    lpbi->bmiHeader.biBitCount = bits_per_pixel;
    lpbi->bmiHeader.biCompression = BI_RGB;

    HDC hScreenDC = GetDC(NULL);
    bool success =
        GetDIBits(
            hScreenDC, hBmp, 0, bmp.bmHeight,
            NULL, lpbi, DIB_RGB_COLORS
            );
    ReleaseDC(NULL, hScreenDC);

    if (!success)
    {
        GlobalUnlock(hDIB);
        GlobalFree(hDIB);
        return;
    }

    const size_t pixels_size =
        lpbi->bmiHeader.biSizeImage != 0 ?
        lpbi->bmiHeader.biSizeImage :
        ((((bmp.bmWidth * bits_per_pixel) + 31) & ~31) >> 3) *
        bmp.bmHeight;

    // on to the next step...
}
```

Step 4: Allocate Memory for the Pixels

Now that you know how much memory to allocate for the pixels, go ahead and allocate the memory. If you're creating an unpacked DIB, you can store the pixels in a separate array. Here, we're going for a packed DIB, so we'll use the **GlobalReAlloc** function to resize our initial memory block:

```
HGLOBAL hDIB = GlobalAlloc(GHND, DIB_size_wo_pixels);
if (hDIB)
{
    LPBITMAPINFO lpbi =
        reinterpret_cast<LPBITMAPINFO>(GlobalLock(hDIB));
    if (!lpbi)
    {
        GlobalFree(hDIB);
        return;
    }
```

```
    // determine the dimensions of the DDB
    BITMAP bmp;
    if (GetObject(hBmp, sizeof(BITMAP), &bmp) != sizeof(BITMAP))
    {
       GlobalUnlock(hDIB);
       GlobalFree(hDIB);
       return;
    }

    // initialize the first six data members of the header
    lpbi->bmiHeader.biSize = sizeof(BITMAPINFOHEADER);
    lpbi->bmiHeader.biWidth = bmp.bmWidth;
    lpbi->bmiHeader.biHeight = -bmp.bmHeight; // top-down DIB
    lpbi->bmiHeader.biPlanes = 1;
    lpbi->bmiHeader.biBitCount = bits_per_pixel;
    lpbi->bmiHeader.biCompression = BI_RGB;

    HDC hScreenDC = GetDC(NULL);
    bool success =
       GetDIBits(
          hScreenDC, hBmp, 0, bmp.bmHeight,
          NULL, lpbi, DIB_RGB_COLORS
          );
    ReleaseDC(NULL, hScreenDC);

    if (!success)
    {
       GlobalUnlock(hDIB);
       GlobalFree(hDIB);
       return;
    }

    const size_t pixels_size =
       lpbi->bmiHeader.biSizeImage != 0 ?
       lpbi->bmiHeader.biSizeImage :
       ((((bmp.bmWidth * bits_per_pixel) + 31) & ~31) >> 3) *
       bmp.bmHeight;

    GlobalUnlock(hDIB);
    hDIB = GlobalReAlloc(
       hDIB, DIB_size_wo_pixels + pixels_size, GMEM_MOVEABLE
       );
    lpbi = reinterpret_cast<LPBITMAPINFO>(GlobalLock(hDIB));

    // on to the next step...
}
```

Step 5: Call GetDIBits to Copy the DDB's Pixel Values

Once you've made room for the pixels, it's time to initialize them with the pixels of the DDB. For this, you call **GetDIBits** again, this time passing the pointer to your array as the **lpvBits** parameter. When **lpvBits** is non-**NULL**, **GetDIBits** will copy the pixels from the DDB. This time, the return value is the number of scan lines that were copied:

```
HGLOBAL hDIB = GlobalAlloc(GHND, DIB_size_wo_pixels);
if (hDIB)
{
   LPBITMAPINFO lpbi =
      reinterpret_cast<LPBITMAPINFO>(GlobalLock(hDIB));
   if (!lpbi)
   {
      GlobalFree(hDIB);
      return;
   }

   // determine the dimensions of the DDB
   BITMAP bmp;
   if (GetObject(hBmp, sizeof(BITMAP), &bmp) != sizeof(BITMAP))
   {
      GlobalUnlock(hDIB);
      GlobalFree(hDIB);
      return;
   }

   // initialize the first six data members of the header
   lpbi->bmiHeader.biSize = sizeof(BITMAPINFOHEADER);
   lpbi->bmiHeader.biWidth = bmp.bmWidth;
   lpbi->bmiHeader.biHeight = -bmp.bmHeight; // top-down DIB
   lpbi->bmiHeader.biPlanes = 1;
   lpbi->bmiHeader.biBitCount = bits_per_pixel;
   lpbi->bmiHeader.biCompression = BI_RGB;

   HDC hScreenDC = GetDC(NULL);
   bool success =
      GetDIBits(
         hScreenDC, hBmp, 0, bmp.bmHeight,
         NULL, lpbi, DIB_RGB_COLORS
         );
   ReleaseDC(NULL, hScreenDC);

   if (!success)
   {
```

```
        GlobalUnlock(hDIB);
        GlobalFree(hDIB);
        return;
    }

    const size_t pixels_size =
        lpbi->bmiHeader.biSizeImage != 0 ?
        lpbi->bmiHeader.biSizeImage :
        ((((bmp.bmWidth * bits_per_pixel) + 31) & ~31) >> 3) *
        bmp.bmHeight;

    GlobalUnlock(hDIB);
    hDIB = GlobalReAlloc(
        hDIB, DIB_size_wo_pixels + pixels_size, GMEM_MOVEABLE
        );
    lpbi = reinterpret_cast<LPBITMAPINFO>(GlobalLock(hDIB));

    // call GetDIBits again, this time to copy the pixel values
    hScreenDC = GetDC(NULL);
    int num_scanlines_copied =
        GetDIBits(
            hScreenDC, hBmp, 0, bmp.bmHeight,
            // see The solution "Accessing The Pixels
            // of a Packed Device-Independent Bitmap"
            PointerToDIBits(lpbi), lpbi, DIB_RGB_COLORS
            );
    ReleaseDC(NULL, hScreenDC);

    if (num_scanlines_copied != bmp.bmHeight)
    {
        GlobalUnlock(hDIB);
        GlobalFree(hDIB);
        return;
    }

    // on to the next step...
}
```


Step 6: Clean Up

After the DIB is created, you can use it as required, or you can pass it on to another part of your application that will use it. For example, you can copy it to the clipboard, or use **StretchDIBits** to render it to a device context. In the former case, you forfeit ownership of the DIB to the clipboard, so there's no need to destroy the DIB. Otherwise, you'll need to manually free its associated memory. In general, you simply free the DIB by using the complement of the allocation routine. For example, if you allocate memory for the DIB via the **new []** operator, you use **delete []** to free its memory. Here we used the **GlobalAlloc** and **GlobalLock** combination, so we use matching calls to **GlobalFree** and **GlobalUnlock**:

```
HGLOBAL hDIB = GlobalAlloc(GHND, total_DIB_size);
if (hDIB)
{
   LPBITMAPINFO lpbi =
      reinterpret_cast<LPBITMAPINFO>(GlobalLock(hDIB));
   if (!lpbi)
   {
      GlobalFree(hDIB);
      return;
   }

   //
   // steps 2, 3, 4, and 5...
   // use the DIB...
   //

   GlobalUnlock(hDIB);
   GlobalFree(hDIB);
}
```

To create DIBs of other bit depths, you follow these same five steps. In fact, if you're creating a DIB that uses more than eight bits per pixel, because no color table will be synthesized, you can simply ignore the color table considerations. In most cases, 24-bit DIBs are the easiest type to work with; for an example of creating a 24-bit DIB from a DDB, see Chapter 6.

Related solutions:	Found on page:
Creating a Color Device-Dependent Bitmap	311
Manipulating the Bits of a Device-Dependent Bitmap	332

Loading a Device-Independent Bitmap from a File

To load a device-independent bitmap from a file, you use the application-defined function **LoadDIBFromFile**:

```
HGLOBAL LoadDIBFromFile(
    IN LPCSTR filename      // name of the bitmap file to load
```

```
    )
{
    HGLOBAL hDIB = NULL;

    // open the file for shared reading
    HANDLE hFile =
        CreateFile(
            filename, GENERIC_READ, FILE_SHARE_READ, NULL,
            OPEN_EXISTING, FILE_ATTRIBUTE_NORMAL, NULL
            );

    if (hFile != INVALID_HANDLE_VALUE)
    {
        DWORD dwRead = 0;
        BITMAPFILEHEADER bmfh;

        // read the file header
        bool read_ok = ReadFile(
            hFile, &bmfh, sizeof(BITMAPFILEHEADER), &dwRead, NULL
            );
        if (read_ok && (dwRead == sizeof(BITMAPFILEHEADER)))
        {
            // check the format
            if (bmfh.bfType == 0x4D42 // BM
            {
                BITMAPINFOHEADER bmih;

                // read the DIB's header
                read_ok = ReadFile(
                    hFile, &bmih, sizeof(BITMAPINFOHEADER), &dwRead, NULL
                    );
                if (read_ok && (dwRead == sizeof(BITMAPINFOHEADER)))
                {
                    // get the number of colors in the color table
                    short num_colors = bmih.biClrUsed;
                    if (num_colors == 0 && bmih.biBitCount <= 8)
                    {
                        num_colors = (1 << bmih.biBitCount);
                    }

                    // compute the size of the color table
                    const size_t color_table_size =
                        sizeof(RGBQUAD) * num_colors;

                    // compute the size of the image
                    const size_t pixels_size =
```

```
   bmih.biSizeImage != 0 ? bmih.biSizeImage :
   abs(bmih.biHeight) *
   ((((bmih.biWidth * bmih.biBitCount) + 31) & ~31) >> 3);

// compute the total size of the packed DIB
const size_t total_DIB_size =
   sizeof(BITMAPINFOHEADER) +
   color_table_size + pixels_size;

// allocate memory for the packed DIB
hDIB = GlobalAlloc(GHND, total_DIB_size);
if (hDIB)
{
   LPVOID lpDIB = GlobalLock(hDIB);
   if (lpDIB)
   {
      // copy the header to the packed DIB
      memcpy(lpDIB, &bmih, sizeof(BITMAPINFOHEADER));

      // offset the pointer
      lpDIB =
         static_cast<unsigned char*>(lpDIB) +
         sizeof(BITMAPINFOHEADER);

      //
      // now for the color table...
      //
      if (color_table_size > 0)
      {
         // read the color table, if present
         read_ok = ReadFile(
            hFile, lpDIB, color_table_size, &dwRead, NULL
            );
         if (!read_ok || (dwRead != color_table_size))
         {
            // upon error, clean up
            GlobalUnlock(hDIB);
            GlobalFree(hDIB);
            CloseHandle(hFile);
            return NULL;
         }

         // offset the DIB's pointer
         lpDIB =
            static_cast<unsigned char*>(lpDIB) +
            color_table_size;
```

```
        }

        //
        // now for the pixels...
        //
        // move to the pixels
        DWORD dwMoved = SetFilePointer(
           hFile, bmfh.bfOffBits, 0, FILE_BEGIN
           );
        if (dwMoved == bmfh.bfOffBits)
        {
           // read the pixels
           read_ok = ReadFile(
              hFile, lpDIB, pixels_size, &dwRead, NULL
              );
           if (!read_ok || (dwRead != pixels_size))
           {
              // upon error, clean up
              GlobalUnlock(hDIB);
              GlobalFree(hDIB);
              CloseHandle(hFile);
              return NULL;
           }

           // offset the DIB's pointer
           lpDIB =
              static_cast<unsigned char*>(lpDIB) +
              pixels_size;
        }
        else
        {
           // upon error, clean up
           GlobalUnlock(hDIB);
           GlobalFree(hDIB);
           CloseHandle(hFile);
           return NULL;
        }
        // unlock the memory
        GlobalUnlock(hDIB);
     }
     else
     {
        // upon error, clean up
        GlobalFree(hDIB);
        hDIB = NULL;
```

```
                        }
                    }
                }
            }
        }
        // close the file
        CloseHandle(hFile);
    }
    return hDIB;
}
```

The **filename** parameter is specified as a pointer to a **NULL**-terminated string that contains the full path of the bitmap file from which the DIB is "created." If the **LoadDIBFromFile** function is successful, it returns a handle to a global memory object that refers to a packed DIB. If the function fails, the return value is **NULL**.

Although the GDI provides no direct means to load a DIB from a file (without going through a DIB section bitmap), the bitmap file format is not complicated. The file simply consists of a file header (a **BITMAPFILEHEADER** structure), plus the regular DIB (header, color table, and pixels). The previous code first reads the file header, checking the **bfType** data member for **'BM'** to ensure that the file is actually a bitmap. Next, the DIB's header is read into a local **BITMAPINFOHEADER**-type variable, and the information from this header is used to determine how much space the DIB requires. When the appropriate size block of memory is determined, the remaining bytes are simply read from the file.

Related solutions:	Found on page:
Loading a Device-Dependent Bitmap from a File	323
Reading an ICM-Aware Bitmap from a File	913

Saving a Device-Independent Bitmap to a File

To save a device-independent bitmap to a file, you use the application-defined function, **SaveDIBToFile**:

```
DWORD SaveDIBToFile(
    IN LPCSTR filename,                    // name of the file to save as
    IN const BITMAPINFO& bmi,              // reference to the DIB
    IN const unsigned char* pBits = NULL   // pointer to the pixels
  )
```

```
{
   DWORD dwBytesWrote = 0;

   // first determine the size (in bytes) of the color table
   short num_colors = bmi.bmiHeader.biClrUsed;
   if (num_colors == 0 && bmi.bmiHeader.biBitCount <= 8)
   {
      num_colors = (1 << bmi.bmiHeader.biBitCount);
   }
   const size_t color_table_size =
      sizeof(RGBQUAD) * num_colors;

   // next, determine the size (in bytes) of the pixels array
   const size_t pixels_size =
      bmi.bmiHeader.biSizeImage != 0 ?
      bmi.bmiHeader.biSizeImage :
      abs(bmi.bmiHeader.biHeight) *
      ((((bmi.bmiHeader.biWidth *
          bmi.bmiHeader.biBitCount) + 31) & ~31) >> 3);

   // initialize the file header
   BITMAPFILEHEADER bmfh;
   bmfh.bfType = 0x4D42
   bmfh.bfSize =
      // size of the file header
      sizeof(BITMAPFILEHEADER) +
      // size of the DIB's header
      sizeof(BITMAPINFOHEADER) +
      // size of the color table
      color_table_size +
      // size of the pixels array
      pixels_size;
   bmfh.bfOffBits = bmfh.bfSize - pixels_size;

   // create the file
   HANDLE hFile =
      CreateFile(
         filename, GENERIC_WRITE, 0, NULL,
         CREATE_ALWAYS, FILE_ATTRIBUTE_NORMAL, NULL
         );
   if (hFile != INVALID_HANDLE_VALUE)
   {
      DWORD dwWritten = 0;

      // write the file header
```

```
bool write_ok = WriteFile(
   hFile, &bmfh, sizeof(BITMAPFILEHEADER), &dwWritten, NULL
   );
if (write_ok && (dwWritten == sizeof(BITMAPFILEHEADER)))
{
    // accrue the number of bytes written
   dwBytesWrote += dwWritten;

   // adjust the size of the header accordingly
   BITMAPINFO bmiCopy = bmi;
   bmiCopy.bmiHeader.biSize = sizeof(BITMAPINFOHEADER);

   // write the DIB header
   write_ok = WriteFile(
      hFile, &bmiCopy.bmiHeader, sizeof(BITMAPINFOHEADER),
      &dwWritten, NULL
      );
   if (write_ok && (dwWritten == sizeof(BITMAPINFOHEADER)))
   {
      // accrue the number of bytes written
      dwBytesWrote += dwWritten;

      // write the color table
      if (color_table_size != 0)
      {
         WriteFile(
            hFile, bmi.bmiColors, color_table_size,
            &dwWritten, NULL
            );
         // accrue the number of bytes written
         dwBytesWrote += dwWritten;
      }

      // write the pixels
      if (!pBits)
      {
         // assume a packed DIB if no pointer is supplied
         pBits = reinterpret_cast<unsigned char*>(
            const_cast<RGBQUAD*>(bmi.bmiColors) + num_colors
            );
      }
      WriteFile(
         hFile, pBits, pixels_size, &dwWritten, NULL
         );
      // accrue the number of bytes written
      dwBytesWrote += dwWritten;
   }
```

```
        }
        CloseHandle(hFile);
    }
    return dwBytesWrote;
}
```

The **filename** parameter identifies the name of the file in which the DIB should be saved. If a file of the same name already exists, it is overwritten. The **bmi** parameter is a reference to the DIB's corresponding **BITMAPINFO** structure. If this parameter refers to a packed DIB, then the **pBits** parameter can be specified as **NULL**. Otherwise, you must specify the **pBits** parameter as a pointer to the DIB's pixels. The **SaveDIBToFile** function returns the number of bytes that have been written to the file.

NOTE: *Because DIB's that contain **WORD**-type color table entries aren't portable, the **SaveDIBToFile** function assumes that the DIB's color table consists of **RGBQUAD**-type entries.*

Although the GDI doesn't provide its own function for saving DIBs, the bitmap file format isn't too complicated. The file simply consists of a file header (a **BITMAPFILEHEADER** structure), plus the regular DIB (header, color table, and pixels). The **SaveDIBToFile** function first initializes a **BITMAPFILE-HEADER** structure (the file header), setting the **bfType** data member to **'BM'** (indicating the Windows bitmap format), setting the **bfSize** data member to the size of the file header plus the size of the DIB, and setting the **bfOffBits** data member to the number of bytes from the beginning of the file header to the DIB's pixels. After the file header is initialized, this data is written to a file, followed by each of the DIB's components (header, color table, and pixels).

Related solutions:	Found on page:
Saving a Device-Dependent Bitmap to a File	329
Saving an ICM-Aware Bitmap to a File	918

Rendering a Device-Independent Bitmap

To render a device-independent bitmap, you use the **StretchDIBits** function:

```
int StretchDIBits(
    IN HDC hdc,                   // handle to the target device context
    IN int XDest,                 // horizontal position of the top-left
                                  // corner of the destination rectangle
```

```
    IN int YDest,                     // vertical position of the top-left
                                      // corner of the destination rectangle
    IN int nDestWidth,                // width of the destination rectangle
    IN int nDestHeight,               // height of the destination rectangle
    IN int XSrc,                      // horizontal position of the top-left
                                      // corner of the source rectangle
    IN int YSrc,                      // vertical position of the top-left
                                      // corner of the source rectangle
    IN int nSrcWidth,                 // width of the source rectangle
    IN int nSrcHeight,                // height of the source rectangle
    IN CONST VOID *lpBits,            // pointer to the DIB's pixels
    IN CONST BITMAPINFO *lpBitsInfo,  // pointer to the DIB's BITMAPINFO
                                      // structure
    IN UINT iUsage,                   // color-table format identifier
    IN DWORD dwRop                    // ternary-raster-operation code
);
```

The **hdc** parameter identifies the destination device context. The **XDest**, **YDest**, **nDestWidth**, and **nDestHeight** parameters specify, in logical coordinates, a bounding rectangle to which the DIB will be rendered. Likewise, the **XSrc**, **YSrc**, **nSrcWidth**, and **nSrcHeight** parameters specify, in pixels, the rectangular portion of the DIB that you want rendered. The **lpBits** parameter specifies the address of the DIB's pixels. The **lpBitsInfo** parameter specifies the address of the DIB's **BITMAPINFO** structure.

The **iUsage** parameter specifies the type of color table that the DIB contains. If the DIB's color table contains **RGBQUAD**-type entries, set this parameter to **DIB_RGB_COLORS** (0). If the DIB's color table contains **WORD**-type entries, set this parameter to **DIB_PAL_COLORS** (1). If the DIB has no color table, **iUsage** is ignored.

The **dwRop** parameter specifies a ROP3 code. In most cases, **dwRop** is specified as **SRCCOPY**, which instructs the function to copy the DIB to the target device, ignoring the colors of the destination and brush.

NOTE: *The **StretchDIBits** function transfers the DIB in a device-independent fashion. Because it is up to the device driver to convert the DIB to a format that's compatible with the device, the results of this function may vary. Moreover, many devices (namely, printers) support only the **SRCCOPY** ROP3 code.*

Upon success, the **StretchDIBits** function returns the number of scan lines that were transferred to the target device; otherwise, the return value is **GDI_ERROR**.

The following code snippet demonstrates how to use the **StretchDIBits** function to render a DIB (**lpbi**) in its original size to a display device context. Here, a non-palettized display is assumed. (For an example that uses a palette, see "Creating a Palette from the Color Table of a Device-Independent Bitmap," later in this chapter.) Here's the code:

```
// determine the number of colors that the DIB uses
short num_colors = lpbi->bmiHeader.biClrUsed;
if (num_colors == 0 && lpbi->bmiHeader.biBitCount <= 8)
{
   num_colors = (1 << lpbi->bmiHeader.biBitCount);
}

// grab a pointer to the DIB's pixels
unsigned char* pBits = reinterpret_cast<unsigned char*>(
   lpbi->bmiColors + num_colors
   /* NOTE: be sure to adjust for WORD-type color tables like so:*/
   /* reinterpret_cast<LPWORD>(lpbi->bmiColors) + num_colors */
   );

HDC hDC = GetDC(hWnd);
try
{
   // render the DIB
   StretchDIBits(
      hDC,
      0, 0, lpbi->bmiHeader.biWidth, abs(lpbi->bmiHeader.biHeight)
      0, 0, lpbi->bmiHeader.biWidth, abs(lpbi->bmiHeader.biHeight)
      pBits, lpbi, DIB_RGB_COLORS,
      SRCCOPY
      );
}
catch (...)
{
   ReleaseDC(hWnd, hDC);
}
ReleaseDC(hWnd, hDC);
```

The **StretchDIBits** function performs best when the color format of the target device is identical to that of the DIB. In any event, **StretchDIBits** is significantly slower than **BitBlt**. If you're just displaying the DIB to the screen, it's better to create a DDB from the DIB first, and then use the **BitBlt** function.

Related solution:	Found on page:
Rendering a Device-Dependent Bitmap	338

Rendering a Device-Independent Bitmap in a Scaled Fashion

To render a device-independent bitmap in a stretched or compacted fashion, you use the **StretchDIBits** function.

***NOTE:** For an explanation of the **StretchDIBits** function, see "Rendering a Device-Independent Bitmap."*

To stretch the DIB, you simply specify the destination rectangle (specified by the **XDest**, **YDest**, **nDestWidth**, and **nDestHeight** parameters) to be larger than the source rectangle (specified by the **XSrc**, **YSrc**, **nSrcWidth**, and **nSrcHeight** parameters). Likewise, to compact (scale down) the DIB, you specify the destination rectangle to be smaller than the source rectangle.

WARNING! When particularly large stretches are required, it's recommended that you use banding (i.e., render the DIB as a series of smaller strips).

The following code snippet demonstrates how to use the **StretchDIBits** function to render a DIB (**lpbi**) to a display device context in twice its original size (assuming a non-palettized display):

```
// determine the number of colors that the DIB uses
short num_colors = lpbi->bmiHeader.biClrUsed;
if (num_colors == 0 && lpbi->bmiHeader.biBitCount <= 8)
{
   num_colors = (1 << lpbi->bmiHeader.biBitCount);
}

// grab a pointer to the DIB's pixels
unsigned char* pBits = reinterpret_cast<unsigned char*>(
   lpbi->bmiColors + num_colors
   /* NOTE: be sure to adjust for WORD-type color tables like so:*/
   /* reinterpret_cast<LPWORD>(lpbi->bmiColors) + num_colors */
   );

HDC hDC = GetDC(hWnd);
try
{
   // ensure a 1:1 mapping mode
   SetMapMode(hDC, MM_TEXT);
   ModifyWorldTransform(hDC, NULL,  MWT_IDENTITY);
```

```
   POINT PRender = {10, 20};
   const int DIB_width = lpbi->bmiHeader.biWidth;
   const int DIB_height = abs(lpbi->bmiHeader.biHeight);

   // render the DIB
   StretchDIBits(
      hDC,
      PRender.x, PRender.y, 2 * DIB_width, 2 * DIB_height,
      0, 0, DIB_width, DIB_height,
      pBits, lpbi, DIB_RGB_COLORS,
      SRCCOPY
      );
}
catch (...)
{
   ReleaseDC(hWnd, hDC);
}
ReleaseDC(hWnd, hDC);
```

Likewise, the following code snippet demonstrates how to use the **StretchDIBits** function to render a DIB to a display device context in half its original size (here, assuming a palettized display):

```
// determine the number of colors that the DIB uses
short num_colors = lpbi->bmiHeader.biClrUsed;
if (num_colors == 0 && lpbi->bmiHeader.biBitCount <= 8)
{
   num_colors = (1 << lpbi->bmiHeader.biBitCount);
}

// grab a pointer to the DIB's pixels
unsigned char* pBits = reinterpret_cast<unsigned char*>(
   lpbi->bmiColors + num_colors
   /* NOTE: be sure to adjust for WORD-type color tables like so:*/
   /* reinterpret_cast<LPWORD>(lpbi->bmiColors) + num_colors */
   );

// create a palette from the DIB's color table
HPALETTE hPal = PaletteFromDIBColorTable(*lpbi);

HDC hDC = GetDC(hWnd);

// select the logical palette into the DC
```

```
HPALETTE hOldPal = SelectPalette(hDC, hPal, false);
try
{
   // realize the logical palette
   RealizePalette(hDC);

   // ensure a 1:1 mapping mode
   SetMapMode(hDC, MM_TEXT);
   ModifyWorldTransform(hDC, NULL,  MWT_IDENTITY);

   POINT PRender = {10, 20};
   const int DIB_width = lpbi->bmiHeader.biWidth;
   const int DIB_height = abs(lpbi->bmiHeader.biHeight);

   // change the stretching mode to preserve colors
   SetStretchBltMode(hDC, COLORONCOLOR);

   // render the DIB
   StretchDIBits(
      hDC,
      PRender.x, PRender.y, 0.5 * DIB_width, 0.5 * DIB_height,
      0, 0, DIB_width, DIB_height,
      pBits, lpbi, DIB_RGB_COLORS,
      SRCCOPY
      );
}
catch (...)
{
   if (hOldPal) DeleteObject(SelectPalette(hDC, hOldPal, false));
   ReleaseDC(hWnd, hDC);
}
if (hOldPal) DeleteObject(SelectPalette(hDC, hOldPal, false));
ReleaseDC(hWnd, hDC);
```

NOTE: *When you're rendering a DIB in a compacted fashion, the current stretching mode of the target device context determines which pixels are discarded. For information on changing the stretching mode of a device context, refer to Chapter 1.*

Related solutions:	Found on page:
Changing the Stretching Mode of a Device Context	60
Rendering a Device-Dependent Bitmap in a Scaled Fashion	341

Creating a Palette from the Color Table of a Device-Independent Bitmap

To create a logical palette from a DIB's color table, you first determine how many entries the color table contains. Then you allocate a block of memory that's large enough to hold a **LOGPALETTE** structure plus an array of **PALETTEENTRY** structures (one **PALETTEENTRY** structure for each color-table entry). Next, you initialize the **LOGPALETTE::palVersion** and **palNumEntries** data members, and then iterate over each color-table entry, copying its color channel information into the corresponding **PALETTEENTRY** structure. Finally, you pass the **LOGPALETTE** structure to the **CreatePalette** function to create the logical palette.

The following application-defined function, **PaletteFromDIBColorTable**, demonstrates how to create a logical palette from a DIB's color table. This function assumes that the color table contains **RGBQUAD**-type entries:

```
HPALETTE PaletteFromDIBColorTable(
   IN const BITMAPINFO& bmi  // reference to the DIB's BITMAPINFO structure
   )
{
   //
   // first see if the DIB has fewer
   // than the maximum color-table entries
   //
   short num_colors = bmi.bmiHeader.biClrUsed;

   //
   // if biClrUsed is zero for a DIB with more
   // than 8-bpp, the DIB has no color table
   //
   if (num_colors == 0 && bmi.bmiHeader.biBitCount > 8)
   {
      return NULL;
   }

   //
   // if the number of colors is zero, use the
   // maximum amount for this bit-depth
   //
   if (num_colors == 0) num_colors = (1 << bmi.bmiHeader.biBitCount);

   // compute the size of the palette
   const int palette_size =
      sizeof(LOGPALETTE) + ((num_colors - 1) * sizeof(PALETTEENTRY));
```

```
    // allocate memory for the palette
    LPLOGPALETTE lpPal = reinterpret_cast<LPLOGPALETTE>(
       new unsigned char[palette_size]
       );

    HPALETTE hPal = NULL;
    try
    {
       // initialize the info. fields
       lpPal->palVersion = 0x300;
       lpPal->palNumEntries = num_colors;

       //
       // copy the entries from the DIB's color table
       // (BITMAPINFO::bmiColors) to entries of lpPal
       //
       for (int index = 0; index < lpPal->palNumEntries; ++index)
       {
          lpPal->palPalEntry[index].peRed =
             bmi.bmiColors[index].rgbRed;
          lpPal->palPalEntry[index].peGreen =
             bmi.bmiColors[index].rgbGreen;
          lpPal->palPalEntry[index].peBlue =
             bmi.bmiColors[index].rgbBlue;
          lpPal->palPalEntry[index].peFlags = NULL;
       }

       // create the logical palette
       hPal = CreatePalette(lpPal);
    }
    catch (...)
    {
       // clean up
       delete [] lpPal;
       return NULL;
    }
    // clean up
    delete [] lpPal;
    return hPal;
}
```

***NOTE:** If your DIB contains **WORD**-type color-table entries, you'll need to use the same logical palette that was used when the DIB was created. If this is the case and you did not create the DIB yourself, the vendor should provide you with palette information. If no palette information is available, your next best bet is to create a logical palette that has a general mix of 256 colors (see Chapter 9).*

The following code snippet demonstrates how to use the **PaletteFromDIBColorTable** function. Here, **lpbi** is a pointer to the DIB's **BITMAPINFO** structure, and **pBits** is a pointer to its pixels (a palettized display is assumed):

```
// create a palette from the DIB's color table
HPALETTE hPal = PaletteFromDIBColorTable(*lpbi);

HDC hDC = GetDC(hWnd);

// select the logical palette into the DC
HPALETTE hOldPal = SelectPalette(hDC, hPal, false);
try
{
   // realize the logical palette
   RealizePalette(hDC);

   // render the DIB
   StretchDIBits(
      hDC,
      0, 0, lpbi->bmiHeader.biWidth, abs(lpbi->bmiHeader.biHeight),
      0, 0, lpbi->bmiHeader.biWidth, abs(lpbi->bmiHeader.biHeight),
      pBits, lpbi, DIB_RGB_COLORS,
      SRCCOPY
      );
}
catch (...)
{
   // clean up
   if (hOldPal) DeleteObject(SelectPalette(hDC, hOldPal, false));
   ReleaseDC(hWnd, hDC);
}
// clean up
if (hOldPal) DeleteObject(SelectPalette(hDC, hOldPal, false));
ReleaseDC(hWnd, hDC);
```


Related solutions:	Found on page:
Creating a Logical Palette	526
Selecting a Logical Palette into a Device Context	527

Accessing the Pixels of a Packed Device-Independent Bitmap

If a packed DIB contains a color table, its pixels are located immediately after the last entry of its color table. In this case, you can grab a pointer to the DIB's pixels by traversing past the last color-table entry. For example, if the DIB's color table contains **RGBQUAD**-type entries, you do the following (here, **lpbi** is a pointer to the DIB's **BITMAPINFO** structure):

```
unsigned char* pBits = NULL;

// determine the number of colors that the DIB uses
short num_colors = lpbi->bmiHeader.biClrUsed;
if (num_colors == 0 && lpbi->bmiHeader.biBitCount <= 8)
{
   num_colors = (1 << lpbi->bmiHeader.biBitCount);
}

// if the DIB doesn't use bit-field masks
if (lpbi->bmiHeader.biCompression != BI_BITFIELDS)
{
   pBits = reinterpret_cast<unsigned char*>(
      lpbi->bmiColors + num_colors
      );
}
else if (
   // only 16- and 32-bit DIBs can use bit-field masks
   lpbi->bmiHeader.biBitCount == 16 ||
   lpbi->bmiHeader.biBitCount == 32
   )
{
   pBits = reinterpret_cast<unsigned char*>(
      lpbi->bmiColors + num_colors + 3
      );
}
```

The previous code relies on pointer arithmetic to locate the pixels. Remember, because the **BITMAPINFO::bmiColors** data member is effectively a pointer to an **RGBQUAD**, simply adding **num_colors** to **bmiColors** will offset the pointer by the product of **num_colors** and **sizeof(RGBQUAD)** bytes. Along these same lines, when the color table contains **WORD**-type entries, you simply cast **bmiColors** to an **LPWORD**, like so:

```
unsigned char* pBits = NULL;
```

```
// determine the number of colors that the DIB uses
short num_colors = lpbi->bmiHeader.biClrUsed;
if (num_colors == 0 && lpbi->bmiHeader.biBitCount <= 8)
{
   num_colors = (1 << lpbi->bmiHeader.biBitCount);
}

// if the DIB doesn't use bit-field masks
if (lpbi->bmiHeader.biCompression != BI_BITFIELDS)
{
   pBits = reinterpret_cast<unsigned char*>(
      reinterpret_cast<LPWORD>(lpbi->bmiColors) + num_colors
      );
}
else if (
   // only 16- and 32-bit DIBs can use bit-field masks
   lpbi->bmiHeader.biBitCount == 16 ||
   lpbi->bmiHeader.biBitCount == 32
   )
{
   pBits = reinterpret_cast<unsigned char*>(
      reinterpret_cast<LPWORD>(lpbi->bmiColors) + num_colors + 6
      );
}
```

If the DIB has no color table, either of the previous techniques will work because **num_colors** will be zero. Remember, when no color table is present, the pixels follow immediately after the DIB's header. You can use the following application-defined function, **PointerToDIBits**, to retrieve a pointer to the pixels of any DIB bit-depth variety:

```
unsigned char* PointerToDIBits(
   IN const BITMAPINFO* pbmi,              // pointer to the DIB
   IN const UINT uUsage = DIB_RGB_COLORS   // color table format
   )
{
   if (!pbmi) return NULL;

   // determine the number of entries in the color table
   short num_color_table_entries = pbmi->bmiHeader.biClrUsed;
   if (num_color_table_entries == 0 && pbmi->bmiHeader.biBitCount <= 8)
   {
      num_color_table_entries = (1 << pbmi->bmiHeader.biBitCount);
   }

   // for non-masked DIB's
```

```
if (pbmi->bmiHeader.biCompression != BI_BITFIELDS)
{
   switch (uUsage)
   {
      // RGBQUAD-type color table entries
      case DIB_RGB_COLORS:
      {
         return reinterpret_cast<unsigned char*>(
            const_cast<BITMAPINFO*>(pbmi)->bmiColors +
            num_color_table_entries
            );
      }

      // WORD-type color table entries
      case DIB_PAL_COLORS:
      {
         return reinterpret_cast<unsigned char*>(
            reinterpret_cast<LPWORD>(
               const_cast<BITMAPINFO*>(pbmi)->bmiColors
               )
            + num_color_table_entries
            );
      }
      default: return NULL;
   }
}
//
// for 16- and 32-bit DIBs that use
// color channel intensity masks
//
else if (
   pbmi->bmiHeader.biCompression == BI_BITFIELDS &&
   (pbmi->bmiHeader.biBitCount == 16 ||
   pbmi->bmiHeader.biBitCount == 32)
   )
{
   switch (uUsage)
   {
      // RGBQUAD-type color table entries
      case DIB_RGB_COLORS:
      {
         return reinterpret_cast<unsigned char*>(
            const_cast<BITMAPINFO*>(pbmi)->bmiColors +
            pbmi->bmiHeader.biClrUsed + 3
            );
      }
```

```
        // WORD-type color table entries
        case DIB_PAL_COLORS:
        {
            return reinterpret_cast<unsigned char*>(
                reinterpret_cast<LPWORD>(
                    const_cast<BITMAPINFO*>(pbmi)->bmiColors
                    ) + pbmi->bmiHeader.biClrUsed + 6
                );
        }
    }
```

Creating a DIB Section Bitmap

To create a DIB section bitmap, you use the **CreateDIBSection** function:

```
HBITMAP CreateDIBSection(
    IN HDC hdc,                  // handle to the target device context
    IN CONST BITMAPINFO *pbmi,   // pointer to a BITMAPINFO structure that
                                 // defines the format of the DIB section
    IN UINT iUsage,              // color-table format identifier
    OUT VOID *ppvBits,           // address of a pointer that will refer to
                                 // the DIB section's pixels
    IN HANDLE hSection,          // handle to a file-mapping object can be
                                 // used to store the pixels
    IN DWORD dwOffset            // position of the DIB section's pixels
                                 // within the memory-mapped file
  );
```

The **hdc** parameter identifies the device context whose currently realized logical palette is used to generate the DIB's color-table entries when the **iUsage** parameter is set to **DIB_PAL_COLORS**. You can set **hdc** to **NULL** when no color table is required or when the **iUsage** parameter is set to **DIB_RGB_COLORS**. The **pbmi** parameter is specified as the address of a **BITMAPINFO** structure that defines the dimensions and color format of the DIB section. The **iUsage** parameter is specified as either **DIB_PAL_COLORS** (1), if you want the DIB section to use **WORD**-type color-table entries, or **DIB_RGB_COLORS** (0) for **RGBQUAD**-type color-table entries. The **ppvBits** parameter is specified as the address of a pointer to a variable that will refer to the DIB section's pixels. You can set this parameter to **NULL** if you don't need a pointer to the pixels.

The **hSection** and **dwOffset** parameters are optional. Typically, they're both set to **NULL**, indicating that the system should manage the memory for the DIB section's pixels. You can specify **hSection** as the handle to a file-mapping object that will be used to store the DIB section's pixels. In this case, the **dwOffset** parameter is specified as the offset, from the beginning of the memory-mapped file, to the DIB section's pixels.

***NOTE:** Even if you pass **CreateDIBSection** a pointer to a packed DIB (as the **pbmi** parameter), the pixel values are not copied. This is by design; the function does not copy pixel values. The color-table entries, on the other hand, are copied.*

If the **CreateDIBitmap** function is successful, it returns a handle to the DIB section bitmap. If the function fails, it sets the variable specified as the **ppvBits** parameter to **NULL**, and then returns **NULL**. When the DIB section is no longer needed, you must destroy it via the **DeleteObject** function. If you specify the handle to a file-mapping object as the **hSection** parameter, you're responsible for that as well.

***TIP:** The system uses user-mode paged memory for the DIB section's pixels. Because of this fact, DIB section bitmaps do not suffer from the size limitations of DDBs.*

WARNING! Because you have direct access to the pixels of a DIB section bitmap, you must ensure that this access is synchronized. You can do this by calling the GDIFlush function (it takes no parameters) before you manipulate a DIB section's pixels (either directly or indirectly by using a GDI rendering function).

The following code snippet demonstrates how to create a 32-bit DIB section bitmap of width 2,000 pixels and height 3,000 pixels. The **pBits** variable receives a pointer to the DIB section's pixels:

```
BITMAPINFO bmi;
memset(&bmi, 0, sizeof(BITMAPINFO));

bmi.bmiHeader.biSize = sizeof(BITMAPINFOHEADER);
bmi.bmiHeader.biWidth = 2000;
bmi.bmiHeader.biHeight = -3000; // top-down DIB section
bmi.bmiHeader.biPlanes = 1;
bmi.bmiHeader.biBitCount = 32;
bmi.bmiHeader.biCompression = BI_RGB;

unsigned char* pBits;
HBITMAP hDIBSection =
    CreateDIBSection(
        NULL, &bmi, 0,
        reinterpret_cast<LPVOID*>(&pBits),
        NULL, 0
        );
```

```
if (pBits)
{
    // ...

    // clean up
    DeleteObject(hDIBSection);
}
```

If the DIB (whose **BITMAPINFO** structure is specified as the **pbmi** parameter) contains a color table, the **CreateDIBSection** function initializes the DIB section's color table with values from the DIB's color table. However, there's an alternative technique to change the color-table entries of a DIB section after it's created and selected into a memory device context (see "Changing the Color-Table Entries of a DIB Section Bitmap"). This latter approach is actually simpler than creating a DIB with a color table.

Related solution:	Found on page:
Creating a Color Device-Dependent Bitmap	311

Creating a DIB Section Bitmap from a Device-Dependent Bitmap

To create a DIB section bitmap from a device-dependent bitmap, you use the **CopyImage** function:

```
HANDLE CopyImage(
    HANDLE hImage,      // handle to the source DDB
    UINT uType,         // set to IMAGE_BITMAP
    int cxDesired,      // set to 0
    int cyDesired,      // set to 0
    UINT fuFlags        // set to LR_CREATEDIBSECTION
   );
```

The **hImage** parameter specifies the handle to the source DDB. The **uType** parameter specifies the type of image to copy; set this parameter to **IMAGE_BITMAP**. The **cxDesired** and **cyDesired** parameters specify the DIB section's width and height. You can simply set both of these parameters to zero to create a DIB section of the same size as the DDB. The **fuFlags** parameter must be set to **LR_CREATEDIBSECTION**.

TIP: *As you might have guessed from the function's name, the* ***CopyImage*** *function can also be used to copy DIB sections. However, don't use this function to copy DDBs; on palettized displays, the new DDB's pixel values are initialized incorrectly.*

If the **CopyImage** function is successful, the return value is a handle to the DIB section bitmap. If the function fails, it returns **NULL**. When you're done with the DIB section, you should destroy it via the **DeleteObject** function.

The following code snippet shows how to create a DIB section bitmap (**hDIBSection**) from a DDB (**hBmp**), and then grab a pointer to the DIB section's pixels:

```
HBITMAP hDIBSection = static_cast<HBITMAP>(
    CopyImage(hBmp, IMAGE_BITMAP, 0, 0, LR_CREATEDIBSECTION)
    );

if (hDIBSection)
{
    DIBSECTION ds;
    const size_t dibSize = sizeof(DIBSECTION);
    if (GetObject(hDIBSection, dibSize, &ds) == dibSize)
    {
        unsigned char* pBits =
            reinterpret_cast<unsigned char*>(
                ds.dsBm.bmBits
                );

        // ...
    }

    // clean up
    DeleteObject(hDIBSection);
}
```

***NOTE:** The **CopyImage** function yields a DIB section bitmap whose pixel format matches that of the DDB. If you want a DIB section of another bit-depth, you'll have to create one manually (see "Creating a DIB Section Bitmap"), select both the DIB section and the DDB into separate memory device contexts, and then **BitBlt** the DDB to the DIB section.*

Loading a DIB Section Bitmap from a File

To load a DIB section bitmap from a file, you use the application-defined **CreateDIBSectionFromFile** function:

```
#include <ole2.h>
#include <olectl.h>
HBITMAP CreateDIBSectionFromFile(
    IN LPCSTR filename,          // name of the image file to load
    OUT HPALETTE* pHPal = NULL   // receives the image's palette,
```

```
    )
{
    HBITMAP hDIBSection = NULL;

    // open the file for shared reading
    HANDLE hFile =
        CreateFile(
            filename, GENERIC_READ, FILE_SHARE_READ, NULL,
            OPEN_EXISTING, FILE_ATTRIBUTE_NORMAL, NULL
            );

    if (hFile != INVALID_HANDLE_VALUE)
    {
        // allocate a global memory object of the file's size
        const DWORD dwSize = GetFileSize(hFile, NULL);
        HGLOBAL hData = GlobalAlloc(GMEM_MOVEABLE, dwSize);
        if (hData)
        {
            LPVOID lpData = GlobalLock(hData);
            if (lpData)
            {
                // read the file
                DWORD dwRead = 0;
                bool read_ok = ReadFile(hFile, lpData, dwSize, &dwRead, NULL);
                if (read_ok && (dwRead == dwSize))
                {
                    GlobalUnlock(hData);
                    CloseHandle(hFile);
                    hFile = NULL;

                    // create an IStream object on hData
                    LPSTREAM pStream;
                    HRESULT hRes = CreateStreamOnHGlobal(
                        hData, false, &pStream
                        );
                    if (SUCCEEDED(hRes))
                    {
                        // load the picture (create an IPicture object)
                        LPPICTURE pPicture;
                        hRes =
                            OleLoadPicture(
                                pStream, 0, false, IID_IPicture,
                                reinterpret_cast<void**>(&pPicture)
                                );
                        if (SUCCEEDED(hRes))
                        {
```

```
// if a palette was requested by the caller
if (pHPal)
{
   // grab a handle to its palette
   pPicture->get_hPal(
      reinterpret_cast<OLE_HANDLE*>(pHPal)
      );

   // copy the palette (since IPicture owns it)
   if (*pHPal)
   {
      const int num_entries =
         GetPaletteEntries(*pHPal, 0, 0, NULL);
      const long size =
         sizeof(LOGPALETTE) +
         (num_entries - 1) * sizeof(PALETTEENTRY);

      LPLOGPALETTE lpLogPal =
         reinterpret_cast<LPLOGPALETTE>(
            GlobalAlloc(GPTR, size)
            );
      if (lpLogPal)
      {
         const int num_got =
            GetPaletteEntries(
               *pHPal, 0, num_entries,
               lpLogPal->palPalEntry
              );
         lpLogPal->palVersion = 0x300;
         lpLogPal->palNumEntries = num_got;

         *pHPal = CreatePalette(lpLogPal);
         GlobalFree(lpLogPal);
      }
   }
}

// grab a handle to IPicture's DIB section
pPicture->get_Handle(
   reinterpret_cast<OLE_HANDLE*>(&hDIBSection)
   );

// make a copy
hDIBSection = static_cast<HBITMAP>(
   CopyImage(
      hDIBSection, IMAGE_BITMAP, 0, 0,
```

```
                                        LR_CREATEDIBSECTION
                                        )
                                    );

                                // release the IPicture object
                                pPicture->Release();
                            }
                            // release the IStream object
                            pStream->Release();
                        }
                    }
                    // clean up
                    else GlobalUnlock(hData);
                }
                // free the global memory object
                GlobalFree(hData);
            }
            // clean up
            if (hFile) CloseHandle(hFile);
        }
        return hDIBSection;
    }
```

The **filename** parameter is specified as a pointer to a **NULL**-terminated string that contains the full path of the image file from which the DIB section bitmap is created. The **pHPal** parameter is specified as the address of a handle to a logical palette. You can set this parameter to **NULL** if a palette is not needed.

***NOTE:** You can alternatively use the **LoadImage** function if you're loading a DIB section bitmap that contains more than 256 colors.*

Upon success, the **CreateDIBSectionFromFile** function returns a handle to a DIB section bitmap that has been initialized with the color data (i.e., the "image") contained in the image file. (You are responsible for destroying this bitmap.) If the function fails, the return value is **NULL**. If a palette is needed and the image exposes a corresponding palette, the variable specified via the **pHPal** parameter will contain a handle to the logical palette (which you are responsible for destroying); if no palette is available, this variable is set to **NULL**.

The following code snippet demonstrates the use of the **CreateDIBSectionFromFile** function to create a DIB section (**hDIBSection**) from a bitmap file (**filename**), and then display the bitmap to the client area of a window (**hWnd**):

```
LPCSTR filename = TEXT("MYBITMAP.BMP\0");
HPALETTE hPal;
HBITMAP hDIBSection = CreateDIBSectionFromFile(filename, &hPal);
if (hDIBSection)
{
   HDC hMemDC = CreateCompatibleDC(NULL);
   HBITMAP hOldBmp = static_cast<HBITMAP>(
      SelectObject(hMemDC, hDIBSection)
      );

   HDC hDC = GetDC(hWnd);
   hPal = SelectPalette(hDC, hPal, false);
   try
   {
      RealizePalette(hDC);

      DIBSECTION ds;
      const size_t DIBSize = sizeof(DIBSECTION);
      if (GetObject(hDIBSection, DIBSize, &ds) != DIBSize + 1) throw;

      BitBlt(
         hDC, 0, 0,
         ds.dsBm.bmWidth, ds.dsBm.bmHeight,
         hMemDC, 0, 0,
         SRCCOPY
         );
   }
   catch (...)
   {
      if (hPal)
      {
         DeleteObject(SelectPalette(hDC, hPal, false));
      }
      DeleteObject(SelectObject(hMemDC, hOldBmp));
      DeleteDC(hMemDC);
   }
   if (hPal)
   {
      DeleteObject(SelectPalette(hDC, hPal, false));
   }
   DeleteObject(SelectObject(hMemDC, hOldBmp));
   DeleteDC(hMemDC);
}
```

As it turns out, the **CreateDIBSectionFromFile** function can be used to load more than just bitmaps—you can also use this function for JPEGs, GIFs, icons, and metafiles. The image decoding task is delegated to the **IPicture** OLE interface. For a non-OLE-based version of this function, see the implementation on the CD-ROM.

Related solution:	Found on page:
Loading a Device-Dependent Bitmap from a File	323

Saving a DIB Section Bitmap to a File

To save a DIB section bitmap to a file, you can simply punt to the **SaveDDBToFile** function (see Chapter 6). In this case, you specify the handle to the DIB section (as the **hBmp** parameter) as if it were a DDB.

Related solution:	Found on page:
Saving a Device-Dependent Bitmap to a File	329

Retrieving Information about a DIB Section Bitmap

As with other GDI graphic objects, you can retrieve information about a DIB section bitmap by using the **GetObject** function:

```
int GetObject(
    IN HGDIOBJ hgdiobj,       // handle to the DIB section bitmap
    IN int cbBuffer,          // number of bytes in the DIBSECTION structure
    OUT LPVOID lpvObject      // address of a DIBSECTION structure
   );
```

The **hgdiobj** parameter is specified as the handle to the DIB section whose attributes you want to retrieve. If the **GetObject** function is successful, these attributes are placed in the **DIBSECTION** structure whose address is specified by the **lpvObject** parameter. The **cbBuffer** parameter is used to specify how many bytes are available in the buffer indicated by **lpvObject**. Here you specify this parameter as **sizeof(DIBSECTION)**.

NOTE: *The **GetObject** function can be used for other graphic objects as well. For a more general discussion of the **GetObject** function, see Chapter 1.*

If the **GetObject** function is successful, it returns the number of bytes that have been copied into the variable referred to by the **lpvObject** parameter. For a DIB section, this return value should be **sizeof(DIBSECTION)**. If the function fails, it returns zero.

TIP: *To obtain a handle to a device context's currently selected DIB section bitmap, use the* ***GetCurrentObject*** *function with the* ***OBJ_BITMAP*** *identifier.*

The following code snippet demonstrates the use of the **GetObject** function to retrieve the width and height of a DIB section bitmap (**hDIBSection**):

```
DIBSECTION ds;
const size_t dibSize = sizeof(DIBSECTION);
if (GetObject(hDIBSection, dibSize, &ds) == dibSize)
{
    const int width = ds.dsBm.bmWidth; // or ds.dsBmih.biWidth;
    const int height = ds.dsBm.bmHeight; // or abs(ds.dsBmih.biHeight);

    // ...
}
```

Likewise, to retrieve the bit-depth of a DIB section bitmap, you use **GetObject**, and then you read the **dsBm::bmBitsPixel** or the **dsBmih::biBitCount** data members:

```
DIBSECTION ds;
const size_t dibSize = sizeof(DIBSECTION);
if (GetObject(hDIBSection, dibSize, &ds) == dibSize)
{
   const int bpp = ds.dsBm.bmBitsPixel; // or ds.dsBmih.biBitCount;
}
```


Related solution:	Found on page:
Retrieving the Dimensions and Color Depth of a Device-Dependent Bitmap	331

Rendering a DIB Section Bitmap

To render a DIB section bitmap, you use the same approach as you would for a DDB. Specifically, you select the DIB section into a memory device context, and then use the **BitBlt** or the **StretchBlt** function. This is one of the main advantages of using a DIB section instead of a true DIB—you can select a DIB section into a memory device context and render it as if it were a DDB. For more information on rendering a DDB, refer to Chapter 6.

The following code snippet demonstrates how to display a DIB section bitmap (**hDIBSection**) to a display device context via the **BitBlt** function:

```
DIBSECTION ds;
const size_t dibSize = sizeof(DIBSECTION);
if (GetObject(hDIBSection, dibSize, &ds) == dibSize)
{
    HDC hDC = GetDC(hWnd);
    HDC hMemDC = CreateCompatibleDC(hDC);
    HBITMAP hOldBmp = static_cast<HBITMAP>(
        SelectObject(hMemDC, hDIBSection)
        );
    try
    {
        //
        // TODO: add palette support as required (see Chapter 9)
        //

        BitBlt(
            hDC, 0, 0,
            ds.dsBm.bmWidth, ds.dsBm.bmHeight,
            hMemDC, 0, 0,
            SRCCOPY
            );
    }
    catch (...)
    {
        SelectObject(hMemDC, hOldBmp);
        DeleteDC(hMemDC);
        ReleaseDC(hWnd, hDC);
    }
    SelectObject(hMemDC, hOldBmp);
    DeleteDC(hMemDC);
    ReleaseDC(hWnd, hDC);

    // if you no longer need the DIB section...
    // DeleteObject(hDIBSection);
}
```


Related solution:	Found on page:
Rendering a Device-Dependent Bitmap	338

Changing the Color-Table Entries of a DIB Section Bitmap

To change the color-table entries of a 1-, 4-, or 8-bit DIB section bitmap, you use the **SetDIBColorTable** function:

```
UINT SetDIBColorTable(
    IN HDC hdc,                   // handle to the memory device context in
                                  // which the DIB section bitmap is selected
    IN UINT uStartIndex,          // index of the first entry to change
    IN UINT cEntries,             // total number of entries to change
    IN CONST RGBQUAD *pColors     // pointer to the new color-table entries
   );
```

The **hdc** parameter identifies the memory device context that's associated with the DIB section bitmap (i.e., the DIB section bitmap must be selected into this device context). The **uStartIndex** parameter specifies the index of the first color-table entry that you want to change. The **cEntries** parameter specifies the total number of color-table entries to change. So, if you want to change every entry in the color table, you set **uStartIndex** to zero and set **cEntries** to the total number of color-table entries. The **pColors** parameter specifies an array of **RGBQUAD** structures that define the new color-table entries.

If successful, the **SetDIBColorTable** function returns the total number of color-table entries that have been changed; otherwise, the function returns zero. For example, to set the color-table entries of an 8-bit DIB section (**hDIBSection**) to grayscale, you'd do the following:

```
// create the new color table
RGBQUAD rgbQ[256];
for (int index = 0; index < 256; ++index)
{
   rgbQ[index].rgbBlue = index;
   rgbQ[index].rgbGreen = index;
   rgbQ[index].rgbRed = index;
   rgbQ[index].rgbReserved = 0;
}

HDC hMemDC = CreateCompatibleDC(NULL);
hDIBSection = static_cast<HBITMAP>(
   SelectObject(hMemDC, hDIBSection)
   );
```

```
// change the color-table entries
const UINT num_changed = SetDIBColorTable(hMemDC, 0, 256, rgbQ);

hDIBSection = static_cast<HBITMAP>(
   SelectObject(hMemDC, hDIBSection)
   );
DeleteDC(hMemDC);
```

The **SetDIBColorTable** function has a counterpart, **GetDIBColorTable**, which can be used to retrieve the color-table entries. The parameters of the two functions are identical. The **GetDIBColorTable** function simply fills the **pColors** parameter instead of changing the DIB's color table to that indicated by **pColors**. For example:

```
// create a color-table container
RGBQUAD rgbQ[256];

HDC hMemDC = CreateCompatibleDC(NULL);
hDIBSection = static_cast<HBITMAP>(
   SelectObject(hMemDC, hDIBSection)
   );

// get the color-table entries
const UINT num_got = GetDIBColorTable(hMemDC, 0, 256, rgbQ);

hDIBSection = static_cast<HBITMAP>(
   SelectObject(hMemDC, hDIBSection)
   );
DeleteDC(hMemDC);
```

Chapter 8

Regions and Paths

In Depth

In the early 1800s, 28-year-old William Clark and 36-year-old Meriwether Lewis led an expedition from St. Louis to the shores of Oregon. They blazed a nearly 4,000-mile trail that's known today as the "Lewis and Clark National Historic Trail." What were these guys after? Thomas Jefferson—who was president at the time—commissioned Lewis and Clark to explore only the territories surrounding the Columbia and Missouri rivers, in the hopes of opening new, more accessible, trade routes. After the United States purchased the Louisiana Territory from France, however, Lewis, Clark, and a team of soldiers and woodsmen were free to explore as far westward as the Pacific Coast, which they did. This journey marked the beginning of an era of westward expansion for the United States.

What do Lewis and Clark have in common with the Windows GDI? Well, not much. The point, however, is that throughout its history, the United States, like many other countries, was divided into several territories or regions. Many of these regions were discovered by pioneers, like Lewis and Clark, who made trails and paths through unknown terrain. If you think of a device context, or even a window, as a country, you, the developer (i.e., president), can define your own territories and trails within this terrain. You accomplish this task through the use of the GDI region and path objects.

In this chapter, we'll explore regions and paths. First, we'll focus on regions, including how to create regions of various shapes, how to use a region for clipping the output of painting and drawing operations, and how to set the shape of a window to match that of a region. Next, we'll examine the process of creating and working with paths. We'll discuss how to open and close a path bracket, how to record the output of different rendering functions to a path, and how to convert a path to a region. We'll even look at a technique for retrieving the geometric description of a path.

A Defined Territory

A *region* is a GDI graphic object that does exactly what its name suggests: it defines a specific territory or "region" within an entity. Most often, this entity is a device context, in which case the region object is called a *clipping region* and the area that it defines is called a *clipping area*. In other cases, regions are used to define the shapes of windows, or they're used for filling irregular areas. Sometimes regions are even used for hit-testing complex shapes.

Clipping Regions

Think back to the last time you used a can of spray paint. You were probably trying to paint a specific object or a specific area within an object. We all know that one of the main problems with spray paint is overspray. Besides the fact that this light mist of paint is awful on the lungs, it dries so quickly that cleanup is more of a chore than is the painting itself. Of course, you probably used a drop cloth and/or a generous amount of masking tape and newspaper. In doing so, you effectively masked off the areas that you didn't want to be painted. Looking at it another way, you effectively defined that area that you *did* want to be painted (i.e., the unmasked portion).

Conceptually, a clipping region is very much like the "inverse" of the newspaper—it defines the unmasked portion of an object (i.e., the clipping area). In this case, the object that's to be painted is a device context, and the masked-off portion is defined by the areas outside the clipping region. For example, consider the following code:

```
HDC hDC = GetWindowDC(hWnd);
Rectangle(hDC, -1000, -1000, 1000, 1000);
ReleaseDC(hWnd, hDC);
```

When this code is executed, will you see a 2000x2000 rectangle on the screen? The answer is no; the **GetWindowDC** function returns a handle to a window DC, and (from Chapter 1) we know that anything drawn to a window DC is clipped to (i.e., limited to) the area of its corresponding window. This scheme is depicted in Figure 8.1.

The "clipping" of any output that's directed to **hWindowDC** is actually performed by a clipping region. Here, the region defines the clipping area, which is exactly the area of the DC that can be rendered to. In this way, a clipping region is like the "on" bits of a mask; it defines the pixels that can be changed. If a specific pixel is contained in the clipping region, then you're free to change its color value. If the pixel is not in this region, then the pixel is effectively "masked off."

As with other GDI graphic objects, there's a specialized set of functions that are designed for working with regions. To create a region, you use the **CreateRectRgn**, **CreateRectRgnIndirect**, **CreateRoundRectRgn**, **CreateEllipticRgn**, **CreateEllipticRgnIndirect**, **CreatePolygonRgn**, or **CreatePolyPolygonRgn** function. As you've probably guessed, each of these functions creates a region of a specific shape.

When these functions succeed, you're given a value of type **HRGN**, a handle to a region. With its handle, you can associate a region with a device context by using the familiar **SelectObject** function or the more convenient **SelectClipRgn** function:

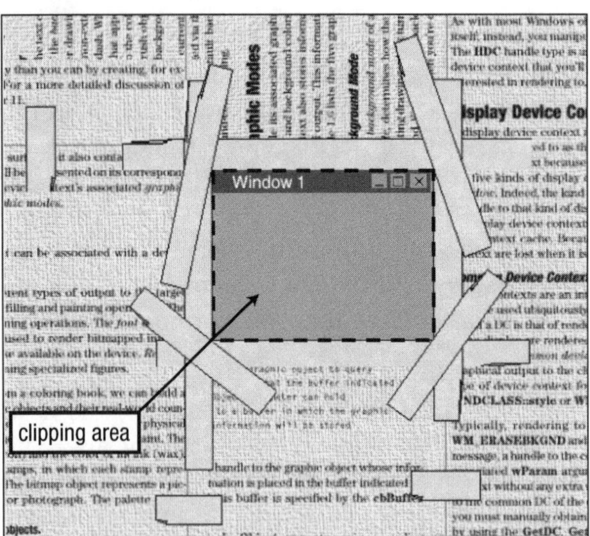

Figure 8.1 **A clipping region limits or "clips" any output to a clipping area in the same way that newspaper and masking tape prevents overspray.**

```
HGDIOBJ SelectObject(hdc, hgdiobj);
int SelectClipRgn(hdc, hrgn);
```

Both of these functions do the same thing—they set the clipping region of the device context to the region created by the intersection of the specified region and the DC's current clipping region (see Figure 8.2). The only difference between the two functions is that **SelectClipRgn** can be used to remove a DC's clipping region, in which case you pass **NULL** as the second (**hRgn**) parameter. You can't do this with the **SelectObject** function—if you pass **NULL** as the **hgdiobj** parameter, **SelectObject** will fail. When the region itself is no longer needed, you destroy it as you would any other GDI graphic object: by using the **DeleteObject** function.

For example, to create a circular region and set it as the clipping region of a device context, you'd do the following:

```
const RECT RCircle = {0, 0, 100, 100};
HRGN hRgn =
   CreateEllipticRgn(
      RCircle.left, RCircle.top,
      RCircle.right, RCircle.bottom
      );
if (hRgn)
{
   HDC hDC = GetDC(hWnd);
```

```
    try
    {
        SelectClipRgn(hDC, hRgn);
        // or SelectObject(hDC, hRgn);

        // draw to hDC...
    }
    catch (...)
    {
        ReleaseDC(hWnd, hDC);
        DeleteObject(hRgn);
    }
    ReleaseDC(hWnd, hDC);
    DeleteObject(hRgn);
}
```

Notice that there's no code to track and restore **hDC**'s original clipping region. This chore isn't required for regions because the device context doesn't actually use the region you select into it. Instead, the device context first makes a copy of the region, and then uses the copy as its clipping region. Because of this fact, when you select a region into a device context via the **SelectObject** or **SelectClipRgn** function, the return value is *not* a handle to the previous region; rather, it's a value that indicates whether the device context's clipping region has been changed. Moreover, the region that you pass to **SelectObject** or **SelectClipRgn** is not linked to the device context; after selecting your region into a DC, you can destroy the region without affecting the DC's clipping region. Therefore, the previous code can be rewritten as:

```
const RECT RCircle = {0, 0, 100, 100};
HRGN hRgn =
    CreateEllipticRgn(
        RCircle.left, RCircle.top,
        RCircle.right, RCircle.bottom
        );
if (hRgn)
{
    HDC hDC = GetDC(hWnd);
    try
    {
        SelectClipRgn(hDC, hRgn);
        // or SelectObject(hDC, hRgn);
        DeleteObject(hRgn); hRgn = NULL;

        // draw to hDC...
    }
```

```
   catch (...)
   {
      ReleaseDC(hWnd, hDC);
      if (hRgn) DeleteObject(hRgn);
   }
   ReleaseDC(hWnd, hDC);
}
```

As I mentioned, both **SelectObject** and **SelectClipRgn** will return a value that indicates whether the device context's clipping region has been changed. Table 8.1 lists the possible return values.

Note that the units for the region-creation functions are dimensionless because there's no device context (and thus no device) involved. When you call the **SelectClipRgn** function or the **SelectObject** function, however, the units of the region are interpreted as device units. All we'll discuss next, this device-specificity also applies when you associate a region with a window.

Regions and Windows

In addition to working with DCs, regions can be used with windows as well. For example, many applications contain windows that aren't limited to the standard rectangular shapes; instead, they appear in the form of circles, diamonds, text, and even custom image-based shapes. This feat is accomplished using regions. That is, a region can be used to define the shape of a window. To associate a region with a window, you use the **SetWindowRgn** function:

```
int SetWindowRgn(hWnd, hRgn, bRedraw);
```

The **hWnd** parameter is a handle to the target window, and the **hRgn** parameter specifies a handle to the region that's used to define this window's shape. Note

Table 8.1 Possible return values for the SelectObject and SelectClipRgn functions.

Identifier	Value	Meaning
SIMPLEREGION	1	The device context's clipping region has been changed; the new clipping region consists of a single rectangular region.
COMPLEXREGION	2	The device context's clipping region has been changed; the new clipping region consists of two or more rectangular regions.
NULLREGION	3	The device context's clipping region has been changed; the new clipping region consists of one or more rectangular regions with zero dimension.
RGN_ERROR	0	The device context's clipping region has not been changed (typically due to an invalid handle).

that the coordinates of this region are relative to the top-left corner of the window, not to that of the window's client area. The **bRedraw** parameter can be set to **TRUE** if you want the window to be redrawn. For example, to create a window in the shape of an ellipse, you use the **SetWindowRgn** function like so:

```
const RECT REllipse = {0, 0, 200, 100};
RGN hRgn =
   CreateEllipticRgn(
      REllipse.left, REllipse.top,
      REllipse.right, REllipse.bottom
      );
if (!SetWindowRgn(hWnd, hRgn, TRUE))
{
   DeleteObject(hRgn);
}
```

Note that the **DeleteObject** function is called only if the **SetWindowRgn** function fails (it returns zero upon failure and non-zero otherwise). That's because the **SetWindowRgn** function forfeits ownership of the region to the window. In this case, it's important not to delete **hRgn** because the window itself will also perform this deletion.

When you call the **SetWindowRgn** function to change the shape of the window, not only does the window appear in the new shape, but mouse-related input is limited to the interior of the shape as well. In this way, the window truly takes on the shape of the region, both in terms of appearance and in terms of accessibility. For this to work, however, Windows must have a mechanism to determine whether the mouse cursor is within a particular region. This is accomplished via the **PtInRegion** function:

```
BOOL PtInRegion(hRgn, pt);
```

Like the **PtInRect** function, **PtInRegion** is used to query a point for inclusion within a region. The function accepts a handle to a region and the address of a **POINT** structure, and returns **TRUE** if the point lies within the region (or on its boundary) and **FALSE** otherwise.

In fact, the **PtInRegion** function provides an alternative method for hit-testing shapes. Namely, to determine if a point lies within an ellipse, you can create an elliptic region and then simply use the **PtInRegion** function. Actually, in this case, the use of a region is overkill because we already have an analytical description of an ellipse. However, for complex shapes that can't be described by a simple equation or even in a parameterized form, using a region is often the simplest solution. Of course, there's always a catch. Although it's easy to create a region of one of the predefined "basic" shapes, such as rectangles, rounded rectangles, and ellipses, there's no simple way to create a region from, say, an arbitrary description, such as a bitmap. Fortunately, the **CombineRgn** function helps us out here.

Complex Regions

As its name suggests, the **CombineRgn** function can be used to combine two regions into a complex or "composite" region, using a set-wise operator (**fnCombineMode**):

```
int CombineRgn(hrgnDest, hrgnSrc1, hrgnSrc2, fnCombineMode);
```

For example, you can call the **CombineRgn** function to create a region that's the intersection of two elliptic regions. Likewise, you can use **CombineRgn** to create the union, the exclusive union, and even the difference of two regions. Figure 8.2 illustrates the results of using different set-wise operators to combine two ellipses. The identifier for each operator is listed in Table 8.2.

How can the **CombineRgn** function be used to create complex regions? The idea is to construct the complex regions from a collection of simpler shapes. For example, to create a (possibly complex) region that's defined by a bitmap, you create, and then combine, a sufficient number of simple pixel-sized regions. The **CreateRectRgn** function can be used to create a region that's one pixel wide by one pixel high.

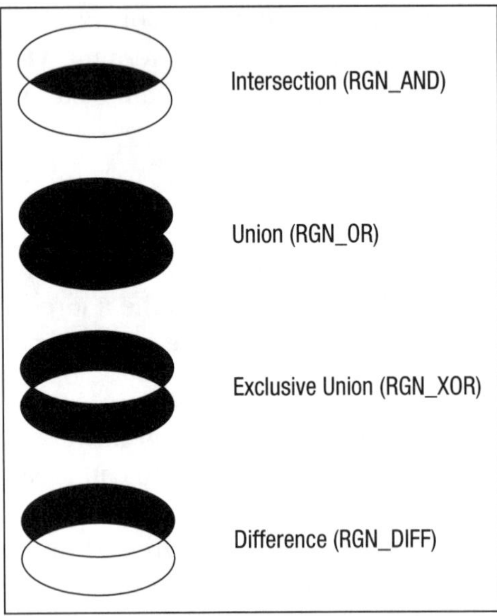

Figure 8.2 Combining regions via the **CombineRgn** function.

Table 8.2 Identifiers used to specify how two regions are combined.

Identifier	Value	Effect
RGN_AND	1	Results in the intersection of **hRgn1** and **hRgn2**
RGN_OR	2	Results in the union of **hRgn1** and **hRgn2**
RGN_XOR	3	Results in the exclusive union of **hRgn1** and **hRgn2**
RGN_DIFF	4	Results in the difference of **hRgn1** and **hRgn2**
RGN_COPY	5	Results in a copy of **hRgn1**

As it turns out, the **CreateRectRgn** function is rather slow when used in an iterative fashion. For example, consider creating a region from a 100x100 bitmap. In this case, depending on which pixels you want to use to define the complex region, you're looking at thousands of calls to **CreateRectRgn**. Although the function won't break when called multiple times, the main drawback is speed or, more correctly, the lack thereof. However, there's another, more flexible function that can be used to create a region: **ExtCreateRgn**:

```
HRGN ExtCreateRgn (pRgnData);
```

The **ExtCreateRgn** function is an "**ext**ended" version of the **CreateRectRgn** function that's specifically designed to create multiple regions via a single function call. The single parameter is a pointer to a **RGNDATA** structure that's used to describe the shape of the new region.

The RGNDATA Structure

The **RGNDATA** structure is used to hold a multirectangular-based description of a region:

```
typedef struct _RGNDATA {
    RGNDATAHEADER rdh;
    char Buffer[1];
} RGNDATA, *PRGNDATA, NEAR *NPRGNDATA, FAR *LPRGNDATA;
```

The **rdh** data member contains the region's "header." The **Buffer** data member contains an array of rectangles that the region is composed of. Although **Buffer** is declared as an array of **char** (for future scalability), for all current versions of Windows you can simply typecast this data member to an **LPRECT**.

The RGNDATAHEADER Structure

The **RGNDATAHEADER** structure is designed to hold information about the array of rectangles that are contained in the **RGNDATA::Buffer** data member:

```
typedef struct _RGNDATAHEADER {
    DWORD dwSize;
    DWORD iType;
    DWORD nCount;
    DWORD nRgnSize;
    RECT rcBound;
} RGNDATAHEADER, *PRGNDATAHEADER;
```

The **dwSize** data member specifies the size of the **RGNDATAHEADER** structure in bytes. The **iType** parameter specifies the type of shape that the region is composed of. For all current versions of Windows, this data member must be set to **RDH_RECTANGLES** (1), indicating that **RGNDATA::Buffer** contains an array of **RECT**s. The **nCount** and **nRgnSize** data members specify the number of **RECT**s and bytes that **RGNDATA::Buffer** contains, respectively. The **rcBound** data member specifies the region's bounding rectangle.

So, given the description of a complex shape, such as a bitmap, you can initialize a corresponding **RGNDATA** structure. In most cases, you can simply pass the address of this structure to the **ExtCreateRgn** function. However, there's a catch. On systems running Windows 95 or Windows 98, the **ExtCreateRgn** function will fail when passed a **RGNDATA** structure that contains a set of numerous rectangles. In this case, you'll need to break the **RGNDATA** structure into smaller batches, then call **ExtCreateRgn** to create each smaller region, and then use the **CombineRgn** function to patch all of the smaller regions into the desired composite region (see **http://codeguru.earthweb.com/bitmap/bmp_to_rgn.shtml** for a code example of this process).

Extracting Information about a Region

The GDI provides a simple method for extracting information about a region. Specifically, the **GetRegionData** function can be used to retrieve a rectangle-based description of a region:

```
BOOL GetRegionData(hRgn, pRgnData);
```

The function takes a handle to a region (**hRgn**) and fills a **RGNDATA** structure (**pRgnData**) with information about the region. For example, the following application-defined function, **CopyRgn**, demonstrates how you can use the **GetRegionData** function, together with the **ExtCreateRegion** function, to create a copy of a region:

```
HRGN CopyRgn(
    IN const HRGN hSrcRgn      // handle to the source region
   )
{
   HRGN hCopyRgn = NULL;
```

```
    const size_t data_size = GetRegionData(hSrcRgn, 0, NULL);
    unsigned char* buffer = new unsigned char[data_size];
    try
    {
       LPRGNDATA lprd = reinterpret_cast<LPRGNDATA>(buffer);
       if (GetRegionData(hSrcRgn, data_size, lprd) == data_size)
       {
          hCopyRgn = ExtCreateRegion(NULL, data_size, lprd);
       }
    }
    catch (...)
    {
       delete [] buffer;
    }
    delete [] buffer;
    return hCopyRgn;
}
```

The logic behind the **CopyRgn** function is straightforward: most of the work is delegated to the **GetRegionData** function, which fills a **RGNDATA** structure with information about the source region. This information is passed directly to the **ExtCreateRegion** function, which actually creates the copy.

The following code snippet demonstrates how to use the **CopyRgn** function to duplicate a region (**hRgn**):

```
HRGN hCopyRgn = NULL;
HRGN hRgn = CreateRectRgn(10, 10, 100, 100);
try
{
   hCopyRgn = CopyRgn(hRgn);

   //
   // see the solution "Testing Regions for Equality"
   // for a description of the EqualRgn function
   //
   BOOL is_copy = EqualRgn(hCopyRgn, hRgn);  // TRUE
}
catch (...)
{
   if (hCopyRgn) DeleteObject(hCopyRgn);
   DeleteObject(hRgn);
}
if (hCopyRgn) DeleteObject(hCopyRgn);
DeleteObject(hRgn);
```

Because the **RGNDATA** structure contains an array of **RECT** structures, the **GetRegionData** function is commonly used with a path object to estimate the area of a region. We'll look at a code example later in this chapter, but first, we'll need to discuss what a path is.

A Recorded Journey

One of the few good things about walking in the snow is that you'll likely be able to find your way back. Assuming that no new snow covers your tracks, you can simply follow your footprints back to where you started. Of course, if it starts to snow and your tracks become covered, there's a chance that you'll get lost. That's why it's a good idea to leave markers along the way to record where you've been.

Think of drawing a series of lines to a window's client area as walking through the snow, where your footprints are marked by the pixels that you change. Unless you're drawing in response to a painting-related message, your journey will be lost the next time your window is covered by another window; that is, your tracks will be covered with snow. Following this analogy, a *path* is the set of trail markers—it's a record of where you've been or the "path" that you took.

Recording

A *path* is special type of GDI graphic object that records a series of drawing routines. Paths are unique in that they're always bound to a device context. You never work directly with the path, not even its handle. Instead, you can access a path only through its associated device context. To initiate the creation of a path—that is, begin a "recording session"—you call the **BeginPath** function. Likewise, to finish the creation process—that is, end the "recording session"—you use the **EndPath** function. Together, these two functions define a "recording session," more commonly known as a *path bracket*. For example:

```
HDC hDC = GetDC(hWnd);
try
{
   if (BeginPath(hDC))  // press the "record button"
   {
      Ellipse(hDC, 0, 0, 100, 100);
      EndPath(hDC);    // press the "stop button"
   }
   // ...
}
catch (...)
{
   ReleaseDC(hWnd, hDC);
}
ReleaseDC(hWnd, hDC);
```

Because you're never provided with a handle to a path, you're probably wondering how a path is selected into a device context. This task is actually performed by the **EndPath** function. After the **EndPath** function closes the path bracket, it selects the path into the specified device context. And, after the path is selected into a device context, you're free to manipulate it as desired.

Editing

Contrary to what you might think, the previous code doesn't actually render an ellipse to **hDC**. Instead, the operation is recorded in memory via the path object. In this way, you can manipulate or "edit" the path before actually displaying the "recording." For example, if you want to widen the path, you use the **WidenPath** function, like so:

```
HDC hDC = GetDC(hWnd);
try
{
   BeginPath(hDC);  // press the "record button"
   Ellipse(hDC, 0, 0, 100, 100);
   EndPath(hDC);    // press the "stop button"

   // widen by five times the current pen width
   const int widen_by = 5;
   WidenPath(hDC, widen_by);

   // ...
}
catch (...)
{
   ReleaseDC(hWnd, hDC);
}
ReleaseDC(hWnd, hDC);
```

Playback

When you want to display your recording (i.e., your drawing), you can use the **StrokePath**, **FillPath**, or **StrokeAndFillPath** function. **StrokePath** is used to trace or "stroke" the boundary of a path. For example, if you want to display the widened outline of the ellipse from the previous code snippet, you use the **StrokePath** function, like so:

```
HDC hDC = GetDC(hWnd);
try
{
   BeginPath(hDC);  // press the "record button"
```

```
    Ellipse(hDC, 0, 0, 100, 100);
    EndPath(hDC);     // press the "stop button"

    // widen by five times the current pen width
    const int widen_by = 5;
    WidenPath(hDC, widen_by);

    // press the "rewind button," then the "play button"
    StrokePath(hDC);
}
catch (...)
{
    ReleaseDC(hWnd, hDC);
}
ReleaseDC(hWnd, hDC);
```

The **FillPath** function is used to fill the interior of a path with a specific brush. For example, if you want to fill the widened interior of the ellipse by using a white brush, you use the **FillPath** function, like so:

```
HDC hDC = GetDC(hWnd);
try
{
    BeginPath(hDC);  // press the "record button"
    Ellipse(hDC, 0, 0, 100, 100);
    EndPath(hDC);     // press the "stop button"

    // widen by five times the current pen width
    const int widen_by = 5;
    WidenPath(hDC, widen_by);

    // press the "rewind button," then the "play button"
    HBRUSH hBrush = static_cast<HBRUSH>(
        GetStockObject(WHITE_BRUSH)
        );
    FillPath(hDC, hBrush);
}
catch (...)
{
    ReleaseDC(hWnd, hDC);
}
ReleaseDC(hWnd, hDC);
```

The **StrokeAndFillPath** function, as its name suggests, simply combines the functionality of the **StrokePath** and **FillPath** functions into a single function call. For example, you can rewrite the previous two code snippets, together, as:

```
HDC hDC = GetDC(hWnd);
try
{
   BeginPath(hDC);  // press the "record button"
   Ellipse(hDC, 0, 0, 100, 100);
   EndPath(hDC);    // press the "stop button"

   // widen by five times the current pen width
   const int widen_by = 5;
   WidenPath(hDC, widen_by);

   // press the "rewind button," then the "play button"
   HBRUSH hBrush = static_cast<HBRUSH>(
      GetStockObject(WHITE_BRUSH)
      );
   StrokeAndFillPath(hDC, hBrush);
}
catch (...)
{
   ReleaseDC(hWnd, hDC);
}
ReleaseDC(hWnd, hDC);
```

It may seem redundant to present the **StrokeAndFillPath** function when you can simply call the **StrokePath** function followed by the **FillPath** function. As it turns out, a call to **StrokePath** followed by a call to **FillPath**, or vice versa, won't work as you might expect. Specifically, whichever function you call first (either **StrokePath** or **FillPath**) is the one that will succeed. The subsequent function will fail. This occurs because both the **StrokePath** and the **FillPath** functions destroy the path after performing their respective operations. For example, after you call the **StrokePath** function to render the outline of a path, assuming that the function succeeds, the path no longer exists. The same goes for the **FillPath** function, and even for the **StrokeAndFillPath** function. Therefore, to render the outline of a path and also fill its interior, you must perform both operations via a single function call. This is the main reason the **StrokeAndFillPath** function exists.

Recordable Functions

Unfortunately, the output of only a limited set of drawing functions is actually recorded to a path. Specifically, on systems running Windows NT or Windows 2000, these drawing functions include the following: **AngleArc**, **Arc**, **ArcTo**, **Chord**, **CloseFigure**, **Ellipse**, **ExtTextOut**, **LineTo**, **MoveToEx**, **Pie**, **PolyBezier**, **PolyBezierTo**, **PolyDraw**, **Polygon**, **Polyline**, **PolylineTo**, **PolyPolygon**, **PolyPolyline**, **Rectangle**, **RoundRect**, and **TextOut**.

In Windows 95 and Windows 98, the output of only the following functions is recorded: **CloseFigure**, **ExtTextOut**, **LineTo**, **MoveToEx**, **PolyBezier**, **PolyBezierTo**, **Polygon**, **Polyline**, **PolylineTo**, **PolyPolygon**, **PolyPolyline**, and **TextOut**.

There's another restriction when you're using the **TextOut** function or the **ExtTextOut** function within a path bracket. The output of these functions is recorded only when the target device context's current font is a TrueType, OpenType, or vector font. Any textual output that's made to the DC using a bitmap font is not recorded.

Keep in mind that because a path is essentially a recorded operation, there is a performance penalty involved during its use. Conceptually, a rendering function that's placed within a path bracket is called twice: once for the target device context and once to record the operation in memory. In general, rendering via the **BeginPath**, **EndPath**, and **StrokePath** function combination is about twice as slow as rendering directly to the target device context (i.e., without the path).

The Description of a Path

Just as you can use the **GetRegionData** function to extract information about a region, you can use the **GetPath** function to extract information about a path:

```
int GetPath(hDC, lpPoints, lpTypes, nSize);
```

The **GetPath** function takes a handle to a device context (that contains a path) and returns an array of **POINT** structures that describes the path as a series endpoints or control points. The **lpPoints** parameter specifies the array in which each point is stored; the **lpTypes** parameter specifies the array in which a description of each point is stored (see Table 8.3). The **nSize** parameter specifies the number of elements in each of these arrays. (They both contain the same number of elements.) Each byte in the **lpTypes** array, which corresponds to the **POINT** at the same position in the **lpPoints** array, can indicate one of the identifiers listed in Table 8.3.

You can pass zero as the **nSize** parameter of the **GetPath** function to determine how much memory to allocate for the **lpPoints** and **lpTypes** arrays. When **nSize** is zero, the **GetPath** function ignores the **lpPoints** and **lpTypes** parameters, and simply returns the number of points that the path contains. You can then allocate enough space for the **lpPoints** and **lpTypes** arrays, and then call the **GetPath** function again, this time specifying **nSize** as the number of points in the path. In this latter case, the **GetPath** function will return the number of points that it copies into the **lpPoints** array (which should be exactly **nSize**).

Table 8.3 Identifiers that indicate the type of each vertex in the lpPoints array.

Identifier	Value	Vertex Type
PT_LINETO	2	The corresponding element in the **lpPoints** array defines the endpoint of a line segment. The starting point of this line segment is defined by the previous element in the **lpPoints** array.
PT_BEZIERTO	4	The corresponding element in the **lpPoints** array defines one of the three control points of a Bézier curve. The curve's starting point is defined by the previous element in the **lpPoints** array.
PT_MOVETO	6	The corresponding point in the **lpPoints** array defines the beginning of a closed figure.

By examining each element in the **lpTypes** array, you can properly interpret each point in the **lpPoints** array. With this information, you can manipulate the path geometrically (e.g., scale each point) or even save the path's information to a file. You can also pass the **lpPoints** and **lpTypes** arrays directly to the **PolyDraw** function (which takes identical parameters as **GetPath**) to render the path to a DC. For example, the following code snippet demonstrates how to use the **GetPath** and **PolyDraw** functions to render the outline of a string of text in a scaled fashion using different colored pens; the result of this code is depicted in Figure 8.3:

```
const double scaleX = 0.75;
const double scaleY = 0.65;
LPCSTR pText = TEXT("The Scaled Text!");

HDC hDC = GetDC(hWnd);

// TIP: use a large TrueType font for better scaling
HFONT hTTFont = font::MakeFont(hDC, "Impact", 72); // from Chapter 4
HFONT hOldFont = static_cast<HFONT>(
   SelectObject(hDC, hTTFont)
   );
try
{
   SetBkMode(hDC, TRANSPARENT);
```

Figure 8.3 Using the **GetPath** and **PolyDraw** functions to render scaled text.

```
// open a path bracket
if (BeginPath(hDC))
{
   // record the text to the path
   TextOut(hDC, 15, 12, pText, lstrlen(pText));

   // close the path bracket and
   // select the path into hDC
   EndPath(hDC);

   // determine the number of endpoints in the path
   const int num_points = GetPath(hDC, NULL, NULL, 0);
   if (num_points > 0)
   {
      // make room for the POINTs and vertex types
      POINT* pPEnds = new POINT[num_points];
      unsigned char* pTypes = new unsigned char[num_points];
      try
      {
         // get the path's description
         int num_got = GetPath(hDC, pPEnds, pTypes, num_points);
         if (num_got > 0)
         {
            // scale each point in the description
            for (int iPoint = 0; iPoint < num_got; ++iPoint)
            {
               pPEnds[iPoint].x = static_cast<LONG>(
                  scaleX * pPEnds[iPoint].x + 0.5
                  );
               pPEnds[iPoint].y = static_cast<LONG>(
                  scaleY * pPEnds[iPoint].y + 0.5
                  );
            }

            // create a wide blue pen
            HPEN hBluePen = CreatePen(
               PS_SOLID, 15, RGB(0, 0, 255)
               );
            HPEN hOldPen = static_cast<HPEN>(
               SelectObject(hDC, hBluePen)
               );

            // pass the data to the PolyDraw function
            PolyDraw(hDC, pPEnds, pTypes, num_got);
```

```
            // clean up
            DeleteObject(SelectObject(hDC, hOldPen));


            // create a less wide yellow pen
            HPEN hYellowPen =
               CreatePen(PS_SOLID, 6, RGB(255, 255, 0)
               );
            hOldPen = static_cast<HPEN>(
               SelectObject(hDC, hYellowPen)
               );

            // pass the data to PolyDraw again
            PolyDraw(hDC, pPEnds, pTypes, num_got);

            // clean up
            DeleteObject(SelectObject(hDC, hOldPen));


            // create a less wide white pen
            HPEN hWhitePen =
               CreatePen(PS_SOLID, 2, RGB(255, 255, 255)
               );
            hOldPen = static_cast<HPEN>(
               SelectObject(hDC, hWhitePen)
               );

            // pass the data to PolyDraw again
            PolyDraw(hDC, pPEnds, pTypes, num_got);

            // clean up
            DeleteObject(SelectObject(hDC, hOldPen));
         }
      }
      catch (...)
      {
         // clean up
         delete [] pTypes;
         delete [] pPEnds;
         throw;
      }
      // clean up
      delete [] pTypes;
      delete [] pPEnds;
   }
}
```

```
    catch (...)
    {
        DeleteObject(SelectObject(hDC, hOldFont));
        ReleaseDC(hWnd, hDC);
    }
    DeleteObject(SelectObject(hDC, hOldFont));
    ReleaseDC(hWnd, hDC);
}
```

Although the **PolyDraw** function is useful for rendering the description of a path, the function won't fill the path's interior. This is especially unfavorable when you want to render scaled text, not just its outline. What you can do, however, is record the output of the **PolyDraw** function to another path, and then use the **StrokeAndFillPath** function to outline and fill this new path. (As it turns out, on Windows NT and Windows 2000, there is an alternative—and better—approach to rendering scaled text that involves coordinate space transformations. We'll discuss this alternative method in Chapter 10, but for now, let's focus on the Windows 9x case.) Unfortunately, on Windows 95 and Windows 98, the **PolyDraw** function is not a recordable function—that is, its output is not recorded to a path. To work around this limitation, you'll have to decode the data that's contained in the **lpPoints** and **lpTypes** arrays (**pPEnds** and **pTypes** in the previous code snippet, respectively), and then manually render the path via the **MoveToEx**, **LineTo**, and **PolyBezierTo** functions. Indeed, these latter three functions are recordable. Listing 8.1 demonstrates this process; Figure 8.4 depicts the result. (You may also want to refer to the solution "Retrieving the Geometric Description of a Path".)

Listing 8.1 Using the GetPath, MoveToEx, LineTo, and PolyBezierTo function to render scaled text.

```
// -----------------------------------------------------------------
// Windows 2000 Graphics API Black Book
// Chapter 8 - Listing 8.1 (Scaled Text Demo)
// -----------------------------------------------------------------

#include <windows.h>
#include <commctrl.h>
#include <cassert>
```

Figure 8.4 Scaled text that was rendered using two paths.

```
HINSTANCE hInst;
const char* WndClassName = "GMainWnd";
LRESULT CALLBACK MainWndProc(HWND hWnd, UINT msg, WPARAM wParam,
   LPARAM lParam);

int APIENTRY WinMain(HINSTANCE hInstance, HINSTANCE, LPTSTR,
   int nCmdShow)
{
   hInst = hInstance;

   WNDCLASS wc;
   memset(&wc, 0, sizeof(WNDCLASS));

   wc.style = CS_HREDRAW | CS_VREDRAW;
   wc.lpszClassName = WndClassName;
   wc.lpfnWndProc = MainWndProc;
   wc.hInstance = hInst;
   wc.hCursor = LoadCursor(NULL, IDC_ARROW);
   wc.hbrBackground = reinterpret_cast<HBRUSH>(
      COLOR_BTNFACE + 1
      );

   if (RegisterClass(&wc))
   {
      HWND hWnd =
         CreateWindow(
            WndClassName, "Scaled Text",
            WS_OVERLAPPEDWINDOW | WS_CAPTION |
            WS_VISIBLE | WS_CLIPCHILDREN,
            CW_USEDEFAULT, CW_USEDEFAULT, 800, 300,
            NULL, NULL, hInst, NULL
            );

      if (hWnd)
      {
         ShowWindow(hWnd, nCmdShow);
         UpdateWindow(hWnd);

         MSG msg;
         while (GetMessage(&msg, NULL, 0, 0))
         {
             TranslateMessage(&msg);
             DispatchMessage(&msg);
         }
      }
    }
    return 0;
}
```

```
HWND hTrackBar = NULL;
HFONT hTTFont = NULL;
double scale = 0.0;
LPCSTR pText = TEXT("The Scaled Text!");

LRESULT CALLBACK MainWndProc(HWND hWnd, UINT msg, WPARAM wParam,
   LPARAM lParam)
{
   switch (msg)
   {
      case WM_CREATE:
      {
         INITCOMMONCONTROLSEX icx;
         icx.dwSize = sizeof(INITCOMMONCONTROLSEX);
         icx.dwICC = ICC_BAR_CLASSES;

         InitCommonControlsEx(&icx);

         hTrackBar =
            CreateWindow(
               TRACKBAR_CLASS, "",
               TBS_HORZ | TBS_BOTH | TBS_AUTOTICKS |
               TBS_FIXEDLENGTH | TBS_ENABLESELRANGE |
               WS_CHILD | WS_VISIBLE,
               10, 260, 375, 40,
               hWnd, NULL, hInst, NULL
               );

         assert(hTrackBar != NULL);
         SNDMSG(hTrackBar, TBM_SETTHUMBLENGTH, 20, 0);
         SNDMSG(hTrackBar, TBM_SETRANGEMAX, TRUE, 100);

         // create the TrueType (scalable) font
         HDC hDC = GetDC(hWnd);
         try
         {
            // see Chapter 4 for the definition of MakeFont
            hTTFont = font::MakeFont(hDC, "Impact", 72);
            if (!hTTFont) throw;
         }
         catch (...)
         {
            ReleaseDC(hWnd, hDC);
         }
         ReleaseDC(hWnd, hDC);
         break;
      }
```

```
case WM_HSCROLL:
{
   if (reinterpret_cast<HWND>(lParam) == hTrackBar)
   {
      //
      // adjust the scaling factor according to
      // the position of the trackbar's slider
      //
      scale = static_cast<double>(
         (SNDMSG(hTrackBar, TBM_GETPOS, 0, 0) + 1) / 50.0
         );
      InvalidateRect(hWnd, NULL, true);
   }
   break;
}
case WM_ERASEBKGND:
{
   LRESULT res = DefWindowProc(hWnd, msg, wParam, lParam);

   HDC hDC = reinterpret_cast<HDC>(wParam);
   HFONT hOldFont = static_cast<HFONT>(
      SelectObject(hDC, hTTFont)
      );
   try
   {
      SetBkMode(hDC, TRANSPARENT);

      // open a path bracket
      if (!BeginPath(hDC)) throw;

      // record the text to the path
      TextOut(hDC, 10, 10, pText, lstrlen(pText));

      // close the path bracket and
      // select the path into hDC
      EndPath(hDC);

      // determine the number of endpoints in the path
      const int num_points = GetPath(hDC, NULL, NULL, 0);
      if (num_points > 0)
      {
         // make room for the POINTs and vertex types
         POINT* pPEnds = new POINT[num_points];
         unsigned char* pTypes = new unsigned char[num_points];
         try
         {
```

```
// get the path's description
int num_got = GetPath(hDC, pPEnds, pTypes, num_points);
if (num_got > 0)
{
   // start a new path bracket
   if (!BeginPath(hDC)) throw;

   // scale each point in the description
   int iPoint;
   for (iPoint = 0; iPoint < num_got; ++iPoint)
   {
      pPEnds[iPoint].x = static_cast<LONG>(
         scale * pPEnds[iPoint].x + 0.5
         );
      pPEnds[iPoint].y = static_cast<LONG>(
         scale * pPEnds[iPoint].y + 0.5
         );
   }

   for (iPoint = 0; iPoint < num_points; ++iPoint)
   {
      // handle the MoveToEx case
      if (pTypes[iPoint] == PT_MOVETO)
      {
         MoveToEx(
           hDC, pPEnds[iPoint].x, pPEnds[iPoint].y, NULL
           );
      }
      // handle the LineTo case
      else if (
         pTypes[iPoint] == PT_LINETO ||
         pTypes[iPoint] == (PT_LINETO | PT_CLOSEFIGURE)
         )
      {
         LineTo(hDC, pPEnds[iPoint].x, pPEnds[iPoint].y);
      }
      // handle the PolyBezierTo case
      else if (
         pTypes[iPoint] == PT_BEZIERTO ||
         pTypes[iPoint] == (PT_BEZIERTO | PT_CLOSEFIGURE)
         )
      {
         PolyBezierTo(hDC, pPEnds + iPoint, 3);
         iPoint += 2;
      }
   }
```

```
                        // close the new path bracket
                        EndPath(hDC);

                        // stroke and fill the new path
                        StrokeAndFillPath(hDC);
                    }
                }
                catch (...)
                {
                    // clean up
                    delete [] pTypes;
                    delete [] pPEnds;
                    throw;
                }
                // clean up
                delete [] pTypes;
                delete [] pPEnds;
            }
        }
        catch (...)
        {
            SelectObject(hDC, hOldFont);
        }
        SelectObject(hDC, hOldFont);
        return res;
    }
    case WM_SIZE:
    {
        MoveWindow(
            hTrackBar,
            0, HIWORD(lParam) - 40, LOWORD(lParam), 40,
            false
            );
        break;
    }
    case WM_DESTROY:
    {
        // clean up
        DeleteObject(hTTFont);
        PostQuitMessage(0);
        break;
    }
  }
  return DefWindowProc(hWnd, msg, wParam, lParam);
}
```

Converting a Path to a Region

Although there's no built-in function that can be used to hit-test a path, the GDI does provide a function for converting a path to a region. The **PathToRegion** function, as its name suggests, accepts a handle to a device context and returns a handle to a region:

```
HDC hDC = GetDC(hWnd);
try
{
   BeginPath(hDC);  // press the "record button"
   LineTo(100, 100);
   EndPath(hDC);    // press the "stop button"

   // convert the path to a region
   HRGN hRgn = PathToRegion(hDC);
   if (hRgn)
   {
      try
      {
         // e.g., if (PtInRegion(hRgn, PMouse)) {...}
      }
      catch (...)
      {
         DeleteObject(hRgn);
      }
      DeleteObject(hRgn);
   }
}
catch (...)
{
   ReleaseDC(hWnd, hDC);
}
ReleaseDC(hWnd, hDC);
```

As with the **StrokePath**, **FillPath**, and **StrokeAndFillPath** functions, the **PathToRegion** function destroys the path. You, however, are responsible for destroying the returned region.

Earlier, I mentioned that a path and a region can be used together to estimate the area of a polygon. To do this, you open a path bracket, render your polygon, close the path bracket, and then convert the path to a region by using the **PathToRegion** function. After you have a handle to the region, you can use the **GetRegionData** function to extract a multiple-rectangle representation of your region, and then sum the areas of each of these rectangles. For example:

```
int total_area = 0;
HDC hDC = GetDC(hWnd);
try
{
   BeginPath(hDC);
   Ellipse(hDC, 10, 10, 100, 100);
   EndPath(hDC);

   HRGN hRgn = PathToRegion(hDC);
   if (hRgn)
   {
      const size_t bytes_needed = GetRegionData(hRgn, 0, NULL);
      const size_t size = bytes_needed + sizeof(RGNDATAHEADER);
      char* buffer = new char[size];
      try
      {
         memset(buffer, 0, size);
         LPRGNDATA lprd = reinterpret_cast<LPRGNDATA>(buffer);
         if (GetRegionData(hRgn, bytes_needed, lprd) == bytes_needed)
         {
            const int num_rects = lprd->rdh.nCount;
            for (int iRect = 0; iRect < num_rects; ++iRect)
            {
               LPRECT lpRect =
                  reinterpret_cast<LPRECT>(
                     lprd->Buffer + (iRect * sizeof(RECT))
                     );

               const int width = lpRect->right - lpRect->left;
               const int height = lpRect->bottom - lpRect->top;
               total_area += (width * height);
            }
         }
      }
      catch (...)
      {
         delete [] buffer;
         DeleteObject(hRgn);
      }
      delete [] buffer;
      DeleteObject(hRgn);
   }
}
catch (...)
{
   ReleaseDC(hWnd, hDC);
}
ReleaseDC(hWnd, hDC);
```

Immediate Solutions

Creating and Managing Regions

In this section, we'll look at various techniques for creating and managing regions.

Creating a Rectangular Region

To create a rectangular region, you use the **CreateRectRgn** function:

```
HRGN CreateRectRgn(
    IN int nLeftRect,       // horizontal location of the region's
                            // top-left corner
    IN int nTopRect,        // vertical location of the region's
                            // top-left corner
    IN int nRightRect,      // horizontal location of the region's
                            // bottom-right corner
    IN int nBottomRect      // vertical location of the region's
                            // bottom-right corner
  );
```

The **nLeftRect**, **nTopRect**, **nRightRect**, and **nBottomRect** parameters specify the rectangle that will define the shape of the new region. If the **CreateRectRegion** function is successful, it returns a handle to this new region. If the **CreateRectRegion** function fails, the return value is **NULL**.

NOTE: *As with many other rectangle-related GDI functions, the rectangular region that's created by the* ***CreateRectRegion*** *function does not contain the rightmost and bottommost edges of the specified rectangle.*

The following code snippet demonstrates the use of the **CreateRectRegion** function to create a rectangular region (**hRectRgn**) that's located at position (10, 20) and whose width and height are 99 and 109 units, respectively:

```
HRGN hRectRgn = CreateRectRgn(10, 20, 110, 130);
assert(hRectRgn != NULL);
try
{
   // ...
}
```

```
catch (...)
{
   DeleteObject(hRectRgn);
}
DeleteObject(hRectRgn);
```

If you want to use the region as a clipping region, you can select it into a device context by using the **SelectObject** function or the **SelectClipRgn** function. And, as demonstrated, when the region is no longer needed, you must destroy it by passing its handle to the **DeleteObject** function. However, don't destroy the region if you've lost ownership of it by, for example, passing its handle to the **SetWindowRgn** function.

An alternative approach is to use the **CreateRectRgnIndirect** function:

```
HRGN CreateRectRgnIndirect(
    IN CONST RECT *lprc     // pointer to a RECT structure
   );
```

The **lprc** parameter is specified as the address of a **RECT** structure whose data members indicate the location and the dimensions of the desired region. If the **CreateRectRgnIndirect** function is successful, it returns a handle to the new region; otherwise, the function returns **NULL**.

The following code snippet demonstrates how to use the **CreateRectRgnIndirect** function to create a 1-by-1 square region (**hSquareRgn**):

```
RECT RSquare = {0, 0, 1, 1};
HRGN hSquareRgn = CreateRectRgnIndirect(&RSquare);
assert(hSquareRgn != NULL);
try
{
   // ...
}
catch (...)
{
   DeleteObject(hSquareRgn);
}
DeleteObject(hSquareRgn);
```


Related solution:	Found on page:
Rendering a Rectangle	247

Creating a Rounded Rectangular Region

To create a rectangular region whose corners are rounded, you use the **CreateRoundRectRgn** function:

```
HRGN CreateRoundRectRgn(
    IN int nLeftRect,       // horizontal location of the region's
                            // top-left corner
    IN int nTopRect,        // vertical location of the region's
                            // top-left corner
    IN int nRightRect,      // horizontal location of the region's
                            // bottom-right corner
    IN int nBottomRect      // vertical location of the region's
                            // bottom-right corner
    IN int nWidthEllipse,   // horizontal extent of rounding
    IN int nHeightEllipse   // vertical extent of rounding
   );
```

The **nLeftRect**, **nTopRect**, **nRightRect**, and **nBottomRect** parameters together specify the top-left and bottom-right corners of the rectangle. The **nWidthEllipse** and **nHeightEllipse** parameters specify the extent to which the corners of this rectangle are rounded. These quantities specify the width and height of an ellipse whose curvature shapes the corners. Figure 8.5 illustrates the role of these parameters.

***NOTE:** As with many other rectangle-related GDI functions, the rounded-rectangular region that's created by the **CreateRoundRectRegion** function does not contain the rightmost and bottommost edges of the specified rectangle.*

If the **CreateRoundRectRgn** function succeeds, it returns a handle to the new region. If the function fails, it returns **NULL**. For example, to create a rectangular

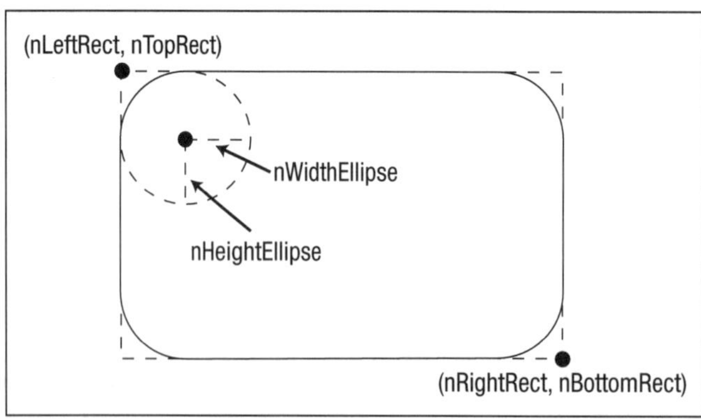

Figure 8.5 The effect of the **nWidthEllipse** and **nHeightEllipse** parameters of the **CreateRoundRectRgn** function.

region (**hRoundRectRgn**) that's located at position (5, 0) with a width and height of 100 and 75 units, respectively, and whose corners are rounded by 50 and 30 units in the horizontal and vertical directions, respectively:

```
const int roundX = 50;
const int roundY = 30;
HRGN hRoundRectRgn =
   CreateRoundRectRgn(5, 0, 106, 76, roundX, roundY);
assert(hRoundRectRgn != NULL);
try
{
   // ...
}
catch (...)
{
   DeleteObject(hRoundRectRgn);
}
DeleteObject(hRoundRectRgn);
```

If you want to use the region as a clipping region, you can use the **SelectObject** function or the **SelectClipRgn** function to select the region into a device context. When the region is no longer needed, and if you haven't forfeited ownership of the region (e.g., by passing its handle to **SetWindowRgn**), you must destroy it by passing its handle to the **DeleteObject** function.

Related solution:	Found on page:
Rendering a Rounded Rectangle	248

Creating an Elliptical Region

To create an elliptical region, you use the **CreateEllipticRgn** function:

```
HRGN CreateEllipticRgn(
    IN int nLeftRect,      // horizontal location of the top-left
                           // corner of the region's bounding rectangle
    IN int nTopRect,       // vertical location of the top-left
                           // corner of the region's bounding rectangle
    IN int nRightRect,     // horizontal location of the bottom-right
                           // corner of the region's bounding rectangle
    IN int nBottomRect     // vertical location of the bottom-right
                           // corner of the region's bounding rectangle
   );
```

The top-left and bottom-right corners of a bounding rectangle are specified by the **nLeftRect**, **nTopRect**, **nRightRect**, and **nBottomRect** parameters. The created region will take the shape of the ellipse that fits just within this rectangle. If the **CreateEllipticRgn** function succeeds, it returns a handle to the new region. If the function fails, it returns **NULL**.

NOTE: *As with many other rectangle-related GDI functions, the rounded-rectangular region that's created by the* ***CreateEllipticRgn*** *function does not contain the rightmost and bottommost edges of the specified rectangle.*

The following code snippet demonstrates the use of the **CreateEllipticRgn** function to create an elliptical region (**hEllipseRgn**) that's located at position (10, 20) with a width and height of 50 and 75 units, respectively:

```
HRGN hEllipseRgn = CreateEllipticRgn(10, 20, 61, 96);
assert(hEllipseRgn != NULL);
try
{
   // ...
}
catch (...)
{
   DeleteObject(hEllipseRgn);
}
DeleteObject(hEllipseRgn);
```

If you want to use the elliptical region as a clipping region, you can use the **SelectObject** function or the **SelectClipRgn** function to select the region into a device context. When the region is no longer needed, and if you haven't forfeited ownership of the region (e.g., by passing its handle to **SetWindowRgn**), you must destroy it by passing its handle to the **DeleteObject** function.

An alternative function, **CreateEllipticRgnIndirect**, can be used to create an elliptical region. The resulting region is identical to that created by the **CreateEllipticRgn** function, except with the **CreateEllipticRgnIndirect** function, you pass the address of a **RECT** structure instead of the individual coordinates of the bounding rectangle. Here's the function declaration:

```
HRGN CreateEllipticRgnIndirect(
    IN CONST RECT *lprc     // pointer to a RECT structure
   );
```

The **lprc** parameter is specified as the address of a **RECT** structure whose data members indicate the location and the dimensions of the elliptical region's bounding rectangle. If the **CreateEllipticRgnIndirect** function is successful, it returns a handle to the new region; otherwise, the return value is **NULL**.

The following code snippet demonstrates the use of the **CreateEllipticRgn** function to create the same elliptical region as that of the previous code snippet:

```
RECT RBounds = {10, 20, 61, 96};
HRGN hEllipseRgn = CreateEllipticRgnIndirect(&RBounds);
assert(hEllipseRgn != NULL);
try
{
   // ...
}
catch (...)
{
   DeleteObject(hEllipseRgn);
}
DeleteObject(hEllipseRgn);
```


Related solution:	Found on page:
Rendering an Ellipse	250

Creating a Polygonal Region

To create a region with the shape of a custom polygon, you use the **CreatePolygonRgn** function:

```
HRGN CreatePolygonRgn(
    CONST POINT *lppt,      // pointer to array of POINT structures that
                            // define the vertices of the polygon
    int cPoints,            // number of POINTS in the array of vertices
    int fnPolyFillMode      // polygon-fill mode identifier
   );
```

The vertices of the polygon are specified by the **lppt** parameter, which is a pointer to an array of **POINT** structures (one for each vertex). Because the **CreatePolygonRgn** function will automatically close the polygon, the last **POINT** structure in this array does not have to be identical to the first **POINT** structure. The **cPoints** parameter specifies the number of **POINT** structures in the **lppt** array. The **fnPolyFillMode** parameter controls the polygon-filling mode. This parameter is specified as either **ALTERNATE** (1) or **WINDING** (2).

If the **CreatePolygonRgn** function is successful, the returned value is a handle to the new region. If the **CreatePolygonRgn** function fails, it returns **NULL**. For example, to create a region that's shaped like a triangle, you use the **CreatePolygonRgn** function like so:

```
const int num_vertices = 3;
const POINT vertices[] = {
    {20, 120}, {120, 20}, {220, 120}
    };
HRGN hTriangleRgn =
    CreatePolygonRgn(vertices, num_vertices, ALTERNATE);
assert(hTriangleRgn != NULL);
try
{
    // ...
}
catch (...)
{
    DeleteObject(hTriangleRgn);
}
DeleteObject(hTriangleRgn);
```

As demonstrated, when the region is no longer needed, you must destroy it by using the **DeleteObject** function. Don't call **DeleteObject**, however, if you've surrendered ownership of the region (e.g., by passing its handle to the **SetWindowRgn** function); in this case, the new owner is responsible for the region's destruction.

If you want to use the polygonal region as a clipping region, you can select it into a device context by using the **SelectObject** function or the **SelectClipRgn** function. For more information on clipping regions, see "Clipping Regions" in the "In Depth" section.

Related solution:	Found on page:
Rendering a Custom Polygon	258

Combining Two Regions

To combine two regions by using a set-wise operator, you use the **CombineRgn** function:

```
int CombineRgn(
    IN HRGN hrgnDest,        // handle to a pre-existing destination region
    IN HRGN hrgnSrc1,        // handle to one of the source regions
    IN HRGN hrgnSrc2,        // handle to the other source region
    IN int fnCombineMode     // combinatorial-operation identifier
  );
```

The **hrgnDest** parameter identifies an existing region to which the result of combining the two source regions, which are specified by the **hrgnSrc1** and **hrgnSrc2** parameters, will be copied. The **fnCombineMode** parameter specifies the fashion in which these two source regions will be combined. This parameter can be passed any one of the values listed in Table 8.2.

TIP: *The **hrgnDest**, **hrgnSrc1**, and **hrgnSrc2** parameters do not have to specify handles to different regions. If you want to overwrite one of the source regions with the combination, you can pass a handle to this source region as the **hrgnDest** parameter.*

If the **CombineRgn** function succeeds, the result of the combination is copied to the region specified by the **hrgnDest** parameter, and the function returns one of the first three identifiers listed in Table 8.1. If the **CombineRgn** function fails, it returns **RGN_ERROR** (0).

The following code snippet demonstrates how to combine two regions, **hRgn1** and **hRgn2**, by using the **CombineRgn** function and the **RGN_OR** identifier (i.e., to create the union of the two regions). The result is stored in the pre-created region, **hRgn3**:

```
HRGN hRgn1 = CreateRectRgn(10, 10, 100, 100);
HRGN hRgn2 = CreateRectRgn(50, 50, 150, 150);
HRGN hRgn3 = CreateRectRgn(0, 0, 0, 0); // NULLREGION
try
{
   // store the union of hRgn1 and hRgn2 in hRgn3
   CombineRgn(hRgn3, hRgn1, hRgn2, RGN_OR);
   // ...
}
catch (...)
{
   DeleteObject(hRgn3);
   DeleteObject(hRgn2);
   DeleteObject(hRgn1);
}
DeleteObject(hRgn3);
DeleteObject(hRgn2);
DeleteObject(hRgn1);
```

The handle specified as the **hrgnDest** parameter must indicate an existing region, but, as mentioned previously, you can pass **hrgnDest** the handle to one of the source regions. It's common practice to come across code similar to the following, which stores the result of combining **hRgn1** and **hRgn2** in the region identified by **hRgn1**:

```
HRGN hRgn1 = CreateRectRgn(10, 10, 100, 100);
HRGN hRgn2 = CreateRectRgn(50, 50, 150, 150);
try
{
   // store the difference of hRgn1 and hRgn2 in hRgn1
   CombineRgn(hRgn1, hRgn1, hRgn2, RGN_DIFF);
   // ...
}
catch (...)
{
   DeleteObject(hRgn2);
   DeleteObject(hRgn1);
}
DeleteObject(hRgn2);
DeleteObject(hRgn1);
```

Copying a Region

To copy a region, you use the **CombineRgn** function, specifying **RGN_COPY** as the **fnCombineMode** parameter:

```
HRGN hRgn = CreateRectRgn(10, 10, 100, 100);
HRGN hCopyRgn = CreateRectRgn(0, 0, 0, 0);  // NULLREGION
try
{
   // copy hRgn to hRgnCopy
   CombineRgn(hCopyRgn, hRgn, NULL, RGN_COPY);
   // ...
}
catch (...)
{
   DeleteObject(hCopyRgn);
   DeleteObject(hRgn);
}
DeleteObject(hCopyRgn);
DeleteObject(hRgn);
```

For more information on the **CombineRgn** function, refer to the Immediate Solution "Combining Two Regions." An alternative approach is to use the application-defined **CopyRgn** function, which uses the **GetRegionData** and **ExtCreateRegion** functions to copy a region (see "Extracting Information about a Region" in the "In Depth" section).

Retrieving the Bounds of a Region

To retrieve a region's bounding rectangle, you use the **GetRgnBox** function:

```
int GetRgnBox(
    IN HRGN hrgn,        // handle to the target region
    OUT LPRECT lprc      // pointer to a RECT structure
   );
```

The **hrgn** parameter identifies the region whose bounding rectangle you want to retrieve. If the **GetRgnBox** function is successful, the coordinates of this rectangle are placed in the **RECT** structure whose address is specified by the **lprc** parameter, and the function returns one of the first three identifiers listed in Table 8.1. If the **GetRgnBox** function fails (e.g., one of the parameters is invalid), the return value is **RGN_ERROR** (0).

The following code snippet demonstrates the use of the **GetRgnBox** function. Here the coordinates of the **RECT** structure indicated by **RBounds** should be equal to those of the **RECT** structure (**RCreate**) that's used to create a region (**hRgn**):

```
const RECT RCreate = {0, 0, 50, 250};
HRGN hRgn = CreateRectRgnIndirect(&RCreate);
try
{
   RECT RBounds = {-1, -1, -1, -1};
   GetRgnBox(hRgn, &RBounds);
   if (!EqualRect(&RBounds, &RCreate)) throw;
   // ...
}
catch (...)
{
   DeleteObject(hRgn);
}
DeleteObject(hRgn);
```

Filling the Interior of a Region

To fill the interior of a region by using a logical brush object, you use the **FillRgn** function:

```
BOOL FillRgn(
    IN HDC hdc,          // handle to the target device context
    IN HRGN hrgn,        // handle to the region that defines
                         // the area to be filled
    IN HBRUSH hbr        // handle to the brush to fill with
   );
```

The **hdc** parameter identifies the device context to which the interior of the region, whose handle is specified by the **hrgn** parameter, is filled using the logical

8. Regions and Paths

brush whose handle is specified by the **hbr** parameter. The dimensions of the region are interpreted in logical units. If the **FillRgn** function is successful, it returns **TRUE**. If **FillRgn** fails, the return value is **FALSE**.

The following code snippet demonstrates the use of the **FillRgn** function to fill the interior of a region (**hRgn**) to **hDC** by using the white stock brush object (**hbr**):

```
HRGN hRgn = CreateRoundRectRgn(10, 20, 200, 100, 15, 15);
HDC hDC = GetDC(hWnd);
try
{
   HBRUSH hBrush = static_cast<HBRUS>(
      GetStockObject(WHITE_BRUSH)
      );
   FillRgn(hDC, hRgn, hBrush);
   // ...
}
catch (...)
{
   DeleteObject(hRgn);
   ReleaseDC(hWnd, hDC);
}
DeleteObject(hRgn);
ReleaseDC(hWnd, hDC);
```

Related solution:	Found on page:
Filling the Interior of a Rectangle with a Custom Brush	261

Outlining a Region

To draw the boundary of a region by using a logical brush object, you use the **FrameRgn** function:

```
BOOL FrameRgn(
    IN HDC hdc,         // handle to the target device context
    IN HRGN hrgn,       // handle to the region whose boundary to draw
    IN HBRUSH hbr,      // handle to the brush to draw the boundary with
    IN int nWidth,      // width of the brush strokes
    IN int nHeight      // height of the brush strokes
   );
```

The **hdc** parameter identifies the device context to which the region's boundary is drawn; the region is identified by the **hrgn** parameter. The region's boundary is interpreted in logical units. The **hbr** parameter is specified as a handle to a brush object that's used to render the boundary. The **nWidth** and **nHeight** parameters specify the desired width and height of the drawn boundary (in logical units), respectively.

Upon success, the **FrameRgn** function returns **TRUE**; otherwise, the return value is **FALSE**. For example, to render the boundary of an elliptic region (**hRgn**) to a display device context (**hDC**) by using the stock black brush object, you use the **FrameRgn** function like so:

```
HRGN hRgn = CreateEllipticRgn(10, 10, 100, 100);
HDC hDC = GetDC(hWnd);
try
{
   HBRUSH hBrush = static_cast<HBRUSH>(
      GetStockObject(BLACK_BRUSH)
      );
   const int stroke_width = 5;
   const int stroke_height = 3;
   FrameRgn(hDC, hRgn, hBrush, stroke_width, stroke_height);
   // ...
}
catch (...)
{
   DeleteObject(hRgn);
   ReleaseDC(hWnd, hDC);
}
DeleteObject(hRgn);
ReleaseDC(hWnd, hDC);
```


Related solution:	Found on page:
Outlining a Rectangle with a Custom Brush	263

Inverting the Pixels within a Region

To invert the color of each pixel within a region (and on its boundary), you use the **InvertRgn** function:

```
BOOL InvertRgn(
    IN HDC hdc,        // handle to the target device context
    IN HRGN hrgn       // handle to the region that defines
                       // the pixels to invert
   );
```

The **hdc** parameter identifies the device context whose pixels are those whose colors you want to invert; these pixels lie in and on the region specified (in logical coordinates) by the **hrgn** parameter. The inverse colors are defined by the **DSTINVERT** raster-operation code. If the **InvertRgn** function is successful, the return value is **TRUE**. If the function fails, it returns **FALSE**.

For example, to invert the colors of the pixels (of **hDC**) that reside in (and on the boundary of) the area defined by the region **hRgn**, you use the **InvertRgn** function like so:

```
HRGN hRgn = CreateEllipticRgn(10, 10, 100, 100);
HDC hDC = GetDC(hWnd);
try
{
   InvertRgn(hDC, hRgn);
   // ...
}
catch (...)
{
   ReleaseDC(hWnd, hDC);
   DeleteObject(hRgn);
}
ReleaseDC(hWnd, hDC);
DeleteObject(hRgn);
```


Related solution:	Found on page:
Inverting the Pixels within a Rectangle	264

Moving a Region

To change the position of a region, you use the **OffsetRgn** function:

```
int OffsetRgn(
    IN HRGN hrgn,        // handle to the region to move
    IN int nXOffset,     // number of units to move in
                         // the horizontal direction
    IN int nYOffset      // number of units to move in
                         // the vertical direction
   );
```

The **hrgn** parameter identifies the region whose position you want to change. The **nXOffset** and **nYOffset** parameters specify the new position of the region relative to its current position. Setting **nXOffset** to a positive value will move the region to the right by **nXOffset** units, while setting this parameter to a negative value will move the region to the left by **nXOffset** units. Similarly, setting **nYOffset** to a positive value will move the region down by **nYOffset** units, while setting this parameter to a negative value will move the region up by **nYOffset** units. If the **OffsetRgn** function is successful, it returns one of the first three values listed in Table 8.1. If the function fails, the return value is **RGN_ERROR** (0).

TIP: *To determine the current position of a region, see "Retrieving the Bounds of a Region."*

The following code snippet demonstrates the use of the **OffsetRgn** function. Here a region (**hRgn**) is moved by 10 units in the horizontal direction and by 50 units in the vertical direction:

```
HRGN hRgn = CreateRectRgn(10, 10, 100, 100);
try
{
   const int x_offset = 10;
   const int y_offset = 50;
   OffsetRgn(hRgn, x_offset, y_offset);  // move to (20, 60)
   // ...
}
catch (...)
{
   DeleteObject(hRgn);
}
DeleteObject(hRgn);
```

Testing Regions for Equality

To determine if two regions are equal (in location, shape, and size), you use the **EqualRgn** function:

```
BOOL EqualRgn(
    HRGN hSrcRgn1,       // handle to one of the regions
    HRGN hSrcRgn2        // handle to the other region
   );
```

The **hRgn1** and **hRgn2** parameters identify the regions that you want to test. If the position or the dimensions of the region indicated by **hRgn1** are identical to those of the region indicated by **hRgn2**, the **EqualRgn** function returns **TRUE**. If the position and/or the dimensions differ, or if an error occurs (e.g., if you pass a handle to a non-region object), the **EqualRgn** function returns **FALSE**.

The following code snippet demonstrates the use of the **EqualRgn** function. Here the variable **regions_equal** should indicate **TRUE**:

```
HRGN hRgn1 = CreateRectRgn(5, 5, 100, 100);
HRGN hRgn2 = CreateRectRgn(5, 5, 100, 100);
try
{
   BOOL regions_equal = EqualRgn(hRgn1, hRgn2);  // TRUE
   // ...
}
catch (...)
{
   DeleteObject(hRgn2);
   DeleteObject(hRgn1);
}
DeleteObject(hRgn2);
DeleteObject(hRgn1);
```

Here's another example, in which the regions (**hRgn1** and **hRgn2**) have the same dimensions but differ in location. In this case, the variable **regions_equal** should indicate **FALSE**:

```
HRGN hRgn1 = CreateEllipticRgn(10, 10, 30, 30);
HRGN hRgn2 = CreateEllipticRgn(10, 11, 30, 31);
try
{
   BOOL regions_equal = EqualRgn(hRgn1, hRgn2);  // FALSE
   // ...
}
catch (...)
{
   DeleteObject(hRgn2);
   DeleteObject(hRgn1);
}
DeleteObject(hRgn2);
DeleteObject(hRgn1);
```

Likewise, if the locations are the same, but the regions differ in shape and/or size, the **EqualRgn** function will return **FALSE**:

```
HRGN hRgn1 = CreateEllipticRgn(10, 10, 30, 30);
HRGN hRgn2 = CreateRectRgn(10, 10, 30, 31);
try
{
```

```
    BOOL regions_equal = EqualRgn(hRgn1, hRgn2);  // FALSE
    // ...
}
catch (...)
{
    DeleteObject(hRgn2);
    DeleteObject(hRgn1);
}
DeleteObject(hRgn2);
DeleteObject(hRgn1);
```

Testing a Point for Inclusion within a Region

To determine whether a specific coordinate lies within (or on the boundary of) a region, you use the **PtInRegion** function:

```
BOOL PtInRegion(
     IN HRGN hrgn,     // handle to the target region
     IN int X,         // horizontal location of the point in question
     IN int Y          // vertical location of the point in question
   )
```

The **hrgn** parameter identifies the region to query. The **X** and **Y** parameters are specified as the horizontal and vertical coordinates of the point to test for inclusion within the region, respectively. If the point is in or on the region, the **PtInRegion** function returns **TRUE**; otherwise, the function returns **FALSE**.

The **PtInRegion** function is useful when you need to hit-test a complex shape. For example, to see if a point (**PTest**) lies within an octagon (defined by **hOctRgn**), you use the **PtInRegion** function like so:

```
const POINT vertices[] = {
    {0, 90}, {90, 0}, {190, 0}, {280, 90},
    {280, 190}, {190, 280}, {90, 280}, {0, 190}
    };
HRGN hOctRgn = CreatePolygonRgn(vertices, 8, WINDING);
try
{
    POINT PTest = {0, 90};
    BOOL in_octagon = PtInRegion(hOctRgn, PTest.x, PTest.y);  // TRUE
    // ...
}
catch (...)
{
    DeleteObject(hOctRgn);
}
DeleteObject(hOctRgn);
```

Related solutions:	Found on page:
Hit-Testing Lines	267
Hit-Testing Bézier Curves	269
Hit-Testing Ellipses	272
Hit-Testing Pie Slices	273
Hit-Testing Arcs	275
Hit-Testing Chords	278

Obtaining the Clipping Region of a Device Context

To retrieve a copy of a device context's clipping region, you use the **GetClipRgn** function:

```
int GetClipRgn(
    IN HDC hdc,         // handle to the target device context
    IN HRGN hrgn        // handle to an existing region to which the device
                        // context's clipping region will be copied
  );
```

The **hdc** parameter identifies the device context whose clipping region you want to copy to the region specified by the **hrgn** parameter. This is somewhat of an odd function because you don't actually retrieve a handle to the clipping region or a handle to its copy. Instead, the **GetClipRgn** function copies the DC's clipping region to a region that you've previously created; you pass a handle to this pre-created region as the **hrgn** parameter. The value of **hrgn** itself won't be changed, but the region that it refers to will.

WARNING! The GetClipRgn function works only for application-defined regions, not for system-defined regions that are created by, for example, the BeginPaint function. To retrieve a copy of a system-defined region, use the GetRandomRgn function (which we'll discuss next).

If the **GetClipRgn** function is successful, it returns 1 if the specified DC has an application-defined clipping region, or 0 if the DC has no application-defined clipping region. If **GetClipRgn** fails, the return value is –1.

The following code snippet demonstrates the use of the **GetClipRgn** function to retrieve a copy of an application-defined clipping region (**hClipRgn**). This clipping region will be copied to a pre-created region (**hCopyClipRgn**):

```
HRGN hClipRgn = CreateRectRgn(10, 10, 100, 100);
HRGN hCopyClipRgn = CreateRectRgn(0, 0, 0, 0);  // NULLREGION
HDC hDC = GetDC(hWnd);
try
```

```
{
   // set the DC's clipping region
   SelectClipRgn(hDC, hClipRgn);

   // grab a copy of the DC's clipping region
   GetClipRgn(hDC, hCopyClipRgn);

   // if successful, the clipping region and the copy should be equal
   BOOL is_clip_copy = EqualRgn(hCopyClipRgn, hClipRgn); // TRUE

   // ...
}
catch (...)
{
   DeleteObject(hCopyClipRgn);
   DeleteObject(hClipRgn);
   ReleaseDC(hWnd, hDC);
}
DeleteObject(hCopyClipRgn);
DeleteObject(hClipRgn);
ReleaseDC(hWnd, hDC);
```

Unfortunately, the **GetClipRgn** function will retrieve a copy of the device context's clipping region only when this clipping region was previously set by an application. The function won't work for system-defined clipping regions that are internally created by the GDI (e.g., via the **BeginPaint** function). To retrieve a copy of a GDI-created clipping region, you should use the **GetRandomRgn** function:

```
int GetRandomRgn(
    IN HDC hdc,         // handle to the target device context
    IN HRGN hrgn        // handle to an existing region to which the device
                        // context's clipping region will be copied
    IN INT iNum         // set to the identifier SYSRGN
);
```

The **hdc** parameter identifies the device context whose system-defined clipping region you want to copy. This clipping region is copied to the pre-created region specified by the **hrgn** parameter. With the **GetRandomRgn** function, as with the **GetClipRgn** function, the value of **hrgn** won't change, but the region that it refers to will. The **iNum** parameter specifies the type of clipping region you're interested in. This parameter must be set to **SYSRGN** (4).

NOTE: *On systems running Windows 95 or Windows 98, the coordinates of the copied clipping region are relative to the client area of the corresponding window. In Windows NT and Windows 2000, the coordinates of the copied clipping region are relative to the screen.*

The possible return values for the **GetRandomRgn** function are identical to those of the **GetClipRgn** function. Namely, if **GetRandomRgn** succeeds and the specified DC has a system-defined clipping region, the function returns 1. If the DC has no system-defined clipping region, the return value is 0. If the **GetRandomRgn** function fails, it returns –1.

The following code snippet demonstrates the use of the **GetRandomRgn** function. Here the **WM_PAINT** case-statement is from a typical window procedure (here, for the window **hWnd**). The **GetRandomRgn** function is used after a call to the **BeginPaint** function to retrieve a copy of a system-defined clipping region (**hCopyClipRgn**):

```
case WM_PAINT:
{
   HRGN hCopyClipRgn = CreateRectRgn(0, 0, 0, 0); // NULLREGION

   PAINTSTRUCT ps;
   HDC hDC = BeginPaint(hWnd, &ps);
   try
   {
      // grab a copy of the DC's system-defined clipping region
      GetRandomRgn(hDC, hCopyClipRgn, SYSRGN);

      // ...
   }
   catch (...)
   {
      EndPaint(hWnd, &ps);
      DeleteObject(hCopyClipRgn);
   }
   EndPaint(hWnd, &ps);
   DeleteObject(hCopyClipRgn);

   return 0;
}
```

Adjusting the Clipping Region of a Device Context

The GDI provides several functions that can be used to manipulate a device context's clipping region. To move a DC's clipping region, you use the **OffsetClipRgn** function:

```
int OffsetClipRgn(
    IN HDC hdc,          // handle to the target device context
    IN int nXOffset,     // number of logical units to move in
                         // the horizontal direction
    IN int nYOffset      // number of logical units to move in
                         // the vertical direction
);
```

The **hdc** parameter identifies the DC that contains the clipping region that you want to move. The **nXOffset** and **nYOffset** parameters specify (in logical units) the new position of this clipping region relative to its current position. If the **OffsetClipRgn** function is successful, it returns one of the first three values listed in Table 8.1; otherwise, the return value is **RGN_ERROR** (0).

TIP: *To determine the current position of a DC's clipping region, see "Retrieving the Bounds of a Device Context's Clipping Region."*

The following code snippet demonstrates the use of the **OffsetClipRgn** function to move the clipping region (**hClipRgn**) of a device context (**hDC**) by 25 logical units in the horizontal direction and by 15 logical units in the vertical direction:

```
HRGN hClipRgn = CreateRectRgn(10, 10, 100, 100);
HDC hDC = GetDC(hWnd);
try
{
   // set the DC's clipping region
   SelectClipRgn(hDC, hClipRgn);

   const int x_offset = 25;
   const int y_offset = 15;
   // move the DC's clipping region
   OffsetClipRgn(hDC, x_offset, y_offset);
}
catch (...)
{
   DeleteObject(hClipRgn);
   ReleaseDC(hWnd, hDC);
}
DeleteObject(hClipRgn);
ReleaseDC(hWnd, hDC);
```

Instead of simply moving a DC's clipping region, you can also combine the DC's current clipping region with another region by using the **ExtSelectClipRgn** function. This function can also be used to completely replace the DC's clipping region:

```
int ExtSelectClipRgn(
    IN HDC hdc,        // handle to the target device context
    IN HRGN hrgn,      // handle to the region to combine with DC's
                       // current clipping region
    IN int fnMode      // set-wise combination operator
   );
```

The **hdc** parameter identifies the device context whose clipping region you want to change. The **hrgn** parameter is specified as a handle to a separate region that you want to combine with the DC's current clipping region. The fashion in which these two regions are combined is specified by the **fnMode** parameter, which can be set to one of the identifiers listed in Table 8.2. If the **ExtSelectClipRgn** function succeeds, it returns one of the first three identifiers listed in Table 8.1. If the **ExtSelectClipRgn** function fails, the return value is **RGN_ERROR** (0).

The following code snippet demonstrates the use of the **ExtSelectClipRgn** function. In this case, the system-defined clipping region (created by the **BeginPaint** function) of the device context (**hDC**) is completely replaced with the new clipping region (**hNewClipRgn**); this is done by specifying the **RGN_COPY** identifier as the **fnMode** parameter:

```
case WM_PAINT:
{
   HRGN hNewClipRgn = CreateEllipticRgn(0, 0, 100, 100);

   PAINTSTRUCT ps;
   HDC hDC = BeginPaint(hWnd, &ps);
   try
   {
      ExtSelectClipRgn(hDC, hNewClipRgn, RGN_COPY);
      DeleteObject(hNewClipRgn); hNewClipRgn = NULL;

      // ...
   }
   catch (...)
   {
      EndPaint(hWnd, &ps);
      if (hNewClipRgn) DeleteObject(hNewClipRgn);
   }
   EndPaint(hWnd, &ps);

   return 0;
}
```

As with the **SelectClipRgn** function (see "Clipping Regions" in the "In Depth" section), the **ExtSelectClipRgn** function does not take ownership of the region that you specify via the **hrgn** parameter. This means that you're still responsible for destroying the separate region. You aren't, however, responsible for destroying the new clipping region that the **ExtSelectClipRgn** function creates.

Retrieving the Bounds of a Device Context's Clipping Region

To retrieve a region's bounding rectangle, you use the **GetClipBox** function:

```
int GetClipBox(
    IN HDC hdc,          // handle to the target device context
    OUT LPRECT lprc      // pointer to a RECT structure
   );
```

The **hdc** parameter identifies the DC that contains the clipping region whose bounding rectangle you want to retrieve. If the **GetClipBox** function is successful, the coordinates of this rectangle are placed in the **RECT** structure whose address is specified by the **lprc** parameter, and the function returns one of the first three identifiers listed in Table 8.1. If the **GetClipBox** function fails, the return value is **RGN_ERROR** (0).

The following code snippet demonstrates the use of the **GetClipBox** function in response to the **WM_PAINT** message. In this case, the clipping region of the device context (**hDC**) is defined by the **BeginPaint** function:

```
case WM_PAINT:
{
   PAINTSTRUCT ps;
   HDC hDC = BeginPaint(hWnd, &ps);
   try
   {
      RECT RBounds;
      GetClipBox(hDC, &RBounds);
      // ...
   }
   catch (...)
   {
      EndPaint(hWnd, &ps);
   }
   EndPaint(hWnd, &ps);

   return 0;
}
```

Creating and Working with Paths

In this section, we'll focus on the GDI path object. We'll examine several techniques for creating and working with paths.

Opening and Closing a Path Bracket

To open a path bracket in a device context, you use the **BeginPath** function:

```
BOOL BeginPath(
    IN HDC hdc      // handle to the target device context
   );
```

The **hdc** parameter identifies the device context in which the path bracket is to be opened. The **BeginPath** function returns a Boolean value indicating success or failure. If the function is indeed successful, any previous paths that are associated with this DC (**hdc**) are destroyed.

Once a path bracket is open, you are free to draw to the device context as usual. However, the output of only a limited number of functions will be recorded to the path. For a list of these so-called recordable functions, see "Recordable Functions" in the "In Depth" section.

To close a previously opened path bracket, you use the **EndPath** function:

```
BOOL EndPath(
    IN HDC hdc     // handle to the target device context
   );
```

The **hdc** parameter identifies the device context in which a path bracket was previously opened. If the **EndPath** function succeeds, it selects the path into this device context and returns **TRUE**. If the **EndPath** function fails, the return value is **FALSE**.

The following code snippet demonstrates the use of the **BeginPath** and **EndPath** functions. Here these functions are used with the **TextOut** and **StrokePath** functions to render outlined text:

```
HDC hDC = GetDC(hWnd);
HFONT hTTFont = font::MakeFont(hDC, "Comic Sans MS", 24); // see Chapter 4
HFONT hOldFont = static_cast<HFONT>(
   SelectObject(hDC, hTTFont)
   );
try
{
```

```
    SetBkMode(hDC, TRANSPARENT);
    // open a path bracket
    if (BeginPath(hDC))
    {
       LPCSTR pText = TEXT("Outlined Text\0");
       // record the text to the path
       TextOut(hDC, 10, 10, pText, lstrlen(pText));

       // close the path bracket and
       // select the path into hDC
       EndPath(hDC);

       // render the outline of the path
       StrokePath(hDC);
    }
    // ...
}
catch (...)
{
    DeleteObject(SelectObject(hDC, hOldFont));
    ReleaseDC(hWnd, hDC);
}
DeleteObject(SelectObject(hDC, hOldFont));
ReleaseDC(hWnd, hDC);
```

For the definition of the application-defined **MakeFont** function, refer to Chapter 4.

Outlining a Path

To render the outline of a path, you use the **StrokePath** function:

```
BOOL StrokePath(
     IN HDC hdc         // handle to the target device context
    );
```

The **hdc** parameter identifies a device context that has a path selected into it. If the **StrokePath** function is successful, it first renders the outline of **hdc**'s path by using the pen that's currently selected into the device context, and then returns **TRUE**. If the function fails, the return value is **FALSE**.

WARNING! After the StrokePath function draws the outline of a path, the path is destroyed.

The following code snippet demonstrates the use of the **StrokePath** function to outline the path that contains the output of the **Ellipse** function:

```
const COLORREF clrRed = PALETTERGB(255, 0, 0);
HPEN hPen = CreatePen(PS_SOLID, 2, clrRed);

HDC hDC = GetDC(hWnd);
HPEN hOldPen = static_cast<HPEN>(
   SelectObject(hDC, hPen)
   );
try
{
   // open a path bracket
   if (BeginPath(hDC))
   {
      // record the ellipse to the path
      Ellipse(hDC, 10, 10, 200, 100);

      // close the path bracket and
      // select the path into hDC
      EndPath(hDC);

      // render the outline of the path
      StrokePath(hDC);
   }
   // ...
}
catch (...)
{
   DeleteObject(SelectObject(hDC, hOldPen));
   ReleaseDC(hWnd, hDC);
}
DeleteObject(SelectObject(hDC, hOldPen));
ReleaseDC(hWnd, hDC);
```

Note that the **StrokePath** function renders only the outline of the path, not the outline of whatever you render to the device context within the path bracket. Specifically, the **StrokePath** function outlines only the output of "recordable functions" that are called within the path bracket. For a list of functions whose output can be recorded to a path, refer to "Recordable Functions" in the "In Depth" section.

Filling the Interior of a Path

To fill the interior of a path, you use the **FillPath** function:

```
BOOL FillPath(
    IN HDC hdc      // handle to the target device context
   );
```

The **hdc** parameter identifies a device context that has a path selected into it. If the **FillPath** function is successful, it first fills the interior of **hdc**'s path by using **hdc**'s current brush, and then returns **TRUE**. If the **FillPath** function fails, the return value is **FALSE**.

WARNING! After the FillPath function fills the interior of a path, the path is destroyed.

One of the (many) limitations of Windows 95 and Windows 98 is the inability to create a geometric pen that exhibits a pen style other than **PS_SOLID**, **PS_NULL**, or **PS_INSIDEFRAME**. A common technique to work around this limitation is to use the **FillPath** function and a (non-solid) brush object to fill the areas that would normally be filled with a (solid) pen. This approach is demonstrated in the following code snippet:

```
const COLORREF clrGreen = PALETTERGB(0, 255, 0);
HPEN hWidePen = CreatePen(PS_SOLID, 20, 0);
HBRUSH hBrush = CreateHatchBrush(HS_CROSS, clrGreen);

HDC hDC = GetDC(hWnd);
HPEN hOldPen = static_cast<HPEN>(
   SelectObject(hDC, hWidePen)
   );
HBRUSH hOldBrush = static_cast<HBRUSH>(
   SelectObject(hDC, hBrush)
   );
try
{
   // open a path bracket
   if (BeginPath(hDC))
   {
      // record the line to the path
      MoveToEx(hDC, 10, 10, NULL);
      LineTo(hDC, 100, 100);

      // close the path bracket and
      // select the path into hDC
      EndPath(hDC);

      // widen the path by one pen width (20 logical units)
      WidenPath(hDC);

      // fill the interior of the path by using hBrush
      FillPath(hDC);
   }
   // ...
}
```

```
catch (...)
{
   DeleteObject(SelectObject(hDC, hOldBrush));
   DeleteObject(SelectObject(hDC, hOldPen));
   ReleaseDC(hWnd, hDC);
}
DeleteObject(SelectObject(hDC, hOldBrush));
DeleteObject(SelectObject(hDC, hOldPen));
ReleaseDC(hWnd, hDC);
```

Widening a Path

To widen a path, you use the **WidenPath** function:

```
BOOL WidenPath(
    IN HDC hdc      // handle to the target device context
   );
```

The **hdc** parameter identifies a device context that has a path selected into it. If the **WidenPath** function is successful, it increases the width of the path by the width of **hdc**'s current pen, and then returns **TRUE**. The only stipulation is that this pen must *not* be an extended cosmetic pen—the **WidenPath** function works only with geometric and non-extended cosmetic pens. If the **WidenPath** function fails, it returns **FALSE**.

WARNING! The WidenPath function internally relies on the FlattenPath and GetPath functions during its process of widening. As a result, the WidenPath function is relatively expensive, especially for complex paths; use this function sparingly.

The following code snippet demonstrates the use of the **WidenPath** function to widen a path that contains the output of the **Ellipse** function:

```
const COLORREF clrBlue = PALETTERGB(0, 0, 255);
HPEN hPen = CreatePen(PS_SOLID, 5, clrBlue);

HDC hDC = GetDC(hWnd);
HPEN hOldPen = static_cast<HPEN>(
   SelectObject(hDC, hPen)
   );
try
{
   // open a path bracket
   if (BeginPath(hDC))
   {
      // record a circle to the path
      Ellipse(hDC, 10, 10, 100, 100);
```

```
        // close the path bracket and
        // select the path into hDC
        EndPath(hDC);

        // widen the path by one pen width (5 logical units)
        WidenPath(hDC);

        // render the outline of the path by using hPen
        StrokePath(hDC);
    }
    // ...
}
catch (...)
{
    DeleteObject(SelectObject(hDC, hOldPen));
    ReleaseDC(hWnd, hDC);
}
DeleteObject(SelectObject(hDC, hOldPen));
ReleaseDC(hWnd, hDC);
```

Converting a Path to a Region

To convert a path to a region, you use the **PathToRegion** function:

```
HRGN PathToRegion(
    IN HDC hdc          // handle to the target device context
   );
```

The **hdc** parameter identifies a device context that has a path selected into it. If the **PathToRegion** function is successful, it returns a handle to the new region; otherwise, the return value is **NULL**.

WARNING! After the PathToRegion function creates a region from a path, the path is destroyed.

The following code snippet demonstrates the use of the **PathToRegion** function to create a region (**hRgn**) that's shaped like the characters of a text string ("Text-Shaped Window"). The handle to this region is then passed to the **SetWindowRgn** function to set the shape of a window (**hWnd**) to that of the region:

```
HDC hDC = GetDC(hWnd);
HFONT hTTFont = font::MakeFont(hDC, "Comic Sans MS", 36); // see Chapter 4
HFONT hOldFont = static_cast<HFONT>(
   SelectObject(hDC, hTTFont)
   );
```

```
try
{
   SetBkMode(hDC, TRANSPARENT);
   // open a path bracket
   if (BeginPath(hDC))
   {
      LPCSTR pText = TEXT("Text-Shaped Window\0");
      // record the text to the path
      TextOut(hDC, 10, 10, pText, lstrlen(pText));

      // close the path bracket and
      // select the path into hDC
      EndPath(hDC);

      // create a region from the path
      HRGN hRgn = PathToRegion(hDC);
      if (hRgn)
      {
         if (!SetWindowRgn(hWnd, hRgn, TRUE))
         {
            DeleteObject(hRgn);
         }
      }
   }
   // ...
}
catch (...)
{
   DeleteObject(SelectObject(hDC, hOldFont));
   ReleaseDC(hWnd, hDC);
}
DeleteObject(SelectObject(hDC, hOldFont));
ReleaseDC(hWnd, hDC);
```


For the definition of the application-defined **MakeFont** function, refer to Chapter 4.

Converting a Path to a Series of Lines

To convert a path's curves to a series of straight-line segments, you use the **FlattenPath** function:

```
BOOL FlattenPath(
    IN HDC hdc         // handle to the target device context
   );
```

The **hdc** parameter identifies a device context that has a path selected into it. If the **FlattenPath** function is successful, it converts the path's curves to a sequence of straight-line segments, and then returns **TRUE**. If the **FlattenPath** function fails, the return value is **FALSE**.

The **FlattenPath** function is especially useful when you want to interpret a path as a sequence of straight-line-segment endpoints instead of Bézier-curve control points. For example, the following code snippet demonstrates the use of the **FlattenPath** function to convert the path's description to only a series of **MoveToEx** and **LineTo** function calls:

```
const COLORREF clrBlue = PALETTERGB(0, 0, 255);
HPEN hPen = CreatePen(PS_SOLID, 5, clrBlue);

HDC hDC = GetDC(hWnd);
HPEN hOldPen = static_cast<HPEN>(
   SelectObject(hDC, hPen)
   );
try
{
   // open a path bracket
   if (BeginPath(hDC))
   {
      // record a circle to the path
      Ellipse(hDC, 10, 10, 100, 100);

      // close the path bracket and
      // select the path into hDC
      EndPath(hDC);

      // "flatten" the path
      FlattenPath(hDC);

      // determine the number of endpoints in the path
      const int num_points = GetPath(hDC, NULL, NULL, 0);
      if (num_points > 0)
      {
         // make room for the POINTs and vertex types
         POINT* pPEnds = new POINT[num_points];
         unsigned char* pTypes = new unsigned char[num_points];
         try
         {
            // get the path's description
            if (GetPath(hDC, pPEnds, pTypes, num_points) == num_points)
            {
```

```
                    for (int iPoint = 0; iPoint < num_points; ++iPoint)
                    {
                       if (pTypes[iPoint] == PT_MOVETO)
                       {
                          MoveToEx(
                            hDC, pPEnds[iPoint].x, pPEnds[iPoint].y, NULL
                            );
                       }
                       else if (
                          pTypes[iPoint] == PT_LINETO ||
                          pTypes[iPoint] == PT_LINETO | PT_CLOSEFIGURE
                          )
                       {
                          LineTo(hDC, pPEnds[iPoint].x, pPEnds[iPoint].y);
                       }
                       //
                       // no need to test for PT_BEZIERTO
                       // because the path is "flat"
                       //
                    }
                 }
              }
              catch (...)
              {
                 delete [] pTypes;
                 delete [] pPEnds;
              }
              delete [] pTypes;
              delete [] pPEnds;
           }
        }
        // ...
     }
     catch (...)
     {
        DeleteObject(SelectObject(hDC, hOldPen));
        ReleaseDC(hWnd, hDC);
     }
     DeleteObject(SelectObject(hDC, hOldPen));
     ReleaseDC(hWnd, hDC);
```


In this example, the **GetPath** function is used to retrieve the points that describe the path. Because the **FlattenPath** function is called before **GetPath**, you don't have to worry about handling the **PT_BEZIERTO** vertex type—it won't be present in the **pTypes** array. For more information on the **GetPath** function, see "Retrieving the Geometric Description of a Path."

Retrieving the Geometric Description of a Path

To convert a path into a series of points—either the endpoints of straight-line segments or the control points of Bézier curves, or both—you use the **GetPath** function:

```
int GetPath(
    IN HDC hdc,               // handle to the target device context
    OUT LPPOINT lpPoints,     // array of POINTs that will receive the
                              // vertices of the path's description
    OUT LPBYTE lpTypes,       // array of values that identifies the
                              // type of each vertex
    IN int nSize              // the number of vertices that lpPoints
                              // (and lpTypes) can hold
  );
```

The **hdc** parameter identifies the device context in which a path is selected. The **lpPoints** parameter is specified as an array of **POINT** structures that will receive the vertices that describe the path. Each vertex in this array is either the endpoint of a straight-line segment or one of the control points of a Bézier curve. It's the job of the array of bytes that's specified by the **lpTypes** parameter to indicate the type of each vertex. Each element of the **lpTypes** array will be filled with one of the vertex type-identifiers listed in Table 8.3.

Both the **PT_LINETO** and the **PT_BEZIERTO** identifiers can be combined with another identifier, **PT_CLOSEFIGURE** (1), which indicates that a figure needs to be closed. However, because the **PT_CLOSEFIGURE** identifier always follows a **PT_MOVETO** identifier, when you're rendering the path manually (i.e., via a series of calls to **LineTo**, **PolyBezierTo**, and **MoveToEx**), you can handle the **PT_CLOSEFIGURE** case as you would if the identifier were not included.

Because each element in the **lpTypes** array indicates the vertex type of each element in the **lpPoints** array, these arrays should contain the same number of elements. To determine how large these arrays should be, you call the **GetPath** function, specifying **NULL** as both of these parameters, and specifying zero as the **nSize** parameter, like so:

```
const int num_points = GetPath(hDC, NULL, NULL, 0);
```

When the **nPoints** parameter is passed a value of zero, the **GetPath** function returns the number of required elements. You can then allocate **num_points** **POINT**s for the **lpPoints** array, allocate **num_points** bytes for the **lpTypes** array, and then call the **GetPath** function again, this time to actually fill both of these arrays, like so:

```
const int num_points = GetPath(hDC, NULL, NULL, 0);
if (num_points > 0)
{
   POINT* pPEnds = new POINT[num_points];
   unsigned char* pTypes = new unsigned char[num_points];
   try
   {
      if (GetPath(hDC, pPEnds, pTypes, num_points) == num_points)
      {
         // ...
      }
   }
   catch (...)
   {
      delete [] pTypes;
      delete [] pPEnds;
   }
   delete [] pTypes;
   delete [] pPEnds;
}
```

When you call the **GetPath** function with a non-zero **nSize** parameter, the returned value is the number of points that were retrieved. If the **GetPath** function fails, it returns –1.

The following code snippet demonstrates how to use the **GetPath** function to retrieve the geometric description of a path that contains the output of the **TextOut** function. This data is scaled and then used to render the text manually:

```
HDC hDC = GetDC(hWnd);
HFONT hTTFont = font::MakeFont(hDC, "Comic Sans MS", 24); // see Chapter 4
HFONT hOldFont = static_cast<HFONT>(
   SelectObject(hDC, hTTFont)
   );
try
{
   SetBkMode(hDC, TRANSPARENT);

   // open a path bracket
   if (BeginPath(hDC))
   {
      LPCSTR pText = TEXT("Scale My Description\0");
      // record the text to the path
      TextOut(hDC, 10, 10, pText, lstrlen(pText));
```

```
// close the path bracket and
// select the path into hDC
EndPath(hDC);

// determine the number of endpoints in the path
const int num_points = GetPath(hDC, NULL, NULL, 0);
if (num_points > 0)
{
   // make room for the POINTs and vertex types
   POINT* pPEnds = new POINT[num_points];
   unsigned char* pTypes = new unsigned char[num_points];
   try
   {
      // get the path's description
      int num_got = GetPath(hDC, pPEnds, pTypes, num_points);
      if (num_got > 0)
      {
         // scale each point in the description
         for (int iPoint = 0; iPoint < num_got; ++iPoint)
         {
            pPEnds[iPoint].x *= 3;
            pPEnds[iPoint].y *= 3;
         }

         //
         // render each segment in the description
         // (you can alternatively pass the data
         // directly to the PolyDraw function---see
         // "The Description of a Path" in the In
         // Depth section)
         //
         for (int iPoint = 0; iPoint < num_got; ++iPoint)
         {
            // test the vertex type
            switch (pTypes[iPoint])
            {
               // handle the MoveToEx case
               case PT_MOVETO:
               {
                  MoveToEx(
                     hDC, pPEnds[iPoint].x, pPEnds[iPoint].y, NULL
                     );
                  break;
               }
               // handle the LineTo case
               case PT_LINETO:
               case PT_LINETO | PT_CLOSEFIGURE:
```

```
                        {
                           LineTo(
                              hDC, pPEnds[iPoint].x, pPEnds[iPoint].y
                              );
                           break;
                        }
                        // handle the PolyBezierTo case
                        case PT_BEZIERTO:
                        case PT_BEZIERTO | PT_CLOSEFIGURE:
                        {
                           PolyBezierTo(hDC, pPEnds + iPoint, 3);
                           iPoint += 2;
                           break;
                        }
                     }
                  }
               }
            }
            catch (...)
            {
               // clean up
               delete [] pTypes;
               delete [] pPEnds;
            }
            // clean up
            delete [] pTypes;
            delete [] pPEnds;
         }
      }
      // ...
   }
   catch (...)
   {
      DeleteObject(SelectObject(hDC, hOldFont));
      ReleaseDC(hWnd, hDC);
   }
   DeleteObject(SelectObject(hDC, hOldFont));
   ReleaseDC(hWnd, hDC);
```

For the definition of the application-defined **MakeFont** function, refer to Chapter 4.

Related solutions:	Found on page:
Rendering a Single Line Segment	241
Rendering a Bézier Curve	245

Chapter 9

Palettes

In Depth

Conceptually, a palette is just like a box of crayons. You're free to place any color in the box; however, the number of crayons the box can hold is determined by the target device. Say, for example, that your box has enough room for 256 crayons. If you know that you're going to use these crayons to draw, say, a red rose, then you'll want to stock your box with as many shades of red as possible. On the other hand, if you don't know what type of image you're going to draw, then it's probably a good idea to fill your box with a wide selection of different colors, perhaps those that are most commonly used by all images. As simple as it may sound, this crayon-based approach is essentially the logic behind a palette.

In this chapter, we'll examine three types of palettes: hardware palettes, system palettes, and logical palettes. We'll discuss how the entries of each of these types of palettes are modified, and how you can retrieve a copy of these entries. In addition, we'll look at the methods that are used to create, select, and realize a logical palette. Finally, we'll examine two palette-specific window messages, **WM_QUERYNEWPALETTE** and **WM_PALETTECHANGED**, and we'll discuss some different techniques for handling these messages and the consequences that result if they're ignored.

A Device-Specific Color Table

A *physical palette*, often called a *hardware palette*, is essentially a device-specific color table that maps indices to red, green, and blue (RGB) intensity values. The device-specificity comes from the fact that the device itself determines how many entries or "slots" are available. For example, on an 8-bit display, each pixel is represented by a single byte, which means that exactly 256 (2^8) unique colors can be displayed at any given time. With only 256 slots available, you'll want to choose the best set of colors to accurately display your image. This is where a palette comes into play—it's an array or "container" of color values that's used to increase the chance of displaying an image in its best light.

Again, it should be stressed that a hardware palette is a device-specific entity. As with the pixels of a device-dependent bitmap, you're never given direct access to the entries of a hardware palette. Indeed, not every device stores and maintains its hardware palette in the same fashion. If we were allowed to manipulate the hardware palette of a specific display adapter, we'd be writing a heck of a lot of code to make sure our application worked on every type of display device. This would obviate the role of the GDI and make our jobs that much more difficult. As you might have guessed, the GDI provides a better solution: the *Palette Manager*.

The Palette Manager

The GDI Palette Manager was designed to serve as a mediator between applications and 8-bit display adapters whose hardware palettes contain 256 entries. The Palette Manager copies this hardware palette and stores the result in an object known as the *system palette*. In turn, applications can indirectly manipulate the hardware palette by changing the entries of this system palette.

The System Palette

The system palette is the Palette Manager's abstraction of a hardware palette. As depicted in Figure 9.1, the system palette is divided into three sections: a static head, a dynamic body, and a static tail. Initially, the static head and tail are filled with the standard 20 VGA colors, and the dynamic body is filled with a general mix of commonly used colors.

The static head and the static tail each consist of 10 colors. These sections are set by the Palette Manager and contain colors that are typically used to render user-interface elements, such as title-bar captions and the background of windows and buttons. These sections are described as "static" because they aren't meant to be changed. In contrast, the term "dynamic" is used to describe the body of the system palette because this section contains colors that are meant to be changed. Specifically, the dynamic body contains 236 entries that you can specify so as to display your application using specific colors. In other words, these entries correspond to the open slots of a crayon box.

The system palette is a shared object that's used by all applications. As we'll discuss later, the foreground application has priority over the system palette's entries. Because of this fact, you can think of the system palette as a common box of crayons that's shared by all applications. The foreground application has first dibs at stocking this box with specific crayons.

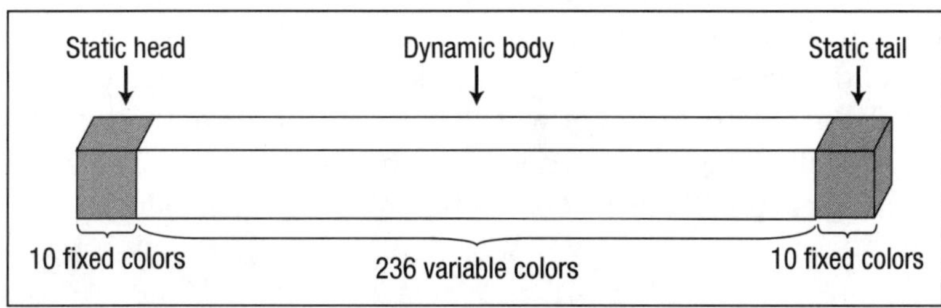

Figure 9.1 The layout of the system palette.

The 20 static entries of the system palette are divided into the static head and the static tail only to allow for better raster operations. Because raster operations on palette-based devices work with indices into the system palette instead of actual RGB color values, the division of the static entries allows, for example, index 0 (black) to **DSTINVERT** to index 255 (white). Although the static colors of the system palette are meant to be fixed, in Windows 2000 the GDI allows you to change all of these entries by using the **SetSystemPaletteUse** function (see "Modifying the System Palette's Static Entries"). In prior Windows versions, you can change only up to 18 of these entries—the entry at index 0 (black) and the entry at index 255 (white) remain fixed.

You can retrieve the entries (both static and dynamic) of the system palette by using the **GetSystemPaletteEntries** function (see "Retrieving the Entries of the System Palette"). However, there's no function, such as "SetSystemPaletteEntries," that can be used to change the dynamic entries (i.e., the 236 colors of the dynamic body) of the system palette. To do this, you'll need to use a *software palette*.

Software Palettes

Consider the case of displaying an image that contains 256 shades of gray on an 8-bit display. If you simply blit this image to the screen, each color in the image will be mapped to a color that's currently in the system palette. Unless the system palette already contains many shades of gray, your image will probably look pretty bad. For example, if you render the grayscale image to the screen when the system palette contains only 16 shades of gray, you're essentially reducing your 8-bit image to a 4-bit image. That is, the image's 256 shades of gray will be mapped to the 16 grayscale shades of the system palette. Clearly, in this situation, you'll want to manipulate the system palette entries beforehand. And, to do this, the GDI provides the *logical palette object*, commonly referred to as a *software palette*.

Logical palettes provide applications with the means of manipulating the entries of the system palette. As with other GDI graphic objects, a logical palette object is a representation of a physical object. In this case, the physical object is a hardware palette. But, as I mentioned earlier, there's a middleman here: the Palette Manager. When you need to display an image on a palette-based device, you fine-tune the entries of the system palette by using a logical palette. When this logical palette is realized, the Palette Manager will change the entries of the system palette, which in turn will change the entries of the hardware palette. In short, it's best to think of a logical palette as an abstraction of the system palette.

As it does with other graphic objects, the GDI provides a function that can be used to create a logical palette, the **CreatePalette** function:

```
HPALETTE CreatePalette(lplgpl);
```

The single argument, **lplgpl**, is a pointer to a **LOGPALETTE** structure (which we'll discuss next). If the **CreatePalette** function is successful, it returns a value of type **HPALETTE**, a handle to a logical palette object. If **CreatePalette** fails, the return value is **NULL**.

The **LOGPALETTE** structure, among other things, holds the entries of a logical palette. In the case of displaying a grayscale image on an 8-bit display, the choice of entries is straightforward; you choose 236 representative shades of gray. Likewise, if you need to display an image of a soccer field, you'll likely want to use a logical palette that contains different shades of green. Or, if you're displaying an image of a banana, you'll want a logical palette that's composed of yellow, brown, and green entries. Whatever your image consists of, on a device that can display only a limited set of colors (at any given time), it's best to use an appropriate logical palette. You can always forgo the use of a palette; your image will still be displayed. But remember, in doing so, you're limiting yourself to the current colors of the system palette. Often these colors are far from what your image requires. Figure 9.2 depicts two applications: one that displays a 256-color image (on an 8-bit display) without the use of a logical palette, and one that displays this same image (on an 8-bit display) with the use of a logical palette.

Figure 9.2 Displaying an image on a palette-based device without (left) and with (right) using a logical palette.

The LOGPALETTE Structure

The **LOGPALETTE** structure is used to describe a logical palette. This structure is composed of three data members:

```
typedef struct tagLOGPALETTE {
   UINT palVersion,
   UINT palNumEntries,
   PALETTEENTRY palEntry[1]
} LOGPALETTE, FAR* LPLOGPALETTE;
```

The **palVersion** data member specifies the version of the logical palette. For all current versions of Windows, this data member is set to a hexadecimal value of 300. The **palNumEntries** data member specifies the number of entries in the palette. Specifically, this data member describes the number of elements in the **palEntry** data member, an array of **PALETTEENTRY** structures.

The PALETTEENTRY Structure

The **PALETTEENTRY** structure is used to describe a single color entry in a logical palette. In fact, this structure is not unlike the **RGBQUAD** structure—it contains four data members:

```
typedef struct tagPALETTEENTRY {
   BYTE palRed,
   BYTE palGreen,
   BYTE palBlue,
   BYTE palUsage
} LOGPALETTE, FAR* LPLOGPALETTE;
```

Notice that unlike the RGB-related data members of the **RGBQUAD** structure, those of the **PALETTEENTRY** structure are ordered "normally"—that is, red, green, and then blue. These intensity values are described by the **palRed**, **palGreen**, and **palBlue** data members, respectively. The **palUsage** data member indicates the "usage" of the palette, describing how the palette entries are mapped when the palette is used in different situations. You can set **palUsage** to 0, indicating default usage (the most common approach), or set it to one of the identifiers listed in Table 9.1.

Ninety-nine percent of the time, you'll want to set the **peFlags** data member for each logical palette entry to 0. The identifiers listed in Table 9.1 are used only to control the way each logical palette entry "changes" the corresponding entry of the system palette. We'll return to this issue later in this chapter (see "Foreground and Background Palette Realization").

So, to create a logical palette, you first allocate enough memory to hold a **LOGPALETTE** structure plus one less than the desired number of **PALETTE-**

Table 9.1 **The possible values for the PALETTEENTRY::palUsage data member.**

Identifier	Value	Meaning
PC_RESERVED	1	The corresponding palette entry is not color-matched to any existing entries in the system palette. If an unused system palette entry is found, it's changed and marked as reserved. If no open slots are available, the color is mapped to black.
PC_EXPLICIT	2	The corresponding palette entry describes a literal index into the system palette.
PC_NOCOLLAPSE	4	The corresponding palette entry is not color-matched to any existing entries in the system palette. If an unused system palette entry is found, it's changed (but not marked as reserved as with **PC_RESERVED**). If no open slots are available, the color is mapped to black.

ENTRY structures. (You need to allocate only one less **PALETTEENTRY** structure than the desired number of entries because the **LOGPALETTE::palEntry** data member already contains one **PALETTEENTRY** structure.) Next, you initialize each palette entry with the desired RGB value, and then you pass this initialized **LOGPALETTE** structure to the **CreatePalette** function. For example, to create a grayscale palette with 256 entries, you do the following:

```
const short num_entries = 256;
const size_t total_size =
   sizeof(LOGPALETTE) +
   sizeof(PALETTENETRY) * (num_entries - 1);

HPALETTE hPal = NULL;
unsigned char* pBuffer = new unsigned char[total_size];
try
{
   LPLOGPALETTE lpLogPal =
      reinterpret_cast<LPLOGPALETTE>(pBuffer);

   lpLogPal->palVersion = 0x300;
   lpLogPal->PalNumEntries = num_entries;

   for (int index = 0; index < num_entries; ++index)
   {
      lpLogPal->palEntry[index].palRed = index;
      lpLogPal->palEntry[index].palGreen = index;
      lpLogPal->palEntry[index].palBlue = index;
      lpLogPal->palEntry[index].palUsage = 0;
   }
```

```
    hPal = CreatePalette(lpLogPal);
    if (!hPal) throw;
    delete [] pBuffer; pBuffer = NULL;
    // ...
}
catch (...)
{
    delete [] pBuffer;
}

// later...
DeleteObject(hPal);
```

As demonstrated, when a logical palette is no longer needed, you must destroy it—just as you would most other graphic objects—by passing its handle to the **DeleteObject** function. Moreover, be sure to deselect the palette from all device contexts before you destroy it.

Associating a Logical Palette with a Device Context

Although a logical palette is a GDI graphic object, selecting a logical palette into a device context is not accomplished with the usual **SelectObject** function. Instead, the GDI provides a specialized function for this purpose, **SelectPalette**:

```
HPALETTE SelectPalette(hDC, hPal, bForceBackground);
```

The **SelectPalette** function takes a handle to a device context as its first parameter, a handle to a logical palette as its second parameter, and a "priority" flag as its third parameter. If the **SelectPalette** function is successful, it returns a handle to the device context's previous palette. If the **SelectPalette** function fails, the return value is **NULL**. The "priority" flag simply determines whether the palette should have foreground or background priority. Let's examine this issue more closely.

Foreground and Background Palette Realization

Unlike the **SelectObject** function, which initiates the process of realization with other graphic objects, the **SelectPalette** function does nothing more than associate a palette with a device context. The process of association and realization is divided into two steps because the system palette is a shared object. Often you'll want to associate a logical palette with a device context but not change the system palette's entries in the process. Likewise, you might sometimes need to re-realize a logical palette that was previously selected into a device context. To actually realize a logical palette, and thus change the entries of the system palette, you use the **RealizePalette** function:

```
UINT RealizePalette(hDC);
```

The **RealizePalette** function returns the number of system palette entries that have been changed. During the process of realization, one of two things can happen: either the logical palette is realized as a foreground palette (*foreground realization*); or it's realized as a background palette (*background realization*). It's the job of the **bForceBackground** parameter of the **SelectPalette** function to specify whether a logical palette will be realized as a foreground or background palette.

During foreground realization, the Palette Manager changes the dynamic entries of the system palette to those of the logical palette. The Palette Manager actually maps the colors of the logical palette to any existing colors in the system palette, taking note of the logical-to-physical index mapping for each entry. The entries of the system palette are changed only when a color is not present. This scheme eliminates any duplicate colors because redundant entries in a logical palette will map to the same index in the system palette. If a foreground logical palette contains more entries than are available in the system palette, the remaining entries of the logical palette are mapped to the system palette's closest matching entry (using the Euclidean distance formula).

NOTE: *The Palette Manager caches its logical-to-physical-index mapping information so that the next time the logical palette is realized in the foreground, the Palette Manager need only use the cached version. As it turns out, even if a logical palette is realized in the background, the Palette Manager will compute, and then store the foreground mapping information so as to speed up the mapping process if and when this logical palette is later realized in the foreground.*

TIP: *You can force the Palette Manager to refresh its cached version of a logical palette's logical-to-physical-index mapping information by using the* ***UnrealizeObject*** *function. This function takes only a single parameter: a handle to the logical palette whose logical-to-physical-index mapping you want redone.*

Unfortunately, this explanation applies only when the entries of the logical palette were created with the **PALETTEENTRY::peFlags** data member specified as 0 (i.e., default behavior). Things aren't as clean-cut when this data member is assigned **PC_EXPLICIT**, **PC_RESERVED**, or **PC_NOCOLLAPSE**:

- In the rare case that the **PC_EXPLICIT** identifier is used, the corresponding palette entry no longer describes a color but instead describes a system palette index. When a logical palette with entries of this type is realized, the system palette is not changed in any way.
- When a logical palette entry has a **peFlags** value of **PC_RESERVED**, no color matching is performed. Instead, the logical palette entry can occupy only an open slot in the system palette, whereupon the system palette entry is marked as "reserved," meaning that no other logical palette entry can be color-matched to it. If there are no open slots lefts, the logical palette entry is mapped to the first system palette entry (0; black).

- The **PC_NOCOLLAPSE** identifier has a similar effect as **PC_RESERVED**. The only difference is that, with **PC_NOCOLLAPSE**, once an open slot in the system palette is occupied by a logical palette entry, that entry in the system palette is not marked as reserved. Therefore, other logical palette entries can be color-matched to this "used, but unreserved" system palette entry.

Keep in mind that the **PC_EXPLICIT**, **PC_RESERVED**, and **PC_NOCOLLAPSE** identifiers are assigned on a per-logical-palette-entry basis; they do not describe the logical palette as a whole.

After the entries of the system palette are changed (or reindexed), all colors that are currently displayed will be changed to the new set of colors. Again, this happens because each logical index no longer refers to the previous physical index. For this reason, foreground realization is performed only when a window (or one of its children) is given keyboard focus (i.e., it's the foreground window). Even if you call the **SelectPalette** function with a **FALSE bForceBackground** parameter, your logical palette will not be realized in the foreground unless your application itself is in the foreground. As we'll discuss next, Windows will actually send a special message, **WM_QUERYNEWPALETTE**, to a window just before it becomes the foreground window. Likewise, after the entries of the hardware palette are changed, Windows will send all top-level windows the **WM_PALETTECHANGED** message.

NOTE: *It's not strictly the foreground status of your window that determines whether or not a logical palette can be realized as a foreground palette. The deciding factor is the* device context *that the palette is selected into. If this DC is the DC of the foreground window, then calling the* ***RealizePalette*** *function (with this DC) will result in a foreground realization, that is, a change in the system palette (assuming you previously called* ***SelectPalette*** *with a* ***FALSE bForceBackground*** *parameter). You can verify this (when your application is in the background) by selecting your palette into the DC of the foreground window (whose handle you retrieve via the* ***GetForegroundWindow*** *function), and then realizing this palette—watch out for recursion!*

During background realization, not all of the entries of the system palette are changed. Instead, if any empty slots are left in the system palette, they'll be filled with entries from the logical palette on a first-come first-served basis. For example, if the system palette contains 25 unused slots, then the next time a background logical palette is realized, its first 25 entries will occupy these 25 empty slots in the system palette. For this reason, when you're creating a logical palette, it's best to place the most important colors first. (Note that this scheme is also governed by the use of the **PC_EXPLICIT**, **PC_RESERVED**, and **PC_NOCOLLAPSE** identifiers.) Conceptually, this first-come first-served approach is similar to buying an airline ticket at the airport—if there's a flight with an available seat, then it's yours; otherwise, you're out of luck. Following this analogy, you can think of background realization as flying standby, and think of foreground realization as reserving the entire plane.

Palette-Related Messages

As I mentioned earlier, the system palette is shared by all applications. When one application changes the entries of the system palette, this also changes the colors that are used by all other applications. To keep all applications in harmony, Windows provides three palette-specific messages: **WM_QUERYNEWPALETTE, WM_PALETTECHANGED**, and **WM_PALETTECHANGING**. The latter is a hangover from the 16-bit days and can simply be ignored. Proper handling of the former two messages, on the other hand, is often crucial. Let's look at these two messages more closely.

The WM_QUERYNEWPALETTE Message

As previously mentioned, the **WM_QUERYNEWPALETTE** message is sent just before a window becomes the foreground window. This is the Palette Manager's way of telling you: "Okay, now it's your turn to change the colors in the system palette." This situation provides a perfect opportunity to realize your logical palette as a foreground palette. For example, if **hPal** is a handle to your logical palette, you might process the **WM_QUERYNEWPALETTE** message like so:

```
case WM_QUERYNEWPALETTE:
{
   // NOTE: wParam and lParam are zero for WM_QUERYNEWPALETTE

   HDC hDC = GetDC(hWnd);
   // select the logical palette
   HPALETTE hOldPal = SelectPalette(hDC, hPal, FALSE);
   try
   {
      // realize the logical palette
      if (RealizePalette(hDC))
      {
         // repaint if the system palette changes
         InvalidateRect(hWnd, NULL, TRUE);
      }
   }
   catch (...)
   {
      SelectPalette(hDC, hOldPal, FALSE);
      ReleaseDC(hWnd, hDC);
   }
   SelectPalette(hDC, hOldPal, FALSE);
   ReleaseDC(hWnd, hDC);
   break;
}
```

A few things need to be mentioned about this code because it's easy to get the wrong impression from it. Perhaps the most confusing thing is that it seems as if we're selecting a palette into a device context, realizing this palette, and then simply selecting the original palette back into the device context. That is, the code doesn't seem to serve any purpose. Indeed, if we were to perform these same steps with a logical brush, for example, there would be no point. For instance, have a look at the following code:

```
// select and realize hBrush
HBRUSH hOldBrush = static_cast<HBRUSH>(
   SelectObject(hDC, hBrush)
   );
// deselect hBrush; select and realize hOldBrush
SelectObject(hDC, hOldBrush);
```

After calling this code, if we were to draw to **hDC** with the **Rectangle** function, for example, the rectangle would not be filled using **hBrush**; instead, the rectangle would be filled with the DC's default brush (**hOldBrush**). Now, if we perform these steps with a logical palette, as we did in the previous code snippet, you might think that the default palette (**hOldPal**) will be used the next time we draw to the window's DC, and you would be correct. But remember, the **WM_QUERYNEWPALETTE** message is a signal that it's our turn to change the system palette. To do this, we need to use the **RealizePalette** function. But to use this function, we need to have the proper logical palette selected into the DC of our window (i.e., the top level window). In short, we select **hPal** into **hDC** *only* so that our subsequent call to the **RealizePalette** function will change the system palette. That is, we first select **hPal** into the device context, storing the original palette as we would with other graphic objects:

```
// STEP 1:
HPALETTE hOldPal = SelectPalette(hDC, hPal, FALSE);
```

We then realize this logical palette by using the **RealizePalette** function:

```
// STEP 2:
RealizePalette(hDC);
```

Finally, we select the original palette (**hOldPal**) back into the device context:

```
// STEP 3:
SelectPalette(hDC, hOldPal, FALSE);
```

Again, the goal of Steps 1, 2, and 3 is only to change the system palette. It's not our intention to change the logical palette of our window's DC (although we must do so temporarily); we'll defer this task to just before we draw to our window's DC.

Note that in Step 3, **hOldPal** is only *selected* into **hDC**; it's not *realized*. That is, in Step 2, we realized the new palette (**hPal**), which instructed the Palette Manager to change the system palette accordingly, but nowhere did we realize **hOldPal**. As a result, any subsequent drawing operations will use **hPal**'s entries until the entries of the system palette are changed again. This is an important concept to keep in mind. Namely, when you select a logical palette into a device context, and then realize this logical palette as a foreground palette, the system palette's entries are changed accordingly; therefore, you can select a different palette back into the device context without worrying about altering the system palette. This is one of the main reasons that the processes of selection and realization are divided into two separate function calls.

Wait; there's another, subtler, thing to note about the final call to the **SelectPalette** function in Step 3. I just mentioned that the previous code snippet works because **hDC**'s original palette is only selected, not realized. As it turns out, the code will still behave as expected if we *were* to realize this original palette (**hOldPal**). For example, many developers prefer the following:

```
case WM_QUERYNEWPALETTE:
{
   HDC hDC = GetDC(hWnd);
   // select the logical palette
   HPALETTE hOldPal = SelectPalette(hDC, hPal, FALSE);
   try
   {
      // realize the logical palette
      if (RealizePalette(hDC))
      {
         // repaint if the system palette changes
         InvalidateRect(hWnd, NULL, TRUE);
      }
   }
   catch (...)
   {
      SelectPalette(hDC, hOldPal, FALSE);
      RealizePalette(hDC);
      ReleaseDC(hWnd, hDC);
   }
   SelectPalette(hDC, hOldPal, FALSE);
   RealizePalette(hDC);
   ReleaseDC(hWnd, hDC);
   break;
}
```

Surely, this code won't work because the final call to the **RealizePalette** function will effectively undo the preceding call to **RealizePalette**. In fact, in most cases, the code won't work (i.e., the **RealizePalette** function *will* effectively undo the preceding call to **RealizePalette**). The only thing saving us in this case is the fact that **hDC** is retrieved from the GDI device-context cache, and as a result, **hOldPal** refers to the *stock default* logical palette. Because of this fact, the **RealizePalette** function does *not* change the system palette. That is, when the stock default logical palette is realized, the system palette isn't changed. This is in contrast to the case when **hOldPal** is a handle to any other logical palette.

TIP: *You can retrieve a handle to the stock default logical palette by calling the* ***GetStockObject*** *function with the* ***DEFAULT_PALETTE*** *(15) identifier.*

Another option is to make the final call to the **RealizePalette** function, but to select the original palette back into the device context with a **TRUE bForceBackground** parameter. In this case, the previous changes to the system palette are still preserved, and the original palette is given secondary priority over the remaining entries (if any are available). This might be useful when you're using, for example, a third-party library to retrieve a handle to a device context because the Palette Manager usually assigns priority to the remaining palette entries according to a window's z-order.

Yet another thing to note about the **WM_QUERYNEWPALETTE** message-handling code is that the **RealizePalette** function returns a value indicating how many of the system's palette entries have changed. For this reason, the **InvalidateRect** function is called only if **RealizePalette** returns non-zero. Indeed, there's no need to force a repaint if no entries have changed. But wait—we've just called the **RealizePalette** function; isn't this function supposed to change the system palette entries? Yes, it does, but only if it has to. Consider the case in which an application displays an image of a penguin. If you open a second instance of this application, the new window becomes the foreground window, but because the images are the same, there's no need to change the system palette. In this case, switching between these two instances should not require a repaint because the system palette itself doesn't require a change.

NOTE: *If you're developing an MDI (Multiple Document Interface) application, your frame window should relay the* ***WM_QUERYNEWPALETTE*** *message to the active MDI child window. In response to this message, the active MDI child window should select and realize its palette into the device context of the* frame window. *(Remember, the* ***WM_QUERYNEWPALETTE*** *message is sent only to top-level windows and foreground realization can take place only if the logical palette is selected into the DC of the foreground window.)*

Although the previous code snippet changes the system palette in response to the **WM_QUERYNEWPALETTE** message, later, when you render to the device context in response to the **WM_PAINT** message, you'll need to select the logical palette into the DC so that indices are correctly mapped to colors (i.e., RGB values), like so:

```
case WM_PAINT:
{
   PAINTSTRUCT ps;
   HDC hDC = BeginPaint(hWnd, &ps);
   HPALETTE hOldPal = SelectPalette(hDC, hPal, FALSE);
   try
   {
      //
      // no call to RealizePalette because we're
      // not changing the system palette here
      //

      BitBlt(
         hDC, 10, 10,
         bmp.bmWidth, bmp.bmHeight,
         hMemDC, 0, 0,
         SRCCOPY
         );
   }
   catch (...)
   {
      SelectPalette(hDC, hOldPal, FALSE);
      EndPaint(hWnd, &ps);
   }
   SelectPalette(hDC, hOldPal, FALSE);
   EndPaint(hWnd, &ps);
   break;
}
```

As indicated in this code, after selecting the logical palette into the DC, you won't need to call **RealizePalette** again because you've already changed the system palette in response to the **WM_QUERYNEWPALETTE** message. In short, you call the **RealizePalette** function only to (indirectly) manipulate the system palette. And the best time to do this is in response to the **WM_QUERYNEWPALETTE** message. In response to the **WM_PAINT** message (or other painting-related messages), you only need to *select* the logical palette (i.e., the one you used to change the system palette) into the target DC before you draw to it. In fact, technically, if you're blitting only a DDB (device-dependent bitmap) in response to the **WM_PAINT** message, you need to select the logical palette into the DC only if your window is in the background (and another application has changed the system palette). In practice, however, this situation is rarely tested because it doesn't hurt to select the logical palette into the DC when the window is in the foreground. Plus, if you need to render a DIB section or you're using another regular drawing function to render a filled shape, you'll need to select the logical palette into the DC regardless of the foreground or background status of your window.

Figure 9.3 depicts a background application that correctly handles the **WM_QUERYNEWPALETTE** message but has failed to select the bitmap's corresponding logical palette into the window's DC in response to the **WM_PAINT** message. In this case, because the foreground application (Microsoft Photo Editor) is displaying the same image, the background application should be able to display the image with fairly accurate colors (assuming that Photo Editor has not severely reindexed the palette entries). Figure 9.4 depicts the same scenario, except this time the background application *has* selected the bitmap's corresponding logical palette into the window's DC in response to the **WM_PAINT** message.

WM_PALETTECHANGED Message

The **WM_PALETTECHANGED** message notifies all top-level windows that a new palette has been realized as a foreground palette. Because this scheme usually results in a new set of colors, this message provides an opportunity for all background windows to deal with the new colors as best as possible. This

Figure 9.3 A background application that has failed to select the bitmap's logical palette in response to the **WM_PAINT** message.

Figure 9.4 A background application that has correctly selected the bitmap's logical palette in response to the WM_PAINT message.

message is sent to the top-level windows according to their z-ordering. Conceptually, this scheme is similar to an airline company sending an email message to all standby passengers informing them that some seats are left. The passenger who's at the top of the list (highest in z-order) will have the best chance of catching the flight (changing the remaining palette entries). Keep in mind, though, that unlike this ticket-notification analogy, the **WM_PALETTECHANGED** message is sent regardless of whether there are any open slots in the system palette.

Unfortunately, as crazy as it may sound, the **WM_PALETTECHANGED** message is also sent to the foreground window (i.e., the window that performed the foreground realization). Therefore, you should test the **wParam** data member, which specifies the handle of the foreground window, before taking any background measures. One example of a background measure is to realize a secondary, lower-priority, palette in response to **WM_PALETTECHANGED** (when the **wParam** data member specifies a different window). In this way, when your window is in the background, you can make the absolute best of a bad situation. In practice, however, most developers simply choose to handle the **WM_PALETTECHANGED** message (when the **wParam** data member specifies a different window) just as they would the **WM_QUERYNEWPALETTE** message, like so:

```
case WM_PALETTECHANGED:
{
   if (reinterpret_cast<HWND>(wParam) == hWnd) break;
   // otherwise, proceed with the WM_QUERYNEWPALETTE code
}
case WM_QUERYNEWPALETTE:
{
   HDC hDC = GetDC(hWnd);
   // select the logical palette
   HPALETTE hOldPal = SelectPalette(hDC, hPal, FALSE);
   try
   {
      // realize the logical palette
      if (RealizePalette(hDC))
      {
         // repaint if the system palette changes
         InvalidateRect(hWnd, NULL, TRUE);
      }
   }
   catch (...)
   {
      SelectPalette(hDC, hOldPal, FALSE);
      ReleaseDC(hWnd, hDC);
   }
   SelectPalette(hDC, hOldPal, FALSE);
   ReleaseDC(hWnd, hDC);
   break;
}
```

Note that even though the initial call to the **SelectPalette** function involves a **FALSE bForceBackground** parameter, when the logical palette is realized in response to the **WM_PALETTECHANGED** message (when the **wParam** data member specifies a different window), the window is in the background, which means that the DC corresponds to a background window; therefore, the result is still a background logical palette realization.

NOTE: *If you're developing an MDI application, your MDI child windows will not receive the **WM_PALETTECHANGED** message; you should handle the **WM_MDIACTIVATE** message instead. You can handle this message as you would the **WM_PALETTECHANGED** message using your same code for the (relayed) **WM_QUERYNEWPALETTE** message, but instead of **break**ing when **wParam** equals **hWnd**, you **break** when **wParam** equals **NULL**.*

What happens if you don't handle the **WM_PALETTECHANGED** message? Well, the answer depends on *when* you receive the message and *how many slots* are open in the system palette. Remember, the **WM_PALETTECHANGED** message is sent to all top-level windows according to their z-ordering. If your window is second highest in z-order (i.e., directly below the foreground window) and there are unused entries in the system palette, the **WM_PALETTECHANGED** message is your prioritized notification that it's your turn to claim these unused entries. If you fail to realize a background logical palette in response to this message, you'll lose your chance of changing the system palette while your window is in the background. Of course, if there aren't any slots open in the system palette, it doesn't really matter whether or not you handle the **WM_PALETTECHANGED** message. Along these same lines, if your window is below, say, 10 other windows, then there's a good chance that, by the time you receive the **WM_PALETTECHANGED** message, there won't be any unused entries left. Figure 9.5 depicts a background application that ignores the **WM_PALETTECHANGED** message. Figure 9.6 depicts this same application, except that it has been modified so that it handles the **WM_PALETTECHANGED** message by using the same code that it uses for the **WM_QUERYNEWPALETTE** message (as demonstrated in the previous code snippet).

Listing 9.1 demonstrates how the **WM_QUERYNEWPALETTE** and **WM_PALETTECHANGED** messages are typically handled (along with the **WM_PAINT** message). The example renders an image (the image of the penguin from the figures in this chapter) to the client area of a window, and for simplicity, a palette-based display is assumed. Keep in mind, however, that in the context of this example, none of the palette-related code is necessary on non-palette-based devices—it will have no effect.

Figure 9.5 A background application that ignores the WM_PALETTECHANGED message.

Figure 9.6 A background application that handles the **WM_PALETTECHANGED** message.

Listing 9.1 Handling the **WM_QUERYNEWPALETTE** and **WM_PALETTECHANGED** messages on a system that uses a palette-based display.

```
// -------------------------------------------------------------------
// Windows 2000 Graphics API Black Book
// Chapter 9 - Listing 9.1 (Palette-Related Messages Demo)
// -------------------------------------------------------------------

#include <windows.h>

HINSTANCE hInst;
const char* WndClassName = "GMainWnd";
LRESULT CALLBACK MainWndProc(HWND HWnd, UINT Msg, WPARAM WParam,
   LPARAM LParam);

int APIENTRY WinMain(HINSTANCE hInstance, HINSTANCE, LPTSTR,
   int nCmdShow)
{
   hInst = hInstance;

   WNDCLASS wc;
   memset(&wc, 0, sizeof(WNDCLASS));

   wc.style = CS_VREDRAW | CS_HREDRAW;
   wc.lpszClassName = WndClassName;
```

```
    wc.lpfnWndProc = MainWndProc;
    wc.hInstance = hInst;
    wc.hCursor = LoadCursor(NULL, IDC_ARROW);
    wc.hbrBackground = reinterpret_cast<HBRUSH>(
       COLOR_BTNFACE + 1
       );

    if (RegisterClass(&wc))
    {
       HWND hWnd =
          CreateWindow(
             WndClassName, "Penguin!",
             WS_OVERLAPPEDWINDOW | WS_CAPTION |
             WS_VISIBLE | WS_CLIPCHILDREN,
             CW_USEDEFAULT, CW_USEDEFAULT, 360, 370,
             NULL, NULL, hInst, NULL
             );

       if (hWnd)
       {
          ShowWindow(hWnd, nCmdShow);
          UpdateWindow(hWnd);

          MSG msg;
          while (GetMessage(&msg, NULL, 0, 0))
          {
              TranslateMessage(&msg);
              DispatchMessage(&msg);
          }
       }
     }
     return 0;
}

BITMAP bmp = {0};        // will hold the DDB's dimensions
HDC hMemDC = NULL;       // memory DC that the DDB is selected into
HBITMAP hOldBmp = NULL; // placeholder DDB
HPALETTE hPal = NULL;    // DDB's associated logical palette

LRESULT CALLBACK MainWndProc(HWND hWnd, UINT msg, WPARAM wParam,
   LPARAM lParam)
{
   switch (msg)
   {
      case WM_CREATE:
      {
```

```
        //
        // see Immediate Solutions in Chapter 6
        // for the CreateDDBFromFile definition
        //
        LPCSTR filename = TEXT("PENGUIN.BMP\0");
        HBITMAP hBmp = CreateDDBFromFile(filename, &hPal);

        if (hBmp)
        {
           // determine the dimensions of the DDB
           GetObject(hBmp, sizeof(BITMAP), &bmp);

           // create a memory DC
           hMemDC = CreateCompatibleDC(NULL);
           if (hMemDC)
           {
              // select the DDB into the memory DC
              hOldBmp = static_cast<HBITMAP>(
                 SelectObject(hMemDC, hBmp)
                 );
           }
           else DeleteObject(hBmp);
        }
        break;
     }
     case WM_PALETTECHANGED:
     {
        if (reinterpret_cast<HWND>(wParam) == hWnd) break;
        // otherwise, proceed with the WM_QUERYNEWPALETTE code
     }
     case WM_QUERYNEWPALETTE:
     {
        HDC hDC = GetDC(hWnd);
        // select hPal as a foreground palette
        HPALETTE hOldPal = SelectPalette(hDC, hPal, FALSE);
        try
        {
           // realize the logical palette
           if (RealizePalette(hDC))
           {
              // repaint if the system palette changes
              InvalidateRect(hWnd, NULL, TRUE);
           }
        }
        catch (...)
        {
```

```
            // clean up
            SelectPalette(hDC, hOldPal, FALSE);
            ReleaseDC(hWnd, hDC);
        }
        // clean up
        SelectPalette(hDC, hOldPal, FALSE);
        ReleaseDC(hWnd, hDC);
        break;
    }
    case WM_PAINT:
    {
        PAINTSTRUCT ps;
        HDC hDC = BeginPaint(hWnd, &ps);
        HPALETTE hOldPal = SelectPalette(hDC, hPal, FALSE);
        try
        {
            //
            // no call to RealizePalette because we're
            // not changing the system palette
            //

            // render the DDB to the window's DC
            BitBlt(
                hDC, 10, 10,
                bmp.bmWidth, bmp.bmHeight,
                hMemDC, 0, 0,
                SRCCOPY
                );
        }
        catch (...)
        {
            SelectPalette(hDC, hOldPal, FALSE);
            EndPaint(hWnd, &ps);
        }
        SelectPalette(hDC, hOldPal, FALSE);
        EndPaint(hWnd, &ps);
        break;
    }
    case WM_DESTROY:
    {
        // clean up
        if (hMemDC)
        {
            if (hOldBmp)
            {
                DeleteObject(SelectObject(hMemDC, hOldBmp));
            }
```

```
            DeleteDC(hMemDC);
        }
        PostQuitMessage(0);
        break;
    }
  }
  return DefWindowProc(hWnd, msg, wParam, lParam);
}
```

Palette-Based vs. Non-Palette-Based Devices

Many developers attempt to use a logical palette on a non-palette-based device and are left in confusion as to why their implementation has no effect. It's important to remember that Windows uses palettes only when necessary. Nowadays, most video displays are set to a bit depth of at least 16 bits per pixel, in which case there's no need for a palette (i.e., the device is a "non-palette-based" device). Typically, palettes are employed only when a device uses eight or fewer bits per pixel, in which case the device is called a "palette-based" device. In short, don't even bother with palettes unless you're sure that they're used. It's not uncommon to see a software package impose a high-color or true-color requirement.

How can you tell whether you're working with a palette-based or non-palette-based device? The GDI provides a simple means: the **GetDeviceCaps** function. As its name suggests, the **GetDeviceCaps** function queries or "GETs" a DEVICE's CAPabilitieS. To determine whether a device uses a palette, you pass the **RASTERCAPS** capability index and look for the **RC_PALETTE** capability flag. For example, to test whether the primary display device is palette-based, you'd use the **GetDeviceCaps** function like so:

```
BOOL IsPaletteBasedDisplay()
{
   HDC hScreenDC = GetDC(NULL);
   BOOL is_palette_based =
      GetDeviceCaps(hScreenDC, RASTERCAPS) & RC_PALETTE;
   ReleaseDC(NULL, hScreenDC);
   return is_palette_based;
}
```

For graphics-intensive projects, it's a good idea to test whether a device is palette-based before calling any palette-specific code. Although it does no harm to simply assume the use of a palette, you might be making a significant number of superfluous function calls at the expense of efficiency. For the majority of projects, however, you can simply leave your palette code in place—your application will work fine even if the display device doesn't use a palette.

In fact, you can call the **IsPaletteBasedDisplay** function at the beginning of your application (e.g., in response to the **WM_CREATE** message of your application's main window), and then simply rely on the initial return value thereafter. And, because the user might later change the display's settings such that its palette-based status changes, you should also call the **IsPaletteBasedDisplay** function in response to the **WM_DISPLAYCHANGE** message. The following code snippet demonstrates this scheme:

```
BOOL uses_palette = FALSE;
LRESULT CALLBACK WndProc(
   HWND hWnd, MSG msg, LPARAM lParam, WPARAM wParam
   )
{
   case WM_CREATE:
   {
      // ...
      uses_palette = IsPaletteBasedDisplay();
      break;
   }
   // ...
   case WM_DISPLAYCHANGE:
   {
      uses_palette = IsPaletteBasedDisplay();
      break;
   }
   // ...
}
```

Palettes, Bitmaps, and Memory Device Contexts

As I pointed out in Chapter 6 (and earlier in this chapter), different rules govern whether you need to use the **SelectPalette** functions when blitting a DDB or a DIB section bitmap to the screen or to a memory DC. In fact, some references claim that a palette isn't needed whenever the **BitBlt** function is used; this is only partially correct. Other texts say to use a palette regardless of the rendering function and destination DC; this is a good rule of thumb, but it's not absolutely necessary. Let's explore these issues more closely.

Blitting from a Memory DC to a Display DC

When you call a blitting function, such as **BitBlt** or **StretchBlt**, to render a (DDB or DIB section) bitmap to a display device context, you must change the system palette beforehand. Remember, when you blit a bitmap to a display DC, your goal is to display the bitmap on the screen. To correctly display the colors of this bitmap, the system palette must itself contain the correct colors. For this reason, when the destination DC is a display DC (e.g., the common DC of your window), you must ensure that you've called the **RealizePalette** function beforehand. Typically, this function is called in response to the **WM_QUERYNEWPALETTE** message or the **WM_PALETTECHANGED** message.

Now, assuming that you've changed the system palette appropriately, do you need to call the **SelectPalette** function before blitting the bitmap to the display DC? As it turns out, the answer depends on the *type* of bitmap that you're going to blit. On the one hand, if your bitmap is a DDB, then you don't need to call the **SelectPalette** function before blitting. Remember, a DDB is a device-specific entity; its pixels refer not to literal RGB values but to palette entries. As a result, if the system palette contains the correct colors, then the pixels of the DDB will also refer to the correct colors, and therefore you don't need to call **SelectPalette** before calling blitting. On the other hand, the pixels of a DIB section bitmap don't refer to palette entries; instead, they are either literal RGB values or indices into the DIB section's color table. For this reason, even if the system palette contains the correct colors, you must call the **SelectPalette** function before you blit a DIB section bitmap to a display DC so that the GDI can map each color of the DIB section to its closest matching system palette entry. (See Chapter 7 for information on retrieving the color table entries of a DIB section bitmap and on creating a logical palette from a color table.)

Blitting from a Memory DC to a Memory DC

When the destination device context is a memory DC that contains a DDB, the need to use a palette depends on what type of bitmap the source (memory) DC contains. If the source DC contains another DDB, and both DDBs use the same palette, then you don't need to bother with calling the **SelectPalette** or **RealizePalette** functions. In this case, the pixels of both DDBs refer to palette entries, and therefore, there's no mapping involved. If the source DC contains a DIB section bitmap, then a palette is required because the GDI must map the pixels of the DIB section to the correct palette entries. In this case, you must call the **SelectPalette** and **RealizePalette** functions before blitting. The **RealizePalette** function instructs the GDI to map the (device-independent) colors of the DIB section to the (device-dependent) entries of the palette that you specify via the **SelectPalette** function; the system palette is not changed in this case. This is the only situation where you'll use the **RealizePalette** function for something other than changing the system palette. (Again, see Chapter 7 for information on creating a logical palette from a color table.)

When the destination device context is a memory DC that contains a DIB section bitmap, the need to use a palette is also governed by what type of bitmap the source (memory) DC contains. If the source DC contains a DDB, then you need to do two things: first, if the DIB section bitmap has a color table, you need to modify it according to the colors of the DDB's palette, like so:

```
#include <cassert>
// NOTE: hPal is a handle to the DDB's palette

PALETTEENTRY palE[256];
if (GetPaletteEntries(hPal, 0, 256, palE) == 256)
{
   RGBQUAD rgbQ[256];
   for (int index = 0; index < 256; ++index)
   {
      rgbQ[index].rgbRed = palE[index].peRed;
      rgbQ[index].rgbGreen = palE[index].peGreen;
      rgbQ[index].rgbBlue = palE[index].peBlue;
      rgbQ[index].rgbReserved = 0;
   }
   assert(
      SetDIBColorTable(hCopyMemDC, 0, 256, rgbQ)
      );
}
```

Next, you need to call the **SelectPalette** function to select the DDB's palette into the destination DC (i.e., the memory DC into which the DIB section bitmap is selected) before blitting. There's no need to call the **RealizePalette** function in this case because the source is a DDB—that is, the pixels of the source already refer to palette entries. In contrast, when the source DC contains a DIB section bitmap, there's no need for a palette. In this case, because both the source and the destination are DIB sections, and thus device-independent entities, you don't have to bother with a (device-specific) palette. You do, however, need to ensure that the color table of the target DIB section contains the same entries as that of the source DIB section (if the destination DIB section uses a color table; the GDI will perform a color-match otherwise).

It's important to keep in mind that, regardless of the type of bitmap you're working with, there's no harm in calling the **SelectPalette** and **RealizePalette** functions. In fact, doing so might save many hours of debugging later down the road. There's a tradeoff here between efficiency and maintainability; in this case, I recommend the latter.

Immediate Solutions

Creating a Logical Palette

To create a logical palette, you use the **CreatePalette** function:

```
HPALETTE CreatePalette(
    IN CONST LOGPALETTE *lplgpl    // pointer to a LOGPALETTE structure
   );
```

The **lplgpl** data member is specified as the address of a **LOGPALETTE** structure. All of the data members of this structure must be properly initialized before its address is passed to the **CreatePalette** function. Upon success, the **CreatePalette** function returns a handle to the new logical palette object. If the **CreatePalette** function fails, the return value is **NULL**.

The following code snippet demonstrates how to properly initialize a **LOGPALETTE** structure and then use this structure with the **CreatePalette** function to create a logical palette that contains a spectrum of green shades:

```
HPALETTE hPal = NULL;

const short num_entries = 256;
const size_t total_size =
   sizeof(LOGPALETTE) +
   (num_entries - 1) * sizeof(PALETTEENTRY);

unsigned char* buffer = new unsigned char[total_size];
try
{
   LPLOGPALETTE lpLogPal =
      reinterpret_cast<LPLOGPALETTE>(buffer);

   lpLogPal->palVersion = 0x300;
   lpLogPal->palNumEntries = num_entries;

   for (int index = 0; index < num_entries; ++index)
   {
      const unsigned char red_intensity = 0;
      const unsigned char green_intensity = index;
      const unsigned char blue_intensity = 0;
```

```
            lpLogPal->palPalEntry[index].peRed = red_intensity;
            lpLogPal->palPalEntry[index].peGreen = green_intensity;
            lpLogPal->palPalEntry[index].peBlue = blue_intensity;
            lpLogPal->palPalEntry[index].peFlags = 0;
        }
        hPal = CreatePalette(lpLogPal);
        if (!hPal) throw;
        delete [] buffer; buffer = NULL;
    }
    catch (...)
    {
        delete [] buffer;
    }
```

When a logical palette is no longer needed, you should destroy it by passing its handle to the **DeleteObject** function. Do not, however, call the **DeleteObject** function on a logical palette while it's selected into a device context; you must deselect the logical palette before destroying it.

Selecting a Logical Palette into a Device Context

To select a logical palette into a device context, you use the **SelectPalette** function:

```
HPALETTE SelectPalette(
    IN HDC hdc,                  // handle to the target device context
    IN HPALETTE hpal,            // handle to the logical palette object
    IN BOOL bForceBackground     // foreground or background realization flag
   );
```

The **hdc** parameter identifies the device context into which the logical palette is selected. The handle of this logical palette is specified by the **hpal** parameter. The **bForceBackground** parameter specifies how the logical palette is to be realized when the **RealizePalette** function is called by a foreground window. If the **bForceBackground** parameter is set to **TRUE**, subsequent calls to the **RealizePalette** function will cause the logical palette to be realized in the background. If **bForceBackground** is set to **FALSE**, subsequent calls to the **RealizePalette** function will cause the logical palette to be realized in the foreground. This parameter has no effect when the **RealizePalette** function is called by a window that's in the background; in this case, the logical palette is always realized as a background palette. This parameter also has no effect when the **hdc** parameter refers to a memory DC; in this case, the system palette is not used.

***NOTE:** You can select a logical palette into more than one device context at a time. However, keep in mind that if you change this logical palette afterward, the colors of all associated device contexts will be affected. This issue is not important with other graphic objects, such as pens and brushes, because (except for **DC_PEN** and **DC_BRUSH**) there's no way to manipulate these types of graphic objects after they've been created. There are, however, functions that can be used to manipulate a logical palette after it has been created (see "Manipulating the Entries of a Logical Palette").*

WARNING! If you plan to select a logical palette into more than one DC at a time, ensure that these DCs are compatible (i.e., they refer to the same device).

If the **SelectPalette** function is successful, it returns a handle to the DC's previously selected palette. If the **SelectPalette** function fails, it returns **NULL**. For example, to select a logical palette (**hPal**) as a background palette into a window's common device context, you use the **SelectPalette** function like so:

```
case WM_PAINT:
{
   PAINTSTRUCT ps;
   HDC hDC = BeginPaint(hWnd, &ps);
   HPALETTE hOldPal = SelectPalette(hDC, hPal, FALSE);
   try
   {
      //
      // be sure to call the RealizePalette function beforehand,
      // such as, in response to the WM_QUERYNEWPALETTE message
      //

      // render to hDC...
   }
   catch (...)
   {
      SelectPalette(hDC, hOldPal, FALSE);
      EndPaint(hWnd, &ps);
   }
   SelectPalette(hDC, hOldPal, FALSE);
   EndPaint(hWnd, &ps);
   break;
}
```

As this code demonstrates, it's customary to track and select the original palette back into the DC after you're done rendering to the DC. This step must be performed before you destroy your logical palette. You can select the original palette back into the DC with a **TRUE** or a **FALSE** **bForceBackground** parameter. However, unless the original palette is the stock default palette (**DEFAULT_PALETTE**), don't call the **RealizePalette** function afterward if you've reselected the original palette with a **FALSE bForceBackground** parameter. The **RealizePalette** function has no effect if the DC contains the stock default palette, but it will change the system palette if the DC contains a non-stock foreground logical palette.

Realizing a Logical Palette

To realize a logical palette, you use the **RealizePalette** function:

```
UINT RealizePalette(
    HDC hdc          // handle to the target device context
   );
```

The **hdc** parameter identifies the device context that contains the logical palette that you want to be realized. This palette must have been selected into **hdc** via the **SelectPalette** function. If **hdc** identifies a display device context, the system palette is changed accordingly. Just how the system palette is changed depends on the **peFlags** data member that corresponds to each entry of **hdc**'s logical palette and on how this palette was selected (see "Foreground and Background Palette Realization" in the "In Depth" section). If the **RealizePalette** function is successful, it returns the number of entries in the logical palette that were mapped to entries in the system palette. (This is not necessarily the number of system palette entries that have been changed.) If the **RealizePalette** function fails, the return value is **GDI_ERROR**.

NOTE: *The **RealizePalette** function has no effect when it's called for a device context that contains the stock default logical palette (**DEFAULT_PALETTE**). In this case, the return value is always zero.*

Typically, the **RealizePalette** function is called immediately after the **SelectPalette** function, as demonstrated in the following code snippet:

```
HDC hDC = GetDC(hWnd);
HPALETTE hOldPal = SelectPalette(hDC, hPal, FALSE);
try
{
   const UINT num_changed = RealizePalette(hDC);
   if (num_changed > 0 && num_changed != GDI_ERROR)
   {
      // ...
   }
}
```

```
catch (...)
{
   SelectPalette(hDC, hOldPal, FALSE);
   ReleaseDC(hWnd, hDC);
}
SelectPalette(hDC, hOldPal, FALSE);
ReleaseDC(hWnd, hDC);
```

Retrieving the Entries of a Logical Palette

To retrieve a copy of the entries of a logical palette, you use the **GetPaletteEntries** function:

```
UINT GetPaletteEntries(
    IN HPALETTE hpal,          // handle to the logical palette
    IN UINT iStart,            // zero-based index of first logical
                               // palette entry to retrieve
    IN UINT nEntries,          // total number of logical palette
                               // entries to retrieve
    IN CONST PALETTEENTRY *lppe // pointer to an array of PALETTEENTRYs
   );
```

The **hpal** parameter identifies the logical palette whose entries you want to retrieve. The **iStart** parameter specifies the zero-based index of the first entry to retrieve. The **nEntries** parameter specifies the total number of entries to retrieve. The **lppe** parameter is specified as a pointer to an array of **PALETTEENTRY** structures that will be filled with a copy of **hpal**'s entries. To determine how much memory to allocate for this array, you first call the **GetPaletteEntries** function with a **NULL lppe** parameter. In this case, the function returns a value indicating the total number of entries in the logical palette. When passed a non-**NULL lppe** parameter, the **GetPaletteEntries** function returns a value indicating the number of palette entries that have been copied to the specified **lppe** array.

TIP: *To change one or more entries of a logical palette, use the* ***SetPaletteEntries*** *function (see "Manipulating the Entries of a Logical Palette").*

The following code snippet demonstrates how to use the **GetPaletteEntries** function to retrieve all 256 entries of a logical palette (**hPal**). The corresponding color of each palette entry is brightened, and then these changes are put into effect via the **SetPaletteEntries** function:

```
//
// first call GetPaletteEntries with a NULL lppe
// parameter to determine the total number of
// entries that the logical palette contains
//
const short num_entries = GetPaletteEntries(hPal, 0, 0, NULL);
if (num_entries == 0) return;

LPPALETTEENTRY pPalEntry = new PALETTEENTRY[num_entries];
try
{
   //
   // call GetPaletteEntries again, this
   // time to actually copy the entries
   //
   const short num_got =
      GetPaletteEntries(hPal, 0, num_entries, pPalEntry);

   const float clip_max = 255.0;
   const float brighten_by = 1.5; // 150%
   for (int index = 0; index < num_got; ++index)
   {
      pPalEntry[index].peRed = static_cast<unsigned char>(
         min(clip_max, pPalEntry[index].peRed * brighten_by)
         );
      pPalEntry[index].peGreen = static_cast<unsigned char>(
         min(clip_max, pPalEntry[index].peGreen * brighten_by)
         );
      pPalEntry[index].peBlue = static_cast<unsigned char>(
         min(clip_max, pPalEntry[index].peBlue * brighten_by)
         );
   }
   // set the entries
   SetPaletteEntries(hPal, 0, num_got, pPalEntry);
   delete [] pPalEntry; pPalEntry = NULL;
}
catch (...)
{
   delete [] pPalEntry;
}
```

Likewise, the following example demonstrates the use of the **GetPaletteEntries** function as part of an application-defined function that copies a logical palette:

```
HPALETTE CopyPalette(
    IN const HPALETTE hPal
   )
```

```
{
   HPALETTE hCopyPal = NULL;

   const short num_entries =
      GetPaletteEntries(hPal, 0, 0, NULL);
   if (num_entries > 0)
   {
      const size_t total_size =
         sizeof(LOGPALETTE) +
         (num_entries - 1) * sizeof(PALETTEENTRY);

      unsigned char* buffer = new unsigned char[total_size];
      try
      {
         LPLOGPALETTE lpLogPal =
            reinterpret_cast<LPLOGPALETTE>(buffer);

         lpLogPal->palVersion = 0x300;
         lpLogPal->palNumEntries =
            GetPaletteEntries(
               hPal, 0, num_entries,
               lpLogPal->palPalEntry
               );
         hCopyPal = CreatePalette(lpLogPal);
      }
      catch (...)
      {
         delete [] buffer;
         return NULL;
      }
      delete [] buffer;
   }
   return hPal;
}
```

Manipulating the Entries of a Logical Palette

To change the entries of a logical palette, you use the **SetPaletteEntries** function:

```
UINT SetPaletteEntries(
    IN HPALETTE hpal,            // handle to the logical palette
    IN UINT iStart,              // zero-based index of first logical
                                 // palette entry to change
```

```
    IN UINT cEntries,             // total number of logical palette
                                  // entries to change
    IN CONST PALETTEENTRY *lppe   // pointer to an array of PALETTEENTRYs
  );
```

The **hpal** parameter identifies the logical palette whose entries you want to change. The **iStart** parameter specifies the zero-based index of the first entry to change. The **cEntries** parameter specifies the total number of entries to change. The **lppe** parameter is specified as a pointer to an array of **PALETTEENTRY** structures that defines the new palette entries. If the **SetPaletteEntries** function is successful, it returns a value indicating how many of the logical palette's entries have been changed. Thus, if the **SetPaletteEntries** function fails, it returns 0.

***TIP:** To retrieve a logical palette's entries, use the **GetPaletteEntries** function (see "Retrieving the Entries of a Logical Palette").*

***NOTE:** Calling the **SetPaletteEntries** function while your logical palette is selected into a display DC will not automatically change the system palette—you must still use the **RealizePalette** function for this purpose.*

The following code snippet demonstrates how to change all 256 entries of a logical palette (**hPal**) to different shades of blue:

```
PALETTEENTRY palEntry[256];
memset(palEntry, 0, 256 * sizeof(PALETTEENTRY));
for (int index = 0; index < 256; ++index)
{
   palEntry[index].peBlue = index;
}
SetPaletteEntries(hPal, 0, 256, palEntry);
```

Retrieving the Entries of the System Palette

To retrieve the entries of the system palette, you use the **GetSystemPaletteEntries** function:

```
UINT GetSystemPaletteEntries(
    HDC hdc,                      // handle to the target device context
    IN UINT iStart,               // zero-based index of first system
                                  // palette entry to retrieve
    IN UINT nEntries,             // total number of system palette
                                  // entries to retrieve
    IN CONST PALETTEENTRY *lppe   // pointer to an array of PALETTEENTRYs
  );
```

The **hdc** parameter is specified as a handle to the device context that identifies the device whose corresponding system palette you want to retrieve. For example, to retrieve the entries of a display's system palette, you pass a handle to a display device context as the **hdc** parameter. The **iStart** parameter specifies the zero-based index of the first entry to retrieve. The **nEntries** parameter specifies the total number of entries to retrieve. The **lppe** parameter is specified as a pointer to an array of **PALETTEENTRY** structures that will be filled with a copy of the system palette's entries. To determine how much memory to allocate for this array, you first call the **GetSystemPaletteEntries** function with a **NULL lppe** parameter, in which case the function returns a value indicating the total number of entries in the system palette. If you pass a non-**NULL lppe** parameter to the **GetSystemPaletteEntries** function, it returns a value indicating the number of palette entries that have been copied to the specified **lppe** array.

TIP: *To change one or more entries of a display's system palette, do the following: first create a logical palette; then select this logical palette into a display device context; and then realize this palette in response to the* ***WM_QUERYNEWPALETTE*** *message (or at another time when your window is in the foreground).*

The following code snippet demonstrates the use of the **GetSystemPaletteEntries** function to retrieve a copy of all of the primary display's system palette entries:

```
HDC hScreenDC = GetDC(NULL);
try
{
   const short num_entries =
      GetSystemPaletteEntries(hScreenDC, 0, 0, NULL);
   if (num_entries > 0)
   {
      LPPALETTEENTRY pPalEntry = new PALETTEENTRY[num_entries];
      try
      {
         const short num_got =
            GetSystemPaletteEntries(
               hScreenDC, 0, num_entries, pPalEntry
               );
         ReleaseDC(NULL, hScreenDC); hScreenDC = NULL;

         //
         // work with pPalEntry...
         //
      }
```

```
      catch (...)
      {
         delete [] pPalEntry;
         throw;
      }
      delete [] pPalEntry;
   }
}
catch (...)
{
   if (hScreenDC) ReleaseDC(NULL, hScreenDC);
}
```

Likewise, the following example demonstrates how to use the **GetSystem-PaletteEntries** function as part of an application-defined function that creates a logical palette that contains the same entries as the current system palette:

```
HPALETTE CopySystemPalette()
{
   HPALETTE hPal = NULL;
   HDC hScreenDC = GetDC(NULL);
   try
   {
      const short num_entries =
         GetSystemPaletteEntries(hScreenDC, 0, 0, NULL);
      if (num_entries > 0)
      {
         const size_t total_size =
            sizeof(LOGPALETTE) +
            (num_entries - 1) * sizeof(PALETTEENTRY);

         unsigned char* buffer = new unsigned char[total_size];
         try
         {
            LPLOGPALETTE lpLogPal =
               reinterpret_cast<LPLOGPALETTE>(buffer);

            lpLogPal->palVersion = 0x300;
            lpLogPal->palNumEntries =
               GetSystemPaletteEntries(
                  hScreenDC, 0, num_entries,
                  lpLogPal->palPalEntry
                  );
            hPal = CreatePalette(lpLogPal);
         }
```

```
            catch (...)
            {
               delete [] buffer;
               throw;
            }
            delete [] buffer;
         }
      }
      catch (...)
      {
         ReleaseDC(NULL, hScreenDC);
         return NULL;
      }
      return hPal;
   }
```

Modifying the System Palette's Static Entries

To modify the system palette's static entries, you use a combination of the **SetSystemPaletteUse** function and the usual **SelectPalette** and **RealizePalette** functions.

WARNING! This operation has the potential to adjust all (Windows 2000) or nearly all (Windows 9x/NT) of the colors on the end user's display, including the colors that are used for standard user-interface elements, such as the Taskbar, the desktop wallpaper, and the text of the system's desktop icons. You should use this technique with caution and ideally warn the end user of your action.

The **SetSystemPaletteUse** function is used to mark all 20 (or 18 in Windows 9x or NT) of the system palette's static entries as dynamic (i.e., non-static):

```
UINT SetSystemPaletteUse(
     IN HDC hdc,          // handle to a display device context
     IN UINT uUsage       // identifier that specifies the number of static
                          // entries the system palette will contain
   );
```

The **hdc** parameter is specified as a handle to a display device context. Typically, this parameter is specified as a handle to the screen's DC. The **uUsage** parameter is used to adjust the number of static palette entries that the system palette will contain. In Windows 2000, you can mark all entries as non-static by specifying this parameter as **SYSPAL_NOSTATIC256** (3). In prior versions of Windows, you can mark all entries except black (index 0) and white (index 255) as non-static by specifying this parameter as **SYSPAL_NOSTATIC** (2). To restore the system palette to its default number of 20 static entries, you specify **uUsage** as **SYSPAL_STATIC** (1).

If the **SetSystemPaletteUse** function is successful, it returns the corresponding identifier (**SYSPAL_STATIC**, **SYSPAL_NOSTATIC**, or **SYSPAL_NOSTATIC256**) for the previous state of the system palette. If the **SetSystemPaletteUse** function fails, the returned value is **SYSPAL_ERROR** (0).

After you've marked the system palette's 20 (or 18) static entries as non-static, you can manipulate all 256 (or 254) entries of the system palette via the usual **SelectPalette** and **RealizePalette** functions. The following code snippet demonstrates the use of the **SetSystemPaletteUse** function in response to the **WM_QUERYNEWPALETTE** message to mark the system palette's static entries as non-static. Later, in response to the **WM_ACTIVATEAPP** message, the **SetSystemPaletteUse** function is used to restore the status of these entries:

```
case WM_QUERYNEWPALETTE:
{
   HDC hDC = GetDC(hWnd);
   HPALETTE hOldPal = SelectPalette(hDC, hPal, FALSE);
   try
   {
      int old_use =  SetSystemPaletteUse(hDC, SYSPAL_NOSTATIC);
      if (RealizePalette(hDC))
      {
         InvalidateRect(hWnd, NULL, TRUE);
      }
   }
   catch (...)
   {
      // clean up
      SetSystemPaletteUse(hDC, SYSPAL_STATIC);
      SelectPalette(hDC, hOldPal, FALSE);
      ReleaseDC(hWnd, hDC);
   }
   // clean up
   SelectPalette(hDC, hOldPal, FALSE);
   ReleaseDC(hWnd, hDC);
   break;
}
case WM_ACTIVATEAPP:
{
   if (!wParam) // if being deactivated
   {
      HDC hScreenDC = GetDC(NULL);
      try
```

```
            {
               SetSystemPaletteUse(hScreenDC, SYSPAL_STATIC);
            }
            catch (...)
            {
               ReleaseDC(NULL, hScreenDC);
            }
            ReleaseDC(NULL, hScreenDC);
         }
         break;
      }
```

***TIP:** After you change the system palette's entries, there's a chance that the user-interface elements will be displayed in colors that make them unrecognizable. In this case, you should retrieve and store the color of each user-interface element by using the **GetSysColor** function, and then match each stored color to one in the new system palette. After you've matched each color, use the **SetSysColors** function to change the color of each user-interface element to its closest match. Also, be sure to restore the previous colors if your application loses foreground status.*

Determining if a Device Uses a Palette

To determine if a device is a palette-based device, you use the **GetDeviceCaps** function:

```
int GetDeviceCaps(
    IN HDC hdc,         // handle to the target device context
    IN int nIndex       // index of device capability to retrieve
   );
```

The **hdc** parameter is specified as a handle to the device context that identifies the device whose palette-based status is in question. The **nIndex** parameter specifies the capability to query; set this parameter to **RASTERCAPS** (38). If the **GetDeviceCaps** function is successful, it returns a value that's packed with bits that indicate all of the device's raster capabilities. You use the bitwise **AND** operator (&) to combine this return value with the **RC_PALETTE** (256) identifier to determine if the device uses a palette.

The following example implements an application-defined function, **IsPaletteBasedDevice**, which demonstrates the use of the **GetDeviceCaps** function to determine if a device is palette-based:

```
BOOL IsPaletteBasedDisplay()
{
   HDC hScreenDC = GetDC(NULL);
```

```
    BOOL is_palette_based =
        GetDeviceCaps(hScreenDC, RASTERCAPS) & RC_PALETTE;
    ReleaseDC(NULL, hScreenDC);
    return is_palette_based;
}
```

TIP: *You can call the application-defined* ***IsPaletteBasedDevice*** *function (see the "In Depth" section) at the start of your application, and update its value only in response to the* ***WM_DISPLAYCHANGE*** *message.*

Handling the WM_QUERYNEWPALETTE Message

The **WM_QUERYNEWPALETTE** message is sent right before a window is brought to the foreground. This is the best time to manipulate the system palette's entries by realizing a foreground logical palette. Specifically, in response to this message, you should perform the following steps:

1. Retrieve a handle to your window's common device context (e.g., by using the **GetDC** function).
2. Select the logical palette into this device context as a foreground palette. You do this by using the **SelectPalette** function and specifying **FALSE** as the function's third (**bForceBackground**) parameter. Store the **SelectPalette** function's return value (of type **HPALETTE**) so that you can use it in Step 5.
3. Realize the foreground logical palette (and thus change the system palette's entries) by using the **RealizePalette** function.
4. If the return value of the **RealizePalette** function (called from Step 3) is greater than zero (indicating that one or more of the system palette's entries have changed), you should repaint the appropriate client areas of your window (e.g., via the **InvalidateRect** function).
5. Select the device context's original palette (whose handle you stored in Step 2) back into the DC by using the **SelectPalette** function. Because the original palette is the stock default logical palette (**DEFAULT_PALETTE**), the **bForceBackground** parameter of the **SelectPalette** function is irrelevant. You can optionally realize this palette by using the **Realize-Palette** function.
6. Release your window's common device context (e.g., by using the **ReleaseDC** function).

The following code snippet demonstrates how to handle the **WM_QUERY-NEWPALETTE** message. Here, **hPal** is a handle to a logical palette:

```
case WM_QUERYNEWPALETTE:
{
   // STEP 1: Retrieve a handle to the window's DC
   HDC hDC = GetDC(hWnd);

   // STEP 2: Select the logical palette
   HPALETTE hOldPal = SelectPalette(hDC, hPal, FALSE);
   try
   {
      // STEP 3: Realize the logical palette
      if (RealizePalette(hDC))
      {
         // STEP 4: Repaint if the system palette changes
         InvalidateRect(hWnd, NULL, TRUE);
      }
   }
   catch (...)
   {
      SelectPalette(hDC, hOldPal, FALSE);
      ReleaseDC(hWnd, hDC);
   }
   // STEP 5: Reselect the original palette back into the DC
   SelectPalette(hDC, hOldPal, FALSE);

   // STEP 6: Clean up
   ReleaseDC(hWnd, hDC);
   break;
}
```

Handling the WM_PALETTECHANGED Message

The **WM_PALETTECHANGED** message is sent when another window has realized a foreground palette (and thus changed the system palette). This is the best time to claim any unused entries in the system palette by realizing a background logical palette. Specifically, in response to this message, you should perform the following steps:

1. Test the **wParam** parameter for equality with your window's handle. If these two quantities are not equal, proceed to Step 2; otherwise, **break**.

2. Retrieve a handle to your window's common device context (e.g., by using the **GetDC** function).
3. Select the logical palette into this device context as a background palette. You do this by using the **SelectPalette** function and specifying **TRUE** as the function's third (**bForceBackground**) parameter. Store the **SelectPalette** function's return value (of type **HPALETTE**) so that you can use it in Step 6.
4. Realize the background logical palette (and thus change any unused entries in the system palette) by using the **RealizePalette** function.
5. If the return value of the **RealizePalette** function (called from Step 4) is greater than zero (indicating that one or more of the system palette's entries have changed), you should repaint the appropriate client areas of your window (e.g., via the **InvalidateRect** function).
6. Select the device context's original palette (whose handle you stored in Step 3) back into the DC by using the **SelectPalette** function. Because the original palette is the stock default logical palette (**DEFAULT_PALETTE**), the **bForceBackground** parameter of the **SelectPalette** function is irrelevant. You can optionally realize this palette by using the **RealizePalette** function.
7. Release your window's common device context (e.g., by using the **ReleaseDC** function).

The following code snippet demonstrates how to handle the **WM_PALETTE-CHANGED** message. Here, **hPal** is a handle to a logical palette:

```
case WM_PALETTECHANGED:
{
   // STEP 1: Make sure your window didn't invoke this message
   if (reinterpret_cast<HWND>(wParam) == hWnd) break;

   // STEP 2: Retrieve a handle to the window's DC
   HDC hDC = GetDC(hWnd);

   // STEP 3: Select the logical palette
   HPALETTE hOldPal = SelectPalette(hDC, hPal, TRUE);
   try
   {
      // STEP 4: Realize the logical palette
      if (RealizePalette(hDC))
      {
         // STEP 5: Repaint if the system palette changes
         InvalidateRect(hWnd, NULL, TRUE);
      }
   }
```

```
    catch (...)
    {
        SelectPalette(hDC, hOldPal, FALSE);
        ReleaseDC(hWnd, hDC);
    }
    // STEP 6: Reselect the original palette back into the DC
    SelectPalette(hDC, hOldPal, FALSE);

    // STEP 7: Clean up
    ReleaseDC(hWnd, hDC);
    break;
}
```

Note that this code is very similar to the code presented in the solution "Handling the **WM_QUERYNEWPALETTE** Message." In fact, you can share the same code for both messages, like so:

```
case WM_PALETTECHANGED:
{
    // STEP 1: Make sure your window didn't invoke this message
    if (reinterpret_cast<HWND>(wParam) == hWnd) break;
    // otherwise, proceed with the WM_QUERYNEWPALETTE code
}
case WM_QUERYNEWPALETTE:
{
    // STEP 2: Retrieve a handle to the window's DC
    HDC hDC = GetDC(hWnd);

    // STEP 3: Select the logical palette
    HPALETTE hOldPal = SelectPalette(hDC, hPal, FALSE);
    try
    {
        // STEP 4: Realize the logical palette
        if (RealizePalette(hDC))
        {
            // STEP 5: Repaint if the system palette changes
            InvalidateRect(hWnd, NULL, TRUE);
        }
    }
    catch (...)
    {
        SelectPalette(hDC, hOldPal, FALSE);
        ReleaseDC(hWnd, hDC);
    }
```

```
    // STEP 6: Reselect the original palette back into the DC
    SelectPalette(hDC, hOldPal, FALSE);

    // STEP 7: Clean up
    ReleaseDC(hWnd, hDC);
    break;
}
```

***NOTE:** Some developers prefer to use the **UpdateColors** function in Step 5 instead of the **InvalidateRect** function. This is an option, but use it only in response to the **WM_PALETTECHANGED** message. You should not use **UpdateColors** in response to the **WM_QUERYNEWPALETTE** message. Also, note that the **UpdateColors** function will result in a loss of color accuracy after subsequent calls. (The **UpdateColors** function accepts a handle to the DC in which the logical palette is selected and returns a Boolean value indicating success or failure.)*

When the code is shared, notice that the initial **SelectPalette** function call (in Step 3) is made with a **FALSE bForceBackground** parameter for both the **WM_PALETTECHANGED** and **WM_QUERYNEWPALETTE** messages. This is still acceptable because the **WM_PALETTECHANGED** message is sent with a **wParam** value that's different from the window's handle only when the window itself is in the background. As a result, in this case, the logical palette will be realized as a background palette (for the **WM_PALETTECHANGED** case) regardless of the **bForceBackground** parameter specification.

Chapter 10

Coordinate Spaces

In Depth

A *coordinate space* is exactly what its name implies: it's a *space* in which each location has a corresponding *coordinate*. Imagine that you have two 12-inch rulers. If you place these rulers on the ground, perpendicular to each other, as depicted in Figure 10.1, you've essentially defined a two-dimensional coordinate space. Here the rulers serve as the *axes* (the lines that serve as references for locations) of your coordinate space.

The *extent* of this coordinate space, which is denoted by the shaded area in Figure 10.1, is the area encompassed by the two rulers. Also, in Figure 10.1, notice that these rulers are oriented such that their zero-inch marks are located in the corner that they form. This corner point is called the *origin* of the coordinate space—it serves as a reference to which all points in the space are relative. In this way, you can denote any position within your coordinate space by exactly two quantities: a position, in inches, along the horizontal ruler, and another position, in inches, along the vertical ruler. So, for example, if a fly lands anywhere within your coordinate space, as depicted in Figure 10.2, you can pinpoint its position by

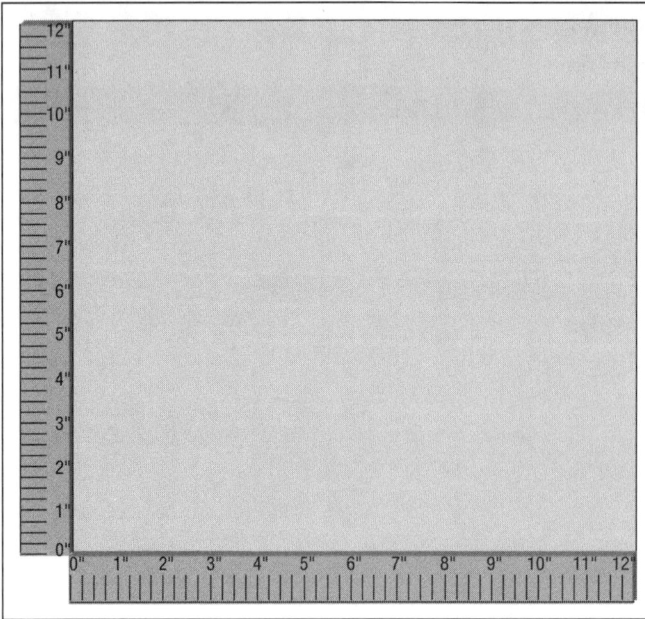

Figure 10.1 A two-dimensional coordinate space is defined by two axes.

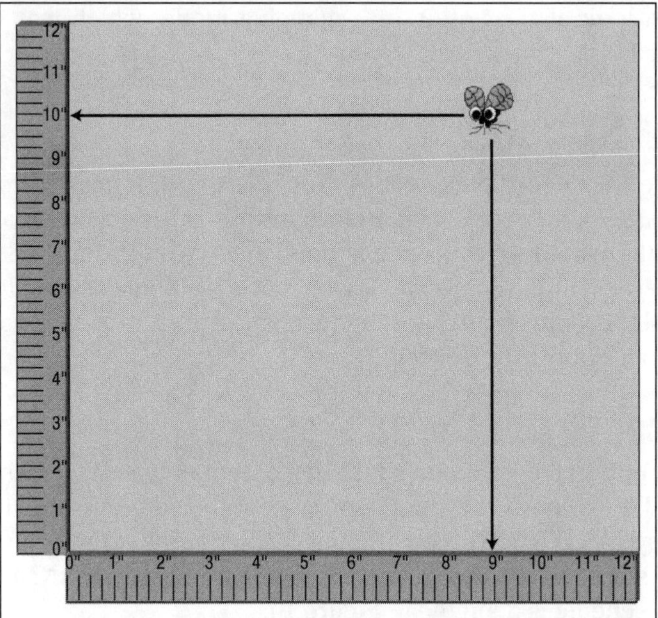

Figure 10.2 In a two-dimensional coordinate space, the position of an object can be described by its horizontal location and its vertical location along the axes.

moving some number of inches along the horizontal ruler and some number of inches along the vertical ruler.

In a *Cartesian* coordinate space, the horizontal ruler is typically denoted by the variable "x" and is called the *x-axis* or the *abscissa*. The vertical ruler is typically denoted by the variable "y" and is called the *y-axis* or the *ordinate*. In this case, you can describe a specific point within a coordinate space by its *x-coordinate* and its *y-coordinate*, like so for the fly:

$$(x_{fly}, y_{fly}) = (\textit{distance along the horizontal ruler, distance along the vertical ruler})$$

$$= (10, 9)$$

This chapter is dedicated to coordinate spaces. We'll start by discussing the standard coordinate spaces that are used by the GDI, and how the points that you pass to a GDI function are interpreted and massaged to produce output on a device. Next, we'll examine several coordinate-space transformations, and how you can use matrices to describe and control the way the GDI maps points in one coordinate space to points in another coordinate space. We'll expand on this topic by looking at several standard transformation matrices that are commonly used to produce effects such as rotation, shearing, scaling, and translation. Finally, we'll take an in-depth look at the notion of a mapping mode, which was first introduced in Chapter 1.

GDI Coordinate Spaces

In Windows, there are four coordinate spaces: a *world space*, a *page space*, a *device space*, and a *physical-device space*. Before output is produced on a device, the GDI must take whatever coordinates you specify (either in world or page units) and convert them into physical-device units. We'll discuss the logic (and the math) behind this conversion later in this chapter, but for now, let's examine each of these four coordinate spaces.

The World Space

The *world space* is an optional coordinate space that's used only in Windows NT and Windows 2000. The extent of the world space in both the vertical and the horizontal direction is **MAXDWORD**. The origin is located right at the center of the coordinate space, so the x-axis and the y-axis both range from –**MAXLONG** to +**MAXLONG**. This scheme is depicted in Figure 10.3.

The world space isn't used by default. Instead, all display device contexts initially use the page space (which we will discuss next). In Windows NT and Windows 2000, you can use the **SetGraphicsMode** function to instruct a device context to use the world space, like so:

```
int old_graphics_mode = SetGraphicsMode(hDC, GM_ADVANCED);
```

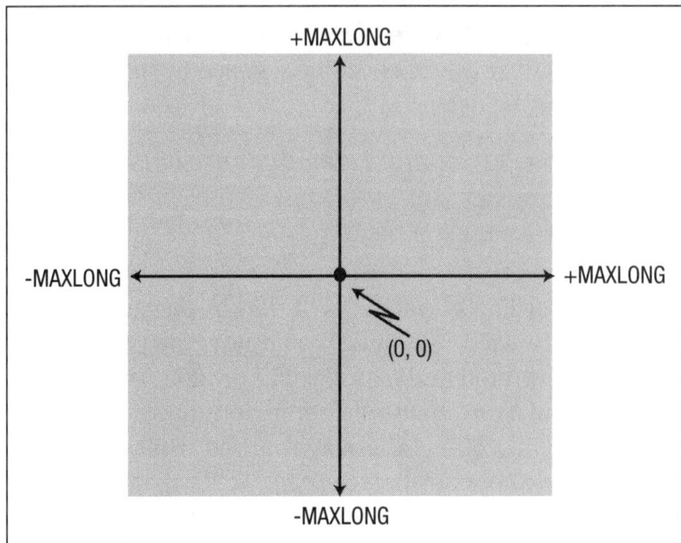

Figure 10.3 The world space.

The **GM_ADVANCED** (2) identifier signals the **SetGraphicsMode** function to switch the device context into *advanced* mode. When a DC is set to the advanced graphics mode, all coordinates are interpreted as being in world-space units. In contrast, when a DC is set to the default graphics mode, which is signified by the **GM_COMPATIBLE** (1) identifier (the default for all display DCs), all coordinates are in page-space units. As we'll discuss shortly, the world space is useful when you need to perform a specific coordinate-space transformation.

Although you can use the **SetGraphicsMode** function in Windows 95 and Windows 98, on these platforms, specifying the **GM_ADVANCED** identifier has no effect. Here the graphics mode of a device context is always **GM_COMPATIBLE**.

The Page Space

The *page space*, which is commonly referred to as the *logical space*, is the default coordinate space of all display device contexts. The extents and origin of the page space are similar to those of the world space: the axes range from –**MAXLONG** to +**MAXLONG**, and the origin is located at the center of the space (see Figure 10.3). As we'll examine later in this chapter (see "Mapping Modes"), the page space is used with the device space to provide a means of working with real physical units, such as inches, centimeters, or twips, just to name a few.

The Device Space

The *device space* is a coordinate space whose units are specific to a device and are thus called *device units*. For the majority of devices, device units refer to pixels. However, the horizontal and vertical extents of the device space have no relation to the physical device itself. Instead, the x-axis and the y-axis of the device space range from –(**MINLONG**/16) to +(**MINLONG**/16). And, as with the world and page spaces, the origin of the device space is located at the center of the space. This scheme is depicted in Figure 10.4.

The Physical Device Space

The *physical device space*, which is often called the *output space*, uses the same units as those of the device space: device units. However, the extents and the origin of the physical device space (unlike those of the device space) depend on the device itself. For example, if the output device is a 1200-dpi printer using 8.5"-by-11" paper, then the horizontal extent of the physical device space is 10,200 (1200x8.5) device units (dots), and the vertical extent of the physical device space is 13,200 (1200x11) device units (dots). Figure 10.5 depicts the layout of the physical device space for this example.

Note that it's up to the printer to decide where the *origin* of the physical device space should be. In other words, such factors as whether the printer uses the

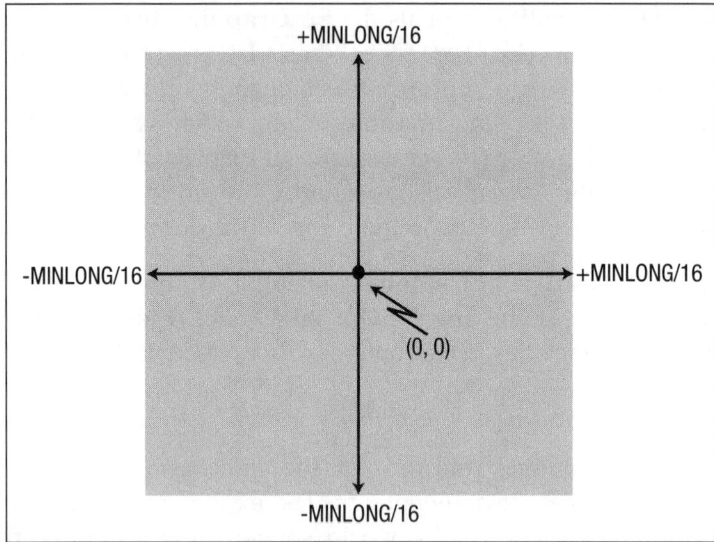

Figure 10.4 The device space.

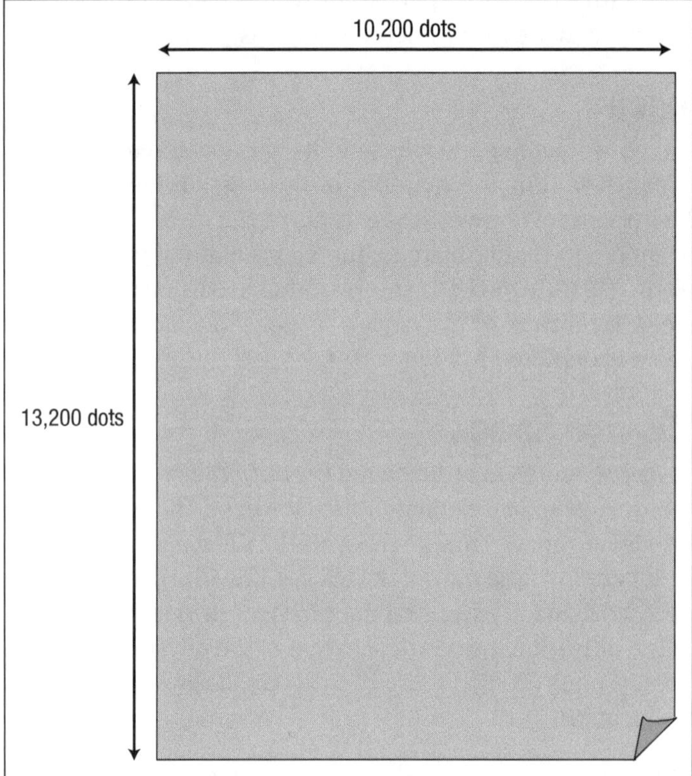

Figure 10.5 The physical device space for an 8.5"-by-11" sheet of paper in a 1200-dpi printer.

front or the back side of the paper and which corner the printer uses as the "top left" location completely depend on the printer itself. If you've ever used letterhead in a laser printer, you're probably all too familiar with this often annoying "variable origin" notion.

Coordinate-Space Transformations

A *coordinate-space transformation* is a mapping from one coordinate space to another. For example, consider the coordinate space that you defined earlier using the two rulers. Now imagine that you flip these rulers over to expose the sides with centimeters (rather than inches). Here you've essentially performed a coordinate-space transformation; that is, you've mapped or "transformed" every point in the original "inches" coordinate space to the new "centimeters" coordinate space. Assuming that you haven't scared the fly off by flipping the rulers over, the fly's new position will be described in centimeters. Although the fly itself didn't move, its coordinates have. Specifically, because the units of the axes have changed, the fly's position is no longer (10, 9) but is instead (25.4, 22.9). In other words, you've mapped the point (10, 9) to the point (25.4, 22.9). That's all a coordinate-space transformation is: a mapping of points from one system to another.

Matrix Notation

The most convenient way to describe a coordinate-space transformation is to use matrices. For example, to convert from inches to centimeters, we use the formula:

$$num\_centimeters = (2.54)(num\_inches)$$

Now, using this formula and using matrix notation, we can write the inch-space to centimeter-space transformation like so:

$$[x_{cm} \;\; y_{cm}] = [x_{inches} \;\; y_{inches}] \cdot M$$

$$\text{where } M = \begin{bmatrix} 2.54 & 0 \\ 0 & 2.54 \end{bmatrix}$$

Here the matrix M serves as a rotation/shear/scale matrix. In this case, the M performs a simple scaling. In general, a coordinate-space transformation involves two matrices: a *rotation/shear/scale matrix* and a *translation matrix*. For example, a transformation from coordinate space A to coordinate space B would be written as follows:

$$[x_B \;\; y_B \;\; 1] = [x_A \;\; y_A \;\; 1] \cdot M + D$$

$$\text{where } M = \begin{bmatrix} m_{11} & m_{12} \\ m_{21} & m_{22} \end{bmatrix} \text{ and } D = [x_{cm} \quad y_{cm}]$$

Here M is the 2x2 (two rows, two columns) rotation/shear/scale matrix, and D is the 1x2 (one row, two columns) translation matrix. If we were to write this using regular algebraic notation, we'd get the following formulae:

$$x_B = (m_{11})(x_A) + (m_{21})(y_A) + d_x$$

$$y_B = (m_{12})(x_A) + (m_{22})(y_A) + d_y$$

Now, to represent both M and D by using only a single matrix, we simply add a placeholder column, like so:

$$[x_B \quad y_B \quad 1] = [x_A \quad y_A \quad 1] \cdot T$$

$$\text{where } T = \begin{bmatrix} m_{11} & m_{12} & 0 \\ m_{21} & m_{22} & 0 \\ d_x & d_y & 1 \end{bmatrix}$$

Here the matrix T is the combined *transformation matrix*, which contains elements of both M and D. The end result is the same, but working with the matrix T is often easier than carrying around both M and D. Nevertheless, although matrices do provide a compact representation, they can sometimes be confusing. If you find this to be the case, you can get up to speed on this topic by working through some of the examples in Appendix A.

The XFORM Structure

The GDI provides a special structure, **XFORM** ("transFORM"), whose data members hold the entries of the transformation matrix T—that is, both the rotation/shear/scale matrix (M) and the translation matrix (D). Here's the declaration of the **XFORM** structure:

```
typedef struct tagXFORM {
   FLOAT eM11;
   FLOAT eM12;
   FLOAT eM21;
   FLOAT eM22;
   FLOAT eDx;
   FLOAT eDy;
} XFORM, *PXFORM, FAR *LPXFORM;
```

As you can see, the data members of the **XFORM** structure directly correspond to the entries of the matrix *T*. And, although this structure is specifically designed for use with coordinate-space transformations, you can use it for general matrix operations.

The GDI provides the **CombineTransform** function to ease the process of working with the **XFORM** structure. As its name suggests, the **CombineTransform** function combines two **XFORM** structures:

```
BOOL CombineTransform(lpxformResult, lpxform1, lpxform2);
```

Here, **lpxformResult** is simply the product of **lpxform1** and **lpxform2**, like so:

[**lpxformResult**] = [**lpxform1**] [**lpxform2**]

The result is the same as it would be if you first applied the coordinate-space transformation described by **lpxform1** and then applied the coordinate-space transformation described by **lpxform2**.

When you render something to a device context, the GDI must carry out a coordinate-space transformation. In fact, the GDI performs several transformations before output is produced on a device. For example, when you draw an ellipse to a display device context whose graphics mode is set to **GM_ADVANCED**, you're working in the world space. That is, the coordinates that you pass to the **Ellipse** function are in world units. Before the ellipse can be shown on the screen, these units must be mapped to device units. In this case, the GDI performs three coordinate-space transformations: a world-space to page-space transformation, a page-space to device-space transformation, and a device-space to physical-device-space transformation. Because of the device-dependent nature of this latter transformation, there are no functions for controlling its behavior—its business is strictly between the GDI and the device driver and usually involves a translation of the origin (e.g., to account for the paper orientation). Let's look at the other two coordinate-space transformations.

The World-Space to Page-Space Transformation

Recall, the world space is used only in Windows NT and Windows 2000, and only for device contexts whose graphics modes are set to **GM_ADVANCED**. In this case, any coordinate-related parameters that specify "logical units" are interpreted as world units. The GDI will map these world units to page units by performing a world-space to page-space transformation.

Earlier, I mentioned that the world space and the page space have identical extents and origins. As a result, the default world-space to page-space transformation is an *identity mapping;* that is, every point in the world space maps to the exact same location in the page space. Returning to matrix notation, this mapping can be written as follows:

$$[x_{page} \quad y_{page} \quad 1]=[x_{world} \quad y_{world} \quad 1]\cdot T$$

$$\text{where } T = \begin{bmatrix} 1 & 0 & 0 \\ 0 & 1 & 0 \\ 0 & 0 & 1 \end{bmatrix}$$

Here *T* is the identity matrix. We can also write this using algebraic notation, which may help make things a bit clearer, like so:

$$x_{page} = (1)(x_{world}) + (0)(y_{world}) + 0 \rightarrow x_{page} = x_{world}$$

$$x_{page} = (1)(x_{world}) + (0)(y_{world}) + 0 \rightarrow y_{page} = y_{world}$$

You can see the *one-to-one* nature of this mapping: every point in the world space maps to a unique point in the page space. Moreover, because *T* is the identity matrix, there's no rotation, shearing, or scaling going on here. And, because the origin of the page space is identical to that of the world space, there's no translation going on here, either.

Well, if the world-space to page-space transformation were limited only to the identity mapping, there would be no point in using the world space; you might as well work directly in the page space. As it turns out, the GDI provides a special function, **SetWorldTransform**, that you can use to change the world-space to page-space transformation:

```
BOOL SetWorldTransform(hdc, lpXform);
```

The **hdc** parameter identifies the device context whose points (for any subsequent rendering operations) will be mapped according to the coordinate-space transformation that you specify in the **lpXform** parameter (a pointer to an **XFORM** structure). Remember, the **SetWorldTransform** function works only if **hdc**'s graphics mode is set to **GM_ADVANCED**.

By using the **SetWorldTransform** function, you gain control over the matrix *T*. In this way, you can fine-tune the world-space to page-space transformation to produce effects such as rotation, shearing, scaling, and translation. Let's work through some examples of each of these transformations.

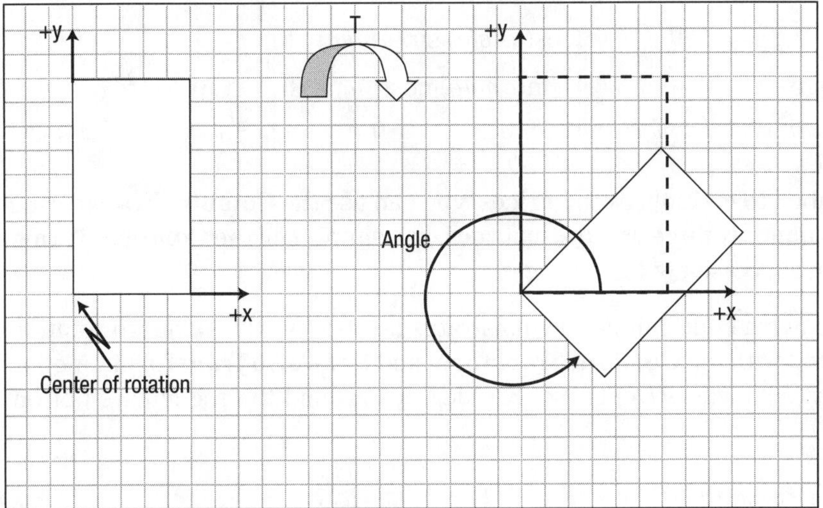

Figure 10.6 A rectangle that's rotated by some *angle* around its lower-left corner.

Rotation Mapping

A *rotation mapping*, as depicted in Figure 10.6, is accomplished by applying the standard rotation matrix (for a derivation, see Appendix A):

$$T = \begin{bmatrix} \cos(angle) & \sin(angle) & 0 \\ -\sin(angle) & \cos(angle) & 0 \\ 0 & 0 & 1 \end{bmatrix}$$

In this case, you initialize the data members of an **XFORM** structure like so:

```
XFORM xf;
xf.eM11 = cos(angle);   xf.eM12 = sin(angle);
xf.eM21 = -sin(angle);  xf.eM22 = cos(angle);
xf.eDx = 0;
xf.eDy = 0;
```

This will perform a rotation around the origin of the coordinate space. To perform a rotation around an arbitrary point, $P_{rotation}$, you first translate by negative $P_{rotation}$, then you use the standard rotation matrix, and then you translate back by positive $P_{rotation}$. In this case, the transformation matrix, T, can be written as a product of three matrices, like so:

$$T = \begin{bmatrix} 1 & 0 & 0 \\ 0 & 1 & 0 \\ -P_{rotation}x & -P_{rotation}y & 1 \end{bmatrix} \begin{bmatrix} \cos(angle) & \sin(angle) & 0 \\ -\sin(angle) & \cos(angle) & 0 \\ 0 & 0 & 1 \end{bmatrix} \begin{bmatrix} 1 & 0 & 0 \\ 0 & 1 & 0 \\ -P_{rotation}x & -P_{rotation}y & 1 \end{bmatrix}$$

Remember, to multiply two matrices, you can use the **CombineTransform** function. To multiply three or more matrices, you simply call the **CombineTransform** function successively.

The following code snippet demonstrates how to use the standard rotation matrix, along with the **CombineTransform** and **SetWorldTransform** functions, to rotate a rectangle (**RDest**) by +320 degrees around the rectangle's bottom-left corner:

```
#include <math.h>
HDC hDC = GetDC(hWnd);
try
{
   const RECT RDest = {20, 50, 100, 300};

   SetMapMode(hDC, MM_ANISOTROPIC);
   SetWindowExtEx(hDC, 1, -1, NULL);
   SetWindowOrgEx(hDC, 0, RDest.bottom, NULL);

   if (SetGraphicsMode(hDC, GM_ADVANCED))
   {
      float angle = 320;           // degrees
      angle *= (M_PI / 180.0);  // radians

      XFORM xf = {
          cos(angle),  sin(angle),
         -sin(angle),  cos(angle),
         0, 0
         };
      XFORM xfTrans1 = {1, 0, 0, 1, -RDest.left, -RDest.top};
      XFORM xfTrans2 = {1, 0, 0, 1, RDest.left, RDest.top};

      CombineTransform(&xf, &xfTrans1, &xf);
      CombineTransform(&xf, &xf, &xfTrans2);

      SetWorldTransform(hDC, &xf);
      Rectangle(
         hDC,
         RDest.left, RDest.top,
```

```
            RDest.right, RDest.bottom
            );
    }
}
catch (...)
{
    ReleaseDC(hWnd, hDC);
}
ReleaseDC(hWnd, hDC);
```

Note the use of the **SetMapMode**, **SetWindowExtEx**, and **SetWindowOrgEx** functions in this code snippet. As we'll discuss later in this chapter (see "Mapping Modes"), together these functions serve to point the positive y-axis in the upward direction (and to move the origin down a bit). This is a crucial step because the rotation matrix *T* expects this type of orientation. Moreover, because the y-axis has been reoriented, the center of rotation is no longer described by the point (**RDest.left**, **RDest.bottom**); instead the center of rotation is described by the point (**RDest.left**, **RDest.top**). This subtlety can become confusing because most of us are used to writing code in which increasing the values of the y-coordinate results in a downward effect.

Shear Mapping

A *shear mapping*, as depicted in Figure 10.7, is accomplished by applying the standard shearing matrix:

$$T = \begin{bmatrix} 1 & shearX & 0 \\ shearY & 1 & 0 \\ 0 & 0 & 1 \end{bmatrix}$$

Here you initialize the data members of an **XFORM** structure as follows:

```
XFORM xf;
xf.eM11 = 1;        xf.eM12 = shearY;
xf.eM21 = shearX;   xf.eM22 = 1;
xf.eDx = 0;
xf.eDy = 0;
```

Note that, contrary to what's depicted in Figure 10.7, the value *shearX* is not the maximum amount of shear in the horizontal direction, nor is the value *shearY* the maximum amount of shear in the vertical direction. Instead, the amount of shear in the horizontal direction is proportional to *shearX* and to the distance from the reference point on the y-axis. Likewise, the amount of shear in the vertical direction is proportional to *shearY* and to the distance from the reference point on the

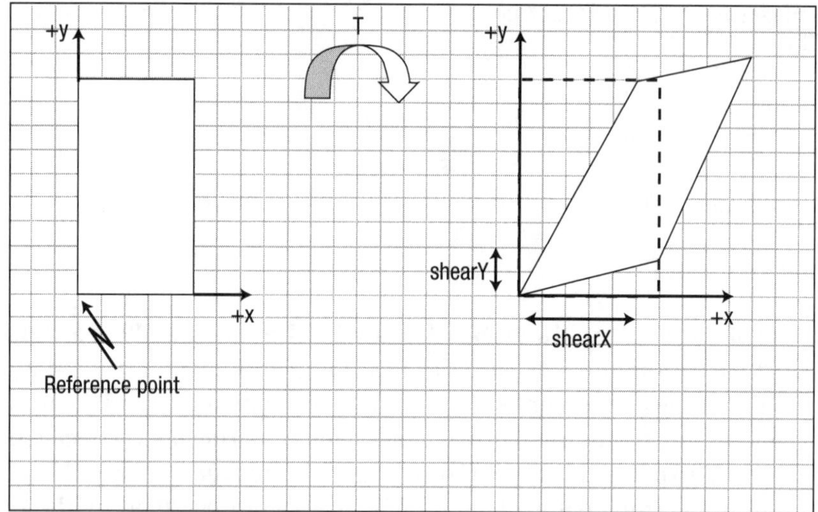

Figure 10.7 A rectangle that's sheared in the horizontal direction.

x-axis. If this description is confusing, just look at the algebraic version of the matrix equation:

$$x_{page} = x_{world} + (shearX)(y_{world})$$

$$y_{page} = y_{world} + (shearY)(x_{world})$$

Also, note that the values of **xf.eDx** (d_x) and **xf.eDy** (d_y) aren't typically set to zero. Instead, they're set to values that will compensate for the translation that's induced by the shearing, like so:

```
xf.eDx = -shearX * ref_point.y;
xf.eDy = -shearY * ref_point.x;
```

In this way, after the transformation, the bottom-left corner of the sheared rectangle will be at the same location as that of the original rectangle.

The following code snippet demonstrates how to use the standard shearing matrix, along with the **SetWorldTransform** function, to shear a rectangle (**RDest**) where the reference point is the rectangle's bottom-left corner (see Figure 10.7):

```
HDC hDC = GetDC(hWnd);
try
{
   const RECT RDest = {20, 50, 100, 300};
```

```
    SetMapMode(hDC, MM_ANISOTROPIC);
    SetWindowExtEx(hDC, 1, -1, NULL);
    SetWindowOrgEx(hDC, 0, RDest.bottom + 50, NULL);

    if (SetGraphicsMode(hDC, GM_ADVANCED))
    {
        const float shearX = 0.5;
        const float shearY = 0.25;

        XFORM xf;
        xf.eM11 = 1;        xf.eM12 = shearY;
        xf.eM21 = shearX;   xf.eM22 = 1;
        xf.eDx = -shearX * RDest.top;
        xf.eDy = -shearY * RDest.left;

        SetWorldTransform(hDC, &xf);
        Rectangle(
            hDC,
            RDest.left, RDest.top,
            RDest.right, RDest.bottom
            );
    }
}
catch (...)
{
    ReleaseDC(hWnd, hDC);
}
ReleaseDC(hWnd, hDC);
```

As with the code snippet for the rotation example, here the **SetMapMode**, **SetWindowExtEx**, and **SetWindowOrgEx** functions are used to point the positive y-axis in the upward direction (and to relocate the origin). For this reason, the reference point (which is also the rectangle's bottom-left corner) is no longer described by (**RDest.left**, **RDest.bottom**); rather, it's described by the point (**RDest.left**, **RDest.top**).

Scale Mapping

A *scale mapping*, as depicted in Figure 10.8, is accomplished by applying the standard scaling matrix:

$$T = \begin{bmatrix} scaleX & 0 & 0 \\ 1 & scaleY & 0 \\ 0 & 0 & 1 \end{bmatrix}$$

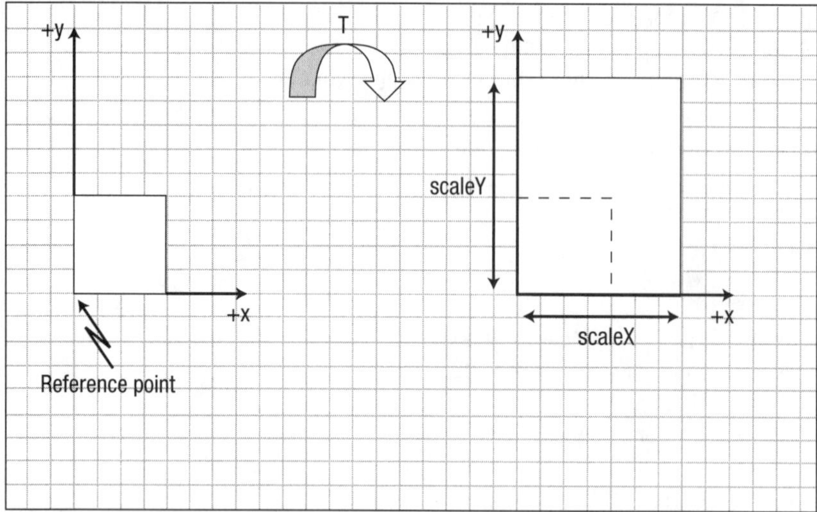

Figure 10.8 A square transformed to a rectangle by using different horizontal (*scaleX*) and vertical (*scaleY*) scaling factors.

In this case, you initialize the data members of an **XFORM** structure like so:

```
XFORM xf;
xf.eM11 = scaleX;  xf.eM12 = 0;
xf.eM21 = 0;       xf.eM22 = scaleY;
xf.eDx = 0;
xf.eDy = 0;
```

Note that, contrary to what's depicted in Figure 10.8, *scaleX* and *scaleY* are scaling factors; they don't describe the final size of the transformed shape. Moreover, as with shearing, scaling induces a translation unless the reference is located at the origin (which is rarely the case). To compensate for this translation, the **XFORM::eDx** and **eDy** data members are typically assigned the following:

```
xf.eDx = -ref_point.x * (scaleX - 1);
xf.eDy = -ref_point.y * (scaleY - 1);
```

Translation Mapping

A *translation mapping*, as depicted in Figure 10.9, is accomplished by applying the standard translation matrix:

$$T = \begin{bmatrix} 1 & 0 & 0 \\ 0 & 1 & 0 \\ d_x & d_y & 1 \end{bmatrix}$$

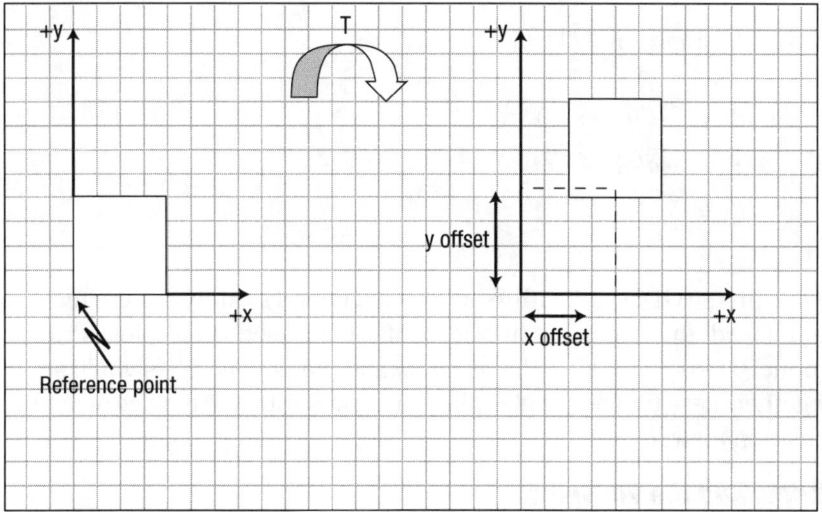

Figure 10.9 A square that's been translated in both the positive-x direction and the positive-y direction.

Here you initialize the data members of an **XFORM** structure as follows:

```
XFORM xf;
xf.eM11 = 1;  xf.eM12 = 0;
xf.eM21 = 0;  xf.eM22 = 1;
xf.eDx = x_offset;
xf.eDy = y_offset;
```

Note that with translation (and even with scaling), how you orient your axes is up to you. The transformation matrix *T* will work regardless.

The Page-Space to Device-Space Transformation

Now that you're probably accustomed to the idea of working with matrices and the **SetWorldTransform** function, let me warn you now: there is no similar function, such as "SetPageTransform," that can be used to control the page-space to device-space transformation. This results from the fact that the page-space to device-space transformation can involve only scaling and translation—you can't perform a rotation or a shear mapping. Okay, then there must be a way to specify the scaling and translation; as it turns out, there is.

Think about how you'd define a scaling and a translation. The intuitive answer would be to use a matrix—a combination of the standard scaling matrix and the standard translation matrix, like so:

$$[xdevice \quad ydevice \quad 1] = [xpage \quad ypage \quad 1] \cdot T$$

$$\text{where } T = \begin{bmatrix} scaleX & 0 & 0 \\ 0 & scaleY & 0 \\ d_x & d_y & 1 \end{bmatrix}$$

Of course, with the GDI (and with Windows in general), rarely are the techniques intuitive. Instead, the engineers at Microsoft abandoned the notion of matrices and introduced two rectangles: the *window* and the *viewport*. As you'll soon discover, together these two rectangles allow us to describe the entries of a different transformation matrix.

The Window and the Viewport

Don't confuse the term "window" with an actual standard top-level or child window, and don't confuse the term "viewport" with a clipping area. In the context of this section, the window and the viewport refer to imaginary rectangles that lie in the page space and in the device space, respectively. These rectangles are depicted in Figure 10.10.

Together, the window and the viewport define both a scaling and a translation. Specifically, the horizontal scaling factor, *scaleX*, is defined by the ratio between the horizontal extent (i.e., the width) of the window and the horizontal extent of the viewport. The vertical scaling factor, *scaleY*, is defined by the ratio between the vertical extent (i.e., the height) of the window and the vertical extent of the viewport. Similarly, the horizontal offset, d_x, is defined by the horizontal difference between the position of the window origin and the position of the

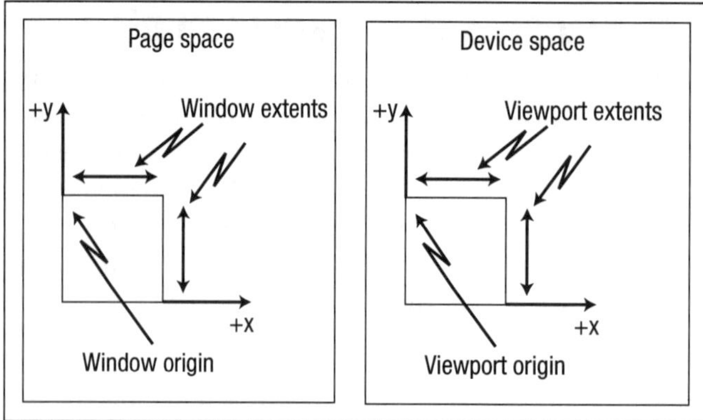

Figure 10.10 The *window* is located in the page space, and the *viewport* is located in the device space.

viewport origin. The vertical offset, d_y, is defined by the vertical difference between the position of the window origin and the position of the viewport origin. Given just the origin and the extents of the window and viewport rectangles, we can write the page-space to device-space transformation by using matrix notation, as follows:

$$[x_{device}\ \ y_{device}\ \ 1] = [x_{page}\ \ y_{page}\ \ 1] \cdot T_1 \cdot T_2$$

$$\text{where } T_1 = \begin{bmatrix} 1 & 0 & 0 \\ 0 & 1 & 0 \\ -origin_{window}x & -origin_{window}y & 1 \end{bmatrix}$$

$$\text{and } T_2 = \begin{bmatrix} \dfrac{width_{viewport}}{width_{window}} & 0 & 0 \\ 0 & \dfrac{height_{viewport}}{height_{window}} & 0 \\ origin_{viewport}x & origin_{viewport}y & 1 \end{bmatrix}$$

The matrix T_1 performs an initial translation, and the matrix T_2 performs both a translation and a scaling. Here the horizontal scaling factor, *scaleX*, is the width of the viewport divided by the width of the window; the vertical scaling factor, *scaleY*, is the height of the viewport divided by the height of the window:

$$scaleX = width_{viewport} \;/\; width_{window}$$

$$scaleY = height_{viewport} \;/\; height_{window}$$

Likewise, the horizontal translation factor, d_x, is the difference between the x-coordinate of the viewport origin and a scaled version of the x-coordinate of the window origin. Similarly, the vertical translation factor, d_y, is the difference between the y-coordinate of the viewport origin and a scaled version of the y-coordinate of the window origin:

$$d_x = origin_{viewport}\,x - (scaleX)(origin_{window}\,x)$$

$$d_y = origin_{viewport}\,y - (scaleY)(origin_{window}\,y)$$

Note that the coordinates of the window origin are scaled because we perform T_1's translation first, and then we scale and translate this intermediate result by T_2. Another way to visualize this is to simply multiply T_1 and T_2. This multiplication results in the following (compare this result with the previous matrix *T* that we defined for the combination of the standard scaling matrix and the standard translation matrix):

$$T = T_1 \cdot T_2 =$$

$$\begin{bmatrix} \frac{width_{viewport}}{width_{window}} & 0 & 0 \\ 0 & \frac{height_{viewport}}{height_{window}} & 0 \\ origin_{viewport}x - \frac{width_{viewport}}{width_{window}} \cdot origin_{window}x & origin_{viewport}y - \frac{height_{viewport}}{height_{window}} \cdot origin_{window}y & 1 \end{bmatrix}$$

It should be clear that because we're dealing just with ratios and differences, the *absolute size* and the *absolute position* of the window or the viewport have little significance. For example, notice in Figure 10.10 that the window and viewport origins are both located in the upper-left corner of each rectangle. Because we're dealing only with the difference in position of these two origins, we could just as well have defined the window and viewport origins to be at, say, the bottom-right corner of each rectangle. The difference in the location of each origin will be the same as long we're consistent with how we define both origins—that is, we pick the same spot on the rectangle for both the window origin and the viewport origin. The same argument applies for the extents. Because we're working with only a ratio, it doesn't matter whether the window is, say, 10 units wide and the viewport is 20 units wide, or the window is 100 units wide and the viewport is 200 units wide—in both of these cases, the result is still a scaling factor of two because the *ratio* between the widths hasn't changed.

When a display device context is created, the dimensions of the window rectangle are set to one page unit wide and one page unit tall. The dimensions of the viewport rectangle are set to one device unit wide and one device unit tall. This means that both scaling factors, *scaleX* and *scaleY*, are exactly 1; that is, there's no scaling. Similarly, the window origin is set to the coordinate (0, 0) in the page space, and the viewport origin is set to the coordinate (0, 0) in the device space. This means that the translation factors, d_x and d_y, are both 0; that is, there's no translation. Put another way, the default page-space to device-space transformation is an *identity mapping*.

Modifying the Window and the Viewport

The GDI provides two functions, **GetWindowOrgEx** and **GetViewportOrgEx**, which you can use to retrieve the location (i.e., the ORiGin) of the window and the viewport, respectively. Likewise, you can use the **GetWindowExtEx** and

GetViewportExtEx function to retrieve the dimensions (i.e., the EXTents) of the window and the viewport, respectively. Each of these four functions takes a handle to the target device context and the address of either a **POINT** structure (when retrieving the origin) or a **SIZE** structure (when retrieving the extents).

The GDI also provides a set of functions that you can use to adjust the window and the viewport, both in terms of position (i.e., the origin) and dimensions (i.e., the extents). To change the origin of the window or the viewport, you use the **SetWindowOrgEx** function or the **SetViewportOrgEx** function, respectively:

```
BOOL SetWindowOrgEx(hdc, X, Y, lpPoint);
BOOL SetViewportOrgEx(hdc, X, Y, lpPoint);
```

The **hdc** parameter identifies the target device context. The **X** parameter and the **Y** parameter specify the x-coordinate and the y-coordinate of the new origin, respectively. If you need to retrieve the previous origins, you can optionally pass the address of a **POINT** structure as the **lpPoint** parameter; if you don't need this information, you can specify this parameter as **NULL**.

To change the extents of the window or the viewport, you use the **SetWindowExtEx** or the **SetViewportExtEx** function, respectively:

```
BOOL SetWindowExtEx(hdc, nXExtent, nYExtent, lpSize);
BOOL SetViewportExtEx(hdc, nXExtent, nYExtent, lpSize);
```

The **hdc** parameter identifies the target device context. The **nXExtent** and **nYExtent** parameters specify the new horizontal and vertical extents, respectively. The **lpSize** parameter is optional. You can pass the address of a **SIZE** structure as **lpSize** to retrieve the DC's previous window or viewport dimensions, or you can pass **NULL** if you don't need this data.

Earlier, I mentioned that the **SetWorldTransform** function works only if the target DC's graphics mode is set to **GM_ADVANCED**. As it turns out, there are similar restrictions to using the **SetWindowExtEx** and **SetViewportExtEx** functions. In this case, the target DC's graphics mode doesn't matter, but its *mapping mode* does.

Mapping Modes

As I pointed out earlier in this chapter, a transformation is simply a mapping from one coordinate system to another. To make it easier to do page-space to device-space transformations, the GDI provides what's called a *mapping mode:* a device context "mode" that controls the "mapping." Moreover, though world-space to page-space transformations are used only (optionally) in Windows NT and Windows 2000, page-space to device-space transformations, and thus mapping modes, are used in all versions of Windows. For this reason, mapping modes are much more ubiquitous than world transformations. Table 10.1 lists the GDI's eight mapping modes.

The GDI provides the **GetMapMode** function, which you can use to retrieve a device context's mapping mode. This function takes a handle to a device context and returns one of the identifiers listed in Table 10.1. To change a device context's mapping mode, you use the **SetMapMode** function:

```
int SetMapMode(hdc, fnMapMode);
```

The **hdc** parameter identifies the target device context. The **fnMapMode** parameter can be specified as one of the identifiers listed in Table 10.1. The **SetMapMode** function returns the DC's previous mapping mode (again, one of the identifiers listed in Table 10.1). See Chapter 1 for more information on the **GetMapMode** and **SetMapMode** functions.

Table 10.1 The eight mapping modes.

Identifier	Value	Effect
MM_TEXT	1	The window and viewport extents are fixed at 1 (i.e., no scaling). The positive x-axis points rightward, and the positive y-axis points downward. This is the default mapping mode for all device contexts.
MM_LOMETRIC	2	The window and viewport extents are fixed such that one page unit maps to 0.1 millimeters in device space. The positive x-axis points rightward, and the positive y-axis points upward.
MM_HIMETRIC	3	The window and viewport extents are fixed such that one page unit maps to 0.01 millimeters in device space. The positive x-axis points rightward, and the positive y-axis points upward.
MM_LOENGLISH	4	The window and viewport extents are fixed such that one page unit maps to 0.01 inches in device space. The positive x-axis points rightward, and the positive y-axis points upward.
MM_HIENGLISH	5	The window and viewport extents are fixed such that one page unit maps to 0.001 inches in device space. The positive x-axis points rightward, and the positive y-axis points upward.
MM_TWIPS	6	The window and viewport extents are fixed such that one page unit maps to 0.0006944 inches in device space. The positive x-axis points rightward, and the positive y-axis points upward.
MM_ISOTROPIC	7	The window and viewport extents can be specified by the user. However, the extents are scaled such that one page unit maps to the same device distance in both the horizontal and vertical directions.
MM_ANISOTROPIC	8	The window and viewport extents can be specified by the user.

The **MM_TEXT** mapping mode is the default for all device contexts; it provides the familiar downward-oriented positive y-axis. The name "MM_TEXT" ("MappingMode_TEXT") originates from the fact that this mapping mode is ideal for displaying textual output—we read text from top to bottom. Scaling is not allowed in this mapping mode, so you can't use the **SetWindowExtEx** or **SetViewportExtEx** functions to adjust the size of the window or the viewport. You can, however, use the **SetWindowOrgEx** or **SetViewportOrgEx** functions to provide a translation.

For the **MM_LOMETRIC**, **MM_HIMETRIC**, **MM_LOENGLISH**, **MM_HIENGLISH**, and **MM_TWIPS** mapping modes, the positive y-axis points in the upward direction, and the viewport and window rectangles are fixed in size. Each of these mapping modes uses a predetermined ratio of window size to viewport size—a ratio that provides a set of real physical units (e.g., twips). Because this ratio is preset, you can't use the **SetWindowExtEx** or **SetViewportExtEx** functions to change the size of the window or the viewport, although you can use the **SetWindowOrgEx** or **SetViewportOrgEx** functions to manipulate the origins.

The **MM_ANISOTROPIC** mapping mode offers the most flexibility. Here the size of the viewport and window rectangles can be adjusted, and as a result, you can define your own customized orientation and working units. The **MM_ISOTROPIC** mapping mode offers nearly as much flexibility, except that the size of the horizontal and vertical extents are always equal (and are adjusted to be that way even if you specify otherwise). In fact, both of these mapping modes are commonly used to provide zooming support when you're drawing output primitives and text. (**StretchBlt** is still the most common means of scaling bitmaps.)

Textual output, of course, requires that the font itself be scalable, but this prerequisite is easily met by using a TrueType (or any other scalable) font. Unfortunately, when the graphics mode of the target device context is set to **GM_COMPATIBLE**, only the height of the font is scaled, not its width. This imposes a severe limitation on systems running Windows 95 or Windows 98, where **GM_COMPATIBLE** is the only graphics mode that's available. You can work around this limitation by using paths (see Chapter 8), but using the **GM_ADVANCED** graphics mode, where both the width and the height of the font are scaled, produces much better (and much faster) results.

Listing 10.1 demonstrates how to use the **MM_ANISOTROPIC** mapping mode (and the **SetWindowExtEx** and **SetViewportExtEx** functions) to produce a scaled ellipse and scaled text. The result of this code is depicted in Figures 10.11 and 10.12. Figure 10.11 depicts the output when the application is run in Windows 2000 (where the **GM_ADVANCED** graphics mode is available). Figure 10.12 depicts the output when the application is run in Windows 98 (where the call to **SetGraphicsMode** has no effect). Notice the difference in the widths of the text

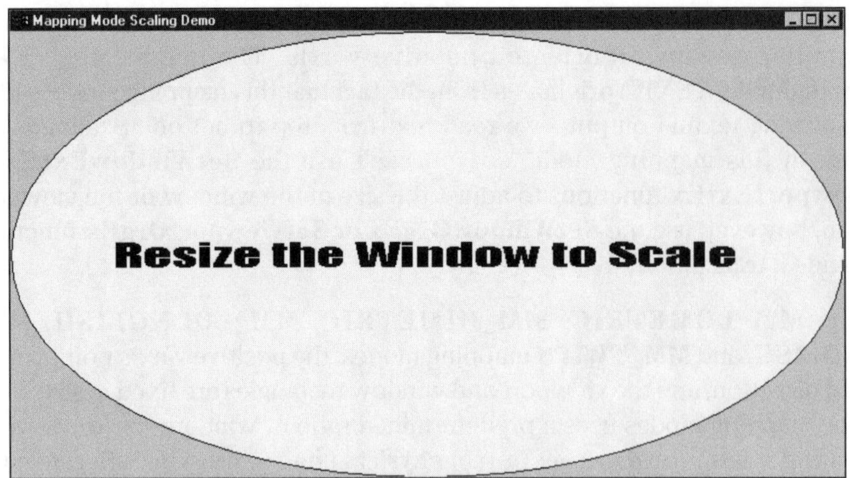

Figure 10.11 The output of Listing 10.1 when run in Windows 2000.

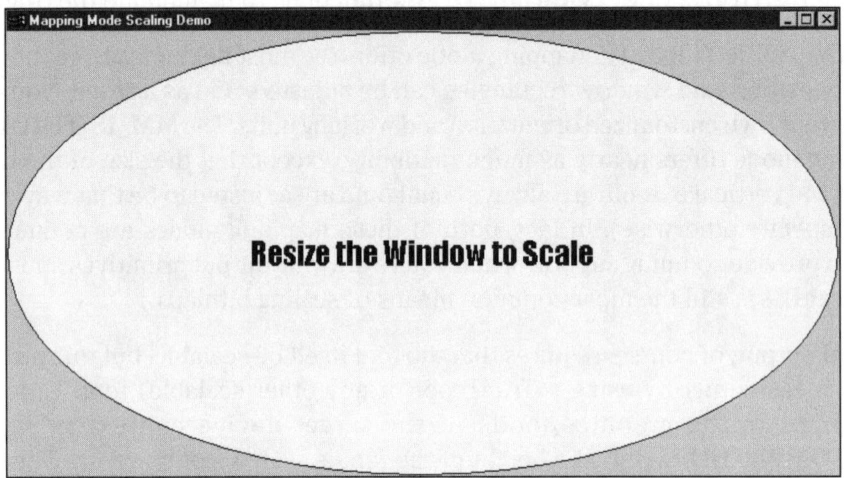

Figure 10.12 The output of Listing 10.1 when run in Windows 98.

(the heights are equal). Also, notice the one-pixel difference in the dimensions of the ellipses. (Remember, the DDK **Output** function, which we discussed in Chapter 5, always renders shapes—that are defined by a bounding rectangle—one device unit within the right and bottom edges.)

Listing 10.1 Using the MM_ANISOTROPIC mapping mode to render a scaled ellipse and scaled text.

```
// ----------------------------------------------------------------
// Windows 2000 Graphics API Black Book
// Chapter 10 - Listing 10.1 (Mapping Mode Scaling Demo)
// ----------------------------------------------------------------
```

```
#include <windows.h>

HINSTANCE hInst;
const char* WndClassName = "GMainWnd";
LRESULT CALLBACK MainWndProc(HWND hWnd, UINT msg, WPARAM wParam,
   LPARAM lParam);

int APIENTRY WinMain(HINSTANCE hInstance, HINSTANCE hPrevInstance,
    LPTSTR lpCmdLine, int nCmdShow)
{
   hInst = hInstance;

   WNDCLASS wc;
   memset(&wc, 0, sizeof(WNDCLASS));

   wc.style = CS_VREDRAW | CS_HREDRAW | CS_DBLCLKS;
   wc.lpfnWndProc = MainWndProc;
   wc.hInstance = hInstance;
   wc.hCursor = LoadCursor(NULL, IDC_ARROW);
   wc.hbrBackground = reinterpret_cast<HBRUSH>(COLOR_BTNFACE + 1);
   wc.lpszClassName = WndClassName;

   if (RegisterClass(&wc))
   {
      HWND hWnd =
         CreateWindow(WndClassName,
                      "Mapping Mode Scaling Demo",
                      WS_OVERLAPPEDWINDOW | WS_CAPTION |
                      WS_VISIBLE | WS_CLIPSIBLINGS,
                      0, 0, 300, 300,
                      NULL, NULL, hInst, NULL);

      if (hWnd)
      {
         ShowWindow(hWnd, nCmdShow);
         UpdateWindow(hWnd);

         MSG msg;
         while (GetMessage(&msg, NULL, 0, 0))
         {
             TranslateMessage(&msg);
             DispatchMessage(&msg);
         }
      }
    }
    return 0;
}
```

```
HFONT hTTFont = NULL;
LPCSTR pText = TEXT("Resize the Window to Scale\0");
RECT RInitialClient = {0};
RECT RCurrentClient = {0};

// main window procedure
LRESULT CALLBACK MainWndProc(HWND hWnd, UINT msg, WPARAM wParam,
   LPARAM lParam)
{
   switch (msg)
   {
      case WM_CREATE:
      {
         // retrieve the initial client area
         GetClientRect(hWnd, &RInitialClient);

         // create the TrueType (scalable) font
         HDC hDC = GetDC(hWnd);
         try
         {
            // see Chapter 4 for the definition of MakeFont
            hTTFont = font::MakeFont(hDC, "Impact", 16);
            if (!hTTFont) throw;
         }
         catch (...)
         {
            ReleaseDC(hWnd, hDC);
         }
         ReleaseDC(hWnd, hDC);
         break;
      }
      case WM_SIZE:
      {
         // update the current client area RECT
         RCurrentClient.right = LOWORD(lParam);
         RCurrentClient.bottom = HIWORD(lParam);
         break;
      }
      case WM_PAINT:
      {
         PAINTSTRUCT ps;
         HDC hDC = BeginPaint(hWnd, &ps);
         HFONT hOldFont = static_cast<HFONT>(
            SelectObject(hDC, hTTFont)
            );
```

```
try
{
   // use GM_ADVANCED graphics mode (no-op in Win9x)
   SetGraphicsMode(hDC, GM_ADVANCED);

   // use the MM_ANISOTROPIC mapping mode
   SetMapMode(hDC, MM_ANISOTROPIC);

   //
   // set the window extents to the
   // initial client area dimensions
   //
   SetWindowExtEx(
      hDC,
      RInitialClient.right - RInitialClient.left,
      RInitialClient.bottom - RInitialClient.top,
      NULL
      );
   //
   // set the viewport extents to the
   // current client area dimensions
   //
   SetViewportExtEx(
      hDC,
      RCurrentClient.right - RCurrentClient.left,
      RCurrentClient.bottom - RCurrentClient.top,
      NULL
      );

   //
   // render the ellipse (notice that we're still
   // using the initial client area, but the
   // ellipse will be scaled by the ratio of the
   // viewport to window extents)
   //
   Ellipse(
      hDC,
      RInitialClient.left, RInitialClient.top,
      RInitialClient.right, RInitialClient.bottom
      );

   //
   // render the text (notice that we're still
   // using the initial client area, but the
   // text will be scaled by the ratio of the
   // viewport to window extents--note the
```

```
            // different effects when the GM_ADVANCED
            // graphics mode is used)
            //
            DrawText(
               hDC, pText, -1, &RInitialClient,
               DT_CENTER | DT_VCENTER | DT_SINGLELINE
               );
         }
         catch (...)
         {
            SelectObject(hDC, hOldFont);
            EndPaint(hWnd, &ps);
         }
         SelectObject(hDC, hOldFont);
         EndPaint(hWnd, &ps);
         break;
      }
      case WM_DESTROY:
      {
         // clean up
         if (hTTFont)
         {
            DeleteObject(hTTFont);
         }
         PostQuitMessage(0);
         return 0;
      }
   }
   return DefWindowProc(hWnd, msg, wParam, lParam);
}
```

Immediate Solutions

Retrieving and Changing a Device Context's Graphics Mode

To retrieve the graphics mode of a device context, you use the **GetGraphicsMode** function (Windows NT/2000 only):

```
int GetGraphicsMode(
    HDC hdc,          // handle to the target device context
   );
```

The **hdc** parameter identifies the device context whose current graphics mode you want to retrieve. If the **GetGraphicsMode** function is successful, it returns either **GM_COMPATIBLE** (1) or **GM_ADVANCED** (2). If the **GetGraphicsMode** function fails, it returns 0. Note that **GM_COMPATIBLE** is the default graphics mode for all device contexts, and it is the only graphics mode that's available in Windows 95 and Windows 98.

To change the graphics mode of a device context, you use the **SetGraphicsMode** function:

```
int SetGraphicsMode(
    HDC hdc,          // handle to the target device context
    int iMode         // new graphics mode identifier
   );
```

The **hdc** parameter identifies the device context whose graphics mode you want to change. This new graphics mode is passed as the **iMode** parameter, which you can specify as either **GM_COMPATIBLE** (1) or **GM_ADVANCED** (2). Note that **GM_COMPATIBLE** is the default graphics mode for all device contexts.

If successful, the **SetGraphicsMode** function returns the DC's previous graphics mode (**GM_COMPATIBLE** or **GM_ADVANCED**). If the **SetGraphicsMode** function fails, it returns 0. For example:

```
HDC hDC = GetDC(hWnd);
try
{
   const int old_graphics_mode = SetGraphicsMode(hDC, GM_ADVANCED);
```

```
    //
    // NOTE: old_graphics_mode should indicate GM_COMPATIBLE
    // because this is the default for all device contexts
    //

    // ...
}
catch (...)
{
    ReleaseDC(hWnd, hDC);
}
ReleaseDC(hWnd, hDC);
```

A device context's graphics mode determines whether the world space is used. When the graphics mode of a DC is set to **GM_ADVANCED**, all GDI functions (aimed at the DC) that accept parameters in logical units will interpret these parameters as being in *world units*. When the graphics mode of a DC is set to **GM_COMPATIBLE**, all GDI functions (aimed at the DC) that accept parameters in logical units will interpret these parameters as being in *page units*. As a result, the world-space to page-space transformation is used only when a DC's graphics mode is set to **GM_ADVANCED**.

NOTE: *Although you can use the **SetGraphicsMode** function in Windows 95 and Windows 98, it has no effect. On these platforms, the graphics mode of a DC is always **GM_COMPATIBLE**.*

Retrieving a Device Context's World-Space to Page-Space Transformation

To retrieve a matrix that describes a device context's current world-space to page-space transformation, you use the **GetWorldTransform** function:

```
BOOL GetWorldTransform(
    IN HDC hdc,              // handle to the target device context
    OUT LPXFORM lpXform      // pointer to an XFORM structure that receives
                             // the transformation matrix
   );
```

The **hdc** parameter identifies the device context whose world-space to page-space transformation you want to retrieve. If the **GetWorldTransform** function succeeds, a matrix that describes this transformation is copied into the **XFORM** structure whose address is specified as the **lpXform** parameter, and the return value is **TRUE**. If the **GetWorldTransform** function fails, it returns **FALSE**.

The following code snippet demonstrates the use of the **GetWorldTransform** function. Note that in this case, the data members of **xf** should indicate an identity matrix because the default world-space to page-space transformation is an identity mapping:

```
HDC hDC = GetDC(hWnd);
try
{
   XFORM xf;
   if (GetWorldTransform(hDC, &xf))
   {
      //
      // xf == {1, 0, 0, 1, 0, 0}
      //

      // ...
   }
}
catch (...)
{
   ReleaseDC(hWnd, hDC);
}
ReleaseDC(hWnd, hDC);
```

Setting a Device Context's World-Space to Page-Space Transformation

To set the world-space to page-space transformation for a device context, you use the **SetWorldTransform** function (Windows NT/2000 only):

```
BOOL SetWorldTransform(
    IN HDC hdc,                 // handle to the target device context
    IN CONST XFORM *lpXform     // pointer to an XFORM structure that holds
                                // the transformation matrix
   );
```

The **hdc** parameter identifies the device context whose world-space to page-space transformation you want to set. The **lpXform** parameter, which is set to the address of an **XFORM** structure, specifies this new transformation.

The default world-space to page-space transformation is an identity mapping. The **SetWorldTransform** function returns **TRUE** if successful, and **FALSE** otherwise.

NOTE: *The world-space to page-space transformation is used only when the target device context's graphics mode is set to* ***GM_ADVANCED****. If you pass the* ***SetWorldTransform*** *function a handle to a DC whose graphics mode is set to* ***GM_COMPATIBLE****, the function will fail. For information on changing a DC's graphics mode, see "Retrieving and Changing a Device Context's Graphics Mode."*

You can use the **SetWorldTransform** function to perform effects such as rotation, shearing, scaling, and translation. For more information on each of these transformations, see "The World-Space to Page-Space Transformation" in the "In Depth" section. The following code snippet demonstrates how to use the **SetWorldTransform** function to perform a scaling:

```
HDC hDC = GetDC(hWnd);
try
{
   const POINT PRef = {20, 50};
   const RECT RDest = {PRef.x, PRef.y, 100, 100};

   if (SetGraphicsMode(hDC, GM_ADVANCED))
   {
      const float scaleX = 4.0;
      const float scaleY = 0.5;

      XFORM xf;
      xf.eM11 = scaleX;  xf.eM12 = 0;
      xf.eM21 = 0;       xf.eM22 = scaleY;
      xf.eDx = -PRef.x * (scaleX - 1);
      xf.eDy = -PRef.y * (scaleY - 1);

      SetWorldTransform(hDC, &xf);
      Ellipse(
         hDC,
         RDest.left, RDest.top,
         RDest.right, RDest.bottom
         );
   }
}
catch (...)
{
   ReleaseDC(hWnd, hDC);
}
ReleaseDC(hWnd, hDC);
```

NOTE: *Although you can use the **SetWorldTransform** function in Windows 95 and Windows 98, it has no effect. On these platforms, the graphics mode of a DC is always **GM_COMPATIBLE**; therefore, the world-space to page-space transformation is not used.*

Modifying a Device Context's World-Space to Page-Space Transformation

To modify the world-space to page-space transformation for a device context, you use the **ModifyWorldTransform** function:

```
BOOL ModifyWorldTransform(
    IN HDC hdc,                 // handle to the target device context
    IN CONST XFORM *lpXform,    // pointer to an XFORM structure that holds
                                // the modification matrix
    IN DWORD iMode              // modification mode
   );
```

The **hdc** parameter identifies the device context whose world-space to page-space transformation you want to adjust. The **lpXform** parameter is set to the address of an **XFORM** structure that holds the entries of the multiplicand matrix. The **iMode** parameter specifies how this matrix is multiplied; this parameter can be assigned one of the identifiers listed in Table 10.2. If the **ModifyWorldTransform** function is successful, it returns **TRUE**; otherwise, the return value is **FALSE**.

NOTE: *The world-space to page-space transformation is used only when the target device context's graphics mode is set to **GM_ADVANCED**. If you pass the **ModifyWorldTransform** function a handle to a DC whose graphics mode is set to **GM_COMPATIBLE**, the function will fail. For information on changing a DC's graphics mode, see "Retrieving and Changing a Device Context's Graphics Mode."*

Note that the GDI defines the x- and y-coordinates (of all coordinate spaces) by using a row matrix (instead of a column matrix). Therefore, multiplying a matrix, *A*, on the left by another matrix, *B*, has the same effect as first performing the transformation described by *A* and then performing the transformation described by *B*. Similarly, multiplying *A* on the right by *B* has the same effect as first performing the transformation described by *B* and then the transformation described by *A*.

The following line of code demonstrates how to use the **ModifyWorldTransform** function to reset a device context's world-space to page-space transformation to its default identity mapping:

```
SetWorldTransform(hDC, NULL, MWT_IDENTITY);
```

Table 10.2 The identifiers that can be specified as the iMode parameter of the ModifyWorldTransform function.

Identifier	Value	Effect
MWT_IDENTITY	1	The device context's world-space to page-space transformation is reset to its default value of an identity mapping. The **lpXForm** parameter is ignored when this identifier is used.
MWT_LEFTMULTIPLY	2	The matrix that defines the device context's current world-space to page-space transformation is multiplied on the left by the matrix specified by the **lpXform** parameter.
MWT_RIGHTMULTIPLY	3	The matrix that defines the device context's current world-space to page-space transformation is multiplied on the right by the matrix specified by the **lpXform** parameter.

The following code snippet shows how to use the **ModifyWorldTransform** function to perform successive translations:

```
HDC hDC = GetDC(hWnd);
try
{
   if (SetGraphicsMode(hDC, GM_ADVANCED))
   {
      const float offsetX = 3;
      XFORM xf = {1, 0, 0, 1, offsetX, 0};

      SetWorldTransform(hDC, &xf);
      for (int index = 0; index < 10; ++index)
      {
         ModifyWorldTransform(
            hDC, &xf, MWT_LEFTMULTIPLY
            );
         Ellipse(hDC, 10, 10, 100, 100);
      }
   }
}
```

***NOTE:** Although you can use the **ModifyWorldTransform** function in Windows 95 and Windows 98, it has no effect. On these platforms, the graphics mode of a DC is always **GM_COMPATIBLE**; therefore, the world-space to page-space transformation is not used.*

For information on the **SetWorldTransform** function, see the Immediate Solution "Setting a Device Context's World-Space to Page-Space Transformation."

Retrieving a Device Context's Window Origin

To retrieve the window origin of a device context, you use the **GetWindowOrgEx** function:

```
BOOL GetWindowOrgEx(
    IN HDC hdc,           // handle to the target device context
    OUT LPPOINT lpPoint   // pointer to a POINT structure that
                          // receives the window origin
   );
```

The **hdc** parameter identifies the device context whose window origin you want to retrieve. The **lpPoint** parameter is specified as the address of a **POINT** structure that receives the x- and y-coordinates of this origin, in page units. If the **GetViewportOrgEx** function is successful, it returns **TRUE**. If the function fails, the return value is **FALSE**.

The following code snippet demonstrates how to use the **GetWindowOrgEx** function to retrieve a device context's window origin. Because a device context's default window origin is (0, 0), the application-defined **POINT**-type variable, **PWindowOrg**, should reflect these coordinates:

```
HDC hDC = GetDC(hWnd);
try
{
   POINT PWindowOrg;
   if (GetWindowOrgEx(hDC, &PWindowOrg))
   {
      //
      // PWindowOrg == {0, 0}
      //

      // ...
   }
}
catch (...)
{
   ReleaseDC(hWnd, hDC);
}
ReleaseDC(hWnd, hDC);
```


Related solution:	Found on page:
Changing the Mapping Mode of a Device Context	63

Changing a Device Context's Window Origin

To change the window origin of a device context, you use the **SetWindowOrgEx** function:

```
BOOL SetWindowOrgEx(
    IN HDC hdc,           // handle to the target device context
    IN int X,             // horizontal position of the new window
                          // origin in page units
    IN int Y,             // vertical position of the new window
                          // origin in page units
    OUT LPPOINT lpPoint   // pointer to an optional POINT structure
                          // that receives the previous origin
   );
```

The **hdc** parameter identifies the device context whose window origin you want to change. You specify this origin, in page units, via the **X** and **Y** parameters. The **lpPoint** parameter is typically specified as **NULL**, but if you need the coordinates of the previous window origin, you can pass the address of a **POINT** structure as this parameter. The default window origin is (0, 0) in page units.

If the **SetWindowOrgEx** function is successful, it returns **TRUE**. If the function fails, the return value is **FALSE**. For example:

```
POINT POldWindowOrg;
POINT PNewWindowOrg = {-100, -200};
bool success =
   SetWindowOrgEx(
      hDC, PNewWindowOrg.x, PNewWindowOrg.y, &POldWindowOrg
      );
```

A device context's window origin is used with the DC's viewport origin and with its window and viewport extents to define the translation factor that's used in the page-space to device-space transformation. For more information on the window and viewport, see "The Window and the Viewport" in the "In Depth" section.

Related solution:	Found on page:
Changing the Mapping Mode of a Device Context	63

Retrieving a Device Context's Viewport Origin

To retrieve the viewpoint origin of a device context, you use the **GetViewportOrgEx** function:

```
BOOL GetViewportOrgEx(
    IN HDC hdc,           // handle to the target device context
    OUT LPPOINT lpPoint   // pointer to a POINT structure that
                          // receives the viewport origin
   );
```

The **hdc** parameter identifies the device context whose viewport origin you want to retrieve. This information is presented in device units and is stored in the **POINT** structure whose address is specified as the **lpPoint** parameter. If the **GetViewportOrgEx** function is successful, it returns **TRUE**. If the function fails, the return value is **FALSE**.

The following code snippet demonstrates how to use the **GetViewportOrgEx** function to retrieve a device context's viewport origin. Here, **PViewOrg** should indicate (0, 0) because this is the default location for the viewport of all device contexts:

```
HDC hDC = GetDC(hWnd);
try
{
   POINT PViewOrg;
   if (GetViewportOrgEx(hDC, &PViewOrg))
   {
      //
      // PViewOrg == {0, 0}
      //

      // ...
   }
}
catch (...)
{
   ReleaseDC(hWnd, hDC);
}
ReleaseDC(hWnd, hDC);
```


Related solution:	***Found on page:***
Changing the Mapping Mode of a Device Context	63

Changing a Device Context's Viewport Origin

To change the viewpoint origin of a device context, you use the **SetViewportOrgEx** function:

```
BOOL SetViewportOrgEx(
    IN HDC hdc,          // handle to the target device context
    IN int X,            // horizontal position of the new window
                         // origin in page units
    IN int Y,            // vertical position of the new window
                         // origin in page units
    OUT LPPOINT lpPoint  // pointer to an optional POINT structure
                         // that receives the previous origin
   );
```

The **hdc** parameter identifies the device context whose viewport origin you want to change. You specify this origin, in device units, via the **X** and **Y** parameters. The **lpPoint** parameter is optional. You can specify **lpPoint** as the address of a **POINT** structure, in which case the **SetViewportOrgEx** function will fill this structure with the coordinates of the previous viewport origin. If you don't need these values, you can specify **lpPoint** as **NULL**. The default viewport origin is (0, 0) in device units.

If the **SetViewportOrgEx** function is successful, it returns **TRUE**. If the function fails, the return value is **FALSE**. For example:

```
POINT POldViewportOrg;
POINT PNewViewportOrg = {5, 10};
bool success =
    SetViewportOrgEx(
        hDC, PNewViewportOrg.x, PNewViewportOrg.y, &POldViewportOrg
        );
```

A device context's viewport origin is used with the DC's window origin and with its window and viewport extents to define the translation factor that's used in the page-space to device-space transformation. For more information on the window and viewport, see "The Window and the Viewport" in the "In Depth" section.

Related solution:	Found on page:
Changing the Mapping Mode of a Device Context	63

Retrieving a Device Context's Window Extents

To retrieve the window extents of a device context, you use the **GetWindowExtEx** function:

```
BOOL GetWindowExtEx(
    IN HDC hdc,             // handle to the target device context
    OUT LPSIZE lpSize       // pointer to a SIZE structure that
                            // receives the window extents
  );
```

The **hdc** parameter identifies the device context whose window extents you want to retrieve. These dimensions are presented in page units and are stored in the **SIZE** structure whose address is specified by the **lpSize** parameter. If the **GetWindowExtEx** function succeeds, it returns **TRUE**. If the function fails, the return value is **FALSE**.

***NOTE:** A device context's window extents are governed by the device context's current mapping mode. For information on mapping modes, see "Mapping Modes" in the "In Depth" section.*

The following code snippet shows how to use the **GetWindowExtEx** function to retrieve the dimensions of a device context's window. Here **SWindow** should indicate a width and height of 1 because the default dimensions of a DC's window are 1-by-1:

```
HDC hDC = GetDC(hWnd);
try
{
   if (SetMapMode(hDC, MM_ANISOTROPIC))
   {
      SIZE SWindow;
      if (GetWindowExtEx(hDC, &SWindow))
      {
         //
         // SWindow == {1, 1}
         //

         //...
      }
   }
}
```

```
catch (...)
{
   ReleaseDC(hWnd, hDC);
}
ReleaseDC(hWnd, hDC);
```

Related solution:	Found on page:
Changing the Mapping Mode of a Device Context	63

Changing a Device Context's Window Extents

To change the window extents of a device context, you use the **SetWindowExtEx** function:

```
BOOL SetWindowExtEx(
    IN HDC hdc,           // handle to the target device context
    IN int nXExtent,      // new width of hdc's window, in page units
    IN int nYExtent,      // new height of hdc's window, in page units
    OUT LPSIZE lpSize     // pointer to an optional SIZE structure that
                          // receives the previous window extents
   );
```

The **hdc** parameter identifies the device context whose window extents you want to change. You specify these extents, in page units, via the **nXExtent** and **nYExtent** parameters. The **nXExtent** parameter specifies the new window width, and the **nYExtent** parameter specifies the new window height. The **lpSize** parameter is typically specified as **NULL**, but if you need the previous dimensions of the window, you can pass the address of a **SIZE** structure as this parameter. The default width of a device context's window is one page unit. The default height of a device context's window is also one page unit.

***NOTE:** The dimensions of a device context's window can be changed to specific values only if the device context's mapping mode is **MM_ANISOTROPIC** or **MM_ISOTROPIC**. If the DC's mapping mode is other than **MM_ANISOTROPIC** or **MM_ISOTROPIC**, the **SetWindowExtEx** function will not fail, but it will have no effect.*

If the **SetWindowExtEx** function is successful, it returns **TRUE**. If the function fails, the return value is **FALSE**. For example, the following code snippet demonstrates how to use the **SetWindowExtEx** function to define a 1-to-5 scaling factor:

```
HDC hDC = GetDC(hWnd);
try
{
   if (SetMapMode(hDC, MM_ANISOTROPIC))
   {
      SIZE SNewWindow = {5, 5};
      bool success = SetWindowExtEx(
         hDC, SNewWindow.cx, SNewWindow.cy, NULL
         );
      if (success)
      {
         Rectangle(hDC, 10, 10, 100, 100);
         //
         // NOTE: this is the same as:
         //    Rectangle(hDC, 2, 2, 20, 20)
         // when in the MM_TEXT mapping mode because
         // the default viewport extents are 1-by-1
         //
      }
   }
}
catch (...)
{
   ReleaseDC(hWnd, hDC);
}
ReleaseDC(hWnd, hDC);
```

The dimensions of a device context's window are used with the dimensions of the DC's viewport to define the horizontal and vertical scaling (and translation) factors that are used in the page-space to device-space transformation. For more information on the window and viewport, see "The Window and the Viewport" in the "In Depth" section.

Related solution:	Found on page:
Changing the Mapping Mode of a Device Context	63

Retrieving a Device Context's Viewport Extents

To retrieve the viewport extents of a device context, you use the **GetViewportExtEx** function:

```
BOOL GetViewportExtEx(
    IN HDC hdc,           // handle to the target device context
```

```
    OUT LPSIZE lpSize      // pointer to a SIZE structure that
                           // receives the viewport extents
   );
```

The **hdc** parameter identifies the device context whose viewport extents you want to retrieve. The **lpSize** parameter is specified as the address of a **SIZE** structure that receives the horizontal and vertical dimensions of **hdc**'s viewport, in device units. If the **GetViewportExtEx** function is successful, it returns **TRUE**. If the function fails, the return value is **FALSE**.

NOTE: *A device context's viewport extents are governed by the device context's current mapping mode. For information on mapping modes, see "Mapping Modes" in the "In Depth" section.*

The following code snippet demonstrates the use of the **GetViewportExtEx** function to retrieve the dimensions of a device context's viewport. Because the default dimensions of a DC's viewport are 1-by-1 device units, **SViewport** should reflect these dimensions:

```
HDC hDC = GetDC(hWnd);
try
{
   if (SetMapMode(hDC, MM_ANISOTROPIC))
   {
      SIZE SViewport;
      if (GetViewportExtEx(hDC, &SViewport))
      {
         //
         // SViewport == {1, 1}
         //

         //...
      }
   }
}
catch (...)
{
   ReleaseDC(hWnd, hDC);
}
ReleaseDC(hWnd, hDC);
```

Related solution:	***Found on page:***
Changing the Mapping Mode of a Device Context	63

Changing a Device Context's Viewport Extents

To change the viewport extents of a device context, you use the **SetViewportExtEx** function:

```
BOOL SetViewportExtEx(
    IN HDC hdc,             // handle to the target device context
    IN int nXExtent,        // new width of hdc's viewport, in page units
    IN int nYExtent,        // new height of hdc's viewport, in page units
    OUT LPSIZE lpSize       // pointer to an optional SIZE structure that
                            // receives the previous viewport extents
   );
```

The **hdc** parameter identifies the device context whose viewport extents you want to change. You specify these extents, in device units, via the **nXExtent** and **nYExtent** parameters. Specifically, the new viewport width is specified by the **nXExtent** parameter, and the new viewport height is specified by the **nYExtent** parameter. If you need the previous dimensions of the viewport, you can pass the address of a **SIZE** structure as the **lpSize** parameter; otherwise, you can simply specify **lpSize** as **NULL**. The default width of a device context's viewport is 1 device unit. The default height of a device context's viewport is also 1 device unit.

NOTE: *The dimensions of a device context's viewport can be changed only if the device context's mapping mode is* ***MM_ANISOTROPIC*** *or* ***MM_ISOTROPIC****. If the DC's mapping mode is other than* ***MM_ANISOTROPIC*** *or* ***MM_ISOTROPIC****, the* ***SetViewportExtEx*** *function will not fail, but it will have no effect.*

The **SetViewportExtEx** function returns **TRUE** if it's successful and **FALSE** otherwise. For example, the following code snippet demonstrates how to use the **SetViewportExtEx** function to define a 2-to-1 scaling factor:

```
HDC hDC = GetDC(hWnd);
try
{
   if (SetMapMode(hDC, MM_ANISOTROPIC))
   {
      SIZE SNewViewport = {2, 2};
      bool success = SetViewportExtEx(
         hDC, SNewViewport.cx, SNewViewport.cy, NULL
         );
      if (success)
      {
         Ellipse(hDC, 10, 20, 100, 50);
```

```
            //
            // NOTE: this is the same as:
            //    Ellipse(hDC, 20, 40, 200, 100)
            // when in the MM_TEXT mapping mode because
            // the default window extents are 1-by-1
            //
         }
      }
   }
   catch (...)
   {
      ReleaseDC(hWnd, hDC);
   }
   ReleaseDC(hWnd, hDC);
```

The dimensions of a device context's viewport are used with the dimensions of the DC's window to define the horizontal and vertical scaling (and translation) factors that are used in the page-space to device-space transformation. For more information on the window and viewport, see "The Window and the Viewport" in the "In Depth" section.

Related solution:	Found on page:
Changing the Mapping Mode of a Device Context	63

Part II

DirectDraw

Chapter 11

The IDirectDraw7 Interface

If you need an immediate solution to:	*See page:*
Using **DirectDrawCreateEx** to Create a DirectDraw Object	613
Using **CoCreateInstance** to Create a DirectDraw Object	614
Working with Previous Versions of DirectDraw	616
Enumerating Available Display Devices	618
Setting the Cooperative Level	623
Setting the Cooperative Level for Multimonitor Applications	624
Handling Task Switches and Display-Mode Changes	625
Setting Up a Windowed Application	628
Setting Up a Full-Screen Application	632
Creating a Surface	634
Creating a Palette	636
Creating a Clipper	637
Determining the Capabilities of the Video Hardware	638
Using the DDCapsViewer Program	641
Retrieving the Driver Name and Version	645
Querying the Amount of Available Video Memory	646
IDirectDraw7-Related Error Codes	648

In Depth

DirectDraw is the high-performance graphics API for Windows. DirectDraw allows your applications to gain direct access to the display memory and to take advantage of some of the advanced features of modern graphics hardware. These features include accelerated blitting and stretching, double-buffering, hardware overlays, and much more. Before DirectDraw was introduced, graphics-intensive games and multimedia applications couldn't run in a Windows environment. It's not surprising that Windows Media Player, NetMeeting, and Internet Explorer all use DirectDraw to drive their graphics.

In this chapter, we'll start with a high-level overview of DirectDraw. We'll discuss the API architecture, we'll talk about hardware acceleration and software emulation, and we'll take a look at the interfaces that make up the API. I will also introduce you to the Component Object Model (COM), which is the foundation for DirectDraw. We'll compare DirectDraw to the GDI, and we'll discuss situations in which your applications could profit from using DirectDraw. After all this, we'll discuss the methods of the main DirectDraw interface, **IDirectDraw7**, in detail. At the end of this chapter, you'll be able to write your first DirectDraw application.

An Overview of DirectDraw

When it comes to speed, DirectDraw easily outperforms the GDI. However, DirectDraw does not replace the GDI. Despite its name, DirectDraw is not a high-level API for drawing. For example, there are no functions to render text or 2D primitives. What DirectDraw does, however, is manage display memory and give applications access to special hardware features that aren't available with the GDI. DirectDraw is part of a set of APIs called *DirectX*, which is also available for Windows 95, 98, and NT. With Windows 2000, DirectX 7 has become an integral part of the operating system.

The DirectX SDK

Many development packages have out-of-the-box support for DirectX programming. These packages include Microsoft Visual C++, Borland C++Builder, and Microsoft Visual Basic. DirectX can be used with any language that supports COM. If you don't have the required header files, libraries, and help files (or if yours are outdated), you can download the DirectX SDK from the MSDN DirectX Developer Center, or you can order it on CD-ROM. (Go to **http://msdn.microsoft.com/directx**.) The DirectX SDK is also part of the Windows Platform SDK.

API Architecture

The DirectDraw API is based on the Component Object Model (COM), which means that it is made up of *COM objects*. Imagine an object as the sum of the program code contained in its DLL files. The object provides its services through the member functions of its *COM interfaces*, with the main DirectDraw interface being **IDirectDraw7**.

In practice, COM interfaces feel like C++ classes, although the header files of the Platform SDK declare them by using the **struct** keyword. There is one important difference between COM interfaces and true classes: Although you would create an instance of a normal C++ class by using the **new** operator, you obtain a pointer to an **IDirectDraw7** interface through a call to the **DirectDrawCreateEx** function. (Often this pointer is stored in a variable named **lpDD**, although the actual variable name is, of course, up to you.) From then on, you can access the interface methods as you would the member functions of a true C++ class. For now, this is enough to know about COM. We'll discuss the specifics of COM later in this chapter (see "COM Essentials").

DirectDraw Interfaces

In most object-oriented languages, you work with a framework of classes that follow a hierarchical structure. This concept is preserved in COM and thus in DirectDraw as well. Naturally, the engineers at Microsoft didn't design the **IDirectDraw7** interface to handle every aspect of DirectDraw. Table 11.1 describes the interfaces that are designed to work with the **IDirectDraw7** interface.

Note that DirectDraw is backward-compatible. The interfaces listed in Table 11.1 will also be supported by future versions of the DirectX Runtime. Similarly, DirectDraw still supports the legacy interfaces, such as **IDirectDraw2** and **IDirectDrawSurface4**. These are not covered in this book, though, because Windows 2000 applications can always assume that the version 7 interfaces are available. See also "Working with Previous Versions of DirectDraw" in the "Immediate Solutions" section.

Device-Independence

DirectDraw is designed to be fast and device-independent. Just like the GDI, DirectDraw provides a consistent interface to the widest possible variety of devices. This is achieved through a layered architecture.

HAL and HEL

The DirectDraw architecture consists of two layers—a hardware abstraction layer (HAL) and a hardware emulation layer (HEL):

Table 11.1 The DirectDraw COM interfaces.

Interface	Description	Chapter Covered In
IDirectDraw7	This is the main DirectDraw interface. It provides methods to initialize DirectDraw, to query the hardware capabilities, and to obtain pointers to some of the other interfaces. The **IDirectDraw7** interface requires Windows 98, Windows 2000, or later to run.	This chapter.
IDirectDrawSurface7	This interface manipulates a surface, which is essentially a bitmap container. This interface provides the **Blt** method. Surfaces are created using the **IDirectDraw7::CreateSurface** method.	This chapter ("Creating a Surface" in "Immediate Solutions") and Chapter 13.
IDirectDrawPalette	DirectDraw palettes encapsulate color information. They are used with surfaces. Palettes are created using the **IDirectDraw7::CreatePalette** method.	This chapter ("Creating a Palette" in "Immediate Solutions") and Chapter 15.
IDirectDrawColorControl and **IDirectDrawGammaControl**	These interfaces are used with surfaces to adjust the gamma correction, hue, saturation, contrast, and other color characteristics.	Chapter 15.
IDirectDrawClipper	Clippers are used during **IDirectDrawSurface7::Blt** operations. Clippers can be created using the **IDirectDraw7::CreateClipper** method.	This chapter ("Creating a Clipper" in "Immediate Solutions") and Chapter 14.

- *Hardware abstraction layer (HAL)*—The HAL is at the lowest level of DirectDraw, closest to the hardware. The HAL provides hardware-accelerated functionality to DirectDraw and is usually implemented in the device driver. Applications do not access the HAL directly.
- *Hardware emulation layer (HEL)*—If (and only if) a requested feature is not supported by the hardware, DirectDraw attempts to emulate it. This emulated functionality is provided through the HEL. This ensures that every application can rely on at least a basic feature set being available. Applications do not access the HEL directly, either.

When calling a DirectDraw function, you don't specify whether you want the HAL or the HEL to perform the task. If the HAL can do it, it does. Otherwise, the HEL is used. (Not all features can be emulated, though.)

NOTE: There are ways to disable either the HAL or the HEL when you're initializing DirectDraw (see "Using DirectDraw" later in this chapter). Disabling a layer can be useful for debugging purposes, but usually it's best to let DirectDraw decide which layer to use.

Determining a Device's Feature Support

Although automatic emulation is convenient, it can be painfully slow. Sometimes you're better off trying to do without a feature if it is not hardware-accelerated. For example, hardware-accelerated stretched blitting is faster than the GDI **StretchBlt** function. But if stretched blitting has to be emulated in software (by the CPU), the frame rate will drop significantly, especially if the source bitmap resides in video memory (which is "far away" from the CPU). You can use the **IDirectDraw7::GetCaps** method to find out whether a specific feature is supported by the hardware or has to be emulated or whether it is not available either way. See "Querying Device Capabilities" later in this chapter.

When to Use DirectDraw

DirectDraw was introduced to make it possible for graphics-intensive games to run in a Windows environment. Before DirectDraw was introduced, it was very hard (if not impossible) to achieve smooth and flicker-free animation in a Windows application.

You should use DirectDraw for the following:

- To create games and multimedia applications. (Feel free to use it for whatever type of application you like, though.)
- To create full-screen applications that need to change the display mode without affecting the Windows desktop. (The standard function **ChangeDisplayMode** always affects the Windows desktop.)
- To create fast, smooth, and flicker-free animation.
- When you want to access the display memory directly. (By using DirectDraw, you can make Windows graphics programming much more DOS-like.)
- When you want to take advantage of hardware acceleration and special hardware features.
- Whenever speed is the primary concern.

DirectDraw vs. the GDI

DirectDraw has a number of advantages but also a number of disadvantages when compared to the GDI. Let's start off with the advantages of using DirectDraw:

- DirectDraw allows lower-level graphics programming than does the GDI. Low-level code is potentially faster because there is no overhead imposed by a high-level interface. On the other hand, low-level access requires more work on your part.
- The GDI doesn't do page flipping, but DirectDraw does. With DirectDraw, you can prepare an image in an off-screen surface and then display it *without any copying*. This technique prevents flicker and is faster than working with GDI memory DCs.
- DirectDraw allows you to synchronize animations with the vertical retrace of the monitor's cathode ray. This synchronizing prevents "tearing artifacts" that traditional GDI animation often suffers from.
- On most systems, DirectDraw applications can take advantage of hardware blitting and color keying. Off-screen surfaces (unlike off-screen DCs) can reside directly in video memory, which makes blitting to the screen faster.
- DirectDraw applications can run full-screen, so they are free to change the resolution and color depth of the screen.
- DirectDraw is compatible with the GDI. GDI functions can also be used on DirectDraw surfaces, although the performance might suffer (see Chapter 13 for more details).
- DirectDraw is also the foundation for Direct3D 7. If you are planning to incorporate 3D graphics into your application, you should also familiarize yourself with DirectDraw. (Direct3D programming deserves a book of its own and is not covered in this book.)

On the other hand, DirectDraw can't do everything the GDI can do. (DirectDraw was never intended to replace the GDI.) These are the limitations:

- DirectDraw can't draw circles, rectangles, Bézier curves, or text. For that, either you can use GDI functions on DirectDraw surfaces, or you have to implement your own (potentially faster) algorithms.
- DirectDraw doesn't perform any color conversion during blits. In this respect, the GDI is more flexible but also slower. GDI conversion services can be combined with DirectDraw.
- Unlike the GDI, DirectX 7 (and thus the **IDirectDraw7** interface) is not available on all systems. However, it's an integral part of Windows 2000 and can be downloaded through Windows Update. You can also redistribute DirectX 7 along with your application free of charge.

WARNING! DirectX 7 does not run on Windows NT. (NT 4 SP 4 supports DirectX 3.) See "Working with Previous Versions of DirectDraw" in the "Immediate Solutions" section.

COM Essentials

The Component Object Model (COM) is a key technology of the Windows platform. COM is also the foundation for OLE (Object Linking and Embedding) and ActiveX. This section will introduce you to those concepts of COM that you'll come across when programming with DirectDraw. If you're already familiar with COM, feel free to skip this section.

GUIDs

"GUID" is an acronym for *globally unique identifier*. With DirectDraw, GUIDs are used to uniquely identify COM objects (in which case they're called CLSIDs or *class identifiers*) and COM interfaces (IIDs or *interface identifiers*). Some examples of DirectDraw GUIDs include **CLSID_DirectDraw**, **IID_IDirectDraw7**, and **IID_IDirectDrawGammaControl**. In addition, GUIDs are used to uniquely identify display devices.

A GUID is a 128-bit data structure. The following extract from the guiddef.h header file shows how a GUID is defined. In the snippet, you can also see that IIDs and CLSIDs are simply alias names for the GUID data type.

```
typedef struct _GUID {
   unsigned long  Data1;
   unsigned short Data2;
   unsigned short Data3;
   unsigned char  Data4[ 8 ];
} GUID;

typedef GUID IID;
typedef GUID CLSID;
```

Objects

COM objects can be compared to DLLs. There are differences and similarities:

- COM objects reside in DLL files.
- Like DLLs, COM objects provide services to client applications.
- Like DLLs, COM objects can be used by multiple applications at the same time. For that purpose, COM objects maintain a reference count.
- Like DLLs, COM objects are language-independent. They can be written in any language, regardless of the language in which the client application is written.
- Unlike DLLs, all COM objects have associated unique identifiers. The objects' identifiers are entered into the system registry so that the COM system can

determine their locations (which might also be on a remote computer in a network) at runtime.

- Unlike DLLs, COM objects do not expose their functions loosely but expose their functions in an object-oriented fashion by using COM interfaces.

Interfaces

A COM *interface* is a collection of functions that together provide the only way to interact with an object. In the Platform SDK header files, interfaces are defined as structures (using the **struct** keyword). However, you can safely think of them as classes. In fact, there is no difference between the **class** and **struct** keywords in C++ (except that structure members are public by default, and class members are private). The member functions of interface structures are *pure virtual*, or *abstract*.

NOTE: *A COM object does not necessarily implement its interfaces as classes internally. For C++ programs, the class is simply a way to keep a bunch of function pointers together.*

Most objects expose more than one interface; this feature allows functions to be grouped logically. For example, color controls are used to adjust the appearance of surfaces. Because of this relationship, both the **IDirectDrawSurface7** interface and the **IDirectDrawColorControl** interface reside in the same object. You can use the **QueryInterface** method of an interface to obtain a pointer to one of the other interfaces residing in the same object. The **QueryInterface** method is described in the following section.

The IUnknown Interface

All COM interfaces are derived from the **IUnknown** interface, which provides the three important methods **AddRef**, **QueryInterface**, and **Release**. Derived interfaces do not actually inherit the *implementation* (as in C++ inheritance); they inherit only the method *declarations*.

- The **AddRef** method is used to have the COM object increase its internal *reference count* (a variable containing the number of clients currently using the object). You will not use **AddRef** often, though, because the reference count of an object is incremented automatically when a function returns a pointer to an interface.

- The **QueryInterface** method returns a pointer to a specific interface of the object. The reference count of the object is automatically increased, which means that, when you call **QueryInterface**, you must also call the returned interface's **Release** method after you're done working with it. For an example of using **QueryInterface**, see "Working with Previous Versions of DirectDraw" in the "Immediate Solutions" section.

- The **Release** method frees an interface. If, after this method is used, no currently running application holds a pointer to any interface of the object, the object's reference count will be zero. In that case, the object reacts by destroying itself, freeing its resources. An interface cannot be used after it has been released, not even if the reference count has not reached zero.

***TIP:** Define a **SAFERELEASE** macro that calls the **Release** method only if the interface pointer is valid. After that, the macro should set the pointer to **NULL** automatically. The code in the "Immediate Solutions" section demonstrates this.*

Retrieving Interface Pointers

The following code snippet initializes the DirectDraw object by using the **CoCreateInstance** function of the COM system and then requests a pointer to an **IDirectDraw7** interface. The code then calls the **Release** member function of the interface, which also uninitializes the DirectDraw object:

```
#define INITGUID
#include <ddraw.h>

LPDIRECTDRAW7 lpDD = NULL;          // pointer to IDirectDraw7

try
{
   CoInitialize(NULL);              // initialize the COM library

   CoCreateInstance(
      CLSID_DirectDraw7,            // identifier of DirectDraw object
      NULL, CLSCTX_ALL,
      IID_IDirectDraw7,             // identifier of IDirectDraw7 interface
      reinterpret_cast<LPVOID*>(&lpDD)
   );

   /*
      work with lpDD
   */

   // release the interface
   if (lpDD) { lpDD->Release(); }

   CoUninitialize();                // free the COM library
}
catch(...)
{
   if (lpDD) { lpDD->Release(); }
   CoUninitialize();
}
```

As you can see in the snippet, calling the methods of an interface is no different from working with your own C++ classes.

HRESULT Values

COM functions return error codes as **HRESULT** data-type values. (In the Platform SDK header files, the type **HRESULT** is mapped to type **LONG**.) These values contain information about the origin, severity, and type of error. However, your application can treat them just like any other numerical error codes. The winerror.h header file defines common error codes and the **FAILED** and **SUCCEEDED** macros that check an **HRESULT** value. In addition, DirectDraw defines its own error codes in the ddraw.h header file.

Using DirectDraw

The remainder of this chapter deals with the **IDirectDraw7** methods in detail. However, some methods are closely related to topics that are covered in their own chapters. Those methods are not discussed here, but chapter references are provided.

The first few sub-sections describe the steps necessary to create a basic DirectDraw application. Here's what we'll do in each of them:

1. "Initializing DirectDraw"—We'll use the **DirectDrawCreateEx** function to set up DirectDraw for use with the primary display device.
2. "Setting Cooperative Levels"—We'll use the **SetCooperativeLevel** method to inform DirectDraw whether our application is a full-screen or a windowed application.
3. "Testing Cooperative Levels"—Although it's not required, we should try to make our DirectDraw application behave well in a multitasking environment. For this purpose, we're going to use the **TestCooperativeLevel** method to react appropriately to task switches and display-mode changes.
4. "Working with Child Objects"—We'll take a look at child objects such as surfaces and clippers. For our basic application, we'll use an **IDirectDrawSurface7** interface obtained through the **CreateSurface** method to perform some rendering.

The complete application can be found on the CD-ROM. More information and additional code listings can also be found in the "Immediate Solutions" section.

Initializing DirectDraw

The starting point for every DirectDraw application is the **IDirectDraw7** interface. The "COM Essentials" section showed you how to use the

CoCreateInstance function to retrieve a pointer to an **IDirectDraw7** interface. The **DirectDrawCreateEx** function obtains an **IDirectDraw7** interface as well. The benefit of using **DirectDrawCreateEx** is that it automatically initializes the display device. The function prototype looks like this:

```
HRESULT WINAPI DirectDrawCreateEx(
    GUID FAR *lpGUID,            // device identifier
    LPVOID *lplpDD,              // variable to receive interface pointer
    REFIID iid,                  // interface ID; must be IID_IDirectDraw7
    IUnknown FAR *pUnkOuter      // reserved for future use; must be NULL
   );
```

***TIP:** Do not forget to link to ddraw.lib when you're using the **DirectDrawCreateEx** function. (ddraw.lib is the import library for ddraw.dll.)*

The **lpGUID** parameter specifies the display device to be used for drawing. In most cases, you can simply pass a **NULL** pointer, and the primary display is used. The next parameter, **lplpDD**, points to a variable of type **LPDIRECTDRAW7** that receives the **IDirectDraw7** interface pointer if the **DirectDrawCreateEx** function returns successfully. The third parameter, **iid**, must be **IID_IDirectDraw7**, and the last parameter, **pUnkOuter**, must be **NULL**. As of DirectDraw 7, all other values would cause an error.

The following code snippet demonstrates how to use the **DirectDrawCreateEx** function to initialize DirectDraw for use with the primary display device:

```
#define INITGUID
#include <ddraw.h>

#define SAFERELEASE(x) if (x) { x->Release(); x = NULL; }

LPDIRECTDRAW7 lpDD = NULL;

try
{
   if (SUCCEEDED(
      DirectDrawCreateEx(
         NULL,                        // use primary display device
         reinterpret_cast<LPVOID*>(&lpDD),
         IID_IDirectDraw7, NULL
      )
   ))
   {
```

```
        /*
            DirectDraw has been successfully initialized.
            You can use lpDD to access the IDirectDraw7 interface methods.
        */
    }

    // clean up
    SAFERELEASE(lpDD);
}
catch (...)
{
    // clean up
    SAFERELEASE(lpDD);
}
```

The **DirectDrawCreateEx** function is actually a wrapper for the following standard COM code:

```
CoCreateInstance(
    CLSID_DirectDraw7,
    NULL, CLSCTX_ALL,
    IID_IDirectDraw7,
    reinterpret_cast<LPVOID*>(&lpDD)
);

lpDD->Initialize(lpGUID);
```

However, there is no reason why you shouldn't use **DirectDrawCreateEx** if possible. See also "Using **DirectDrawCreateEx** to Create a DirectDraw Object" and "Using **CoCreateInstance** to Create a DirectDraw Object" in the "Immediate Solutions" section.

Setting Cooperative Levels

In a multitasking environment like Windows, applications must not interfere with each other—they must behave cooperatively. Therefore, they are usually not given direct access to the system resources. DirectDraw, however, provides low-level access to the display device. By setting the cooperative level, a DirectDraw application tells DirectDraw how cooperative it wants to be. Applications with a normal cooperative level (as specified with the **DDSCL_NORMAL** flag) behave like normal Windows applications. Applications with an exclusive cooperative level (also called *full-screen exclusive* applications because of the **DDSCL_EXCLUSIVE | DDSCL_FULLSCREEN** flag combination), on the other hand, have the following characteristics:

- They cover the entire screen. While they are active, neither the Taskbar nor any "stay-on-top" windows are visible.
- Full-screen applications can take advantage of *double-buffering*, also called *surface flipping*. Double-buffering is a technique that prevents flicker and tearing artifacts during animations. For more information about flipping, see Chapter 13.
- Full-screen applications are allowed to change the resolution and bit depth of the screen. Such changes do not influence the Windows desktop, nor are they persistent.
- While a full-screen application is active (has focus), no other application is allowed to change the display mode, whether through the standard function **ChangeDisplayMode** or through DirectDraw services.
- A full-screen application does not prevent the user from task-switching between applications. While a full-screen application is inactive (doesn't have focus), the display mode is temporarily restored.

The cooperative level is set with the **IDirectDraw7::SetCooperativeLevel** method. Every application *must* set the cooperative level before it can perform any drawing. If the application fails to do so, most **IDirectDraw7** methods will return with an error. The following code sets an exclusive cooperative level:

```
// lpDD is assumed to be a valid pointer to an IDirectDraw7 interface

lpDD->SetCooperativeLevel(
   hMainWnd,                    // the main window of the application
   DDSCL_FULLSCREEN | DDSCL_EXCLUSIVE
);
```

For details, see "Setting the Cooperative Level" and "Setting the Cooperative Level for Multimonitor Applications" in the "Immediate Solutions" section.

Testing Cooperative Levels

DirectDraw applications should be written in a way that allows them to survive task switches and display-mode changes. If a display mode is changed (e.g., when a user task-switches from a full-screen application to the desktop), or if another application gains direct access to the display device, surfaces that reside in display memory might lose their memory and have to be restored. The **IDirectDraw7::TestCooperativeLevel** method can be helpful when you're trying to determine whether special action has to be taken and, if so, which action.

Windowed Applications

A normal cooperative level does not prevent other applications from changing the screen resolution. Whenever the screen resolution is changed, a **WM_DISPLAYCHANGE** message is sent. The **TestCooperativeLevel** method returns **DDERR_WRONGMODE** if the new display mode is different from the mode used when the application created its surfaces. In that case, it is recommended that you destroy and re-create all surfaces.

When the user switches from a windowed application to a full-screen exclusive application, the **TestCooperativeLevel** method, when called by the windowed application, returns **DDERR_EXCLUSIVEMODEALREADYSET**. The windowed application should wait until **TestCooperativeLevel** returns **DD_OK** again, meaning that the application can continue rendering. It's best to simply return from the rendering routine if the **DDERR_EXCLUSIVEMODEALREADYSET** error code is returned. The following code does this:

```
// lpDD is assumed to be a valid pointer to an IDirectDraw7 interface

void RenderingRoutine()
{
   HRESULT hr;
   hr = lpDD->TestCooperativeLevel();
   if (hr == DDERR_EXCLUSIVEMODEALREADYSET)
   {  return; }

   // ...
}
```

Full-Screen Applications

When a full-screen exclusive application loses focus, the **TestCooperativeLevel** method returns **DDERR_NOEXCLUSIVEMODE**. The rendering routine should simply return:

```
// lpDD is assumed to be a valid pointer to an IDirectDraw7 interface

void RenderingRoutine()
{
   HRESULT hr;
   hr = lpDD->TestCooperativeLevel();
   if (hr == DDERR_NOEXCLUSIVEMODE)
   {  return; }

   // ...
}
```

When focus is returned to a full-screen application, its surfaces are almost always lost. (Subsequent surface operations return **DDERR_SURFACELOST**.) Therefore, an application should call the **IDirectDraw7::RestoreAllSurfaces** method upon receiving a **WM_ACTIVATEAPP** message. For details about restoring surfaces, see Chapter 13.

See also "Handling Task Switches and Display-Mode Changes" in the "Immediate Solutions" section.

Working with Child Objects

Now that you have a pointer to the **IDirectDraw7** interface, and you've set the cooperative level, you're free to work with DirectDraw at your heart's desire. As I mentioned earlier, however, the **IDirectDraw7** interface does not handle every aspect of DirectDraw. For many tasks, you need to work with child objects. For example, the actual rendering is performed through the methods of the surface interface, **IDirectDrawSurface7**. Palettes and clippers are encapsulated in their own objects as well.

The **IDirectDraw7** interface provides several methods that create child objects. These methods are **CreateClipper**, **CreatePalette**, and **CreateSurface**. In addition, the **IDirectDraw7** interface can be queried for the **IDirect3D7** interface, which is used by Direct3D-enabled applications; surface interfaces can be queried for the **IDirectDrawColorControl** and **IDirectDrawGammaControl** interfaces. This section discusses child object lifetimes.

NOTE: *When I'm referring to child* objects, *I'm actually talking about* interfaces. *Child objects are not necessarily objects in a COM sense. However, they are closely related to the object that creates them, which can therefore be viewed as their parent.*

Child Object Lifetimes

Whenever an interface pointer is obtained, the reference count of the owning COM object is increased. We've already talked about the reference count in the "COM Essentials" section. Recall that a COM object is not destroyed before all of its interfaces are released by the applications that retrieved them. The same is true for child objects. For example, a DirectDraw application that creates surfaces must call the **IDirectDrawSurface7::Release** method for all of them. Otherwise, the DirectDraw object isn't going to be destroyed because its reference count won't reach zero.

In earlier versions of DirectDraw, child objects were released by their parents. For example, if the **IDirectDraw::Release** method was called, **Release** was automatically called for every child object that had been created through the methods of that **IDirectDraw** interface. Following COM rules, programmers nevertheless used to release all child interfaces separately. Programmers had to make sure that child interfaces were released *before* the parent interface was released so that no invalid pointers were dereferenced after the child interfaces had already been released by the parents.

In the current version of DirectDraw, child objects are not released by their parents. As long as the application holds a reference to an interface, the DirectDraw object is not destroyed. The order in which child objects are released doesn't matter. Consider the following code snippet:

```
#define INITGUID
#include <ddraw.h>

#define SAFERELEASE(x) if (x) { x->Release(); x = NULL; }

LPDIRECTDRAW7 lpDD = NULL;
LPDIRECTDRAWSURFACE7 lpDDSFirstSurface = NULL;
LPDIRECTDRAWSURFACE7 lpDDSSecondSurface = NULL;

try
{
   // Step 1: Create IDirectDraw7
   DirectDrawCreateEx(
      NULL,
      reinterpret_cast<LPVOID*>(&lpDD),
      IID_IDirectDraw7, NULL
   );

   // Step 2: Create a surface
   DDSURFACEDESC2 ddsd;
   /*
      initialize ddsd
   */
   lpDD->CreateSurface(&ddsd, &lpDDSFirstSurface, NULL);

   // Step 3: Create a second surface
   /*
      initialize ddsd
   */
   lpDD->CreateSurface(&ddsd, &lpDDSSecondSurface, NULL);


   // Step 4: Release IDirectDraw7 interface
   SAFERELEASE(lpDD);
```

```
    // Step 5: Use surfaces
    lpDDSFirstSurface->BltFast(0, 0, lpDDSSecondSurface, NULL, 0);

    // Step 6: Release surfaces
    SAFERELEASE(lpDDSFirstSurface);
    SAFERELEASE(lpDDSSecondSurface);
}
catch (...)
{
    SAFERELEASE(lpDD);
    SAFERELEASE(lpDDSFirstSurface);
    SAFERELEASE(lpDDSSecondSurface);
}
```


After Step 1, the reference count of the DirectDraw object is 1. This count is increased twice by the **CreateSurface** calls (in Steps 2 and 3) and is then 3. In Step 4, the **IDirectDraw7** interface is released, but the DirectDraw object is not destroyed because its reference count is still 2. Therefore, it's okay to use the surface interfaces (pointed to by the **lpDDSFirstSurface** and **lpDDSSecondSurface** parameters) in Step 5. Step 6 finally releases both **IDirectDrawSurface7** interfaces. The reference count of the DirectDraw object reaches 0 and the object is automatically destroyed.

The reference count is increased not only when a new interface pointer is obtained (be it through one of the **Create...** functions or by calling the **IUnknown::QueryInterface** method) but also in other circumstances. The reference count is also increased, for example, when a clipper is attached to a surface. The following code is often found in DirectDraw applications:

```
// lpDD and lpDDSurface are assumed to be valid pointers

LPDIRECTDRAWCLIPPER lpClipper = NULL;

try
{
    // Step 1: Create a clipper object
    if (SUCCEEDED(lpDD->CreateClipper(0, &lpClipper, NULL)))
    {
        // specify the clipping area
        lpClipper->SetHWnd(0, hWnd);

        // Step 2: Attach clipper to surface
        lpDDSurface->SetClipper(lpClipper);
```

```
        // Step 3: Release clipper
        SAFERELEASE(lpClipper);
    }
}
catch (...)
{
    SAFERELEASE(lpClipper);
}
```

After Step 1, the reference count of the newly created clipper object is 1. After the clipper object is attached to the surface in Step 2, this reference count is increased to 2. (The reference count of the surface's DirectDraw object is not changed.)

If the clipper does not have to be manipulated anymore, the **IDirectDrawClipper** interface can be released, as is done in Step 3. The reference count of the clipper object is decreased but is still 1. (The surface still holds a reference to the clipper object.) Therefore, the application can perform clipped blits as long as the clipper is not detached from the surface (by calling the **SetClipper** method with a **NULL** pointer). If the **IDirectDrawSurface7** interface is released itself, the reference count of the currently attached clipper object is also decreased.

Child Object Compatibility

Child objects created by one DirectDraw object can't be used with the methods of another DirectDraw object. For example, you can't attach an **IDirectDrawPalette** object created by using one **IDirectDraw7** interface to a surface created by using another **IDirectDraw7** interface. Clippers, however, can be created as independent COM objects which can be used with any surface, no matter which DirectDraw object created them. However, the only time you should create multiple DirectDraw objects is when you're writing a MultiMon (multimonitor) application.

Device Enumeration

In the section "Initializing DirectDraw," I demonstrated how to use DirectDraw with the primary display device (the desktop device). As it turns out, DirectDraw can be used on any display device that the computer is equipped with, and it can be used on several devices simultaneously. If you don't want to hard-code your application to always work with the primary display, you have to use the **DirectDrawEnumerateEx** helper function to retrieve a list of available devices:

```
HRESULT WINAPI DirectDrawEnumerateEx(
    LPDDENUMCALLBACKEX lpCallback,  // pointer to callback function
    LPVOID lpContext,               // value to be passed to the callback
    DWORD  dwFlags                  // option flags
   );
```

The **dwFlags** parameter specifies which devices to enumerate. The **DirectDrawEnumerateEx** function can enumerate devices that are attached to the desktop (i.e., devices on which the Windows desktop is displayed), devices that are not attached to the desktop, and stacked 3D accelerators that have no 2D capabilities (this is useful for Direct3D applications). For every available device, the **DirectDrawEnumerateEx** function invokes the callback function pointed to by the **lpCallback** parameter.

The callback is application-defined. It is declared as follows:

```
BOOL WINAPI DDEnumCallbackEx(
    GUID FAR *lpGUID,               // device identifier
    LPSTR     lpDriverDescription, // string containing driver description
    LPSTR     lpDriverName,        // string containing driver name
    LPVOID    lpContext,           // value passed to DirectDrawEnumerateEx
    HMONITOR  hm                   // monitor handle
   );
```

The **lpGUID** parameter is a pointer to the device identifier that will be passed to the **DirectDrawCreateEx** function (or to the **IDirectDraw7::Initialize** method). The strings **lpDriverDescription** and **lpDriverName** are typically presented to the user in a "Please select a device" list box. The fifth parameter, **hm**, is a handle to the monitor that is attached to the device. This is useful in a multimonitor environment.

It is noteworthy that the **lpContext** parameter of the callback function is the value that was passed as the **lpContext** parameter of the **DirectDraw-EnumerateEx** function. DirectDraw does not interpret the **lpContext** parameter in any way. You can, for example, use it to pass the handle of the list box that the callback should add the device names to.

The following code snippet demonstrates how to use the **DirectDraw-EnumerateEx** function:

```
#include <ddraw.h>

BOOL WINAPI MyDDEnumCallback(
    GUID FAR *lpGUID,
    LPSTR lpDriverDescription,
    LPSTR lpDriverName,
    LPVOID lpContext,
    HMONITOR hm
   )
{
try
```

```
{
   // prepare a message
   char Buf[100];
   wsprintf(Buf,
      "Device: \"%s\"; Description: \"%s\"\nContinue?",
      lpDriverName, lpDriverDescription);

   // display the message
   return (MessageBox(NULL, Buf, "Device Enumerated", MB_YESNO) == IDYES);
}
catch (...)
{
   return true;
}
}

void DoEnumeration()
{
   // call DirectDrawEnumerateEx
   DirectDrawEnumerateEx(
      MyDDEnumCallback,
      NULL,
      DDENUM_ATTACHEDSECONDARYDEVICES
   );
}
```

See also "Enumerating Available Display Devices" in the "Immediate Solutions" section.

Querying Device Capabilities

The **IDirectDraw7::GetCaps** method can be used to find out whether specific DirectDraw features are supported by the hardware, by the software emulator, or not at all. The function prototype looks like this:

```
HRESULT IDirectDraw7::GetCaps(
    LPDDCAPS lpDDDriverCaps,      // pointer to DDCAPS to receive HAL caps
    LPDDCAPS lpDDHELCaps          // pointer to DDCAPS to receive HEL caps
   );
```

If the **GetCaps** method is successful, it fills the two **DDCAPS** structures with information about the capabilities of the driver and of the HEL, respectively. One of the pointers can be **NULL**. If both are **NULL**, the method returns with an error. The **dwSize** member of the **DDCAPS** structure must be initialized before you call the **GetCaps** method:

```
DDCAPS HardwareCaps;
DDCAPS EmulationCaps;
HardwareCaps.dwSize = sizeof(HardwareCaps);
EmulationCaps.dwSize = sizeof(EmulationCaps);

// lpDD is assumed to be a valid pointer to an IDirectDraw7 interface

lpDD->GetCaps(&HardwareCaps, &EmulationCaps);
```

The **DDCAPS** structure members are discussed in "Determining the Capabilities of the Video Hardware" in the "Immediate Solutions" section.

Retrieving Driver and Device Information

This section discusses the **GetDeviceIdentifier** and **GetAvailableVidMem** methods. They can be used to detect specific hardware configurations and driver versions.

Retrieving Driver Information

The **IDirectDraw7::GetDeviceIdentifier** method is very simple: It expects a pointer to a **DDDEVICEIDENTIFIER2** structure that it fills with information about the display device that was initialized with the **DirectDrawCreateEx** function. The structure contains the following fields (among others): the file name of the driver; a descriptive name for the device (which can be different from what is passed to the callback of **DirectDrawEnumerateEx**); the driver version; and information about the hardware manufacturer. This information can be used to track problematic driver-and-chipset pairs in your DirectDraw application. For a programming example, see "Retrieving the Driver Name and Version" in the "Immediate Solutions" section.

Video Memory

You can use the **IDirectDraw7::GetAvailableVidMem** method to find out how much memory is available on the graphics card:

```
HRESULT IDirectDraw7::GetAvailableVidMem(
    LPDDSCAPS2 lpDDSCaps2,
    LPDWORD    lpdwTotal,
    LPDWORD    lpdwFree
   );
```

With the **GetAvailableVidMem** method, you can retrieve either the total amount of video memory (**lpdwTotal**) or the amount of free video memory (**lpdwFree**) that can be used to create a given type of surface (as specified by the **DDSCAPS2** structure pointed to by **lpDDSCaps2**).

WARNING! The lpdwTotal parameter is not the physical amount of memory on the graphics card. The lpdwTotal parameter does not include the amount of memory currently reserved for the primary surface (the screen).

The following code snippet can be used to find out how much memory is available for off-screen surfaces:

```
// lpDD is assumed to be a valid pointer to an IDirectDraw7 interface

// prepare DDSCAPS2
DDSCAPS2 DDSCaps;
ZeroMemory(&DDSCaps, sizeof(DDSCaps));
DDSCaps.dwCaps = DDSCAPS_OFFSCREENPLAIN;

DWORD dwFree;

// call GetAvailableVidMem
if (SUCCEEDED(
   lpDD->GetAvailableVidMem(
      &DDSCaps,
      NULL,                    // we don't need dwTotal
      &dwFree
   )
))
{
   // on success, format a message
   char Message[100];
   wsprintf(Message,
      "Display memory free for off-screen surfaces: %lu bytes",
      dwFree
   );

   // present message to user
   MessageBox(NULL,
      Message,
      "GetAvailableVidMem Results",
      MB_OK | MB_ICONINFORMATION
   );
}
```

See also “Querying the Amount of Available Video Memory” in the “Immediate Solutions” section.

Immediate Solutions

Using DirectDrawCreateEx to Create a DirectDraw Object

The **DirectDrawCreateEx** function creates an instance of a DirectDraw object, initializes the display device, and returns an **IDirectDraw7** interface. The function is declared as follows:

```
HRESULT WINAPI DirectDrawCreateEx(
    GUID FAR *lpGUID,              // display device identifier
    LPVOID *lplpDD,                // variable to receive interface pointer
    REFIID iid,                    // interface ID; must be IID_IDirectDraw7
    IUnknown FAR *pUnkOuter        // reserved for future use; must be NULL
   );
```

The following programming example uses the **DirectDrawCreateEx** function to initialize DirectDraw for the primary display device and to retrieve an **IDirectDraw7** interface. The first parameter to pass to the **DirectDrawCreateEx** function is the identifier of the display device, which is either obtained through enumeration or **NULL** for the primary display. The second parameter is going to receive the interface pointer if the **DirectDrawCreateEx** function is successful:

```
#define INITGUID
#include <windows.h>
#include <ddraw.h>
// ...

LPDIRECTDRAW7 lpDD = NULL;

// create and initialize DirectDraw object
if (SUCCEEDED(
   DirectDrawCreateEx(
      NULL,                        // NULL = primary display device
      reinterpret_cast<LPVOID*>(&lpDD),
      IID_IDirectDraw7, NULL       // do not change these!
   )
))
```

```
{
   /*
      lpDD is valid.
   */
}
```


Don't forget to link to ddraw.lib, the import library for ddraw.dll, if you want to use **DirectDrawCreateEx**. If you don't **#define INITGUID** in one (and only one) of your source code modules, you will also have to link to dxguid.lib.

Before shutting down your program, call the **IDirectDraw7::Release** method. It's best to call the **Release** method through an application-defined **SAFERELEASE** macro that checks whether the interface pointer is valid before it dereferences the pointer. Here is how you can define the macro:

```
#define SAFERELEASE(x) if (x) { x->Release(); x = NULL; }
// ...
// Instead of lpDD->Release(), you'd call:
SAFERELEASE(lpDD);
```

For related information, see the following sections: "Using **CoCreateInstance** to Create a DirectDraw Object"; "Working with Previous Versions of DirectDraw"; and "Enumerating Available Display Devices."

Using CoCreateInstance to Create a DirectDraw Object

You can use the standard COM function **CoCreateInstance** to retrieve an **IDirectDraw7** interface. The function is declared in objbase.h as follows:

```
STDAPI CoCreateInstance(
    REFCLSID rclsid,        // class identifier (CLSID) of the object
    LPUNKNOWN pUnkOuter,    // reserved for "COM aggregation"
    DWORD dwClsContext,     // context for running executable code
    REFIID riid,            // interface identifier
    LPVOID *ppv             // variable to receive interface pointer
   );
```

When you're working with DirectDraw 7, the **rclsid** parameter is **CLSID_DirectDraw7**, the **dwClsContext** parameter is **CLSCTX_ALL**, the **riid** parameter is **IID_IDirectDraw7**, and the **ppv** parameter is the pointer to an **LPDIRECTDRAW7** variable. The **pUnkOuter** parameter is unused and must be **NULL**.

The following code calls the **CoCreateInstance** function to obtain an **IDirectDraw7** interface:

```
#define INITGUID
#include <windows.h>
#include <ddraw.h>
// ...

CoInitialize(NULL);              // initialize the COM library

LPDIRECTDRAW7 lpDD = NULL;

// create DirectDraw object
if (FAILED(
   CoCreateInstance(
      CLSID_DirectDraw7,
      NULL, CLSCTX_ALL,
      IID_IDirectDraw7,
      reinterpret_cast<LPVOID*>(&lpDD)
   )
))
{
   return;                       // CoCreateInstance failed
}
```

Before you can do anything else, you are required to call the **IDirectDraw7::Initialize** method, which is declared as follows:

```
HRESULT Initialize(
    GUID FAR *lpGUID             // identifier of device used for rendering
);
```

The following code initializes DirectDraw for use with the primary display device:

```
if (SUCCEEDED(lpDD->Initialize(NULL)))
{
   /*
      DirectDraw is ready.
   */
}
```

NOTE: *The* ***DirectDrawCreateEx*** *helper function encapsulates these two steps in one call. See the previous Immediate Solution.*

When you're shutting down the application, release the **IDirectDraw7** interface and free the COM library:

```
#define SAFERELEASE(x) if (x) { x->Release(); x = NULL; }
// ...
SAFERELEASE(lpDD);

CoUninitialize();
```

For related information, see the following sections: "Using **DirectDrawCreateEx** to Create a DirectDraw Object"; "Working with Previous Versions of DirectDraw"; and "Enumerating Available Display Devices."

Working with Previous Versions of DirectDraw

The **IDirectDraw7** interface is not available on all systems. Your starting point for making your application compatible with earlier versions of DirectX is the **IDirectDraw** interface. Using the **DirectDrawCreate** function is the most convenient way to retrieve a pointer to such an interface:

```
HRESULT WINAPI DirectDrawCreate(
    GUID FAR *lpGUID,           // display device identifier
    LPDIRECTDRAW FAR *lplpDD,   // variable to receive interface pointer
    IUnknown FAR *pUnkOuter     // must be NULL
   );
```

The **lpGUID** parameter specifies which device to use; this can be **NULL** for the primary display. The variable pointed to by the **lplpDD** parameter receives the interface pointer. The **pUnkOuter** parameter must be **NULL**. See the following code:

```
#define INITGUID
#include <windows.h>
#define DIRECTDRAW_VERSION 0x0600       // specify the target version
#include <ddraw.h>
// ...

LPDIRECTDRAW lpDD = NULL;

// create and initialize DirectDraw object
if (FAILED(
   DirectDrawCreate(
```

```
      NULL,            // pass device GUID. NULL = primary display device
      reinterpret_cast<LPVOID*>(&lpDD),
      NULL
   )
))
{
   return false;
}
```

You can also use the **CoCreateInstance** function to retrieve a pointer to an **IDirectDraw** interface (see "Using **CoCreateInstance** to Create a DirectDraw Object"):

```
if (FAILED(
   CoCreateInstance(
      CLSID_DirectDraw,         // always CLSID_DirectDraw
      NULL, CLSCTX_ALL,
      IID_IDirectDraw,          // always IID_IDirectDraw
      reinterpret_cast<LPVOID*>(&lpDD)
   )
))
{
   return false;
}

// initialize DirectDraw for the given display device
// NULL = primary display device
if (FAILED(lpDD->Initialize(NULL))) { return false; }
```

Once you have a valid **IDirectDraw** interface pointer, you can use the **IDirectDraw::QueryInterface** method to query for newer interfaces. **QueryInterface** takes as parameters the identifier of the interface to query for and the address of a variable to receive the interface pointer:

```
HRESULT QueryInterface(
     REFIID riid,            // identifier of interface to query for
     LPVOID *obp             // variable to receive interface pointer
   );
```

You can query for the following interfaces: **IID_IDirectDraw**, **IID_IDirectDraw2**, **IID_IDirectDraw4**, and **IID_IDirectDraw7**.

The following code demonstrates how to retrieve a pointer to an **IDirectDraw4** interface, which was introduced with DirectDraw 6:

```
LPDIRECTDRAW4 lpDDNew = NULL;

if (SUCCEEDED(
   lpDD->QueryInterface(
      IID_IDirectDraw4,
      reinterpret_cast<LPVOID*>(&lpDDNew)
   )
))
{
   /*
      lpDDNew is valid.
   */
}

// you can release lpDD. lpDDNew will have to be released separately.
SAFERELEASE(lpDD);
```

For related information, see the following sections: "Using **DirectDrawCreateEx** to Create a DirectDraw Object"; "Using **CoCreateInstance** to Create a DirectDraw Object"; and "Enumerating Available Display Devices."

Enumerating Available Display Devices

Enumeration is required if your application must be able to work with devices other than the primary display device (**NULL** device). For example, enumeration is required when you want to support multiple monitors. The **DirectDrawEnumerateEx** function returns a list of GUIDs that can be passed to the **DirectDrawCreateEx** function (or to the **IDirectDraw7::Initialize** method). The declaration for **DirectDrawEnumerateEx** looks like this:

```
HRESULT WINAPI DirectDrawEnumerateEx(
    LPDDENUMCALLBACKEX lpCallback,  // pointer to callback function
    LPVOID lpContext,               // value to be passed to the callback
    DWORD  dwFlags                  // option flags
   );
```

NOTE: *The **DirectDrawEnumerateEx** function requires DirectX 6 or later in Windows 95, and requires DirectX 5 or later in Windows 98.*

For every available device, the **DirectDrawEnumerateEx** function invokes the callback function pointed to by the **lpCallback** parameter. The **lpContext** parameter is application-defined and has no predefined meaning attached to it. It is simply forwarded to the callback function as the fourth parameter of the callback. The **dwFlags** parameter specifies which devices to enumerate. If it is set to zero, only the primary display device is enumerated. The other possible values are:

- **DDENUM_ATTACHEDSECONDARYDEVICES**—Enumerates the primary display device and all devices that are attached to the Windows desktop.
- **DDENUM_DETACHEDSECONDARYDEVICES**—Enumerates the primary display device and all devices that are *not* attached to the Windows desktop.
- **DDENUM_NONDISPLAYDEVICES**—Enumerates the primary display device and all devices that have no 2D capabilities, such as stacked 3D accelerators. This value is used primarily in Direct3D applications.

Following is the function prototype of the callback used with **DirectDraw-EnumerateEx** (note that the function name is application-defined; it does not have to be **DDEnumCallbackEx**):

```
BOOL WINAPI DDEnumCallbackEx(
    GUID FAR *lpGUID,               // device identifier
    LPSTR     lpDriverDescription,  // string containing driver description
    LPSTR     lpDriverName,         // string containing driver name
    LPVOID    lpContext,            // value passed to DirectDrawEnumerateEx
    HMONITOR  hm                    // monitor handle
   );
```

The **lpGUID** parameter is a pointer to the device identifier. The strings **lpDriverDescription** and **lpDriverName** are typically presented to the user. The **lpContext** parameter of this callback function is the value that was passed to the **DirectDrawEnumerateEx** function as its **lpContext** parameter. You are free to change the parameter name as well as the data type, as long as the size of the parameter is 4 bytes. Finally, the **hm** parameter specifies the monitor that is attached to the graphics card. This parameter can be **NULL** for the primary device, detached devices, and non-display devices. If the callback returns **TRUE**, the enumeration is continued; otherwise, it is stopped.

The remainder of this Immediate Solution demonstrates how to display a list of available devices to the user and how to initialize a display device based on the user's selection. Figure 11.1 shows an example of a list box containing the available display devices.

The next programming example uses the following **struct** to store information about a single device as passed to the callback:

```
struct SDeviceInfo
{
   GUID DeviceGuid;                // GUID to be passed to DirectDrawCreateEx
```

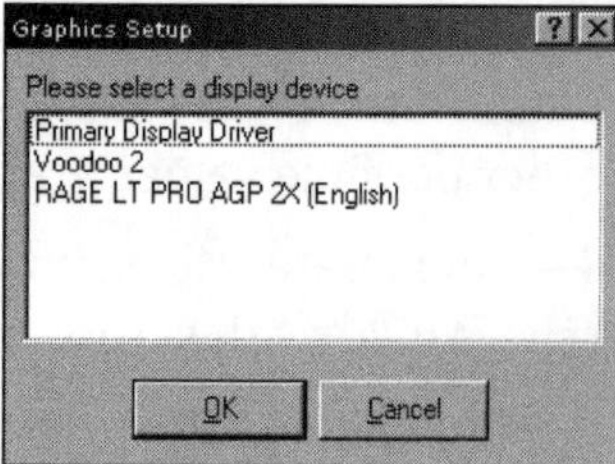

Figure 11.1 This is what the device selector could look like.

```
   bool NullDevice;              // If true, DeviceGuid is invalid. Pass
                                 // NULL to DirectDrawCreateEx instead.
   char DriverName[100];         // short name of device
   char DriverDescription[100];  // longer name of device
   HMONITOR hMonitor;            // monitor that the device is attached to
};
```

The callback places these structures into the array **AvailableDevices**, which can hold up to 16 **SDeviceInfo** structures. The global variable **NumAvailableDevices** specifies how many entries of the array are valid:

```
int NumAvailableDevices = 0;
SDeviceInfo AvailableDevices[16];

// ...

BOOL WINAPI DDEnumCallbackEx(
    GUID FAR *lpGUID,             // device identifier
    LPSTR     lpDriverDescription, // string containing driver description
    LPSTR     lpDriverName,        // string containing driver name
    LPVOID    lpContext,           // value passed to DirectDrawEnumerateEx
    HMONITOR  hm                   // monitor handle
   )
{
   SDeviceInfo *di = &AvailableDevices[NumAvailableDevices];

try
{
   // The GUID must be copied. Saving the pointer would not work.
   // If lpGUID is NULL, nothing is copied but di->NullDevice is set
   // to true.
   if (lpGUID)
   {
      memcpy(&di->DeviceGuid, lpGUID, sizeof(GUID));
      di->NullDevice = false;
   }
```

```
        else
        {  di->NullDevice = true; }

        // fill the other fields as well
        strcpy(di->DriverName, lpDriverName);
        strcpy(di->DriverDescription, lpDriverDescription);
        di->hMonitor = hm;

        NumAvailableDevices++;
        if (NumAvailableDevices == 16)    // array is full
        {  return false; }                // stop enumeration

        return true;                      // continue enumeration
    }
    catch (...)
    {
        return false;                     // stop enumeration
    }
}
```

The **DoEnumeration** function performs the device enumeration:

```
bool DoEnumeration()
{
    // call DirectDrawEnumerateEx
    NumAvailableDevices = 0;    // mark array AvailableDevices as empty

    if (SUCCEEDED(
        DirectDrawEnumerateEx(
            DDEnumCallbackEx,
            NULL,
            DDENUM_ATTACHEDSECONDARYDEVICES |     // enum all devices
            DDENUM_DETACHEDSECONDARYDEVICES |
            DDENUM_NONDISPLAYDEVICES
        )
    ))
    {
        return true;
    }
    else
    {
        return false;
    }
}
```

The following code snippet shows how to fill a list box with the names of the available devices. The code uses the **LB_SETITEMDATA** message to associate a pointer to the corresponding **SDeviceInfo** structure with each item. You can display the list in a dialog box and ask the user to select a device:

```
// HWND hListBox is assumed to be the handle of the list box
// Use GetDlgItem to retrieve it if the list box is in a dialog box.

for (int i=0; i < NumAvailableDevices; i++)
{
   // add device description
   SendMessage(
      hListBox,
      LB_ADDSTRING,
      0,
      reinterpret_cast<LPARAM>(AvailableDevices[i].DriverDescription)
   );
   // associate item with SDeviceInfo
   SendMessage(
      hListBox,
      LB_SETITEMDATA,
      i,
      reinterpret_cast<LPARAM>(&AvailableDevices[i])
   );
}
```

When the user has selected a device from the list box, you can initialize DirectDraw as follows:

```
LPDIRECTDRAW7 InitSelectedDevice(HWND hListBox)
{
   LPDIRECTDRAW7 lpDD = NULL;

try
{
   int SelIndex;                  // index of selected item

   // get index of selected item
   if ((SelIndex = SendMessage(hListBox, LB_GETCURSEL, 0, 0)) != LB_ERR)
   {
      SDeviceInfo *SelDevice;

      // retrieve pointer to SDeviceInfo associated with the item
      SelDevice = reinterpret_cast<SDeviceInfo*>(
         SendMessage(hListBox, LB_GETITEMDATA, SelIndex, 0)
      );

      GUID *lpGUID = NULL;
```

```
    if (SelDevice != reinterpret_cast<SDeviceInfo*>(LB_ERR))
      if (SelDevice->NullDevice)          // DeviceGuid is NULL
      {  lpGUID = NULL; }
      else                                // DeviceGuid is valid
      {  lpGUID = &SelDevice->DeviceGuid; }

    DirectDrawCreateEx(
      lpGUID,
      reinterpret_cast<LPVOID*>(&lpDD),
      IID_IDirectDraw7, NULL
    );
  }

  return lpDD;
}
catch (...)
{
  return lpDD;
}
}
```


Setting the Cooperative Level

Setting the cooperative level is required by all DirectDraw applications. By doing so, you specify whether your application is a normal (windowed) application or a full-screen application. The **IDirectDraw7::SetCooperativeLevel** method is declared as follows:

```
HRESULT SetCooperativeLevel(
   HWND hWnd,                  // handle of application's main window
   DWORD dwFlags               // cooperative level and option flags
  );
```

The first parameter is an **HWND** that specifies the handle of the application's top-level window. The second one, **dwFlags**, is a bit field. One of the following mutually exclusive flags is required:

- **DDSCL_NORMAL**—Used for windowed applications. Windowed applications behave like standard Windows applications. The **hWnd** parameter can be **NULL**.
- **DDSCL_FULLSCREEN | DDSCL_EXCLUSIVE**—Used for full-screen exclusive applications. Such applications are allowed to change the display mode. The **hWnd** parameter must be a valid window handle.

These flags can be combined with any of the following bits:

- **DDSCL_ALLOWMODEX**—This flag must be specified if you're planning to use the **SetDisplayMode** function to initialize the special display mode called Mode X. See Chapter 12.
- **DDSCL_ALLOWREBOOT**—This flag allows the use of Ctrl+Alt+Del to kill applications while the DirectDraw application is in full-screen mode.
- **DDSCL_CREATEDEVICEWINDOW**, **DDSCL_SETDEVICEWINDOW**, and **DDSCL_SETFOCUSWINDOW**—These flags can be used only in Windows 98 and Windows 2000, which support multiple-monitor ("MultiMon") systems. See "Setting the Cooperative Level for Multimonitor Applications."
- **DDSCL_FPUPRESERVE** and **DDSCL_FPUSETUP**—These flags are used only with Direct3D.
- **DDSCL_MULTITHREADED**—This flag makes DirectDraw multithread-safe. Used with Direct3D.
- **DDSCL_NOWINDOWCHANGES**—Usually, full-screen applications are maximized when they're activated and minimized when they lose focus. Setting this bit prevents that behavior.

The following code snippet sets the cooperative level for a full-screen application that is going to use Mode X:

```
// lpDD is assumed to be a valid pointer to an IDirectDraw7 interface
// hWnd is the application's main window handle

lpDD->SetCooperativeLevel(hWnd,
   DDSCL_FULLSCREEN | DDSCL_EXCLUSIVE | DDSCL_ALLOWMODEX);
```

For related information, see the following sections: "Setting the Cooperative Level for Multimonitor Applications"; "Setting Up a Windowed Application"; and "Setting Up a Full-Screen Application."

Setting the Cooperative Level for Multimonitor Applications

Windowed applications do not have to be changed in order to work on MultiMon (multimonitor) systems as long as DirectDraw is initialized using the **NULL** device. Like any other Windows application, multimonitor applications can be dragged and sized across monitors.

Full-screen exclusive applications, on the other hand, do not support multiple monitors automatically. Follow these steps to allow your full-screen application to span several monitors:

1. Create one main application window.
2. Enumerate available display devices. The enumeration callback receives the handles of the monitors that are attached to the devices.
3. For every monitor that your application should use, create a separate DirectDraw object.
4. For every DirectDraw object, call **IDirectDraw7::SetCooperativeLevel** with the following parameters:

```
// lpDD is assumed to be a valid pointer to an IDirectDraw7 interface

lpDD->SetCooperativeLevel(
   hMainWnd,                    // your application's main window
   DDSCL_FULLSCREEN | DDSCL_EXCLUSIVE |
   DDSCL_CREATEDEVICEWINDOW |   // DirectDraw creates a window that it uses
                                // for display
   DDSCL_SETFOCUSWINDOW         // your main window receives input messages
);
```

Because every DirectDraw object is independent, blit operations do not span multiple monitors automatically. It's the responsibility of your application to retrieve information about the physical arrangement of monitors. You can use the standard Win32 multimonitor API for that.

***TIP:** For the best performance, you should create multiple DirectDraw objects for windowed applications as well. If you don't, hardware acceleration will be available only if the application window resides fully within the primary monitor.*

For related information, see "Setting the Cooperative Level."

Handling Task Switches and Display-Mode Changes

This section shows how to use the **IDirectDraw7::TestCooperativeLevel** method to handle task switches and display-mode changes. The method has no parameters and returns one of four possible **HRESULT** values:

- **DDERR_EXCLUSIVEMODEALREADYSET**—This error code is returned to a windowed application while another application has exclusive access to the display. The application should wait.

- **DDERR_NOEXCLUSIVEMODE**—This error code is returned to a full-screen exclusive application while it doesn't have focus. The application should wait.
- **DDERR_WRONGMODE**—This error code is returned to a windowed application after the desktop display mode has been changed. All surfaces must be re-created.
- **DD_OK**—The application can continue normal execution.

If you're creating a windowed application, add the following code to your main window procedure:

```
// lpDD is assumed to be a valid pointer to an IDirectDraw7 interface

LRESULT CALLBACK MainWndProc(
    HWND hwnd,                    // handle of window
    UINT uMsg,                    // message identifier
    WPARAM wParam,                // first message parameter
    LPARAM lParam                 // second message parameter
   )
{
   switch (uMsg)
   {
   // ...

   case WM_DISPLAYCHANGE:
   {
      if (!lpDD) { break; }
      if (lpDD->TestCooperativeLevel() == DDERR_WRONGMODE)
      {
         destroy_all_directdraw_surfaces();        // application-defined
         recreate_all_directdraw_surfaces();       // application-defined
      }
      break;
   }

   case WM_ACTIVATEAPP:
   {
      if (!lpDD) { break; }
      if (static_cast<BOOL>(wParam) == TRUE)
      {
         lpDD->RestoreAllSurfaces();
         reload_all_graphics();  // application-defined function that blits
                                 // all bitmap graphics to their surfaces
      }
```

```
        break;
    }

    // ...
```

In your rendering routine, check whether another application currently has exclusive access. If so, simply return. The following code does this:

```
void Render()
{
    if (lpDD->TestCooperativeLevel() == DDERR_EXCLUSIVEMODEALREADYSET)
    {  return; }

    // do the rendering
    // ...
```

If you're creating a full-screen application, add the following code to your main window procedure:

```
// lpDD is assumed to be a valid pointer to an IDirectDraw7 interface

    case WM_ACTIVATEAPP:
    {
        if (!lpDD) break;
        if (static_cast<BOOL>(wParam) == TRUE)
        {
            lpDD->RestoreAllSurfaces();
            reload_all_graphics();  // application-defined function that blits
                                    // all bitmap graphics to their surfaces
        }
        break;
    }
```

In your rendering routine, check whether your application currently has exclusive access. If not, simply return. The following code does this:

```
void Render()
{
    if (lpDD->TestCooperativeLevel() == DDERR_NOEXCLUSIVEMODE)
    {  return; }

    // do the rendering
    // ...
```

See also "Testing Cooperative Levels" in the "In Depth" section and "Setting Up a Windowed Application" and "Setting Up a Full-Screen Application" in the "Immediate Solutions" section.

Setting Up a Windowed Application

This section demonstrates how to set up a minimal windowed DirectDraw application. A primary surface is created. Let's begin with the **#includes**, **#defines**, and global variables:

```
#define INITGUID             // Alternatively, you can link to dxguid.lib.
#include <windows.h>
#include <ddraw.h>           // Don't forget to link to ddraw.lib!

// SAFERELEASE: macro to release COM interfaces
#define SAFERELEASE(x) if (x) { x->Release(); x = NULL; }


HWND hMainWnd;
LPDIRECTDRAW7 lpDD = NULL;
LPDIRECTDRAWSURFACE7 lpDDSPrimary = NULL;
```

Following is the **WinMain** function that creates a window, initializes DirectDraw, and enters a message loop:

```
WINAPI WinMain(HINSTANCE hInst, HINSTANCE, LPSTR, int)
{
   try
   {
      WNDCLASS wc;

      wc.style = CS_HREDRAW | CS_VREDRAW;    // redraw if size changes
      wc.lpfnWndProc = MainWndProc;          // points to window procedure
      wc.cbClsExtra = 0;                     // no extra class memory
      wc.cbWndExtra = 0;                     // no extra window memory
      wc.hInstance = hInst;                  // handle of instance
      wc.hIcon = LoadIcon(NULL,
         IDI_APPLICATION);                   // predefined app. icon
      wc.hCursor = LoadCursor(NULL,
         IDC_ARROW);                         // predefined arrow
      wc.hbrBackground = reinterpret_cast<HBRUSH>(COLOR_BTNFACE+1);
                                             // gray background brush
      wc.lpszMenuName = NULL;                // name of menu resource
      wc.lpszClassName = "MainWClass";       // name of window class

      // Register the window class.
      RegisterClass(&wc);
```

```
      // Create the main window.
      hMainWnd = CreateWindow(
         "MainWClass",                 // class name
         "Main Window",                // window name
         WS_OVERLAPPEDWINDOW,          // overlapped window
         CW_USEDEFAULT,                // default horizontal position
         CW_USEDEFAULT,                // default vertical position
         CW_USEDEFAULT,                // default width
         CW_USEDEFAULT,                // default height
         (HWND)NULL,                   // no parent or owner window
         (HMENU)NULL,                  // no class menu
         hInst,                        // instance handle
         NULL                          // no window creation data
      );

      // show the window
      ShowWindow(hMainWnd, SW_SHOWDEFAULT);
      UpdateWindow(hMainWnd);

      // initialize DirectDraw
      InitDirectDraw(hMainWnd);

      MSG msg;
      while (GetMessage(&msg, static_cast<HWND>(NULL), 0, 0))
      {
         TranslateMessage(&msg);
         DispatchMessage(&msg);
      }

      return msg.wParam;
   }
   catch (...)
   {
      DoneDirectDraw();
      return 0;
   }
}
```

The **InitDirectDraw** function creates the DirectDraw object and sets the cooperative level to **DDSCL_NORMAL**. This function also creates a primary surface. (For details about surface creation, see Chapter 13.)

```
bool InitDirectDraw(HWND hWnd)
{
   // create and initialize DirectDraw object
   DirectDrawCreateEx(
```

```
        NULL,                                    // primary display device
        reinterpret_cast<LPVOID*>(&lpDD),
        IID_IDirectDraw7, NULL
    );

    // set cooperative level to normal
    lpDD->SetCooperativeLevel(hWnd, DDSCL_NORMAL);

    // prepare a DDSURFACEDESC2 structure
    DDSURFACEDESC2 ddsd;
    ZeroMemory(&ddsd, sizeof(ddsd));
    ddsd.dwSize = sizeof(ddsd);
    ddsd.dwFlags = DDSD_CAPS;  // mark ddsCaps as valid
    ddsd.ddsCaps.dwCaps = DDSCAPS_PRIMARYSURFACE;

    // create the primary surface
    if (FAILED(lpDD->CreateSurface(&ddsd, &lpDDSPrimary, NULL)))
    {  return false; }

    // set a clipper
    LPDIRECTDRAWCLIPPER lpDDClipper=NULL;
    if (SUCCEEDED(lpDD->CreateClipper(0, &lpDDClipper, NULL)))
    {
        lpDDClipper->SetHWnd(0, hWnd);
        lpDDSPrimary->SetClipper(lpDDClipper);
    }
    SAFERELEASE(lpDDClipper);

}
```

The highlighted code attaches a clipper to the application window. DirectDraw applications can always draw to the entire primary surface (the screen), even when their cooperative level is set to **DDSCL_NORMAL**. The clipper ensures that overlapping windows are not overdrawn. You can use the highlighted code unchanged in any of your windowed applications. For more information about clippers, see Chapter 14.

The **WinMain** function calls the **DoneDirectDraw** function to release the DirectDraw interfaces:

```
void DoneDirectDraw()
{
    SAFERELEASE(lpDDSPrimary);
    SAFERELEASE(lpDD);
}
```

Finally, there's **MainWndProc**, the window procedure. DirectDraw applications don't receive any messages that normal Windows applications wouldn't receive. The following example reacts to the **WM_PAINT** message by clearing the primary surface to a random color. (If we hadn't attached a clipper to the primary surface, the entire screen would be cleared.) Of course, you don't have to perform rendering in the **WM_PAINT** message handler. Whenever the display mode is changed, a **WM_DISPLAYCHANGE** message is sent. A DirectDraw windowed application should react by releasing and re-creating its surfaces. The following code does this:

```
LRESULT CALLBACK MainWndProc(
    HWND hwnd,                     // handle of window
    UINT uMsg,                     // message identifier
    WPARAM wParam,                 // first message parameter
    LPARAM lParam                  // second message parameter
   )
{
   switch (uMsg)
   {
   case WM_PAINT:
   {
      if (!lpDD | !lpDDSPrimary) { break; }

      // perform a color fill
      DDBLTFX bltfx;
      ZeroMemory(&bltfx, sizeof(bltfx));
      bltfx.dwSize = sizeof(bltfx);
      bltfx.dwFillColor = rand();
      lpDDSPrimary->Blt(NULL, NULL, NULL, DDBLT_COLORFILL, &bltfx);
      break;
   }

   case WM_DISPLAYCHANGE:
   {
      if (lpDD)
      {
         if (lpDD->TestCooperativeLevel() == DDERR_WRONGMODE)
         {
            DoneDirectDraw();              // destroy...
            InitDirectDraw(hMainWnd);      // ...and re-create all surfaces
         }
      }
      break;
   }
```

```
    case WM_ACTIVATEAPP:
    {
        if (!lpDD) break;
        if (static_cast<BOOL>(wParam) == TRUE)
        {
            lpDD->RestoreAllSurfaces();
        }
        break;
    }

    case WM_DESTROY:
    {
        DoneDirectDraw();
        PostQuitMessage(0);
        break;
    }

    default:
    {
        return DefWindowProc(hwnd, uMsg, wParam, lParam);
    }
    }

    return 0;
}
```

Related solutions:	Found on page:
Creating a Non-Flipping Primary Surface	737
Creating Clippers	782

Setting Up a Full-Screen Application

This section demonstrates how to set up a minimal DirectDraw full-screen application. I will present the code only where it differs from the preceding section.

Because the main window of a full-screen application should always cover the entire screen, the main window is created without a caption or border. The following code from the **WinMain** function creates a window with the **WS_POPUP** style:

```
// Create the main window.
hMainWnd = CreateWindow(
   "MainWClass",                  // class name
   "Main Window",                 // window name
   WS_POPUP,                      // overlapped window
   CW_USEDEFAULT,                 // default horizontal position
   CW_USEDEFAULT,                 // default vertical position
   CW_USEDEFAULT,                 // default width
   CW_USEDEFAULT,                 // default height
   (HWND)NULL,                    // no parent or owner window
   (HMENU)NULL,                   // no class menu
   hInst,                         // instance handle
   NULL                           // no window creation data
);
```


The **InitDirectDraw** function creates the DirectDraw object and sets the cooperative level to **DDSCL_FULLSCREEN | DDSCL_EXCLUSIVE**. The primary surface creation is the same as for windowed applications:

```
bool InitDirectDraw(HWND hWnd)
{
   // create and initialize DirectDraw object
   DirectDrawCreateEx(
      NULL,                      // primary display device
      reinterpret_cast<LPVOID*>(&lpDD),
      IID_IDirectDraw7, NULL
   );

   // set cooperative level to normal
   lpDD->SetCooperativeLevel(hWnd, DDSCL_FULLSCREEN | DDSCL_EXCLUSIVE);

   // the remainder did not change from "Setting Up a Windowed Application"
```

You can also remove the clipper creation code if you wish. In full-screen mode, there are no windows that could overlap. Therefore, a clipper is not required. However, a clipper *is* required if you want to perform blit operations with destination rectangles that are partially outside the screen.

The **MainWndProc** function has changed slightly as well. The **WM_DISPLAYCHANGE** message is not handled in full-screen applications because an exclusive cooperative level prevents other applications from changing the display mode. Instead, the application restores all surfaces with the **IDirectDraw7::RestoreAllSurfaces** method when focus is returned to it, and it receives a **WM_ACTIVATEAPP** message with **wParam** set to **TRUE**:

```
LRESULT CALLBACK MainWndProc(
    HWND hwnd,                    // handle of window
    UINT uMsg,                    // message identifier
    WPARAM wParam,                // first message parameter
    LPARAM lParam                 // second message parameter
   )
{
   switch (uMsg)
   {
   // ...

   case WM_ACTIVATEAPP:
   {
      // focus is returned
      if (static_cast<BOOL>(wParam) == TRUE)
      {
         lpDD->RestoreAllSurfaces();
         reload_all_graphics();  // application-defined function that blits
                                 // all bitmap graphics to their surfaces
         break;
      }
   }

   // ...

   default:
   {
      return DefWindowProc(hwnd, uMsg, wParam, lParam);
   }
   }

   return 0;
}
```

Creating a Surface

Pointers to DirectDraw surface interfaces are retrieved by calling the **IDirectDraw7::CreateSurface** method:

```
HRESULT CreateSurface(
    LPDDSURFACEDESC2 lpDDSurfaceDesc2,          // surface characteristics
    LPDIRECTDRAWSURFACE7 FAR *lplpDDSurface,    // interface pointer
    IUnknown FAR *pUnkOuter                     // reserved; must be NULL
);
```

The first parameter is a pointer to a **DDSURFACEDESC2** structure that describes the surface characteristics. Its **dwSize** member must have been initialized. The **dwFlags** parameter specifies which of the structure members are valid. The second parameter, **lplpDDSurface**, points to the variable that is going to receive the interface pointer. The last parameter, **pUnkOuter**, must be **NULL**.

The following code creates the primary surface for a DirectDraw object:

```
// lpDD is assumed to be a valid pointer to an IDirectDraw7 interface

// prepare surface description
DDSURFACEDESC2 ddsd;
ZeroMemory(&ddsd, sizeof(ddsd));    // clear all unused members
ddsd.dwSize = sizeof(ddsd);         // set dwSize
ddsd.dwFlags = DDSD_CAPS;           // specify which members are valid
                                    // DDSD_CAPS means ddsd.ddsCaps is valid
ddsd.ddsCaps.dwCaps = DDSCAPS_PRIMARYSURFACE; // every application has one
                                    // primary surface that represents
                                    // the screen

LPDIRECTDRAWSURFACE7 lpDDSPrimary = NULL;

if (SUCCEEDED(
   lpDD->CreateSurface(
      &ddsd,
      &lpDDSPrimary,
      NULL                           // must be NULL
   )
))
{
   /*
      lpDDSPrimary is valid
   */

   SAFERELEASE(lpDDSPrimary);
}
```


Related solution:	Found on page:
Creating a Non-Flipping Primary Surface	737

Creating a Palette

Pointers to DirectDraw palette interfaces are retrieved by calling the **IDirectDraw7::CreatePalette** method:

```
HRESULT CreatePalette(
   DWORD dwFlags,                          // palette options
   LPPALETTEENTRY lpDDColorArray,          // color table
   LPDIRECTDRAWPALETTE FAR *lplpDDPalette, // interface pointer
   IUnknown FAR *pUnkOuter                 // reserved; must be NULL
);
```

The **dwFlags** parameter specifies the type of palette (e.g., how many entries). The palette is initialized with the colors in the array of **PALETTEENTRY** structures pointed to by the **lpDDColorArray** parameter. The **lplpDDPalette** parameter points to an **LPDIRECTDRAWPALETTE** variable that will receive the **IDirectDrawPalette** interface pointer.

The following code retrieves an array of 256 colors from the system palette and creates a DirectDraw palette from them:

```
// lpDD is assumed to be a valid pointer to an IDirectDraw7 interface

LPDIRECTDRAWPALETTE lpDDPal = NULL;
HDC DesktopDC = NULL;

try
{
   PALETTEENTRY Entries[256];
   DesktopDC = GetDC(GetDesktopWindow());
   GetSystemPaletteEntries(DesktopDC, 0, 256, Entries);
   ReleaseDC(GetDesktopWindow(), DesktopDC);

   // create DirectDrawPalette
   lpDD->CreatePalette(
      DDPCAPS_8BIT |               // 256 colors
      DDPCAPS_ALLOW256,            // no reserved colors for Windows
      Entries,                     // init. with these colors
      &lpDDPal,
      NULL
   );

   SAFERELEASE(lpDDPal);
}
```

```
catch (...)
{
   SAFERELEASE(lpDDPal);
   if (DesktopDC) { ReleaseDC(GetDesktopWindow(), DesktopDC); }
}
```

Related solution:	Found on page:
Creating a Palette	819

Creating a Clipper

A pointer to a DirectDraw clipper interface can be retrieved by calling the **IDirectDraw7::CreateClipper** method. The interface pointer can then be passed to the **IDirectDrawSurface7::SetClipper** method to attach the clipper to a surface. The method is declared as follows:

```
HRESULT CreateClipper(
   DWORD dwFlags,                              // reserved; must be 0
   LPDIRECTDRAWCLIPPER FAR *lplpDDClipper,     // interface pointer
   IUnknown FAR *pUnkOuter                     // reserved; must be NULL
);
```

Only the second parameter, **lplpDDClipper**, is used. It points to an **LPDIRECTDRAWCLIPPER** variable that will receive the interface pointer. Here's a usage example:

```
// lpDD is assumed to be a valid pointer to an IDirectDraw7 interface

LPDIRECTDRAWCLIPPER lpClipper = NULL;

try
{
   if (SUCCEEDED(lpDD->CreateClipper(0, &lpClipper, NULL)))
   {
      /*
         set clipping area
         attach clipper to surface
      */

      SAFERELEASE(lpClipper);
   }
}
```

```
catch (...)
{
   SAFERELEASE(lpClipper);
}
```

Related solutions:	Found on page:
Using **CoCreateInstance** to Create a Clipper Object	791
Creating an Independent Clipper Object	792

Determining the Capabilities of the Video Hardware

The **IDirectDraw7::GetCaps** method is used to retrieve the capabilities of the hardware and of the DirectDraw hardware emulation layer (HEL). The method is declared as follows:

```
HRESULT GetCaps(
    LPDDCAPS lpDDDriverCaps,     // pointer to DDCAPS to receive HAL caps
    LPDDCAPS lpDDHELCaps         // pointer to DDCAPS to receive HEL caps
   );
```

The **dwSize** members of the **DDCAPS** structures must have been initialized with **sizeof(DDCAPS)**. At least one of the pointers must be valid. See the following example:

```
// lpDD is assumed to be a valid pointer to an IDirectDraw7 interface

DDCAPS HardwareCaps;
DDCAPS EmulationCaps;
HardwareCaps.dwSize = sizeof(DDCAPS);
EmulationCaps.dwSize = sizeof(DDCAPS);

if (SUCCEEDED(lpDD->GetCaps(&HardwareCaps, &EmulationCaps)))
{
   // the structures have been filled
}
```

The **DDCAPS** structure is too complex to present it in its entirety here. (It has 57 members, some of which are structures or bit fields themselves.) The following is a selection of frequently used members:

- **dwCaps**—This is a bit field containing lots of useful information about general capabilities. Among others, any of the following bits can be set:

    - **DDCAPS_BLT**—Blit operations are hardware-accelerated (assuming that the **DDCAPS** structure represents the hardware capabilities).
    - **DDCAPS_BLTSTRETCH**—Hardware is capable of stretching during blit operations.
    - **DDCAPS_CANBLTSYSMEM**—The hardware blitter can be used on system-memory surfaces.
    - **DDCAPS_CANCLIP** and **DDCAPS_CANCLIPSTRETCHED**—During blits, nonvisible areas are clipped in hardware.
    - **DDCAPS_COLORKEY**—Hardware supports blitting bitmaps with transparent pixels. (See the description of the **dwCKeyCaps** bit field.)
    - **DDCAPS_NOHARDWARE**—There is no hardware acceleration whatsoever.
    - **DDCAPS_OVERLAY**—The hardware supports overlays. (For more information about overlay surfaces, see Chapter 13.)
    - **DDCAPS_PALETTE**—The hardware supports palettes for off-screen surfaces.
    - **DDCAPS_PALETTEVSYNC**—The updating of the palettes can be synchronized with the monitor's vertical retrace. This feature provides cleaner palette animation without visual artifacts.
- **dwCaps2**—This is another bit field. Among others, any of the following bits can be set:
    - **DDCAPS2_NONLOCALVIDMEM**—The hardware supports surfaces in nonlocal (AGP) video memory. AGP (Accelerated Graphics Port) memory is a special area of system memory that the hardware can access very fast.
    - **DDCAPS2_NONLOCALVIDMEMCAPS**—The blit capabilities for AGP surfaces are different from the blit capabilities in the **dwCaps** bit field. Your application should check the **dwNLVB...** bit fields for details.
    - **DDCAPS2_PRIMARYGAMMA**—The primary surface supports gamma ramps (see Chapter 15 for more information about gamma controls).
    - **DDCAPS2_STEREO**—The hardware supports stereo vision.
    - **DDCAPS2_WIDESURFACES**—The hardware supports off-screen surfaces that are wider than the screen.
- **dwCKeyCaps**—This bit field contains information about the color-keying capabilities of the device during blits. If **DDCKEYCAPS_DESTBLT** is set, the device supports *destination color keys;* that is, only areas of a specified color are overwritten by the blit. If **DDCKEYCAPS_SRCBLT** is set, the device supports *source color keys;* that is, the source pixels of a specified

color are treated as if they are transparent. For more information about color-keyed blits, see Chapter 13.

- **dwFXCaps**—This bit field provides information about the supported effects during blit operations. Shrinking, stretching, and mirroring, for example, are widely supported by hardware devices and are emulated by the DirectDraw HEL otherwise. Rotation, on the other hand, can be performed only when the hardware supports this effect. For more information about blitting effects, see Chapter 13.
- **dwSVBCaps**, **dwSVBCaps2**, **dwSVBCKeyCaps**, **dwSVBFXCaps**—These are the same as **dwCaps**, **dwCaps2**, **dwCKeyCaps**, and **dwFXCaps**, respectively, but are used specifically for blits from system-memory surfaces to video-memory surfaces. (The normal bit fields represent video-to-video blits.) Not all blit operations that are accelerated in video-to-video blits are necessarily accelerated in system-to-video blits.
- **dwVSB...**, **dwSSB...**, and **dwNLVB...** bit fields—These are the same as the **dwSVB...** bit fields but are used specifically for video-to-system, system-to-system, and nonlocal-to-video blits.

The **HardwareCaps** structure describes the hardware-acceleration capabilities of the device that the DirectDraw object was created for. If a feature is marked as unsupported in the **HardwareCaps** structure, you should check whether the DirectDraw HEL is capable of emulating it. The HEL capabilities are contained in the **EmulationCaps** structure. If neither the hardware nor the HEL support a given feature, all DirectDraw methods requesting that feature will fail.

The following programming example demonstrates how to work with the **DDCAPS** structure. The example determines whether transparent blitting from system-memory surfaces to video-memory surfaces is supported:

```
if (HardwareCaps.dwSVBCKeyCaps & DDCKEYCAPS_SRCBLT)
{
   /*
      blitting from system-memory surfaces to video-memory surfaces
      with a source color key is ACCELERATED
   */
}
else
   if (EmulationCaps.dwSVBCKeyCaps & DDCKEYCAPS_SRCBLT)
   {
      /*
         blitting from system-memory surfaces to video-memory surfaces
         with a source color key is EMULATED
      */
```

```
    }
    else
    {
        /*
            blitting from system-memory surfaces to video-memory surfaces
            with a source color key is NOT SUPPORTED
        */
    }
```


Using the DDCapsViewer Program

It is important to know which features you can expect to be supported by current graphics cards and by the DirectDraw HEL (hardware emulation layer). The DDCapsViewer utility can help you with this. It formats the **DDCAPS** structures and writes the results into a text file. The heart of the program is a set of seven arrays containing the names of the bits in the **DDCAPS** bit fields. Each array has 32 entries so that it can be indexed using the bit positions of a **DWORD**. Undefined bits are assigned the name **Unknown**.

***NOTE:** The following code snippets provide part, but not all, of the source code of the DDCapsViewer program. Omissions are marked with comment marks and ellipses ("// ..."). For your convenience, all 420 lines of source code can be found on the CD-ROM.*

The following code snippets provide part of the source code of the DDCapsViewer program:

```
char* DDCAPS_Bits[] = {          // The names of the bits in DDCAPS::dwCaps
    "DDCAPS_3D",
    "DDCAPS_ALIGNBOUNDARYDEST",
    "DDCAPS_ALIGNSIZEDEST",
    // ...
    "DDCAPS_CANBLTSYSMEM"
};

char* DDCAPS2_Bits[] = {         // The names of the bits in DDCAPS::dwCaps2
    "DDCAPS2_CERTIFIED",
    "DDCAPS2_NO2DDURING3DSCENE",
    "DDCAPS2_VIDEOPORT",
    // ...
    "Unknown"
};

// ...
```

The DDCapsViewer program uses the application-defined **PrintBitField** function to format a **DWORD** bit field as a list of bit names. The string **BitFieldName** ends up in the file as a string of the form "<BitFieldName> =". The names of the set bits are printed indented below that line:

```
void PrintBitField(
    fstream &os,                 // stream to output to
    DWORD BitField,              // the bit field
    char *BitFieldName,          // the name of the bit field
    char **BitNames              // array containing the names of the bits
   )
{
   os << BitFieldName << "=" << endl;   // Print name of bit field

   for (int bit=0; bit < 32; bit++)     // Iterate through bits
   {
      try
      {
         if (BitField & (1 << bit))  // if bit is set
         {
            os << "    " << BitNames[bit] << endl;  // print name of bit
         }
      }
      catch (...)
      {
         os << "    Exception at bit " << bit << endl;
      }
   }
}
```

The **PrintDDCaps** function uses **PrintBitField** to format every bit field in the passed **DDCAPS** structure (e.g., **dwCaps**, **dwCKeyCaps**, **dwSVBCaps2**, and so on). The **PRINTDW** macro is a shortcut to format single **DWORD** values:

```
// PRINTDW: Macro that outputs a DWORD to a stream
#define PRINTDW(dw) os << #dw << " = " << dw << endl

void PrintDDCaps(fstream &os, DDCAPS &DDCaps)
{
   PrintBitField(os, DDCaps.dwCaps, "dwCaps", DDCAPS_Bits);
   PrintBitField(os, DDCaps.dwCaps2, "dwCaps2", DDCAPS2_Bits);
   PrintBitField(os, DDCaps.dwCKeyCaps, "dwCKeyCaps", DDCKEYCAPS_Bits);
   // ...
   PRINTDW(DDCaps.dwVidMemTotal);
   PRINTDW(DDCaps.dwVidMemFree);
```

```
    PRINTDW(DDCaps.dwMaxVisibleOverlays);
    // ...
}
```

In the following code, the **WinMain** function initializes DirectDraw and queries the capabilities by using the **IDirectDraw7::GetCaps** method. A text file is created and filled by **PrintDDCaps** with information about both hardware and emulation capabilities. Finally, the file is opened with the associated viewer (usually Notepad):


```
#define INITGUID                // Alternatively, you can link to dxguid.lib
#include <windows.h>
#include <ddraw.h>              // Don't forget to link to ddraw.lib!
#include <iostream>
#include <fstream.h>

// SAFERELEASE: macro to release COM interfaces
#define SAFERELEASE(x) if (x) { x->Release(); x = NULL; }


WINAPI WinMain(HINSTANCE, HINSTANCE, LPSTR, int)
{
   LPDIRECTDRAW7 lpDD=NULL;

try
{
   // create and initialize DirectDraw object
   DirectDrawCreateEx(
      NULL,                    // primary display device
      reinterpret_cast<LPVOID*>(&lpDD),
      IID_IDirectDraw7, NULL
   );

   // prepare DDCAPS structures
   DDCAPS HardwareCaps;
   DDCAPS EmulationCaps;
   HardwareCaps.dwSize = sizeof(HardwareCaps);
   EmulationCaps.dwSize = sizeof(EmulationCaps);

   // query capabilities
   if (SUCCEEDED(lpDD->GetCaps(&HardwareCaps, &EmulationCaps)))
   {
      // open a file
      fstream f("ddcaps.txt", ios_base::out | ios_base::trunc);

      // ...
```

```
        // print hardware caps
        f << "Hardware capabilities" << endl;
        f << "--------------------" << endl;
        PrintDDCaps(f, HardwareCaps);
        f << endl;
        f << endl;

        // print emulation caps
        f << "Emulation capabilities" << endl;
        f << "----------------------" << endl;
        PrintDDCaps(f, EmulationCaps);

        f.close();

        // try to display ddcaps.txt:
        if (MessageBox(
           NULL,
           "GetCaps returned successfully. Report was generated.\n"
           "Open ddcaps.txt with associated program?",
           "Display GetCaps Results?",
           MB_YESNO | MB_ICONQUESTION
        ) == IDYES)
        {
           ShellExecute(NULL, NULL, "ddcaps.txt", NULL, NULL, SW_SHOWNORMAL);
        }
     }

     // call IDirectDraw7::Release
     SAFERELEASE(lpDD);

  }
  catch (...)
  {
     MessageBox(NULL, "Exception caught", "There was a fatal exception.",
        MB_OK | MB_ICONERROR);
     SAFERELEASE(lpDD);
  }

     return 0;
  }
```

For related information, see “Retrieving the Driver Name and Version” and “Querying the Amount of Available Video Memory.”

Retrieving the Driver Name and Version

The **IDirectDraw7::GetDeviceIdentifier** method can be used to gather information about the display driver. This kind of information is often presented to the user in an "About" box. This information can also be used to identify configurations that might cause problems (if there are any known issues with those configurations). The **GetDeviceIdentifier** method is declared as follows:


```
HRESULT IDirectDraw7::GetDeviceIdentifier(
    LPDDDEVICEIDENTIFIER2 lpdddi,    // pointer to DDDEVICEIDENTIFIER2
    DWORD dwFlags                    // option flags
   );
```

The **lpdddi** parameter points to a **DDDEVICEIDENTIFIER2** structure that will receive information about the device. The **dwFlags** parameter can be set to **DDGDI_GETHOSTIDENTIFIER** to retrieve information about only the host adapter of a stacked secondary device (such as a 3D accelerator with no 2D capabilities). You can alternatively set **dwFlags** to zero, in which case the **GetDeviceIdentifier** function retrieves information about the secondary device. For example:

```
// lpDD is assumed to be a valid pointer to an IDirectDraw7 interface

// retrieve device identifier
DDDEVICEIDENTIFIER2 di;
if (SUCCEEDED(lpDD->GetDeviceIdentifier(&di, 0)))
{
   /*
      interpret di
   */
}
```

The members of the **DDDEVICEIDENTIFIER2** structure are interpreted as follows:

- **szDriver** and **szDescription**—Present these to the user. The **szDriver** member is the driver file name, and the **szDescription** member is the name of the device as it appears in the Control Panel.
- **liDriverVersion**—A version string of the form "x.xx.xx.xxxx" is assembled as follows:

```
char Buf[100];
wsprintf(
   Buf,
```

```
    "%d.%02d.%02d.%04d",
    HIWORD(di.liDriverVersion.HighPart),
    LOWORD(di.liDriverVersion.HighPart),
    HIWORD(di.liDriverVersion.LowPart),
    LOWORD(li.liDriverVersion. LowPart)
);
```

- **dwVendorId**, **dwDeviceId**, **dwSubSysId**, **dwRevision**—Compare these to known identifiers. These are not reliable when you're trying to identify a driver/chipset pair.
- **guidDeviceIdentifier**—Use this to identify specific driver/chipset pairs. You can use the COM helper function **StringFromGUID2** to convert **guidDeviceIdentifier** into a string of printable characters:

```
OLECHAR GuidStr[50];
StringFromGUID2(di.guidDeviceIdentifier, GuidStr, 50);
char Str[50];
wsprintf(Str, "%ls", GuidStr);

// present Str to the user
```

- **dwWHQLLevel**—This specifies the level of Windows Hardware Quality Labs certification. Compare this to known values or decode with **GET_WHQL_YEAR**, **GET_WHQL_MONTH**, and **GET_WHQL_DAY** macros.

See also "Determining the Capabilities of the Video Hardware" and "Querying the Amount of Available Video Memory."

Querying the Amount of Available Video Memory

You can use the **IDirectDraw7::GetAvailableVidMem** method to retrieve either the total amount of video memory or the amount of free video memory for a given type of surface. The **GetAvailableVidMem** method uses the following parameters:

```
HRESULT IDirectDraw7::GetAvailableVidMem(
    LPDDSCAPS2 lpDDSCaps2,      // pointer to DDCAPS2 structure
    LPDWORD    lpdwTotal,       // total amount of memory
    LPDWORD    lpdwFree         // amount of free memory
  );
```

The **lpDDSCaps2** parameter is a pointer to a **DDSCAPS2** structure that describes the surface type for which the amount of free memory is to be queried. The **lpdwTotal** parameter receives the total amount of memory if the **GetAvailableVidMem** function is successful. This does not include the amount of memory currently reserved for the screen. The **lpdwFree** parameter receives the amount of memory that can be used to create the specified type of surface. One of these two pointers can be **NULL**.

WARNING! The lpDDSCaps2 parameter must be a valid pointer even if lpdwFree is NULL.

The following code snippet can be used to find out how much memory is available for off-screen surfaces. This code also estimates the amount of memory physically installed on the graphics card:

```
// lpDD is assumed to be a valid pointer to an IDirectDraw7 interface

LPDIRECTDRAWSURFACE7 lpDDSPrimary = NULL;

try
{
   // prepare DDSCAPS2
   DDSCAPS2 DDSCaps;
   ZeroMemory(&DDSCaps, sizeof(DDSCaps));
   DDSCaps.dwCaps = DDSCAPS_OFFSCREENPLAIN;

   DWORD dwTotal;
   DWORD dwFree;

   // call GetAvailableVidMem
   lpDD->GetAvailableVidMem(
      &DDSCaps,
      &dwTotal,
      &dwFree
   );

   // dwFree gives the amount of memory for off-screen surfaces
   // dwTotal gives the total amount of (not necessarily free) memory

   // estimate amount of on-board memory

   // we need a primary surface
   // (see Chapter 13)
   DDSURFACEDESC2 ddsd;
   ZeroMemory(&ddsd, sizeof(ddsd));
   ddsd.dwSize = sizeof(ddsd);
```

```
    ddsd.dwFlags = DDSD_CAPS;         // mark ddsCaps as valid
    ddsd.ddsCaps.dwCaps = DDSCAPS_PRIMARYSURFACE;

    lpDD->CreateSurface(&ddsd, &lpDDSPrimary, NULL);

    // query surface characteristics
    lpDDSPrimary->GetSurfaceDesc(&ddsd);

    SAFERELEASE(lpDDSPrimary);

    // surface size in bytes = bytes per scan line * number of scan lines
    DWORD SurfaceSizeInBytes = ddsd.lPitch * ddsd.dwHeight;

    // amount of on-board memory = dwTotal + size of primary surface
    DWORD PhysicalVideoMemory = dwTotal + SurfaceSizeInBytes;
}
catch (...)
{
    SAFERELEASE(lpDDSPrimary);
}
```

See also "Determining the Capabilities of the Video Hardware" and "Retrieving the Driver Name and Version."

IDirectDraw7-Related Error Codes

Table 11.2 lists the error codes that are frequently returned by the **IDirectDraw7** methods.

Table 11.2 Error codes that are frequently returned by the IDirectDraw7 methods.

Error Code Probable Cause	Suggested Solution
DDERR_ALREADYINITIALIZED	
You called the **IDirectDraw7::Initialize** method twice or after a call to the **DirectDrawCreateEx** function.	Call **Initialize** only once. **DirectDrawCreateEx** initializes DirectDraw automatically.
DDERR_EXCLUSIVEMODEALREADYSET	
You were trying to set the cooperative level to **DDSCL_NORMAL** but exclusive mode had been set before. This error code can also be a return value of the **TestCooperativeLevel** method.	You can't change the cooperative level from full-screen exclusive to normal. Destroy and re-create the DirectDraw object instead. This code is not an error when returned by the **TestCooperativeLevel** method.

(continued)

Table 11.2 Error codes that are frequently returned by the IDirectDraw7 methods *(continued)*.

Error Code Probable Cause	Suggested Solution
DDERR_INCOMPATIBLEPRIMARY This is caused by the **CreateSurface** method when you're creating the primary surface. The passed **DDSURFACEDESC2** structure does not accurately describe the current display mode.	To create a primary surface, specify only the **DDSCAPS_PRIMARYSURFACE** flag in **ddsCaps.dwCaps**. Set the **dwFlags** member to **DDSD_CAPS**.
DDERR_INVALIDDIRECTDRAWGUID You passed an invalid GUID to the **DirectDrawCreateEx** function.	Enumerate devices every time your application is started, or use the **NULL** GUID. Devices can be removed from the system or drivers updated between sessions.
DDERR_INVALIDPARAMS You passed **NULL** when a valid pointer was required, or you forgot to set the **dwSize** member of a structure, or one of the flags is not allowed in this context.	Use **ZeroMemory** to reset a structure before setting its members. If the structure has a **dwSize** member, set it to the size of the structure (not to the size of a pointer to it). Check the reference manual to determine whether the flags are valid.
DDERR_INVALIDPIXELFORMAT When calling the **CreateSurface** method, the **ddpfPixelFormat** member of the **DDSURFACEDESC2** structure contained invalid values.	Use **ZeroMemory** to clear the entire **DDSURFACEDESC2** structure (which clears the **ddpfPixelFormat** member as well) before setting individual members of the structure. Make sure that the specified values and value combinations are allowed. See Chapter 13 for more information.
DDERR_NOCOOPERATIVELEVELSET You forgot to call the **SetCooperativeLevel** method.	**SetCooperativeLevel** should be the first **IDirectDraw7** method you call.
DDERR_NODIRECTDRAWHW You tried to use **DDCREATE_HARDWAREONLY** with the **DirectDrawCreateEx** function, but no hardware support is available.	Try the **NULL** GUID in calls to **DirectDraw-CreateEx** and **IDirectDraw7::Initialize**.
DDERR_NODIRECTDRAWSUPPORT The display driver does not support DirectDraw.	Ask the user to update the drivers.
DDERR_NOEXCLUSIVEMODE You tried to use a method that requires an exclusive cooperative level to be set while the cooperative level was **DDSCL_NORMAL**, or you called the **TestCooperativeLevel** method.	Set the cooperative level to **DDSCL_FULLSCREEN | DDSCL_EXCLUSIVE**. This is not an error when returned by the **TestCooperativeLevel** method.

(continued)

Table 11.2 Error codes that are frequently returned by the IDirectDraw7 methods *(continued)*.

Error Code Probable Cause	Suggested Solution
DDERR_NOFOCUSWINDOW You tried to set the device window before the focus window was set.	Call the **SetCooperativeLevel** method with the **DDSCL_SETFOCUSWINDOW** flag before using **DDSCL_SETDEVICEWINDOW** or together with **DDSCL_CREATEDEVICEWINDOW**.
DDERR_NOTINITIALIZED You tried to use an **IDirectDraw7** method before calling the **Initialize** method of the interface.	When using the **CoCreateInstance** function, call **Initialize** first. The **DirectDrawCreateEx** function does this automatically.
DDERR_OUTOFMEMORY There was not enough memory for DirectDraw to complete an operation.	Warning the user is probably the only thing you can do.
DDERR_OUTOFVIDEOMEMORY The surface could not be created because there was not enough video memory.	Check whether there is enough memory to create a surface of the specified size (e.g., with the **GetAvailableVidMem** method). Specify smaller values for the **dwWidth** and **dwHeight** members of the **DDSURFACEDESC2** structure.
DDERR_PRIMARYSURFACEALREADYEXISTS You tried to create multiple primary surfaces.	The primary surface represents the screen. There can be only one primary surface per display device at any given time.
DDERR_UNSUPPORTED This is returned by the **CreatePalette** method when the specified palette can't be created.	Use **IDirectDraw7::GetCaps** to query the palette capabilities.
DDERR_UNSUPPORTEDMODE The screen is currently set to an unsupported mode.	Create a full-screen application and use the **SetDisplayMode** method, or ask the user to change the desktop settings.
DDERR_WRONGMODE This is returned by the **TestCooperativeLevel** method when the display mode has changed while a windowed application was active.	Destroy and re-create all DirectDraw surfaces.

Chapter 12

DirectDraw Display Modes

In Depth

The Windows operating system supports a wide variety of graphics cards. Therefore, Windows applications must be written in a way that allows them to handle various resolutions and color depths. For example, a spreadsheet must work at 640×480 equally as well as at 800×600. Usually, this can be achieved by simply adding scroll bars, implementing word wrap, scaling child windows, and the like.

With games and multimedia applications, it's different. Their graphics are often pre-rendered for a specific resolution. If the desktop resolution is lower than that, the graphics won't fit. If it's higher, the graphics don't fill up the screen and video memory is wasted. The situation is similar with color depths: One application requires a true-color mode to be set; another one requires a palettized mode. In short, sometimes it's necessary that (or at least convenient if) your application can choose its own display mode. That's possible with DirectDraw.

An Overview of Display Modes

A display mode is defined by a resolution, a color depth, and—optionally—a refresh rate. The resolution specifies how many pixels the screen is divided into. It has a horizontal and a vertical component. For example, at a resolution of 640×480 there are 640 pixels along the physical width of the screen and 480 pixels along its physical height. The color depth, or "bit depth," specifies how many bits are used to store the color of each pixel—the more bits, the higher the visual fidelity. Finally, the refresh rate, or "monitor frequency," specifies how often the screen is refreshed per second.

Bit Depths

There is a fundamental difference between 4- and 8-bit modes on the one hand and 16-, 24-, and 32-bit modes on the other hand. The former are palettized; the latter are true-color modes.

In a palettized mode, every pixel is stored as an index into a color table, the palette. An 8-bit palette has 256 entries, a 4-bit palette has 16 entries. These entries, in turn, store the red, green, and blue intensities of the color. The number of different colors that can be visible *at the same time* is limited by the size of the palette. However, the choice of colors is completely up to you.

True-color modes, on the other hand, store the complete color information for every single pixel. In the 24- and 32-bit modes, there are 8 bits for every color component. In a 16-bit mode (sometimes referred to as "high-color"), there are 16 bits for all 3 color components together. Usually, but not necessarily, that's five bits each and an unused bit. The benefit of higher bit depths is obvious: There are 16.8 million possible shades in a 24-bit mode (2^{3*8}) but only 65,536 in a 16-bit mode (2^{16}). The drawback is obvious as well: 32-bit modes take up twice as much memory as 16-bit modes.

***NOTE:** The only purpose of the 8 unused bits in 32-bit modes is to speed up memory operations. **DWORD**-aligned data is easier to process than data aligned on a 3-byte (24-bit) boundary.*

Refresh Rates

The screen is not updated every time you set the color of a pixel. Rather, this is done at a fixed refresh rate. Traditional monitors are equipped with a cathode ray tube (CRT), where a cathode ray scans the screen and lights up phosphor particles. These particles lose their brightness almost immediately, which makes it necessary that the cathode ray returns to every single one of them multiple times per second. Figure 12.1 illustrates this process.

The cathode ray starts at the upper left corner of the screen and moves to the right. When it reaches the end of a scan line, it moves to the beginning of the next

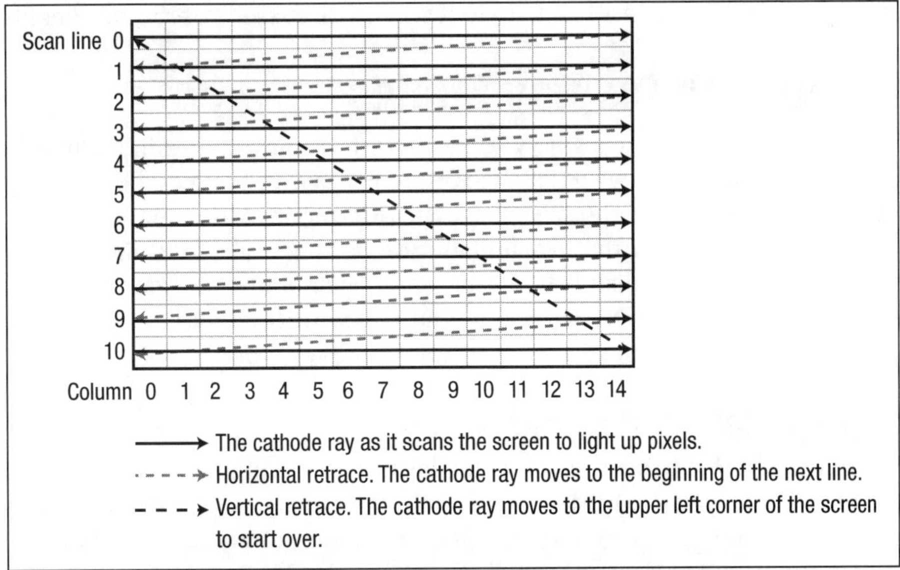

Figure 12.1 The cathode ray at work at a hypothetical 15×11 resolution.

one. This movement is called "horizontal retrace." When the ray reaches the lower right corner of the screen, it moves back up to the upper left corner. That moving back up is the "vertical retrace."

NOTE: *I'm going to use the terms "retrace" and "blank" interchangeably, although they are not exactly the same thing. The vertical blank includes the period when the cathode ray scans a few lines above and below the visible area without lighting up pixels. The vertical and horizontal blanks are the cause for the thin black border around the screen.*

The graphics card takes the color information from the frame buffer and feeds it to the monitor as the ray moves by the pixels. Changes to the contents of the frame buffer won't be visible before the next refresh. This behavior can be exploited to prevent tearing artifacts. See "Working with the Vertical Blank," later in this chapter.

Mode 13 and Mode X

In 1987, the original VGA graphics card introduced a 256-color display mode with a resolution of 320 by 200 pixels. Because of the 256 colors, this mode soon became very popular among MS-DOS game developers. Its resolution was only about a fifth of the maximum VGA resolution, but 256 colors was four times as many as had been supported before. The mode's BIOS number is a hexadecimal 13. By tweaking the VGA registers, one can enable up to three off-screen buffers in which graphics can be prepared before they are displayed. The tweaked Mode 13 is called Mode X. These modes can still be used with DirectDraw when low resolutions are required. Mode 13 and Mode X will be discussed later in this chapter.

Working with Display Modes

In this section, we'll discuss how to work with display modes in a DirectDraw application. First of all, we'll use the **EnumDisplayModes** method to retrieve a list of supported modes. Next, we'll use the **SetDisplayMode** method to change the display mode. After that, we'll elaborate on the Mode 13 vs. Mode X topic. We'll discuss what the deal is with these modes and how you can use them. Finally, we'll use the **GetDisplayMode** and **GetMonitorFrequency** methods to retrieve information about the currently set display mode.

Display Mode Enumeration

Before you attempt to set a specific display mode, you should check whether it's available. Either you can retrieve a list of all supported modes, or you can provide a mode description and have only matching modes enumerated. In both cases, the method to call is **IDirectDraw7::EnumDisplayModes**.

Among the parameters of the **EnumDisplayModes** method is a pointer to an application-defined callback function. This callback is invoked by DirectDraw for every available display mode. The characteristics of the enumerated mode are passed to the callback in a **DDSURFACEDESC2** structure. As the name suggests, this structure is used primarily in conjunction with DirectDraw surfaces. However, surfaces have similar characteristics as display modes: a horizontal and a vertical dimension and a bit depth. Therefore, the structure can easily be used for display modes as well.

Here's how you should implement the callback:

```
HRESULT WINAPI MyEnumModesCallback(      //
    LPDDSURFACEDESC2 lpDDSurfaceDesc,    // mode description
    LPVOID lpContext                     // application-defined value as
                                         // passed to EnumDisplayModes
   )
{
try
{
   /*
     Extract information from the DDSURFACEDESC2 structure here
     and store it in an array, write it into a list box, or the like.
     See also "Retrieving Information about the Current Mode,"
     later in this chapter.
   */

   return DDENUMRET_OK;         // continue enumeration
}
catch (...)
{
   return DDENUMRET_CANCEL;     // stop enumeration
}
}
```

The return value of the callback function specifies whether enumeration should be stopped (**DDENUMRET_CANCEL**) or continued (**DDENUMRET_OK**).

Now you can use **MyEnumModesCallback** with the **IDirectDraw7::EnumDisplayModes** method. Following is a typical usage example:

```
// lpDD is assumed to be a valid pointer to an IDirectDraw7 interface

if (FAILED(lpDD->EnumDisplayModes(
   DDEDM_REFRESHRATES,       // enumerate possible refresh rates for the
                             // different resolutions
```

```
    NULL,                   // enumerate all resolutions
    NULL,        // application-defined value to be passed to the callback
    MyEnumModesCallback     // pointer to our callback
)))
{
    throw "Display mode enumeration failed.";
}
```


The first parameter specifies optional flags. We set this to **DDEDM_REFRESH-RATES**. This instructs DirectDraw to enumerate all possible refresh rates for the different resolutions. For example, when the 640×480×16 mode (640×480 pixels at 16 bits per pixel) supports a refresh rate of 100 Hz as well as a refresh rate of 85 Hz, the callback is invoked twice for the 640×480×16 mode—once with the **dwRefreshRate** member of the **DDSURFACEDESC2** structure set to 100, and once with **dwRefreshRate** set to 85. However, some drivers are not capable of enumerating refresh rates, in which case each mode is enumerated only once with **dwRefreshRate** being set to 0.

The second parameter of the **EnumDisplayModes** method is a pointer to a **DDSURFACEDESC2** structure. This parameter can be used to find out whether a specific resolution or bit depth is supported. For this purpose, the **DDSURFACEDESC2** structure must be initialized with the desired characteristics. The **dwFlags** parameter of the structure is used to indicate which members contain valid data. Before the **EnumDisplayModes** method passes information about a display mode to the callback, it checks whether the mode has the desired characteristics. The mode is enumerated only if the characteristics match. The following example demonstrates how you can instruct **EnumDisplayModes** to enumerate all modes with a horizontal resolution of 800 pixels:

```
// lpDD is assumed to be a valid pointer to an IDirectDraw7 interface

// prepare mode description
DDSURFACEDESC2 ModeDescription;
ZeroMemory(&ModeDescription, sizeof(ModeDescription));
ModeDescription.dwSize = sizeof(ModeDescription);
ModeDescription.dwFlags = DDSD_WIDTH;        // mark dwWidth as valid
ModeDescription.dwWidth = 800;

// enumerate modes
if (FAILED(lpDD->EnumDisplayModes(
    DDEDM_REFRESHRATES,
    &ModeDescription,            // check modes against this description
                                 // before enumerating them
    NULL,
```

```
   MyEnumModesCallback
)))
{
   throw "Enumerating display modes failed.";
}
```

If you do not pass a mode description, all display modes are enumerated.

Setting Display Modes

Once you have retrieved a list of supported modes and have chosen one, you are free to switch to that mode at any time, regardless of the desktop settings. The changes in resolution and bit depth take effect immediately and are not persistent, i.e., the desktop mode is restored when your application terminates. To set the display mode, you simply call the **IDirectDraw7::SetDisplayMode** method with the new resolution, the new bit depth, and the new refresh rate as its parameters. The following example shows how this might look:

```
// lpDD is assumed to be a valid pointer to an IDirectDraw7 interface

lpDD->SetDisplayMode(
   Width,        // new horizontal...
   Height,       // ...and vertical resolution
   BPP,          // new bit depth
   0,            // use the default refresh rate
   0             // no special flags
);
```

In most cases, you will want to set the fourth parameter of the **SetDisplayMode** method—the one that specifies the refresh rate—to zero. This instructs DirectDraw to use the driver's default refresh rate. Some drivers will always use the default anyway, regardless of the value that you specify. The flags parameter, finally, is used to switch to Mode 13, which we'll discuss in the next section.

Both full-screen and windowed applications are allowed to use **SetDisplayMode**. However, there are some advantages to using this method when you're creating a full-screen application. For example, when a full-screen application loses focus, the display mode is automatically restored to the desktop setting. The word processor, or other program, that is running in the background doesn't even notice that the display mode has been changed. In a windowed application, on the other hand, the new mode remains set until **IDirectDraw7::RestoreDisplayMode** is called or the **IDirectDraw7** interface is released. Other currently running applications might resize and rearrange their windows according to the new resolution, which might be an undesired effect.

Setting and Enumerating Mode 13 and Mode X

Earlier in this chapter, I mentioned that DirectDraw supports Mode 13 and Mode X. I said that Mode 13 has a resolution of 320×200×8 and that Mode X supports two resolutions: 320×200×8 and 320×240×8. Today, 320×200 sounds as low a resolution as it is. Nevertheless, low-resolution modes can still be useful. Think, for example, about a video player: There is no better resolution to play back one of those postage-stamp-sized Internet videos than 320×200.

As it turns out, however, Mode 13 and Mode X are handled slightly differently than other display modes. In particular, Mode X imposes limitations that might cause applications to fail if they're not specifically written to support Mode X modes. (We'll get back to these limitations soon.) Therefore, applications must "register" themselves as Mode X-aware by specifying the **DDSCL_ALLOWMODEX** flag in the call to the **SetCooperativeLevel**. (See Chapter 11 for more information about setting cooperative levels.) To set one of the Mode X modes (either 320×200×8 or 320×240×8), you simply specify its resolution and bit depth when calling the **SetDisplayMode** method. To set Mode 13, on the other hand, you must specify the **DDSDM_STANDARDVGAMODE** flag to distinguish it from the 320×200×8 Mode X mode:

```
// lpDD is assumed to be a valid pointer to an IDirectDraw7 interface

lpDD->SetDisplayMode(
   320, 200, 8,              // resolution
   0,                        // default refresh rate
   DDSDM_STANDARDVGAMODE     // request Mode 13
);
```

Mode X modes have one severe limitation: They do not allow applications to access the primary surface (the screen), neither through **IDirectDrawSurface7::Lock** nor through **IDirectDrawSurface7::Blt** nor by using GDI functions on it. Only the back buffers of the primary surface flipping chain can be accessed. Their contents are then displayed by calling the **IDirectDrawSurface7::Flip** method. Mode 13, on the other hand, does allow direct access to the primary surface, but it does not support real page flipping. In Mode 13, the **Flip** method is emulated through a blit operation. For more information about the **IDirectDrawSurface7** interface and page flipping, see Chapter 13.

When calling the **EnumDisplayModes** method, you must specify the **DDEDM_STANDARDVGAMODES** flag to enumerate Mode 13. When Mode 13 is enumerated, the **ddsCaps.dwCaps** field of the **DDSURFACEDESC2** structure that is passed to the callback contains the **DDSCAPS_STANDARDVGAMODE** flag. When a Mode X mode is enumerated, that field contains the

DDSCAPS_MODEX flag. If neither flag is set for a 320×200×8 or a 320×240×8 mode, a so-called linear accelerated mode is enumerated. Linear accelerated modes do not have the limitations of Mode X and Mode 13. Their primary surface can be accessed directly and page flipping is supported. When calling the **SetDisplayMode** method, linear accelerated modes always override Mode 13 and Mode X modes, regardless of any flags that you specify.

For a programming example, see "Using Mode X and Mode 13" in the "Immediate Solutions" section.

Retrieving Information about the Current Mode

With DirectDraw, you cannot only *change* display modes, but you can also *query* the characteristics of the currently set mode. In this section, we'll use the **IDirectDraw7::GetDisplayMode** method to do this. Furthermore, we'll discuss how to extract the relevant information from the **DDSURFACEDESC2** structure that the method fills.

TIP: DDSURFACEDESC2 *structures are also used by the* ***EnumDisplayModes*** *method and its callback function. Therefore, the information presented in this section applies to the section on "Display Mode Enumeration" as well.*

The only parameter of the **GetDisplayMode** method is a pointer to a **DDSURFACEDESC2** structure. This structure is filled with information about the currently set display mode when the method returns. Before **GetDisplayMode** is called, you must initialize the **dwSize** member of the structure. The following code snippet demonstrates this:

```
// lpDD is assumed to be a valid pointer to an IDirectDraw7 interface

DDSURFACEDESC2 ModeDescription;
ZeroMemory(&ModeDescription, sizeof(ModeDescription));
ModeDescription.dwSize = sizeof(ModeDescription);

if (FAILED(lpDD->GetDisplayMode(&ModeDescription)))
{  throw "Querying the current mode failed."; }
```

When **GetDisplayMode** returns successfully, the **ModeDescription** structure contains information about the resolution and bit depth of the current mode. The resolution, in pixels, is given in the **dwWidth** and **dwHeight** members of the structure. The refresh rate is contained in the **dwRefreshRate** member and can be zero to indicate a driver default. The bit depth is given in the **ddpfPixelFormat** member, which is a structure of type **DDPIXELFORMAT**. First of all, you should find out whether the mode is a palettized mode or a true-color mode. For this, you check whether the **dwFlags** member of the **ddpfPixelFormat** structure contains the **DDPF_RGB** flag. If it does, the mode is a true-color mode and the bit depth is contained in the **ddpfPixelFormat.dwRGBBitCount** member. Otherwise, the **dwFlags** member contains one of the **DDPF_PALETTEINDEXED*n*** flags. If **DDPF_PALETTEINDEXED8** is set, the mode is an 8-bit (256-color) mode. If **DDPF_PALETTEINDEXED4** is set, the mode is a 4-bit (16-color) mode.

NOTE: *There are also* ***DDPF_PALETTEINDEXED1*** *and* ***DDPF_PALETTEINDEXED2*** *flags, but in practice, you won't encounter such display modes.*

The following code demonstrates how you would fill a variable with the bit depth of the display mode:

```
// create a shortcut for the flags member of the pixel format structure
DWORD dwFlags = ModeDescription.ddpfPixelFormat.dwFlags;

DWORD BitDepth;
if (dwFlags & DDPF_RGB)
{
   BitDepth = ModeDescription.ddpfPixelFormat.dwRGBBitCount;
}
else if (dwFlags & DDPF_PALETTEINDEXED4)
{  BitDepth = 8; }
else if (dwFlags & DDPF_PALETTEINDEXED8)
{  BitDepth = 4; }
else
{
   throw "Unexpected mode.";
}
```

Finally, you can find out whether the current mode is Mode 13 or Mode X. To do this, examine the **dwCaps** member of the **DDSCAPS2** structure that is part of the **DDSURFACEDESC2** structure. If the bit field contains the **DDSCAPS_MODEX** flag, a Mode X is set. If it contains the **DDSCAPS_STANDARDVGAMODE** flag, Mode 13 is set. Otherwise, the display mode is a linear accelerated mode. The following code demonstrates how you would check for Mode X and Mode 13:

```
// mode type constants
static const int MODE_13 = 1;
static const int MODE_X = 2;
static const int LINEAR_ACCELERATED = 3;

int ModeType;           // this variable will be filled
```

```
// create a shortcut for the dwCaps member of the surface caps structure
DWORD dwCaps = ModeDescription.ddsCaps.dwCaps;

if (dwCaps & DDSCAPS_STANDARDVGAMODE)
{  ModeType = MODE_13; }
else if (dwCaps & DDSCAPS_MODEX)
{  ModeType = MODE_X; }
else
{  ModeType = LINEAR_ACCELERATED; }
```

As a final note, you shouldn't save the information returned by the **GetDisplayMode** method for the purpose of restoring the default mode at a later time. Otherwise, when the user changes the desktop settings while your application is running, you'd restore a display mode that isn't the default mode anymore. You should use the **IDirectDraw7::RestoreDisplayMode** method instead.

Working with the Vertical Blank

At the beginning of this chapter, when we discussed the cathode ray, I mentioned that the vertical blank has something to do with tearing artifacts. First of all, let's discuss what tearing artifacts actually are.

Take a look at Figure 12.2. Initially, all pixels in the frame buffer are white. The screen, of course, is white as well. At time index 1, you issue a DirectDraw command that sets all pixels to a gray color. The cathode ray (represented by the

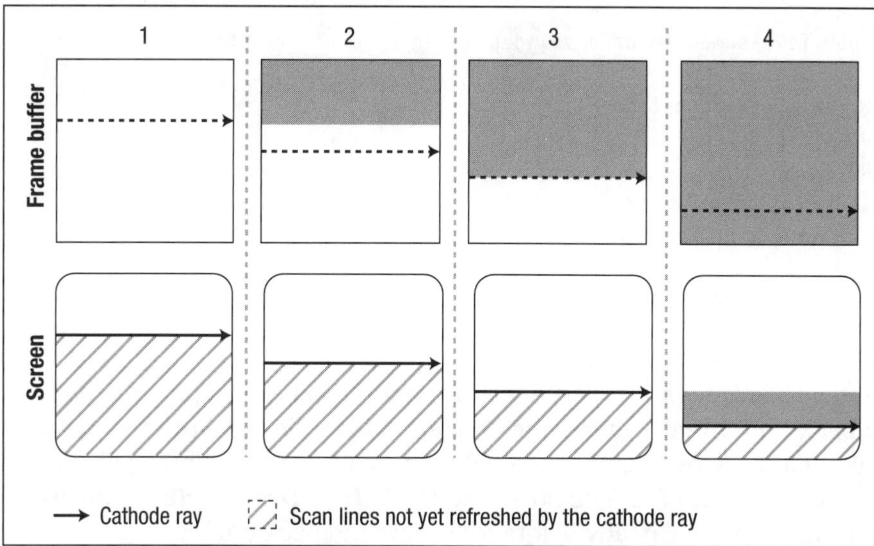

Figure 12.2 The cause of tearing artifacts.

arrow) is currently at a scan line in the upper half of the screen. At time index 2, the pixels in the upper third of the frame buffer have been set. In the meantime, the cathode ray has moved down a few lines. On its way from position 1 to position 2, however, it didn't come across any gray pixels. Therefore, the screen is still all white. At time index 3, another third of the frame buffer has been filled. At this point, the filling catches up with the cathode ray. Still, the cathode ray hasn't come across any gray pixels. Between time index 3 and time index 4, the frame buffer is filled ahead of the cathode ray. All pixels that the ray comes across are light gray. When, sometime after time index 4, the ray has reached the bottom scan line, the upper two thirds of the screen are white and the lower third is gray. This effect is called a tearing artifact.

Another example involves a moving sprite: When it's blitted to the screen while the cathode ray lights up pixels, the upper half of the sprite might appear at its old position while the lower half is already at its new position. Until the cathode ray returns to the upper half of the screen, the sprite appears torn apart (therefore *tearing artifact*). The artifact is especially noticeable at high frame rates, i.e., when the frame buffer is updated very often.

The trick is to blit to the frame buffer while the cathode ray moves back up to the upper left corner—during the vertical retrace. Before you blit to the primary surface, simply call the **IDirectDraw7::WaitForVerticalBlank** method with the **DDWAITVB_BLOCKBEGIN** flag. When the method returns and the blit command is executed, the vertical blank interval has just begun. The following code demonstrates how a blit operation is synchronized with the vertical blank:

```
// lpDD is assumed to be a valid pointer to an IDirectDraw7 interface

lpDD->WaitForVerticalBlank(
   DDWAITVB_BLOCKBEGIN,
   NULL
);

/*
   perform the blit here
*/
```

A vertical blank interval is very short. Therefore, you should prepare the graphics in a back buffer that you can then display with a single blit during the vertical blank. In a full-screen application with a primary surface flipping chain, you do not have to call **WaitForVerticalBlank**. The **IDirectDrawSurface7::Flip** method synchronizes automatically before it displays the back buffer.

Dialog Boxes in Full-Screen Mode

Windows GUI elements, such as windows and dialog boxes, are automatically drawn to the screen. You don't specify the rendering destination when, say, displaying a dialog box with the **ShowWindow** function. When a DirectDraw full-screen application is active, however, it's not always possible for Windows to access the screen. When page flipping is used, for example, the GDI surface (the GDI's canvas) becomes invisible after every other flip (see also Chapter 13). Some display devices can't be used by the GDI at all. This section demonstrates how standard dialog boxes can nevertheless be used in DirectDraw full-screen applications.

It's all very simple if the device is shared with the GDI (which is always the case for the **NULL** device). In that case, an application calls the **IDirectDraw7::FlipToGDISurface** method once to make the display memory area visible that the GDI draws GUI elements to. To find out whether this is supported, you should check whether the device capabilities contain the **DDCAPS2_CANRENDERWINDOWED** flag. The following code demonstrates this:

```
// lpDD is assumed to be a valid pointer to an IDirectDraw7 interface

// query hardware capabilities
DDCAPS HardwareCaps;
HardwareCaps.dwSize = sizeof(HardwareCaps);
lpDD->GetCaps(&HardwareCaps, NULL);

// check whether the DDCAPS2_CANRENDERWINDOWED flag is set
bool CanFlipToGDI;
if (HardwareCaps.dwCaps2 & DDCAPS2_CANRENDERWINDOWED)
{  CanFlipToGDI = true; }
else
{  CanFlipToGDI = false; }
```

For more information about querying the device capabilities, see Chapter 11.

As long as the dialog box is used, the application must not use page flipping. If it did, the dialog box would flicker or blink. The reason is that every other flip makes the back buffer visible, which the GDI doesn't draw GUI elements to. After another flip, the GDI surface becomes visible again. Instead of flipping, an application uses a blit operation to make the contents of the back buffer visible. An attached clipper ensures that the dialog box is not overwritten. See "Displaying a Dialog Box in Full-Screen Mode" in the "Immediate Solutions" section for an example of how this could be done.

Some devices, namely those that are enumerated by the **DirectDrawEnumerateEx** function when the **DDENUM_NONDISPLAYDEVICES** flag is used, do not support the **FlipToGDISurface** method. These devices do not have the **DDCAPS2_CANRENDERWINDOWED** flag set. On these devices, you have to grab an image of the invisible dialog box using GDI functions. You can obtain a DC to the dialog box by using the **GetWindowDC** function. Then, you use the **IDirectDrawSurface7::GetDC** method to obtain a GDI device context for the DirectDraw back buffer surface. You can then use the GDI function **BitBlt** to transfer the image from the hidden GDI surface to the DirectDraw surface.

WARNING! You can't use this approach on devices that have the DDCAPS2_CANRENDERWINDOWED capability. On these devices, you* must *use the FliptoGDISurface function.

For a complete code listing of both the **FlipToGDISurface** approach and the **GetWindowDC** approach, see "Displaying a Dialog Box in Full-Screen Mode" in the "Immediate Solutions" section.

Immediate Solutions

Setting the Display Mode

To temporarily change the resolution, bit depth, and refresh rate of the screen, call the **IDirectDraw7::SetDisplayMode** method. This method changes the display mode immediately. The new settings are not persistent, i.e., the display mode is restored when the application terminates. The **SetDisplayMode** method is declared as follows:

```
HRESULT IDirectDraw7::SetDisplayMode(
    DWORD dwWidth,              // horizontal resolution
    DWORD dwHeight,             // vertical resolution
    DWORD dwBPP,                // bit depth
    DWORD dwRefreshRate,        // monitor refresh rate
    DWORD dwFlags               // option flags
   );
```

The **dwWidth** and **dwHeight** parameters specify the desired resolution in pixels. The **dwBPP** parameter specifies the desired bit depth. To retrieve a list of supported modes, call the **IDirectDraw7::EnumDisplayModes** method. (See also "Enumerating the Supported Display Modes" and "Checking Whether a Mode Is Available.")

The **dwRefreshRate** parameter can be used to force a specific refresh rate. If this parameter is set to zero, the driver's default refresh rate is chosen. (Supported refresh rates can also be enumerated.) Otherwise, the **dwRefreshRate** parameter specifies the desired refresh rate in Hz (times per second). Please note that some drivers will ignore this parameter.

The **dwFlags** parameter is used to distinguish between Mode X and Mode 13 when a 320×200×8 display mode is requested. In this case, specify **DDSDM_STANDARDVGAMODE** to use Mode 13. The **DDSDM_STANDARDVGAMODE** flag is ignored for resolutions other than 320×200×8 (see "Mode 13 and Mode X" in the "In Depth" section).

The following code snippet sets a display mode with a resolution of 640 by 480 pixels, a bit depth of 8 (256 colors), and the default refresh rate:

```
// lpDD is assumed to be a valid pointer to an IDirectDraw7 interface

// set 640×480×8 mode
if (FAILED(lpDD->SetDisplayMode(
   640, 480,                    // resolution
   8,                           // bit depth
   0,                           // default refresh rate
   0                            // no special flags
)))
{
   throw "Display mode could not be set.";
}
```

Note that an exclusive cooperative level is not required to use the **SetDisplayMode** method.

Enumerating the Supported Display Modes

To retrieve a list of display modes supported by the device that DirectDraw was initialized for, use the **IDirectDraw7::EnumDisplayModes** method (along with an application-defined callback function). Here's the method's declaration:

```
HRESULT IDirectDraw7::EnumDisplayModes(
    DWORD dwFlags,                                  // option flags
    LPDDSURFACEDESC2 lpDDSurfaceDesc2,              // mode description
    LPVOID lpContext,                               // application-defined value
    LPDDENUMMODESCALLBACK2 lpEnumModesCallback      // callback function
   );
```

The **dwFlags** parameter can be zero or one of the following flags:

- **DDEDM_REFRESHRATES** causes **EnumDisplayModes** to enumerate the same resolution and bit depth more than once if more than one refresh rate is available for it. (Some drivers can't enumerate refresh rates, in which case the **dwRefreshRate** member of the mode description that is passed to the callback will be zero.)
- **DDEDM_STANDARDVGAMODES** causes Mode 13 to be enumerated in addition to the Mode X modes. To use this flag, you must have passed the **DDSCL_ALLOWMODEX** flag to the **IDirectDraw7::SetCooperativeLevel** method (see "Mode 13 and Mode X" in the "In Depth" section).

The **lpDDSurfaceDesc2** parameter is a pointer to a **DDSURFACEDESC2** structure describing a display mode. Only those modes will be enumerated that match the description. See "Checking Whether a Mode Is Available" later in this section. This parameter can be **NULL** if all available modes should be enumerated.

The **lpContext** parameter is an application-defined value that will be passed to the callback. It has no predefined meaning attached to it.

The **lpEnumModesCallback** parameter is a pointer to a callback routine that will be invoked for every enumerated mode.

The prototype of the enumeration callback looks like this: (The function name is user-defined.)

```
HRESULT WINAPI EnumModesCallback2(
    LPDDSURFACEDESC2 lpDDSurfaceDesc,     // mode description
    LPVOID lpContext                      // application-defined value
   );
```


The **lpDDSurfaceDesc** parameter is a pointer to a **DDSURFACEDESC2** structure that contains information about the resolution, bit depth, and refresh rate of the enumerated mode. The **lpContext** parameter is the 4-byte value that was passed to **EnumDisplayModes** as the **lpContext** parameter.

DDSURFACEDESC2 structures are also used in conjunction with DirectDraw surfaces. For a complete description of the structure, please refer to Chapter 13. Following is a list of display mode-related members of the **DDSURFACEDESC2** structure:

- **dwWidth** and **dwHeight**—Specify the resolution of the enumerated mode in pixels.
- **ddpfPixelFormat**—This is a **DDPIXELFORMAT** structure with information about the pixel format of the enumerated mode. If the **dwFlags** member of this structure contains the **DDPF_RGB** flag, the enumerated mode is a true-color mode and its bit depth is contained in the **dwRGBBitCount** member of this structure. Otherwise, either **DDPF_PALETTEINDEXED4** (4-bit) or **DDPF_PALETTEINDEXED8** (8-bit) is set.
- **dwRefreshRate**—Specifies the refresh rate of the display mode in Hz.
- **ddsCaps.dwCaps**—This bit field can be examined to distinguish between Mode X and Mode 13. If the bit field contains the **DDSCAPS_MODEX** flag, the enumerated mode is a Mode X mode. If it contains **DDSCAPS_STANDARD VGAMODE**, the enumerated mode is Mode 13. For all other modes, these flags are not set.

The callback function must return **DDENUMRET_OK** to continue the enumeration and return **DDENUMRET_CANCEL** otherwise.

The following programming example demonstrates how display mode enumeration is performed. The callback fills a list box with the mode descriptions. For this purpose, the callback re-declares the **lpContext** parameter as **HWND hListBox**:

```
#define INITGUID
#include <windows.h>
#include <ddraw.h>

#define SAFERELEASE(x) if (x) { x->Release(); x = NULL; }

// mode type constants
static const int MODE_13 = 1;
static const int MODE_X = 2;
static const int LINEAR_ACCELERATED = 3;

// enumeration callback
HRESULT WINAPI MyEnumModesCallback(
    LPDDSURFACEDESC2 lpDDSurfaceDesc,   // mode description
    HWND hListBox                       // list box handle
   )
{
try
{
   DWORD HorizontalResolution = lpDDSurfaceDesc->dwWidth;
   DWORD VerticalResolution = lpDDSurfaceDesc->dwHeight;
   DWORD RefreshRate = lpDDSurfaceDesc->dwRefreshRate;

   // create a shortcut for the flags member of the pixel format structure
   DWORD dwFlags = ModeDescription.ddpfPixelFormat.dwFlags;

   DWORD BitsPerPixel;
   if (dwFlags & DDPF_RGB)
   {
      BitsPerPixel = ModeDescription.ddpfPixelFormat.dwRGBBitCount;
   }
   else if (dwFlags & DDPF_PALETTEINDEXED4)
   {  BitsPerPixel = 8; }
   else if (dwFlags & DDPF_PALETTEINDEXED8)
   {  BitsPerPixel = 4; }

   // create a shortcut for the dwCaps member of the surface caps structure
   DWORD dwCaps = ModeDescription.ddsCaps.dwCaps;
```

```
    int ModeType;           // Mode 13, Mode X, or linear accelerated?
    if (dwCaps & DDSCAPS_STANDARDVGAMODE)
    {  ModeType = MODE_13; }
    else if (dwCaps & DDSCAPS_MODEX)
    {  ModeType = MODE_X; }
    else
    {  ModeType = LINEAR_ACCELERATED; }

    // format the mode description
    // (ex.: "640x480, 16 bits (85 Hz)")
    char Buf[100];
    wsprintf(
       Buf,
       "%lux%lu, %lu bits (%lu Hz)",
       HorizontalResolution,
       VerticalResolution,
       BitsPerPixel,
       RefreshRate
    );

    // append information about mode type
    if (ModeType == MODE_13)
    {  strcat(Buf, ", Mode 13"); }
    else if (ModeType == MODE_X)
    {  strcat(Buf, ", Mode X"); }

    // add string to list box
    SendMessage(
       hListBox,
       LB_ADDSTRING,
       0,
       reinterpret_cast<LPARAM>(Buf)
    );

    return DDENUMRET_OK;
 }
 catch (...)
 {
    return DDENUMRET_CANCEL;              // stop enumeration
 }
}

void DoModeEnumeration(HWND hListBox)
{
    LPDIRECTDRAW7 lpDD = NULL;
```

```
try
{
   // initialize the device for which display modes are to be enumerated
   if (FAILED(DirectDrawCreateEx(
      NULL,
      reinterpret_cast<LPVOID*>(&lpDD),
      IID_IDirectDraw7,
      NULL
   )))
   {
      throw "Initializing DirectDraw failed.";
   }

   // enumerate all display modes and all refresh rates for each mode
   if (FAILED(lpDD->EnumDisplayModes(
      DDEDM_REFRESHRATES,
      NULL,                        // don't check whether mode matches
                                   // description before enumerating it
      reinterpret_cast<LPVOID>(hListBox),   // pass hListBox as lpContext
      reinterpret_cast<LPDDENUMMODESCALLBACK2>(MyEnumModesCallback)
   )))
   {
      throw "Display mode enumeration failed.";
   }

   SAFERELEASE(lpDD);
}
catch(...)
{
   SAFERELEASE(lpDD);
}
}
```

Checking Whether a Mode Is Available

This Immediate Solution is closely related to "Enumerating the Supported Display Modes." It demonstrates the use of the **lpDDSurfaceDesc2** parameter in calls to **EnumDisplayModes**. We'll write an **IsModeAvailable** function that returns **true** or **false** upon passing a resolution and a bit depth. For this purpose, the function fills a **DDSURFACEDESC2** structure with the display mode characteristics that are passed to the function. It then passes this structure to the **EnumDisplayModes** function. The callback simply sets a Boolean variable to **true** if it is called. If the Boolean variable is still **false** when **EnumDisplayModes** returns, the callback hasn't been called, which means that a matching mode isn't available. The **IsModeAvailable** function is implemented as follows:

```
bool IsModeAvailable(
    LPDIRECTDRAW7 lpDD,          // IDirectDraw7 interface pointer
    DWORD dwWidth,               // horizontal resolution
    DWORD dwHeight,              // vertical resolution
    DWORD dwBitDepth             // bit depth
   )
{
   bool bIsAvail = false;        // so far, we haven't seen the mode

try
{
   // prepare a mode description
   DDSURFACEDESC2 ModeDescription;
   ZeroMemory(&ModeDescription, sizeof(ModeDescription));
   ModeDescription.dwSize = sizeof(ModeDescription);
   // mark dwWidth, dwHeight, and ddpfPixelFormat as valid
   ModeDescription.dwFlags = DDSD_WIDTH | DDSD_HEIGHT | DDSD_PIXELFORMAT;
   // specify resolution
   ModeDescription.dwWidth = dwWidth;
   ModeDescription.dwHeight = dwHeight;
   // specify bit depth
   ModeDescription.ddpfPixelFormat.dwSize = sizeof(DDPIXELFORMAT);
   if (dwBitDepth > 8)
   {
      ModeDescription.ddpfPixelFormat.dwFlags = DDPF_RGB;
      ModeDescription.ddpfPixelFormat.dwRGBBitCount = dwBitDepth;
   }
   else if (dwBitDepth == 8)
   {  ModeDescription.ddpfPixelFormat.dwFlags = DDPF_PALETTEINDEXED8; }
   else if (dwBitDepth == 4)
   {  ModeDescription.ddpfPixelFormat.dwFlags = DDPF_PALETTEINDEXED4; }

   // perform the enumeration
   if (FAILED(lpDD->EnumDisplayModes(
      DDEDM_REFRESHRATES,
      &ModeDescription,
      reinterpret_cast<bool*>(&bIsAvail),   // pass bIsAvail as lpContext
      reinterpret_cast<LPDDENUMMODESCALLBACK2>(CheckModeAvailCallback)
   )))
   {
      throw "Display mode enumeration failed.";
   }
```

```
        // if callback has found a matching mode, bIsAvail is true,
        // otherwise it's false
        return bIsAvail;
    }
    catch(...)
    {
        return bIsAvail;
    }
}
```


The above function specifies **CheckModeAvailCallback** as the application-defined enumeration callback function. This function is implemented as follows:

```
HRESULT WINAPI CheckModeAvailCallback(
        LPDDSURFACEDESC2 lpDDSurfaceDesc,   // mode description
        bool *lpbIsAvail                    // pointer to boolean variable
                                            // indicating availability of mode
    )
{
try
{
    // The fact that this callback is invoked tells us that
    // a matching mode is available. Set bool to true...
    *lpbIsAvail = true;

    // ...and stop
    return DDENUMRET_CANCEL;
}
catch (...)
{
    return DDENUMRET_OK;
}
}
```

In your own programs, you can use the **IsModeAvailable** function as demonstrated in the following programming example:

```
// lpDD is assumed to be a valid pointer to an IDirectDraw7 interface

if (IsModeAvailable(lpDD, 800, 600, 32))
{
    MessageBox(
        NULL,
        "An 800x600x32 display mode is available.",
        "IsModeAvailable Result",
        MB_OK | MB_ICONINFORMATION
```

```
        );
    }
    else
    {
        MessageBox(
            NULL,
            "An 800x600x32 display mode is not available.",
            "IsModeAvailable Result",
            MB_OK | MB_ICONINFORMATION
        );
    }
```


Using Mode X and Mode 13

This Immediate Solution is meant to help you support Mode X and Mode 13 in your DirectDraw applications. Please note that these modes are special flavors of 320×200×8 and 320×240×8 modes. For a conceptual overview, see "Mode 13 and Mode X" in the "In Depth" section.

Using Mode X

DirectDraw provides two Mode X modes for all display devices: 320×200 and 320×240 (both 8-bit). Follow these steps when working with them:

1. Request a full-screen exclusive cooperative level and specify the **DDSCL_ALLOWMODEX** flag.

```
lpDD->SetCooperativeLevel(
    hMainWnd,
    DDSCL_FULLSCREEN | DDSCL_EXCLUSIVE | DDSCL_ALLOWMODEX
);
```

2. During display mode enumeration, you can recognize a Mode X mode by examining the **ddsCaps.dwCaps** member of the mode description. If this member contains the **DDSCAPS_MODEX** flag, a Mode X mode is enumerated.

```
HRESULT WINAPI EnumModesCallback2(
     LPDDSURFACEDESC2 lpDDSurfaceDesc,    // mode description
     LPVOID lpContext                     // application-defined value
    )
{
    // ...
```

```
    if (lpDDSurfaceDesc->ddsCaps.dwCaps & DDSCAPS_MODEX)
    {
        /* This is a Mode X mode. */
    }
    else
    {
        /* This is not a Mode X mode. */
    }

    // ...
}
```

3. To set a Mode X mode, use one of the following **SetDisplayMode** calls:

```
// either
lpDD->SetDisplayMode(320, 200, 8, dwRefreshRate, 0);
// or
lpDD->SetDisplayMode(320, 240, 8, dwRefreshRate, 0);
```

NOTE: *If supported by the device, linear low-resolution modes override Mode X modes at this point. You can't force the Mode X mode to be used.*

4. Do not attempt to lock the primary surface and do not blit to it. Instead, create a primary surface flipping chain, draw to the back buffer, and make it visible through the **IDirectDrawSurface7::Flip** method. See Chapter 13 for more information about this method.

Using Mode 13

Follow these steps when working with Mode 13:

1. As with Mode X, specify the **DDSCL_ALLOWMODEX** flag when calling **SetCooperativeLevel**.
2. Use the **GetCaps** method as described in Chapter 11 to find out whether Mode 13 is supported. If Mode 13 is available, the **DDSCAPS_STANDARD-VGAMODE** flag is set in the **DDSCAPS2** structure that is part of the **DDCAPS** structure:

```
DDCAPS HardwareCaps;
HardwareCaps.dwSize = sizeof(HardwareCaps);

lpDD->GetCaps(&HardwareCaps, NULL);

if (HardwareCaps.ddsCaps.dwCaps & DDSCAPS_STANDARDVGAMODE)
{
```

```
   /* Mode 13 is available. */
}
else
{
   /* Mode 13 is not available. */
}
```

3. To enumerate Mode 13 in addition to Mode X, specify the **DDEDM_STANDARDVGAMODES** flag when calling the **EnumDisplayMode** function.

```
lpDD->EnumDisplayModes(
   DDEDM_REFRESHRATES,
   ...
);
```


4. During display mode enumeration, you can recognize Mode 13 by examining the **ddsCaps.dwCaps** member of the mode description. If this member contains the **DDSCAPS_STANDARDVGAMODE** flag, the enumerated mode is Mode 13.

```
HRESULT WINAPI EnumModesCallback2(
    LPDDSURFACEDESC2 lpDDSurfaceDesc,    // mode description
    LPVOID lpContext                     // application-defined value
   )
{
   // ...

   if (lpDDSurfaceDesc->ddsCaps.dwCaps & DDSCAPS_STANDARDVGAMODE)
   {
      /* This is Mode 13. */
   }
   else
   {
      /* This is not Mode 13. */
   }

   // ...
}
```

5. To set Mode 13, use the following **SetDisplayMode** call:

```
lpDD->SetDisplayMode(320, 200, 8, dwRefreshRate, DDSDM_STANDARDVGAMODE);
```

__NOTE:__ If supported by the device, the linear 320×200×8 mode overrides Mode 13 at this point. You can't force the true Mode 13 to be used.

6. In Mode 13, you can access the primary surface directly. The **IDirect-DrawSurface7::Flip** method is emulated through a copy operation.

Determining which Mode Is Currently Set

The **IDirectDraw7::GetDisplayMode** method retrieves a description of the current display mode. The method is declared as follows:

```
HRESULT IDirectDraw7::GetDisplayMode(
    LPDDSURFACEDESC2 lpDDSurfaceDesc2       // display mode description
   );
```

The **lpDDSurfaceDesc** parameter is a pointer to a **DDSURFACEDESC2** structure that is going to be filled with information about the resolution, bit depth, and refresh rate of the current mode. Its **dwSize** member must have been initialized with **sizeof(DDSURFACEDESC2)**. See "Enumerating the Supported Display Modes" for a description of the relevant structure members.

Here's an example of calling the **GetDisplayMode** method:

```
// lpDD is assumed to be a valid pointer to an IDirectDraw7 interface

// prepare structure
DDSURFACEDESC2 ddsd;
ZeroMemory(&ddsd, sizeof(ddsd));
ddsd.dwSize = sizeof(ddsd);

// retrieve mode description
if (SUCCEEDED(lpDD->GetDisplayMode(&ddsd)))
{
   /*
      ddsd contains information about the currently set mode
   */
   // ...
}
```

WARNING! Do not save the information returned by GetDisplayMode to restore the display mode upon termination. For this purpose, use RestoreDisplayMode. See the following Immediate Solution.

Restoring the Display Mode

After calling **SetDisplayMode**, use **IDirectDraw7::RestoreDisplayMode** to return to the desktop resolution.

```
HRESULT IDirectDraw7::RestoreDisplayMode();
```

The display mode is restored automatically when the **IDirectDraw7** interface is released.

Retrieving the Refresh Rate

You can query the refresh rate of the monitor by calling **IDirectDraw7::Get-MonitorFrequency**, which is declared like this:

```
HRESULT IDirectDraw7::GetMonitorFrequency(
    LPDWORD lpdwFrequency                  // variable to receive the
                                              result
   );
```

The **lpdwFrequency** parameter is a pointer to a **DWORD** variable that is going to receive the monitor frequency if the **GetMonitorFrequency** function is successful. The following is a programming example:

```
// lpDD is assumed to be a valid pointer to an IDirectDraw7 interface

DWORD Frequency;
if (SUCCEEDED(lpDD->GetMonitorFrequency(&Frequency)))
{
   // Frequency is valid.
}
else
{
   // The function call failed.
}
```

If the driver is not capable of retrieving the refresh rate, the return value of the method is **DDERR_UNSUPPORTED**. In that case, you can calculate the refresh rate manually by querying the status of the vertical retrace. See "Calculating the Refresh Rate."

Calculating the Refresh Rate

If the driver is not capable of reporting the refresh rate (**dwRefreshRate** is always zero or **GetMonitorFrequency** returns with **DDERR_UNSUPPORTED**), you can calculate it by monitoring the vertical retrace. What you have to do is count the number of vertical blanks per second. The following is only an example of how this could be done. It uses the **IDirectDraw7::GetVerticalBlankStatus** method, which is described in detail in "Querying the Vertical Blank Status." The program queries the vertical blank status in a loop for one second. When a new vertical blank occurs, a counter is increased. The program temporarily sets its scheduling priority to "REALTIME" so that not a single vertical blank period is missed.

Listing 12.1 A program that calculates the monitor frequency.

```
// -------------------------------------------------------------------
// Windows 2000 Graphics API Black Book
// Chapter 12 - Immediate Solutions
// "Calculating the Refresh Rate"
// -------------------------------------------------------------------

#define INITGUID                // Alternatively, you can link to dxguid.lib.
#include <windows.h>
#include <ddraw.h>              // Don't forget to link to ddraw.lib!
#include <mmsystem.h>           // We need this for the timeGetTime function.
                                // Don't forget to link to winmm.lib!

#define SAFERELEASE(x) if (x) { x->Release(); x = NULL; }

//----------------------------------------------------------------------

WINAPI WinMain(HINSTANCE, HINSTANCE, LPSTR, int)
{
   LPDIRECTDRAW7 lpDD = NULL;
   HANDLE hProcess = GetCurrentProcess();

try
{
   // initialize DirectDraw
   DirectDrawCreateEx(
      NULL,
      reinterpret_cast<LPVOID*>(&lpDD),
      IID_IDirectDraw7, NULL
   );
```

```
// display startup message
if (MessageBox(
   NULL,
   "The program will now calculate the current refresh rate "
      "(monitor frequency). This will take 1 second.",
   "Calculating the Refresh Rate",
   MB_OKCANCEL | MB_ICONQUESTION
) == IDOK)
{
   DWORD Time = timeGetTime();
   DWORD NumVerticalBlanks = 0;
   BOOL VerticalBlankInProgress;
   bool VBPeriodHasEnded = true;

   // set priority of process to "REALTIME"
   // so that we don't miss a single blank
   SetPriorityClass(hProcess, REALTIME_PRIORITY_CLASS);

   // for 1 second...
   while (timeGetTime() < Time + 1000)
   {
      // ...monitor the vertical blank
      lpDD->GetVerticalBlankStatus(&VerticalBlankInProgress);

      // if we're in the vertical blank period...
      if (VerticalBlankInProgress)
      {
         // ...increase counter if it's a new vertical blank period
         if (VBPeriodHasEnded)
         {
            NumVerticalBlanks++;
            VBPeriodHasEnded = false;
         }
      }
      // otherwise, mark vertical blank period as ended
      else
      {
         VBPeriodHasEnded = true;
      }
   }

   // restore process priority
   SetPriorityClass(hProcess, NORMAL_PRIORITY_CLASS);
```

```
        // prepare a message
        char Buf[100];
        wsprintf(
           Buf,
           "The refresh rate is %i Hz.",
           NumVerticalBlanks
        );

        // display message
        MessageBox(
           NULL,
           Buf,
           "Refresh Rate Calculated",
           MB_OK | MB_ICONINFORMATION
        );
     }

     SAFERELEASE(lpDD);

  }
  catch (...)
  {
     SetPriorityClass(hProcess, NORMAL_PRIORITY_CLASS);
     MessageBox(NULL, "There was a fatal exception.", "Exception caught",
        MB_OK | MB_ICONERROR);
  }

      return 0;
  }
```

Synchronizing with the Vertical Blank

Windowed applications or those that draw directly to the primary surface can use the **IDirectDraw7::WaitForVerticalBlank** method to synchronize display operations with the vertical retrace. The method does not return before the specified condition is met, which can be either the beginning or the end of a vertical blank period. The method is declared as follows:

```
HRESULT IDirectDraw7::WaitForVerticalBlank(
    DWORD dwFlags,              // option flags
    HANDLE hEvent               // unused
   );
```

The possible values for the **dwFlags** parameter are:

- **DDWAITVB_BLOCKBEGIN**—When this flag is specified, the method does not return before a new vertical-blank interval begins and blit operations can take place without causing tearing artifacts.
- **DDWAITVB_BLOCKEND**—When this flag is specified, the method does not return before the vertical-blank interval ends and the display begins.
- **DDWAITVB_BLOCKBEGINEVENT**—This flag is not currently supported. The related **hEvent** parameter isn't supported either.

The following **RenderToScreen** function draws directly to the primary surface. Before it does so, it waits for the vertical blank period to begin.

```
// lpDD is assumed to be a valid pointer to an IDirectDraw7 interface

void RenderToScreen()
{
   lpDD->WaitForVerticalBlank(DDWAITVB_BLOCKBEGIN, 0);

   /*
      Rendering to the primary surface should take place here.
   */
}
```

The **WaitForVerticalBlank** function does not have to be called, of course, when you're rendering to off-screen surfaces. Furthermore, if the primary surface is updated through a call to **IDirectDrawSurface7::Flip** (full-screen applications only), synchronization is performed automatically. See also "Querying the Vertical Blank Status."

The **IDirectDraw7::GetVerticalBlankStatus** method fills a Boolean variable with the status of the vertical blank. If a vertical blank is in progress while the method is called, the method sets the variable to **TRUE**. Otherwise, the method sets the variable to **FALSE**. The method is declared as follows:

```
HRESULT IDirectDraw7::GetVerticalBlankStatus(
    LPBOOL lpbIsInVB            // BOOL variable to receive status
   );
```

The Boolean variable pointed to by the **lpbIsInVB** parameter receives the vertical blank status if the **GetVerticalBlankStatus** function is successful. The following code snippet demonstrates this by emulating the **WaitForVerticalBlank** function. First, the code waits until a vertical blank that is currently in progress is finished. It then waits for the next vertical blank to begin. This is to ensure that subsequent blit operations have the full interval to do their work.

```
// lpDD is assumed to be a valid pointer to an IDirectDraw7 variable

BOOL bIsInVB;
lpDD->GetVerticalBlankStatus(&bIsInVB);

// wait for currently running vertical blank to finish
if (bIsInVB)
{
   while (bIsInVB) { lpDD->GetVerticalBlankStatus(&bIsInVB); }
}

// wait for new vertical blank to begin
while (!bIsInVB) { lpDD->GetVerticalBlankStatus(&bIsInVB); }

// you can now perform drawing without causing tearing artifacts
```


WaitForVerticalBlank can also be used to calculate the monitor frequency. See "Calculating the Refresh Rate."

Displaying a Dialog Box in Full-Screen Mode

This Immediate Solution is related to "Dialog Boxes in Full-Screen Mode" in the "In Depth" section. You can use the following code in your own programs if you wish to use standard dialog boxes in full-screen mode. The code is taken from the FSDlgBox source code module, which can be found on the CD-ROM. The code that is not directly related to this Immediate Solution (such as helper functions and initialization code) is omitted.

First of all, you should determine whether the **IDirectDraw7::FlipToGDISurface** method is supported or whether the dialog box must be displayed and updated manually. The following code does this by calling the **IDirectDraw7::GetCaps** method and checking for the presence of the **DDCAPS2_CANRENDER-WINDOWED** flag:

```
// g_lpDD is assumed to be a valid pointer to an IDirectDraw7 interface

bool CanFlipToGDI;
// ...
```

```
// query hardware capabilities
DDCAPS HardwareCaps;
HardwareCaps.dwSize = sizeof(HardwareCaps);
g_lpDD->GetCaps(&HardwareCaps, NULL);

// check whether FlipToGDISurface is possible
if (HardwareCaps.dwCaps2 & DDCAPS2_CANRENDERWINDOWED)
{
   CanFlipToGDI = true;
}
else
{
   CanFlipToGDI = false;
}
}
```


When a dialog box is displayed, you call the **DlgBoxShown** function. This function attaches a clipper to the primary surface, so that the dialog box is not overwritten when the contents of the back buffer are blitted to the screen. This is required only if **FlipToGDISurface** is used. The **DlgBoxShown** function is implemented as follows:

```
// g_lpDDSPrimary is a pointer to the primary surface
// g_hMainWnd is the HWND handle for the application's main window

HWND g_hDlgBox;
// ...

void DlgBoxShown(HWND hDlgBox)
{
   g_hDlgBox = hDlgBox;          // store dialog box handle for future use

   if (!CanFlipToGDI) return;    // for non-display devices, the following
                                 // is not required

   LPDIRECTDRAWCLIPPER lpClipper = NULL;

try
{
   g_lpDD->CreateClipper(0, &lpClipper, NULL);
   lpClipper->SetHWnd(0, g_hMainWnd);

   g_lpDDSPrimary->SetClipper(lpClipper);
```

```
        SAFERELEASE(lpClipper);
    }
    catch (...)
    {
        SAFERELEASE(lpClipper);
    }
}
```

As long as the dialog box is visible, your application should call the **UpdateScreen** function to update the screen. This function handles all the details of displaying the dialog box. If **CanFlipToGDI** is **true**, the function calls the **FlipToGDISurface** method and uses **IDirectDrawSurface7::Blt** to make the contents of the back buffer visible. If **CanFlipToGDI** is **false**, the function grabs an image of the dialog box, blits it over the contents of the back buffer, and makes the back buffer visible by calling the **IDirectDrawSurface7::Flip** method. The **UpdateScreen** function is implemented as follows:


```
// g_lpDDSBackBuffer is a pointer to the back buffer surface

void UpdateScreen()
{
try
{
    // if FlipToGDISurface is possible
    if (CanFlipToGDI)
    {
        // synchronize with the vertical blank
        g_lpDD->WaitForVerticalBlank(DDWAITVB_BLOCKBEGIN, 0);

        // Blit back buffer to primary. Because of an attached clipper
        // (see the DlgBoxShown function), the dialog box is not overwritten.
        g_lpDDSPrimary->Blt(
            NULL,                  // use entire destination surface
            g_lpDDSBackBuffer,     // blit from back buffer
            NULL,                  // use entire source surface
            DDBLT_WAIT,            // wait until blitter is ready
            NULL                   // no effects
        );
    }
    // if FlipToGDISurface is not possible
    else
    {
        HDC hdcBackBuffer = NULL;
```

```
        try
        {
           // retrieve back buffer HDC
           if (SUCCEEDED(g_lpDDSBackBuffer->GetDC(&hdcBackBuffer)))
           {
              // render dialog box to back buffer
              RenderDialogBox(g_hDlgBox, hdcBackBuffer);

              g_lpDDSBackBuffer->ReleaseDC(hdcBackBuffer);
           }

           // bring back buffer to front
           g_lpDDSPrimary->Flip(NULL, DDFLIP_WAIT);
        }
        catch (...)
        {
           if (hdcBackBuffer)
           {  g_lpDDSBackBuffer->ReleaseDC(hdcBackBuffer); }
        }
    }
}
catch (...)
{
}
}
```

For rendering the dialog box to the back buffer, **UpdateScreen** uses the **RenderDialogBox** function. **RenderDialogBox** retrieves the handle to the GDI device context of the dialog box, and then calls **BitBlt** to blit to the device context of the DirectDraw surface, which **UpdateScreen** has obtained. See the following code snippet:

```
bool RenderDialogBox(
     HWND hDlgBox,            // window handle of the dialog box
     HDC SurfaceDC            // GDI device context of the DirectDraw surface
    )
{
   HDC WindowDC = NULL;

try
{
   RECT WindowRect;
   // retrieve dialog box position
   if (!GetWindowRect(hDlgBox, &WindowRect))
   {  throw "GetWindowRect"; }
```

```
    // calculate dimensions
    int WndWidth = WindowRect.right - WindowRect.left + 1;
    int WndHeight = WindowRect.bottom - WindowRect.top + 1;

    // get dialog box DC
    WindowDC = GetWindowDC(hDlgBox);
    if (WindowDC == NULL)
    {  throw "GetWindowDC"; }

    // blit from the dialog box DC to the surface DC
    if (!BitBlt(
       SurfaceDC,           // destination = DirectDraw surface
       WindowRect.left,     // dest. horz. position
       WindowRect.top,      // dest. vert. position
       WndWidth,            // dialog box width
       WndHeight,           // dialog box height
       WindowDC,            // source = window DC
       0, 0,                // window is at 0,0 within its own DC
       SRCCOPY              // perform a straight copy
    ))
    {  throw "BitBlt"; }

    // release dialog box DC
    if (WindowDC) ReleaseDC(hDlgBox, WindowDC);

    return true;            // report success to caller
}
catch (...)
{
    if (WindowDC) ReleaseDC(hDlgBox, WindowDC);
    return false;           // report failure to caller
}
}
```

For your convenience, the complete source code of the FSDlgBox module can be found on the accompanying CD-ROM. You can readily use it in your own programs.

Chapter 13

DirectDraw Surfaces

(continued)

In Depth

After all the initialization and preparation in the previous two chapters, we're now ready to bring up some graphics. For this, we'll use DirectDraw surface objects. Surfaces are as important to DirectDraw programming as device contexts are to GDI programming. Surfaces, however, can be used for a number of things that the GDI isn't capable of. Among these things are page flipping, overlays, and stereo vision, all of which will be covered in this chapter.

First we'll discuss the surface basics, including what surfaces are and what they are used for, and we'll explain related terminology. After that, we'll elaborate on the introduction to creating surfaces that we had in Chapter 11. We'll create a primary surface that will allow us to access the screen, and we'll create off-screen surfaces. Then we'll discuss the different ways to draw to surfaces—by using the GDI, by using the **Blt** and **BltFast** methods, and by accessing the video memory directly. Then there's a section about page flipping, in which we'll also discuss stereo vision. We'll also use overlays to create composite images of different pixel formats. At the end, we'll talk about situations in which surface memory might be lost, and we'll discuss ways to restore the surfaces.

What's a DirectDraw Surface?

A DirectDraw surface contains some graphics—either what is currently visible on screen or what is going to be displayed sometime in the future. A surface "represents a linear area of display memory," as the *DirectX Programmer's Reference* puts it. If I had to compare a DirectDraw surface to a known GDI entity, I'd say that the DirectDraw surface is like a device-dependent bitmap that is selected into a device context. The bitmap (represented by an **HBITMAP** handle) provides the memory. The device context (represented by an **HDC** handle) provides the interface to the device driver. The **HDC** handle is passed to the rendering functions so that the GDI knows where to draw to. A DirectDraw surface object, on the other hand, encapsulates the memory, the interface to the device driver, and the rendering functions in one object-oriented construct.

The only rendering a DirectDraw surface supports is blitting. These blits between DirectDraw surfaces can be hardware-accelerated if the graphics card supports that. The frame buffer (the linear area of display memory that contains the graphics) of any DirectDraw surface can reside in video memory, which speeds up blit operations.

Types of Surfaces

The following list outlines the characteristics of the different types of surfaces that are supported by DirectDraw:

- *The primary surface* represents the screen. Whatever is blitted or drawn to it becomes visible immediately. For obvious reasons, there can be only one primary surface per display device.
- *Off-screen surfaces* are used to hold graphics that are going to be blitted to the screen (e.g., moving sprites). In a windowed application, an entire animation frame is prepared in an off-screen surface before it is displayed with a single blit. Off-screen surfaces can reside in video memory as well as in system memory.
- *Complex surfaces* consist of several surfaces that are attached to a root surface. They are created with a single function call and are destroyed by releasing the root. In this chapter, we'll use a special type of complex surface—the flipping chain.
- *Flipping chains* are complex surfaces that support the **IDirectDrawSurface7::Flip** method. Flipping has the same effect as blitting between surfaces, but flipping is many times faster. How this is achieved and how flipping chains are used will be explained in the "Concepts and Terminology" section. In full-screen applications, the primary surface is usually created as a flipping chain.
- *Overlay surfaces* are visible above everything else on the screen, but they do not modify the contents of the primary surface (the screen). They are displayed on-the-fly while the cathode ray scans the screen. Their pixel format does not have to match the format of the primary surface. Overlays are available only if the hardware supports them.

Concepts and Terminology

In this section, I will introduce you to the terminology that we're going to use throughout the remainder of this chapter. This section covers the different types of memory, the concepts of pixel formats, the difference between width and pitch, and color keying and page flipping.

Memory Locations

Surfaces can reside in three memory locations: local video memory, system memory, and, if the system supports it, AGP (Accelerated Graphics Port) memory. The characteristics of these locations are listed here:

- *Local video memory* refers to the RAM chips on the graphics card. Surfaces are automatically created in local video memory as long as enough video memory is available and unless a different location is explicitly requested.

Blitting between video-memory surfaces is usually accelerated and therefore very fast.

- *System memory* refers to the Windows virtual memory space. Surfaces are automatically created in system memory if not enough local video memory is available. Blitting to, from, or between system-memory surfaces is often not accelerated and is therefore slower than video memory blits. However, when the CPU is used to read data from the surface, system memory is faster than video memory (see "Accessing Surface Memory Directly").
- *AGP memory* is also referred to as *non-local video memory*. You can think of it as a special system-memory area that the graphics card can access faster than it can access normal system memory. Non-local video memory must be explicitly requested when you're creating a surface. On some systems, AGP surfaces have the same acceleration level (regarding blit operations) as local video-memory surfaces. (Otherwise, the **DDCAPS2_NONLOCALVIDMEMCAPS** flag is set in the **DDCAPS** structure. See Chapter 11 for more information about querying device capabilities.)

Pixel Formats

The pixel format describes how the bits in the surface's frame buffer are to be translated to color information. We've already touched upon pixel formats—namely bit depth, which is one component of the pixel format—in Chapter 12. In this section, we'll discuss the other components of the pixel format.

***NOTE:** In DirectDraw, information about the pixel format is stored in **DDPIXELFORMAT** structures. Where it is appropriate, I will refer to the structure in the following sections. For detailed information about the **DDPIXELFORMAT** structure, please refer to "Interpreting the **DDPIXELFORMAT** Structure" in the "Immediate Solutions" section.*

Color Spaces

A *color space* is a model for representing colors by splitting up the color information into three or more components. The RGB model—which stores color in terms of red, green, and blue intensities—is most common. (You will hardly ever use anything else with DirectDraw.) The YUV model (used in the PAL analog broadcast television standard) is also supported for DirectDraw surfaces (usually overlays). In the YUV model, color is stored in terms of luminance (Y) and two levels of chrominance (U and V). In the **DDPIXELFORMAT** structure, the **DDPF_RGB** and **DDPF_YUV** flags designate the color space.

Bit Depth and Bit Masks

The *bit depth* specifies how many bits are used per pixel. Common bit depths are 16, 24, and 32 bpp (bits per pixel). When you access the surface memory directly, you need to have more detailed information about the layout of the bits. For that purpose, the **DDPIXELFORMAT** structure stores bit masks. Applications interpret these masks to determine the order of color components (whether it's red-green-blue or blue-green-red) and the number of bits per component. For example, **dwRBitMask** is a **DWORD** that has all bits set that are reserved for the red channel of the pixel. When reading data from or writing data to the surface directly, an application counts these bits and determines the position of the lowest-order bit so that it can convert pixels to and from the surface's format. For more information, see "Accessing Surface Memory Directly," later in this chapter.

Alpha Channels

Some pixel formats contain an *alpha channel*, which gives the opacity of the pixels, ranging from fully transparent to translucent to fully opaque. If the **DDPF_ALPHAPIXELS** flag is set in the **DDPIXELFORMAT** structure, some of the bits of the pixel format (e.g., the 8 unused bits of a 32-bit format) are reserved for the alpha channel.

Alpha-blended blit operations are not currently supported. The **IDirectDrawSurface7::Blt** method will ignore any alpha-related flags. Nevertheless, you can use the alpha bits in your own emulation routines. Some devices might also support alpha pixel formats in conjunction with overlay surfaces.

FOURCCs

An alternative way of describing a pixel format is through a *four-character code*, or FOURCC. FOURCCs are also used in the headers of image or video files—for example, in the **biCompression** member of the **BITMAPINFOHEADER** structure—to identify the pixel layout of the images. You can use the **IDirectDraw7::GetFourCCCodes** method to find out whether a particular layout is supported by the display device. The actual format of the data in the frame buffer is implied; i.e., the other **DDPIXELFORMAT** members are ignored. FOURCCs are frequently used for overlay surfaces. See "Working with Overlay Surfaces," later in this chapter, and "Accessing FOURCC Surfaces Directly," in the "Immediate Solutions" section.

NOTE: *Video CODECs (compressors-decompressors) are also represented by four-character codes. However, FOURCCs such as MSVC (Video 1), CVID (CinePak), or IV50 (Indeo 5.0) are never supported for surfaces.*

Pitch vs. Width

The *width* of a surface specifies its horizontal dimension in pixels. A surface's *pitch*, on the other hand, is the number of bytes between the beginning of a scan line and the beginning of the next line. This is not necessarily equal to the width multiplied by the number of bytes per pixel. Devices might reserve additional bytes for a cache or simply to align scan lines in memory for optimal performance. Figure 13.1 illustrates the difference between pitch and width.

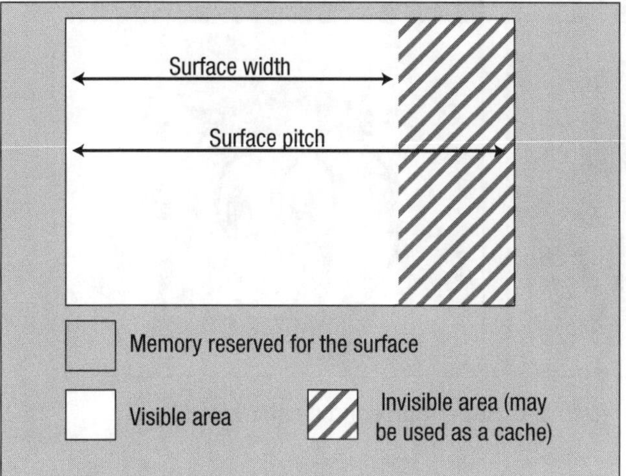

Figure 13.1 Pitch and width of a surface.

The byte address of a scan line must therefore be calculated as follows:

```
lpScanLine = lpFrameBuffer + NumScanLine * Pitch
```

See "Accessing Surface Memory Directly," for more details.

Color-Keyed Blitting

Bitmaps are always perfectly rectangular. Sprites aren't. Imagine a "Flying Heads" screen saver. (See Figure 13.2.) The picture of the head is our sprite. It resides in its own off-screen surface, which, of course, is rectangular. The area surrounding the head is dark gray. If we blitted the sprite onto the background as is, we'd end up with a dark gray rectangle with the picture of a head at its center. To achieve transparency, DirectDraw lets us choose a *source color key,* which specifies the color (or range of colors) to be treated as transparent. (You will want to choose some infrequently used color, such as pink, for the transparent area.) Figure 13.2 illustrates blitting without (left) and with (right) color keying.

Another kind of color keying is *destination color keying.* If a destination color key is used, only the destination pixels of the specified color (or range of colors) can be overwritten by the blit. In fact, blitting a sprite onto a background with a destination color key has the same effect as blitting the sprite first and then blitting the background with a source color key.

Color keys are directly associated with the surface and can be overridden on a per-blit basis. Most display devices provide hardware acceleration for color keying. To find out whether color keying is accelerated, emulated, or not supported

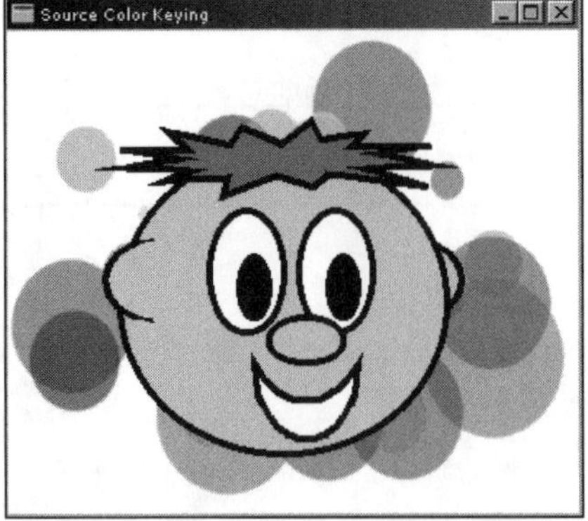

Figure 13.2 Blitting without (left) and with (right) source color keying.

at all, you can use the **IDirectDraw7::GetCaps** method (see Chapter 11 for more information).

For more information, see "Surface Blit Operations," later in this chapter.

Page Flipping

To prevent flicker artifacts, animation cells are typically prepared off-screen before they are displayed. Page flipping speeds up the process of displaying the off-screen image because, unlike blitting, flipping does not require a copy operation. Instead, the involved surfaces simply exchange their frame-buffer pointers.

To be able to take advantage of flipping, a surface must be explicitly created as a *flipping chain*. Such a flipping chain consists of at least two surfaces: a front buffer and one or more back buffers. Full-screen applications can create their primary surface as a flipping chain so that the contents of the back buffer become visible immediately after a flip. Here's how it works:

1. You create the primary surface as a flipping chain by requesting the **DDSCAPS_COMPLEX** and **DDSCAPS_FLIP** capabilities in the call to the **IDirectDraw7::CreateSurface** method.
2. The application obtains pointers to the **IDirectDrawSurface7** interfaces of the front buffer and of the back buffer. Let's call these pointers **lpFrontBuffer** and **lpBackBuffer**.
3. The application draws to the back buffer pointed to by **lpBackBuffer**.
4. The **lpFrontBuffer->Flip()** method is called. The surface interface pointed to by **lpFrontBuffer** has its internal frame-buffer pointer point to the frame buffer of **lpBackBuffer** and vice versa. In other words, the frame-buffer pointers are swapped. Because the surface pointed to by

lpFrontBuffer is also the primary surface, the screen is immediately updated with the new contents.

5. The application continues at Step 3. Note that **lpFrontBuffer** and **lpBackBuffer** still point to the same interfaces, but the interfaces manage different frame buffers now.

Page flipping can also be used on off-screen surfaces if they have been created as flipping chains. For more details, see the section on "Working with Flipping Chains," later in this chapter.

Surface Creation

You can create a surface and obtain a pointer to its **IDirectDrawSurface7** interface by calling the **IDirectDraw7::CreateSurface** method. Before calling the method, you have to prepare a **DDSURFACEDESC2** structure that specifies the desired surface characteristics. The following sections demonstrate this technique for the primary surface and for off-screen surfaces. For detailed information about the **DDSURFACEDESC2** structure, see "Interpreting the **DDSURFACEDESC2** Structure" in the "Immediate Solutions" section.

The **CreateSurface** method is declared as follows:

```
HRESULT IDirectDraw7::CreateSurface(
    LPDDSURFACEDESC2 lpDDSurfaceDesc2,          // surface characteristics
    LPDIRECTDRAWSURFACE7 FAR *lplpDDSurface,    // interface pointer
    IUnknown FAR *pUnkOuter                     // reserved; must be NULL
   );
```

The **lpDDSurfaceDesc2** parameter points to the initialized **DDSURFACEDESC2** structure. The variable pointed to by the **lplpDDSurface** parameter receives the **IDirectDrawSurface7** interface when the method is successful. The **pUnkOuter** parameter is unused.

Creating the Primary Surface

To create the primary surface, you must set the **ddsCaps.dwCaps** member of the **DDSURFACEDESC2** structure to **DDSCAPS_PRIMARYSURFACE**. The pixel format and dimensions of the primary surface are dictated by the currently set display mode. If you specify a different width, height, or pixel format, the **CreateSurface** method will fail. Similarly, you must not specify a memory location other than local video memory.

The following code snippet demonstrates how to create the primary surface:

```
// lpDD is assumed to be a valid pointer to an IDirectDraw7 interface

// prepare surface description
DDSURFACEDESC2 ddsd;
ZeroMemory(&ddsd, sizeof(ddsd));
ddsd.dwSize = sizeof(ddsd);
ddsd.dwFlags = DDSD_CAPS;                // ddsCaps is valid
ddsd.ddsCaps.dwCaps = DDSCAPS_PRIMARYSURFACE;

// create the surface
LPDIRECTDRAWSURFACE7 lpDDSPrimary = NULL;
if (FAILED(lpDD->CreateSurface(
   &ddsd,
   &lpDDSPrimary,
   NULL
)))
{
   throw "The primary surface could not be created.";
}

/*
   lpDDSPrimary is now a valid pointer to the primary surface interface.
   Before shutting down your program, you must release the interface.
*/
```

See also "Creating a Non-Flipping Primary Surface" in the "Immediate Solutions" section. Please note that the primary surface can also be created as a flipping chain. For more information, see "Working with Flipping Chains," later in this chapter.

Creating Off-Screen Surfaces

To create an off-screen surface, you must set the **ddsCaps.dwCaps** parameter of the **DDSURFACEDESC2** structure to **DDSCAPS_OFFSCREENPLAIN**. In addition, the **dwCaps** member is used to request a specific memory location. By default, DirectDraw attempts to create the surface in local video memory. Table 13.1 discusses when you should request which memory location.

When creating an off-screen surface, you must specify the surface dimensions. For this purpose, set the **DDSD_WIDTH** and **DDSD_HEIGHT** flags in the **dwFlags** member of the surface description, and set **dwWidth** and **dwHeight** to arbitrary values. Some devices might not allow video-memory surfaces that are wider than the screen. To determine whether wide surfaces are supported, call the **GetCaps** method and check whether the hardware capabilities include

Table 13.1 Memory locations and when to use them.

Memory Location	When to Use
Not specified	Not specifying any of the memory location flags is the best choice for most purposes. DirectDraw attempts to use local video memory and, if that's not possible, falls back to system memory. DirectDraw does not attempt to use AGP memory.
DDSCAPS_VIDEOMEMORY	Use this flag to force local video memory. (The **DDSCAPS_LOCAL-VIDMEM** flag is implied.) Local video memory will provide the best performance, but the **CreateSurface** method will fail if not enough local video memory is available.
DDSCAPS_SYSTEMMEMORY	Use this flag to force system memory. This results in better performance when you're using the CPU (as opposed to the hardware blitter) to read data from the surface (see "Accessing Surface Memory Directly"). The CPU is also used when a feature is emulated by the HEL (hardware emulation layer). For example, if stretched blitting is not hardware-accelerated, you should create the source surface in system memory for better performance (see Chapter 11 for more information about determining feature support). Surfaces with a pixel format different from that of the primary surface must also reside in system memory.
DDSCAPS_VIDEOMEMORY | DDSCAPS_NONLOCALVIDMEM	Use this flag if not enough local video memory is available and the display device supports AGP memory. First, you should use the **GetCaps** method, as described in Chapter 11, to find out whether AGP is supported. If the **DDCAPS2_NONLOCALVIDMEMCAPS** flag is *not* reported, the device provides the same acceleration for AGP surfaces that it does for local video-memory surfaces. The **dwNLVB...** members contain detailed information.

DDCAPS2_WIDESURFACES. Wide surfaces are always supported in system memory.

You can also request a pixel format other than the format of the primary surface. To do this, set the **DDSD_PIXELFORMAT** flag in the **dwFlags** member of the surface description and initialize the **ddpfPixelFormat** child structure. The **DDSCAPS_SYSTEMMEMORY** flag must also be specified. Be warned, though, that, unlike the GDI, DirectDraw doesn't perform any pixel format conversion during blit operations. For example, blitting from an 8-bit off-screen surface to a 24-bit primary surface would cause an error. To create a compatible off-screen surface, do not use the **ddpfPixelFormat** member of the **DDSURFACEDESC2** structure.

The following example creates a 100×100 off-screen surface:

```
// lpDD is assumed to be a valid pointer to an IDirectDraw7 interface

// prepare surface description
DDSURFACEDESC2 ddsd;
ZeroMemory(&ddsd, sizeof(ddsd));
ddsd.dwSize = sizeof(ddsd);
ddsd.dwFlags = DDSD_CAPS |          // ddsCaps, ...
   DDSD_WIDTH | DDSD_HEIGHT;        // ...dwWidth, and dwHeight are valid
ddsd.ddsCaps.dwCaps = DDSCAPS_OFFSCREENPLAIN;
ddsd.dwWidth = 100;
ddsd.dwHeight = 100;

// create the surface
LPDIRECTDRAWSURFACE7 lpDDSOffScreen = NULL;
if (FAILED(lpDD->CreateSurface(
   &ddsd,
   &lpDDSOffScreen,
   NULL
)))
{
   throw "The off-screen surface could not be created.";
}

/*
   lpDDSOffScreen is now a valid pointer to the surface interface.
   Before shutting down your program, you must release the interface.
*/
```

See also "Creating an Off-Screen Surface" in the "Immediate Solutions" section.

Creating Client Memory Surfaces

DirectDraw allows you to create off-screen surfaces from previously allocated memory blocks. For example, you might have loaded an image file into a memory block that had been reserved using the **new** operator. You can instruct the **CreateSurface** method to have the surface use this memory block for its frame buffer so that you don't have to copy the data in a separate pass. In addition to width, height, and pixel format, you have to pass the pitch and the pointer to the memory to the **CreateSurface** function. The pitch must be an 8-byte multiple. Common bitmap widths such as 160, 320, or 256 pixels will always result in a pitch that is an 8-byte multiple. The memory pointer is passed in the **lpSurface** member of the **DDSURFACEDESC2** structure. DirectDraw does not attempt to free the memory when the surface is released. For a programming example, see "Creating an Off-Screen Surface from an Existing Block of Memory" in the "Immediate Solutions" section.

Combining DirectDraw and the GDI

Before we discuss blit operations in the next section, we should fill our surfaces with images that are worth being blitted. The easiest way to do this is to use GDI functions, which you are already familiar with. The GDI can be used to draw 2D primitives or text to DirectDraw surfaces, and it can be used to load bitmaps of any pixel format into DirectDraw surfaces. The **IDirectDrawSurface7** interface provides the **GetDC** method to retrieve an **HDC** handle for the surface. The following is a usage example of the **GetDC** method:

```
// lpDDSurface is assumed to be a valid pointer to
// an IDirectDrawSurface7 interface

HDC hdc = NULL;

try
{
   if (SUCCEEDED(lpDDSurface->GetDC(&hdc)))
   {
      // hdc is valid
      // You can call GDI functions to draw to the surface:
      Ellipse(hdc, 16, 16, 100, 100);

      // release the DC
      lpDDSurface->ReleaseDC(hdc);
   }

}
catch (...)
{
   if (hdc)
   {
      lpDDSurface->ReleaseDC(hdc);
   }
}
```

When you use the **GetDC** method, you should keep a number of things in mind:

- The GDI wasn't designed for high-performance multimedia applications. Using GDI functions can slow down your DirectDraw applications significantly. If possible, prepare the GDI graphics in an off-screen surface and reuse them; i.e., simply blit the off-screen surface to the screen instead of redrawing the graphics.
- You can't use a surface as the source or the destination of DirectDraw blit operations while you have an **HDC** handle to it. You must call the **ReleaseDC** method of the surface before you can call **IDirectDrawSurface7::Blt** again.

- Be careful when you're debugging DirectDraw code that uses the **GetDC** method. Your debugger and Windows might hang when you enter a breakpoint between calls to **GetDC** and **ReleaseDC**. You should always embed **GetDC** in a **try-catch** block. The exception handler should call **ReleaseDC** when an exception occurs.

Loading a Bitmap

One of the most common uses of calling GDI functions on surface DCs is for loading bitmaps. Blitting between DirectDraw surfaces isn't interesting as long as we don't have some nice graphics to blit. Therefore, this section will show you how to use GDI functions to load a bitmap from a file into a DirectDraw surface.

The central function is **LoadImage**, which loads a Windows bitmap file and returns an **HBITMAP** handle to the bitmap. After the file is loaded, the bitmap is selected into a memory DC. The application calls **IDirectDrawSurface7::GetDC** and uses the GDI function **BitBlt** to blit the image from the DC to the surface. The following code demonstrates this:


```
// lpDDSurface is assumed to be a valid pointer to
// an IDirectDrawSurface7 interface

HBITMAP hBmp = NULL;
HDC hMemDC = NULL;
HDC hSurfaceDC = NULL;

try
{
   // load the image
   hBmp = reinterpret_cast<HBITMAP>(LoadImage(
      0,
      lpszImageFileName,     // name of .bmp file
      IMAGE_BITMAP,
      0, 0,                  // take dimensions from file
      LR_LOADFROMFILE
   ));
   if (hBmp == NULL)
   {  throw "LoadImage failed."; }

   // create a GDI memory DC
   hMemDC = CreateCompatibleDC(NULL);
   if (hMemDC == NULL)
   {  throw "Creating memory DC failed."; }
```

```
    // select bitmap into memory DC
    SelectObject(hMemDC, hBmp);

    // retrieve bitmap dimensions
    BITMAP BmpInfo;
    if (!GetObject(
       reinterpret_cast<HGDIOBJ>(hBmp),
       sizeof(BITMAP),
       reinterpret_cast<LPVOID>(&BmpInfo)
    ))
    {  throw "Retrieving bitmap dimensions failed."; }

    // get surface DC
    if (SUCCEEDED(lpDDSurface->GetDC(&hSurfaceDC)))
    {
       // blit from memory DC to surface DC
       BitBlt(
          hSurfaceDC,
          0, 0, BmpInfo.bmWidth, BmpInfo.bmHeight,
          hMemDC,
          0, 0,
          SRCCOPY
       );

       // release surface DC
       lpDDSurface->ReleaseDC(hSurfaceDC);
    }

    if (hMemDC) { DeleteDC(hMemDC); }
    if (hBmp) { DeleteObject(reinterpret_cast<HGDIOBJ>(hBmp)); }

}
catch (...)
{
    if (hSurfaceDC) { lpDDSurface->ReleaseDC(hSurfaceDC); }
    if (hMemDC) { DeleteDC(hMemDC); }
    if (hBmp) { DeleteObject(reinterpret_cast<HGDIOBJ>(hBmp)); }
}
```

Surface Blit Operations

The **IDirectDrawSurface7** interface provides two methods that can perform hardware-accelerated blit operations. These methods are **Blt** and **BltFast**. Although the **Blt** method is more flexible, **BltFast** is faster in some situations. The **IDirectDrawSurface7::Blt** method has the following characteristics:

- The **Blt** method performs shrinking and stretching if the source and destination rectangles are not the same size.
- The **Blt** method supports DirectDraw clippers. Those areas that are outside the clipping region are not drawn.
- The **Blt** method can perform color keying. The source and destination color keys that are currently set for the surface object can be overridden on a per-blit basis.
- The **Blt** method supports additional blitting effects such as mirroring and color fills.

The **BltFast** method has the following characteristics:

- The **BltFast** method is 10 percent faster than the **Blt** method if the blit operation is emulated. If the hardware blitter can be used, there is no speed difference. You can use the **GetCaps** method, as described in Chapter 11, to find out whether or not a blit operation is accelerated.
- The **BltFast** method does not use a destination rectangle, but uses a destination position. Therefore, no shrinking or stretching can be performed.
- The **BltFast** method fails if a DirectDraw clipper is attached to the surface.
- The **BltFast** method can perform color keying. Unlike the **Blt** method, **BltFast** will always use the color keys specified for the surface with the **SetColorKey** method.
- The **BltFast** method does not support additional blitting effects.

Both methods can be used for video-to-video, video-to-system, system-to-system, and system-to-video blits. The **DDCAPS** structure that is filled by the **IDirectDraw7::GetCaps** method provides more information about the general blitting capabilities of the system. See Chapter 11 for more information.

Performing Blits

The **IDirectDrawSurface7::Blt** method is declared as follows:

```
HRESULT IDirectDrawSurface7::Blt(
    LPRECT lpDestRect,                      // destination rectangle
    LPDIRECTDRAWSURFACE7 lpDDSrcSurface,    // source surface
    LPRECT lpSrcRect,                       // source rectangle
    DWORD dwFlags,                          // blit flags
    LPDDBLTFX lpDDBltFx                     // blit effects
   );
```

The surface that provides the **Blt** method will be the destination of the blit. The **lpDestRect** parameter points to a **RECT** structure that specifies the destination rectangle on the surface. Please note that the **right** and **bottom** members of the structure are exclusive; i.e., **right** minus **left** equals the width of the rectangle, not one less than the width. The **lpDDSrcSurface** parameter is a pointer to the **IDirectDrawSurface7** interface of the source surface. The **lpSrcRect** parameter specifies the source rectangle. If an **LPRECT** pointer is **NULL**, the entire surface is used. Unless clippers are attached to the surfaces, both source and destination rectangles must be entirely contained within their respective surfaces. Otherwise, nothing will be copied.

The following programming example copies the contents of the entire source surface into a 90×80 destination rectangle:

```
// lpDDSDestination and lpDDSSource are assumed to be valid pointers to
// IDirectDrawSurface7 interfaces

// copy to an area that is 90 pixels wide and 80 pixels high
RECT DestRect = { 10, 20, 100, 100 };

lpDDSDestination->Blt(
   &DestRect,           // rectangle on lpDDSDestination
   lpDDSSource,         // source surface
   NULL,                // use the entire source surface. If lpDDSSource
                        // is not 90x80, the bitmap is scaled
   0,                   // no flags
   NULL                 // no effects
);
```

The parameters of the **BltFast** method are similar, except that there is no destination rectangle and no pointer to a **DDBLTFX** structure:

```
HRESULT BltFast(
    DWORD dwX,                                // destination x-coordinate
    DWORD dwY,                                // destination y-coordinate
    LPDIRECTDRAWSURFACE7 lpDDSrcSurface,      // source surface
    LPRECT lpSrcRect,                         // source rectangle
    DWORD dwTrans                             // flags
   );
```

The **dwX** and **dwY** parameters together specify the upper-left corner of the destination rectangle. The width and height of the destination rectangle are the same as the width and height of the source rectangle pointed to by the **lpSrcRect** parameter. As with the **Blt** method, the source and destination rectangles must be entirely contained within their respective surfaces. The following code snippet copies the entire source surface to the upper-left corner of the destination surface:

```
// lpDDSDestination and lpDDSSource are assumed to be valid pointers to
// IDirectDrawSurface7 interfaces

lpDDSDestination->BltFast(
   0, 0,                  // destination coordinates
   lpDDSSource,           // source surface
   NULL,                  // use the entire source surface
   0                      // no flags
);
```

For more information, see "Blitting by Using the **Blt** Method" and "Blitting by Using the **BltFast** Method" in the "Immediate Solutions" section.

Performing Color-Keyed Blits

We've already discussed the concept of color keying in the "Concepts and Terminology" section earlier in this chapter. In this section, we'll discuss how to use the **Blt** and **BltFast** methods to perform color-keyed blits.

Every surface can have an associated source color key and an associated destination color key. The source color key is used during blit operations *from* the surface, and the destination color key is used during blit operations *to* the surface. The **IDirectDrawSurface7::SetColorKey** method can be used to set both color keys. The following code snippet demonstrates how to use this method:

```
// lpDDSurface is assumed to be a valid pointer to
// an IDirectDrawSurface7 interface

DDCOLORKEY ColorKey;
ColorKey.dwColorSpaceLowValue = 0x00000000;     // 0 is always black,
                           // regardless of the pixel format of the surface

// set the source color key
lpDDSurface->SetColorKey(DDCKEY_SRCBLT, &ColorKey);
// set the destination color key
lpDDSurface->SetColorKey(DDCKEY_DESTBLT, &ColorKey);
```

WARNING! The color key must be given in the pixel format of the surface. For information about converting an RGB triple into the surface's pixel format, see "Converting an RGB Triple into the Surface's Pixel Format" in the "Immediate Solutions" section.

You can use the **SetColorKey** method to set a color range instead of a single color key. For this purpose, specify the **DDCKEY_COLORSPACE** flag in addition to the **DDCKEY_DESTBLT** or **DDCKEY_SRCBLT** method. However, many display devices do not support color ranges, and the HEL does not emulate them.

To perform a color-keyed blit, specify the **DDBLT_KEYDEST** or **DDBLT_KEY-SRC** flag in the **dwFlags** parameter of the **IDirectDrawSurface7::Blt** method. The blit will use the color key specified with a call to the **SetColorKey** method. If no color key has been set, or if you want to override the current setting, you can use the **DDBLT_KEYSRCOVERRIDE** or **DDBLT_KEYDESTOVERRIDE** flags and the **lpDDBltFx** parameter. The following code instructs the **Blt** method to ignore the currently set source color key and use a blue color instead:

```
// lpDDSDestination and lpDDSSource are assumed to be valid pointers to
// IDirectDrawSurface7 interfaces

DDBLTFX BltFx;
ZeroMemory(&BltFx, sizeof(BltFx));
BltFx.dwSize = sizeof(BltFx);
// set color key to blue (provided that the surface is a 24- or 32-bit RGB
// surface)
BltFx.ddckSrcColorkey.dwColorSpaceLowValue = 0x00ff0000;

lpDDSDestination->Blt(
   NULL,                    // use the entire destination surface
   lpDDSSource,             // source surface
   NULL,                    // use the entire source surface
   DDBLT_KEYSRCOVERRIDE,    // take source color key from DDBLTFX
   &BltFx                   // DDBLTFX structure containing source color key
);
```

Using the **BltFast** method, you perform a color-keyed blit by specifying the **DDBLTFAST_DESTCOLORKEY** or **DDBLTFAST_SRCCOLORKEY** flags in the **dwTrans** parameter. The following code snippet demonstrates this:

```
// lpDDSDestination and lpDDSSource are assumed to be valid pointers to
// IDirectDrawSurface7 interfaces

lpDDSDestination->BltFast(
   0, 0,                         // destination coordinates
   lpDDSSource,                  // source surface
   NULL,                         // use the entire source surface
   DDBLTFAST_SRCCOLORKEY         // perform source color keying
);
```

When using the **BltFast** method, you can't override the color key set with the **SetColorKey** method.

See also the following Immediate Solutions: "Setting the Color Key of a Surface," "Blitting by Using the **Blt** Method," and "Blitting by Using the **BltFast** method."

Performing Color Fills

DirectDraw provides a fast way to perform *color filling*—the process of clearing an entire surface to an arbitrary color. If a display device has a hardware blitter, that device can probably use the blitter to perform accelerated color fills. A color fill is performed with the **Blt** method and the **DDBLT_COLORFILL** flag. Only the destination surface (the one that provides the **Blt** method) is involved. Therefore, source surface and source rectangle are ignored. The fill color is specified in the **dwFillColor** member of the **DDBLTFX** structure that is passed to the method. Just as with color keying, the fill color is specified in the pixel format of the surface.

See also "Requesting Blit Effects with the **DDBLTFX** Structure" in the "Immediate Solutions" section.

Performing Blit Effects

In addition to color keying and color filling, the **IDirectDrawSurface7::Blt** method supports a number of blit effects:

- *Mirroring*—The **Blt** method can mirror the source rectangle along the x-axis or along the y-axis during a blit. Mirroring is emulated by the HEL if the hardware does not support it.
- *Arithmetic stretching*—You can instruct the **Blt** method to interpolate pixels when scaling along the y-axis. Arithmetic scaling along the x-axis cannot be explicitly requested, although some drivers might support it by default.
- *Raster operations*—You can use raster operations (ROPs) during blits. These ROPs are the same as the ROPs supported by the GDI **BitBlt** function.
- *Rotation*—The **DDBLTFX** structure has members that control rotation during blits. Unfortunately, rotation can't be emulated by the HEL, and hardware support is not common.

Although there are flags that control alpha-blended blits, these flags are always ignored by the **Blt** method.

When you call the **Blt** method, the **dwFlags** parameter specifies whether an effect should be performed. Arithmetic stretching, mirroring, and rotation by 90, 180, or 270 degrees is controlled with the **DDBLT_DDFX** flag. This flag indicates that the **dwDDFX** member of the **BLTFX** structure is used. The **DDBLT_ROP** flag marks the **dwROP** member of the structure as valid, and the **DDBLT_-ROTATIONANGLE** flag marks the **dwRotationAngle** member as valid.

For more information, see "Blitting by Using the **Blt** Method" and "Requesting Blit Effects with the **DDBLTFX** Structure" in the "Immediate Solutions" section.

Accessing Surface Memory Directly

Sometimes you will want to read or modify single pixels, not rectangular areas, on a surface. There are different ways to do this. For example, you could call the GDI functions **GetPixel** and **SetPixel** for every single pixel. However, this would be very slow. You could also use the **GetDIBits** function to create a device-independent bitmap from the contents of the surface, work with the DIB, and then have the **SetDIBits** function write the DIB back to the surface. This might be faster than the **GetPixel/SetPixel** approach, but it would still be a waste of resources and CPU cycles.

With DirectDraw, it's possible to gain direct access to the surface memory, so you can access the surface's frame buffer just like an array allocated with the **new** operator. This works regardless of the surface's memory location. In this section, you will learn how this can be done. For demonstration purposes, we'll write a DirectDraw **SetPixel** routine for RGB true-color surfaces. (In a real-world application, you wouldn't want to have a separate routine that repeats preparation and cleanup tasks for every single pixel. Rather, you'd insert the **SetPixel** code right into the routine that needs to access the pixels.) Writing the **SetPixel** routine involves the following steps:

1. *Lock the surface*—Use the **IDirectDrawSurface7::Lock** method to gain direct access to the surface's frame buffer.
2. *Calculate the pixel offset*—Calculate the byte address of the pixel within the frame buffer.
3. *Interpret the pixel format*—Convert an RGB triple into the pixel format of the surface.
4. *Write the pixel to the frame buffer*—Store the pixel that you converted in Step 3 to the frame buffer.
5. *Release the surface*—Use the **IDirectDrawSurface7::Unlock** method to release the surface.

Locking the Surface

Your starting point for accessing a surface's frame buffer directly is the **IDirect-DrawSurface7::Lock** method. Calling this method serves several purposes:

- It ensures that the surface memory can't be moved or lost before you call the **Unlock** method. This is similar to the way you call the standard function **GlobalLock** on a memory handle returned by the **GlobalAlloc** function.
- It returns a pointer to the surface's frame buffer.
- It returns information about the layout of the data in the frame buffer.

Calling the **Lock** method is easy. All you have to do is initialize a **DDSURFACEDESC2** structure and pass it to the method. Optionally, you can pass a pointer to a **RECT** structure that specifies the area that you want to have locked. To lock the entire surface, simply pass a **NULL** pointer, as shown in the following programming example:

```
// lpDDSurface is assumed to be a valid pointer to
// an IDirectDrawSurface7 interface

DDSURFACEDESC2 ddsd;
ZeroMemory(&ddsd, sizeof(ddsd));
ddsd.dwSize = sizeof(ddsd);

if (SUCCEEDED(lpDDSurface->Lock(
   NULL,                        // no rectangle; lock entire surface
   &ddsd,                       // DDSURFACEDESC2 structure to be filled
   0,                           // no flags
   NULL                         // unused; must be NULL
)))
{
   /*
      ddsd.lpSurface points to the upper left pixel on the surface
   */
}
```

If the **Lock** method is successful, it fills the **DDSURFACEDESC2** structure with all the information you need to access the frame buffer directly. The **lpSurface** member of the structure, for example, contains the memory address of the upper-left pixel in the locked area. The frame buffer presents itself to the application as a contiguous block of memory, which you can access just like an array allocated with the **new** operator.

WARNING! As discussed in Chapter 12, the primary surface of a Mode X mode can't be locked.

Calculating Pixel Offsets

The **lpSurface** pointer points to the upper-left pixel in the locked area. The offset of the pixel at position (x,y) is **y(LengthOfScanLineInBytes)+x(PixelSize-InBytes)**. Recall that the pitch is the number of bytes between the beginning of a scan line and the beginning of the next line. That's our **LengthOfScanLine-InBytes**. Recall also that the bit depth of the pixel format specifies the size of a single pixel in bytes. Therefore, **PixelSizeInBytes** equals the bit depth divided by 8. The following code snippet calculates the address of a pixel:

```
// ddsd is a DDSURFACEDESC2 structure that has been filled by
// the IDirectDrawSurface7::Lock method
// x and y contain the coordinates of the pixel

LONG LengthOfScanLineInBytes = ddsd.lPitch;
DWORD PixelSizeInBytes = ddsd.ddpfPixelFormat.dwRGBBitCount / 8;

LPVOID lpPointerToPixel = reinterpret_cast<LPVOID>(
   reinterpret_cast<DWORD>(ddsd.lpSurface) +
   y * LengthOfScanLineInBytes +
   x * PixelSizeInBytes
);
```

NOTE: *When you're working with a 256-color surface or an 8-bit alpha-only surface, calculating the pixel offset is all you have to do. Simply cast **lpPointerToPixel** to type **LPBYTE** and write or read the pixel.*

Interpreting the Pixel Format

In the RGB model (as well as in the YUV model), a color consists of three components. In device-independent image files, these components are typically stored as bytes—their values range from 0 to 255. When writing pixels to a surface's frame buffer, you have to convert these byte triples into the surface's pixel format. Our starting point is a **COLORREF** value, which is a **DWORD** created with the GDI **RGB** macro. In the end, we want to have a **DWORD** containing a single pixel in the surface's format. The following list outlines the steps required to reach our goal:

1. Extract the red, green, and blue components from the **COLORREF** value.
2. If the surface's pixel format doesn't use the full 8 bits to store each color component, scale the color components down.
3. Write the scaled color components to the **DWORD** in the right order.

Although the following sub-sections do not explicitly mention YUV surfaces, the presented code will also work, without modifications, for these surfaces. The reason is that the YUV and RGB members of the **DDPIXELFORMAT** structure are contained in unions (declared with the **union** keyword). Therefore, members such as **dwRGBBitCount** and **dwYUVBitCount** share the same memory location.

Decoding a COLORREF Value

The GDI provides the **GetRValue**, **GetGValue**, and **GetBValue** macros, which we can use to decode the **COLORREF** value. If your implementation of the **SetPixel** routine does not use a **COLORREF** value but uses three separate **BYTE** values, please skip this step. Otherwise, see the following code:

```
// rgb is the COLORREF value that was passed to our SetPixel routine

BYTE Red = GetRValue(rgb);
BYTE Green = GetGValue(rgb);
BYTE Blue = GetBValue(rgb);
```

Scaling Down the Color Components

For this step, we need to know how many bits are reserved for each color component. We'll use the bit masks stored in the **ddpfPixelFormat** member of the **DDSURFACEDESC2** structure to find out. Let's assume we have a 16-bit pixel format. The pixel masks could look like the illustration shown in Figure 13.3.

In **dwRBitMask**, all bits that are reserved for the red component are set. In hexadecimal format, **dwRBitMask** contains the value 0x1F. Looking at Figure 13.3, you can see that there are five bits for each component. The C++ code to calculate this number looks like this:

```
WORD GetNumberOfBits(DWORD dwMask)
{
   WORD wBits = 0;              // our bit counter
   while (dwMask != 0)          // as long as there are bits in the mask...
   {
      // ...mask off the least-significant bit
      dwMask = dwMask & (dwMask - 1);
      wBits++;                  // ...and increase our bit counter
   }
   return wBits;
}
```

We calculate the number of bits for every color component as shown in the following code snippet:

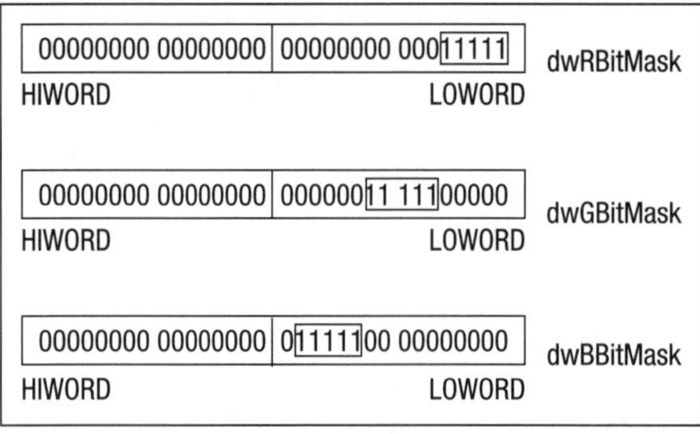

Figure 13.3 Illustration of the pixel format's bit masks.

```
// ddsd is a DDSURFACEDESC2 structure that has been filled by
// the IDirectDrawSurface7::Lock method

WORD NumRedBits = GetNumberOfBits(ddsd.ddpfPixelFormat.dwRBitMask);
WORD NumGreenBits = GetNumberOfBits(ddsd.ddpfPixelFormat.dwGBitMask);
WORD NumBlueBits = GetNumberOfBits(ddsd.ddpfPixelFormat.dwBBitMask);
```

Once we know how many bits we're *allowed* to use, we can scale down the bytes that we extracted from the **COLORREF** value. We do this by shifting the bytes to the right by the number of surplus bits. The following code does this:

```
BYTE ScaledRed = static_cast<BYTE>(Red >> (8 - NumRedBits));
BYTE ScaledGreen = static_cast<BYTE>(Green >> (8 - NumGreenBits));
BYTE ScaledBlue = static_cast<BYTE>(Blue >> (8 - NumBlueBits));
```

Assembling a Pixel

The 16-bit format depicted in Figure 13.3 is an RGB format—i.e., first red, then green, then blue. In some formats, however, it's the other way around—first blue, then green, then red. We have to take this difference into account when assembling the **DWORD** that is to be stored to the frame buffer. What we'll do is calculate the position of the least-significant bit of the color component, and then shift the scaled byte to the left by that number before we use a bitwise **OR** to combine it with the **DWORD**. The bit positions of the color components can be calculated with the following function:

```
WORD GetMaskPos(DWORD dwMask)
{
   WORD wPos = 0;                     // the bit position
   while (!(dwMask & (1 << wPos)))  // as long as we haven't encountered
                                      // the first set bit...

   {
      wPos++;                         // ...go to the next bit
      if (wPos > 31) break;
   }   return wPos;
}
```

The following code snippet retrieves the bit position of each color mask and assembles the bytes **ScaledRed**, **ScaledGreen**, and **ScaledBlue** to the **DWORD ConvertedPixel**, which is going to be written into the frame buffer in the next step:

```
WORD RedBitsPos = GetMaskPos(ddsd.ddpfPixelFormat.dwRBitMask);
WORD GreenBitsPos = GetMaskPos(ddsd.ddpfPixelFormat.dwGBitMask);
WORD BlueBitsPos = GetMaskPos(ddsd.ddpfPixelFormat.dwBBitMask);
```

```
// assemble a DWORD
DWORD ConvertedPixel = 0;
ConvertedPixel |= ScaledRed << RedBitsPos;      // add the red bits
ConvertedPixel |= ScaledGreen << GreenBitsPos;  // add the green bits
ConvertedPixel |= ScaledBlue << BlueBitsPos;    // add the blue bits
```

TIP: *Because color keys are specified in the surface's pixel format as well, you can also use the* ***DWORD ConvertedPixel*** *for the members of the* ***DDCOLORKEY*** *structure. See also "Converting an RGB Triple into the Surface's Pixel Format" in the "Immediate Solutions" section.*

Handling Pixel Formats that Contain Alpha Information

Some surfaces embed alpha channel information in the pixels. These surfaces are created with the **DDPF_ALPHAPIXELS** flag in the **dwFlags** member of the **DDPIXELFORMAT** structure. When this flag is set, the **dwRGBAlphaBitMask** member of the structure is valid. You can add the following code to the **SetPixel** routine to have it handle alpha channels:

```
// alpha_value_of_pixel is either a separate parameter of the function
// or contained in the most-significant byte of the COLORREF value

BYTE Alpha = alpha_value_of_pixel;

WORD NumAlphaBits = GetNumberOfBits(
   ddsd.ddpfPixelFormat.dwRGBAlphaBitMask);
BYTE ScaledAlpha = Alpha >> (8 - NumAlphaBits);
WORD AlphaBitsPos = GetMaskPos(ddsd.ddpfPixelFormat.dwRGBAlphaBitMask);

// add alpha to the pixel
ConvertedPixel |= ScaledAlpha << AlphaBitsPos;  // add the red bits
```

Writing Pixels to the Frame Buffer

Let us summarize what we have done: We have calculated the memory address of the pixel to set. The address is stored in the pointer **lpPointerToPixel**. We have converted the color that was passed to our **SetPixel** routine into the surface's pixel format. The converted pixel is waiting in the variable **ConvertedPixel**. What we can't do (except in a 32-bit pixel format) is write the **DWORD ConvertedPixel** to the frame buffer. If we did this, we'd overwrite part or all of the subsequent pixel. We have to ensure that we don't write more bits than a pixel uses in this format. A straightforward way of doing this would be to introduce a **switch** statement that handles every bit depth individually. The following code snippet is an example of how this could be done:

```
// ddsd, ConvertedPixel, and lpPointerToPixel have been
// prepared in the preceding steps

try
{
   switch (ddsd.ddpfPixelFormat.dwRGBBitCount / 8)
   {
   case 32:                // 32-bit format
   {
      // write DWORD as is
      *(reinterpret_cast<LPDWORD>(lpPointerToPixel)) = ConvertedPixel;
      break;
   }

   case 16:                // 16-bit format
   {
      // write the lower 16-bits of the DWORD
      *(reinterpret_cast<LPWORD>(lpPointerToPixel)) =
         LOWORD(ConvertedPixel);
      break;
   }

   case 24:                // 24-bit format
   {
      // split up the DWORD into a WORD...
      *(reinterpret_cast<LPWORD>(lpPointerToPixel)) =
         LOWORD(ConvertedPixel);
      // ...and a BYTE
      *(reinterpret_cast<LPBYTE>(
         reinterpret_cast<DWORD>(lpPointerToPixel) + 2)
      ) = LOBYTE(HIWORD(ConvertedPixel));
      break;
   }

   default:                // other formats
   {
      throw "This is an invalid bit depth.";
   }
   }

}
catch (...)
{
   throw "An exception occurred in the SetPixel routine.";
}
```

Of course, you don't have to place the **switch** statement into the **SetPixel** routine. You could also write separate **SetPixel** routines for every bit depth—e.g., **SetPixel16**, **SetPixel24**, and **SetPixel32**.

Releasing the Surface

When you're done working with the surface, you must call the **Unlock** method. Until you do so, you can't use the surface in blit operations, and you can't retrieve an **HDC** to the surface. GUI debuggers can't operate while a surface is locked. (This is due to the Win16Mutex, which DirectDraw often holds while a surface is locked. For more information about the Win16Mutex, see the Platform SDK.) Therefore, make sure that **Unlock** is always called, even when an exception occurs. See also the section about "Combining DirectDraw and the GDI."

Writing a GetPixel Function

A **GetPixel** function reads a pixel from a locked surface and converts it back into an RGB triple. In a **GetPixel** function, you would use the following code to convert the pixel that you read from the surface into a **COLORREF** value:

```
// OriginalPixel has been read from the surface.
// ddsd has been filled by the Lock method.

COLORREF rgb;
BYTE Red, Green, Blue;

Red = static_cast<BYTE>(
   ((OriginalPixel & ddsd.ddpfPixelFormat.dwRBitMask)
      >> RedBitsPos) << (8 - NumRedBits));
Green = static_cast<BYTE>(
   ((OriginalPixel & ddsd.ddpfPixelFormat.dwGBitMask)
      >> GreenBitsPos) << (8 - NumGreenBits));
Blue = static_cast<BYTE>(
   ((OriginalPixel & ddsd.ddpfPixelFormat.dwBBitMask)
      >> BlueBitsPos) << (8 - NumBlueBits));
```

The code to actually read the pixel is very similar to the code from the **SetPixel** routine and is therefore not listed here.

Working with Flipping Chains

In this section, we'll discuss how to create and use flipping chains. We'll set up the primary surface of a DirectDraw application as a flipping chain, we'll discuss the benefits and drawbacks of triple buffering, and we'll use an off-screen flipping chain to display a simple animation. We'll also address stereo vision flipping chains. The **IDirectDrawSurface7** interface methods that we'll cover are **Flip** and **GetAttachedSurface**.

Using a Primary Surface Flipping Chain

Creating the primary surface as a flipping chain is possible only when an exclusive cooperative level is set, i.e., in full-screen exclusive applications. Full-screen applications can prepare their graphics in the back buffer (the non-visible surface). When they're done, they display the contents of the back buffer by calling the **IDirectDrawSurface7::Flip** method. To create a flipping chain, you have to include the **DDSCAPS_COMPLEX** and **DDSCAPS_FLIP** flags in the **dwCaps** member of the **DDSCAPS2** structure that is passed to the **IDirectDraw::CreateSurface** method. In addition, the **dwBackBufferCount** member of the **DDSURFACEDESC2** structure must be set to a value greater than zero. The following code demonstrates this:


```
// lpDD is assumed to be a valid pointer to an IDirectDraw7 interface

// prepare surface description
DDSURFACEDESC2 ddsd;
ZeroMemory(&ddsd, sizeof(ddsd));
ddsd.dwSize = sizeof(ddsd);
ddsd.dwFlags = DDSD_CAPS |              // ddsCaps...
   DDSD_BACKBUFFERCOUNT;                // ...and dwBackBufferCount are valid
ddsd.ddsCaps.dwCaps = DDSCAPS_PRIMARYSURFACE |
   DDSCAPS_COMPLEX | DDSCAPS_FLIP;
ddsd.dwBackBufferCount = 1;             // one back buffer

// create the surface
LPDIRECTDRAWSURFACE7 lpDDSPrimary = NULL;
if (FAILED(lpDD->CreateSurface(
   &ddsd,
   &lpDDSPrimary,
   NULL
)))
{
   throw "The primary flipping chain could not be created.";
}
```

Retrieving a Pointer to the Back Buffer

To gain access to the back buffer, you have to retrieve its **IDirectDrawSurface7** interface by calling the **GetAttachedSurface** method of the front buffer. The **GetAttachedSurface** method takes a **DDSCAPS2** structure as input; this structure specifies the requested surface's characteristics. In our case, we only set the **dwCaps** member of the structure to **DDSCAPS_BACKBUFFER**. The following code demonstrates how to retrieve a pointer to the back buffer interface from the **lpDDSPrimary** interface:

```
DDSCAPS2 ddsCaps;
ddsCaps.dwCaps = DDSCAPS_BACKBUFFER;

LPDIRECTDRAWSURFACE7 lpDDSBackBuffer;
if (SUCCEEDED(lpDDSPrimary->GetAttachedSurface(
    &ddsCaps,
    &lpDDSBackBuffer
)))
{
    /*
        lpDDSBackBuffer is a valid pointer to the back buffer interface
    */
}
```


You will always draw to the surface pointed to by **lpDDSBackBuffer**, and you will always use the **Flip** method provided by the surface pointed to by **lpDDSPrimary**. Before shutting down your application, you must release the flipping chain by calling **lpDDSPrimary->Release()**. This will release the back buffer implicitly. You do not have to call **lpDDSBackBuffer->Release()**.

See also "Creating a Primary Surface Flipping Chain" in the "Immediate Solutions" section.

Using the Flip Method

The interface pointed to by **lpDDSPrimary** provides the **Flip** method. A flip is performed like this:

```
lpDDSPrimary->Flip(NULL, 0);
```

In the call to the **Flip** method, the first parameter specifies which surface you want to make visible. The **NULL** pointer causes the next surface in the chain to be displayed. The second parameter is a flags parameter. A value of zero defaults to the **DDFLIP_WAIT** flag, which instructs the **Flip** method not to return before the flip has been set up. After the first call to the **Flip** method, you will most likely see garbage on the screen. This occurs because the back buffer has not been cleared yet. In addition, dialog boxes, menu bars, and window captions are not visible on the back buffer. After a second flip, you'll see the main window of your full-screen application again.

Flipping to the Desktop

A special **Flip** method can be used to switch back to the front buffer—i.e., the surface on which Windows GUI elements (such as your application's main window) are visible. This method is **IDirectDraw7::FlipToGDISurface**. This method works only if the **GetCaps** method reports the **DDCAPS2_CANRENDERWINDOWED** capability for the hardware. For more information about querying hardware capabilities, see Chapter 11. For a usage example of **FlipToGDISurface**, see Chapter 12.

Triple Buffering

A blit operation fails if it is called while an asynchronous flip is still in progress. For this reason, the **Flip** method is usually called with the **DDFLIP_WAIT** flag, which causes the method to wait until the flip is completed and subsequent blit operations can be performed. This causes some idling time that could be better used to prepare the next frame. To be able to blit to the back buffer while a flip is still in progress, you can create a primary flipping chain with two back buffers (a triple-buffering scheme). To do this, set **dwBackBufferCount** to 2. (Creating more than two back buffers is a waste of memory—the performance will not be better.) With triple buffering, you can safely specify the **DDFLIP_DONOTWAIT** flag in calls to **IDirectDrawSurface7::Flip**. Figure 13.4 illustrates how the **Flip** method cycles through the buffers of a triple-buffering scheme.

The biggest disadvantage of triple buffering is that it requires 50 percent more video memory than does a primary surface with one back buffer.

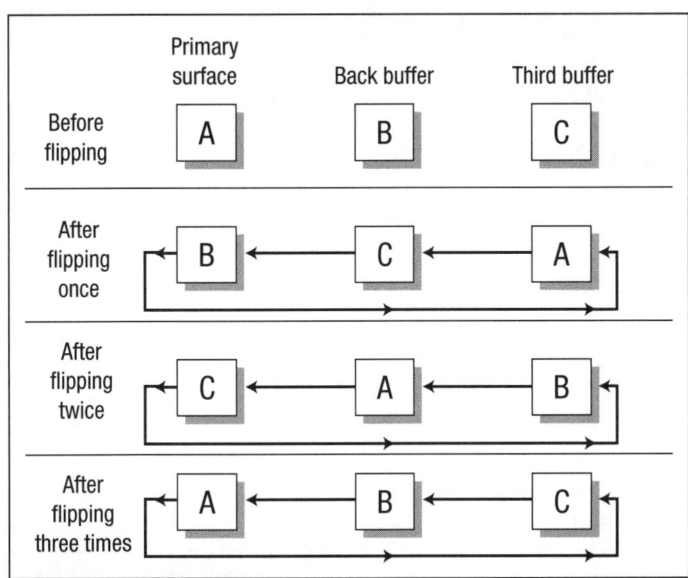

Figure 13.4 Triple buffering.

Using Stereo Vision Flipping Chains

Stereo vision is one of the most exciting features of DirectDraw 7. Equipped with special hardware—namely, 3D glasses and a display device that supports them—users can perceive a scene as having depth, not as flat. LCD shutter glasses are very common for this purpose. An application prepares two views of a scene: one for the left eye and one for the right eye. The display hardware switches between these views many times per second. Whenever the left view is displayed, the shutter glasses shut the right eye. Whenever the right view is displayed, they shut the left eye. This way, each eye sees only those views that are intended for it. This section demonstrates how you can set up a stereo vision primary surface with DirectDraw.

First of all, your application should determine whether stereo vision is supported. To do this, you have to enumerate available display modes as described in Chapter 12. The enumeration callback receives pointers to **DDSURFACEDESC2** structures describing the display modes. If the **DDSCAPS2_STEREOSURFACELEFT** flag is set in the **ddsCaps.dwCaps2** member of the structure, stereo vision is supported in that mode.

Next, you have to set one of the display modes that supports stereo vision. When creating the stereo vision flipping chain, you include the **DDSCAPS2_STEREOSURFACELEFT** flag in the **dwCaps2** member of the **DDSCAPS2** structure that you pass to **CreateSurface** as part of the surface description. Here's the code to do this:

```
// lpDD is assumed to be a valid pointer to an IDirectDraw7 interface

// prepare surface description
DDSURFACEDESC2 ddsd;
ZeroMemory(&ddsd, sizeof(ddsd));
ddsd.dwSize = sizeof(ddsd);
ddsd.dwFlags = DDSD_CAPS |           // ddsCaps...
   DDSD_BACKBUFFERCOUNT;             // ...and dwBackBufferCount are valid
ddsd.ddsCaps.dwCaps = DDSCAPS_PRIMARYSURFACE |
   DDSCAPS_COMPLEX | DDSCAPS_FLIP;
ddsd.ddsCaps.dwCaps2 = DDSCAPS2_STEREOSURFACELEFT;
ddsd.dwBackBufferCount = 1;          // one back buffer

// create the surface
LPDIRECTDRAWSURFACE7 lpDDSPrimary = NULL;
if (FAILED(lpDD->CreateSurface(
   &ddsd,
   &lpDDSPrimary,
   NULL
```

```
)))
{
   throw "The stereo vision flipping chain could not be created.";
}
```

This code results in the creation of four surfaces—a front buffer and a back buffer, each consisting of a left-eye surface and a right-eye surface.

After you have retrieved a pointer to the back buffer as described in "Using a Primary Surface Flipping Chain," you use the **GetAttachedSurface** method on the back buffer interface to retrieve a pointer to the left-eye surface. Again, you must set the **dwCaps2** member of the **DDSCAPS2** structure to **DDSCAPS2_STEREOSURFACELEFT**. The following code does this:

```
// lpDDSBackBuffer has been retrieved from lpDDSPrimary
// by using the GetAttachedSurface method

DDSCAPS2 ddsCaps;
ddsCaps.dwCaps2 = DDSCAPS2_STEREOSURFACELEFT;

LPDIRECTDRAWSURFACE7 lpDDSLeftBackBuffer;
if (SUCCEEDED(lpDDSBackBuffer->GetAttachedSurface(
   &ddsCaps,
   &lpDDSLeftBackBuffer
)))
{
   /*
      lpDDSLeftBackBuffer is a valid pointer to the
      back buffer surface for the left eye
   */
}
```

The **lpDDSBackBuffer** pointer is now a pointer to the surface for the right eye, and **lpDDSLeftBackBuffer** is a pointer to the surface for the left eye. The images that you render to these surfaces should be taken from slightly different angles to produce a 3D effect. When the images are prepared, call the **Flip** method with the **DDFLIP_STEREO** flag. This flag instructs the hardware to automatically flip between the left and right buffers. You do not have to call the **Flip** method again before you have prepared a new back buffer. See the following code:

```
lpDDSPrimary->Flip(
   NULL,                    // flip to next buffer in the chain
   DDFLIP_STEREO            // enable stereo autoflipping
);
```

See also "Creating a Stereo Vision Flipping Chain" in the "Immediate Solutions" section.

Using Off-Screen Flipping Chains

You can use off-screen flipping chains to play back short looping animations. Every surface in the chain contains one animation frame. You need one **IDirectDrawSurface7** interface pointer for the entire animation instead of one pointer per frame. The following steps are required to set up such a flipping animation:

1. *Create the flipping chain*—Use the **CreateSurface** method to set up an off-screen flipping chain.
2. *Load the animation*—Use the **GetAttachedSurface** method to iterate through the back buffers of the flipping chain and to load the animation frames from image files.
3. *Play back the animation*—Use the **Flip** and **Blt** methods to display the animation.

Creating the Flipping Chain

An off-screen flipping chain is created just like a primary flipping chain, except that with an off-screen flipping chain, the **DDSCAPS_OFFSCREENPLAIN** flag is used instead of the **DDSCAPS_PRIMARYSURFACE** flag. Because it is an off-screen surface, the width and height must also be specified. The number of back buffers is limited only by the amount of available memory. The following code snippet demonstrates the creation of an off-screen flipping chain:

```
// lpDD is assumed to be a valid pointer to an IDirectDraw7 interface

DDSURFACEDESC2 ddsd;
ZeroMemory(&ddsd, sizeof(ddsd));
ddsd.dwSize = sizeof(ddsd);
ddsd.dwFlags = DDSD_CAPS |
   DDSD_BACKBUFFERCOUNT |
   DDSD_WIDTH | DDSD_HEIGHT;
ddsd.ddsCaps.dwCaps = DDSCAPS_COMPLEX | DDSCAPS_FLIP |
   DDSCAPS_OFFSCREENPLAIN;
ddsd.dwBackBufferCount = NumberOfFrames;
   ddsd.dwWidth = FrameWidth;
   ddsd.dwHeight = FrameHeight;

LPDIRECTDRAWSURFACE7 lpDDSAnimation = NULL;
```

```
if (FAILED(lpDD->CreateSurface(
   &ddsd,
   &lpDDSAnimation,
   NULL
)))
{
   throw "Off-screen flipping chain creation failed.";
}
```

Loading the Animation

In a flipping chain, the surfaces are attached to each other; i.e., the first back buffer is attached to the front buffer, the second back buffer is attached to the first back buffer, and so on. The following code snippet uses the **GetAttachedSurface** method to iterate through the flipping chain:

```
// lpDDSAnimation is a valid pointer to the
// front buffer of the flipping chain

try
{
   int FrameNum = 0;            // frame count

   LPDIRECTDRAWSURFACE7 lpCurrSurf;
   lpCurrSurf = lpDDSAnimation; // start with the front buffer

   // prepare DDSCAPS2 structure to pass to GetAttachedSurface
   DDSCAPS2 ddsCaps;
   ZeroMemory(&ddsCaps, sizeof(ddsCaps));
   ddsCaps.dwCaps = DDSCAPS_COMPLEX | DDSCAPS_FLIP; // the attached surface
                                                    // has these capabilities

   while (true)
   {
      /*
         load bitmap #FrameNum into lpCurrSurf here
      */

      // increment frame number
      FrameNum++;

      // get pointer to next surface in chain (overwrites lpCurrSurf)
      if (FAILED(lpCurrSurf->GetAttachedSurface(&ddsCaps, &lpCurrSurf)))
      {
         throw "GetAttachedSurface failed.";
      }
```

```
        // break if we're through (the next surface is the front buffer)
        if (lpCurrSurf == lpDDSAnimation)
        {  break; }
    }

    return true;

}
catch (...)
{
    return false;
}
```

The code to load a bitmap from a file can be found in the "Immediate Solutions" section.

Playing Back the Animation

To display an animation frame, you have to blit from the surface pointed to by **lpDDSAnimation** to the primary surface (or to the back buffer if you're using double buffering). The display routine doesn't have to care about which animation frame is currently contained in the front buffer of the off-screen flipping chain. To cycle through the animation frames, you call **lpDDSAnimation->Flip()**—for example, as a reaction to a timer event. The cycle routine, in turn, doesn't have to know how the animation must be displayed. When the last frame of the animation has been reached, the next flip automatically returns to the first frame.

The CD-ROM contains the complete source code of the sample program.

Working with Overlay Surfaces

This section describes how to use DirectDraw overlay surfaces. First of all, let's see why overlay surfaces can be useful:

- They are displayed above everything else on the screen, similar to the OSDs (on-screen displays) of TV sets and computer monitors.
- The graphics card displays an overlay without modifying the contents of the primary surface (see Figure 13.5). When you remove the overlay, nothing has to be redrawn.
- Displaying an overlay does not involve any blitting. The hardware is completely responsible for displaying overlay surfaces.
- Overlays can have a different pixel format than the primary surface. If the hardware supports it, you can display a 32-bit video on a 16-bit primary surface without having to convert the pixels.

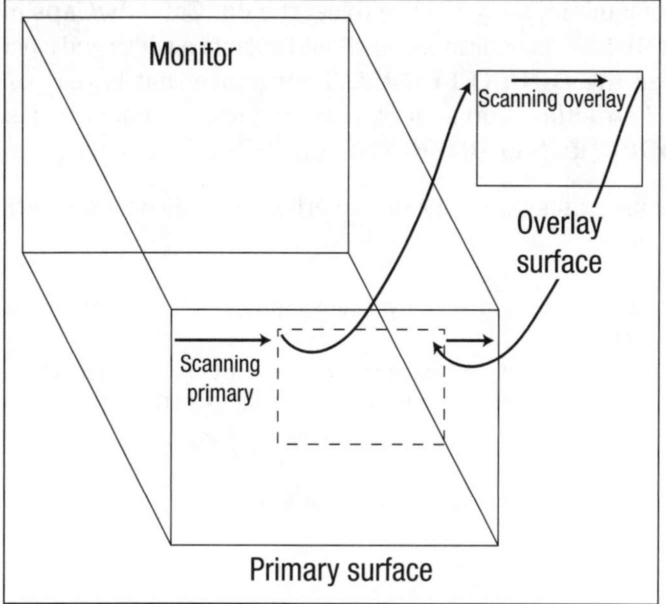

Figure 13.5 The process of displaying an overlay surface.

Figure 13.5 illustrates how the process of displaying an overlay works. As the cathode ray scans the monitor, the graphics card reads the color information of the pixels from the primary surface. If a pixel is covered by an overlay, the graphics card reads the color information from the overlay surface instead.

Determining Hardware Support for Overlays

Before you start creating overlay surfaces, you should check whether the hardware supports them. You do this by calling the **IDirectDraw7::GetCaps** method, as described in Chapter 11, and checking the members of the **DDCAPS** structure that represents the hardware capabilities. (Checking the emulation capabilities is superfluous because DirectDraw never attempts to emulate overlay functionality.) If overlays are supported, the **dwCaps** member of the **DDCAPS** structure contains the **DDCAPS_OVERLAY** flag. The **dwMaxVisibleOverlays** member of the structure is greater than zero.

Finding a Supported Overlay Format

Display hardware might not support overlays of a specific pixel format or any overlays at all in every display mode. You can use the **IDirectDraw7::EnumSurfaces** method with the **DDENUMSURFACES_CANBECREATED** flag to find a supported format. One of the parameters of the **EnumSurfaces** method is a **DDSURFACEDESC2** structure that describes the general characteristics of the desired surface. At a minimum, you have to set the **ddsCaps.dwCaps** member to **DDSCAPS_OVERLAY**. In addition, you should specify a width and a height. You can also initialize the **DDPIXELFORMAT** structure that is part of the **DDSURFACEDESC2** structure. You should, however, specify only the desired color space (either **DDPF_RGB** or **DDPF_YUV**) or a FOURCC code.

The following code enumerates the supported overlay surfaces with a width and a height of 64:

```
// This is the callback that is invoked by EnumSurfaces:
HRESULT WINAPI EnumSurfacesCallback(
    LPDIRECTDRAWSURFACE7,        // This parameter is not valid when the
                                 // DDENUMSURFACES_CANBECREATED flag was
                                 // passed to EnumSurfaces.
    LPDDSURFACEDESC2 ddsd,       // surface description
    int *Count                   // application-defined
   )
{
try
{
   (*Count)++;                   // count enumerated surfaces

   /*
      In your application, you might wish to save the
      DDSURFACEDESC2 structure for future use (e.g.,
      to pass it to the CreateSurface method).
   */

   // ...

}
catch (...)
{
   return DDENUMRET_CANCEL;
}
}


// This is the routine that calls EnumSurfaces:
void EnumerateOverlayFormats()
{
try
{
   // prepare DDSURFACEDESC2 structure
   DDSURFACEDESC2 ddsd;
   ZeroMemory(&ddsd, sizeof(ddsd));
```

```
    ddsd.dwSize = sizeof(ddsd);
    ddsd.dwFlags = DDSD_CAPS |
       DDSD_WIDTH | DDSD_HEIGHT |              // these are...
       DDSD_PIXELFORMAT;                       // ...optional
    ddsd.ddsCaps.dwCaps = DDSCAPS_OVERLAY;
    ddsd.dwWidth = 64;
    ddsd.dwHeight = 64;
    ddsd.ddpfPixelFormat.dwSize = sizeof(DDPIXELFORMAT);
    ddsd.ddpfPixelFormat.dwFlags = DDPF_RGB; // enumerate all RGB formats

    // call EnumSurfaces
    int Count = 0;

    if (FAILED(lpDD->EnumSurfaces(
       DDENUMSURFACES_CANBECREATED | DDENUMSURFACES_MATCH,
       &ddsd,
       reinterpret_cast<LPVOID>(&Count),
       reinterpret_cast<LPDDENUMSURFACESCALLBACK7>(EnumSurfacesCallback)
    )))
    {
       throw "EnumSurfaces failed.";
    }
    else
    {
       /*
          int Count contains the number of enumerated surfaces.
       */
    }

 }
 catch (...)
 {
    throw "An exception occurred.";
 }
 }
```

***NOTE:** Many display devices will support FOURCC formats for overlay surfaces. You can use the **IDirectDraw7::GetFourCCCodes** method to retrieve a list of FOURCC codes that you can test with the **EnumSurfaces** method. See also "Retrieving Supported FOURCC Formats" in the "Immediate Solutions" section.*

Creating an Overlay Surface

Creating overlay surfaces is straightforward. All you have to do is include the **DDSCAPS_OVERLAY** and **DDSCAPS_VIDEOMEMORY** flags in the **ddsCaps.dwCaps** member of the **DDSURFACEDESC2** structure that you pass to the **CreateSurface** method. You can also create an overlay flipping chain by making the **dwBackBufferCount** member valid and setting it to a value greater than zero. For more information, see "Creating an Overlay Surface" in the "Immediate Solutions" section.

Displaying Overlay Surfaces

Overlays are displayed with the **IDirectDrawSurface7::UpdateOverlay** method. The method takes a pointer to the **IDirectDrawSurface7** interface that is to be overlaid and pointers to the source and destination rectangles. Many display devices impose restrictions on the positions and dimensions of the rectangles. Let's first take a look at these restrictions.

Determining Hardware Restrictions

The **DDCAPS** structure contains a number of members that provide information about hardware restrictions for overlay surfaces. Table 13.2 lists these members.

Calling the UpdateOverlay Method

After you have adjusted the source and destination rectangles according to the hardware restrictions, you can call the **UpdateOverlay** method of the overlay

Table 13.2 DDCAPS members containing overlay information.

Member	Meaning
dwAlignBoundarySrc	The value specifying the x-coordinate of the source rectangle must be a multiple of the value of **dwAlignBoundarySrc**. This member is valid if the **DDCAPS_ALIGNBOUNDARYSRC** flag is set.
dwAlignBoundaryDest	The value specifying the x-coordinate of the destination rectangle must be a multiple of the value of **dwAlignBoundaryDest**. This member is valid if the **DDCAPS_ALIGNBOUNDARYDEST** flag is set.
dwAlignSizeSrc	The width of the source rectangle must be a multiple of the value of **dwAlignSizeSrc**. This member is valid if the **DDCAPS_ALIGNSIZESRC** flag is set.
dwAlignSizeDest	The width of the destination rectangle must be a multiple of the value of **dwAlignSizeDest**. This member is valid if the **DDCAPS_ALIGNSIZEDEST** flag is set.
dwMinOverlayStretch and **dwMaxOverlayStretch**	These members contain the minimum and maximum stretch factors multiplied by 1,000. For example, if **dwMaxOverlayStretch** is 2,000, the destination rectangle must not be more than twice as wide as the source rectangle. The height of destination rectangles does not have to be adjusted. If both members are zero, you can assume that there are no restrictions regarding stretch factors. The **DDCAPS_OVERLAYSTRETCH** flag is set. Otherwise, the hardware does not support stretching during overlay operations.

surface interface. You must specify the **DDOVER_SHOW** flag. The following code simply displays the overlay without stretching it:

```
// lpDDSOverlay is assumed to be a valid pointer to
// the IDirectDrawSurface7 interface of an overlay surface.
// lpDDSPrimary is assumed to be a valid pointer to
// the IDirectDrawSurface7 interface of the primary surface.

RECT SrcRect = { 0, 0, 64, 64 };
RECT DestRect = { 0, 0, 64, 64 };

if (FAILED(lpDDSOverlay->UpdateOverlay(
   &SrcRect,
   lpDDSPrimary,
   &DestRect,
   DDOVER_SHOW,
   NULL
)))
{
   throw "Displaying the overlay surface failed.";
}
```

See also “Displaying or Hiding an Overlay Surface” in the “Immediate Solutions” section.

Losing and Restoring Surfaces

In some situations, the frame-buffer memory of a surface might be freed before the surface interface is released. This happens when the display mode is changed and sometimes when the user performs a task switch to another application. In Chapter 11, we used the **IDirectDraw7::RestoreAllSurfaces** method to restore the surfaces again. In this chapter, we'll enumerate all surfaces that the application created. For each of them, we'll call the **IsLost** method to check whether the surface is lost. If it is, we can restore the surface by using the **IDirectDraw-Surface7::Restore** method. In addition, we can reload the surface's graphics.

The first step is to call the **IDirectDraw7::EnumSurfaces** method with the **DDENUMSURFACES_DOESEXIST** and **DDENUMSURFACES_ALL** flags. This is demonstrated in the following code snippet:

```
// lpDD is assumed to be a valid pointer to an IDirectDraw7 interface

if (FAILED(lpDD->EnumSurfaces(
   DDENUMSURFACES_DOESEXIST | DDENUMSURFACES_ALL,
   NULL,                          // no description that surfaces must match
```

```
      NULL,                          // pass this to the callback
      RestoreCallback                // see next section
)))
{
      throw "Enumerating existing surfaces failed.";
}
```

The **EnumSurfaces** method invokes the application-defined callback function **RestoreCallback** for every surface that has been created. In that callback, we call the **IsLost** method of the surface. If the method returns **DDERR_SURFACELOST**, the surface memory has been lost. We solve this problem by calling the **Restore** method of the surface. The following is the source code of the callback function:


```
HRESULT WINAPI RestoreCallback(
     LPDIRECTDRAWSURFACE7 lpDDSurface,   // pointer to the enumerated
                                         // surface's interface
     LPDDSURFACEDESC2 ,                  // we don't use these...
     LPVOID                              // ...two parameters
   )
{
try
{
   // check whether surface is lost
   if (lpDDSurface->IsLost() == DDERR_SURFACELOST)
   {
      // if so, restore it
      lpDDSurface->Restore();
      /*
         Reload the graphics here
      */
   }

   // EnumSurfaces has increased the reference count of the surface,
   // so we must decrease it again:
   SAFERELEASE(lpDDSurface);

   // continue enumeration
   return DDENUMRET_OK;

}
catch (...)
{
```

```
        // EnumSurfaces has increased the reference count of the surface,
        // so we must decrease it again:
        SAFERELEASE(lpDDSurface);
        return DDENUMRET_CANCEL;
    }
}
```

After restoring a surface, you have to reload the graphics that it contained. This is not done automatically.

For more information, see "Enumerating Surfaces," "Determining Whether a Surface Is Lost," and "Restoring a Surface" in the "Immediate Solutions" section.

Immediate Solutions

Interpreting the DDSURFACEDESC2 Structure

The **DDSURFACEDESC2** structure is used by DirectDraw functions to store information about surfaces. In some contexts, the structure is used to pass information to DirectDraw functions (e.g., to **IDirectDraw7::CreateSurface**). In other contexts, it is used by DirectDraw functions (e.g., **IDirectDrawSurface7::Lock** or **IDirectDraw7::EnumDisplayModes**) to return information to the caller. Following is the declaration of the **DDSURFACEDESC2** structure:


```
typedef struct _DDSURFACEDESC2 {
    DWORD          dwSize;
    DWORD          dwFlags;
    DWORD          dwHeight;
    DWORD          dwWidth;
    union
    {
        LONG       lPitch;
        DWORD      dwLinearSize;
    } DUMMYUNIONNAMEN(1);
    DWORD          dwBackBufferCount;
    union
    {
        DWORD      dwMipMapCount;
        DWORD      dwRefreshRate;
    } DUMMYUNIONNAMEN(2);
    DWORD          dwAlphaBitDepth;
    DWORD          dwReserved;
    LPVOID         lpSurface;
    union
    {
        DDCOLORKEY     ddckCKDestOverlay;
        DWORD          dwEmptyFaceColor;
    } DUMMYUNIONNAMEN(3);
    DDCOLORKEY     ddckCKDestBlt;
    DDCOLORKEY     ddckCKSrcOverlay;
    DDCOLORKEY     ddckCKSrcBlt;
```

```
    DDPIXELFORMAT ddpfPixelFormat;
    DDSCAPS2      ddsCaps;
    DWORD         dwTextureStage;
} DDSURFACEDESC2, FAR* LPDDSURFACEDESC2;
```

The following list provides detailed information about each of the structure members:

- **dwSize**—Before you pass the structure to one of the DirectDraw methods, set this member to **sizeof(DDSURFACEDESC2)**. The following function template can be used to initialize any structure containing a **dwSize** member:

```
template <class DirectDrawStruct>
void PrepareDDrawStruct(DirectDrawStruct &s)
{
   ZeroMemory(&s, sizeof(DirectDrawStruct));
   s.dwSize = sizeof(DirectDrawStruct);
}
```

- **dwFlags**—This bit field indicates which of the structure members are valid. Don't read from invalid members, and don't forget to initialize **dwFlags** before passing the structure to one of the DirectDraw member functions. Table 13.3 lists the defined constants. These constants can be combined using a bitwise **OR**.
- **dwHeight** and **dwWidth**—These **DWORDs** contain the dimensions of the surface, in pixels.
- **lPitch**—This long integer contains the surface pitch—i.e., the length of the scan lines in bytes. See "Concepts and Terminology" in the "In Depth" section.
- **dwLinearSize**—This member is used with Direct3D.
- **dwBackBufferCount**—This specifies the number of back buffers of a complex surface or flipping chain.
- **dwMipMapCount**—This member is used with Direct3D.
- **dwRefreshRate**—When the **DDSURFACEDESC2** structure is returned by one of the display-mode-related methods, this member specifies the monitor frequency. See Chapter 12.
- **dwAlphaBitDepth**—This member contains the bit depth of an alpha-only surface. The **ddsCaps.dwCaps** member contains the **DDSCAPS_ALPHA** flag.
- **dwReserved**—Reserved.

Table 13.3 Valid flags for the dwFlags member of the DDSURFACEDESC2 structure.

Flag	Meaning
DDSD_ALL	All members are valid.
DDSD_ALPHABITDEPTH	The **dwAlphaBitDepth** member is valid.
DDSD_BACKBUFFERCOUNT	The **dwBackBufferCount** member is valid.
DDSD_CAPS	The **ddsCaps** member is valid.
DDSD_CKDESTBLT	The **ddckCKDestBlt** member is valid.
DDSD_CKDESTOVERLAY	The **ddckCKDestOverlay** member is valid.
DDSD_CKSRCBLT	The **ddckCKSrcBlt** member is valid.
DDSD_CKSRCOVERLAY	The **ddckCKSrcOverlay** member is valid.
DDSD_HEIGHT	The **dwHeight** member is valid.
DDSD_LINEARSIZE	The **dwLinearSize** member is valid.
DDSD_LPSURFACE	The **lpSurface** member is valid.
DDSD_MIPMAPCOUNT	The **dwMipMapCount** member is valid.
DDSD_PITCH	The **lPitch** member is valid.
DDSD_PIXELFORMAT	The **ddpfPixelFormat** member is valid.
DDSD_REFRESHRATE	The **dwRefreshRate** member is valid.
DDSD_TEXTURESTAGE	The **dwTextureStage** member is valid.
DDSD_WIDTH	The **dwWidth** member is valid.

- **lpSurface**—This member contains a pointer to the beginning of the surface's frame buffer, i.e., to its upper-left pixel. The **lpSurface** member is a return value of the **IDirectDrawSurface7::Lock** method and an input value with the **IDirectDrawSurface7::SetSurfaceDesc** method. See "Accessing Surface Memory Directly" in the "In Depth" section and "Creating an Off-Screen Surface from an Existing Block of Memory" in the "Immediate Solutions" section.
- **ddckCKDestOverlay**—This is a **DDCOLORKEY** structure containing the destination color key for an overlay surface.
- **dwEmptyFaceColor**—This member is used with Direct3D.
- **ddckCKDestBlt**—This is a **DDCOLORKEY** structure containing the destination color key for blit operations.
- **ddckCKSrcOverlay**—This is a **DDCOLORKEY** structure containing the source color key for an overlay surface.
- **ddckCKSrcBlt**—This is a **DDCOLORKEY** structure containing the source color key for blit operations.

- **ddpfPixelFormat**—This is a **DDPIXELFORMAT** structure containing information about the pixel format of the surface. See "Interpreting the **DDPIXELFORMAT** Structure."
- **ddsCaps**—This is a **DDSCAPS2** structure specifying the capabilities of the surface. See "Interpreting the **DDSCAPS2** Structure" in the "Immediate Solutions" section.
- **dwTextureStage**—This member is used with Direct3D.

Interpreting the DDPIXELFORMAT Structure

The **DDPIXELFORMAT** structure contains information about the pixel format of a surface. The structure is declared as follows:

```
typedef struct _DDPIXELFORMAT{
    DWORD dwSize;
    DWORD dwFlags;
    DWORD dwFourCC;
    union
    {
        DWORD dwRGBBitCount;
        DWORD dwYUVBitCount;
        DWORD dwZBufferBitDepth;
        DWORD dwAlphaBitDepth;
        DWORD dwLuminanceBitCount;
        DWORD dwBumpBitCount;
    } DUMMYUNIONNAMEN(1);
    union
    {
        DWORD dwRBitMask;
        DWORD dwYBitMask;
        DWORD dwStencilBitDepth;
        DWORD dwLuminanceBitMask;
        DWORD dwBumpDuBitMask;
    } DUMMYUNIONNAMEN(2);
    union
    {
        DWORD dwGBitMask;
        DWORD dwUBitMask;
        DWORD dwZBitMask;
        DWORD dwBumpDvBitMask;
    } DUMMYUNIONNAMEN(3);
```

```
    union
    {
        DWORD dwBBitMask;
        DWORD dwVBitMask;
        DWORD dwStencilBitMask;
        DWORD dwBumpLuminanceBitMask;
    } DUMMYUNIONNAMEN(4);
    union
    {
        DWORD dwRGBAlphaBitMask;
        DWORD dwYUVAlphaBitMask;
        DWORD dwLuminanceAlphaBitMask;
        DWORD dwRGBZBitMask;
        DWORD dwYUVZBitMask;
    } DUMMYUNIONNAMEN(5);
} DDPIXELFORMAT, FAR* LPDDPIXELFORMAT;
```


The following list provides detailed information about each of the structure members:

- **dwSize**—Before you pass the structure to one of the DirectDraw methods, set this member to **sizeof(DDPIXELFORMAT)**. This is also required for the **DDPIXELFORMAT** structure that is part of the **DDSURFACEDESC2** structure. If the **DDSURFACEDESC2** structure does not have the **DDSD_PIXELFORMAT** flag set in its **dwFlags** member, the entire **DDPIXELFORMAT** structure (including the **dwSize** member) is ignored.
- **dwFlags**—This bit field indicates which of the structure members are valid. Don't read from invalid members, and don't forget to initialize **dwFlags** before passing the structure to one of the DirectDraw member functions. Table 13.4 lists the defined constants. These constants can be combined using a bitwise **OR**.
- **dwFourCC**—The pixel layout of the surface is described by this four-character code. A list of codes can be retrieved through **IDirectDraw7::GetFour CCCodes**. See also the solution "Retrieving Supported FOURCC Formats."
- **dwRGBBitCount**—This specifies the number of bits per pixel (16, 24, or 32) for an RGB surface.
- **dwYUVBitCount**—This specifies the number of bits per pixel (16, 24, or 32) for a YUV surface.
- **dwAlphaBitDepth**—This specifies the bit depth of an alpha-only surface. (Check the **dwFlags** member of the structure for the presence of the **DDPF_ALPHA** flag to find out whether this is an alpha-only surface.)

Table 13.4 Valid flags for the dwFlags member of the DDPIXELFORMAT structure.

Flag	Meaning
DDPF_ALPHA	This is an alpha-only surface. The **dwAlphaBitDepth** member is valid.
DDPF_ALPHAPIXELS	The surface has alpha-channel information in the pixel format. The **dwRGBAlphaBitMask** (or **dwYUVAlphaBitMask**) member is valid.
DDPF_ALPHAPREMULT	The surface uses the premultiplied alpha format. That is, the color components in each pixel are premultiplied by the alpha component.
DDPF_FOURCC	The pixel format is implied by the four-character code in the **dwFourCC** member.
DDPF_PALETTEINDEXED1, **DDPF_PALETTEINDEXED2**, **DDPF_PALETTEINDEXED4**, **DDPF_PALETTEINDEXED8**	The surface is 1-, 2-, 4-, or 8-bit color-indexed.
DDPF_PALETTEINDEXEDTO8	The surface is 1-, 2-, or 4-bit color-indexed to an 8-bit palette.
DDPF_RGB	This is an RGB surface. The **dwRGBBitCount**, **dwRBitMask**, **dwGBitMask**, and **dwBBitMask** members are valid.
DDPF_RGBTOYUV	Data is written to the surface in RGB format and is automatically translated to YUV format. The **DDPF_RGB** flag is also set.
DDPF_YUV	This is a YUV surface. The **dwYUVBitCount**, **dwYBitMask**, **dwUBitMask**, and **dwVBitMask** members are valid.

- **dwRBitMask**—This is the mask for the red bits. All bits that are reserved for the red channel are set.
- **dwYBitMask**—This is the mask for the Y bits. All bits that are reserved for the Y channel are set.
- **dwGBitMask**—This is the mask for the green bits. All bits that are reserved for the green channel are set.
- **dwUBitMask**—This is the mask for the U bits. All bits that are reserved for the U channel are set.
- **dwBBitMask**—This is the mask for the blue bits. All bits that are reserved for the blue channel are set.
- **dwVBitMask**—This is the mask for the V bits. All bits that are reserved for the V channel are set.
- **dwRGBAlphaBitMask** and **dwYUVAlphaBitMask**—These are the masks for the alpha channel of RGB and YUV surfaces, respectively. All bits that are reserved for the alpha channel are set. This is valid only if **dwFlags** contains the **DDPF_ALPHAPIXELS** flag.

Interpreting the DDSCAPS2 Structure

The **DDSCAPS2** structure describes the general capabilities of a DirectDraw surface. The structure is declared as follows:

```
typedef struct _DDSCAPS2 {
    DWORD    dwCaps;
    DWORD    dwCaps2;
    DWORD    dwCaps3;
    DWORD    dwCaps4;
} DDSCAPS2, FAR* LPDDSCAPS2;
```

Currently, only the **dwCaps** and **dwCaps2** members of the structure are used. Table 13.5 lists the possible flags for the **dwCaps** member. They can be combined using a bitwise **OR**. Please note that unused members and those that are used only with Direct3D are omitted from the table.

There is only one flag for the **dwCaps2** member that is of interest to us—**DDSCAPS2_STEREOSURFACELEFT**. (All other flags are used either with Direct3D or with video ports, which are not covered in this book.) The **DDSCAPS2_-STEREOSURFACELEFT** flag is specified for that surface in a stereo vision flipping chain that contains the image for the left eye. For details about stereo flipping chains, see "Working with Flipping Chains" in the "In Depth" section.

Table 13.5 Possible flags for the dwCaps member of the DDSCAPS2 structure.

Flag	Meaning
DDSCAPS_ALPHA	This is an alpha-only surface that stores no color information.
DDSCAPS_BACKBUFFER	This is the first back buffer of a flipping chain. All other back buffers have only the **DDSCAPS_FLIP** flag set and neither the **DDSCAPS_BACKBUFFER** flag nor the **DDSCAPS_FRONT-BUFFER** flag.
DDSCAPS_COMPLEX	This is a complex surface. Flipping chains have this flag set as well.
DDSCAPS_FLIP	This is a flipping surface. The front buffer has the **DDSCAPS_-FRONTBUFFER** flag set. The first back buffer has the **DDSCAPS_BACKBUFFER** flag set. When you're creating a flipping chain, **DDSCAPS_COMPLEX** must also be set, and the **dwBackBufferCount** member of the **DDSURFACEDESC2** structure must be 1 or greater.
DDSCAPS_FRONTBUFFER	This is the front buffer of a flipping chain.
DDSCAPS_LOCALVIDMEM	This surface resides in local video memory. **DDSCAPS_VIDEO-MEMORY** must be specified as well.

(continued)

Table 13.5 Possible flags for the dwCaps member of the DDSCAPS2 structure *(continued)*.

Flag	Meaning
DDSCAPS_MODEX	This is a Mode X surface. For more information about Mode X, see Chapter 12.
DDSCAPS_NONLOCALVIDMEM	This surface resides in AGP memory. The **DDSCAPS_VIDEO-MEMORY** flag must be specified as well.
DDSCAPS_OFFSCREENPLAIN	This is an off-screen surface.
DDSCAPS_OVERLAY	This is an overlay surface. For more information, see "Working with Overlay Surfaces" in the "In Depth" section.
DDSCAPS_OWNDC	This surface has a device context (DC) association for a long period of time.
DDSCAPS_PALETTE	A DirectDraw palette can be attached to the surface. For more information about palettes, see Chapter 15.
DDSCAPS_PRIMARYSURFACE	This is the primary surface. Its contents are always visible on screen.
DDSCAPS_STANDARDVGAMODE	This is a standard VGA mode surface. For more information, see Chapter 12.
DDSCAPS_SYSTEMMEMORY	This surface resides in system memory.
DDSCAPS_VIDEOMEMORY	This surface resides in local or non-local video memory. See also the **DDSCAPS_LOCALVIDMEM** and **DDSCAPS_NONLOCAL-VIDMEM** flags.
DDSCAPS_VISIBLE	Whatever is drawn to this surface becomes visible immediately. This is always true for the primary surface (**DDSCAPS_PRIMARY-SURFACE**) and for an overlay surface (**DDSCAPS_OVERLAY**) after the **IDirectDrawSurface7::UpdateOverlay** method has been called with the **DDOVER_SHOW** flag.
DDSCAPS_WRITEONLY	This surface is write-only. Read access from the surface can cause a general protection (GP) fault.

Creating a Non-Flipping Primary Surface

To create a non-flipping primary surface for your windowed or full-screen DirectDraw application, use the **IDirectDraw7::CreateSurface** method. The **DDSURFACEDESC2** structure must be initialized as follows:

```
DDSURFACEDESC2 ddsd;
ZeroMemory(&ddsd, sizeof(ddsd));
ddsd.dwSize = sizeof(ddsd);
```

```
ddsd.dwFlags = DDSD_CAPS;        // ddsCaps is valid
ddsd.ddsCaps.dwCaps = DDSCAPS_PRIMARYSURFACE;
```

You can use the following function to create the primary surface in your programs:

```
// CreatePrimarySurface function
//    lpDD is a valid pointer to an IDirectDraw7 interface.
//    The function returns a pointer to the IDirectDrawSurface7 interface
//    of the newly created primary surface.
//
LPDIRECTDRAWSURFACE7 CreatePrimarySurface(LPDIRECTDRAW7 lpDD)
{
try
{
   // prepare surface description
   DDSURFACEDESC2 ddsd;
   ZeroMemory(&ddsd, sizeof(ddsd));
   ddsd.dwSize = sizeof(ddsd);
   ddsd.dwFlags = DDSD_CAPS;                // ddsCaps is valid
   ddsd.ddsCaps.dwCaps = DDSCAPS_PRIMARYSURFACE;

   // create the surface
   LPDIRECTDRAWSURFACE7 lpDDSPrimary = NULL;
   lpDD->CreateSurface(
      &ddsd,
      &lpDDSPrimary,
      NULL
   );

   // return IDirectDrawSurface7 interface pointer
   // (is still NULL if CreateSurface failed)
   return lpDDSPrimary;
}
catch (...)
{
   return NULL;
}
}
```

See also the next solution.

Related solution:	Found on page:
Creating a Surface	634

Creating a Primary Surface Flipping Chain

To create a primary surface flipping chain for your full-screen DirectDraw application, use the **IDirectDraw7::CreateSurface** method. The **DDSURFACE DESC2** structure must be initialized as follows:

```
DDSURFACEDESC2 ddsd;
ZeroMemory(&ddsd, sizeof(ddsd));
ddsd.dwSize = sizeof(ddsd);
ddsd.dwFlags = DDSD_CAPS |       // ddsCaps and...
   DDSD_BACKBUFFERCOUNT;         // ...dwBackBufferCount are valid
ddsd.ddsCaps.dwCaps = DDSCAPS_PRIMARYSURFACE |
   DDSCAPS_COMPLEX | DDSCAPS_FLIP;
ddsd.dwBackBufferCount = NumberOfBackBuffers;   // specify 1 (double
                                 // buffering) or 2 (triple buffering)
```

The following code creates a primary surface flipping chain and uses the **GetAttachedSurface** method to retrieve a pointer to the first back buffer (see also "Retrieving a Pointer to an Attached Surface"):

```
// lpDD is assumed to be a valid pointer to an IDirectDraw7 interface

LPDIRECTDRAWSURFACE7 lpDDSPrimary = NULL;
LPDIRECTDRAWSURFACE7 lpDDSBackBuffer = NULL;

try
{
   // prepare surface description
   DDSURFACEDESC2 ddsd;
   ZeroMemory(&ddsd, sizeof(ddsd));
   ddsd.dwSize = sizeof(ddsd);
   ddsd.dwFlags = DDSD_CAPS |       // ddsCaps and...
      DDSD_BACKBUFFERCOUNT;         // ...dwBackBufferCount are valid
   ddsd.ddsCaps.dwCaps = DDSCAPS_PRIMARYSURFACE |
      DDSCAPS_COMPLEX | DDSCAPS_FLIP;
   ddsd.dwBackBufferCount = NumberOfBackBuffers;   // specify 1 (double
                                    // buffering) or 2 (triple buffering)

   // create the surface
   if (FAILED(lpDD->CreateSurface(
      &ddsd,
      &lpDDSPrimary,
      NULL
   )))
```

```
        {
            throw "Primary surface flipping chain could not be created.";
        }

        // retrieve a pointer to the first back buffer
        DDSCAPS2 ddsCaps;
        ZeroMemory(&ddsCaps, sizeof(ddsCaps));
        ddsCaps.dwCaps = DDSCAPS_BACKBUFFER;
        if (FAILED(lpDDSPrimary->GetAttachedSurface(
            &ddsCaps,
            &lpDDSBackBuffer
        )))
        {
            throw "Retrieving the pointer to the back buffer failed.";
        }

    }
    catch (...)
    {
        SAFERELEASE(lpDDSPrimary);
    }
```


WARNING! The primary surface of a windowed application (cooperative level is DDSCL_NORMAL) can't be created as a flipping chain. Instead, you create the back buffer as a separate off-screen surface with the same dimensions as the application window's client area. The back buffer is displayed by blitting it to the primary surface. See also "Creating a Non-Flipping Primary Surface" and "Creating an Off-Screen Surface."

Related solution:	Found on page:
Creating a Surface	634

Using the Flip Method

The **IDirectDrawSurface7::Flip** method is used to cycle through the buffers of a flipping chain. The method is declared as follows:

```
HRESULT IDirectDrawSurface7::Flip(
    LPDIRECTDRAWSURFACE7 lpDDSurfaceTargetOverride,  // surface to flip to
    DWORD dwFlags                                    // flags
);
```

In most cases, the **lpDDSurfaceTargetOverride** parameter is **NULL**. This instructs DirectDraw to flip to the next buffer in the flipping chain. Otherwise, the specified surface is made visible. The specified surface must be part of the flipping chain. For the **dwFlags** parameter, you can use any of the constants listed in Table 13.6.

For more information, see "Working with Flipping Chains" in the "In Depth" section.

Table 13.6 Constants for the dwFlags parameter of the IDirectDrawSurface7::Flip method.

Flag	Meaning
DDFLIP_DONOTWAIT	When this flag is specified, the **Flip** method returns immediately with an error (**DDERR_WASSTILLDRAWING**) if the hardware is busy.
DDFLIP_EVEN and **DDFLIP_ODD**	These flags are used only when you're displaying video on an overlay surface.
DDFLIP_STEREO	This flag instructs the hardware to perform stereo autoflipping. See also "Working with Flipping Chains" in the "In Depth" section.
DDFLIP_INTERVAL2, **DDFLIP_INTERVAL3**, and **DDFLIP_INTERVAL4**	These flags specify how many vertical retraces should pass between flips. If none of these flags is specified, the flip is performed during the next vertical blank period.
DDFLIP_NOVSYNC	This flag instructs DirectDraw not to synchronize the flip with the vertical blank.
DDFLIP_WAIT	When this flag is specified, the **Flip** method waits until the flip can be successfully set up. **DDERR_WASSTILLDRAWING** is never reported. This is the default.

Retrieving a Pointer to an Attached Surface

In a flipping chain, several surfaces are attached to each other. You can use the **IDirectDrawSurface7::GetAttachedSurface** method to retrieve a pointer to an attached surface. The method is declared as follows:

```
HRESULT IDirectDrawSurface7::GetAttachedSurface(
    LPDDSCAPS2 lpDDSCaps,       // capabilities of the attached surface
    LPDIRECTDRAWSURFACE7 FAR *lplpDDAttachedSurface     // variable to
                                                 // receive interface pointer
  );
```

The **lpDDSCaps** parameter points to an initialized **DDSCAPS2** structure that specifies the characteristics of the surface to retrieve. The structure must contain enough information to uniquely identify an attached surface. In a flipping chain, for example, the **dwCaps** member of the structure is set to **DDSCAPS_-COMPLEX | DDSCAPS_FLIP**. The **lplpDDAttachedSurface** parameter points to a variable that will receive the **IDirectDrawSurface7** interface pointer of the attached surface when the method is successful.

The following programming example retrieves a pointer to the first back buffer in a flipping chain:

```
// lpDDSFrontBuffer is assumed to be a valid pointer to
// an IDirectDrawSurface7 interface

// retrieve a pointer to the first back buffer
DDSCAPS2 ddsCaps;
ZeroMemory(&ddsCaps, sizeof(ddsCaps));
ddsCaps.dwCaps = DDSCAPS_BACKBUFFER;      // the first back buffer has
                                          // this flag set
if (FAILED(lpDDSFrontBuffer->GetAttachedSurface(
   &ddsCaps,
   &lpDDSBackBuffer
)))
{
   throw "Retrieving the pointer to the back buffer failed.";
}
```


See also the following solutions: "Creating a Primary Surface Flipping Chain," "Loading a Sequence of Bitmaps into a Flipping Chain," and "Creating a Stereo Vision Flipping Chain."

Creating an Off-Screen Surface

To create an off-screen surface, use the **IDirectDraw7::CreateSurface** method. Table 13.7 lists the members of the **DDSURFACEDESC2** structure that are most frequently used for creating off-screen surfaces.

You can use the following function in your programs to create an off-screen surface with the same pixel format as the primary surface:

```
// CreateOffScreenSurface function
//    lpDD is a valid pointer to an IDirectDraw7 interface.
//    dwWidth and dwHeight specify the desired dimensions of the surface.
//
```

Table 13.7 Members of the DDSURFACEDESC2 structure that are used most frequently for creating off-screen surfaces.

DDSURFACEDESC2 structure member	Meaning
dwFlags	This must be set to **DDSD_CAPS I DDSD_WIDTH I DDSD_HEIGHT** to mark the **ddsCaps**, **dwWidth**, and **dwHeight** members as valid. You can also specify other flags as needed.
dwCaps	This bit field must contain the **DDSCAPS_OFFSCREENPLAIN** flag. In addition, you can specify the desired memory location of the surface with the **DDSCAPS_VIDEOMEMORY**, **DDSCAPS_LOCALVIDMEM**, **DDSCAPS_NONLOCALVIDMEM**, and **DDSCAPS_SYSTEMMEMORY** flags.
dwWidth and **dwHeight**	Set these to the desired size of the surface.
ddpfPixelFormat	You must initialize this **DDPIXELFORMAT** structure when you include the **DDSD_PIXELFORMAT** flag in the **dwFlags** member of the **DDSURFACEDESC2** structure. If the specified pixel format does not match the format of the primary surface, the surface must be created with the **DDSCAPS_SYSTEMMEMORY** capability.


```
LPDIRECTDRAWSURFACE7 CreateOffScreenSurface(
    LPDIRECTDRAW7 lpDD,
    DWORD dwWidth,
    DWORD dwHeight
   )
{
try
{
   // prepare surface description
   DDSURFACEDESC2 ddsd;
   ZeroMemory(&ddsd, sizeof(ddsd));
   ddsd.dwSize = sizeof(ddsd);
   ddsd.dwFlags = DDSD_CAPS |       // ddsCaps, ...
      DDSD_WIDTH | DDSD_HEIGHT;     // ...dwWidth, and dwHeight are valid
   ddsd.ddsCaps.dwCaps = DDSCAPS_OFFSCREENPLAIN;
   ddsd.dwWidth = dwWidth;
   ddsd.dwHeight = dwHeight;

   // create the surface
   LPDIRECTDRAWSURFACE7 lpDDSOffScreen = NULL;
   lpDD->CreateSurface(
      &ddsd,
      &lpDDSOffScreen,
      NULL
   );
```

```
        // return IDirectDrawSurface7 interface pointer
        // (is still NULL if CreateSurface failed)
        return lpDDSOffScreen;

    }
    catch (...)
    {
        return NULL;
    }
}
```

See also "Surface Creation" in the "In Depth" section and "Creating an Off-Screen Flipping Chain" in the "Immediate Solutions" section.

Related solution:	Found on page:
Creating a Surface	634

Creating an Off-Screen Surface from an Existing Block of Memory

You can instruct DirectDraw to create a surface from a memory block that was previously allocated by the application. For this, you have to store the pointer to the memory block in the **lpSurface** member of the **DDSURFACEDESC2** structure that you pass to the **CreateSurface** method. In addition, the **DDSCAPS_SYSTEMMEMORY** flag must be specified. You can specify a width, height, and pixel format. The **lPitch** member of the structure must be set to an 8-byte multiple. Of course, the memory block must be big enough for the specified surface.

The following programming example demonstrates this process:

```
// lpDD is assumed to be a valid pointer to an IDirectDraw7 interface

LPDIRECTDRAWSURFACE7 lpDDSurface = NULL;
LPVOID lpClientMemory = NULL;

try
{
    // prepare surface description
    DDSURFACEDESC2 ddsd;
    ZeroMemory(&ddsd, sizeof(ddsd));
```

```
    ddsd.dwSize = sizeof(ddsd);
    ddsd.dwCaps = DDSD_CAPS |
       DDSD_WIDTH | DDSD_HEIGHT |
       DDSD_PIXELFORMAT |
       DDSD_PITCH;
    ddsd.ddsCaps.dwCaps = DDSCAPS_SYSTEMMEMORY;
    ddsd.dwWidth = 53;
    ddsd.dwHeight = 100;
    ddsd.ddpfPixelFormat.dwSize = sizeof(DDPIXELFORMAT);
    ddsd.ddpfPixelFormat.dwFlags = DDPF_RGB;
    ddsd.ddpfPixelFormat.dwRGBBitCount = 16;    // two bytes per pixel
    ddsd.lPitch = 112;      // 112 is the next 8-byte boundary after 53 * 2

    // allocate memory for the surface
    lpClientMemory = reinterpret_cast<LPVOID>(new char[112 * 100]);
    if (lpClientMemory == NULL)
    {  throw "Could not allocate memory for the surface."; }

    // create the surface
    if (FAILED(lpDD->CreateSurface(
       &ddsd,
       &lpDDSurface,
       NULL
    )))
    {
       throw "Surface could not be created.";
    }

    // release surface
    SAFERELEASE(lpDDSurface);
    // free memory block afterwards
    if (lpClientMemory)
    {  delete[] lpClientMemory; }

 }
 catch (...)
 {
    SAFERELEASE(lpDDSurface);
    if (lpClientMemory)
    {  delete[] lpClientMemory; }
 }
```

Related solution:	***Found on page:***
Creating a Surface	634

Creating an Off-Screen Flipping Chain

Off-screen flipping chains are created like single off-screen surfaces. In addition, the **DDSD_BACKBUFFERCOUNT** flag is added to the **dwFlags** member of the **DDSURFACEDESC2** structure, and **dwBackBufferCount** is set to a value greater than zero. The **DDSCAPS_COMPLEX** and **DDSCAPS_FLIP** flags are added to the **ddsCaps.dwCaps** member.

You can use the following function in your programs to create off-screen flipping chains:

```
// CreateOffScreenFlip function
//    lpDD is a valid pointer to an IDirectDraw7 interface.
//    dwWidth and dwHeight specify the desired dimensions of the surface.
//    NumBuffers specifies the total number of buffers.
//
LPDIRECTDRAWSURFACE7 CreateOffScreenFlip(
     LPDIRECTDRAW7 lpDD,
     DWORD dwWidth,
     DWORD dwHeight,
     DWORD NumBuffers
   )
{
   if (NumBuffers < 2)
   {
      throw "Can't create a flipping chain with less than 2 buffers.";
   }

try
{
   // prepare surface description
   DDSURFACEDESC2 ddsd;
   ZeroMemory(&ddsd, sizeof(ddsd));
   ddsd.dwSize = sizeof(ddsd);
   ddsd.dwFlags = DDSD_CAPS |          // ddsCaps, ...
      DDSD_WIDTH | DDSD_HEIGHT |       // ...dwWidth, dwHeight, and...
      DDSD_BACKBUFFERCOUNT;            // ...dwBackBufferCount are valid
   ddsd.ddsCaps.dwCaps = DDSCAPS_OFFSCREENPLAIN |
      DDSCAPS_COMPLEX | DDSCAPS_FLIP;
   ddsd.dwWidth = dwWidth;
   ddsd.dwHeight = dwHeight;
   ddsd.dwBackBufferCount = NumBuffers - 1;     // (excluding front buffer)
```

```
    // create the surface
    LPDIRECTDRAWSURFACE7 lpDDSOffScreen = NULL;
    lpDD->CreateSurface(
        &ddsd,
        &lpDDSOffScreen,
        NULL
    );

    // return IDirectDrawSurface7 interface pointer
    // (is still NULL if CreateSurface failed)
    return lpDDSOffScreen;

}
catch (...)
{
    return NULL;
}
}
```

See also "Creating an Off-Screen Surface" and "Loading a Sequence of Bitmaps into a Flipping Chain."

Related solution:	Found on page:
Creating a Surface	634

Retrieving an HDC Handle for a Surface

You can use GDI functions on a DirectDraw surface when you retrieve an **HDC** handle for the surface by using the **IDirectDrawSurface7::GetDC** method. The method is declared as follows:

```
HRESULT IDirectDrawSurface7::GetDC(
    HDC FAR *lphDC              // pointer to variable to receive HDC handle
  );
```

Use the **IDirectDrawSurface7::ReleaseDC** method to release the **HDC** handle when you're done working with it. The **ReleaseDC** method is declared as follows:

```
HRESULT IDirectDrawSurface7::ReleaseDC(
    HDC hDC                     // HDC handle to release
  );
```

The following is a programming example:

```
// lpDDSurface is assumed to be a valid pointer to
// an IDirectDrawSurface7 interface

HDC hdc = NULL;

try
{
   if (SUCCEEDED(lpDDSurface->GetDC(&hdc)))
   {
      /*
         Use GDI functions here
      */

      // release the DC
      lpDDSurface->ReleaseDC(hdc);
   }

}
catch (...)
{
   if (hdc)
   {
      lpDDSurface->ReleaseDC(hdc);
   }
}
```


Loading a Bitmap File into a Surface

This Immediate Solution presents the application-defined **LoadBitmapToSurface** function. You can use this function in your programs to load an image from a Windows bitmap file into a surface. The function uses the **LoadImage** function to obtain an **HBITMAP** handle to the bitmap. The function then selects the bitmap into a memory DC and uses the **BitBlt** function to blit it to the DirectDraw surface. The function uses the **IDirectDrawSurface7::GetDC** method to obtain an **HDC** handle for the surface. For more information, see "Retrieving an **HDC** Handle for a Surface" in the "Immediate Solutions" section.

The following is the complete code listing of the **LoadBitmapToSurface** function:

```
// LoadBitmapToSurface function
//    lpDDSurface points to the destination surface.
//    lpszImageFileName contains the file name of the .bmp file.
//
bool LoadBitmapToSurface(
    LPDIRECTDRAWSURFACE7 lpDDSurface,
    char *lpszImageFileName
   )
{
   HBITMAP hBmp = NULL;
   HDC hMemDC = NULL;
   HDC hSurfaceDC = NULL;

try
{
   // load the image
   hBmp = reinterpret_cast<HBITMAP>(LoadImage(
      0,
      lpszImageFileName,    // name of .bmp file
      IMAGE_BITMAP,
      0, 0,                 // take dimensions from file
      LR_LOADFROMFILE
   ));
   if (hBmp == NULL)
   {  throw "LoadImage failed."; }

   // create a GDI memory DC
   hMemDC = CreateCompatibleDC(NULL);
   if (hMemDC == NULL)
   {  throw "Creating memory DC failed."; }

   // select bitmap into memory DC
   SelectObject(hMemDC, hBmp);

   // retrieve bitmap dimensions
   BITMAP BmpInfo;
   if (!GetObject(
      reinterpret_cast<HGDIOBJ>(hBmp),
      sizeof(BITMAP),
      reinterpret_cast<LPVOID>(&BmpInfo)
   ))
   {  throw "Retrieving bitmap dimensions failed."; }

   // get surface DC
   if (SUCCEEDED(lpDDSurface->GetDC(&hSurfaceDC)))
   {
```

```
        // blit from memory DC to surface DC
        BitBlt(
           hSurfaceDC,
           0, 0, BmpInfo.bmWidth, BmpInfo.bmHeight,
           hMemDC,
           0, 0,
           SRCCOPY
        );

        // release surface DC
        lpDDSurface->ReleaseDC(hSurfaceDC);
     }

     if (hMemDC) { DeleteDC(hMemDC); }
     if (hBmp) { DeleteObject(reinterpret_cast<HGDIOBJ>(hBmp)); }


     return true;

  }
  catch (...)
  {
     if (hSurfaceDC) { lpDDSurface->ReleaseDC(hSurfaceDC); }
     if (hMemDC) { DeleteDC(hMemDC); }
     if (hBmp) { DeleteObject(reinterpret_cast<HGDIOBJ>(hBmp)); }

     return false;
  }
  }
```


Related solutions:	Found on page:
Creating a Memory Device Context	64
Rendering to a Device Context by Using the **BitBlt** Function	68

Loading a Sequence of Bitmaps into a Flipping Chain

This solution demonstrates how to load a sequence of bitmaps into the buffers of a flipping chain. This solution uses code from the Immediate Solution "Loading a Bitmap File into a Surface" and is related to "Retrieving a Pointer to an Attached Surface."

You can use the following function to load a series of bitmap files into the buffers of a flipping chain. The **lpDDSFlip** parameter is a pointer to the **IDirectDraw-**

Surface7 interface of the front buffer (the pointer filled by the **CreateSurface** method). The **lpszAniFiles** parameter is a string containing the file-name mask of the bitmap files. This string must contain an **%s** sequence (as used by the **wsprintf** function) where the number of the animation frame appears in the file name. There must be as many bitmap files as there are buffers in the flipping chain. Here's the code for the **LoadFlippingAnimation** function:

```
bool LoadFlippingAnimation(
     LPDIRECTDRAWSURFACE7 lpDDSFlip,
     const char *lpszAniFiles
    )
{
try
{
   int FrameNum = 0;

   LPDIRECTDRAWSURFACE7 lpCurrSurf;
   lpCurrSurf = lpDDSFlip;

   // prepare DDSCAPS2 structure to pass to GetAttachedSurface
   DDSCAPS2 ddsCaps;
   ZeroMemory(&ddsCaps, sizeof(ddsCaps));
   ddsCaps.dwCaps = DDSCAPS_COMPLEX | DDSCAPS_FLIP;
   while (true)
   {
      // combine lpszAniFileName and FrameNum to file name
      char FileName[MAX_PATH];
      wsprintf(FileName, lpszAniFiles, FrameNum);

      // increment frame number
      FrameNum++;

      // load bitmap into surface
      LoadBitmapToSurface(lpCurrSurf, FileName);

      if (FAILED(lpCurrSurf->GetAttachedSurface(&ddsCaps, &lpCurrSurf)))
      {
         throw "GetAttachedSurface failed.";
      }

      // if we're through...
      if ((lpCurrSurf == lpDDSFlip))
      {  break; }
   }

   return true;
```

```
    }
    catch (...)
    {
        return false;
    }
}
```

See the CD-ROM for a sample program that uses the **LoadFlippingAnimation** function. See also "Using Off-Screen Flipping Chains" in the "In Depth" section, and "Loading a Bitmap File into a Surface" and "Retrieving a Pointer to an Attached Surface" in the "Immediate Solutions" section.

Blitting by Using the Blt Method

The **IDirectDrawSurface7::Blt** method performs a blit operation from a source surface to the surface that provides the **Blt** method. The **Blt** method can perform stretched blits, clipped blits, color-keyed blits, and blit effects. The method is declared as follows:

```
HRESULT IDirectDrawSurface7::Blt(
    LPRECT lpDestRect,                      // destination rectangle
    LPDIRECTDRAWSURFACE7 lpDDSrcSurface,    // source surface
    LPRECT lpSrcRect,                       // source rectangle
    DWORD dwFlags,                          // flags
    LPDDBLTFX lpDDBltFx                     // blit effects
  );
```

The surface that provides the **Blt** method is the destination of the blit operation. The **lpDestRect** parameter points to a **RECT** structure that specifies the rectangular area that will be filled by the blit. The column that is specified in the **right** member of the structure will not be filled; neither will the scan line that is specified in the **bottom** member. (This is similar to the way the GDI function **FillRect** treats the **RECT** structure.) The rectangle must be entirely contained within the destination surface unless a DirectDraw clipper is attached to the surface. If the **lpDestRect** parameter is **NULL**, the entire destination surface is filled by the blit.

The **lpDDSrcSurface** parameter specifies the source of the blit operation. This can be identical to the destination surface, even if source and destination rectangles overlap. If this parameter is **NULL**, the entire source surface is used.

Table 13.8 lists the flags that can be used for the **dwFlags** parameter. These flags can be combined by using the bitwise **OR** operator.

Table 13.8 Valid flags for the dwFlags parameter of the Blt method.

Flag	Meaning
DDBLT_COLORFILL	This flag is used for color fills. The **dwFillColor** member of the **DDBLTFX** structure pointed to by the **lpDDBltFx** parameter specifies the color that the destination rectangle will be filled with. The source surface is not used.
DDBLT_DDFX	The **dwDDFX** member of the **DDBLTFX** structure specifies a blit effect.
DDBLT_DDROPS	The **dwDDROP** member of the **DDBLTFX** structure specifies a DirectDraw raster operation (ROP) that the blit operation will use.
DDBLT_KEYDESTOVERRIDE	This flag is used when a blit operation with a destination color key will be performed. The color key is given in the **ddckDestColorkey** member of the **DDBLTFX** structure. The color key set with the **SetColorKey** method is ignored.
DDBLT_KEYSRCOVERRIDE	This flag is used when a blit operation with a source color key will be performed. The color key is given in the **ddckSrcColorkey** member of the **DDBLTFX** structure. The color key set with the **SetColorKey** method is ignored.
DDBLT_ROP	The **dwROP** member of the **DDBLTFX** structure specifies a raster operation that the blit operation will use.
DDBLT_ROTATIONANGLE	The **dwRotationAngle** member of the **DDBLTFX** structure specifies, in 1/100ths of a degree, the angle by which the source will be rotated.
DDBLT_KEYDEST	The destination color key set with the **SetColorKey** method will be used for this blit.
DDBLT_KEYSRC	The source color key set with the **SetColorKey** method will be used for this blit.
DDBLT_ASYNC	When this flag is specified, the blit operation is performed asynchronously; i.e., the blit is queued.
DDBLT_DONOTWAIT	When this flag is specified, the **Blt** method returns immediately with an error (**DDERR_WASSTILLDRAWING**) if another blit is still in progress.
DDBLT_WAIT	When this flag is specified, the **Blt** method waits until the blit can be successfully set up. **DDERR_WASSTILLDRAWING** is never reported. This is the default.

The **lpDDBltFx** parameter can be **NULL** if no blit effect is requested. Otherwise, the **DDBLTFX** structure must have been properly initialized.

The following programming example performs a stretched blit:

```
// lpDDSDest and lpDDSSrc are assumed to be valid pointers to
// IDirectDrawSurface7 interfaces
```

```
try
{
   // source rectangle
   RECT SrcRect = { 0, 0, 100, 100 };
   // destination rectangle
   RECT DestRect = { 10, 10, 210, 60 };

   if (FAILED(lpDDSDest->Blt(
      &DestRect,
      lpDDSSrc,
      &SrcRect,
      DDBLT_WAIT,
      NULL
   )))
   {
      throw "The blit could not be performed.";
   }

}
catch(...)
{
   throw "An exception occurred.";
}
```


For more information about color-keyed blits, see "Setting the Color Key of a Surface." For more information about the **DDBLTFX** structure and related flags, see "Requesting Blit Effects with the **DDBLTFX** Structure."

Blitting by Using the BltFast Method

The **IDirectDrawSurface7::BltFast** method performs a blit operation from a source surface to the surface that provides the **BltFast** method. The **BltFast** method can perform color-keyed blits. It cannot perform stretched blits, clipped blits, or blit effects. The method is declared as follows:

```
HRESULT IDirectDraw7::BltFast(
    DWORD dwX,                          // destination x-coordinate
    DWORD dwY,                          // destination y-coordinate
    LPDIRECTDRAWSURFACE7 lpDDSrcSurface, // source surface
    LPRECT lpSrcRect,                   // source rectangle
    DWORD dwTrans                       // flags
);
```

The **dwX** and **dwY** coordinates together specify the upper-left corner of the destination rectangle. The width and height of the destination rectangle are the same as the width and height of the source rectangle. Both destination and source rectangles must be entirely contained within their surfaces. Otherwise, nothing will be copied. The **lpDDSrcSurface** parameter specifies the source surface. The **lpSrcRect** parameter points to a **RECT** structure that specifies the source rectangle of the blit. If it is **NULL**, the entire source surface is copied. The **dwTrans** parameter is used to control color keying. It can be either **DDBLTFAST_DESTCOLORKEY**, **DDBLTFAST_SRCCOLORKEY**, or **DDBLTFAST_NOCOLORKEY** (the default). The **BltFast** method always uses the color key set with the **SetColorKey** method. When **dwTrans** contains the **DDBLTFAST_WAIT** flag, the **BltFast** method waits until the blit can be successfully set up. **DDERR_WASSTILLDRAWING** is never reported.

The following programming example copies the contents of the entire source surface to the upper-left corner of the destination surface:

```
// lpDDSDest and lpDDSSrc are assumed to be valid pointers to
// IDirectDrawSurface7 interfaces

try
{
   if (FAILED(lpDDSDest->BltFast(
      0, 0,
      lpDDSSrc,
      NULL,
      DDBLTFAST_WAIT
   )))
   {
      throw "The blit could not be performed.";
   }

}
catch(...)
{
   throw "An exception occurred.";
}
```

See also “Blitting by Using the **Blt** Method.”

Related solution:	Found on page:
Performing Clipped Blits with the **BltFast** Method	800

Setting the Color Key of a Surface

To associate source and destination color keys with a DirectDraw surface, you call the surface's **SetColorKey** method. The method is declared as follows:

```
HRESULT IDirectDrawSurface7::SetColorKey(
    DWORD dwFlags,              // flags
    LPDDCOLORKEY lpDDColorKey   // pointer to new color key values
);
```

The **dwFlags** parameter specifies which color key is to be set. Table 13.9 describes the valid flags.

The **lpDDColorKey** parameter points to an initialized **DDCOLORKEY** structure that contains the new color key values. The **dwColorSpaceLowValue** member of the structure specifies the low value of the color range, and the **dwColorSpaceHighValue** member specifies the high value of the color range. If **DDCKEY_COLORSPACE** is not specified in the call to **SetColorKey**, only the low value is used. The color must be given in the current pixel format of the surface. The code to convert an RGB triple into the surface's pixel format can be found in the Immediate Solution "Converting an RGB Triple into the Surface's Pixel Format."

The following code snippet sets the source color key of a surface to black:

```
// lpDDSurface is assumed to be a valid pointer to
// an IDirectDrawSurface7 interface
```

Table 13.9 Valid flags for the dwFlags parameter of the SetColorKey method.

Flag	Meaning
DDCKEY_COLORSPACE	The **DDCOLORKEY** structure pointed to by the **lpDDColorKey** parameter specifies a range of colors rather than a single color. Not all devices support this.
DDCKEY_DESTBLT	The **DDCOLORKEY** structure specifies the destination color key for blit operations.
DDCKEY_DESTOVERLAY	The **DDCOLORKEY** structure specifies the destination color key for overlay operations.
DDCKEY_SRCBLT	The **DDCOLORKEY** structure specifies the source color key for blit operations.
DDCKEY_SRCOVERLAY	The **DDCOLORKEY** structure specifies the source color key for overlay operations.

```
// initialize DDCOLORKEY structure
DDCOLORKEY ColorKey;
ColorKey.dwColorSpaceLowValue = 0x00000000; // black in all formats

// set the color key
lpDDSurface->SetColorKey(
   DDCKEY_SRCBLT,
   &ColorKey
);
```

See also "Retrieving the Color Key of a Surface."

Retrieving the Color Key of a Surface

To retrieve the color key that has been associated with a surface by using the **SetColorKey** method, you can use the surface's **GetColorKey** method. The method is declared as follows:

```
HRESULT IDirectDrawSurface7::GetColorKey(
    DWORD dwFlags,             // flags
    LPDDCOLORKEY lpDDColorKey  // pointer to color key values
);
```

The **dwFlags** parameter specifies which color key is to be retrieved. Table 13.10 describes the valid flags.

When the method is successful, the **DDCOLORKEY** structure pointed to by the **lpDDColorKey** parameter is filled with the current color key values. The **dwColorSpaceLowValue** member of the structure specifies the low value of the color range, and the **dwColorSpaceHighValue** member specifies the high value

Table 13.10 Valid flags for the dwFlags parameter of the GetColorKey method.

Flag	Meaning
DDCKEY_DESTBLT	The **DDCOLORKEY** structure receives the destination color key for blit operations.
DDCKEY_DESTOVERLAY	The **DDCOLORKEY** structure receives the destination color key for overlay operations.
DDCKEY_SRCBLT	The **DDCOLORKEY** structure receives the source color key for blit operations.
DDCKEY_SRCOVERLAY	The **DDCOLORKEY** structure receives the source color key for overlay operations.

of the color range. Both color values are given in the current pixel format of the surface. The code to convert these values into an RGB triple can be found in the Immediate Solution “Decoding a Pixel into an RGB Triple.”

See also “Setting the Color Key of a Surface.”

Requesting Blit Effects with the **DDBLTFX** Structure

The **DDBLTFX** structure is used with the **IDirectDrawSurface7::Blt** method to perform blit effects. These are the structure members:

- **dwSize**—Set this to **sizeof(DDBLTFX)** before passing a pointer to the structure to the **Blt** method.
- **dwDDFX**—When the **DDBLT_DDFX** flag is passed to **Blt**, this member specifies the effect that is to be performed. Table 13.11 lists these effects.
- **dwROP**—When the **DDBLT_ROP** flag is passed to **Blt**, this member specifies the Win32 raster operation to be used. These raster operations are the same as the ROPs used with the GDI **BitBlt** function.
- **dwDDROP**—When the **DDBLT_DDROPS** flag is passed to **Blt**, this member specifies the DirectDraw-specific raster operation to be used. Currently no such ROPs are defined.
- **dwRotationAngle**—When the **DDBLT_ROTATIONANGLE** is passed to **Blt**, this member specifies, in 1/100ths of a degree, the angle by which the source is to be rotated.
- **dwFillColor**—When the **DDBLT_COLORFILL** flag is passed to **Blt**, the destination rectangle will be filled with the color given in this member. The color must be specified in the surface’s current pixel format. (See “Converting an RGB Triple into the Surface’s Pixel Format.”)
- **lpDDSPattern**—This is a pointer to a surface that contains a pattern that will be used in certain blit operations that combine a source and a destination.
- **ddckDestColorkey**—When the **DDBLT_KEYDESTOVERRIDE** flag is passed to **Blt**, the color value in this **DDCOLORKEY** structure is used as the destination color key of the blit operation.
- **ddckSrcColorkey**—When the **DDBLT_KEYSRCOVERRIDE** flag is passed to **Blt**, the color value in this **DDCOLORKEY** structure is used as the source color key of the blit operation.

For information about using this structure with the **IDirectDrawSurface7::Blt** method, see “Blitting by Using the **Blt** Method.”

Table 13.11 Flags for the dwDDFX member of the DDBLTFX structure.

Flag	Meaning
DDBLTFX_ARITHSTRETCHY	This flag instructs DirectDraw to interpolate pixels along the y-axis when performing stretched blits.
DDBLTFX_MIRRORLEFTRIGHT	When this flag is specified, the source bitmap is mirrored horizontally during the blit.
DDBLTFX_MIRRORUPDOWN	When this flag is specified, the source bitmap is mirrored vertically during the blit.
DDBLTFX_NOTEARING	When this flag is specified, the blit is synchronized with the vertical blank.
DDBLTFX_ROTATE180	When this flag is specified, the source is rotated 180 degrees clockwise during the blit.
DDBLTFX_ROTATE270	When this flag is specified, the source is rotated 90 degrees counterclockwise during the blit.
DDBLTFX_ROTATE90	When this flag is specified, the source is rotated 90 degrees clockwise during the blit.

Locking a Surface to Access its Frame Buffer Directly

The **IDirectDrawSurface7::Lock** method is used to gain direct access to a surface's frame buffer. The method is declared as follows:

```
HRESULT IDirectDrawSurface7::Lock(
    LPRECT lpDestRect,                   // rectangular area to be locked
    LPDDSURFACEDESC2 lpDDSurfaceDesc,    // structure to receive surface
                                         // description
    DWORD dwFlags,                       // flags
    HANDLE hEvent                        // unused; must be NULL
  );
```

The **lpDestRect** parameter can be used to lock only a portion of the surface. If the parameter is **NULL**, the entire surface is locked. The **lpDDSurfaceDesc** parameter is a pointer to a **DDSURFACEDESC2** structure that will be filled with information about the surface when the method is successful. The **dwSize** member of the structure must have been set to **sizeof(DDSURFACEDESC2)**. Table 13.12 lists the flags that can be used for the **dwFlags** parameter.

The **hEvent** parameter of the **Lock** method is not currently used.

When the method returns successfully, the **DDSURFACEDESC2** structure is filled. The **lpSurface** member of the structure contains a pointer to the upper-left

Table 13.12 Flags for the dwFlags parameter of the IDirectDrawSurface7::Lock method.

Flag	Meaning
DDLOCK_DONOTWAIT	When this flag is specified, the **Lock** method returns with an error (**DDERR_WASSTILLDRAWING**) when it is called before a blit operation has been completed. Otherwise, the **Lock** method waits until the blit operation has finished.
DDLOCK_NOSYSLOCK	This flag instructs the **Lock** method not to take the Win16Mutex. The Win16Mutex is used to serialize access to the GDI and USER libraries. This flag is ignored when the primary surface is locked.
DDLOCK_READONLY	Use this flag when you do not want to write to the surface. DirectDraw might be able to optimize the memory access when write access is not required.
DDLOCK_SURFACEMEMORYPTR	This flag specifies that a pointer to the upper-left corner of the rectangle (or the entire surface) should be returned in the **lpSurface** member of the **DDSURFACEDESC2** structure. This is the default.
DDLOCK_WAIT	When this flag is specified, the **Lock** method waits until a blit operation that is currently in progress has finished. It does not return **DDERR_WASSTILLDRAWING**.
DDLOCK_WRITEONLY	Use this flag when you do not want to read from the surface. DirectDraw might be able to optimize the memory access when read access is not required.

pixel of the locked rectangle. While the surface is locked, no blit operations involving the surface can be performed, and the **IDirectDrawSurface7::GetDC** method can't be used.

The following programming example locks an entire surface:

```
// lpDDSurface is assumed to be a valid pointer to
// an IDirectDrawSurface7 interface

try
{
   DDSURFACEDESC2 ddsd;
   ZeroMemory(&ddsd, sizeof(ddsd));
   ddsd.dwSize = sizeof(ddsd);

   if (SUCCEEDED(lpDDSurface->Lock(
      NULL,                    // lock entire surface
      &ddsd,
      0,                       // no flags
      NULL
```

```
    )))
    {
        /*
            You can use ddsd.lpSurface to access the surface's frame buffer.
        */

        lpDDSurface->Unlock(NULL);
    }
}
catch (...)
{
    lpDDSurface->Unlock(NULL);
}
```

See also "Unlocking a Surface."

Unlocking a Surface

You must call the **IDirectDrawSurface7::Unlock** method when you're done working with a surface that was locked by using the **Lock** method. The **Unlock** method takes as its only parameter the rectangle that was passed to the **Lock** method:

```
HRESULT IDirectDrawSurface7::Unlock(
    LPRECT lpRect               // rectangle to unlock
  );
```

Every call to the **Lock** method must have a corresponding call to the **Unlock** method with the same rectangle. See also "Locking a Surface to Access its Frame Buffer Directly."

Converting an RGB Triple into the Surface's Pixel Format

This solution presents the **RGBToPixel** function, which you can use in your programs to convert **COLORREF** values created with the **RGB** macro into the pixel format of a specific DirectDraw surface. The parameters of the function are a pointer to the **IDirectDrawSurface7** interface surface and a **COLORREF** value. The function returns a **DWORD** that you can use in the **DDCOLORKEY** structure, in the **dwFillColor** member of the **DDBLTFX** structure, or when accessing the surface directly. The function uses the **GetSurfaceDesc** function to retrieve information about the surface's pixel format.

The following is the complete source code of the **RGBToPixel** function:

```
DWORD RGBToPixel(
    LPDIRECTDRAWSURFACE7 lpDDSurface,
    COLORREF rgb
   )
{
   // retrieve DDSURFACEDESC2 structure
   DDSURFACEDESC2 ddsd;
   ZeroMemory(&ddsd, sizeof(ddsd));
   ddsd.dwSize = sizeof(ddsd);
   if (FAILED(lpDDSurface->GetSurfaceDesc(&ddsd)))
   {  throw "GetSurfaceDesc failed."; }

   // decode COLORREF value
   BYTE Red = GetRValue(rgb);
   BYTE Green = GetGValue(rgb);
   BYTE Blue = GetBValue(rgb);

   // calculate the number of bits for each color component
   WORD NumRedBits = GetNumberOfBits(ddsd.ddpfPixelFormat.dwRBitMask);
   WORD NumGreenBits = GetNumberOfBits(ddsd.ddpfPixelFormat.dwGBitMask);
   WORD NumBlueBits = GetNumberOfBits(ddsd.ddpfPixelFormat.dwBBitMask);

   // scale the color accordingly
   BYTE ScaledRed = static_cast<BYTE>(Red >> (8 - NumRedBits));
   BYTE ScaledGreen = static_cast<BYTE>(Green >> (8 - NumGreenBits));
   BYTE ScaledBlue = static_cast<BYTE>(Blue >> (8 - NumBlueBits));

   // calculate the bit positions of the color components
   WORD RedBitsPos = GetMaskPos(ddsd.ddpfPixelFormat.dwRBitMask);
   WORD GreenBitsPos = GetMaskPos(ddsd.ddpfPixelFormat.dwGBitMask);
   WORD BlueBitsPos = GetMaskPos(ddsd.ddpfPixelFormat.dwBBitMask);

   // assemble a DWORD
   DWORD ConvertedPixel = 0;
   ConvertedPixel |= ScaledRed << RedBitsPos;       // add the red bits
   ConvertedPixel |= ScaledGreen << GreenBitsPos;   // add the green bits
   ConvertedPixel |= ScaledBlue << BlueBitsPos;     // add the blue bits

   return ConvertedPixel;
}
```

The **RGBToPixel** function uses the following two helper functions, **GetNumberOfBits** and **GetMaskPos**:

```
WORD GetNumberOfBits(DWORD dwMask)
{
   WORD wBits = 0;              // our bit counter
   while (dwMask != 0)          // as long as there are bits in the mask...
   {
      // ...mask off the least-significant bit
      dwMask = dwMask & (dwMask - 1);
      wBits++;                  // ...and increase our bit counter
   }
   return wBits;
}

WORD GetMaskPos(DWORD dwMask)
{
   WORD wPos = 0;                      // the bit position
   while (!(dwMask & (1 << wPos)))     // as long as we haven't encountered
                                       // the first set bit...
   {
      wPos++;                          // ...go to the next bit
      if (wPos > 31) break;
   }   return wPos;
}
```

See also "Decoding a Pixel into an RGB Triple."

Decoding a Pixel into an RGB Triple

This solution presents the **PixelToRGB** function, which you can use in your programs to convert a pixel in the pixel format of a specific DirectDraw surface into a **COLORREF** value. You can use the function when accessing surfaces directly and to decode the color values given in **DDCOLORKEY** structures and in the **dwFillColor** member of the **DDBLTFX** structure. The parameters of the function are a pointer to the **IDirectDrawSurface7** interface surface and a **DWORD** value. The function returns a **COLORREF** value that gives the intensities of red, green, and blue in the specified pixel. The intensities range from 0 to 255. The function uses the **GetSurfaceDesc** function to retrieve information about the surface's pixel format.

The following is the complete source code of the **PixelToRGB** function:

```
COLORREF PixelToRGB(
    LPDIRECTDRAWSURFACE7 lpDDSurface,
    DWORD OriginalPixel
   )
{
   // retrieve DDSURFACEDESC2 structure
   DDSURFACEDESC2 ddsd;
   ZeroMemory(&ddsd, sizeof(ddsd));
   ddsd.dwSize = sizeof(ddsd);
   if (FAILED(lpDDSurface->GetSurfaceDesc(&ddsd)))
   {  throw "GetSurfaceDesc failed."; }

      // calculate bit counts and bit positions
   WORD NumRedBits = GetNumberOfBits(ddsd.ddpfPixelFormat.dwRBitMask);
   WORD NumGreenBits = GetNumberOfBits(ddsd.ddpfPixelFormat.dwGBitMask);
   WORD NumBlueBits = GetNumberOfBits(ddsd.ddpfPixelFormat.dwBBitMask);
   WORD RedBitsPos = GetMaskPos(ddsd.ddpfPixelFormat.dwRBitMask);
   WORD GreenBitsPos = GetMaskPos(ddsd.ddpfPixelFormat.dwGBitMask);
   WORD BlueBitsPos = GetMaskPos(ddsd.ddpfPixelFormat.dwBBitMask);

   BYTE Red, Green, Blue;

   Red = ((OriginalPixel & ddsd.ddpfPixelFormat.dwRBitMask)
      >> RedBitsPos) << (8 - NumRedBits);
   Green = ((OriginalPixel & ddsd.ddpfPixelFormat.dwGBitMask)
      >> GreenBitsPos) << (8 - NumGreenBits);
   Blue = ((OriginalPixel & ddsd.ddpfPixelFormat.dwBBitMask)
      >> BlueBitsPos) << (8 - NumBlueBits);

   return RGB(Red, Green, Blue);
}
```

The **PixelToRGB** function uses the **GetNumberOfBits** function from the previous Immediate Solution.

Querying Surface Characteristics

The **IDirectDrawSurface7::GetSurfaceDesc** method is used to retrieve information about a surface. The method is declared as follows:

```
HRESULT IDirectDrawSurface7::GetSurfaceDesc(
    LPDDSURFACEDESC2 lpDDSurfaceDesc        // structure to be filled with
                                            // surface description
   );
```

The method fills the **DDSURFACEDESC2** structure pointed to by the **lpDDSurfaceDesc** parameter. The **dwSize** member of the structure must have been set to **sizeof(DDSURFACEDESC2)**.

For more information about the **DDSURFACEDESC2** structure, see "Interpreting the **DDSURFACEDESC2** Structure" in the "Immediate Solutions" section.

Creating a Stereo Vision Flipping Chain

Creating a stereo vision flipping chain is similar to creating a primary surface flipping chain. After you have initialized the **DDSURFACEDESC2** structure for a primary surface flipping chain, the **ddsCaps.dwCaps2** member of the structure is set to **DDSCAPS2_STEREOSURFACELEFT**. The following code creates a stereo vision flipping chain with one back buffer:


```
// lpDD is assumed to be a valid pointer to an IDirectDraw7 interface

// prepare surface description
DDSURFACEDESC2 ddsd;
ZeroMemory(&ddsd, sizeof(ddsd));
ddsd.dwSize = sizeof(ddsd);
ddsd.dwFlags = DDSD_CAPS |          // ddsCaps...
   DDSD_BACKBUFFERCOUNT;            // ...and dwBackBufferCount are valid
ddsd.ddsCaps.dwCaps = DDSCAPS_PRIMARYSURFACE |
   DDSCAPS_COMPLEX | DDSCAPS_FLIP;
ddsd.ddsCaps.dwCaps2 = DDSCAPS2_STEREOSURFACELEFT;
ddsd.dwBackBufferCount = 1;         // one back buffer

// create the surface
LPDIRECTDRAWSURFACE7 lpDDSPrimary = NULL;
if (FAILED(lpDD->CreateSurface(
   &ddsd,
   &lpDDSPrimary,
   NULL
)))
{
   throw "The stereo vision flipping chain could not be created.";
}
```

After this, you can retrieve a pointer to the first back buffer of the flipping chain:

```
DDSCAPS2 ddsCaps;
ZeroMemory(&ddsCaps, sizeof(ddsCaps));
ddsCaps.dwCaps = DDSCAPS_BACKBUFFER;
```

```
LPDIRECTDRAWSURFACE7 lpDDSBackBuffer = NULL;
if (FAILED(lpDDSPrimary->GetAttachedSurface(
   &ddsCaps,
   &lpDDSBackBuffer
)))
{
   throw "Retrieving the pointer to the back buffer failed.";
}
```

This code retrieves a pointer to the right back buffer. To retrieve a pointer to the left back buffer, call **GetAttachedSurface** on the back buffer interface and set the **dwCaps2** member of the **DDSCAPS2** structure to **DDSCAPS2_STEREO-SURFACELEFT**. The following code does this:


```
DDSCAPS2 ddsCaps;
ddsCaps.dwCaps2 = DDSCAPS2_STEREOSURFACELEFT;

LPDIRECTDRAWSURFACE7 lpDDSLeftBackBuffer;
if (SUCCEEDED(lpDDSBackBuffer->GetAttachedSurface(
   &ddsCaps,
   &lpDDSLeftBackBuffer
)))
{
   /*
      lpDDSLeftBackBuffer is a valid pointer to the
      back buffer surface for the left eye
   */
}
```

For more information about stereo vision, see "Working with Flipping Surfaces" in the "In Depth" section. See also the following Immediate Solutions: "Creating a Primary Surface Flipping Chain" and "Retrieving a Pointer to an Attached Surface."

Creating an Overlay Surface

Overlay surfaces are created with the **IDirectDraw7::CreateSurface** method. The **ddsCaps.dwCaps** member of the **DDSURFACEDESC2** structure must contain the **DDSCAPS_OVERLAY | DDSCAPS_VIDEOMEMORY** flag combination. The following code demonstrates this:

```
// prepare surface description
DDSURFACEDESC2 ddsd;
```

```
ZeroMemory(&ddsd, sizeof(ddsd));
ddsd.dwSize = sizeof(ddsd);
ddsd.dwFlags = DDSD_CAPS |
   DDSD_WIDTH | DDSD_HEIGHT |
   DDSD_PIXELFORMAT;
ddsd.ddsCaps.dwCaps = DDSCAPS_OVERLAY |
   DDSCAPS_VIDEOMEMORY;
ddsd.dwWidth = DesiredWidth;
ddsd.dwHeight = DesiredHeight;
ddsd.ddpfPixelFormat = DesiredPixelFormat;

// create the surface
LPDIRECTDRAWSURFACE7 lpDDSOverlay;
if (FAILED(lpDD->CreateSurface(
   &ddsd,
   &lpDDSOverlay,
   NULL
)))
{
   throw "Creating overlay surface failed.";
}
```


Using the UpdateOverlay Method

The **IDirectDrawSurface7::UpdateOverlay** method is used to display overlay surfaces, to specify their position on the screen, and to perform overlay effects. The method is declared as follows:

```
HRESULT UpdateOverlay(
    LPRECT lpSrcRect,                       // source rectangle
    LPDIRECTDRAWSURFACE7 lpDDDestSurface,   // destination surface
    LPRECT lpDestRect,                      // destination rectangle
    DWORD dwFlags,                          // flags
    LPDDOVERLAYFX lpDDOverlayFx             // overlay effects
);
```

The **UpdateOverlay** method is supported only for overlay surfaces. The **lpSrcRect** parameter points to a **RECT** structure that specifies a rectangular area within the overlay surface that should be displayed. If **lpSrcRect** is **NULL**, the entire overlay surface is used. The **lpDDDestSurface** parameter specifies the surface that will be overlaid. The **lpDestRect** parameter points to a **RECT** structure that specifies the rectangular area on the destination surface that will be overlaid. If **lpDestRect** is **NULL**, the entire destination surface is used.

The **lpDDOverlayFx** parameter points to a **DDOVERLAYFX** structure. This parameter can be **NULL** if no overlay effect is requested.

Table 13.13 lists the most frequently used constants that are defined for the **dwFlags** parameter. These constants can be combined using a bitwise **OR**.

The following list describes those members of the **DDBLTFX** structure that are required by the flags listed in Table 13.13:

- **dwSize**—This member must always be set to **sizeof(DDOVERLAYFX)** for the **UpdateOverlay** method to be successful.
- **dwAlphaSrcConst**—This member is used when the **DDOVER_ALPHASRCCONSTOVERRIDE** flag is specified. This member specifies the desired opacity of the overlay surface.

Table 13.13 The most frequently used constants defined for the dwFlags parameter of the UpdateOverlay method.

Flag	Meaning
DDOVER_ALPHASRC	When this flag is specified, the overlay will be displayed as translucent. The overlay surface must have alpha-channel information in its pixel format.
DDOVER_ALPHASRCCONSTOVERRIDE	When this flag is specified, the **dwAlphaSrcConst** member of the **DDOVERLAYFX** structure pointed to by the **lpDDOverlayFx** parameter is used as a constant alpha value for the overlay.
DDOVER_DDFX	When this flag is specified, the **lpDDOverlayFx** parameter of the **DDOVERLAYFX** structure contains more information about the overlay effect to be performed.
DDOVER_HIDE	This flag instructs DirectDraw to hide a currently visible overlay.
DDOVER_KEYDEST	This flag requests that destination color keying be performed. The destination color key set with the **SetColorKey** method is used.
DDOVER_KEYDESTOVERRIDE	This flag requests that destination color keying be performed. The **dckDestColorkey** member of the **DDOVERLAYFX** structure specifies the color key to use.
DDOVER_KEYSRC	This flag requests that source color keying be performed. The source color key set with the **SetColorKey** method is used.
DDOVER_KEYSRCOVERRIDE	This flag requests that destination color keying be performed. The **dckSrcColorkey** member of the **DDOVERLAYFX** structure specifies the color key to use.
DDOVER_SHOW	This flag instructs DirectDraw to make the overlay visible.

- **dwAlphaSrcConstBitDepth**—This member specifies how many bits of the **dwAlphaSrcConst** member are used for the alpha information.
- **ddckDestColorkey**—This **DDCOLORKEY** structure specifies the destination color key to be used when the **DDOVER_KEYDESTOVERRIDE** flag is specified.
- **ddckSrcColorkey**—This **DDCOLORKEY** structure specifies the source color key to be used when the **DDOVER_KEYSRCOVERRIDE** flag is specified.
- **dwDDFX**—This member specifies an overlay effect to be performed. Valid flags are **DDOVERFX_ARITHSTRETCHY**, **DDOVERFX_MIRROLEFTRIGHT**, and **DDOVERFX_MIRRORUPDOWN**. These flags have the same meaning as the related **DDBLTFX_...** flags of the **DDBLTFX** structure.

You should query the hardware capabilities before requesting any of these effects. See Chapter 11 for more information.

Displaying or Hiding an Overlay Surface

You can use the **IDirectDrawSurface7::UpdateOverlay** method to display an overlay surface. To do this, include the **DDOVER_SHOW** flag in the **dwFlags** parameter of the method. The following code demonstrates this:

```
// lpDDSOverlay is assumed to be a valid pointer to
// the IDirectDrawSurface7 interface of an overlay surface.
// lpDDSPrimary is assumed to be a valid pointer to
// the IDirectDrawSurface7 interface of the primary surface.

RECT SrcRect = { 0, 0, 64, 64 };
RECT DestRect = { 0, 0, 64, 64 };

if (FAILED(lpDDSOverlay->UpdateOverlay(
   &SrcRect,
   lpDDSPrimary,
   &DestRect,
   DDOVER_SHOW,
   NULL
)))
{
   throw "Displaying the overlay surface failed.";
}
```

To hide an overlay surface, simply pass the **DDOVER_HIDE** flag to the **UpdateOverlay** method.

See also "Using the **UpdateOverlay** Method."

Enumerating Surfaces

The **IDirectDraw7::EnumSurfaces** method can be used to enumerate all surfaces that have been created by the application. In addition, this method can be used to enumerate those surfaces that *can* be created. The method is declared as follows:


```
HRESULT EnumSurfaces(
    DWORD dwFlags,                          // flags specifying the type of
                                            // enumeration
    LPDDSURFACEDESC2 lpDDSD2,               // surface description to check
                        // surfaces against before they're enumerated
    LPVOID lpContext,   // application-defined value to pass to the callback
    LPDDENUMSURFACESCALLBACK7 lpEnumSurfacesCallback   // callback function
   );
```

The **dwFlags** parameter specifies which type of enumeration should be performed. Table 13.14 lists the valid flags.

The **lpDDSD2** parameter points to a (partially) initialized **DDSURFACEDESC2** structure. If either **DDENUMSURFACES_MATCH** or **DDENUMSURFACES_-NOMATCH** is specified, the valid members of this structure are compared to the corresponding characteristics of each surface before the callback is invoked.

The **lpEnumSurfacesCallback** parameter points to the callback function. The **lpContext** parameter is passed to the callback as is; i.e., DirectDraw does not interpret its value in any way.

The following callback is used with the **EnumSurfaces** method:

```
HRESULT WINAPI EnumSurfacesCallback(
    LPDIRECTDRAWSURFACE7 lpDDSurface,   // pointer to surface if existing
                                        // surfaces are enumerated
    LPDDSURFACEDESC2 lpDDSurfaceDesc,   // characteristics of the enumerated
                                        // surface
    LPVOID lpContext                    // application-defined value
   );
```

Table 13.14 Valid flags for the dwFlags parameter of the IDirectDraw7::EnumSurfaces method.

Flag	Meaning
DDENUMSURFACES_DOESEXIST	When this flag is specified, the method enumerates currently existing surfaces. This flag cannot be used with the **DDENUMSURFACES_CANBECREATED** flag.
DDENUMSURFACES_CANBECREATED	When this flag is used, the method enumerates the descriptions of surfaces that the application can create. This flag cannot be used with the **DDENUMSURFACES_DOESEXIST** flag.
DDENUMSURFACES_ALL	This flag is used with **DDENUMSURFACES_DOESEXIST** when all currently existing surfaces should be enumerated.
DDENUMSURFACES_MATCH	This flag instructs **EnumSurfaces** to check a surface against the description pointed to by the **lpDDSD2** parameter before it invokes the callback. The surface is enumerated only if the description matches.
DDENUMSURFACES_NOMATCH	This flag instructs **EnumSurfaces** to check a surface against the description pointed to by the **lpDDSD2** parameter before it invokes the callback. The surface is enumerated only if the description does not match.

If the **EnumSurfaces** method was called with the **DDENUMSURFACES_DOESEXIST** flag, the **lpDDSurface** parameter of the callback is a valid interface pointer of the enumerated surface. The interface must be released before the callback returns. The **lpDDSurfaceDesc** parameter points to the surface description as it is passed to the **CreateSurface** method or retrieved by calling the **GetSurfaceDesc** method on the surface. The **lpContext** parameter contains the value that was passed to **EnumSurfaces** as the **lpContext** parameter.

Finding Out which Surfaces Can Be Created

You can use the **IDirectDraw7::EnumSurfaces** method to find out whether a surface with specific characteristics can be created. The desired characteristics are passed to the method in a **DDSURFACEDESC2** structure, which may be only partially initialized. The **EnumSurfaces** method invokes a callback and passes complete **DDSURFACEDESC2** structures to it. The callback is invoked for every possible surface. You must specify the **DDENUMSURFACES_CANBECREATED** and **DDENUMSURFACES_MATCH** flags to use this feature. The following programming example demonstrates how to use the method to find out which pixel formats are supported for an off-screen surface of the given dimensions:

```
HRESULT WINAPI EnumSurfacesCallback(
    LPDIRECTDRAWSURFACE7,        // This parameter is not valid when the
                                 // DDENUMSURFACES_CANBECREATED flag was
                                 // passed to EnumSurfaces.
    LPDDSURFACEDESC2 ddsd,       // surface description
    LPVOID lpContext             // application-defined value
   )
{
try
{
   /*
      ddsd is a completely initialized DDSURFACEDESC2 structure
      with information about the surface.
   */

   // ...

}
catch (...)
{
   return DDENUMRET_CANCEL;
}
}

void SomeFunction()
{
try
{
   // prepare DDSURFACEDESC2 structure
   // we're interested in 100x100 off-screen surfaces
   DDSURFACEDESC2 ddsd;
   ZeroMemory(&ddsd, sizeof(ddsd));
   ddsd.dwSize = sizeof(ddsd);
   ddsd.dwFlags = DDSD_CAPS |
      DDSD_WIDTH | DDSD_HEIGHT;
   ddsd.ddsCaps.dwCaps = DDSCAPS_OFFSCREENPLAIN;
   ddsd.dwWidth = 100;
   ddsd.dwHeight = 100;

   // call EnumSurfaces
   if (FAILED(lpDD->EnumSurfaces(
      DDENUMSURFACES_CANBECREATED | DDENUMSURFACES_MATCH,
      &ddsd,
      NULL,
      reinterpret_cast<LPDDENUMSURFACESCALLBACK7>(EnumSurfacesCallback)
   )))
```

```
    {
        throw "EnumSurfaces failed.";
    }

}
catch (...)
{
    throw "An exception occurred.";
}
}
```

***NOTE:** When the **DDENUMSURFACES_CANBECREATED** flag is specified, the **EnumSurfaces** method attempts to temporarily create a surface of the desired format. The **EnumSurfaces** method can't be used to find out whether a specific surface is* supported. *It determines only whether the surface can be created* at the time of the function call.

For more information about the **IDirectDraw7::EnumSurfaces** method and its callback, see "Enumerating Surfaces" in the "Immediate Solutions" section.

Retrieving Supported FOURCC Formats

The **IDirectDraw7::GetFourCCCodes** method can be used to retrieve a list of FOURCC formats that the device supports for surfaces. You can then use the **EnumSurfaces** method to find out whether a surface (usually an overlay surface) with a particular FOURCC format can be created.

The following code calls the **GetFourCCCodes** method twice. The first call is used to retrieve the number of supported codes. The second call fills an array with the supported codes. The array is dynamically allocated according to the result of the first call:

```
// lpDD is assumed to be a valid pointer to an IDirectDraw7 interface

LPDWORD lpCodes = NULL;

try
{
    DWORD NumCodes;

    if (FAILED(lpDD->GetFourCCCodes(&NumCodes, NULL)))
    {  throw "First GetFourCCCodes failed."; }

    if (NumCodes == 0) { return; }
```

```
    lpCodes = new DWORD[NumCodes];
    if (lpCodes == NULL)
    {  throw "Array could not be allocated."; }

    if (FAILED(lpDD->GetFourCCCodes(&NumCodes, lpCodes)))
    {  throw "Second GetFourCCCodes failed."; }

    /*
       lpCodes contains a list of all supported FOURCC codes.
    */

    delete[] lpCodes;

}
catch (...)
{
    if (lpCodes) { delete[] lpCodes; }
}
```


Accessing a FOURCC Surface Directly

This Immediate Solution demonstrates how to load a bitmap into a FOURCC surface. FOURCC surfaces are created by setting the **ddpfPixelFormat.dwFourCC** member of the **DDSURFACEDESC2** structure that is passed to the **CreateSurface** method. The format of the data in the frame buffer is implied by the FOURCC code. DirectDraw surfaces use packed YUV formats. The most common formats are UYVY and YUY2, which store two pixels in one **DWORD**. Every pixel has its own Y component, but both pixels share the same U and V components.

The following code snippet copies a bitmap from a GDI device context into a locked FOURCC surface. **ddsd** is a **DDSURFACEDESC2** structure that has been filled by the **IDirectDrawSurface7::Lock** method. **SourceDC** is the GDI device context that is used to access the bitmap. The bitmap and the surface have the same dimensions. Their width in pixels is a multiple of two.

```
COLORREF Pixel;              // stores the return value of GetPixel
BYTE R, G, B;                // the color components of Pixel
BYTE Y0, Y1, U, V;           // the converted Y, U, and V components
DWORD PackedPixels;          // two packed YUV pixels

for (DWORD y = 0; y < ddsd.dwHeight; y++)
{
```

```
// set an LPDWORD pointer to the beginning of the scan line
LPDWORD lpdwSurface = reinterpret_cast<LPDWORD>(
   reinterpret_cast<DWORD>(ddsd.lpSurface) + y * ddsd.lPitch
);

for (DWORD x = 0; x < ddsd.dwWidth; x += 2)
{
   // read pixel and extract color components
   Pixel = GetPixel(SourceDC, x, y);
   R = GetRValue(Pixel);
   G = GetGValue(Pixel);
   B = GetBValue(Pixel);

   // calculate Y and U from this first pixel
   Y0 = static_cast<BYTE>(0.299 * R + 0.587 * G + 0.114 * B);
   U = static_cast<BYTE>(-0.146 * R - 0.288 * G + 0.434 * B + 128);

   // read adjacent pixel and extract color components
   Pixel = GetPixel(SourceDC, x + 1, y);
   R = GetRValue(Pixel);
   G = GetGValue(Pixel);
   B = GetBValue(Pixel);

   // calculate Y and V from this second pixel
   Y1 = static_cast<BYTE>(0.299 * R + 0.587 * G + 0.114 * B);
   V = static_cast<BYTE>(0.617 * R - 0.517 * G - 0.100 * B + 128);

   // pack pixels
   PackedPixels = 0;
   switch (ddsd.ddpfPixelFormat.dwFourCC)
   {
   // YUY2 format
   case MAKEFOURCC('Y','U','Y','2'):
   {
      // order of color components: Y0, U, Y1, V
      PackedPixels = Y0 | (U << 8) | (Y1 << 16) | (V << 24);
      break;
   }

   // UYVY format
   case MAKEFOURCC('U','Y','V','Y'):
   {
      // order of color components: U, Y0, V, Y1
      PackedPixels = U | (Y0 << 8) | (V << 16) | (Y1 << 24);
      break;
   }
```

```
        // other formats
        default:
        {
            /*
                For information about the data layout of other FOURCC formats,
                contact the vendor of the respective technology.
                Also, search the Internet for "FOURCC" and "YUV".
            */
        }
        }

        // write the two pixels to the surface
        *lpdwSurface = PackedPixels;
        lpdwSurface++;

    }
}
```


Determining Whether a Surface Is Lost

To find out whether a surface can be used in a blit operation or otherwise accessed without causing the **DDERR_SURFACELOST** error, call the **IsLost** method of the surface interface. The method is declared as follows:

```
HRESULT IDirectDrawSurface7::IsLost();
```

The return value of the method is **DDERR_SURFACELOST** when the surface has to be restored. Otherwise, it is **DD_OK**. When a surface is lost, call the **IDirectDraw7::RestoreAllSurfaces** method or the **IDirectDrawSurface7::Restore** method. For more information, see the next solution.

Restoring a Surface

When a surface is lost (as indicated by the **DDERR_SURFACELOST** error), it must be restored. Restoring a surface reassigns frame-buffer memory to the surface. This can be done with one of two methods. The **IDirectDraw7::RestoreAllSurfaces** method restores all surfaces that the application created. The method is declared as follows:

```
HRESULT IDirectDraw7::RestoreAllSurfaces();
```

The **IDirectDrawSurface7::Restore** method, on the other hand, restores only the surface for which the method is called. The method is declared as follows:

```
HRESULT IDirectDrawSurface7::Restore();
```

After you restore a surface, the graphics that the surface contained must be reloaded.

Chapter 14

DirectDraw Clippers

In Depth

By default, the primary surface covers the entire screen, not only in full-screen applications but also in windowed mode. So, when you can access the entire screen, how do you prevent blit operations from drawing outside your application window? The answer is by attaching a DirectDraw clipper to the surface.

When working with the GDI, you use clipping regions to define the areas in which painting and drawing are permitted. You'll notice that DirectDraw clippers are very similar to clipping regions—in the way they work and in the way they are manipulated. In this chapter, we'll even reuse some of the GDI functions that were discussed in Chapter 8. We'll begin with an overview of clipped blits and of the **IDirectDrawClipper** interface. After creating a clipper object, we'll discuss how to manipulate its clip list by using the **SetClipList** and **GetClipList** methods. In this context, we'll also come across the **SetHWnd** method, which is very important for windowed applications. Next, we'll use the initialized clipper to restrict the output of blit operations. We'll also discuss how to use clippers with DirectDraw methods that do not support clipping by default.

An Overview of Clippers

In Chapter 13, we discussed DirectDraw blit operations. I mentioned that the **IDirectDrawSurface7::Blt** method fails when the source and destination rectangles are not entirely contained within their respective surfaces. That's a limitation that most applications can't live with. Often you'll want a sprite to enter the screen from an edge. For a few frames, then, the sprite would be partially outside the screen. Figure 14.1 shows what this could look like.

Let's assume that, in the figure, the destination surface of the blit operation has the same dimensions as the client area of the window (which is usually the case for the back buffer of a windowed application). If DirectDraw performed a straight copy from the sprite surface to the destination surface, the invisible pixels would wrap around to the beginning of the next scan line. If there were no next line, an access violation would probably occur. To avoid these problems, DirectDraw does not blit anything if the destination rectangle is outside the surface.

This is not the case when a clipper is attached to the surface. To allow our sprite to be partially outside the screen, we can attach a clipper with a rectangular clipping region. Then, when we call the **Blt** method, DirectDraw ensures that nothing is drawn outside the clipping region, which, in this case, covers the entire surface.

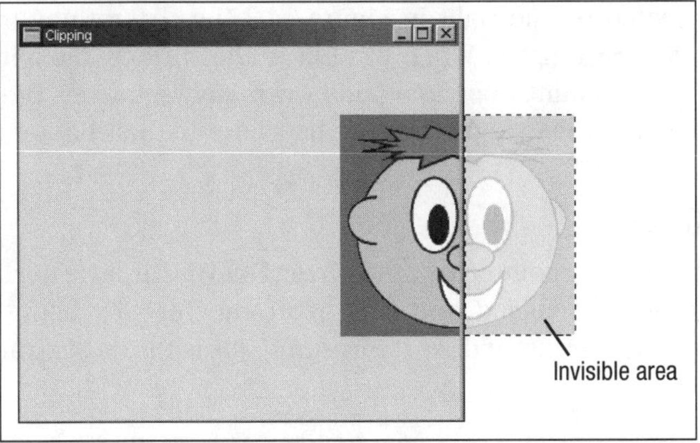

Figure 14.1 A sprite entering a surface from the right edge.

***NOTE:** The source surface can't be clipped. Blit operations will fail if the source rectangle is partially outside the surface, regardless of any attached clippers.*

But clippers are far more flexible than that. With a clipper, you can also mask off areas *within* a surface. This is especially useful for the primary surface of a windowed application. In these applications, blit operations are usually restricted to the client area of the application window. The point is that the client area is not always a simple rectangle. The application window can be overlapped by other windows, in which case the clipping region becomes more complex. Figure 14.2 shows what such a clipping region could look like. On the left, you can see that parts of the application window are obscured by other windows and by a button control within the window. On the right, you can see how the corresponding clipping region looks.

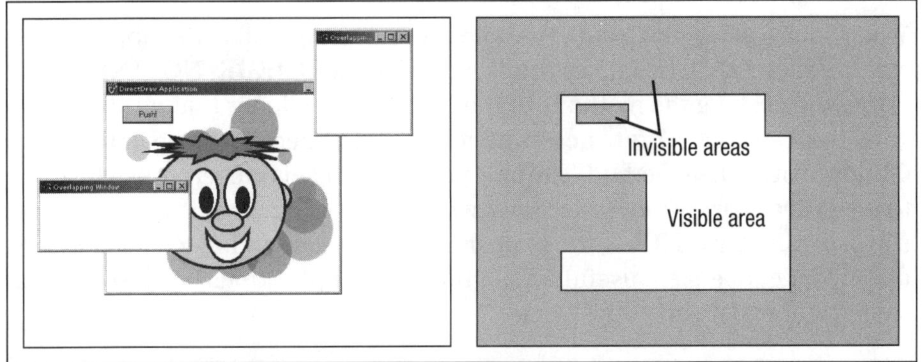

Figure 14.2 A complex clipping region (white areas are inside the region, and gray areas are outside).

The clipping region depicted on the right in Figure 14.2 (i.e., everything that's white) is made up of seven rectangles. When you blit to the surface, the blit operation is split up into several blits, depending on how many rectangles the blit affects. We'll get back to this when we discuss clip lists later in this chapter.

Creating Clippers

In this section, we'll retrieve a pointer to an **IDirectDrawClipper** interface. In Chapter 11, we already discussed one way of doing this—by using the **IDirectDraw7::CreateClipper** method. As it turns out, this is the most straightforward way.

However, you can also use the COM (Component Object Model) library function **CoCreateInstance** to create a clipper object. The COM object is represented by the **CLSID_DirectDrawClipper** GUID, and the interface is represented by **IID_IDirectDrawClipper**. The call to the **CoCreateInstance** function is similar to the one we used in Chapter 11 to obtain a pointer to an **IDirectDraw7** interface. Here's an example:


```
LPDIRECTDRAWCLIPPER lpClipper = NULL;

if (FAILED(CoCreateInstance(
   CLSID_DirectDrawClipper,  // identifier of DirectDraw clipper object
   NULL, CLSCTX_ALL,
   IID_IDirectDrawClipper,   // identifier of IDirectDrawClipper interface
   reinterpret_cast<LPVOID*>(&lpClipper)
)))
{
   throw "Retrieving an IDirectDrawClipper interface failed.";
}
```

When you're using **CoCreateInstance**, you must initialize the object in a separate function call. Otherwise, you will receive the **DDERR_NOTINITIALIZED** error when calling the methods of the interface. A clipper that has been created with the **CoCreateInstance** function is initialized with the **IDirectDrawClipper::Initialize** method. The only parameter that is currently used is a pointer to the **IDirectDraw7** interface with which the clipper object will be associated. If this parameter is **NULL**, the clipper is initialized as an independent object. Independent clippers are useful for multimonitor applications because they can be shared among DirectDraw objects.

NOTE: *Only clippers that are explicitly created as independent clippers can be used with more than one DirectDraw object.*

You'd use the following code to initialize the clipper object that we created in the preceding code snippet:

```
// lpDD is assumed to be a valid pointer to an IDirectDraw7 interface

lpClipper->Initialize(reinterpret_cast<LPDIRECTDRAW>(lpDD), 0);
```

To create an independent clipper, you can also use the **DirectDrawCreateClipper** method, which wraps the calls to **CoCreateInstance** and **IDirectDrawClipper::-Initialize**. For a usage example, see "Creating an Independent Clipper Object" in the "Immediate Solutions" section.

After you have an initialized **IDirectDrawClipper** interface, you can set the clipper's clipping region. This step is discussed in the following section.

Working with the Clip List

The GDI, as well as DirectDraw, can clip blit operations to regions of any shape, whether these regions are elliptical, triangular, banana-shaped, fish-shaped, or whatever. Internally, complex shapes are split up into rectangles. The list of rectangles in which drawing is permitted is called a *clip list*.

In this section, we'll discuss how you can manipulate the clipping region associated with a DirectDraw clipper. We'll use the **SetClipList** method to initialize the clip list with a GDI region, and we'll use the **GetClipList** method to convert the clip list back into a GDI region. Furthermore, we'll take a look at the **SetHWnd** method.

Setting the Clip List

When you have a set of rectangles in which drawing is permitted, you can call the **IDirectDrawClipper::SetClipList** method to have the clipper use these rectangles as its clip list. The rectangles are passed to the method in a **RGNDATA** structure, which is the same **RGNDATA** structure that was discussed in Chapter 8. Later in this section, we'll use the **GetRegionData** function to fill a **RGNDATA** structure. But first, let's initialize one ourselves.

Often you'll simply want to clip the output of blits to the bounds of a surface. To do this, you have to set the clipping region of the DirectDraw clipper to a single rectangle that has the same dimensions as the surface. The following code snippet uses the **IDirectDrawSurface7::GetSurfaceDesc** method to retrieve the width and height of the surface. These values are then stored in the **RECT** structure **SurfaceRect**:

```
// lpDDSurface is assumed to be a valid pointer to
// an IDirectDrawSurface7 interface

// prepare a DDSURFACEDESC2 structure
DDSURFACEDESC2 ddsd;
ZeroMemory(&ddsd, sizeof(ddsd));
ddsd.dwSize = sizeof(ddsd);

// retrieve surface dimensions
if (FAILED(lpDDSurface->GetSurfaceDesc(&ddsd)))
{
   throw "Retrieving surface dimensions failed.";
}

// initialize RECT structure
RECT SurfaceRect;
SurfaceRect.left = 0;
SurfaceRect.top = 0;
SurfaceRect.right = ddsd.dwWidth;
SurfaceRect.bottom = ddsd.dwHeight;
```


The **RECT** structure that we just initialized must be passed to the **SetClipList** method as part of a **RGNDATA** structure, which is merely a list of rectangles with information about the size of the list. The following code demonstrates how you would initialize such a structure (and its **RGNDATAHEADER** child structure) for a single rectangle. (For more information about the **RGNDATA** structure, see Chapter 8.) Here's the code:

```
LPRGNDATA lpRgnData = NULL;

// allocate memory for the RGNDATA structure so that
// there's enough space for one RECT structure
lpRgnData = reinterpret_cast<LPRGNDATA>(
   new char[sizeof(RGNDATA) + sizeof(RECT)]);

// initialize the RGNDATAHEADER child structure
lpRgnData->rdh.dwSize = sizeof(RGNDATAHEADER);  // size of the structure
lpRgnData->rdh.iType = RDH_RECTANGLES;
lpRgnData->rdh.nCount = 1;                      // number of rectangles
lpRgnData->rdh.nRgnSize = 1 * sizeof(RECT); // size of the list, in bytes
lpRgnData->rdh.rcBound = SurfaceRect;       // this member must be set to
                       // the bounding rectangle of the entire region.
                       // In our case, that's the surface rectangle itself.

// copy our rectangle to the clip list
CopyMemory(&lpRgnData->Buffer, &SurfaceRect, sizeof(SurfaceRect));
```

You could also use the GDI function **GetRegionData** to fill the **RGNDATA** structure. The **GetRegionData** function requires you to pass an **HRGN** handle of a GDI region as one of its parameters. (To create a rectangular region, you'd use the **CreateRectRgn** function.) You can use the **GetRegionData** function to initialize a DirectDraw clipper with any GDI region. For a programming example, see "Initializing the Clip List with a GDI Region" in the "Immediate Solutions" section.

As soon as the buffer pointed to by the **lpRgnData** structure has been filled with a valid **RGNDATA** structure, we can call the **SetClipList** method:

```
lpClipper->SetClipList(lpRgnData, 0);
```

The clipper works with a copy of the clip list. Therefore, you can safely free the allocated memory at this point.

Setting the Clip List to a Window's Client Area

In Figure 14.2, you can see what the clipping region of the primary surface of a windowed application could look like. The good news is that you don't have to manage the clip list for a windowed application yourself. Instead, you call the **SetHWnd** method of the **IDirectDrawClipper** interface to associate the DirectDraw clipper with the **HWND** handle of your application's main window. Not only does this method set the clip list to the current clipping region of the window, but it also instructs DirectDraw to update the clip list automatically when the clipping region changes. For a programming example, see "Associating a Clipper with a Window" in the "Immediate Solutions" section.

Retrieving the Clip List

In some situations, you might want to retrieve the clip list that is currently set for the clipper object, for example, when you want to add a rectangle to the clip list instead of simply replacing the list. The **IDirectDrawClipper** interface provides the **GetClipList** method to do this. The method fills a **RGNDATA** structure, which you can then pass to the **SetClipList** method or to the GDI function **ExtCreateRgn** (to obtain an **HRGN** handle for the clip list).

The **GetClipList** method requires you to provide a buffer that is big enough for the returned **RGNDATA** structure. If you pass **NULL** as the address of that buffer, the method does not attempt to fill the structure, but it sets a variable (to which you pass a pointer) to the required size of the buffer. This value is then used to allocate memory for the buffer. The following code demonstrates this:

```
// lpClipper is assumed to be a valid pointer to
// an IDirectDrawClipper interface
```

```
DWORD RequiredSize;

if (FAILED(lpClipper->GetClipList(
   NULL,           // retrieve entire clip list
   NULL,           // no buffer provided; fill variable with required size
   &RequiredSize   // this variable will be filled with the required size
)))
{
   throw "Retrieving required buffer size failed.";
}
```

The required size of the buffer is now contained in the **DWORD** variable **RequiredSize**. The following code passes this value to the **new** operator to allocate a byte array. After this, the **GetClipList** method can be called again. This time, the buffer is filled:

```
RGNDATA *lpRgnData = reinterpret_cast<RGNDATA*>(
   new char[RequiredSize]);

if (FAILED(lpClipper->GetClipList(
   NULL,           // retrieve entire clip list
   lpRgnData,      // this buffer will be filled
   &RequiredSize   // size of the buffer at lpRgnData
)))
{
   throw "Getting the clip list failed.";
}
```


The **Buffer** member of the **RGNDATA** structure is a pointer to an array of **RECT** structures that together define the area in which drawing is permitted. The number of rectangles in the array is given in the **rdh.nCount** member of the **RGNDATA** structure. Cast the **Buffer** member to type **LPRECT** before you access the array. The **rdh.rcBound** member, finally, contains the bounding rectangle for the region. For a detailed description of the **RGNDATA** structure, see Chapter 8.

For a programming example of how the **RGNDATA** structure would be used to create a GDI region, see Chapter 8 and "Creating a GDI Region from a Clip List" in the "Immediate Solutions" section of this chapter.

Performing Clipped Blits

In this section, we'll discuss how clipped blits are performed. In fact, there's not much to it: All you have to do is attach the clipper to a surface and call the surface's **Blt** method. Clippers are attached to surfaces by using the **IDirectDraw-Surface7::SetClipper** method. The following code snippet demonstrates this:

```
// lpDDSurface is an IDirectDrawSurface7 interface pointer
// lpClipper is an IDirectDrawClipper interface pointer

// attach the clipper to the surface
if (FAILED(lpDDSurface->SetClipper(lpClipper)))
{
   throw "Couldn't attach the clipper to the surface.";
}

// it is safe to release the clipper
lpClipper->Release();
```

When the **SetClipper** method is called, the COM reference count of the clipper object is incremented. Therefore, after calling **SetClipper**, you can call the clipper's **Release** method without losing the clipper object. When the **SetClipper** method is called several times for the same clipper object, however, the reference count is incremented only once. When a clipper is attached to the surface, it remains attached until the surface is released or until you call the **SetClipper** method again with **NULL** as the pointer to the clipper interface. In both cases, the reference count of the clipper object is decremented.

When a clipper is attached to the destination surface, the **IDirectDraw-Surface7::Blt** method clips its output automatically, whether you perform a normal blit, a stretched blit, a color fill, or any other blit effect. The **BltFast** method, on the other hand, fails if a clipper is attached to the surface. In the following section, we'll discuss a workaround for this.

Clipping without a Clipper

In this section, we'll discuss how you can emulate clipping. This way, you'll be able to use the **BltFast** method—which doesn't support DirectDraw clipper objects—to have a sprite smoothly enter or leave a surface. We won't perform any fancy clipping to complex shapes, but we'll prevent the blit operation from failing when the destination rectangle (as defined by the destination position and the width and height of the source rectangle) is not entirely contained within the surface.

Take another look at Figure 14.1. The destination position (the upper-left corner of the sprite) lies within the surface, which is okay. However, the sprite is too wide to fit the screen, i.e., part of the destination rectangle is outside the destination surface. What we have to do is exclude the invisible parts of the sprite from being blitted. We do this by moving the right edge of the source rectangle to the left. This instructs DirectDraw not to blit the right-most columns of the sprite. In the end, the width of the source rectangle should equal the width of the destination surface minus the x-coordinate of the sprite position.

***NOTE:** The width of the destination rectangle is implicitly reduced as well. Therefore, the sprite is not compressed.*

The following code checks whether the destination position is too far to the right for the sprite to fit the screen. If it is, the width of the source rectangle is reduced by moving the right edge of the rectangle to the left:

```
if (X > DestSurfaceWidth - SpriteWidth)     // sprite exceeds right edge
{
   SrcRect.right -= X + (SrcRect.right - SrcRect.left) -
      DestSurfaceWidth;
}
```

When the sprite enters the screen from the left edge, on the other hand, you have to move the left edge of the source rectangle to the right. The amount by which you have to move the left edge equals the distance from the x-position of the sprite to the left edge of the screen. In code, this would look something like this:

```
if (X < 0)                                  // sprite exceeds left edge
{  SrcRect.left += abs(X); NewX = 0; }
```


***NOTE:** After you adjust the width of the sprite, the x-position of the destination rectangle is still outside the screen. Therefore, we have to pass zero as the new x-position (as stored in the variable **NewX**) to the **BltFast** method.*

The code that clips vertically looks similar:

```
if (Y < 0)                                  // sprite exceeds top edge
{  SrcRect.top += abs(Y); NewY = 0; }
if (Y > DestSurfaceHeight - SpriteHeight)   // sprite exceeds bottom edge
{
   SrcRect.bottom -= Y + (SrcRect.bottom - SrcRect.top) -
      DestSurfaceHeight;
}
```

See also "Performing Clipped Blits with the **BltFast** Method" in the "Immediate Solutions" section.

Clipping When Accessing Surface Memory Directly

Another method, besides **IDirectDrawSurface7::BltFast**, that doesn't support clippers is **IDirectDrawSurface7::Lock**. The **Lock** method doesn't fail when a clipper is attached to the surface, but the clipper doesn't affect write operations to the frame buffer either. This section presents a way you can add support for DirectDraw clippers to the **SetPixel** routine that we wrote in Chapter 13.

In fact, it's all very easy. At the beginning of the **SetPixel** function, we have to check whether the specified coordinates are within the clipping region. For this hit test, we can use the GDI function **PtInRegion**. If this function returns **FALSE**, we can immediately return from the **SetPixel** function. Nothing has to be drawn.

The **PtInRegion** function requires an **HRGN** handle to work with. As I've already mentioned, we can obtain such a handle for the clip list of a DirectDraw clipper by using the **ExtCreateRgn** function. This function, in turn, requires an initialized **RGNDATA** structure, which we'll fill with the **IDirectDrawClipper::GetClipList** method. Finally, we obtain the **IDirectDrawClipper** interface from the destination surface by calling the **IDirectDrawSurface7::GetClipper** method. Here's what we have to do:

1. Call the **GetClipper** method of the surface interface to obtain an **IDirectDrawClipper** interface. If no clipper is attached, set the pixel as usual.
2. Call the **IDirectDrawClipper::GetClipList** method to fill a **RGNDATA** structure with the clip list.
3. Call the GDI function **ExtCreateRgn** to obtain an **HRGN** handle for the clip list.
4. Call the GDI function **PtInRegion** to check whether the pixel to set is within the region. If it isn't, return from the function without setting the pixel.

Here's how the new **SetPixel** function could look:

```
HRESULT SetPixel(
    LPDIRECTDRAWSURFACE7 lpDDSurface,
    DWORD dwX, DWORD dwY,
    COLORREF rgb
   )
{
   LPDIRECTDRAWCLIPPER lpClipper = NULL;
   HRGN hRgn = NULL;
   // ...

try
{
   // obtain clipper interface
   if (SUCCEEDED(lpDDSurface->GetClipper(&lpClipper)))
   {
      // convert the clipper's clip list into a GDI region
      hRgn = CreateRgnFromClipper(lpClipper);
```

14. DirectDraw Clippers

```
        /*
           The CreateRgnFromClipper function wraps Steps 2 and 3. The
           complete source code of the function can be found in "Creating a
           GDI Region from a Clip List" in the "Immediate Solutions" section.
        */

        // hit-test the point
        BOOL bIsInRegion = PtInRegion(hRgn, dwX, dwY))

        // release everything
        SAFERELEASE(lpClipper);
        if (hRgn) { DeleteObject(reinterpret_cast<HGDIOBJ>(hRgn)); }

        if (!bIsInRegion)
        { return S_FALSE; }       // successful but nothing to do
     }

     // go on with normal SetPixel code
     // ...

  }
  catch (...)
  {
     SAFERELEASE(lpClipper);
     if (hRgn) { DeleteObject(reinterpret_cast<HGDIOBJ>(hRgn)); }
     // ...
  }
  }
```

WARNING! In a real-world application, you wouldn't convert the clip list into a GDI region every time you called the SetPixel function. Instead, you could create the region up front and pass the HRGN handle to the function. In addition, you could use the RectInRegion function to find out whether any of the pixels (within the area that you are going to access) are within the region.

14. DirectDraw Clippers

Immediate Solutions

Using CoCreateInstance to Create a Clipper Object

You can use the standard COM function **CoCreateInstance** to retrieve an **IDirectDrawClipper** interface. The function is declared as follows:

```
STDAPI CoCreateInstance(
    REFCLSID rclsid,        // class identifier (CLSID) of the object
    LPUNKNOWN pUnkOuter,    // reserved for "COM aggregation"
    DWORD dwClsContext,     // context for running executable code
    REFIID riid,            // interface identifier
    LPVOID *ppv             // variable to receive interface pointer
   );
```

To create a DirectDraw clipper object, pass **CLSID_DirectDrawClipper** as the **rclsid** parameter, **CLSCTX_ALL** as the **dwClsContext** parameter, and **IID_IDirectDrawClipper** as the **riid** parameter. The **ppv** parameter points to a variable that will receive the **IDirectDrawClipper** interface pointer when the function returns successfully. The **pUnkOuter** parameter is unused and must be **NULL**.

The following code calls the **CoCreateInstance** function to obtain an **IDirectDrawClipper** interface:

```
#define INITGUID
#include <windows.h>
#include <ddraw.h>
// ...

CoInitialize(NULL);              // initialize the COM library

LPDIRECTDRAWCLIPPER lpClipper = NULL;

// create DirectDraw clipper
if (FAILED(
   CoCreateInstance(
      CLSID_DirectDrawClipper,
      NULL, CLSCTX_ALL,
```

```
        IID_IDirectDrawClipper,
        reinterpret_cast<LPVOID*>(&lpClipper)
    )
))
{
    throw "CoCreateInstance failed.";
}
```

Before you can use the clipper object, you are required to call the **IDirectDrawClipper::Initialize** method. This method is declared as follows:

```
HRESULT Initialize(
    LPDIRECTDRAW lpDD,          // IDirectDraw interface pointer
    DWORD dwFlags               // unused; must be NULL
   );
```

The **lpDD** parameter is used to associate the clipper with a DirectDraw object. If you pass a **NULL** pointer, an independent clipper is created. Independent clippers can be attached to the surfaces of any DirectDraw object. See also "Creating an Independent Clipper Object."

The following code associates the clipper with a DirectDraw object:

```
// lpDD is assumed to be a valid IDirectDraw7 interface pointer

if (SUCCEEDED(lpClipper->Initialize(
    reinterpret_cast<LPDIRECTDRAW>(lpDD),
    0
)))
{
    /*
        Clipper is ready.
    */
}
```

Related solution:	Found on page:
Creating a Clipper	637

Creating an Independent Clipper Object

Independent clipper objects, which can be attached to the surfaces of any DirectDraw object, can be created by using the **DirectDrawCreateClipper** function. The **DirectDrawCreateClipper** function is declared as follows:

```
HRESULT WINAPI DirectDrawCreateClipper(
    DWORD dwFlags,                          // unused; must be 0
    LPDIRECTDRAWCLIPPER FAR *lplpDDClipper, // variable to receive
                                            // interface pointer
    IUnknown FAR *pUnkOuter                 // unused; must be NULL
   );
```

The only parameter that is used is **lplpDDClipper**, which points to a variable of type **LPDIRECTDRAWCLIPPER** that will receive the **IDirectDrawClipper** interface pointer when the function returns successfully.

The following code snippet demonstrates how the **DirectDrawCreateClipper** method is used:

```
LPDIRECTDRAWCLIPPER lpClipper = NULL;

if (SUCCEEDED(DirectDrawCreateClipper(0, &lpClipper, NULL)))
{
   /*
      Clipper is ready.
   */
}
```

You can also create an independent clipper object by using the **CoCreateInstance** function. See the previous Immediate Solution.

Attaching a Clipper to a Surface

To be able to perform clipped blit operations, you must attach a clipper to the surface that is the destination of the blit. The **IDirectDrawSurface7** interface provides the **SetClipper** method to attach a clipper object to a surface. The method is declared as follows:

```
HRESULT IDirectDrawSurface7::SetClipper(
    LPDIRECTDRAWCLIPPER lpDDClipper     // pointer to DirectDraw clipper
   );
```

The **SetClipper** method attaches the clipper pointed to by the **lpDDClipper** parameter to the surface. If this parameter is **NULL**, the currently attached clipper (if any) is detached. Attaching a clipper increments the reference count of the clipper object, but only if the clipper is not already attached.

Detaching a Clipper from a Surface

The following code snippet uses the **IDirectDrawSurface7::SetClipper** method to detach the clipper from the surface:

```
// lpDDSurface is assumed to be a valid pointer to
// an IDirectDrawSurface7 interface

lpDDSurface->SetClipper(NULL);
```

See also the previous Immediate Solution.

Retrieving the Currently Attached Clipper

You can use the **IDirectDrawSurface7::GetClipper** method to obtain the **IDirectDrawClipper** interface pointer of the clipper that is currently attached to the surface. The method is declared as follows:

```
HRESULT IDirectDrawSurface7::GetClipper(
    LPDIRECTDRAWCLIPPER FAR *lplpDDClipper  // variable to receive
                                            // interface pointer
   );
```

When the function is successful, the variable pointed to by the **lplpDDClipper** parameter receives a pointer to the **IDirectDrawClipper** interface of the currently attached clipper object. The reference count of the clipper object is incremented. When you're done working with the clipper, call the **Release** method of the clipper interface.

The following is a usage example of the **GetClipper** method:

```
// lpDDSurface is assumed to be a valid pointer to
// an IDirectDrawSurface7 interface

LPDIRECTDRAWCLIPPER lpClipper = NULL;

try
{
   if (SUCCEEDED(lpDDSurface->GetClipper(&lpClipper)))
   {
      /*
         work with lpClipper
      */
```

```
        SAFERELEASE(lpClipper);
    }
}
catch (...)
{
    SAFERELEASE(lpClipper);
}
```

Setting the Clip List

The clip list of a DirectDraw clipper object defines the rectangular areas in which blitting is permitted. The clip list is set with the **IDirectDrawClipper::SetClipList** method. This method is declared as follows:

```
HRESULT IDirectDrawClipper::SetClipList(
    LPRGNDATA lpClipList,       // new clip list
    DWORD dwFlags               // unused; must be 0
   );
```

The **lpClipList** parameter of the method points to an initialized **RGNDATA** structure that contains the list of rectangular areas. The **RGNDATA** structure is discussed in Chapter 8. The following Immediate Solution demonstrates how you can use GDI functions to initialize a **RGNDATA** structure from an **HRGN** handle.

Initializing the Clip List with a GDI Region

In this section, we'll use the GDI function **GetRegionData** to convert a region (represented by an **HRGN** handle) into a **RGNDATA** structure that we can use with the **IDirectDrawClipper::SetClipList** method. We'll write a function that you can use in your own programs to set a DirectDraw clipper to a GDI clipping region. The function is declared as follows:

```
HRESULT InitClipperWithHRgn(
    LPDIRECTDRAWCLIPPER lpClipper,      // clipper to initialize
    HRGN hRgn                           // handle of GDI region
   )
{
   RGNDATA *lpRgnData = NULL;

try
{
```

```
    // retrieve size of RGNDATA structure
    DWORD ReqSize = 0;
    if ((ReqSize = GetRegionData(hRgn, 0, NULL)) == 0)
    {  throw 0; }

    // allocate RGNDATA structure
    lpRgnData = reinterpret_cast<RGNDATA*>(new char[ReqSize]);
    if (!lpRgnData) { throw 1; }

    // get region data
    if (!GetRegionData(hRgn, ReqSize, lpRgnData))
    {  throw 2; }

    // set clip list to RGNDATA
    HRESULT hr = lpClipper->SetClipList(lpRgnData, 0);

    // free the memory allocated for the RGNDATA structure
    delete[] lpRgnData;

    return hr;

  }
  catch (...)
  {
    if (lpRgnData)
    {  delete[] lpRgnData; }
    return E_FAIL;
  }
  }
```


Associating a Clipper with a Window

You can instruct a DirectDraw clipper object to set its clip list to the clipping region of a window's client area. To do this, pass the **HWND** handle of the window to the **IDirectDrawClipper::SetHWnd** method. The method is declared as follows:

```
HRESULT IDirectDrawClipper::SetHWnd(
    DWORD dwFlags,      // unused; must be 0
    HWND hWnd           // window handle
   );
```

The clip list is automatically updated every time the clipping region of the window's client area changes.

Retrieving the Clip List

You can retrieve a copy of the clip list of a DirectDraw clipper by calling the **IDirectDrawClipper::GetClipList** method. This method fills a **RGNDATA** structure, which you can then pass to GDI functions or to the **IDirectDraw-Clipper::SetClipList** method. The **GetClipList** method is declared as follows:

```
HRESULT IDirectDrawClipper::GetClipList(
  LPRECT lpRect,                // rectangle specifying the part of the
                                // clip list to retrieve
  LPRGNDATA lpClipList,         // buffer to receive RGNDATA structure
  LPDWORD lpdwSize              // size of the lpClipList buffer
);
```

The **lpRect** parameter of the method points to a rectangle that is used to clip the clip list; i.e., only those parts of the clip list that are within the rectangle are copied to the **RGNDATA** structure. If this parameter is **NULL**, the entire clip list is retrieved.

The **lpClipList** parameter points to the buffer that will receive the **RGNDATA** structure when the method is successful. The **lpdwSize** parameter points to a **DWORD** variable containing the size of the buffer. If **lpClipList** is **NULL**, that variable is set to the required size of the buffer.

Here's a programming example:

```
// lpClipper is assumed to be a valid pointer to
// an IDirectDrawClipper interface

RGNDATA *lpRgnData = NULL;

try
{
   // retrieve required size of buffer
   DWORD RequiredSize;
   if (FAILED(lpClipper->GetClipList(
      NULL,         // retrieve entire clip list
      NULL,         // no buffer provided; fill variable with required size
      &RequiredSize // this variable will be filled with the required size
   )))
   {
      throw "Retrieving required buffer size failed.";
   }
```

```
   // allocate memory for the buffer
   RGNDATA *lpRgnData = reinterpret_cast<RGNDATA*>(
      new char[RequiredSize]);
   if (!lpRgnData)
   {  throw "Allocating memory for the RGNDATA structure failed."; }

   // copy the clip list to the buffer
   if (FAILED(lpClipper->GetClipList(
      NULL,          // retrieve entire clip list
      lpRgnData,     // this buffer will be filled
      &RequiredSize // size of the buffer at lpRgnData
   )))
   {
      throw "Getting the clip list failed.";
   }

   /*
      lpRgnData points to a valid RGNDATA structure that you
      can pass to ExtCreateRgn or IDirectDrawClipper::SetClipList.
      See also the following Immediate Solution.
   */

   delete[] lpRgnData;

}
catch (...)
{
   if (lpRgnData) { delete[] lpRgnData; }
}
```


Creating a GDI Region from a Clip List

You can use the following function in your own programs to create an **HRGN** handle for the clip list of a DirectDraw clipper. The code uses the **IDirectDraw-Clipper::GetClipList** method to fill a **RGNDATA** structure that can then be passed to the GDI function **ExtCreateRgn**:

```
HRGN CreateRgnFromClipper(LPDIRECTDRAWCLIPPER lpClipper)
{
   RGNDATA *lpRgnData = NULL;

try
{
```

```
    // retrieve required size of buffer
    DWORD RequiredSize;
    if (FAILED(lpClipper->GetClipList(
       NULL,         // retrieve entire clip list
       NULL,         // no buffer provided; fill variable with required size
       &RequiredSize // this variable will be filled with the required size
    )))
    {
       throw "Retrieving required buffer size failed.";
    }

    // allocate memory for the buffer
    RGNDATA *lpRgnData = reinterpret_cast<RGNDATA*>(
       new char[RequiredSize]);
    if (!lpRgnData)
    {  throw "Allocating memory for the RGNDATA structure failed."; }

    // copy the clip list to the buffer
    if (FAILED(lpClipper->GetClipList(
       NULL,         // retrieve entire clip list
       lpRgnData,    // this buffer will be filled
       &RequiredSize // size of the buffer at lpRgnData
    )))
    {
       throw "Retrieving the clip list failed.";
    }

      // create HRGN from RGNDATA structure
    HRGN hRgn = ExtCreateRegion(
       NULL,                   // no transformation
       RequiredSize,           // size of buffer pointed to by lpRgnData
       lpRgnData               // buffer containing the RGNDATA structure
    );

    delete[] lpRgnData;

    return hRgn;

 }
 catch (...)
 {
    if (lpRgnData) { delete[] lpRgnData; }
    return NULL;
 }
 }
```

See Chapter 8 for more information about the **ExtCreateRgn** function.

Performing Clipped Blits with the BltFast Method

This Immediate Solution contains the complete source code of the **ClippedBltFast** function. This function is a wrapper for the **IDirectDrawSurface7::BltFast** method. **BltFast** fails when the destination rectangle (as defined by the destination position and the width and height of the source rectangle) is partially outside the destination surface. The **ClippedBltFast** function circumvents this limitation: Before it calls the **BltFast** method, **ClippedBltFast** adjusts the source rectangle so that the destination rectangle becomes valid and the invisible parts of the sprite are accurately clipped.

The **lpDDDestSurface** parameter of the function is a pointer to the **IDirectDrawSurface7** interface of the destination surface. The other parameters have the same meaning as the corresponding parameters of the **BltFast** method.

***NOTE:** The destination position is given in integers, not in **DWORD**s, so that negative coordinates are possible.*


```
HRESULT ClippedBltFast(
    LPDIRECTDRAWSURFACE7 lpDDDestSurface,    // destination surface
    int X, int Y,                            // destination position
    LPDIRECTDRAWSURFACE7 lpDDSrcSurface,     // source surface
    LPRECT lpSrcRect,                        // source rectangle
    DWORD dwTrans                            // flags (e.g., color keying)
   )
{
try
{
   // get dimensions of destination surface
   // (the GetSurfaceRect function is application-defined)
   RECT DestRect;
   GetSurfaceRect(DestRect, lpDDDestSurface);

   // get dimensions of source surface
   RECT SrcRect;
   if (!lpSrcRect)                           // handle a NULL source rect.
   {  GetSurfaceRect(SrcRect, lpDDSrcSurface); }
   else
   {  SrcRect = *lpSrcRect; }

   int SrcWidth = SrcRect.right - SrcRect.left;
   int SrcHeight = SrcRect.bottom - SrcRect.top;
```

```
    // adjust source rectangle and destination position so that the
    // destination rectangle is entirely contained within its surface

    int NewX = X;
    int NewY = Y;

    if (X < 0)                              // sprite exceeds left edge
    {  SrcRect.left += abs(X); NewX = 0; }
    if (X > DestRect.right - SrcWidth)      // sprite exceeds right edge
    {  SrcRect.right -= X + SrcWidth - DestRect.right; }

    if (Y < 0)                              // sprite exceeds top edge
    {  SrcRect.top += abs(Y); NewY = 0; }
    if (Y > DestRect.bottom - SrcHeight)    // sprite exceeds bottom edge
    {  SrcRect.bottom -= Y + SrcHeight - DestRect.bottom; }


    // perform the blit
    return lpDDDestSurface->BltFast(
       NewX, NewY,
       lpDDSrcSurface,
       &SrcRect,
       dwTrans
    );

}
catch (...)
{
    return DDERR_EXCEPTION;
}
}
```

ClippedBltFast can only clip the output to the boundaries of the surface. It does not support DirectDraw clipper objects.

Chapter 15

DirectDraw Colors and Palettes

In Depth

In this chapter, we'll discuss how you can influence the appearance of color on DirectDraw surfaces. The chapter is divided into three parts. The first part deals with DirectDraw palette objects and with the **IDirectDrawPalette** interface. We'll discuss how palettized display modes work and how palettes are used with these modes. You'll find out that palettized display modes are not simply relics from a distant past when video RAM was too expensive to allow for true-color modes. Even nowadays, palettized modes have their merits when you want to achieve visual effects with little CPU overhead.

In the second part of this chapter, we'll use DirectDraw color controls (the **IDirectDrawColorControl** interface) to adjust the color characteristics of DirectDraw surfaces, just as you would adjust the characteristics of a television screen display. We'll talk about brightness, contrast, saturation, hue, and the like.

At the end of this chapter, we'll discuss DirectDraw gamma controls (the **IDirectDrawGammaControl** interface) and how they can be used to achieve effects similar to those produced by palettes and color controls.

Working with DirectDraw Palettes

As you know, there are two major types of display modes—true-color modes and palettized modes. In a true-color mode, up to 16,777,216 colors can be visible at the same time. (You'd need a resolution of 4096×4096 pixels to display that many colors.) In an 8-bit palettized mode, on the other hand, the number of visible colors drops to 256.

Now, why would you want to use a palettized mode? First of all, surfaces consume significantly less memory in a palettized mode. Therefore, more sprites fit into local video memory, which means better blit performance. And second, palettized modes allow for interesting, yet computationally inexpensive, effects through palette animation. These effects include blending and fading. With palettes you can also adjust color characteristics, such as brightness, contrast, saturation, and the like, without having to modify the bitmap data pixel by pixel.

In this section, we'll discuss the steps necessary to work with palettized surfaces (i.e., with palettized display modes). These are the topics and the steps that we'll cover:

1. *Creating Palettes*—This section discusses the **IDirectDraw7::Create-Palette** method in detail and provides an overview of the **IDirectDraw-Palette** interface.
2. *Attaching Palettes to Surfaces*—This section explains how palettes and surfaces work together. We'll use the **IDirectDrawSurface7::SetPalette** method to apply the palette that we created in Step 1 to the primary surface.
3. *Dynamically Modifying Palettes*—This section deals with the **SetEntries** method of the **IDirectDrawPalette** interface. We'll discuss the basics of palette animation, and we'll produce a few simple effects, such as fading out an image.

Creating Palettes

A palette is a set of colors that are used for rendering. An 8-bit palette, for example, contains 256 colors; a 4-bit palette contains 16 colors. A DirectDraw palette object is an encapsulation of this set of colors and of the methods that are used to manipulate the set. These methods, **GetEntries** and **SetEntries**, are provided through the **IDirectDrawPalette** interface. A pointer to such an interface can be obtained by calling the **IDirectDraw7::CreatePalette** method. In this section, we'll use the **CreatePalette** method to create and initialize a 256-color palette.

NOTE: *In addition to 8-bit (256-color) palettes, DirectDraw supports 1-bit, 2-bit, and 4-bit palettes. However, working with these palette types is very similar to working with 8-bit palettes. Therefore, we will not discuss the other types separately.*

When a palette object is created, it is automatically initialized with a list of colors that you provide. This list of colors is passed to the **CreatePalette** method as an array of **PALETTEENTRY** structures. When you're creating a 256-color palette, the array must contain 256 elements. Every element stores the red, green, and blue components of the color as well as an optional flag. In a windowed application, you can use this flag to control how the respective colors should be mapped to the system palette. As a rule of thumb, you should use the **PC_EXPLICIT** flag for the 20 reserved colors of the system palette; use **PC_RESERVED** for palette entries that you are planning to use for palette animation; and use **PC_NO-COLLAPSE** for all other entries. In a full-screen application, you don't have to share the system palette with other applications. Therefore, you can safely set the flag to zero.

The **CreatePalette** method itself has a flags parameter as well. This parameter specifies the type of palette to create—**DDPCAPS_8BIT** requests an 8-bit palette, **DDPCAPS_4BIT** requests a 4-bit palette, and so on. When you create an 8-bit palette, DirectDraw reserves palette entries 0 and 255. To be allowed to use these two entries as well, you must specify the **DDPCAPS_ALLOW256** flag. That's basically all there is to it. The following programming example demonstrates how to create a palette for a full-screen application:

```
// lpDD is assumed to be a valid pointer to an IDirectDraw7 interface

PALETTEENTRY Entries[256];      // we need 256 entries for an 8-bit palette

// initialize the entries with a standard 3:3:2 palette
for (int i = 0; i < 256; i++)
{
   Entries[i].peRed = static_cast<BYTE>(((i >> 5) & 7) * 255 / 7);
   Entries[i].peGreen = static_cast<BYTE>(((i >> 2) & 7) * 255 / 7);
   Entries[i].peBlue = static_cast<BYTE>((i & 3) * 255 / 3);
   Entries[i].peFlags = 0;
}

// create the palette
LPDIRECTDRAWPALETTE lpPalette = NULL;
if (FAILED(lpDD->CreatePalette(
   DDPCAPS_8BIT | DDPCAPS_ALLOW256,      // flags
   Entries,                              // the array of palette entries
   &lpPalette,                   // variable to receive interface pointer
   NULL                          // unused; must be NULL
)))
{
   throw "Creating the palette failed.";
}
```

For a complete description of the parameters of the **CreatePalette** method, see "Creating a Palette" in the "Immediate Solutions" section.

In a windowed application, you don't want to change the appearance of GUI elements when you set the palette. (*Creating* a palette is not the same as *setting* a palette. We'll get back to this soon.) But the appearance of GUI elements *will* change when you overwrite one of those entries that Windows uses to draw window frames, caption bars, menus, and so on. Windows reserves the first 10 and the last 10 entries of the system palette for GUI elements. One way of leaving these entries untouched is to initialize them with the current contents of the system palette. However, when the user changes the color scheme, the results might be wrong. To avoid this, you can specify the **PC_EXPLICIT** flag to "link" entries to the system palette. When this flag is set, the system ensures that the entry always contains the same color as the system palette entry at the same index, regardless of color scheme changes. See also "Setting Up a Palette for a Windowed Application" in the "Immediate Solutions" section.

Creating a palette does not affect the display yet. First, you have to attach the palette to the primary surface. This is discussed in the following section.

Attaching Palettes to Surfaces

Once you have a pointer to an **IDirectDrawPalette** interface, you can attach the palette to a palettized surface. The palette format must match the pixel format of the surface, of course. For example, you can attach an 8-bit palette only to a surface that has the **DDPF_PALETTEINDEXED8** flag set in the **dwFlags** member of the **DDPIXELFORMAT** structure. The primary surface of an 8-bit display mode, for example, is always 8-bit palettized. The off-screen surfaces are usually 8-bit palettized as well, unless you explicitly request a different pixel format.

You attach palettes to surfaces by using the **SetPalette** method of the **IDirectDrawSurface7** interface. Here's how you would attach the palette that we created in the previous section to the primary surface:

```
if (FAILED(lpDDSPrimary->SetPalette(lpPalette)))
{
   throw "Setting the palette failed.";
}
```

The next time the surface is displayed (this happens when the cathode ray refreshes the screen), the surface appears in the new colors. Every pixel is stored as a single byte (eight bits). The graphics card uses this byte as an index into the system palette to look up the color of the pixel.

For a detailed description of the **IDirectDrawSurface7::SetPalette** method, see "Attaching a Palette to a Surface" in the "Immediate Solutions" section.

So far, we've talked only about the primary surface. Though it is possible to attach a palette to an off-screen surface, this usually doesn't make sense. Recall, DirectDraw does not perform any color conversion or color matching when it blits from an off-screen surface to the screen. The pixels are simply copied. A pixel that uses palette entry 37 is always a pixel that uses palette entry 37, even if palette entry 37 contains different colors in the primary palette and in the off-screen palette. The ability to use palettes with surfaces other than the primary surface is used primarily by Direct3D applications.

Dynamically Modifying Palettes

You can modify palette entries after the palette object has been created. To do this, call the **IDirectDrawPalette::SetEntries** method. This method—just like the **CreatePalette** method—takes a pointer to an array of **PALETTEENTRY** structures as one of its parameters. This array contains the new palette entries, which the **SetEntries** method applies to the palette object immediately. With the **SetEntries** method, you can update only a part of the palette. For example, say you want to change the color of the sky in a picture from blue to orange. Here's how you could do this:

```
// lpPalette is assumed to be a valid pointer to
// an IDirectDrawPalette interface

PALETTEENTRY Orange;
Orange.peRed = 255;
Orange.peGreen = 165;
Orange.peBlue = 0;

if (FAILED(lpPalette->SetEntries(
   0,                // unused; must be 0
   IndexOfSkyBlue,   // palette index of the blue color (application-defined)
   1,                // change a single entry
   &Orange           // new color for entry IndexOfSkyBlue
)))
{
   throw "Couldn't change the color of the sky.";
}
```


Instead of simply replacing the color, you could also blend colors smoothly. For this, you would first set up an array of **PALETTEENTRY** structures containing the destination colors. Then you would slowly increment or decrement the color intensities of the colors in the DirectDraw palette until the colors in the palette matched the destination colors.

The following programming example demonstrates this by fading the image to black. First, the code queries the palette for the current entries. These entries are saved in an array of **PALETTEENTRY** structures:

```
// lpPalette is assumed to be a valid pointer to
// an IDirectDrawPalette interface

// save the current palette
PALETTEENTRY SrcPal[256];
lpPalette->GetEntries(0, 0, 256, SrcPal);
```

Then the destination palette is set up. For the purpose of fading the image to black, we simply fill an array of **PALETTEENTRY** structures, **DestPal**, with binary zeros:

```
// set up destination palette
PALETTEENTRY DestPal[256];
ZeroMemory(DestPal, sizeof(DestPal));
```

Of course, you can initialize the palette as you like—for example, with the grayscale version of the original palette.

After this, we enter a **while** loop in which we'll animate the palette. We specify that the animation should last three seconds. Furthermore, we save the current system time and set a progress meter (the **Progress** variable) to zero. Another array of **PALETTEENTRY** structures, **CurrentPal**, will serve as our working palette:

```
PALETTEENTRY CurrentPal[256];
DWORD FadeDuration = 3000;          // fade duration is 3 seconds
float Progress = 0.0f;
DWORD StartTime = timeGetTime();

while (Progress < 1.0f)
{
// ...
```

In the loop, we go through the 256 entries and blend the colors from the source palette and the destination palette according to the current progress of the animation. (The **Progress** variable will be updated later in the loop.) Here's the code for the blending:

```
//...
   for (int i = 0; i < 255; i++)        // we assume that we can animate
                                        // all 256 entries
   {
      CurrentPal[i].peRed = SrcPal[i].peRed * (1.0f - Progress) +
         DestPal[i].peRed * Progress;
      CurrentPal[i].peGreen = SrcPal[i].peGreen * (1.0f - Progress) +
         DestPal[i].peGreen * Progress;
      CurrentPal[i].peBlue = SrcPal[i].peBlue * (1.0f - Progress) +
         DestPal[i].peBlue * Progress;
   }

 lpPalette->SetEntries(
      0,                        // unused; must be 0
      0, 256,                   // change 256 entries starting at index 0
      CurrentPal                // new colors
   );
// ...
```

***TIP:** To avoid visual artifacts when you're constantly updating the palette, you should call **IDirectDraw7::WaitFor-VerticalBlank** before calling the **SetEntries** method. See Chapter 12 for details.*

At the end of the loop, we update the **Progress** variable so that it is 1.0 after three seconds:

```
// ...
   Progress = 1.0f / FadeDuration * (timeGetTime() - StartTime);
}
```

See also "Blending Between Palettes" in the "Immediate Solutions" section.

Working with Color Controls

In this section, we'll discuss how you use the **IDirectDrawColorControl** interface to adjust the color characteristics of DirectDraw surfaces. Color controls provide controls similar to the controls on TV sets. With DirectDraw color controls, you can adjust settings such as brightness, contrast, and saturation. Color controls work on palettized surfaces as well as on true-color surfaces, on the primary surface, and on overlay surfaces. This section is divided into the following sub-sections:

- *Obtaining a Color Control Interface*—After determining whether color controls are supported on the device, we'll use the **QueryInterface** method on a surface object to obtain a pointer to an **IDirectDrawColorControl** interface.
- *Determining which Controls Are Supported*—We'll use the **GetColorControls** method to find out whether particular controls (such as brightness or contrast) are supported.
- *Adjusting Color Characteristics*—Here we'll discuss the **SetColorControls** method and the related **DDCOLORCONTROL** structure, as well as the effects that particular controls have on the appearance of color.

Obtaining a Color Control Interface

Color controls are very closely related to DirectDraw surfaces. It makes sense that the functionality of color controls is implemented right in the surface object. The color control methods, however, are encapsulated in their own interface—the **IDirectDrawColorControl** interface. A pointer to such an interface can be obtained by calling the **QueryInterface** method of the **IDirectDrawSurface7** interface. (For more information about the **QueryInterface** method, see Chapter 11.) The following code demonstrates how you can retrieve a color control interface:

```
// lpDDSurface is assumed to be a valid pointer to
// an IDirectDrawSurface7 interface

LPDIRECTDRAWCOLORCONTROL lpDDColorControl = NULL;

try
{
   if (FAILED(lpDDSurface->QueryInterface(
      IID_IDirectDrawColorControl,
      reinterpret_cast<LPVOID*>(&lpDDColorControl)
   )))
   {
      throw "Couldn't retrieve color control interface.";
   }

   /*
      adjust color characteristics here
   */

   // release color control interface
   SAFERELEASE(lpDDColorControl);

}
catch (...)
{
   SAFERELEASE(lpDDColorControl);
}
```

You can query the primary surface and the overlay surfaces for the **IDirectDrawColorControl** interface. If the **QueryInterface** call fails, color controls are not available for that kind of surface. A more elegant way of finding out whether color controls are supported is to use the **IDirectDraw7::GetCaps** method. The relevant member of the **DDCAPS** structure that is filled by that method is the **dwCaps2** bit field. If **dwCaps2** contains the **DDCAPS2_COLORCONTROLPRIMARY** flag, then color controls are supported for the primary surface; if it contains the **DDCAPS2_COLORCONTROLOVERLAY** flag, then color controls are supported for overlay surfaces.

Determining which Controls Are Supported

A device might not support all color characteristics that are defined by DirectDraw. For example, a device might allow the adjustment of brightness, but might not support changing the hue. To find out which controls are supported, you can use the **IDirectDrawColorControl::GetColorControls** method. This method is usually called to retrieve the current color settings. The method fills a

DDCOLORCONTROL structure. The **dwFlags** member of the structure indicates which structure members are valid and thus which color controls are supported.

The following programming example queries the color control interface for support of the saturation setting:

```
// lpDDColorControl is assumed to be a valid pointer to
// an IDirectDrawColorControl interface

// prepare the DDCOLORCONTROL structure
DDCOLORCONTROL ColorCtrl;
ZeroMemory(&ColorCtrl, sizeof(ColorCtrl));
ColorCtrl.dwSize = sizeof(ColorCtrl);

// have DirectDraw fill the structure
if (SUCCEEDED(lpDDColorControl->GetColorControls(&ColorCtrl)))
{
   // check saturation flag
   if (ColorCtrl.dwFlags & DDCOLOR_SATURATION)
   {
      /* adjusting the saturation is supported */
   }
}
```

See also “Querying the Color Controls” in the “Immediate Solutions” section.

Adjusting Color Characteristics

After you have a pointer to an **IDirectDrawColorControl** interface (and have verified that the desired controls are available), you can call the **SetColorControls** method to adjust the color settings. The method takes a pointer to a **DDCOLORCONTROL** structure as its only parameter. The structure is declared as follows:

```
typedef struct _DDCOLORCONTROL {
    DWORD   dwSize;
    DWORD   dwFlags;
    LONG    lBrightness;
    LONG    lContrast;
    LONG    lHue;
    LONG    lSaturation;
    LONG    lSharpness;
    LONG    lGamma;
    LONG    lColorEnable;
    DWORD   dwReserved1;
} DDCOLORCONTROL, FAR *LPDDCOLORCONTROL;
```

In the remainder of this section, we'll discuss the seven available controls and their effect on the appearance of the surface.

The **lBrightness** member of the **DDCOLORCONTROL** structure influences the luminance of the colors on the surface. The brightness is specified in IRE (International Radio Engineers) units times 100, ranging from 0 to 20,000 (200 IRE).

The contrast is specified in the **lContrast** member. At the lowest theoretically possible contrast, all colors appear as gray. At the highest theorectically possible contrast, the colors are either black or white, depending on their initial luminance. For example, a color with a luminance level of 34 percent will be mapped to black, regardless of its color. A color with a luminance value of 75 percent will be mapped to white. For DirectDraw color controls, possible values for the contrast range from 0 to 20,000 (200 IRE).

The hue—as specified by the **lHue** member—influences the dominant wavelength of each color. The hue is specified in degrees, ranging from –180° to 180°. To understand hue, see Figure 15.1.

In Figure 15.1, the colors of the spectrum are arranged in a circle. Red is at the top, green is at 120°, and blue is at –120°. When you modify the hue by setting the **lHue** member, all colors are rotated around this circle. For example, when you specify 120°, all yellow pixels (yellow is at 60°, between red and green) become cyan (cyan is at 180°, between blue and green).

The saturation specifies the color intensity. The possible values for the **lSaturation** member range from 0 to 20,000 (200 IRE). If the saturation is zero, the pixels contain only brightness information; i.e., the image appears in grayscale. Instead of setting the saturation to zero, you can also use the **lColorEnable** member to disable color. If **lColorEnable** is 1, color is used. If it is 0, color is not used.

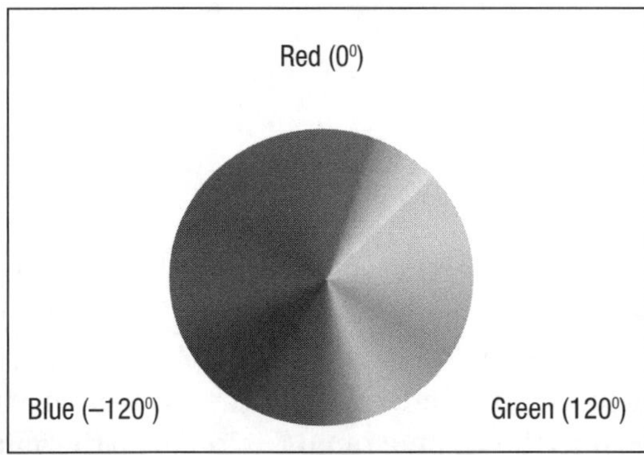

Figure 15.1 Illustration of hue.

Finally, the **DDCOLORCONTROL** structure contains members to adjust the sharpness (**lSharpness**) and the overall gamma correction (**lGamma**) of the image. Possible values for **lSharpness** range from 0 to 10. Possible values for **lGamma** range from 1 to 500.

Calling the **IDirectDrawColorControl::SetColorControls** method does not affect the data in the surface's frame buffer. Color settings are applied on the fly while the graphics card sends the color information to the monitor.

For more information about adjusting the color controls, see also "Setting the Color Controls" in the "Immediate Solutions" section.

Working with Gamma Controls

The DirectDraw surface object exposes one more interface that allows applications to change the appearance of the primary surface easily—the gamma control interface **IDirectDrawGammaControl**. Gamma controls operate with three lookup tables, called *gamma ramps*. The red, green, and blue intensities of the colors in the frame buffer are mapped to the values in these gamma ramps before the color information is sent to the monitor. For example, you could specify that a red intensity of 50 percent should be replaced with a red intensity of 25 percent. This would darken the red channel of all pixels with a red component of 50 percent. In the following sections, we'll discuss how gamma controls are used.

An Overview of Gamma Ramps

DirectDraw gamma controls manage one gamma ramp for each color component—i.e., one for the red channel, one for the green channel, and one for the blue channel. In DirectDraw, these gamma ramps are represented by **DDGAMMARAMP** structures. These structures are declared as follows:

```
typedef struct _DDGAMMARAMP {
    WORD red[256];
    WORD green[256];
    WORD blue[256];
} DDGAMMARAMP, FAR * LPDDGAMMARAMP;
```

As you can see, each gamma ramp is an array of 256 values of type **WORD**. These values correspond to the possible color intensities of the pixels. For example, **red[192]** contains the red intensity that should be used for all pixels with a red intensity of 192. Before a pixel is displayed, DirectDraw uses the intensities of the pixel's color components as indices into the gamma ramps. It looks up the values at these indices and replaces the color intensities with the new values that it retrieves from the gamma ramps.

Take a look at the linear gamma ramp in Figure 15.2. When this ramp is used for one of the color channels, nothing happens. An intensity of zero will be mapped to an intensity of zero. An intensity of 100 percent will be replaced with an intensity of 100 percent.

***NOTE:** Input intensities (the array indices of the values in the **DDGAMMARAMP** structure) range from 0 to 255. Output intensities (the values in the arrays in the **DDGAMMARAMP** structure) range from 0 to 65,535.*

By adjusting the gamma ramps, you can produce a number of interesting effects. The most common (but least interesting) use of gamma ramps is to adjust the brightness of the display. With gamma ramps, you can also adjust the contrast of an image, flash colors, or produce a negative image. In Figure 15.3, you can see three examples of gamma ramps.

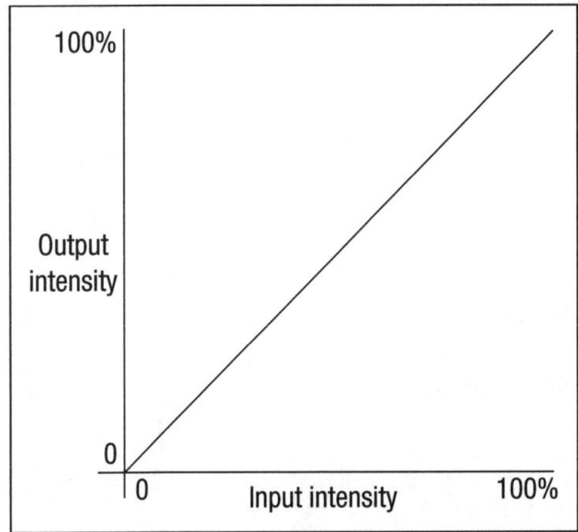

Figure 15.2 A linear gamma ramp.

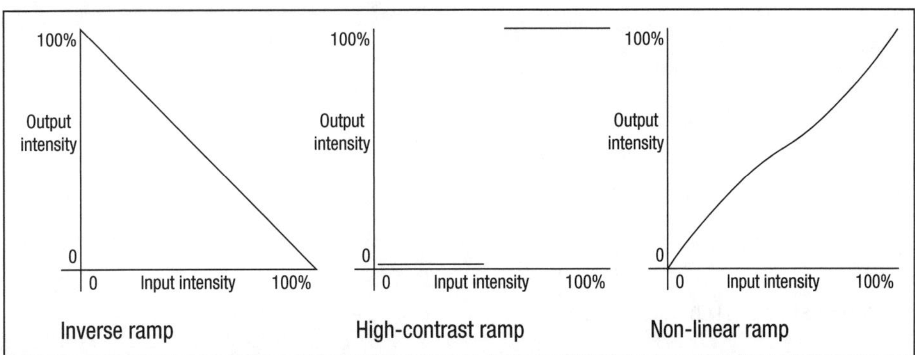

Figure 15.3 Gamma ramp examples.

In the left ramp, the color intensities are inverted. An intensity of 100 percent is mapped to an intensity of 0 percent and vice versa. When you use this gamma ramp for all three color channels, the screen is inverted. When you use the second ramp, the screen has the highest possible contrast. There are only two intensities—full or none. The third ramp demonstrates that you are not limited to linear ramps.

In the next two sections, we'll discuss how gamma controls are programmed.

Obtaining a Gamma Control Interface

Pointers to **IDirectDrawGammaControl** interfaces are obtained just like pointers to **IDirectDrawColorControl** interfaces—by calling the **QueryInterface** method of an **IDirectDrawSurface7** interface. The following example demonstrates this:

```
// lpDDSPrimary is assumed to be a valid pointer to
// the IDirectDrawSurface7 interface of the primary surface

LPDIRECTDRAWGAMMACONTROL lpDDGammaControl = NULL;

try
{
   if (FAILED(lpDDSPrimary->QueryInterface(
      IID_IDirectDrawGammaControl,
      reinterpret_cast<LPVOID*>(&lpDDGammaControl)
   )))
   {
      throw "Couldn't retrieve gamma control interface.";
   }

   /*
      set or query gamma ramps here
   */

   // release gamma control interface
   SAFERELEASE(lpDDGammaControl);

}
catch (...)
{
   SAFERELEASE(lpDDGammaControl);
}
```

***NOTE:** Only the primary surface exposes a gamma control interface.*

You can find out whether gamma controls are supported before you call the **QueryInterface** method. To do this, call the **IDirectDraw7::GetCaps** method as described in Chapter 11. The **GetCaps** method fills a **DDCAPS** structure with information about the capabilities of the device. If gamma controls are supported, the **dwCaps2** member of that structure contains the **DDCAPS2_PRIMARYGAMMA** flag. Just like color controls, gamma controls are not emulated by the DirectDraw HEL (hardware emulation layer) if the hardware does not support them.

Setting and Querying Gamma Ramps

Now that you have a pointer to an **IDirectDrawGammaControl** interface, you are free to adjust the red, green, and blue gamma ramps. The new ramp data is passed to the **SetGammaRamp** method in a **DDGAMMARAMP** structure. To map an intensity to a new value, take the intensity as an index into one of the member arrays of the structure. The new intensity is specified by the value of the array element at that index. Possible values range from 0 to 65,535.

The **GetGammaRamp** method is used to have DirectDraw fill a **DDGAMMARAMP** structure with the current ramp data. The following programming example demonstrates how you can use the **SetGammaRamp** method with the **GetGammaRamp** method to darken the screen:

```
// lpDDGammaControl is assumed to be a valid pointer to
// an IDirectDrawGammaControl interface

DDGAMMARAMP GammaRamps;

if (SUCCEEDED(lpDDGammaControl->GetGammaRamp(0, &GammaRamps)))
{
   // darken the screen by dividing the gamma values by 2
   WORD Gamma;
   for (int i = 0; i < 256; i++)
   {
      GammaRamps.red[i] = GammaRamps.red[i] >> 1;
      GammaRamps.green[i] = GammaRamps.green[i] >> 1;
      GammaRamps.blue[i] = GammaRamps.blue[i] >> 1;
   }

   // apply the new gamma ramps
   if (FAILED(lpDDGammaControl->SetGammaRamp(0, &GammaRamps)))
   {
      throw "Setting the gamma ramps failed.";
   }
}
```

```
else
{
   throw "Retrieving the gamma ramps failed.";
}
```

For detailed descriptions of the **GetGammaRamp** and **SetGammaRamp** methods, see the "Immediate Solutions" section.

Of course, gamma ramps can also be animated. See the companion CD-ROM for additional programming examples.

Immediate Solutions

Creating a Palette

You can use the **IDirectDraw7::CreatePalette** method to retrieve an **IDirectDrawPalette** interface pointer. The method is declared as follows:

```
HRESULT IDirectDraw7::CreatePalette(
   DWORD dwFlags,                              // palette options
   LPPALETTEENTRY lpDDColorArray,              // color table
   LPDIRECTDRAWPALETTE FAR *lplpDDPalette,     // interface pointer
   IUnknown FAR *pUnkOuter                     // reserved; must be NULL
);
```

The **dwFlags** parameter is typically set to **DDPCAPS_8BIT** to create a 256-color palette. By default, palette entries 0 and 255 of an 8-bit palette are reserved. You can combine the **DDPCAPS_8BIT** flag with the **DDPCAPS_ALLOW256** flag if you want to use these two entries as well. Other valid flags are **DDPCAPS_1BIT**, **DDPCAPS_2BIT**, and **DDPCAPS_4BIT**.

NOTE: *Obsolete flags and those used only with Direct3D are not listed here.*

The **lpDDColorArray** parameter is a pointer to an array of **PALETTEENTRY** structures. When the palette is created, it is automatically initialized with these entries. **PALETTEENTRY** structures are also used with the GDI (see Chapter 9). With DirectDraw palettes, the **peFlags** member can be set to one of the values listed in Table 15.1.

The **lplpDDPalette** parameter is a pointer to an **LPDIRECTDRAWPALETTE** variable that will receive the **IDirectDrawPalette** interface pointer. The last parameter, **pUnkOuter**, is reserved for future use and must be **NULL**.

For a programming example, see the next solution.

Related solution:	Found on page:
Creating a Palette	636

Table 15.1 Valid flags for the peFlags member of the PALETTEENTRY structure.

Flag	Meaning
PC_EXPLICIT	The palette entry is an index into the system palette. The index is stored in the **peRed** member. The other members are ignored. Typically, you'll use this flag in a windowed application for palette entries 0 through 9 and 246 through 255. See also "Setting Up a Palette for a Windowed Application."
PC_RESERVED	No other application is allowed to map its logical palette entries to this physical entry. This flag is used for palette entries that are going to be used for palette animation.
PC_NOCOLLAPSE	Use this flag for normal, non-animated palette entries.

Setting Up a Palette for a Windowed Application

This Immediate Solution demonstrates how to use the **IDirectDraw7::CreatePalette** method in a windowed application. The palette is initialized so that the first 10 and the last 10 entries are mapped to the corresponding entries of the system palette. Entries 10 through 25 are reserved for palette animation. Here's the code:


```
// lpDD is assumed to be a valid pointer to an IDirectDraw7 interface

PALETTEENTRY DDColorArray[256];

// map first 10 and last 10 entries to the system palette
int i;
for (i = 0; i < 10; i++)
{
   DDColorArray[i].peFlags = PC_EXPLICIT;
   DDColorArray[i].peRed = i;
   DDColorArray[i].peGreen = DDColorArray[i].peBlue = 0;

   DDColorArray[246 + i].peFlags = PC_EXPLICIT;
   DDColorArray[246 + i].peRed = i;
   DDColorArray[246 + i].peGreen = DDColorArray[246 + i].peBlue = 0;
}

// reserve entries 10 through 25 for palette animation (optional)
for (i = 10; i < 26; i++)
{
   DDColorArray[i].peFlags = PC_RESERVED;
```

```
    /*
       set peRed, peGreen, and peBlue to the desired values
    */
}

// the remaining entries are normal, non-animated entries
for (i = 26; i < 246; i++)
{
    DDColorArray[i].peFlags = PC_NOCOLLAPSE;
    /*
       set peRed, peGreen, and peBlue to the desired values
    */
}

// create the palette object
LPDIRECTDRAWPALETTE lpPalette = NULL;
if (SUCCEEDED(lpDD->CreatePalette(
    DDPCAPS_8BIT,
    DDColorArray,
    &lpPalette,
    NULL
)))
{
    /*
       the palette can be attached to the primary surface
    */
}
```

For a description of the **IDirectDraw7::CreatePalette** method, see "Creating a Palette."

Changing the Palette Entries

The entries of DirectDraw palettes can be modified dynamically. For this purpose, the **IDirectDrawPalette** interface provides the **SetEntries** method. The method is declared as follows:

```
HRESULT IDirectDrawPalette::SetEntries(
    DWORD dwFlags,              // unused; must be 0
    DWORD dwStartingEntry,      // first entry to be set
    DWORD dwCount,              // number of entries to be set
    LPPALETTEENTRY lpEntries    // new palette entries
   );
```

The **dwStartingEntry** parameter specifies the index of the first entry to be set. The number of entries is specified by the **dwCount** parameter. The **lpEntries** parameter is a pointer to an array of **PALETTEENTRY** structures containing the new color values. The first element of the array will be used for the palette entry at index **dwStartingEntry**. See the solution "Creating a Palette" for more information about the **PALETTEENTRY** structure.

The following programming example sets 10 palette entries starting at index 16:

```
// lpPalette is assumed to be a valid pointer to
// an IDirectDrawPalette interface

PALETTEENTRY NewEntries[10];
/*
   Set palette entries here.
*/

if (FAILED(lpPalette->SetEntries(0, 16, 10, NewEntries)))
{
   throw "Setting the palette entries failed.";
}
```

If the palette is currently attached to the primary surface, the changes become visible immediately.

***TIP:** When you use the **SetEntries** method in windowed mode to modify a subset of the palette entries, make sure to change only those entries that have the **PC_RESERVED** or **PC_NOCOLLAPSE** flags set.*

Querying the Palette Entries

The **IDirectDrawPalette::GetEntries** method fills an array of **PALETTEENTRY** structures with the current contents of the palette. The method is declared as follows:

```
HRESULT IDirectDrawPalette::GetEntries(
    DWORD dwFlags,              // unused; must be 0
    DWORD dwBase,               // first entry to be retrieved
    DWORD dwNumEntries,         // number of entries to be retrieved
    LPPALETTEENTRY lpEntries    // array to be filled with the entries
   );
```

The **dwBase** parameter specifies the index of the first entry to be retrieved. The number of entries is specified by the **dwNumEntries** parameter. The **lpEntries** parameter is a pointer to an array of **PALETTEENTRY** structures. This array will receive the retrieved palette entries when the method is successful.

The following code snippet demonstrates how to use the **GetEntries** method:

```
// lpPalette is assumed to be a valid pointer to
// an IDirectDrawPalette interface

PALETTEENTRY Entries[10];

if (FAILED(lpPalette->GetEntries(0, 16, 10, Entries)))
{
   throw "Querying the palette entries failed.";
}
```

Attaching a Palette to a Surface

You can attach a DirectDraw palette object to a DirectDraw surface by using the **IDirectDrawSurface7::SetPalette** method. For this method to succeed, the format of the palette must match the format of the surface. For example, a palette that was created with the **DDPCAPS_8BIT** flag can be attached only to a surface with a pixel format of **DDPF_PALETTEINDEXED8**. If a palette is attached to the primary surface, the display is updated immediately with the new colors.

Following is the prototype of the **SetPalette** method:

```
HRESULT IDirectDrawSurface7::SetPalette(
    LPDIRECTDRAWPALETTE lpDDPalette     // IDirectDrawPalette interface
   );
```

The **lpDDPalette** parameter points to the **IDirectDrawPalette** interface of the palette object. If the palette is not already attached to the surface, the palette object's reference count is incremented. If the parameter is **NULL**, the currently attached palette is detached and its reference count decremented.

Blending Between Palettes

In this solution, you can find the complete source code of the **BlendPalettes** function, which you can use in your own programs to blend between palettes. The function uses the following parameters:

- The **lpPalette** parameter is a pointer to the **IDirectDrawPalette** interface of the palette to be animated. The palette must be currently attached to the primary surface for the changes to be visible.
- The **StartIndex** and **NumEntries** parameters specify which entries should be animated.
- The **DestPal** parameter points to an array of **PALETTEENTRY** structures describing the destination palette. The array should contain as many elements as are specified by the **NumEntries** member.
- The **AnimationDuration** parameter specifies the length of the animation in milliseconds.

Here's the complete source code of the **BlendPalettes** function:

```
void BlendPalettes(
    LPDIRECTDRAWPALETTE lpPalette,   // palette to be animated; must be
                                     // attached to the primary surface
    LPPALETTEENTRY DestPal,          // destination palette
    BYTE StartIndex,                 // first entry to be animated
    BYTE NumEntries,                 // number of entries to animate
                                     // (array DestPal must be big enough)
    DWORD AnimationDuration          // length of animation in milliseconds
   )
{
try
{
   // save the current palette
   PALETTEENTRY SrcPal[256];
   lpPalette->GetEntries(0, StartIndex, NumEntries, SrcPal);

   PALETTEENTRY CurrentPal[256];    // working palette
   float Progress = 0.0f;
   DWORD StartTime = timeGetTime();

   while (Progress < 1.0f)
   {
      // calculate the palette for this time index
      for (int i = 0; i < NumEntries; i++)
      {
```

15. DirectDraw Colors and Palettes

```
            CurrentPal[i].peRed = SrcPal[i].peRed * (1.0f - Progress) +
               DestPal[i].peRed * Progress;
            CurrentPal[i].peGreen = SrcPal[i].peGreen * (1.0f - Progress) +
               DestPal[i].peGreen * Progress;
            CurrentPal[i].peBlue = SrcPal[i].peBlue * (1.0f - Progress) +
               DestPal[i].peBlue * Progress;
         }

         /*
            Optionally, you can wait for the vertical blank here.
         */

         // set the new palette entries
         lpPalette->SetEntries(
            0,                           // unused; must be 0
            StartIndex, NumEntries,
            CurrentPal                   // new colors
         );

         // update the Progress variable according to the system time
         Progress = 1.0f / AnimationDuration * (timeGetTime() - StartTime);
      }

   }
   catch (...)
   {
      throw "An exception occurred.";
   }
   }
```

WARNING! The application will not respond to Windows messages while the animation is in progress. You can change this behavior by inserting calls to the Windows functions PeekMessage and DispatchMessage within the while loop.

See also “Working with DirectDraw Palettes” in the “In Depth” section.

Obtaining a Pointer to an IDirectDrawColorControl Interface

The **IDirectDrawColorControl** interface is exposed by DirectDraw surface objects. You can use the **IDirectDrawSurface7::QueryInterface** method to retrieve an **IDirectDrawColorControl** interface pointer. The following code snippet demonstrates this:

```
// lpDDSurface is assumed to be a valid pointer to
// an IDirectDrawSurface7 interface

LPDIRECTDRAWCOLORCONTROL lpDDColorControl = NULL;
if (SUCCEEDED(lpDDSurface->QueryInterface(
   IID_IDirectDrawColorControl,
   reinterpret_cast<LPVOID*>(&lpDDColorControl)
)))
{
   /*
      lpDDColorControl can be used to change the appearance of the surface.
      Don't forget to release the interface when you don't need it anymore.
   */
}
```

NOTE: *The* ***IDirectDrawSurface7::QueryInterface*** *method is inherited from the* ***IUnknown*** *interface. See Chapter 11 for more information.*

The **QueryInterface** method will fail if color controls are not supported for the surface. You can use the **IDirectDraw7::GetCaps** method to query hardware support for color controls. If color controls are supported for the primary surface, the **dwCaps2** member of the **DDCAPS** structure contains the **DDCAPS2_COLORCONTROLPRIMARY** flag; if color controls are supported for the overlay surfaces, the **dwCaps2** member contains the **DDCAPS2_COLORCONTROLOVERLAY** flag.

Related solution:	Found on page:
Determining the Capabilities of the Video Hardware	638

Setting the Color Controls

The **IDirectDrawColorControl** interface exposes the **SetColorControls** method to adjust the color controls associated with a surface. The method is declared as follows:

```
HRESULT IDirectDrawColorControl::SetColorControls(
    LPDDCOLORCONTROL lpColorControl // pointer to DDCOLORCONTROL structure
   );
```

The **DDCOLORCONTROL** structure pointed to by the **lpColorControl** parameter contains the new color control settings. The structure is declared as follows:

```
typedef struct _DDCOLORCONTROL {
    DWORD   dwSize;
    DWORD   dwFlags;
    LONG    lBrightness;
    LONG    lContrast;
    LONG    lHue;
    LONG    lSaturation;
    LONG    lSharpness;
    LONG    lGamma;
    LONG    lColorEnable;
    DWORD   dwReserved1;
} DDCOLORCONTROL, FAR *LPDDCOLORCONTROL;
```

The following list describes the structure members in detail:

- **dwSize**—This member must be set to **sizeof(DDCOLORCONTROL)** before the structure is passed to one of the DirectDraw member functions.
- **dwFlags**—This bit field indicates which of the structure members are valid. Initialize **dwFlags** before passing the structure to the **SetColorControls** method, and don't read from invalid members when you're using the structure with the **GetColorControls** method. Table 15.2 lists the defined constants. These constants can be combined using a bitwise **OR**.
- **lBrightness**—This value specifies the brightness. Possible values range from 0 to 10,000. The brightness is given in IRE (International Radio Engineers) units times 100.
- **lContrast**—This value specifies the contrast. Possible values range from 0 to 20,000 (200 IRE). The contrast specifies the difference in brightness between darker and brighter colors.
- **lHue**—This value specifies the hue in degrees. Possible values range from –180 to 180. For additional information, see the "In Depth" section.

Table 15.2 Valid flags for the dwFlags member of the DDCOLORCONTROL structure.

Flag	Meaning
DDCOLOR_BRIGHTNESS	The **lBrightness** member is valid.
DDCOLOR_COLORENABLE	The **lColorEnable** member is valid.
DDCOLOR_CONTRAST	The **lContrast** member is valid.
DDCOLOR_GAMMA	The **lGamma** member is valid.
DDCOLOR_HUE	The **lHue** member is valid.
DDCOLOR_SATURATION	The **lSaturation** member is valid.
DDCOLOR_SHARPNESS	The **lSharpness** member is valid.

- **lSaturation**—This value specifies the color intensity. Possible values range from 0 to 20,000 (200 IRE). A saturation of zero results in a grayscale image.
- **lSharpness**—This value specifies the sharpness, ranging from 0 to 10.
- **lGamma**—This value controls the amount of gamma correction applied to the luminance values. Possible values range from 1 to 500.
- **lColorEnable**—If this flag is 1, color is used. If it is 0, color is not used.
- **dwReserved1**—Reserved.

See "Working with Color Controls" in the "In Depth" section for additional information about the meaning of the structure members.

The following programming example demonstrates how to set the brightness to an arbitrary value:

```
// lpDDColorControl is assumed to be a valid pointer to
// an IDirectDrawColorControl interface

// prepare a DDCOLORCONTROL structure
DDCOLORCONTROL ColorCtrl;
ZeroMemory(&ColorCtrl, sizeof(ColorCtrl));
ColorCtrl.dwSize = sizeof(ColorCtrl);
ColorCtrl.dwFlags = DDCOLOR_BRIGHTNESS;     // mark lBrightness as valid
ColorCtrl.lBrightness = 3000;               // set to 30 IRE units

// pass the structure to the color control
if (FAILED(lpDDColorControl->SetColorControls(&ColorCtrl)))
{
   throw "Setting the color controls failed.";
}
```


Querying the Color Controls

You can use the **IDirectDrawColorControl::GetColorControls** method to query the color controls associated with a surface. The method is declared as follows:

```
HRESULT IDirectDrawColorControl::GetColorControls(
    LPDDCOLORCONTROL lpColorControl // pointer to DDCOLORCONTROL structure
   );
```

The **DDCOLORCONTROL** structure pointed to by the **lpColorControl** parameter will receive the color control data. When the method returns, the **dwFlags** member of the structure indicates which controls are supported. See "Setting the Color Controls" for a detailed description of the **DDCOLORCONTROL** structure.

Obtaining a Pointer to an IDirectDrawGammaControl Interface

The **IDirectDrawGammaControl** interface is exposed by DirectDraw surface objects. You can use the **IDirectDrawSurface7::QueryInterface** method to retrieve an **IDirectDrawGammaControl** interface pointer. The following code snippet demonstrates this:

```
// lpDDSurface is assumed to be a valid pointer to
// the IDirectDrawSurface7 interface of the primary surface

LPDIRECTDRAWGAMMACONTROL lpDDGammaControl = NULL;
if (SUCCEEDED(lpDDSurface->QueryInterface(
   IID_IDirectDrawGammaControl,
   reinterpret_cast<LPVOID*>(&lpDDGammaControl)
)))
{
   /*
      lpDDGammaControl can be used to change the appearance of the surface.
      Don't forget to release the interface when you don't need it anymore.
   */
}
```

***NOTE:** The **IDirectDrawSurface7::QueryInterface** method is inherited from the **IUnknown** interface. See Chapter 11 for more information.*

The **QueryInterface** method will fail if gamma controls are not supported by the display device. You can use the **IDirectDraw7::GetCaps** method to find out whether gamma controls are supported. If they are, the **dwCaps2** member of the **DDCAPS** structure contains the **DDCAPS2_PRIMARYGAMMA** flag. See Chapter 11 for more information about querying device capabilities.

Setting the Gamma Ramps

You can use the **IDirectDrawGammaControl::SetGammaRamp** method to set the red, green, and blue gamma ramps of the primary surface. The method is declared as follows:

```
HRESULT IDirectDrawGammaControl::SetGammaRamp(
    DWORD dwFlags,              // option flags
    LPDDGAMMARAMP lpRampData    // new gamma ramps
   );
```

The **dwFlags** parameter can be zero or **DDSGR_CALIBRATE**. If the **DDSGR_-CALIBRATE** flag is specified, the gamma ramps are adjusted so that the results are identical on all display devices that support calibration. If calibration is not supported, the flag is ignored but the method succeeds. You can use the **IDirect-Draw7::GetCaps** method as described in Chapter 11 to query for calibration support.

The **lpRampData** parameter points to a **DDGAMMARAMP** structure. This structure is declared as follows:

```
typedef struct _DDGAMMARAMP {
    WORD red[256];
    WORD green[256];
    WORD blue[256];
} DDGAMMARAMP, FAR * LPDDGAMMARAMP;
```

The arrays **red**, **green**, and **blue** contain the values that color intensities should be replaced with before they are sent to the screen. For example, a red intensity of zero will be replaced with the value given in **red[0]**. Please note that the values range from 0 to 65,535 (not to 255).

Here's a usage example:

```
// lpDDGammaControl is assumed to be a valid pointer to
// an IDirectDrawGammaControl interface

DDGAMMARAMP GammaRamps;

// set up inverse gamma ramps (to produce a negative image)
WORD Gamma;
for (int i = 0; i < 256; i++)
{
   Gamma = 65535 - (i * 256);
   GammaRamps.red[i] = Gamma;
```

```
    GammaRamps.green[i] = Gamma;
    GammaRamps.blue[i] = Gamma;
}

// apply gamma ramps
if (FAILED(lpDDGammaControl->SetGammaRamp(0, &GammaRamps)))
{
    throw "Setting the gamma ramps failed.";
}
```

See “Working with Gamma Controls” in the “In Depth” section for more information about gamma ramps.

Querying the Gamma Ramps

You can use the **IDirectDrawGammaControl::GetGammaRamp** method to retrieve the gamma ramps for the primary surface. The method is declared as follows:

```
HRESULT IDirectDrawGammaControl::GetGammaRamp(
    DWORD  dwFlags,             // unused; must be 0
    LPDDGAMMARAMP lpRampData    // structure to receive gamma ramp data
   );
```

The **lpRampData** parameter is a pointer to a **DDGAMMARAMP** structure. This structure will be filled with the current gamma ramps when the method returns successfully.

The following code snippet demonstrates how to use the **GetGammaRamp** method:

```
// lpDDGammaControl is assumed to be a valid pointer to
// an IDirectDrawGammaControl interface

DDGAMMARAMP GammaRamps;

if (SUCCEEDED(lpDDGammaControl->GetGammaRamp(0, &GammaRamps)))
{
   /*
      The structure GammaRamps has been filled. See "Setting
      the Gamma Ramps" for information about how to interpret
      the structure.
   */
}
```

Part III

Image Support

Chapter 16

Image Color Management

In Depth

If you've ever studied modern art, you've probably seen, or at least heard of, Kasimir Malevich's famous 1918 painting, "White on White." The two predominant reactions to this painting are either: "It's a masterpiece!" or "You call that art?!" Whichever reaction you side with, the point is that art, like many perceived phenomena, is a *subjective* matter. Your opinion of Malevich's work is likely different from that of your colleagues. What is consistent, however, is the combination of physics and physiology that underlie the mechanisms of perception. Though your judgment of an image's aesthetic quality is yours alone, the way this image is transformed into neuronal impulses is inherent to all humans; this aspect is governed by the physics of light and the physiology of the *human visual system* (HVS).

The HVS has recently become a hot topic in many areas of computer graphics and image processing research. In fact, as we'll discuss in Chapter 18, most state-of-the-art image compression strategies rely on well-known HVS characteristics to achieve optimal compression ratios. Color-related research is particularly dependent on properties of the HVS. An understanding of how we see colors is vital when you're designing capture devices such as scanners and digital cameras, output devices such as monitors and printers, and even the output medium such as the paper on which an image is printed. Still, these devices are man-made contraptions that can only mimic *how* (HVS) and *what* (light reflected off a physical scene) we see in the physical world. Because different devices produce colors in different ways, you can't blindly assume than an image will look the same when it's displayed on different devices. With proper color management, however, this assumption is not out of the question.

This chapter is unlike any other chapter in this text simply because there's a great deal of background information to cover. Much of this information is on color science, but we'll also discuss a bit of physiology and, of course, math. Surprisingly, all of these fields work well together, at least in the context of color management. After the prerequisites are out of the way, we'll examine a brief history of image color management, and then we'll get right to work with some coding.

Colors and the HVS

Human vision is accomplished through the interaction of light and two types of photoreceptor cells in the retina: *rods* and *cones*. (These names come from the apparent shape of each type of cell.) The rods contribute mostly to our perception of an object's form and brightness, but contribute little to our perception of an object or any of its fine details. Rods are used in low-illumination conditions (which explains why we can't see fine details in the dark) and are responsible for our *scoptopic* or "night" vision. The cones, on the other hand, contribute mostly to our perception of detail and color. Cones are used in high-illumination conditions (in daylight, for example) and are responsible for our *photopic* or "day" vision.

The Trichromatic Theory of Color Vision

Even before the physiology of the eye or of its photoreceptor cells was known, researchers made claims about the mechanisms behind color vision. The *trichromatic theory* of color vision—first made famous by Thomas Young in the early 1800s, and later perfected by Hermann von Helmholtz in the mid-1800s—states that there are three types of receptors in the eye that are responsible for our perception of color. This theory was supported in the 1920s by the results of psychophysical (color-matching) experiments; it was indeed proved correct more than a century later.

Modern biomedical research has shown that there are three types of cones; each type is most sensitive to light of a particular wavelength. The "S" cones, which are most sensitive to *short* wavelengths of light, have a maximum sensitivity at about 440nm (nanometers). The "M" cones, which are most sensitive to *medium* wavelengths of light, have a maximum sensitivity at about 535nm. The "L" cones, which are most sensitive to *long* wavelengths of light, have a maximum sensitivity at about 565nm. Figure 16.1 illustrates the normalized (i.e., scaled) sensitivity of each type of cone.

The fact that there are three types of cones not only governs how we *see* different colors, but also plays a part in how we *describe* different colors. If you think about it, there are very few unique names for colors. Most languages have names for black, white, red, green, blue, brown, and so on, but imagine trying to describe every single color in a photograph by using only a small set of unique color names. You'll probably end up using combined names such as "bluish-green" or reference names such as "sky blue." Of course, you can't simply instruct a printer to print the color "sky blue." Even if this were possible, the color of the sky varies greatly. It's situations like this in which a *color space* (sometimes called a *color model*) proves invaluable. Because there are three types of cones, a color space usually has three dimensions.

Three-Dimensional Color Spaces

In Chapter 10, we discussed the notion of a two-dimensional coordinate space. Recall, the main advantage of such a system is that you can describe the location of an object within the space by using exactly two coordinates (usually an "x" and

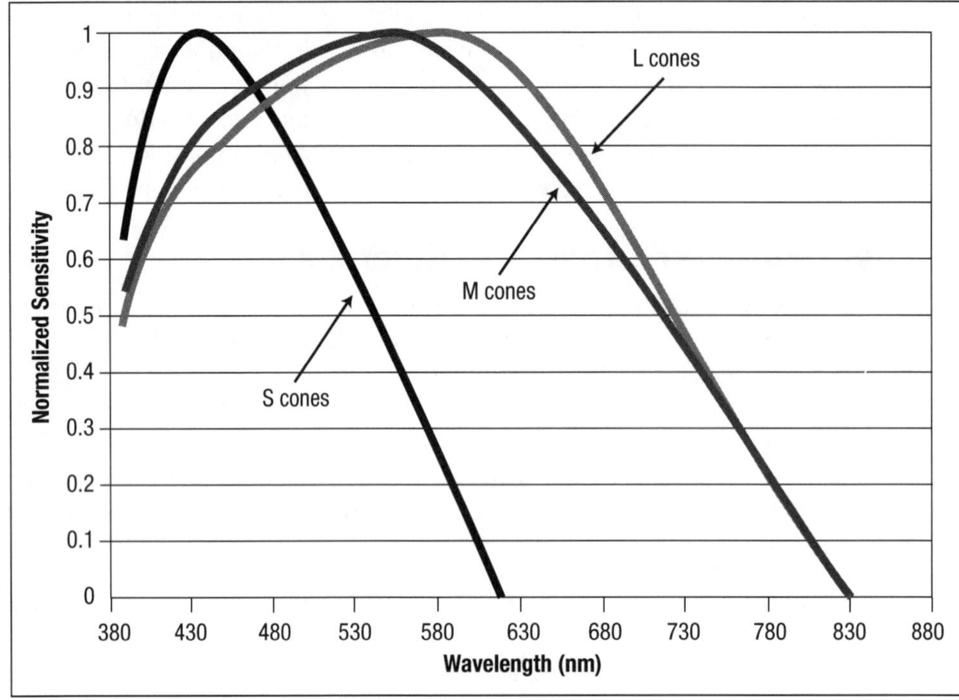

Figure 16.1 The normalized sensitivities of the S, M, and L cones to different wavelengths of light.

a "y" coordinate). The idea behind a color space is similar—to describe a particular color, you simply indicate its location within the color space. In contrast to a two-dimensional coordinate space, however, most color spaces are defined in three dimensions. Indeed, the trichromatic theory of color vision lends support to the notion that you can describe any color that can be perceived (by humans) by using only three dimensions (coordinate-space axes) or *primaries* (primary colors).

The RGB Color Space

We're all familiar with the *RGB* color space, in which the three primary colors are red, green, and blue. When graphed, this three-dimensional color space takes the form of a cube in which each axis ranges from 0 to 1 (normalized). Figure 16.2 depicts the RGB color space.

The RGB color space is based on the idea that colors mix *additively*. That is, an equal mixture of the three primaries produces white; and in the absence of color, you have black. In Figure 16.2, the point (0, 0, 0) corresponds to black—the absence of color. Likewise, the point (1, 1, 1) corresponds to white—an equal mixture of red, green, and blue. The line that connects these two points is called the

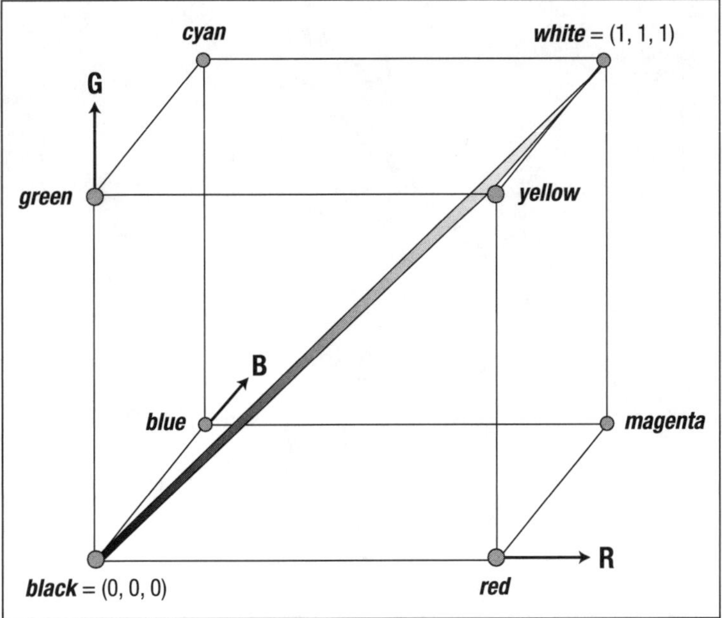

Figure 16.2 The RGB color space.

neutral axis or the *gray axis*. Most monitors use the RGB color space because in the absence of color, the background (i.e., a blank screen) is black.

You'll often see diagrams similar to Figure 16.2 in which the cube is colored. Although this may help you visualize the space, these colors have little bearing on the actual color that will be represented on a device. This is one of the main problems with the RGB color space—it's device-dependent. More precisely, it's *primary-dependent*. For example, the color of the point (R, G, B) = (1, 0, 0) depends on the definition of the red primary. One device might represent red using a combination of wavelengths in the 680nm range, while another device might use a combination of wavelengths in the 700nm range. In other words, there's an inherent variability in how different devices represent the red primary; the same argument applies for the green and blue primaries.

The CMY Color Space

The CMY color space is another three-dimensional color space; in this one, the three primary colors are cyan, magenta, and yellow. Figure 16.3 depicts the CMY color space.

Unlike the RGB color space, the CMY color space is based on a *subtractive* color system in which an equal mixture of all three primaries produces black, and the absence of color produces white. It's not surprising that many printers use the CMY color space—most often, the output medium itself is white. To produce black,

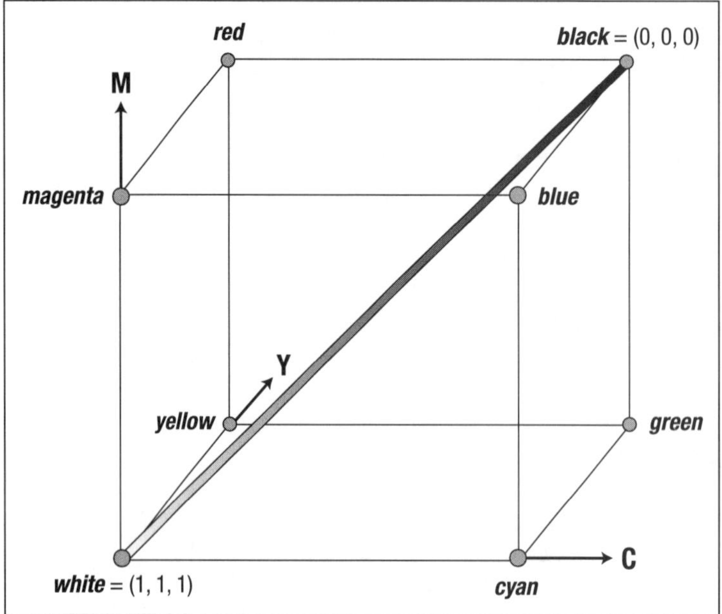

Figure 16.3 The CMY color space.

a CMY printer combines pure cyan, pure magenta, and pure yellow. Because colored inks are often more expensive than black ink, however, most modern ink jet printers use black as a fourth primary color; these types of printers are sometimes called CMYK printers, where the letter K denotes black. (K is used instead of B to avoid confusion with blue from the RGB color space.)

As with the RGB color space, the CMY(K) color space is device-dependent. There's an inconsistency in how different devices represent cyan, magenta, and yellow. With printers, there's another degree of variability imposed by the output medium. Different types of papers possess different color-handling capabilities.

Clearly, describing a color isn't a straightforward process. Though specifying a three-dimensional coordinate rather than a reference name is a bit more accurate, we still have this device-dependence factor at play. In a sense, an RGB or CMY color coordinate is also merely a reference—in this case, a color is described in reference to the primaries of a specific device. In other words, instead of using the reference name "sky blue," we're now using the reference coordinate "my monitor's RGB (0.62, 0.77, 1.00)" or "my printer's CMY (0.38, 0.23, 0.00)." Fortunately, there's an alternative, device-independent way to describe a color; the Commission Internationale de l'Éclairage (CIE) has introduced several device-independent color spaces that are based on the results of psychophysical experiments.

The 1931 CIEXYZ and 1976 CIELAB Color Space

The CIEXYZ color space is based on the results of color-matching experiments that were performed in the 1920s by John Guild and W.D. Wright. I won't go into the details here of how to derive this color space, but you can see Appendix B for some references. The main thing to note is that the CIEXYZ color space isn't based on perceptually realizable primary colors such as red, green, and blue, or cyan, magenta, and yellow; instead this color space is based on "imaginary" primaries (axes) denoted by the boldface letters **X**, **Y**, and **Z**. Values along the Y-axis correspond to luminance (i.e., perceived brightness). With these new primary "colors," the CIEXYZ color space takes the form not of a cube but of a slanted and slightly rounded cone that's flat on one side. Coordinates within this space are called *tristimulus values* and are denoted by the italicized letters X, Y, and Z.

Specifying a color as a location within an oddly shaped cone isn't very convenient (or intuitive). Instead, the cone is projected onto a two-dimensional (x, y)-plane, where x and y are computed as follows:

$$x = X / (X + Y + Z)$$

$$y = Y / (X + Y + Z)$$

$$z = Z / (X + Y + Z)$$

$$x + y + z = 1$$

The result of this projection, called an (x, y)-chromaticity diagram, is depicted in Figure 16.4. Because the CIE (x, y)-chromaticity diagram is only a two-dimensional projection of a three-dimensional space, in addition to specifying an x- and a y-coordinate, you also need to specify a *luminance value* (i.e., the y-coordinate), or a *white point* (i.e., another chromaticity coordinate pair that denotes the position of the (x, y) = plane within the CIEXYZ space). The line that bounds the projection is called the *spectral locus*—we can't perceive any colors outside this line.

NOTE: *A white point is usually specified in reference to a standard light source (called a standard illuminant). Two common standard illuminants are D50, which denotes that the light source is a tungsten lamp, and D65, which denotes that the light source is daylight. Each of these white points has a corresponding (x, y) pair that's used to denote the whitest white in the associated (x, y)-plane.*

Although the CIEXYZ color space is a truly device-independent model, it still suffers from the fact that it's not "perceptually uniform." I'll punt the specifics of this color space to the color-related references listed in Appendix B; just keep in mind that moving some arbitrary distance in the XYZ color space doesn't produce the same relative change in the perceived color. It's just like the power specification of a light bulb—a 100-watt bulb is not perceived as being twice as bright as a 50-watt bulb.

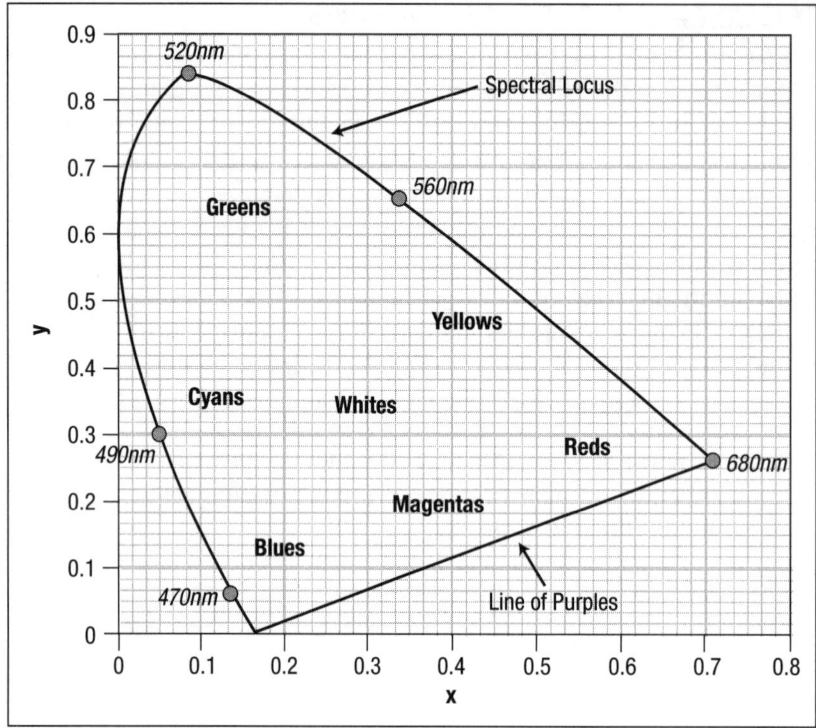

Figure 16.4 The 1931 CIEXYZ (x, y)-chromaticity diagram.

To transform the CIEXYZ color space into a more perceptually homogeneous form, the CIE created the CIELAB color space. I'll save the specifics of this color space for Appendix B; for now, just keep in mind that CIELAB is another device-independent color space that differs from CIEXYZ mainly in that it has perceptually uniform units.

If the CIEXYZ and CIELAB color spaces are device-independent, why are most images stored in RGB coordinates? The simple answer is that it's more efficient to code RGB values; remember, x- and y-coordinates (from the CIEXYZ space) are both floating-point numbers. Plus, RGB is a bit more intuitive to work with, and what's more important, most monitors, scanners, and digital cameras use the RGB color space. Recall from our discussion of the RGB color space that the main problem with specifying a color in terms of red, green, and blue intensities is that not all devices conform to a standard definition of the red, green, and blue primaries. Because most television sets conform to a specific standard, there should be a similar protocol for computer monitors. Well, the folks at Microsoft and Hewlett-Packard decided to take the initiative and propose such a standard; the result is what's known as the *sRGB* or *standard RGB* color space.

The sRGB Color Space

The sRGB color space is identical to the generic RGB color space except that the primary colors (red, green, and blue) are defined. Specifically, these colors—which are provided as a set of chromaticity coordinates and a white point—are identical to the reference primaries that are defined in the HDTV (high-definition television) standard (ITU-R BT.709). These coordinates are listed in Table 16.1.

Is the sRGB the fix-all for the color variations that exist among different devices? Well, no, of course not. What it does do, however, is statistically increase your chances of viewing an image in its true (intended) colors. Remember, the sRGB model makes many assumptions (e.g., a particular white point; particular chromaticity coordinates). These values are supposed to represent those of the "average" device. And, as it turns out, most devices come pretty close; on a calibrated sRGB device, these colors should be as intended (i.e., accurate). Still, the sRGB color space is no substitute for an integrated system that can deal with color variations. As we'll discuss next, a *color management system* is vital for displaying accurate colors.

Color Management Systems

The goal of a color management system (CMS) is to provide an accurate display of colors on any output device. For example, say that your cousin emails you a picture of his or her puppy. You decide to print this picture using your new, color ink jet printer. You adjust the colors of the image (using your favorite image manipulation software) so that it looks pretty good on the screen. Unfortunately, when you print the image, even using the expensive photographic-quality paper, you find that the colors are a bit off—the puppy appears to have green fur! What happened? Remember, most monitors use the RGB color space, whereas most ink jet printers use the CMYK color space. Both of these are device-dependent spaces, and without the knowledge of the actual chromaticity coordinates of the primaries and the white points of both the monitor and the printer, there's bound to be some colors that will be converted inaccurately. It's situations like this that a CMS is designed to solve. Macs use a CMS called ColorSync; Solaris workstations use a CMS called KCMS (Kodak Color Management System); Windows machines use a CMS called ICM (Image Color Management).

Table 16.1 The chromaticity coordinates for the sRGB model.

Primary	x	y
Red	0.6400	0.3300
Green	0.3000	0.1000
Blue	0.1500	0.0600
White (D65)	0.3127	0.3291

An Overview of ICM

ICM version 1 was Microsoft's first attempt at integrating a color management system into Windows (namely Windows 95; ICM isn't available in Windows NT). The basic idea was simple: Device manufacturers supply a special file known as an *ICC* (International Color Consortium) *device profile*, which usually has the extension .icm and which provides the CMS with information that's specific to the device. With this information, the CMS can accurately convert color values from, for example, a monitor's RGB color space to, for example, a printer's CMYK color space. In this way, you know that what you see on the screen will be as close as possible (color-wise) to what will be printed (within the capabilities of the output device and medium).

In fact, ICC device profiles caught on very rapidly; many device manufacturers began to ship model-specific ICM files. The only problem with this scheme is that device profiles are, of course, device-dependent. This means that the colors you see on one system's monitor (or printed page) will likely be different from the colors you see on another system's monitor (or printed page). When someone emails you a bitmap, for example, there's no way to know if the colors displayed on your monitor are the same as those displayed on the sender's monitor. Who knows—your cousin's puppy may very well have green fur!

The problem with most images is that the pixels are usually specified as device-dependent RGB values. There are only two ways to convey the actual colors: either use a device-independent color space, or provide a device profile with the image. In fact, many image file formats allow device profiles to be embedded. Neither of these solutions, however, is well suited for low-bandwidth transmissions. Device profiles themselves aren't very large, but for smaller images, this data (typically on the order of 1K) can contribute to a large portion of the overall file size. We all know how slowly some Web pages load (regardless of the speed of your Internet connection). Who wants to wait an extra 30 seconds just to see a dancing monkey and a boxing glove appear in their "true" colors?

Another major drawback of ICM 1, from a development standpoint, is that most of the color management functions require a handle to a device context. This so-called within device context scheme prevents the use of a color management function without the intervention of a DC. Moreover, ICM 1 provides very few functions for working with device profiles, and there's no user interface support. For these reasons, ICM 1 never really caught on with application developers, so very few applications used ICM. In short, ICM 1 wasn't very successful—it's the CMS equivalent of a LaserDisc player.

ICM version 2 is Microsoft's latest color management system, and it's available in Windows 98, Windows ME, and Windows 2000. This new version removes many of the limitations of its predecessor. ICM 2 offers support for a wider variety of color spaces, some user interface features, and a whole slew of functions that can be used without a device context (i.e., "outside device context").

As with version 1, ICM 2 relies on ICC device profiles. Again, a device profile serves as a crucial link between the CMS and a specific device (whether it's the output device or the device on which the source image was created or captured). In fact, if a device profile isn't present, ICM 2 assumes that the color coordinates of the image or of the output device (or both, if necessary) lie in the sRGB color space. Let's take a closer look at what a color matching strategy entails.

The Color Matching Process

I pointed out earlier that different types of devices use different color spaces. When you send an RGB image to a printer, for example, the printer driver must transform RGB coordinates to CMY(K) coordinates. This color-space transformation is the first step in any color matching process. The second step involves a color gamut mapping. Let's take a closer look at each of these steps.

Color-Space Transformations

We first discussed coordinate-space transformations in Chapter 10. Recall, a coordinate-space transformation is simply a mapping of points from one coordinate space to another. Well, a color-space transformation is no different. Instead of altering axes (e.g., flipping rulers over) as we did in Chapter 10, to perform a color-space transformation, you simply change the primary colors. And, as with coordinate-space transformations, most color-space transformations are performed using 3-by-3 matrices. For example, to convert from CIEXYZ coordinates to ITU-R BT.709 RGB coordinates for HDTV, you'd perform the following (for a D65 white point):

$$\begin{bmatrix} R_{(709)} \\ G_{(709)} \\ B_{(709)} \end{bmatrix} = \begin{bmatrix} 3.240 & -1.537 & -0.499 \\ -0.969 & 1.876 & 0.042 \\ 0.056 & -0.204 & 1.057 \end{bmatrix} \begin{bmatrix} X \\ Y \\ Z \end{bmatrix}$$

Similarly, to convert from sRGB coordinates to CIEXYZ coordinates, you'd use the following formulation (for a D50 white point):

$$\begin{bmatrix} X \\ Y \\ Z \end{bmatrix} = \begin{bmatrix} 0.436 & 0.358 & 0.181 \\ 0.223 & 0.715 & 0.072 \\ 0.019 & 0.119 & 0.951 \end{bmatrix} \begin{bmatrix} R_{(sRGB)} \\ G_{(sRGB)} \\ B_{(sRGB)} \end{bmatrix}$$

Note that both the XYZ-to-BT.709-RGB conversion matrix and the sRGB-to-XYZ conversion matrix are special cases in which the RGB color space can work in a device-independent fashion. In general, the matrix to convert from an arbitrary monitor's RGB space to another color space is unknown; such information must be provided through a device profile. (This is exactly why a color management system is needed.)

Color Gamut Mapping and Rendering Intents

A color gamut is nothing more than a range of colors. For example, the color gamut of an image is the range of colors that it possesses. The color gamut of the HVS is the range of colors that we can see, usually wavelengths of light between 380 and 750nm. The color gamuts of monitors and printers are usually much less. Figure 16.5 illustrates the color gamut that's defined by the standard STMPE (Society of Motion Picture & Television Engineers) chromaticity coordinates.

When you instruct a device to display a color that it can't produce, the device has to substitute this color with one that it can produce. This process of "color substitution" is called *color gamut mapping*—any color that falls outside the gamut of a device is mapped to the next best color that the device can produce (i.e., a color that's within the device's color gamut). This scheme is depicted in Figure 16.6.

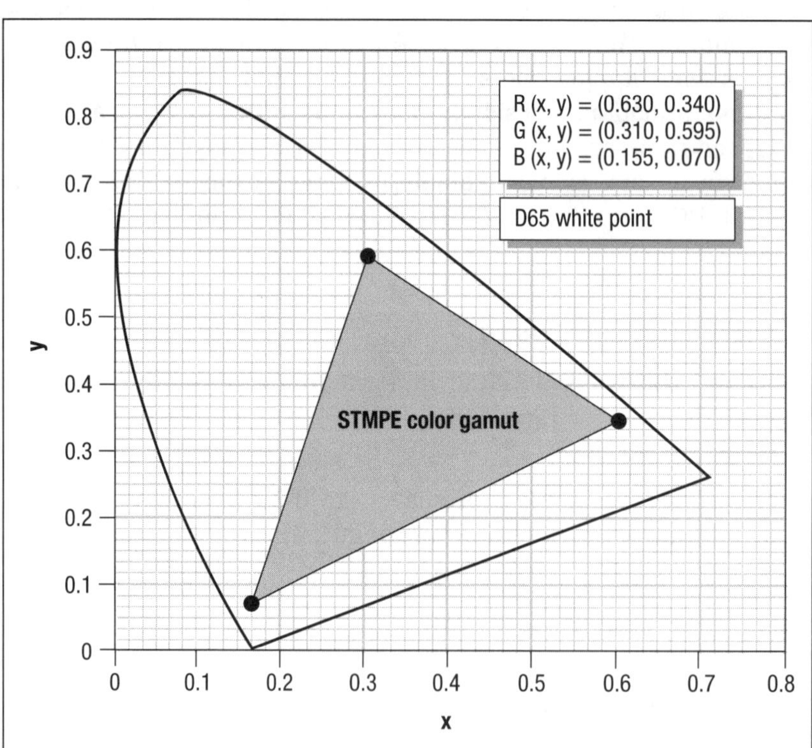

Figure 16.5 The STMPE color gamut is the area inside the triangle.

16. Image Color Management

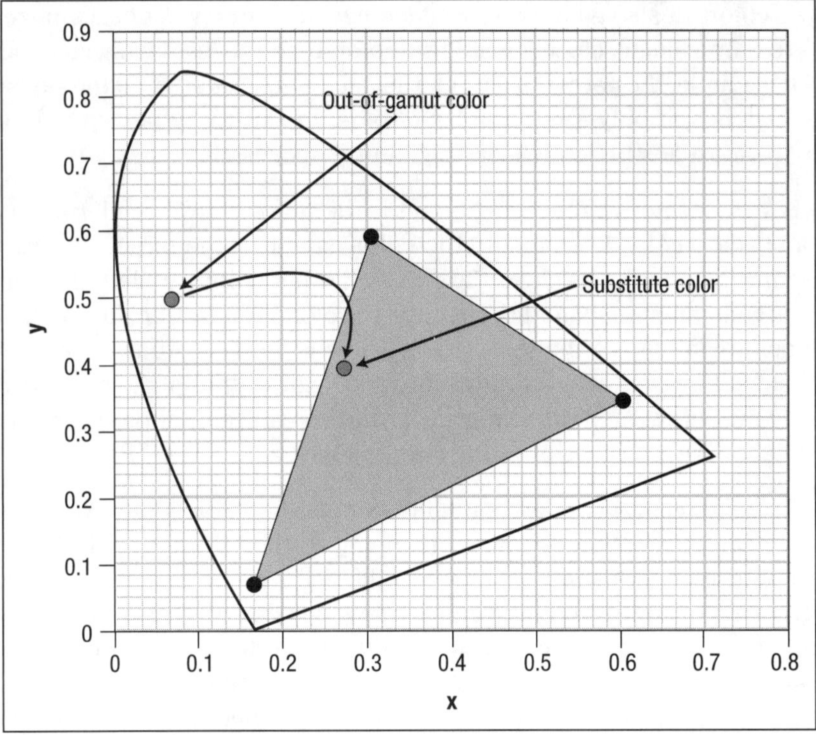

Figure 16.6 Color gamut mapping—when a color lies outside the color gamut of a device, the color must be mapped to a point inside the gamut.

Color gamut mapping is easier said than done. The biggest question is, how do we choose the "next best color"? This problem has been researched for years—CIE has its own technical committee (TC8-03) on gamut mapping. The general consensus is that the next best color depends on the color's context—that is, on the *type of image* that's being represented. This leads to the notion of a *rendering intent*, which specifies the type of information that the color "intends" to convey. In this way, an image's author can specify a rendering intent, which is later used by a CMS to govern the type of color-gamut-mapping strategy that's used. The latest ICC color profile specification (ICC.1:1998-09) defines four rendering intents: *perceptual*, *absolute colorimetric*, *relative colorimetric*, and *saturation*. (For your convenience, Specification ICC.1:1998-09 is included on the companion CD-ROM; see page 34 of that document for the rendering intents.)

The *perceptual* rendering intent is used mostly for displaying natural images, such as photographs. In this case, if a specific color lies outside the color gamut of the target device, *all* of the image's colors are adjusted so that the color gamut of the image fits within the color gamut of the device. Although the gamut mapping method that's used for the perceptual rendering intent results in a shift of all of the image's colors, it also guarantees that a range of colors won't be quantized or "clipped" to only a single, closest matching color. If you're displaying an image of the sky, for example, the perceptual rendering intent guarantees that the sky won't appear as patches of only a few shades of blue. In short, the perceptual intent produces the most aesthetically pleasing natural images.

The *absolute colorimetric* rendering intent is the "poor man's" rendering intent. Here, if a specific color lies outside the color gamut of the target device, that color is simply mapped to its closest match—all other colors are left unchanged. Clearly, this gamut mapping method is prone to color quantization, in which more than one color can map to the same color. The absolute colorimetric rendering intent is useful, however, when you want to proof the output of a device without considering the output medium (e.g., paper) and viewing conditions (namely, the source of light). We'll discuss proofing later in this chapter (see "Proofing").

The *relative colorimetric* rendering intent is similar to the absolute colorimetric rendering intent, except that the gamut mapping method that's used for the relative colorimetric rendering intent preserves the white point. Specifically, when a specific color lies outside the color gamut of the target device, that color is mapped to its closest match; in addition, the whitest white in the image is scaled to the whitest white that the target device can produce (i.e., the whitest white in the target device's color gamut) and all other colors are scaled *relative* to this (new) white point. The relative colorimetric rendering intent also suffers from quantization, but this method is useful when you want the output medium and light source taken into account during proofing. Again, we'll discuss proofing later in this chapter (see "Proofing").

The *saturation* rendering intent is used when what needs to be preserved is the *contrast between colors* (rather than a range of perceptually similar colors). For example, if you're displaying an image that contains pale-blue text on a deep-blue background, the most important feature to preserve is the visibility of the text, not its exact color. The gamut mapping method that's used for the saturation rendering intent guarantees that the color of the background is not mapped to a less-saturated blue that might mask the pale-blue text; instead, the deep-blue background will perhaps map to a deep purple. The saturation rendering intent is used mainly for images that convey data (e.g., a chart), rather than scenes.

The Profile Connection Space

A profile connection space (PCS) serves as an intermediate, device-independent color space that connects the color spaces of two devices. The actual transformation of color coordinates and gamut mapping is performed by a *color management module* (CMM). This scheme is depicted in Figure 16.7.

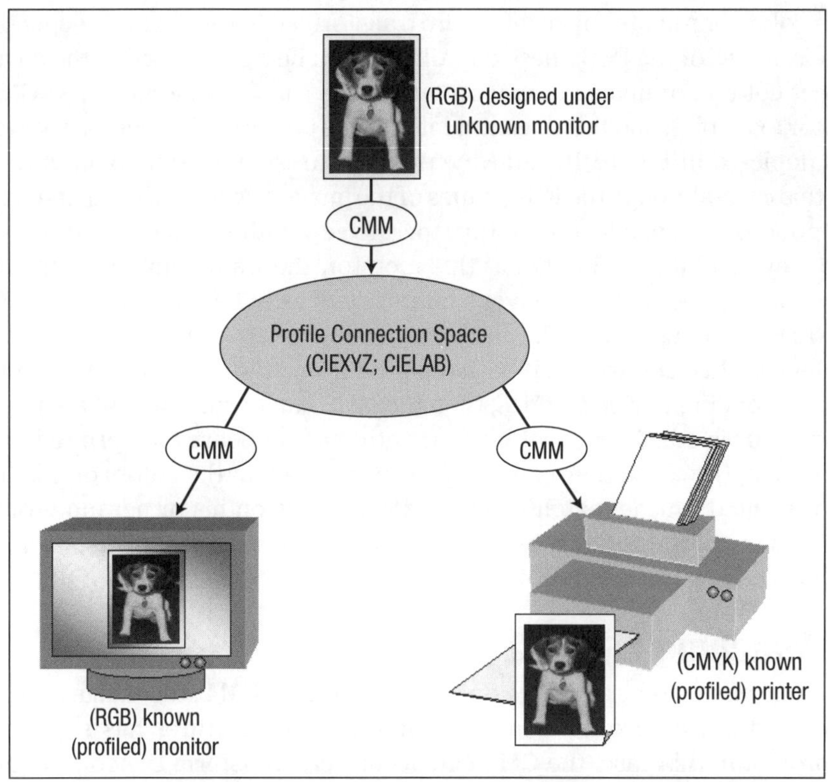

Figure 16.7 The PCS serves as the intermediate (device-independent) color space; all other (device-dependent) color spaces are translated to and from this space via a CMM.

Often, you'll see CMM more accurately referred to as a *color management method* or a *color matching method*. The interpretation, however, is more or less the same—a CMM is responsible for converting device-dependent coordinates to (and from) the coordinates of the PCS (profile connection space) by using information in a device profile. Whether these device-dependent coordinates are transformed to CIEXYZ or CIELAB is up to the device profile. The CMM must be able to convert to both.

CMMs can be supplied by device manufacturers, or the conversion can be delegated to the default CMM. ICM 2 uses the LimoColor CMM as its default. (ICM 1 used a proprietary Kodak-based color matching method to convert between color spaces.) In fact, LimoColor technology, developed by the German company Heidelberg CPS, has been used by ColorSync (on Macs) for many years. (Windows is clearly behind when it comes to color management.)

After the color coordinates of an image are transformed to the device-independent color coordinates of the PCS, these coordinates can be transformed to the device-dependent color coordinates of any output device (an RGB monitor or a CMYK printer, for example), and then a gamut mapping is performed, if necessary. However, as depicted in Figure 16.7, device profiles are seldom embedded into images. In this case, although the RGB values of the image might have been fine-tuned to look good on the sender's monitor (the image's author), because the image itself conveys no information about this monitor, there's no guarantee that the image will look good on the receiver's output devices. What is guaranteed, however, is that this image will look *consistent* among any of the receiver's profiled output devices. In other words, if both the printer and the monitor of Figure 16.7 have corresponding device profiles, then the CMS can ensure that what appears on the monitor is consistent (color-wise) with what appears on a printed page, and vice versa. However, there's no way to guarantee that the colors of this (displayed or printed) image match what the sender sees on his or her monitor (or printer). This is, perhaps, the most common situation when you're displaying an image that's created on another machine.

Color Matching in ICM 2

Ideally, when you display an image on a monitor using ICM 2, the image contains an embedded device profile, and the monitor's manufacturer has supplied a device profile. In this case, the CMS can accurately transform the color coordinates of the image to PCS device-independent coordinates (using the embedded profile), and then accurately transform these device-independent coordinates to device-dependent coordinates of the monitor (using the monitor's profile). The same argument applies when the image is to be printed. However, what happens when the image has no profile? What happens when the output device (e.g., a monitor or printer) has no profile?

- When *neither* the source image nor the destination device has a device profile, the CMS assumes that the color coordinates of the image and the destination device are both in the sRGB color space.
- When the *source image* has a device profile, but the destination device doesn't, the CMS uses the device profile of the image and assumes the sRGB color space for the destination device.
- When the source image doesn't have a device profile, but the *destination device* does, the CMS assumes that the color coordinates of the image are in the sRGB color space, and it uses the device profile of the destination device.
- When *both* the source image and the destination device have a device profile, the CMS uses the device profile of the image and the device profile of the destination device.

Clearly, with all these assumptions, the accuracy of the conversions can vary. Although Microsoft, Hewlett-Packard, and the World Wide Web Consortium are all encouraging the standardization of the sRGB color space, at this point its use is scattered, at best. This may change in the near future, but for the time being, let's gauge what the image will look like under different scenarios (adapted from the sRGB technical specifications IEC/3WD 61966-2.1).

Scenario 1: The Destination Device Doesn't Have an ICC Device Profile

As I pointed out earlier, support of device profiles was, perhaps, the best thing that came out of ICM 1. Still, many output devices were created before the advent of ICM, and worse yet, many end users fail to install a device profile even if one is provided. What will the image look like when the output device has no corresponding device profile?

If the source image has an embedded device profile, then the transformation from the image's device-dependent coordinates to device-independent PCS coordinates can be carried out according to the information in the image's device profile. This transformation will be accurate. There's no guarantee, however, that this image will look correct (color-wise) when it's displayed on the output device. Although the CMS knows the color space of the image's colors, it does not know the color space of the output device. In this case, the CMS assumes that the output device uses the sRGB color space:

- If the destination device uses the sRGB color space, then the colors of the image will look accurate.
- If the destination device doesn't use the sRGB color space, then the accuracy of the displayed image's colors will vary according to how closely the output device conforms to the sRGB standard.

If the source image doesn't have an embedded profile, but its color values are in sRGB coordinates, then the transformation from the image's sRGB coordinates to device-independent PCS coordinates will be accurate. But again, because the output device doesn't have a corresponding device profile, there's no guarantee that the colors of this image will look correct when displayed on the output device. The CMS will simply assume that the output device uses the sRGB color space:

- If the destination device uses the sRGB color space, then the colors of the image will look accurate.
- If the destination device doesn't use the sRGB color space, then the accuracy of the displayed image's colors will vary according to how closely the output device conforms to the sRGB standard.

If the source image doesn't have an embedded profile, and its color values aren't in sRGB coordinates, then the CMS will assume the sRGB color space for the image. In this case, the accuracy of the transformation from the image's device-dependent coordinates to device-independent PCS coordinates will vary according to how closely the image's colors conform to the sRGB standard. (Often the accuracy depends on how closely the device on which the image was created or captured conforms to the sRGB standard.) Moreover, there's no guarantee that this image will look correct (color-wise) when it's displayed on the output device. As before, the CMS will just assume that the output device uses the sRGB color space:

- If the destination device uses the sRGB color space, then the accuracy of the displayed image's colors will vary according to how closely the original image's colors conform to the sRGB standard.
- If the destination device doesn't use the sRGB color space, then the accuracy of the displayed image's colors will vary in two ways. The colors will vary according to how closely the output device conforms to the sRGB standard and according to how closely the source image's colors conform to the sRGB standard.

Scenario 2: The Destination Device Has an ICC Device Profile

If the destination device has a corresponding device profile (and it's installed), then the CMS will not assume the sRGB color space for the device. Instead, the CMS will use the information in the output device's profile to accurately transform device-independent PCS coordinates to device-dependent coordinates. Now the only possible limiting factor is the image itself.

If the source image has an embedded device profile, then the transformation from the image's device-dependent coordinates to device-independent PCS coordinates can be carried out according to the information in the image's device profile. This transformation will be accurate. In addition, the colors of the image will be accurate when the image is displayed on the output device because the transformation from device-independent PCS coordinates to device-dependent coordinates is performed according to the output device's device profile.

If the source image doesn't have an embedded profile, but its color values are in sRGB coordinates, then the transformation from the image's sRGB coordinates to device-independent PCS coordinates will be accurate. Also, the colors of this image will look correct when displayed on the output device because the CMS can accurately transform device-independent PCS coordinates to device-dependent coordinates by using the information in the output device's profile.

If the source image doesn't have an embedded profile, and its color values aren't in sRGB coordinates, then the CMS will assume the sRGB color space for the image. The accuracy of the transformation from the image's device-dependent coordinates to device-independent PCS coordinates will vary according to how closely the image's colors conform to the sRGB standard. When displayed, the colors of the image might not look correct, but they will at least be consistent when the image is displayed on different profiled devices.

Summary of Color Management Systems

There's a lot of information to absorb in this chapter, so before we get our hands dirty with coding, let's recap some of the main concepts from this section. Recall, because different devices have different operating characteristics (e.g., gamut, white point, colorants), a *color management system* (CMS) is needed to ensure that colors will be displayed accurately regardless of the output device. In Windows, this CMS is called *ICM* (Image Color Management). The newest version of ICM, version 2, is available only in Windows 98, Windows ME, and Windows 2000.

Device manufacturers convey the particulars of their devices through an ICC *device profile*, which is often model-specific. Images can also contain a device profile—usually one that's specific to the monitor on which the image was created or to the input device (e.g., a scanner or a digital camera) with which the image was captured.

Using information in the image's device profile, the CMS uses a *color management module* (CMM, or *color management method*, or *color matching method*) to convert the image's device-dependent coordinates (color values) to the device-independent coordinates of the *profile connection space* (PCS). When this image is to be displayed on a monitor, the color management system uses a CMM and the monitor's device profile to convert from PCS device-independent coordinates to the monitor's device-dependent coordinates. Likewise, when the image is to be printed, the color management system uses a CMM and the printer's device profile to convert from PCS device-independent coordinates to the printer's device-dependent coordinates.

If the destination device doesn't have a corresponding device profile, the CMS assumes that the destination device uses the sRGB color space. If this assumption is incorrect, then the accuracy of the displayed (or printed) image's colors will vary according to how closely the destination device conforms to the sRGB standard. If the source image doesn't have an embedded profile, as is often the case, the CMS assumes that the colors of the image are in sRGB coordinates. If this assumption is incorrect, then the accuracy of the displayed (or printed) image's colors will vary according to how closely the image's colors conform to the sRGB standard.

Keep in mind that ICM doesn't work without the support of applications. Although ICM is the official color management system for Windows, you, as an application developer, must utilize ICM technology to take advantage of the aforementioned benefits. Because very few applications are ICM-aware, Windows has been criticized in many research, academic, and professional communities for its lack of color management support. As we'll discuss next, however, it's not at all difficult to extend your application to be ICM-aware. In fact, now that we've got all of the nitty-gritty, often intimidating, terminology out of the way, the rest is gravy.

Using ICM 2

One of the main reasons ICM 1 didn't catch on was because it didn't really have too much to offer. It didn't support many color spaces; of the few functions that were available for color matching, none worked without the use of a device context; and perhaps most of all, color printers weren't as ubiquitous during the Windows 95 era as they are today.

Earlier I mentioned that the "within device context" design of ICM 1 is undesirable, but let me tell you exactly why. The GDI functions that can utilize ICM technology are called *ICM-enabled* functions. The problem is, not all GDI functions are ICM-enabled. For example, **BitBlt** and **StretchBlt**, the two most commonly used bitmap-related rendering functions, aren't ICM-enabled. In fact, the only bitmap-related rendering functions that are ICM-enabled are those that are designed to work with DIBs; namely, **StretchDIBits** and **SetDIBitsToDevice**. If you recall from Chapter 7, the main problem with these two functions is that they're considerably slower than **BitBlt** and **StretchBlt**. So there's a Catch-22 situation in ICM 1—if you want to use ICM technology, you'll have to work with DIBs at the cost of rendering speed; and if you want optimal rendering speed (using DDBs or DIB section bitmaps), then you'll have to forfeit ICM. Though you can always create a DIB section bitmap, and then use the **StretchDIBits** function to render a color-matched DIB to the DIB section bitmap, ICM 2 offers a better solution.

It's not surprising that things have changed a bit in ICM 2. The bad news is, **BitBlt** and **StretchBlt** still aren't ICM-enabled. The good news is, ICM 2 offers a modular design that allows you to convert the colors of your bitmap *before* passing it to a blitting function. Because you can convert the colors beforehand, the bitmap-related rendering functions don't really have to be ICM-enabled. It's just like asking your local photo shop to develop a roll of film containing pictures that were taken in a low-light setting. The photo shop (i.e., ICM 1) can adjust the colors for you, but it will take an extra week to produce the prints. But if your camera has features (i.e., ICM 2) that can automatically adjust the colors before the film is even exposed, then you won't need to rely on the photo shop's adjustments. Similarly, because ICM 2 provides functions that can be used to color-match the pixels of a bitmap, the bitmap itself is, in a sense, ICM-enabled.

Of course, before you can color-match the colors of a bitmap, you'll need to gauge the color space of the bitmap and the color space of the output device on which the bitmap will be displayed. To determine this information, you need to work with the device profile of both the image and the output device. (Remember, if these profiles aren't present, you should assume the sRGB color space.) Once you have this information, the fun begins. You can punt all of the hard work to the LimoColor CMM by using the **TranslateBitmapBits** function (which we'll discuss shortly). This function instructs the CMS to transform the colors of your bitmap to the color space of the output device. At this point, you're free to render the bitmap as usual. In fact, as simple as this explanation may sound, from an application developer's standpoint, 90 percent of color management is based on this one function.

NOTE: *Most ICM-related functions are declared in the header file icm.h. Most color management functions also require that you statically link with mscms.lib or you dynamically link with mscms.dll.*

Here's how the remainder of this chapter is laid out. First we'll examine the various functions that are available in ICM 2 for working with device profiles. We'll focus strictly on the case in which the output device is the primary display monitor, and we'll assume that this monitor is profiled. Moreover, we'll assume, for the moment, that the colors of the source bitmap are defined in sRGB coordinates. (I'll show you how to work with embedded profiles later in this chapter.) Next, using information in the output device's profile, we'll examine how to use the **TranslateBitmapBits** function to color-match the pixels of a bitmap. In later sections, we'll look at more advanced techniques such as proofing and extracting embedded profiles. Don't worry; I'll summarize things along the way to help reinforce the main concepts. So let's get to work.

Working with ICC Device Profiles

Recall, the first step toward accurately displaying an image's colors is to determine the color space and the gamut of the output device. This information is conveyed by an ICC device profile. In fact, in addition to its robust "outside device context" design, ICM 2 offers a multitude of functions that can be used to manage device profiles. Most of these functions are designed to work with a special object known as a color profile object.

Color Profile Objects

A *color profile object* is an abstraction of an ICC device profile. Recall, there are two common ways in which an ICC device profile is stored. For output devices, the device profile is usually stored in an ICM file. For images, the device profile is commonly embedded in the image's file. You can create a device profile object from an ICC device-profile (.icm) file or from the raw device-profile data that you extract from an image's file. In this way, a color profile object is similar to both a file object (**HANDLE**; **HFILE**) and a global memory object (**HGLOBAL**). Either way, don't confuse a color profile object with a GDI graphic object—you can't select a color profile object into a device context. Remember, one of the aims of ICM 2 is to separate color management from the GDI (namely, device contexts).

NOTE: *As with most Windows entities, there's a specialized type,* ***HPROFILE****, which denotes a handle to a color profile object.*

As it turns out, the majority of the device-profile-management functions are seldom used. The **OpenColorProfile**, **IsColorProfileValid**, and **CloseColorProfile** functions are the exceptions. You can probably guess what each of these functions does. Here's what they look like:

```
HPROFILE OpenColorProfile(
   pProfile, dwDesiredAccess, dwShareMode, dwCreationMode
   );
BOOL IsColorProfileValid(hProfile, pbValid);
BOOL CloseColorProfile(hProfile);
```

The **OpenColorProfile** function creates a color profile object from information in a memory buffer or from an ICC-device-profile file. The **IsColorProfileValid** function checks to see if the information in a color profile object constitutes a valid ICC device profile. The **CloseColorProfile** function destroys the color profile object (and closes the corresponding device-profile file, if present).

The **OpenColorProfile** function might look complicated, but it's not. The **pProfile** parameter is a pointer to a **PROFILE** structure (which we'll discuss next). The other three parameters simply control how the profile data should be accessed. You set the **dwDesiredAccess** parameter to **PROFILE_READ** (1) if you plan to only read the data, or you set this parameter to **PROFILE_READWRITE** (2) if you also need to change the data. The other two parameters, **dwShareMode** and **dwCreationMode**, are exactly like the **dwShareMode** and **dwCreationDisposition** parameters of the **CreateFile** function. These parameters, of course, have no meaning (and are ignored) if the profile data is already in memory (i.e., not stored in an ICM file).

If successful, the **OpenColorProfile** function returns a handle to a color profile object, which you can then validate (via **IsColorProfileValid**), and later close (**CloseColorProfile**). I'll demonstrate how to use these functions shortly, but first we need to examine the **PROFILE** structure.

The PROFILE Structure

The **PROFILE** structure is designed to hold information about an ICC device profile. This structure doesn't actually convey the specifics of the device profile itself; rather it holds information about the device profile's location (on disk or in memory). Here's the declaration of this structure:

```
typedef struct tagPROFILE {
    DWORD dwType;            // identifies pProfileData's data
    PVOID pProfileData;      // the file name or memory location of
                             // the device profile's data
    DWORD cbDataSize;        // the number of bytes in pProfileData
} PROFILE;
typedef PROFILE *PPROFILE, *LPPROFILE;
```

The **dwType** data member identifies the type of information that's conveyed by the **pProfileData** data member. If the **pProfileData** data member is a pointer to a **NULL**-terminated string that holds the name of the device profile's file, then you set **dwType** to **PROFILE_FILENAME** (1). If the **pProfileData** data member is a pointer to a memory buffer that contains the device profile's data, then you set **dwType** to **PROFILE_MEMBUFFER** (2). Accordingly, you set the **cbDataSize** data member to the number of bytes contained in **pProfileData**'s corresponding string or memory buffer.

An Example of Creating a Color Profile Object

Now that we've examined the **PROFILE** structure, let's look at a simple example of opening, validating, and then closing an ICC device profile's file. Here we'll assume that this file is located on disk and in the current directory. (Later I'll show you how to determine where these files are usually stored.) Here's the code:

```
LPTSTR profile_filename = TEXT("MyProfile.ICM\0");

// STEP 1: Initialize the PROFILE structure
PROFILE profile;
profile.dwType = PROFILE_FILENAME;
profile.pProfileData = static_cast<void*>(profile_filename);
profile.cbDataSize =
   // "+ 1" for the NULL-termination
   (lstrlen(profile_filename) + 1) * sizeof(TCHAR);

// STEP 2: Create a color profile object
HPROFILE hProfile =
   OpenColorProfile(
      &profile, PROFILE_READ, FILE_SHARE_READ, OPEN_EXISTING
      );
```

```
if (hProfile)
{
   //
   // STEP 3: Validate the profile's contents
   // (this code reads: IsColorProfileValid function is successful
   // and the device profile is a valid ICC device profile)
   //
   BOOL is_valid;
   if (IsColorProfileValid(hProfile, &is_valid) && is_valid)
   {
      //
      // work with the device profile...
      //
   }

   // STEP 4: Close the device profile's file
   CloseColorProfile(hProfile);
}
```

***NOTE:** A device-profile file doesn't have to be installed with the system or associated with any device for the **OpenColorProfile**, **IsColorProfileValid**, and **CloseColorProfile** functions to work.*

For most output devices, the corresponding ICC device profile is stored in an ICM file. For images, however, this data (if present) is embedded in the image's file and must be extracted manually. I'll show you how to do this with bitmaps later in this chapter (see "Profiled Bitmaps"). For now, just keep in mind that the **OpenColorProfile**, **IsColorProfileValid**, and **CloseColorProfile** functions also work with a device profile that's stored in a memory buffer.

Locating Device Profiles

In the previous code snippet, we assumed that the ICM device-profile file ("MyProfile.icm") was stored in the current directory. In most cases, however, unless you provide your own profile, you'll need to determine where the device-profile files are stored. In Windows 98, these files are stored in the folder \Windows\System\Color. In Windows 2000, they're stored in the folder \Winnt\System32\Spool\Drivers\Color. Naturally, you won't want to hard-code these paths into your application; instead, ICM 2 provides the **GetColorDirectory** function (see the solution, "Locating the Color Folder").

In most cases, you won't need to locate the Color folder. Instead, either you use the target device's default device profile or you display the ICM common dialog. Either approach yields an absolute path to a specific ICM file, which you can then simply pass to the **OpenColorProfile** function. To locate a device's default profile, you use the **GetICMProfile** function:

```
BOOL GetICMProfile(hDC, lpcbName, lpszFilename);
```

The **hDC** parameter specifies the device whose corresponding (default) device profile you want to find. The **lpcbName** parameter specifies a pointer to a **DWORD**-type variable that specifies and receives the number of characters that the buffer, specified by the **lpszFilename** parameter, contains and receives a copy of, respectively. Note the use of a device context here—that's right, **GetICMProfile** is an ICM-1-related function and a very useful one at that. Here's how you'd use the **GetICMProfile** function to retrieve the location of the primary monitor's default profile:

```
HDC hScreenDC = GetDC(NULL);
try
{
   // get the file name of the monitor's default profile
   DWORD num_chars = MAX_PATH;
   bool got_profile =
      GetICMProfile(hScreenDC, &num_chars, monitor_profilename);
   if (!got_profile) throw;
}
catch (...)
{
   ReleaseDC(NULL, hScreenDC);
}
ReleaseDC(NULL, hScreenDC);
```

If you're intent on sticking with ICM 2, you can use the **SetupColorMatching** function to display the ICM common dialog. As depicted in Figure 16.8, the ICM common dialog is useful when you want the user to choose a specific profile and rendering intent. I'll save the specifics of the **SetupColorMatching** function for the solution, "Using the ICM Common Dialog."

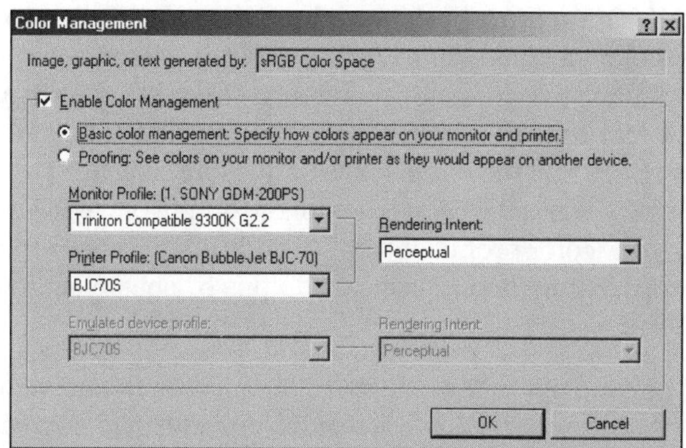

Figure 16.8 The ICM common dialog.

Summary of Device Profiles

Again, there are a lot of concepts to grasp in this chapter, so I'll summarize the main points of this section to help reiterate the high-level picture. Recall, all of the ICM 2 functions are designed to work *without* a device context. Because color matching is performed "outside" a DC, you work with ICC device profiles to determine the color space and characteristics of the output device and the source image. To ease this process, ICM 2 provides what's known as a *color profile object;* it's an abstraction of an ICC device profile. There's one set of functions that work strictly with color profile objects, and there's another set of functions that work strictly with ICM device-profile files.

Again, the main advantage of the "outside device context" scheme is that you can perform color matching on the pixels of a bitmap before passing the bitmap to a blitting function. This way, you're not required to use DIBs and the **StretchDIBits** or **SetDIBitsToDevice** functions; instead, you can use a DIB section bitmap and the faster **BitBlt** and **StretchBlt** functions. In fact, as we'll discuss next, you can use ICM 2 to color-match any arbitrary array of colors—they don't have to correspond to the pixels of a bitmap.

I've demonstrated how to work with the device profile of an output device. Specifically, we examined how to create a color profile object (whose handle you store in a variable of type **HPROFILE**) from an ICM file. This is the first step. The next step is to color-match the colors of the source image. Let's see how this is done.

Color Matching

Once you've created a color profile object for the output device, the next step is to color-match the colors of your image. Remember, you don't have to perform the color matching manually—ICM 2 provides a set of functions that allow you to delegate this chore to a CMM (most often the LimoColor CMM). You do, however, need to specify how this color matching is to be carried out. (Remember, the LimoColor CMM can handle a variety of color matching schemes.) Specifically, you need to instruct the CMM how the *color-space transformation* should be performed. You do this by specifying the color space of the source image (which for now we'll assume to be sRGB) and the color space of the output device (whose specifics are conveyed by your color profile object). In addition, you need to tell the CMM which *gamut mapping* method to use; you do this by specifying a rendering intent.

In the previous section, I pointed out that a color profile object is an abstraction of an ICC device profile. As it turns out, there's an equivalent entity called a *color transform object*, which is an abstraction of both a color-space transformation and a gamut mapping.

Color Transform Objects

The ICM 2 functions that perform color matching (using a CMM) require you to specify exactly how this matching process should be performed. This information is conveyed by using a color transform object. A color transform object holds information about both a color-space transformation and a gamut mapping. As with the **HPROFILE** type, which is used for color profile objects, you store a handle to a color transform object in a variable of type **HTRANSFORM**. This color transform object is not a GDI graphic object, so you can't select it into a device context (which you shouldn't need to do anyway).

There are two functions for managing the lifetime of a color transform object: **CreateColorTransform** and **DeleteColorTransform**. Here's what they look like:

```
HTRANSFORM CreateColorTransform(
   pLogColorSpace, hDestProfile, hTargetProfile, dwFlags
   );
BOOL DeleteColorTransform(hColorTransform);
```

The **CreateColorTransform** function creates a color transform object from information that you specify by its three parameters. The **pLogColorSpace** parameter is a pointer to a **LOGCOLORSPACE** structure, which we'll discuss shortly. The **hDestProfile** parameter is a handle to a color profile object that specifies the profile of the output device. The **hTargetProfile** parameter is a handle to a color profile object that specifies the profile of the device on which the colors will be proofed. (I'll explain this parameter in more detail when we discuss proofing; for now, just set it to **NULL**.) The **dwFlags** parameter is a **DWORD**-type value that specifies both the quality of the color matching and whether or not gamut mapping should be performed. You set the lower 16 bits (**LOWORD**) of this parameter to one of the identifiers from Table 16.2, and you set the upper 16 bits (**HIWORD**) to one of the identifiers from Table 16.3.

Table 16.2 The possible identifiers for the lower 16 bits of the dwFlags parameter of the CreateColorTransform function.

Identifier	Value	Effect
PROOF_MODE	1	A low-quality color matching scheme is performed when the resulting image will be used only for proofing (previewing). Use of this identifier results in the fastest color matching at the expense of quality.
NORMAL_MODE	2	An average-quality color matching scheme is performed when the resulting image will be used for general display purposes.
BEST_MODE	3	A high-quality color matching scheme is performed when the resulting image will be used for production. Use of this identifier results in the best color matching at the expense of speed.

Table 16.3 The possible identifiers for the upper 16 bits of the dwFlags parameter of the CreateColorTransform function.

Identifier	Value	Effect
ENABLE_GAMUT_CHECKING	65536	Gamut mapping is enabled. If a color lies outside the gamut of the destination color space, the color is mapped according to the rendering intent that's specified by the **LOGCOLORSPACE::lcsIntent** data member.
USE_RELATIVE_COLORIMETRIC	131072	Minimal gamut mapping is enabled. If a color lies outside the gamut of the destination color space, the color is mapped using the proof intent.
FAST_TRANSLATE	262144	Minimal gamut mapping is enabled. If a color lies outside the gamut of the destination color space, the color is mapped to the next nearest neighbor that lies within the gamut.

The LOGCOLORSPACE Structure

The **LOGCOLORSPACE** structure is used to describe a logical color space object. Because a color space object is a true GDI graphic object, you can select it into a device context and use it with the legacy color matching functions from ICM 1. Moreover, because color space objects aren't needed in ICM 2, we won't discuss them. We will, however, discuss the **LOGCOLORSPACE** structure because it's used with the **CreateColorTransform** function. Here's what the structure looks like:

```
typedef struct tagLOGCOLORSPACE {
    DWORD lcsSignature;
    DWORD lcsVersion;
    DWORD lcsSize;
    LCSCSTYPE lcsCSType;
    LCSGAMUTMATCH lcsIntent;
    CIEXYZTRIPLE lcsEndpoints;
    DWORD lcsGammaRed;
    DWORD lcsGammaGreen;
    DWORD lcsGammaBlue;
    CHAR lcsFilename[MAX_PATH];
} LOGCOLORSPACE, *LPLOGCOLORSPACE;
```

The first three data members of this structure specify the structure's signature, version, and size, respectively. You must set the **lcsSignature** data member to **LCS_SIGNATURE** ('PSOC'). Likewise, you must set the **lcsVersion** data member to a hexadecimal value of 400. And you must set the **lcsSize** data member to the number of bytes that the structure requires. Because there are no variations in the values that can be assigned to these first three data members, they're customarily initialized like so:

```
LOGCOLORSPACE lcs = {LCS_SIGNATURE, 0x400, sizeof(LOGCOLORSPACE)};
```

The rest of the data members of the **LOGCOLORSPACE** structure are used to describe the characteristics of a color space. When you use this structure with the **CreateColorTransform** function, these data members describe the color space of the source image along with the desired rendering intent. The **lcsCSType** data member specifies the color space type (e.g., sRGB); you assign this data member one of the identifiers listed in Table 16.4. The **lcsIntent** data member specifies the desired rendering intent. Recall, the rendering intent governs how the gamut mapping is carried out. You assign this data member one of the identifiers listed in Table 16.5.

The **lcsEndpoints**, **lcsGammaRed**, **lcsGammaGreen**, and **lcsGammaBlue** data members are used only when the **lcsCSType** data member is set to **LCS_CALIBRATED_RGB**. The **lcsEndpoints** data member is a

Table 16.4 The possible identifiers for use with the lcsCSType data member of the LOGCOLORSPACE structure.

Identifier	Value	Meaning
LCS_CALIBRATED_RGB	0	The colors of the source image lie in a calibrated RGB color space. The calibration information is stored in the **lcsEndpoints**, **lcsGammaRed**, **lcsGammaGreen**, and **lcsGammaBlue** data members.
LCS_sRGB	'sRGB'	The colors of the source image lie in the sRGB color space.
LCS_WINDOWS_COLOR_SPACE	'Win'	The colors of the source image lie in the system's default color space (also sRGB in Windows 98, ME, and 2000).

Table 16.5 The possible identifiers for use with the lcsIntent data member of the LOGCOLORSPACE structure.

Identifier	Value	Meaning
LCS_GM_BUSINESS	1	Specifies the saturation rendering intent.
LCS_GM_GRAPHICS	2	Specifies the relative colorimetric rendering intent.
LCS_GM_IMAGES	4	Specifies the perceptual rendering intent.
LCS_GM_ABS_COLORIMETRIC	8	Specifies the absolute colorimetric rendering intent.

CIEXYZTRIPLE structure that describes the endpoints of the three primaries (i.e., the axes of the color space). Recall, one of the problems with the RGB color space is that different devices use slightly different definitions of the primary colors. The **lcsEndpoints** data member specifies the tristimulus values (*X*, *Y*, *Z*) of the device's definition of pure red (**CIEXYZTRIPLE::ciexyzRed**), pure green (**CIEXYZTRIPLE::ciexyzGreen**), and pure blue (**CIEXYZTRIPLE::ciexyz-Blue**). The **lcsGammaRed**, **lcsGammaGreen**, and **lcsGammaBlue** data members specify the gamma curves for the red, green, and blue axes, respectively. Note that these gamma and tristimulus values are meaningful only if the **lcsCSType** data member is set to **LCS_CALIBRATED_RGB**. (We'll look at the **CIEXYZTRIPLE** structure later in this chapter.)

WARNING! Microsoft's documentation incorrectly uses lowercase x, y, and z in the description of the CIEXYZTRIPLE structure. In reality, the CIEXYZTRIPLE::ciexyzRed, ciexyzGreen, and ciexyzBlue data members specify tristimulus values—that is, uppercase X, Y, and Z.

NOTE: *You might have noticed that the* ***LOGCOLORSPACE*** *structure has no data member that specifies the white point of the corresponding color space. Indeed, when the* ***lcsCSType*** *data member indicates* ***LCS_CALIBRATED_RGB****, the white point is assumed D50. See Chapter 18 for more information on adjusting the values of the* ***lcsEndpoints*** *data member to conform to a D50 white point.*

The **lcsFilename** data member is specified when the **LOGCOLORSPACE** structure should correspond to the color space (and the characteristics) defined by an ICM device-profile file. In this case, the **lcsCSType** data member should be set to **LCS_CALIBRATED_RGB**; all of the other color-space-related data members are ignored.

An Example of Creating a Color Transform Object

After you properly initialize a **LOGCOLORSPACE** structure, you can pass its address to the **CreateColorTransform** function (as the **pLogColorSpace** parameter). This will provide the CMM with information about the source image's color space and characteristics. Again, information about the output device's color space and characteristics is specified via the color profile object whose handle you specify as the **hDestProfile** parameter of the **CreateColorTransform** function.

Let's look at a simple example of creating a color transform object. Because we're assuming that the colors of the source image lie in the sRGB color space, we can leave most of the data members of our **LOGCOLORSPACE** structure at zero. Here, **hMonitorProfile** is a handle to a color profile object that corresponds to the device profile of the monitor:

16. Image Color Management

```
// STEP 1: Declare and initialize a LOGCOLORSPACE structure
LOGCOLORSPACE lcs = {LCS_SIGNATURE, 0x400, sizeof(LOGCOLORSPACE)};
lcs.lcsCSType = LCS_sRGB;
lcs.lcsIntent = LCS_GM_IMAGES;

// STEP 2: Create the color transform object
HTRANSFORM hColorTransform =
   CreateColorTransform(
      &lcs, hMonitorProfile, NULL,
      MAKELONG(BEST_MODE, ENABLE_GAMUT_CHECKING)
      );
if (hColorTransform)
{
   //
   // work with hColorTransform...
   //

   // STEP 3: Destroy the color transform object
   DeleteColorTransform(hColorTransform);
}
```

Because we assumed that the source image uses the sRGB color space, initializing the **LOGCOLORSPACE** structure in this example was trivial. And, although the color space of your source image won't always be sRGB, usually the image won't have an embedded device profile, so the sRGB assumption is your best bet. Simply put, in most situations you'll initialize the **LOGCOLORSPACE** structure as in Step 1. You get a glimpse here of why Microsoft is pushing for the sRGB color space—not only does it reduce the size of an image's file, but it also makes our jobs as developers a bit easier.

Performing the Color Matching: The TranslateBitmapBits Function

Now that we've discussed how to create a color transform object, let's put it to good use. Remember, our goal is to color-match the colors of a bitmap before passing it to a blitting function. To do this, we use the **TranslateBitmapBits** function:

```
BOOL TranslateBitmapBits(
    IN HTRANSFORM hColorTransform,  // handle to a color transform object
    IN PVOID pSrcBits,              // pointer to the source pixels array
    IN BMFORMAT bmInput,            // format ID for the source pixels
    IN DWORD dwWidth,               // width of the source pixels array
    IN DWORD dwHeight,              // height of the source pixels array
    IN DWORD dwInputStride,         // number of bytes per scan line in the
                                    // source pixels array
    OUT PVOID pDestBits,            // pointer to the destination (color-
```

```
                                    // matched) pixels array
    IN BMFORMAT bmOutput,           // format ID for the destination pixels
    IN DWORD dwOutputStride,        // number of bytes per scan line in the
                                    // destination pixels array
    IN PBMCALLBACKFN pfnCallback,   // pointer to an optional application-
                                    // defined callback function
    IN ULONG ulCallbackData         // optional data to pass to the
                                    // optional callback function
);
```

Don't let the sheer number of parameters intimidate you; using the **TranslateBitmapBits** function is the simplest part of the color management process. Let's start with the three most straightforward parameters: **hColorTransform**, **pScrBits,** and **pDestBits**. The **hColorTransform** parameter specifies a handle to a color transform object. The **pScrBits** parameter is a pointer to the source ("to be color-matched") pixels. The **pDestBits** parameter is a pointer to the destination (color-matched) pixels. Using these three parameters, you tell the **TranslateBitmapBits** function *which* pixels to color-match (**pSrcBits**), *how* this color matching should be carried out (**hTransform**), and *where* to store the results (**pDestBits**). Note that the **pSrcBits** and the **pDestBits** parameters can be specified as pointers to the same buffer, in which case the **TranslateBitmapBits** function will perform in-place color matching.

The next step is to tell the **TranslateBitmapBits** function how many pixels the source and destination arrays contain. This is where the **dwWidth**, **dwHeight**, **dwInputStride**, and **dwOutputStride** parameters come in. The **dwWidth** and **dwHeight** parameters specify the width and the height, respectively, of the array that contains the source pixels. Because the number of pixels in the source array must equal the number of pixels in the destination array, the **dwWidth** and **dwHeight** parameters also specify the width and the height of the array that contains the destination pixels. Moreover, because the number of pixels in an array is not necessarily the number of bytes that the array can hold, there are two separate parameters, **dwInputStride** and **dwOutputStride**, that specify the number of bytes per scan line in the source and destination arrays, respectively. Most often, you'll set both of these parameters to zero, indicating that each array is **DWORD**-aligned. (See Chapter 7 if this terminology is ambiguous.)

Remember, the **TranslateBitmapBits** function (as its name suggests) was designed to work with bitmaps—namely, DIB section bitmaps. Because bitmaps come in a wide variety of color formats, you must tell the **TranslateBitmapBits** function the format of the source and destination pixels (e.g., 24 bits per pixel). This is the role of the **bmInput** and **bmOutput** parameters. The **bmInput** parameter specifies the format of the source pixels, and the **bmOutput** parameter specifies the format of the destination pixels. Both of these parameters are of the

BMFORMAT enumeration type and can be specified as one of the enumerators listed in Table 16.6.

Table 16.6 Enumerators of the BMFORMAT enumeration data type for use with RGB bitmaps.

Identifier	Value	Meaning
BM_x555RGB	0	Specifies that the pixels of the bitmap are in the RGB color space; 16 bits are used for each pixel; 5 bits are allocated to each color channel; and the most significant bit isn't used.
BM_565RGB	1	Specifies that the pixels of the bitmap are in the RGB color space; 16 bits are used for each pixel; 5 bits are allocated for the red and blue color channels; and 6 bits are used for the green color channel.
BM_RGBTRIPLETS	2	Specifies that the pixels of the bitmap are in the RGB color space; 24 bits are used for each pixel; 8 bits are allocated to each color channel. Within each pixel, the color channel information is packed in the order blue, green, and then red.
BM_BGRTRIPLETS	4	Specifies that the pixels of the bitmap are in the RGB color space; 24 bits are used for each pixel; 8 bits are allocated to each color channel. Within each pixel, the color channel information is packed in the order red, green, and then blue.
BM_xRGBQUADS	8	Specifies that the pixels of the bitmap are in the RGB color space; 32 bits are used for each pixel; 8 bits are allocated to each color channel; and the most significant byte isn't used. Within each pixel, the color channel information is packed in the order blue, green, and then red.
BM_xBGRQUADS	16	Specifies that the pixels of the bitmap are in the RGB color space; 32 bits are used for each pixel; 8 bits are allocated to each color channel; and the most significant byte isn't used. Within each pixel, the color channel information is packed in the order red, green, and then blue.
BM_10b_RGB	9	Specifies that the pixels of the bitmap are in the RGB color space; 32 bits are used for each pixel; 10 bits are allocated to each color channel; and the two most significant bits aren't used. Within each pixel, the color channel information is packed in the order blue, green, and then red.
BM_16b_RGB	10	Specifies that the pixels of the bitmap are in the RGB color space; 64 bits are used for each pixel; 16 bits are allocated to each color channel; and the two most significant bytes are used for a grayscale intensity value. Within each pixel, the color channel information is packed in the order blue, green, red, and then gray.

WARNING! The TranslateBitmapBits function won't work unless the format of your source and destination arrays are compatible with the color spaces that are defined by the color transform object.

In most cases, you'll specify the same enumerator as the **bmInput** parameter and the **bmOutput** parameter. Usually, these parameters are both set to **BM_x555RGB**, **BM_RGBTRIPLETS**, or **BM_xRGBQUADS**. You specify **BM_x555RGB** if your source image is a 16-bit bitmap; you specify **BM_RGBTRIPLETS** if your source image is a 24-bit bitmap; or you specify **BM_xRGBQUADS** if your source image is a 32-bit bitmap. You also use the **BM_xRGBQUADS** enumerator if you're working with an 8-bit (or less) bitmap. In this case, instead of color-matching the bitmap's pixels, you color-match its color table.

NOTE: *Don't be confused into thinking that you should use an enumerator whose name more closely reflects the actual layout of the red, green, and blue color channels in each pixel (or color-table entry). For example, each pixel of a 24-bit bitmap contains the blue intensity, followed by the green intensity, followed by the red intensity (i.e., BGR). In this case, you might be tempted to specify* ***BM_BGRTRIPLETS*** *as the* ***bmInput*** *and* ***bmOutput*** *parameters. You don't want to do this. Remember, the* ***TranslateBitmapBits*** *function was designed to work with bitmaps—the odd (BGR) ordering is automatically taken into account.*

The **pfnCallback** and **ulCallbackData** parameters are optional; you can simply set both of these parameters to **NULL**, and the **TranslateBitmapBits** function will still work. However, in some cases, depending on the speed of the machine, the format of the source pixels, and the characteristics of the output device, the color matching process might take some time. In this case, you can pass a pointer to an application-defined callback function as the **pfnCallback** parameter. This way, you can use your callback function to display a progress dialog, for example. And if you want to pass any application-defined data to this callback function, you can use the **ulCallbackData** parameter. Here's the signature of the callback function:

```
BOOL WINAPI ICMProgressProcCallback(
  IN ULONG ulMax,
  IN ULONG ulCurrent,
  IN LPARAM ulCallbackData
);
```

The **ulMax** parameter tells you the total "amount" of color matching that needs to be done. The **ulCurrent** parameter tells you the current "amount" of color matching that has been done. Both of these parameters reveal only a number, so they're not too meaningful when used separately. However, as you might have guessed, you can divide **ulCurrent** by **ulMax** to ascertain the *percentage* of color matching that has been completed. This is ideal for a dialog containing a progress bar. Moreover, because your callback function can return a Boolean value that instructs the **TranslateBitmapBits** function to continue (**TRUE**) or terminate (**FALSE**), your dialog can contain a button that allows the user to cancel the color matching process.

Usually, the following conditions will be true: your source image will be a 24-bit DIB section bitmap (or converted to this color depth, if necessary) that's smaller than the size of the screen; the color gamut of the monitor or printer will be sufficiently large; and the end user's machine will be sufficiently fast so that your callback function is never called. In other words, don't worry if your progress dialog never appears—the LimoColor CMM is highly optimized.

Believe it or not, that's all there is to adding basic color management support to your application; the **TranslateBitmapBits** function is the last ICM-related step. Listing 16.1 demonstrates how to create a bare-bones ICM-aware image viewer (as depicted in Figure 16.9). This example assumes the sRGB color space for the source image and uses the default ICC device profile of the monitor; the rendering intent is set to perceptual (**LCS_GM_IMAGES**).

Figure 16.9 A simple ICM-aware image viewer.

Listing 16.1 Building a bare-bones ICM-aware image viewer.

```
// -----------------------------------------------------------------
// Windows 2000 Graphics API Black Book
// Chapter 16 - Listing 16.1 (TranslateBitmapBits Demo)
// -----------------------------------------------------------------

#include <windows.h>
#include <cassert>
#include <icm.h>
// NOTE: link to "mscms.lib"

HINSTANCE hInst;
const char* WndClassName = "GMainWnd";

LRESULT CALLBACK MainWndProc(HWND HWnd, UINT Msg, WPARAM WParam,
   LPARAM LParam);

int APIENTRY WinMain(HINSTANCE hInstance, HINSTANCE, LPTSTR,
   int nCmdShow)
{
   hInst = hInstance;

   WNDCLASS wc;
   memset(&wc, 0, sizeof(WNDCLASS));

   wc.lpszClassName = WndClassName;
   wc.lpfnWndProc = MainWndProc;
   wc.hInstance = hInst;
   wc.hCursor = LoadCursor(NULL, IDC_ARROW);
   wc.hbrBackground = reinterpret_cast<HBRUSH>(
      COLOR_BTNFACE + 1
      );

   if (RegisterClass(&wc))
   {
      HWND hWnd =
         CreateWindow(
            WndClassName, "TranslateBitmapBits Demo",
            WS_OVERLAPPED | WS_MINIMIZEBOX | WS_SYSMENU |
            WS_CAPTION | WS_VISIBLE | WS_CLIPCHILDREN,
            CW_USEDEFAULT, CW_USEDEFAULT, 380, 355,
            NULL, NULL, hInst, NULL
            );

      if (hWnd)
```

```
        {
            ShowWindow(hWnd, nCmdShow);
            UpdateWindow(hWnd);

            MSG msg;
            while (GetMessage(&msg, NULL, 0, 0))
            {
                TranslateMessage(&msg);
                DispatchMessage(&msg);
            }
        }
    }
    return 0;
}

// UI-related...
bool use_ICM = false;                   // ICM enabled/disabled flag
HWND hCheckBox = NULL;                  // ICM enabled/disabled checkbox

// image-related...
DIBSECTION ds = {0};                    // DIB section information
HDC hSourceMemDC = NULL;                // handle to a memory DC
HDC hMatchedMemDC = NULL;               // handle to a memory DC
HBITMAP hSourceDIBSection = NULL;       // handle to a DIB section
HBITMAP hMatchedDIBSection = NULL;      // handle to a DIB section
unsigned char* pSourceBits = NULL;      // pointer to original pixels
unsigned char* pMatchedBits = NULL;     // pointer to color-matched pixels

// profile-related...
TCHAR monitor_profilename[MAX_PATH];    // display's profile file name

LRESULT CALLBACK MainWndProc(HWND hWnd, UINT msg, WPARAM wParam,
   LPARAM lParam)
{
   switch (msg)
   {
      case WM_CREATE:
      {
         // create the color management checkbox
         hCheckBox =
            CreateWindow(
               "BUTTON", "Use Color Management",
               WS_CHILD | WS_VISIBLE | BS_PUSHLIKE | BS_AUTOCHECKBOX,
               8, 295, 200, 25,
               hWnd, NULL, hInst, NULL
```

```
        );

    //
    // load the source DIB section from a file
    // (see Chapter 7 for the definition of the
    // CreateDIBSectionFromFile function)
    //
    LPCSTR filename = TEXT("Squirrel.bmp\0");
    hSourceDIBSection = CreateDIBSectionFromFile(filename, NULL);
    assert(hSourceDIBSection != NULL);

    //
    // create a copy of the source DIB section
    // to be used as the color-matched DIB section
    //
    hMatchedDIBSection = static_cast<HBITMAP>(
       CopyImage(hSourceDIBSection, IMAGE_BITMAP,
                 0, 0, LR_CREATEDIBSECTION)
       );
    if (!hMatchedDIBSection)
    {
       DeleteObject(hSourceDIBSection);
       assert(false);
    }

    try
    {
       // get the bitmap information for each DIB section
       const size_t dibSize = sizeof(DIBSECTION);
       if (GetObject(hSourceDIBSection, dibSize, &ds) == dibSize)
       {
          // grab a pointer to the source pixels
          pSourceBits = static_cast<unsigned char*>(ds.dsBm.bmBits);
       }
       else throw;
       if (GetObject(hMatchedDIBSection, dibSize, &ds) == dibSize)
       {
          // grab a pointer to the color-matched pixels
          pMatchedBits = static_cast<unsigned char*>(ds.dsBm.bmBits);
       }
       else throw;

       // resize the window and the checkbox
       SetWindowPos(
          hWnd, NULL,
```

```
            0, 0, 30 + ds.dsBm.bmWidth, 80 + ds.dsBm.bmHeight,
            SWP_NOMOVE | SWP_NOZORDER
            );
         SetWindowPos(
            hCheckBox, NULL,
            8, 20 + ds.dsBm.bmHeight, ds.dsBm.bmWidth + 4, 25,
            SWP_NOZORDER
            );

         //
         // create the first memory DC and then
         // select the source DIB section into it
         //
         hSourceMemDC = CreateCompatibleDC(NULL);
         if (hSourceMemDC)
         {
            hSourceDIBSection = static_cast<HBITMAP>(
               SelectObject(hSourceMemDC, hSourceDIBSection)
               );
         }

         //
         // create the second memory DC and then
         // select the color-matched DIB section into it
         //
         hMatchedMemDC = CreateCompatibleDC(NULL);
         if (hMatchedMemDC)
         {
            hMatchedDIBSection = static_cast<HBITMAP>(
               SelectObject(hMatchedMemDC, hMatchedDIBSection)
               );
         }
      }
      catch (...)
      {
         // clean up
         DeleteObject(hSourceDIBSection);
         DeleteObject(hMatchedDIBSection);
      }
      break;
   }
   case WM_PAINT:
   {
      PAINTSTRUCT ps;
      HDC hDC = BeginPaint(hWnd, &ps);
      try
      {
```

```
            // decide which image to render
            HDC hMemDC = (use_ICM ? hMatchedMemDC : hSourceMemDC);

            // render the image
            const bool blt_source_ok =
               BitBlt(
                  hDC, 10, 10,
                  ds.dsBm.bmWidth, ds.dsBm.bmHeight,
                  hMemDC, 0, 0,
                  SRCCOPY
                  );
            if (!blt_source_ok) throw;

            // render a border around the image
            RECT RImage =
               {8, 8, 12 + ds.dsBm.bmWidth, 12 + ds.dsBm.bmHeight};
            DrawEdge(hDC, &RImage, EDGE_SUNKEN, BF_RECT);
         }
         catch (...)
         {
            EndPaint(hWnd, &ps);
         }
         EndPaint(hWnd, &ps);
         return 0;
      }
      case WM_COMMAND:
      {
         // when the "Use Color Management" checkbox is clicked...
         if (HIWORD(wParam) == BN_CLICKED &&
             reinterpret_cast<HWND>(lParam) == hCheckBox)
         {
            // is the "Use Color Management" checkbox checked?
            use_ICM =
               (SNDMSG(hCheckBox, BM_GETCHECK, 0, 0) == BST_CHECKED);
            if (!use_ICM)
            {
               // redraw the source bitmap
               RECT RImage =
                  {10, 10, 10 + ds.dsBm.bmWidth, 10 + ds.dsBm.bmHeight};
               InvalidateRect(hWnd, &RImage, false);
               break;
            }

            //
            // otherwise, proceed with color matching...
```

```
//
HDC hDC = GetDC(hWnd);
try
{
   // get the file name of the monitor's default profile
   DWORD num_chars = MAX_PATH;
   bool got_profile =
      GetICMProfile(hDC, &num_chars, monitor_profilename);
   if (!got_profile) throw;
}
catch (...)
{
   ReleaseDC(hWnd, hDC);
}
ReleaseDC(hWnd, hDC);

// initialize a PROFILE structure for the monitor
PROFILE monitor_profile;
monitor_profile.dwType = PROFILE_FILENAME;
monitor_profile.pProfileData =
   static_cast<void*>(monitor_profilename);
monitor_profile.cbDataSize =
   // "+ 1" for the NULL-termination
   (lstrlen(monitor_profilename) + 1) * sizeof(TCHAR);

// create a color profile object for the monitor's profile
HPROFILE hMonitorProfile =
   OpenColorProfile(
      &monitor_profile, PROFILE_READ,
      FILE_SHARE_READ, OPEN_EXISTING
      );
try
{
   // validate the contents of the monitor's profile
   BOOL is_monitor_valid = FALSE;
   IsColorProfileValid(hMonitorProfile, &is_monitor_valid);
   if (!is_monitor_valid) throw;

   //
   // initialize a LOGCOLORSPACE structure for the
   // source image, using the sRGB color space and
   // the perceptual rendering intent
   //
   LOGCOLORSPACE lcs =
      {LCS_SIGNATURE, 0x400, sizeof(LOGCOLORSPACE)};
   lcs.lcsCSType = LCS_sRGB;       // sRGB color space
```

```
        lcs.lcsIntent = LCS_GM_IMAGES; // perceptual intent

        // create a color transform object
        HTRANSFORM hColorTransform =
           CreateColorTransform(
              &lcs, hMonitorProfile, NULL,
              MAKELONG(BEST_MODE, ENABLE_GAMUT_CHECKING)
              );
        if (hColorTransform)
        {
           // stay in sync
           GdiFlush();

           //
           // if the DIB section is <= 8bpp, color-match
           // its color table instead of its pixels
           //
           BOOL match_ok = FALSE;
           const unsigned char bpp = ds.dsBm.bmBitsPixel;
           if (bpp <= 8)
           {
              // extract the color table's size
              short num_colors = ds.dsBmih.biClrUsed;
              if (num_colors == 0) num_colors = 1 << bpp;

              // get the color-table entries
              RGBQUAD rgbQ[256];
              short num_got = GetDIBColorTable(
                 hSourceMemDC, 0, num_colors, rgbQ
                 );
              if (num_got == num_colors)
              {
                 // color-match the color table
                 match_ok =
                    TranslateBitmapBits(
                       hColorTransform,
                       rgbQ, BM_xRGBQUADS,
                       num_colors, 1, NULL,
                       rgbQ, BM_xRGBQUADS, NULL,
                       NULL, NULL
                       );

                 // update the color-matched image's color table
                 num_got = SetDIBColorTable(
                    hMatchedMemDC, 0, num_colors, rgbQ
                    );
```

16. Image Color Management

```
                match_ok &= (num_got == num_colors);
             }
          }
          else  // the DIB section is > 8bpp
          {
             // color-match the pixels
             match_ok =
                TranslateBitmapBits(
                   hColorTransform,
                   pSourceBits, BM_RGBTRIPLETS,
                   ds.dsBm.bmWidth, ds.dsBm.bmHeight, NULL,
                   pMatchedBits, BM_RGBTRIPLETS, NULL,
                   NULL, NULL
                   );
          }
          if (!match_ok)
          {
             MessageBox(
                hWnd, "Error Matching Colors!", "Error",
                MB_OK | MB_ICONERROR
                );
             throw;
          }

          // redraw the color-matched image
          RECT RImage =
             {10, 10, 10 + ds.dsBm.bmWidth, 10 + ds.dsBm.bmHeight};
          InvalidateRect(hWnd, &RImage, false);

          // clean up
          DeleteColorTransform(hColorTransform);
       }
       else
       {
          MessageBox(
             hWnd, "Error Creating Transform!", "Error",
             MB_OK | MB_ICONERROR
             );
          throw;
       }
    }
    catch (...)
    {
       // clean up
       CloseColorProfile(hMonitorProfile);
    }
    // clean up
```

```
            CloseColorProfile(hMonitorProfile);
         }
         break;
      }
      case WM_DESTROY:
      {
         // clean up
         if (hSourceMemDC)
         {
            DeleteObject(SelectObject(hSourceMemDC, hSourceDIBSection));
            DeleteDC(hSourceMemDC);
         }
         if (hMatchedMemDC)
         {
            DeleteObject(SelectObject(hMatchedMemDC, hMatchedDIBSection));
            DeleteDC(hMatchedMemDC);
         }

         PostQuitMessage(0);
         break;
      }
   }
   return DefWindowProc(hWnd, msg, wParam, lParam);
}
```

Other Color-Matching Functions

ICM 2 offers three other color matching functions: **CheckBitmapBits**, **CheckColors**, and **TranslateColors**. The former two functions are used only to determine whether specific colors fall outside the color gamut of a target device. The **TranslateColors** function is similar to the **TranslateBitmapBits** function; the only difference is that **TranslateColors** is designed for color-matching an arbitrary array of colors rather than the pixels of a bitmap. I won't discuss these functions because they are rarely used.

Summary of Color Matching

The process of color matching involves a color space transformation and a mapping of colors into the color gamut of the output device. This process ensures that you don't instruct the output device to display colors that it can't represent accurately. This process also ensures that colors will be represented accurately regardless of the output device.

In ICM 2, the process of color matching is performed by using a **LOGCOLORSPACE** structure, a color profile object, a color transform object, and the **TranslateBitmapBits** function. The **LOGCOLORSPACE** structure tells the CMM about the color space of the source image, and it conveys the desired rendering intent (the gamut mapping method). The color profile object tells the CMM about the color space and the gamut of the output device. The color transform object—which is created from a **LOGCOLORSPACE** structure and one (or two) color profile object(s)—tells the CMM what type of color matching to perform and how accurate this color matching should be (i.e., proof-, normal-, or high-quality). To instruct the CMM to carry out the color matching, you call the **TranslateBitmapBits** function.

Here's a recap of the steps necessary to add basic ICM support to your application:

1. Use the **OpenColorProfile** function to create a color profile object for the output device.
2. Initialize a **LOGCOLORSPACE**-type variable according to the color space of the source image. (Use the sRGB color space if the source image doesn't reveal any color-space information.)
3. Using the color profile object from Step 1 and the **LOGCOLORSPACE**-type variable from Step 2, create a color transform object by passing these data to the **CreateColorTransform** function.
4. Use the **TranslateBitmapBits** function to color-match the pixels of the source image.
5. Display or print the image as you would normally.

Note that for Step 1, you'll need the name of the output device's ICM file. As demonstrated in Listing 16.1, you can retrieve this information by using the **GetICMProfile** function, or you can use the **EnumColorProfiles** function that we discussed earlier. Ideally, however, you should allow the user to specify which profile to use; for this, you can use the **SetupColorMatching** function to display the ICM common dialog box. This way, not only does the user have more control over the device profile, but he or she can also specify which rendering intent to use.

When an image is displayed on a monitor, adjusting the profile and the rendering intent is a cheap operation—you need only color-match the pixels and then redraw the image. When the output device is a printer, however, reprinting an image can become an expensive operation, especially if photographic-quality paper is used. It would be nice if there were a way to preview the printer's output on the monitor before printing. This is the idea behind *proofing;* as we'll discuss next, ICM 2 provides native support for this facility.

Proofing

Imagine that you need to print a hundred copies of a full-color brochure using an ink jet printer and expensive, high-quality paper. With the brochure correctly laid out in your desktop-publishing application, you press the Print button and after about 30 minutes, you have 100 brochures that display your company's logo in the wrong colors. Of course, no one in their right mind would blindly print 100 copies; instead, most of us would print only a single page, just to make sure everything looks okay. Only after verifying or *proofing* the output can we be sure that we won't be wasting ink, paper, and ultimately, money.

Industrial Proofing

Proofing is the process of previewing a printed product (called a *proof page*) before the product is mass-produced. In the production industry, proofing is sometimes performed using a computer and a thermal-wax or dye-sublimation printer, although high-quality ink jet printers are also becoming popular. This type of proofing (using a computer and a printer) is called *digital proofing* because the source image itself is digitized. In fact, for most of us, this type of proof page would actually surpass the quality of the final output. When compared to the quality of a page that's printed from the press, however, the quality of a thermal-wax or dye-sublimation proof page is generally poor. In contrast, *analog proofing* involves the use of the same film that's used to make the printing plates. For this reason, analog proofing is typically used near the final stages of production when superior accuracy is essential.

Continuing advancements in printing technologies—and the rapid decrease in the cost of color printers—have made it possible for the average consumer to produce mid- to high-quality prints from their home computers. Nowadays you can buy a decent ink jet printer for less than $100 (or even less after a manufacturer's rebate). Of course, there's always a catch—although the printer itself is inexpensive, it's the cost of the supplies that gets you. If you use the expensive photographic-quality paper, for example, there's absolutely no room for error. What's more, in this case, even proofing is expensive. It's situations like this in which ICM technology proves indispensable; it allows the user to proof an image on the monitor before the image is printed.

Adding Proofing to Your Application

Recall from its declaration that the **CreateColorTransform** function takes four parameters: **pLogColorSpace**, **hDestProfile**, **hTargetProfile**, and **dwFlags**. We've already discussed the first, second, and fourth parameters; the third parameter, **hTargetProfile**, is used for proofing.

When you create a color transform object by passing the **CreateColorTransform** function a **NULL hTargetProfile** parameter, and then use this transform object with a color matching function (e.g., **TranslateBitmapBits**), the returned transform object tells the CMM to color-match the colors of the source image to the color space of the output device. Remember, the color space of the source image is specified by the **pLogColorSpace** parameter, and the color space of the output device is specified by the **hDestProfile** parameter. In Listing 16.1, the color space of the source image was assumed to be sRGB, and the output device was the monitor whose color space was defined by the monitor's corresponding ICC device profile. We could just as easily have used the printer as the output device, in which case, we would have used the printer's corresponding ICC device profile. Still, either approach involves only one color-matching step. To view the printer's output on the monitor (instead of on paper), we need to perform two color-matching steps: first we need to match the source image's colors to the printer's color space, and then we need to match the resulting colors to the monitor's color space. This scheme is depicted in Figure 16.10.

To add proofing to your application, you simply specify a non-**NULL** value as the **hTargetProfile** parameter of the **CreateColorTransform** function. For example, to proof the printer's output on the monitor, you specify **hTargetProfile** as a handle to the printer's corresponding color profile object, and, as usual, you specify **hDestProfile** as a handle to the monitor's corresponding color profile object. Conversely, in the rare case that you want to proof the monitor's output on a printed page, you specify **hTargetProfile** as a handle to the monitor's corresponding color profile object, and you specify **hDestProfile** as a handle to the printer's color profile object. In short, you always specify the **hTargetProfile** parameter as a handle to a color profile object that corresponds to the device whose output you want to proof (normally the printer), and you always specify the **hDestProfile** parameter as a handle to a color profile object that corresponds to the device on which this output will be proofed (normally the monitor).

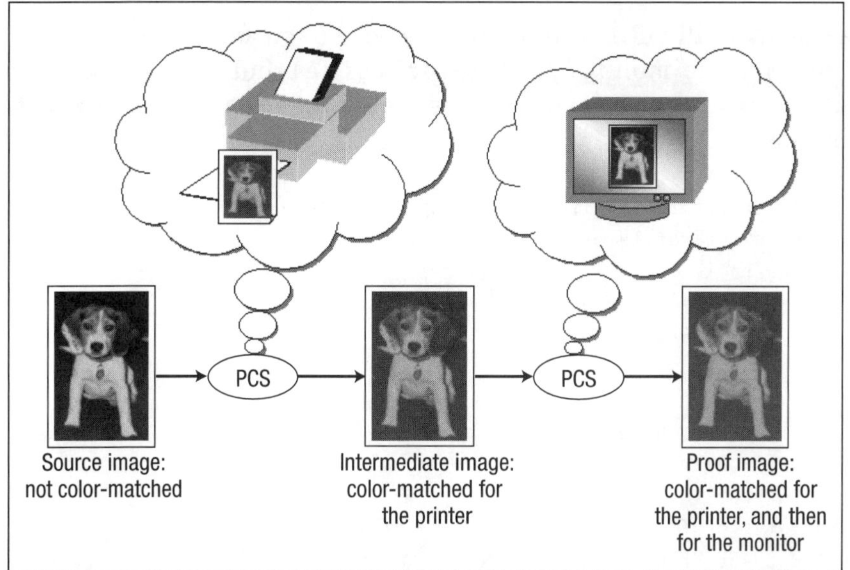

Figure 16.10 Proofing the printer's output on the monitor involves two color-matching steps.

Let's work through an example. For simplicity, we'll assume that we know the path and file name of both the monitor's and the printer's ICM files. As before, the first step is to initialize a **PROFILE** structure. This time we need to initialize two **PROFILE** structures—one for the monitor and one for the printer—like so:

```
LPTSTR monitor_profilename = TEXT("MonitorProfile.icm\0");
LPTSTR printer_profilename = TEXT("PrinterProfile.icm\0");

// STEP 1A: Initialize the monitor's PROFILE structure
PROFILE monitor_profile;
monitor_profile.dwType = PROFILE_FILENAME;
monitor_profile.pProfileData =
   static_cast<void*>(monitor_profilename);
monitor_profile.cbDataSize =
   // "+ 1" for the NULL-termination
   (lstrlen(monitor_profilename) + 1) * sizeof(TCHAR);

// STEP 1B: Initialize the printer's PROFILE structure
PROFILE printer_profile;
printer_profile.dwType = PROFILE_FILENAME;
printer_profile.pProfileData =
   static_cast<void*>(printer_profilename);
printer_profile.cbDataSize =
   // "+ 1" for the NULL-termination
   (lstrlen(printer_profilename) + 1) * sizeof(TCHAR);
```

Now, using these **PROFILE** structures, we need to create two color profile objects: one for the monitor (**hMonitorProfile**) and one for the printer (**hPrinterProfile**). Remember, to do this, we use the **CreateColorProfile** function, like so:

```
// STEP 2A: Create the monitor's color profile object
HPROFILE hMonitorProfile =
   OpenColorProfile(
      &monitor_profile, PROFILE_READ,
      FILE_SHARE_READ, OPEN_EXISTING
      );

// STEP 2B: Create the printer's color profile object
HPROFILE hPrinterProfile =
   OpenColorProfile(
      &printer_profile, PROFILE_READ,
      FILE_SHARE_READ, OPEN_EXISTING
      );
```

The next step is to validate the contents of each of the ICM files. As before, this is done by using the **IsColorProfileValid** function. The only difference now is that we need to call the **IsColorProfileValid** function two times—once for **hMonitorProfile** and once for **hPrinterProfile**:

```
// STEP 3A: Validate the contents of the monitor's profile
BOOL is_monitor_profile_valid = FALSE;
IsColorProfileValid(
   hMonitorProfile, &is_monitor_profile_valid
   );
if (!is_monitor_profile_valid) throw;

// STEP 3B: Validate the contents of the printer's profile
BOOL is_printer_profile_valid = FALSE;
IsColorProfileValid(
   hPrinterProfile, &is_printer_profile_valid
   );
if (!is_printer_profile_valid) throw;
```

Now we simply declare and initialize a **LOGCOLORSPACE** structure that describes the color space of the source image. Because this step doesn't involve the printer's profile, the procedure is identical to that which we performed earlier in this chapter. Here it is again (assuming the sRGB color space):

```
// STEP 4: Initialize a LOGCOLORSPACE for the source image
LOGCOLORSPACE lcs =
   {LCS_SIGNATURE, 0x400, sizeof(LOGCOLORSPACE)};
lcs.lcsCSType = LCS_sRGB;
lcs.lcsIntent = LCS_GM_IMAGES;
```


The next step is to create a multistage color transform object. To do this, we call the **CreateColorTransform** function specifying a non-**NULL hTargetProfile** parameter. Remember, the color profile object that's passed as the **hTargetProfile** parameter specifies the color space (and the characteristics) of the device whose output we want to proof. The color profile object that's passed as the **hDestProfile** parameter specifies the color space (and the characteristics) of the device on which the image will be proofed. In this case, because we want to proof the printer's output on the monitor, we specify **hPrinterProfile** as the **hTargetProfile** parameter and specify **hMonitorProfile** as the **hDestProfile** parameter, like so:

```
// STEP 5: Create a multistage color transform object
HTRANSFORM hColorTransform =
   CreateColorTransform(
      &lcs,
```

```
      hMonitorProfile,
      hPrinterProfile,
      MAKELONG(BEST_MODE, ENABLE_GAMUT_CHECKING)
      );
```

After the multistage color transform object is created, the final step is to perform the color matching. We do this, as usual, with the **TranslateBitmapBits** function:

```
// STEP 6: Perform the multistage color match
bool match_ok =
   TranslateBitmapBits(
      hColorTransform,
      pSourceBits, BM_RGBTRIPLETS,
      bmp.bmWidth, bmp.bmHeight, NULL,
      pMatchedBits, BM_RGBTRIPLETS, NULL,
      NULL, NULL
      );
```

It turns out that proofing is not at all difficult once you've implemented the code for standard (single-stage) color matching. All you need to do is create another color profile object—one that corresponds to the device whose output you want to proof. (In most cases, this device will be the printer.) Just keep in mind that you don't want to print an image whose colors have been matched using a multistage transform in which the last (second) stage involves a color match to the monitor's color space. Remember, when you use a multistage color transform, the source image's colors are first matched to the color space of the device whose output needs proofing, and then these colors are matched to the color space of the device on which the image will be proofed. If this latter device is the monitor, the image is no longer well-suited for printing. Because there are two color-matching steps, you're essentially limiting the image's colors to the color spaces of two devices. If you want to print a color-matched image, you simply create a regular (single-stage) color transform object, specifying a handle to the printer's color profile object as the **hDestProfile** parameter (of the **CreateColorTransform** function), and specifying **NULL** as the **hTargetProfile** parameter (of the **CreateColorTransform** function), like so:

```
HTRANSFORM hColorTransform =
   CreateColorTransform(
      &lcs,
      hPrinterProfile,
      NULL, // use NULL because we're printing, not proofing
      MAKELONG(BEST_MODE, ENABLE_GAMUT_CHECKING)
      );
```

On the other hand, if you want to proof one printer's output on another printer, then you indeed need a multistage color transform. For example, if a user has two color ink jet printers—one that uses relatively inexpensive ink and another that uses very expensive ink—he or she might want to proof the output of the expensive printer by printing the image on the inexpensive printer. In this case, you'd create a multistage color transform object by specifying a handle to the expensive printer's color profile object as the **hDestProfile** parameter (of the **CreateColorTransform** function), and by specifying a handle to the inexpensive printer's color profile object as the **hTargetProfile** parameter (of the **CreateColorTransform** function), like so:

```
HTRANSFORM hColorTransform =
   CreateColorTransform(
      &lcs,
      hExpensivePrinterProfile,
      hCheapPrinterProfile,
      MAKELONG(BEST_MODE, ENABLE_GAMUT_CHECKING)
      );
```

How accurate is the proofed image as compared to the actual (single-stage) version? Well, to a large extent, the answer depends on the size of the color gamuts of both output devices (i.e., the proofed and the proofing device). For proofing on the monitor to be successful (i.e., the proofed image looks close to the printed image), the monitor's color gamut should be a superset of the printer's color gamut. Likewise, when you're proofing the output of one printer by using another printer, the color gamut of the proofing printer (i.e., the printer that's used to proof the output of another printer) should be a superset of the proofed printer's color gamut. Following this notion, and intuition, it makes little sense to proof the output of, say, an expensive dye-sublimation printer on, say, an inexpensive ink jet printer. Similarly, it makes no sense to proof the output of a high-resolution color printer on, for example, a low-resolution grayscale printer.

Also bear in mind that manufacturers create ICC device profiles based on devices that have been properly calibrated; these profiles are usually based on devices that are fresh off the assembly line. When a device has many hours of operation under its belt, chances are good that its operating characteristics have strayed a bit from when the device was first manufactured (and tested). In other words, the color accuracy of a displayed image depends not only on a precise ICC device profile but also—and to a greater extent—on how well this device is *calibrated*. Unfortunately, there's no programmatic way to accurately calibrate a monitor. Proper calibration requires special equipment (the most expensive of which is a spectrophotometer).

Profiled Bitmaps

Up until this point, we've assumed that the colors of all source images have been defined in sRGB coordinates. Clearly, this isn't always an accurate assumption. The truth is, most images provide no color space information at all. Although some modern file formats provide specifications for embedded profiles, no one really uses them. (PNGs—which we'll discuss in Chapter 18—are the exception.) Even with the recent abundance of high-speed (broadband) modems, we're still at a stage where bandwidth comes at a premium. This is especially true for many international users who pay outrageous, often per-minute, dial-up fees. Looked at this way, embedded profiles cost not only bytes but also money. This is one of the main benefits of the sRGB standard—there's no need for an embedded profile.

For most ICM-aware applications, simply assuming that all source images use the sRGB space is sufficient. If you want to implement extra functionality that can handle embedded profiles (or other embedded information), then this is the section to read. We'll examine both embedded and linked profiles, along with other calibration information that's sometimes embedded into an image. Let's start with the new DIB headers: **BITMAPV4HEADER** and **BITMAPV5HEADER**.

ICM-Aware DIB Headers

The bitmap (DIB) file format is one of the simplest image file formats out there. Extending the bitmap file format to support ICM-related information was an entirely straightforward venture—the engineers at Microsoft simply added more data members to the **BITMAPINFOHEADER** structure. The result is the **BITMAPV4HEADER** and **BITMAPV5HEADER** structures.

TIP: *When you're designing an API, avoid the use of numbers in the names of capitalized data structures—they're cumbersome to type.*

The BITMAPV4HEADER Structure

The **BITMAPV4HEADER** structure is not actually new—it's been available since ICM version 1. This structure illustrates Microsoft's first attempt at supporting embedded color-management-related information. Here's what it looks like:

```
typedef struct {
    DWORD bV4Size;
    LONG bV4Width;
    LONG bV4Height;
    WORD bV4Planes;
    WORD bV4BitCount;
    DWORD bV4V4Compression;
    DWORD bV4SizeImage;
```

```
    LONG bV4XPelsPerMeter;
    LONG bV4YPelsPerMeter;
    DWORD bV4ClrUsed;
    DWORD bV4ClrImportant;
    DWORD bV4RedMask;
    DWORD bV4GreenMask;
    DWORD bV4BlueMask;
    DWORD bV4AlphaMask;
    DWORD bV4CSType;
    CIEXYZTRIPLE bV4Endpoints;
    DWORD bV4GammaRed;
    DWORD bV4GammaGreen;
    DWORD bV4GammaBlue;
} BITMAPV4HEADER, FAR *LPBITMAPV4HEADER, *PBITMAPV4HEADER;
```

Note that most of the data members of the **BITMAPV4HEADER** structure are straight from the **BITMAPINFOHEADER** structure; namely, the first 11 data members of **BITMAPV4HEADER** correspond directly to the 11 data members of the **BITMAPINFOHEADER** structure. (See Chapter 7 for an explanation of these data members.) The remaining nine data members (the highlighted ones) are exclusive to the **BITMAPV4HEADER** structure.

Of the nine new data members, the first four (**bV4RedMask**, **bV4GreenMask**, **bV4BlueMask**, and **bV4AlphaMask**) have nothing to do with ICM. The **bV4RedMask**, **bV4GreenMask**, and **bV4BlueMask** data members are provided only to ease the process of working with 16- and 32-bit DIBs whose **BITMAPV4HEADER::biCompression** data member specifies **BI_BITFIELDS**. Recall from Chapter 7 that these 16- and 32-bit DIB varieties require that you extract the three **DWORD**-type bit-field masks from the first three entries of the DIB's color table. If you thought then (in Chapter 7) that this design was ridiculous, you're not alone. The **BITMAPV4HEADER** structure fixes this nonsense by providing the **bV4RedMask**, **bV4GreenMask**, and **bV4BlueMask** data members; these data members correspond directly to these three bit-field masks, respectively. Also recall from Chapter 7 that in the 16-bit case, the most significant bit is usually ignored; in the 32-bit case, the most significant byte is usually ignored. In the (common) event that there's extra space (i.e., one or more bits) in each pixel, you can use the new **bV4AlphaMask** data member to specify which bit or bits are unused. This way, you can store—and easily extract—extra information, such as a translucency percentage (alpha channel information).

The remaining data members are ICM-related. The **bV4CSType** data member specifies the color space of the bitmap; this member can be assigned one of the identifiers listed in Table 16.4. When **bV4CSType** is set to **LCS_CALIBRATED_RGB**, the header must also contain information about the characteristics of the device on which the image was created or captured. This information is presented via the **bV4Endpoints**, **bV4GammaRed**, **bV4GammaGreen**, and **bV4GammaBlue** data members. Note that if the **bV4CSType** data member is set to **LCS_sRGB** or **LCS_WINDOWS_COLOR_SPACE**, then the **bV4Endpoints**, **bV4GammaRed**, **bV4GammaGreen**, and **bV4GammaBlue** data members aren't used.

The **bV4Endpoints** data member is a **CIEXYZTRIPLE** structure that specifies the tristimulus values of the image's primaries. (These values actually refer to the device on which the image was created or captured.) Here's the declaration of the **CIEXYZTRIPLE** structure:

```
typedef struct tagCIEXYZTRIPLE {
    CIEXYZ ciexyzRed;
    CIEXYZ ciexyzGreen;
    CIEXYZ ciexyzBlue;
} CIEXYZTRIPLE;
typedef CIEXYZTRIPLE FAR *LPCIEXYZTRIPLE;
```

The **ciexyzRed**, **ciexyzGreen**, and **ciexyzBlue** data members are **CIEXYZ** structures that denote the tristimulus values of the red, green, and blue primaries, respectively. Recall, CIEXYZ tristimulus values are specified as floating-point numbers; for this reason, the data members of the **CIEXYZ** structure are specified using 2.30 fixed-point notation. Here's the declaration of the **CIEXYZ** structure:

```
typedef struct tagCIEXYZ {
    FXPT2DOT30 ciexyzX;
    FXPT2DOT30 ciexyzY;
    FXPT2DOT30 ciexyzZ;
} CIEXYZ;
typedef CIEXYZ FAR *LPCIEXYZ;
```


The **ciexyzX**, **ciexyzY**, and **ciexyzZ** data members specify the *X*, *Y*, and *Z* tristimulus values, respectively, of a specific point in the 1931 **CIEXYZ** color space. Note that the **FXPT2DOT30** data type is simply an alternative type-definition (**typdef**) of the **long** data type. (See Chapter 18 for an example that converts floating-point values to 16.16 fixed-point values.)

The **bV4GammaRed**, **bV4GammaGreen**, and **bV4GammaBlue** data members specify gamma compensation factors in 16.16 fixed-point notation. These data members should be set to the inverse of the gamma of the device on which the image was created or captured. For example, if an image was created on a monitor with a red, green, and blue channel gamma of 2.0, then these data members should all reveal 0.5.

You may have noticed that the **BITMAPV4HEADER** structure contains no specification for an embedded or linked profile. This is one of the major limitations of the **BITMAPV4HEADER** structure and is the primary reason that it's rarely used. As we'll discuss next, this limitation has been lifted in the **BITMAPV5HEADER** structure.

The BITMAPV5HEADER Structure

The **BITMAPV5HEADER** structure is a recent extension of the **BITMAPV4HEADER** structure. Here's the declaration of the **BITMAPV5HEADER** structure:

```
typedef struct {
    DWORD bV5Size;
    LONG bV5Width;
    LONG bV5Height;
    WORD bV5Planes;
    WORD bV5BitCount;
    DWORD bV5Compression;
    DWORD bV5SizeImage;
    LONG bV5XPelsPerMeter;
    LONG bV5YPelsPerMeter;
    DWORD bV5ClrUsed;
    DWORD bV5ClrImportant;
    DWORD bV5RedMask;
    DWORD bV5GreenMask;
    DWORD bV5BlueMask;
    DWORD bV5AlphaMask;
    DWORD bV5CSType;
    CIEXYZTRIPLE bV5Endpoints;
    DWORD bV5GammaRed;
    DWORD bV5GammaGreen;
    DWORD bV5GammaBlue;
    DWORD bV5Intent;
    DWORD bV5ProfileData;
    DWORD bV5ProfileSize;
    DWORD bV5Reserved;
} BITMAPV5HEADER, FAR *LPBITMAPV5HEADER, *PBITMAPV5HEADER;
```

The first 20 data members of the **BITMAPV5HEADER** structure correspond directly to the 20 data members of the **BITMAPV4HEADER** structure, the first 11 of which also correspond directly to the 11 data members of the **BITMAPINFOHEADER** structure. The **BITMAPV5HEADER** structure extends its predecessors by providing four new data members: **bV5Intent**, **bV5ProfileData**, **bV5ProfileSize**, and **bV5Reserved**. The **bV5Reserved** data member, as its name suggests, isn't currently used. The former three data members, on the other hand, provide crucial information about the color space of the image (i.e., the device on which the image was created or captured).

The **bv5Intent** data member specifies the desired rendering intent. This data member can be assigned one of the identifiers listed in Table 16.5. The **bv5ProfileData** data member specifies the location of the profile data within the DIB. Specifically, **bv5ProfileData** specifies an offset, in bytes, from the beginning of the **BITMAPV5HEADER** structure to the location (in the file or in memory) of the embedded profile data or of the linked profile's file name. If the profile data is embedded, the **bV5ProfileSize** data member specifies the size of this data (in bytes).

How can you tell whether a profile is embedded or linked? You examine the **bV5CSType** data member. There's an important difference between the **bV5CSType** data member of the **BITMAPV5HEADER** structure and the **bV4CSType** data member of the **BITMAPV4HEADER** structure. In addition to the possible identifiers (in Table 16.3) that can be assigned to the **bV4CSType** data member, the **bV5CSType** data member can alternatively be set to either **PROFILE_EMBEDDED** ('MBED'), indicating that the image contains an embedded profile, or **PROFILE_LINKED** ('LINK'), indicating that the image contains a string that denotes the path and file name of a profile. Let's take a closer look at how to work with an image's profile.

Extracting a Bitmap's Profile

Before I get into the nitty-gritty of extracting a bitmap's profile data, let's see how this data is laid out in the bitmap's file and how it should be laid out in memory. There is, unfortunately, a subtle difference between these two layouts.

Recall from Chapter 7 that a DIB is composed of three parts: a header, an optional color table, and an array of pixels. When a DIB is written to a file, these parts are placed in that order: first the header, then the color table (if present), and then the pixels. Also recall from Chapter 7 that, when stored in a file, the DIB's header is preceded by the file's header, a **BITMAPFILEHEADER** structure. Where in this file is the profile information? The logical choice would be right after the pixels; and as it turns out, this is exactly where the profile data is located. The profile data, if present, should always follow the bitmap's pixels when stored in a file. This layout is depicted in Figure 16.11.

You can use the layout depicted in Figure 16.11 as a guide when you're reading a bitmap's file, but there are a few things to note before you store this information in memory (i.e., to constitute a DIB). If you're creating a packed DIB, then there's no need to shuffle the data around; the layout (in memory) of a packed DIB is identical to the layout depicted in Figure 16.11 (without the file header). On the other hand, if you're creating a "regular" (non-packed) DIB, then the profile data no longer follows the pixels; rather, you should place this data right after the color table. Remember, the pixels of a non-packed DIB can be located anywhere in memory. When you're given a non-packed DIB from, say, a third-party library, a pointer to the DIB's pixels is usually provided in a separate variable. To avoid the

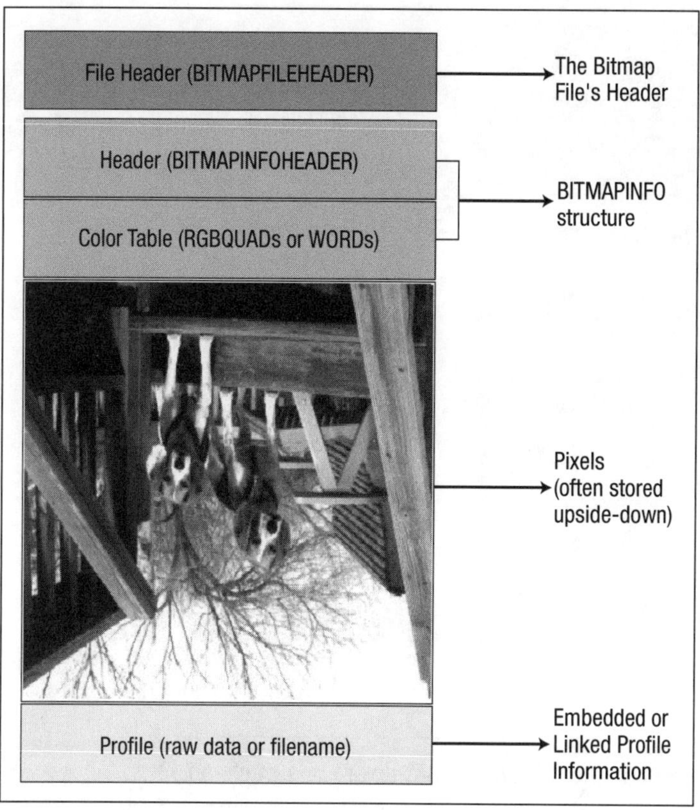

Figure 16.11 The layout of an ICM-aware bitmap file.

hassle of yet another variable for the profile data, non-packed DIBs (in memory), always store the profile data right after the color table. This layout is illustrated in Figure 16.12.

Keep in mind that these layouts are just guidelines to provide a bit of consistency when you're working with ICM-aware DIBs and DIB files. When extracting profile information, you should always rely on **BITMAPV5HEADER::bv5-ProfileData** to tell you where the profile data is located. Accordingly, if you read a non-packed DIB from a file, and then correctly place the profile data (in memory) as depicted in Figure 16.12, you should assign a *new* value to the **bv5ProfileData** data member—a value that denotes the new location of the profile's data. That is, when a bitmap's file contains an embedded profile, the profile data is located right after the pixels, and the **bv5ProfileData** data member indicates this location. However, after you read the bitmap into memory and place the profile data as indicated in Figure 16.12, the profile data is no longer located after the pixels; instead, it's located right after the color table. Because you've changed the location of the profile data, you also need to update the **bv5ProfileData** data member so that it reflects this new location.

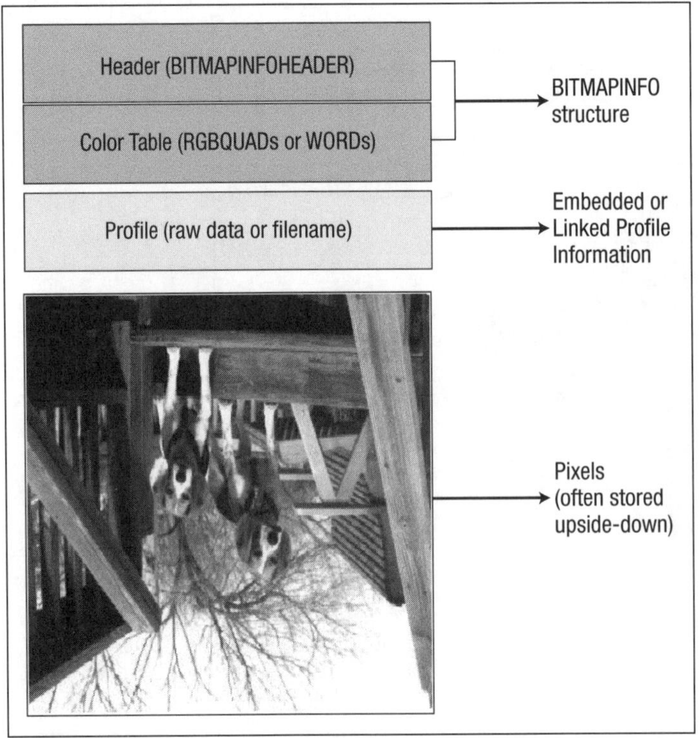

Figure 16.12 The layout, in memory, of an ICM-aware non-packed DIB.

Using an Image's Profile

After you've extracted the (linked or embedded) profile information, the next step is to initialize a **LOGCOLORSPACE** structure with information from this profile. Recall, the color space and the characteristics of an output device are specified by using a color profile object; if you want to proof an image, then you need to use two color profile objects. The image's color space, on the other hand, is specified by using a **LOGCOLORSPACE** structure.

As it turns out, the **LOGCOLORSPACE** structure isn't well-suited for working with embedded profile data. If you re-examine the declaration of the **LOGCOLORSPACE** structure (which we discussed earlier), you'll notice that **lcsFilename** is the only data member that has anything to do with a profile. Remember, this data member is a **NULL**-terminated string that specifies the name and path of the profile's file. If you're working with a linked profile, then this is perfect—you simply set the **lcsFilename** data member to the **NULL**-terminated string that's embedded in the bitmap's file, like so:

```
LOGCOLORSPACE lcs = {LCS_SIGNATURE, 0x400, sizeof(LOGCOLORSPACE)};
lcs.lcsCSType = LCS_CALIBRATED_RGB;
lcs.lcsIntent = bmV5h.bV5Intent;    // bmV5h is the DIB's header
lcs.lcsFilename = pProfileData;     // extracted from the bitmap's file
```

If you're working with embedded profile data, on the other hand, you must first save this data to a file, and then assign the location of this file to the **lcsFilename** data member. Don't worry; you don't need to understand the file format of an ICC device profile to create such a file from raw profile data. Just use the **CreateFile** function and dump the entire chunk of data to the file, like so:

```
//
// note the use of the BITMAPV5HEADER::bV5ProfileSize
// data member; this tells us how many bytes to write
// to the file
//
TCHAR image_profilename[MAX_PATH];
DWORD path_len = MAX_PATH;
GetTempPath(path_len, image_profilename);
lstrcat(image_profilename, TEXT("embedded_profile.icm\0"));
HANDLE hFile =
   CreateFile(
      image_profilename, GENERIC_READ | GENERIC_WRITE,
      0, NULL, CREATE_ALWAYS, FILE_ATTRIBUTE_NORMAL, NULL
      );
if (hFile != INVALID_HANDLE_VALUE)
{
   DWORD dwWrote;

   // dump the embedded profile data to the file
   bool write_ok = WriteFile(
      hFile, pProfileData, bmV5h.bV5ProfileSize, &dwWrote, NULL
      );
   //
   // add error checking...
   //

   // close the file
   CloseHandle(hFile);
}
```

NOTE: *The latest ICC color profile specification (ICC.1:1998-09) requires that all embedded color profiles be in complete form (with all tags left intact).*

After you've created the profile's file, you simply assign the name of this file to the **LOGCOLORSPACE::lcsFilename** data member, like so:

```
LOGCOLORSPACE lcs = {LCS_SIGNATURE, 0x400, sizeof(LOGCOLORSPACE)};
lcs.lcsCSType = LCS_CALIBRATED_RGB;
lcs.lcsIntent = bmV5h.bV5Intent;
lcs.lcsFilename = image_profilename;
```

WARNING! You must assign a fully qualified (i.e., absolute) file name to the LOGCOLORSPACE::lcsFilename data member (and you should ensure that this file indeed exists). If you assign the lcsFilename data member the name of a file without a full path, or if you specify the name of a non-existent file, you won't be given any indication of your error. Specifically—and unfortunately—subsequent calls to the CreateColorTransform function (and the TranslateBitmapBits function) will still succeed.

At this point, you have a properly initialized **LOGCOLORSPACE** structure, which you can then pass to the **CreateColorTransform** function. You implement the remaining steps in exactly the same fashion as we did in previous code snippets (where we assumed the sRGB color space).

What if the DIB doesn't contain an embedded profile? Well, in this case, you should see if the bitmap's colors lie in the sRGB color space. Specifically, you examine the **BITMAPV5HEADER::bV5CSType** data member to see if it's set to **LCS_sRGB**. If the bitmap's color space is indeed sRGB, then you're good to go—you simply initialize your **LOGCOLORSPACE** structure as we've done throughout this chapter. On the other hand, if the **BITMAPV5HEADER::bV5CSType** data member is set to **LCS_CALIBRATED_RGB** (as opposed to **PROFILE_EMBEDDED**, **PROFILE_LINKED**, or **LCS_sRGB**), then you need to initialize the data members of your **LOGCOLORSPACE** structure according to the corresponding data members of the **BITMAPV5HEADER** structure. See the companion CD-ROM and Chapter 18 for some examples of this.

Immediate Solutions

Creating a Color Profile Object

To create a color profile object, you use the **OpenColorProfile** function:

```
HPROFILE OpenColorProfile(
    IN PPROFILE pProfile,           // pointer to a PROFILE structure
    IN DWORD dwDesiredAccess,       // desired access rights
    IN DWORD dwShareMode,           // share privileges
    IN DWORD dwCreationMode         // creation options
   );
```

The **pProfile** parameter specifies a pointer to an initialized **PROFILE** structure that describes the location of the ICC device profile's disk file or location in memory. The **dwDesiredAccess** parameter specifies how the profile's data should be accessed. You can set this parameter to **PROFILE_READ** (1) for read-only access, or you can set it to **PROFILE_READWRITE** (2) for read/write access.

If the profile's data is contained in memory (instead of in a file), the **dwShareMode** and **dwCreationMode** parameters are ignored—simply set them both to zero. If the profile's data is contained in a file, the **dwShareMode** parameter specifies how to treat subsequent requests for access to this file. You can set **dwShareMode** to **FILE_SHARE_READ** (1), indicating that the file can be accessed only for reading, or to **FILE_SHARE_WRITE** (2), indicating that the file can be accessed only for writing, or you can specify a combination of these two identifiers by using the bitwise **OR** (|) operator. In addition (if the profile's data is contained in a file), the **dwCreationMode** parameter specifies general creation options. You can set this parameter to one of the identifiers listed in Table 16.7.

If the **OpenColorProfile** function is successful, it returns a handle to a color profile object (of type **HPROFILE**). If the function fails, the return value is **NULL** (not **INVALID_HANDLE_VALUE**, as is returned by an unsuccessful call to the **CreateFile** function). When the color profile object is no longer needed, you must destroy it by passing its handle to the **CloseColorProfile** function.

The following code snippet demonstrates how to use the **OpenColorProfile** function to create a color profile corresponding to the primary display's device-profile file (whose name and path are stored in the user-defined variable, **monitor_profilename**):

Table 16.7 Possible identifiers for the dwCreationMode parameter of the OpenColorProfile function.

Identifier	Value	Effect
CREATE_NEW	1	Indicates that a new file should be created. (The name of this file is specified by the **PROFILE::pProfileData** data member.) If a file of the same name already exists, the **OpenColorProfile** function fails.
CREATE_ALWAYS	2	Indicates that a new file should be created. (The name of this file is specified by the **PROFILE::pProfileData** data member.) If a file of the same name already exists, it's overwritten.
OPEN_EXISTING	3	Indicates that the file (whose name is specified by the **PROFILE::pProfileData** data member) should be opened. If this file doesn't exist, the **OpenColorProfile** function fails.
OPEN_ALWAYS	4	Indicates that the file (whose name is specified by the **PROFILE::pProfileData** data member) should be opened. If this file doesn't exist, a new file is created.
TRUNCATE_EXISTING	5	Indicates that the file (whose name is specified by the **PROFILE::pProfileData** data member) should be opened and then cleared. If this file doesn't exist, the **OpenColorProfile** function fails.

```
PROFILE profile;
profile.dwType = PROFILE_FILENAME;
profile.pProfileData = static_cast<void*>(monitor_profilename);
profile.cbDataSize =
   // "+ 1" for the NULL-termination
   (lstrlen(monitor_profilename) + 1) * sizeof(TCHAR);

// create a color profile object for the monitor's profile
HPROFILE hMonitorProfile =
   OpenColorProfile(
      &profile, PROFILE_READ,
      FILE_SHARE_READ, OPEN_EXISTING
      );
if (hMonitorProfile)
{
   //
   // work with hMonitorProfile...
   //

   CloseColorProfile(hMonitorProfile);
}
```

Creating a Color Transform Object

To create a color transform object that's to be used in a color matching scheme, you use the **CreateColorTransform** function:

```
HTRANSFORM CreateColorTransform(
    IN LPLOGCOLORSPACE pLogColorSpace,
    IN HPROFILE hDestProfile,
    IN HPROFILE hTargetProfile,
    IN DWORD dwFlags
   );
```

The **pLogColorSpace** parameter specifies a pointer to an initialized **LOGCOLORSPACE** structure that describes the characteristics of the source color space. The **hDestProfile** parameter specifies a handle to a color profile object that describes the characteristics of the destination color space. The **hTargetProfile** parameter is optional and is usually set to **NULL**. If you want to proof the output of one device on another device, you specify **hTargetProfile** as a handle to a color profile object that corresponds to the device whose output is to be proofed. The **dwFlags** parameter specifies the desired quality of the color matching when the color transform object is used with a color matching function; this parameter also specifies if, and how, the gamut mapping should be performed. The **LOWORD** of **dwFlags** can be set to one of the identifiers from Table 16.2. The **HIWORD** of **dwFlags** can be set to one of the identifiers from Table 16.3.

The following list describes how to specify the **hDestProfile** and **hTargetProfile** parameters for the most common situations:

- If you're displaying an image on a monitor, specify the **hDestProfile** parameter as a handle to a color profile object that was created from the monitor's ICC device profile. Set the **hTargetProfile** parameter to **NULL**.
- If you're printing an image, specify the **hDestProfile** parameter as a handle to a color profile object that was created from the printer's ICC device profile. Set the **hTargetProfile** parameter to **NULL**.
- If you're viewing (proofing) the output of a printer on a monitor, specify the **hDestProfile** parameter as a handle to a color profile object that was created from the monitor's ICC device profile. Specify the **hTargetProfile** parameter as a handle to a color profile object that was created from the printer's ICC device profile.

If the **CreateColorTransform** function is successful, it returns a handle to a new color transform object; otherwise, the return value is **NULL**. When the color transform object is no longer needed, you must destroy it by passing its handle to the **DeleteColorTransform** function. Note that color transform objects are used only with the **TranslateBitmapBits** function (most common), the **TranslateColors** function, the **CheckBitmapBits** function, or the **CheckColors** function.

WARNING! Not all ICC device profiles can be used for color matching. Even if the IsColorProfileValid function indicates that a particular device profile is valid, this does not guarantee that the CreateColorTransform function will succeed. Specifically, to create a color transform object, the specified profile must contain information about how to convert colors from the PCS to the color space of the destination device. The presence of the BToA0, BToA1, and BToA2 tag signatures (in the ICM file itself) indicates that this information is available for the perceptual, colorimetric, or saturation rendering intents, respectively.

The following code snippet demonstrates how to use the **CreateColorTransform** function to create a color transform object; this object is then used with the **TranslateBitmapBits** function to color-match a bitmap image. The color space of this image is assumed to be sRGB; **pBits** is a pointer to the bitmap's pixels; and **hMonitorProfile** is a handle to an existing color profile object. Here's the code:

```
//
// initialize a LOGCOLORSPACE structure
// for the source image (assume sRGB)
//
LOGCOLORSPACE lcs = {LCS_SIGNATURE, 0x400, sizeof(LOGCOLORSPACE)};
lcs.lcsCSType = LCS_sRGB;
lcs.lcsIntent = LCS_GM_IMAGES;

// create a color transform object
HTRANSFORM hColorTransform =
   CreateColorTransform(
      &lcs, hMonitorProfile, NULL,
      MAKELONG(BEST_MODE, ENABLE_GAMUT_CHECKING)
      );
if (hColorTransform)
{
   // perform the color matching
   bool match_ok =
      TranslateBitmapBits(
         hColorTransform,
         pBits, BM_RGBTRIPLETS,
         // bmp is an initialized BITMAP structure
         bmp.bmWidth, bmp.bmHeight, 0,
         pBits, BM_RGBTRIPLETS, 0,
         NULL, NULL
         );
```

```
    // clean up
    DeleteColorTransform(hColorTransform);
}
```

For more information on the **TranslateBitmapBits** function, see the next solution.

Color-Matching a Bitmap

To color-match the pixels of a bitmap, you use the **TranslateBitmapBits** function:

```
BOOL TranslateBitmapBits(
    IN HTRANSFORM hColorTransform,  // handle to a color transform object
    IN PVOID pSrcBits,              // pointer to the bitmap's pixels
    IN BMFORMAT bmInput,            // format ID for the source pixels
    IN DWORD dwWidth,               // width of the source bitmap
    IN DWORD dwHeight,              // height of the source bitmap
    IN DWORD dwInputStride,         // number of bytes per scan line in the
                                    // source pixels array
    OUT PVOID pDestBits,            // pointer to an array in which the
                                    // color-matched pixels will be placed
    IN BMFORMAT bmOutput,           // format ID for the destination pixels
    IN DWORD dwOutputStride,        // number of bytes per scan line in the
                                    // destination pixels array
    IN PBMCALLBACKFN pfnCallback,   // pointer to an optional application-
                                    // defined callback function
    IN ULONG ulCallbackData         // optional data to pass to the
                                    // callback function
  );
```

The **hColorTransform** parameter specifies a handle to a color transform object; this object describes the overall color-space transformation, which governs the way the pixels are color-matched. These pixels are denoted by using the **pSrcBits** parameter, which specifies a pointer to the pixels of the bitmap whose colors should be matched ("source array"). The **pDestBits** parameter specifies a pointer to a previously allocated array ("destination array") in which the output of this color match should be stored. Often **pDestBits** is specified as a pointer to the pixels of a second bitmap. Alternatively, you can pass a pointer to the original bitmap's pixels as both the **pSrcBits** and **pDestBits** parameters, in which case the **TranslateBitmapBits** function will store the color-matched results in the original bitmap. Note that in this case, the source pixels will be overwritten.

The **bmInput** and **bmOutput** parameters specify the format of the source and destination pixels, respectively. You can specify each of these parameters as one of the identifiers listed in Table 16.6. Note that both of these parameters are usually set to the same identifier—usually **BM_x555RGB** (for 16-bit bitmaps), **BM_RGBTRIPLETS** (for 24-bit bitmaps), or **BM_xRGBQUADS** (for 32-bit bitmaps).

The **dwWidth** and **dwHeight** parameters specify the width and height of the source bitmap. Note that because each scan line of a bitmap is usually **DWORD**-aligned, the product of the **dwWidth** and **dwHeight** parameters is not necessarily the size of the source array. Instead, the **dwInputStride** parameter specifies the number of bytes (rather than pixels) contained in each scan line of the source array. You can set this parameter to zero, in which case the **TranslateBitmapBits** function will assume **DWORD**-alignment. Likewise, the **dwOutputStride** parameter specifies the number of bytes contained in each scan line of the destination array; this parameter can also be set to zero to denote **DWORD**-alignment.

The **pfnCallback** parameter specifies a pointer to an optional application-defined callback function. The **ulCallbackData** parameter specifies optional application-defined information that will be passed to the callback function. This callback function should have the following signature:

```
BOOL WINAPI ICMProgressProcCallback(
  IN ULONG ulMax,
  IN ULONG ulCurrent,
  IN LPARAM ulCallbackData
);
```


The **ulMax** parameter indicates the total amount of color matching that needs to be done. The **ulCurrent** parameter indicates the amount of color matching that has already been done. The **ulCallbackData** parameter indicates the same value that's specified as the **TranslateBitmapBits** function's **ulCallbackData** parameter. This way, you can use the **TranslateBitmapBits** function to send application-defined data to the callback function.

If the **TranslateBitmapBits** function is successful, the return value is **TRUE**; otherwise, the function returns **FALSE**. For example, the following code snippet demonstrates how to use the **TranslateBitmapBits** function to color-match the pixels of a 24-bit DIB section bitmap (**hDIBSection**); **hColorTransform** is a handle to an existing color transform object:

```
BITMAP bmp;
const size_t bmpSize = sizeof(BITMAP);
if (GetObject(hDIBSection, bmpSize, &bmp) == bmpSize)
```

```
{
   // stay in sync
   GdiFlush();

   // perform the color matching
   bool match_ok =
      TranslateBitmapBits(
         hColorTransform,
         bmp.bmBits, BM_RGBTRIPLETS,
         bmp.bmWidth, bmp.bmHeight, NULL,
         bmp.bmBits, BM_RGBTRIPLETS, NULL,
         NULL, NULL
         );
   assert(match_ok);

   //
   // display, print, or save hDIBSection...
   //
}
```

Note that if you need to color-match an 8-bit (or less) DIB or DIB section bitmap, use the **TranslateBitmapBits** function on the bitmap's color table instead of on its pixels. (In this case, you specify **BM_xRGBQUADS** as the **bmInput** and **bmOutput** parameters.)

Proofing a Bitmap

To proof the colors of a bitmap on a particular device, you perform the following steps:

1. Initialize a **PROFILE** structure for the proofing device—i.e., the device on which the bitmap will be proofed (such as a monitor).
2. Initialize a **PROFILE** structure for the proof device—i.e., the device whose output will be proofed (such as a printer).
3. Using the proofing device's **PROFILE** structure that you initialized in Step 1, create a color profile object for the proofing device by using the **OpenColorProfile** function.
4. Using the proof device's **PROFILE** structure that you initialized in Step 2, create a color profile object for the proof device by using the **OpenColorProfile** function.
5. Validate the contents of the proofing device's profile by using the **IsColorProfileValid** function. If this profile is not valid, proceed to Step 10.

6. Validate the contents of the proof device's profile by using the **IsColorProfileValid** function. If this profile is not valid, proceed to Step 10.
7. Initialize a **LOGCOLORSPACE** structure with information about the bitmap's profile. If this information is unknown, assume the sRGB color space.
8. Using the proofing device's color profile object (from Step 3), the proof device's color profile object (from Step 4), and the **LOGCOLORSPACE** structure (from Step 7), create a multistage color transform object by using the **CreateColorTransform** function.
9. Using the color transform object that you created in Step 8 and the bitmap's pixels, perform the multistage color matching by using the **TranslateBitmapBits** function.
10. Display the color-matched bitmap on the proofing device.
11. Use the **DeleteColorTransform** function to destroy the color transform object that you created in Step 8.
12. Use the **CloseColorProfile** function twice—once to destroy the proof device's color profile object that you created in Step 4, and again to destroy the proofing device's color profile object that you created in Step 3.

Listing 16.2 demonstrates how to proof the colors of a bitmap on the primary display monitor. This example uses the **ColorMatchSetup** function to display the ICM common dialog, from which the user can choose the desired profiles and rendering intents. These selections are then used to initialize the two **PROFILE** structures (one for the monitor and one for the proof device). Two DIB section bitmaps are used—one to hold the source image, and another to hold the color-matched image. The color space of the source image is assumed to be sRGB. The output of this example is depicted in Figure 16.13.

Listing 16.2 Creating a multistage color transform object for proofing.

```
// -------------------------------------------------------------
// Windows 2000 Graphics API Black Book
// Chapter 16 - Listing 16.2 (Proofing Demo)
// -------------------------------------------------------------

#include <windows.h>
#include <cassert>
#include <icm.h>

HINSTANCE hInst;
const char* WndClassName = "GMainWnd";
```

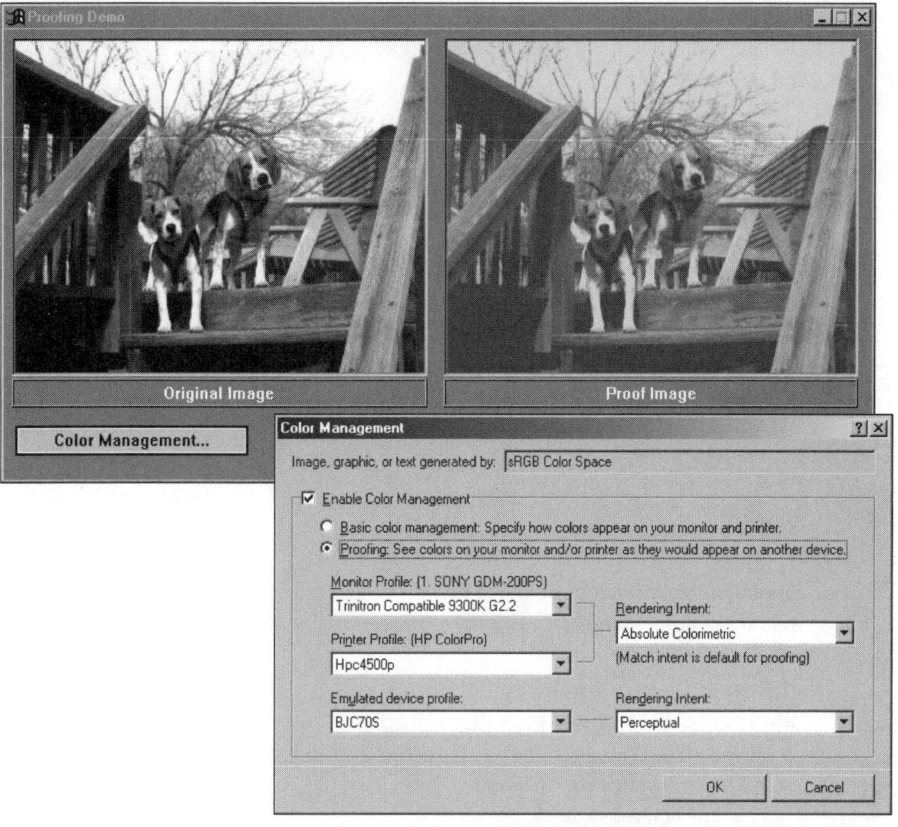

Figure 16.13 Proofing the colors of a bitmap on the monitor; the proof device profile is for a Canon Bubble-Jet BJC-70 printer.

```
LRESULT CALLBACK MainWndProc(HWND HWnd, UINT Msg, WPARAM WParam,
   LPARAM LParam);
BOOL WINAPI MyICMProgressProcCallback(ULONG ulMax, ULONG ulCurrent,
   LPARAM ulCallbackData);

int APIENTRY WinMain(HINSTANCE hInstance, HINSTANCE, LPTSTR,
   int nCmdShow)
{
   hInst = hInstance;

   WNDCLASS wc;
   memset(&wc, 0, sizeof(WNDCLASS));

   wc.lpszClassName = WndClassName;
   wc.lpfnWndProc = MainWndProc;
   wc.hInstance = hInst;
```

```
    wc.hCursor = LoadCursor(NULL, IDC_ARROW);
    wc.hbrBackground = reinterpret_cast<HBRUSH>(
       COLOR_APPWORKSPACE + 1
       );

    if (RegisterClass(&wc))
    {
       HWND hWnd =
          CreateWindow(
             WndClassName, "Proofing Demo",
             WS_OVERLAPPED | WS_MINIMIZEBOX | WS_SYSMENU |
             WS_CAPTION | WS_VISIBLE | WS_CLIPCHILDREN,
             CW_USEDEFAULT, CW_USEDEFAULT, 750, 400,
             NULL, NULL, hInst, NULL
             );

       if (hWnd)
       {
          ShowWindow(hWnd, nCmdShow);
          UpdateWindow(hWnd);

          MSG msg;
          while (GetMessage(&msg, NULL, 0, 0))
          {
              TranslateMessage(&msg);
              DispatchMessage(&msg);
          }
       }
     }
     return 0;
}


// color-matching related...
bool is_proofing = false;                // flag for proofing
BITMAP bmp = {0};                        // bitmap information
HDC hSourceMemDC = NULL;                 // handle to a memory DC
HDC hMatchedMemDC = NULL;                // handle to a memory DC
HBITMAP hSourceDIBSection = NULL;        // handle to a DIB section
HBITMAP hMatchedDIBSection = NULL;       // handle to a DIB section
unsigned char* pSourceBits = NULL;       // pointer to original pixels
unsigned char* pMatchedBits = NULL;      // pointer to color-matched pixels

HWND hButton;   // handle to the color management button
```

16. Image Color Management

```
// color-matching dialog variables...
TCHAR monitor_profile_filename[MAX_PATH];
TCHAR printer_profile_filename[MAX_PATH];
TCHAR proofing_profile_filename[MAX_PATH];
COLORMATCHSETUP cms = {sizeof(COLORMATCHSETUP), COLOR_MATCH_VERSION};

LRESULT CALLBACK MainWndProc(HWND hWnd, UINT msg, WPARAM wParam,
   LPARAM lParam)
{
   switch (msg)
   {
      case WM_CREATE:
      {
         // create the color management button
         hButton =
            CreateWindow(
               "BUTTON", "Color Management...",
               WS_CHILD | WS_VISIBLE | BS_FLAT | BS_DEFPUSHBUTTON,
               10, 330, 200, 25,
               hWnd, NULL, hInst, NULL
               );

         // initialize the COLORMATCHSETUP structure
         cms.dwFlags = CMS_ENABLEPROOFING;
         cms.hwndOwner = hWnd;
         cms.pMonitorProfile = monitor_profile_filename;
         cms.pPrinterProfile = printer_profile_filename;
         cms.pTargetProfile = proofing_profile_filename;
         cms.ccMonitorProfile = MAX_PATH;
         cms.ccPrinterProfile = MAX_PATH;
         cms.ccTargetProfile = MAX_PATH;

         // load the source DIB section from a file
         LPCSTR filename = TEXT("OnDeck.BMP\0");
         hSourceDIBSection =
            CreateDIBSectionFromFile(filename, NULL); // from Chapter 7
         assert(hSourceDIBSection != NULL);

         //
         // create a copy of the source DIB section
         // for the color-matched DIB section
         //
         hMatchedDIBSection = static_cast<HBITMAP>(
            CopyImage(hSourceDIBSection, IMAGE_BITMAP,
                      0, 0, LR_CREATEDIBSECTION)
            );
```

```
if (!hMatchedDIBSection)
{
   DeleteObject(hSourceDIBSection);
   assert(false);
}

try
{
   // get the bitmap information for each DIB section
   const size_t bmpSize = sizeof(BITMAP);
   if (GetObject(hSourceDIBSection, bmpSize, &bmp) == bmpSize)
   {
      // grab a pointer to the source pixels
      pSourceBits = static_cast<unsigned char*>(bmp.bmBits);
   }
   else throw;
   if (GetObject(hMatchedDIBSection, bmpSize, &bmp) == bmpSize)
   {
      // grab a pointer to the color-matched pixels
      pMatchedBits = static_cast<unsigned char*>(bmp.bmBits);
   }
   else throw;

   //
   // create the first memory DC and then
   // select the source DIB section into it
   //
   hSourceMemDC = CreateCompatibleDC(NULL);
   if (hSourceMemDC)
   {
      hSourceDIBSection = static_cast<HBITMAP>(
         SelectObject(hSourceMemDC, hSourceDIBSection)
         );
   }

   //
   // create the second memory DC and then
   // select the color-matched DIB section into it
   //
   hMatchedMemDC = CreateCompatibleDC(NULL);
   if (hMatchedMemDC)
   {
      hMatchedDIBSection = static_cast<HBITMAP>(
         SelectObject(hMatchedMemDC, hMatchedDIBSection)
         );
```

16. Image Color Management

```
        }
    }
    catch (...)
    {
        // clean up
        DeleteObject(hSourceDIBSection);
        DeleteObject(hMatchedDIBSection);
    }
    break;
}
case WM_PAINT:
{
    PAINTSTRUCT ps;
    HDC hDC = BeginPaint(hWnd, &ps);
    try
    {
        // define where to render the images
        RECT RImage1 =
            {10, 10, bmp.bmWidth + 10, bmp.bmHeight + 10};
        RECT RImage2 = RImage1;
        OffsetRect(&RImage2, bmp.bmWidth + 20, 0);

        // render the source DIB section
        bool blt_source_ok =
            BitBlt(
                hDC, RImage1.left, RImage1.top,
                bmp.bmWidth, bmp.bmHeight,
                hSourceMemDC, 0, 0,
                SRCCOPY
                );
        InflateRect(&RImage1, 3, 3);
        blt_source_ok &= static_cast<bool>(
            DrawEdge(hDC, &RImage1, EDGE_SUNKEN, BF_RECT)
            );
        if (!blt_source_ok) throw;

        // render the color-matched DIB section
        bool blt_matched_ok =
            BitBlt(
                hDC, RImage2.left, RImage2.top,
                bmp.bmWidth, bmp.bmHeight,
                hMatchedMemDC, 0, 0,
                SRCCOPY
                );
        InflateRect(&RImage2, 3, 3);
        blt_matched_ok &= static_cast<bool>(
```

```
            DrawEdge(hDC, &RImage2, EDGE_SUNKEN, BF_RECT)
            );
         if (!blt_matched_ok) throw;

         // adjust the text color and the background mode
         SetTextColor(hDC, RGB(255, 255, 255));
         SetBkMode(hDC, TRANSPARENT);

         // determine the height of the text
         SIZE SText;
         GetTextExtentPoint32(hDC, TEXT("A"), 1, &SText);
         SText.cy += 10;

         // render the source image's label
         RECT RLabel1 = {
            RImage1.left, RImage1.bottom + 2,
            RImage1.right, RImage1.bottom + SText.cy
            };
         DrawText(
            hDC, TEXT("Original Image\0"), -1, &RLabel1,
            DT_CENTER | DT_VCENTER | DT_SINGLELINE
            );
         DrawEdge(hDC, &RLabel1, EDGE_BUMP, BF_RECT);

         // render the color-matched image's label
         RECT RLabel2 = {
            RImage2.left, RImage2.bottom + 2,
            RImage2.right, RImage2.bottom + SText.cy
            };
         DrawText(
            hDC, TEXT("Proof Image\0"), -1, &RLabel2,
            DT_CENTER | DT_VCENTER | DT_SINGLELINE
            );
         DrawEdge(hDC, &RLabel2, EDGE_BUMP, BF_RECT);
      }
      catch (...)
      {
         EndPaint(hWnd, &ps);
      }
      EndPaint(hWnd, &ps);
      return 0;
   }
   case WM_COMMAND:
   {
      if (HIWORD(wParam) == BN_CLICKED &&
```

```
     reinterpret_cast<HWND>(lParam) == hButton)
{
   // display the color matching setup dialog
   bool setup_ok = SetupColorMatching(&cms);
   if (!setup_ok) break;

   bool no_ICM = (cms.dwFlags & CMS_DISABLEICM);
   is_proofing = (cms.dwFlags & CMS_ENABLEPROOFING);

   // if the user has disabled ICM or is not proofing...
   if (no_ICM || !is_proofing)
   {
      // copy the source bitmap to the color-matched bitmap
      BitBlt(
         hMatchedMemDC, 0, 0,
         bmp.bmWidth, bmp.bmHeight,
         hSourceMemDC, 0, 0,
         SRCCOPY
         );

      // redraw the restored bitmap
      RECT RMatched = {bmp.bmWidth + 30, 5};
      RMatched.right = RMatched.left + bmp.bmWidth;
      RMatched.bottom = RMatched.top + bmp.bmHeight;
      InvalidateRect(hWnd, &RMatched, false);
      break;
   }

   //
   // otherwise, let's proceed with color matching
   // only if the user decides to proof the output...
   //
   if (is_proofing)
   {
      //
      // STEP 1: Initialize a PROFILE
      // structure for the monitor
      //
      PROFILE monitor_profile;
      monitor_profile.dwType = PROFILE_FILENAME;
      monitor_profile.pProfileData =
         static_cast<void*>(monitor_profile_filename);
      monitor_profile.cbDataSize =
         // "+ 1" for the NULL-termination
         (lstrlen(monitor_profile_filename) + 1) * sizeof(TCHAR);
```

```
//
// STEP 2: Initialize a PROFILE
// structure for the target device
//
PROFILE target_profile;
target_profile.dwType = PROFILE_FILENAME;
target_profile.pProfileData =
   static_cast<void*>(proofing_profile_filename);
target_profile.cbDataSize =
   // "+ 1" for the NULL-termination
   (lstrlen(proofing_profile_filename) + 1) * sizeof(TCHAR);


//
// STEP 3: Create a color profile
// object for the monitor's profile
//
HPROFILE hMonitorProfile =
   OpenColorProfile(
      &monitor_profile, PROFILE_READ,
      FILE_SHARE_READ, OPEN_EXISTING
      );

//
// STEP 4: Create a color profile
// object for the target profile
//
HPROFILE hTargetProfile =
   OpenColorProfile(
      &target_profile, PROFILE_READ,
      FILE_SHARE_READ, OPEN_EXISTING
      );
try
{
   // STEP 5: Validate the contents of the monitor's profile
   BOOL is_monitor_valid = FALSE;
   IsColorProfileValid(hMonitorProfile, &is_monitor_valid);
   if (!is_monitor_valid) throw;

   // STEP 6: Validate the contents of the target profile
   BOOL is_target_valid = FALSE;
   IsColorProfileValid(hTargetProfile, &is_target_valid);
   if (!is_target_valid) throw;
```

```
//
// STEP 7: Initialize a LOGCOLORSPACE structure for
// the source image, using the proper rendering intent
//
LOGCOLORSPACE lcs = {
   LCS_SIGNATURE, 0x400, sizeof(LOGCOLORSPACE), LCS_sRGB
   };
lcs.lcsIntent = cms.dwProofingIntent;

// STEP 8: Create a multistage color transform object
HTRANSFORM hColorTransform =
   CreateColorTransform(
      &lcs, hMonitorProfile, hTargetProfile,
      MAKELONG(NORMAL_MODE, ENABLE_GAMUT_CHECKING)
      );
if (hColorTransform)
{
   // stay in sync
   GdiFlush();

   // STEP 9: Color-match the bitmap
   bool match_ok =
      TranslateBitmapBits(
         hColorTransform,
         pSourceBits, BM_RGBTRIPLETS,
         bmp.bmWidth, bmp.bmHeight, NULL,
         pMatchedBits, BM_RGBTRIPLETS, NULL,
         NULL, NULL
         );
   if (!match_ok)
   {
      MessageBox(
         hWnd, "Error Matching Colors!", "Error",
         MB_OK | MB_ICONERROR
         );
   }

   // STEP 10: Redraw the color-matched bitmap
   RECT RMatched = {bmp.bmWidth + 30, 5};
   RMatched.right = RMatched.left + bmp.bmWidth;
   RMatched.bottom = RMatched.top + bmp.bmHeight;
   InvalidateRect(hWnd, &RMatched, false);
```

```
                    // STEP 11: Clean up
                    DeleteColorTransform(hColorTransform);
                 }
                 else
                 {
                    MessageBox(
                       hWnd, "Error Creating Transform!", "Error",
                       MB_OK | MB_ICONERROR
                       );
                 }
              }
              catch (...)
              {
                 // clean up
                 CloseColorProfile(hMonitorProfile);
                 CloseColorProfile(hTargetProfile);
              }
              // STEP 12: Clean up
              CloseColorProfile(hMonitorProfile);
              CloseColorProfile(hTargetProfile);
           }
        }
        break;
     }
     case WM_DESTROY:
     {
        // clean up
        if (hSourceMemDC)
        {
           DeleteObject(SelectObject(hSourceMemDC, hSourceDIBSection));
           DeleteDC(hSourceMemDC);
        }
        if (hMatchedMemDC)
        {
           DeleteObject(SelectObject(hMatchedMemDC, hMatchedDIBSection));
           DeleteDC(hMatchedMemDC);
        }

        PostQuitMessage(0);
        break;
     }
  }
  return DefWindowProc(hWnd, msg, wParam, lParam);
}
```

Reading an ICM-Aware Bitmap from a File

To read an ICM-aware DIB from a file, you use the application-defined **LoadICMDIBFromFile** function:

```
HGLOBAL LoadICMDIBFromFile(
    IN LPCSTR filename,       // name of the bitmap file to load
    OUT LPVOID& pProfileInfo  // receives a pointer to the profile
                              // information (data or file name)
   )
{
   HGLOBAL hDIB = NULL;

   // open the file for shared reading
   HANDLE hFile =
      CreateFile(
         filename, GENERIC_READ, FILE_SHARE_READ, NULL,
         OPEN_EXISTING, FILE_ATTRIBUTE_NORMAL, NULL
         );

   if (hFile != INVALID_HANDLE_VALUE)
   {
      DWORD dwRead = 0;
      BITMAPFILEHEADER bmfh;

      // read the file header
      bool read_ok = ReadFile(
         hFile, &bmfh, sizeof(BITMAPFILEHEADER), &dwRead, NULL
         );
      if (read_ok && (dwRead == sizeof(BITMAPFILEHEADER)))
      {
         // check the format
         if (bmfh.bfType == 0x4D42)
         {
            BITMAPV5HEADER bmV5h;

            // read the DIB's header
            read_ok = ReadFile(
               hFile, &bmV5h, sizeof(BITMAPV5HEADER), &dwRead, NULL
               );
            if (read_ok && (dwRead == sizeof(BITMAPV5HEADER)))
            {
               // get the number of colors in the color table
               short num_colors = bmV5h.bV5ClrUsed;
               if (num_colors == 0 && bmV5h.bV5BitCount <= 8)
```

```
{
   num_colors = (1 << bmV5h.bV5BitCount);
}

// compute the size of the color table
const size_t color_table_size =
   sizeof(RGBQUAD) * num_colors;

// compute the size of the image
const size_t pixels_size =
   bmV5h.bV5SizeImage != 0 ? bmV5h.bV5SizeImage :
   abs(bmV5h.bV5Height) *
   ((((bmV5h.bV5Width *
       bmV5h.bV5BitCount) + 31) & ~31) >> 3);

// extract the size of the profile data
const size_t profile_size = bmV5h.bV5ProfileSize;

// compute the total size of the packed DIB
const size_t total_DIB_size =
   sizeof(BITMAPV5HEADER) +   // size of the header
   color_table_size +         // size of the color table
   pixels_size +              // size of the pixels array
   profile_size;              // size of the profile

// allocate memory for the packed DIB
hDIB = GlobalAlloc(GHND, total_DIB_size);
if (hDIB)
{
   LPVOID lpDIB = GlobalLock(hDIB);
   if (lpDIB)
   {
      // copy the header to the packed DIB
      memcpy(lpDIB, &bmV5h, sizeof(BITMAPV5HEADER));

      // offset the DIB's pointer
      lpDIB =
         static_cast<unsigned char*>(lpDIB) +
         sizeof(BITMAPV5HEADER);

      //
      // now for the color table...
      //
      if (color_table_size > 0)
      {
```

```
        // read the color table, if present
        read_ok = ReadFile(
           hFile, lpDIB, color_table_size, &dwRead, NULL
           );
        if (!read_ok || (dwRead != color_table_size))
        {
           // upon error, clean up
           pProfileInfo = NULL;
           GlobalUnlock(hDIB);
           GlobalFree(hDIB);
           CloseHandle(hFile);
           return NULL;
        }

        // offset the DIB's pointer
        lpDIB =
           static_cast<unsigned char*>(lpDIB) +
           color_table_size;
     }

     //
     // now for the pixels...
     //
     // move to the pixels
     DWORD dwMoved = SetFilePointer(
        hFile, bmfh.bfOffBits, 0, FILE_BEGIN
        );
     if (dwMoved == bmfh.bfOffBits)
     {
        // read the pixels
        read_ok = ReadFile(
           hFile, lpDIB, pixels_size, &dwRead, NULL
           );
        if (!read_ok || (dwRead != pixels_size))
        {
           // upon error, clean up
           pProfileInfo = NULL;
           GlobalUnlock(hDIB);
           GlobalFree(hDIB);
           CloseHandle(hFile);
           return NULL;
        }

        // offset the DIB's pointer
        lpDIB =
           static_cast<unsigned char*>(lpDIB) +
           pixels_size;
```

```
}
else
{
   // upon error, clean up
   pProfileInfo = NULL;
   GlobalUnlock(hDIB);
   GlobalFree(hDIB);
   CloseHandle(hFile);
   return NULL;
}

//
// now for the profile data...
//
if (bmV5h.bV5CSType == PROFILE_EMBEDDED ||
    bmV5h.bV5CSType == PROFILE_LINKED)
{
   // compute the location of the profile data
   const size_t profile_pos =
      sizeof(BITMAPFILEHEADER) + bmV5h.bV5ProfileData;

   // move to the profile
   dwMoved = SetFilePointer(
      hFile, profile_pos, 0, FILE_BEGIN
      );
   if (dwMoved == profile_pos)
   {
      // assign the profile info pointer
      pProfileInfo = lpDIB;

      // read the embedded profile data
      read_ok = ReadFile(
         hFile, lpDIB, profile_size, &dwRead, NULL
         );
      if (!read_ok || (dwRead != profile_size))
      {
         // upon error, clean up
         pProfileInfo = NULL;
         GlobalUnlock(hDIB);
         GlobalFree(hDIB);
         CloseHandle(hFile);
         return NULL;
      }
   }
   else
   {
```

16. Image Color Management

```
                        // upon error, clean up
                        pProfileInfo = NULL;
                        GlobalUnlock(hDIB);
                        GlobalFree(hDIB);
                        hDIB = NULL;
                     }
                  }
                  else pProfileInfo = NULL;

                  // unlock the global memory object
                  GlobalUnlock(hDIB);
               }
               else
               {
                  // upon error, clean up
                  pProfileInfo = NULL;
                  GlobalFree(hDIB);
                  hDIB = NULL;
               }
            }
         }
      }
   }
   // close the file
   CloseHandle(hFile);
  }
  return hDIB;
}
```

The **filename** parameter specifies a pointer to a **NULL**-terminated string that contains the full path of the bitmap file from which the DIB is loaded. Note that this bitmap must use the **BITMAPV5HEADER** structure, although you can easily modify the **LoadICMDIBFromFile** function to accommodate the **BITMAPV4HEADER** structure. The **pProfileInfo** parameter is specified as a pointer that will be initialized either with the name and path of the image's linked profile file or with the address (within the packed DIB) of the image's embedded profile data. (Recall, in a packed DIB, the embedded profile data, if present, must follow the pixels.) If no profile information is present (it's neither linked nor embedded), **pProfileInfo** is set to **NULL**.

Upon success, the **LoadICMDIBFromFile** function returns a handle to a global memory object that refers to a packed DIB. If the function fails, the return value is **NULL**. For more information on the layout of an ICM-aware DIB, see "Extracting a Bitmap's Profile" in the "In Depth" section.

Saving an ICM-Aware Bitmap to a File

To save an ICM-aware DIB to a file, or to save a non-ICM-aware DIB, DIB section bitmap, or DDB with either embedded or linked profile data, you use the application-defined **SaveICMDIBToFile** function:

```
DWORD SaveICMDIBToFile(
    IN LPCSTR filename,                      // name of the file to save as
    IN const BITMAPV5HEADER& dibHeader,      // reference to the DIB's header
    IN const unsigned char* pBits = NULL,    // pointer to the pixels
    IN LPCVOID pProfileInfo = NULL,          // pointer to profile data to
                                             // embed in the bitmap's file
    IN size_t profile_data_size = 0,         // size of the profile data
    IN BOOL embed_profile = TRUE
   )
{
   DWORD dwBytesWrote = 0;

   // first make a copy of the DIB's header
   BITMAPV5HEADER bmV5h = dibHeader;
   hmV5h.bV5Size = sizeof(BITMAPV5HEADER); // fix the size just in case

   // determine the size (in bytes) of the color table
   short num_colors = bmV5h.bV5ClrUsed;
   if (num_colors == 0 && bmV5h.bV5BitCount <=8)
   {
      num_colors = (1 << bmV5h.bV5BitCount);
   }
   const size_t color_table_size = sizeof(RGBQUAD) * num_colors;

   // next, determine the size (in bytes) of the pixels array
   const size_t pixels_size =
      bmV5h.bV5SizeImage != 0 ? bmV5h.bV5SizeImage :
      abs(bmV5h.bV5Height) *
      ((((bmV5h.bV5Width * bmV5h.bV5BitCount) + 31) & ~31) >> 3);
```

16. Image Color Management

```
// update the DIB's header
if (pProfileInfo)
{
   // specify the location of the profile data
   bmV5h.bV5ProfileData =
      sizeof(BITMAPV5HEADER) +
      color_table_size +
      pixels_size;

   //
   // specify the size of the profile data
   // and/or the type of profile data
   //
   if (embed_profile)
   {
      bmV5h.bV5ProfileSize = profile_data_size;
      bmV5h.bV5CSType = PROFILE_EMBEDDED;
   }
   else bmV5h.bV5CSType = PROFILE_LINKED;
}

// initialize the file header
BITMAPFILEHEADER bmfh;
bmfh.bfType = 0x4D42;
bmfh.bfSize =
   // size of the file header
   sizeof(BITMAPFILEHEADER) +
   // size of the DIB's header
   sizeof(BITMAPV5HEADER) +
   // size of the color table
   color_table_size +
   // size of the pixels array
   pixels_size +
   // size of the profile data
   bmV5h.bV5ProfileSize;

// offset to the pixels
bmfh.bfOffBits = bmfh.bfSize - pixels_size - bmV5h.bV5ProfileSize;

// create the file
HANDLE hFile =
   CreateFile(
      filename, GENERIC_WRITE, 0, NULL,
      CREATE_ALWAYS, FILE_ATTRIBUTE_NORMAL, NULL
      );
```

```
if (hFile != INVALID_HANDLE_VALUE)
{
   DWORD dwWritten = 0;

   // write the file header
   bool write_ok = WriteFile(
      hFile, &bmfh, sizeof(BITMAPFILEHEADER), &dwWritten, NULL
      );
   if (write_ok && (dwWritten == sizeof(BITMAPFILEHEADER)))
   {
      // accrue the number of bytes written
      dwBytesWrote += dwWritten;

      //
      // write the DIB header...
      //
      write_ok = WriteFile(
         hFile, &bmV5h, sizeof(BITMAPV5HEADER), &dwWritten, NULL
         );
      if (write_ok && (dwWritten == sizeof(BITMAPV5HEADER)))
      {
         // accrue the number of bytes written
         dwBytesWrote += dwWritten;

         //
         // write the color table, if present...
         //
         if (color_table_size != 0)
         {
            // grab a pointer to the color table
            LPRGBQUAD pColorTable = reinterpret_cast<LPRGBQUAD>(
               reinterpret_cast<unsigned char*>(&bmV5h)
               + bmV5h.bV5Size
               );
            // write the color table
            write_ok = WriteFile(
               hFile, pColorTable, color_table_size,
               &dwWritten, NULL
               );
            if (!write_ok || (dwWritten != color_table_size))
            {
               // abort upon error
               CloseHandle(hFile);
               return 0;
            }
            else
```

16. Image Color Management

```
        {
            // accrue the number of bytes written
            dwBytesWrote += dwWritten;
        }
    }

    //
    // write the pixels...
    //
    if (!pBits)
    {
        // assume a packed DIB if no pointer is supplied
        pBits = reinterpret_cast<const unsigned char*>(
            reinterpret_cast<const unsigned char*>(&dibHeader)
            + bmV5h.bV5Size + color_table_size
            );
    }
    // write the pixels
    write_ok = WriteFile(
        hFile, pBits, pixels_size, &dwWritten, NULL
        );
    if (!write_ok || (dwWritten != pixels_size))
    {
        // abort upon error
        CloseHandle(hFile);
        return 0;
    }
    else
    {
        // accrue the number of bytes written
        dwBytesWrote += dwWritten;
    }

    //
    // write the profile data, if present...
    //
    // if profile info was supplied
    if (pProfileInfo)
    {
        if (embed_profile && (profile_data_size > 0))
        {
            // write the profile
            write_ok = WriteFile(
                hFile, pProfileInfo, profile_data_size,
                &dwWritten, NULL
                );
```

```
            if (!write_ok || (dwWritten != profile_data_size))
            {
               // abort upon error
               CloseHandle(hFile);
               return 0;
            }
            else
            {
               // accrue the number of bytes written
               dwBytesWrote += dwWritten;
            }
         }
         else // linked
         {
            const size_t length =
               lstrlen(static_cast<LPCSTR>(pProfileInfo));

            // write the profile
            write_ok = WriteFile(
               hFile, pProfileInfo, length, &dwWritten, NULL
               );
            if (!write_ok || (dwWritten != length))
            {
               // abort upon error
               CloseHandle(hFile);
               return 0;
            }
            else
            {
               // accrue the number of bytes written
               dwBytesWrote += dwWritten;
            }
         }
      }
      // otherwise, is profile info indicated in the header?
      else if (bmV5h.bV5ProfileSize > 0)
      {
         // grab a pointer to the profile
         pProfileInfo =
            reinterpret_cast<unsigned char*>(&bmV5h) +
            bmV5h.bV5ProfileData;

         // write the profile
         write_ok = WriteFile(
            hFile, pProfileInfo, bmV5h.bV5ProfileSize,
```

16. Image Color Management

```
                        &dwWritten, NULL
                        );
                    if (!write_ok || (dwWritten != bmV5h.bV5ProfileSize))
                    {
                        // abort upon error
                        CloseHandle(hFile);
                        return 0;
                    }
                    else
                    {
                        // accrue the number of bytes written
                        dwBytesWrote += dwWritten;
                    }
                    // accrue the number of bytes written
                    dwBytesWrote += dwWritten;
                }
            }
        }
        // close the file
        CloseHandle(hFile);
    }
    //
    // return the total number of bytes
    // that was written to the file
    //
    return dwBytesWrote;
}
```

The **filename** parameter specifies the name of the file in which the ICM-aware DIB should be saved. If a file of the same name already exists, it is overwritten. The **bmV5h** parameter is a reference to the DIB's corresponding **BITMAPINFO** structure. If this parameter refers to a packed DIB, then the **pBits** parameter can be specified as **NULL**. Otherwise, you must specify the **pBits** parameter as a pointer to the DIB's pixels. The optional **pProfileInfo** parameter specifies a pointer to a buffer that contains any profile data that you want to place in the file. This buffer can contain either raw profile data or a **NULL**-terminated string that specifies the name of the file to link. If the **pProfileData** parameter specifies raw profile data, the **profile_data_size** parameter must indicate the size of the data buffer. The **embed_profile** parameter is a Boolean value that specifies whether the profile should be embedded or linked.

***NOTE:** Because DIBs that contain **WORD**-type color-table entries aren't portable, the **SaveICMDIBToFile** function assumes that the DIB's color table, if present, consists of **RGBQUAD**-type entries.*

If the **SaveICMDIBToFile** function is successful, it returns the number of bytes that have been written to the file; otherwise, the return value is zero. The following code snippet demonstrates how to use to the **SaveICMDIBToFile** function to save an ICM-aware packed DIB (**lpPackedbV5h**) to a file:

```
LPCSTR filename = TEXT("MyICMBitmap.BMP\0");
DWORD bytes_wrote = SaveICMDIBToFile(filename, *lpPackedbV5h);
assert(bytes_wrote != NULL);
```


Related solutions:	Found on page:
Saving a Device-Dependent Bitmap to a File	329
Saving a Device-Independent Bitmap to a File	409
Saving a DIB Section Bitmap to a File	432

Embedding Profile Information in a Bitmap

To embed profile information (raw profile data or a file name for a profile file), you use the **SaveICMDIBToFile** function (see the previous solution).

The following code snippet demonstrates how to save a non-packed ICM-aware DIB (**lpbV5h**) to a file with embedded profile information (**pProfileInfo**) that's read directly from an ICM file:

```
DWORD profile_size = 0;
unsigned char* profile_data = NULL;

LPTSTR profilename = TEXT("sRGB.ICM\0");
HANDLE hFile = CreateFile(
   profilename, GENERIC_READ, FILE_SHARE_READ, NULL,
   OPEN_EXISTING, FILE_ATTRIBUTE_NORMAL, NULL
   );
if (hFile != INVALID_HANDLE_VALUE)
{
   profile_size = GetFileSize(hFile, NULL);
   profile_data = new unsigned char[profile_size];
   try
   {
      DWORD dwRead;
      ReadFile(hFile, profile_data, profile_size, &dwRead, NULL);
      if (dwRead != profile_size) throw;
      CloseHandle(hFile); hFile = NULL;
```

```
        LPCSTR bitmap_filename = TEXT("MyICMBitmap.bmp\0");
        DWORD dwWrote =
           SaveICMDIBToFile(
              bitmap_filename, lpbV5h, pBits, profile_data, profile_size
              );
        if (dwWrote == 0) throw;
     }
     catch (...)
     {
        CloseHandle(hFile);
        delete [] profile_data;
     }
     delete [] profile_data;
}
```

In addition, you can save a non-ICM-aware DIB, DIB section bitmap, or DDB into an ICM-aware format with or without profile information. Although ICM is seldom used with DDBs, you can use the **GetDIBits** function (see Chapter 6) to retrieve a copy of a DDB's pixels. If you're working with a DIB section bitmap, the process is much less involved because you can readily access the DIB section's pixels. This approach is demonstrated in the following code snippet; **hDIBSection** is a handle to a non-ICM-aware DIB section bitmap:

```
DWORD profile_size = 0;
unsigned char* profile_data = NULL;

LPTSTR profilename = TEXT("sRGB.ICM\0");
HANDLE hFile = CreateFile(
   profilename, GENERIC_READ, FILE_SHARE_READ, NULL,
   OPEN_EXISTING, FILE_ATTRIBUTE_NORMAL, NULL
   );
if (hFile != INVALID_HANDLE_VALUE)
{
   profile_size = GetFileSize(hFile, NULL);
   profile_data = new unsigned char[profile_size];
   try
   {
      DWORD dwRead;
      ReadFile(hFile, profile_data, profile_size, &dwRead, NULL);
      if (dwRead != profile_size) throw;
      CloseHandle(hFile); hFile = NULL;

      DIBSECTION ds;
      const size_t dibSize = sizeof(DIBSECTION);
      if (GetObject(hDIBSection, dibSize, &ds) == dibSize)
```

```
      {
         BITMAPV5HEADER bmV5h = {0};
         memcpy(&bmV5h, &ds.dsBmih, sizeof(BITMAPINFOHEADER));
         bmV5h.bV5Size = sizeof(BITMAPV5HEADER);

         LPCSTR bitmap_filename = TEXT("MyICMBitmap.bmp\0");
         DWORD dwWrote =
            SaveICMDIBToFile(
               bitmap_filename, bmV5h, ds.dsBm.bmBits,
               profile_data, profile_size
               );
      }
   }
   catch (...)
   {
      CloseHandle(hFile);
      delete [] profile_data;
   }
   delete [] profile_data;
}
```

Locating the Color Folder

To determine the location of the system Color folder, you use the **GetColorDirectory** function:

```
BOOL GetColorDirectory(
    IN PCTSTR pMachineName,      // not currently used; set to NULL
    OUT PTSTR pBuffer,           // pointer to a buffer that receives
                                 // the Color folder's location
    IN OUT PDWORD pdwSize        // specifies the number of bytes in
                                 // the pBuffer array
);
```

The **pMachineName** parameter is currently ignored; set this parameter to **NULL**. The **pBuffer** parameter specifies a pointer to a buffer that will receive a string that identifies an absolute path to the system Color folder. The **pdwSize** parameter specifies the number of bytes that **pBuffer** contains; upon success, the **GetColorDirectory** function changes the value of **pdwSize** to reflect the number of bytes that have been copied to **pBuffer**.

The **GetColorDirectory** function returns a Boolean value indicating success or failure. The following code snippet demonstrates how to use the **GetColorDirectory** function to locate the system Color folder:

```
TCHAR color_folder[MAX_PATH];
DWORD num_bytes = MAX_PATH;

if (GetColorDirectory(NULL, color_folder, &num_bytes))
{
   MessageBox(hWnd, color_folder, "", MB_OK);
}
```

Using the ICM Common Dialog

To display the ICM common dialog box, you use the **SetupColorMatching** function:

```
BOOL SetupColorMatching(
    IN OUT PCOLORMATCHSETUP pcms   // pointer to an initialized
                                   // COLORMATCHSETUP structure
   );
```

The single parameter, **pcms**, specifies a pointer to an initialized **COLORMATCHSETUP** structure. The data members of this structure serve as your means of communication with the **SetupColorMatching** function. Before you call the **SetupColorMatching** function, you initialize the data members of this structure to set various display and storage options. If the **SetupColorMatching** function is successful, it shows the ICM common dialog box, and then changes the data members of the **COLORMATCHSETUP** structure according to the user's selections (unless the user cancels the dialog box).

Table 16.8 describes the data members of the **COLORMATCHSETUP** structure. You don't have to initialize all of these data members, but at a minimum, you must initialize at least the following: **dwSize**, **dwVersion**, **pMonitorProfile**, **pPrinterProfile**, **pTargetProfile**, **ccMonitorProfile**, **ccPrinterProfile**, and **ccTargetProfile**. The other data members can simply be set to zero. Table 16.9 describes the identifiers that can be assigned to the **dwFlags** data member (combinations are allowed).

***NOTE:** To use the **ColorMatchSetup** function, you must either statically link with icmui.lib or dynamically link with icmui.dll.*

See also "Color Gamut Mapping and Rendering Intents" in the "In Depth" section.

Table 16.8 The data members of the COLORMATCHSETUP structure.

Member If Set by the Developer...	If Set by the ColorMatchSetup Function...
dwSize Specifies the structure's size; set to **sizeof(COLORMATCHSETUP)**.	N/A
dwVersion Specifies the structure's version; set to **COLOR_MATCH_VERSION** (512).	N/A
dwFlags Specifies display options; see Table 16.9.	Specifies the user's chosen options; see Table 16.9.
hwndOwner Specifies the dialog's owner window.	N/A
pSourceName Specifies an application-defined string that describes the color space of the source image—this is meant only for display purposes; see Figure 16.9. If set to **NULL**, the string "sRGB Color Space" is displayed.	N/A
pDisplayName Specifies the name of the monitor to be used with the Monitor Profile combo box. If set to **NULL**, the primary monitor is used.	N/A
pPrinterName Specifies the name of the printer to be used with the Printer Profile combo box. If set to **NULL**, the default printer is used.	N/A
dwRenderIntent Specifies the initial rendering intent to be displayed in the non-proofing Rendering Intent combo box (see Table 16.10). If set to **NULL**, the Picture intent is used. This data member is ignored unless the **dwFlags** data member contains the **CMS_SETRENDERINTENT** flag.	Specifies the rendering intent that the user has chosen from the non-proofing Rendering Intent combo box.
dwProofingIntent Specifies the initial proofing intent to be displayed in the proofing Rendering Intent combo box (see Table 16.10). If set to **NULL**, the Picture intent is used. This data member is ignored unless the **dwFlags** data member contains a combination of the **CMS_ENABLEPROOFING** and **CMS_SETRENDERINTENT** flags.	If the user chooses proofing, this data member specifies the rendering intent that the user has chosen from the proofing Rendering Intent combo box.

(continued)

Table 16.8 The data members of the COLORMATCHSETUP structure *(continued)*.

Member If Set by the Developer...	If Set by the ColorMatchSetup Function...
pMonitorProfile Specifies a pointer to a previously allocated buffer that will hold the name of the profile chosen from the Monitor Profile combo box. If the **dwFlags** data member contains the **CMS_SETMONITORPROFILE** flag, **pMonitorProfile** can be initialized to a string that specifies the profile that should be displayed initially in the Monitor Profile combo box.	Specifies the name of the profile that the user has chosen from the Monitor Profile combo box.
ccMonitorProfile Specifies the number of characters in the buffer referred to by the **pMonitorProfile** data member.	N/A
pPrinterProfile Specifies a pointer to a previously allocated buffer that will hold the name of the profile chosen from the Printer Profile combo box. If the **dwFlags** data member contains the **CMS_SETPRINTERPROFILE** flag, **pPrinterProfile** can be initialized to a string that specifies the profile that should be displayed initially in the Printer Profile combo box.	Specifies the name of the profile that the user has chosen from the Printer Profile combo box.
ccPrinterProfile Specifies the number of characters in the buffer referred to by the **pPrinterProfile** data member.	N/A
pTargetProfile Specifies a pointer to a previously allocated buffer that will hold the name of the profile chosen from the Emulated Device Profile combo box. If the **dwFlags** data member contains the **CMS_SETTARGETPROFILE** flag, **pTargetProfile** can be initialized to a string that specifies the profile that should be displayed initially in the Emulated Device Profile combo box.	Specifies the name of the profile that the user has chosen from the Emulated Device Profile combo box.
ccTargetProfile Specifies the number of characters in the buffer referred to by the **pTargetProfile** data member.	N/A
lpfnHook Specifies a pointer to an optional application-defined hook procedure. If set to **NULL**, no hook procedure is used.	N/A

(continued)

Table 16.8 The data members of the COLORMATCHSETUP structure *(continued).*

Member If Set by the Developer...	If Set by the ColorMatchSetup Function...
lParam Specifies optional application-defined data that's passed to the **lpfnHook** hook procedure as the **lParam** parameter that accompanies the **WM_INITDIALOG** message. If set to **NULL**, no application-defined information is sent to the hook procedure.	N/A
lpfnApplyCallback Specifies a pointer to an optional application-defined callback function that's invoked when the user clicks on the Apply button. This data member is ignored unless the **dwFlags** data member contains the **CMS_USEAPPLYCALLBACK** flag. If set to **NULL**, no callback function is used.	N/A
lParamApplyCallback Specifies optional application-defined data that's passed to the **lpfnApplyCallback** callback function. If set to **NULL**, no application-defined information is sent to the callback function.	N/A

Table 16.9 Possible identifiers that can be assigned to the COLORMATCHSETUP::dwFlags data member.

Identifier Value	If Set by the Developer...	If Set by the ColorMatchSetup Function...
CMS_DISABLEICM 1	Specifies that the Enable Color Management checkbox should be unchecked initially.	Specifies that the user has unchecked the Enable Color Management checkbox.
CMS_ENABLEPROOFING 2	Specifies that the Proofing checkbox should be checked initially.	Specifies that the user has checked the Proofing checkbox.
CMS_SETRENDERINTENT 4	Specifies that the non-proofing Rendering Intent combo box should be set initially to the intent indicated by the **dwRenderIntent** data member.	Specifies that the user has checked the Enable Color Management checkbox.

(continued)

16. Image Color Management

Table 16.9 Possible identifiers that can be assigned to the COLORMATCHSETUP::dwFlags data member *(continued)*.

Identifier Value	If Set by the Developer...	If Set by the ColorMatchSetup Function...
CMS_SETPROOFINTENT		
8	Specifies that the non-proofing Rendering Intent combo box should be set initially to the intent indicated by the **dwProofingIntent** data member. This identifier is ignored unless the **CMS_ENABLEPROOFING** flag is also set.	Specifies that the user has checked the Proofing checkbox.
CMS_SETMONITORPROFILE		
0x10	Specifies that the **pMonitorProfile** data member contains a string indicating the profile that should be selected initially in the Monitor Profile combo box.	N/A
CMS_SETPRINTERPROFILE		
0x20	Specifies that the **pPrinterProfile** data member contains a string indicating the profile that should be selected initially in the Printer Profile combo box.	N/A
CMS_SETTARGETPROFILE		
0x40	Specifies that the **pTargetProfile** data member contains a string indicating the profile that should be selected initially in the Emulated Device Profile combo box.	N/A
CMS_USEHOOK		
0x80	Specifies that the **lpfnHook** and **lParam** data members are valid.	N/A
CMS_USEAPPLYCALLBACK		
0x100	Specifies that the **lpfnApplyCallback** and **lParamApplyCallback** data members are valid; this causes the dialog box to display an Apply button.	N/A
CMS_USEDESCRIPTION		
0x200	Specifies that the Monitor Profile, Printer Profile, and Emulated Device Profile combo boxes should contain profile description tags instead of profile file names.	N/A

(continued)

Table 16.9 Possible identifiers that can be assigned to the COLORMATCHSETUP::dwFlags data member *(continued)*.

Identifier Value	If Set by the Developer...	If Set by the ColorMatchSetup Function...
CMS_DISABLEINTENT		
0x400	Specifies that both Rendering Intent combo boxes should be disabled.	N/A
CMS_DISABLERENDERINTENT		
0x800	Specifies that the non-proofing Rendering Intent combo box should be disabled when the Proofing checkbox is checked.	N/A
CMS_MONITOROVERFLOW		
0x80000000L	N/A	Specifies that the buffer indicated by the **pMonitorProfile** data member is not large enough to hold the name of the chosen monitor profile.
CMS_PRINTEROVERFLOW		
0x40000000L	N/A	Specifies that the buffer indicated by the **pPrinterProfile** data member is not large enough to hold the name of the chosen printer profile.
CMS_TARGETOVERFLOW		
0x20000000L	N/A	Specifies that the buffer indicated by the **pProofingProfile** data member is not large enough to hold the name of the chosen proofing profile.

16. Image Color Management

Table 16.10 Possible identifiers that can be assigned to the dwRenderIntent and dwProofingIntent data members of the COLORMATCHSETUP structure.

Identifier	Value	Meaning
INTENT_PERCEPTUAL	0	Specifies the perceptual rendering intent.
INTENT_SATURATION	1	Specifies the saturation rendering intent.
INTENT_RELATIVE_COLORIMETRIC	2	Specifies the relative colorimetric rendering intent.
INTENT_ABSOLUTE_COLORIMETRIC	3	Specifies the absolute colorimetric rendering intent.

If the **SetupColorMatching** function fails, no dialog box is shown and the function returns **FALSE**. If the **SetupColorMatching** function is successful, the ICM common dialog box is shown, and the return value is a Boolean value that indicates whether or not the user canceled the dialog box. If the user accepts the dialog box (clicks on the OK button), the **SetupColorMatching** function returns **TRUE**. If the user cancels the dialog box, the return value is **FALSE**.

The following code snippet demonstrates how to use the **ColorMatchSetup** function to display a bare-bones ICM common dialog box. The names of the chosen profiles are then displayed:

```
TCHAR monitor_profilename[MAX_PATH];
TCHAR printer_profilename[MAX_PATH];
TCHAR proofing_profilename[MAX_PATH];

COLORMATCHSETUP cms = {
   sizeof(COLORMATCHSETUP), COLOR_MATCH_VERSION
   };
cms.pMonitorProfile = monitor_profilename;
cms.pPrinterProfile = printer_profilename;
cms.pTargetProfile = proofing_profilename;
cms.ccMonitorProfile = MAX_PATH;
cms.ccPrinterProfile = MAX_PATH;
cms.ccTargetProfile = MAX_PATH;

// display the ICM common dialog
if (SetupColorMatching(&cms))
{
   // if the user has not disabled ICM
   if (!(cms.dwFlags & CMS_DISABLEICM))
   {
      MessageBox(
         NULL, monitor_profilename,
         TEXT("Chosen Monitor Profile..."),
         MB_OK
         );
      MessageBox(
         NULL, printer_profilename,
         TEXT("Chosen Printer Profile..."),
         MB_OK
         );
```

```
        // if the user has enabled proofing
        if (cms.dwFlags & CMS_ENABLEPROOFING)
        {
           MessageBox(
              NULL, proofing_profilename,
              TEXT("Chosen Proofing Profile..."),
              MB_OK
              );
        }
     }
  }
```

See the companion CD-ROM for an example that uses a callback function within the ICM dialog.

Chapter 17

Image Manipulation

In Depth

In this chapter, we'll examine several image-processing-based techniques that you can use to manipulate images. We'll first focus on an area of image processing called *point processing*, which is used to adjust an image's brightness, contrast, and other intensity-based attributes. Next, we'll discuss a technique called *filtering*, which is used to manipulate an image's frequency components. We'll examine two techniques that can be used to filter an image: frequency-domain filtering and spatial-domain filtering. In addition, we'll discuss the fundamentals of signal processing and how you can apply signal processing theory to create special effects. Next, we'll shift gears and discuss a technique called *image warping*, which can be used to manipulate an image's geometry. We'll look at the math behind image warping and how it relates to other geometric transformations. Later, we'll examine how image warping plays a central role in morphing two images.

This chapter is unique in that there's no inherent link to Windows. That is, you can use all of the algorithms that we'll discuss with any (ANSI-compliant) C++ compiler, on any platform. When possible, it's best to avoid mixing front-end and back-end code—image processing definitely falls in the latter category. So, before we discuss any actual image processing, let me introduce the **GBuffer** and **GBufferList** classes.

The GBuffer Class

The **GBuffer** class is a parameterized (template-based) C++ class that's designed to serve as an abstraction of a general image—i.e., a two-dimensional array. Although most of the examples in this chapter use the **GBuffer** class, you certainly don't have to. You can use one of the many varieties of the **CDIB** class that are available on the Internet; you can use the **TBitmap** class if you're working with C++Builder (or Delphi); or you can use the **QPixmap** class if you're working with Qt. I do, however, recommend that you avoid using a raw DIB or DIB section bitmap. Many of the algorithms that we'll examine are complicated enough on their own—there's no point in adding extra confusion by worrying about bit-shifting or pointer arithmetic.

Now let's look at the declaration of the **GBuffer** class:

```
#include <stdexcept>

template<class Type>
class GBuffer
{
public:
   // default constructor
   GBuffer(int width = 0, int height = 0);
   // copy constructor
   GBuffer(const GBuffer<Type> &copy);
   // destructor
   ~GBuffer();

   // assignment operator
   GBuffer<Type>& operator =(const GBuffer<Type>& rhs);
   // element-by-element multiplication operator
   GBuffer<Type> operator *(const GBuffer<Type>& rhs);

   // read-only member functions
   int Width() const;
   int Height() const;
   unsigned long Size() const;
   unsigned long SizeOf() const;
   const Type* Data() const;
   Type* Data();
   Type Pixels(int X, int Y) const
      {
         if (X >= 0 && X < width_ && Y >= 0 && Y < height_)
         {
            return *(data_ + X + (width_ * Y));
         }
         return blank_pixel_;
      }
   Type PixelsCE(int X, int Y) const
      {
         // perform inline circular extension
         if (X < 0) X = X + width_;
         else if (X >= width_) X = X - width_;
         if (Y < 0) Y = Y + height_;
         else if (Y >= height_) Y = Y - height_;

         return *(data_ + X + (width_ * Y));
      }
   Type PixelsSE(int X, int Y) const
      {
```

```
            // perform inline symmetric extension
            if (X < 0) X = -X;
            else if (X >= width_) X = 2 * width_ - X - 2;
            if (Y < 0) Y = -Y;
            else if (Y >= height_) Y = 2 * height_ - Y - 2;

            return *(data_ + X + (width_ * Y));
        }

    // write-only member functions
    void SetBlankPixel(Type value);
    void Width(int value);
    void Height(int value);
    void Pixels(int X, int Y, Type value)
    {
            if (X >= 0 && X < width_ && Y >= 0 && Y < height_)
            {
               *(data_ + X + (width_ * Y)) = value;
            }
            else throw std::out_of_range("Pixels");
    }

    // utility member functions
    void ZeroData();
    void FillData(Type value);

private:
    int width_;
    int height_;
    Type* data_;
    Type blank_pixel_;
};
```


Again, the **GBuffer** class is meant to represent any arbitrary two-dimensional array of pixels. Because **GBuffer** is parameterized, these pixels can be of type **unsigned char**, **RGBTRIPLE**, **RGBQUAD**, and so on. You use the **Height** and **Width** member functions to get and set the height and the width of the image. To read the value of each pixel, you use the version of the **Pixels** member function that takes two parameters: an x-coordinate and a y-coordinate. Likewise, you set the value of each pixel by using the version of the **Pixels** member function that accepts three parameters: an x-coordinate, a y-coordinate, and a new pixel value.

The **PixelsCE** and **PixelsSE** member functions are used to perform circular extension and symmetric extension, respectively. As we'll discuss later, many of the algorithms require special processing at an image's boundaries. The **PixelsCE** member function is useful when an image is assumed to be periodic. If you read the pixel that's located 10 pixels beyond the rightmost edge of the image, for example, the **PixelsCE** member function will return the value of the pixel that's located at 10 pixels from the image's leftmost edge. The **PixelsSE** member function, on the other hand, assumes that the image is reflected across its edges. In this case, if you read the pixel that's located 10 pixels beyond the rightmost edge of the image, the **PixelsSE** member function will return the value of the pixel that's located at 10 pixels from the image's rightmost edge.

If you need direct access to the underlying data, you use the **Data** member function. The **Size** and **SizeOf** member functions report the size of this data in pixels and in bytes, respectively. The rest of the member functions should be self-explanatory.

In the "Immediate Solutions" sections, you'll find the definition of the **DIBSectionToBuffer** and **BufferToDIBSection** functions. The **DIBSectionToBuffer** is used to initialize a **GBuffer** object with the pixels of a 24-bpp DIB section bitmap. Likewise, the **BufferToDIBSection** function is used to initialize the pixels of a DIB section bitmap with those of a **GBuffer** object. Although both of these functions are used by many of the code snippets in this chapter, you don't really need to know their definitions to understand the image-processing-related material. For more information on DIB section bitmaps, you can refer to Chapter 7; in this chapter, we'll focus mainly on image processing.

The GBufferList Class

Any element class (**GBuffer**) should have a corresponding container class. This is the role of the **GBufferList** class—it's designed to maintain a list of **GBuffer** objects. Here's its declaration:

```
#include <vector>
#include "gbuffer.h"

template<class Type>
class GBufferList
{
typedef std::vector<GBuffer<Type>*> Container;
typedef Container::iterator Iterator;

public:
   // default constructor
   GBufferList();
   // copy constructor
   GBufferList(const GBufferList<Type>& copy);
```

```
    // destructor
    ~GBufferList();

    // assignment operator
    GBufferList<Type>& operator =(const GBufferList<Type>& rhs);

    // general member functions
    int Count() const;
    const GBuffer<Type>& Items(int index) const;
    GBuffer<Type>& Items(int index);
    GBuffer<Type>& Add(int width = 0, int height = 0);
    GBuffer<Type>& Add(const GBuffer<Type>& Item);
    GBuffer<Type>& Insert(int index, int AWidth = 100, int height = 100);
    GBuffer<Type>& Insert(int index, const GBuffer<Type>& Item);
    void Replace(int index, const GBuffer<Type>& Item);
    void Delete(int index);
    void Clear();

    // utility member functions
    void ZeroItems(int count);
    void ZeroItems(const int* pIndices, int count);

private:
    Container items_;
};
```

The **GBufferList** class uses the **vector** class from the Standard C++ Library to maintain an internal list of **GBuffer** objects. You add a new **GBuffer** object to the list by using the version of the **Add** member function that accepts width and height parameters. These parameters, which are zero by default, define the dimensions of the new **GBuffer** object. (If you want to add an existing **GBuffer** object to the list, you use the version of the **Add** member function that accepts a reference to a **GBuffer** object.) Later, to access these **GBuffer** objects, you use the **Items** member function. The **Items** member function returns a reference to the **GBuffer** object that's located at the zero-based position specified by the **index** parameter. To remove a specific **GBuffer** object from the list, you use the **Delete** member function. The rest of the member functions are either seldom used or self-explanatory.

Point Processing

The term *point processing* is used to describe a set of image processing algorithms that rely only on a single point—i.e., pixel—of an image. (Here, we'll focus strictly on point processing techniques that rely on the *value* of each pixel as opposed to its position within the image.) Because each pixel is treated independently, point processing is useful when you want to tweak an image's colors. For example, point processing is most often used to produce effects such as brightening, darkening, contrast enhancement, and the like. In this section, we'll discuss five "must know" point processing techniques: *grayscale approximation*, *thresholding*, *brightness adjustment*, *contrast stretching*, and *histogram equalization*. Before we get into the details, however, there's an important (albeit obvious) shortcut that you can use to significantly reduce the number of flops involved in most point processing computations; this involves the use of a so-called *result table*.

Imagine that you have an image that's 1,000 pixels wide and 1,000 pixels high. Suppose that, for each pixel, you need to perform some (potentially expensive) computation using only that pixel's value. For example, say that you need to compute the cubed-root of each value, scaled by some factor. One way to implement this—which we'll do by using a **GBuffer** object called **imgBuffer**—is as follows:

```
#define CLIP(x) x > 255 ? 255 : x < 0 ? 0 : x
const double one_third = 1 / 3.0;
const double norm_scale = 40.21241170178;

// for each pixel...
for (int y = 0; y < 1000; ++y)
{
   for (int x = 0; x < 1000; ++x)
   {
      RGBTRIPLE pixel = imgBuffer.Pixels(x, y);

      pixel.rgbtRed = static_cast<unsigned char>(
         CLIP(norm_scale * pow(pixel.rgbtRed, one_third) + 0.5)
         );
      pixel.rgbtGreen = static_cast<unsigned char>(0.5 +
         CLIP(norm_scale * pow(pixel.rgbtGreen, one_third) + 0.5)
         );
      pixel.rgbtBlue = static_cast<unsigned char>(
         CLIP(norm_scale * pow(pixel.rgbtBlue, one_third) + 0.5)
         );

      imgBuffer.Pixels(x, y, pixel);
   }
}
```

In this case, because the image's dimensions are 1000x1000 and because the image contains three color planes, we're making 3,000,000 calls to the **pow** function. Notice, however, that we're calling the **pow** function with a fixed second parameter (1/3), and with only a limited range of values for the first parameter. Namely, because the red, green, and blue components (of each pixel) are each of only a single byte, the value of each color component will always be in the range 0 to 255. Because we're passing only 256 different values to the **pow** function, there will be only 256 different outputs. Therefore, instead of calling the **pow** function 3,000,000 times, we really need to call the **pow** function only 256 times, storing the results in a 256-element look-up table. In this way, instead of calling **pow** for each pixel, we simply "look up" the appropriate result. This approach is demonstrated in the following code snippet:

```
#define CLIP(x) x > 255 ? 255 : x < 0 ? 0 : x
const double one_third = 1 / 3.0;
const double norm_scale = 40.21241170178;

// compute the result table
unsigned char result_table[256];
for (int value = 0; value < 256; ++value)
{
   result_table[value] = static_cast<unsigned char>(
      CLIP(norm_scale * pow(value, one_third) + 0.5)
      );
}

// for each pixel...
for (int y = 0; y < height; ++y)
{
   for (int x = 0; x < width; ++x)
   {
      RGBTRIPLE pixel = imgBuffer.Pixels(x, y);

      // look up the pre-computed result
      pixel.rgbtRed = result_table[pixel.rgbtRed];
      pixel.rgbtGreen = result_table[pixel.rgbtGreen];
      pixel.rgbtBlue = result_table[pixel.rgbtBlue];

      imgBuffer.Pixels(x, y, pixel);
   }
}
```

It's important to note that this result-table-based approach works only because each pixel is treated independently, and only because the size of the result table (i.e., range of inputs) is most often less than the size of the image. If you're working with a 24-bpp image that contains only 50 pixels, for example, it makes no sense to call the **pow** function 256 times when the direct approach involves only

150 calls to **pow**. Of course, very few images contain only 50 pixels; most images contain tens of thousands of pixels. So, for most (but not all) situations, a result table is a good thing.

Histograms

A *histogram* is a graphical representation of a frequency distribution. The histogram of an image is a graphical representation that describes the frequency of occurrence of each of the possible values that the image may contain. An image's histogram is composed of a series of bins in which each bin holds a value that represents the number of pixels in the image that match a certain value. Figure 17.1 depicts an 8-bpp-grayscale image and its corresponding histogram. In this case, the histogram contains 256 bins because each pixel of an 8-bpp image can represent one of 256 possible values.

For color images, a separate histogram can be created for each color channel. In many situations, however, it's most useful to create a single histogram in which each bin represents a specific luminance (i.e., luminous intensity per unit projected area). For an RGB image, you can use the following NTSC (National Television Systems Committee) formulation to compute the luminance, Y, of each pixel, $f(x, y)$:

$$Y = 0.299 f_{red}(x, y) + 0.587 f_{green}(x, y) + 0.114 f_{blue}(x, y)$$

Each color component—$f_{red}(x, y)$, $f_{green}(x, y)$, $f_{blue}(x, y)$—is weighted by a value that's related to our sensitivity (i.e., the sensitivity of the human visual system) to different colors. This formula is also useful if you want to convert a color image into its grayscale equivalent.

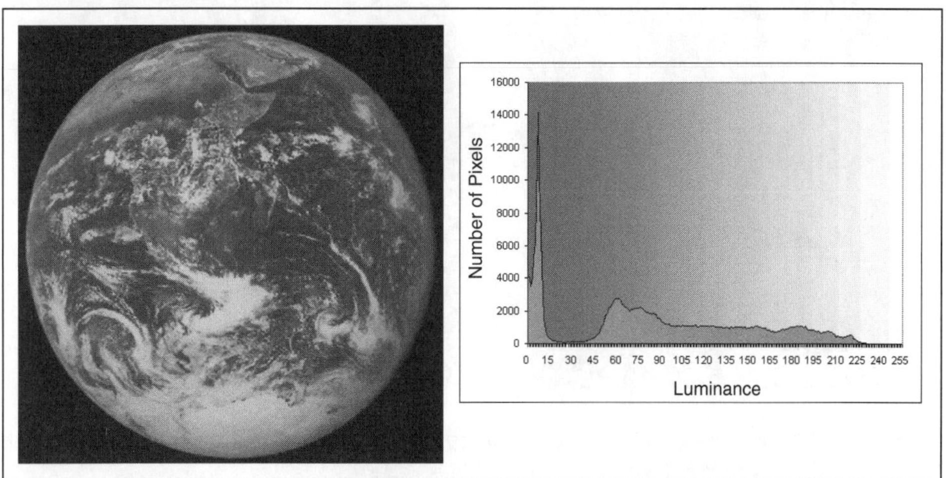

Figure 17.1 The histogram of an image.

Single-level Thresholding

Single-level thresholding is the process of transforming an image into a binary form, in which each pixel can take on one of two values (usually, 0 or 255). This type of thresholding is accomplished by examining each pixel in an image and testing whether its value lies above or below a certain *threshold value*. All pixels whose values fall below the threshold are mapped to zero while values above (or equal to) the threshold are mapped to 255. Figure 17.2 depicts an image and its processed counterpart.

For color images, you first convert the image to a grayscale form, and then perform the thresholding operation. As we'll discuss later, thresholding is commonly used as the final step in a technique called *segmentation* in which the objects of an image are demarcated. (You might be able to see this from Figure 17.2.)

Brightness Adjustment

An image's brightness can be adjusted in either a linear or a non-linear fashion. The linear approach involves offsetting each pixel's value by some fixed constant, clipping all results that are greater than 255 to 255 and all results that are less than 0 to 0. Because each pixel's value is adjusted by the same amount, linear brightness-adjustment results in a shift of the image's histogram; namely, a shift toward white for brightening and a shift toward black for darkening. Figure 17.3 depicts three images and their corresponding histograms. The first image is the original; the second and third images depict the effects of offsetting each pixel's value by positive and negative 20 units, respectively.

Figure 17.2 An image (left) and the result of performing a thresholding operation (right) with the threshold value of 205.

Linear brightness-adjustment is fast, simple, and it generally produces good results. However, notice from the second histogram of Figure 17.3 that the brightened image no longer contains an intensity value of zero. Likewise, the third histogram no longer contains an intensity value of 255. Non-linear brightness-

Figure 17.3 Brightening and darkening an image via linear brightness adjustment.

adjustment is useful when you want to preserve the values of 0 and 255. The nonlinear adjustment to each pixel's value, $f(x, y)$, is computed as follows:

$$f_{adjusted}(x, y) = 255 \left(\frac{f(x, y)}{255}\right)^{\gamma}$$

where $f_{adjusted}(x, y)$ is the adjusted (i.e., brightened or darkened) value.

NOTE: *For a grayscale image, f(x, y) represents a pixel's value. For a color image, f(x, y) represents the value of one color channel of a pixel. You should compute $f_{adjusted}(x, y)$ separately for each color plane.*

When the value of the exponent γ is less than 1, the result is a brightening. When γ is greater than 1, the result is a darkening. (And, when γ is equal to 1, there's no change because you're just dividing and then multiplying each pixel's value by 255.) Notice that this technique preserves the values of 0 and 255 because when $f(x, y)$ is 0, $f_{adjusted}(x, y)$ is just 255 times 0 raised to some power—i.e., the result is 0. Similarly, when $f(x, y)$ is 255, $f_{adjusted}(x, y)$ is just 255 times 1 raised to some power—i.e., the result is 255. (For a code snippet that uses this equation, see the solution "Brightening or Darkening an Image.")

Contrast Stretching

Contrast stretching is a technique that's used to increase an image's contrast and dynamic range. The term "stretching" refers to the fact that the histogram of the resulting image is stretched out. This stretching effect is useful because the histogram of a low contrast image is usually very compact (i.e., skinny).

Consider, for example, an image that has a dynamic range of 10; specifically, suppose the image contains only 10 unique intensity values that range from 125 to 134. Clearly, the histogram of this (extremely low contrast) image is very compact; therefore, we'd like to stretch the histogram out. The idea behind contrast stretching is to take the lowest intensity value (125) and map or "pull" it down to zero, and to take the highest intensity value (134) and map or "pull" it up to 255. Mathematically, this scheme is written as follows:

$$f_{stretched}(x, y) = 255 \left(\frac{f(x, y) - I_{\min}}{I_{\max} - I_{\min}}\right)$$

where $f(x, y)$ is the pixel's original value, $f_{stretched}(x, y)$ is the adjusted value, I_{min} is the lowest intensity value (125 in our case), and I_{max} is the highest intensity value (134 in our case). You can see from this equation that when a pixel's value, $f(x, y)$, is 125, the numerator will be zero, and thus the pixel's new value, $f_{stretched}(x, y)$, will also be zero. Similarly, when $f(x, y)$ is 134, the numerator and the denominator will be equal, and thus $f_{stretched}(x, y)$ will be 255. Also note that if you use this equation on an image with a full dynamic range—that is, an image whose I_{min} value is 0 and whose I_{max} value is 255—the denominator will evaluate to 255, which will cancel the 255 out front, and because I_{min} is zero, $f_{stretched}(x, y)$ will just equal $f(x, y)$.

To compute $f_{stretched}(x, y)$, you first need to establish the values of the I_{min} and I_{max}. One approach (as just mentioned) is to assign I_{min} and I_{max} the lowest and highest intensity values of your image, respectively. Unfortunately, this approach doesn't work in practice because it's very sensitive to outliers. For example, if you have a relatively large image that contains only a single black pixel and only a single white pixel, I_{min} will be 0, I_{max} will be 255, and therefore the contrast of the image won't be adjusted at all. To combat this sensitivity to outliers, what's commonly done is to examine the histogram of the image. Specifically, you first determine the highest value (i.e., the peak) of the histogram—that is, the count of the most prevalent intensity value. Next, you find the bin that contains (i.e., whose count is) some small percentage (say, 10 percent) of the highest count, and then you assign this intensity value (i.e., the ordinal position or "index" of the bin) to I_{min}. Similarly, you find the bin that contains some large percentage (say, 90 percent) of the highest count, and then you assign this intensity value (the ordinal position or "index" of the bin) to I_{max}.

Unfortunately, although the histogram-based approach (to determine the values of the I_{min} and I_{max}) does work, it's not robust to images with very low contrast. In 1994, Paul Haeberli and Douglas Voorhies published a simple, fast, and effective method for adjusting an image's contrast. This scheme, which is based on extrapolation, is defined as follows:

$$f_{stretched}(x, y) = 128 + \alpha(f(x, y) - 128)$$

The value of α determines the extent of the contrast adjustment. Values of α less than 1 reduce the image's contrast, while values of α greater than 1 increase the image's contrast. This equation is based on the notion that an image with no contrast contains only one color—in this case, the color is assumed gray (thus the value 128). When α is less than 1, this expression computes an interpolation between the original image and a gray image, thus reducing the original image's contrast. When α is greater than 1, this expression computes an extrapolation of the original image from a gray image, thus increasing the original image's contrast. (See the solution "Contrast-Stretching an Image" for a code snippet that uses this equation.)

Figure 17.4 depicts a low-contrast image (the launch of Atlantis for mission STS-106) and its histogram; depicted below this image is the result of performing

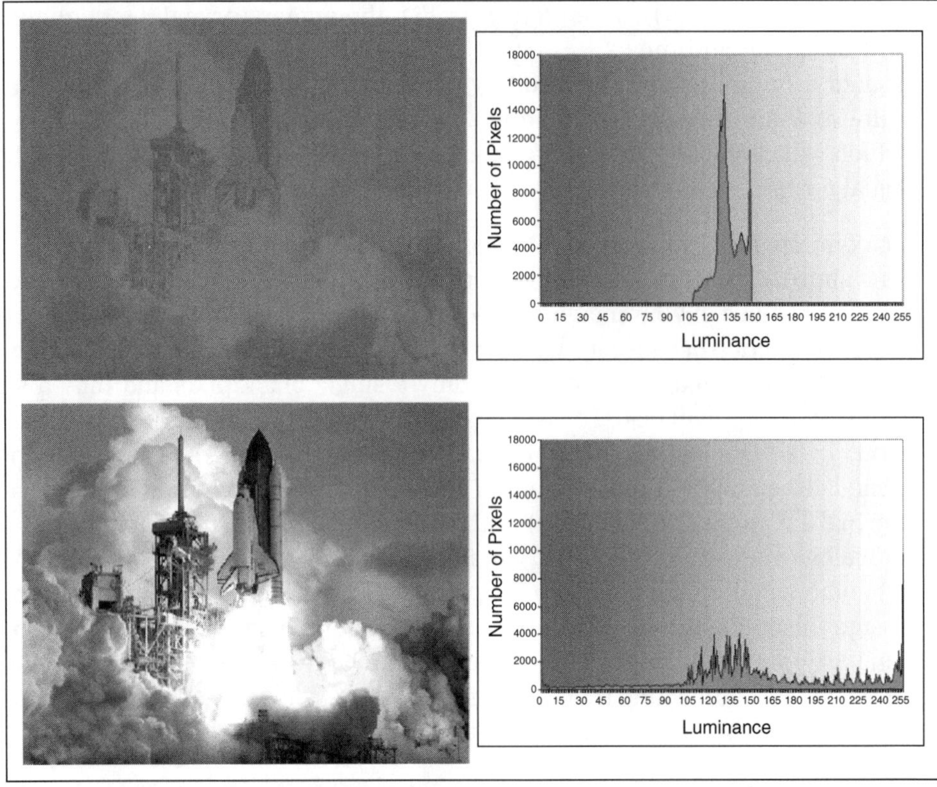

Figure 17.4 A low contrast image (top) and the result of applying contrast stretching (bottom).

Haeberli and Voorhies's contrast stretching technique with an α value of 7 (along with the new histogram). Notice that the histogram of the processed image is indeed "stretched out."

Histogram Equalization

Histogram equalization is a point processing technique that's similar to contrast stretching. As with contrast stretching, the goal of histogram equalization is to increase the contrast and dynamic range of an image. As opposed to contrast stretching, however, histogram equalization is automated—it's designed not only to "stretch out" an image's histogram, but also to make this histogram more uniform. The intuition here is that an image with a uniform histogram (i.e., a flat histogram with equal values for all bins) should also have good contrast.

Earlier, I mentioned that a histogram is nothing more than a table that denotes the frequency-of-occurrence of each intensity value. Well, in essence, this description is equivalent to saying that a histogram specifies a probability distribution.

That is, if you take the count of each bin and divide it by the total number of pixels in the image, you'll have the probability that a specific intensity value (i.e., the intensity value that the bin stands for) is represented in the image. Following this notion, if an image's histogram is uniform, then each bin has the same count, which means that each intensity value has the same probability.

How do you make an image's histogram uniform? It turns out that the desired transformation is exactly the cumulative distribution function of the image's intensity values. (For a derivation, see R. Gonzalez and R. Woods, *Digital Image Processing*, Reading, MA: Addison-Wesley, 1992.) Formally, this is written as follows:

$$f_{equalized}(x, y) = 255\left(\frac{\sum_{i=0}^{f(x,y)}\left(\frac{histogram[i]}{N}\right) - \frac{histogram[0]}{N}}{1 - \frac{histogram[0]}{N}}\right)$$

where *histogram* is the histogram of the image and N is the total number of pixels. Note that the quantity,

$$\sum_{i=0}^{f(x,y)}\left(\frac{histogram[i]}{N}\right)$$

represents an estimation of the cumulative distribution function evaluated at the value $f(x, y)$. Also note that the quantity,

$$\left(\frac{histogram[0]}{N}\right)$$

is just the probability that a given pixel's value is equal to zero. This quantity, along with the quantity in the denominator, is used to map the cumulative distribution function from the range [0, 1] to the range [0, 255]. (See the solution "Histogram-Equalizing an Image" for an example that uses this equation.)

Figure 17.5 depicts the results of performing histogram equalization on a low contrast image, along with the new "equalized" histogram. Note that the histogram, while more uniform, is not perfectly uniform. Also note the graininess of the processed image; although histogram equalization is fully automatic (i.e., we didn't have to specify any extra parameters such as α, I_{min}, or I_{max}), the resulting image is often less aesthetically pleasing than that of contrast stretching.

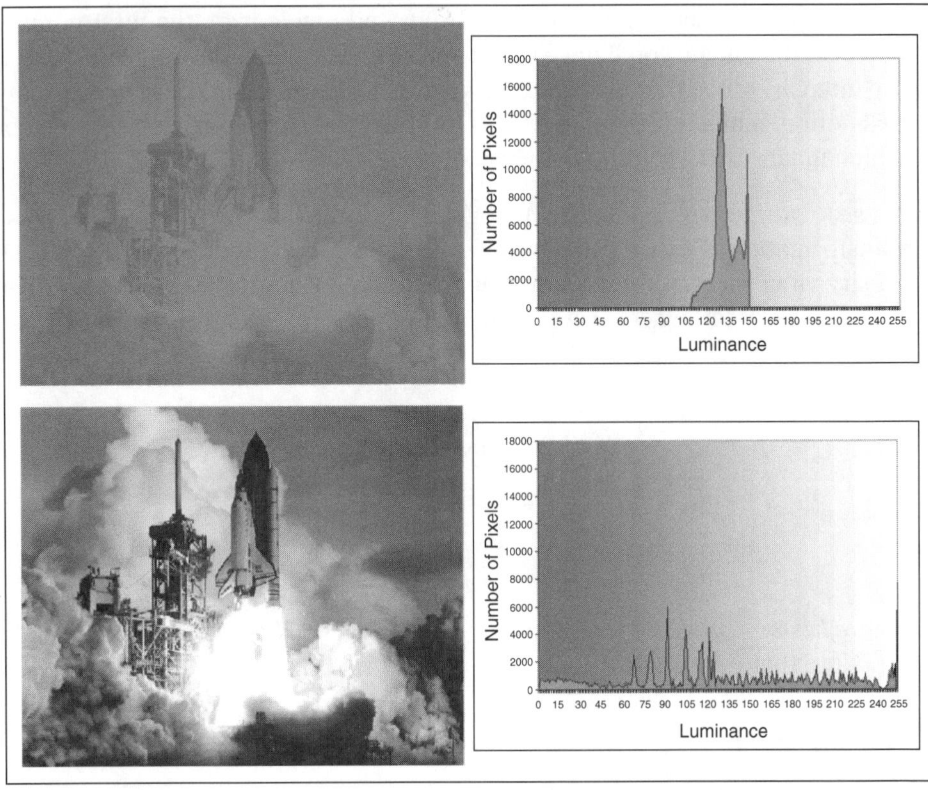

Figure 17.5 A low contrast image (top) and the result of applying histogram equalization (bottom).

Filtering

What meaning does the word "filter" bring to mind? Well, a coffee filter separates coffee grinds from the actual coffee. A fuel filter separates foreign particles from the fuel. The ozone layer separates harmful UV rays from sunlight. The list goes on and on. It seems, however, that whatever type of filter you consider, there's an underlying notion of *separation* going on—you use a filter to separate a composite entity into its ingredients; and in most cases, at least one of these ingredients is discarded. If you're baking a cake that requires egg whites, for example, you first separate the yolk (and the shell) from the whites, and you then discard the yolk (and the shell). The act of filtering an image is no different. When you filter an image, the ingredients that you want to keep or discard are specific *frequencies*.

An Image's Frequencies

Visualizing a still image in terms of its frequency components might, at first, seem awkward. What we actually need is a more concrete definition of the word "frequency." In fact, frequency is most frequently used with a time interval, in which case the denotation is a *temporal* frequency (usually measured in Hertz—cycles per second). For example, if you drink three cups of coffee every five hours (as most developers do), your temporal frequency (of drinking coffee) is 1.67×10^{-4} Hz. Although no one ever speaks this mumbo-jumbo to describe how often they drink coffee, temporal frequency is commonly used to describe sounds.

Although there's no time component involved with a still image, there is a position. In this case, the word "frequency" is used to refer to an image's *spatial* frequencies—the number of cycles per *distance* (usually measured in degrees of visual angle). Figure 17.6 depicts two images; the one on the left has a relatively high spatial frequency in the horizontal direction, and the one on the right has a lower spatial frequency in the vertical direction.

Of course, in natural images, rarely will you see "clean-cut" spatial frequencies such as those depicted in Figure 17.6. The concept, however, is the same. If you have an image of someone wearing a plaid shirt, for example, the shirt will consist of relatively high vertical and horizontal spatial frequencies. This is in contrast to, say, an image of the sky, which contains predominantly low frequencies. In general, edge regions and detailed regions of an image are classified as high-frequency areas, whereas smooth regions (such as the sky) are classified as low-frequency areas. As we'll discuss later (and in Chapter 18), this scheme of labeling an image in terms of its smooth, edge, and detailed regions is of paramount importance to image compression.

What's the point of filtering an image's (spatial) frequency components? Well, because you can classify an image's smooth, edge, and detailed regions in terms of the image's spatial frequencies, you can indirectly manipulate these regions by directly manipulating the corresponding frequencies. For example, if you want to

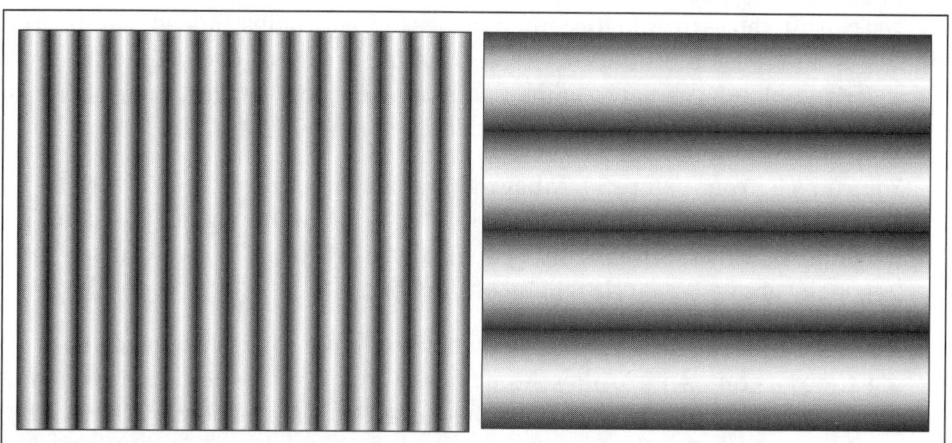

Figure 17.6 Images with different spatial frequencies.

blur an image, you need to eliminate its details. Because an image's detailed regions correspond to its higher spatial frequencies, you can eliminate the details by simply filtering out the high frequencies. In this case, you'd use a low-pass filter—i.e., a filter that blocks the high frequencies while allowing the lower frequencies to pass through. Other types of filters work in a similar fashion—they're designed to manipulate (and often eliminate) certain frequencies. In fact, the field of filter design is enough to fill a text on its own. We won't discuss this subject, but Appendix B lists some references if you're interested. We will, however, discuss how you can apply different types of filters to an image and, more generally, to a signal.

An Overview of Signal Processing

Think back to the last time you wore a pair of sunglasses. What purpose did these sunglasses serve? Unless you had a late night or a black eye, you likely wore the sunglasses to protect your eyes. The lenses supplied this protection by *processing a signal;* in this case, the signal was electromagnetic radiation—that is, light. Signal processing is a large field of study that has its foundations in several disciplines, including mathematics and statistics. Used extensively by electrical engineers, signal processing underpins most of the electrical gadgets that drive the modern world (including your computer).

How does signal processing relate to image filtering? Well, an image is just another type of signal; the only difference is that an image is a two-dimensional variety. An audio clip, on the other hand, is an example of a one-dimensional signal. (In fact, it's much easier to understand filtering by first considering the one-dimensional case.) If you've ever used a graphic equalizer to fine-tune your music, you already have an idea of what filtering can do. For example, consider the 10-band graphic equalizer that's depicted in Figure 17.7. By using the sliders, you can attenuate or amplify certain ranges of frequencies; indeed, a graphic equalizer is an adjustable filter. If we plot the frequency of each slider against that slider's amplitude, we get an amplitude-frequency plot that illustrates the frequency response of the filter. This plot is also depicted in Figure 17.7.

You can see from Figure 17.7 that the graphic equalizer is set to work as a low-pass filter. If you apply the low-pass filter to an audio signal, the signal's high frequencies will be attenuated. Specifically, in Figure 17.7, we can see that any frequency above 12,000 Hz will be filtered out.

How exactly is the filter applied to the audio signal? This is where signal processing theory comes into play. Most audio signals are depicted by using an amplitude-time plot. The problem is, here our x-axis corresponds to *time*, whereas in the plot of the filter's frequency response, the x-axis corresponds to *frequency*. This discrepancy in x-axis units proves to be a significant roadblock. Although

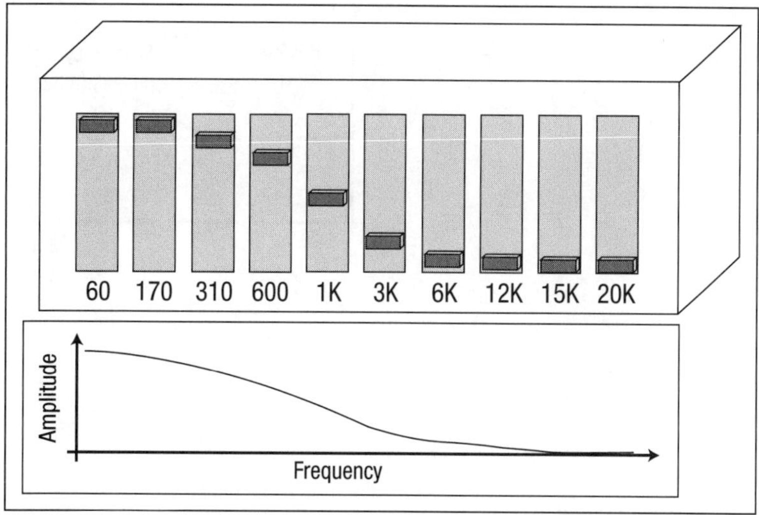

Figure 17.7 Frequency of a one-dimensional low-pass filter.

it's easy to characterize a one-dimensional signal by considering how its amplitude varies with time, it's not so straightforward to examine a signal's frequency response. Similarly, although it's easy to characterize a filter by considering its frequency response, it's not as easy to describe a filter's amplitude-time behavior. If these x-axis units were both expressed in terms of frequency, then we could simply multiply the signal by the response of the filter to get a filtered signal. But, again, this isn't the case. So somehow we need to make these x-axis units equal. To do this, we have two choices:

- One approach is to determine the signal's frequency response, multiply this response with the filter's frequency response, and then determine the amplitude-time behavior of this product to retrieve the filtered signal. This approach—called *frequency-domain filtering*—is depicted in Figure 17.8.
- Alternatively, we could determine the filter's amplitude-time response, and then convolve (more on this term later) this response with the signal. This approach—called *spatial-domain filtering*—is depicted in Figure 17.9.

Frequency-Domain Filtering

Determining a signal's frequency response from the signal's amplitude-time behavior is easier said than done. The solution to this problem actually involves a coordinate-space transformation similar to those discussed in Chapters 10 and 16. Recall, in Chapter 10, the axes of our coordinate space were two rulers, and in Chapter 16, our axes were three colors. Well, now, instead of denoting a location or a color, we want to describe a signal's frequencies. We already have an axis that corresponds to time; thus, in this case, we need a transformation that will convert

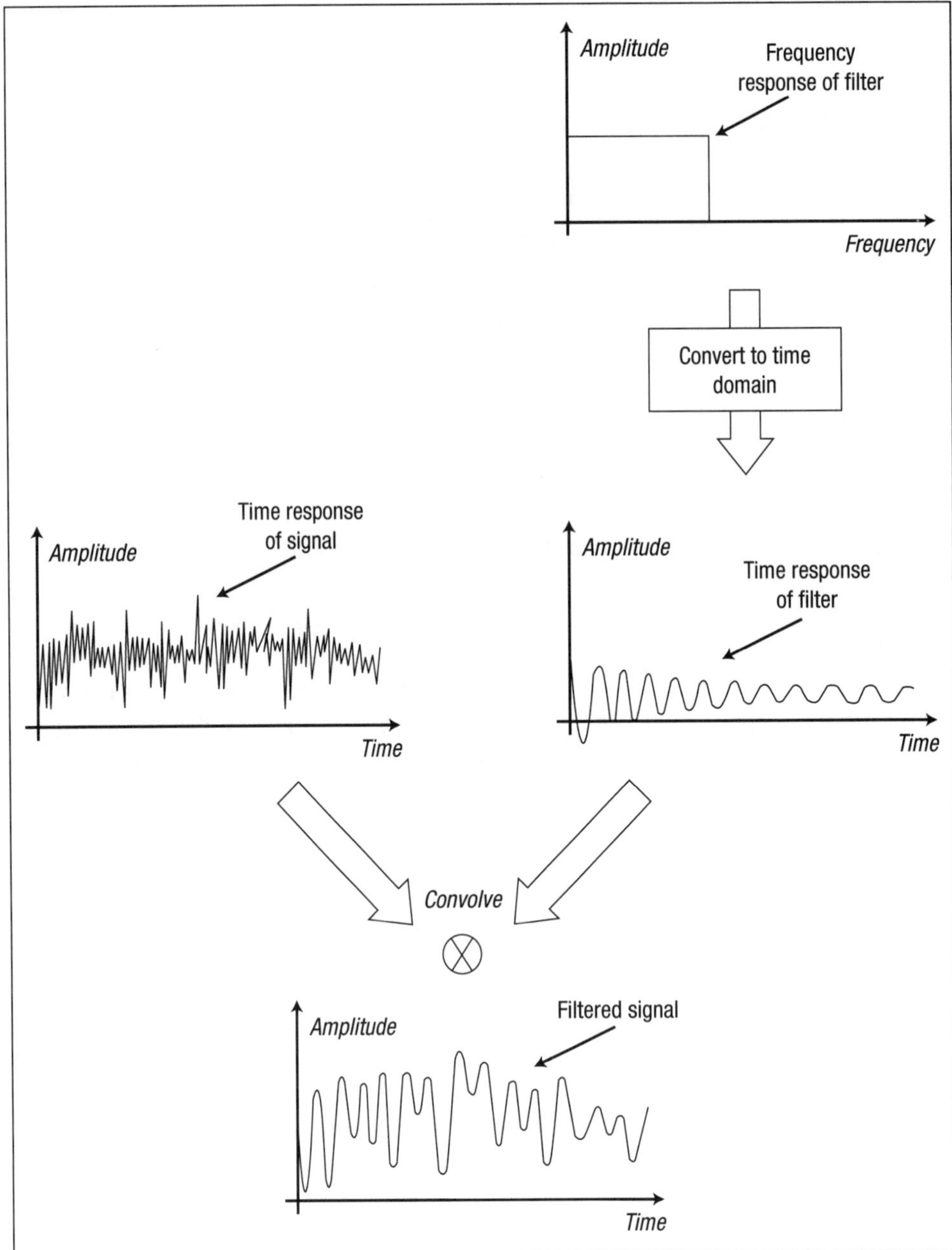

Figure 17.8 Frequency-domain filtering.

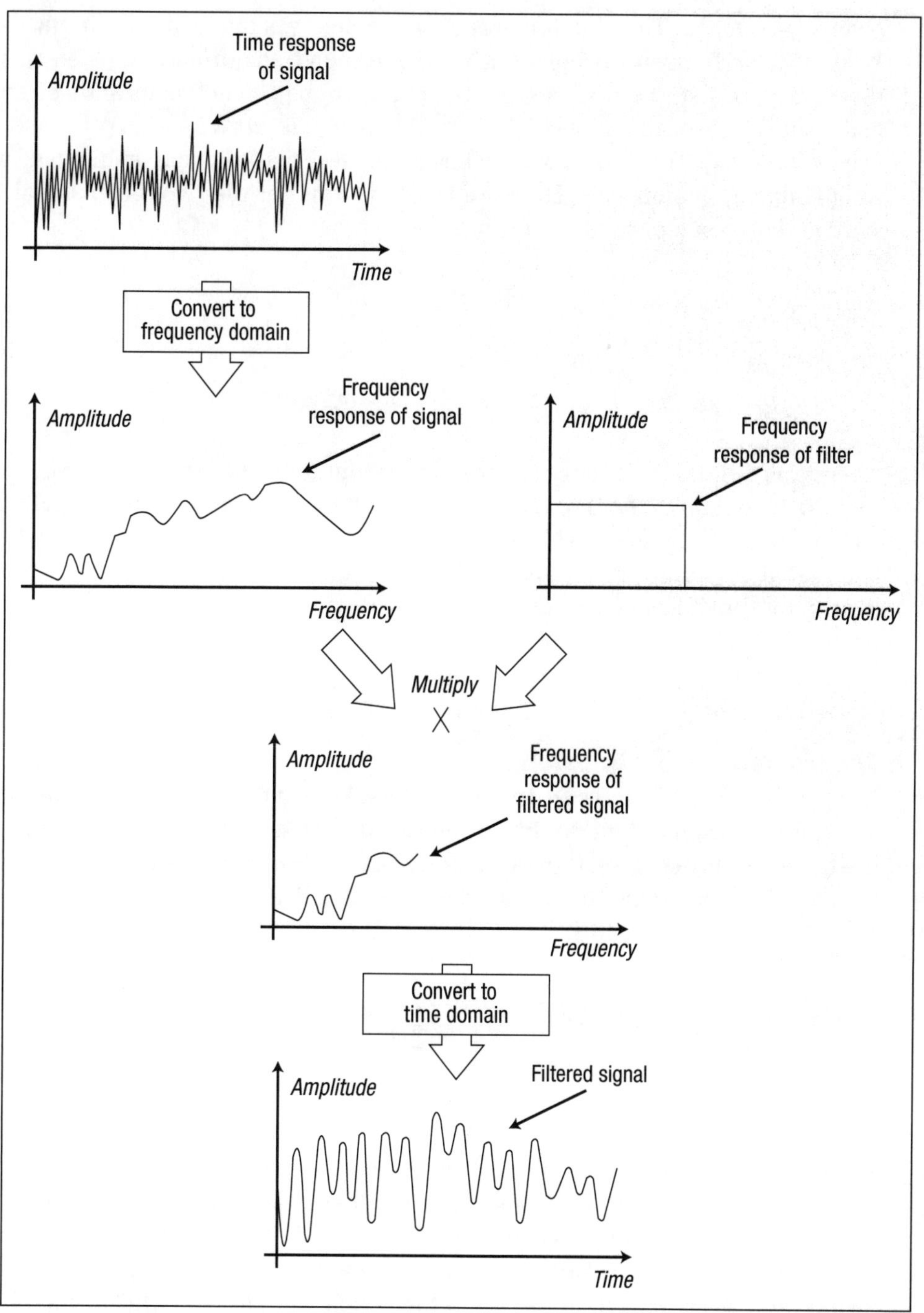

Figure 17.9 Spatial-domain filtering.

time to *frequency*. The *Fourier transform*, which was made famous in the early 1800s by Jean-Baptiste-Joseph Fourier, is one such transformation. When we use the Fourier transform, our axes, so to speak, are sines and cosines; these sines and cosines are more commonly referred to as *basis functions*. In other words, using the Fourier transform, we can base (i.e., describe) a signal or an image as a weighted sum of sinusoids. Here are the equations for the two-dimensional forward and inverse Fourier transform:

$$\Im\{f(x, y)\} = F(u,v) = \int\int_{-\infty}^{\infty} f(x, y) \exp[-j2\pi(ux + vy)]dxdy$$

$$\Im^{-1}\{F(u, v)\} = f(x,y) = \int\int_{-\infty}^{\infty} F(u, v) \exp[j2\pi(ux + vy)]dudv$$

As it turns out, the Fourier transform isn't commonly used in image processing. The first problem is that computing the Fourier transform requires integration, which is something that can be approximated only on a computer. Although there is a digital version of the Fourier transform (called the discrete Fourier transform), the transformed image, $F(u, v)$, often contains imaginary (i.e., complex) numbers. Because it is the sines (as opposed to the cosines) that introduce these imaginary components, images are commonly transformed using the *discrete cosine transform* (DCT).

The Discrete Cosine Transform

As we'll discuss in Chapter 18, the DCT is best known for its use in creating JPEG (Joint Photographic Experts Group) images. Because the DCT represents an image by using only cosines, the transformed image, $F(u, v)$—often called the transform coefficient—consists of only real numbers. The two-dimensional forward DCT is computed as follows:

$$F(u,v) = \alpha(u)\alpha(v)\sum_{x=0}^{N-1}\sum_{y=0}^{N-1} f(x, y) \cos\left[\frac{(2x + 1)u\pi}{2N}\right] \cos\left[\frac{(2y + 1)v\pi}{2N}\right]$$

for u, v = 0, 1, 2, ... N-1

After you transform an image into the frequency domain, you apply a filter by performing a simple multiplication. However, because the DCT involves the computation of cosines, transforming an image as a whole (by using the DCT) is a relatively expensive operation. Instead, an image is usually divided into several smaller (equal-sized) sub-images, and then each sub-image is transformed independently. The value N in the DCT equation is chosen to be equal to the dimension (i.e., the width and the height) of each sub-image. The most common

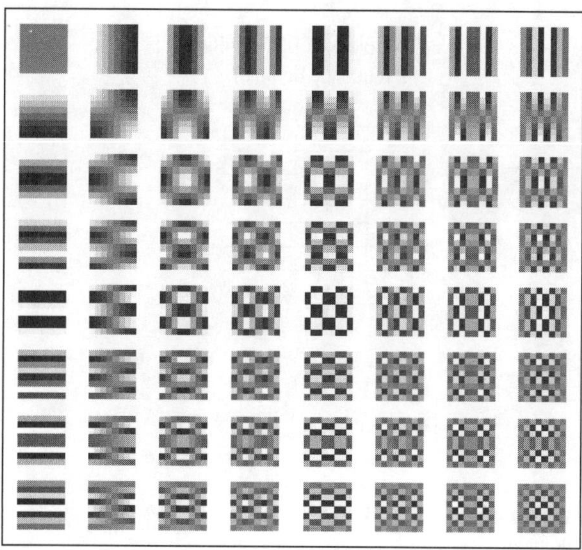

Figure 17.10 The 64 basis images for the discrete cosine transform when $N = 8$.

sub-image dimensions are 8x8 (i.e., 64 pixels; $N = 8$). Figure 17.10 depicts the two-dimensional basis functions (commonly referred to as *basis images*) that are used for the two-dimensional DCT when $N = 8$.

In essence, when you perform a two-dimensional DCT (when $N = 8$) on an image, you're describing the image in terms of (i.e., based on) the 64 basis functions of Figure 17.10. It's the same concept as using Morse code to write a message. When you use Morse code, your "basis functions" are the dots and the dashes. However, there's a key difference between Morse code and the DCT. In Figure 17.10, notice that each of the basis functions represents a different spatial frequency. Because of this fact, when you describe an image in terms of the 64 basis functions of Figure 17.10, you're representing the image's spatial frequencies. Remember, this is exactly the reason that the DCT is used in the first place—we want to transform time (or position, in two-dimensions) into frequency. So, given an 8x8 sub-image, you use the DCT ($N = 8$) to transform the sub-image, and you end up with an 8x8 "image" of coefficients. This process is depicted in Figure 17.11.

Okay, so you have an 8x8 block of coefficients; how is this used for filtering? Well, think of each basis function (in Figure 17.10) as a slider on a graphic equalizer. If you want to attenuate a certain frequency, you simply multiply the corresponding coefficient by a value that's less than one. For example, if you want to filter out all of the high spatial frequencies, you can multiply $F(u, v)$ by $H(u, v)$ as depicted in Figure 17.12. (Remember, because you're filtering in the frequency domain, you can use simple multiplication.)

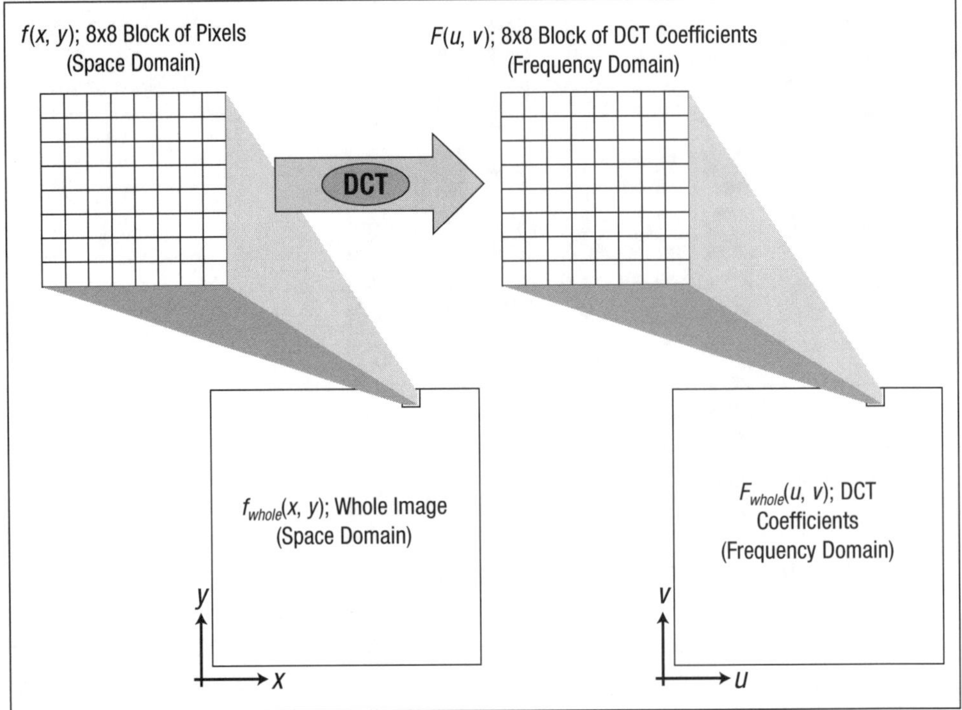

Figure 17.11 Transforming an 8x8 block of pixels to an 8x8 block of DCT coefficients.

F(*u*, *v*); 8x8 Block of DCT Coefficients (Frequency Domain)

F_{11}	F_{12}	F_{13}	F_{14}	F_{15}	F_{16}	F_{17}	F_{18}
F_{21}	F_{22}	F_{23}	F_{24}	F_{25}	F_{26}	F_{27}	F_{28}
F_{31}	F_{32}	F_{33}	F_{34}	F_{35}	F_{36}	F_{37}	F_{38}
F_{41}	F_{42}	F_{43}	F_{44}	F_{45}	F_{46}	F_{47}	F_{48}
F_{51}	F_{52}	F_{53}	F_{54}	F_{55}	F_{56}	F_{57}	F_{58}
F_{61}	F_{62}	F_{63}	F_{64}	F_{65}	F_{66}	F_{67}	F_{68}
F_{71}	F_{72}	F_{73}	F_{74}	F_{75}	F_{76}	F_{77}	F_{78}
F_{81}	F_{82}	F_{83}	F_{84}	F_{85}	F_{86}	F_{87}	F_{88}

X

H(*u*, *v*); 8x8 Filter (Frequency Domain)

1	1	0.5	0	0	0	0	0
1	1	0.5	0	0	0	0	0
0.5	0.5	0.5	0	0	0	0	0
0	0	0	0	0	0	0	0
0	0	0	0	0	0	0	0
0	0	0	0	0	0	0	0
0	0	0	0	0	0	0	0
0	0	0	0	0	0	0	0

=

G(*u*, *v*); 8x8 Block of DCT Coefficients (Frequency Domain)

G_{11}	G_{12}	G_{13}	0	0	0	0	0
G_{21}	G_{22}	G_{23}	0	0	0	0	0
G_{31}	G_{32}	G_{33}	0	0	0	0	0
0	0	0	0	0	0	0	0
0	0	0	0	0	0	0	0
0	0	0	0	0	0	0	0
0	0	0	0	0	0	0	0
0	0	0	0	0	0	0	0

Figure 17.12 Filtering in the frequency domain by manipulating the DCT coefficients.

The Inverse Discrete Cosine Transform

After $F(u, v)$ is multiplied appropriately, you're still left with a block of transform coefficients (denoted by $G(u, v)$ in Figure 17.7). To retrieve a sub-image from each 8x8 block of transform coefficients, you need to perform what's called an *inverse DCT*. The inverse DCT serves the opposite role of the DCT; namely, the inverse DCT transforms frequency back into time (or space in 2-D). Here's the equation for the two-dimensional inverse DCT:

$$F(x,y) = \sum_{x=0}^{N-1} \sum_{y=0}^{N-1} \alpha(u)\alpha(v)F(u, v) \cos\left[\frac{(2x+1)u\pi}{2N}\right] \cos\left[\frac{(2y+1)v\pi}{2N}\right]$$

for $x, y = 0, 1, 2, \ldots N\text{-}1$

After you perform an inverse DCT on each 8x8 block of coefficients, you're left with a series of sub-images; you can then "patch" these sub-images together to reconstruct the entire image. Figure 17.13 depicts the results of reconstructing an image from each 8x8 block of coefficients $G(u, v)$—that is, the image has been filtered by the filter, $H(u, v)$, of Figure 17.12. In Figure 17.13, notice that because $H(u, v)$ is a low-pass filter, the reconstructed image (on the right) appears slightly blurred as compared to the original (on the left); pay particular attention to high-frequency areas such as the flag and the footprints. If you want a more pronounced blurring effect, you simply lower the cut-off frequency of the filter—i.e., you remove more high-frequency components. Figure 17.14 depicts the results of reconstructing an image in which only the lowest-frequency component, $F(0, 0)$, has

Figure 17.13 Low-pass-filtering an image by directly manipulating its DCT coefficients; the original is depicted on the left, and the reconstructed (filtered) image is depicted on the right.

Figure 17.14 Reconstructing an image from only its lowest-frequency DCT coefficient; the original is depicted on the left, and the reconstructed (filtered) image is depicted on the right.

been preserved. ($F(0, 0)$ is the coefficient that corresponds to the top-left basis image. This zero-frequency coefficient is commonly called the *D.C. coefficient.*)

Notice the presence of blocking artifacts in the filtered image of Figure 17.14. These artifacts are a direct result of performing the DCT on sub-images (e.g., 8x8 blocks). You've probably noticed these blocking artifacts in JPEG images as well. Although most JPEG decoders try to combat this effect by using a post-processing step, the block-based nature of the DCT hinders its usefulness when it comes to filtering. The DCT is most useful when you need to analyze the frequency content of an image. You can, however, use the DCT to produce some special effects, such as those depicted in Figure 17.15. Use the basis functions in Figure 17.12 as a guide to determine which coefficients you need to manipulate to create specific effects. (Again, think of each basis function as a slider on a graphic equalizer.) Bear in mind, however, that if you manipulate $F(0, 0)$ (the zero-frequency coefficient), you'll need to re-adjust the dynamic range of the reconstructed image (e.g., via contrast stretching or histogram-equalization).

You can see the solutions "Computing the Discrete Cosine Transform of an Image" and "Computing the Inverse Discrete Cosine Transform" for code examples of how to perform a DCT and inverse DCT, respectively. If you simply need to smooth or sharpen an image, however, you're better off filtering in the spatial domain. (It's often much faster.)

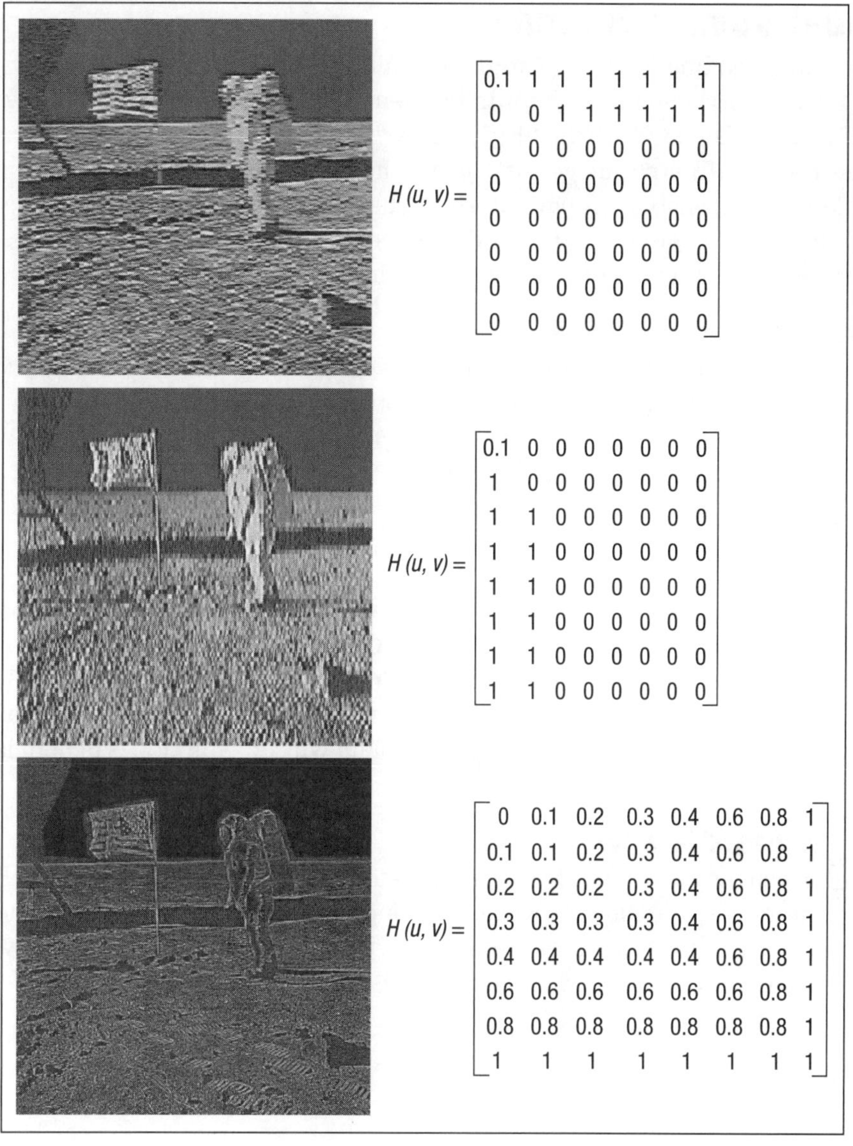

Figure 17.15 Special effects created by manipulating the DCT coefficients.

Spatial-Domain Filtering

We've examined one method of applying a filter to an image; namely, we use the DCT to transform the image into its frequency representation, we multiply the transform coefficients with the filter, and we then inverse-transform this result to reconstruct the filtered image. As I mentioned, however, there's an alternative technique called spatial-domain filtering. The idea here is to first determine the filter's amplitude-time response, and then compute the *convolution* of this response with the image to produce a filtered image.

Convolution

To compute the convolution of two signals, you integrate one of the signals with a time-reversed and shifted version of the other signal. Specifically, to compute the convolution of the signal $f(x)$ with the signal $h(x)$, you compute the following integral (called the *convolution integral*):

$$f(x) \otimes h(x) = \int_{\infty}^{\infty} f(u)h(x-u)du$$

As opposed to the symbol "×" or "·", which is used to denote multiplication, the symbol "⊗" is used to denote the convolution of two signals. The colloquial phrase "to convole" two signals simply means "to compute the convolution" of those signals. Before we get into the details of computing the convolution integral for an image (i.e., in two dimensions), let me explain why convolution is beneficial in the first place.

The Principle of Duality

As with frequency-domain filtering, spatial-domain filtering is based on the Fourier transform—specifically, on a special property of the Fourier transform known as *duality*. This property states that multiplying two signals in the frequency domain is equivalent to convolving those signals in the time domain, and vice versa. Formally, this principle is written as follows:

$$F(u, v)\ H(u, v) \Leftrightarrow f(x, y) \otimes h(x, y)$$

$$F(u, v) \otimes H(u, v) \Leftrightarrow f(x, y)\ h(x, y)$$

Here, $H(u, v)$ is the amplitude-frequency response of the filter, and $h(x, y)$ is the filter's amplitude-time response (often called the *convolution kernel* or just the *kernel*). That is to say, $H(u, v)$ is the result of performing a Fourier transform on $h(x, y)$, and $h(x, y)$ is the result of performing an inverse Fourier transform on $H(u, v)$. Likewise, $F(u, v)$ is the result of performing a Fourier transform on $f(x, y)$—the original image—and $f(x, y)$ is the result of performing an inverse Fourier transform on $F(u, v)$—the transform coefficients.

What does all of this mean? Simply put, we can use convolution to filter an image without first transforming the image into its frequency representation—that is, we can avoid computing the Fourier transform or the DCT of an image.

Convolving an Image

To convolve an image with a filter, you simply multiply each pixel of the image with the corresponding coefficient (called a *tap*) of the filter, summing each product along the way. You then assign this sum to the pixel at the center of the filter. Here's the two-dimensional, discrete version of the convolution integral:

$$f_{filtered}(x, y) = F(x, y) \otimes h(x, y) = \sum_{m} \left(\sum_{n} f(n, m)\, h(x - n, y - m) \right)$$

Here, $f_{filtered}(x, y)$ represents a pixel of the filtered image, $f(x, y)$ represents a pixel of the original image, and $h(x, y)$ is the convolution kernel (i.e., the filter's amplitude-time response).

In theory, it's often easier to compute the Fourier transform of a signal, especially when the signal has a simple form in which its Fourier transform is well-known. For example, nearly all signal processing texts have a table that lists the Fourier transforms of sines, cosines, exponentials, impulse functions, and the like. Therefore, you can convolve two signals by simply multiplying their respective Fourier transforms (which you simply look up). In practice, the situation is reversed. Rarely does the signal have a simple form, and thus rarely is its Fourier transform known beforehand. What is the Fourier transform of some random image? You can't simply look this up in the table of an image processing text. Without manual computation, there's just no way to know. What is well-known, however, is the amplitude-time response of a wide variety of filters. That is, you can open almost any image processing text and find $h(x, y)$ for many common filters, including blurring, sharpening, and edge-detection filters. Figure 17.16 depicts the amplitude-time response—that is, $h(x, y)$—of several filters along with their respective effects when applied to an image.

Note that, in contrast to the low-pass kernels, many of the high-pass kernels sum to zero. For this reason, high-pass filtering operations, such as sharpening, are usually followed by applying a point processing technique (e.g., contrast stretching or histogram equalization). Remember, this same post-processing approach was also required after we manipulated the high-frequency DCT coefficients. This requirement lends support to the duality principle—that is, in both cases we're altering the low-frequency content of the image. The only difference is that with spatial-domain filtering, we're using convolution, whereas with frequency-domain filtering, we're using multiplication.

Blurring (variable-sized matrix)

$$h(x,y) = \begin{bmatrix} 1/N & 1/N & 1/N & 1/N & 1/N \\ 1/N & 1/N & 1/N & 1/N & 1/N \\ 1/N & 1/N & 1/N & 1/N & 1/N \\ 1/N & 1/N & 1/N & 1/N & 1/N \\ 1/N & 1/N & 1/N & 1/N & 1/N \end{bmatrix} \text{ ; } N = \text{number of taps}$$

Gaussian Smoothing

$$h(x,y) = \begin{bmatrix} 0 & 0 & 1/20 & 0 & 0 \\ 0 & 1/20 & 1/10 & 1/20 & 0 \\ 1/20 & 1/10 & 1/5 & 1/10 & 1/20 \\ 0 & 1/20 & 1/10 & 1/20 & 0 \\ 0 & 0 & 1/20 & 0 & 0 \end{bmatrix}$$

Sharpening (Unsharp Masking)

$$h(x,y) = \begin{bmatrix} -1/9 & -1/9 & -1/9 \\ -1/9 & 17/9 & -1/9 \\ -1/9 & -1/9 & -1/9 \end{bmatrix}$$

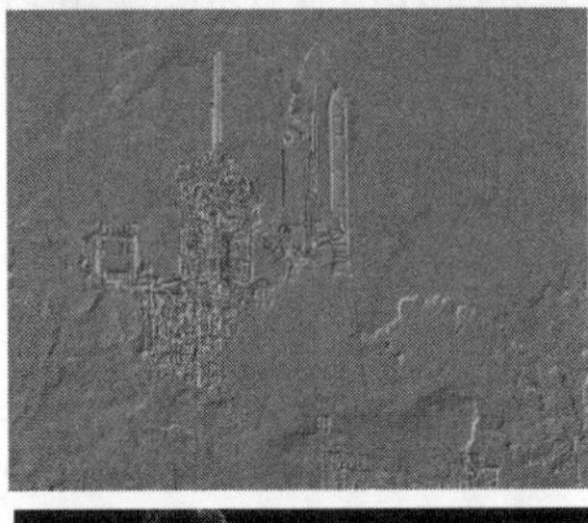

Emboss (135 degrees)

$$h(x,y) = \begin{bmatrix} -1 & 0 & 0 \\ 0 & 0 & 0 \\ 0 & 0 & 1 \end{bmatrix} \text{ ; } offset = 128$$

Sobel Edge Detectors

$$h_x(x,y) = \begin{bmatrix} -1 & 0 & 1 \\ -2 & 0 & 2 \\ -1 & 0 & 1 \end{bmatrix} \qquad h_y(x,y) = \begin{bmatrix} 1 & 2 & 1 \\ 0 & 0 & 0 \\ -1 & -2 & -1 \end{bmatrix}$$

Figure 17.16 The effects of several common filters.

Filtering an Image in the Spatial Domain

Let's work through an example of filtering an image in the spatial domain—that is, convolving an image, $f(x, y)$, with a filter's amplitude-time response, $h(x, y)$. As before, we'll use the **GBuffer** class to simplify things a bit. The first step is to define the filter taps; for this example, we'll use the 3x3 (low-pass) mean filter, like so:

```
// define the filter kernel
const int kernel[][3] = {
      {1, 1, 1},
      {1, 1, 1},
      {1, 1, 1}
      };
```

Now, for each pixel in the image, we center the filter kernel over that pixel, and then perform the convolution, like so (**hDIBSectionSrc** is a handle to a 24-bpp DIB section bitmap):

```
// create a GBuffer object corresponding to the source image
GBuffer<RGBTRIPLE> imgBufferSrc;
DIBSectionToBuffer(imgBufferSrc, hDIBSection);

// extract the dimensions
const int width = imgBufferSrc.Width();
const int height = imgBufferSrc.Height();

// create a GBuffer object for the filtered image
GBuffer<RGBTRIPLE> imgBufferDst(width, height);

for (int y = 0; y < height; ++y)
{
   for (int x = 0; x < width; ++x)
   {
      // keep a running sum for the convolution
      int sumR = 0, sumG = 0, sumB = 0;

      // for each tap in the filter
      for (int row = -1; row <= 1; ++row)
      {
         for (int col = -1; col <= 1; ++col)
         {
            // perform the convolution using symmetric extension
            RGBTRIPLE pixel = imgBufferSrc.PixelsSE(x + col, y + row);
            sumR += (pixel.rgbtRed * kernel[col + 1][row + 1]);
```

```
                sumG += (pixel.rgbtGreen * kernel[col + 1][row + 1]);
                sumB += (pixel.rgbtBlue * kernel[col + 1][row + 1]);
            }
        }

        // assign the filtered pixel to the destination
        RGBTRIPLE filtered_pixel = {
            static_cast<unsigned char>(sumB / 9.0 + 0.5),
            static_cast<unsigned char>(sumG / 9.0 + 0.5),
            static_cast<unsigned char>(sumR / 9.0 + 0.5)
            };
        imgBufferDst.Pixels(x, y, filtered_pixel);
    }
}

// update hDIBSection's pixels
BufferToDIBSection(hDIBSection, imgBufferDst);
```

Note that we used symmetric extension in this example because it tends to produce the most natural-looking results. You could alternatively use circular extension or pixel replication. Also, keep in mind that you can use a larger filter—say, 7x7—to achieve a greater blurring effect. Although the size is up to you, most filters have an odd number of taps to prevent an *end-to-end delay* (a shift in one direction). Moreover, many two-dimensional filters can be written as an outer product of two one-dimensional filters. For example, consider our 3x3 mean filter. In matrix notation, the kernel looks like the following:

$$h(x, y) = \begin{bmatrix} 1/9 & 1/9 & 1/9 \\ 1/9 & 1/9 & 1/9 \\ 1/9 & 1/9 & 1/9 \end{bmatrix}$$

When we convolve this filter with an image, for each pixel we're performing nine multiplications and eight additions. So the number of flops per pixel is on the order of $2n^2$, where n is the length of the filter (3 in this case). Notice, however, that $h(x, y)$ can be written as an outer product of two one-dimensional vectors, $h_{col}(x, y)$ and $h_{row}(x, y)$, like so:

$$h(x, y) = h_{col}(x, y) \times h_{row}(x, y) = \begin{bmatrix} 1/3 \\ 1/3 \\ 1/3 \end{bmatrix} [1/3 \quad 1/3 \quad 1/3]$$

Because we can separate $h(x, y)$ into two single-dimensional vectors, $h(x, y)$ is called a *separable filter*. Now instead of convolving $h(x, y)$ with each 3x3 block of pixels, we need only convolve $h_{col}(x, y)$ with each column of the image and convolve $h_{row}(x, y)$ with each row of the image. Here's the code for this separable implementation:

```
// define the filter kernel
const int kernel[] = {1, 1, 1};

// create a GBuffer object for the source image
GBuffer<RGBTRIPLE> imgBufferSrc;
DIBSectionToBuffer(imgBufferSrc, hDIBSection);

// extract the dimensions
const int width = imgBufferSrc.Width();
const int height = imgBufferSrc.Height();

// create a GBuffer object for the filtered image
GBuffer<RGBTRIPLE> imgBufferDst(width, height);

// first filter each column...
for (int y = 0; y < height; ++y)
{
   for (int x = 0; x < width; ++x)
   {
      // keep a running sum for the convolution
      int sumR = 0, sumG = 0, sumB = 0;

      // for each tap in the filter
      for (int iTap = -1; iTap <= 1; ++iTap)
      {
         RGBTRIPLE pixel = imgBufferSrc.PixelsSE(x, y + iTap);
         sumR += (pixel.rgbtRed * kernel[iTap + 1]);
         sumG += (pixel.rgbtGreen * kernel[iTap + 1]);
         sumB += (pixel.rgbtBlue * kernel[iTap + 1]);
      }
      RGBTRIPLE filtered_pixel = {
         static_cast<unsigned char>(sumB / 3.0 + 0.5),
         static_cast<unsigned char>(sumG / 3.0 + 0.5),
         static_cast<unsigned char>(sumR / 3.0 + 0.5)
         };
      imgBufferDst.Pixels(x, y, filtered_pixel);
   }
}
```

```
// then filter each row...
for (int y = 0; y < height; ++y)
{
   for (int x = 0; x < width; ++x)
   {
      // keep a running sum for the convolution
      int sumR = 0, sumG = 0, sumB = 0;

      // for each tap in the filter
      for (int iTap = -1; iTap <= 1; ++iTap)
      {
         RGBTRIPLE pixel = imgBufferDst.PixelsSE(x + iTap, y);
         sumR += (pixel.rgbtRed * kernel[iTap + 1]);
         sumG += (pixel.rgbtGreen * kernel[iTap + 1]);
         sumB += (pixel.rgbtBlue * kernel[iTap + 1]);
      }
      RGBTRIPLE filtered_pixel = {
         static_cast<unsigned char>(sumB / 3.0 + 0.5),
         static_cast<unsigned char>(sumG / 3.0 + 0.5),
         static_cast<unsigned char>(sumR / 3.0 + 0.5)
         };
      imgBufferDst.Pixels(x, y, filtered_pixel);
   }
}

// update hDIBSection's pixels
BufferToDIBSection(hDIBSection, imgBufferDst);
```

By separating $h(x, y)$ into $h_{col}(x, y)$ and $h_{row}(x, y)$, for each pixel we're performing only 2x3 multiplications and 2x2 additions. In this case, the number of flops per pixel is on the order of $4n$, where n is the length of the filter. This means that the longer the filter, the more flops you'll save by capitalizing on the filter's separability. There are some situations, however, in which $h(x, y)$ is separable, but the filtering operation is not well-suited to be implemented as a separable operation. Edge detection is one example of this situation.

Edge Detection

Edge detection is but one approach in a process called *segmentation*, in which the objects of an image are demarcated. This process is helpful, for example, when you need to locate significant local intensity changes. Edge detection is typically composed of four stages:

1. A grayscale transformation, if required
2. Noise reduction

3. Enhancement
4. Thresholding

The noise reduction is often accomplished by using a mean or a median filter. However, because the more you blur an image, the less strong its edges become, this step is often skipped. Enhancement is carried out by computing the intensity gradient of a local neighborhood of pixels. This process is typically implemented by filtering an image with one of the edge-detection-related kernel pairs of Figure 17.16; the Sobel kernels are the most commonly used filters for this process.

Let's look at an example of performing an edge detection. As before, we'll use the **GBuffer** class. Specifically, given that **hDIBSection** is a handle to a DIB section bitmap, we'll create a corresponding **GBuffer** object (**imgBufferSrc**), and then perform the grayscale transformation, like so:

```
// create a GBuffer object for the source image
GBuffer<RGBTRIPLE> imgBufferSrc;
DIBSectionToBuffer(imgBufferSrc, hDIBSection);

// extract the dimensions
const int width = imgBufferSrc.Width();
const int height = imgBufferSrc.Height();

//
// convert the GBuffer image to grayscale
//
for (int y = 0; y < height; ++y)
{
   for (int x = 0; x < width; ++x)
   {
      RGBTRIPLE pixel = imgBufferSrc.Pixels(x, y);
      unsigned char intensity =
         static_cast<unsigned char>(0.5 +
            0.299 * pixel.rgbtRed +
            0.587 * pixel.rgbtGreen +
            0.114 * pixel.rgbtBlue
            );
      pixel.rgbtRed = intensity;
      pixel.rgbtGreen = intensity;
      pixel.rgbtBlue = intensity;
      imgBufferSrc.Pixels(x, y, pixel);
   }
}
```

Next, we define the horizontal and vertical gradient kernels; then we create a **GBuffer** object (**imgBufferDst**) to hold the results; and then we perform the spatial-filtering operation by using convolution. Here's the code for that:

```
// define the horizontal gradient kernel
const int hx[][3] = {
   {-1, 0, 1},
   {-2, 0, 2},
   {-1, 0, 1}
   };

// define the vertical gradient kernel
const int hy[][3] = {
   { 1,  2,  1},
   { 0,  0,  0},
   {-1, -2, -1}
   };

// create a GBuffer object for the filtered image
GBuffer<RGBTRIPLE> imgBufferDst(width, height);

// perform the convolution...
for (int y = 0; y < height; ++y)
{
   for (int x = 0; x < width; ++x)
   {
      int gradX = 0, gradY = 0;
      for (int row = -1; row <= 1; ++row)
      {
         for (int col = -1; col <= 1; ++col)
         {
            const unsigned char intensity =
               imgBufferSrc.PixelsSE(x + col, y + row).rgbtBlue;
            gradX += (intensity * hx[col + 1][row + 1]);
            gradY += (intensity * hy[col + 1][row + 1]);
         }
      }

      const unsigned char gradMag =
         0.5 + sqrt(gradX * gradX + gradY * gradY);
      RGBTRIPLE pixel = {gradMag, gradMag, gradMag};
      imgBufferDst.Pixels(x, y, pixel);
   }
}
```

The last step is to perform a single-level thresholding operation. Remember, this operation converts the image into a binary form; so, depending on the activity content of the image, you need to choose the cut-off value appropriately (often by trial and error). Here, we'll simply use a value of 128—that is, any intensity that's below this value is mapped to zero, and any intensity that's greater than or equal to 128 is mapped to 255. Here's the code:

```
// threshold the image at 128...
for (int y = 0; y < height; ++y)
{
   for (int x = 0; x < width; ++x)
   {
      unsigned char intensity =
         imgBufferDst.Pixels(x, y).rgbtBlue;

      intensity = intensity < 128 ? 0 : 255;

      RGBTRIPLE pixel = {intensity, intensity, intensity};
      imgBufferDst.Pixels(x, y, pixel);
   }
}

// update hDIBSection's pixels
BufferToDIBSection(hDIBSection, imgBufferDst);
```

Figure 17.17 depicts the results of using this edge detection code on an image from NASA's archives. The image on the left is the original, and the image on the right is the edge-detected version.

Figure 17.17 The image on the right demonstrates the results of using Sobel edge detection (with a threshold value of 128) on the image on the left.

Filtering an image in the spatial domain is fast and simple, but not always intuitive. The important thing to remember is that $h(x, y)$ is not the frequency response of the filter; it's the filter's amplitude-time response. For this reason, examining the taps of $h(x, y)$ tells you little about the specific frequencies that the filter is designed to manipulate. Remember, to get at this information, you need to compute the Fourier transform of the filter's amplitude-time response. For example, if you plot $h(x, y)$ for a one-dimensional mean filter, you'll get a one-dimensional box (called a *rect function*). This tells you nothing about the frequency response of the filter—that is, you can't assume that the bounds of this box define the frequencies that will be passed (or attenuated). What you need to do is take the Fourier transform of this rect function, and then examine this result (which is the *sinc function*) to determine the filter's frequency response. In short, in terms of manipulating an image's frequency components, spatial-domain filtering is useful for only a limited set of operations such as blurring, sharpening, edge detection, and the like.

So now we've examined two approaches to filtering an image. One approach involves direct manipulation of an image's frequency components by performing a DCT, followed by multiplication and then an inverse DCT. The other approach involves indirect manipulation of an image's frequency components by using convolution to filter the image in the spatial domain. The DCT-based approach is superior to spatial-domain filtering in the sense that you have greater control over the frequency content. However, as we discussed earlier, the DCT suffers from blocking artifacts; this is one of the main reasons that many JPEG images look horrible at low bit rates. In fact, JPEG-2000, the next-generation version of JPEG, is based not on the DCT but on the DWT—the *discrete wavelet transform*.

Wavelets

What does the word "wavelet" bring to mind? Well, Piglet is a little pig, so a wavelet must be a little wave. In fact, that's exactly how the word "wavelet" is defined in Webster's dictionary (although this definition tells you little about what wavelets are used for). If you've read Chapters 10 and 16 and the previous discussion on the Fourier transform and the DCT, you may have noticed that the underlying theme of these sections is this notion of axes—that is, basis functions. Remember, using basis functions is just another way to represent a quantity. In Chapter 10, we used two rulers; in Chapter 16, we used three primary colors; with the DCT, we used cosines; and with the Fourier transform, we used both cosines and sines. As you might have guessed, with the DWT (discrete wavelet transform), our basis functions are a set of little waves.

The DWT is simply another "recipe" to transform an image or, more generally, an N-dimensional signal into its frequency components. The DWT is superior to the DCT in several respects. The main advantage of the DWT over the DCT is that we get information about both *frequency* and *orientation*. That is, the wavelet basis functions are localized in both frequency and space. This type of representation is useful for a wide variety of applications—most notably, image compression.

Wavelets and Image Compression

The ultimate goal of data compression is to represent information by using only a minimal number of information-carrying units (e.g., bits). Transmitting a message in Morse code, for example, requires far fewer bits than does transmitting an audio clip of someone saying that message. Compression usually comes in one of two varieties: lossless or lossy.

Lossless compression is an invertible process; because there's no loss of information, the decompressed data is identical (within round-off tolerance) to the original data. This invertibility criterion is crucial when you're transmitting, say, a binary executable, because the decompressed data must match, bit-for-bit, the original data. In contrast, the pixels of a decompressed digital image or the samples of a decompressed audio stream do not have to be identical to the original data—in most cases, the reconstructed version is close enough to the original such that the overall result is quite acceptable.

Lossy compression is typically carried out in three stages:

1. A transformation of the image into its frequency components
2. Quantization of the transform coefficients
3. Entropy encoding of the quantized transform coefficients

Information is discarded in the second (quantization) stage. The degree of quantization affects various aspects of the reconstructed image, including its objective measures (such as the mean-squared error and the peak signal-to-noise ratio), subjective measures, and storage space requirements. Lossless compression schemes omit this quantization stage, and as a result, lossless compression is an invertible process—the reconstructed digital image is identical to the original digital image. This is not the case with an image that is compressed in a lossy fashion; lossy compression is a non-invertible process in which the reconstructed image is not identical to the original image. The advantage, however, is that lossy compression affords significantly larger compression ratios and thus significantly smaller file sizes. (This is one of the main reasons that JPEG images and MP3 audio files are so popular.) In contrast, the storage space requirements of an image that is compressed in a lossless fashion can typically be reduced by only a factor of two.

Because it is the quantization stage (of a lossy compression scheme) that affects the visual quality of the reconstructed image, quantization is not performed in an arbitrary fashion. Instead, characteristics of the human visual system (HVS) are often taken into account. Most quantization strategies exploit the differing degrees of HVS sensitivities to various spatial frequencies. Such information is conveyed via the *contrast sensitivity function* (CSF), which has been assessed and is well-known for humans. This function shows that we are most sensitive to low frequencies (smooth regions) and less sensitive to high frequencies (edge and detail regions). Therefore, more quantization is typically applied to an image's high-frequency components, whereas less quantization is applied to an image's low-frequency components. Clearly, the success of this strategy depends on the performance of the first stage—that is, on how well an image is decomposed into its frequency components. The discrete wavelet transform has proved to be the superlative choice for this task.

Earlier, I mentioned that the main advantage of the DWT is that it provides information not only about an image's frequency content, but also about how these frequencies are oriented in space. As it turns out, this type of representation is ideal for images because our *visual cortex contains cells that are tuned to specific frequencies at specific orientations*. Why exactly is this useful? Well, think back to the DCT. When you compute the DCT of an image, you're left with a set of DCT coefficients. And, as I related earlier, if you manipulate one (or more) of these coefficients, it's as if you're adjusting the corresponding slider(s) of a 2-D graphic equalizer—i.e., the "amounts" of the DCT basis images. Although these basis images are useful, they serve as only a *rough* guide as to how the resulting image will look. With the DWT, on the other hand, you get a much greater level of control. When you manipulate a DWT coefficient, in essence, you're adjusting the amount of stimulus that a specific *type of cell* in the visual cortex receives. It's this extraordinary level of control that makes wavelets so popular for image compression and analysis.

Wavelets and Subband Coding

Recall that the DCT is usually performed on 8x8 sub-image blocks. The primary reason for this block-based approach is speed; the smaller the size of each block, the fewer flops it requires to transform the entire image. The main drawback, however, is that quantizing the DCT coefficients often leads to blocking artifacts. The DWT, on the other hand, operates on the image as a whole; as a result, quantization of the DWT coefficients doesn't introduce blocking artifacts. However, you might be thinking that computing the DWT for an entire image is computationally expensive, and yes, this is generally true. However, because the DWT can be implemented as a *subband decomposition*, the number of flops can be reduced significantly.

When you use the DCT to transform an image into frequency components, you're actually representing the image as a weighted sum of cosines—i.e., in terms of the DCT basis functions. As a result, you can determine "how much" (i.e., the

DCT coefficient) of a specific spatial frequency (i.e., the corresponding DCT basis function) an image contains. You can see that the DCT actually performs a *fullband decomposition*, in which each spatial frequency band is represented equally. It's argued, however, that this type of representation isn't well-suited with how we see images. Remember, the CSF implies that our visual system is not as sensitive to high frequencies, so there's no need to compute the high-frequency information so precisely. It's much better to compute only a rough estimate of the high-frequency information and devote most of the flops to computing a more precise representation of the low-frequency information. This is exactly the idea behind a subband decomposition. You take an image and decompose it into its low-frequency and high-frequency components; then you take only the low-frequency components, and you perform the same type of decomposition again. Each time you split an image into its low-frequency and high-frequency components, you're performing a new *level of decomposition*. This scheme is depicted for an image in Figure 17.18.

Subband decomposition is typically implemented by using a spatial filtering operation. This practice follows from the work of Ingrid Daubiches, who proved that by using special wavelet filters, you can implement a DWT as a spatial filtering operation. (Remember, spatial filtering is often much faster than performing a "brute-force" Fourier-based transformation.) Different types of wavelet filters give rise to different wavelet transforms (i.e., wavelet basis functions). The most popular wavelet filter is the 9-7 biorthogonal pair, which uses a 9-tap low-pass filter and a 7-tap high-pass filter; this filter pair will be used in the upcoming JPEG-2000 standard. The FBI also uses the 9-7 biorthogonal filters for compressing images

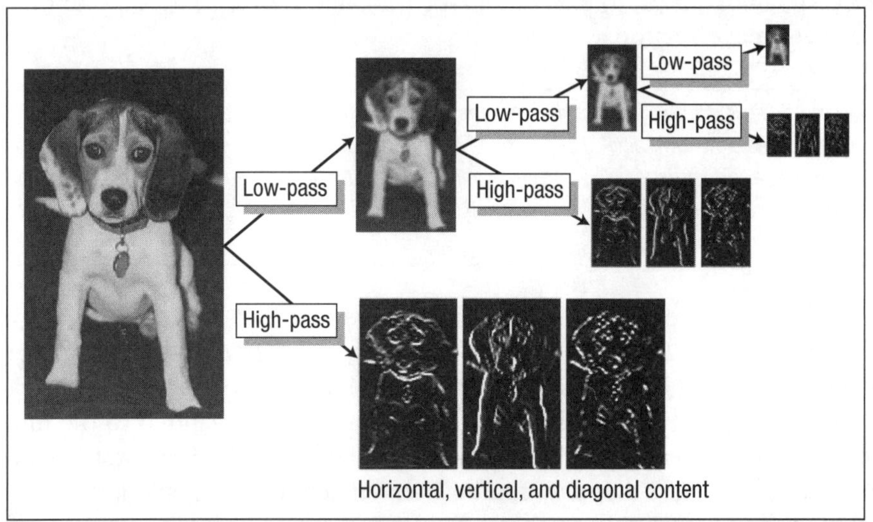

Figure 17.18 Subband coding an image with three levels of decomposition.

of fingerprints. Other common filters include the CREW, the Haar, the S+P, the TS, and the 5-3 filter pair.

A Recipe for Computing the DWT

Regardless of the actual wavelet filters that are used, the underlying subband coding scheme is the same: you implement the DWT by using a separable spatial filtering operation. This process uses four filters: low-pass and high-pass analysis or "decomposition" filters, and low-pass and high-pass synthesis or "reconstruction" filters. To compute the DWT, you use the analysis filters. The algorithm for one level of decomposition is as follows:

1. Filter the rows of the image by using the low-pass analysis filter to get a two-dimensional array of coefficients called $L(u, v)$.
2. Filter the rows of the image by using the high-pass analysis filter to get a two-dimensional array of coefficients called $H(u, v)$.
3. Downsample $L(u, v)$ and $H(u, v)$ by a factor of 2 in the horizontal direction.
4. Filter the columns of $L(u, v)$ by using the low-pass analysis filter to get a two-dimensional array of coefficients called $LL(u, v)$.
5. Filter the columns of $L(u, v)$ by using the high-pass analysis filter to get a two-dimensional array of coefficients called $LH(u, v)$.
6. Filter the columns of $H(u, v)$ by using the low-pass analysis filter to get a two-dimensional array of coefficients called $HL(u, v)$.
7. Filter the columns of $H(u, v)$ by using the high-pass analysis filter to get a two-dimensional array of coefficients called $HH(u, v)$.
8. Downsample $LL(u, v)$, $LH(u, v)$, $HL(u, v)$, and $HH(u, v)$ by a factor of 2 in the vertical direction.

NOTE: *To downsample an image by a factor of N in the horizontal direction, you keep one out of every N columns of the image. An image that has been downsampled by a factor of N in the horizontal direction should be 1/N times as wide as the original image. Likewise, to downsample an image by a factor of N in the vertical direction, you keep one out of every N rows of the image. An image that has been downsampled by a factor of N in the vertical direction should be 1/N times as tall as the original image.*

After performing Steps 1 through 8, you'll have four two-dimensional arrays of DWT coefficients: $LL(u, v)$, $LH(u, v)$, $HL(u, v)$, and $HH(u, v)$. These arrays are called the *subbands* of the image. The LL coefficients correspond to the image's low spatial frequencies. The LH and HL coefficients correspond to the image's horizontal and vertical spatial frequencies, respectively. The HH coefficients correspond to the image's diagonal spatial frequencies. To perform another level of decomposition, you simply perform Steps 1 through 8, using the LL subband as the input image. Figure 17.19 illustrates this process.

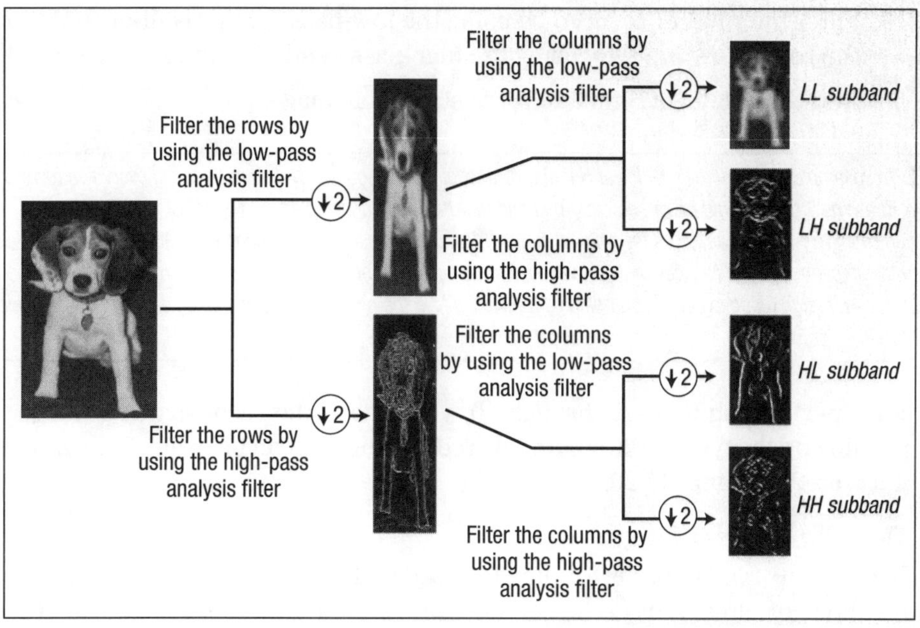

Figure 17.19 The forward DWT implemented as a filtering operation.

A Recipe for Computing the Inverse DWT

To reconstruct an image from the *LL*, *LH*, *HL*, and *HH* subbands, you perform another spatial filtering operation, this time using the synthesis filters. The algorithm for one level of reconstruction is as follows:

1. Upsample $LL(u, v)$, $LH(u, v)$, $HL(u, v)$, and $HH(u, v)$ by a factor of 2 in the vertical direction.
2. Filter the columns of $LL(u, v)$ by using the low-pass synthesis filter to get a two-dimensional array of coefficients called $LL^*(u, v)$.
3. Filter the columns of $LH(u, v)$ by using the high-pass synthesis filter to get a two-dimensional array of coefficients called $LH^*(u, v)$.
4. Filter the columns of $HL(u, v)$ by using the low-pass synthesis filter to get a two-dimensional array of coefficients called $HL^*(u, v)$.
5. Filter the columns of $HH(u, v)$ by using the high-pass synthesis filter to get a two-dimensional array of coefficients called $HH^*(u, v)$.
6. Add $LL^*(u, v)$ and $LH^*(u, v)$ to get a two-dimensional array of coefficients called $L^*(u, v)$.
7. Add $HL^*(u, v)$ and $HH^*(u, v)$ to get a two-dimensional array of coefficients called $H^*(u, v)$.
8. Upsample $L^*(u, v)$ and $H^*(u, v)$ by a factor of 2 in the horizontal direction.

9. Filter the rows of $L^*(u, v)$ by using the low-pass synthesis filter, and filter the rows of $H^*(u, v)$ by using the high-pass synthesis filter.
10. Add the results of Step 9 to reconstruct the image.

NOTE: *To upsample an image by a factor of N in the vertical direction, you add N-1 rows between every two rows of the image. These new rows should be zeroed out. An image that has been upsampled by a factor of N in the vertical direction should be N times as tall as the original image. Similarly, to upsample an image by a factor of N in the horizontal direction, you add N-1 columns between every two columns of the image. These new columns should be zeroed out. An image that has been upsampled by a factor of N in the horizontal direction should be N times as wide as the original image.*

After performing Steps 1 through 10, you'll have the reconstructed image. Depending on the type of filter pair, this reconstruction can be exact. This process is illustrated in Figure 17.20.

The GTransform Class

Because the recipe for performing forward and inverse DWTs doesn't depend on the types of filters that are used, an implementation of this scheme can be presented by using an abstract base class. On the companion CD-ROM, you'll find the **GTransform** class that demonstrates this process. Here's the declaration of the **GTransform** class:

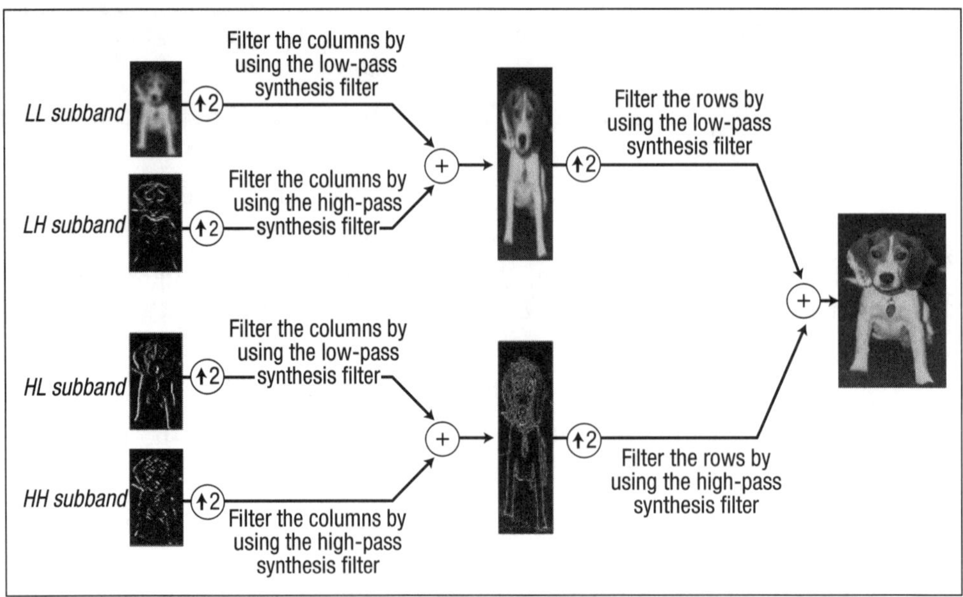

Figure 17.20 The inverse DWT implemented as a filtering operation.

17. Image Manipulation

```
template <class Type>
class GTransform
{
protected:
   // pure virtual functions (must be defined)
   virtual void TransformRows(const GBuffer<Type>& Buffer,
      GBuffer<Type>& LBuffer, GBuffer<Type>& HBuffer) = 0;
   virtual void TransformColumns(const GBuffer<Type>& Buffer,
      GBuffer<Type>& LBuffer, GBuffer<Type>& HBuffer) = 0;
   virtual void UntransformRows(GBuffer<Type>& Buffer,
      const GBuffer<Type>& LBuffer, const GBuffer<Type>& HBuffer) = 0;
   virtual void UntransformColumns(GBuffer<Type>& Buffer,
      const GBuffer<Type>& LBuffer, const GBuffer<Type>& HBuffer) = 0;

   virtual void DoDecompose(GBufferList<Type>& BufferList, int num_levels);
   virtual void DoReconstruct(GBufferList<Type>& BufferList, int
num_levels);

public:
   void Decompose(GBufferList<Type>& BufferList, int num_levels);
   void Reconstruct(GBufferList<Type>& BufferList);

public:
   GTransform();
   virtual ~GTransform();
};
```

The **GTransform** class provides two private member functions: **DoDecompose** and **DoReconstruct**. The **DoDecompose** member function is designed to perform a single level of decomposition. This function is defined as follows:

```
template<class Type>
void GTransform<Type>::DoDecompose(
    GBufferList<Type>& BufferList,
    int index
   )
{
   //
   // extract the source image (or the LL subband
   // from the previous level of decomposition)
   //
   const GBuffer<Type>& Buffer = BufferList.Items(index);
   const int width = Buffer.Width();
   const int height = Buffer.Height();
```

17. Image Manipulation

```
    // make room for the L and H subbands
    GBuffer<Type>& LBuffer = BufferList.Add(width / 2, height);
    GBuffer<Type>& HBuffer = BufferList.Add(width / 2, height);
    // filter the rows and upsample horizontally
    TransformRows(Buffer, LBuffer, HBuffer);

    // make room for the LL, LH, HL, and HH subbands
    GBuffer<Type>& HHBuffer = BufferList.Add(width / 2, height / 2);
    GBuffer<Type>& HLBuffer = BufferList.Add(width / 2, height / 2);
    GBuffer<Type>& LHBuffer = BufferList.Add(width / 2, height / 2);
    GBuffer<Type>& LLBuffer = BufferList.Add(width / 2, height / 2);
    // filter the columns and upsample vertically
    TransformColumns(LBuffer, LLBuffer, LHBuffer);
    TransformColumns(HBuffer, HLBuffer, HHBuffer);
}
```

The **BufferList** parameter specifies a reference to a **GBufferList** object that must contain at least one **GBuffer** object. This **GBuffer** object is used as the "source" image; the zero-based position (within the list) of this **GBuffer** object is specified by the **index** parameter. For example, to compute only one level of decomposition, the **BufferList** parameter should specify a **GBufferList** object whose zeroeth element is (a **GBuffer** object that corresponds to) the source image. Accordingly, in this case, the **index** parameter should be set to zero. Notice from its definition that the **DoDecompose** member function will use this "source" image and compute its forward DWT, placing the results in six new **GBuffer** objects (which are added to the list after the "source" image). So, after one call to the **DoDecompose** member function (i.e., after one level of decomposition), the **GBufferList** object (**BufferList**) will contain the following:

```
BufferList.Items(0) contains the original "source" image
BufferList.Items(1) contains the computed L subband
BufferList.Items(2) contains the computed H subband
BufferList.Items(3) contains the computed HH subband
BufferList.Items(4) contains the computed HL subband
BufferList.Items(5) contains the computed LH subband
BufferList.Items(6) contains the computed LL subband
```

If you want to compute another level of decomposition, you call the **DoDecompose** member function again (in a derived class because the function is protected), this time, by using the LL subband as the "source" image—that is, you pass the same **GBufferList** object as before, but you specify 6 as the **index** parameter. You can iterate this process to perform multiple levels of decomposition; in fact, that's exactly what the public **Decompose** member function does.

The **DoReconstruct** member function is designed to perform a single level of reconstruction. The definition of the **DoReconstruct** member function is as follows:

```
template<class Type>
void GTransform<Type>::DoReconstruct(
    GBufferList<Type>& BufferList,
    int index
   )
{
   // extract the LH and LL subbands from the list
   const GBuffer<Type>& LHBuffer = BufferList.Items(index + 5);
   const GBuffer<Type>& LLBuffer = BufferList.Items(index + 6);
   //
   // extract the L subband from the list
   // (this buffer will be overwritten with L*)
   //
   GBuffer<Type>& LBuffer = BufferList.Items(index + 1);
   LBuffer.ZeroData();
   //
   // upsample vertically, filter the columns, and then
   // sum the results (which are stored in LBuffer)
   //
   UntransformColumns(LBuffer, LLBuffer, LHBuffer);

   // extract the HH and HL subbands from the list
   const GBuffer<Type>& HHBuffer = BufferList.Items(index + 3);
   const GBuffer<Type>& HLBuffer = BufferList.Items(index + 4);
   //
   // extract the H subband from the list
   // (this buffer will be overwritten with H*)
   //
   GBuffer<Type>& HBuffer = BufferList.Items(index + 2);
   HBuffer.ZeroData();
   //
   // upsample vertically, filter the columns, and then
   // sum the results (which are stored in HBuffer)
   //
   UntransformColumns(HBuffer, HLBuffer, HHBuffer);

   //
   // extract the buffer for the reconstructed image
   //
   GBuffer<Type>& Buffer = BufferList.Items(index);
   Buffer.ZeroData();
```

```
    //
    // upsample horizontally, filter the rows, and then
    // sum the results (which are stored in Buffer)
    //
    UntransformRows(Buffer, LBuffer, HBuffer);
}
```

The **BufferList** parameter specifies a **GBufferList** object that contains the original image's subbands. The **DoReconstruct** member function will use these subbands to reconstruct the original image (or the LL subband that's used for the next level of reconstruction). This result is placed in the **GBuffer** object (within the list) whose zero-based position is specified by the **index** parameter. For example, after you use the **DoDecompose** member function to perform one level of decomposition, recall that the *HH*, *HL*, *LH*, and *LL* subbands are stored in the third, fourth, fifth, and sixth (zero-based) positions of your **GBufferList** object, respectively. Now, if you call the **DoReconstruct** member function, passing this same **GBufferList** object as the **BufferList** parameter and zero as the **index** parameter, the reconstructed image will be placed in the zeroeth position of this **GBufferList** object, like so:

```
BufferList.Items(6) contains the previously computed LL subband
BufferList.Items(5) contains the previously computed LH subband
BufferList.Items(4) contains the previously computed HL subband
BufferList.Items(3) contains the previously computed HH subband
BufferList.Items(2) contains the computed H* subband
BufferList.Items(1) contains the computed L* subband
BufferList.Items(0) contains the reconstructed image
```

If you've used the **DoDecompose** member function to compute more than one level of decomposition, you can call the **DoReconstruct** member function in an iterative fashion. Just remember, you should call the **DoReconstruct** member function the same number of times that you've called the **DoDecompose** member function. This is exactly what the public **Reconstruct** member function does. The **Reconstruct** member function is designed to wrap the process of reconstruction. The number of decomposition levels, and thus the number of required reconstruction levels, are inferred from the length of (i.e., the number of **GBuffers** contained within) the supplied **GBufferList** object.

Notice that the **GTransform** class contains four pure virtual member functions: **TransformRows**, **TransformColumns**, **UntransformRows**, and **UntransformColumns**. All classes that descend from the **GTransform** class must provide a definition for these functions. On the companion CD-ROM, you'll find two **GTransform** descendant classes: **GWavelet** and **G97**. Both of these classes define the **TransformRows**, **TransformColumns**, **UntransformRows**, and

UntransformColumns functions in a way that's specific to each type of transform. For example, the **GWavelet** class—which uses the 9-7 biorthogonal filter pair in a non-optimized fashion (which is useful to learn from)—defines these functions as follows (**lo_a**, **hi_a**, **lo_s**, and **hi_s** are the low-pass and high-pass analysis and synthesis filter kernels):

```
template<class Type>
void GWavelet<Type>::TransformRows(
    const GBuffer<Type>& Buffer,
    GBuffer<Type>& LBuffer,
    GBuffer<Type>& HBuffer
   )
{
   const int height = Buffer.Height();
   const int width = Buffer.Width();

   // filter the rows and downsample horizontally...
   for (int y = 0; y < height; ++y)
   {
      for (int x = 0; x < width; x += 2) // +2 to downsample
      {
         int s_pos = 4;
         int d_pos = 4;

         Type s_res = 0, d_res = 0;
         for (int iTap = 0; iTap < MAX_FILTER_LENGTH; ++iTap)
         {
            s_res += (lo_a[iTap] * Buffer.PixelsSE(x + s_pos--, y));
            d_res += (hi_a[iTap] * Buffer.PixelsSE(x + d_pos--, y));
         }
         LBuffer.Pixels(
            static_cast<int>(x / 2.0 + 0.5), y, s_res
            );
         HBuffer.Pixels(
            static_cast<int>(x / 2.0 + 0.5), y, d_res
            );
      }
   }
}

template<class Type>
void GWavelet<Type>::TransformColumns(
    const GBuffer<Type>& Buffer,
    GBuffer<Type>& LBuffer,
    GBuffer<Type>& HBuffer
   )
```

```
{
   const int height = Buffer.Height();
   const int width = Buffer.Width();

   // filter the columns and downsample vertically...
   for (int x = 0; x < width; ++x)
   {
      for (int y = 0; y < height; y += 2) // +2 to downsample
      {
         int s_pos = 4;
         int d_pos = 4;

         Type s_res = 0, d_res = 0;
         for (int iTap = 0; iTap < MAX_FILTER_LENGTH; ++iTap)
         {
            s_res += (lo_a[iTap] * Buffer.PixelsSE(x, y + s_pos--));
            d_res += (hi_a[iTap] * Buffer.PixelsSE(x, y + d_pos--));
         }
         LBuffer.Pixels(
            x, static_cast<int>(y / 2.0 + 0.5), s_res
            );
         HBuffer.Pixels(
            x, static_cast<int>(y / 2.0 + 0.5), d_res
            );
      }
   }
}

template<class Type>
void GWavelet<Type>::UntransformColumns(
    GBuffer<Type>& Buffer,
    const GBuffer<Type>& LBuffer,
    const GBuffer<Type>& HBuffer
   )
{
   //
   // NOTE: all widths are the same, but Buffer's
   // height is 2x that of LBuffer and HBuffer
   //

   const int height = LBuffer.Height();
   const int width = LBuffer.Width();

   GBuffer<Type> LBuffer2(width, height * 2);
   GBuffer<Type> HBuffer2(width, height * 2);
```

```
    // upsample by 2 in the vertical direction...
    for (int x = 0; x < width; ++x)
    {
       for (int y = 0; y < height; ++y)
       {
          LBuffer2.Pixels(x, y * 2, LBuffer.Pixels(x, y));
          HBuffer2.Pixels(x, y * 2 + 1, HBuffer.Pixels(x, y));
       }
    }

    // filter the columns...
    for (int x = 0; x < width; ++x)
    {
       for (int y = 0; y < height * 2; ++y)
       {
          int s_pos = 5;
          int d_pos = 5;

          Type s_res = 0, d_res = 0;
          for (int iTap = 0; iTap < MAX_FILTER_LENGTH; ++iTap)
          {
             s_res += (lo_s[iTap] * LBuffer2.PixelsSE(x, y + s_pos--));
             d_res += (hi_s[iTap] * HBuffer2.PixelsSE(x, y + d_pos--));
          }
          Buffer.Pixels(x, y, s_res + d_res);
       }
    }
}

template<class Type>
void GWavelet<Type>::UntransformRows(
     GBuffer<Type>& Buffer,
     const GBuffer<Type>& LBuffer,
     const GBuffer<Type>& HBuffer
    )
{
    //
    // NOTE: widths and heights are the same for
    // Buffer, Lbuffer, and HBuffer
    //

    const int height = LBuffer.Height();
    const int width = LBuffer.Width();

    GBuffer<Type> LBuffer2(width * 2, height);
    GBuffer<Type> HBuffer2(width * 2, height);
```

```
    // upsample by 2 in the horizontal direction...
    for (int y = 0; y < height; ++y)
    {
       for (int x = 0; x < width; ++x)
       {
          LBuffer2.Pixels(x * 2, y, LBuffer.Pixels(x, y));
          HBuffer2.Pixels(x * 2 + 1, y, HBuffer.Pixels(x, y));
       }
    }

    // filter the rows...
    for (int y = 0; y < height; ++y)
    {
       for (int x = 0; x < width * 2; ++x)
       {
          int s_pos = 5;
          int d_pos = 5;

          Type s_res = 0, d_res = 0;
          for (int iTap = 0; iTap < MAX_FILTER_LENGTH; ++iTap)
          {
             s_res += (lo_s[iTap] * LBuffer2.PixelsSE(x + s_pos--, y));
             d_res += (hi_s[iTap] * HBuffer2.PixelsSE(x + d_pos--, y));
          }
          Buffer.Pixels(x, y, s_res + d_res);
       }
    }
 }
```

As I mentioned, the **GWavelet** class is useful only for learning how to implement a wavelet transform by using a spatial filtering operation. The **G97** class uses an optimization technique called *lifting*, which requires about half the time necessary to perform a DWT. See Appendix B for a few references on lifting and wavelets in general.

Geometric Manipulations

Up until now, we've discussed only pixel-value-based manipulations. Specifically, all of the aforementioned techniques rely not on a pixel's spatial location but on its intensity value. For example, histogram equalization relies on the probability distribution of intensities. Likewise, the mean filter relies on the average intensity of a group of pixels. In short, none of these algorithms relies on the *geometry* of the image or on the geometry of the objects that the image contains. In Chapter 10, we looked at some standard transformation matrices that can be used to perform so-called basic geometric transformations. In this section, we'll examine a more versatile technique called *image warping*. Later I'll show you how warping can be combined with intensity-value manipulations to create an image metamorphosis.

Image Warping

Image warping is a general term used to describe a combination of the basic geometric transformations: rotation, shearing, scaling, and translation. Warping is closely related to a technique called *texture mapping*, in which a specific texture is mapped pixel-for-pixel to a given shape. You can think of texture mapping as taking a burlap cloth, for example, and wrapping it around some three-dimensional object. With warping, the idea is similar, except the shape of the texture and/or the shape of the object that's being mapped isn't necessarily predefined.

Several warping algorithms are available; the one we'll discuss, which is by far the most popular (and intuitive), is called *field warping*. Field warping was first introduced by Beier and Neely in their 1992 SIGGRAPH (Special Interest Group—Graphics) publication on feature-based image morphing. Because of its computational simplicity, field warping has since become the warping method of choice. If you're interested in other warping algorithms, Appendix B lists a few other references.

An Overview of Field Warping

For an image, you normally have two coordinates—a horizontal coordinate and a vertical coordinate. Each pixel in the image is defined by its position, (x, y), and its intensity value, $f(x, y)$. Because warping is only a geometric transformation, the intensity value of each pixel is of no concern. The position of each pixel, on the other hand, is important; we saw this with the basic geometric transformations. The problem with these basic transformations, however, is that they're all based on only one set of axes. If you rotate these axes to perform a rotation, for example, *every* pixel in the image is rotated by the same angle. Likewise, if you scale these axes to perform an expansion, you have a similar *global* effect. The purpose of field warping is to define a set of *local* miniature two-dimensional coordinate systems so that the global effect is minimized. This concept is depicted in Figure 17.21.

Note that each pair of axes in Figure 17.21 is mutually independent—that is, if you want to rotate a specific area of an image, you can rotate one pair of axes without affecting the other mini-coordinate systems. What isn't independent, however, is the influence of each mini-coordinate system on every pixel of the image. One way to visualize this is to think of an image as a rubber sheet whose corners are pinned down. If you twist a specific area on this sheet, the laws of physics tells us that all surrounding areas will also be twisted or stretched in some way. The extent to which a certain pixel is affected depends on how far away that

Figure 17.21 By using multiple pairs of local axes, field warping allows specific areas of an image to be geometrically transformed.

pixel is from the area that you deformed. This is where the adjective "field" comes into play—each mini-coordinate system has a *field of influence* on each pixel. It's just like a magnetic field—the closer you move a metal object to a magnet, the stronger the magnet's pull on the object.

The Field Warping Algorithm

The first step to performing a field warp is to define a set of mini-coordinate systems and define how each of these systems should be transformed. You do this by using a set of vectors (i.e., directed line segments). Each mini-coordinate system is specified by using one vector. The length and orientation of this vector define one axis; the other axis is assumed to be orthogonal (perpendicular) to this first axis. So, defining a set of mini-coordinate systems is straightforward. Now the question is, how do you specify the transformation? Specifying the transformation is similar to defining the page-space to device-space transformation that was discussed in Chapter 10. Namely, in Chapter 10, to define the page-space to device-space transformation, you altered the window and the viewport rectangles. Well, in field warping, instead of using a window and a viewport, you use two mini-coordinate systems—that is, two vectors. One vector defines the original coordinate system (compare with the window), and the other vector defines the transformed coordinate system (compare with the viewport).

Let's examine the case of using only one pair of vectors. The first vector defines the "source" mini-coordinate system, and the second vector defines the "destination" mini-coordinate system—that is, these two vectors define a transformation. (I'll use notation similar to that which Beier and Neely used in their paper just in case you want to compare notes later on.) Assume that the source vector, $P_{src}Q_{src}$, is defined by the endpoints P_{src} and Q_{src} (directed from P_{src} to Q_{src}). Assume that the destination vector, $P_{dst}Q_{dst}$, is defined by the endpoints P_{dst} and Q_{dst} (directed from P_{dst} to Q_{dst}). Again, these two vectors define a transformation as depicted in Figure 17.22.

Now, for a given pixel, X_{dst}, in the destination coordinate space, the first thing we need to do is determine its location, u, along the destination vector. We do this by projecting the vector $P_{dst}X_{dst}$ onto $P_{dst}Q_{dst}$, like so:

$$u = \frac{(X_{dst} - P_{dst}) \bullet (Q_{dst} - P_{dst})}{\| Q_{dst} - P_{dst} \|^2}$$

Note that the projection of $P_{dst}X_{dst}$ onto the destination vector is normalized by the squared length of the destination vector. In this way, u is equal to 0 when X_{dst}

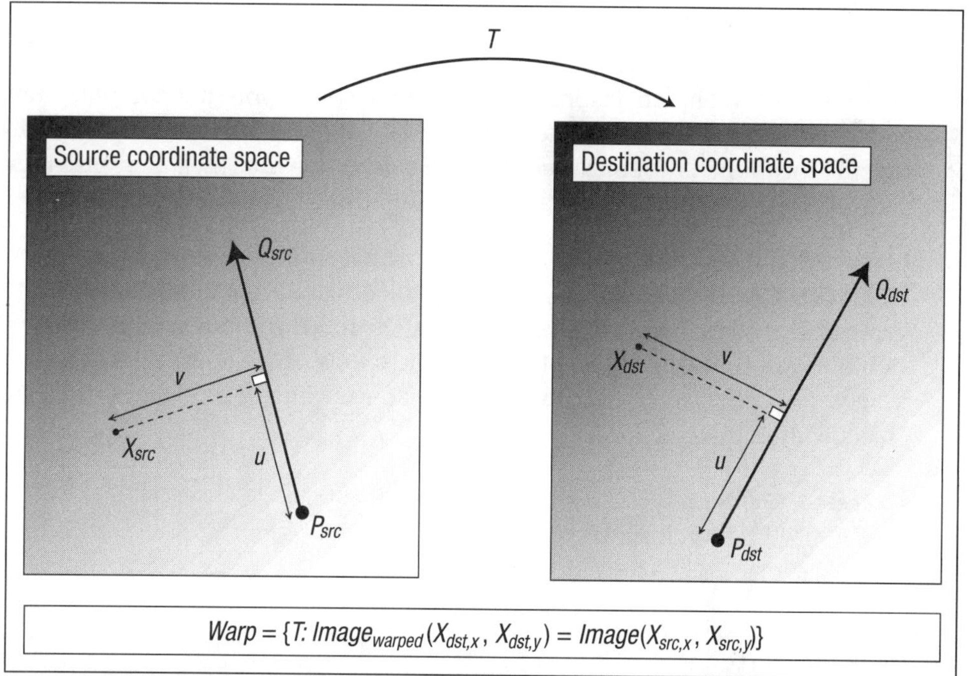

Figure 17.22 Each pair of corresponding vectors defines a coordinate-space transformation.

is located perpendicular to P_{dst}, and is equal to 1 when X_{dst} is located perpendicular to Q_{dst} (and u is less than 0 or greater than 1 when X_{dst} is beyond P_{dst} or Q_{dst}, respectively). In short, u indicates the position of the destination pixel along the axis $P_{dst}Q_{dst}$. For the other axis of the destination coordinate space, we compute a similar value, v, like so:

$$v = \frac{(X_{dst} - P_{dst}) \bullet \perp (Q_{dst} - P_{dst})}{\|Q_{dst} - P_{dst}\|}$$

In this equation, the $\perp$ operator denotes that the projection is made onto the vector that's perpendicular to the vector $P_{dst}Q_{dst}$. Because the length of this projection is divided only by the length of the destination vector (not by its squared length), the units of v are in pixels. Specifically, v indicates the distance, in pixels, of X_{dst} to the line that's defined by the destination vector.

After u and v are defined, the next task is to compute the location of X_{dst} in the source coordinate space; we'll call this location X_{src}. This point is computed as follows:

$$X_{src} = u \cdot (Q_{src} - P_{src}) + \frac{v \cdot \perp (Q_{src} - P_{src})}{\|Q_{src} - P_{src}\|} + P_{src}$$

So, for each pixel in the destination coordinate space, you first compute u and v, and then you use these values to compute X_{src}. Again, this latter value indicates a specific location in the source coordinate space. The final step is to assign to the pixel at X_{dst} the color value of the pixel at X_{src}; that is, you use a reverse mapping.

Let's work through an example. In the following code snippet, **Psrc** and **Qsrc** are **POINT**s that correspond to P_{src} and Q_{src}, respectively. **Pdst** and **Qdst** are **POINT**s that correspond to P_{dst} and Q_{dst}, respectively. The **imgBufferSrc** and **imgBufferDst** variables are **GBuffer** objects that hold the pixels of the source and destination images, respectively. The **hDIBSection** variable is a handle to a DIB section bitmap object. Here's the code:

```
// create GBuffers for the source and destination
GBuffer<RGBTRIPLE> imgBufferSrc, imgBufferDst;
DIBSectionToBuffer(imgBufferSrc, hDIBSection);

// set the background color
RGBTRIPLE white_pixel = {255, 255, 255};
imgBufferSrc.SetBlankPixel(white_pixel);
```

```
// extract the dimensions of the source
const int width = imgBufferSrc.Width();
const int height = imgBufferSrc.Height();

// initialize the dimensions of the destination
imgBufferDst.Width(width);
imgBufferDst.Height(height);

// define the source and destination vectors
POINT Psrc = {width / 2, 0};
POINT Qsrc = {width / 2, height};
POINT Pdst = {width / 2, 30};
POINT Qdst = {width / 2, height - 30};

//
// for each pixel in the destination image...
//
for (int y = 0; y < height; ++y)
{
   for (int x = 0; x < width; ++x)
   {
      POINT Xdst = {x, y};

      // compute the distance from Pdst to Qdst
      int dx = Qdst.x - Pdst.x;
      int dy = Qdst.y - Pdst.y;
      const double dist_PQdst = sqrt(dx * dx + dy * dy);

      // compute u
      const double u =
         ((Xdst.x - Pdst.x) * dx + (Xdst.y - Pdst.y) * dy) /
         (dist_PQdst * dist_PQdst);

      // compute v
      const double v =
         ((Xdst.x - Pdst.x) * dy + (Xdst.y - Pdst.y) * -dx) /
         dist_PQdst;

      // compute the distance from Psrc to Qsrc
      dx = Qsrc.x - Psrc.x;
      dy = Qsrc.y - Psrc.y;
      const double dist_PQsrc = sqrt(dx * dx + dy * dy);

      // compute Xsrc
      POINT Xsrc;
      Xsrc.x = static_cast<LONG>(0.5 +
```

```
            (u * dx) + (v * dy) / dist_PQsrc + Psrc.x
            );
        Xsrc.y = static_cast<LONG>(0.5 +
            (u * dy) - (v * dx) / dist_PQsrc + Psrc.y
            );

        // copy the source to the destination
        RGBTRIPLE src_pixel = imgBufferSrc.Pixels(Xsrc.x, Xsrc.y);
        imgBufferDst.Pixels(Xdst.x, Xdst.y, src_pixel);
    }
}

// update hDIBSection's pixels
BufferToDIBSection(hDIBSection, imgBufferDst);
```

Note that in this code snippet, **Psrc**, **Qsrc**, **Pdst**, and **Qdst** together define a vertical scaling (a contraction in the vertical direction). You can see this effect in Figure 17.23, which depicts the result (on the right) of executing this code on an image (on the left).

In Figure 17.23, notice that there's no field of influence going on—that is, the transformation had a global effect. The thing to remember is that with only one source vector and one destination vector, in contrast to the rubber sheet that we talked about earlier, the corners of our image aren't pinned down. In this case, it's like placing the rubber sheet on an air-hockey table. Because there's no friction, so to speak, when we move a point in the rubber sheet, the entire sheet is going to move. Clearly, what we need to do is constrain the edges of the image. To do this,

Figure 17.23 Warping via a single vector pair—the vectors used to generate the warped image together define a vertical scaling. (The original image is on the left; the warped image is on the right.)

we need to use eight additional vectors—four vectors for the source coordinate space, and four corresponding vectors for the destination coordinate space. Specifically, we place these vectors around the bounds of the image as depicted in Figure 17.24.

Because we now have a total of 10 vectors—5 for each image, 4 of which constrain the corners of the image—we'll need to modify the previous code snippet to handle multiple vector pairs. Because there's more than one vector pair, however, each destination vector will likely give rise to a different reverse mapping. This is where the field of influence comes into play. Specifically, we first determine how much influence each of the five destination vectors has on each pixel, and then we use these weights to compute a weighted average of where X_{src} should lie in the source coordinate space. This weight is computed for the ith destination vector as follows:

$$weight_i = \left(\frac{\|Q_{dst,i} - P_{dst,i}\|^p}{a + s_i} \right)^b$$

where i ranges from 1 to the number of vector pairs.

Okay, so what do all these variables denote? Well, the numerator of the equation is just the squared length of the ith destination vector raised to the pth power. Therefore, if p is zero, then the length of the ith destination vector plays no part in

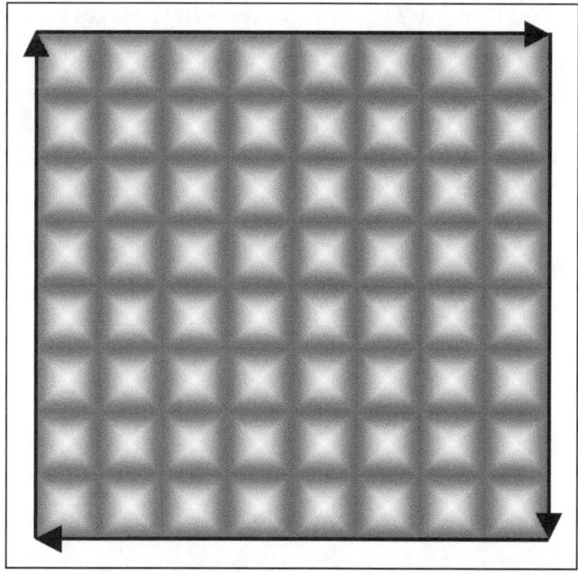

Figure 17.24 Constraining the edges of an image reduces the global effect of each vector pair.

how much weight that vector is assigned (i.e., the numerator is always 1). Conversely, if p is greater than zero, then the weight of the ith vector will be scaled by a value that's proportional to that vector's length. The variable b controls how the influence of each destination vector decreases with the vector's distance to each pixel. Because the variable s_i denotes the shortest distance from each pixel to the ith vector, b is most often set to 2 to follow the inverse square law. Accordingly, p is most often set to 0.5 to cancel the b's squaring effect on the numerator. The variable a is added to s_i only to avoid division by zero. Usually, a is set to a small value (say, 0.1) so that if a pixel lies on top of a vector ($s_i = 0$), that vector's weight will be extremely large. Larger values of a increase the smoothness of the warp but at the cost of precision.

Note that the variable s_i is the same as the absolute value of v only when the corresponding pixel, X_{dst}, is between $P_{dst,i}$ and $Q_{dst,i}$. Remember, s_i is the shortest distance to the ith destination vector, $P_{dst,i}Q_{dst,i}$, whereas v is the signed (shortest) distance to the *line* that's defined by $P_{dst,i}Q_{dst,i}$. If X_{dst} is beyond $P_{dst,i}$, then you should set s_i to the distance from X_{dst} to $P_{dst,i}$. Similarly, if X_{dst} is beyond $Q_{dst,i}$, then you should set s_i to the distance from X_{dst} to $Q_{dst,i}$.

So, using the formula for the weight of each vector, we can rewrite the previous code snippet by using three nested loops. The innermost loop iterates over each vector pair, keeping a running sum of the weight and a running sum of weighted reverse-mapped location, $X_{src,i}$, within the source coordinate space. Remember, because each vector pair defines its own transformation, we need to compute a weighted average of each $X_{src,i}$ so that we can determine where to reverse-map the pixel X_{dst} from. Here's the code:

```
// create GBuffers for the source and destination
GBuffer<RGBTRIPLE> imgBufferSrc, imgBufferDst;
DIBSectionToBuffer(imgBufferSrc, hDIBSection);

// set the background color
RGBTRIPLE gray_pixel = {156, 156, 156};
imgBufferSrc.SetBlankPixel(gray_pixel);

// extract the dimensions of the source
const int width = imgBufferSrc.Width();
const int height = imgBufferSrc.Height();

// initialize the dimensions of the destination
imgBufferDst.Width(width);
imgBufferDst.Height(height);
```

```
// define the source and destination vectors...
const int num_vectors = 5;
const POINT Psrc[] = {
   // constrain the edges
   {0, 0}, {width, 0}, {width, height}, {0, height},
   // our deformation vector
   {width / 2, 0}
   };
const POINT Qsrc[] = {
   // constrain the edges
   {width, 0}, {width, height}, {0, height}, {0, 0},
   // our deformation vector
   {width / 2, height}
   };
const POINT Pdst[] = {
   // constrain the edges
   {0, 0}, {width, 0}, {width, height}, {0, height},
   // our deformation vector
   {width / 2, 30}
   };
const POINT Qdst[] = {
   // constrain the edges
   {width, 0}, {width, height}, {0, height}, {0, 0},
   // our deformation vector
   {width / 2, height - 30}
   };

//
// for each pixel in the destination image...
//
for (int y = 0; y < height; ++y)
{
   for (int x = 0; x < width; ++x)
   {
      double DSUMx = 0.0;      // Xsrc.x's weighted displacement sum
      double DSUMy = 0.0;      // Xsrc.y's weighted displacement sum
      double weightsum = 0.0; // weight sum
      POINT Xdst = {x, y};     // current point

      //
      // for each pair of vectors...
      //
      for (int i = 0; i < num_vectors; ++i)
      {
         // compute the distance from Pdst to Qdst
         int dx = Qdst[i].x - Pdst[i].x;
```

17. Image Manipulation

```
int dy = Qdst[i].y - Pdst[i].y;
const double dist_PQdst = sqrt(dx*dx + dy*dy);

// compute the displacement from Xdst to Pdst
const int dx_XPdst = Xdst.x - Pdst[i].x;
const int dy_XPdst = Xdst.y - Pdst[i].y;

// compute u
const double u =
   (dx_XPdst * dx + dy_XPdst * dy) / (dist_PQdst * dist_PQdst);

// compute v
const double v =
   (dx_XPdst * dy - dy_XPdst * dx) / dist_PQdst;

// compute the shortest distance to the vector
double shortest_dist;
if (u < 0.0)
{
   shortest_dist =
      sqrt(dx_XPdst * dx_XPdst + dy_XPdst * dy_XPdst);
}
else if (u > 1.0)
{
   const int dx = x - Qdst[i].x;
   const int dy = y - Qdst[i].y;
   shortest_dist = sqrt(dx * dx + dy * dy);
}
else shortest_dist = (v < 0.0 ? -v : v);

//
// compute this vector's influence (weight)
// (use a = 0.1, b = 2, and p = 0.5)
//
double weight = sqrt(dist_PQdst) / (0.1 + shortest_dist);
weight *= weight;

// compute the distance from Psrc to Qsrc
dx = Qsrc[i].x - Psrc[i].x;
dy = Qsrc[i].y - Psrc[i].y;
const double dist_PQsrc = sqrt(dx*dx + dy*dy);

// compute Xsrc
POINT current_Xsrc;
current_Xsrc.x = static_cast<LONG>(0.5 +
   (u * dx) + (v * dy) / dist_PQsrc + Psrc[i].x
```

17. Image Manipulation

```
            );
        current_Xsrc.y = static_cast<LONG>(0.5 +
            (u * dy) - (v * dx) / dist_PQsrc + Psrc[i].y
            );

        // accrue the weighted displacement
        DSUMx += ((current_Xsrc.x - x) * weight);
        DSUMy += ((current_Xsrc.y - y) * weight);
        weightsum += weight;
    }

    // compute the location of the pixel to reverse-map
    POINT Xsrc = {
        static_cast<LONG>(0.5 + x + (DSUMx / weightsum)),
        static_cast<LONG>(0.5 + y + (DSUMy / weightsum))
        };

    // copy the source to the destination
    RGBTRIPLE src_pixel = imgBufferSrc.Pixels(Xsrc.x, Xsrc.y);
    imgBufferDst.Pixels(Xdst.x, Xdst.y, src_pixel);
  }
}

// update hDIBSection's pixels
BufferToDIBSection(hDIBSection, imgBufferDst);
```

Figure 17.25 depicts the result of using this code snippet on an image. In this case, because we constrained the edges, the contraction is localized to only the areas surrounding the fifth vector pair (i.e., the fifth mini-coordinate system).

Figure 17.25 Warping using five vector pairs; four of the vector pairs constrain the edges.

17. Image Manipulation

Some Warping Examples

The images in Figures 17.24 and 17.25 don't do justice to the actual capabilities of warping. By far, the biggest advantage of warping an image (rather than performing a basic geometric transformation) is that you can manipulate localized areas of an image—namely, the *objects* that an image contains. For example, if you've ever seen a caricature, you've probably noticed that the subject's distinct features are exaggerated (often to a great extent). In fact, many psychologists claim that we remember a person's face mainly by how far his or her face deviates from that of the "average" male or female. With warping, you can exaggerate things even more. Although I won't show any warped faces, I do encourage you to try this technique on images of your friends. I will, however, show some images of our feathered friend from Chapter 9; I don't think he'll mind too much. Figures 17.26, 17.27, and 17.28 depict some common warps of the image "Penguin."

The GWarp Class

On the companion CD-ROM is a C++ template class called **GWarp**, which encapsulates the process of warping an image. The **GWarp** class is designed to be used with **GBuffer** objects, and, as with the **GBuffer** class, there's no inherent link to Windows. The implementation is similar to previous code snippets but with a few tweaks in place for enhanced performance. The underlying algorithm, however, is identical. Here's the declaration of the **GWarp** class:

Figure 17.26 Warping to exaggerate a feature: make the penguin look like a pelican.

Figure 17.27 Warping to exaggerate a feature: Super Penguin!

Figure 17.28 Warping to exaggerate a feature: "Honestly, it looked like a regular mushroom!" said the penguin.

```
#include <vector>
#include "gbuffer.h"

struct GPoint {
   int x;
   int y;
};

template <class Type>
class GWarp
{
typedef std::vector<GPoint*> GPoints;
typedef std::vector<double> GLengths;

public:
   // default constructor
   GWarp();
   // destructor
   ~GWarp();

   // warping member function
   void Warp(GBuffer<Type>& imgBufferDst,
      const GBuffer<Type>& imgBufferSrc);
```

```
    // read-only member functions
    int NumLinesSrc() const { return pPsrc_.size(); }
    int NumLinesDst() const { return pPdst_.size(); }
    void GetLineSrc(int index, int& x1, int& y1, int& x2, int& y2) const;
    void GetLineDst(int index, int& x1, int& y1, int& x2, int& y2) const;

    // write-only member functions
    void AddLineSrc(int x1, int y1, int x2, int y2);
    void AddLineDst(int x1, int y1, int x2, int y2);
    void InsertLineSrc(int index, int x1, int y1, int x2, int y2);
    void InsertLineDst(int index, int x1, int y1, int x2, int y2);
    void RemoveLineSrc(int index);
    void RemoveLineDst(int index);

protected:
    // internal warping member function
    virtual void DoWarp(GBuffer<Type>& imgBufferDst,
       const GBuffer<Type>& imgBufferSrc);

    // internal read-only member functions
    virtual void DoGetLineSrc(
       int index, int& x1, int& y1, int& x2, int& y2) const;
    virtual void DoGetLineDst(
       int index, int& x1, int& y1, int& x2, int& y2) const;

    // internal write-only member functions
    virtual void DoAddLineSrc(int x1, int y1, int x2, int y2);
    virtual void DoAddLineDst(int x1, int y1, int x2, int y2);
    virtual void DoInsertLineSrc(int index, int x1, int y1, int x2, int y2);
    virtual void DoInsertLineDst(int index, int x1, int y1, int x2, int y2);
    virtual void DoRemoveLineSrc(int index);
    virtual void DoRemoveLineDst(int index);

private:
    GPoints pPsrc_; GPoints pQsrc_;
    GPoints pPdst_; GPoints pQdst_;
    GLengths src_dists_;
    GLengths dst_dists_;
    double a_;
};
```


The **GWarp** class maintains a list of the source and destination vectors in its private **pPsrc_**, **pQsrc_**, **pPdst_**, and **pQsrc_** members. Each of these members is of type **GPoints**, a **vector** of **GPoint** structures. You specify the source and destination vectors by using the **AddLineSrc** and **AddLineDst** member functions, respectively. (To minimize the number of flops required during warping, the **GWarp** class computes and stores the length of each vector as you add it.) After the source and destination vectors are defined, you instruct the **GWarp** class to perform the warp by using the **Warp** member function. The **Warp** member function accepts two parameters: a reference to a **GBuffer** object that holds the warped image (**imgBufferDst**), and a reference to a **const GBuffer** object that contains the source image (**imgBufferSrc**).

Image Metamorphosis

Image metamorphosis, often referred to as just *morphing*, is the process of blending two or more images, in terms of both their colors and their geometries. Although morphing is used mainly for animations and special effects, it does have some practical applications in several fields, including medical imaging and forensic science. Morphing is actually an extension of warping—that is, we can use warping to blend the geometries of two images. The other step, blending the colors of two images, is actually a much simpler task. This process is performed by using a technique called *cross-dissolving*.

Blending the Colors of Two Images

After tackling all those crazy P's, Q's, x's, and y's from the previous section on image warping, you'll find cross-dissolving a welcome relief. The idea is entirely straightforward. To blend the colors of two images, you simply perform a weighted average—that is, you interpolate the intermediate colors. Specifically, for each pixel in the first image, you find the corresponding pixel in the second image, and then you interpolate the intermediate color by using the colors of these two pixels. You then assign this interpolated color to the corresponding pixel in the "destination" image. As with most image-processing-based techniques, the only stipulation is that you must compute the interpolation separately for each color plane.

Let's look at an example. Suppose that you want to create an image (**imgBufferDst**) that's blended halfway between two images (**imgBuffer1** and **imgBuffer2**). In this case, you'd do the following (**hDIBSection1** and **hDIBSection2** are handles to the two source DIB section bitmaps):

```
// create GBuffer objects for the source images
GBuffer<RGBTRIPLE> imgBuffer1, imgBuffer2;
DIBSectionToBuffer(imgBuffer1, hDIBSection1);
DIBSectionToBuffer(imgBuffer2, hDIBSection2);

// extract the dimensions
const int width = min(imgBuffer1.Width(), imgBuffer2.Width());
const int height = min(imgBuffer1.Height(), imgBuffer2.Height());
```

```
// create a GBuffer object for the destination image
GBuffer<RGBTRIPLE> imgBufferDst(width, height);

for (int y = 0; y < height; ++y)
{
   for (int x = 0; x < width; ++x)
   {
      // extract the pixels of the source images
      RGBTRIPLE pixel1 = imgBuffer1.Pixels(x, y);
      RGBTRIPLE pixel2 = imgBuffer2.Pixels(x, y);

      // perform the 50/50 blending
      RGBTRIPLE blended_pixel;
      blended_pixel.rgbtRed = static_cast<unsigned char>(
         0.5 + (pixel1.rgbtRed + pixel2.rgbtRed) / 2.0
         );
      blended_pixel.rgbtGreen = static_cast<unsigned char>(
         0.5 + (pixel1.rgbtGreen + pixel2.rgbtGreen) / 2.0
         );
      blended_pixel.rgbtBlue = static_cast<unsigned char>(
         0.5 + (pixel1.rgbtBlue + pixel2.rgbtBlue) / 2.0
         );

      // assign the blended pixel to the destination image
      imgBufferDst.Pixels(x, y, blended_pixel);
   }
}
```

This code blends 50 percent of the color of each of **imgBuffer1's** pixels with 50 percent of the color of **imgBuffer2's** corresponding pixels. To blend two images by using some arbitrary percentage, you use a probability weighting, like so:

```
for (int y = 0; y < height; ++y)
{
   for (int x = 0; x < width; ++x)
   {
      // extract the pixels of the source images
      RGBTRIPLE pixel1 = imgBuffer1.Pixels(x, y);
      RGBTRIPLE pixel2 = imgBuffer2.Pixels(x, y);

      // e.g., 25% image1 and 75% image2
      const double prob1 = 0.75; // in the range [0.0, 1.0]
      const double prob2 = 1.0 - prob1;
```

```
      // perform the blending
      RGBTRIPLE blended_pixel;
      blended_pixel.rgbtRed = static_cast<unsigned char>(
         0.5 + (prob1 * pixel1.rgbtRed + prob2 * pixel2.rgbtRed)
         );
      blended_pixel.rgbtGreen = static_cast<unsigned char>(
         0.5 + (prob1 * pixel1.rgbtGreen + prob2 * pixel2.rgbtGreen)
         );
      blended_pixel.rgbtBlue = static_cast<unsigned char>(
         0.5 + (prob1 * pixel1.rgbtBlue + prob2 * pixel2.rgbtBlue)
         );

      // assign the blended pixel to the destination image
      imgBufferDst.Pixels(x, y, blended_pixel);
   }
}
```

Figure 17.29 depicts the results of performing this code with **prob1** set to values of 100 percent, 75 percent, 50 percent, 25 percent, and 0 percent (from top to bottom). In this figure, notice that, although there is a transition from the colors of the eagle (**imgBufferSrc**) to those of the squirrel (**imgBufferDst**), this sequence doesn't suggest a realistic metamorphosis because we're used to seeing a change in geometries as well as a change in colors. This is where the warping comes into play.

Blending the Geometries of Two Images

As I pointed out earlier, you can use warping to blend the geometries of two images. To do this, you use a method similar to that of blending the colors of two images; namely, you use interpolation. In this case, however, instead of interpolating an intermediate color, you interpolate an intermediate vector by using each pair of vectors (a vector from the first image and a corresponding vector from the second image). The simplest way to compute this intermediate vector is to interpolate between the endpoints of the first image's and second image's vectors. Figure 17.30 illustrates this process for a single vector pair. Remember, to perform the interpolation, you use a probability weighting, like so:

```
const double prob1 = 0.45; // 45% for example
const double prob2 = 1.0 - prob1;

POINT Pintermediate = {
   static_cast<LONG>(0.5 + (prob1 * Psrc.x + prob2 * Pdst.x)),
   static_cast<LONG>(0.5 + (prob1 * Psrc.y + prob2 * Pdst.y))
   };
```

Figure 17.29 Cross-dissolving two images.

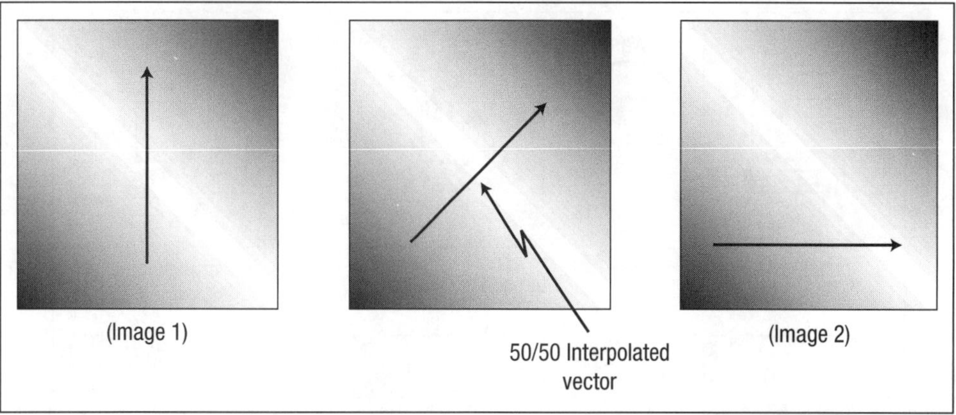

Figure 17.30 Interpolating endpoints.

```
POINT Qintermediate = {
   static_cast<LONG>(0.5 + (prob1 * Qsrc.x + prob2 * Qdst.x)),
   static_cast<LONG>(0.5 + (prob1 * Qsrc.y + prob2 * Qdst.y))
   };
```

By computing the intermediate vectors, you're actually defining two sets of transformations—one set that's described by the vectors of the first image and the intermediate vectors, and another set that's described by the vectors of the second image and the intermediate vectors. Now all that's left is to warp the first image to the intermediate image by using the first set of transformations, and to warp the second image to the intermediate image by using the second set of transformations. This scheme is depicted in Figure 17.31.

As you might have guessed, the most time-consuming part of this process is defining the vector pairs; typically, this job is delegated to an animator. In most cases, these vectors are placed along *features* that both images share. (This is why Beier and Neely's paper is titled "Feature-Based Image Metamorphosis.") For example, if you're morphing two faces, you'll want to place corresponding vectors around all of the important facial features, especially the eyes. The more vectors you use, the more realistic the metamorphosis will look.

Creating a Morph Sequence

Once all of the vectors are in place, you interpolate the intermediate vectors, and then warp each image according to these intermediate vectors (and according to each image's own vectors). This process will yield two intermediate images—a warped version of the first image, and a warped version of the second image. Both of these intermediate images should contain features (the ones that you

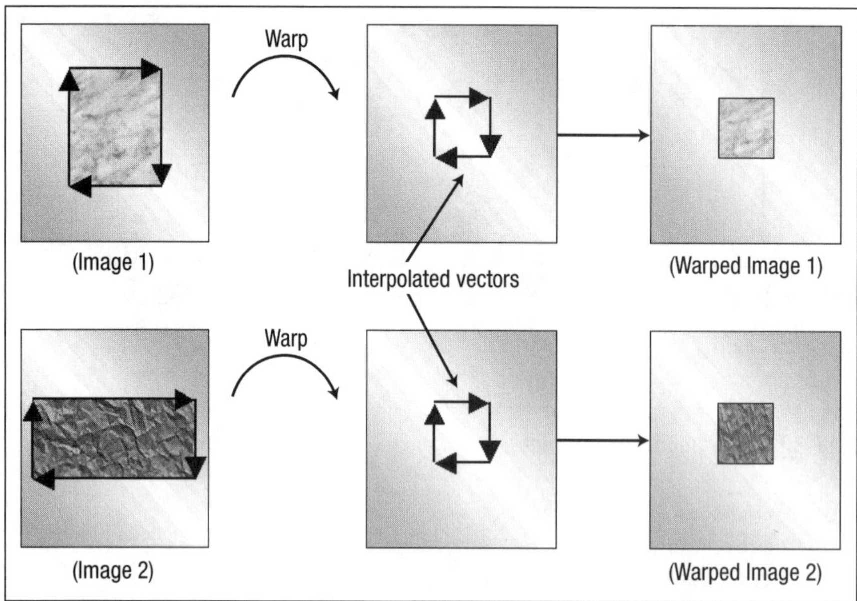

Figure 17.31 Blending the geometries of two images requires two warps: one from the first image to the interpolated coordinate space, and another from the second image to the interpolated coordinate space.

marked with the vectors) that are similar in position and size. Finally, you blend the colors of these intermediate images to create a single intermediate frame. To morph the shapes depicted in Figure 17.31, for example, you take Warped Image 1 and cross-dissolve it with Warped Image 2; this will yield a morphed image as illustrated in Figure 17.32.

This process will also work when you need to create a morphing sequence with more than one intermediate frame. In this case, you need to perform multiple interpolations, where the amount of each image's "contribution" is based on the position of each frame in the sequence. Bear in mind, however, that because each intermediate frame is computed using interpolation, the geometric transitions might look unrealistic.

The GMorph Class

The **GMorph** class (included on the companion CD-ROM) is a parameterized class that's designed to work with the **GWarp** class. (In fact, most of the work is punted to the **GWarp** class.) The **GMorph** class handles the task of blending the colors and geometries of the two images. The class is designed to be used with the **GBufferList** class to create a multiframe morph sequence. Here's the declaration of the **GMorph** class:

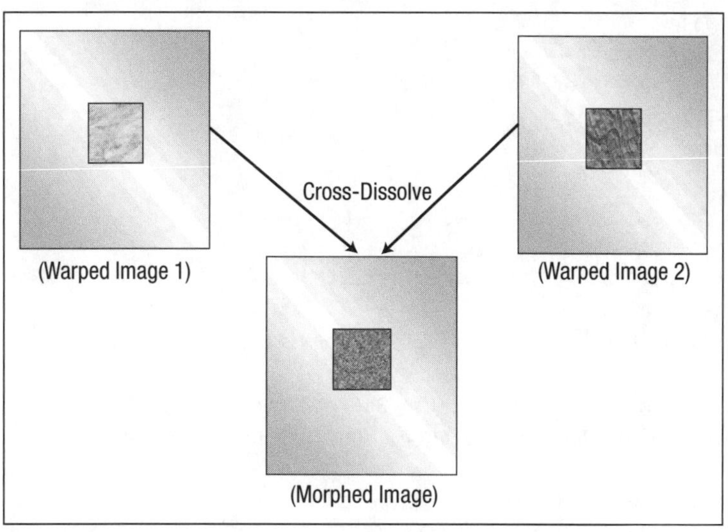

Figure 17.32 Morphing requires two warps followed by cross-dissolving.

```
template<class Type>
class GMorph
{
public:
   GMorph();
   ~GMorph();

   void Morph(GBufferList<Type>& BufferList, const GWarp<Type>& Warp,
      int num_frames);

protected:
   virtual void DoMorph(GBufferList<Type>& BufferList,
      const GWarp<Type>& Warp, int num_frames);
   virtual void DoCrossDissolve(GBuffer<Type>& BufferResult,
      const GBuffer<Type>& Buffer1, const GBuffer<Type>& Buffer2,
      double ratio1_to_2);
};
```

The public **Morph** member function simply calls the protected **DoMorph** member function, which uses the **GWarp** class and the protected **DoCrossDissolve** member function to create the metamorphosis. We won't examine the definition of the **DoCrossDissolve** member function because it's virtually identical to the previous code snippet that demonstrated how to blend the colors of two images. (You can examine the source code on the CD-ROM if you're interested.) The definition of the **DoMorph** member function, on the other hand, provides valuable insight into how to create a morph sequence. Here's what it looks like:

```
template <class Type>
void GMorph<Type>::DoMorph(
    GBufferList<Type>& BufferList,
    const GWarp<Type>& Warp,
    int num_frames
   )
{
   // extract the first image
   const GBuffer<Type>& Buffer1 = BufferList.Items(0);
   // extract the second image
   const GBuffer<Type>& Buffer2 = BufferList.Items(1);

   const int width = min(Buffer1.Width(), Buffer2.Width());
   const int height = min(Buffer1.Height(), Buffer2.Height());

   GBuffer<Type> TempBuffer1(width, height);
   GBuffer<Type> TempBuffer2(width, height);

   for (int iFrame = 1; iFrame <= num_frames; ++iFrame)
   {
      // compute the probability weighting
      const double prob2 = iFrame / (num_frames + 1.0);
      const double prob1 = 1.0 - prob2;

      // extract the number of vectors
      const int num_lines = min(Warp.NumLinesSrc(), Warp.NumLinesDst());

      // create two temporary warp objects
      GWarp<Type> TempWarp1, TempWarp2;

      // for each vector pair...
      for (int iLine = 0; iLine < num_lines; ++iLine)
      {
         GPoint Psrc, Qsrc, Pdst, Qdst;

         // extract image1's and image2's vectors
         Warp.GetLineSrc(iLine, Psrc.x, Psrc.y, Qsrc.x, Qsrc.y);
         Warp.GetLineDst(iLine, Pdst.x, Pdst.y, Qdst.x, Qdst.y);

         // interpolate between the endpoints of each vector pair
         GPoint Pint = {
            static_cast<int>(0.5 + prob1 * Psrc.x + prob2 * Pdst.x),
            static_cast<int>(0.5 + prob1 * Psrc.y + prob2 * Pdst.y)
            };
```

```
            GPoint Qint = {
               static_cast<int>(0.5 + prob1 * Qsrc.x + prob2 * Qdst.x),
               static_cast<int>(0.5 + prob1 * Qsrc.y + prob2 * Qdst.y)
               };

            //
            // add image1's vectors and the interpolated
            // vectors to the first temporary GWarp object
            //
            TempWarp1.AddLineSrc(Psrc.x, Psrc.y, Qsrc.x, Qsrc.y);
            TempWarp1.AddLineDst(Pint.x, Pint.y, Qint.x, Qint.y);

            //
            // add image2's vectors and the interpolated
            // vectors to the second temporary GWarp object
            //
            TempWarp2.AddLineSrc(Pdst.x, Pdst.y, Qdst.x, Qdst.y);
            TempWarp2.AddLineDst(Pint.x, Pint.y, Qint.x, Qint.y);
         }

         // warp the source image to the intermediate image
         TempWarp1.Warp(TempBuffer1, Buffer1);
         // warp the destination image to the intermediate image
         TempWarp2.Warp(TempBuffer2, Buffer2);

         // add a new GBuffer to the end of list
         GBuffer<Type>& BufferResult = BufferList.Add(width, height);
         // cross-dissolve the two warped images
         DoCrossDissolve(BufferResult, TempBuffer1, TempBuffer2, prob1);
      }

      // move the second image to the end
      BufferList.Insert(BufferList.Count() - 1, Buffer2);
      BufferList.Delete(1);
   }
```

Immediate Solutions

Converting an Image to Grayscale

To convert the colors of an image to grayscale, you implement the following pseudo-code:

```
For each pixel P in the image:
   Set luminance = (0.299 * P.red) + (0.587 * P.green) + (0.114 * P.blue)
   Set P.red = luminance
   Set P.green = luminance
   Set P.blue = luminance
```

The following code snippet demonstrates how to convert the colors of a 24-bpp DIB section bitmap (**hDIBSection**) to grayscale by using a **GBuffer** object and the application-defined **DIBSectionToBitmap** and **BufferToDIBSection** functions:

```
// create a GBuffer object for the image
GBuffer<RGBTRIPLE> imgBuffer;
DIBSectionToBuffer(imgBuffer, hDIBSection);

// extract the image's dimensions
const int width = imgBuffer.Width();
const int height = imgBuffer.Height();

// for each pixel in the image...
for (int y = 0; y < height; ++y)
{
   for (int x = 0; x < width; ++x)
   {
      // extract the pixel
      RGBTRIPLE pixel = imgBuffer.Pixels(x, y);

      // convert to grayscale
      unsigned char luminance =
         static_cast<unsigned char>(0.5 +
```

```
                0.299 * pixel.rgbtRed +
                0.587 * pixel.rgbtGreen +
                0.114 * pixel.rgbtBlue
                );

        // assign the value back to the image
        pixel.rgbtRed = luminance;
        pixel.rgbtGreen = luminance;
        pixel.rgbtBlue = luminance;
        imgBuffer.Pixels(x, y, pixel);
    }
}

// update hDIBSection's pixels
BufferToDIBSection(hDIBSection, imgBuffer);
```

For more information on the **GBuffer** class, see the "In Depth" section and the source code that's included on the companion CD-ROM. For more information on the **DIBSectionToBitmap** function, see the solution "Initializing a **GBuffer** Object with the Pixels of a DIB Section Bitmap." For more information on the **BufferToDIBSection** function, see the solution "Initializing a DIB Section Bitmap with the Pixels of a **GBuffer** Object."

Thresholding an Image

To threshold an image at a specific value T, you implement the following pseudocode:

```
For each pixel P in the image:
   If P is not grayscale, convert P to grayscale
   If P's value is less than T, set P = 0
   Otherwise, set P = 255
```

The following code snippet demonstrates how to threshold a 24-bpp DIB section bitmap (**hDIBSection**) at a value of 192 by using a **GBuffer** object and the application-defined **DIBSectionToBitmap** and **BufferToDIBSection** functions:

```
// threshold value
const unsigned char T = 192;
```

```
// create a GBuffer object for the image
GBuffer<RGBTRIPLE> imgBuffer;
DIBSectionToBuffer(imgBuffer, hDIBSection);

// extract the image's dimensions
const int width = imgBuffer.Width();
const int height = imgBuffer.Height();

// for each pixel in the image...
for (int y = 0; y < height; ++y)
{
   for (int x = 0; x < width; ++x)
   {
      // extract the pixel
      RGBTRIPLE pixel = imgBuffer.Pixels(x, y);

      // convert to grayscale
      unsigned char luminance =
         static_cast<unsigned char>(0.5 +
            0.299 * pixel.rgbtRed +
            0.587 * pixel.rgbtGreen +
            0.114 * pixel.rgbtBlue
            );

      // threshold the pixel
      luminance = luminance < T ? 0 : 255;

      // assign the value back to the image
      pixel.rgbtRed = luminance;
      pixel.rgbtGreen = luminance;
      pixel.rgbtBlue = luminance;
      imgBuffer.Pixels(x, y, pixel);
   }
}

// update hDIBSection's pixels
BufferToDIBSection(hDIBSection, imgBuffer);
```

For more information on the **GBuffer** class, see the "In Depth" section and the source code that's included on the companion CD-ROM. For more information on the **DIBSectionToBitmap** function, see the solution "Initializing a **GBuffer** Object with the Pixels of a DIB Section Bitmap." For more information on the **BufferToDIBSection** function, see the solution "Initializing a DIB Section Bitmap with the Pixels of a **GBuffer** Object."

Brightening or Darkening an Image

To brighten or darken an image, you implement the following pseudo-code:

```
1. Define a gamma value:
       0.0 < gamma < 1.0 defines a brightening
       gamma > 1.0 defines a darkening

2. For each pixel P in the image:
       Set P.red =   255 * pow(P.red / 255.0, gamma)
       Set P.green = 255 * pow(P.green / 255.0, gamma)
       Set P.blue =  255 * pow(P.blue / 255.0, gamma)
```

The following code snippet demonstrates how to brighten a 24-bpp DIB section bitmap (**hDIBSection**) by using a **GBuffer** object and the application-defined **DIBSectionToBitmap** and **BufferToDIBSection** functions:

```
#define CLIP(x) x > 255 ? 255 : x < 0 ? 0 : x

// create a GBuffer object for the image
GBuffer<RGBTRIPLE> imgBuffer;
DIBSectionToBuffer(imgBuffer, hDIBSection);

// define the gamma value
const double gamma = 0.75;

// create the result table
unsigned char result_table[256];
for (int index = 0; index < 256; ++index)
{
   result_table[index] = CLIP(255 * pow(index / 255.0, gamma));
}

// create a GBuffer object for the image
GBuffer<RGBTRIPLE> imgBuffer;
DIBSectionToBuffer(imgBuffer, hDIBSection);

// extract the image's dimensions
const int width = imgBuffer.Width();
const int height = imgBuffer.Height();
```

```
// for each pixel in the image...
for (int y = 0; y < height; ++y)
{
   for (int x = 0; x < width; ++x)
   {
      // extract the pixel
      RGBTRIPLE pixel = imgBuffer.Pixels(x, y);

      // look up the result
      pixel.rgbtRed = result_table[pixel.rgbtRed];
      pixel.rgbtGreen = result_table[pixel.rgbtGreen];
      pixel.rgbtBlue = result_table[pixel.rgbtBlue];

      // assign the pixel back to the image
      imgBuffer.Pixels(x, y, pixel);
   }
}

// update hDIBSection's pixels
BufferToDIBSection(hDIBSection, imgBuffer);
```

For more information on the **GBuffer** class, see the "In Depth" section and the source code that's included on the companion CD-ROM. For more information on the **DIBSectionToBitmap** function, see the solution "Initializing a **GBuffer** Object with the Pixels of a DIB Section Bitmap." For more information on the **BufferToDIBSection** function, see the solution "Initializing a DIB Section Bitmap with the Pixels of a **GBuffer** Object."

Computing the Histogram of an Image

To compute the histogram of an image, you implement the following pseudocode:

```
1. Create an Nx256 array, "hist", where N is
    at least the total number of pixels in your image

2. For each pixel P in the image:
       If P is not grayscale, convert P to grayscale
       Increment hist[P's value] by 1
```

The following application-defined function, **ComputeHistogram**, demonstrates how to compute the histogram of a 24-bpp DIB section bitmap (**hDIBSection**) by using a **GBuffer** object:

```
void ComputeHistogram(
    IN const GBuffer<RGBTRIPLE>& imgBuffer,
    // pointer to a previously allocated array
    OUT LPUINT pHistogram
   )
{
   // zero-out the histogram
   memset(pHistogram, 0, 256 * sizeof(UINT));

   // extract the image's dimensions
   const int width = imgBuffer.Width();
   const int height = imgBuffer.Height();

   // compute the histogram
   for (int y = 0; y < height; ++y)
   {
      for (int x = 0; x < width; ++x)
      {
         RGBTRIPLE pixel = imgBuffer.Pixels(x, y);

         // convert the pixel to grayscale
         unsigned char intensity =
            static_cast<unsigned char>(0.5 +
               0.299 * pixel.rgbtRed +
               0.587 * pixel.rgbtGreen +
               0.114 * pixel.rgbtBlue
               );

         // increment the intensity-th bin
         ++pHistogram[intensity];
      }
   }
}
```

For more information on the **GBuffer** class, see the “In Depth” section and the source code that’s included on the companion CD-ROM.

Contrast-Stretching an Image

To contrast-stretch an image, you implement either of the following blocks of pseudo-code:

```
Method 1: The Classical Approach

1. Compute the image's histogram.

2. Determine the histogram's maximum count.

3. Determine which bin of the histogram has the maximum count.

4. Define low-end and high-end cut-off values at certain percentages
   (say, 10 percent and 90 percent) of the maximum count.

5. Determine the bins whose count satisfies these cut-off values
   ("min_hist_bin" and "max_hist_bin").

6. For each pixel P in the image:
       Set P.red =   255 * (P.red - min_hist_bin) /
                     (max_hist_bin - min_hist_bin)
       Set P.green = 255 * (P.green - min_hist_bin) /
                     (max_hist_bin - min_hist_bin)
       Set P.blue =  255 * (P.blue - min_hist_bin) /
                     (max_hist_bin - min_hist_bin)


Method 2: Haeberli and Voorhies's algorithm

1. Choose a value of alpha (alpha < 1 decreases contrast;
   alpha > 1 increases contrast).

2. For each pixel P in the image:
       Set P.red   = 128 + alpha * (P.red - 128)
       Set P.green = 128 + alpha * (P.green - 128)
       Set P.blue  = 128 + alpha * (P.blue - 128)
```

The following code snippet demonstrates how to use the classical approach to contrast-stretch a 24-bpp DIB section bitmap (**hDIBSection**) by using a **GBuffer** object and the application-defined **ComputeHistogram**, **DIBSectionToBitmap**, and **BufferToDIBSection** functions:

```
#define CLIP(x) x > 255 ? 255 : x < 0 ? 0 : x

// create a GBuffer object for the image
GBuffer<RGBTRIPLE> imgBuffer;
DIBSectionToBuffer(imgBuffer, hDIBSection);

// extract the image's dimensions
const int width = imgBuffer.Width();
const int height = imgBuffer.Height();

// compute the image's histogram
UINT histogram[256];
ComputeHistogram(imgBuffer, histogram);

// find the bin with the maximum count
UINT max_count = 0;
unsigned char bin_with_max_count = 0;
for (int iBin = 0; iBin < 256; ++iBin)
{
   if (histogram[iBin] > max_count)
   {
      bin_with_max_count = iBin;
      max_count = histogram[iBin];
   }
}

// find the bins with cutoff values at 10 and 90 percentiles
unsigned char min_hist_bin = 0, max_hist_bin = 255;
for (int iBin = 0; iBin < bin_with_max_count; ++iBin)
{
   if (histogram[iBin] >
        static_cast<UINT>(0.10 * max_count + 0.5))
   {
      min_hist_bin = iBin;
      break;
   }
}
for (int iBin = 255; iBin > bin_with_max_count; --iBin)
{
   if (histogram[iBin] >
        static_cast<UINT>(0.10 * max_count + 0.5))
   {
      max_hist_bin = iBin;
      break;
   }
}
```

```
// create a result table
unsigned char result_table[256];
for (int index = 0; index < 256; ++index)
{
   // perform the contrast stretching
   result_table[index] = CLIP(
      255 * (index - min_hist_bin) / (max_hist_bin - min_hist_bin)
      );
}

// for each pixel in the image...
for (int y = 0; y < height; ++y)
{
   for (int x = 0; x < width; ++x)
   {
      // extract the pixel
      RGBTRIPLE pixel = imgBuffer.Pixels(x, y);

      // look up the result
      pixel.rgbtRed = result_table[pixel.rgbtRed];
      pixel.rgbtGreen = result_table[pixel.rgbtGreen];
      pixel.rgbtBlue = result_table[pixel.rgbtBlue];

      // assign the pixel back to the image
      imgBuffer.Pixels(x, y, pixel);
   }
}

// update hDIBSection's pixels
BufferToDIBSection(hDIBSection, imgBuffer);
```

The following code snippet demonstrates how to use Haeberli and Voorhies's algorithm to contrast-stretch a 24-bpp DIB section bitmap (**hDIBSection**) by using a **GBuffer** object and the application-defined **ComputeHistogram**, **DIBSectionToBitmap**, and **BufferToDIBSection** functions:

```
// create a GBuffer object for the image
GBuffer<RGBTRIPLE> imgBuffer;
DIBSectionToBuffer(imgBuffer, hDIBSection);

// extract the image's dimensions
const int width = imgBuffer.Width();
const int height = imgBuffer.Height();
```

```
// create a result table
const float alpha = 3; // adjustable
unsigned char result_table[256];
for (int index = 0; index < 22; ++index)
{
   for (int value = 0; value < 256; ++value)
   {
      // perform the constrast stretching
      result_table[value] = CLIP(
         128 + alpha * (value - 128)
         );
   }
}

// for each pixel in the image...
for (int y = 0; y < height; ++y)
{
   for (int x = 0; x < width; ++x)
   {
      // extract the pixel
      RGBTRIPLE pixel = imgBuffer.Pixels(x, y);

      // look-up the result
      pixel.rgbtRed = result_table[pixel.rgbtRed];
      pixel.rgbtGreen = result_table[pixel.rgbtGreen];
      pixel.rgbtBlue = result_table[pixel.rgbtBlue];

      // assign the pixel back to the image
      imgBuffer.Pixels(x, y, pixel);
   }
}

// update hDIBSection's pixels
BufferToDIBSection(hDIBSection, imgBuffer);
```

For the definition of the **ComputeHistogram** function, refer to the solution "Computing the Histogram of an Image." For more information on the **GBuffer** object and class, see the "In Depth" section and the source code that's included on the companion CD-ROM. For more information on the **DIBSectionToBitmap** function, see the solution "Initializing a **GBuffer** Object with the Pixels of a DIB Section Bitmap." For more information on the **BufferToDIBSection** function, see the solution "Initializing a DIB Section Bitmap with the Pixels of a **GBuffer** Object."

Histogram-Equalizing an Image

To histogram-equalize an image, you perform the following steps:

```
1. Compute the image's histogram.

2. Compute the image's probability distribution function.

3. Compute the image's cumulative distribution function ("cdf").

4. For each pixel P in the image:
       Set P.red =   255 * (cdf[P.red] - cdf[0]) / (1.0 - cdf[0])
       Set P.green = 255 * (cdf[P.green] - cdf[0]) / (1.0 - cdf[0])
       Set P.blue =  255 * (cdf[P.blue] - cdf[0]) / (1.0 - cdf[0])
```

The following code snippet demonstrates how to histogram-equalize a 24-bpp DIB section bitmap (**hDIBSection**) by using a **GBuffer** object and the application-defined **ComputeHistogram**, **DIBSectionToBitmap**, and **BufferToDIBSection** functions:

```
// create a GBuffer object for the image
GBuffer<RGBTRIPLE> imgBuffer;
DIBSectionToBuffer(imgBuffer, hDIBSection);

// extract the image's dimensions
const int width = imgBuffer.Width();
const int height = imgBuffer.Height();

// compute the image's histogram
UINT histogram[256];
ComputeHistogram(imgBuffer, histogram);

// compute the image's probability distribution function
double pdf[256];
const UINT total_num_pixels = imgBuffer.Size();
for (int iBin = 0; iBin < 256; ++iBin)
{
   pdf[iBin] =
      static_cast<double>(histogram[iBin]) /
      static_cast<double>(total_num_pixels);
}

// compute the image's cumulative distribution function
double cdf[256];
for (int iBin = 0; iBin < 256; ++iBin)
{
```

```
    cdf[iBin] = 0.0;
    for (int index = 0; index <= iBin; ++index)
    {
        cdf[iBin] += pdf[index];
    }
}

// compute a result table
unsigned char result_table[256];
for (int index = 0; index < 256; ++index)
{
    // perform the histogram-equalization
    result_table[index] = static_cast<unsigned char>(
        0.5 + 255 * (cdf[index] - cdf[0]) / (1.0 - cdf[0])
        );
}

// for each pixel in the image...
for (int y = 0; y < height; ++y)
{
    for (int x = 0; x < width; ++x)
    {
        // extract the pixel
        RGBTRIPLE pixel = imgBuffer.Pixels(x, y);

        // look up the result
        pixel.rgbtRed = result_table[pixel.rgbtRed];
        pixel.rgbtGreen = result_table[pixel.rgbtGreen];
        pixel.rgbtBlue = result_table[pixel.rgbtBlue];

        // assign the pixel back to the image
        imgBuffer.Pixels(x, y, pixel);
    }
}

// update hDIBSection's pixels
BufferToDIBSection(hDIBSection, imgBuffer);
```

For the definition of the **ComputeHistogram** function, refer to the solution "Computing the Histogram of an Image." For more information on the **GBuffer** object and class, see the "In Depth" section and the source code that's included on the companion CD-ROM. For more information on the **DIBSectionToBitmap** function, see the solution "Initializing a **GBuffer** Object with the Pixels of a DIB Section Bitmap." For more information on the **BufferToDIBSection** function, see the solution "Initializing a DIB Section Bitmap with the Pixels of a **GBuffer** Object."

Computing the Discrete Cosine Transform of an Image

To transform an image into the frequency domain by using the DCT, you use the application-defined **ComputeForwardDCT** function:

```
struct DCTTRIPLE {double dctRed, dctGreen, dctBlue;};

void ComputeForwardDCT(
    OUT GBuffer<DCTTRIPLE>& dctBuffer,       // F(u, v); DCT coefficients
    IN const GBuffer<RGBTRIPLE>& imgBuffer,  // f(x, y); source image
    IN const GBuffer<double> cosBuffer       // DCT basis functions
   )
{
   static const int N = 8;

   // extract the dimensions of the image
   const int width = imgBuffer.Width();
   const int height = imgBuffer.Height();
   dctBuffer.Width(width);
   dctBuffer.Height(height);

   // intermediate result (an NxN block)
   GBuffer<DCTTRIPLE> dctBlock(N, N);

   //
   // for every NxN block of the image
   //
   for (int y = 0; y < height; y += N)
   {
      for (int x = 0; x < width; x += N)
      {
         //
         // do the first matrix multiplication
         // ([cosBuffer]' [imgBuffer)
         // and store the results in dctBlock
         //
         for (int col = 0; col < N; ++col)
         {
            for (int row = 0; row < N; ++row)
            {
               DCTTRIPLE result = {0.0, 0.0, 0.0};
               for (int index = 0; index < N; ++index)
               {
                  // note the use of symmetric extension
```

```
                    RGBTRIPLE pixel = imgBuffer.PixelsSE(x + index, y + row);
                    double cosVal_transpose = cosBuffer.Pixels(index, col);

                    result.dctRed += cosVal_transpose * pixel.rgbtRed;
                    result.dctGreen += cosVal_transpose * pixel.rgbtGreen;
                    result.dctBlue += cosVal_transpose * pixel.rgbtBlue;
                }
                dctBlock.Pixels(col, row, result);
            }
        }
        //
        // do the second matrix multiplication
        // ([dctBlock [cosBuffer])
        // and store the results in result_block
        //
        for (int col = 0; col < N; ++col)
        {
            for (int row = 0; row < N; ++row)
            {
                DCTTRIPLE result = {0.0, 0.0, 0.0};
                for (int index = 0; index < N; ++index)
                {
                    DCTTRIPLE coeff = dctBlock.Pixels(col, index);
                    double cosVal = cosBuffer.Pixels(index, row);

                    result.dctRed += coeff.dctRed * cosVal;
                    result.dctGreen += coeff.dctGreen * cosVal;
                    result.dctBlue += coeff.dctBlue * cosVal;
                }
                dctBuffer.Pixels(x + col, y + row, result);
            }
        }
      }
   }
}
```

The **dctBuffer** parameter specifies a reference to a **GBuffer** object that will be filled with the DCT coefficients. The elements of **dctBuffer** must be of type **DCTTRIPLE**. These coefficients are computed from the source image, which is specified by the **imgBuffer** parameter (a reference to a **GBuffer** object that contains the source image). The pixels of **imgBuffer** must be of type **RGBTRIPLE**. The **cosBuffer** parameter specifies a reference to a **GBuffer** object that holds the DCT basis functions for the case in which the sub-image size is 8x8 pixels (i.e., $N = 8$). These basis functions can be computed as follows:

```
//
// compute the table of basis functions and
// store the result in the GBuffer cosBuffer
//
GBuffer<double> cosBuffer(N, N);
for (int m = 0; m < N; ++m)
{
   for (int n = 0; n < N; ++n)
   {
      double result;
      if (n == 0)
      {
         result =
            sqrt(1.0 / N) *
            cos(((2 * m + 1) * n * M_PI) / (2.0 * N));
      }
      else
      {
         result =
            sqrt(2.0 / N) *
            cos(((2 * m + 1) * n * M_PI) / (2.0 * N));
      }
      cosBuffer.Pixels(m, n, result);
   }
}
```

For more information on the **GBuffer** class, see the "In Depth" section and the source code that's included on the companion CD-ROM.

Computing the Inverse Discrete Cosine Transform

To compute the inverse DCT of a previously DCT-transformed image (i.e., an "image of DCT coefficients"), you use the application-defined **ComputeInverseDCT** function:

```
struct DCTTRIPLE {double dctRed, dctGreen, dctBlue;};

void ComputeInverseDCT(
    OUT GBuffer<RGBTRIPLE>& imgBuffer,      // f(x, y); source image
    IN const GBuffer<DCTTRIPLE>& dctBuffer, // F(u, v); DCT coefficients
    IN const GBuffer<double> cosBuffer      // DCT basis functions
   )
```

```
{
   static const int N = 8;

   const int width = dctBuffer.Width();
   const int height = dctBuffer.Height();
   imgBuffer.Width(width);
   imgBuffer.Height(height);

   // intermediate result (an NxN block)
   GBuffer<DCTTRIPLE> dctBlock(N, N);

   //
   // for every NxN block of the coefficients
   //
   for (int y = 0; y < height; y += N)
   {
      for (int x = 0; x < width; x += N)
      {
         //
         // do the first matrix multiplication
         // ([cosBuffer][dctBuffer])
         // and store the results in dctBlock
         //
         for (int col = 0; col < N; ++col)
         {
            for (int row = 0; row < N; ++row)
            {
               DCTTRIPLE result = {0.0, 0.0, 0.0};
               for (int index = 0; index < N; ++index)
               {
                  DCTTRIPLE coeff = dctBuffer.Pixels(x + index, y + row);
                  double cosVal = cosBuffer.Pixels(col, index);

                  result.dctRed += cosVal * coeff.dctRed;
                  result.dctGreen += cosVal * coeff.dctGreen;
                  result.dctBlue += cosVal * coeff.dctBlue;
               }
               dctBlock.Pixels(col, row, result);
            }
         }
         //
         // do the second matrix multiplication
         // ([dctBlock][cosBuffer]')
```

```
        // and store the results in imgBuffer
        //
        for (int col = 0; col < N; ++col)
        {
           for (int row = 0; row < N; ++row)
           {
              DCTTRIPLE result = {0.0, 0.0, 0.0};
              for (int index = 0; index < N; ++index)
              {
                 DCTTRIPLE coeff = dctBlock.Pixels(col, index);
                 double cosVal_transpose = cosBuffer.Pixels(row, index);

                 result.dctRed += coeff.dctRed * cosVal_transpose;
                 result.dctGreen += coeff.dctGreen * cosVal_transpose;
                 result.dctBlue += coeff.dctBlue * cosVal_transpose;
              }

              //
              // assign the computed value back to the image
              // (note the BGR ordering)
              //
              RGBTRIPLE new_pixel = {
                 CLIP(result.dctBlue + 0.5),
                 CLIP(result.dctGreen + 0.5),
                 CLIP(result.dctRed + 0.5)
                 };
              imgBuffer.Pixels(x + col, y + row, new_pixel);
           }
        }
     }
  }
}
```


The **imgBuffer** parameter specifies a reference to a **GBuffer** object that will be filled with the reconstructed pixels. The elements of **imgBuffer** must be of type **RGBTRIPLE**. These pixels are computed from the DCT coefficients, which are specified by the **dctBuffer** parameter (a reference to a **GBuffer** object that contains the DCT coefficients of a previously DCT-transformed image). The elements of **dctBuffer** must be of type **DCTTRIPLE**. The **cosBuffer** parameter specifies a reference to a **GBuffer** object that holds the DCT basis functions for the case in which the sub-image size is 8x8 pixels (i.e., $N = 8$). These basis functions can be computed as follows:

```
//
// compute the table of basis functions and
// store the result in the GBuffer cosBuffer
//
GBuffer<double> cosBuffer(N, N);
for (int m = 0; m < N; ++m)
{
   for (int n = 0; n < N; ++n)
   {
      double result;
      if (n == 0)
      {
         result =
            sqrt(1.0 / N) *
            cos(((2 * m + 1) * n * M_PI) / (2.0 * N));
      }
      else
      {
         result =
            sqrt(2.0 / N) *
            cos(((2 * m + 1) * n * M_PI) / (2.0 * N));
      }
      cosBuffer.Pixels(m, n, result);
   }
}
```

For more information on the **GBuffer** class, see the "In Depth" section and the source code that's included on the companion CD-ROM.

Filtering an Image in the Spatial Domain

To filter an image in the spatial domain, you compute the two-dimensional convolution between the image and one of the filter kernels depicted in Figure 17.16. If the filter kernel is separable, you need only compute two one-dimensional convolutions.

Blurring an Image

The following code snippet demonstrates how to blur an image (i.e., attenuate the image's high-frequency components) by computing the convolution between the image (**hDIBSection**; **imgBuffer**) and the low-pass Gaussian filter kernel (**kernel**):

```
#define CLIP(x) x > 255 ? 255 : x < 0 ? 0 : x

// define the filter kernel
const int kernel[][5] = {
   {0, 0, 1, 0, 0},
   {0, 1, 2, 1, 0},
   {1, 2, 4, 2, 1},
   {0, 1, 2, 1, 0},
   {0, 0, 1, 0, 0},
   };

// create a GBuffer object corresponding to the source image
GBuffer<RGBTRIPLE> imgBufferSrc;
DIBSectionToBuffer(imgBufferSrc, hDIBSection);

// extract the dimensions
const int width = imgBufferSrc.Width();
const int height = imgBufferSrc.Height();

// create a GBuffer object for the filtered image
GBuffer<RGBTRIPLE> imgBufferDst(width, height);

for (int y = 0; y < height; ++y)
{
   for (int x = 0; x < width; ++x)
   {
      //
      // keep a running sum for the convolution
      // (using the offset value of 128)
      //
      int sumR = 0, sumG = 0, sumB = 0;

      // for each tap in the filter
      for (int row = -2; row <= 2; ++row)
      {
         for (int col = -2; col <= 2; ++col)
         {
            // perform the convolution using symmetric extension
            RGBTRIPLE pixel = imgBufferSrc.PixelsSE(x + col, y + row);
            sumR += (pixel.rgbtRed * kernel[col + 2][row + 2]);
            sumG += (pixel.rgbtGreen * kernel[col + 2][row + 2]);
            sumB += (pixel.rgbtBlue * kernel[col + 2][row + 2]);
         }
      }
```

```
        // assign the filtered pixel to the destination
        RGBTRIPLE filtered_pixel = {
            static_cast<unsigned char>(CLIP(sumB / 20.0 + 0.5)),
            static_cast<unsigned char>(CLIP(sumG / 20.0 + 0.5)),
            static_cast<unsigned char>(CLIP(sumR / 20.0 + 0.5))
            };
        imgBufferDst.Pixels(x, y, filtered_pixel);
    }
}

// update hDIBSection's pixels
BufferToDIBSection(hDIBSection, imgBufferDst);
```

Sharpening an Image

The following code snippet demonstrates how to sharpen an image (i.e., boost an image's high-frequency components) by computing the convolution between the image (**hDIBSection**; **imgBuffer**) and the high-pass unsharp masking filter kernel (**kernel**):

```
#define CLIP(x) x > 255 ? 255 : x < 0 ? 0 : x

// define the filter kernel
const int kernel[][3] = {
    {-1, -1, -1},
    {-1, 17, -1},
    {-1, -1, -1},
    };

// create a GBuffer object corresponding to the source image
GBuffer<RGBTRIPLE> imgBufferSrc;
DIBSectionToBuffer(imgBufferSrc, hDIBSection);

// extract the dimensions
const int width = imgBufferSrc.Width();
const int height = imgBufferSrc.Height();

// create a GBuffer object for the filtered image
GBuffer<RGBTRIPLE> imgBufferDst(width, height);

for (int y = 0; y < height; ++y)
{
    for (int x = 0; x < width; ++x)
    {
```

```
        //
        // keep a running sum for the convolution
        // (using the offset value of 128)
        //
        int sumR = 0, sumG = 0, sumB = 0;

        // for each tap in the filter
        for (int row = -1; row <= 1; ++row)
        {
            for (int col = -1; col <= 1; ++col)
            {
                // perform the convolution using symmetric extension
                RGBTRIPLE pixel = imgBufferSrc.PixelsSE(x + col, y + row);
                sumR += (pixel.rgbtRed * kernel[col + 1][row + 1]);
                sumG += (pixel.rgbtGreen * kernel[col + 1][row + 1]);
                sumB += (pixel.rgbtBlue * kernel[col + 1][row + 1]);
            }
        }

        // assign the filtered pixel to the destination
        RGBTRIPLE filtered_pixel = {
            static_cast<unsigned char>(CLIP(sumB / 9.0 + 0.5)),
            static_cast<unsigned char>(CLIP(sumG / 9.0 + 0.5)),
            static_cast<unsigned char>(CLIP(sumR / 9.0 + 0.5))
            };
        imgBufferDst.Pixels(x, y, filtered_pixel);
    }
}

// update hDIBSection's pixels
BufferToDIBSection(hDIBSection, imgBufferDst);
```

Embossing an Image

The following code snippet demonstrates how to emboss an image by computing the convolution between the image (**hDIBSection**; **imgBuffer**) and the embossing filter kernel (**kernel**):

```
// define the filter kernel
const int kernel[][3] = {
    {-1, 0, 0},
    { 0, 0, 0},
    { 0, 0, 1}
    };
```

```
// create a GBuffer object corresponding to the source image
GBuffer<RGBTRIPLE> imgBufferSrc;
DIBSectionToBuffer(imgBufferSrc, hDIBSection);

// extract the dimensions
const int width = imgBufferSrc.Width();
const int height = imgBufferSrc.Height();

// create a GBuffer object for the filtered image
GBuffer<RGBTRIPLE> imgBufferDst(width, height);

for (int y = 0; y < height; ++y)
{
   for (int x = 0; x < width; ++x)
   {
      //
      // keep a running sum for the convolution
      // (using the offset value of 128)
      //
      int sumR = 128, sumG = 128, sumB = 128;

      // for each tap in the filter
      for (int row = -1; row <= 1; ++row)
      {
         for (int col = -1; col <= 1; ++col)
         {
            // perform the convolution using symmetric extension
            RGBTRIPLE pixel = imgBufferSrc.PixelsSE(x + col, y + row);
            sumR += (pixel.rgbtRed * kernel[col + 1][row + 1]);
            sumG += (pixel.rgbtGreen * kernel[col + 1][row + 1]);
            sumB += (pixel.rgbtBlue * kernel[col + 1][row + 1]);
         }
      }

      // assign the filtered pixel to the destination
      RGBTRIPLE filtered_pixel = {
         static_cast<unsigned char>(sumB),
         static_cast<unsigned char>(sumG),
         static_cast<unsigned char>(sumR)
         };
      imgBufferDst.Pixels(x, y, filtered_pixel);
   }
}

// update hDIBSection's pixels
BufferToDIBSection(hDIBSection, imgBufferDst);
```

Computing the Discrete Wavelet Transform of an Image

To compute the DWT of an image, you use the **GTransform::Decompose** member function:

```
void GTransform::Decompose(
    IN OUT GBufferList<Type>& BufferList,
    IN int num_levels
  );
```

The **BufferList** parameter specifies a **GBufferList** object that will be filled with the DWT subbands of the image. The first image in this list defines the source image (i.e., the image that you want to compute the DWT of). The **num_levels** parameter specifies the number of decomposition levels that will be performed. The number of decomposition levels is limited only by the size of the source image. If successful, the **Decompose** member function fills the specified **GBufferList** object as follows:

```
-----------------------------------------------------------------
 LL0 | L1 | H1 | HH1 | HL1 | LH1 | LL1 | L2 | H2 | HH2 | ... | LHN
-----------------------------------------------------------------
```

LL0 denotes the source image, and **N** is the number of decomposition levels (**num_levels**). If the **Decompose** member function fails, an exception is thrown.

NOTE: *For color images, you should separate the image into its individual color planes before you use the **Decompose** member function.*

Bear in mind that the **GTransform** class is an abstract base class. To use the **Decompose** member function, you must create an instance of the **GWavelet** or **G97** class. Each of these classes is a descendant of the **GTransform** class (and thus, they inherit the **Decompose** member function). The following code snippet demonstrates how to compute the DWT by using the **Decompose** member function of the **G97** class:

```
#include "g97.h"

// create a GBuffer object for the image
GBuffer<RGBTRIPLE> imgBuffer;
DIBSectionToBuffer(imgBuffer, hDIBSection);

const int width = imgBuffer.Width();
const int height = imgBuffer.Height();
```

```
// create a separate buffer for each color plane
GBuffer<int> redBuffer(width, height);
GBuffer<int> greenBuffer(width, height);
GBuffer<int> blueBuffer(width, height);

// extract the image's color planes into the separate buffers
for (int y = 0; y < height; ++y)
{
   for (int x = 0; x < width; ++x)
   {
      RGBTRIPLE pixel = imgBuffer.Pixels(x, y);
      redBuffer.Pixels(x, y, pixel.rgbtRed);
      greenBuffer.Pixels(x, y, pixel.rgbtGreen);
      blueBuffer.Pixels(x, y, pixel.rgbtBlue);
   }
}

// create three GBufferList objects (one for each color plane)
GBufferList<int> redBufferList, greenBufferList, blueBufferList;
redBufferList.Add(redBuffer);
greenBufferList.Add(greenBuffer);
blueBufferList.Add(blueBuffer);

// create a G97 object
G97<int> wave97;

// perform the decomposition
const int num_levels = 2;
wave97.Decompose(redBufferList, num_levels);
wave97.Decompose(greenBufferList, num_levels);
wave97.Decompose(blueBufferList, num_levels);

//
// work with the subbands...
//

// source image's red, green, and blue color planes
GBuffer<int>& redLL0 = redBufferList.Items(0);
GBuffer<int>& greenLL0 = greenBufferList.Items(0);
GBuffer<int>& blueLL0 = blueBufferList.Items(0);

// first level of decomposition of the red color plane
GBuffer<int>& redHH1 = redBufferList.Items(3);
GBuffer<int>& redHL1 = redBufferList.Items(4);
GBuffer<int>& redLH1 = redBufferList.Items(5);
GBuffer<int>& redLL1 = redBufferList.Items(6);
```

```
// first level of decomposition of the green color plane
GBuffer<int>& greenHH1 = greenBufferList.Items(3);
GBuffer<int>& greenHL1 = greenBufferList.Items(4);
GBuffer<int>& greenLH1 = greenBufferList.Items(5);
GBuffer<int>& greenLL1 = greenBufferList.Items(6);

// first level of decomposition of the blue color plane
GBuffer<int>& blueHH1 = blueBufferList.Items(3);
GBuffer<int>& blueHL1 = blueBufferList.Items(4);
GBuffer<int>& blueLH1 = blueBufferList.Items(5);
GBuffer<int>& blueLL1 = blueBufferList.Items(6);

// second level of decomposition of the red color plane
GBuffer<int>& redHH2 = redBufferList.Items(9);
GBuffer<int>& redHL2 = redBufferList.Items(10);
GBuffer<int>& redLH2 = redBufferList.Items(11);
GBuffer<int>& redLL2 = redBufferList.Items(12);

// second level of decomposition of the green color plane
GBuffer<int>& greenHH2 = greenBufferList.Items(9);
GBuffer<int>& greenHL2 = greenBufferList.Items(10);
GBuffer<int>& greenLH2 = greenBufferList.Items(11);
GBuffer<int>& greenLL2 = greenBufferList.Items(12);

// second level of decomposition of the blue color plane
GBuffer<int>& blueHH2 = blueBufferList.Items(9);
GBuffer<int>& blueHL2 = blueBufferList.Items(10);
GBuffer<int>& blueLH2 = blueBufferList.Items(11);
GBuffer<int>& blueLL2 = blueBufferList.Items(12);

//
// later, reconstruct the image (see the next solution)...
//
```

For more information on the **GBuffer** and **GBufferList** classes, see the "In Depth" section and the source code that's included on the companion CD-ROM. For more information on the **DIBSectionToBitmap** function, see the solution "Initializing a **GBuffer** Object with the Pixels of a DIB Section Bitmap." For more information on the **BufferToDIBSection** function, see the solution "Initializing a DIB Section Bitmap with the Pixels of a **GBuffer** Object."

Computing the Inverse Discrete Wavelet Transform

To compute the inverse DWT from the subbands of a previously transformed image, you use the **GTransform::Reconstruct** member function:

```
void GTransform::Reconstruct(
    IN OUT GBufferList<Type>& BufferList
   );
```

The **BufferList** parameter specifies a **GBufferList** object that contains the DWT subbands. These subbands must be arranged as follows:

```
-----------------------------------------------------------------
 LL0 | L1 | H1 | HH1 | HL1 | LH1 | LL1 | L2 | H2 | HH2 | ... | LHN
-----------------------------------------------------------------
```

LL0 denotes the source image, and **N** is the number of decomposition levels (**num_levels**). If the **Reconstruct** member function is successful, it will use the subbands in the specified **GBufferList** object to reconstruct the image. This reconstructed image is then placed in the first position of the list (**LL0**; **BufferList.Items(0)**). The number of decomposition levels is inferred from the size of the list. If the **Reconstruct** member function fails, an exception is thrown.

Note that the **GTransform** class is an abstract base class. To use the **Reconstruct** member function, you must create an instance of the **GWavelet** or **G97** class. Both of these classes descend from the **GTransform** class, and they inherit the **Reconstruct** member function. The following code snippet demonstrates how to compute the inverse DWT by using the **Reconstruct** member function of the **GSplusP** class:

```
#include "g97.h"

// create a GBuffer object for the image
GBuffer<RGBTRIPLE> imgBuffer;
DIBSectionToBuffer(imgBuffer, hDIBSection);

const int width = imgBuffer.Width();
const int height = imgBuffer.Height();

// create separate buffer for each color plane
GBuffer<float> redBuffer(width, height);
GBuffer<float> greenBuffer(width, height);
GBuffer<float> blueBuffer(width, height);
```

```
// extract the color planes into separate buffers
for (int y = 0; y < height; ++y)
{
   for (int x = 0; x < width; ++x)
   {
      RGBTRIPLE pixel = imgBuffer.Pixels(x, y);
      redBuffer.Pixels(x, y, pixel.rgbtRed);
      greenBuffer.Pixels(x, y, pixel.rgbtGreen);
      blueBuffer.Pixels(x, y, pixel.rgbtBlue);
   }
}

// create three GBufferList objects
GBufferList<float> redBufferList, greenBufferList, blueBufferList;
redBufferList.Add(redBuffer);
greenBufferList.Add(greenBuffer);
blueBufferList.Add(blueBuffer);

// create a G97 object
G97<float> wave97;

// perform the decomposition
const int num_levels = 2;
wave97.Decompose(redBufferList, num_levels);
wave97.Decompose(greenBufferList, num_levels);
wave97.Decompose(blueBufferList, num_levels);

//
// work with the subbands...
//

// discard the high-frequency information from the red color plane
redBufferList.Items(3).ZeroData();  // HH1
redBufferList.Items(4).ZeroData();  // HL1
redBufferList.Items(5).ZeroData();  // LH1
redBufferList.Items(9).ZeroData();  // HH2
redBufferList.Items(10).ZeroData(); // HL2
redBufferList.Items(11).ZeroData(); // LH2

// discard the high-frequency information from the green color plane
greenBufferList.Items(3).ZeroData();  // HH1
greenBufferList.Items(4).ZeroData();  // HL1
greenBufferList.Items(5).ZeroData();  // LH1
greenBufferList.Items(9).ZeroData();  // HH2
greenBufferList.Items(10).ZeroData(); // HL2
greenBufferList.Items(11).ZeroData(); // LH2
```

```
// discard the high-frequency information from the blue color plane
blueBufferList.Items(3).ZeroData();  // HH1
blueBufferList.Items(4).ZeroData();  // HL1
blueBufferList.Items(5).ZeroData();  // LH1
blueBufferList.Items(9).ZeroData();  // HH2
blueBufferList.Items(10).ZeroData(); // HL2
blueBufferList.Items(11).ZeroData(); // LH2

// perform the reconstruction
wave97.Reconstruct(redBufferList);
wave97.Reconstruct(greenBufferList);
wave97.Reconstruct(blueBufferList);

for (int y = 0; y < height; ++y)
{
   for (int x = 0; x < width; ++x)
   {
      // extract the reconstructed color planes
      unsigned char red = CLIP(
         redBufferList.Items(0).Pixels(x, y)
         );
      unsigned char green = CLIP(
         greenBufferList.Items(0).Pixels(x, y)
         );
      unsigned char blue = CLIP(
         blueBufferList.Items(0).Pixels(x, y)
         );

      // copy the color back to the original buffer
      RGBTRIPLE pixel = {blue, green, red};
      imgBuffer.Pixels(x, y, pixel);
   }
}

// copy the GBuffer back to the DIB section bitmap
BufferToDIBSection(hDIBSection, imgBuffer);
```

For more information on the **GBuffer** and **GBufferList** classes, see the "In Depth" section and the source code that's included on the companion CD-ROM. For more information on the **DIBSectionToBitmap** function, see the solution "Initializing a **GBuffer** Object with the Pixels of a DIB Section Bitmap." For more information on the **BufferToDIBSection** function, see the solution "Initializing a DIB Section Bitmap with the Pixels of a **GBuffer** Object."

Warping an Image

To warp an image, you use the **GWarp::Warp** member function:

```
void GWarp::Warp(
    OUT GBuffer<Type>& BufferDst,
    IN const GBuffer<Type>& BufferSrc
   );
```

The **BufferDst** parameter specifies a **GBuffer** object that will be filled with the pixels of the warped image. The **BufferSrc** parameter specifies a **GBuffer** object that defines the image that you want to warp. If the **Warp** member function fails, an exception is thrown.

Before you can use the **Warp** member function, you need to define how the deformation will be performed. You do this by using the **GWarp::AddLineSrc** and **AddLineDst** member functions to specify matching vector pairs. The following code snippet demonstrates this process (**width** and **height** denote the dimensions of **hDIBSection**):

```
// create the source and destination buffers
GBuffer<RGBTRIPLE> imgBufferSrc(width, height);
GBuffer<RGBTRIPLE> imgBufferDest(width, height);

// initialize the source buffer
DIBSectionToBuffer(imgBufferSrc, hDIBSection);

// create a GWarp object
GWarp<RGBTRIPLE> warp;

// specify the "source" vectors
warp.AddLineSrc(width / 2, 0, width / 2, height);
warp.AddLineSrc(0, 0, width, 0);
warp.AddLineSrc(width, 0, width, height);
warp.AddLineSrc(width, height, 0, height);
warp.AddLineSrc(0, height, 0, 0);

// specify the "destination" vectors
warp.AddLineDst(width / 2, 0, width / 2, height - 100);
warp.AddLineDst(0, 0, width, 0);
warp.AddLineDst(width, 0, width, height);
warp.AddLineDst(width, height, 0, height);
warp.AddLineDst(0, height, 0, 0);
```

```
// warp the image
warp.Warp(imgBufferDest, imgBufferSrc);

// update the DIB section with the imgBufferDest's pixels
BufferToDIBSection(hDIBSection, imgBufferDest);
```

For more information on the **GBuffer** and **GWarp** classes, see the "In Depth" section and the source code that's included on the companion CD-ROM. For more information on the **DIBSectionToBitmap** function, see the solution "Initializing a **GBuffer** Object with the Pixels of a DIB Section Bitmap." For more information on the **BufferToDIBSection** function, see the solution "Initializing a DIB Section Bitmap with the Pixels of a **GBuffer** Object."

Morphing Two Images

To morph two images, you use the **GMorph::Morph** member function:

```
void GMorph::Morph(
    IN OUT GBufferList<Type>& BufferList,
    IN const GWarp<Type>& Warp,
    IN int num_frames
  );
```

The **BufferList** parameter specifies the **GBufferList** object whose first two elements (**GBuffer** objects) define the two images that you want to morph. The **Warp** parameter specifies a **GWarp** object that defines how the geometries of these images should be transformed. The **num_frames** parameter specifies the number of intermediate frames that should be generated. If the **Morph** member function is successful, the morph sequence will be contained in the **GBufferList** object that's specified as the **BufferList** parameter. The images in this list are ordered to match the sequence. (Specifically, the original "second" image will be moved to the end of the list.) If the **Morph** function fails, an exception is thrown.

To use the **Morph** member function, you perform the following steps:

1. Create a **GBuffer** object, and initialize it with information from your first image.
2. Create a **GBuffer** object, and initialize it with information from your second image.
3. Create a **GBufferList** object, and add the **GBuffers** from Steps 1 and 2 to the list.

4. Create a **GWarp** object, and use the **GWarp::AddLineSrc** and **AddLineDst** member functions to define the matching pairs of feature vectors.
5. Create a **GMorph** object, and call the **GMorph::Morph** member function, passing the **GBufferList** object from Step 3 as the **BufferList** parameter, passing the **GWarp** object from Step 4 as the **Warp** parameter, and specifying the number of intermediate frames as the **num_frames** parameter.

After Step 5, the **GBufferList** object from Step 3 will contain the morph sequence as you'd normally display it. That is, the first position of the list is still occupied by the **GBuffer** object from Step 1, but the **GBuffer** object from Step 2 will be moved to the end of the list. The intermediate images will be located between the first and last images in the list. The following code snippet demonstrates how to use the **Morph** member function:

```
GBufferList<RGBTRIPLE> BufferList;
GBuffer<RGBTRIPLE>& Buffer1 = BufferList.Add(width, height);
GBuffer<RGBTRIPLE>& Buffer2 = BufferList.Add(width, height);

DIBSectionToBuffer(Buffer1, hDIBSection1);  // first image
DIBSectionToBuffer(Buffer2, hDIBSection2);  // second image

// set the background colors
RGBTRIPLE white_pixel = {255, 255, 255};
Buffer1.SetBlankPixel(white_pixel);
Buffer2.SetBlankPixel(white_pixel);

// create a GWarp object
GWarp<RGBTRIPLE> Warp;

// specify the source vectors
Warp.AddLineSrc(17, 14, 249, 14);
Warp.AddLineSrc(249, 14, 249, 235);
Warp.AddLineSrc(249, 235, 17, 235);
Warp.AddLineSrc(17, 235, 17, 14);

// specify the destination vectors
Warp.AddLineDst(70, 70, 190, 70);
Warp.AddLineDst(190, 70, 190, 190);
Warp.AddLineDst(190, 190, 70, 190);
Warp.AddLineDst(70, 190, 70, 70);

// create a GMorph object
GMorph<RGBTRIPLE> Morph;
```

```
// perform the morph (with 3 intermediate frames)
Morph.Morph(BufferList, Warp, 3);

// display the results...
for (int index = 0; index < BufferList.Count(); ++index)
{
   BufferToDIBSection(hDIBSection, BufferList.Items(index));
   //
   // display hDIBSection...
   // delay...
   //
}
```

For more information on the **GBuffer**, **GBufferList**, **GWarp**, and **GMorph** classes, see the "In Depth" section and the source code that's included on the companion CD-ROM. For more information on the **DIBSectionToBitmap** function, see the solution "Initializing a **GBuffer** Object with the Pixels of a DIB Section Bitmap." For more information on the **BufferToDIBSection** function, see the solution "Initializing a DIB Section Bitmap with the Pixels of a **GBuffer** Object."

Initializing a GBuffer Object with the Pixels of a DIB Section Bitmap

To initialize a **GBuffer** object with the pixels of a 24-bpp DIB section bitmap, you use the **DIBSectionToBuffer** function:

```
void DIBSectionToBuffer(
    OUT GBuffer<RGBTRIPLE>& Buffer,
    IN HBITMAP hDIBSection
   )
{
   BITMAP bmp = {0};
   GetObject(hDIBSection, sizeof(BITMAP), &bmp);
   assert(bmp.bmBitsPixel == 24);
   assert(bmp.bmBits != NULL);

   Buffer.Width(bmp.bmWidth);
   Buffer.Height(bmp.bmHeight);

   const unsigned int aligned_bytes_per_scanline =
      (((bmp.bmWidth * bmp.bmBitsPixel) + 31) & ~31) >> 3;
```

```
    unsigned char* pBits = static_cast<unsigned char*>(bmp.bmBits);
    for (int y = 0; y < bmp.bmHeight; ++y)
    {
       // assume a bottom-up DIB section bitmap
       RGBTRIPLE* pScanLine = reinterpret_cast<RGBTRIPLE*>(
          pBits + ((bmp.bmHeight - y - 1) * aligned_bytes_per_scanline)
          );
       for (int x = 0; x < bmp.bmWidth; ++x)
       {
          Buffer.Pixels(x, y, pScanLine[x]);
       }
    }
}
```

The **Buffer** parameter specifies the **GBuffer** object that you want to initialize with information from a 24-bpp DIB section bitmap. The handle to this DIB section is specified by the **hDIBSection** parameter. If the **DIBSectionToBuffer** function fails, an exception is thrown.

The **DIBSectionToBuffer** function demonstrates how to initialize a **GBuffer** object with the dimensions and pixels of a bottom-up 24-bpp DIB section bitmap. You can easily extend this function to work with DIB sections (or DIBs) of other bit depths. For more information on DIB section bitmaps, see Chapter 7. For more information on the **GBuffer** object and class, see the "In Depth" section and the source code that's included on the companion CD-ROM.

Initializing a DIB Section Bitmap with the Pixels of a GBuffer Object

To initialize the pixels of a 24-bpp DIB section bitmap with those of a **GBuffer** object, you use the **BufferToDIBSection** function:

```
void BufferToDIBSection(
     OUT HBITMAP hDIBSection,
     IN const GBuffer<RGBTRIPLE>& Buffer
   )
{
   BITMAP bmp = {0};
   GetObject(hDIBSection, sizeof(BITMAP), &bmp);
   assert(bmp.bmBitsPixel == 24);
   assert(bmp.bmBits != NULL);
```

```
    const unsigned int aligned_bytes_per_scanline =
        (((bmp.bmWidth * bmp.bmBitsPixel) + 31) & ~31) >> 3;

    unsigned char* pBits = static_cast<unsigned char*>(bmp.bmBits);
    for (int y = 0; y < bmp.bmHeight; ++y)
    {
        // assume a bottom-up DIB section bitmap
        RGBTRIPLE* pScanLine = reinterpret_cast<RGBTRIPLE*>(
            pBits + ((bmp.bmHeight - y - 1) * aligned_bytes_per_scanline)
            );
        for (int x = 0; x < bmp.bmWidth; ++x)
        {
            pScanLine[x] = Buffer.Pixels(x, y);
        }
    }
}
```

The **hDIBSection** parameter specifies a handle to the DIB section bitmap whose pixels you want to initialize with information from a **GBuffer** object. This **GBuffer** object is specified by the **Buffer** parameter. If the **BufferToDIBSection** function fails, an exception is thrown.

The **BufferToDIBSection** function demonstrates how to initialize the pixels of a bottom-up 24-bpp DIB section bitmap with those of an **RGBTRIPLE**-type **GBuffer** object. You can easily extend this function to work with DIB sections (or DIBs) of other bit depths. For more information on DIB section bitmaps, see Chapter 7. For more information on the **GBuffer** object and class, see the "In Depth" section and the source code that's included on the companion CD-ROM.

Chapter 18

Image File Formats

In Depth

Throughout this text, we've worked strictly with bitmaps—device-dependent bitmaps, device-independent bitmaps, and DIB section bitmaps. Indeed, the Windows API provides native support for most anything you'd want to do with a bitmap. In fact, bitmaps play such a key role in Windows-based applications for one simple reason: the only efficient way to display a pixel-based image in Windows is to use a bitmap. In a sense, this is good because the format of a bitmap isn't too complicated. From an end user's perspective, however, bitmaps are pretty much useless. How many Web pages have you seen that contain bitmaps? Probably very few—bitmaps are huge compared to other image formats. Even with the prevalence of broadband modems, no one in their right mind would transfer an image as a bitmap unless it's absolutely necessary. Instead, most people use JPEGs, GIFs, or PNGs.

For developers, the popularity of JPEGs, GIFs, and PNGs (along with the bad reputation of bitmaps) puts us in somewhat of a tough situation. The Windows API provides innate support only for bitmaps, so if we want to support other formats (as most developers do), we have to first convert these other image types into the bitmap format. Moreover, once we have a bitmap, in order to produce images of other formats, we have to perform yet another conversion. Aside from providing the **IPicture** interface, which affords only minimal support for reading JPEGs and GIFs, the Windows API leaves us high and dry. And, although it's not impossible to perform these format conversions manually, it's quite an undertaking, to say the least.

In this chapter we'll examine two image file formats: JPEG and PNG. I choose these specific formats for several reasons. JPEG was an obvious choice because JPEG images are so ubiquitous. The JPEG format is popular because JPG files can be extremely small. This results from the fact that JPEG compression is a non-invertible or *lossy* process—that is, the decompressed image is not identical to the original. Indeed, for many types of images, lossy compression is the best choice. But there are a fair number of situations in which you need an exact reconstruction. If an image is to be analyzed for its frequency content, for example, you'll likely get erroneous results if the image has been compressed in a lossy fashion. It's situations like this in which an invertible or *lossless* compression scheme comes in handy.

GIF and PNG are the two most popular formats that use lossless compression. In fact, both of these formats use a compression algorithm that's derived from the earlier work of Abraham Lempel and Jacob Ziv. GIFs are compressed by using an algorithm called LZW (Lempel-Ziv-Welch) that's currently patented by Unisys Corporation. For this reason, many developers, and thus applications, don't support the GIF format. The PNG format, on the other hand, was specifically designed to avoid patent issues; PNGs are compressed by using an algorithm called *deflate*—a variation of the LZ77 (Lempel-Ziv-1977) algorithm. (The LZ77 algorithm also underpins many popular compression programs, including gzip, ARJ, and PKZIP.) Plus the PNG format is trendy—support it, and you'll future-proof your application.

JPEG Images

The term JPEG—pronounced "jay peg"—stands for Joint Photographic Experts Group. JPEG represents a compression method that's used to compress natural (namely, photographic) images. JPEG itself is not a file format—there's a dedicated format for that called JFIF (JPEG File Interchange Format). The JFIF file format was created as a means of storing JPEG-compressed images. Released to the public by C-Cube Microsystems, the JFIF format is best known by the file extension JPG. I won't get into the specifics of the JFIF format because it's rather complicated and somewhat open-ended. There are, however, some references in Appendix B if you're interested. Fortunately, if you use Intel's JPEG library, you don't need to know much about the JFIF format. The key thing to note is that a JFIF file is made up of segments called *markers*, a compressed data stream (i.e., the pixels are stored in a top-down fashion), and quantization and entropy tables. These data are meant to support the JPEG compression method.

JPEG Compression

The Joint Photographic Experts Group was formed in 1986 to devise a technique for encoding and decoding digital photographic images. The JPEG compression format was standardized by ISO (International Standards Organization) in 1990, and since then (due partly to the spread of increased computing power) it has become the de facto method for compressing natural images. JPEG compression is based on the notion that photographic images usually represent a natural scene that's meant to be viewed by humans. Because the human visual system (HVS) has limitations of its own, the reconstructed (i.e., decompressed) image doesn't have to be identical to the original image—that is, there's extra information in the image that we can't see anyway. Moreover, as we discussed in Chapter 17, our visual system isn't as sensitive to errors in the high-frequency (spatial-frequency) areas of an image. For these reasons, JPEG compression was designed to be a lossy process. This is how JPEG can achieve such great compression ratios—it discards information that corresponds to the parts of an image that our visual system is less sensitive to. Figure 18.1 outlines the steps involved in compressing (encoding) and decompressing (decoding) a JPEG image.

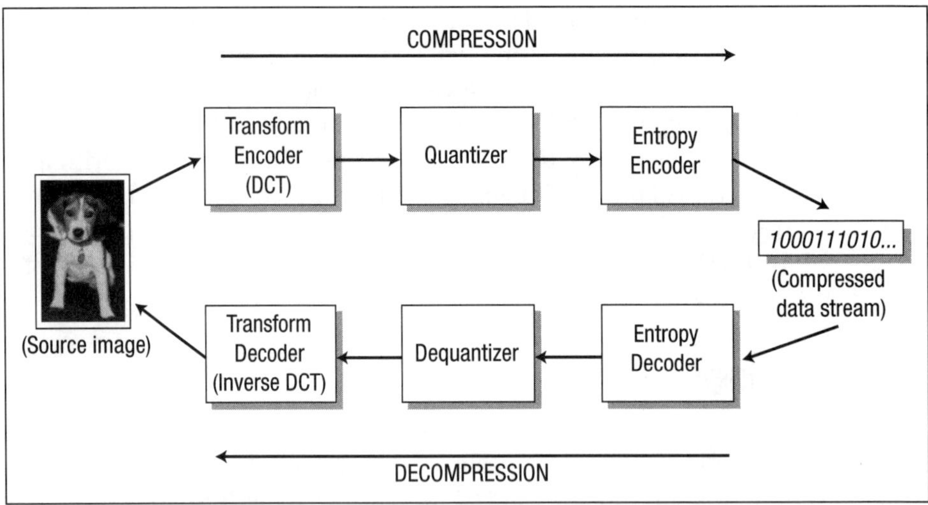

Figure 18.1 The JPEG compression process consists of three steps; decompression is accomplished by reversing these steps.

Transform Coding

Recall from Chapter 17 that the discrete cosine transform (DCT) is used to represent an image in terms of its (spatial) frequency components. The DCT is but one approach in a general scheme called *transform coding* that's designed to reduce the spatial redundancy between neighboring pixels. This type of coding is ideal for photographic images because most natural scenes follow the principal of *self-similarity*, which states that neighboring points in space will likely have similar intensity values. Note that the DCT isn't the best transform method available; the discrete wavelet transform (DWT) has been proved superior and will be used in the forthcoming JPEG-2000 standard.

For color images, there's also the issue of *spectral redundancy*, in which different color planes represent the same information. Because the RGB color space is notorious for its high degree of spectral redundancy, before the pixels are sent to the DCT engine, they're (most often) transformed into the YCrCb color space. The YCrCb color space is another three-dimensional color space that represents the luminance information—which is stored in the Y plane—separately from the color (chrominance) information—which is stored in the Cr and Cb planes. Because our visual system is most sensitive to luminance (i.e., perceived brightness; the Y plane), the chrominance planes (Cr and Cb) are often downsampled by a factor of two or four. This scheme is referred to as 4:2:2 or 4:1:1 chrominance subsampling, respectively.

So, the first step in JPEG compression is to reduce both the spectral and the spatial redundancy. This is the job of a module called the *source encoder*, which

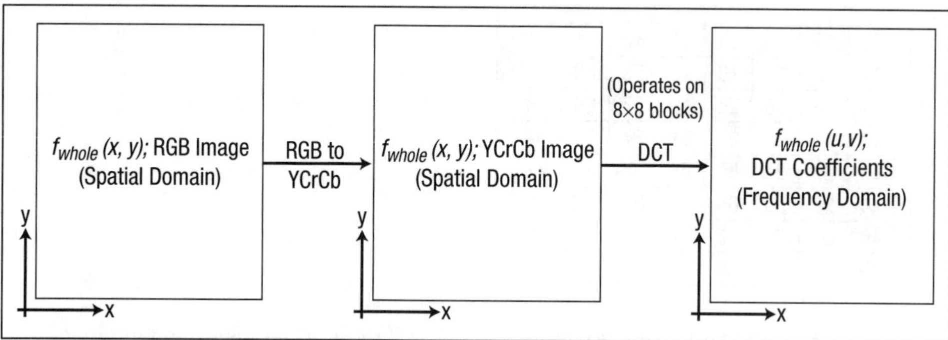

Figure 18.2 The source encoder is designed to reduce spectral and spatial redundancy.

performs the RGB-to-YCrCb conversion, if necessary, and then uses the DCT to transform the pixels into DCT coefficients. (Recall from Chapter 17 that the DCT operates on 8x8 blocks of pixels.) This scheme is outlined in Figure 18.2.

Quantization

After the source encoder comes the quantizer. Quantizing is the primary step in which information is discarded (aside from the optional chrominance subsampling), so quantization is really what makes JPEG a lossy compression method. Recall from Chapter 17 that each coefficient within an 8x8 DCT-coefficient block corresponds to one of the 64 DCT basis images. Because we have this spatial frequency layout, we can use properties of the human visual system to perform a so-called visually optimal quantization. That is, because our visual system is less sensitive to high-frequency errors, we can use fewer bits to represent the coefficients that correspond to the higher spatial frequencies. In a sense, the quantizer is designed to reduce psychovisual redundancy.

The quantization stage is where the notion of the JPEG "quality setting" comes into play. The lower the quality setting, the more quantization is performed on the high-frequency components, and thus the less accurate the reconstructed image will look. (See Chapter 17 for some representative images.) The quality setting actually determines the entries of a *quantization table* (or quantization matrix), whose 64 values denote how many bits to use for each DCT coefficient within each 8x8 block. Although the JPEG standard doesn't require the use of a specific quantization table, again, most quantization tables are designed to be visually optimal. Figure 18.3 depicts the quantization table that's suggested in the JPEG standard. Note the use of higher values (suggesting greater quantization—i.e., fewer bits) for the entries that correspond to the higher spatial frequencies.

Just how do these numbers translate to quantization values? Well, each entry in the quantization table actually denotes what's called a *quantization step size*. Within an 8x8 block of DCT coefficients, each coefficient is divided by its

16	11	10	16	24	40	51	61
12	12	14	19	26	58	60	55
14	13	16	24	40	57	69	56
14	17	22	29	51	87	80	62
18	22	37	56	68	109	103	77
24	35	55	64	81	104	113	92
49	64	78	87	103	121	120	101
72	92	95	98	112	100	103	99

Figure 18.3 The suggested quantization matrix for the DCT-transformed luminance (Y) values.

corresponding quantization step size (table entry) and then rounded to the nearest integer. For example, suppose that within an 8x8 block of DCT coefficients, the top-left DCT coefficient (called the D.C. coefficient) holds a value of 125.9. This value is to be quantized by using the quantization step size that's located in the top-left entry of the quantization table. In Figure 18.3, this value is 16, so we'd get the following:

$$F(0,0) = 125.9$$

$$Q(0,0) = 16$$

$$F_{quantized}(0,0) = round\left(\frac{F(0,0)}{Q(0,0)}\right) = round\left(\frac{125.9}{16}\right) = 8$$

Later, during the decoding process, the original DCT coefficients are "dequantized" (estimated) by multiplying the quantized coefficients by the corresponding quantization step size, like so:

$$F_{reconstructed}(0,0) = F_{quantized}(0,0) \bullet Q(0,0) = 8 \bullet 16 = 128$$

Clearly, 128 is not equal to 125.9, so when the decoder performs an inverse DCT, there's a good chance that the reconstructed pixel value won't be exact. Remember, though, the idea is that the HVS can tolerate such small errors, and thus the overall aesthetic quality of the image is preserved.

Entropy Coding

After the DCT coefficients are quantized, they are ordered in a zigzag fashion and then sent to the entropy encoder. The idea behind entropy encoding is to further compress the data stream (i.e., the quantized coefficients) by capitalizing on the statistics of the data.

Consider the word "abracadabra." What's the most efficient way to represent this word as a series of bits? Well, the word contains only five unique letters, so we could represent each letter by using 3 bits. In this case, because there are 11 letters total, we need a total of 33 bits to represent the entire word. Notice, however, that the letter "a" is very prevalent in "abracadabra," whereas the letters "c" and "d" are used only once. Instead of using 3 bits for each letter, we can represent each letter by using a unique variable-length code word. This way, we can use shorter code words for the letters that occur frequently and longer code words for those that don't. For example, if we compute the probability of each letter in "abracadabra," we get the following:

```
"a" occurs 5 times  →  prob(a) = 5/11
"b" occurs 2 times  →  prob(b) = 2/11
"r" occurs 2 times  →  prob(r) = 2/11
"c" occurs 1 time   →  prob(c) = 1/11
"d" occurs 1 time   →  prob(d) = 1/11
```

Now we need to choose a code word for each letter. Because about half of "abracadabra" is the letter "a," let's choose the shortest possible code word for this letter. Well, that's exactly 1 bit, so let's choose the code word 1. The letters "b" and "r" are the next most prevalent letters, so let's choose a short code word for these as well. We can't use only 1 bit because we have to be able to distinguish "b" and "r" from "a." Therefore, let's use 2 bits for "b" and 3 bits for "r"; specifically, let's use the code words 00 and 011 for "b" and "r," respectively. Remember, we have to be able to distinguish these code words from each other, so when the decoder sees the bit stream 011, it'll know that 011 isn't "a" because the first bit is 0, and it'll know that 011 isn't "b" because the second bit is 1. Following this notion, let's use the 4-bit code words 0100 and 0101 for the letters "c" and "d," respectively. So here's what we have so far:

```
"a"  →  code word = 1
"b"  →  code word = 00
"r"  →  code word = 011
"c"  →  code word = 0100
"d"  →  code word = 0101
```

Using this code-word alphabet, we'll need 5x1 bits to represent all occurrences of the letter "a," 2x2 bits to represent all occurrences of the letter "b," 2x3 bits to represent all occurrences of the letter "r," and 1x4 bits each for the letters "c" and "d." In this case, we'll need only a total of 23 (5+4+6+4+4) bits to represent the word "abracadabra." In short, we've saved a total of 10 bits. This is the basic idea behind entropy encoding.

Sophisticated entropy encoders use a more complicated algorithm, but the underlying concept is, nonetheless, the same; the idea is to compress the data stream by taking advantage of the statistics of the data itself. Huffman coding and arithmetic coding are the two most popular entropy coding methods. Either of these methods can be used in JPEG compression.

Setting Up the Intel JPEG Library

The Intel JPEG Library (IJL) is a free, high-performance C-based package that significantly eases the process of reading and writing JPEG files. The code is highly optimized and easy to use, and it comes with extensive documentation and a demo application. Perhaps the strongest aspect of the IJL, at least from a development standpoint, is that it's designed for Windows developers. If you're used to programming for Windows, you'll find the IJL entirely straightforward.

***NOTE:** An Intel-based processor is* not *required to use the Intel JPEG library. IJL is also extremely fast on systems with non-Intel-based processors.*

You can download the latest version (1.5) of the IJL from Intel's Web site (the IJL page is currently at **http://developer.intel.com/software/products/perflib/ijl/**). After you download the library, the next step is to install it. And it turns out that the folks at Intel made this process easy—the IJL comes with its own foolproof setup program, whose first screen is depicted in Figure 18.4.

After the library is installed, your installation folder will contain the following subfolders: bin, doc, examples, include, and lib. The bin folder contains the main DLL file: ijl15.dll. The doc folder contains all of the library's documentation in PDF format. The examples folder contains the source code for the JPEGView demo application (using MFC-based code). The include folder contains the single

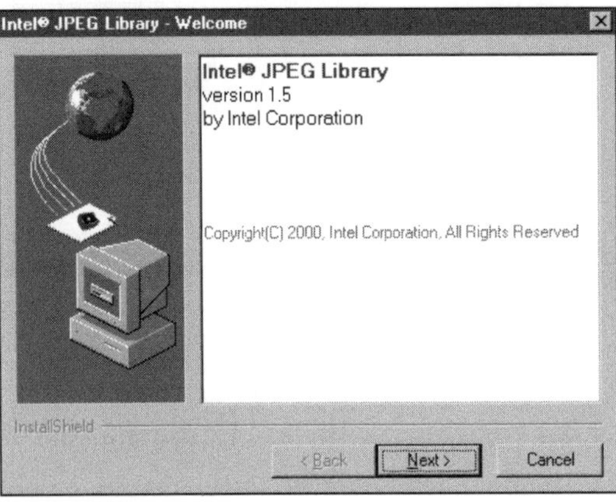

Figure 18.4 Installing the Intel JPEG Library.

header file: ijl.h. And the lib folder contains the single import library file: ijl15.lib. To use the IJL, all you need to do is **#include** the ijl.h header file in your code, statically link with ijl15.lib, and copy the ijl15.dll file to any folder that's in your system's path.

Reading JPEG Images

The first step to reading a JPEG image from a file is to allocate and initialize a **JPEG_CORE_PROPERTIES** structure. This is, in fact, the only IJL structure that you'll have to work with. Here's what it looks like:

```
typedef struct _JPEG_CORE_PROPERTIES {
    int UseJPEGPROPERTIES;

    // DIB-image-parameters-specific data members
    unsigned char* DIBBytes;
    int DIBWidth;
    int DIBHeight;
    int DIBPadBytes;
    int DIBChannels;
    IJL_COLOR DIBColor;
    IJL_DIBSUBSAMPLING DIBSubsampling;

    // JPEG-image-parameters-specific data members
    const char* JPGFile;
    unsigned char* JPGBytes;
    int JPGSizeBytes;
    int JPGWidth;
    int JPGHeight;
    int JPGChannels;
    IJL_COLOR JPGColor;
    IJL_JPGSUBSAMPLING JPGSubsampling;
    int JPGThumbWidth;
    int JPGThumbHeight;

    // JPEG-compression-related data members
    int cconversion_reqd;
    int upsampling_reqd;
    int jquality;
    JPEG_PROPERTIES jprops;
} JPEG_CORE_PROPERTIES;
```

We'll discuss most of these data members as they're used. For now, you can simply create an instance of the **JPEG_CORE_PROPERTIES** structure on the stack, and then use the **iljInit** function to initialize it, like so:

```
// declare and initialize a JPEG_CORE_PROPERTIES structure
JPEG_CORE_PROPERTIES jcProps;
IJLERR result = ijlInit(&jcProps);
if (result != IJL_OK)
{
   MessageBox(
      hWnd, ijlErrorStr(result), TEXT("Error initializing!"),
      MB_OK | MB_ICONERROR
      );
   assert(false);
}
try
{
   // all other reading code that follows...
}
```

The **ijlInit** function takes only one parameter: the address of a **JPEG_CORE_PROPERTIES** structure. If the **ijlInit** function is successful, it returns an enumerated value of type **IJLERR**. The **IJL_OK**, **IJL_INTERRUPT_OK**, and **IJL_ROI_OK** enumerators, which are all positive values, indicate success. All other **IJLERR**-type enumerators are negative, indicating an error condition. (The **ijlInit** function will return **IJL_OK** upon success.) As demonstrated, you can use the **ijlErrorStr** function to retrieve a **char***-type message indicating the type of error that occurred.

The next step is to specify which JPG file to read, and then instruct the IJL to extract the image's parameters (e.g., dimensions, color channels, and so on) from the file. The IJL will handle all of the details of opening and reading from the file; all you have to do is tell it which file to read. You do this by assigning a file name to the **JPEG_CORE_PROPERTIES::JPGFile** data member, like so:

```
// specify input file name
LPCSTR filename = TEXT("planes.jpg");
jcProps.JPGFile = filename;
```

Next, you use the **ijlRead** function to instruct the IJL to initialize the JPEG-related data members of the **JPEG_CORE_PROPERTIES** structure with information from the JPG file. Here's the code for that:

```
// read JPEG parameters from the file
result = ijlRead(&jcProps, IJL_JFILE_READPARAMS);
if (result != IJL_OK)
{
   throw std::runtime_error("Error reading file info!");
}
```

As we'll discuss shortly, the **ijlRead** function is used not only to read the image's parameters, but also to read the image's pixels. As its first parameter, the **ijlRead** function accepts the address of a **JPEG_CORE_PROPERTIES** structure; as its second parameter, the function accepts an identifier that specifies what part of the JPG file to read. In this case, because we want to read the image's parameters from the JPG file, we pass **IJL_JFILE_READPARAMS** as the second parameter. Alternatively, we can use the **IJL_JBUFF_READPARAMS** identifier if the JPEG is located in a memory buffer instead of a file.

At this point, the JPEG-image-related data members of the **JPEG_CORE_-PROPERTIES** structure have been initialized, and you can proceed with allocating the proper amount of memory to hold the JPEG image. Here, we'll simply create a DIB section bitmap to hold the image so that we can display it. To do this, we need only query the **JPEG_CORE_PROPERTIES::JPGWidth** and **JPGHeight** data members to initialize a **BITMAPINFO** structure, and then use this **BITMAPINFO** structure to create the DIB section bitmap. Here's the code:

```
// initialize the DIB section's header
BITMAPINFO bmi = {0};
bmi.bmiHeader.biSize = sizeof(BITMAPINFOHEADER);
bmi.bmiHeader.biWidth = jcProps.JPGWidth;
bmi.bmiHeader.biHeight = -jcProps.JPGHeight; // top-down
bmi.bmiHeader.biPlanes = 1;
bmi.bmiHeader.biBitCount = 24;
bmi.bmiHeader.biCompression = BI_RGB;

unsigned char* pBits;
HBITMAP hDIBSection =
   CreateDIBSection(
      NULL, &bmi, 0,
      reinterpret_cast<LPVOID*>(&pBits),
      NULL, 0
      );
if (!pBits)
{
   throw std::runtime_error("Error reading file info!");
}
```

Now that you have a place to store the JPEG image, you need to tell the IJL some information about this buffer (i.e., the DIB section bitmap). To do this, you use the DIB-related data members of the **JPEG_CORE_PROPERTIES** structure. Specifically, you initialize the **DIBWidth**, **DIBHeight**, **DIBColor**, **DIBChannels**, and **DIBPadBytes** data members like so:

```
// compute the number of DIB bytes per scan line
unsigned int dib_bytes_per_scanline =
   (((bmi.bmiHeader.biWidth * bmi.bmiHeader.biBitCount)
     + 31) & ~31) >> 3;

// set up the DIB info for the JPEG decoder
jcProps.DIBWidth = bmi.bmiHeader.biWidth;
jcProps.DIBHeight = -bmi.bmiHeader.biHeight;
jcProps.DIBColor = IJL_BGR;
jcProps.DIBChannels = 3;
jcProps.DIBPadBytes =
   dib_bytes_per_scanline -
   (jcProps.DIBChannels * bmi.bmiHeader.biWidth);
```

The **DIBWidth** and **DIBHeight** data members specify the dimensions of the destination buffer (in our case, the DIB section's pixels). The **DIBColor** data member specifies the color space of the destination buffer (the DIB section's pixels); we use the **IJL_BGR** identifier to denote that the color channels of the DIB's pixels are ordered blue, then green, and then red. Accordingly, the **DIBChannels** data member specifies the number of color channels that the destination buffer can hold (three in our case). The IJL will convert the pixels of the JPEG image into the color space that you specify in the **DIBColor** and **DIBChannels** data members. The **DIBColor** data member's other valid values, which are actually enumerators of type **IJL_COLOR**, are listed in Table 18.1.

Table 18.1 Possible identifiers for the JPEG_CORE_PROPERTIES::DIBColor data member.

Identifier	Value	Meaning
IJL_RGB	1	RGB color space; three color channels ordered red, green, and then blue.
IJL_BGR	2	RGB color space; three color channels ordered blue, green, and then red.
IJL_YCBCR	3	YCrCb color space; three color channels ordered Y, Cb, and then Cr.
IJL_G	4	Grayscale.
IJL_RGBA_FPX	5	FlashPix RGB color space; four channels ordered red, green, blue, and then alpha.
IJL_YCBCRA_FPX	6	FlashPix YCrCb color space; four channels ordered Y, Cb, Cr, and then alpha.
IJL_OTHER	255	Undefined color space; IJL will not perform any conversion.

The **DIBPadBytes** data member specifies the number of "padding" bytes that are added to the end of each scan line. Because our DIB section's pixels are **DWORD**-aligned, we computed this value manually—note, however, that we could have alternatively used the IJL's **IJL_DIB_PAD_BYTES** macro, like so:

```
jcProps.DIBPadBytes =
   IJL_DIB_PAD_BYTES(bmi.bmiHeader.biWidth, jcProps.DIBChannels);
```

Now it's time to read the JPEG's pixels. Before you do this, however, there's one more data member of the **JPEG_CORE_PROPERTIES** structure that needs to be set. Namely, you tell the IJL where to store the JPEG's pixels; you do this by specifying a pointer to the destination buffer. This is the role of the **JPEG_CORE_PROPERTIES::DIBBytes** data member. Because we want the JPEG's pixels to be copied to the DIB section's pixels, we assign the **DIBBytes** data member a pointer to our DIB section's pixels:

```
   // tell IJL where to store the image
   jcProps.DIBBytes = pBits;
```

After the DIB-related data members of the **JPEG_CORE_PROPERTIES** structure have been initialized, you can proceed with reading the JPEG's pixels. To do this, you again use the **ijlRead** function, this time specifying **IJL_JFILE_READWHOLEIMAGE** as the function's second parameter, like so:

```
   // read data from the JPEG image into the DIB section
   result = ijlRead(&jcProps, IJL_JFILE_READWHOLEIMAGE);
   if (result != IJL_OK)
   {
      DeleteObject(hDIBSection);
      throw std::runtime_error("Error reading bits!");
   }
```

***NOTE:** You can alternatively specify the **IJL_JBUFF_READPARAMS** identifier as the second parameter to the **ijlRead** function if the JPEG image is located in a memory buffer instead of a file.*

Alternatively, if you want to read one or more scan lines at a time, you can use the **ijlRead** function in an iterative fashion, specifying **IJL_JFILE_READENTROPY** as the function's second parameter. Using this approach, however, you'll also need to tell the IJL which part of the JPEG image to read (e.g., how many scan lines at a time). You do this by using the **JPEG_PROPERTIES::roi** (region of interest) data member, which you can access through the **JPEG_CORE_PROPERTIES::-jprops** data member. Here's the code:

```
    // specify the region of interest (entire width)
    jcProps.jprops.roi.left = 0;
    jcProps.jprops.roi.right = jcProps.JPGWidth;

    // instruct IJL to read the JPEG into the DIB section
    for (int y = 0; y < jcProps.DIBHeight; y += 32)
    {
       // specify the region of interest (32 lines at a time)
       jcProps.jprops.roi.top = y;
       jcProps.jprops.roi.bottom = y + 32;

       // specify a pointer to the bits
       jcProps.DIBBytes = pBits + (y * dib_bytes_per_scanline);

       // read data from the JPEG image into the DIB section
       result = ijlRead(&jcProps, IJL_JFILE_READENTROPY);
       if (result != IJL_ROI_OK)
       {
          throw std::runtime_error("Error reading bits!");
       }
    }
```

At this point, you can display the DIB section, save it to a file, or the like. There is one final issue though—you need to free the memory that the IJL used to read the image. This step involves only a single call to the **ijlFree** function, like so:

```
    // clean up
    ijlFree(&jcProps);
}
catch (std::runtime_error& e)
{
    // clean up
    ijlFree(&jcProps);

    // display the error message
    MessageBox(
       hWnd, TEXT(ijlErrorStr(result)), TEXT(e.what()),
       MB_OK | MB_ICONERROR
       );
}
```

That's all that's involved in reading a JPEG image from a file and converting it to a DIB section bitmap. Let's now go the other way around—let's convert a DIB section bitmap to a JPEG, and then save the JPEG image to a JPG file.

Writing JPEG Images

Writing a JPEG image to a file is pretty much the reverse of reading a JPEG image from a file. As with the reading process, the Intel JPEG Library (IJL) significantly simplifies the process of writing a JPEG to a file. The first step is to allocate and initialize a **JPEG_CORE_PROPERTIES** structure—this is the same as before:

```
// initialize the JPEG structure
JPEG_CORE_PROPERTIES jcProps;
IJLERR result = ijlInit(&jcProps);
if (result != IJL_OK)
{
   MessageBox(
      hWnd, ijlErrorStr(result), TEXT("Error initializing!"),
      MB_OK | MB_ICONERROR
      );
   assert(false);
}
try
{
   // all other writing code that follows...
}
```

Now that the **JPEG_CORE_PROPERTIES** structure is set up, the next step is to initialize its DIB-related data members. Recall, in the reading process, we used the **ijlRead** function to initialize the **JPEG_CORE_PROPERTIES** structure's JPEG-related data members with information from the JPG file. This time, because you're interested in converting a bitmap to a JPEG image, and then writing the JPEG to a file, you need to do the reverse. You need to first manually initialize the **JPEG_CORE_PROPERTIES** structure's DIB-related data members like so:

```
   // get the DIB section info
   DIBSECTION ds;
   const size_t dibSize = sizeof(DIBSECTION);
   assert(GetObject(hDIBSection, dibSize, &ds) == dibSize);

   // compute the number of bytes per scan line
   unsigned int dib_bytes_per_scanline =
      (((ds.dsBm.bmWidth * ds.dsBm.bmBitsPixel)
        + 31) & ~31) >> 3;

   //
   // set up the DIB section info for the JPEG encoder,
   // including a pointer to the DIB section's bits
   //
```

```
jcProps.DIBWidth = ds.dsBm.bmWidth;
jcProps.DIBHeight = ds.dsBm.bmHeight;
jcProps.DIBColor = IJL_BGR;
jcProps.DIBChannels = 3;
jcProps.DIBPadBytes =
   dib_bytes_per_scanline -
   (jcProps.DIBChannels * ds.dsBm.bmWidth);
jcProps.DIBBytes =
   reinterpret_cast<unsigned char*>(ds.dsBm.bmBits);
```

After you've initialized the **JPEG_CORE_PROPERTIES** structure's DIB-related data members, you need to initialize the structure's JPEG-related data members; in this way, you can tell the IJL's decoder how the resultant JPEG image should be created. You don't have to set all of the JPEG-related data members—you're required to initialize only **JPGFile**, **JPEGWidth**, and **JPEGHeight**. You'll probably also want to control the amount of quantization; you do this by specifying a value between 0 and 100 for the **JPEG_CORE_PROPERTIES::jquality** data member:

```
// initialize the JPEG info for the JPEG encoder
jcProps.JPGFile = TEXT("my_jpg.jpg");
jcProps.JPGWidth = ds.dsBm.bmWidth;
jcProps.JPGHeight = ds.dsBm.bmHeight;
jcProps.jquality = 85;  // percentage [0, 100];
```

Because, in this case, we're writing a 24-bpp JPEG, we don't have to worry about initializing the **JPGChannels**, **JPGColor**, and **JPGSubsampling** data members. The IJL will use the default values of **3**, **IJL_YCBCR**, and **IJL_411**, respectively. The **JPGChannels** and **JPGColor** data members specify the desired number of color channels and the desired color space for the resulting JPEG image, respectively. The **JPGSubsampling** data member specifies the type of chrominance subsampling that should be used. This data member can be assigned one of the identifiers from Table 18.2. If you're writing a grayscale JPEG, you should set the **JPGChannels** data member to **1**, set the **JPGColor** data member to **IJL_G**, and set the **JPGSubsampling** data member to **IJL_NONE**. It's important that you specify these values when writing a grayscale JPEG—remember, a grayscale image has no chrominance planes.

Now you're ready to instruct the IJL to perform the bitmap-to-JPEG conversion, and write the image to a JPG file. To do this, you use the **ijlWrite** function, which has the same signature as its counterpart, **ijlRead**. For writing to a file, however, you specify **IJL_JFILE_WRITEWHOLEIMAGE** as the second parameter, like so:

Table 18.2 Possible identifiers for the JPEG_CORE_PROPERTIES::JPGSubsampling data member.

Identifier	Value	Meaning
IJL_NONE	0	No chrominance subsampling.
IJL_411	1	4:1:1 chrominance subsampling; for 3-channel (24-bpp) JPEGs.
IJL_422	2	4:2:2 chrominance subsampling; for 3-channel (24-bpp) JPEGs.
IJL_4114	3	4:1:1:4 chrominance subsampling; for 4-channel (32-bpp) JPEGs (the alpha channel is preserved).
IJL_4224	4	4:2:2:4 chrominance subsampling; for 4-channel (32-bpp) JPEGs (the alpha channel is preserved).

```
    // write the entire JPEG image
    result = ijlWrite(&jcProps, IJL_JFILE_WRITEWHOLEIMAGE);
    if (result != IJL_OK)
    {
       throw std::runtime_error("Error writing image!");
    }
```

NOTE: *You can alternatively specify the* ***IJL_JBUFF_WRITEWHOLEIMAGE*** *identifier as the second parameter to the* ***ijlWrite*** *function if you want to write the JPEG image to a memory buffer. In this case, you set the* ***JPGFile*** *data member to* ***NULL****, and you initialize the* ***JPGBytes*** *and* ***JPGSizeBytes*** *data members with a pointer to your buffer and its size (in bytes), respectively.*

At this point, assuming that the **ijlWrite** function succeeded, you should have a newly created JPG file. The last step is to clean up; as before, you do this by using the **ijlFree** function:

```
    // clean up
    ijlFree(&jcProps);
 }
 catch (std::runtime_error& e)
 {
    // clean up
    ijlFree(&jcProps);

    // display the error message
    MessageBox(
       hWnd, TEXT(ijlErrorStr(result)), TEXT(e.what()),
       MB_OK | MB_ICONERROR
       );
 }
```

That's all there is to writing a JPEG image. As advertised, the Intel JPEG Library makes this process trivial (well, not completely trivial). Perhaps the best aspect of the IJL is its accompanying documentation, which includes a reference manual (in PDF format) with plenty of examples. (You can also see the solution "Writing a JPEG Image to a File" in the "Immediate Solutions" section.)

PNG Images

The Portable Network Graphics (PNG; pronounced "ping") format was designed to replace and extend the GIF format. The PNG format isn't as widely utilized as is its predecessor; however, due to the licensing issues that surround the use of LZW compression in GIFs, the use of PNGs is expected to surpass that of GIFs within the next couple of years. In this section, we'll look at how a PNG file is laid out, how to read and write a PNG file by using the libpng library, and how to convert a PNG to and from a bitmap.

An Overview of the PNG Format

Like many audio file formats, a PNG file is composed of a series of chunks. Each chunk is designed to hold information about a specific attribute of the PNG image. In fact, the only part of a PNG file that's not a chunk is its signature. Specifically, the first 8 bytes of a PNG file must appear as depicted in Figure 18.5.

The values of the signature were not chosen arbitrarily. Instead, the signature's values are designed to detect common network transmission problems. For example, the first byte (137) is designed to detect whether the file was transferred over a 7-bit channel. Specifically, because a binary representation of the number 137 has its most significant bit set, it would be obvious if the PNG file was transferred by a file-transfer program that strips the eighth bit. Moreover, because 137 has no meaningful ASCII equivalent, there's no mistaking a PNG file for a text file. The second, third, and fourth bytes of the 8-byte signature denote the format of the file; namely, 80, 78, and 71 simply represent "PNG" in ASCII. The fifth byte (13) and the sixth byte (10) represent a carriage-return/linefeed combination, and the eighth byte (10) represents only a linefeed. If a PNG file is transferred in text mode, these bytes will be altered according to how the target platform interprets new line sequences, thus indicating a transmission error (i.e., text-mode transmission versus binary-mode transmission). The seventh byte in the signature (26)

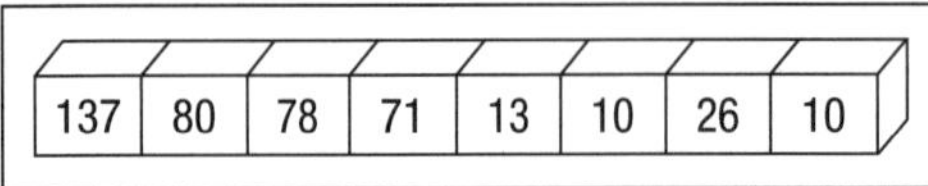

Figure 18.5 The 8-byte PNG signature (in decimal notation).

represents CTRL-Z, which translates to an end-of-file character or a stop sequence, depending on the platform. This byte is designed to eliminate the display of nonsensical data when an attempt is made to view a PNG file in a text-based console. For example, using the MS-DOS **TYPE** command on a PNG file yields the following:

```
C:\> TYPE E:\Images\Red_Brush.png
ëPNG

C:\>_
```

After the signature come the chunks. Although the PNG format allows a wide variety of chunks, decoders aren't required (or expected) to interpret and understand every chunk that a PNG file might contain. Instead, the chunks are designed to allow decoders to easily examine the type of chunk in question, make a yes/no decision on whether or not the chunk is meaningful to the decoder, and then process or skip the data accordingly. Figure 18.6 illustrates the layout of a chunk.

The Data Length field (the first four bytes of the chunk) specifies the length (in bytes) of only the chunk's Data field; this length can be as small as zero and as large as 2^{31}-1. The Chunk Type field specifies the type of information that the chunk's Data field contains. Specifically, the Type field contains four bytes, each of which represents a lowercase or uppercase ASCII character (on most computers; these bytes should, however, be interpreted as binary values). Table 18.3 lists the various chunk-type names as of version 1.2 of the PNG format specification.

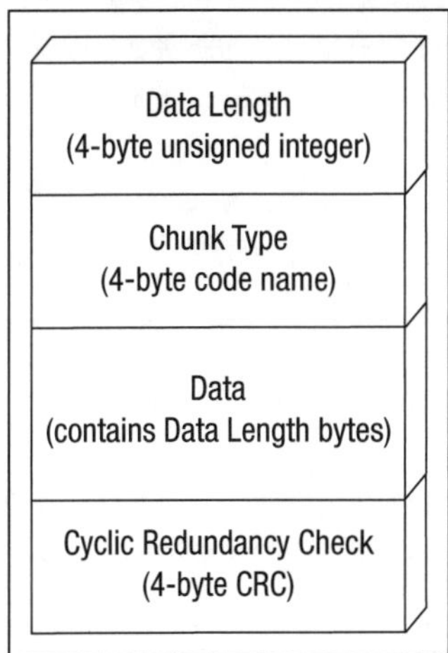

Figure 18.6 The layout of a PNG chunk.

Table 18.3 Various type names of critical and ancillary PNG chunks.

Type Name	Common Name	Indication/Contents
IHDR	Image header	Contains vital information about the PNG image, including its dimensions, bit depth, color type, compression method, filter method, and interlace method. This chunk is required and must immediately follow the signature.
PLTE	Palette	Contains a color table for palettized images. The color table contains anywhere from 1 to 256 entries, each of which is a 3-byte value that specifies the red, green, and blue intensities (in that order). This chunk is required for palettized images (color type 3), is optional for RGB and RGBA images (color types 2 and 6, respectively), and prohibited for grayscale images with or without alpha information (color types 0 and 4, respectively). If present, this chunk must precede the first **IDAT** chunk.
IDAT	Image data	Contains the filtered and compressed image data. Multiple **IDAT** chunks are permitted, but they must be placed consecutively. The data from multiple chunks is assumed to be continuous.
IEND	Image trailer	Denotes the end of the PNG file. This chunk contains no information in its Data field.
tRNS	Transparency	Specifies that the image uses simple transparency (as opposed to a full alpha channel). For palette-based images, the Data field of this chunk contains an array of single-byte alpha values, with one value for each palette entry. For grayscale or RGB images, the Data field of this chunk contains a single gray or color value that denotes the transparent color.
gAMA	Gamma	Contains a value that specifies the inverse of the gamma of the device on which the image was created or captured.
cHRM	Primary chromaticities	Contains chromaticity coordinates and the coordinates of the white point of the device on which the image was created or captured.
sRGB	Standard RGB color space	Specifies that the image uses the sRGB color space. The Data field of this chunk contains a value that denotes the rendering intent.
iCCP	Embedded ICC profile	Specifies that the image contains an embedded ICC device profile. The Data field of this chunk contains a compressed version of the embedded profile.

(continued)

Table 18.3 Various type names of critical and ancillary PNG chunks *(continued)*.

Type Name	Common Name	Indication/Contents
tEXT	Textual data	Contains uncompressed textual data from the Latin-1 character set.
zTXt	Compressed textual data	Contains compressed textual data from the Latin-1 character set.
iTXt	International textual data	Contains compressed textual data from the UTF-8 (Unicode) character set.
bKGD	Background color	Specifies the background color of the image. For palette-based images, the Data field of this chunk contains a single-byte palette index. For grayscale, grayscale with alpha, RGB, and RGBA images, the Data field of this chunk contains a 16-bit gray or color value.
pHYs	Physical pixel dimensions	Contains two 32-bit values that specify the intended physical pixel size in the horizontal and vertical directions. An additional bit represents the units of these values (0 for unknown; 1 for meters).
sBIT	Significant bits	Contains a variable-length value that specifies the number of significant bits per sample.
sPLT	Suggested palette	Contains a palette that can be used when the image is displayed on a device that's capable of displaying only a limited number of simultaneous colors.
hIST	Palette histogram	Contains a histogram (made up of 16-bit values) of the image's palette.
tIME	Image last-modification time	Specifies the time at which the image was last modified. The Data field of this chunk contains a 16-bit value for the year followed by single-byte values for the month, day, hour, minute, and second.

The case (bit 5) of each character in a chunk's type name denotes specific properties of the chunk. For example:

- If the first character is uppercase, then the chunk is required for the proper display of the image; these chunks are called *critical*. If the first character is lowercase, then the chunk is an *ancillary* chunk, and its data can be safely ignored.
- If the second character is uppercase, then the chunk is *public* (i.e., in the PNG specs or officially registered). If the second character is lowercase, then the chunk contains *private* (e.g., application-specific) data.
- The third character is reserved for future use and must be uppercase.

- The fourth character's case is useful only when you're writing a PNG file and only for ancillary chunks that are unrecognized. Specifically, if the fourth character is lowercase, then the unknown ancillary chunk can simply be copied to the output PNG file, as is, without restriction. If the fourth character is uppercase and any critical chunks have been added, reordered, or otherwise modified, then the unknown ancillary chunk must *not* be copied, as is, to the output PNG file; in this case, the encoder should omit the unknown ancillary chunk.

  On the other hand, if the ancillary chunk in question is known, it can be modified accordingly and then written to the output file. For example, if you modify an image's colors (i.e., the data of the **IDAT** or **PLTE** chunks), there's a good chance that the original contents of the **hIST** chunk are no longer valid. In this case, as denoted by the capital "T," it wouldn't make sense to simply copy the original **hIST** chunk to the output PNG file. Instead, you must either omit the **hIST** chunk altogether (if your software doesn't recognize it) or modify its contents accordingly.

At a bare minimum, a PNG file must contain the **IHDR**, **IDAT**, and **IEND** chunks. If the image is palette-based, then the **PLTE** chunk is also required. Let's take a closer look at each of these critical chunks.

The IHDR Chunk

The **IHDR** or *image header* chunk is a critical chunk (note the capital "I") that's designed to hold general (but vital) information about the PNG image. Specifically, the **IHDR** chunk's Length field always specifies a value of 13, which indicates that the Data field contains exactly 13 bytes. These bytes are as follows (in the following order):

- *Width* (4 bytes)—Specifies the number of pixels in the horizontal direction. Valid values are in the range 1 to 2^{31}-1.
- *Height* (4 bytes)—Specifies the number of pixels in the vertical direction. Valid values are in the range 1 to 2^{31}-1.
- *Bit depth* (1 byte)—Specifies the number of bits per color channel or palette index (not per pixel). Valid values are 1, 2, 4, 8, and 16.
- *Color type* (1 byte)—Specifies the format of the pixels. Valid values are listed in Table 18.4.
- *Compression method* (1 byte)—Specifies the type of compression that's used. Currently, the only valid value is 0, indicating LZ77-type compression.
- *Filter method* (1 byte)—Specifies the type of filtering that's applied to each scan line before compression. Currently, the only valid value is 0, indicating that each byte of each scan line is filtered by using one of the five basic

Table 18.4 Color-type constants and libpng identifiers for the PNG IHDR chunk.

Value	libpng Identifier	Pixel Format
0	**PNG_COLOR_TYPE_GRAY**	The image is a grayscale image in which each pixel is represented by using 1, 2, 4, 8, or 16 bits.
2	**PNG_COLOR_TYPE_RGB**	The image is an RGB image in which each pixel is represented by using 24 or 48 bits (8 or 16 bits per color channel). The data for each pixel is packed in RGB order (red, then green, and then blue).
3	**PNG_COLOR_TYPE_PALETTE**	The image is a palette-based image in which each pixel is represented by using 1, 2, 4, or 8 bits. The **PLTE** chunk is required for images of this color type, and each pixel denotes a location within the palette (color table).
4	**PNG_COLOR_TYPE_GRAY_ALPHA**	The image is a grayscale image with an alpha channel. Each pixel in the image is represented by using 8 or 16 bits (4 or 8 bits for the gray level, and 4 or 8 bits for the alpha information).
6	**PNG_COLOR_TYPE_RGB_ALPHA**	The image is an RGB image with an alpha channel. Each pixel is represented by using 32 or 64 bits (8 or 16 bits per color channel, and 8 or 16 bits for the alpha information). The data for each pixel is packed in RGBA order (red, then green, then blue, and then alpha).

predictive filtering methods: None, Sub, Up, Average, and Paeth. See "The **IDAT** Chunk" later in this chapter.

- *Interlace method* (1 byte)—Specifies the type of interlacing that's used, if any. Currently, the only valid values are 0 (no interlacing) and 1 (Adam7 interlacing); see "The **IDAT** Chunk" later in this chapter.

The information in the **IHDR** chunk is just like any other image header, and as with most image file formats, the header must be located right after the signature. The important thing to remember—which can be a bit confusing if you're used to working only with bitmaps—is that the bit depth indicates the number of bits per *sample* (i.e., per color channel or palette index), not the number of bits per pixel. Moreover, the bit depth alone tells you little about how to interpret the pixels. If the bit depth indicates a value of 8, then you know that the number of bits per sample is 8, but you'll still need to examine the color type to determine the number of bits per pixel.

The PLTE Chunk

The **PLTE** or *palette* chunk is a critical chunk whose corresponding data represents the PNG equivalent of a DIB's color table. Unlike the DIB's color table, however, a PNG's color table contains a series of RGB triplets in which each color channel (red, green, and blue, in that order) is represented by 8 bits (for a total of 3 bytes per color-table entry). In contrast, recall that a DIB's color table contains **RGBQUAD**s. Although each color-table entry is always made up of 3 bytes regardless of the bit depth, the bit depth does govern the maximum number of entries that the color table can contain (the minimum number of entries is 1). Specifically, palette-based images with bit depths of 1, 2, 4, and 8 can contain color tables with up to 2, 4, 16, and 256 entries, respectively.

As indicated in Table 18.3, the **PLTE** chunk is required for palette-based images (i.e., images of color type 3), and is optional for RGB images (color types 2 and 6). Grayscale images (color types 0 and 4), however, cannot contain a **PLTE** chunk, although you might come across a palette-based image in which the color table contains strictly grayscale entries. Although it's rare for an RGB image to contain a **PLTE** chunk, images of this type can contain anywhere from 1 to 256 entries. This might be useful when the image is to be displayed on a palettized device, but again, it's rare because the PNG format provides a dedicated chunk (**sPLT** or *suggested palette*) for this purpose.

The IDAT Chunk

The **IDAT** or *image data* chunk is a critical chunk that contains the pixels. The image is composed of scan lines that are laid out from top to bottom, and each scan line contains pixels that run from left to right. In contrast to the layout of a bottom-up DIB, the layout of a PNG is just as you'd picture it. This layout, of course, applies only to non-interlaced PNGs. The only type of interlacing that's currently specified is *Adam7 interlacing*, which is named after its creator Adam Costello, and which uses seven passes over the image. Adam7 interlacing works by dividing an image into 8x8 blocks and then filling in selected pixels of each block during each pass. Figure 18.7 illustrates this scheme.

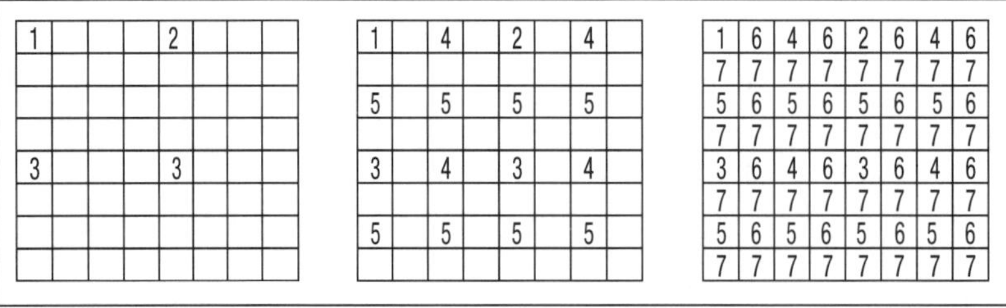

Figure 18.7 Adam7 interlacing for an 8x8 block; each sub-image illustrates the pixels that are filled in after the third, fifth, and seventh passes (pictured from left to right).

During the encoding process, the pixels of a PNG image are optionally filtered and then compressed. Unfortunately, "filtering" is a poor choice of words because no data is actually discarded. Instead, each byte is "filtered" by using a predictive coding scheme that's based on one of the following: the corresponding byte of the pixel to the left (*Sub* filtering); the corresponding byte of the pixel on the top (*Up* filtering); the values of the pixels to the left and top (*Average* filtering); or the value of the pixels to the left, top, and top-left (*Paeth* filtering).

The same type of filtering must be used for each byte of a single scan line, but each scan line can be coded by using a different filtering (predictive) algorithm. For example, you can use Sub filtering for every odd scan line and Paeth filtering for every even scan line. Before the filtered scan lines are sent to the compressor, an extra byte is tacked on to the front of each scan line to denote the type of filtering that was used. After the pixels are filtered, LZ77-type compression is used to compress the filtered data.

During the decoding process, the information in the data field of the **IDAT** chunk is extracted (and concatenated if more than one **IDAT** chunk is present), decompressed, and then "unfiltered." You can refer to the PNG specs for the specifics of interlacing, (un)filtering, and (de)compression, but you don't really need to be concerned with the particulars. The libpng library handles all the details of decoding and encoding the pixels. In fact, as we'll discuss shortly, this entire process boils down to just a few function calls.

The IEND Chunk

The **IEND** or *image trailer* chunk is a critical chunk that denotes the end of the PNG data stream. The Length field of this chunk always specifies zero, indicating that the chunk's data field is empty. The **IEND** chunk must be the last chunk in a PNG file.

Setting Up the libpng Library

Libpng is a free, C-based library that was created (and is currently maintained) by many of the original designers of the PNG format. Needless to say, libpng is the de facto reference library for reading and writing PNG files. Unfortunately, installing and using libpng is not as simple as installing and using the IJL; libpng was designed by Unix types, so we Windows developers are forced to work around those pesky **printf** statements. Still, libpng is extremely versatile and robust; once you get used to it, you'll likely find its API refreshing.

The libpng is an open-source venture whose compression functionality is afforded through the use of the free zlib compression library. You can download the latest version of libpng (1.0.8., as of this writing), along with zlib, from the libpng Web site (currently at **http://www.libpng.org/pub/png/libpng.html**). After you've unpacked the ZIP files, you should have two folders: lpng108 and zlib.

At this point, if you're using Microsoft Visual C++, perform the following steps:

1. Open the lpng108 folder.
2. Open the msvc folder.
3. Open the workspace file libpng.dsw in the Visual C++ IDE (Integrated Development Environment).
4. Within the Visual C++ IDE, choose Build|Rebuild All from the main menu.

After Step 4, the msvc folder will contain a new folder called win32. Within this folder, you'll find two subfolders—one that contains a subfolder with the import library file libpng.lib, and another that contains a subfolder with the import library file zlib.lib. You should copy these files to your main lib folder (or another suitable folder that you can refer to from within your project).

If you're using Borland C++Builder, perform the following steps:

1. Open the zlib folder.
2. Open the contrib folder.
3. Open the delphi2 folder.
4. Open the project file zlib.bpr in the C++Builder IDE.
5. Within the C++Builder IDE, choose Project|Build Zlib from the main menu.

After Step 5, the delphi2 folder will contain the import library file zlib.lib. You should copy this file to your main lib folder (or another suitable folder that you can refer to from within your project).

If you're using Borland C++Builder, you still need to create the libpng.lib import library file. You do this by performing the following steps:

1. Open the lpng108 folder.
2. Open the scripts folder.
3. Copy the makefile makefile.bc32 to the lpng108 folder.
4. At a command prompt in the lpng108 directory, type: **make -f makefile.bc32**. For example:

```
C:\ lpng108\>make -f makefile.bc32
```

After Step 4, the lpng108 folder will contain the import library file libpng.lib. You need to copy this file to your main lib folder (or another suitable folder that you can refer to from within your project).

Now, whichever development environment you're using, you need to copy the required header files. Specifically, copy the following header files from the lpng108 folder to your main include folder (or another suitable folder that you can refer to from within your project):

deflate.h, infblock.h, infcodes.h, inffast.h, inffixed.h, inftrees.h, infutil.h, png.h, pngasmrd.h, pngconf.h, trees.h

Finally, copy the following header files from the zlib folder to your main include folder (or another suitable folder that you can refer to from within your project):

zconf.h, zlib.h, zutil.h

At this point, you need only **#include** the png.h header file in your application, and statically link with the import library files libpng.lib and zlib.lib.

Reading PNG Files

The libpng library offers a set of functions that you can use to read PNG images from a file. Most of these functions are designed to read specific chunks; a fair number of functions are dedicated specifically to decoding the **IDAT** chunk (i.e., the pixels). Although you can store the image data in an arbitrary block of memory, I'll focus strictly on the steps necessary to convert this data into the form of a DIB section bitmap. This process begins with reading the PNG file's signature.

Opening the File for Reading

The first step to reading a PNG image from a file is to verify that you actually have a PNG file. You do this by examining the header; specifically, you use the libpng function: **png_check_sig**. The first step, of course, is to actually open the file and read in the signature (i.e., the first 8 bytes). Because libpng's input/output routines are designed to work with C-type file streams (although you can override this aspect), we'll perform this task by using the **fopen** and **fread** functions, like so:

```
// open the file for reading in binary mode
LPCSTR filename = TEXT("owl.png");
FILE* pFile = fopen(filename, "rb");
assert(pFile != NULL);

// read the signature
const size_t num_sig_bytes = 8;
unsigned char sig[num_sig_bytes];
fread(sig, 1, num_sig_bytes, pFile);
```

Now that the signature has been read and is contained in the buffer **sig**, we can use the **png_check_sig** function to verify the signature. Here's the code for that:

```
bool is_png = png_check_sig(sig, num_sig_bytes);
if (!is_png)
{
   // clean up
   fclose(pFile);
   assert(false);
}
```

The **png_check_sig** function returns a Boolean value, indicating whether or not the signature denotes a valid PNG file. Well, now that the signature's out of the way, let's move on to decoding the rest of the file.

Creating the Read and Info Structures

Aside from the **png_check_sig** function, most libpng functions that are designed to read data from a PNG file do so by using instances of two special structures: **png_struct** and **png_info**. The **png_struct** structure holds the information necessary to read and write from a PNG file. This structure is used internally by libpng, and it contains well over 100 data members. In short, you never need to concern yourself with the specifics of this structure (although you can see the png.h header file for its declaration). All you need to know is how to create and destroy an instance of **png_struct**. You do this by using the **png_create_read_struct** and **png_destroy_read_struct** functions.

The **png_create_read_struct** function allocates and initializes a **png_struct** structure for use in reading from a PNG file. Here's how you use the **png_create_-read_struct** function:

```
// set up an error pointer
PNGERROR PNGError = {hWnd};

// create a png_struct structure for reading
png_structp pRead =    // png_structp <=> png_struct*
   png_create_read_struct(
      PNG_LIBPNG_VER_STRING, // must be PNG_LIBPNG_VER_STRING
      &PNGError,             // optional app-defined callback data
      PNGErrorHandler,       // optional error callback function
      NULL                   // optional warning callback function
      );
if (!pRead)
{
   // clean up
   fclose(pFile);
   assert(false);
}
```

The first parameter of the **png_create_read_struct** function specifies the version of libpng. Set this parameter to **PNG_LIBPNG_VER_STRING**, which is defined in the png.h header file according to the version of libpng that you're using. The other three parameters are optional; they're used for error handling, and if you want libpng to use its default error-handling functions, you can specify these parameters as **NULL**. However, because libpng provides feedback by using the **fprintf** function, you'll almost always want to use your own error-handling function. Accordingly, you'll want to pass appropriate data (e.g., a **jmp_buf** address) to the callback function so that you can recover from the error. The error-handling callback function and the application-defined data structure are declared as follows:

```
struct PNGERROR {
   HWND hWnd;
   jmp_buf pErrorJump;
};
typedef PNGERROR *PPNGERROR;

static void PNGErrorHandler(
    png_structp pStruct,      // pointer to a png_struct structure
    png_const_charp pMessage  // error message string
   )
{
   PPNGERROR pPNGError = reinterpret_cast<PPNGERROR>(
      png_get_error_ptr(pStruct)
      );
   if (!pPNGError) throw std::runtime_error(pMessage);
   else
   {
      MessageBox(
         pPNGError->hWnd, pMessage, TEXT("libpng Error"),
         MB_OK | MB_ICONERROR
         );
      longjmp(pPNGError->pErrorJump, 1);
   }
}
```

The error-handling callback function will be passed a pointer to the **png_struct** structure and a **char***-type message that indicates the type of error. This way, instead of relying on libpng's **fprintf** function call, you can use a better-suited means of reporting the error to the user (e.g., via the **MessageBox** function). Note, however, that the callback function doesn't have a parameter that corresponds to the application-defined data. Instead, libpng requires that you retrieve this data manually by using the **png_get_error_ptr** function. If this function returns **NULL**, then a fatal error occurred, and there's little more you can do. Otherwise, you can log or display the supplied error message and then use the application-defined data to recover from the error. In this code snippet, we simply use the **longjmp** function along with the application-defined **PNGERROR::pErrorJump** data member to "jump" back up to the rest of the application (whereupon we'll clean up).

After the **png_struct** structure is allocated and initialized, and the error-handling function is set up, the next step is to create the **png_info** structure. The **png_info** structure is designed to hold information about the PNG image itself; you indirectly initialize its data members by using libpng's file-reading functions. To create an instance of the **png_info** structure, you use libpng's **png_create_info_struct** function:

```
// create a png_info structure
png_infop pInfo =  // png_infop <=> png_info*
   png_create_info_struct(pRead);
if (!pInfo)
{
   // clean up
   png_destroy_read_struct(&pRead, NULL, NULL);
   fclose(pFile);
   assert(false);
}
```

Using the **png_create_info_struct** function is entirely straightforward: you simply pass it a pointer to an initialized **png_struct** structure. If the function fails (at which point it returns **NULL**), you must destroy the **png_struct** instance that you allocated in the previous step; you do this by using the **png_destroy_-read_struct** function. In fact, the **png_destroy_read_struct** function is designed to destroy both the **png_struct** structure and the two **png_info** structures. (A second **png_info** structure is optional if you want to store the chunks that follow the pixels—i.e., **IDAT**—in a separate structure.) To clean up after the **png_info** structure has been allocated, you use the **png_destroy_read_struct** function as demonstrated in the following **setjmp** block:

```
// set the jump point
if (setjmp(PNGError.pErrorJump))
{
   // clean up
   png_destroy_read_struct(&pRead, &pInfo, NULL);
   fclose(pFile);
   return 0;
}
```

***NOTE:** If you're unfamiliar with **setjmp** and **longjmp**, here's how they work: The first time the **setjmp** function is called, it stores the current task state in the **PNGERROR::pErrorJump** data member (a **jump_buf**), and then returns zero. Later, when the **longjmp** function is called with this data member (as it is in our error-handling callback function), the application returns to the code inside the **if**-block as if the **setjmp** function returned non-zero. This scheme is similar to a cross between using a **catch** statement and a **goto** statement. Instead of using the **longjmp** function (in the callback function), you can define a structure that holds the file pointer (**pFile**) and the **png_info** pointer (**pInfo**), and then pass this structure as the application-defined callback data. This way, you can call the **png_destroy_read_struct** and **fclose** functions from within the callback function itself.*

After you've allocated the **png_struct** and **png_info** pointers (and you've properly set up the error-handling code), the next task is to initialize libpng's input/output routines. You do this by using the **png_init_io** function, like so:

```
// initialize the I/O routines
png_init_io(pRead, pFile);
```

And finally, before you start reading the image, you need to let libpng know that you've already read the file's signature. This way, libpng won't try to advance the file pointer (**pFile**) past the first eight bytes (which you've already done). The **png_set_sig_bytes** function is designed to convey this information:

```
// tell libpng that we've already read the signature
png_set_sig_bytes(pRead, num_sig_bytes);
```

Reading the Header and Other pre-IDAT Chunks

Now that all of the initializations are out of the way, let's actually start reading the image. The first step is to use the **png_read_info** function, which is designed to read all chunks up to (but not including) the first **IDAT** chunk—that is, everything before the pixels. This way, we can assess how much memory to allocate for the image before actually reading the pixels. Here's how to use the **png_read_info** function:

```
// read all pre-IDAT chunks
png_read_info(pRead, pInfo);
```

After the call to the **png_read_info** function, the **png_info** structure (**pInfo**) is initialized with information from all the chunks before the first **IDAT** chunk. At this point, you can query the **png_info** structure for information about the image. However, libpng offers the capability to perform *transformations*—that is, to convert grayscale, palette-based, and other cumbersome formats into the friendlier RGB and RGBA formats. So, the next step is to determine the bit depth and color type of the image. To do this, you use the **png_get_bit_depth** and **png_get_color_type** functions, like so:

```
// get the bit depth and color type
const unsigned char bit_depth =
   png_get_bit_depth(pRead, pInfo);
const unsigned char color_type =
   png_get_color_type(pRead, pInfo);
```

After you've assessed the bit depth and color type, you can use this data to decide which transformations to perform. Here we'll work strictly with 24-bpp and 32-bpp DIB section bitmaps, so we'll use the following transformations to convert all other pixel types to 24-bpp or 32-bpp varieties:

```
// expand to RGB if palette-based
if (color_type == PNG_COLOR_TYPE_PALETTE)
{
   png_set_palette_to_rgb(pRead);
}
// expand to RGB if grayscale
if (color_type == PNG_COLOR_TYPE_GRAY ||
    color_type == PNG_COLOR_TYPE_GRAY_ALPHA)
{
   if (bit_depth < 8) png_set_gray_1_2_4_to_8(pRead);
   png_set_gray_to_rgb(pRead);
}
// expand to RGBA if transparency chunk is present
if (png_get_valid(pRead, pInfo, PNG_INFO_tRNS))
{
   png_set_tRNS_to_alpha(pRead);
}
// set to BGR instead of RGB
if (color_type & PNG_COLOR_MASK_COLOR)
{
   png_set_bgr(pRead);
}
// reduce 16-bit images down to 8 bits per sample
if (bit_depth == 16)
{
   png_set_strip_16(pRead);
}
```

Note that we haven't instructed libpng to perform the actual transformations yet; we'll do this shortly. For now, there's one other transformation that you'll want to use: *interlace expansion.* As I pointed out earlier, you don't need to know the specifics of Adam7 interlacing—libpng will handle the interlace expansion (i.e., "deinterlacing" the interlaced image) for you. You do, however, need to instruct libpng to handle this task. To do this, you use the **png_set_interlace_handling** function, like so:

```
// instruct libpng to handle the interlacing
const int num_passes = png_set_interlace_handling(pRead);
```

The **png_set_interlace_handling** function simply tells libpng that you want it to handle all the details of interlace expansion. The function will return 7 if the image is interlaced, or 1 if the image isn't interlaced.

Although there are many other transformations that you can instruct libpng to perform, we've pretty much covered all the crucial ones. The next step is to update the **png_info** structure so that its data members will correspond to the transformed parameters, not to the actual image parameters. You do this by using the **png_read_update_info** function:

```
// update pInfo according to the transformations
png_read_update_info(pRead, pInfo);
```

At this point, the **png_info** structure (**pInfo**) has been updated, and the interlace handler has been set. We're now ready to read the pixels.

Reading the Pixels

Before you actually read the pixels, you'll need somewhere to put them. Because you'll usually want to display the image, we'll read the PNG image into a DIB section bitmap. Of course, we'll need to know how big to make this bitmap and how many bits to use for each pixel (24 or 32). So, before we read the PNG's pixels, we extract the dimensions, the number of color channels, and the (now transformed) bit depth by using the **png_get_image_width**, **png_get_image_-height**, **png_get_channels**, and **png_get_bit_depth** functions, like so:

```
// initialize the DIB section's header
BITMAPINFO bmi = {0};
bmi.bmiHeader.biSize = sizeof(BITMAPINFOHEADER);
bmi.bmiHeader.biWidth =
   png_get_image_width(pRead, pInfo);
bmi.bmiHeader.biHeight =
   -png_get_image_height(pRead, pInfo); // top-down
bmi.bmiHeader.biBitCount =
   png_get_channels(pRead, pInfo) *
   png_get_bit_depth(pRead, pInfo);
bmi.bmiHeader.biPlanes = 1;
bmi.bmiHeader.biCompression = BI_RGB;
```

Note that because we previously specified the transformation to RGB(A), and because we updated **pInfo** by using the **png_read_update_info** function, the **BITMAPINFOHEADER::biBitCount** data member will always be 24 (or 32). The **biBitCount** data member will indicate 24 if, prior to our transformations, either the PNG image was a grayscale or palette-based image without a **tRNS** (transparency) chunk, or the PNG image was actually a true RGB image. The **biBitCount** data member will indicate 32 if, prior to our transformations, the PNG image was a grayscale or palette-based image with a **tRNS** (transparency) chunk, the PNG image was a grayscale image with an alpha channel, or the PNG image was actually a true RGBA image.

After the DIB section's header is initialized, the next step is to create the DIB section bitmap, grab a pointer to the DIB section's pixels, iterate over the interlace passes (**num_passes**; either 1 or 7), and then read each scan line from the PNG file into the bitmap by using the **png_read_row** function. Here's the code for that:

```
// create a DIB section bitmap
unsigned char* pBits;
HBITMAP hDIBSection =
   CreateDIBSection(
      NULL, &bmi, 0,
      reinterpret_cast<LPVOID*>(&pBits),
      NULL, 0
      );
if (!pBits) longjmp(PNGError.pErrorJump, 1);

// compute the number of bytes per scan line
unsigned int dib_bytes_per_scanline =
   (((bmi.bmiHeader.biWidth * bmi.bmiHeader.biBitCount)
     + 31) & ~31) >> 3;

// for each interlaced scan
for (int iPass = 0; iPass < num_passes; ++iPass)
{
   // for each scan line
   for (int y = 0; y < -bmi.bmiHeader.biHeight; ++y)
   {
      unsigned char* pScanLine =
         reinterpret_cast<unsigned char*>(
         pBits + (y * dib_bytes_per_scanline)
         );

      // fill the DIB section with PNG data
      png_read_row(pRead, pScanLine, NULL);
   }
}
```

At this point, the PNG image has been converted to a DIB section bitmap, and you're free to display it, copy it to the clipboard, and so on. However, if the bitmap is a 32-bpp variety, this indicates that the PNG image contains a full alpha channel or a transparency chunk that has been transformed to an alpha channel. In either case, before displaying the 32-bpp DIB section bitmap, we'll need to perform the alpha blending.

Handling the Alpha Channel

Alpha blending is similar to the cross-dissolving step of image morphing, which we discussed in Chapter 17. In fact, libpng provides a macro, **png_composite**, that handles all the details for you. This macro, which appears in the png.h header file, has the following signature:

```
#define png_composite(composite, fg, alpha, bg)
```

So if you have a 32-bpp DIB section bitmap, before you display it, you can use the **png_composite** macro to perform the alpha blending as follows:

```
// if the image has an alpha channel
if (bmi.bmiHeader.biBitCount == 32)
{
   //
   // extract the app's background color
   // and alpha-blend the pixels
   //
   const COLORREF clrApp = GetSysColor(COLOR_BTNFACE);
   png_color_16 BkColor;
   BkColor.red = GetRValue(clrApp);
   BkColor.green = GetGValue(clrApp);
   BkColor.blue = GetBValue(clrApp);

   // set the background color
   for (int y = 0; y < -bmi.bmiHeader.biHeight; ++y)
   {
      RGBQUAD* pScanLine =
         reinterpret_cast<RGBQUAD*>(
            pBits + (y * dib_bytes_per_scanline)
            );
      for (int x = 0; x < bmi.bmiHeader.biWidth; ++x)
      {
         unsigned char alpha =
            pScanLine[x].rgbReserved;
```

```
                png_composite(
                    pScanLine[x].rgbRed,
                    pScanLine[x].rgbRed,
                    alpha, BkColor.red
                    );
                png_composite(
                    pScanLine[x].rgbGreen,
                    pScanLine[x].rgbGreen,
                    alpha, BkColor.green
                    );
                png_composite(
                    pScanLine[x].rgbBlue,
                    pScanLine[x].rgbBlue,
                    alpha, BkColor.blue
                    );
        }
    }
}
```

Finishing Up

For the most part, the primary goal is to read the PNG image itself. However, if you want to read the chunks that follow the **IDAT** chunk, now's the time to do so. Usually, the post-**IDAT** chunks are only text- or time-related, but if you need this information, you use the **png_read_end** function like so:

```
// read any post-IDAT chunks  (including IEND)
png_read_end(pRead, pInfo);
```

If you don't need any information from the chunks that follow the pixels, you still have to call the **png_read_end** function to read at least the **IEND** chunk. In this case, you pass **NULL** as the second parameter, like so:

```
// read the IEND chunk
png_read_end(pRead, NULL);
```

Finally, you use the **png_destroy_read_struct** function to destroy the **png_struct** and **png_info** structures, and you use the **fclose** function to close the file:

```
// clean up
png_destroy_read_struct(&pRead, &pInfo, NULL);
fclose(pFile);
```

For an uninterrupted version of the steps involved in reading a PNG image from a file, see the solution "Loading a PNG Image from a File."

18. Image File Formats

Writing a PNG Image

As with the steps involved in reading a PNG image from a file, the libpng library offers a set of functions that are designed to write a PNG image to a file. In fact, the steps involved are similar to the reverse of those involved in the reading process.

Opening the File for Writing

As before, the first step is to open the target file in binary mode, this time with Write privileges, like so:

```
// open the file for writing
LPCSTR filename = TEXT("my_png.png");
FILE* pFile = fopen(filename, "wb");
assert(pFile != NULL);
```

Creating the Write and Info Structures

The next task is to allocate and initialize a **png_struct** structure and a **png_info** structure. This time, instead of using the **png_create_read_struct** function to create the **png_struct** structure, you use the **png_create_write_struct** function. The **png_create_write_struct** function has the same signature as the **png_create_read_struct** function except that the former initializes the **png_struct** structure for writing. You create the **png_info** structure by using the same function as before: **png_create_info_struct**. Here's the code:

```
// set up an error pointer
PNGERROR PNGError = {hWnd};

// create a png_struct structure for writing
png_structp pWrite =
   png_create_write_struct(
      PNG_LIBPNG_VER_STRING,
      &PNGError,
      PNGErrorHandler,
      NULL
      );
if (!pWrite)
{
   fclose(pFile);
   assert(false);
}

// create a png_info structure
png_infop pInfo = png_create_info_struct(pWrite);
```

```
if (!pInfo)
{
  png_destroy_write_struct(&pWrite, NULL);
  fclose(pFile);
  assert(false);
}

// set the jump point
if (setjmp(PNGError.pErrorJump))
{
  png_destroy_write_struct(&pWrite, &pInfo);
  fclose(pFile);
  return 0;
}
```

Note the use of the **png_destroy_write_struct** function; this function destroys both the **png_struct** structure and the **png_info** structure. Also note that the error-handling callback function, **PNGErrorHandler**, is the same function that we used to handle the read-related errors.

After you've created the **png_struct** and **png_info** structures and you've set up the error-handling code, you need to initialize the input/output routines. As before, you do this by using the **png_init_io** function, like so:

```
// initialize the I/O routines
png_init_io(pWrite, pFile);
```

Now that the preliminaries are taken care of, you're ready to write the signature, the header, and all other chunks that come before the pixels. The methods are similar to those involved for reading, but this time, instead of reading data from the file into the **png_info** structure, you modify the **png_info** structure and then instruct libpng to write this information to the file. Before doing this, however, you'll likely want to set the compression level; libpng provides an easy way to do this.

Setting the Compression Level

Because PNG images are always compressed in a lossless fashion, there's no quality factor involved in the compression setting—the reconstructed image will always look identical to the original image. You can, however, specify the amount of compression that you want libpng to perform. You do this by using the **png_set_compression_level** function:

```
const int compression_level = 3;  // [-1, 9]
png_set_compression_level(pWrite, compression_level);
```

The libpng library uses the compression-level value that you pass to the **png_set_compression_level** function and punts the work to the zlib library. Higher values of **compression_level** denote greater compression. A value of 0, which corresponds to the zlib identifier **Z_NO_COMPRESSION**, specifies no compression. A value of –1, which corresponds to the zlib identifier **Z_DEFAULT_COMPRESSION**, specifies that zlib should choose the compression level. Keep in mind, however, that these compression levels won't affect the size of the PNG image as much as the "compression quality" setting of JPEG will.

Writing the Header and Other Pre-IDAT Chunks

Whereas the **png_read_info** function is used to initialize a **png_info** structure from information in a PNG file, the **png_write_info** function is used to write the information that's contained in a **png_info** structure to a PNG file. The first step, however, is to properly initialize the data members of the **png_info** structure.

For simplicity, we'll focus strictly on writing 24-bpp RGB or 32-bpp RGBA images. (In practice, you won't want to do this because there's a fair chance that you'll end up with a bloated image. Nonetheless, it's easiest to learn from a simplified example.) So, assuming that you have a DIB section bitmap that you want to save as a PNG file, you first need to determine the properties of the bitmap, like so:

```
// get the bitmap info
DIBSECTION ds;
const size_t dibSize = sizeof(DIBSECTION);
if (GetObject(hDIBSection, dibSize, &ds) != dibSize)
{
   longjmp(PNGError.pErrorJump, 1);
}
```

Next, you compute the color type of the PNG image based on the color depth of the DIB section bitmap. Then you update the **png_info** structure's **IHDR** field by using the **png_set_IHDR** function:

```
// determine the color type
unsigned char color_type;
switch (ds.dsBm.bmBitsPixel)
{
   case 24:
      color_type = PNG_COLOR_TYPE_RGB;
      break;
   case 32:
      color_type = PNG_COLOR_TYPE_RGB_ALPHA;
      break;
}
```

```
// initialize the IHDR information
png_set_IHDR(
   pWrite, pInfo,
   ds.dsBm.bmWidth, ds.dsBm.bmHeight,
   8, color_type,
   PNG_INTERLACE_NONE,  // or PNG_INTERLACE_ADAM7
   PNG_COMPRESSION_TYPE_DEFAULT, // must be PNG_COMPRESSION_TYPE_DEFAULT
   PNG_FILTER_TYPE_DEFAULT       // must be PNG_FILTER_TYPE_DEFAULT
   );
```

At this point, the **png_info** structure's **IHDR**-related data members have been initialized (although nothing has been written to the file yet), and because we're not creating a palette-based PNG image, there's no need to create a **PLTE** chunk. It's customary, however, to include a **bKGD** chunk, just in case the viewing application doesn't have its own background color. You include this chunk by using the **png_set_bKGD** function:

```
// set the background color
png_color_16 BkColor = {0, 255, 255, 255}; // white
png_set_bKGD(pWrite, pInfo, &BkColor);
```

The next step is to instruct libpng to write the file's signature, the **IHDR** chunk, and the **bKGD** chunk to the file. Again, you do this by using the **png_write_info** function, like so:

```
// write the info chunks
png_write_info(pWrite, pInfo);
```

Writing the Pixels

After the signature, the header, and any other pre-**IDAT** chunks have been written to the file, it's time to write the pixels. If you need to transform the pixels to match a certain format, now's the time to do it. For example, because the color channels of the DIB section's pixels are stored in BGR order, we'll need to instruct libpng to switch them back to RGB. We do this by using the **png_set_bgr** transformation function:

```
// instruct libpng to switch back to RGB
png_set_bgr(pWrite);
```

After you've indicated (or manually performed) all the desired transformations, the next step is to actually write the pixels to the file. If you've specified **PNG_INTERLACE_ADAM7** in the call to the **png_set_IHDR** function, you need to instruct libpng to handle the interlacing. As before, you do this by using the **png_set_interlace_handling** function:

```
// set up interlacing...
const int num_passes = png_set_interlace_handling(pWrite);
```

Note that the call to the **png_set_interlace_handling** function is still valid for non-interlaced images because the function will simply return 1 if you've specified **PNG_INTERLACE_NONE** in the call to the **png_set_IHDR** function. Now you grab a pointer to the DIB section's pixels, iterate over each pass, and then iterate over each scan line, using the **png_write_row** function along the way to write each scan line to the file. Here's the code:

```
// compute the number of bytes per scan line
unsigned int dib_bytes_per_scanline =
   (((ds.dsBm.bmWidth * ds.dsBm.bmBitsPixel)
     + 31) & ~31) >> 3;

// grab a pointer to the DIB section's bits
unsigned char* pBits =
   static_cast<unsigned char*>(ds.dsBm.bmBits);

// for each interlaced scan
for (int iPass = 0; iPass < num_passes; ++iPass)
{
   // for each scan line
   for (int y = 0; y < ds.dsBm.bmHeight; ++y)
   {
      unsigned char* pScanLine =
         reinterpret_cast<unsigned char*>(
         pBits + (y * dib_bytes_per_scanline)
         );

      // write each scan line to the PNG file
      png_write_row(pWrite, pScanLine);
   }
}
```

Finishing Up

The last step is to write the **IEND** chunk, destroy the **png_struct** and **png_info** structures, and then close the PNG file. Whereas you use the **png_read_end** function to read the **IEND** chunk, you use the **png_write_end** function to write the **IEND** chunk, like so:

```
// write the IEND chunk
png_write_end(pWrite, pInfo);
```

Finally, you use the **png_destroy_write_struct** function to destroy the **png_struct** and **png_info** structures, and you use the **fclose** function to close the PNG file:

```
// clean up
png_destroy_write_struct(&pWrite, &pInfo);
fclose(pFile);
```

See the solution "Saving a PNG Image to a File" for an uninterrupted version of the steps involved in writing a PNG image to a file.

PNG Color Management Support

Perhaps the strongest aspect of the PNG format is its extensive support for color management. Although bitmaps also provide support for color-management-related data—recall the **BITMAPV5HEADER** structure from Chapter 16—in today's bandwidth-hungry market, transmitting a bitmap just isn't practical. Note from Table 18.3 that the PNG specifications (1.2) provide four color-management-related ancillary chunks: *iCCP*, *sRGB*, *cHRM*, and *gAMA*. These chunks are analogous to the color-management-related data members of the **BITMAPV5HEADER** structure:

- *iCCP*—the presence of the iCCP chunk indicates that the PNG file contains an embedded profile. Accordingly, the data field of the iCCP chunk contains a compressed version of this profile data, a couple of bytes that are used to decode the data, and a character string (1–79 bytes) that specifies the name of the profile. The iCCP chunk is similar to the **BITMAPV5HEADER::bV5ProfileData** and **bV5ProfileSize** data members.
- *sRGB*—the presence of the sRGB chunk indicates that the image's color space is sRGB. Accordingly, the data field of the sRGB chunk specifies one of the four rendering intents: perceptual, absolute colorimetric, relative colorimetric, or saturation. In this way, the sRGB chunk is similar to both the **BITMAPV5HEADER::bV5Intent** and **bV5CSType** data members (with the latter set to **LCS_sRGB**).
- *cHRM*—the data field of the cHRM chunk specifies the chromaticity coordinates and the white point of the image's color space (i.e., the chromaticity coordinates and white point of the device on which the image was created or captured). The cHRM chunk is similar to both the **BITMAPV5HEADER::bV5EndPoints** and **bV5CSType** data members (with the latter set to **LCS_CALIBRATED_RGB**).
- *gAMA*—the data field of the gAMA chunk specifies the image's gamma—that is, the inverse of the gamma of the device on which the image was created or

captured. The gAMA chunk is similar to a combination of the **BITMAPV5-HEADER::bV5GammaRed**, **bV5GammaGreen**, and **bV5GammaBlue** data members.

Fortunately, the libpng library provides functions for reading and writing the iCCP, sRGB, cHRM, and gAMA chunks. By extracting the data from these chunks, and by using ICM 2 technology that we discussed in Chapter 16, you can read, write, and display PNG images with full color-management support.

Reading the iCCP Chunk

The iCCP chunk takes precedence over all other color-management-related chunks. If a PNG file contains an iCCP chunk, you should disregard the sRGB, cHRM, and gAMA chunks. You can determine if a PNG file contains an iCCP chunk and extract an uncompressed version of its data field by using the **png_get_iCCP** function, like so:

```
int compress_type;
png_charp pTitle, pProfile;
png_uint_32 profile_length;

// check for an embedded profile (and extract it, if it's present)...
bool has_iCCP =
    png_get_iCCP(
        pRead, pInfo, &pTitle, &compress_type,
        &pProfile, &profile_length
        );
```

The first two parameters to the **png_get_iCCP** function are the **png_struct** and **png_info** structures that you used to open and read the PNG file. The third parameter specifies the address of a pointer to a string (of type **png_charp**) that will receive the embedded profile's name; this information is usually disregarded. The fourth parameter specifies the address of an **int**-type variable that receives an identifier for the type of compression that's used. As of the current PNG specs (version 1.2), this identifier will always be zero, indicating that the profile data is compressed via the deflate algorithm. The fourth parameter specifies the address of a **png_charp**-type variable that receives the location (in memory) of the decompressed profile data. (The libpng library handles the decompression and the memory management of this data.) The last parameter specifies the address of a **png_uint_32**-type variable that receives the length (in bytes) of the decompressed profile data.

After you've extracted the profile data, you can save it to a file (just dump the entire chunk of data that the **pProfile** variable points to), and then use this file with ICM 2. Remember, this profile specifies the color space of the image. To use this profile with ICM 2, you simply copy the name of the profile's file to the **LOGCOLORSPACE::lcsFilename** data member, like so:

```
LOGCOLORSPACE lcs = {LCS_SIGNATURE, 0x400, sizeof(LOGCOLORSPACE)};
lcs.lcsCSType = LCS_CALIBRATED_RGB;
lstrcpy(lcs.lcsFilename, image_profilename);
```

***NOTE:** In this code snippet, **image_profilename** is the name of the file that you saved the profile data to. This must be an absolute (i.e., full path included) filename.*

Remember, you use a **LOGCOLORSPACE** structure to specify the color space of the image. (This is the **LOGCOLORSPACE** structure that you use with ICM 2's **CreateColorTransform** function.) In Chapter 16 we mostly assumed this color space to be sRGB. If the iCCP chunk is present, however, you no longer need to make this assumption. (See Listing 18.1 for a complete example.)

Reading the sRGB Chunk

If the iCCP chunk isn't present, you should look next for the sRGB chunk. This chunk signifies that the image's colors lie in the sRGB color space. You can use the **png_get_sRGB** function to locate the sRGB chunk, and then read its data (an identifier for the rendering intent). Here's how it's done:

```
int rendering_intent;

// check for sRGB (and extract the rendering intent)...
if (png_get_sRGB(pRead, pInfo, & rendering_intent))
{
   LCSGAMUTMATCH sRGBIntent;
   switch (rendering_intent)
   {
      case 0: sRGBIntent = LCS_GM_IMAGES; break;
      case 1: sRGBIntent = LCS_GM_GRAPHICS; break;
      case 2: sRGBIntent = LCS_GM_BUSINESS; break;
      case 3: sRGBIntent = LCS_GM_ABS_COLORIMETRIC; break;
      default: sRGBIntent = LCS_GM_IMAGES; break;
   }

   //
   // proceed with color management...
   //
}
```

The data field of the sRGB chunk contains a single byte that specifies the rendering intent. A value of 0 specifies the perceptual intent; a value of 1 specifies the relative colorimetric intent; a value of 2 specifies the saturation intent; and a value of 3 specifies the absolute colorimetric intent. To use this data with ICM 2, you should initialize your **LOGCOLORSPACE** structure like so:

```
LOGCOLORSPACE lcs = {LCS_SIGNATURE, 0x400, sizeof(LOGCOLORSPACE)};
lcs.lcsCSType = LCS_sRGB;
lcs.lcsIntent = sRGBIntent;
```

Reading the cHRM Chunk

If neither the iCCP chunk nor the sRGB chunk is present in the PNG file, the next chunk to look for is cHRM. This chunk signifies that image's colors lie in some device-dependent RGB color space, but that the chromaticity coordinates and the white point of this device are provided (in the chunk's data field). To locate the cHRM chunk and subsequently read its data, you use the **png_get_cHRM** function, like so:

```
struct xyz_ {
   double x, y, z;
} white, red, green, blue;  // used for cHRM

// check for cHRM (and extract the calibration info)...
if (
   png_get_cHRM(
      pRead, pInfo,
      &white.x, &white.y,
      &red.x, &red.y,
      &green.x, &green.y,
      &blue.x, &blue.y
      )
   )
{
   white.z = 1.0 - white.x - white.y;
   red.z = 1.0 - red.x - red.y;
   green.z = 1.0 - green.x - green.y;
   blue.z = 1.0 - blue.x - blue.y;

   // convert xyz to XYZ and compensate for the white
   // point (see the sidebar "Chromatic Adaptation")
   WhitePointAdapt(white, red, green, blue);

   // grab the gAMA info (see the next section)
   double image_gamma = 0;
   png_get_gAMA(pRead, pInfo, &image_gamma);
```

```
    //
    // proceed with color management...
    //
}
```

Aside from your **png_struct** and **png_info** structures, the **png_get_cHRM** function takes eight **double**-type parameters that correspond to the x-coordinate and the y-coordinate of the white, red, green, and blue primaries within the projected CIEXYZ color space. The **png_get_cHRM** function doesn't retrieve the z-coordinate because this data is redundant—remember, x+y+z must equal 1.

Unfortunately, as opposed to the **bV5Endpoints** data member of the **BITMAPV5HEADER** structure, the chromaticity coordinates within the cHRM chunk (and thus, what the **png_get_cHRM** function retrieves) are *lowercase* x and y. Remember, the lowercase x and y are chromaticity coordinates that denote a location within the *projected* CIEXYZ color space—that is, x and y are coordinates within the CIE 1931 (x, y) chromaticity plane. Why is this unfortunate? Well, if we want to use these values with ICM 2, we'll need to initialize a **LOGCOLORSPACE** structure. We can initialize the first few data members like so:

```
LOGCOLORSPACE lcs = {LCS_SIGNATURE, 0x400, sizeof(LOGCOLORSPACE)};
lcs.lcsCSType = LCS_CALIBRATED_RGB;
lcs.lcsIntent = LCS_GM_IMAGES;
```

But, we still need to initilialize the **LOGCOLORSPACE::lcsEndpoints** data member with information that corresponds to the chromaticity coordinates. Recall from Chapter 16 that the **lcsEndpoints** data member requires *capital X, Y*, and *Z* values (called *tristimulus values*), not the lowercase x, y, and z that we've extracted from the cHRM chunk. This is the first problem. The second problem is, where does this white point specification come into play? It's obviously embedded in the file, so we somehow need to use it. Again, recall from Chapter 16 that the **LOGCOLORSPACE::lcsEndpoints** data member assumes that the tristimulus values are specified according to the D50 white point—that is, a white point of (x, y, z) = (0.3457, 0.3585, 0.2958). So, before we can initialize the **LOGCOLORSPACE::lcsEndpoints** data member, we need to do two things: we first we need to convert the lowercase x, y, and z chromaticity coordinates to uppercase *X*, *Y*, and *Z* tristimulus values; and then, we need to adjust these *X*, *Y*, and *Z* values—by using the specified white point—so that they refer to the D50 white point. This is the job of the application-defined **WhitePointAdapt** from the previous code snippet; let's digress for the moment and examine how this function works.

Chromatic Adaptation

All lights aren't created equal. You might have noticed that many paint stores have displays that allow you to view the color of the paints under different lighting conditions. Indeed, the type of illuminant (i.e., light source) plays an important role in how the colors will appear. If you view an image under sunlight, for example, the image's colors will likely appear different than if you were to view the image under, say a fluorescent bulb.

Chromatic adaptation is the process of adjusting the primary colors (e.g., red, green, and blue) so that the resulting colors (e.g., the colors of the image) will appear as they're viewed under a different illuminant. The most popular chromatic adaptation algorithm, called the *Bradford Transform*, actually takes into account some properties of the human visual system. Let's see how this works by examining the definition of our **WhitePointAdapt** function:

```
void WhitePointAdapt(
    IN const xyz& white,  // white point from the cHRM chunk
    IN OUT xyz& red,      // red chrom. coords./tristimulus values
    IN OUT xyz& green,    // green chrom. coords./tristimulus values
    IN OUT xyz& blue      // blue chrom. coords./tristimulus values

    //
    // NOTE: red, green, and blue come in as lowercase
    // x, y, and z (chromaticity coordinates), and they
    // go out as uppercase X, Y, and Z (tristimulus values)
    //
   )
{
   //
   // First, convert (x, y, z) to (X, Y, Z).
   // Recall (from Chapter 16) the formulas that are
   // used to project the 3-D CIEXYZ space onto a 2-D
   // (x,y)-plane:
   //
   //    X = x * (X + Y + Z)
   //    Y = y * (X + Y + Z)
   //    Z = z * (X + Y + Z)
   //

   //
   // Next, temporarily assume Y = 1, and then use the fact that:
   //
   //    x/y = X/Y  ->  X = Y*(x/y) = (x/y) because Y = 1
   // and
   //    z/y = Z/Y  ->  Z = Y*(z/y) = (z/y) because Y = 1
```

```
//
// to solve for X and Z (for red, green, blue, and white).
// Also, the Y value of white is guaranteed to be one
// (remember, Y is luminance).
//
assert(red.y != 0);
double Xred = red.x / red.y,
       Zred = red.z / red.y;

assert(green.y != 0);
double Xgreen = green.x / green.y,
       Zgreen = green.z / green.y;

assert(blue.y != 0);
double Xblue = blue.x / blue.y,
       Zblue = blue.z / blue.y;

assert(white.y != 0);
double Xwhite = white.x / white.y,
       Ywhite = 1.0,
       Zwhite = white.z / white.y;

//
// Now we need to find the correct values for
// Yred, Ygreen, and Yblue, as follows:
//
//  | Yred   |      | Xred  Xgreen  Xblue |   | Xwhite |
//  | Ygreen | = inv|  1      1       1   | * | Ywhite |
//  | Yblue  |      | Zred  Zgreen  Zblue |   | Zwhite |
//

//
// So, solve for Yred, Ygreen, and Yblue by using
// Cramer's rule (for simplicity):
//
double c11 = Zblue - Zgreen;
double c12 = Zred - Zblue;
double c13 = Zgreen - Zred;

double c21 = Xblue * Zgreen - Xgreen * Zblue;
double c22 = Xred * Zblue - Xblue * Zred;
double c23 = Xgreen * Zred - Xred * Zgreen;
```

```
double c31 = Xgreen - Xblue;
double c32 = Xblue - Xred;
double c33 = Xred - Xgreen;

const double detA = c11 * Xred + c21 + c31 * Zred;

double Yred =
   Xwhite * c11 / detA +
   Ywhite * c21 / detA +
   Zwhite * c31 / detA;
double Ygreen =
   Xwhite * c12 / detA +
   Ywhite * c22 / detA +
   Zwhite * c32 / detA;
double Yblue =
   Xwhite * c13 / detA +
   Ywhite * c23 / detA +
   Zwhite * c33 / detA;

//
// Now compute the corrected values for Xred, Zred,
// Xgreen, Zgreen, Xblue, and Zblue:
//
Xred *= Yred;  Xgreen *= Ygreen;  Xblue *= Yblue;
Zred *= Yred;  Zgreen *= Ygreen;  Zblue *= Yblue;

//
// At this point, we have XYZ tristimulus values for
// for red, green, blue, and white.  Now, we need to
// perform the "to D50" white-point adjustment...
//

//
// First multiply our D65 white point vector by
// the Bradford cone-response matrix:
//
// | Xwhite_adj |   |  0.8961   0.2664  -0.1614 |   | Xwhite |
// | Ywhite_adj | = | -0.7502   1.7135   0.0367 | * | Ywhite |
// | Zwhite_adj |   |  0.0389  -0.0685   1.0296 |   | Zwhite |
//
double Xwhite_adj =
   0.8961 * Xwhite + 0.2664 * Ywhite + -0.1614 * Zwhite;
```

```
double Ywhite_adj =
   -0.7502 * Xwhite + 1.7135 * Ywhite + 0.0367 * Zwhite;
double Zwhite_adj =
   0.0389 * Xwhite + -0.0685 * Ywhite + 1.0296 * Zwhite;

//
// Now scale these values by the adjusted XYZ
// tristimulus values for the D50 white point:
//
assert(Xwhite_adj != 0);
Xwhite_adj = 0.997333473 / Xwhite_adj;

assert(Ywhite_adj != 0);
Ywhite_adj = 1.020366722 / Ywhite_adj;

assert(Zwhite_adj != 0);
Zwhite_adj = 0.818538801 / Zwhite_adj;

//
// Next, scale the corresponding columns of the inverse
// Bradford matrix by these values. Here's the
// inverse of the Bradford matrix:
//
// |  0.986019711  -0.146909258   0.159804925 |
// |  0.431879008   0.518423781   0.049222144 |
// | -0.008520255   0.040041569   0.968488059 |
//
double Binv_11 =  0.986019711 * Xwhite_adj;
double Binv_21 =  0.431879008 * Xwhite_adj;
double Binv_31 = -0.008520255 * Xwhite_adj;

double Binv_12 = -0.146909258 * Ywhite_adj;
double Binv_22 =  0.518423781 * Ywhite_adj;
double Binv_32 =  0.040041569 * Ywhite_adj;

double Binv_13 =  0.159804925 * Zwhite_adj;
double Binv_23 =  0.049222144 * Zwhite_adj;
double Binv_33 =  0.968488059 * Zwhite_adj;

//
// Now multiply the scaled inverse Bradford matrix
// by the original Bradford matrix to get the
// white-point adjustment matrix:
//
```

```
double white_11 =
   Binv_11 * 0.8961 + Binv_12 * -0.7502 + Binv_13 * 0.0389;
double white_12 =
   Binv_11 * 0.2664 + Binv_12 * 1.7135 + Binv_13 * -0.0685;
double white_13 =
   Binv_11 * -0.1614 + Binv_12 * 0.0367 + Binv_13 * 1.0296;

double white_21 =
   Binv_21 * 0.8961 + Binv_22 * -0.7502 + Binv_23 * 0.0389;
double white_22 =
   Binv_21 * 0.2664 + Binv_22 * 1.7135 + Binv_23 * -0.0685;
double white_23 =
   Binv_21 * -0.1614 + Binv_22 * 0.0367 + Binv_23 * 1.0296;

double white_31 =
   Binv_31 * 0.8961 + Binv_32 * -0.7502 + Binv_33 * 0.0389;
double white_32 =
   Binv_31 * 0.2664 + Binv_32 * 1.7135 + Binv_33 * -0.0685;
double white_33 =
   Binv_31 * -0.1614 + Binv_32 * 0.0367 + Binv_33 * 1.0296;

//
// Finally, to compute the adapted tristimulus values,
// we multiply this white-point adjustment matrix by the
// matrix of XYZ values. That is:
//
//  | white_11  white_12  white_13 |   | Xred  Xgreen  Xblue |
//  | white_21  white_22  white_23 | * | Yred  Ygreen  Yblue |
//  | white_31  white_32  white_33 |   | Zred  Zgreen  Zblue |
//
red.x =
   white_11 * Xred + white_12 * Yred + white_13 * Zred;
red.y =
   white_21 * Xred + white_22 * Yred + white_23 * Zred;
red.z =
   white_31 * Xred + white_32 * Yred + white_33 * Zred;

green.x =
   white_11 * Xgreen + white_12 * Ygreen + white_13 * Zgreen;
green.y =
   white_21 * Xgreen + white_22 * Ygreen + white_23 * Zgreen;
green.z =
   white_31 * Xgreen + white_32 * Ygreen + white_33 * Zgreen;
```

```
    blue.x =
        white_11 * Xblue + white_12 * Yblue + white_13 * Zblue;
    blue.y =
        white_21 * Xblue + white_22 * Yblue + white_23 * Zblue;
    blue.z =
        white_31 * Xblue + white_32 * Yblue + white_33 * Zblue;

    //
    // (Special thanks to Charles Cowens for these equations.)
    //
}
```

After you call the **WhitePointAdapt** function, the **red**, **green**, and **blue** parameters will be overwritten with capital *X*, *Y*, and *Z* values that have been adapted to the D50 white point. You can then assign these values to the **ciexyzRed**, **ciexyzGreen**, and **ciexyzBlue** data members of the **LOGCOLORSPACE::lcsEndpoints** data member, like so:

```
LOGCOLORSPACE lcs = {LCS_SIGNATURE, 0x400, sizeof(LOGCOLORSPACE)};
lcs.lcsCSType = LCS_CALIBRATED_RGB;
lcs.lcsIntent = LCS_GM_IMAGES;

// X, Y, and Z for the red primary
lcs.lcsEndpoints.ciexyzRed.ciexyzX = DoubleToFixPt230(red.x);
lcs.lcsEndpoints.ciexyzRed.ciexyzY = DoubleToFixPt230(red.y);
lcs.lcsEndpoints.ciexyzRed.ciexyzZ = DoubleToFixPt230(red.z);

// X, Y, and Z for the green primary
lcs.lcsEndpoints.ciexyzGreen.ciexyzX = DoubleToFixPt230(green.x);
lcs.lcsEndpoints.ciexyzGreen.ciexyzY = DoubleToFixPt230(green.y);
lcs.lcsEndpoints.ciexyzGreen.ciexyzZ = DoubleToFixPt230(green.z);

// X, Y, and Z for the blue primary
lcs.lcsEndpoints.ciexyzBlue.ciexyzX = DoubleToFixPt230(blue.x);
lcs.lcsEndpoints.ciexyzBlue.ciexyzY = DoubleToFixPt230(blue.y);
lcs.lcsEndpoints.ciexyzBlue.ciexyzZ = DoubleToFixPt230(blue.z);
```

The application-defined **DoubleToFixPt230** function simply converts a **double**-type value to its 2.30 fixed point equivalent (see Listing 18.1).

Reading the gAMA Chunk

If neither the iCCP chunk nor the sRGB chunk is present, and regardless of whether or not the cHRM chunk is present, you should look for the gAMA chunk. You can use libpng's **png_get_gAMA** function to determine if a gAMA chunk is present, and if so, read its data field. Here's how you use the **png_get_gAMA** function:

```
double image_gamma;
if (png_get_gAMA(pRead, pInfo, &image_gamma))
{
   //
   // image_gamma holds the floating point gamma value;
   // compensate accordingly...
   //
}
```

If the gAMA chunk is present, you should take the provided value into account and compensate the pixel values accordingly. The easiest way to do this is to let libpng handle the gamma correction for you by using the **png_set_gamma** function:

```
double image_gamma;
if (png_get_gAMA(pRead, pInfo, &image_gamma))
{
   const double screen_gamma = 2.2; // for PCs
   png_set_gamma(pRead, screen_gamma, image_gamma);
}
```

The **png_set_gamma** function is another one of those "transformation" functions that you should call before reading the pixels from the file. (This function is also used to set the gAMA chunk in a PNG file.) A good place to call this function is right before you call the **png_read_update_info** function to update the **png_info** structure. Alternatively, if you're using ICM, you can assign the inverse of the retrieved gamma value (**image_gamma**) to the **lcsGammaRed**, **lcsGammaGreen**, and **lcsGammaBlue** data members of the **LOGCOLORSPACE** structure that defines the color space of the bitmap. We'll look at an example of this shortly (see Listing 18.1).

Writing Color-Management-Related Chunks

All of the aforementioned color-management-related libpng functions have counterparts that you can use to write the iCCP, sRGB, cHRM, and gAMA chunks to a PNG file. For example, to embed a profile with a PNG, you use the **png_set_iCCP** function. Similarly, to set the sRGB, cHRM, and gAMA chunks, you use the **png_set_sRGB**, **png_set_cHRM**, and **png_set_gAMA** functions, respectively. Because each of these "setter" functions has a signature that's almost identical to its "getter" function counterpart, there's really no need to discuss the specifics.

NOTE: *See my changes to the* ***png_write_iCCP*** *function in the libpng file, pngwutil.c (on the CD-ROM). These changes work around a problem with using the* ***png_set_iCCP*** *function.*

An ICM-Enabled PNG Image Viewer

Listing 18.1 demonstrates how to use libpng's color-management-related functions and ICM 2 technology to view PNG images in their true colors (and light, thanks to the chromatic adaptation). For a definition of the **WhitePointAdapt** function, see the sidebar "Chromatic Adaptation."

Listing 18.1 Using libpng and ICM 2 to provide color management support.

```
// -----------------------------------------------------------------
// Windows 2000 Graphics API Black Book
// Chapter 18 - Listing 18.1 (PNG Color Management Demo)
// -----------------------------------------------------------------

#include <windows.h>
#include <cassert>
#include <stdexcept>
#include <icm.h>
#include <math.h>
#include "png.h"
// NOTE: link with mscms.lib

//
// converts floating point values to
// their 2.30 fixed point equivalents...
//
DWORD DoubleToFixPt230(double value)
{
   return (
      (static_cast<DWORD>(value) << 30) |
      static_cast<DWORD>(ldexp(value - static_cast<DWORD>(value), 30))
      );
}
//
// converts floating point values to
// their 16.16 fixed point equivalents...
//
DWORD DoubleToFixPt1616(double value)
{
   return (
      (static_cast<DWORD>(value) << 16) |
      static_cast<DWORD>(ldexp(value - static_cast<DWORD>(value), 16))
      );
}

struct xyz {double x, y, z;};
void WhitePointAdapt(
   const xyz& white, xyz& red, xyz& green, xyz& blue
```

```
   );
BOOL ColorMatchBitmap(
   HBITMAP hDIBSection, LCSGAMUTMATCH sRGBIntent,
   double image_gamma, const LPCIEXYZTRIPLE pEndpoints = NULL,
   LPCSTR image_profilename = NULL, LPCSTR monitor_profilename = NULL
   );

static void PNGErrorHandler(png_structp pStruct, png_const_charp pMessage);

HINSTANCE hInst;
const char* WndClassName = "GMainWnd";
LRESULT CALLBACK MainWndProc(HWND HWnd, UINT Msg, WPARAM WParam,
   LPARAM LParam);

int APIENTRY WinMain(HINSTANCE hInstance, HINSTANCE, LPTSTR,
   int nCmdShow)
{
   hInst = hInstance;

   WNDCLASS wc;
   memset(&wc, 0, sizeof(WNDCLASS));

   wc.lpszClassName = WndClassName;
   wc.lpfnWndProc = MainWndProc;
   wc.hInstance = hInst;
   wc.hCursor = LoadCursor(NULL, IDC_ARROW);
   wc.hbrBackground = reinterpret_cast<HBRUSH>(
      COLOR_BTNFACE + 1
      );

   if (RegisterClass(&wc))
   {
      HWND hWnd =
         CreateWindow(
            WndClassName, "PNG Color Management Demo",
            WS_OVERLAPPED | WS_MINIMIZEBOX | WS_SYSMENU |
            WS_CAPTION | WS_VISIBLE | WS_CLIPCHILDREN,
            CW_USEDEFAULT, CW_USEDEFAULT,
            CW_USEDEFAULT, CW_USEDEFAULT,
            NULL, NULL, hInst, NULL
            );

      if (hWnd)
      {
         ShowWindow(hWnd, nCmdShow);
         UpdateWindow(hWnd);
```

```
            MSG msg;
            while (GetMessage(&msg, NULL, 0, 0))
            {
                TranslateMessage(&msg);
                DispatchMessage(&msg);
            }
        }
    }
    return 0;
}

// used with the DIB section bitmap...
HDC hMemDC = NULL;
HBITMAP hDIBSection = NULL;
HBITMAP hOldDIBSection = NULL;
BITMAPINFO bmi = {0};

// used to hold the embedded profile, if present
TCHAR profile_filename[MAX_PATH];

// used with libpng...
struct PNGERROR {
   HWND hWnd;
   jmp_buf pErrorJump;
};
typedef PNGERROR *PPNGERROR;

LRESULT CALLBACK MainWndProc(HWND hWnd, UINT msg, WPARAM wParam,
   LPARAM lParam)
{
   switch (msg)
   {
      case WM_CREATE:
      {
         LPCSTR filename = TEXT("earth.png");
         FILE* pFile = fopen(filename, "rb");
         assert(pFile != NULL);

         const size_t num_sig_bytes = 8;
         unsigned char sig[num_sig_bytes];
         fread(sig, 1, num_sig_bytes, pFile);

         // verify the signature
         bool is_png = png_check_sig(sig, num_sig_bytes);
         if (!is_png)
```

```
{
   // clean up
   fclose(pFile);
   assert(false);
}

// set up an error pointer
PNGERROR PNGError = {hWnd};

// create a png_struct structure for reading
png_structp pRead =
   png_create_read_struct(
      PNG_LIBPNG_VER_STRING, // must be PNG_LIBPNG_VER_STRING
      &PNGError,             // pointer to app-defined data
      PNGErrorHandler,       // error callback function
      NULL                   // warning callback function
      );
if (!pRead)
{
   // clean up
   fclose(pFile);
   assert(false);
}

// create a png_info structure
png_infop pInfo = png_create_info_struct(pRead);
if (!pInfo)
{
   // clean up
   png_destroy_read_struct(&pRead, NULL, NULL);
   fclose(pFile);
   assert(false);
}

// set the jump point
if (setjmp(PNGError.pErrorJump))
{
   // clean up
   png_destroy_read_struct(&pRead, &pInfo, NULL);
   fclose(pFile);
   DeleteFile(profile_filename);
   return 0;
}

// initialize the I/O routines
png_init_io(pRead, pFile);
```

```
// tell libpng that we've already read the signature
png_set_sig_bytes(pRead, num_sig_bytes);

// read all pre-IDAT chunks
png_read_info(pRead, pInfo);

// get the bit depth and color type
const unsigned char bit_depth =
   png_get_bit_depth(pRead, pInfo);
const unsigned char color_type =
   png_get_color_type(pRead, pInfo);

//
// indicate the desired transformations...
//
// expand to RGB if palette-based
if (color_type == PNG_COLOR_TYPE_PALETTE)
{
   png_set_palette_to_rgb(pRead);
}
// expand to RGB if grayscale
if (color_type == PNG_COLOR_TYPE_GRAY ||
    color_type == PNG_COLOR_TYPE_GRAY_ALPHA)
{
   if (bit_depth < 8) png_set_gray_1_2_4_to_8(pRead);
   png_set_gray_to_rgb(pRead);
}
// expand to RGBA if transparency chunk is present
if (png_get_valid(pRead, pInfo, PNG_INFO_tRNS))
{
   png_set_tRNS_to_alpha(pRead);
}
// set to BGR instead of RGB
if (color_type & PNG_COLOR_MASK_COLOR)
{
   png_set_bgr(pRead);
}
// reduce to 16 bit images down to 8 bits per sample
if (bit_depth == 16)
{
   png_set_strip_16(pRead);
}

// instruct lipng to handle the interlacing
const int num_passes = png_set_interlace_handling(pRead);
```

```
// update pInfo according to the transformations
png_read_update_info(pRead, pInfo);

// initialize the DIB section's header
bmi.bmiHeader.biSize = sizeof(BITMAPINFOHEADER);
bmi.bmiHeader.biWidth =
   png_get_image_width(pRead, pInfo);
bmi.bmiHeader.biHeight =
   -png_get_image_height(pRead, pInfo); // top-down
bmi.bmiHeader.biBitCount =
   png_get_channels(pRead, pInfo) *
   png_get_bit_depth(pRead, pInfo);
bmi.bmiHeader.biPlanes = 1;
bmi.bmiHeader.biCompression = BI_RGB;

// create a DIB section bitmap
if (hDIBSection)
{
   DeleteObject(SelectObject(hMemDC, hOldDIBSection));
}
unsigned char* pBits;
hDIBSection =
   CreateDIBSection(
      NULL, &bmi, 0,
      reinterpret_cast<LPVOID*>(&pBits),
      NULL, 0
      );
if (!pBits) longjmp(PNGError.pErrorJump, 1);

// compute the number of bytes per scanline
unsigned int dib_bytes_per_scanline =
   (((bmi.bmiHeader.biWidth * bmi.bmiHeader.biBitCount)
     + 31) & ~31) >> 3;

// for each interlaced scan
for (int iPass = 0; iPass < num_passes; ++iPass)
{
   // for each scan line
   for (int y = 0; y < -bmi.bmiHeader.biHeight; ++y)
   {
      unsigned char* pScanLine =
         reinterpret_cast<unsigned char*>(
         pBits + (y * dib_bytes_per_scanline)
         );
```

```
            // fill the DIB section with PNG data
            png_read_row(pRead, pScanLine, NULL);
        }
    }

    //
    // handle the color-management-related chunks...
    //
    png_charp pTitle, pProfile;    // used for iCCP
    png_uint_32 profile_length;    // used for iCCP
    int compress_type;             // used for iCCP
    int intent;                    // used for sRGB
    xyz white, red, green, blue;   // used for cHRM

    // first, check for an embedded profile...
    if (
        png_get_iCCP(
            pRead, pInfo, &pTitle, &compress_type,
            &pProfile, &profile_length
            )
        )
    {
        //
        // now dump the embedded profile to disk...
        // (we'll use the Temp folder just in case we crash)
        //
        DWORD path_len = MAX_PATH;
        GetTempPath(path_len, profile_filename);

        //
        // call the file the title of the profile
        // (NOTE: this is not required)
        //
        lstrcat(profile_filename, pTitle);
        lstrcat(profile_filename, TEXT(".icm"));

        // create the profile file
        HANDLE hFile =
            CreateFile(
                profile_filename, GENERIC_READ | GENERIC_WRITE,
                0, NULL, CREATE_ALWAYS, FILE_ATTRIBUTE_NORMAL, NULL
                );
        if (hFile != INVALID_HANDLE_VALUE)
        {
            DWORD dwWritten = 0;
```

```
            // write the profile to disk
            BOOL write_ok = WriteFile(
               hFile, pProfile, profile_length, &dwWritten, NULL
               );
            if (!write_ok || (dwWritten != profile_length))
            {
               CloseHandle(hFile);
               PNGErrorHandler(pRead, "error writing profile data");
            }
            CloseHandle(hFile);
         }
         else PNGErrorHandler(pRead, "error creating profile file");

         // perform the color matching
         ColorMatchBitmap(
            hDIBSection, 0, 0, NULL, profile_filename, NULL
            );
      }
      // next, check for sRGB...
      else if (png_get_sRGB(pRead, pInfo, &intent))
      {
         LCSGAMUTMATCH sRGBIntent;
         switch (intent)
         {
            case 1: sRGBIntent = LCS_GM_GRAPHICS; break;
            case 2: sRGBIntent = LCS_GM_BUSINESS; break;
            case 3: sRGBIntent = LCS_GM_ABS_COLORIMETRIC; break;
            default: sRGBIntent = LCS_GM_IMAGES; break;
         }

         // perform the color matching
         ColorMatchBitmap(hDIBSection, sRGBIntent, 0);
      }
      // next check for cHRM...
      else if (
         png_get_cHRM(
            pRead, pInfo,
            &white.x, &white.y,
            &red.x, &red.y,
            &green.x, &green.y,
            &blue.x, &blue.y
            )
         )
      {
         white.z = 1.0 - white.x - white.y;
         red.z = 1.0 - red.x - red.y;
```

```
        green.z = 1.0 - green.x - green.y;
        blue.z = 1.0 - blue.x - blue.y;

        // perform the chromatic adaptation
        WhitePointAdapt(white, red, green, blue);

        CIEXYZTRIPLE endpoints;
        // X, Y, and Z for the red primary
        endpoints.ciexyzRed.ciexyzX = DoubleToFixPt230(red.x);
        endpoints.ciexyzRed.ciexyzY = DoubleToFixPt230(red.y);
        endpoints.ciexyzRed.ciexyzZ = DoubleToFixPt230(red.z);
        // X, Y, and Z for the green primary
        endpoints.ciexyzGreen.ciexyzX = DoubleToFixPt230(green.x);
        endpoints.ciexyzGreen.ciexyzY = DoubleToFixPt230(green.y);
        endpoints.ciexyzGreen.ciexyzZ = DoubleToFixPt230(green.z);
        // X, Y, and Z for the blue primary
        endpoints.ciexyzBlue.ciexyzX = DoubleToFixPt230(blue.x);
        endpoints.ciexyzBlue.ciexyzY = DoubleToFixPt230(blue.y);
        endpoints.ciexyzBlue.ciexyzZ = DoubleToFixPt230(blue.z);

        // grab the gAMA info
        double image_gamma = 0;
        png_get_gAMA(pRead, pInfo, &image_gamma);

        // perform the color matching
        ColorMatchBitmap(
           hDIBSection, LCS_GM_IMAGES, image_gamma, &endpoints
           );
    }
    // otherwise, default to sRGB...
    else
    {
        // grab the gAMA info
        double image_gamma = 0;
        png_get_gAMA(pRead, pInfo, &image_gamma);

        // perform the color matching
        ColorMatchBitmap(hDIBSection, LCS_GM_IMAGES, image_gamma);
    }
    // if the image supports transparency
    if (bmi.bmiHeader.biBitCount == 32)
    {
        //
        // extract the app's background color
        // and alpha blend the pixels
        //
```

```
        const COLORREF clrApp = GetSysColor(COLOR_BTNFACE);
        png_color_16 BkColor;
        BkColor.red = GetRValue(clrApp);
        BkColor.green = GetGValue(clrApp);
        BkColor.blue = GetBValue(clrApp);

        // set the background color
        for (int y = 0; y < -bmi.bmiHeader.biHeight; ++y)
        {
            RGBQUAD* pScanLine =
                reinterpret_cast<RGBQUAD*>(
                    pBits + (y * dib_bytes_per_scanline)
                    );
            for (int x = 0; x < bmi.bmiHeader.biWidth; ++x)
            {
                unsigned char alpha =
                    pScanLine[x].rgbReserved;

                png_composite(
                    pScanLine[x].rgbRed,
                    pScanLine[x].rgbRed,
                    alpha, BkColor.red
                    );
                png_composite(
                    pScanLine[x].rgbGreen,
                    pScanLine[x].rgbGreen,
                    alpha, BkColor.green
                    );
                png_composite(
                    pScanLine[x].rgbBlue,
                    pScanLine[x].rgbBlue,
                    alpha, BkColor.blue
                    );
            }
        }
    }

    // clean up
    png_read_end(pRead, pInfo);
    png_destroy_read_struct(&pRead, &pInfo, NULL);

    // clean up
    fclose(pFile);

    // resize the window
    SetWindowPos(
```

```
            hWnd, NULL, 0, 0,
            32 + bmi.bmiHeader.biWidth,
            50 - bmi.bmiHeader.biHeight,
            SWP_NOMOVE | SWP_NOZORDER
            );

        // associate the DIB section with a memory DC
        hMemDC = CreateCompatibleDC(NULL);
        hOldDIBSection = static_cast<HBITMAP>(
            SelectObject(hMemDC, hDIBSection)
            );
        break;
    }
    case WM_PAINT:
    {
        PAINTSTRUCT ps;
        HDC hDC = BeginPaint(hWnd, &ps);
        try
        {
            if (hDIBSection)
            {
                // render the image
                const bool blt_source_ok =
                    BitBlt(
                        hDC, 12, 12,
                        bmi.bmiHeader.biWidth, -bmi.bmiHeader.biHeight,
                        hMemDC, 0, 0,
                        SRCCOPY
                        );
                if (!blt_source_ok) throw std::runtime_error("!");
            }

            // render a border around the image
            RECT RImage = {
                10, 10,
                14 + bmi.bmiHeader.biWidth,
                14 - bmi.bmiHeader.biHeight
                };
            DrawEdge(hDC, &RImage, EDGE_SUNKEN, BF_RECT);

            RECT RClient = {0};
            GetClientRect(hWnd, &RClient);
        }
        catch (std::runtime_error&)
        {
```

```
            EndPaint(hWnd, &ps);
         }
         EndPaint(hWnd, &ps);
         break;
      }
      case WM_DESTROY:
      {
         DeleteFile(profile_filename);
         if (hDIBSection)
         {
            DeleteObject(SelectObject(hMemDC, hOldDIBSection));
         }
         PostQuitMessage(0);
         break;
      }
   }
   return DefWindowProc(hWnd, msg, wParam, lParam);
}

static void PNGErrorHandler(
    png_structp pStruct,      // pointer to a png_struct structure
    png_const_charp pMessage  // error message string
   )
{
   PPNGERROR pPNGError = reinterpret_cast<PPNGERROR>(
      png_get_error_ptr(pStruct)
      );
   if (!pPNGError) throw std::runtime_error(pMessage);
   else
   {
      MessageBox(
         pPNGError->hWnd, pMessage, TEXT("libpng Error"),
         MB_OK | MB_ICONERROR
         );
      longjmp(pPNGError->pErrorJump, 1);
   }
}

BOOL ColorMatchBitmap(
    IN HBITMAP hDIBSection,
    IN LCSGAMUTMATCH sRGBIntent,
    IN double image_gamma,
    IN LPCIEXYZTRIPLE pEndpoints,
    IN LPCSTR image_profilename,
    IN LPCSTR monitor_profilename
   )
```

```
{
   // get info about the DIB section
   BITMAP bmp;
   const size_t bmpSize = sizeof(BITMAP);
   assert(GetObject(hDIBSection, bmpSize, &bmp) == bmpSize);
   assert(bmp.bmBits != NULL);
   assert(bmp.bmBitsPixel == 24 || bmp.bmBitsPixel == 32);

   //
   // get the filename of the primary
   // monitor's profile if one wasn't supplied
   //
   TCHAR default_monitor_profilename[MAX_PATH];
   if (!monitor_profilename)
   {
      HDC hScreenDC = GetDC(NULL);
      try
      {
         DWORD len = MAX_PATH;
         bool got_profile = GetICMProfile(
            hScreenDC, &len, default_monitor_profilename
            );
         if (!got_profile) throw std::runtime_error("no profile!");
      }
      catch (std::runtime_error& e)
      {
         ReleaseDC(NULL, hScreenDC);
         MessageBox(
            GetForegroundWindow(),
            TEXT(e.what()), TEXT("ColorMatchBitmap Exception..."),
            MB_OK | MB_ICONERROR
            );
      }
      ReleaseDC(NULL, hScreenDC);
   }

   // initialize a PROFILE structure for the monitor
   PROFILE monitor_profile = {PROFILE_FILENAME};
   monitor_profile.pProfileData =
      (monitor_profilename != NULL) ?
         static_cast<void*>(const_cast<LPSTR>(monitor_profilename)) :
         static_cast<void*>(default_monitor_profilename);
   monitor_profile.cbDataSize =
      (monitor_profilename != NULL) ?
         (lstrlen(monitor_profilename) + 1) * sizeof(TCHAR) :
         (lstrlen(default_monitor_profilename) + 1) * sizeof(TCHAR);
```

```
// create a color profile object for the monitor
HPROFILE hMonitorProfile =
   OpenColorProfile(
      &monitor_profile, PROFILE_READ,
      FILE_SHARE_READ, OPEN_EXISTING
      );
try
{
   // validate the monitor profile
   BOOL is_valid_monitor = FALSE;
   IsColorProfileValid(hMonitorProfile, &is_valid_monitor);
   if (!is_valid_monitor) throw std::runtime_error("invalid profile");

   //
   // initialize a LOGCOLORSPACE structure for the
   // source image according to the supplied info
   //
   LOGCOLORSPACE lcs = {
      LCS_SIGNATURE, 0x400, sizeof(LOGCOLORSPACE)
      };
   if (image_profilename)
   {
      lcs.lcsCSType = LCS_CALIBRATED_RGB;
      lcs.lcsIntent = LCS_GM_IMAGES;
      lstrcpy(lcs.lcsFilename, image_profilename);
   }
   //
   // if the chromaticty coordinates are
   // provided, use them...
   //
   else if (pEndpoints)
   {
      lcs.lcsCSType = LCS_CALIBRATED_RGB;
      lcs.lcsIntent = LCS_GM_IMAGES;
      lcs.lcsEndpoints = *pEndpoints;

      //
      // if no gamma is specified, guess a
      // value of 0.4545 (i.e., 1.0 / 0.45455 = 2.2)
      //
      if (image_gamma == 0) image_gamma = 0.45455;

      lcs.lcsGammaRed =
         lcs.lcsGammaGreen =
            lcs.lcsGammaBlue = DoubleToFixPt1616(1.0 / image_gamma);
   }
```

18. Image File Formats

```
//
// otherwise, if only a gamma value is
// provided, use the sRGB XYZ(D50) tristimulus
// values with the supplied gamma...
// (see http://www.srgb.com/hpsrgbprof/sld006.htm)
//
else if (image_gamma)
{
   lcs.lcsCSType = LCS_CALIBRATED_RGB;
   lcs.lcsIntent = LCS_GM_IMAGES;

   // X, Y, and Z for the red primary
   lcs.lcsEndpoints.ciexyzRed.ciexyzX = DoubleToFixPt230(0.4361);
   lcs.lcsEndpoints.ciexyzRed.ciexyzY = DoubleToFixPt230(0.2225);
   lcs.lcsEndpoints.ciexyzRed.ciexyzZ = DoubleToFixPt230(0.0139);
   // X, Y, and Z for the green primary
   lcs.lcsEndpoints.ciexyzGreen.ciexyzX = DoubleToFixPt230(0.3851);
   lcs.lcsEndpoints.ciexyzGreen.ciexyzY = DoubleToFixPt230(0.7169);
   lcs.lcsEndpoints.ciexyzGreen.ciexyzZ = DoubleToFixPt230(0.0971);
   // X, Y, and Z for the blue primary
   lcs.lcsEndpoints.ciexyzBlue.ciexyzX = DoubleToFixPt230(0.1431);
   lcs.lcsEndpoints.ciexyzBlue.ciexyzY = DoubleToFixPt230(0.0606);
   lcs.lcsEndpoints.ciexyzBlue.ciexyzZ = DoubleToFixPt230(0.7141);

   lcs.lcsGammaRed =
      lcs.lcsGammaGreen =
         lcs.lcsGammaBlue = DoubleToFixPt1616(1.0 / image_gamma);
}
//
// otherwise, our next best guess
// is the sRGB color space...
//
else
{
   lcs.lcsCSType = LCS_sRGB;
   lcs.lcsIntent = sRGBIntent;
}

//
// proceed with the color matching...
//
// create a color transform object
HTRANSFORM hColorTransform =
   CreateColorTransform(
      &lcs, hMonitorProfile, NULL,
```

```
            MAKELONG(BEST_MODE, ENABLE_GAMUT_CHECKING)
            );
      if (hColorTransform)
      {
         // perform the color matching
         BMFORMAT pixel_format =
            (bmp.bmBitsPixel == 24 ? BM_RGBTRIPLETS : BM_xBGRQUADS);

         bool match_ok =
            TranslateBitmapBits(
               hColorTransform,
               bmp.bmBits, pixel_format,
               bmp.bmWidth, bmp.bmHeight, 0,
               bmp.bmBits, pixel_format,
               0, NULL, NULL
               );

         if (!match_ok)
         {
            DeleteColorTransform(hColorTransform);
            throw std::runtime_error("Error in TranslateBitmapBits()");
         }
         // clean up
         DeleteColorTransform(hColorTransform);
      }
      // clean up
      CloseColorProfile(hMonitorProfile);

      return TRUE;
   }
   catch (std::runtime_error& e)
   {
      // clean up
      CloseColorProfile(hMonitorProfile);

      // display the error message
      MessageBox(
         GetForegroundWindow(),
         TEXT(e.what()), TEXT("ColorMatchBitmap Exception..."),
         MB_OK | MB_ICONERROR
         );
      return FALSE;
   }
   return FALSE;
}
```

Immediate Solutions

Reading a JPEG Image from a File

To read a JPEG image from a file, you use the Intel JPEG Library. Specifically, you perform the following steps:

1. Install the Intel JPEG Library. (See "Setting Up the Intel JPEG Library" in the "In Depth" section.)
2. **#include** the header file ijl.h in your source code, and statically link with the import library file ijl15.lib.
3. Declare a variable of type **JPEG_CORE_PROPERTIES**.
4. Initialize the **JPEG_CORE_PROPERTIES**-type variable from Step 3 by using the **ijlInit** function. Ensure that the return value of this function (of type **IJLERR**) is equal to **IJL_OK**.
5. Assign the name of the JPG file to the **JPGFile** data member of the **JPEG_CORE_PROPERTIES**-type variable from Step 3.
6. Read the JPEG image parameters from the file by using the **ijlRead** function. For the **ijlRead** function, you pass the address of the **JPEG_CORE_PROPERTIES**-type variable from Step 3 as the first parameter, and pass **IJL_JFILE_READPARAMS** as the second parameter. Ensure that the return value of this function (of type **IJLERR**) is equal to **IJL_OK**.
7. Use the **JPGWidth**, **JPGHeight**, and **JPGChannels** data members of the **JPEG_CORE_PROPERTIES**-type variable from Step 3 to determine how much memory to allocate to hold the pixels of the JPEG image. Then allocate that much memory. (For example, you can use the **JPGWidth**, **JPGHeight**, and **JPGChannels** data members to initialize a **BITMAPINFOHEADER** structure, and then create a DIB or a DIB section bitmap to hold the JPEG image.)
8. After you've allocated memory for the JPEG's pixels (e.g., after you've created a DIB section bitmap), initialize the **DIBWidth**, **DIBHeight**, **DIBColor**, **DIBChannels**, and **DIBPadBytes** data members of the **JPEG_CORE_PROPERTIES**-type variable from Step 3 according to the properties of your buffer (DIB section bitmap). The **DIBWidth** and **DIBHeight** data members specify the dimensions (in pixels) of your

destination buffer. The **DIBColor** data member can be assigned one of the identifiers listed in Table 18.1. The **DIBChannels** data member specifies the number of color channels in the destination buffer; this data member must be set according to the identifier that you assign to the **DIBColor** data member. The **DIBPadBytes** data member specifies the number of extra bytes that are added to each scan line.

9. Assign a pointer to your destination buffer (e.g., the DIB section's pixels) to the **DIBBytes** data member of the **JPEG_CORE_PROPERTIES**-type variable from Step 3.
10. Read the JPEG image from the file into your destination buffer by using the **ijlRead** function. For this function, you pass the address of the **JPEG_CORE_PROPERTIES**-type variable from Step 3 as the first parameter, and pass **IJL_JFILE_READWHOLEIMAGE** as the second parameter. Ensure that the return value of this function (of type **IJLERR**) is equal to **IJL_OK**.
11. Free the resources used by the Intel JPEG Library by using the **ijlFree** function. You pass the **ijlFree** function the address of the **JPEG_CORE_PROPERTIES**-type variable from Step 3.

In Listing 18.2, the example function **CreateDIBSectionFromJPGFile** demonstrates how to use these 11 steps to read a JPEG image from a file and place the results in a DIB section bitmap. The resulting DIB section bitmap (whose handle is returned if the **CreateDIBSectionFromJPGFile** function is successful) will be either a 24-bpp variety if the JPEG image itself is 24-bpp or an 8-bpp variety if the JPEG image is grayscale. Here's the code:

Listing 18.2 Reading a JPEG image from a file and placing the results in a DIB section bitmap.

```
// -------------------------------------------------------------------
// Windows 2000 Graphics API Black Book
// Chapter 18 - Listing 18.2 (CreateDIBSectionFromJPGFile Definition)
// -------------------------------------------------------------------

#include <stdexcept>
HBITMAP CreateDIBSectionFromJPGFile(IN LPCSTR filename)
{
//
// STEP 1: Install the Intel JPEG Library
// STEP 2: #include "ijl.h" and link with "ijl15.lib"
//

   assert(filename != NULL);
   HBITMAP hDIBSection = NULL;
```

```
//
// STEP 3: Declare a JPEG_CORE_PROPERTIES structure
//
JPEG_CORE_PROPERTIES jcProps;

//
// STEP 4: Initialize jcProps
//
IJLERR result = ijlInit(&jcProps);
if (result != IJL_OK)
{
   MessageBox(
      GetForegroundWindow(),
      TEXT(ijlErrorStr(result)), TEXT("Error initializing!"),
      MB_OK | MB_ICONERROR
      );
   assert(false);
}
try
{
   //
   // STEP 5: Specify input file name
   //
   jcProps.JPGFile = TEXT(filename);

   //
   // STEP 6: Read JPEG parameters from the file
   //
   result = ijlRead(&jcProps, IJL_JFILE_READPARAMS);
   if (result != IJL_OK)
   {
      throw std::runtime_error("Error reading file info!");
   }

   //
   // STEP 7: Initialize a corresponding DIB header
   //
   BITMAPINFO bmi = {0};
   bmi.bmiHeader.biSize = sizeof(BITMAPINFOHEADER);
   bmi.bmiHeader.biWidth = jcProps.JPGWidth;
   bmi.bmiHeader.biHeight = -jcProps.JPGHeight; // top-down
   bmi.bmiHeader.biPlanes = 1;
   bmi.bmiHeader.biCompression = BI_RGB;
   switch (jcProps.JPGChannels)
```

```
{
    case 1: bmi.bmiHeader.biBitCount = 8; break;
    case 3: bmi.bmiHeader.biBitCount = 24; break;
    /* if desired, handle FlashPix format here with a case 4: */
    default: throw std::runtime_error("Invalid JPG file!"); break;
}

// create a DIB section bitmap
unsigned char* pBits;
hDIBSection =
   CreateDIBSection(
      NULL, &bmi, 0,
      reinterpret_cast<LPVOID*>(&pBits),
      NULL, 0
      );
if (!pBits)
{
   throw std::runtime_error("Error reading file info!");
}

// compute the number of bytes per scan line
unsigned int dib_bytes_per_scanline =
   (((bmi.bmiHeader.biWidth * bmi.bmiHeader.biBitCount)
     + 31) & ~31) >> 3;

//
// STEP 8: Set up the DIB info for the JPEG decoder
//
jcProps.DIBWidth = bmi.bmiHeader.biWidth;
jcProps.DIBHeight = -bmi.bmiHeader.biHeight;
jcProps.DIBChannels = jcProps.JPGChannels;
switch (bmi.bmiHeader.biBitCount)
{
   case 8: jcProps.DIBColor = IJL_G; break;
   case 24: jcProps.DIBColor = IJL_BGR; break;
}
jcProps.DIBPadBytes =
   dib_bytes_per_scanline -
   (jcProps.DIBChannels * bmi.bmiHeader.biWidth);

// set up a grayscale color table for the 8-bpp case
if (jcProps.DIBColor == IJL_G)
{
   RGBQUAD rgbQ[256];
```

```
    for (int index = 0; index < 256; ++index)
    {
        rgbQ[index].rgbRed =
            rgbQ[index].rgbGreen =
                rgbQ[index].rgbBlue = index;
        rgbQ[index].rgbReserved = 0;
    }

    HDC hMemDC = CreateCompatibleDC(NULL);
    hDIBSection = static_cast<HBITMAP>(
        SelectObject(hMemDC, hDIBSection)
        );
    if (SetDIBColorTable(hMemDC, 0, 256, rgbQ) != 256)
    {
        hDIBSection = static_cast<HBITMAP>(
            SelectObject(hMemDC, hDIBSection)
            );
        DeleteDC(hMemDC);
        DeleteObject(hDIBSection);
        throw std::runtime_error("Error setting color table!");
    }
    hDIBSection = static_cast<HBITMAP>(
        SelectObject(hMemDC, hDIBSection)
        );
    DeleteDC(hMemDC);
}

//
// STEP 9: Tell IJL where to store the image
//
jcProps.DIBBytes = pBits;

//
// STEP 10: Read data from the JPEG image into the DIB section
//
result = ijlRead(&jcProps, IJL_JFILE_READWHOLEIMAGE);
if (result != IJL_OK)
{
    DeleteObject(hDIBSection);
    throw std::runtime_error("Error reading bits!");
}

//
// STEP 11: Clean up
//
```

```
        ijlFree(&jcProps);
    }
    catch (std::runtime_error& e)
    {
        // clean up
        ijlFree(&jcProps);

        // display the error message
        MessageBox(
            GetForegroundWindow(),
            TEXT(ijlErrorStr(result)), TEXT(e.what()),
            MB_OK | MB_ICONERROR
            );
        return NULL;
    }
    return hDIBSection;
}
```

For more information on reading a JPEG image from a file, see "Reading a JPEG Image" in the "In Depth" section. For more information on using the Intel JPEG Library, refer to the *Developer's Guide* (the PDF file ijlman.pdf) that accompanies the Intel JPEG Library.

Writing a JPEG Image to a File

To write a JPEG image to a file, you use the Intel JPEG Library. Specifically, you perform the following steps:

1. Install the Intel JPEG Library. (See "Setting Up the Intel JPEG Library" in the "In Depth" section.)
2. **#include** the header file ijl.h in your source code, and statically link with the import library file ijl15.lib.
3. Declare a variable of type **JPEG_CORE_PROPERTIES**.
4. Initialize the **JPEG_CORE_PROPERTIES**-type variable from Step 3 by using the **ijlInit** function. Ensure that the return value of this function (of type **IJLERR**) is equal to **IJL_OK**.
5. Initialize the **DIBWidth**, **DIBHeight**, **DIBColor**, **DIBChannels**, and **DIBPadBytes** data members of the **JPEG_CORE_PROPERTIES**-type variable from Step 3 with information from your source buffer (e.g., DIB section bitmap). The **DIBWidth** and **DIBHeight** data members specify the dimensions (in pixels) of your source buffer. The **DIBColor** data

member can be assigned one of the identifiers listed in Table 18.1. The **DIBChannels** data member specifies the number of color channels in the destination buffer; this data member must be set according to the identifier that you assign to the **DIBColor** data member. The **DIBPadBytes** data member specifies the number of extra bytes that are added to each scan line.

6. Assign a pointer to your source buffer (e.g., the DIB section's pixels) to the **DIBBytes** data member of the **JPEG_CORE_PROPERTIES**-type variable from Step 3.
7. Initialize the **JPGWidth**, **JPGHeight**, **JPGColor**, and **JPGChannels** data members of the **JPEG_CORE_PROPERTIES**-type variable from Step 3. In most situations, you'll want to assign these data members the same values as the **DIBWidth**, **DIBHeight**, **DIBColor**, and **DIBChannels** data members, respectively, from Step 6 in order to write a JPEG image that corresponds to the DIB section's properties. You can assign different values, however, if you want the Intel JPEG Library to create a JPEG image of a different size and/or format. The **JPGWidth** and **JPGHeight** data members specify the dimensions (in pixels) of the resulting JPEG image in the file. The **JPGColor** data member can be assigned one of the identifiers listed in Table 18.1. The **JPGChannels** data member specifies the number of color channels; this data member must be set according to the identifier that you assign to the **JPGColor** data member. In addition, if you're creating a grayscale JPEG—that is, the **JPGColor** data member is set to **IJL_G**—you need to set the **JPGSubsampling** data member to **IJL_NONE**.
8. If you want to control the "compression quality," assign a value between 0 and 100 to the **jquality** data member of the **JPEG_CORE_PROPERTIES**-type variable from Step 3. The default value is 75.
9. Assign the name of the output file to the **JPGFile** data member of the **JPEG_CORE_PROPERTIES**-type variable from Step 3.
10. Create the JPG file by using the **ijlWrite** function. For this function, you pass the address of the **JPEG_CORE_PROPERTIES**-type variable from Step 3 as the first parameter, and pass **IJL_JFILE_WRITEWHOLEIMAGE** as the second parameter. Ensure that the return value of this function (of type **IJLERR**) is equal to **IJL_OK**.
11. Free the resources used by the Intel JPEG Library by using the **ijlFree** function. You pass the **ijlFree** function the address of the **JPEG_CORE_PROPERTIES**-type variable from Step 3.

In Listing 18.3, the example function **SaveDIBSectionToJPGFile** demonstrates how to use these 11 steps to write a JPG file from the pixels of a DIB section bitmap. The resulting JPEG image (that's contained in the file) will be either a 24-bpp variety if the DIB section itself is 24-bpp, or an 8-bpp variety if the DIB section is grayscale. Here's the code:

Listing 18.3 Writing a JPG file from the pixels of a DIB section bitmap.

```
// -------------------------------------------------------------------
// Windows 2000 Graphics API Black Book
// Chapter 18 - Listing 18.3 (SaveDIBSectionToJPGFile Definition)
// -------------------------------------------------------------------

#include <stdexcept>
BOOL SaveDIBSectionToJPGFile(
     IN LPCSTR filename, IN HBITMAP hDIBSection, IN int quality = 75
   )
{
//
// STEP 1: Install the Intel JPEG Library
// STEP 2: #include "ijl.h" and link with "ijl15.lib"
//

   assert(filename != NULL);
   assert(hDIBSection != NULL);

   //
   // STEP 3: Declare a JPEG_CORE_PROPERTIES structure
   //
   JPEG_CORE_PROPERTIES jcProps;

   //
   // STEP 4: Initialize jcProps
   //
   IJLERR result = ijlInit(&jcProps);
   if (result != IJL_OK)
   {
      MessageBox(
         GetForegroundWindow(),
         TEXT(ijlErrorStr(result)), TEXT("Error initializing!"),
         MB_OK | MB_ICONERROR
         );
      assert(false);
   }
```

```
try
{
   // get the bitmap info
   BITMAP bmp;
   const size_t bmpSize = sizeof(BITMAP);
   if (GetObject(hDIBSection, bmpSize, &bmp) != bmpSize)
   {
      throw std::runtime_error("Error getting bitmap info!");
   }
   if (!bmp.bmBits)
   {
      throw std::runtime_error("Invalid DIB section! (DDB?)");
   }

   // compute the number of bytes per scan line
   unsigned int dib_bytes_per_scanline =
      (((bmp.bmWidth * bmp.bmBitsPixel) + 31) & ~31) >> 3;

   //
   // STEP 5: Set up the DIB info for the JPEG encoder
   //
   jcProps.DIBWidth = bmp.bmWidth;
   jcProps.DIBHeight = bmp.bmHeight;
   jcProps.DIBChannels = bmp.bmBitsPixel / 8;
   switch (bmp.bmBitsPixel)
   {
      case 8: jcProps.DIBColor = IJL_G; break;
      case 24: jcProps.DIBColor = IJL_BGR; break;
      default: throw std::runtime_error("Invalid color depth!"); break;
   }
   jcProps.DIBPadBytes =
      dib_bytes_per_scanline -
      (jcProps.DIBChannels * bmp.bmWidth);

   //
   // STEP 6: Assign a pointer to the source pixels
   //
   jcProps.DIBBytes =
      reinterpret_cast<unsigned char*>(bmp.bmBits);

   //
   // STEP 7: Initialize the desired JPEG properties
   //
   jcProps.JPGWidth = bmp.bmWidth;
   jcProps.JPGHeight = bmp.bmHeight;
```

```
        switch (jcProps.DIBColor)
        {
            case IJL_G:
                jcProps.JPGColor = jcProps.DIBColor;
                jcProps.JPGSubsampling = IJL_NONE;
                break;
            case IJL_BGR:
                jcProps.JPGColor = IJL_YCBCR;
                break;
        }
        jcProps.JPGChannels = jcProps.DIBChannels;

        //
        // STEP 8: Set the compression quality
        //
        jcProps.jquality = quality;  // percentage [0, 100];

        //
        // STEP 9: Specify the destination file name
        //
        jcProps.JPGFile = TEXT(filename);

        //
        // STEP 10: Write the entire JPEG image to the file
        //
        result = ijlWrite(&jcProps, IJL_JFILE_WRITEWHOLEIMAGE);
        if (result != IJL_OK)
        {
            throw std::runtime_error("Error writing image!");
        }

        //
        // STEP 11: Clean up
        //
        ijlFree(&jcProps);

        return TRUE;
    }
    catch (std::runtime_error& e)
    {
        // clean up
        ijlFree(&jcProps);

        // display the error message
        MessageBox(
            GetForegroundWindow(),
```

```
            TEXT(ijlErrorStr(result)), TEXT(e.what()),
            MB_OK | MB_ICONERROR
            );
    }
    return FALSE;
}
```

For more information on writing a JPEG image from a file, see "Writing a JPEG Image" in the "In Depth" section. For more information on using the Intel JPEG Library, refer to the *Developer's Guide* (the PDF file ijlman.pdf) that accompanies the Intel JPEG Library.

Reading a PNG Image from a File

To read a PNG image from a file, you use the libpng library. Specifically, you perform the following steps:

1. Install the libpng library. (See "Setting Up the libpng Library" in the "In Depth" section.)
2. **#include** the header file png.h in your source code, and statically link with the import library file libpng.lib.
3. Open the input PNG file in binary mode with Read access privileges by using the **fopen** function; store the return value (which is a pointer to the file stream of type **FILE***).
4. Allocate an 8-byte buffer, and use the **fread** function to read the first 8 bytes (the signature) of the PNG file into the buffer.
5. Verify the signature of the PNG file by using the **png_check_sig** function. Specifically, specify the buffer from Step 4 as the first parameter of the **png_check_sig** function, and specify 8 as the second parameter. If the signature is valid, the **png_check_sig** function will return **true** and you can proceed to Step 6. If the signature is invalid, the **png_check_sig** function will return **false**, and you should proceed to Step 19.
6. Allocate and initialize a **png_struct** structure for reading by using the **png_create_read_struct** function. You must specify **PNG_LIBPNG_-VER_STRING** as the first parameter of the **png_create_read_struct** function; the other three parameters can be set to **NULL**. In most cases, however, you'll want to provide an error-handling callback function. To do this, you specify a pointer to your callback function as the third parameter of the **png_create_read_struct** function, and you specify a pointer to any additional application-defined data that you want to access from within the

callback function as the second parameter of the **png_create_read_struct** function. (From within your callback function, you can access the application-defined data by using the **png_get_error_ptr** function.) If it's successful, the **png_create_read_struct** function will return a pointer to an allocated (and initialized) **png_struct** structure. If the function fails, it returns **NULL** and you should proceed to Step 19.

7. Allocate and initialize a **png_info** structure by using the **png_create_-info_struct** function. You pass this function a pointer to the **png_struct**-type variable from Step 6. If the **png_create_info_struct** function is successful, it will return a pointer to an allocated (and initialized) **png_info** structure. If the function fails, it will return **NULL** and you should proceed to Step 18.
8. Initialize libpng's input/output routines by using the **png_init_io** function. For this function, you pass a pointer to the **png_struct**-type variable from Step 6 as the first parameter, and pass the **png_info**-type variable from Step 7 as the second parameter.
9. Tell libpng that you've already read the signature (which you did in Step 4) by using the **png_set_sig_bytes** function. For this function, you pass a pointer to the **png_struct**-type variable from Step 6 as the first parameter, and pass 8 as the second parameter.
10. Read all of the chunks that precede the first **IDAT** chunk by using the **png_read_info** function. For this function, you pass a pointer to the **png_struct**-type variable from Step 6 as the first parameter, and pass the **png_info**-type variable from Step 7 as the second parameter.
11. Extract and store the bit depth and the color type of the PNG image by using the **png_get_bit_depth** and **png_get_color_type** functions. Both of these functions have the same signature. For each function, you pass a pointer to the **png_struct**-type variable from Step 6 as the first parameter, and pass the **png_info**-type variable from Step 7 as the second parameter.
12. Use the bit-depth and color-type values from Step 11 to determine which types of image-related transformations to perform. In most cases, you'll want to convert the PNG image to an RGB or RGBA variety, and you'll want to order the color channels in BGR order (to display the image as a bitmap). See "Reading a PNG Image" in the "In Depth" section for more information on this step.
13. Instruct libpng to handle the expansion of the interlaced images by using the **png_set_interlace_handling** function. You pass this function a pointer to the **png_struct**-type variable from Step 6, and the function will return the number of interlaced passes that are required to read the entire

image. You should store this return value; it will be either 1 (no interlacing) or 7 (the image is interlaced).

14. Instruct libpng to handle the specified transformations (and interlace expansion) by using the **png_read_update_info** function. For this function, you pass a pointer to the **png_struct**-type variable from Step 6 as the first parameter, and pass the **png_info**-type variable from Step 7 as the second parameter.
15. Extract and store the dimensions and pixel depth of the PNG image by using the **png_get_image_width**, **png_get_image_height**, **png_get_channels**, and **png_get_bit_depth** functions. All of these functions have the same signature. For each function, you pass a pointer to the **png_struct**-type variable from Step 6 as the first parameter, and pass the **png_info**-type variable from Step 7 as the second parameter. Use the dimensions and pixel depth to determine how much memory to allocate for the buffer that's to hold the PNG image. Then allocate the buffer (e.g., create a DIB section bitmap).
16. In an outer loop, iterate over the required number of interlacing passes (the value you stored in Step 13). Within this loop, create an inner loop that iterates over the number of scan lines (the PNG image's height, which you stored in Step 15). For each iteration of the inner loop (i.e., for each scan line), read a scan line of the PNG image from the file into your buffer by using the **png_read_row** function. You pass this function the following: a pointer to the **png_struct**-type variable from Step 6 as the first parameter; a pointer to a specific scan line as the second parameter; and **NULL** as the third parameter.
17. Read the **IEND** chunk by using the **png_read_end** function. For this function, you pass a pointer to the **png_struct**-type variable from Step 6 as the first parameter, and pass **NULL** as the second parameter.
18. Destroy the **png_struct**-type variable from Step 6 and the **png_info**-type variable from Step 7 by using the **png_destroy_read_struct** function. You pass this function the following: the address of a pointer to the **png_struct**-type variable from Step 6 as the first parameter; the address of a pointer to the **png_info**-type variable from Step 7 as the second parameter; and **NULL** as the third parameter.
19. Close the file stream (from Step 3) by using the **fclose** function.

In Listing 18.4, the example function **CreateDIBSectionFromPNGFile** demonstrates how to use these 19 steps to read a PNG image from a file and place the results in a DIB section bitmap. The resulting DIB section bitmap (whose handle is returned if the **CreateDIBSectionFromPNGFile** function is successful) will be either a 24-bpp variety if the PNG image contains no alpha or transparency information, or a 32-bpp variety if the PNG image is RGBA (or can be converted to RGBA—e.g., if the original image is grayscale with an alpha channel or has transparency information). Here's the code:

Listing 18.4 Reading a PNG image from a file and placing the results in a DIB section bitmap.

```
// -------------------------------------------------------------------
// Windows 2000 Graphics API Black Book
// Chapter 18 - Listing 18.4 (CreateDIBSectionFromPNGFile Definition)
// -------------------------------------------------------------------

struct PNGERROR {
   HWND hWnd;
   jmp_buf pErrorJump;
};
typedef PNGERROR *PPNGERROR;

static void PNGErrorHandler(
    png_structp pStruct,      // pointer to a png_struct structure
    png_const_charp pMessage  // error message string
   )
{
   PPNGERROR pPNGError = reinterpret_cast<PPNGERROR>(
      png_get_error_ptr(pStruct)
      );
   if (!pPNGError) throw std::runtime_error(pMessage);
   else
   {
      MessageBox(
         pPNGError->hWnd, pMessage, TEXT("libpng Error"),
         MB_OK | MB_ICONERROR
         );
      longjmp(pPNGError->pErrorJump, 1);
   }
}

HBITMAP CreateDIBSectionFromPNGFile(IN LPCSTR filename)
{
//
// STEP 1: Install the libpng library
// STEP 2: #include "png.h" and link with "libpng.lib" and "zlib.lib"
//

   //
   // STEP 3: Open the file for binary reading
   //
```

```
FILE* pFile = fopen(filename, "rb");
assert(pFile != NULL);

//
// STEP 4: Read the file's signature
//
const size_t num_sig_bytes = 8;
unsigned char sig[num_sig_bytes];
fread(sig, 1, num_sig_bytes, pFile);

//
// STEP 5: Verify the signature
//
bool is_png = png_check_sig(sig, num_sig_bytes);
if (!is_png)
{
   // clean up
   fclose(pFile);
   assert(false);
}

// set up an error pointer
PNGERROR PNGError = {GetForegroundWindow()};

//
// STEP 6: Create a png_struct structure for reading
//
png_structp pRead =
   png_create_read_struct(
      PNG_LIBPNG_VER_STRING, // must be PNG_LIBPNG_VER_STRING
      &PNGError,             // pointer to app-defined data
      PNGErrorHandler,       // error callback function
      NULL                   // warning callback function
      );
if (!pRead)
{
   // clean up
   fclose(pFile);
   assert(false);
}

//
// STEP 7: Create a png_info structure
//
png_infop pInfo = png_create_info_struct(pRead);
```

```
if (!pInfo)
{
   // clean up
   png_destroy_read_struct(&pRead, NULL, NULL);
   fclose(pFile);
   assert(false);
}

// set the jump point
if (setjmp(PNGError.pErrorJump))
{
   // clean up
   png_destroy_read_struct(&pRead, &pInfo, NULL);
   fclose(pFile);
   return NULL;
}

//
// STEP 8: Initialize the I/O routines
//
png_init_io(pRead, pFile);

//
// STEP 9: Tell libpng that we've already read the signature
//
png_set_sig_bytes(pRead, num_sig_bytes);

//
// STEP 10: Read all pre-IDAT chunks
//
png_read_info(pRead, pInfo);

//
// STEP 11: Get the bit depth and color type
//
const unsigned char bit_depth =
   png_get_bit_depth(pRead, pInfo);
const unsigned char color_type =
   png_get_color_type(pRead, pInfo);

//
// STEP 12: Specify the desired transformations...
//
// expand to RGB if palette-based
if (color_type == PNG_COLOR_TYPE_PALETTE)
```

```
{
    png_set_palette_to_rgb(pRead);
}
// expand to RGB if grayscale
if (color_type == PNG_COLOR_TYPE_GRAY ||
     color_type == PNG_COLOR_TYPE_GRAY_ALPHA)
{
    if (bit_depth < 8) png_set_gray_1_2_4_to_8(pRead);
    png_set_gray_to_rgb(pRead);
}
// expand to RGBA if transparency chunk is present
if (png_get_valid(pRead, pInfo, PNG_INFO_tRNS))
{
    png_set_tRNS_to_alpha(pRead);
}
// set to BGR instead of RGB
if (color_type & PNG_COLOR_MASK_COLOR)
{
    png_set_bgr(pRead);
}
// reduce 16-bit images down to 8 bits per sample
if (bit_depth == 16)
{
    png_set_strip_16(pRead);
}
// handle the gAMA chunk
double image_gamma = 1 / 2.2;
png_get_gAMA(pRead, pInfo, &image_gamma);
png_set_gamma(pRead, 2.2, image_gamma);

//
// STEP 13: Instruct libpng to handle the interlacing
//
const int num_passes = png_set_interlace_handling(pRead);

//
// STEP 14: Update pInfo according to the transformations
//
png_read_update_info(pRead, pInfo);


//
// STEP 15: Initialize the DIB section's header
// according to the dimensions and pixel format
// of the PNG image
//
```

```
BITMAPINFO bmi = {0};
bmi.bmiHeader.biSize = sizeof(BITMAPINFOHEADER);
bmi.bmiHeader.biWidth =
   png_get_image_width(pRead, pInfo);
bmi.bmiHeader.biHeight =
   -png_get_image_height(pRead, pInfo); // top-down
bmi.bmiHeader.biBitCount =
   png_get_channels(pRead, pInfo) *
   png_get_bit_depth(pRead, pInfo);
bmi.bmiHeader.biPlanes = 1;
bmi.bmiHeader.biCompression = BI_RGB;

// create a DIB section bitmap
unsigned char* pBits;
HBITMAP hDIBSection =
   CreateDIBSection(
      NULL, &bmi, 0,
      reinterpret_cast<LPVOID*>(&pBits),
      NULL, 0
      );
if (!pBits) longjmp(PNGError.pErrorJump, 1);

// compute the number of bytes per scan line
unsigned int dib_bytes_per_scanline =
   (((bmi.bmiHeader.biWidth * bmi.bmiHeader.biBitCount)
     + 31) & ~31) >> 3;

//
// STEP 16: Read the image from the file...
//
// for each interlaced scan
for (int iPass = 0; iPass < num_passes; ++iPass)
{
   // for each scan line
   for (int y = 0; y < -bmi.bmiHeader.biHeight; ++y)
   {
      unsigned char* pScanLine =
         reinterpret_cast<unsigned char*>(
         pBits + (y * dib_bytes_per_scanline)
         );

      // fill the DIB section with PNG data
      png_read_row(pRead, pScanLine, NULL);
   }
}
```

```
// if the image supports transparency
if (bmi.bmiHeader.biBitCount == 32)
{
   //
   // extract the app's background color
   // and alpha-blend the pixels
   //
   const COLORREF clrApp = GetSysColor(COLOR_BTNFACE);
   png_color_16 BkColor;
   BkColor.red = GetRValue(clrApp);
   BkColor.green = GetGValue(clrApp);
   BkColor.blue = GetBValue(clrApp);

   // set the background color
   for (int y = 0; y < -bmi.bmiHeader.biHeight; ++y)
   {
      RGBQUAD* pScanLine =
         reinterpret_cast<RGBQUAD*>(
            pBits + (y * dib_bytes_per_scanline)
            );
      for (int x = 0; x < bmi.bmiHeader.biWidth; ++x)
      {
         unsigned char alpha =
            pScanLine[x].rgbReserved;

         png_composite(
            pScanLine[x].rgbRed,
            pScanLine[x].rgbRed,
            alpha, BkColor.red
            );
         png_composite(
            pScanLine[x].rgbGreen,
            pScanLine[x].rgbGreen,
            alpha, BkColor.green
            );
         png_composite(
            pScanLine[x].rgbBlue,
            pScanLine[x].rgbBlue,
            alpha, BkColor.blue
            );
      }
   }
}
```

```
    //
    // STEP 17: Read the IEND chunk
    //
    png_read_end(pRead, pInfo);

    //
    // STEP 18: Clean up
    //
    png_destroy_read_struct(&pRead, &pInfo, NULL);

    //
    // STEP 19: Clean up
    //
    fclose(pFile);

    return hDIBSection;
}
```

For more information on reading a PNG image from a file, see "Reading a PNG Image" in the "In Depth" section. For more information on using the libpng library, refer to the file libpng.txt, which accompanies the libpng library.

Writing a PNG Image to a File

To read a PNG image from a file, you use the libpng library. Specifically, you perform the following steps:

1. Install the libpng library. (See "Setting Up the libpng Library" in the "In Depth" section.)
2. **#include** the header file png.h in your source code, and statically link with the import library file libpng.lib.
3. Open the output PNG file in binary mode with Write access privileges by using the **fopen** function; store the return value (which is a pointer to the file stream of type **FILE***).
4. Allocate and initialize a **png_struct** structure for writing by using the **png_create_write_struct** function. You must specify **PNG_LIBPNG_-VER_STRING** as the first parameter of the **png_create_ write_struct** function; the other three parameters can be set to **NULL**. In most cases, however, you'll want to provide an error-handling callback function. To do this, you specify a pointer to your callback function as the third parameter of the **png_create_ write_struct** function, and you specify a pointer to

any additional application-defined data that you want to access from within the callback function as the second parameter of the **png_create_ write_-struct** function. (From within your callback function, you can access the application-defined data by using the **png_get_error_ptr** function.) If it's successful, the **png_create_ write_struct** function will return a pointer to an allocated (and initialized) **png_struct** structure. If the function fails, it will return **NULL** and you should proceed to Step 15.

5. Allocate and initialize a **png_info** structure by using the **png_create_info_struct** function. You pass this function a pointer to the **png_struct**-type variable from Step 4. If the **png_create_info_struct** function is successful, it will return a pointer to an allocated (and initialized) **png_info** structure. If the function fails, it will return **NULL,** and you should proceed to Step 14.
6. Initialize libpng's input/output routines by using the **png_init_io** function. For this function, you pass a pointer to the **png_struct**-type variable from Step 4 as the first parameter, and pass the **png_info**-type variable from Step 5 as the second parameter.
7. Specify the amount of compression by using the **png_set_compression_-level** function. For this function, you pass a pointer to the **png_struct**-type variable from Step 4 as the first parameter, and specify a value ranging from –1 to 9 as the second parameter. (Higher values indicate more compression; –1 indicates default compression.)
8. Initialize the **IHDR**-related information in the **png_info**-type variable (that you created in Step 6) by using the **png_set_IHDR** function. You pass this function the following: a pointer to the **png_struct**-type variable from Step 4 as the first parameter; a pointer to the **png_info**-type variable from Step 5 as the second parameter; the width and height of your source image as the third and fourth parameters, respectively; the number of bits per sample (usually 8) as the fifth parameter; a corresponding color-type identifier (from Table 18.4) as the sixth parameter; an interlacing-related identifier (**PNG_INTERLACE_NONE** or **PNG_INTERLACE_ADAM7**) as the seventh parameter; and **PNG_COMPRESSION_TYPE_DEFAULT** and **PNG_FILTER_TYPE_DEFAULT** as the eighth and ninth parameters, respectively.
9. If your source image is palette-based, initialize the **PLTE**-related information in the **png_info**-type variable (that you created in Step 5) by using the **png_set_PLTE** function. You pass this function the following: a pointer to the **png_struct**-type variable from Step 4 as the first parameter; a pointer to the **png_info**-type variable from Step 5 as the second parameter; an array of **png_color** structures (i.e., the palette entries) as the third parameter; and the number of palette entries as the fourth parameter.

10. Instruct libpng to write all of the pre-**IDAT** chunks by using the **png_write_info** function. For this function, you pass a pointer to the **png_struct**-type variable from Step 4 as the first parameter, and pass the **png_info**-type variable from Step 5 as the second parameter.
11. If the color channels of your source image are ordered BGR, use the **png_set_bgr** function to instruct libpng to switch back to RGB. You pass the **png_set_bgr** function a pointer to the **png_struct**-type variable from Step 4.
12. Instruct libpng to handle the expansion of the interlaced images by using the **png_set_interlace_handling** function. You pass this function a pointer to the **png_struct**-type variable from Step 4, and the function will return the number of interlaced passes that are required to write the entire image. You should store this return value; it will be either 1 (if you specified **PNG_INTERLACE_NONE** in Step 8) or 7 (if you specified **PNG_INTERLACE_ADAM7** in Step 8).
13. In an outer loop, iterate over the required number of interlacing passes (the value you stored in Step 12). Within this loop, create an inner loop that iterates over the number of scan lines (the height of your source image). For each iteration of the inner loop (i.e., for each scan line), write a scan line to the PNG file by using the **png_write_row** function. For this function, you pass a pointer to the **png_struct**-type variable from Step 4 as the first parameter, and pass a pointer to a specific scan line of your source image as the second parameter.
14. Write the **IEND** chunk by using the **png_write_end** function. For this function, you pass a pointer to the **png_struct**-type variable from Step 4 as the first parameter, and pass a pointer to the **png_info**-type variable from Step 5 as the second parameter.
15. Destroy the **png_struct**-type variable from Step 4 and the **png_info**-type variable from Step 5 by using the **png_destroy_write_struct** function. For this function, you pass the address of a pointer to the **png_struct**-type variable from Step 4 as the first parameter, and pass the address of a pointer to the **png_info**-type variable from Step 5 as the second parameter.
16. Close the file stream (from Step 3) by using the **fclose** function.

In Listing 18.5, the example function **SaveDIBSectionToPNGFile** demonstrates how to use these 16 steps to write a PNG file from the pixels of a 24-bpp or 32-bpp DIB section bitmap. The resulting PNG image (that's contained in the file) will be either a 24-bpp variety if the DIB section itself is 24-bpp, or a 32-bpp variety if the DIB section is 32-bpp. Here's the code:

Listing 18.5 Writing a PNG file from the pixels of a 24-bpp or 32-bpp DIB section bitmap.

```
// -----------------------------------------------------------------
// Windows 2000 Graphics API Black Book
// Chapter 18 - Listing 18.5 (SaveDIBSectionToPNGFile Definition)
// -----------------------------------------------------------------

struct PNGERROR {
   HWND hWnd;
   jmp_buf pErrorJump;
};
typedef PNGERROR *PPNGERROR;

static void PNGErrorHandler(
    png_structp pStruct,      // pointer to a png_struct structure
    png_const_charp pMessage  // error message string
   )
{
   PPNGERROR pPNGError = reinterpret_cast<PPNGERROR>(
      png_get_error_ptr(pStruct)
      );
   if (!pPNGError) throw std::runtime_error(pMessage);
   else
   {
      MessageBox(
         pPNGError->hWnd, pMessage, TEXT("libpng Error"),
         MB_OK | MB_ICONERROR
         );
      longjmp(pPNGError->pErrorJump, 1);
   }
}

BOOL SaveDIBSectionToPNGFile(
    IN LPCSTR filename,
    IN HBITMAP hDIBSection,
    IN int compression_level = -1
   )
{
//
// STEP 1: Install the libpng library
// STEP 2: #include "png.h" and link with "libpng.lib" and "zlib.lib"
//

   //
   // STEP 3: Open the file for binary writing
   //
```

```
FILE* pFile = fopen(filename, "wb");
assert(pFile != NULL);

// set up an error pointer
PNGERROR PNGError = {GetForegroundWindow()};

//
// STEP 4: Create a png_struct structure for writing
//
png_structp pWrite =
   png_create_write_struct(
      PNG_LIBPNG_VER_STRING, // must be PNG_LIBPNG_VER_STRING
      &PNGError,             // pointer to app-defined data
      PNGErrorHandler,       // error callback function
      NULL                   // warning callback function
      );
if (!pWrite)
{
   fclose(pFile);
   assert(false);
}

//
// STEP 5: Create a png_info structure
//
png_infop pInfo = png_create_info_struct(pWrite);
if (!pInfo)
{
   png_destroy_write_struct(&pWrite, NULL);
   fclose(pFile);
   assert(false);
}

// set the jump point
if (setjmp(PNGError.pErrorJump))
{
   png_destroy_write_struct(&pWrite, &pInfo);
   fclose(pFile);
   return FALSE;
}

//
// STEP 6: Initialize the I/O routines
//
png_init_io(pWrite, pFile);
```

```
// get the bitmap info
BITMAP bmp;
const size_t bmpSize = sizeof(BITMAP);
if (GetObject(hDIBSection, bmpSize, &bmp) != bmpSize || !bmp.bmBits)
{
   longjmp(PNGError.pErrorJump, 1);
}

// determine the color type...
unsigned char color_type;
switch (bmp.bmBitsPixel)
{
   case 8:
      color_type = PNG_COLOR_TYPE_PALETTE;
      break;
   case 24:
      color_type = PNG_COLOR_TYPE_RGB;
      break;
   case 32:
      color_type = PNG_COLOR_TYPE_RGB_ALPHA;
      break;
   default:
      PNGErrorHandler(pWrite, "Unsupported bitmap color depth!");
      break;
}

//
// STEP 7: Set the compression level
//
png_set_compression_level(pWrite, compression_level);

//
// STEP 8: Initialize the IHDR information
//
png_set_IHDR(
   pWrite, pInfo,
   bmp.bmWidth, bmp.bmHeight,
   8, color_type,
   PNG_INTERLACE_ADAM7,
   PNG_COMPRESSION_TYPE_DEFAULT,
   PNG_FILTER_TYPE_DEFAULT
   );
```

```
//
// initialize any other chunks, if required...
//
// set the background color and gamma
png_color_16 BkColor = {0, 255, 255, 255}; // white
png_set_bKGD(pWrite, pInfo, &BkColor);
png_set_gAMA(pWrite, pInfo, 1 / 2.2);

//
// STEP 9: Initialize the PLTE information
// if the source image is palette-based
//
// NOTE: Be sure to keep the memory for the array
// of png_color until after the image is written
//
png_color palette[256];
if (bmp.bmBitsPixel <= 8)
{
   //
   // get the DIB section's color-table entries...
   //
   RGBQUAD rgbQ[256];
   HDC hMemDC = CreateCompatibleDC(NULL);
   hDIBSection = static_cast<HBITMAP>(
      SelectObject(hMemDC, hDIBSection)
      );
   const int num_colors = GetDIBColorTable(hMemDC, 0, 256, rgbQ);
   hDIBSection = static_cast<HBITMAP>(
      SelectObject(hMemDC, hDIBSection)
      );
   DeleteDC(hMemDC);

   if (num_colors > 0)
   {
      // copy the color table to the png_info array
      for (int index = 0; index < num_colors; ++index)
      {
         palette[index].red = rgbQ[index].rgbRed;
         palette[index].green = rgbQ[index].rgbGreen;
         palette[index].blue = rgbQ[index].rgbBlue;
      }
      // initialize pInfo's PLTE-related info
      png_set_PLTE(pWrite, pInfo, palette, num_colors);
   }
}
```

```
//
// STEP 10: Write the info chunks
//
png_write_info(pWrite, pInfo);

//
// STEP 11: Instruct libpng to switch back to RGB
//
png_set_bgr(pWrite);

//
// STEP 12: Instruct libpng to handle the interlacing
//
const int num_passes = png_set_interlace_handling(pWrite);

// compute the number of bytes per scan line
unsigned int dib_bytes_per_scanline =
   (((bmp.bmWidth * bmp.bmBitsPixel)
     + 31) & ~31) >> 3;

// grab a pointer to the DIB section's bits
unsigned char* pBits = static_cast<unsigned char*>(bmp.bmBits);

//
// STEP 13: Write the image to the file...
//
// for each interlaced scan
for (int iPass = 0; iPass < num_passes; ++iPass)
{
   // for each scan line
   for (int y = 0; y < bmp.bmHeight; ++y)
   {
      unsigned char* pScanLine =
         reinterpret_cast<unsigned char*>(
         // assuming a top-down DIB section
         pBits + (y * dib_bytes_per_scanline)
         );

      // fill the DIB section with PNG data
      png_write_row(pWrite, pScanLine);
   }
}
```

```
    //
    // STEP 14: Write the IEND chunk
    //
    png_write_end(pWrite, pInfo);

    //
    // STEP 15: Clean up
    //
    png_destroy_write_struct(&pWrite, &pInfo);

    //
    // STEP 16: Clean up
    //
    fclose(pFile);

    return TRUE;
}
```

For more information on writing a PNG image from a file, see "Writing a PNG Image" in the "In Depth" section. For more information on using the libpng library, refer to the file libpng.txt, which accompanies the libpng library.

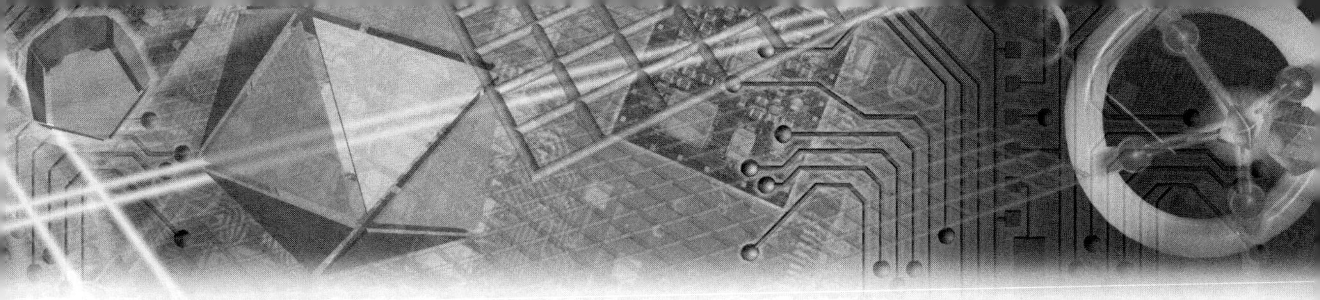

Part IV

Appendixes

Appendix A

A Brief Review of Matrices and Vectors

Matrices and Matrix Algebra

A *matrix* is a two-dimensional array of numbers, equations, or functions. A matrix T has m rows and n columns and can be written as:

$$T = \begin{bmatrix} t_{11} & t_{12} & \Lambda & t_{1n} \\ t_{21} & t_{22} & \Lambda & t_{2n} \\ \mathrm{M} & \mathrm{M} & & \mathrm{M} \\ t_{m1} & t_{m2} & \Lambda & t_{mn} \end{bmatrix}$$

If you want to access the element in the second column of the first row, for example, you'd query the value of t_{12}. Note that a matrix is not necessarily square; in other words, the number of rows, m, and the number of columns, n, are not necessarily equal.

A matrix that consists of only a single row is generally called a *row vector*. Likewise, a matrix that consists of only a single column is called a *column vector*.

Matrix Addition

The addition of two matrices is possible only if these matrices have the same dimensions—that is, they have the same number of rows *and* columns. To compute the sum, you simply add each of the corresponding elements. For example:

$$\begin{bmatrix} 1 & 2 \\ 0 & -1 \end{bmatrix} + \begin{bmatrix} 5 & 4 \\ 3 & 2 \end{bmatrix} = \begin{bmatrix} 1+5 & 2+4 \\ 0+3 & -1+2 \end{bmatrix} = \begin{bmatrix} 6 & 6 \\ 3 & 1 \end{bmatrix}$$

With respect to matrix addition, the distributive property does hold. That is, for three matrices A, B, and C:

$$A(B + C) = AB + CD$$

Matrix Multiplication

You can multiply two matrices only if the number of columns in the matrix on the left is equal to the number of rows in the matrix on the right. Here's a simple example:

$$\text{If} \quad A = \begin{bmatrix} 1 & 0 \\ 2 & 2 \\ -2 & 0 \end{bmatrix} \quad \text{and } B = \begin{bmatrix} 3 & 0 & 2 & 1 \\ 1 & 0 & 0 & -1 \end{bmatrix}$$

then,

$$AB = \begin{bmatrix} 1 & 0 \\ 2 & 2 \\ -2 & 0 \end{bmatrix} \begin{bmatrix} 3 & 0 & 2 & 1 \\ 1 & 0 & 0 & -1 \end{bmatrix}$$

$$= \begin{bmatrix} 1 \cdot 3 + 0 \cdot 1 & 1 \cdot 0 + 0 \cdot 0 & 1 \cdot 2 + 0 \cdot 0 & 1 \cdot 1 + 0 \cdot -1 \\ 2 \cdot 3 + 2 \cdot 1 & 2 \cdot 0 + 2 \cdot 0 & 2 \cdot 2 + 2 \cdot 0 & 2 \cdot 1 + 2 \cdot -1 \\ -2 \cdot 3 + 0 \cdot 1 & -2 \cdot 0 + 0 \cdot 0 & -2 \cdot 2 + 0 \cdot 0 & -2 \cdot 1 + 0 \cdot -1 \end{bmatrix}$$

$$= \begin{bmatrix} 3 & 1 & 2 & 1 \\ 8 & 0 & 4 & 0 \\ -6 & 0 & -4 & -2 \end{bmatrix}$$

The multiplication is done with each of the rows in A to each of the columns in B, producing a matrix C with the same number of rows as A and the same number of columns as B. Note that although we can compute the product AB, we cannot compute the product BA because the number of columns in B, which is 4, does not match the number of rows in A, which is 3. Also note that matrix multiplication is *not* always commutative. That is, for two matrices, A and B, in general:

$AB \neq BA$.

The Transpose of a Matrix

By interchanging the rows and columns of a matrix, T, you get its transposition (called the transpose), T'. For example:

$$T = \begin{bmatrix} 1 & 4 \\ 2 & 5 \\ 3 & 6 \end{bmatrix}$$

$$T' = \begin{bmatrix} 1 & 2 & 3 \\ 4 & 5 & 6 \end{bmatrix}$$

A useful property involving transposition and products is:

$(AB)' = B'A'$

The Determinant of a Matrix

The determinant of a matrix is useful for many reasons, one of which is the cross product of vectors, which we'll examine a little later. The determinant of a 2x2 matrix is computed as follows:

$$\begin{bmatrix} a & b \\ c & d \end{bmatrix} = ad - cb$$

Finding the determinant of any higher-order matrix is much more difficult, however. You can recursively calculate higher-order determinants by choosing any column j of an nxn matrix. The determinant can be computed as:

$$\det(T) = \sum_{i=1}^{n} (-1)^{i+j}\, t_{ij} \det T_{ij}$$

Bear in mind that you can compute the determinant of a matrix only if it's a *square* matrix.

The Inverse of a Matrix

As with the determinant, we're dealing only with square matrices when we're talking about inverses; however, not all matrices have inverses. We can use determinants to determine whether or not a matrix has an inverse. The inverse of an nxn matrix T exists if and only if the determinant of T is nonzero. The inverse of T is written as T^{-1} and has the following property:

$T\,T^{-1} = T^{-1}\,T = I_n$

where I_n is the nxn identity matrix (1's on the diagonal and 0 everywhere else).

Finding the inverse of a matrix is often necessary when you need to solve a set of linear equations. You can write a system of equations in matrix form:

$AX = B$

For example, if you wanted to solve the following system:

$2x_1 + 3x_2 + 5x_3 = 16$

$14x_2 + 3x_3 = 9$

$10x_1 + 2x_2 + x_3 = 2$

You can first represent it as follows:

$$AX = B \begin{bmatrix} 2 & 3 & 5 \\ 0 & 14 & 3 \\ 10 & 2 & 1 \end{bmatrix} \begin{pmatrix} x_1 \\ x_2 \\ x_3 \end{pmatrix} = \begin{pmatrix} 16 \\ 9 \\ 2 \end{pmatrix}$$

To solve this, we want the values of X, so the solution can be expressed as:

$X = A^{-1}B$

Thus, the solution depends on finding the inverse of A. This system of equations can be solved by using the *Gaussian elimination* method to find A^{-1}. The idea is to reduce A to the identity matrix (from the property that a matrix times its inverse gives the identity matrix), leaving only values for x_1, x_2, and x_3.

Vectors and Vector Algebra

Given the positions of any two points in space, the vector, $\underline{v}$, can be found by taking the difference of the two points. This scheme is depicted in Figure A.1.

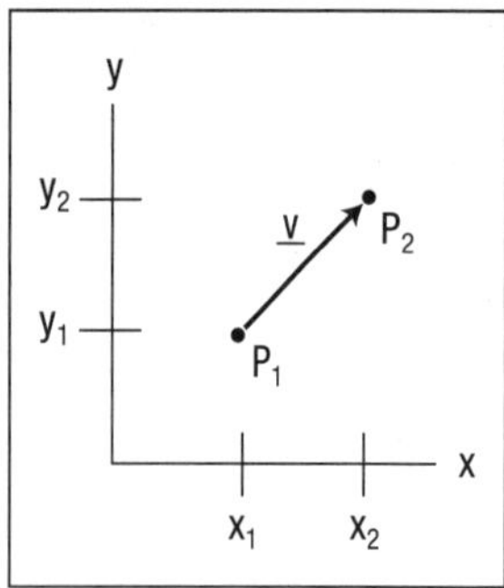

Figure A.1 A vector is a directed line segment that's defined by two points.

In two dimensions, as depicted in Figure A.1, the vector $\underline{v}$ is written as follows:

$$\begin{aligned}\underline{v} &= P_2 - P_1 \\ &= (x_2 - x_1,\ y_2 - y_1) \\ &= (v_x,\ v_y)\end{aligned}$$

This is equivalent to the following ($\underline{x}$ and $\underline{y}$ are the basis vectors—i.e., the axes of the coordinate space):

$$\underline{v} = v_x\,\underline{x} + v_y\,\underline{y}$$

A vector has two defining features: *magnitude* and *direction.* In 2D Cartesian space, a vector's magnitude can be found using the Pythagorean theorem:

$$\begin{aligned}|\underline{v}| &= \sqrt{(x_1 - x_2)^2 + (y_1 - y_2)^2} \\ &= \sqrt{(v_x^{\,2} + v_y^{\,2})}\end{aligned}$$

A vector's direction can be found in terms of its angular position from the x-axis using this relationship:

$$\vartheta = \tan^{-1}\left(\frac{v_x}{v_y}\right)$$

The key thing to remember about vectors is that the magnitude and direction are *independent* of its position within a specific reference frame. You can move a vector from place to place, within the same coordinate system, and its magnitude and direction remain the same.

A vector's magnitude is also independent of its frame of reference. You can move a vector into a different coordinate system, and although the values of the vector components will change accordingly, the vector's magnitude remains the same.

Because of these properties, vectors are used to describe anything that has a magnitude and a direction. Typical vectors are velocity and force vectors, which are used to describe the earth's orbit around the sun.

As I said earlier, the direction of a vector is an angular measurement relative to the axis. The angle that a vector makes with each of the positive coordinate axes is called the *direction angle.* So, in 3D Cartesian space, the magnitude vector is:

$$|\underline{v}| = \sqrt{v_x^{\,2} + v_y^{\,2} + v_z^{\,2}}$$

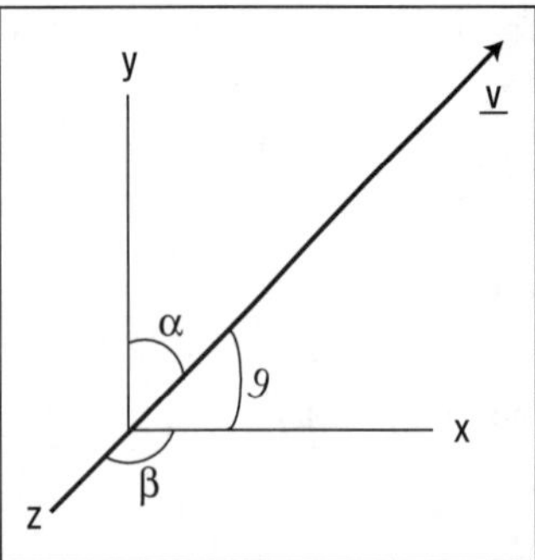

Figure A.2 The direction angles of a three-dimensional vector.

And the *direction angles*, which are illustrated in Figure A.2, can be calculated as follows:

$$\cos \vartheta = \frac{v_x}{|\underline{v}|},$$

$$\cos \alpha = \frac{v_y}{|\underline{v}|},$$

$$\cos \beta = \frac{v_z}{|\underline{v}|}$$

Vector Addition

To add two vectors, you simply sum up the same components from each:

$$\underline{v}_1 + \underline{v}_2 = (v_{1x} + v_{2x}, v_{1y} + v_{2y})$$

By this definition, you cannot add a vector to a scalar because a scalar has only one component, whereas the number of components a vector has depends on what dimension of space that vector is in. You can, however, multiply a vector by a scalar as follows:

$$c\underline{v} = c(v_x, v_y, v_z) = (cv_x, cv_y, cv_z)$$

And so each component is multiplied by the scalar. You can see that if c equals 0.5, $\underline{v}$ would just be half of its original length.

Vector Multiplication: The Dot Product

The *dot product*, or the inner product of two vectors, is defined as:

$$\underline{a} \bullet \underline{b} = |\underline{a}|\ |\underline{b}|\ \cos(\theta)$$

where θ is the angle between $\underline{a}$ and $\underline{b}$.

The result of a dot product is a scalar, so sometimes dot products are called *scalar products*. A good way to think of a dot product conceptually is that you're looking at how much of $\underline{a}$ is *parallel* to $\underline{b}$. A dot product is a product of the *parallel components* of the two vectors. So, if you take the dot product of a vector with itself, you get the magnitude of the vector, squared:

$$\underline{a} \bullet \underline{a} = |\underline{a}|^2$$

Because dot products measure the parallel components, a dot product will be equal to zero if and only if the two vectors are *orthogonal* (i.e., perpendicular).

Dot Product Properties

The following are properties of the vector dot product:

- *Commutative Property:* [ceo6] $\underline{a} \bullet \underline{b} = \underline{b} \bullet \underline{a}$
- *Distributive Property:* $\underline{v} \bullet (\underline{a} + \underline{b}) = \underline{v} \bullet \underline{a} + \underline{v} \bullet \underline{b}$

Vector Multiplication: The Cross Product

When you multiply two vectors and the product yields another vector, it is called a *cross product* or a *vector product*. It's written as:

$$\underline{a} \times \underline{b} = \underline{c}$$

$$|\underline{c}| = |\underline{a}||\underline{b}| \sin(\theta)$$

where θ is the angle between $\underline{a}$ and $\underline{b}$.

The direction of $|\underline{c}|$ depends on the *right-hand rule*. If you extend your right hand along the axis of $\underline{a}$ and curl your fingers toward the axis of $\underline{b}$, your thumb now points in the direction of $\underline{c}$. The direction of $\underline{c}$ is always perpendicular to the plane of $\underline{a}$ and $\underline{b}$, with a magnitude defined by the area of the parallelogram formed by $\underline{a}$ and $\underline{b}$, as depicted in Figure A.3.

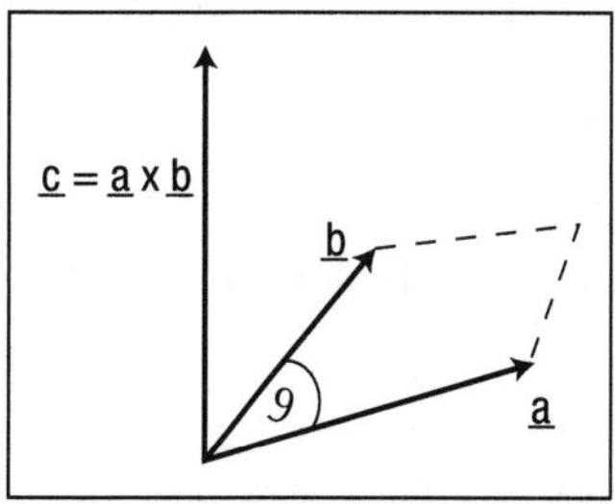

Figure A.3 The cross product ($\underline{c}$) of two vectors ($\underline{a}$ and $\underline{b}$).

Analogous to the interpretation of the dot product, we can think of the cross product as looking for how much of vector $\underline{a}$ is *perpendicular* to vector $\underline{b}$. The cross product of any two *parallel* vectors is zero, and so is the cross product of any vector with itself.

The cross product can also be expressed as the determinant of a matrix to calculate the components of the cross product as:

$$\underline{a} \times \underline{b} = \begin{vmatrix} x & y & z \\ a_1 & a_2 & a_3 \\ b_1 & b_2 & b_3 \end{vmatrix}$$

$$\underline{a} \times \underline{b} = (a_2 b_3 - a_3 b_2)\ \underline{x} + (a_3 b_1 - a_1 b_3)\ \underline{y} + (a_1 b_2 - a_2 b_1)\ \underline{z}$$

Cross Product Properties

The following are properties of the vector cross product:

- *NOT Commutative Property:* $\underline{a} \times \underline{b} = -(\underline{b} \times \underline{a})$
- *NOT Associative Property:* $\underline{a} \times (\underline{b} \times \underline{c}) \neq (\underline{a} \times \underline{b}) \times \underline{c}$
- *Distributive Property:* $\underline{a} \times (\underline{b} + \underline{c}) = (\underline{a} \times \underline{b}) + (\underline{a} \times \underline{c})$

The Transpose of a Vector

As I mentioned earlier, any vector $\underline{v}$ can be written using a matrix representation, and that matrix can actually be written in two ways. You can have a 1x3 matrix or a 3x1 matrix for a 3D vector. In Cartesian coordinates, this would be:

$$[\underline{v}] = \begin{bmatrix} a \\ b \\ c \end{bmatrix}$$

$$[\underline{v}]' = [a \ \ b \ \ c]$$

The notation, $[\ \underline{v}\ ]'$, is the transpose of $[\ \underline{v}\ ]$, which means that the rows and columns have been interchanged.

Vector Rotation

Let's do a simple rotation of a 2D vector in a Cartesian coordinate system. We'll begin with a vector, $\underline{v}$, which is at some angleθ from the x-axis. Vector $\underline{v}$ can be written as follows:

$$\underline{v} = (v_x, v_y)$$

where

$$v_x = \cos(\theta)$$

$$v_y = \sin(\theta)$$

and

$$v = |\underline{v}| = \sqrt{v_x^2 + v_y^2}$$, as mentioned earlier.

Vector $\underline{w}$ can be created by rotating vector $\underline{v}$ counterclockwise by some angle, ϕ. As described previously, the magnitude of $\underline{v}$ is preserved; just the orientation changes (see Figure A.4). Thus, $\underline{w}$ can be written as follows:

$$\underline{w} = (w_x, w_y)$$

where

$$w_x = v\cos(\theta + \emptyset) = v\cos(\theta)\cos(\emptyset) - v\sin(\theta)\sin(\emptyset)$$

$$w_y = v\cos(\theta - \emptyset) = v\cos(\theta)\sin(\emptyset) + v\sin(\theta)\cos(\emptyset)$$

In matrix form, these equations can be rewritten as follows:

$$\begin{bmatrix} w_x \\ w_y \end{bmatrix} = \begin{bmatrix} \cos\emptyset & -\sin\emptyset \\ \sin\emptyset & \cos\emptyset \end{bmatrix} \begin{bmatrix} v_x \\ v_y \end{bmatrix}$$

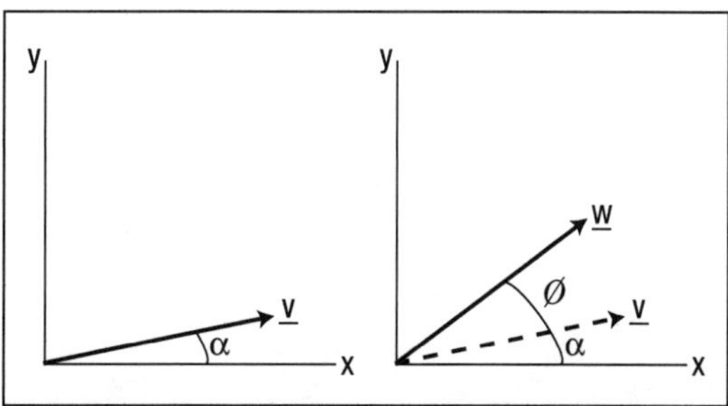

Figure A.4 Rotating a vector $\underline{v}$ by an angle Ø in the counterclockwise direction.

This expression can be abbreviated:

$$\underline{w} = R(\text{Ø})\ \underline{v}$$

where the matrix $R(\text{Ø})$ is called the *rotation matrix*, defined as follows:

$$R(\text{Ø}) = \begin{bmatrix} \cos \text{Ø} & -\sin \text{Ø} \\ \sin \text{Ø} & \cos \text{Ø} \end{bmatrix}$$

Appendix B

Other Resources

Computer Graphics

- Arvo, J. *Graphics Gems II*. Boston: Academic Press, 1991.
- Foley, J. D., A. van Dam, S. K. Feiner, and J. F. Hughes. *Computer Graphics: Principles and Practice, Second Edition in C*. Reading, Mass.: Addison-Wesley, 1996.
- Glassner, A. S. *Graphics Gems*. Boston: Academic Press, 1990.
- Hearn, D., and M. P. Baker. *Computer Graphics, C Version*. 2nd ed. Upper Saddle River, NJ: Prentice Hall, 1997.
- Heckbert, P. S. *Graphics Gems IV*. Boston: Academic Press, 1994.
- Kirk, D. *Graphics Gems III*. Boston: Academic Press, 1992.
- Paeth, A. W. *Graphics Gems V*. Boston: Academic Press, 1995.
- *Feature-Based Image Metamorphosis*—**http://www.hammerhead.com/thad/morph.html**
- *Graphics Algorithms FAQ*—**http://www.faqs.org/faqs/graphics/algorithms-faq/**
- *Graphics Gems Online*—**http://www.graphicsgems.org/**
- *UC Davis Graphics Group On-Line Notes*—**http://graphics.cs.ucdavis.edu/GraphicsNotes/Graphics-Notes.html**

Image Processing

- Castleman, K. R. *Digital Image Processing*. Englewood Cliffs, NJ: Prentice Hall, 1996.
- Gonzalez, R. C., and R. E. Woods. *Digital Image Processing*. 3rd ed. Reading, Mass.: Addison-Wesley, 1992.

- Jain, A. K. *Fundamentals of Digital Image Processing*. Englewood Cliffs, NJ: Prentice Hall, 1989.
- Lim, J. S. *Two-Dimensional Signal and Image Processing*. Prentice Hall Signal Processing Series. Englewood Cliffs, NJ: Prentice-Hall, 1990.
- *HP-ISE Image Processing Fundamentals*—**http://www.ph.tn.tudelft.nl/Courses/FIP/#course**

Wavelets

- Akansu, A. N., and M. J. T. Smith, editors. *Subband and Wavelet Transforms: Design and Applications*. Boston: Kluwer Academic Publishers, 1996.
- Calderbank, R., I. Daubechies, W. Sweldens, and B. L. Yeo. *Wavelet Transforms That Map Integers to Integers*. Technical report. Princeton: Princeton University, Department of Mathematics, 1996.
- Kaiser, G. *A Friendly Guide to Wavelets*. Boston: Birkhäuser, 1994.
- Louis, A. K., P. Maab, and A. Rieder. *Wavelets: Theory and Applications*. Chichester, England: John Wiley & Sons, 1997.
- Stollnitz, E. J., T. D. DeRose, and D. H. Salesin. "Wavelets for Computer Graphics: A Primer, Part 1." *IEEE Computer Graphics and Applications* 15, no. 3 (1995): 76–84.
- Stollnitz, E. J., T. D. DeRose, and D. H. Salesin. "Wavelets for Computer Graphics: A Primer, Part 2." *IEEE Computer Graphics and Applications* 15, no. 4 (1995): 75–85.
- Strang, G., and T. Nguyen. *Wavelets and Filter Banks*. Wellesley: Wellesley-Cambridge Press, 1996.
- *Amara's Wavelet Page*—**http://www.amara.com/IEEEwave/IEEEwavelet.html**
- *The Wavelet Digest*—**http://www.wavelet.org/**

Image Compression

- Ahmed, N., T. Natarajan, and K. R. Rao. "Discrete Cosine Transform." *IEEE Transactions on Computers* C-23, no. 1 (1974): 90–93.
- Huffman, D. A. "A Method for the Construction of Minimum-Redundancy Codes." *Proceedings of the IRE* 40, no.9 (1952): 1098–1101.
- Langdon, G. G., Jr. "An Introduction to Arithmetic Coding." *IBM Journal of Research and Development* 28, no. 2 (1984):135–149.

- Pennebaker, W. B., and J. L. Mitchell. *JPEG Still Image Data Compression Standard*. New York: Van Nostrand Reinhold, 1993.
- Wallace, G. K. "The JPEG Still Picture Compression Standard." *Communications of the ACM* 34, no. 4 (1991): 30–44.
- Ziv, J., and A. Lempel. "A Universal Algorithm for Sequential Data Compression." *IEEE Transactions on Information Theory* IT-23, no. 3 (1977): 337–343.
- *Image Compression FAQ*—**http://www.faqs.org/faqs/compression-faq/**
- *JPEG FAQ*—**http://www.faqs.org/faqs/jpeg-faq/**

Color Science

- Berns, R. S., F. W. Billmeyer, and M. Saltzman. *Principles of Color Technology*. 3rd ed. New York: John Wiley & Sons, 2000.
- Fairchild, M. D. *Color Appearance Models*. Reading, Mass.: Addison-Wesley, 1997.
- Giorgianni, E. J., and T. E. Madden. *Digital Color Management: Encoding Solutions*. Reading, Mass.: Addison-Wesley, 1998.
- Has, M., and T. Newman. "Color Management: Current Practice and the Adoption of a New Standard"—**http://www.color.org/wpaper1.html**
- Sangwine, S. J., and R. E. N. Horne. *The Colour Image Processing Handbook*. London: Chapman & Hall, 1998.
- Stokes, M., M. Anderson, S. Chandrasekar, and R. Motta. "A Standard Default Color Space for the Internet—sRGB"—**http://www.color.org/sRGB.html**
- Wyszecki, G., and W. S. Stiles. *Color Science: Concepts and Methods, Quantitative Data and Formula*. 2nd ed. New York: John Wiley & Sons, 1982.
- *Color Matters*—**http://www.colormatters.com/**
- *Colorspace FAQ*—**http://www.landfield.com/faqs/graphics/colorspace-faq/**
- *CVRL Color & Vision Database*—**http://cvision.ucsd.edu/**
- *International Color Consortium* (ICC)—**http://www.color.org/**
- *sRGB*—**http://www.sRGB.com/**

Image Databases

- *Caltech Vision Group Image Database*—**http://www.vision.caltech.edu/html-files/archive.html**
- *Carnegie Mellon VASC Image Database*—**http://www.vasc.ri.cmu.edu/idb/**

- *Dryden Research Aircraft Photo Gallery*—**http://www.dfrc.nasa.gov/gallery/photo/photoServer.html**
- *Michigan State PRIP Image Database*—**ftp://ftp.cps.msu.edu/pub/prip/**
- *NASA Photo Gallery*—**http://www.nasa.gov/gallery/photo/**
- *NSSDC Photo Gallery*—**http://nssdc.gsfc.nasa.gov/photo_gallery/**
- *University of Minnesota APS Image Database*—**http://spihr.spa.umn.edu/**
- *USC-SIPI Image Database*—**http://sipi.usc.edu/services/database/Database.html**
- *Vision 1 Image Database*—**http://www.vision1.com/imagedb.html**

Imaging Support

- *Graphics File Formats FAQ*—**http://www.faqs.org/faqs/graphics/fileformats-faq/**
- *ImageLib* (C++ image processing class library)—**http://www.dip.ee.uct.ac.za/~brendt/srcdist/**
- *ImageMagick* (Image file I/O library)—**http://www.simplesystems.org/ImageMagick/**
- *Intel Image Processing Library*—**http://developer.intel.com/software/products/perflib/ipl/index.htm**
- *Intel JPEG Library*—**http://developer.intel.com/software/products/perflib/ijl/index.htm**
- *lcms* (Color management library)—**http://www.littlecms.com/**
- *libjpg* (JPEG library)—**ftp://ftp.uu.net/graphics/jpeg/**
- *libmng* (MNG library)—**http://www.libmng.com/**
- *libpng* (PNG library)—**http://www.libpng.org/pub/png/libpng.html**
- *libtiff* (TIFF library)—**http://www.libtiff.org/**
- *Microsoft Vision SDK*—**http://research.microsoft.com/visionsdk/**
- *PNGSuite* (PNG test images)—**http://www.schaik.com/pngsuite/pngsuite.html**

General Development Resources

- *C FAQ*—**http://www.faqs.org/faqs/C-faq/**
- *C++ FAQ Lite*—**http://marshall-cline.home.att.net/cpp-faq-lite/**
- *C++ FAQ*—**http://www.faqs.org/faqs/C++-faq/**

- *C++Builder Developer's Journal*—**http://www.reisdorph.com/**
- *CodeGuru*—**http://codeguru.earthweb.com/**
- *Dr. Dobb's Journal*—**http://www.ddj.com/**
- *Journal of Object-Oriented Programming*—**http://joopmag.com/**
- *The C++ Report*—**http://www.creport.com/**
- *Thinking in C++* (B. Eckel's free online text)—**http://www.mindview.net/ThinkingInCPP2e.html**
- *Visual C++ Developer's Journal*—**http://www.vcdj.com/**
- *Windows Developer Journal*—**http://www.wdj.com/**

Index

A

B

C

D

E

F

G

H

I

J

K

L

M

N

O

P

Q

R

S

T

U

V

W

X

Y

Z

Related Coriolis Technology Press Titles

Active Server Pages Solutions

By Al Williams, Kim Barber, and Paul Newkirk
ISBN: 1-57610-608-X
Price: $49.99 U.S. • $74.99 CAN
Media: CD-ROM • Available Now

Explores all the components that work with Active Server Pages, such as HTML (including Dynamic HTML), scripting, Java applets, Internet Information Server, Internet Explorer and server-side scripting for VBScript, Jscript, and ActiveX controls. Offers practical examples using commonly used tools.

HTML Black Book

By Steven Holzner
ISBN: 1-57610-617-9
Price: $59.99 U.S. • $89.99 CAN
Media: CD-ROM • Available Now

Explores HTML programming thoroughly, from the essentials up through issues of security, providing step-by-step solutions to everyday challenges. This comprehensive guide discusses HTML in-depth, as well as covering XML, dynamic XML, JavaScript, Java, Perl, and CGI programming, to create a full Web site programming package.

Java Black Book

By Steven Holzner
ISBN: 1-57610-531-8
Price: $49.99 U.S. • $74.99 CAN
Media: CD-ROM • Available Now

A comprehensive reference filled with examples, tips, and solved problems. Discusses the Java language, Abstract Windowing Toolkit, Swing, Java 2D, advanced java beans, the Java Database Connectivity Package, servlets, internalization and security, streams and sockets, and more.

C++ Black Book

NEW

By Steven Holzner
ISBN: 1-57610-777-9
Price: $59.99 U.S. • $89.99 CAN
Media: CD-ROM • Available: December 2000

From the basics to the most advanced topics, this book provides complete coverage of everything needed to master C++, including all C++ compilers. The book explores working with data and C++ operators, storing data in strings and arrays, creating functions, and standard library functions for data processing and I/O, plus much more.

Visual Basic 6 Black Book

By Steven Holzner
ISBN: 1-57610-283-1
Price: $49.99 U.S. • $69.99 CAN
Media: CD-ROM • Available Now

Completely explains the crucial Visual Basic tool set in detail. Jam-packed with insight, programming tips and techniques, and real-world solutions. Covers everything from graphics and image processing, to ActiveX controls, database development and data-bound controls, multimedia, OLE automation, Registry handling, error handling and debugging, Windows API, and more.

Visual Basic 6 Core Language Little Black Book

By Steven Holzner
ISBN: 1-57610-390-0
Price: $24.99 U.S. • $36.99 CAN
Available Now

Provides a detailed reference on all Basic control structures, data types, and other code mechanisms. Includes step-by-step instructions on how to build common code structures in VB, from simple if statements to objects and ActiveX components. Not merely a syntax summary, but a detailed reference on creating code structures with VB6 code and data elements.

THE CORIOLIS GROUP, LLC

Telephone: 800.410.0192 • www.coriolis.com
Coriolis books are also available at bookstores and computer stores nationwide.

What's On The CD-ROM 

The *Windows 2000 Graphics API Black Book*'s companion CD-ROM contains elements specifically selected to enhance the usefulness of this book, including:

- Source code for nearly all of the code listings.
- Sample applications that fortify the concepts from the complex chapters—You can adapt these real-world programs based on your needs.
- 30 DirectDraw sample applications.
- A PDF document of the latest ICC device profile specifications.
- C++ classes that you can reuse and/or expand upon.

To supplement the material on the CD-ROM, we have established the following online Web site for this text: http://graphicsBB.itgo.com.

System Requirements

Software

- To compile the sample projects, you need either Microsoft Visual C++ version 6.0 (or later) or Borland C++Builder version 5.0 (or later).
- Most of the sample projects will run on Windows 95, 98, NT, Me, and 2000. The following are the exceptions:
  - The trackbar project of Chapter 6 requires version 4.70 (or later) of comctl32.dll.
  - The ICM-related projects of Chapter 16 and Chapter 18 require Windows 98, Me, or 2000.
  - The DirectDraw demos of Chapters 11-15 require DirectX 7 (or later) which is available only on Windows 95, 98, Me, and 2000. You can download the latest version of DirectX (version 8 as of this writing), along with the DirectX SDK from http://www.microsoft.com/directx/.
- The JPEG projects of Chapter 18 require Microsoft Visual C++ and the Intel JPEG Library. You can download the latest version of the Intel JPEG Library from http://developer.intel.com/software/products/perflib/ijl/index.htm.
- The PNG projects of Chapter 18 require libpng version 1.08 (or later). You can download the latest version of libpng from ftp://ftp.freesoftware.com/pub/png/libpng.html.

Hardware

- Your system must meet the hardware requirements of the following: (1) your development environment, (2) your compiler, and (3) the required libraries. None of the sample projects require special hardware.